Lecture Notes in Artificial Intelligence 3642

Edited by J. G. Carbonell and J. Siekmann

Subseries of Lecture Notes in Computer Science

T0189711

Dominik Ślęzak   JingTao Yao
James F. Peters   Wojciech Ziarko
Xiaohua Hu (Eds.)

Rough Sets, Fuzzy Sets, Data Mining, and Granular Computing

10th International Conference, RSFDGrC 2005
Regina, Canada, August 31 – September 3, 2005
Proceedings, Part II

 Springer

Series Editors

Jaime G. Carbonell, Carnegie Mellon University, Pittsburgh, PA, USA
Jörg Siekmann, University of Saarland, Saarbrücken, Germany

Volume Editors

Dominik Ślęzak
JingTao Yao
Wojciech Ziarko
University of Regina, Department of Computer Science
3737 Wascana Parkway, Regina, SK S4S 0A2, Canada
E-mail: {slezak, jtyao, ziarko}@cs.uregina.ca

James F. Peters
University of Manitoba, Department of Electrical and Computer Engineering
Winnipeg, MB R3T 5V6, Canada
E-mail: jfpeters@ee.umanitoba.ca

Xiaohua Hu
Drexel University, College of Information Science and Technology
Philadelphia, PA 19104, USA
E-mail: thu@cis.drexel.edu

Library of Congress Control Number: 2005931253

CR Subject Classification (1998): I.2, H.2.4, H.3, F.4.1, F.1, I.5, H.4

ISSN   0302-9743
ISBN-10   3-540-28660-8 Springer Berlin Heidelberg New York
ISBN-13   978-3-540-28660-8 Springer Berlin Heidelberg New York

Springer is a part of Springer Science+Business Media

springeronline.com

© Springer-Verlag Berlin Heidelberg 2005
Printed in Germany

Typesetting: Camera-ready by author, data conversion by Scientific Publishing Services, Chennai, India
Printed on acid-free paper   SPIN: 11548706   06/3142   5 4 3 2 1 0

Preface

This volume contains the papers selected for presentation at the Tenth International Conference on Rough Sets, Fuzzy Sets, Data Mining, and Granular Computing, RSFDGrC 2005, organized at the University of Regina, August 31st - September 3rd, 2005. This conference follows in the footsteps of international venues devoted to the subject of rough sets, held so far in Canada, China, Japan, Poland, Sweden, and the USA. RSFDGrC achieved the status of bi-annual international conference, starting from the year of 2003 in Chongqing, China.

The theory of rough sets, proposed by Zdzisław Pawlak in 1982, is a model of approximate reasoning. The main idea is based on indiscernibility relations that describe indistinguishability of objects. Concepts are represented by approximations. In applications, rough set methodology focuses on approximate representation of knowledge derivable from data. It leads to significant results in many areas such as finance, industry, multimedia, medicine.

The RSFDGrC conferences put an emphasis on connections between rough sets and fuzzy sets, granular computing, as well as knowledge discovery and data mining, both at the level of theoretical foundations and real-life applications. In the case of this venue, additional effort was made to establish a linkage towards a broader range of applications. We achieved it by including in the conference program the workshops on bioinformatics, security engineering, and embedded systems, as well as tutorials and sessions related to other application areas.

Revision Process

There were 277 submissions, excluding the invited, workshop, and special session papers. Every paper was examined by at least three reviewers. Out of the papers initially selected, some were approved subject to major revision and then additionally evaluated by the advisory board and program committee members. 119 papers were finally accepted. This gives an acceptance ratio equal to 43.0%.

In the case of workshops, 22 out of 130 submissions were finally approved to be published in the proceedings. This gives an acceptance ratio equal to 16.9%.

The reviewing process for the special session included into the proceedings was conducted independently by its organizers. 5 papers were finally accepted.

Final versions of all invited, regular, workshop, and special session papers were thoroughly revised by editors, often with several iterations of corrections.

Layout of Proceedings

The regular, invited, workshop, and special session papers are published within 30 chapters, grouped with respect to their topics. The conference materials are split onto two volumes (LNAI 3641 and 3642), both consisting of 15 chapters.

This volume contains 77 papers. 3 invited papers are gathered in chapter 1. 47 regular papers are gathered in chapters 2-8,10,11,13, related to rough set software, data mining, hybrid and hierarchical methods, information retrieval, image recognition and processing, multimedia applications, medical applications, web content analysis, business applications, and industrial applications. 22 workshop papers are gathered in chapters 9,12,14. 5 papers accepted for the special session on intelligent and sapient systems are gathered in chapter 15.

Acknowledgements

We wish to thank Zdzisław Pawlak and Lotfi A. Zadeh for acting as honorary chairs of the conference. We are also very grateful to the scientists who kindly agreed to give the keynote, plenary, and tutorial lectures: Vladimir Vapnik and Ronald Yager, Salvatore Greco, Hung Son Nguyen, Witold Pedrycz, Dimiter Vakarelov, Julio Valdés, and Ning Zhong, as well as Andrzej Czyżewski, Stephané Demri, Ivo Düntsch, Igor Jurisica, Bożena Kostek, and Piotr Wasilewski.

Our special thanks go to Andrzej Skowron for presenting the keynote lecture on behalf of Zdzisław Pawlak, Ewa Orłowska for organizing and chairing the invited workshop on foundations of rough sets, René V. Mayorga for co-organizing the special session, as well as Jiman Hong, Tai-hoon Kim, and Sung Y. Shin for organizing three workshops at RSFDGrC 2005.

We are grateful for support given by the University of Regina, Faculty of Science, and Department of Computer Science. We would like to express our gratitude to all the people who helped in organization of the conference in Regina: Brien Maguire and Lois Adams for coordinating all the arrangements, as well as Donalda Kozlowski, Connie Novitski, and Janice Savoie for support at various stages of conference preparations; Cory Butz for serving as a publicity chair; Robert Cowles and Peng Yao for administrating and improving the conference software systems; Hong Yao for launching the conference homepage, as well as Shan Hua for its updating and taking care of email correspondence; All other students of Computer Science who helped during the conference preparations.

We would like to thank to the authors who contributed to this volume. We are very grateful to the chairs, advisory board, and program committee members who helped in the revision process. We also acknowledge all the reviewers not listed in the conference committee. Their list is presented on a separate page, including also those who evaluated the workshop paper submissions.

Last but not least, we are thankful to Alfred Hofmann and Anna Kramer at Springer-Verlag for support and cooperation during preparation of this volume.

Regina, June 2005

Dominik Ślęzak
JingTao Yao
James F. Peters
Wojciech Ziarko
Xiaohua Hu

RSFDGrC 2005 Conference Committee

Honorary Chairs	Zdzisław Pawlak, Lotfi A. Zadeh
Conference Chairs	Wojciech Ziarko, Yiyu Yao, Xiaohua Hu
Program Chair	Dominik Ślęzak
Program Co-Chairs	Ivo Düntsch, James F. Peters, Guoyin Wang
Workshop Chair	JingTao Yao
Tutorial Chair	Marcin Szczuka
Publicity Chair	Cory Butz
Local Organizing Chair	Brien Maguire
Conference Secretary	Lois Adams

Advisory Board

Nick Cercone	Stan Matwin	Roman Słowiński
Salvatore Greco	Ewa Orłowska	Zbigniew Suraj
Jerzy Grzymała-Busse	Sankar K. Pal	Shusaku Tsumoto
Masahiro Inuiguchi	Witold Pedrycz	Julio Valdes
Jan Komorowski	Lech Polkowski	Jue Wang
Tsau Young Lin	Zbigniew Raś	Bo Zhang
Qing Liu	Andrzej Skowron	Ning Zhong

Program Committee

Mohua Banerjee	Jiye Liang	Henryk Rybiński
Jan Bazan	Churn-Jung Liau	Hiroshi Sakai
Malcolm Beynon	Pawan Lingras	Zhongzhi Shi
Hans-Dieter Burkhard	Chunnian Liu	Arul Siromoney
Gianpiero Cattaneo	Benedetto Matarazzo	Jerzy Stefanowski
Chien-Chung Chan	Ernestina Menasalvas-Ruiz	Jarosław Stepaniuk
Juan-Carlos Cubero	Duoqian Miao	Roman Świniarski
Andrzej Czyżewski	Sadaaki Miyamoto	Piotr Synak
Jitender S. Deogun	John Mordeson	Gwo-Hshiung Tzeng
Didier Dubois	Mikhail Moshkov	Dimiter Vakarelov
Maria C. Fernandez-Baizan	Hiroshi Motoda	Alicja Wakulicz-Deja
Günther Gediga	Tetsuya Murai	Hui Wang
Anna Gomolińska	Michinori Nakata	Lipo Wang
Shoji Hirano	Hung Son Nguyen	Paul P. Wang
Ryszard Janicki	Sinh Hoa Nguyen	Anita Wasilewska
Jouni Jarvinen	Piero Pagliani	Jakub Wróblewski
Licheng Jiao	Frederick Petry	Keming Xie
Janusz Kacprzyk	Henri Prade	Zongben Xu
Jacek Koronacki	Mohamed Quafafou	Wen-Xiu Zhang
Bożena Kostek	Vijay Raghavan	Yanqing Zhang
Marzena Kryszkiewicz	Sheela Ramanna	Zhi-Hua Zhou

Non-committee Reviewers

Adam Ameur
Robin Andersson
Ryan Benton
Steffen Bickel
Fuyuan Cao
Jesus Cardenosa
Yoojin Chung
Piotr Dałka
Agnieszka Dardzińska
Anca Doloc-Mihu
Isabel Drost
Eugene Eberbach
Santiago Eibe Garcia
Stefan Enroth
František Franek
Alicja Grużdź
Junyoung Heo
Jiman Hong
Piotr Hońko
Torgeir Hvidsten
Aleksandra Ihnatowicz
Gangil Jeon
Guang Jiang
Bo Jin

Andrzej Kaczmarek
Wolfram Kahl
Katarzyna Kierzkowska
Hanil Kim
Jung-Yeop Kim
Sung-Ryul Kim
Tai-hoon Kim
Maciej Koutny
Sangjun Lee
Jiye Li
Gabriela Lindemann
Krzysztof Marasek
Óscar Marbán
René V. Mayorga
Dagmar Monett Díaz
Lalita Narupiyakul
Jose Negrete Martinez
Phu Chien Nguyen
Atorn Nuntiyagul
Kouzou Ohara
J. Orzechowski-Westholm
Tianjie Pang
Puntip Pattaraintakorn
Jiming Peng

Concepción Pérez Llera
Skip Poehlman
Yuhua Qian
Kenneth Revett
Tobias Scheffer
Kay Schröter
Biren Shah
Charlie Shim
Sung Y. Shin
Chang O. Sung
Robert Susmaga
Piotr Szczuko
Yu Tang
Yuchun Tang
Alexandre Termier
Tinko Tinchev
Uma Maheswari V.
Junhong Wang
Haibin Wang
Ying Xie
Sangho Yi
Yan Zhao
Marta Zorrilla
Włodek Zuberek

Table of Contents – Part II

Hybrid and Hierarchical Methods

Information Retrieval

Image Recognition and Processing

Multimedia Applications

Medical Applications

Bioinformatic Applications

Web Content Analysis

Business Applications

Security Applications

Industrial Applications

Embedded Systems and Networking

Intelligent and Sapient Systems

Generalizing Rough Set Theory Through Dominance-Based Rough Set Approach

Salvatore Greco[1], Benedetto Matarazzo[1], and Roman Słowiński[2]

[1] Faculty of Economics, University of Catania,
Corso Italia, 55, 95129 - Catania, Italy
[2] Institute of Computing Science, Poznań University of Technology,
60-965 Poznań, and Institute for Systems Research,
Polish Academy of Sciences, 01-447 Warsaw, Poland

Abstract. Ordinal properties of data related to preferences have been taken into account in the Dominance-based Rough Set Approach (DRSA). We show that DRSA is also relevant in case where preferences are not considered but a kind of monotonicity relating attribute values is meaningful for the analysis of data at hand. In general terms, monotonicity concerns relationship between different aspects of a phenomenon described by data: for example, "the larger the house, the higher its price" or "the closer the house to the city centre, the higher its price". In this perspective, the DRSA gives a very general framework in which the classical rough set approach based on indiscernibility relation can be considered as a special case.

1 Introduction

Dominance-based Rough Set Approach (DRSA) [3] has been proposed to deal with ordinal properties of data related to preferences in decision problems [4]. In this paper, we show that the concept of dominance-based rough approximation includes the classical rough set concept, based on indiscernibility or a kind of similarity. This is because the monotonicity, which is crucial for DRSA, is also meaningful for problems where preferences are not considered. Generally, monotonicity concerns relationship between different aspects of a phenomenon described by data. More specifically, it concerns mutual trends between different variables like distance and gravity in physics, or inflation rate and interest rate in economics. Whenever we discover a relationship between different aspects of a phenomenon, this relationship can be represented by a monotonicity with respect to some specific measures of the considered aspects. So, in general, the monotonicity is a property translating in a formal language a primitive intuition of interaction between different concepts of our knowledge. As discovering is an inductive process, it is illuminating to remember the following Proposition 6.363 of Wittgenstein [8]: *"The process of induction is the process of assuming the simplest law that can be made to harmonize with our experience"*. We claim that this simplest law is just monotonicity and, therefore, each data analysis methodology can be seen as a specific way of dealing with monotonicity.

D. Ślęzak et al. (Eds.): RSFDGrC 2005, LNAI 3642, pp. 1–11, 2005.

Rough set philosophy is based on an approximation describing relationships between concepts. For example, in medical diagnosis the concept of "disease Y" can be represented in terms of concepts such as "low blood pressure and high temperature" or "muscle pain and headache". The classical rough approximation is based on a very coarse representation in the sense that, for each aspect characterizing concepts ("low blood pressure", "high temperature", "muscle pain", etc.), only its presence or its absence is considered relevant. In this case, the rough approximation involves a very primitive idea of monotonicity related to a scale with only two values: "presence" and "absence".

Monotonicity gains importance when a finer representation of the concepts is considered. A representation is finer when for each aspect characterizing concepts, not only its presence or its absence is taken into account, but also the *degree* of its presence or absence is considered relevant. Due to graduality, the idea of monotonicity can be exploited in the whole range of its potential. Graduality is typical for fuzzy set philosophy [9] and, therefore, a joint consideration of rough sets and fuzzy sets is worthwhile. In fact, rough sets and fuzzy sets capture the two basic complementary aspects of monotonicity: rough sets deal with relationships between different concepts and fuzzy sets deal with expression of different dimensions in which the concepts are considered. For this reason, many approaches have been proposed to combine fuzzy sets with rough sets (cf. [1]).

In this paper we show how the framework of DRSA can be extended to represent any relationship of monotonicity in reasoning about data. In this context, we envisage a knowledge representation model composed of a set of decision rules with the following syntax:

"If object y presents feature f_{i1} in degree at least h_{i1}, and feature f_{i2} in degree at least h_{i2}, and ..., and feature f_{im} in degree at least h_{im}, then object y belongs to set X in degree at least α".

We will show that the classical rough set approach [6,7] can be seen as a specific case of our general model. This is important for several reasons; in particular, this interpretation of DRSA gives an insight into fundamental properties of the classical rough set approach and permits to further generalize it.

The paper is organized as follows. Section 2 introduces rough approximation of a fuzzy set, based on monotonicity property. Section 3 compares monotonic rough approximation of a fuzzy set with the classical rough set; we prove that the latter is a special case of the former. Section 4 contains conclusions.

2   Monotonicity Property-Based Fuzzy Set Approximations

In this section we show how the dominance-based rough set approach can be used for rough approximation of fuzzy sets.

A *fuzzy information base* is the 3-tuple $\boldsymbol{B} = < U, F, \varphi >$, where U is a finite set of *objects* (universe), $F = \{f_1, f_2, ..., f_m\}$ is a finite set of *features*, and $\varphi : U \times F \to [0, 1]$ is a function such that $\varphi(x, f_h) \in [0, 1]$ expresses the credibility that object x has feature f_h. Each object x from U is described by a vector

$$Des_F(x)=[\varphi(x,\ f_1),\ \ldots,\ \varphi(x,\ f_m)]$$

called *description* of x in terms of the evaluations of the features from F; it represents the available information about x. Obviously, $x \in U$ can be described in terms of any non-empty subset $E \subseteq F$ and in this case we have

$$Des_E(x)=[\varphi(x,\ f_h),\ f_h \in F].$$

For any $E \subseteq F$, we can define the dominance relation D_E as follows: for any $x,y \in U$, x dominates y with respect to E (denotation xD_Ey) if for any $f_h \in E$

$$\varphi(x,f_h) \geq \varphi(y,f_h).$$

Given $E \subseteq F$ and $x \in U$, let

$$D_E^+(x) = \{y \in U : yD_Ex\}, \quad D_E^-(x) = \{y \in U : xD_Ey\}.$$

Let us consider a fuzzy set X in U, given its membership function $\mu_X : U \to [0,1]$. For each cutting level $\alpha \in [0,1]$ and for $* \in \{\geq,>\}$, we can define the E-lower and the E-upper approximation of $X^{*\alpha}=\{y \in U : \mu_X(y) * \alpha\}$ with respect to $E \subseteq F$ (denotation $\underline{E}(X^{*\alpha})$ and $\overline{E}(X^{*\alpha})$, respectively), as:

$$\underline{E}(X^{*\alpha}) = \{x \in U : D_E^+(x) \subseteq X^{*\alpha}\} \quad = \bigcup_{x \in U}\{D_E^+(x) : D_E^+(x) \subseteq X^{*\alpha}\},$$
$$\overline{E}(X^{*\alpha}) = \{x \in U : D_E^-(x) \cap X^{*\alpha} \neq \emptyset\} = \bigcup_{x \in U}\{D_E^+(x) : D_E^-(x) \cap X^{*\alpha} \neq \emptyset\}.$$

Analogously, for each cutting level $\alpha \in [0,1]$ and for $* \in \{\leq,<\}$, we define the E-lower and the E-upper approximation of $X^{*\alpha}=\{y \in U : \mu_X(y)*\alpha\}$, with respect to $E \subseteq F$ (denotation $\underline{E}(X^{*\alpha})$ and $\overline{E}(X^{*\alpha})$, respectively), as:

$$\underline{E}(X^{*\alpha}) = \{x \in U : D_E^-(x) \subseteq X^{*\alpha}\} \quad = \bigcup_{x \in U}\{D_E^-(x) : D_E^-(x) \subseteq X^{*\alpha}\},$$
$$\overline{E}(X^{*\alpha}) = \{x \in U : D_E^+(x) \cap X^{*\alpha} \neq \emptyset\} = \bigcup_{x \in U}\{D_E^-(x) : D_E^+(x) \cap X^{*\alpha} \neq \emptyset\}.$$

Let us remark that we can rewrite the rough approximations $\underline{E}(X^{\geq\alpha})$, $\overline{E}(X^{\geq\alpha})$, $\underline{E}(X^{\leq\alpha})$ and $\overline{E}(X^{\leq\alpha})$ as follows:

$$\underline{E}(X^{\geq\alpha}) = \{x \in U : \forall w \in U, wD_Ex \Rightarrow w \in X^{\geq\alpha}\},$$
$$\overline{E}(X^{\geq\alpha}) = \{x \in U : \exists w \in U \text{ such that } wD_Ex \text{ and } w \in X^{\geq\alpha}\},$$
$$\underline{E}(X^{\leq\alpha}) = \{x \in U : \forall w \in U, xD_Ew \Rightarrow w \in X^{\leq\alpha}\},$$
$$\overline{E}(X^{\leq\alpha}) = \{x \in U : \exists w \in U \text{ such that } xD_Ew \text{ and } w \in X^{\leq\alpha}\}.$$

Rough approximations $\underline{E}(X^{>\alpha})$, $\overline{E}(X^{>\alpha})$, $\underline{E}(X^{<\alpha})$ and $\overline{E}(X^{<\alpha})$ can be rewritten analogously by the simple substitution of "$\geq$" with "$>$" and "$\leq$ "with "$<$".

This reformulation of the rough approximations is concordant with the syntax of decision rules obtained in DRSA. For example $\underline{E}(X^{\geq\alpha})$ is concordant with decision rules of the type

"If object w presents feature f_{i1} in degree at least h_{i1}, and feature f_{i2} in degree at least h_{i2}, $\ldots$, and feature f_{im} in degree at least h_{im}, then object w belongs to set X in degree at least α", where $\{i1,\ldots,im\} = E$ and $h_{i1} = \varphi(x,f_{i1})$, $\ldots$, $h_{im} = \varphi(x,f_{im})$.

Let us remark that in the above approximations, even if $X^{\geq \alpha} = X^{\leq \alpha}$, their approximations are different due to the different directions of cutting the membership function of X. Of course, a similar remark holds also for $X^{<\alpha}$ and $X^{>\alpha}$. Considerations of the directions in the cuts $X^{\leq \alpha}$, $X^{<\alpha}$ and $X^{\geq \alpha}$, $X^{>\alpha}$ are important in the definition of the rough approximations of unions and intersection of cuts. Let us consider n fuzzy sets $X_1, \ldots, X_n$ in U such that $\mu_{X_1}(\cdot), \ldots, \mu_{X_n}(\cdot)$ are their membership functions.

Let us also consider n cutting levels $\alpha_1, \ldots, \alpha_n \in [0,1]$ and n "directions" $*_1, \ldots, *_n \in \{\geq, \leq, >, <\}$. In this way, we can define a cut for each considered fuzzy set obtaining $X_1^{*_1 \alpha_1}, \ldots, X_n^{*_n \alpha_n}$. For example, if $*_1 = "\geq"$, then $X_1^{*_1 \alpha_1} = X_1^{\geq \alpha_1}$; if $*_2 = "<"$, then $X_2^{*_2 \alpha_2} = X_1^{<\alpha_2}$, and so on. We define the rough approximations of the union $X_1^{*_1 \alpha_1} \cup \ldots \cup X_n^{*_n \alpha_n}$ and intersection $X_1^{*_1 \alpha_1} \cap \ldots \cap X_n^{*_n \alpha_n}$ with respect to $E \subseteq F$ as follows:

$$\underline{E}(\textstyle\bigcup_i X_i^{*_i \alpha_i}) = \{x \in U : D_E^+(x) \subseteq \bigcup_{i : *_i \in \{\geq, >\}} X_i^{*_i} \vee D_E^-(x) \subseteq \bigcup_{i : *_i \in \{\leq, <\}} X_i^{*_i}\},$$

$$\underline{E}(\textstyle\bigcap_i X_i^{*_i \alpha_i}) = \{x \in U : D_E^+(x) \subseteq \bigcap_{i : *_i \in \{\geq, >\}} X_i^{*_i} \wedge D_E^-(x) \subseteq \bigcap_{i : *_i \in \{\leq, <\}} X_i^{*_i}\},$$

$$\overline{E}(\textstyle\bigcup_i X_i^{*_i \alpha_i}) = \{x \in U : D_E^-(x) \cap \bigcup_{i : *_i \in \{\geq, >\}} X_i^{*_i} \neq \emptyset \vee D_E^+(x) \cap \bigcup_{i : *_i \in \{\leq, <\}} X_i^{*_i} \neq \emptyset\},$$

$$\overline{E}(\textstyle\bigcap_i X_i^{*_i \alpha_i}) = \{x \in U : D_E^-(x) \cap \bigcap_{i : *_i \in \{\geq, >\}} X_i^{*_i} \neq \emptyset \wedge D_E^+(x) \cap \bigcap_{i : *_i \in \{\leq, <\}} X_i^{*_i} \neq \emptyset\}.$$

We consider also fuzzy rough approximations $\underline{X}_E^{\uparrow}$, $\underline{X}_E^{\downarrow}$, $\overline{X}_E^{\uparrow}$, $\overline{X}_E^{\downarrow}$, which are fuzzy sets with memberships defined, respectively, as follows: for any $y \in U$,

$$\mu_{\underline{X}_E^{\uparrow}}(y) = max\{\alpha \in [0,1] : y \in \underline{E}(X^{\geq \alpha})\},$$
$$\mu_{\underline{X}_E^{\downarrow}}(y) = min\{\alpha \in [0,1] : y \in \underline{E}(X^{\leq \alpha})\},$$
$$\mu_{\overline{X}_E^{\uparrow}}(y) = max\{\alpha \in [0,1] : y \in \overline{E}(X^{\geq \alpha})\},$$
$$\mu_{\overline{X}_E^{\downarrow}}(y) = min\{\alpha \in [0,1] : y \in \overline{E}(X^{\leq \alpha})\}.$$

$\mu_{\underline{X}_E^{\uparrow}}(y)$ is defined as the upward lower fuzzy rough approximation of X with respect to E and can be interpreted in the following way. For any $\alpha, \beta \in [0,1]$ we have that $\alpha < \beta$ implies $X^{\geq \alpha} \supseteq X^{\geq \beta}$. Therefore, the greater the cutting level α, the smaller $X^{\geq \alpha}$ and, consequently, the smaller also its lower approximation $\underline{E}(X^{\geq \alpha})$. Thus, for each $y \in U$ and for each fuzzy set X there is a threshold $k(y)$, $0 \leq k(y) \leq \mu_X(y)$, such that $y \in \underline{E}(X^{\geq \alpha})$ if $\alpha \leq k(y)$, and $y \notin \underline{E}(X^{\geq \alpha})$ if $\alpha > k(y)$. Since $k(y) = \mu_{\underline{X}_E^{\uparrow}}(y)$, this explains the interest of $\mu_{\underline{X}_E^{\uparrow}}(y)$. Analogous interpretation holds for $\mu_{\overline{X}_E^{\uparrow}}(y)$ defined as the upward upper fuzzy rough approximation of X with respect to E.

$\mu_{\underline{X}_E^{\downarrow}}(y)$ is defined as the downward lower fuzzy rough approximation of X with respect to E and can be interpreted as follows. For any $\alpha, \beta \in [0,1]$ we have that $\alpha < \beta$ implies $X^{\leq \alpha} \subseteq X^{\leq \beta}$. Therefore, the greater the cutting level α, the greater $X^{\leq \alpha}$ and, consequently, its lower approximation $\underline{E}(X^{\geq \alpha})$. Thus, for each $y \in U$ and for each fuzzy set X there is a threshold $h(y)$, $\mu_X(y) \leq h(y) \leq 1$, such that $y \in \underline{E}(X^{\leq \alpha})$ if $\alpha \geq h(y)$, and $y \notin \underline{E}(X^{\leq \alpha})$ if $\alpha < h(y)$. We have that $h(y) = \mu_{\underline{X}_E^{\downarrow}}(y)$. Analogous interpretation holds for $\mu_{\overline{X}_E^{\downarrow}}(y)$ defined as the upward upper fuzzy rough approximation of X with respect to E.

Proposition 1. *For any $y \in U$,*

$$\mu_{\underline{X}_E^{\uparrow}}(y) = min\{\mu_X(z) : z \in D_E^+(y)\}, \qquad \mu_{\overline{X}_E^{\uparrow}}(y) = max\{\mu_X(z) : z \in D_E^-(y)\},$$
$$\mu_{\underline{X}_E^{\downarrow}}(y) = max\{\mu_X(z) : z \in D_E^-(y)\}, \qquad \mu_{\overline{X}_E^{\downarrow}}(y) = min\{\mu_X(z) : z \in D_E^+(y)\}. \diamond$$

Proposition 1 gives alternative formulation of fuzzy rough approximation which has been introduced and investigated by Greco, Inuiguchi and Słowiński [2] .

We consider, moreover, the fuzzy rough "approximations of approximations" defined as second order fuzzy rough approximations. Let us take the fuzzy rough approximation $\underline{X}_E^{\uparrow}$ with its membership function $\mu_{\underline{X}_E^{\uparrow}}(y)$. For each cutting level $\alpha \in [0,1]$ and $E \subseteq F$, we define the E-lower and E-upper approximation of

$$\underline{X}_E^{\uparrow \geq \alpha} = \{y \in U : \mu_{\underline{X}_E^{\uparrow}}(y) \geq \alpha\} \quad \text{and} \quad \overline{X}_E^{\uparrow \geq \alpha} = \{y \in U : \mu_{\overline{X}_E^{\uparrow}}(y) \geq \alpha\}$$

as: $\quad \underline{E}(\underline{X}_E^{\uparrow \geq \alpha}) = \{x \in U : D_E^+(x) \subseteq \underline{X}_E^{\uparrow \geq \alpha}\} = \bigcup_{x \in U} \{D_E^+(x) : D_E^+(x) \subseteq \underline{X}_E^{\uparrow \geq \alpha}\},$

$$\overline{E}(\underline{X}_E^{\uparrow \geq \alpha}) = \{x \in U : D_E^-(x) \cap \underline{X}_E^{\uparrow \geq \alpha} \neq \emptyset\} = \bigcup_{x \in U} \{D_E^+(x) : D_E^-(x) \cap \underline{X}_E^{\uparrow \geq \alpha} \neq \emptyset\},$$

$$\underline{E}(\overline{X}_E^{\uparrow \geq \alpha}) = \{x \in U : D_E^+(x) \subseteq \overline{X}_E^{\uparrow \geq \alpha}\} = \bigcup_{x \in U} \{D_E^+(x) : D_E^+(x) \subseteq \overline{X}_E^{\uparrow \geq \alpha}\},$$

$$\overline{E}(\overline{X}_E^{\uparrow \geq \alpha}) = \{x \in U : D_E^-(x) \cap \overline{X}_E^{\uparrow \geq \alpha} \neq \emptyset\} = \bigcup_{x \in U} \{D_E^+(x) : D_E^-(x) \cap \overline{X}_E^{\uparrow \geq \alpha} \neq \emptyset\}.$$

Now, we define the second order fuzzy rough approximations (fuzzy rough "approximations of approximations") related to the above sets. The upward fuzzy rough *lower / upper* approximation of the upward *lower / upper* approximation of fuzzy set X is defined as

lower ... of ... lower $\quad \mu_{(\underline{X}_E^{\uparrow})^{\uparrow}}(y) = max\{\alpha \in [0,1] : y \in \underline{E}(\underline{X}_E^{\uparrow \geq \alpha})\},$

upper ... of ... lower $\quad \mu_{\overline{(\underline{X}_E^{\uparrow})^{\uparrow}}}(y) = max\{\alpha \in [0,1] : y \in \overline{E}(\underline{X}_E^{\uparrow \geq \alpha})\},$

lower ... of ... upper $\quad \mu_{(\overline{X}_E^{\uparrow})^{\uparrow}}(y) = max\{\alpha \in [0,1] : y \in \underline{E}(\overline{X}_E^{\uparrow \geq \alpha})\},$

upper ... of ... upper $\quad \mu_{\overline{(\overline{X}_E^{\uparrow})^{\uparrow}}}(y) = max\{\alpha \in [0,1] : y \in \overline{E}(\overline{X}_E^{\uparrow \geq \alpha})\}.$

The above second order fuzzy rough approximations are "upward" with respect to the first order approximations of upward cuts $X^{\geq \alpha}$, and the second order approximations of upward cuts $\underline{X}_E^{\uparrow \geq \alpha}$. Analogous definitions can be given for the second order fuzzy rough approximations being "downward" (i.e. based on downward cuts $X^{\leq \alpha}$ and $\underline{X}_E^{\downarrow \leq \alpha}$). For each cutting level $\alpha \in [0,1]$ and for each $E \subseteq F$, we can define the E-lower and the E-upper approximation of

$$\underline{X}_E^{\downarrow \leq \alpha} = \{y \in U : \mu_{\underline{X}_E^{\downarrow}}(y) \leq \alpha\} \quad \text{and} \quad \overline{X}_E^{\downarrow \leq \alpha} = \{y \in U : \mu_{\overline{X}_E^{\downarrow}}(y) \leq \alpha\}$$

as: $\underline{E}(\underline{X}_E^{\downarrow \le \alpha}) = \{x \in U : D_E^-(x) \subseteq \underline{X}_E^{\downarrow \le \alpha}\} = \bigcup_{x \in U} \{D_E^-(x) : D_E^-(x) \subseteq \underline{X}_E^{\downarrow \le \alpha}\},$

$\overline{E}(\underline{X}_E^{\downarrow \le \alpha}) = \{x \in U : D_E^-(x) \cap \underline{X}_E^{\downarrow \le \alpha} \neq \emptyset\} = \bigcup_{x \in U} \{D_E^-(x) : D_E^+(x) \cap \underline{X}_E^{\downarrow \le \alpha} \neq \emptyset\},$

$\underline{E}(\overline{X}_E^{\downarrow \le \alpha}) = \{x \in U : D_E^-(x) \subseteq \overline{X}_E^{\downarrow \le \alpha}\} = \bigcup_{x \in U} \{D_E^-(x) : D_E^-(x) \subseteq \overline{X}_E^{\downarrow \le \alpha}\},$

$\overline{E}(\overline{X}_E^{\downarrow \le \alpha}) = \{x \in U : D_E^-(x) \cap \overline{X}_E^{\downarrow \le \alpha} \neq \emptyset\} = \bigcup_{x \in U} \{D_E^-(x) : D_E^+(x) \cap \overline{X}_E^{\downarrow \le \alpha} \neq \emptyset\}.$

The downward fuzzy rough *lower / upper* approximation of the downward *lower / upper* approximation of fuzzy set X is defined as

lower ... of ... lower $\mu_{(\underline{X}_E^\downarrow)^\downarrow}(y) = min\{\alpha \in [0,1] : y \in \underline{E}(\underline{X}_E^{\downarrow \le \alpha})\},$

upper ... of ... lower $\mu_{\overline{(\underline{X}_E^\downarrow)^\downarrow}}(y) = min\{\alpha \in [0,1] : y \in \overline{E}(\underline{X}_E^{\downarrow \le \alpha})\},$

lower ... of ... upper $\mu_{(\overline{X}_E^\downarrow)^\downarrow}(y) = min\{\alpha \in [0,1] : y \in \underline{E}(\overline{X}_E^{\downarrow \le \alpha})\},$

upper ... of ... upper $\mu_{\overline{(\overline{X}_E^\downarrow)^\downarrow}}(y) = min\{\alpha \in [0,1] : y \in \overline{E}(\overline{X}_E^{\downarrow \le \alpha})\}.$

Let us also remark that "upwardness" or "downwardness" of the second order approximation is independent of "upwardness" or "downwardness" of the first order fuzzy rough approximation. Thus, for example, the downward fuzzy rough lower approximation of the upward upper approximation of X is defined as

$$\mu_{\underline{(\overline{X}_E^\uparrow)^\downarrow}}(y) = min\{\alpha \in [0,1] : y \in \underline{E}(\overline{X}_E^{\uparrow \le \alpha})\}.$$

The third, fourth and further order fuzzy rough approximations can be defined analogously.

The following theorem states some properties of the dominance-based rough and fuzzy rough approximations.

Theorem 1. *Given a fuzzy information base* $\mathbf{B} =< U, F, \varphi >$ *and a fuzzy set* X *in* U *with membership function* $\mu_X(\cdot)$, *the following properties hold:*

1. *For any* $0 \le \alpha \le 1$ *and for any* $E \subseteq F$,

$$\underline{E}(X^{\ge \alpha}) \subseteq X^{\ge \alpha} \subseteq \overline{E}(X^{\ge \alpha}), \quad \underline{E}(X^{\le \alpha}) \subseteq X^{\le \alpha} \subseteq \overline{E}(X^{\le \alpha}),$$
$$\underline{E}(X^{< \alpha}) \subseteq X^{< \alpha} \subseteq \overline{E}(X^{< \alpha}), \quad \underline{E}(X^{> \alpha}) \subseteq X^{> \alpha} \subseteq \overline{E}(X^{> \alpha}).$$

2. *For any* $0 \le \alpha \le 1$ *and for any* $E \subseteq F$,

$$\underline{E}(X^{\ge \alpha}) = U - \overline{E}(X^{< \alpha}), \quad \underline{E}(X^{\le \alpha}) = U - \overline{E}(X^{> \alpha}),$$
$$\underline{E}(X^{< \alpha}) = U - \overline{E}(X^{\ge \alpha}), \quad \underline{E}(X^{> \alpha}) = U - \overline{E}(X^{\le \alpha}).$$

3. *For any* $0 \le \alpha \le \beta \le 1$ *and for any* $E \subseteq F$,

$$\underline{E}(X^{\ge \beta}) \subseteq \underline{E}(X^{\ge \alpha}), \quad \underline{E}(X^{> \beta}) \subseteq \underline{E}(X^{> \alpha}),$$
$$\underline{E}(X^{\le \alpha}) \subseteq \underline{E}(X^{\le \beta}), \quad \underline{E}(X^{< \alpha}) \subseteq \underline{E}(X^{< \beta}),$$
$$\overline{E}(X^{\ge \beta}) \subseteq \overline{E}(X^{\ge \alpha}), \quad \overline{E}(X^{> \beta}) \subseteq \overline{E}(X^{> \alpha}),$$
$$\overline{E}(X^{\le \alpha}) \subseteq \overline{E}(X^{\le \beta}), \quad \overline{E}(X^{< \alpha}) \subseteq \overline{E}(X^{< \beta}).$$

4. For any $E \subseteq F$,

$$\underline{E}(X^{>1}) = \overline{E}(X^{>1}) = \underline{E}(X^{<0}) = \overline{E}(X^{<0}) = \emptyset,$$
$$\underline{E}(X^{\geq 0}) = \overline{E}(X^{\geq 0}) = \underline{E}(X^{\leq 1}) = \overline{E}(X^{\leq 1}) = U.$$

5. For any $0 \leq \alpha \leq 1$ and for any $E \subseteq F$,

$$\underline{E}(X^{>\alpha}) \subseteq \underline{E}(X^{\geq \alpha}), \quad \overline{E}(X^{>\alpha}) \subseteq \overline{E}(X^{\geq \alpha}),$$
$$\underline{E}(X^{<\alpha}) \subseteq \underline{E}(X^{\leq \alpha}), \quad \overline{E}(X^{<\alpha}) \subseteq \overline{E}(X^{\leq \alpha}).$$

6. For any $x, y \in U$, for any $0 \leq \alpha \leq 1$ and for any $E \subseteq F$,

   (a) $[y D_E x$ and $x \in \underline{E}(X^{\geq \alpha})] \Rightarrow y \in \underline{E}(X^{\geq \alpha})$,

   (b) $[y D_E x$ and $x \in \underline{E}(X^{>\alpha})] \Rightarrow y \in \underline{E}(X^{>\alpha})$,

   (c) $[y D_E x$ and $x \in \overline{E}(X^{\geq \alpha})] \Rightarrow y \in \overline{E}(X^{\geq \alpha})$,

   (d) $[y D_E x$ and $x \in \overline{E}(X^{>\alpha})] \Rightarrow y \in \overline{E}(X^{>\alpha})$,

   (e) $[x D_E y$ and $x \in \underline{E}(X^{\leq \alpha})] \Rightarrow y \in \underline{E}(X^{\leq \alpha})$,

   (f) $[x D_E y$ and $x \in \underline{E}(X^{<\alpha})] \Rightarrow y \in \underline{E}(X^{<\alpha})$,

   (g) $[x D_E y$ and $x \in \overline{E}(X^{\leq \alpha})] \Rightarrow y \in \overline{E}(X^{\leq \alpha})$,

   (h) $[x D_E y$ and $x \in \overline{E}(X^{<\alpha})] \Rightarrow y \in \overline{E}(X^{<\alpha})$.

7. For any $E_1 \subseteq E_2 \subseteq F$ and for any $0 \leq \alpha \leq 1$,

$$\underline{E}_1(X^{\leq \alpha}) \subseteq \underline{E}_2(X^{\leq \alpha}), \quad \underline{E}_1(X^{<\alpha}) \subseteq \underline{E}_2(X^{<\alpha}),$$
$$\underline{E}_1(X^{\geq \alpha}) \subseteq \underline{E}_2(X^{\geq \alpha}), \quad \underline{E}_1(X^{>\alpha}) \subseteq \underline{E}_2(X^{>\alpha}),$$
$$\overline{E}_1(X^{\leq \alpha}) \supseteq \overline{E}_2(X^{\leq \alpha}), \quad \overline{E}_1(X^{<\alpha}) \supseteq \overline{E}_2(X^{<\alpha}),$$
$$\overline{E}_1(X^{\geq \alpha}) \supseteq \overline{E}_2(X^{\geq \alpha}), \quad \overline{E}_1(X^{>\alpha}) \supseteq \overline{E}_2(X^{>\alpha}).$$

8. Given n fuzzy sets $X_1, \ldots, X_n$ in U, n levels $\alpha_1, \ldots, \alpha_n \in [0,1]$, as well as n "directions" $*_1, \ldots, *_n \in \{\geq, \leq, >, <\}$, for any $E \subseteq F$,

$$\underline{E}(X_1^{*_1 \alpha_1} \cap \ldots \cap X_n^{*_n \alpha_n}) = \bigcap_{i=1}^{n} \underline{E}(X_i^{*_i \alpha_i}),$$
$$\overline{E}(X_1^{*_1 \alpha_1} \cup \ldots \cup X_n^{*_n \alpha_n}) = \bigcup_{i=1}^{n} \overline{E}(X_i^{*_i \alpha_i}),$$
$$\underline{E}(X_1^{*_1 \alpha_1} \cup \ldots \cup X_n^{*_n \alpha_n}) \supseteq \bigcup_{i=1}^{n} \underline{E}(X_i^{*_i \alpha_i}),$$
$$\overline{E}(X_1^{*_1 \alpha_1} \cap \ldots \cap X_n^{*_n \alpha_n}) \subseteq \bigcap_{i=1}^{n} \overline{E}(X_i^{*_i \alpha_i}).$$

9. For any $E \subseteq F$ and for any $\alpha \in [0,1]$,

   (a) $\underline{E}(X_E^{\uparrow \geq \alpha}) = \overline{E}(X_E^{\uparrow \geq \alpha}) = \underline{E}(\overline{X}_E^{\downarrow \geq \alpha}) = \overline{E}(\overline{X}_E^{\downarrow \geq \alpha}) = \underline{E}(X^{\geq \alpha})$,

   (b) $\underline{E}(X_E^{\uparrow > \alpha}) = \overline{E}(X_E^{\uparrow > \alpha}) = \underline{E}(\overline{X}_E^{\downarrow > \alpha}) = \overline{E}(\overline{X}_E^{\downarrow > \alpha}) = \underline{E}(X^{> \alpha})$,

   (c) $\underline{E}(X_E^{\downarrow \leq \alpha}) = \overline{E}(X_E^{\downarrow \leq \alpha}) = \underline{E}(\overline{X}_E^{\uparrow \leq \alpha}) = \overline{E}(\overline{X}_E^{\uparrow \leq \alpha}) = \underline{E}(X^{\leq \alpha})$,

   (d) $\underline{E}(X_E^{\downarrow < \alpha}) = \overline{E}(X_E^{\downarrow < \alpha}) = \underline{E}(\overline{X}_E^{\uparrow < \alpha}) = \overline{E}(\overline{X}_E^{\uparrow < \alpha}) = \underline{E}(X^{< \alpha})$,

   (e) $\overline{E}(\overline{X}_E^{\uparrow \geq \alpha}) = \underline{E}(\overline{X}_E^{\uparrow \geq \alpha}) = \overline{E}(\underline{X}_E^{\downarrow \geq \alpha}) = \underline{E}(\underline{X}_E^{\downarrow \geq \alpha}) = \overline{E}(X^{\geq \alpha})$,

   (f) $\overline{E}(\overline{X}_E^{\uparrow > \alpha}) = \underline{E}(\overline{X}_E^{\uparrow > \alpha}) = \overline{E}(\underline{X}_E^{\downarrow > \alpha}) = \underline{E}(\underline{X}_E^{\downarrow > \alpha}) = \overline{E}(X^{> \alpha})$,

   (g) $\overline{E}(\overline{X}_E^{\downarrow \leq \alpha}) = \underline{E}(\overline{X}_E^{\downarrow \leq \alpha}) = \overline{E}(\underline{X}_E^{\uparrow \leq \alpha}) = \underline{E}(\underline{X}_E^{\uparrow \leq \alpha}) = \overline{E}(X^{\leq \alpha})$,

   (h) $\overline{E}(\overline{X}_E^{\downarrow < \alpha}) = \underline{E}(\overline{X}_E^{\downarrow < \alpha}) = \overline{E}(\underline{X}_E^{\uparrow < \alpha}) = \underline{E}(\underline{X}_E^{\uparrow < \alpha}) = \overline{E}(X^{< \alpha})$.

10. For any $y \in U$ and for any $E \subseteq F$,

$$\mu_{\underline{X}_E^\uparrow}(y) \le \mu_X(y) \le \mu_{\overline{X}_E^\uparrow}(y), \quad \mu_{\overline{X}_E^\downarrow}(y) \le \mu_X(y) \le \mu_{\underline{X}_E^\downarrow}(y).$$

11. For any $y \in U$ and for any $E \subseteq F$,

$$\mu_{\underline{X}_E^\uparrow}(y) = \mu_{\overline{X}_E^\downarrow}(y), \quad \mu_{\underline{X}_E^\downarrow}(y) = \mu_{\overline{X}_E^\uparrow}(y).$$

12. For any $\alpha \in [0,1]$ and for any $E \subseteq F$,

$$\alpha \le \mu_{\underline{X}_E^\uparrow}(y) \Rightarrow y \in \underline{E}(X^{\ge\alpha}), \quad \alpha \ge \mu_{\underline{X}_E^\downarrow}(y) \Rightarrow y \in \underline{E}(X^{\le\alpha})$$
$$\alpha \le \mu_{\overline{X}_E^\uparrow}(y) \Rightarrow y \in \overline{E}(X^{\ge\alpha}), \quad \alpha \ge \mu_{\overline{X}_E^\downarrow}(y) \Rightarrow y \in \overline{E}(X^{\le\alpha})$$

13. For any $x, y \in U$ and for any $E \subseteq F$,

$$yD_Ex \Rightarrow \mu_{\underline{X}_E^\uparrow}(y) \ge \mu_{\underline{X}_E^\uparrow}(x), \quad yD_Ex \Rightarrow \mu_{\overline{X}_E^\uparrow}(y) \ge \mu_{\overline{X}_E^\uparrow}(x),$$
$$yD_Ex \Rightarrow \mu_{\underline{X}_E^\downarrow}(y) \ge \mu_{\underline{X}_E^\downarrow}(x), \quad yD_Ex \Rightarrow \mu_{\overline{X}_E^\downarrow}(y) \ge \mu_{\overline{X}_E^\downarrow}(x).$$

14. For any $E_1 \subseteq E_2 \subseteq F$ and for any $y \in U$,

$$\mu_{\underline{X}_{E_1}^\uparrow}(y) \le \mu_{\underline{X}_{E_2}^\uparrow}(y), \quad \mu_{\underline{X}_{E_1}^\downarrow}(y) \ge \mu_{\underline{X}_{E_2}^\downarrow}(y),$$
$$\mu_{\overline{X}_{E_1}^\uparrow}(y) \ge \mu_{\overline{X}_{E_2}^\uparrow}(y), \quad \mu_{\overline{X}_{E_1}^\downarrow}(y) \le \mu_{\overline{X}_{E_2}^\downarrow}(y).$$

15. For any pair of fuzzy sets X and Y in U with membership function $\mu_X(\cdot)$ and $\mu_Y(\cdot)$, such that for any $w \in U$, $\mu_{X\cap Y}(w) = min(\mu_X(w), \mu_Y(w))$ and $\mu_{X\cup Y}(w) = max(\mu_X(w), \mu_Y(w))$, for any $E \subseteq F$ we have,

(a) $\mu_{\underline{X\cap Y}_E^\uparrow}(w) = min(\mu_{\underline{X}_E^\uparrow}(w), \mu_{\underline{Y}_E^\uparrow}(w))$,

(b) $\mu_{\underline{X\cap Y}_E^\downarrow}(w) \le min(\mu_{\underline{X}_E^\downarrow}(w), \mu_{\underline{Y}_E^\downarrow}(w))$,

(c) $\mu_{\overline{X\cup Y}_E^\uparrow}(w) = max(\mu_{\overline{X}_E^\uparrow}(w), \mu_{\overline{Y}_E^\uparrow}(w))$,

(d) $\mu_{\overline{X\cup Y}_E^\downarrow}(w) \ge max(\mu_{\overline{X}_E^\downarrow}(w), \mu_{\overline{Y}_E^\downarrow}(w))$,

(e) $\mu_{\underline{X\cup Y}_E^\uparrow}(w) \ge max(\mu_{\underline{X}_E^\uparrow}(w), \mu_{\underline{Y}_E^\uparrow}(w))$,

(f) $\mu_{\underline{X\cup Y}_E^\downarrow}(w) = max(\mu_{\underline{X}_E^\downarrow}(w), \mu_{\underline{Y}_E^\downarrow}(w))$,

(g) $\mu_{\overline{X\cap Y}_E^\uparrow}(w) \le min(\mu_{\overline{X}_E^\uparrow}(w), \mu_{\overline{Y}_E^\uparrow}(w))$,

(h) $\mu_{\overline{X\cap Y}_E^\downarrow}(w) = min(\mu_{\overline{X}_E^\downarrow}(w), \mu_{\overline{Y}_E^\downarrow}(w))$.

16. For any $E \subseteq F$ and for any $y \in U$ we have,

(a) $\mu_{\underline{(\underline{X}_E^\uparrow)}^\uparrow}(y) = \mu_{\overline{(\underline{X}_E^\uparrow)}^\uparrow}(y) = \mu_{\underline{(\underline{X}_E^\uparrow)}^\downarrow}(y) = \mu_{\overline{(\underline{X}_E^\uparrow)}^\downarrow}(y) = \mu_{\underline{X}_E^\uparrow}(y)$,

(b) $\mu_{\underline{(\underline{X}_E^\downarrow)}^\downarrow}(y) = \mu_{\overline{(\underline{X}_E^\downarrow)}^\downarrow}(y) = \mu_{\underline{(\underline{X}_E^\downarrow)}^\uparrow}(y) = \mu_{\overline{(\underline{X}_E^\downarrow)}^\uparrow}(y) = \mu_{\underline{X}_E^\downarrow}(y)$,

(c) $\mu_{\overline{(\overline{X}_E^\uparrow)}^\uparrow}(y) = \mu_{\underline{(\overline{X}_E^\uparrow)}^\uparrow}(y) = \mu_{\overline{(\overline{X}_E^\uparrow)}^\downarrow}(y) = \mu_{\underline{(\overline{X}_E^\uparrow)}^\downarrow}(y) = \mu_{\overline{X}_E^\uparrow}(w)$,

(d) $\mu_{\overline{(\overline{X}_E^\downarrow)}^\downarrow}(y) = \mu_{\underline{(\overline{X}_E^\downarrow)}^\downarrow}(y) = \mu_{\overline{(\overline{X}_E^\downarrow)}^\uparrow}(y) = \mu_{\underline{(\overline{X}_E^\downarrow)}^\uparrow}(y) = \mu_{\overline{X}_E^\downarrow}(w)$. $\lozenge$

Most of the results given in Theorem 1 correspond to well known properties of classical rough sets. For example,

- property 1) says that the set we are approximating includes its lower approximation and is included in its upper approximation;
- property 10) has an analogous interpretation with respect to fuzzy rough approximations $\underline{X}_E^{\uparrow}$, $\underline{X}_E^{\downarrow}$, $\overline{X}_E^{\uparrow}$ and $\overline{X}_E^{\downarrow}$.

3 Monotonic Rough Approximations of Fuzzy/Rough Sets

In this section we show that the classical rough approximation is a specific case of the rough approximation of a fuzzy set presented in the previous section.

Let us remember that in classical rough set approach [6,7], the original information is expressed by means of an *information table*, that is the 4-tuple $S=<U,Q,V,f>$, where U is a finite set of *objects* (universe), $Q=\{q_1,q_2,...,q_m\}$ is a finite set of *attributes*, V_q is the domain of attribute q, $V = \bigcup_{q\in Q} V_q$ and $f : U \times Q \to V$ is a total function such that $f(x,q) \in V_q$ for each $q \in Q$, $x \in U$, called *information function*.

Therefore, each object x from U is described by a vector $Des_Q(x) = [f(x,q_1), f(x,q_2), ..., f(x,q_m)]$, called *description* of x in terms of the evaluations of the attributes from Q; it represents the available information about x. Obviously, $x \in U$ can be described in terms of any non-empty subset $P \subseteq Q$.

To every (non-empty) subset of attributes P is associated an *indiscernibility relation* on U, denoted by I_P:

$$I_P = \{(x,y) \in U \times U: f(x,q) = f(y,q), \forall q \in P\}.$$

If $(x,y) \in I_P$, it is said that the objects x and y are P-indiscernible. Clearly, the indiscernibility relation thus defined is an equivalence relation (reflexive, symmetric and transitive). The family of all the equivalence classes of the relation I_P is denoted by $U|I_P$, and the equivalence class containing an element $x \in U$ is denoted by $I_P(x)$, i.e.

$$I_P(x) = \{y \in U: f(y,q) = f(y,q), \forall q \in P\}.$$

The equivalence classes of the relation I_P are called P-*elementary sets.*

Let S be an information table, X a non-empty subset of U and $\emptyset \neq P \subseteq Q$. The P-*lower approximation* and the P-*upper approximation* of X in S are defined, respectively, by:

$$\underline{P}(X) = \{x \in U : I_P(x) \subseteq X\}, \quad \overline{P}(X) = \{x \in U : I_P(x) \cap X \neq \emptyset\}.$$

The elements of $\underline{P}(X)$ are all and only those objects $x \in U$ which belong to the equivalence classes generated by the indiscernibility relation I_P, *contained* in X; the elements of $\overline{P}(X)$ are all and only those objects $x \in U$ which belong to the equivalence classes generated by the indiscernibility relation I_P, *containing at least one* object x belonging to X. In other words, $\underline{P}(X)$ is the largest union of the P-elementary sets included in X, while $\overline{P}(X)$ is the smallest union of the P-elementary sets containing X.

Now, we prove that any information table can be expressed in terms of a specific type of information base. An *information base* is called *Boolean* if $\varphi : U \times F \rightarrow \{0,1\}$. A partition $\boldsymbol{F}=\{F_1,\ldots,F_r\}$ of F, with $card(F_k) \geq 2$ for all $k=1, \ldots, r$, is called *canonical* if, for each $x \in U$ and for each $F_k \subseteq F$, $k=1,\ldots,r$, there exists only one $f_j \in F_k$ for which $\varphi(x,f_j)=1$ (and thus, for all $f_i \in F_k\text{-}\{f_j\}$, $\varphi(x, f_i)=0$). The condition $card(F_k) \geq 2$ for all $k=1, \ldots, r$, is necessary because, otherwise, we would have at least one element of the partition $F_k=\{f'\}$ such that $\varphi(x,f')=1$ for all $x \in U$, and this would mean that feature f' gives no information and can be removed. Now, we can see that any *information table* $\boldsymbol{S}=< U,Q,V,f >$ can be interpreted as a Boolean information base $\boldsymbol{B}=< U, F, \varphi >$ such that to each $v \in V_q$ corresponds one feature $f_{qv} \in F$ for which $\varphi(x,f_{qv})=1$ if $f(x,q) = v$, and $\varphi(x,f_{qv})=0$ otherwise. Let us remark that $\boldsymbol{F}=\{F_1,\ldots,F_m\}$, with $F_q = \{f_{qv}, v \in V_q\}$, $q \in Q$, is a canonical partition of F. In other words, this means that each information system can be viewed as an information base where each possible value $v \in V$ of attribute q corresponds to a specific feature f_{qv}. Let us remark that the vice versa is not true, i.e. there are Boolean information bases which cannot be transformed into information systems because their set of attributes does not admit any canonical partition.

The above considerations say that the rough approximation in the context of a Boolean information base is more general than the rough approximation in the context of an information system. This means, of course, that the rough approximation in the context of a fuzzy information system is still more general.

The following theorem states what are the relationships between the rough approximations in the context of a fuzzy information base and the classical definition of rough approximations in the context of an information system.

Theorem 2. *Consider an information system and the corresponding Boolean information base; for each $P \subseteq Q$ let E^P be the set of all the features corresponding to values v of attributes in P. Let X be a crisp set in U, i.e. $\mu_X : U \rightarrow \{0,1\}$ and, therefore, for any $y \in U$, $\mu_X(y)=1$ or $\mu_X(y)=0$. Then, we have:*

$$\underline{E}^P(X^{\geq 1}) = \underline{P}(X^{\geq 1}), \qquad \overline{E^P}(X^{\geq 1}) = \overline{P}(X^{\geq 1}),$$
$$\underline{E}^P(X^{\leq 0}) = \underline{P}(U - X^{\geq 1}), \qquad \overline{E^P}(X^{\leq 0}) = \overline{P}(U - X^{\geq 1}). \quad \Diamond$$

The above theorem proves that the rough approximation of a crisp set X within a Boolean information base admitting a canonical partition is equivalent to the classical rough approximation of set X within the corresponding information system. Therefore, the classical rough approximation is a particular case of the rough approximation within a fuzzy information system.

4   Conclusions

We presented a general model of rough approximations based on ordinal properties of membership functions of fuzzy sets. In this very general framework, the classical rough set theory can be considered as a special case. This direction of research seems very promising and we envisage developments with respect to three following issues:

1) algebraic properties of the proposed rough approximations;
2) generalizations of other rough set fundamental concepts such as reducts, core, and decision rules;
3) application of the absolute and relative rough membership concept (see [5]) in a generalized variable precision model based on the proposed rough approximations.

Acknowledgements

The research of the first two authors has been supported by the Italian Ministry of Education, University and Scientific Research (MIUR). The third author wishes to acknowledge financial support from the State Committee for Scientific Research (KBN).

References

1. Dubois, D., Prade, H., Putting rough sets and fuzzy sets together, in: R. Słowiński (ed.), *Intelligent Decision Support: Handbook of Applications and Advances of the Sets Theory*, Kluwer, Dordrecht, 1992, pp. 203-232
2. Greco, S., Inuiguchi, M., Słowiński, R., Fuzzy rough sets and multiple-premise gradual decision rules, *International Journal of Approximate Reasoning* (2005) to appear
3. Greco, S., Matarazzo, B., Słowiński R., Rough sets theory for multicriteria decision analysis, *European Journal of Operational Research*, 129 (2001) 1-47
4. Greco, S., Matarazzo, B., Słowiński R., Decision rule approach, in: J. Figueira, S. Greco, M. Erghott (eds.) *Multiple Criteria Decision Analysis: State of the Art Surveys*, Springer, Berlin, 2005, pp. 507-563
5. Greco, S., Matarazzo, B., Słowiński R., Rough Membership and Bayesian Confirmation Measures for Parametrized Rough Sets, in Proc. of RSFDGrC 2005, LNAI 3641, Springer (2005) 312-322
6. Pawlak, Z., Rough Sets, *International Journal of Computer and Information Sciences*, 11 (1982) 341-356
7. Pawlak, Z., *Rough Sets*, Kluwer, Dordrecht, 1991
8. Wittgenstein, L., *Tractatus Logico-Philosophicus*, Routledge and Kegan Paul, London, 1922; fifth impression 1951
9. Zadeh, L., Fuzzy Set, *Information Control*, 8 (1965) 338-353

Approximate Boolean Reasoning Approach to Rough Sets and Data Mining

Hung Son Nguyen

Institute of Mathematics, Warsaw University,
Banacha 2, 02-097 Warsaw, Poland
son@mimuw.edu.pl

Abstract. Many problems in rough set theory have been successfully solved by boolean reasoning (BR) approach. The disadvantage of this elegant methodology is based on its high space and time complexity. In this paper we present a modified BR approach that can overcome those difficulties. This methodology is called the approximate boolean reasoning (ABR) approach. We summarize some most recent applications of ABR approach in development of new efficient algorithms in rough sets and data mining.

Keywords: Rough sets, data mining, boolean reasoning.

1 Introduction

Concept approximation problem is one of most important issues in machine learning and data mining. Classification, clustering, association analysis or regression are examples of well known problems in data mining that can be formulated as concept approximation problems. A great effort of many researchers has been done to design newer, faster and more efficient methods for solving concept approximation problem.

Rough set theory has been introduced by [14] as a tool for concept approximation under uncertainty. The idea is to approximate the concept by two descriptive sets called *lower and upper approximations*. The lower and upper approximations must be extracted from available training data. The main philosophy of rough set approach to concept approximation problem is based on minimizing the difference between upper and lower approximations (also called the *boundary region*). This simple, but brilliant idea, leads to many efficient applications of rough sets in machine learning and data mining like feature selection, rule induction, discretization or classifier construction [4].

As boolean algebra has a fundamental role in computer science, the boolean reasoning approach is also an ideological method in Artificial Intelligence. In recent years, boolean reasoning approach shows to be a powerful tool for designing effective and accurate solutions for many problems in rough set theory. This paper presents a more generalized approach to modern problems in rough set theory as well as their applications in data mining. This generalized method is called the *approximate boolean reasoning* (ABR) approach.

D. Ślęzak et al. (Eds.): RSFDGrC 2005, LNAI 3642, pp. 12–22, 2005.

2   Boolean Reasoning Approach

Boolean reasoning approach is a general framework for solving decision and optimization problems. This method comes from the great idea of George Boole to whom we owe a possibility of using symbolic notation in mathematics. He proposed to solve a problem by (1) converting it to a boolean formula, (2) solving a corresponding problem for boolean formula and (3) decoding the solution for boolean function to obtain the solution of the original problem.

By boolean function we denote any function $f : \{0,1\}^n \to \{0,1\}$. Boolean functions can be described by boolean formulas, i.e., expressions constructed by boolean variables from a set $VAR = \{x_1, ..., x_k\}$, and boolean operators like conjunction ($\land$), disjunction ($\lor$), and negation ($\neg$).

The most famous problem related to boolean functions is the satisfiability problem (SAT). It is based on checking, for a given boolean function, whether there exists such an evaluation of variables that the function becomes satisfied. In other words, the problem is to solve the equation $f(x_1, ..., x_n) = 1$. SAT is the first problem which has been proved to be NP-complete (the Cook's theorem). This important result is used to prove the NP-hardness of many other problems by showing the polynomial transformation of SAT to the studied problem. From practical point of view, any SAT-solver (heuristical algorithm for SAT) can be used to design heuristic solutions for all problems in the class NP. Therefore, instead of solving a couple of hard problems, the main effort may be limited to create efficient heuristics for the SAT problem.

One of possible solutions for scheduling problem is based on SAT-solver. In this method, the specification of scheduling problem is formulated by a boolean function, where each variable encodes one possible assignment of tasks, resources, time slots, etc. The encoding function is satisfiable if and only if there exists a correct schedule for the given specification [17].

The following steps should be taken into account when applying boolean reasoning approach:

- **Encoding:** this is the most important step in BR scheme. It begins with determining the set of boolean variables and their meanings in the original problem. Later, the specification of the studied problem and input data are encoded by boolean expressions over selected variables.
- **Solving the corresponding problem for boolean function:** this step is independent with the original problem. The problem is to select the relevant solution for the encoding boolean function. Selection criteria may be related to the complexity and efficiency of existing solutions for the problem over boolean function.
- **Decoding:** in this step, the solution for the problem over boolean function is converted into the solution of the original problem.

SAT is more useful for solving decision problems. In this paper we consider another problem for boolean functions called *minimal prime implicant problem* that is more suitable for optimization problems. Let us briefly describe this problem in more details.

2.1   Prime Implicant Problems

The boolean function $\phi : \{0,1\}^n \rightarrow \{0,1\}$ is called "*monotone*" if

$$\forall_{\mathbf{x},\mathbf{y}\in\{0,1\}^n}(\mathbf{x} \leqslant \mathbf{y}) \Rightarrow (\phi(\mathbf{x}) \leqslant \phi(\mathbf{y}))$$

It has been shown that monotone functions can be represented by a boolean expression without negations.

Let ϕ be a monotone boolean function which can be expressed as a boolean formula over the set of boolean variables $VAR = \{x_1, ..., x_n\}$. The term $\mathbf{T} = x_{i_1} \wedge ... \wedge x_{i_k}$ is called *implicant* of ϕ if $\mathbf{T}(\mathbf{x}) \leq \phi(\mathbf{x})$ for any $\mathbf{x} \in \{0,1\}^n$. The term $\mathbf{T}$ is called *prime implicant* of ϕ if (1) $\mathbf{T}$ is an implicant and (2) any term $\mathbf{T}'$, which is obtained from $\mathbf{T}$ by removing some variables, is not implicant of ϕ. If the set of all prime implicants of ϕ is denoted by $PI(\phi)$, then $f(\mathbf{x}) = \bigvee_{\mathbf{T}\in PI(\phi)} \mathbf{T}$.

Let us consider the following problem:

MINIMAL PRIME IMPLICANT PROBLEM:
Input: Monotone boolean function f of n variables.
Output: A prime implicant of f with the minimal length.

It has been shown that the minimal prime implicant problem is NP-hard and the corresponding decision problem, e.g., checking the existence of prime implicant of a given length, is NP-complete [3].

2.2   Boolean Reasoning Approach to Optimization Problems

Most problems in data mining are formulated as optimization problems. We will show in the next Section that prime implicant problem is very useful for application of boolean reasoning approach to optimization problem. The general boolean reasoning scheme (BR-scheme) for optimization problems is presented in Figure 1.

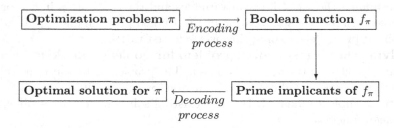

Fig. 1. The boolean reasoning scheme for solving optimization problems

Since the minimal prime implicant problem is NP-hard, it cannot be solved (in general case) by exact methods only. It is necessary to create some heuristics to search for short prime implicants of large and complicated boolean functions.

Usually, the input boolean function is given in the CNF form, i.e., it is presented as a conjunction of clauses, and the minimal prime implicant problem is equivalent to the problem of searching for minimal set of variables that has nonempty intersection with each clause of the given function. Let us mention some well known heuristics that have been proposed for prime implicant problem:

1. **Greedy algorithm:** the prime implicant can be treated as a set covering problem, where a set of variables X is said to cover a clause C if X contains at least one variable of C. Therefore, in each step, greedy method selects the variable that most frequently occurs within clauses of the given function and removes all those clauses which contain the selected variable.
2. **Linear programming:** the minimal prime implicant can also be resolved by converting the given function into a system of linear inequations and applying the Integer Linear Programming (ILP) approach to this system. More details are described in [15].
3. **Simulated annealing:** many optimization problems are resolved by a Monte-Carlo search method called simulated annealing. In case of minimal prime implicant problem, the search space consists of subsets of variables and the cost function for a given subset X of variables is defined by the size of X and the number of clauses that are uncovered by X, see [16].

3   Boolean Reasoning Approach to Rough Set Problems

As we have introduced before, searching for approximation of a concept is a fundamental problem in machine learning and data mining. Classification, clustering, association analysis, and many other tasks in data mining can be formulated as concept approximation problems. Let $\mathcal{X}$ be a given universe of objects, and let $\mathcal{L}$ be a predefined descriptive language consisting of such formulas that are interpretable as subsets of $\mathcal{X}$. Concept approximation problem can be understood as a problem of searching for a description ψ of a given concept $C \subset \mathcal{X}$ such that (i) ψ expressible in $\mathcal{L}$ and (ii) the interpretation of ψ should be as close to the original concept as possible. Usually, the concept to be approximated is given on a *finite set of examples* $U \subset \mathcal{X}$, called the training set, only.

The main idea of rough set theory is based on approximating the unknown concept by a pair sets called lower and upper approximations. The lower approximation contains those objects which certainly – according to the actual knowledge of the learner – belong to the concept, the upper approximation contains those objects which possibly belong to the concept.

Let $C \subseteq \mathcal{X}$ be a concept and let $U \subseteq \mathcal{X}$ be a training set. Any pair $\mathbb{P} = (\mathbf{L}, \mathbf{U})$ is called *rough approximation of* C (see [2]) if it satisfies the following conditions:

1. $\mathbf{L} \subseteq \mathbf{U} \subseteq \mathcal{X}$;
2. $\mathbf{L}, \mathbf{U}$ are expressible in the language $\mathcal{L}$;
3. $\mathbf{L} \cap U \subseteq C \cap U \subseteq \mathbf{U} \cap U$;
4. $\mathbf{L}$ is maximal and $\mathbf{U}$ is minimal among those $\mathcal{L}$-definable sets satisfying 3.

The sets $\mathbf{L}$ and $\mathbf{U}$ are called the *lower approximation* and the *upper approximation* of the concept C, respectively. The set $\mathbf{BN} = \mathbf{U} - \mathbf{L}$ is called the *boundary region of approximation* of C. For objects $x \in \mathbf{U}$, we say that "probably, x is in C". The concept C is called *rough* with respect to its approximations $(\mathbf{L}, \mathbf{U})$ if $\mathbf{L} \neq \mathbf{U}$, otherwise C is called *crisp* in $\mathcal{X}$.

The input data for concept approximation problem is given by *decision table* which is a tuple $\mathbb{S} = (U, A, dec)$, where U is a non-empty, finite set of *training objects*, A is a non-empty, finite set of *attributes* and $dec \notin A$ is a distinguished attribute called *decision*. Each attribute $a \in A$ corresponds to the function $a : \mathcal{X} \to V_a$ where V_a is called the *domain* of a. For any non-empty set of attributes $B \subseteq A$ and any object $x \in \mathcal{X}$, we define the *B-information vector* of x by: $inf_B(x) = \{(a, a(x)) : a \in B\}$. The language $\mathcal{L}$, which is used to describe approximations of concepts, consists of boolean expressions over descriptors of the form $(attribute = value)$ or $(attribute \in set\_of\_values)$. If $C \subset \mathcal{X}$ is a concept to be approximated, then the decision attribute dec is a characteristic function of concept C, i.e., if $x \in C$ we have $dec(x) = yes$, otherwise $dec(x) = no$. In general, the decision attribute dec can describe several disjoint concepts.

The first definition of rough approximation was introduced by Pawlak in his pioneering book on rough set theory [14]. For any subset of attributes $B \subset A$, the set of objects U is divided into *equivalence classes* by the *indiscernibility relation* and the upper and lower approximations are defined as unions of corresponding equivalence classes. This definition can be called *the attribute-based rough approximation*. A great effort of many researchers in RS Society has been investigated to modify and to improve this classical approach. One can find many interesting methods for rough approximation like Variable RS Model [24], Tolerance-based Rough Approximation [22], Approximation Space [21], or Classifier-based Rough Approximations [2].

The condition (4) in the above list can be substituted by inclusion to a degree to make it possible to induce approximations of higher quality of the concept on the whole universe $\mathcal{X}$. In practical applications, it is hard to fulfill the last condition. Hence, by using some heuristics we construct sub-optimal instead of maximal or minimal sets. This condition is the main inspiration for all applications of rough sets in data mining and decision support systems.

Let $\mathbb{S} = (U, A \cup \{dec\})$ be a given decision table, where $U = \{u_1, ..., u_n\}$, and $A = \{a_1, ..., a_m\}$. The following rough set methods have been successfully solved by boolean reasoning approach:

Attribute Reduction: *Reducts* are subsets of attributes that preserve the same amount of information. In rough set theory a subset of attributes $B \subset A$ is called a decision reduct, if B preserves the same rough approximation of a concept likes A. It has been shown in [20] that the problem of searching for minimal reduct of a decision system is equivalent to the minimal prime implicant problem. BR approach has been applied to minimal reduct problem as follows:

- **Boolean Variables:** We associate with each attribute $a_i \in A$ a boolean variable a_i^* for $i = 1, ..., m$.

- **Encoding:** for any pair of objects $u_i, u_j \in U$, where $i, j = 1, ..., n$ we define a discernibility function between u_i, u_j by

$$\psi_{i,j} = \bigvee_{a \in A: a(u_i) \neq a(u_j)} a^*$$

A *discernibility function* $f_\mathbb{S}$ for $\mathbb{S}$ is defined by

$$f_\mathbb{S}(a_1^*, ..., a_m^*) = \bigwedge_{dec(u_i) \neq dec(u_j)} \psi_{i,j} \tag{1}$$

- **Heuristics:** in the greedy algorithm for reduct problem, quality of a subset of attributes B is measured by the number of pairs of objects that are discerned by B. More efficient algorithm based on genetic algorithm was presented in [23].

Decision Rule Induction: decision rules are logical formulas that indicate the relationship between conditional and decision attributes. Let us consider those decision rules **r** whose the premise is a boolean monomial of descriptors, i.e.,

$$\mathbf{r} \equiv (a_{i_1} = v_1) \wedge ... \wedge (a_{i_m} = v_m) \Rightarrow (dec = k) \tag{2}$$

In the rough set approach to concept approximation, decision rules are used to define finer rough approximation comparing to attribute-base rough approximation. Each decision rule is supported by some objects and, inversely, the information vector of each object can be reduced to obtain a minimal consistent decision rule. The boolean reasoning approach to decision rule construction from a given decision table $\mathbb{S} = (U, A \cup \{dec\})$ is very similar to the minimal reduct problem. The only difference occurs in the encoding step, i.e.:

- **Encoding:** For any object $u \in U$ in , we define a function $f_u(a_1^*, ..., a_m^*)$, called *discernibility function for u* by

$$f_u(a_1^*, ..., a_m^*) = \bigwedge_{v: dec(v) \neq dec(u)} \psi_{u,v}(x_1, ..., x_k) \tag{3}$$

- **Heuristics:** all heuristics for minimal prime implicant problem can be applied to boolean functions in Equation 3. Because there are n such functions, where n is a number of objects in the decision table, the well known heuristics may show to be time consuming.

Discretization: In [6], boolean reasoning approach to real value attribute discretization problem was presented. The problem is to search for a minimal set of cuts on real value attributes that preserve the discernibility between objects. Given a decision table $\mathbb{S} = (U, A \cup \{dec\})$ and a set of candidate cuts **C** the discretization problem is encoded as follows:

- **Variables:** Each cut $(a, c) \in \mathbf{C}$ is associated with a boolean variable $x_{(a,c)}$
- **Encoding:** similarly to the reduct problem, a discernibility function between $u_i, u_j \in U$, where $i, j = 1, ..., n$, is defined by

$$\phi_{i,j} = \bigvee_{(a,c)discernsu_iandu_j} x_{(a,c)}$$

and the discretization problem is encoded by the following boolean function

$$\phi = \bigwedge_{dec(u_i) \neq dec(u_j)} \phi_{i,j} \qquad (4)$$

- **Heuristics:** again all mentioned heuristics for prime implicant problem can be applied to optimal discretization problem, but we have to take under our attention their computational complexity.

4   Approximate Boolean Reasoning Approach

In [6], [18], [9] we have presented few more feature extraction methods based on rough sets and BR approach. Let us mention the following ones:

- **Symbolic value grouping problem:** the idea is to create new features by partition of attribute domains into as less as possible groups of attribute values. This method leads to construction of generalized decision rule of form

$$(a_{i_1} \subset S_1) \wedge ... \wedge (a_{i_m} = S_m) \Rightarrow (dec = k)$$

Each boolean variable encodes a a group of symbolic values in the domain of an attribute.
- **Oblique hyperplanes extraction:** new features are defined by linear combination of the existing ones.

All mentioned problems can be encoded by boolean functions but the complexity of heuristic solutions are very different. Table 1 compares the complexity of encoding functions for the mentioned above problems.

Table 1. Complexity of encoding boolean functions for basic problems in rough sets (n, m are numbers of objects and attributes of the given decision table, respectively)

Problem	Complexity of encoding function
minimal reduct	$O(m)$ variables, $O(n^2)$ clauses
decision rules	$O(n)$ functions containing $O(m)$ variables and $O(n)$ clauses each
discretiztion	$O(mn)$ variables, $O(n^2)$ clauses
grouping	$O(\sum_{a \in A} 2^{|V_a|})$ variables, $O(n^2)$ clauses
hyperplanes	$O(n^m)$ variables , $O(n^2)$ clauses

The problem with computational complexity becomes more serious in data mining applications on very large databases. We have proposed a novel solution called *approximate boolean reasoning approach*. Figure 2 presents a general scheme of this method. The idea is to approximate every step in the BR-scheme. Let us discuss some possible techniques that were applied in rough set methods.

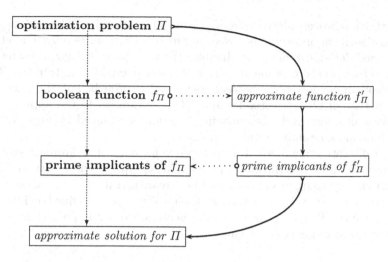

Fig. 2. General scheme of approximate boolean reasoning approach

4.1   The α-Reduct Problem

One method for computation time reduction is based on weakening the requirement of a problem. α-reducts are example of this technique, see [7].

The set B of attributes is called α-reduct if B has nonempty intersection with at least $\alpha \cdot N$ clauses of the discernibility function (1), where N is the total number of clauses occurring in (1) and $\alpha \in [0,1]$ is a real parameter.

In some applications (see [19]), e.g., rough classifier construction, α-reducts produce much shorter and more accurate classifiers comparing with original reducts. Practical experiments show that in some cases, the 95%-reducts are two times shorter than 100%-reducts.

Let $\mathbb{S} = (U, A)$ be a given information system and let $\mathbf{T} = D_1 \wedge D_2 ... \wedge D_k$ be an extracted pattern (or frequent itemset [1]). Consider the set of descriptors $\mathbf{P} \subset \{D_1, D_2..., D_k\}$, the implication

$$\bigwedge_{D_i \in \mathbf{P}} D_i \Rightarrow \bigwedge_{D_j \notin \mathbf{P}} D_j$$

1. is 100%-irreducible association rule from $\mathbf{T}$ if and only if $\mathbf{P}$ is reduct in $\mathbb{S}|_\mathbf{T}$.
2. is c-irreducible association rule from $\mathbf{T}$ if and only if $\mathbf{P}$ is α-reduct in $\mathbb{S}|_\mathbf{T}$, where $\alpha = 1 - (\frac{1}{c} - 1)/(\frac{n}{s} - 1)$, n is the total number of objects from U and $s = support(\mathbf{T})$.

One can show that for a given α, the problems of searching for shortest α-reducts and for all α-reducts are also NP-hard [10].

4.2   Discretization Problem

Two solutions based on approximate boolean reasoning approach have been proposed for discretization problem.

Discretization process always effects on a lost of information. The optimal discretization algorithm preserves the discernibility of all attributes only. Therefore, the discretized decision table is irreducible. We have proposed for a discretization method that preserves some more reducts for a given decision table [5]. This method also can be solved by boolean reasoning approach, but the encoding function consists of $O(mn)$ variables and $O(n^2 2^n)$ clauses. In the approximate boolean reasoning approach the encoding function is replaced by approximate encoding function containing $O(n^2)$ clauses only.

Another discretization method was proposed for relational database systems [8]. This method minimizes the number of simple SQL queries necessary to search for the best cuts by using "divide and conquer" search strategy. To make it possible, we develop some novel "approximate measures" which are defined on intervals of attribute values. Proposed measures are necessary to evaluate a chance that a given interval contains the best cut.

4.3   Symbolic Value Grouping Problem

This method is the best demonstration of approximate boolean reasoning approach. This problem can be encoded by a boolean function containing $O(n^2)$ clauses and $O(\sum_{a \in A} 2^{|V_a|})$ variables. We have proposed an approximate encoding function containing $O(\sum_{a \in A} |V_a|^2)$ variables (and still $O(n^2)$ clauses) only [18]. In this application, the decoding process was not trivial, since it is equivalent to a well-known graph vertex coloring problem which is NP-hard. One more heuristical algorithm for this graph coloring problem is necessary to construct a whole solution for symbolic value grouping problem.

5   Applications in Data Mining

Rough sets and approximate boolean reasoning approach to data mining has been presented in [11], [9], [7]. Both discretization and symbolic value grouping methods can be used to construct accurate decision trees from large databases.

In the decision tree construction method based on rough sets and boolean reasoning approach, the quality of a split (defined either by a cut on a continuous attribute or by a partition symbolic values) is measured by the number of pairs of objects from different classes that are discerned by the split. In case of large data sets, an application of approximate boolean reasoning approach makes a search for semi-optimal cuts very efficient, particularly when the data set is stored in a relational database system [11]. We have proposed a concept of soft cuts and soft decision trees which have many advantages. Comparing with the standard decision tree concept, soft decision tree model maintains the high classification accuracy, but it can be constructed very fast [12].

The latest applications of approximate boolean reasoning approach is related to the concept of layered learning [13]. This method allows improving the accuracy of concept approximation by utilizing the domain knowledge in the learning process. In cases, when the domain knowledge is given in form of concept ontology, we have proposed a layered learning method based on rough sets and boolean reasoning approach [13].

6 Conclusions

We have presented a boolean reasoning approach and its extension called approximate boolean reasoning approach as general methods for designing efficient solutions for rough sets and data mining. Recently, we are working on an application of boolean reasoning approach to decision tables with continuous decision. The method is called the differential calculus for pseudo boolean functions, and some first experiments are showing that this method is quite promising. We are also planning to apply the approximate boolean reasoning method in layered learning algorithms that make approximation of concept from data and domain knowledge possible.

Acknowledgement. The research has been partially supported by the grant 3T11C00226 from Ministry of Scientific Research and Information Technology of the Republic of Poland.

References

1. Agrawal R., Imiclinski T., Suami A.: Mining Assocation Rules Between Sets of Items in Large Datatabes, ACM SIGMOD. Conference on Management of Data, Washington, D.C., 1993, pp. 207–216.
2. Bazan J., Nguyen H.S., Skowron A., Szczuka M.: A view on rough set concept approximation. In proceedings of the 9th International Conference on Rough Sets, Fuzzy Sets, Data Mining and Granular Computing (RSFDGrC'2003),Chongqing, China. LNAI 2639, Heidelberg, Germany, Springer-Verlag, 2003, pp. 181–188
3. Brown E.M.: *Boolean Reasoning*, Kluwer Academic Publishers, Dordrecht, 1990.
4. Kloesgen W., Żytkow J., eds.: *Handbook of Knowledge Discovery and Data Mining*. Oxford University Press, Oxford, 2002.
5. Nguyen H. S.: Discretization problems for rough set methods. In L. Polkowski and A. Skowron, editors, *New Direction in Rough Sets, Data Mining and Granular-Soft Computing (Proc. of RSCTC'98, Warsaw, Poland)*, LNAI 1424, Springer-Verlag, Berlin Heidelberg, 1998, pp. 545–552.
6. Nguyen H. S., Nguyen S. H.: Discretization methods for data mining. In L. Polkowski and A. Skowron, editors, *Rough Sets in Knowledge Discovery*, Physica-Verlag, Heidelberg New York, 1998, pp. 451–482.
7. Nguyen H. S., Nguyen S. H.: Rough sets and association rule generation. *Fundamenta Informaticae*, 40(4), 1999, pp. 310–318.
8. Nguyen H. S.: Efficient sql-querying method for data mining in large data bases. In *Proc. of Sixteenth International Joint Conference on Artificial Intelligence, IJCAI-99*, Stockholm, Sweden, Morgan Kaufmann, 1999, pp. 806–811.
9. Nguyen H. S.: From optimal hyperplanes to optimal decision trees. *Fundamenta Informaticae*, 34(1–2), 1998, pp. 145–174.
10. Nguyen H. S., Slezak D.: Approximate reducts and association rules – correspondence and complexity results. In Proc. of RSFDGrC'99, Yamaguchi, Japan, LNAI 1711, Springer-Verlag, Berlin Heidelberg, 1999, pp. 107–115.

11. Nguyen H. S.: On efficient handling of continuous attributes in large data bases. *Fundamenta Informaticae*, 48(1), 2001, pp. 61–81.
12. Nguyen H. S.: On exploring soft discretization of continuous attributes. In Sankar K. Pal, Lech Polkowski, and Andrzej Skowron, editors, *Rough-Neural Computing Techniques for Computing with Words*, chapter 13, Springer, 2004, pages 333–350.
13. Nguyen S. H., Bazan J., Skowron A., and Nguyen H.S.: Layered learning for concept synthesis. In Peters at al. (eds), *Transactions on Rough Sets I*, volume LNCS 3100, Springer, 2004, pages 187–208.
14. Pawlak Z.: Rough Sets: Theoretical Aspects of Reasoning about Data. Volume 9 of System Theory, Knowledge Engineering and Problem Solving. Kluwer Academic Publishers, Dordrecht, The Netherlands (1991)
15. Pizzuti C.: Computing Prime Implicants by Integer Programming. In Proceedings of IEEE International Conference on Tools with Artificial Intelligence, 1996.
16. Sen S.: Minimal cost set covering using probabilistic methods In Proceedings 1993 ACM/SIGAPP Symposium on Applied Computing, 1993, pp. 157–194.
17. Selman B., Kautz H., McAllester D.: Ten Challenges in Propositional Reasoning and Search. In *Proc. IJCAI'97*, Japan, 1997.
18. Skowron A., Nguyen H. S.: Boolean reasoning schema with some applications in data mining. In J. Zytkow and J. Rauch, editors, Principple of Data Mining and Knowledge Discovery (Proc. of PKDD'1999, Praga, Czech), LNAI 1704, Springer-Verlag, Berlin Heidelberg, 1999, pp. 107–115.
19. Skowron A. Synthesis of adaptive decision systems from experimental data. In A. Aamodt, J. Komorowski (eds), Proc. of the 5th Scandinavian Conference on AI (SCAI'95), IOS Press, May 1995, Trondheim, Norway, pp. 220–238.
20. Skowron A., Rauszer C.: The discernibility matrices and functions in information systems. In: R. Słowiński (Ed.), *Intelligent decision support: Handbook of applications and advances of the rough sets theory*, Kluwer Academic Publishers, Dordrecht, 1992, pp. 331-362.
21. Skowron A., Stepaniuk J.: Tolerance approximation spaces. Fundamenta Informaticae **27**, 1996, pp. 245–253
22. Słowiński R., Vanderpooten D., 1995. *Similarity Relation as a Basis for Rough Approximations*. In: P. Wang (Ed.): Advances in Machine Intelligence & Soft Computing, Bookwrights, Raleigh NC, 1997, pp. 17–33.
23. Wróblewski J.: Covering with reducts - a fast algorithm for rule generation. In: Polkowski L., Skowron A.(eds.): Proc. of RSCTC'98, Warsaw, Poland. Springer-Verlag, Berlin, 1998, pp. 402–407.
24. Ziarko W.: Variable Precision Rough Set Model. In Journal of Computer and System Sciences, Vol. 46, 1993, pp. 39-59.

Towards Human-Level Web Intelligence

Ning Zhong

The International WIC Institute & Department of Information Engineering,
Maebashi Institute of Technology,
460-1 Kamisadori-Cho, Maebashi-City 371-0816, Japan
zhong@maebashi-it.ac.jp

The concept of Web Intelligence (WI for short) was first introduced in our papers and books [4,13,16,17,19]. Broadly speaking, Web Intelligence is a new direction for scientific research and development that explores the fundamental roles as well as practical impacts of Artificial Intelligence (AI)[1] and advanced Information Technology (IT) on the next generation of Web-empowered systems, services, and environments. The WI technologies revolutionize the way in which information is gathered, stored, processed, presented, shared, and used by virtualization, globalization, standardization, personalization, and portals.

As more detailed blueprints and issues of Web Intelligence (WI) are being evolved and specified [4,13,17,19,24], it has been recognized that one of the fundamental goals of WI research is to understand and develop Wisdom Web based intelligent systems that integrate all the human-level capabilities such as real-time response, robustness, autonomous interaction with their environment, communication with natural language, commonsense reasoning, planning, learning, discovery and creativity.

Turing gave the first scientific discussion of human level machine intelligence [12]. Newell and Simon made a start on programming computers for general intelligence [8]. McCarthy argued that reaching human-level AI requires programs that deal with the commonsense informative situation, in which the phenomena to be taken into account in achieving a goal are not fixed in advance [6]. Laird and Lent proposed using interactive computer games that are the killer application for human-level AI research, because they can provide the environments for research on the right kinds of problem that lead to the type of incremental and integrative research needed to achieve human-level AI [2].

The new generation of WI research and development needs to understand multiple natures of intelligence in depth, by studying integrately the three intelligence related research areas: machine intelligence, human intelligence, and social intelligence, as shown in Figure 1, towards developing truly human-level Web intelligence. Machine intelligence (also called Artificial Intelligence (AI)) has been mainly studied as computer based technologies for the development of intelligent knowledge based systems; Human intelligence studies the nature of intelligence towards our understanding of intelligence; Social intelligence needs

---

[1] Here the term of AI includes classical AI, computational intelligence, and soft computing etc.

D. Ślęzak et al. (Eds.): RSFDGrC 2005, LNAI 3642, pp. 23–28, 2005.
© Springer-Verlag Berlin Heidelberg 2005

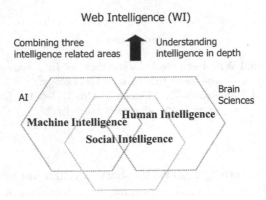

Fig. 1. The relationship between WI and other three intelligence related research areas

a combination of machine intelligence and human intelligence for establishing social networks that contain communities of people, organizations, or other social entities [18]. Furthermore, the Web can be regarded as a social network in which it connects a set of people (or organizations or other social entities). People are connected by a set of social relationships, such as friendship, co-working or information exchange with common interests. In other words, it is a Web-supported social network or called virtual community. In this sense, the study of Web Intelligence is of social network intelligence (social intelligence for short).

In previous paper [24], we gave a new perspective of WI research from the viewpoint of *Brain Informatics*. Brain Informatics (BI) is a new interdisciplinary field to study human information processing mechanism systematically from both macro and micro points of view by cooperatively using experimental brain/cognitive technology and WI centric advanced information technology. In particular, it attempts to understand human intelligence in depth, towards a holistic view at a long-term, global field of vision, to understand the principles, models and mechanisms of human multi-perception, reasoning and inference, problem solving, learning, discovery and creativity [22].

As mentioned by McCarthy [6], if we understood enough about how the human intellect works, we could simulate it. However, we, so far, did not have sufficient ability to observe ourselves or others to understand directly how our intellects work. Understanding the human brain well enough to imitate its function therefore requires theoretical and experimental success in cognitive science and neuroscience.

Fortunately, now neuroscience, the study of the brain and nervous system, is beginning to allow direct measurement and observation of ourselves or others to understand directly how our intellects work. These measurements and observations are, in turn, challenging our understanding of the relation between mind and action, leading to new theoretical constructs and calling old ones into question. New instrumentation (fMRI etc.) and advanced information technology are causing an impending revolution in WI and Brain Sciences [7,21,22,23,24]. This revolution is bi-directional:

- WI based portal techniques will provide a new powerful platform for Brain Sciences.
- New understanding and discovery of human intelligence models in Brain Sciences will yield a new generation of WI research and development.

Figure 2 shows the relationship between Brain Informatics and other brain sciences related disciplines as well as the WI centric IT. On one hand, although brain sciences have been studied from different disciplines such as cognitive science and neuroscience, Brain Informatics (BI) represents a potentially revolutionary shift in the way that research is undertaken. It attempts to capture new forms of collaborative and interdisciplinary work. In this vision, new kinds of Brain Informatics methods and global research communities will emerge, through infrastructure on the Wisdom Web and Knowledge Grids that enables high speed and distributed, large-scale analysis and computations, and radically new ways of sharing data/knowledge repositories. On the other hand, some of these lessons in cognitive science and neuroscience are applicable to novel technological developments in Brain Informatics, yet others may need to be enhanced or transformed in order to manage and account for the complex and possibly more innovative practices of sharing data/knowledge that are made technically possible by the Wisdom Web and Knowledge Grids [1,3,4,22].

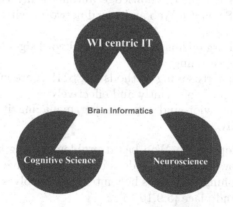

Fig. 2. The relationship between Brain Informatics and other brain sciences related disciplines as well as the WI centric IT

Figure 3 shows the relationship between WI research and Brain Informatics research. The synergy between WI with BI will yield profound advances in our analyzing and understanding of the mechanism of data, knowledge, intelligence and wisdom, as well as their relationship, organization and creation process. It means that fundamental and implementation of Web intelligence will be studied as a central topic and in a unique way. It will fundamentally change the nature of information technology in general and artificial intelligence in particular.

A good example is the development and use of a Web-based problem-solving system for portal-centralized, adaptable Web services [4,10,11,15,18,19]. The core

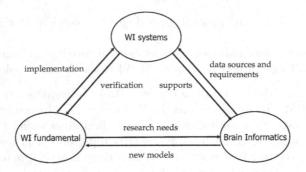

Fig. 3. The relationship between WI research and Brain Informatics research

of such a system is the Problem Solver Markup Language (PSML) and PSML-based distributed Web inference engines, in which the following support functions should be provided since this is a must for developing intelligent portals.

- The expressive power and functional support in PSML for complex adaptive, distributed problem solving;
- Performing automatic reasoning on the Web by incorporating globally distributed contents and meta-knowledge automatically collected and transformed from the Semantic Web and social networks with locally operational knowledge-data bases;
- Representing and organizing multiple, huge knowledge-data sources for distributed network reasoning;
- Combining multiple reasoning methods in PSML representation and distributed inference engines, efficiently and effectively;
- Modeling user behavior and representing/managing it as a personalized model dynamically.

In order to develop such a Web based problem-solving system, we need to better understand how human being does complex adaptive (distributed) problem solving and reasoning, as well as how intelligence evolves for individuals and societies, over time and place [5,9,10,15].

More specifically, we will investigate ways by discussing the following issues:

- How to design fMRI/EEG experiments to understand the principle of human inference/reasoning and problem solving in depth?
- How to understand and predict user profile and usage behavior?
- How to implement human-level inference/reasoning and problem solving on the Web based portals that can serve users wisely?

We will describe our endeavor in this direction, in particular, we will show that grid-based multi-aspect analysis in multiple knowledge and data sources on the Wisdom Web is an important way to investigate human intelligence mechanism, systematically. The ultimate goal is to establish the foundations of Web Intelligence by studying Brain Informatics for developing Wisdom Web based intelligent systems that integrate all the human-level capabilities.

Acknowledgments

I am grateful to all my research collaborators, assistants, and students who have, over the years, together contributed to the development of Web Intelligence (WI) and Brain Informatics (BI). I would like to express my gratitude to Jiming Liu, Yiyu Yao, and Jinglong Wu for our joint projects and discussions. I am very grateful to people who have joined or supported the WI community, members of the WIC advisory board, WIC technical committee, and WIC research centres, as well as keynote/invited speakers of WI-IAT conferences, in particular, N. Cercone, J. Bradshaw, B.B. Faltings, E.A. Feigenbaum, G. Gottlob, J. Hendler, W.L. Johnson, C. Kesselman, V. Lesser, J. McCarthy, T.M. Mitchell, S. Ohsuga, P. Raghavan, Z.W. Ras, A. Skowron, K. Sycara, B. Wah, P.S.P. Wang, M. Wooldridge, X. Wu, P.S. Yu, and L.A. Zadeh. I thank them for their strong support. Special thanks to Dominik Slezak, Wojciech Ziarko and other organizers of RSFDGrC 2005 for the kind invitation and the excellent organization.

References

1. J. Hu, and N. Zhong, "Organizing Dynamic Multi-level Workflows on Multi-layer Grids for e-Business Portals Development", *Proc. 2005 IEEE International Conference on e-Technology, e-Commerce and e-Service (EEE'05)*, IEEE Press (2005) 196-201.
2. J.E. Laird and M. van Lent, "Human-Level AI's Killer Application Interactive Computer Games", *AI Magazine* (Summer 2001) 15-25.
3. J. Liu, N. Zhong, Y.Y. Yao, and Z.W. Ras, "The Wisdom Web: New Challenges for Web Intelligence (WI)", *Journal of Intelligent Information Systems*, 20(1) Kluwer (2003) 5-9.
4. J. Liu, "Web Intelligence (WI): What Makes Wisdom Web?", *Proc. Eighteenth International Joint Conference on Artificial Intelligence (IJCAI'03)* (2003) 1596-1601.
5. J. Liu, X. Jin, and Y. Tang, "Multi-agent Collaborative Service and Distributed Problem Solving", *Cognitive Systems Research*, 5(3), Elsevier (2004)191-206 .
6. J. McCarthy, "Roads to Human Level AI?", Keynote Talk at Beijing University of Technology, Beijing, China (September 2004).
7. T.M. Mitchell, R. Hutchinson, M. Just, R.S. Niculescu, F. Pereira, and X. Wang, "Classifying Instantaneous Cognitive States from fMRI Data", *Proc. American Medical Informatics Association Annual Symposium* (2003) 465-469.
8. A. Newell and H.A. Simon, *Human Problem Solving*, Prentice-Hall (1972).
9. R.J. Sternberg, J. Lautrey, and T.I. Lubart, *Models of Intelligence*, American Psychological Association (2003).
10. Y. Su, L. Zheng, N. Zhong, C. Liu, and J. Liu, "Distributed Reasoning Based on Problem Solver Markup Language (PSML): A Demonstration through Extended OWL", *Proc. 2005 IEEE International Conference on e-Technology, e-Commerce and e-Service (EEE'05)*, IEEE Press (2005) 208-213.
11. K. Tomita, N. Zhong, and H. Yamauchi, "Coupling Global Semantic Web with Local Information Sources for Problem Solving", *Proc. First International Workshop on Semantic Web Mining and Reasoning (SWMR'04)* (2004) 66-74.

12. A. Turing, "Computing Machinery and Intelligence", Mind LIX(236) (1950) 433-460.
13. Y.Y. Yao, N. Zhong, J. Liu, and S. Ohsuga, "Web Intelligence (WI): Research Challenges and Trends in the New Information Age", N. Zhong, Y.Y. Yao, J. Liu, S. Ohsuga (eds.) *Web Intelligence: Research and Development*, LNAI 2198, Springer (2001) 1-17.
14. Y.Y. Yao, "Web Intelligence: New Frontiers of Exploration", *Proc. 2005 International Conference on Active Media Technology (AMT'05)* (2005) 1-6.
15. L.A. Zadeh, "Precisiated Natural Language (PNL)", *AI Magazine*, 25(3) (Fall 2004) 74-91.
16. N. Zhong, J. Liu, Y.Y. Yao, and S. Ohsuga, "Web Intelligence (WI)", *Proc. 24th IEEE Computer Society International Computer Software and Applications Conference (COMPSAC 2000)*, IEEE Press (2000) 469-470.
17. N. Zhong, "Representation and Construction of Ontologies for Web Intelligence", *International Journal of Foundations of Computer Science*, 13(4), World Scientific (2002) 555-570.
18. N. Zhong, J. Liu, and Y.Y. Yao, "In Search of the Wisdom Web", *IEEE Computer*, 35(11) (2002) 27-31.
19. N. Zhong, J. Liu, and Y.Y. Yao (eds.) *Web Intelligence*, Springer (2003).
20. N. Zhong, "Developing Intelligent Portals by Using WI Technologies", J.P. Li et al. (eds.) *Wavelet Analysis and Its Applications, and Active Media Technology*, Vol. 2, World Scientific (2004) 555-567.
21. N. Zhong, J.L. Wu, A. Nakamaru, M. Ohshima, and H. Mizuhara, "Peculiarity Oriented fMRI Brain Data Analysis for Studying Human Multi-Perception Mechanism", *Cognitive Systems Research*, 5(3), Elsevier (2004) 241-256.
22. N. Zhong, J. Hu, S. Motomura, J.L. Wu, and C. Liu, "Building a Data Mining Grid for Multiple Human Brain Data Analysis", *Computational Intelligence*, 21(2), Blackwell Publishing (2005) 177-196.
23. N. Zhong, S. Motomura, and J.L. Wu, "Peculiarity Oriented Multi-Aspect Brain Data Analysis for Studying Human Multi-Perception Mechanism", *Proc. SAINT 2005 Workshops (Workshop 8: Computer Intelligence for Exabyte Scale Data Explosion)*, IEEE Computer Society Press (2005) 306-309.
24. N. Zhong, J. Liu, Y.Y. Yao, and J. Wu, "Web Intelligence (WI) Meets Brain Informatics (BI)", *Proc. First International Conference on Complex Medical Engineering (CME'05)* (2005).

Credibility Coefficients in ARES Rough Set Exploration System

Roman Podraza[1], Mariusz Walkiewicz[1], and Andrzej Dominik[2]

[1] Warsaw University of Technology, Institute of Computer Science,
Nowowiejska 15/19, 00-665 Warsaw, Poland
{R.Podraza, M.Walkiewicz}@ii.pw.edu.pl
[2] Warsaw University of Technology, Institute of Radioelectronics,
Nowowiejska 15/19, 00-665 Warsaw, Poland
A.Dominik@elka.pw.edu.pl

Abstract. This paper presents ARES Rough Set Exploration System. This system is a complex data analyzing application. The program lets the user to discretize real data, find relative static and dynamic reducts, find frequent sets, find decision rules and calculate credibility coefficients for objects from a decision table. Some information about logical and technical aspects of the system architecture is provided as well.

1 Introduction

In the past few years rapid growth of data can be observed and a demand for new tools for processing them into a concise form is emerging. Data mining and knowledge acquisition projects have gained a lot of interests and applications. In the paper ARES Rough Set Exploration System is presented. Its basis lies in the rough set theory. The system provides functionality similar to existing rough set tools but also introduce some new features.

There are many commercial as well as free to use systems [1] which use rough set theory for data analysis. Some of them are versatile (eg. RSES2, ROSETTA and some of them are specialized, goal-oriented (eg. LERS, PRIMEROSE - only inducing rules, RoughFuzzyLab - specially designed for image recognition).

The most important and unique feature of ARES system is ability to calculate credibility coefficients for every object from decision table using different methods. This feature can be very useful in detecting either corrupted data or abnormal and distinctive situations. Such functionality can be applied in different fields of science, especially in medicine [2], [3]. By evaluating credibility coefficients the system can recognize objects that are exceptions to the "typical" description and draw attention of an expert to them. If in a medical application the objects represent patients then the low values of credibility coefficients can identify the set of them requiring a special consideration as not fitting to the usual explanation.

Improper data in the information system can be blamed for corrupting relationships between the other objects. This situation can be exposed when elimination of the improper data results in improving the outcome of the system

D. Ślęzak et al. (Eds.): RSFDGrC 2005, LNAI 3642, pp. 29–38, 2005.

denoted by better quality of generated rules or uncovering some new ones. Credibility coefficients can recommend candidates for elimination from a decision table.

The main functionality of this system was originally presented in [4]. A multi-document architecture of the system facilitates performing parallel analysis of different steps or aspects of data processing and analyzing.

2   System Overview

System has been implemented in Java and supplied with a user-friendly graphic environment. The main application window consists of two views:

– **Tree view** - A list of all elements currently available for user (e.g. workspaces, decision tables, analysis results).
– **Workspace view** - Panel where windows are opened according to user selection from the tree view (e.g. window with decision table or window with list of all found reducts).

A sample screenshot from ARES Rough Set Exploration System is shown in Fig. 1. In the next section basic system functionality is shortly described.

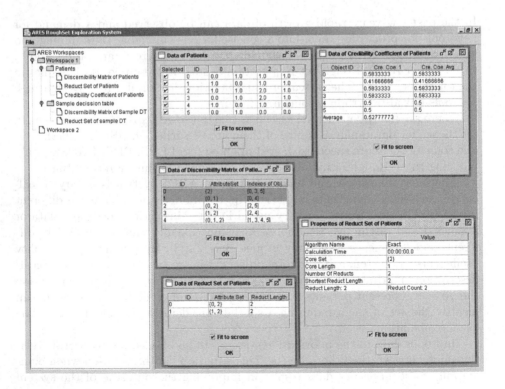

Fig. 1. Sample screenshot from Ares Rough Set Exploration System

The main goal of such a design is easy management of the whole process of data analysis. Each data-mining operation is presented as a new item in a tree-view section (the relationships between the items are user dependent and usually are denoted by similarity of item names). This feature enables carrying out parallel analysis of different aspects of the same information system (or related ones). Additionally, multi document architecture allows comparing gained data in an easy way.

The user may display in separate windows information associated with every node in tree view. The nodes usually store the following information:

- **Node type (kind)** - Structure or process represented by node (e.g. information system, reduct set, rule set, summary of execution of an algorithm).
- **Node data** - Data associated with the node (e.g. for an information system the window presents information on the set of objects).
- **Processing algorithm basic information** - Some basic information of data-mining operation (e.g. algorithm name, execution time).
- **Processing algorithm extended information** - It contains some algorithm specific information (e.g. minimal reduct length and number of reducts are provided for reduct finding algorithm).

3   System Functionality

3.1   Data Discretization

Discretization [5] is one of the methods of data preprocessing. Usually, vast data mining algorithms do not work on real values, which makes discretization so important phase of data analyses.

This module supports five algorithms of discretization assigning a given value to a class representing it (the last two were originally designed for ARES system):

- **Naive Discretizer** [5] - Each unique value denotes a different class.
- **Equal Width Discretizer** [5] - A class is an interval and all classes have equal widths; number of classes is a parameter. A value from an interval belongs to its class.
- **Equal Frequency Discretizer** [5] - A class is an interval and all classes have equal widths; number of elements in each class is a parameter. A value from an interval belongs to its class.
- **Equal Support Discretizer** - Each class consists of the same number of elements (values).
- **Upper Bound of Ranges Discretizer** - After naive discretization the number of classes is reduced by merging the classes to get the required number of classes.

ARES system provides discretization preview which presents information about discretization process (i.e. number of objects in each range).

Each attribute of an information system is discretized separately using one of available methods according to user needs and preferences. The discretization results (obtained by the described algorithms) can be arbitrary customized to expert knowledge. Discretized information system is saved as a new one.

3.2 Rough Set Primary Analyses

This module enables to work out basic rough set [6] components such as:

- **Class approximation** - Lower and upper approximation, positive and negative region, boundary for each decision class.
- **Approximation accuracy and quality**
- **Indiscernibility matrix**
- **Indiscernibility function**

These elements may contain some important information themselves or they may be used in further analyses of information system.

3.3 Reducts

Reduct is a subset of attributes which allow to classify the data as satisfactory as the whole set of attributes. Reducts are usually applied to reduce size of information system (by removing the dependent attributes) without a loss of classification capabilities. This may, for instance directly influence the speed of rule generation or credibility coefficients calculation algorithms.

ARES system provides a wide variety of different algorithms for finding reducts. They are divided into two basic types: methods which calculate only one (minimal or almost minimal) reduct and methods which calculate a set of reducts (all reducts) for a given decision table. The following algorithms may be used for achieving the goal:

- **Complete (exhaustive) method** [7] is based on indiscernibility matrix and indiscernibility function. This method finds all reducts of a given decision table. Its time complexity is very high, so it can be applied only for relatively small sets of data.
- **Random algorithm** [8] tries to find reducts by random guesses.
- **Johnson algorithm** [7] is heuristic and discovers only one reduct (minimal or almost minimal) from indiscernibility matrix.
- Set of **simple greedy algorithms** [8] which find one reduct. They are very fast and may be used as start point in more advanced heuristic methods.
- Set of **genetic algorithms** [9], which differ from each other in chromosome representation and applied genetic operators. They may be used either for finding minimal reduct or set of reducts. All genetic methods can be parameterized by parameters typical for evolutionary algorithms (i.e. crossover probability, number of individuals, and so on).
- **Space decompositions algorithms** [8] work together with genetic algorithms (Genetic Space) but may be used with random search as well. These algorithms take advantage of reduction of optimization problem to a series of decision problems. Genetic Space is faster than other known genetic algorithms for finding reducts. It provides better results as well. This target is achieved by effective chromosome coding and specially designed genetic operators. Algorithms based on decomposition of search space are important and unique feature of ARES system and currently are not provided in any other rough set data analyzing application.

Dynamic reducts [7] calculation is parameterized by the following parameters:

- **Number of decision sub-tables**
- **Percentage of all original objects in each decision sub-table**
- **Static reduct finding algorithm** - One of algorithms presented in the preceding section

Dynamic reducts are almost the same as static reducts. In some cases (especially when new data is being added to information system) calculation of dynamic reduct is more suitable.

For each reduct set ARES also calculates following parameters:

- **Core set** comprising the most important attributes of a given decision tables regarding classification purposes.
- **Reduct stability**, which is a ratio of all objects from decision table discernible by this attribute set. It is only important when dynamic reducts are considered (for static reducts this value is always equal to 100%).

Reducts may be used for the next steps of inducing rules process to simplify and speed it up.

We consider medical data as a special case of information system in which the essential operation is to detect whether an analyzed object fits or, even more important, do not fit to the rest of the objects. The latter should be immediately reconsidered as a suspect for a medical mistake or an item requiring special investigation as an exception to the rule.

If using reducts can speed up the whole processing without blurring the decision by partial data elimination then obviously reducts will be generated. The most probably approach will incorporate analyses with and without finding the reducts and then some comparisons to get experience for further adjusting the methodology of exploiting the system.

3.4 Frequent Sets

A frequent set is a set of variable-value pairs that occur in objects of information system more often than other pairs. It is also the base for some data-mining algorithms.

This module enables to generate set of frequent sets with a standard Apriori algorithm [10]. There are 3 parameters of this algorithm:

- **Minimal support** - the minimal number of objects in which the considered set of variable-value pairs are required to be present.
- **Hash value** (hash tree parameter) is the parameter of a hash function associated with all non-terminal nodes.
- **Leaf node capacity** (hash tree parameter) is the maximal capacity of terminal nodes.

Both hash tree parameters can only effect in speed efficiency of finding the frequent sets. The default values for the hash tree parameters are provided and only an experienced user can benefit from adjusting their values to the specific needs.

3.5 Rules

Decision rules are one of the most popular methods of representing knowledge gained from a considered information system. Rules can be immediately applied to the inferring processes. Rules may be generated with 2 types of algorithms:

- **Apriori**
- **Based on extraction**

Both algorithms [11] allow to create certain and possible rules. Apriori based algorithm generates rules directly from the information system, whereas extraction algorithm can be used on previously generated frequent sets (generally, it can be used on previously generated set of rules).

There are two main parameters: minimal support and minimal confidence. Minimal support is the minimal number of objects in which the considered rules are correct (it is possible that there are objects for which the considered rules are incorrect). Confidence is the ratio of correctness of the rule. Maximal value (100%) means that whenever the rule is applied, the decision part of the rule is correct.

Rule analyzer provides following functionality:

- **Object coverage** selects a subset of generated rules that covers a specified object. Taking analyzed object as a starting point, it provides the user with a small decision system of reliable (in respect to the object) rules.
- **Rules coverage** selects a subset of information system covered by specified rules. It provides a proof of reliability of decision rules in form of properly identified association in the selected objects.
- **Rules investigator** selects list of objects covered by the predecessor of specified rule. It can be used to detailed analyses of the specified rule by providing user with a list of objects covered by the rule and those for which the rule is incorrect. Potentially, it can lead to either disproving of the considered rule or, if rule is believed reliable, finding in-correct objects.

3.6 Credibility Coefficients Calculation

Credibility coefficient of object is a measure of its similarity with respect to the rest of the objects in the considered information system. There is no common way to define the relation of similarity, so it is strictly connected with the implemented method.

All credibility coefficients implemented in ARES system are normalized to range $<0, 1>$. Value 0 represents the least level of credibility of a given object, while value 1 is the maximum representing perfect relationship of similarity to other objects in the decision table. This normalization is very useful especially when we want to compare results returned by different algorithms.

This module allows calculation of credibility coefficients with one of the following methods:

- **Statistical/frequency method** (C_{SF}) - This is a very simple and fast algorithm. It calculates credibility coefficients based on number of objects having the same value for each attribute. Coefficient for each object is proportional to the number of objects having the same values for given attributes. Credibility coefficient $C_{SF}(u, d)$ for object u of decision table $S =< U, C \cup \{d\}, V, p >$ is calculated according to the following formula:

$$C_{SF}(u, d) = \frac{\sum_{a \in C} \frac{card(W_{u,d,a})}{card(K_{u,d})}}{card(C)} \tag{1}$$

where:

$$\begin{aligned} K_{u,d} &= \{y \in U : p(y, d) = p(u, d)\} \\ W_{u,d,a} &= \{y \in U : p(y, d) = p(u, d) \wedge p(y, a) = p(u, a)\} \end{aligned} \tag{2}$$

- **Based on class approximation** (C_{CA}) - This credibility coefficient is based on rough set theory. The value of coefficient is calculated using measures of positive and negative regions of each decision class. Credibility coefficient $C_{CA}(u, d)$ for object u of decision table $S =< U, C \cup \{d\}, V, p >$ is calculated according to the following formula:

$$C_{CA}(u, d) = \frac{\sum_{h \in H} def(u, d, h)}{card(H)} \tag{3}$$

where:

$$\begin{aligned} H &= \{v \in V_d\}; X_{d,h} = \{u \in U : p(u, d) = h\} = X \\ K_{pos} &= \{u \in U : u \in POS_C(X)\}; K_{neg} = \{u \in U : u \in NEG_C(X)\} \\ W_{pos_{u,a}} &= \{y \in U : y \in POS_C(X) \wedge p(y, a) = p(u, a)\} \\ W_{neg_{u,a}} &= \{y \in U : y \in NEG_C(X) \wedge p(y, a) = p(u, a)\} \\ def(u, d, h) &= \begin{cases} 1 & for\ u \in \{POS_C(X) \cup NEG_C(X)\} \\ \frac{\sum_{a \in A} addCoef(u,d,h,a)}{card(C)} & for\ u \in BN_C(X) \end{cases} \\ addCoef(u, d, h, a) &= \begin{cases} \frac{card(Wpos_{u,a})}{card(Kpos)} & for\ p(u, d) = h \\ \frac{card(Wneg_{u,a})}{card(Kneg)} & for\ p(u, d) \neq h \end{cases} \end{aligned} \tag{4}$$

- **Hybrid** (C_{HM}) - This is an assemblage of the most significant features of frequency method and class approximation method. Credibility coefficient $C_{HM}(u, d)$ for object u of decision table $S =< U, C \cup \{d\}, V, p >$ is calculated according to the following formula:

$$C_{HM}(u, d) = \frac{\sum_{h \in H} def2(u, d, h)}{card(H)} \tag{5}$$

where:

$$def2(u, d, h) = \begin{cases} 1 & for\ u \in \{POS_C(X) \cup NEG_C(X)\} \\ \frac{\sum_{a \in C} \frac{card(W_{u,d,a})}{card(K_{u,d})}}{card(C)} & for\ u \in BN_C(X) \end{cases} \tag{6}$$

All other parameters are defined in previous methods.

Example

Sample decision table $(S =< U, C \cup \{d\}, V, p >, U = \{1, 2, 3, 4, 5, 6\}, C = \{c1, c2, c3\}, d = dec)$ and credibility coefficients (C_{SF}, C_{CA}, C_{HM}) calculated for every object are presented in Table 1.

Table 1. Sample decision table and values of credibility coefficient for every object

Object Id	c1	c2	c3	dec	C_{SF}	C_{CA}	C_{HM}
1	0	1	0	1	0.44	1.00	1.00
2	1	0	0	1	0.22	0.22	0.21
3	1	1	1	1	0.44	1.00	1.00
4	0	1	1	1	0.00	1.00	1.00
5	1	0	0	0	0.00	0.00	0.25
6	0	1	2	0	0.44	1.00	1.00

3.7   Data Elimination

This module enables to change information systems' structure by eliminating selected objects and/or attributes. The elimination may be done arbitrary by user. User decisions may be also supported by results generated by different modules of the ARES system. For instance: using reduct sets only the least meaningful attributes may be removed or using credibility coefficients can indicate the least reliable objects for elimination. Modified information system is saved as a new one and it may be used as input data for all presented algorithms (presumably to be compared with the original one's outcomes).

4   Technical Aspects of ARES System

ARES Rough Set Exploration System was developed using only free tools and free software. It was entirely written in JAVA programming language. Graphic user interface was implemented using standard JAVA graphic library - Swing. The GUI of ARES system is equipped with some elements of MDI (Multiple Document Interface) architecture. It means that the user can work simultaneously on a few projects (the user may use number of independent workspaces).

Whole system was designed in such a way that it is very easy to add additional functionality to it (e.g. new algorithms for finding reducts or mining rules). It could be achieved by employing abstract classes and interfaces, which build framework of this application.

ARES can be launched on every operating system on which Java Virtual Machine is provided (e.g. Windows, Linux, Unix, Solaris). ARES system is easy to install and operate. The user has to copy application files and execute the prepared batch file, which sets up the system environment.

The most crucial parameter of a computer system is the amount of RAM memory installed. The bigger decision tables we want to analyze, the more memory we need for efficient work. Huge data sets will require fast CPU as well. Minimal requirements are: 128MB of RAM, CPU of 500 MHz, 1MB of free disc space and Java Runtime Environment (JRE) 1.4.

5   Conclusions

The paper presents ARES Rough Set Exploration System functional capabilities. All typical stages of data exploration based on the rough set theory can be performed and presented with support of ARES system. This application is similar to other versatile rough set tools [1] but it also provides some unique and useful features:

- **Credibility coefficient calculation** - A set of algorithms which estimate reliability of data stored in decision tables. More on this topic (algorithms description, samples, etc...) can be found in [4].
- **Reduct finding algorithm based on decomposition of the search space** - Very fast and effective algorithm for finding minimal reduct and set of reducts of given size. Comparison of this method with other algorithms is presented in [8].
- **New discretization algorithms** - ARES system introduces two new approaches to this problem.

The first feature introduces new capabilities to rough set tools functionality and the next two ones can improve efficiency of the appropriate data analysis steps. Some preliminary experiments on credibility coefficients were carried out and the results seem to be promising. To the original data set some randomly generated elements were added and it was possible to detect them by low values of credibility coefficients. We hope the proposed credibility coefficients may be successfully used in detecting corrupted data or abnormal and distinctive situations.

The methodology of handling credibility coefficients should be worked out. We do believe that a knowledge consisting of rules and exceptions to them is complete. The significance of identifying improper data may vary in different applications, nevertheless credibility coefficients introduce a new quality to data analysis.

A multi-document architecture of the ARES System allows for detailed analysis of the data exploration process, what makes the system a perfect and easy to use learning tool.

The ARES system has been implemented in Java and is portable. Its architecture enables permanent development by adding new items with appropriate algorithms to the documents presented and processed by the system. The module structure of ARES Rough Set Exploration System makes its development very easy - new functional items inherit structure features of the system. In the nearest future we plan to provide more functionality to the system e.g. reduct finding algorithm using simulated annealing and ant colony, support for other data sources (database servers).

ARES system was aimed at medical application to exploit its ability to recognize exceptional cases by employing credibility coefficients, but, generally, it can be used on any kind of data, e.g. engineering purposes.

Acknowledgement

This work has been partially supported by the Polish State Committee for Scientific Research under Grant 7 T11C 012 20 and by the Dean of Faculty of Electronics and Information Technology, Warsaw University of Technology, Warsaw, Poland.

References

1. Rough Set Database System page, http://www.rsds.wsiz.rzeszow.pl
2. Podraza, R., Podraza, W.: Rough Set System with Data Elimination. Proc. of the 2002 Int. Conf. on Mathematics and Engineering Techniques in Medicine and Biological Sciences (METMBS'2002), Las Vegas, Nevada, USA (2002) 493–499
3. Podraza, R., Dominik, A., Walkiewicz, M.: Decision Support System for Medical Applications. Proc. of the IASTED International Conference on Applied Simulations and Modeling, Marbella, Spain (2003) 329–334
4. Podraza, R., Dominik, A., Walkiewicz, M.: Application of ARES Rough Set Exploration System for Data Analysis. Conf. Computer Science - Research and Applications, Kazimierz Dolny, Poland (2005), to appear in Annales Universitatis Mariae Curie-Skłodowska, Sectio AI Informatica, Vol. III (2005)
5. Risvik, K.M.: Discretization of Numerical Attributes, Preprocessing for Machine Learning. Norwegian University of Science and Technology, Department of Computer and Information Science (1997)
6. Pawlak, Z.: Rough Sets. Theoretical Aspects of Reasoning about Data. Kluwer, Dordrecht (1991)
7. Bazan, J.G., Nguyen, H.S., Nguyen, S.H., Synak, P., Wróblewski, J.: Rough Set Algorithms in Classification Problem. In: Polkowski, L., Tsumoto, S., Lin, T.Y. (eds), Rough Set Methods and Applications, Physica-Verlag (2000) 49–88
8. Walczak, Z., Dominik, A., Terlecki, P.: Space Decomposition in the Problem of Finding Minimal Reducts. Proc. of the VII National Conference on Genetic Algorithms and Global Optimization, Kazimierz Dolny, Poland (2004) 193–201
9. Wróblewski, J.: Finding minimal reducts using genetic algorithm. Second Annual Joint Conference on Information Sciences (JCIS'95), University of Warsaw - Institute of Mathematics (1995) 186–189
10. Agrawal, R., Srikant, R.: Fast Algorithms for Mining Association Rules in Large Databases. Proc. of XX International Conference on VLDB, Santiago, Chile (1994) 487–499
11. Kryszkiewicz, M.: Strong Rules in Large Databases. Proc. of VII International Conference on Information Processing and Management of Uncertainty in Knowledge-based Systems (IPMU), Paris, France (1998) 1520–1527

DIXER – Distributed Executor
for Rough Set Exploration System

Jan G. Bazan[1], Rafał Latkowski[2], and Marcin Szczuka[3]

[1] Institute of Mathematics, University of Rzeszów,
ul. Rejtana 16A, 35-959 Rzeszów, Poland
bazan@univ.rzeszow.pl
[2] Institute of Informatics, Warsaw University,
ul. Banacha 2, 02-097 Warszawa, Poland
R.Latkowski@mimuw.edu.pl
[3] Institute of Mathematics, Warsaw University,
ul. Banacha 2, 02-097 Warszawa, Poland
szczuka@mimuw.edu.pl

Abstract. We present the Distributed Executor for RSES (DIXER) which is a supplementary software for the Rough Set Exploration System (RSES). It takes an advantage of grid computing paradigm and allows to shorten the time necessary for experiments by employing all available workstations to run a scenario of experiments. DIXER software includes most important rough set classification algorithms from RSES and also other algorithms for distributed machine learning. It creates an easy to operate and utilize platform for grid computations and provides a robust and fault tolerant environment for computation-heavy experiments. We provide also experimental evaluation of DIXER that proves at least 96% efficiency in parallelization.

1 Introduction

Machine Learning researchers commonly face a problem of carrying out a huge number of experiments or one, but very time-consuming. The two main reasons of that is the demand for completeness of experimental evaluation and complexity of the machine learning methods themselves.

Let us take, for example, an imaginary algorithm with three parameters. Each of these parameters may take one of three discrete values. This makes $3 \cdot 3 \cdot 3 = 27$ different configurations for our algorithm and if we would like to do a complete empirical evaluation we should provide experimental results for all 27 possibilities. Let's also assume that we have an implementation of this algorithm that requires one minute of execution time to complete single run. To get results of ten experiments using ten-fold cross-validation (CV10) with this algorithm we have to wait $27 \cdot 10 \cdot 10 = 2700$ minutes (45 hours).

The example above is only imaginary, but in real cases we usually face much more demanding problems. If we could acquire four times more computational power then instead of 45 hours we would obtain results overnight. That is why for carrying out experiments we would like to utilize not one, but several computers.

D. Ślęzak et al. (Eds.): RSFDGrC 2005, LNAI 3642, pp. 39–47, 2005.

There are several ways to get more computational power through balancing the load over a number of computational units. The first and the simplest way to do this is just by dividing the work manually and then, by going from machine to machine, put parts of work on all available computers. This approach can be improved by using remote access to another computer but, unfortunately, this method is not available on some software platforms. Obviously, in such an approach we waste a lot of effort on manual partitioning of work, not-automated process of experiment execution, result gathering, and execution monitoring.

Another approach is to use specially designed parallel computers or clusters of computers. However, these machines are extremely expensive and efficient utilization of such resources require re-implementation of software used in experiments (or manual partitioning of work as above).

In late 90's another approach has been proposed, namely the grid computing (cf. [5]). This approach is constantly gaining popularity in academic and commercial circles. In contrast to cluster computing, the grid computing does not require highly efficient and very expensive inter-computer connections and assumes utilization of regular network of workstations, exactly like those available at every university or company. Probably the first widely known grid computing scientific application is the Seti@Home (cf. [10]). In this project every computer connected to the Internet can participate in searching for extra-terrestrial civilization by analyzing data from a radio-telescope.

In this paper we present a grid computing platform dedicated to machine learning experiments. The *Distributed Executor* (*DIXER*) software system is designed to meet the need for a tool that makes it possible to perform series of complex experiments by employing the *grid computing* paradigm. It provides an easy to operate environment that automates execution of tasks in heterogeneous, commonly available networks of workstations. The DIXER is a supplementary software for the *Rough Set Exploration System* (RSES, see [1,2]). It is mainly suited for experiments based on RSES-Lib software [1], but as an open architecture it facilitates a plug-in mechanism, so that new modules can be added without modification of the main program.

The DIXER had to be written from scratch, as existing solutions proved to be not suitable for our purposes. We considered utilization of existing clustering/concurrency support systems, such as *PVM* or *MPI*, but they are either not efficient enough in machine learning applications or provide too low-level solutions. It is not a surprise, as these approaches are designed to work with specialized parallel computers or very expensive equipment like Myrinet network in the case of Network of Workstations (NOW) project (cf. [3]). In the case of grid computing applications in data analysis we should avoid implementations that assume too frequent synchronization between concurrent processes. In general, we would like to make the use of the machine standing in the office next door after hours, or to employ a student lab as a grid machine, when there are no classes.

In the second section we provide a very brief description of DIXER. Next, (Section 3) we describe two modules bundled with DIXER. In Section 4 we describe our experimental evaluation of the efficiency boost achieved through the use of DIXER. Finally, conclusions and bibliography close the paper.

2   Description

The DIXER software consist of two applications: Manager and Node. As they are written in Java, it is possible to install them on variety of operating systems including Linux, MS-Windows, Mac-OS, and various flavors of Unix. *DIXER-Node* has to be installed and run on all computers that cooperate in distributed computation. *DIXER-Manager* should run on one machine only (see Fig. 1). DIXER-Manager schedules experiments (jobs) for all nodes in the grid of computers, i.e., those, where DIXER-Node is executed. DIXER-Node performs all experiments (jobs) scheduled by DIXER-Manager.

The DIXER software creates an easy to operate and utilize platform for grid computing and provides a robust and fault tolerant environment for computation-heavy experiments. At the moment it is bundled with two modules for distributed computations. The *RSES Parallel Experimenter* (RSParallel) allows performing experiments with classifiers available in RSES-Lib. The *Branch-and-Bound* DIXER module makes it possible to perform feature selection with use of wrapper attribute evaluation and strategies similar to well known branch-and-bound search algorithm.

The DIXER-Manager has a graphical user interface (GUI, see Fig. 2) that provides the console for managing all cooperating computers. Playing the boss, for most of the time DIXER-Manager consumes only a small fraction of system resources, both CPU time and system memory. This load, however, depends on the number of nodes in grid and the task at hand. DIXER-Manager requires some additional data files to be created. These files are necessary to store experiment control data.

The DIXER-Node contains simplistic graphical user interface (GUI, see Fig. 2) on which one can supervise the program status. On demand this GUI can be disabled and then DIXER-Node runs silently in background. Usually, DIXER-Node consumes a lion share of system resources, both CPU time and system memory. DIXER-Node can also require some disc space in order to store data files needed in experiments, which are sent by DIXER-Manager together with job descriptions.

DIXER also provides mechanisms for recovery from failure. Execution of all experiments can be easily stopped and restarted without loss of any already computed results. This property is used also for assuring robustness. Should one or more nodes crash because of the hardware or software failure, the already

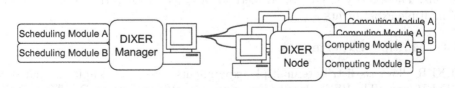

Fig. 1. Architecture of the grid of computers running DIXER-Manager and DIXER-Nodes

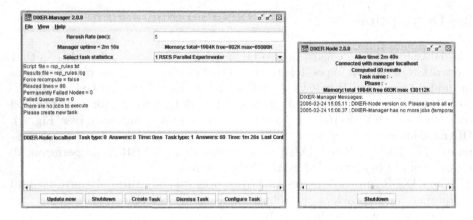

Fig. 2. Graphical User Interface of DIXER-Manager and DIXER-Node

computed results are preserved. If crash occurs only on the computers that run DIXER-Node, then the whole system is still working, but with less computational power due to reduced grid size. If crash touches the computer that runs DIXER-Manager then the DIXER-Manager should be restarted from the point of last delivered result.

There are several advantages of using DIXER for machine learning experiments. The obvious benefit from DIXER is the automation of processing multiple experiments using several computers. If it is necessary to test, e.g., which discretization or which decision rule shortening factor gives the best classification for particular data set, then DIXER can help in automation of experiment series. Another advantage is that DIXER architecture offers the platform that efficiently utilize power of available computers. DIXER is entirely written in Java™ programming language, what makes possible the construction of the grid in heterogenous hardware and software environments. DIXER, as well as the RSES is distributed free of charge for non-commercial purposes. It can be downloaded from the RSES Web page [9].

3   Implemented Methods

The DIXER software is distributed with two built-in modules. Apart from them it is possible to plug-in new modules that implement other distributed algorithms. The already implemented methods are: feature selection and execution of multiple experiments.

3.1   Multiple Experiments

DIXER allows to distribute multiple experiments across all computers that run DIXER-Node. The RSES Parallel Experimenter (RSParallel) is a DIXER module that makes it possible to carry out experiments based on methods implemented in Rough Set Exploration System (RSES), and particularly in RSES-Lib (c.f.

[1]). It processes a special script language, described in DIXER User Manual [7], that is used to prepare individual scenarios for experiments. This script language is interpreted line by line from the beginning of the file to its end, and each line contains description of a separate experiment.

While preparing the scenario file user can choose between several classification algorithms implemented in RSES-Lib. The description of each experiment includes the selection of algorithm, its parameters, and reference to data files used in training and testing phases. The results of experiments are written to a special file that can be used for generating description of results in the form of tables and/or statistics. These results are easy to analyze and support reporting.

Currently RSParallel provides the following RSES-Lib methods in experiment scenarios: discretization, decision rule induction, decision rule shortening and decomposition-based classifiers. A given experiment scenario can be stopped and restarted without loss of already computed partial results. User can also force DIXER to recalculate all results from the beginning.

3.2 Feature Selection

The feature selection problem is one of the most important problems in Data Mining as well as one of the most computationally expensive. The *Branch-and-Bound* DIXER module allows to carry out experiments with very expensive and accurate feature selection based on the wrapper method (see, e.g., [4]), which is a non-rough set feature selection approach. The strategy for searching the space of the possible attribute subsets is similar to the branch-and-bound search. Here, however, this strategy is not complete and is used rather in selection of the first candidate to visit within the lattice of the possible feature subsets. The results are saved in the special file that can be viewed both manually and with a help of text processing tools. As a wrapper classifier the decision tree from RSES-Lib is used. This decision tree algorithm can perform clustering of symbolic values using the indiscernibility as a measure for heuristic split.

This algorithm is an example of method that cannot be manually partitioned in order to distribute work among several machines. It cannot be prepared beforehand as the search strategy is modified on the basis of partial results. The integrated solutions for distributed computing give the advantage over manual methods, because implementation of more sophisticated experiments becomes viable.

The details on using these two methods are provided in the DIXER User Manual [7] bundled with the software.

4   Experimental Illustration

DIXER is available for download since 2003 (see [9]) and already has been used in several research experiments. As an example of such experiment we refer the reader to [8] where research on flexible indiscernibility relations and, particularly, on attribute limited indiscernibility relations is presented. The attribute limited indiscernibility relations are modifications of the indiscernibility relations that enable different treatment of missing attribute values for each attribute. The experimental work consisted of discretization and induction of decision rules over train part of data using all possible attribute limited indiscernibility relations and calculating classification accuracy over test part of data. Since the RSES-Lib does not support decision rule induction using attribute limited indiscernibility relations a special data preprocessing routine was used to simulate it. Generally speaking, there were two possible treatments of missing values for each attribute, so the number of all possible attribute limited indiscernibility relations is 2^N, where N is the number of conditional attributes in data. The experiments were carried out for five data sets, three of them with six conditional attributes and two of them with eight conditional attributes. Every data set was partitioned into ten pairs of train and test samples in order to use ten fold cross-validation (CV10), so in total there were $10 \cdot (3 \cdot 2^6 + 2 \cdot 2^8) = 7040$ experiments. The execution of those experiments took about a week on heterogeneous grid of computers consisting of up to three computers with Pentium 4 2.6GHz CPU and one computer with Pentium M 1GHz CPU, connected with 100Mb switched network. Some of computers were detached from the grid because of network failure or other user actions, but as it was mentioned before, it did not break the computation, it only reduced the computational power of the grid.

For the purpose of this paper we repeated a part of the experiments described above on a homogeneous grid of computers. The experiments were carried out with use of up to ten identical computers with a 733Mhz Pentium III CPU connected to 100Mb non-switched network. We took one pair of train and test data that has the shortest time of discretization and decision rule induction. The selected data — head injury data (hin), 3 classes, 6 categorical attributes, 1000 observations, 40.5% incomplete cases, 9.8% missing values — requires less than 7 seconds on a computer mentioned above to complete a single decision rule induction procedure. The number of possible attribute limited indiscernibility relations, thus the number of experiments is $2^6 = 64$. We selected this set of data because with so small execution time the effect of communication and synchronization overhead will be most visible. We may say, that this experiment is the worst case as the potential communication overhead is significant.

The results of experiments are presented in Table 1. The experiments were carried out using separate machine for manager and separate machines for nodes of the grid. We decided to measure the execution time in that way, because the execution of all 64 experiments on exactly the same computer acting as manager and node requires up to two seconds more than the execution on separate computers. In the first row of Table 1 the number of computers acting as nodes is presented, in the second — the execution time in seconds, and in the third row — the relative speed-up factor.

We have to take into account that on some configurations, where 64 is not divisible by the number of nodes in grid, DIXER-Manager has to wait for the last computer to collect all results. This implies that on configurations where 64 is divisible by the number of computers cooperating in grid the efficiency of grid should be slightly better. The worst result, i.e., result with largest difference

Table 1. Execution time and observed speed-up of DIXER grid consisting of up to ten computers

Number of computers	1	2	3	4	5	6	7	8	9	10
Time	440.32	220.17	148.28	115.13	92.81	75.52	65.72	55.79	50.87	46.3
Speed-up	1.00	2.00	2.97	3.82	4.74	5.83	6.70	7.89	8.66	9.51

from the expected speed-up is the result with ten computers acting as grid nodes. In this case we have 9.51 speed-up ratio instead of 10. That corresponds to two wasted seconds. In order to measure the scalability more accurately, we also performed a linear regression on the presented results. The results are linearly approximated by line with factor 0.9636 with goodness of fit $R^2 = 0.999$. It corresponds to 96% efficiency in computational resources utilization.

Figure 3 presents two charts with results of experiments. On that figure the execution time and speed-up for first 16, 32 and 48 experiments is presented for reference purposes. On the execution time chart (left) we can notice that the reduction of computation time is inversely proportional to the resources (number of computers). On the right, speed-up chart a reference line with ideal speed-up is presented for comparison. We can observe that the lowest speed-up curve correspond to the execution of first 16 experiments. It suggests that the DIXER achieves worst parallelization efficiency is at the beginning of distributed computation. However, overall efficiency is never lower than 95% of the ideal speed-up.

The excellent results of experiments are partially caused by the fact, that on mentioned computers we carried out multiple experiments utilizing always the same 64 pairs of data. This means, that on those computers we needed to download the input data to local hard disk only once. However, if the data for scheduled experiment is not present on the remote computer then they have to be sent from the Manager to Node using DIXER internal mechanism for data

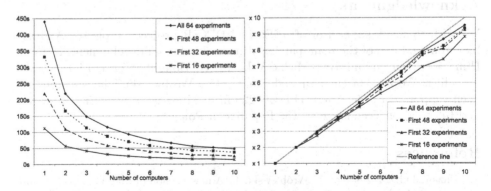

Fig. 3. The left chart presents execution time of the experiments on DIXER grid with parition to first 16, 32, 48 and all 64 experiments. The right chart presents observed speed-up of the execution.

transfer. We have not tested in detail the influence of data transfer on execution time, but this influence should not be significant. There are two arguments supporting such statement. Firstly, the size of the data is somehow proportional to the execution time of the experiment. In this particular case each pair of files have total size of about 19KB, so the transfer time is negligible. Secondly, even when the data is on local hard disk, DIXER performs additional test by comparing properties of these files on the DIXER-Manager computer with originals stored on the DIXER-Node computer. It checks such values as: last modification time, total size and CRC16 of the first 4KB of the file. Such a verification is very similar to the data transfer, as it employs both local hard drive and network connection. This verification is, of course, included in the results presented in Table 1 and Figure 3. After all, not all experiments done with help of DIXER utilize different data files. More typical use is to test different methods or different parameters on relatively small set of data files.

5 Conclusions

The DIXER software provides a platform for grid-like computations supporting Machine Learning and Data Mining experiments. The computational core, with respect to the Machine Learning algorithms, is based on renewed RSES-Lib library that implements several Rough Set based algorithms. The flexibility of DIXER software makes it possible to extend its functionality without modification of the essential source code. The DIXER is easy to operate and provides a robust and fault tolerant environment for computational-heavy experiments. Especially in an academic environment, where usually a number of standard workstations is available, it is the cheapest way to access an enlarged computational power. The minimization of communication overhead and grid management (load balancing) makes it possible to obtain the computational throughput that almost equals the sum of computational powers of cooperating computers.

Acknowledgments

We wish to thank supervisor of RSES and DIXER projects, professor Andrzej Skowron, and rest of the team participating in design and development: Nguyen Hung Son, Nguyen Sinh Hoa, Michał Mikołajczyk, Dominik Ślęzak, Piotr Synak, Arkadiusz Wojna, Marcin Wojnarski, and Jakub Wróblewski. The research has been supported by the grant 3T11C00226 from Ministry of Scientific Research and Information Technology of the Republic of Poland.

References

1. Bazan, J.G., Szczuka, M.S., Wróblewski, J.: A new version of rough set exploration system. In Alpigini, J.J., Peters, J.F., Skowron, A., Zhong, N., eds.: Rough Sets and Current Trends in Computing, Third International Conference, RSCTC 2002, Malvern, PA, USA, October 14-16, 2002, Proceedings. Volume 2475 of Lecture Notes in Computer Science., Springer (2002) 397–404

2. Bazan, J.G., Szczuka, M., Wojna, A., Wojnarski, M.: On the evolution of rough set exploration system. In Tsumoto, S., Słowiński, R., Komorowski, H.J., Grzymała-Busse, J.W., eds.: Rough Sets and Current Trends in Computing, RSCTC 2004. Volume 3066 of Lecture Notes in Computer Science., Springer (2004) 592–601
3. Culler, D., Arpaci-Dusseau, A., Arpaci-Dusseau, R., Chun, B., Lumetta, S., Mainwaring, A., Martin, R., Yoshikawa, C., Wong, F.: Parallel computing on the Berkeley NOW. In: Proceedings of the 9th Joint Symposium on Parallel Processing, JSPP'97. (1997)
4. Dash, M., Liu, H.: Feature selection for classification. Intelligent Data Analysis **1** (1997) 131–156
5. Forester, I., Kesselman, C. (Eds.): The Grid: Blueprint for a New Computing Infrastructure. Morgan-Kaufmann. (1998)
6. Groupp, W., Lusk, E.: Why are PVM and MPI so different? Report of Mathematics and Computer Science Division of Aragonne National Laboratory ANL/MCS-P667-0697. (1997)
7. Latkowski, R.: DIXER User Manual. Warsaw University. (2003) (refer to [9])
8. Latkowski, R.: Flexible Indiscernibility Relations for Missing Attribute Values. Fundamenta Informaticae **66:2** (2005), In print.
9. The RSES WWW homepage at http://logic.mimuw.edu.pl/~rses
10. SETI@home WWW homepage at http://setiathome.ssl.berkeley.edu/

$\mathcal{R}o\mathcal{S}y$: A Rough Knowledge Base System

Robin Andersson[1], Aida Vitória[2], Jan Małuszyński[3], and Jan Komorowski[1]

[1] The Linnaeus Centre for Bioinformatics,
Uppsala University, Box 598, SE-751 24 Uppsala, Sweden
{Robin.Andersson, Jan.Komorowski}@lcb.uu.se
[2] Dept. of Science and Technology,
Linköping University, SE-601 74 Norrköping, Sweden
aidvi@itn.liu.se
[3] Dept. of Computer and Information Science,
Linköping University, SE-581 83 Linköping, Sweden
janma@ida.liu.se

Abstract. This paper presents a user-oriented view of $\mathcal{R}o\mathcal{S}y$, a $\mathcal{R}$ough Knowledge Base $\mathcal{S}$ystem. The system tackles two problems not fully answered by previous research: the ability to define rough sets in terms of other rough sets and incorporation of domain or expert knowledge. We describe two main components of $\mathcal{R}o\mathcal{S}y$: knowledge base creation and query answering. The former allows the user to create a knowledge base of rough concepts and checks that the definitions do not cause what we will call a model failure. The latter gives the user a possibility to query rough concepts defined in the knowledge base. The features of $\mathcal{R}o\mathcal{S}y$ are described using examples. The system is currently available on a web site for online interactions.

1 Introduction

The rough set framework [1] is relevant from the knowledge representation and data mining perspectives. The ability to handle vague and contradictory knowledge makes rough sets an important technique that can be incorporated in knowledge base systems. In addition, rough set methods can also be used to perform data exploration, which makes them relevant from a data mining point of view.

This paper presents a $\mathcal{R}$ough Knowledge Base $\mathcal{S}$ystem, called $\mathcal{R}o\mathcal{S}y$. The system is accessible on the web page: http://www.ida.liu.se/rkbs .

$\mathcal{R}o\mathcal{S}y$ tackles two problems not fully answered by previous research in the field of rough set theory. The first problem is related to defining rough sets in terms of other rough sets. For instance, we may wish to express that a rough set is obtained as a projection of another rough set over a subset of its attributes. The second problem deals with incorporation of domain or expert knowledge. A question arises of how concept approximations can be derived by taking into account not only the examples provided explicitly by one or more tables but also domain knowledge.

In $\mathcal{R}o\mathcal{S}y$, the user can create a knowledge base of (non-recursive) vague concepts. Vague concepts are represented as implicitly or explicitly defined rough

D. Ślęzak et al. (Eds.): RSFDGrC 2005, LNAI 3642, pp. 48–58, 2005.

sets. Implicitly defined rough sets are obtained by combining different regions of other rough sets, e.g. lower approximations, upper approximations, and boundaries. The system also allows defining rough sets in terms of explicit examples. An important feature is that $\mathcal{R}o\mathcal{S}y$ handles some basic numerical measures and that they can be used in the implicit definition of rough sets. The system detects whether the defined vague concepts do not introduce "conflicts" leading to a so-called model failure. Finally, a knowledge base of rough concepts can be queried. Hence, the system supports the user in reasoning about the defined rough concepts and in data exploration.

As we show in this paper through some examples[1], $\mathcal{R}o\mathcal{S}y$ allows users to describe in an declarative and concise way solutions to problems that otherwise would require constructing specific programs in some language.

To our knowledge, besides $\mathcal{R}o\mathcal{S}y$, only the *CAKE* system [2] addresses the problem of implicitly defining rough sets. There are two major differences between the two systems. Firstly, our system distinguishes tuples for which there is no information available from the tuples for which there is contradictory evidence. The latter case corresponds to tuples in the boundary region. *CAKE* does not support this distinction: the boundary region includes tuples about which there is no information at all and tuples about which there is contradictory information. Secondly, $\mathcal{R}o\mathcal{S}y$ supports quantitative measures. This feature seems less obvious to achieve in *CAKE*. A more detailed comparison between both systems is included in [3].

2 A Knowledge Base System for Rough Sets

In this section we present the rough knowledge base system $\mathcal{R}o\mathcal{S}y$. We start with presenting the online user interface of $\mathcal{R}o\mathcal{S}y$. The notion of rough sets used in our framework and a proposed language for defining rough sets are presented in Section 2.2. Finally, a rough query language is discussed in Section 2.3. For a detailed and technical description of the system and its main components consult [4].

2.1 The Online User Interface

The online user interface of $\mathcal{R}o\mathcal{S}y$ is a simple tab-navigation system, where each tab corresponds to a different mode. The main mode is **Compile Rules or Queries**, described below. Besides this mode, $\mathcal{R}o\mathcal{S}y$ provides a mode for overviewing the defined rough knowledge base and a tool for query construction. Fig. 1 shows the main page of $\mathcal{R}o\mathcal{S}y$'s web interface.

The first step in using the system (Fig. 1) is to create a rough knowledge base (RKB). An RKB can be typed directly in $\mathcal{R}o\mathcal{S}y$ in the text area or loaded from local or remote files. The second step is to compile the RKB by clicking the **Compile Rules** button. Errors detected during compilation, such as syntax

---

[1] All examples presented in this paper are available from:
http://www.ida.liu.se/rkbs/examples.html .

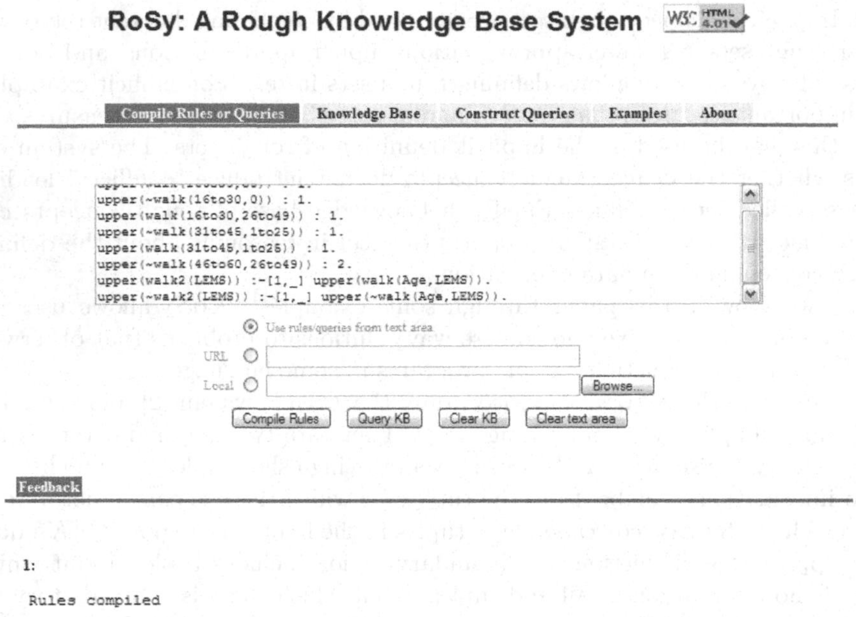

RoSy: A Rough Knowledge Base System   W3C HTML 4.01

Compile Rules or Queries	Knowledge Base	Construct Queries	Examples	About

```
upper(~walk(16to30,0)) : 1.
upper(walk(16to30,26to49)) : 1.
upper(~walk(31to45,1to25)) : 1.
upper(walk(31to45,1to25)) : 1.
upper(~walk(46to60,26to49)) : 2.
upper(walk2(LEMS)) :-[1,_] upper(walk(Age,LEMS)).
upper(~walk2(LEMS)) :-[1,_] upper(~walk(Age,LEMS)).
```

⊙ Use rules/queries from text area

URL ○

Local ○   [Browse...]

[Compile Rules] [Query KB] [Clear KB] [Clear text area]

Feedback

1:

    Rules compiled

Fig. 1. $\mathcal{R}o\mathcal{S}y$'s web interface, http://www.ida.liu.se/rkbs

errors, are displayed in the **Feedback** area. If the compilation procedure succeeds then the message *Rules compiled* is displayed in the feedback area. An RKB can be deleted from the system via the **Clear KB** button. The third step is to reason with the knowledge in the (compiled) RKB by querying it. Queries can be typed directly in the text area or loaded from local or remote files. Queries are evaluated via the **Query KB** button and answers to the queries are output in table format in the feedback area.

2.2 Defining Rough Relations in $\mathcal{R}o\mathcal{S}y$

We start with presenting the notion of rough sets used in our framework [3, 5]. Consider an information system $\mathcal{I} = (U, A)$, in the sense of [6], where U is a universe of objects and A is a set of attributes. Every object in U is associated with a tuple of conditional attributes. We assume that such a tuple is the only way of referring to an object. Hence, different individuals described by the same tuple are indiscernible. For simplicity, we write t to designate a general tuple $\langle t_1, \ldots, t_n \rangle$. Let k be a positive integer. A pair $t : k$ is called a *supported tuple*, where k is called the *support*. Intuitively, $t : k$ represents k individuals which all have their conditional attribute values as indicated by the tuple t. A *rough set* (or *rough relation*[2]) S is a pair of sets $(\overline{S}, \neg S)$ of supported tuples, such that for any tuple t at most one supported tuple $t : k$ appears in each of the sets $\overline{S}$

---

[2] The expressions "rough set" and "rough relation" are used interchangeably in this paper.

and $\overline{\neg S}^3$. An element $t : k \in \overline{S}$ or $t : k \in \overline{\neg S}$ indicates that the indiscernibility class described by t belongs to the *upper approximation* of a rough set S or $\neg S$, respectively, and that this class contains $k > 0$ individuals that are positive examples of the concept described by S or $\neg S$.

The *lower approximation* and the *boundary region* of a rough set S is defined as:

$$\underline{S} = \{t : k_1 \in \overline{S} \mid \forall k_2 > 0, t : k_2 \notin \overline{\neg S}\} \tag{1}$$

$$\underline{\overline{S}} = \{t : k_1 : k_2 \mid \exists k_1, k_2 > 0, t : k_1 \in \overline{S} \text{ and } t : k_2 \in \overline{\neg S}\} \tag{2}$$

A *decision table* $\mathcal{D} = (U, A = \{a_1, \ldots, a_n\}, \{d\})$, where $d \notin A$ is a binary decision attribute, represents a rough set $D = (\overline{D}, \overline{\neg D})$. Any decision table can be encoded by *rough facts* that describe the rows in the table. A rough fact describes a tuple in the upper approximation of a rough relation D and is in one of the following forms:

$$\texttt{upper(d(t}_1\texttt{,...,t}_n\texttt{))} \; : \; \texttt{k.} \tag{3}$$

$$\texttt{upper(}\sim\texttt{d(t}_1\texttt{,...,t}_n\texttt{))} \; : \; \texttt{k.} \tag{4}$$

where the predicate symbols $\texttt{d}$ and $\sim\texttt{d}$ denote the positive and negative outcome of the decision attribute respectively, each $\texttt{t}_i$ $(1 \le \texttt{i} \le \texttt{n})$ is an attribute value corresponding to attribute a_i, and $\texttt{k}$ denotes the support of the tuple.

As an example, consider decision table $\mathcal{W}alk$ [6] and its corresponding rough facts encoding rough relation $Walk$ in Table 1.

Table 1. Decision table $\mathcal{W}alk$ and its corresponding collection of rough facts defining rough relation $Walk$

	Age	LEMS	Walk	
o1	16to30	50	Yes	⇒ upper(walk(16to30,50)) : 1.
o2	16to30	0	No	⇒ upper(∼walk(16to30,0)) : 1.
o3	16to30	26to49	Yes	⇒ upper(walk(16to30,26to49)) : 1.
o4	31to45	1to25	No	⇒ upper(∼walk(31to45,1to25)) : 1.
o5	31to45	1to25	Yes	⇒ upper(walk(31to45,1to25)) : 1.
o6	46to60	26to49	No	⎫ ⇒ upper(∼walk(46to60,26to49)) : 2.
o7	46to60	26to49	No	⎭

Note that objects o6 and o7 are indiscernible and they belong to the same decision class, which yields the support 2. From Table 1 it is easy to see that:

$$\underline{Walk} = \{\langle 16\text{to}30, 50\rangle \; : \; 1, \langle 16\text{to}30, 26\text{to}49\rangle \; : \; 1\} \tag{5}$$

$$\underline{\neg Walk} = \{\langle 16\text{to}30, 0\rangle \; : \; 1, \langle 46\text{to}60, 26\text{to}49\rangle \; : \; 2\} \tag{6}$$

$$\overline{Walk} = \{\langle 31\text{to}45, 1\text{to}25\rangle \; : \; 1 \; : \; 1\} \tag{7}$$

---

[3] Intuitively, this restriction requires that the support of each tuple t is specified only once, rather than as the sum of different supports.

Rough facts explicitly define the upper approximation of a rough relation. However, the lower approximation and the boundary region of that relation are implicitly derived from (1) and (2). $\mathcal{RoSy}$ also allows specific regions of rough relations to be defined implicitly by regions of other rough relations. This can be accomplished by *rough clauses*.

Consider again decision table $\mathcal{W}$alk in Table 1. Its corresponding rough relation *Walk* can be used to define a new rough relation *Walk2*, which corresponds to *Walk* but ignores the attribute Age. The following rough clauses define *Walk2*:

$$upper(walk2(LEMS)) :-[1,\_] \; upper(walk(Age,LEMS)). \tag{8}$$

$$upper(\sim walk2(LEMS)) :-[1,\_] \; upper(\sim walk(Age,LEMS)). \tag{9}$$

A rough clause is an implication on the general form *Head* ← *Body*, e.g. upper(walk2(LEMS)) ← upper(walk(Age,LEMS))., meaning that the tuples of $\overline{Walk}$ are defined to be members of $\overline{Walk2}$. The body and head of clause (8) contain *rough literals* that denote upper approximations of rough relations. A head rough literal refers to the rough relation being defined and can denote either the upper or lower approximation of that relation, while the body can contain one or more rough literals that can also denote boundary regions. A general rough literal is on the form reg(p(T$_1$,...,T$_n$)) , where p (possibly negated) denotes a rough relation P, reg $\in$ {upper, lower, boundary}, and T$_i$ $(1 \leq i \leq n)$ denotes an attribute term representing attribute i in that relation. *Attribute terms* can either be constants, starting with lower-case letters or digits, or variables, starting with upper-case letters. A constant denotes a specific attribute value, e.g. 16to30, while a variable can denote any attribute value in the domain of the corresponding attribute, e.g. variable Age above can denote any of the values 16to30, 31to45, or 46to60.

Besides rough literals, certain *quantitative measures*, such as support (supp), accuracy (acc), coverage (cov), and strength (strength) can optionally be included in the body as constraints. All variables occurring as their arguments should also appear in some rough literal in the body.

The body and the head of a rough clause is separated by the implication operator :-[τ,F]. F is the support-combining function sum, min or max, that specifies how the support of the newly defined rough relation is obtained from the support of the rough relations in the body of the clause. If the body only has one rough literal then F is auxiliary and often set to _ ([τ,_]). The constant $\tau \in [0,1]$ (often set to 1) is a rational number representing the *trust* in the body of the clause. The trust is the fraction of the calculated support of the body that should be considered as support for the rough region being defined.

A rough clause defining the lower approximation of a rough relation must fulfill condition (1). If the user tries to define a rough relation P such that a tuple $t \in \underline{P}$ and $t \in \overline{\neg P}$ then, $\mathcal{RoSy}$ reports a *model failure* [4], the current compilation stops, and the definition is retracted. For more details see [4].

2.3   Querying RoSy

RoSy provides a rough query language for retrieving information about defined rough relations. For instance, it may be desirable to monitor the changes in the regions of *Walk* when excluding the attribute Age. Such information may be retrieved by, for example, asking the following rough query.

```
boundary(walk2(LEMS)), K1 = supp(walk2(LEMS)), K2 = supp(~walk2(LEMS)).
```

The above compound query asks for all the tuples in the boundary region of *Walk2* and their support. In other words, the query requests all instantiations of the variables LEMS, K1 and K2 for the tuples in the boundary of *Walk2*. The received answer is given below.

K1	K2	LEMS
1	1	1to25
1	2	26to49

The answer states that tuples $\langle 1to25 \rangle : 1 : 1$ and $\langle 26to49 \rangle : 1 : 2$ are members of $\overline{Walk2}$.

A rough query can be any combination of rough literals and quantitative measures (constraints or assignments). Moreover, RoSy provides a classification procedure written on the form K = classify(p(T_1,...,T_n)), where K denotes a variable to be instantiated with the classification results, p denotes some (defined) rough relation P, and T_i ($1 \le i \le n$) denotes an attribute term representing attribute i of P. The classification query requests a prediction for the decision class to which a new individual described by tuple $\langle T_1,...,T_n \rangle$ may belong. The answer to such a query is either yes, no or unknown together with the certainty of the prediction. For more details see [3].

A rough query can either be ground (all attribute terms are constants) or non-ground (some attribute terms are variables). If a query is ground then it requests the truth value, yes or no, of the query. If the query on the other hand is non-ground then it requests all instantiations of the attribute variables in the query that make it true.

3   A Medical Informatics Application in RoSy

We now illustrate the use of RoSy with a data set that previously was analyzed with classical rough sets in [7].

Study [8] has shown that the single most important independent predictor for future hard cardiac events (cardiac death or non-fatal myocardial infarction) is an abnormal scintigraphic scan pattern. However, performing such a test is expensive, and may sometimes be redundant with respect to making a prognosis. It is therefore desirable to identify patients who are in need of a scintigraphic scan and avoid it for patients who can be prognosticated without such a test.

Table 2 describes information about patients observed in [8][4]. A group of 417 patients has been examined and each patient has an associated set of medical

---

[4] The number of attributes were reduced by Komorowski and Øhrn in [7] from the original data in [8].

Table 2. Attribute definitions

Attribute	Definition
Age	> 70 years old
Oldmi	Prior Infarction
Hypert	Hypertension
Dm	Diabetes
Smok	Smoking
Chol	Hypercholesterolemia
Gender	Male or female
Hfmed	History of dec. cordis
Angp	History of angina
Apstress	Angina during stress
Stt	Level of ST-T changes
Scanabn	Abnormal scintigraphic scan
Deathmi	Cardiac death or infarction

information. Attribute Deathmi is the decision attribute. The data is captured by rough relation *Deathmi* that is encoded by 335 rough facts.

Following the approach suggested in [7], identification of the patients who are in need of a scintigraphic scan requires monitoring changes in $\overline{Deathmi}$ when considering only the set of attributes $A \setminus \{\text{Scanabn}\}$, i.e. removing the attribute Scanabn. Next, we show how the problem can be formulated and solved in $\mathcal{R}o\mathcal{S}y$. A detailed comparison between our approach and the approach by [7] is outside the limits of this paper, but can be found in [3].

3.1 Avoiding the Expensive Test

The knowledge of a scintigraphic scan outcome is strictly required for the patients for whom excluding conditional attribute Scanabn causes migration into the boundary region from either *Deathmi* or ¬*Deathmi*. In the following rough clauses in Fig. 2, we shorten the sequence of attributes for readability reasons, e.g. we write Age,...,Scanabn instead of Age,Oldmi,Hypert,Dm,Smok,Chol, Gender,Hfmed,Angp,Apstress,Stt,Scanabn[5].

First, the set of attributes is reduced to not include Scanabn. The new rough relations D and its explicit negation $\neg D$ are defined by *Deathmi*, ignoring the last attribute, through rough clauses (10) and (11). The set of patients migrating into the boundary region of D from either *Deathmi* or ¬*Deathmi* corresponds to the rough relation *Migrate* defined by (12) and (13). These clauses state that the set of migrating individuals are the patients who are members of *Deathmi* (clause (12)) or ¬*Deathmi* (clause (13)) and also members of $\overline{D}$. If a patient is captured by either of these rules, one cannot make a reliable prognosis of future cardiac events without including the knowledge of the outcome of a scintigraphic scan. Rough clauses (14), (15) and (16) capture the set of non-migrating patients. Clause (14) captures those patients who were originally in the boundary region of

---

[5] This kind of abbreviation is, however, not allowed in the $\mathcal{R}o\mathcal{S}y$ system.

```
upper(d(Age,...,Stt)) :-[1,_] upper(deathmi(Age,...,Stt,Scanabn)).        (10)
upper(~d(Age,...,Stt)) :-[1,_] upper(~deathmi(Age,...,Stt,Scanabn)).       (11)
upper(migrate(Age,...,Stt)) :-[1,min] boundary(d(Age,...,Stt)),            (12)
     lower(deathmi(Age,...,Stt,Scanabn)).
upper(migrate(Age,...,Stt)) :-[1,min] boundary(d(Age,...,Stt)),            (13)
     lower(~deathmi(Age,...,Stt,Scanabn)).
upper(~migrate(Age,...,Stt)) :-[1,sum]                                     (14)
     upper(deathmi(Age,...,Stt,Scanabn)),
     upper(~deathmi(Age,...,Stt,Scanabn)).
upper(~migrate(Age,...,Stt)) :-[1,_] lower(d(Age,...,Stt)).                (15)
upper(~migrate(Age,...,Stt)) :-[1,_] lower(~d(Age,...,Stt)).               (16)
```

Fig. 2. A rough program for identification of migrating patients

Deathmi. These patients obviously remain in the boundary region after removing the Scanabn attribute. sum is used for combining the support of those tuples t such that $t : k_1 \in \overline{Deathmi}$ and $t : k_2 \in \overline{\neg Deathmi}$, into $sum(k_1, k_2) = k_1 + k_2$, since $k_1 + k_2$ is the total number of individuals in the indiscernibility class t.

We want to know for which patients the scintigraphic scan test is needed for a reliable prognosis. The answer to the following query is given in Table 3.

```
upper(migrate(Age,...,Stt)),
K1 = strength(migrate(Age,...,Stt)),
K2 = strength(~migrate(Age,...,Stt)).
```
For which patients is it useful to request the scintigraphic scan and what is the percentage of patients for whom the test is needed?

Table 3. Migrating patients

K1	K2	Age	Oldmi	Hypert	Dm	Smok	Chol	Gender	Hfmed	Angp	Apstress	Stt
0.0024	0.0073	0	0	0	0	0	0	0	0	0	0	0
0.0024	0.0049	0	0	0	0	0	0	1	1	1	2	0
0.0049	0.0000	0	1	0	0	0	0	1	0	0	0	0

For any tuple t, strength(migrate(t)) (strength($\neg$migrate(t))) represents the proportion of patients of the universe who belong to the indiscernibility class described by t and have positive (negative) outcome for migrate. Hence, the percentage of patients for whom the scintigraphic test is needed can be computed by the formula
$$\Phi = 100 \cdot \sum_{t \in \overline{Migrate}} (\text{strength}(\text{migrate}(t)) + \text{strength}(\neg\text{migrate}(t))).$$

```
upper(deathmiApprox(Attrs)) :-[1,_] lower(deathmi(Attrs)).        (17)

upper(~deathmiApprox(Attrs)) :-[1,_] lower(~deathmi(Attrs)).      (18)

lower(deathmiApprox(Attrs)) :-[1,sum] upper(deathmi(Attrs)),      (19)
        upper(~deathmi(Attrs)), acc(deathmi(Attrs)) >= 0.7.

lower(~deathmiApprox(Attrs)) :-[1,sum] upper(deathmi(Attrs)),     (20)
        upper(~deathmi(Attrs)), acc(deathmi(Attrs)) =< 0.3.

upper(deathmiapprox(Attrs)) :-[1,_] upper(deathmi(Attrs)),        (21)
        acc(deathmi(Attrs)) > 0.3, acc(deathmi(Attrs)) < 0.7.

upper(~deathmiapprox(Attrs)) :-[1,_] upper(~deathmi(Attrs)),      (22)
        acc(deathmi(Attrs)) > 0.3, acc(deathmi(Attrs)) < 0.7.
```

Fig. 3. A rough program approximating *Deathmi*

The answer indicates that if only the migrating patients, given by Table 3, undergo the expensive scintigraphic scan, then one may expect to avoid the test for approximately 98% of all the patients. Non-migrating patients who are members of $\overline{D}$ cannot be reliably prognosticated. For these patients it may still be needed to perform the scintigraphic scan procedure, if that is the opinion of a medical expert.

3.2   VPRSM in $\mathcal{R}o\mathcal{S}y$

Quantitative measures in the body of rough clauses can be used as constraints to build more generalized rough approximations of a relation in the same spirit as with *precision control parameters* in the *variable precision rough set model* (VPRSM) [9], as discussed in [5]. This means that it is possible to define new rough relations by other ones stating that a certain constraint must be fulfilled. The new rough relation *DeathmiApprox*, see Fig. 3, can be defined by the boundary region of *Deathmi* and the constraint stating that the accuracy of *Deathmi* should be above a certain threshold, say 70% (clause (19)). ¬*DeathmiApprox* is then defined by the boundary region of *Deathmi* and the constraint stating that the accuracy of *Deathmi* should be below 30% (clause (20)). In the rough clauses of Fig. 3, we write `Attrs` to denote the sequence `Age,Oldmi,Hypert,Dm,Smok, Chol,Gender,Hfmed,Angp,Apstress,Stt,Scanabn`[6].
      Rough clauses (17) and (18) state that the indiscernibility classes in $\underline{Deathmi}$ and ¬$\underline{Deathmi}$ are members of the upper approximation of respective approximate rough relation. The decision rules corresponding to these indiscernibility classes have 100% accuracies and are therefore included in the same region of the new rough relation. Rough clauses (21) and (22) state that any indiscernibility class t in the boundary such that `0.3 < acc(deathmi(t)) < 0.7` remains in the boundary.

---

[6] As previously, such a notation is used here only for readability reasons and is not allowed in the $\mathcal{R}o\mathcal{S}y$ system.

To see that the previously defined *DeathmiApprox* in fact approximates the rough relation *Deathmi* one can ask the following query to RoSy.

```
lower(~deathmiApprox(Age,...,Scanabn)),
upper(deathmi(Age,...,Scanabn)),
K1 = acc(~deathmi(Age,...,Scanabn)),
K2 = acc(deathmi(Age,...,Scanabn)).
```

Which indiscernibility classes are both in ¬DeathmiApprox and in Deathmi, and what are the corresponding accuracies?

The answer, given in Table 4, shows that two indiscernibility classes of *Deathmi* are members of the concept ¬*DeathmiApprox*. Since K2 ≤ 0.3, by rough clause (20), those classes are included in ¬*DeathmiApprox*.

Table 4. Patients who are members of ¬$\overline{DeathmiApprox}$ and $\overline{Deathmi}$

K1	K2	Age	Oldmi	Hypert	Dm	Smok	Chol	Gender	Hfmed	Angp	Apstress	Stt	Scanabn
0.8000	0.2000	0	1	0	0	0	0	1	0	0	1	0	1
0.8000	0.2000	0	1	1	0	0	0	1	0	0	0	0	1

4 Conclusions

This paper presents an overview of a system, called RoSy, that allows users to create knowledge bases of vague concepts. The main novel aspect of this system is that concepts can be represented by intensionally defined rough relations.

The main strengths of RoSy can be summarized as follows.

- RoSy makes it possible to capture and to integrate in a uniform way vague knowledge obtained directly from experimental data and encoded as rough facts with domain or expert knowledge expressed as rough clauses. This contrasts with most of current rough set techniques that only allow definition of (vague) concepts to be obtained from experimental data.
- The expressive power of RoSy makes it possible to formulate in the same language several useful techniques and extensions to rough sets reported in the literature, such as [7, 9]. Section 3 illustrates this point with two concrete examples.

Another important aspect of RoSy is the possibility of using queries to retrieve information about the defined rough sets and patterns implicit in the data.

The functionalities of RoSy can be improved in several ways. Firstly, RoSy does not handle recursive rough programs. This extension requires compilation of rough programs to extended logic programs whose semantics is captured by paraconsistent stable models [3]. Secondly, the query language may need extensions. For instance, assume that danger(Roadcond, Speed) is a rough concept indicating whether a traffic situation is dangerous in terms of road conditions (e.g. ice, wet) and vehicle speed (e.g. high, medium). The user may want to find out whether for an icy road, it is definitely dangerous to drive at any speed (based on this information a road may then be temporarily closed for safety reasons). The actual query capabilities of $\mathcal{RoSy}$ do not allow a direct formulation of this query. Thirdly, $\mathcal{RoSy}$ may be extended to find candidate hypothesis that explain observed facts, given a rough knowledge base. In this way we could combine abductive reasoning with rough relations. A possible application is reasoning about incomplete networks of chemical reactions represented in a rough knowledge base. Exploration of $\mathcal{RoSy}$ on a wide range of applications is crucial for further demonstration of its usefulness and for making relevant improvements. Among others, rough mereology [10] applications seem to be promising in that respect.

References

[1] Pawlak, Z.: Rough sets. International Journal of Computer and Information Sciences **11** (1982) 341–356
[2] Doherty, P., Łukaszewicz, W., Szałas, A.: CAKE: A computer-aided knowledge engineering technique. Proceedings of the 15th European Conference on Artificial Intelligence ECAI'2002 (2002) 220–224
[3] Vitória, A.: A framework for reasoning with rough sets. Licentiate thesis, Linköping University, Dept. of Science and Technology (2005) LiU-TEK-LIC-2004:73, Thesis No. 1144.
[4] Andersson, R.: Implementation of a rough knowledge base system supporting quantitative measures. Master's thesis, Linköping University (2004)
[5] Vitória, A., Damásio, C.V., Małuszyński, J.: Toward rough knowledge bases with quantitative measures. In Tsumoto, S., Slowinski, R., Komorowski, H.J., Grzymala-Busse, J.W., eds.: Rough Sets and Current Trends in Computing. Volume 3066 of Lecture Notes in Computer Science., Springer (2004) 153–158
[6] Komorowski, J., Pawlak, Z., Polkowski, L., Skowron, A.: Rough sets: A tutorial. In Pal, S., Skowron, A., eds.: Rough-Fuzzy Hybridization: A New Method for Decision Making. Springer Verlag, Singapore (1998) 3–98
[7] Komorowski, J., Øhrn, A.: Modelling prognostic power of cardiac tests using rough sets. Artificial Intelligence in Medicine **15** (1999)
[8] Geleijnse, M., Elhendy, A., van Domburg, R.: Prognostic value of dobutamine-atropine stress technetium-99m sestamibi perfusion scintigraphy in patients with chest pain. J Am Coll Cardiol **28** (1996) 447–454
[9] Ziarko, W.: Variable precision rough set model. Journal of Computer and Systems Science **46** (1993) 39–59
[10] Polkowski, L., Skowron, A.: Rough mereological calculi of granules: A rough set approach to computation. Journal of Computational Intelligence **17** (2001) 472–492

A Classification Model: Syntax and Semantics for Classification

Anita Wasilewska[1] and Ernestina Menasalvas[2]

[1] Department of Computer Science, State University of New York,
Stony Brook, NY, USA
anita@cs.sunysb.edu
[2] Departamento de Lenguajes y Sistemas Informaticos
Facultad de Informatica, U.P.M, Madrid, Spain
ernes@fi.upm.es

Abstract. We present here Semantic and Descriptive Models for Classification as components of our Classification Model (definition 17). We do so within a framework of a General Data Mining Model (definition 4) which is a model for Data Mining viewed as a generalization process and sets standards for defining syntax and semantics and its relationship for any Data Mining method. In particular, we define the notion of truthfulness, or a degree of truthfulness of syntactic descriptions obtained by any classification algorithm, represented within the Semantic Classification Model by a classification operator. We use our framework to prove (theorems 1 and 3) that for any classification operator (method, algorithm) the set of all discriminant rules that are fully true form semantically the lower approximation of the class they describe. The set of characteristic rules describes semantically its upper approximation. Similarly, the set of all discriminant rules for a given class that are partially true is semantically equivalent to approximate lower approximation of the class. The notion of the approximate lower approximation extends to any classification operator (method, algorithm) the ideas first expressed in 1986 by Wong, Ziarko, Ye [9], and in the VPRS model of Ziarko [10].

1 Introduction

One of the main goals of Data Mining is to provide a comprehensible description of information we extract from the data bases. The description comes in different forms. It might be a decision tree or a neural network, or a set of neural networks with fixed set of weights. It might be, as in Rough Set analysis ([5], [10], [11]) a decision table, or a set of reducts. In case of association analysis it is a set of associations, or association rules (with accuracy parameters). In case of cluster analysis it is a set of clusters, each of which has its own description and name.

In presented work we concentrate on, and describe in detail a special case of the General DM Model, namely a Classification Model. The Classification Model defined here includes a general method how to build a formal syntax and semantics for any classification problem, algorithm, or method. In this sense

D. Ślęzak et al. (Eds.): RSFDGrC 2005, LNAI 3642, pp. 59–68, 2005.

our Model encompasses all known (and future) classification algorithms and semantical and syntactical meaning of their results. In order to achieve this level of generality we assume that syntactically all algorithms have sets of rules as their outputs. We assume in particular that whatever the descriptive output of a given algorithm is (decision tree, neural network, decision table or others) it has been translated into a proper set of discriminant or characteristic rules, or both, with uncertainty or other measures, when needed. Hence our Descriptive Model (definition 14) is a rule based model.

The details of the Data Mining Model viewed as generalization process are presented in [7], [8]. The General DM Model framework is a subject of section 2. The details of the Descriptive Model and Semantic Model for Classification and their relationship to within the Classification Model (definition 17) are presented in sections 4, 3, and section 5.

2   The General Data Mining Model Framework

We build the General DM Model on two levels: syntactic and semantic. On syntactic level we define how to construct a formal description language and its components. The language is always based on the input data and the form of the output of a given algorithm used in the data mining process. The descriptive (syntactical) quality of information generalization performed by a given algorithm, or method is defined by its connection with the semantics of the algorithm which is being established by the Semantic Model (definition 2). The algorithms, or different DM methods are represented in the Semantic and Data Mining (definition 3) Models by proper generalization operators, as defined and The generalization investigated in [4], [7], [8].

The syntactic view of Data Mining as information generalization is modelled in our General Model by a Descriptive Model defined below. The definition of a Semantic Model follows.

Definition 1. *A* **Descriptive Model** *is a system* $\mathcal{DM} = (\mathcal{L}, \mathcal{E}, \mathcal{DK})$, *where*

- $\mathcal{L} = (\mathcal{A}, \mathcal{E})$ *is called a* **descriptive language**.
- $\mathcal{A}$ *is a countably infinite set called the* alphabet.
- $\mathcal{E} \neq \emptyset$ *and* $\mathcal{E} \subseteq \mathcal{A}^*$ *is the set of* descriptive expressions *of* $\mathcal{L}$.
- $\mathcal{DK} \neq \emptyset$ *and* $\mathcal{DK} \subseteq \mathcal{P}(\mathcal{E})$ *is a set of* **descriptions of knowledge states**.

For a given Data Mining application or method one defines in detail all the components of the model but in the General Model we only assume existence and a form of such definitions.

We usually view Data Mining results and present them to the user in their syntactic form as it is the most natural form of communication. The algorithms process records finding similarities which are then presented in a corresponding descriptive i.e. syntactic form. But the Data Mining process is deeply semantical in its nature and in order to capture this fact we not only define a semantic model but also its relationship with the syntactic descriptions. It means that we have to assign a semantic meaning to descriptive generalization operators and this is done in the General Model by the satisfiability relation.

Definition 2. *A* **Semantic Model** *is a system* $\mathbf{M} = (U, \mathcal{K}, \mathcal{G}, \preceq)$, *where*

- $U \neq \emptyset$ *is the* **universe**,
- $\mathcal{K} \neq \emptyset$ *is the set of* **generalization states**,
- $\preceq \subseteq \mathcal{K} \times \mathcal{K}$ *is a* **generalization relation**; *we assume that* $\preceq$ *is transitive.*
- $\mathcal{G} \neq \emptyset$ *is the set of* **generalizations operators** *such that for every* $G \in \mathcal{G}$, *for every* $K, K' \in \mathcal{K}$, $G(K) = K'$ *if and only if* $K \preceq K'$.

Data Mining process consists of two phases: preprocessing and data mining proper. We concentrate here on the Data Mining phase. The detailed definitions and discussion of its generalization operators is published in [7]. The preprocessing operators and preprocessing phase can also be expressed within our Semantic Model and are presented in a separate paper [8].

Data Mining Model defined below is a special case of the Semantic Model, with generalization relation being a special, non-reflexive data mining relation $\prec_{dm} \subseteq \preceq$.

Definition 3. *A* **Data Mining Model** *is a system* $\mathbf{DM} = (U, \mathcal{K}, \mathcal{G}_{dm}, \prec_{dm})$, *where the set* $\mathcal{G}_{dm}$ *is the set of data mining generalization operators.*

The detailed definitions of the above notions and motivation for them are the subject of [7] and [8]. Let $\mathcal{D}M$ and $\mathbf{DM}$ be descriptive (definition 1) and Data Mining (definition 3) Models. We define our General Model as follows.

Definition 4. *A* **General Data Mining Model** *is a system* $\mathbf{GM} = (\mathcal{D}\mathbf{M}, \mathbf{DM}, \models)$, *where*

- $\mathcal{D}\mathbf{M}$ *is a* **descriptive model**,
- $\mathbf{DM}$ *is the Data Mining Model model (definition 3)*,
- $\models \subseteq \mathcal{E} \times U$ *is called a* **satisfaction relation**. *It establishes relationship between expressions of the descriptive model* $\mathcal{D}\mathbf{M}$, *and the data mining model* $\mathbf{DM}$.

The notion of satisfaction depends on the Data Mining algorithm one works with and consequently, on the appropriate choice of the Descriptive Language. The definition of our notion of a satisfaction relation (definition 15) is a generalization of Pawlak's definition, as it appears in [5].

3 Semantic Classification Model

In the classification process we are given a data set (set of records) with a special attribute C, called a class attribute. The values $c_1, c_2, ...c_n$ of the class attribute C are called class labels. The classification process is both semantical (grouping objects in sets that would fit into the classes) and syntactical (finding the descriptions of those sets in order to use them for testing and future classification).

In fact all data mining techniques share the same characteristics of semantical-syntactical duality. The formal definitions of classification data and classification operators are as follows.

Definition 5 (Classification Information System). *Any information system $I = (U, A \cup \{C\}, V_A \cup V_C, f)$ with a distinguished class attribute C and with the class attribute values $V_C = \{c_1, c_2, ...c_m\}$, $m \geq 2$, is called a classification information system, or shortly,* **a classification system** *if and only if the sets $C_n = \{x \in U : \ f(x, C) = c_n\}$ form a partition of U.*

The classification information system is called in the Rough Set community and literature ([10], [5], [11]) a decision information system with the decision attribute C.

Definition 6. *Let $I = (U, A \cup \{C\}, V_A \cup V_C, f)$ be the initial database with the class attribute C. The sets $C_{n,I} = \{x \in U : \ f(x, C) = c_n\}$, for $n = 1, 2, .., m$, are called the* **object classification classes***.*

In the data analysis, preprocessing and data mining in general and in classification process in particular we start the process with the input data. We assume here that they are represented in a format of information system table. We hence define the lowest level of information generalization as the relational table. The meaning of the intermediate and final results are considered to be of a higher level of generalization. We represent those levels of generalization by a sets of objects of the given (data mining) universe U, as in [2], and [7], [8].

This approach follows the granular view of the data mining and is formalized within a notion of knowledge generalization system, defined as follows.

Definition 7. *A* **generalization system** *based on the information system $I = (U, A, V_A, f)$, or classification system $I = (U, A \cup \{C\}, V_A \cup V_C, f)$ is a system $K_I = (\mathcal{P}(U), A, E, V_A, V_E, g)$, where*

- *E is a finite set of* **groups attributes**, *called also* **granules attributes** *such that $A \cap E = \emptyset$.*
- *V_E is a finite set of* **values of granules attributes***.*
- *g is a partial function called* **knowledge information function** *$g : \mathcal{P}(U) \times (A \cup E) \longrightarrow (V_A \cup V_E)$, such that*
  - (i) $g \mid (\bigcup_{x \in U} \{x\} \times A) = f$
  - (ii) $\forall_{S \in \mathcal{P}(U)} \forall_{a \in A} ((S, a) \in dom(g) \ \Rightarrow \ g(S, a) \in V_A)$
  - (iii) $\forall_{S \in \mathcal{P}(U)} \forall_{e \in E} ((S, e) \in dom(g) \ \Rightarrow \ g(S, e) \in V_E)$

Classification system: *the generalization system K_I a classification system if and only if I is a classification system and the following additional condition holds. $\forall S \in \mathcal{P}(U)(\forall a \in A((S, a) \in dom(g)) \Rightarrow (S, C) \in dom(g)$).*

We denote by $\mathcal{K}^{clf}$ the set of all classification systems based on any subsystem of the initial classification system I.

Definition 8. *For any $K \in \mathcal{K}^{clf}$ the sets $\mathbf{C}_{n,K} = \{X \in \mathcal{P}(U) : \ g(X, C) = c_n\}$, for $n = 1, 2, .., m$ are called* **granule classes** *of K.*

The knowledge system K represents a state of knowledge after some algorithm (represented by a generalization operator) had been applied to the initial data base represented by the initial information system I. Hence if we apply a classification algorithm (operator) to initial classification system we obtain a classification knowledge system, with its own classification classes (as computed by the algorithm). To assure the correctness of the operation we must relate obtained (computed) classes to the initial (real) ones. We adopt hence the following definition.

Definition 9. *Let* $\mathbf{DM} = (U, \mathcal{K}^{clf}, \mathcal{G}_{dm}, \prec_{dm})$ *be a Data Mining Model. A generalization operator* $G \in \mathcal{G}_{dm}$ *is called a* **classification operator** *if and only if* G *is a partial function* $G : \mathcal{K}^{clf} longrightarrow \mathcal{K}^{clf}$, *such that for any* $K' \in domG$, *any* $K \in \mathcal{K}^{clf}$ *such that* $K = G(K')$ *the following* **classification condition** *holds.* $\forall X (X \in \mathbf{C}_{n,K} \Rightarrow (X \subseteq C_{n,I} \cup X \subseteq_K C_{n,I}), \text{ for } n = 1, 2, .., m.$

The sets $C_{n,I}, \mathbf{C}_{n,K}$ are the sets from definitions 6, 8, respectively and $\subseteq_K$ is an **approximate set inclusion** defined in terms of granules-attributes of K, i.e. the attributes from E. We denote the set of classification operators based on the initial system I by $\mathcal{G}_{clf}$.

Definition 10. A Semantic Classification Model *is a system*
$\mathbf{SC} = (U, \mathcal{K}^{clf}, \mathcal{G}_{clf}, \prec_{dm})$.

4   Descriptive Classification Model

Given a Semantic Classification Model $\mathbf{SC} = (U, \mathcal{K}^{clf}, \mathcal{G}_{dm}, \prec_{dm})$. We associate with any and any $K \in \mathcal{K}^{clf}$ its Descriptive Language $\mathcal{L}_K$. We adopt here the Rough Sets community tradition and write $a = v$ to denote that v is a value of an attribute a.

Definition 11. *For any* $K \in \mathcal{K}^{clf}$ *of* **SC** *of definition 10, we define the* **Description Language** $\mathcal{L}_K = (\mathcal{A}_K, \mathcal{E}_K, \mathcal{F}_K)$, *where* $\mathcal{A}_K$ *is called an* **alphabet**, $\mathcal{E}_K$ *the set of descriptive expressions, or* **descriptions***, and* $\mathcal{F}_K$ *is the set of all* **formulas** *of the language* $\mathcal{L}_K$.

Let $K = (\mathcal{P}(U), A \cup \{C\}, E, V_A \cup V_C, V_E, g)$ be a system based on the initial classification data $I = (U, A \cup \{C\}, V_A \cup V_C, f)$ (definition 6). The components of the language $\mathcal{L}_K$ are defined as follows.

$\mathcal{A}_K = VAR \cup CONN$, for $VAR = VAR_A \cup VAR_E \cup VAR_C$, where
$VAR_A = \{(a = v) : a \in A, v \in V_A,$
$VAR_E = \{(a = v) : a \in E, v \in V_E\},$
$VAR_C = \{(C = c) : C \in \{C\}, c \in V_C\}.$

Elements of VAR are called **variables** and represent minimal "blocks" of semantical description. They also are called **atomic descriptions**. Elements of VAR_A are atomic descriptions of minimal blocks build with use of non-classification attributes of the initial database. Elements of VAR_E are atomic descriptions of minimal blocks build with use of group attributes used (if any) during the process of constructing a classifier. Elements of VAR_C are atomic descriptions of minimal blocks build with use of classification attribute of the initial database. The set of connectives $CONN = \{\cap, \Rightarrow\}$ contains two classical connectives. We use them to build the set $\mathcal{E}_K$ descriptions, and the set $\mathcal{F}_K$ of all formulas.

Definition 12. *The set* $\mathcal{E}_K \subset \mathcal{A}_K^*$ *is a set of all* **descriptions** *of the language* $\mathcal{L}_K$ *and* $\mathcal{E}_K = DES_A \cup DES_E \cup DES_C$.

DES_A is called the set of descriptions by attributes of I, DES_E is the set of descriptions by granule attributes of K, and DES_C is the set of class descriptions. $DES_A \subset \mathcal{A}_K^*$ is the smallest set such that $VAR_A \subseteq DES_A$ (atomic object descriptions), and if $D_1, D_2 \in DES_A$, then $D_1 \cap D_2 \in DES_A$. $DES_E \subset \mathcal{A}_K^*$ is the smallest set such that $VAR_K \subseteq DES_K$ (atomic group attributes descriptions), and if $D_1, D_2 \in DES_E$, then $D_1 \cap D_2 \in DES_E$. $DES_C = VAR_C$ (class descriptions).

Definition 13. *The set* $\mathcal{F}_K \subset \mathcal{A}_K^*$ *of all* **formulas** *of the language* $\mathcal{L}_K$ *is defined as* $\mathcal{F}_K = D\mathcal{F}_I \cup D\mathcal{F}_K \cup CH\mathcal{F}$.

$D\mathcal{F}_I$ is called a set of **discriminant formulas** based on I and
$$D\mathcal{F}_I = \{(D \Rightarrow D_C): \ D \in DES_I, D_C \in DES_C\}.$$
The set $D\mathcal{F}_K$ is the set of K-**discriminant formulas** and contains discriminant formulas that incorporate the information expressed by the granules attributes of K. These attributes usually denote uncertainty measures. We put
$$D\mathcal{F}_K = \{(D \Rightarrow D_C) \cap B: \ D \in DES_K, D_C \in DES_C, B \in DES_K\}.$$
The set $CH\mathcal{F}$ is called a set of **characteristic formulas** for K and
$$CH\mathcal{F} = \{(D_C \Rightarrow D): \ D \in DES_I, D_C \in DES_C\}.$$

Definition 14. *A* **Descriptive Classification Model** *based on a classification system* K *and initial classification data* $I = (U, A \cup \{C\}, V_A \cup V_C, f)$ *is a system* $\mathcal{DC} = (\ \mathcal{L}_K, \ D\mathcal{F}_I, \ D\mathcal{F}_K, \ CH\mathcal{F})$.

Remark that the formulas of the language $\mathcal{L}_K$ **are not** data mining **rules.** They only describe a syntactical form of appropriate discriminant of characteristic rules. Formulas from $\mathcal{F}_K$ become **rules determined by** K only when they do relate semantically to K, i.e. reflect the properties of K and in this case we say that they are **true**, or **true with some certainty** in K. In the next section we define the satisfaction relation $\models$ that establishes the relationship between formulas of the descriptive language determined by K with what K semantically represents. We use it to define what does it mean that "F **is true**" in K, and "F **is partially true**" in K, with the the measures of truthfulness described by granule attributes of K, and hence by a description $B \in DES_K$.

4.1   Satisfaction, Truth

Let $K = (\mathcal{P}(U), A \cup \{C\}, E, V_A \cup V_C, V_E, g)$ and is based on $I = (U, A \cup \{C\}, V_A \cup V_C, f)$. Let $\mathcal{L}_K = (\mathcal{A}_K, \mathcal{E}_K, \mathcal{F}_K)$ be the description language defined by K and I.

Definition 15. *A* **satisfaction relation** *is a binary relation* $\models \mathcal{P}(U) \times (\mathcal{E}_K \cup \mathcal{F}_K)$ *defined in stages, by induction over level of complexity of* $F \in (\mathcal{E}_K \cup \mathcal{F}_K)$.

Step 1.   *Let* $a = v \in VAR_A$, $C = c \in DES_C$, *and* $S \in \mathcal{P}(U)$ *we define*
$S \models a = v$ *iff* $((S, a) \in dom(g)$ *and* $g(S, a) = v$.
Step 2.   *Let* $D_C = C = c$, *we say that* $S \models D_C$ *iff* $((S, C) \in dom(g)$ *and*
$g(S, C) = c$.
Step 3.   *We extend* $\models$ *to the set* DES_A *as follows. For any* $D = D_1 \cap .. \cap D_n \in$
DES_A, $S \models D$ *iff* $\forall (1 \le i \le n)(S \models D_i)$.
Step 4. *We extend* $\models$ *to the set* $D\mathcal{F}_I$ *of discriminant and characteristic formulas based on* I *as follows. For any* $(D \Rightarrow D_C) \in D\mathcal{F}_I$,
$S \models (D \Rightarrow D_C), S \models (D_C \Rightarrow D)$ *iff* $S \models D$ *and* $S \models D_C$.

Denote $\mathcal{E}_I = DES_A \cup DES_C$ and $\mathcal{F}_I = D\mathcal{F}_I \cup CH\mathcal{F}_I$.

Definition 16. *A description, or a formula* $F \in \mathcal{E}_I \cup \mathcal{F}_I$ *is* **satisfiable in** K *if there is* S, *such that* $S \models F$.

5   The Model

Now we are ready to define our classification model as a particular case of the General DM Model of definition 4.

Definition 17. *A* **Classification Model** *based on a classification system* K *and initial classification data* $I = (U, A \cup \{C\}, V_A \cup V_C, f)$ *is a system* **CM** $=$ $(\mathbf{SC}, \mathcal{DC}, \models)$ *for the components defined by definitions 10, 14, and definition 16, respectively.*

Let us now assume that $K = G(K')$, i.e. K is a result of application of any classification operator G (algorithm). Satisfiability means that the semantics and then syntax of the application of a classification algorithm described within the system K can be, and are related to each other. It shows that the **semantics-syntax duality** inherent to all Data Mining applications is well reflected within our General Data Mining model **GM** and in the Classification Model **CM** in particular.

The definitions of descriptive language (definition 11) and of satisfiability relation (definition 15) is hence setting a standard how to define syntax for a semantic model. As we pointed before, satisfiability of F in K does not yet mean that a given formula is true. In order to define the notion of "true in K" we need to point out two properties of classifications systems. Directly from the definition 7 we get that the following holds.

Lemma 1. *For any classification system* $K = (\mathcal{P}(U), A \cup \{C\}, E, V_A \cup V_C, V_E, g)$ *the following holds.*

$$\forall S \in \mathcal{P}(U) \forall a \in A((S, a) \in dom(g) \Rightarrow \exists (1 \le n \le m) \exists X \in \mathbf{C}_{n,K}(S \subseteq X)),$$

where $\mathbf{C}_{n,K}$ *is a granule class of* K *as in the definition 8.*

Directly from the above lemma 1 and the definition 9 we obtain the following.

Lemma 2. *For any classification system K such that $K = G(K')$ for certain $K' \in \mathcal{K}^{clf}$ and classification operator $G \in \mathcal{G}_{clf}$ the following holds.*

$$\forall S \in \mathcal{P}(U) \forall a \in A((S, a) \in dom(g) \Rightarrow$$
$$\Rightarrow \exists(1 \leq n \leq m) \exists C_{n,I}(S \subseteq C_{n,I} \cup S \subseteq_K C_{n,I})),$$

where $C_{n,I}$ is the object class from definitions 6 and $\subseteq_K$ is an approximate set inclusion defined in terms of granules attributes of K.

Now we are ready to define the notion of truthfulness of formulas of $\mathcal{L}_K$ in K.

Definition 18. *For any discriminant formula $F = (D \Rightarrow C = c_n)$ we say that F is **true in K** and is **a discriminant rule** determined by K iff there is $S \in \mathcal{P}(U)$, such that $S \models F$ and $S \subseteq C_{n,I}$.*

Definition 19. *For any discriminant formula $F = (D \Rightarrow C = c_n)$ we say that F is **partially true in K** iff there is $S \in \mathcal{P}(U)$, such that $S \models F$ and $S \subseteq_K C_{n,I}$, and $\subseteq_K$ is an approximate set inclusion defined in terms of granules attributes of K.*

The approximate set inclusion defined in terms of granules attributes of K is usually represented by a formula $B \in DES_K$ a formula $(D \Rightarrow C = c_n) \cap B \in D\mathcal{F}_K$ is used instead of F. We hence adopt the following definition.

Definition 20. *For any discriminant formula $F = (D \Rightarrow C = c_n) \cap B$ for $B \in DES_K$ we say that F is partially true in K and is **a partially certain discriminant rule** determined by K iff there is $S \in \mathcal{P}(U)$, such that $S \models F$ and $S \subseteq_K C_{n,I}$, where $\subseteq_K$ is an approximate set inclusion defined by $B \in DES_K$.*

We define, in a similar way true **characteristic formulas**, i.e. characteristic rules.

Definition 21. *For any characteristic formula $F = (C = C_n \Rightarrow D)$ we say that F is **true in K** and is **a characteristic rule** determined by K iff there is $S \in \mathcal{P}(U)$, such that $S \models F$ and $S \cap C_{n,I} \neq \emptyset$.*

Denote by $D\mathcal{R}_I$, $CH\mathcal{R}$ the sets of all discriminant rules (definition 18) and characteristics rules (definition 21), respectively.

Let $C_{n,I}$ be an object classification class (definition 6). We denote

$$(D\mathcal{R}_{n,I})^* = \{S : \; S \models (D \Rightarrow C = c_n), \; (D \Rightarrow C = c_n) \in D\mathcal{R}_I\},$$

$$(CH\mathcal{R}_{n,I})^* = \{S : \; S \models (C = c_n \Rightarrow D), \; (C = c_n \Rightarrow D) \in CH\mathcal{R}\}.$$

Directly from the definitions 18, 21 and lemma 2 and the definition of lower and upper rough set approximations ([5]) we obtain the following relationship between any classification algorithms (as expressed in our model by the classification operator) and the Rough Set methodology.

Theorem 1. *Let* **SC** $= (U, \mathcal{K}^{clf}, \mathcal{G}_{clf}, \prec_{dm})$ *be a Semantic Classification Model (definition 10). For any* $G \in \mathcal{G}_{clf}$ *and* $K \in \mathcal{K}^{clf}$, *such that* $K = G(K')$ *for some* $K' \in \mathcal{K}^{clf}$ *the following holds.*

$$\bigcup (D\mathcal{R}_{n,I})^* = lower(C_{n,I}),$$

$$\bigcup (CH\mathcal{R}_{n,I})^* = upper(C_{n,I}),$$

where $lower(A)$, $upper(A)$ *are lower and upper approximations of the set* A, *as defined in [5].*

The meaning of the above theorem 1 expressed in "plain words" is the following.

Theorem 2 (Plain Statement of theorem 1). *Let* $(D\mathcal{R}_{n,I})$ *be a set of discriminant rules describing a class (concept)* $C = c_n$ *of the initial data base obtained an application of a classification algorithm, as represented by classification operator* G.

The union of all sets described by these rules, i.e. sets in which the rules are true, is the lower approximation of the class (concept) $C = c_n$.

Similar property holds for the characteristic rules; semantically they describe the upper approximation of the class (concept) $C = c_n$.

Consider now the set of discriminant formulas based on K, namely $D\mathcal{F}_K = \{(D \Rightarrow D_C) \cap B : D \in DES_K, D_C \in DES_C, B \in DES_K\}$. As we said before some of them become partially true discriminant rules generated by an application of a classification operator G and describing a class $C = c_n$ of the initial database I. Denote by $PD\mathcal{R}_I \subseteq D\mathcal{F}_K$ the sets of all partially certain discriminant rules (definition 20) as obtained by an application of an classification operator G, i.e. by $K = G(K')$. We denote $(PD\mathcal{R}_{n,I})^* = \{S : S \models (D \cap B \Rightarrow C = c_n), (D \Rightarrow C = c_n) \in D\mathcal{R}_I, B \in DES_K\}$. Directly from the definition 20 and lemma 2 and the we obtain the following.

Theorem 3. *Let* **CM** $= (U, \mathcal{K}^{clf}, \mathcal{G}_{clf}, \prec_{dm})$ *be a Semantic Classification Model (definition 10). For any* $G \in \mathcal{G}_{clf}$ *and* $K \in \mathcal{K}^{clf}$, *such that* $K = G(K')$ *for some* $K' \in \mathcal{K}^{clf}$ *the following holds.*

$$\bigcup (PD\mathcal{R}_{n,I})^* = lower_K(C_{n,I}),$$

where $lower$ *is an approximate lower approximation defined in terms of* $B \in DES_K$ *and* $\subseteq_K$.

6   Conclusions

Classification, or machine learning as they used to be called, algorithms and methods such as Neural Networks, Bayesian Networks, Genetic Algorithms have a long history dating early 1960ties. Then in the mid-70ties and mid-80ties came Decision Tree Induction and Rough Sets approaches and algorithms. All these methods and algorithms had been developed and implemented by thousands researches and practitioners for long before they were incorporated and extended to the large databases and hence became a part of a field that is now called Data Mining. The appearance and a vide spread and rapid development of the Rough Sets methodology brought a foundational and not only algorithmic investigations into the picture. We follow this foundational trend by proving that our extension of the language of Rough Sets provides a common ground to any Data Mining foundational investigations.

References

1. Lin, T.Y.: *Database Mining on Derived Attributes. Proceedings of Third International Conference RSCTC'02*, Malvern, PA, USA, October. Springer Lecture Notes in Artificial Intelligence (2002) 14-32
2. Menasalvas, E., Wasilewska, A., Fernández, C.: *The lattice structure of the KDD process: Mathematical expression of the model and its operators.* International Journal of Information Systems and Fundamenta Informaticae; special issue (2001) 48-62
3. Menasalvas, E., Wasilewska, A., Fernández-Baizan, M.C., Martinez, J.F.: *Data Mining - A Semantical Model.* Proceedings of 2002 World Congres on Computational Intelligence, Honolulu, Hawai, USA, May 11- 17 (2002) 435-441
4. Menasalvas, E., Wasilewska, A.: *Data Mining as Generalization Process: A Formal MOdel.* In: Foundation of Data Mining, Kluwer (2005) to appear
5. Pawlak, Z.: *Rough Sets - theoretical Aspects Reasoning About Data* Kluwer Academic Publishers (1991)
6. Wasilewska, A., Menasalvas, E., Fernández-Baizan, M.C.: *Modelization of rough set functions in the KDD frame.* 1st International Conference on Rough Sets and Current Trends in Computing (RSCTC'98) June 22 - 26 (1998)
7. Wasilewska, A., Menasalvas, E.: *Data Mining Operators.* newblock Proceedings of Foundations of Data Mining Workshop in Fourth IEEE International Conference on Data Mining, Brighton, UK, 1-4 November (2004)
8. Wasilewska, A., Menasalvas, E.: *Data Preprocessing and Data Mining as Generalization Process.* Proceedings of Foundations of Data Mining Workshop in Fourth IEEE International Conference on Data Mining, Brighton, UK, 1-4 November (2004)
9. Wong, S.K.M., Ziarko, W., Ye, R.L.: *On Learning and Evaluation of Decision Rules in Context of Rough sets.* Proceedings of the first ACM SIGART International Symposium on Methodologies for Intelligent Systems, Knoxville, Tenn (1986) 308-324
10. Ziarko, W.: *Variable Precision Rough Set Model.* Journal of Computer and Systen Sciences, 46(1) (1993) 39-59
11. Yao, J.T., Yao, Y.Y.: *Induction of Classification Rules by Granular Computing.* Proceedings of Third International RSCTC'02 Conference, Malvern, PA, USA, October. Springer Lecture Notes in Artificial Intelligence (2002) 331-338

"Rule + Exception" Strategies for Knowledge Management and Discovery

Yiyu Yao[1], Fei-Yue Wang[2], and Jue Wang[3]

[1] Department of Computer Science, University of Regina,
Regina, Saskatchewan, Canada S4S 0A2
yyao@cs.uregina.ca
[2] Systems and Industrial Engineering Department,
University of Arizona, Tucson, Arizona 85721
feiyue@sie.arizona.edu
[3] Institute of Automation, Chinese Academy of Sciences,
Beijing, China 10080
Jue.wang@mail.ia.ac.cn

Abstract. A common practice of human learning and knowledge management is to use general rules, exception rules, and exceptions to rules. One of the crucial issues is to find a right mixture of them. For discovering this type of knowledge, we consider "rule + exception", or rule-plus-exception, strategies. Results from psychology, expert systems, genetic algorithms, and machine learning and data mining are summarized and compared, and their implications to knowledge management and discovery are examined. The study motivates and establishes a basis for the design and implementation of new algorithms for the discovery of "rule + exception" type knowledge.

1 Introduction

Many theories and algorithms have been proposed and studied extensively for understanding and summarizing data, and discovering knowledge from data. The spectrum ranges from classical statistical analysis, cluster analysis, and data analysis to recent machine learning, data mining, and knowledge discovery [1,18,19]. For simplicity, we use the term knowledge discovery to cover all those approaches by highlighting their high-level shared commonalities and ignoring their low-level detailed differences.

From the vast amount of studies, we identify two related fundamental problems that have not received enough attention.

Problem 1: Diverse user requirements. Every user may try to make sense of a set of data by seeing it from different angles, in different aspects, and under different views. There exists a wide range of users with great diversity of needs. On the other hand, there may not exist a universally applicable theory or method to serve the needs of all users. This justifies the co-existence of many theories and methods, and motivates the exploration of new theories and methods.

D. Ślęzak et al. (Eds.): RSFDGrC 2005, LNAI 3642, pp. 69–78, 2005.

Problem 2: Roles of knowledge discovery systems and users. The huge volume of raw data is far beyond a user's processing capacity. A goal of knowledge discovery is to discover, summarize and present the information and knowledge in the data in concise and human understandable forms. It should be realized that, at least in the near future, the insights about the data, as well as its semantics, may not be brought out by a knowledge discovery system alone. A user, in fact, uses knowledge discovery systems as research tools to browse, explore, understand the data, and to search for knowledge and insights from the data.

A careful examination of the two problems would provide guidelines for the design of viable knowledge discovery systems. We need to consider a number of fundamental issues, such as different views of the same data, different aspects of the same data, different presentations of the same data, different interpretations of the same data, and different types of knowledge embedded in the same data, as well as their associated construction and discovery methods. In fact, a majority of studies of knowledge discovery is devoted to the investigation of novel approaches that analyze and interpret data differently.

In this paper, we take a user-centered view of knowledge discovery. It is emphasized that the *knowledge discovery problem must be related to the ways in which the discovered knowledge is to be used by human users*. More specifically, the knowledge discovered by a system must be easily understood and organized, and subsequently used, by a human user. Potential solutions to the problem may be obtained by examining how human users learn and use knowledge in real world problem solving. This motivates the study of "rule + exception", or rule-plus-exception, strategies, as they are commonly employed by human [5,7,21,24,27].

The main objective of the paper is to prepare the groundwork and to establish a basis for "rule + exception" strategies for knowledge discovery. To achieve such a goal, the rest of the paper is organized as follows. Section 2 briefly discusses "rule + exception" strategies and their essential role in human problem solving. Section 3 presents a review and comparison of three "rule + exception" models. Section 4 examines applications of "rule + exception" strategies in knowledge discovery. The emphasis of this paper is on the understanding of the problem, rather than proposing new knowledge discovery algorithms. As future research, we are planning to design and evaluate new or modified algorithms for knowledge discovery based on "rule + exception" strategies.

2   "Rule + Exception" Strategies

The central idea of "rule + exception" strategies is the representation, understanding, and organization of knowledge at different levels of detail and accuracy. A higher level consists of simple, generally applicable, and almost correct rules. They are amended by exception rules and exceptions at a lower level. That is, the knowledge is gradually made more accurate through the introduction of exceptions, and possibly exceptions to exceptions, and so on.

There are many reasons for the study of the "rule + exception" strategies. First, they provide more realistic models by capturing the nature of the real world. Second, they are consistent with the ways in which human understands, organizes, and utilizes knowledge. Third, they offer the economy in knowledge representation in the sense that a smaller set of simpler rules are used. Consequently, they lead to easy communication and understanding of knowledge.

Natural things and phenomena normally have exceptions. Generalizations have exceptions, or have the status of a default when more exact information is not available [24]. It may be impossible to have general rules without exceptions. An important topic of knowledge representation in artificial intelligence is to study the notions of defaults and exceptions, in order to handle partial knowledge and real world problems [22,24]. One uses rules to represent the main characteristics, most common features and properties, and general, common-sense knowledge, and uses exceptions to represent particulars and special cases. The "rule + exception" models provide a realistic description of the real world.

In real world problem solving, we often have general rules of what we normally do, as well as exceptions to the rules. A typical example is the grammar rules of natural languages such as English [11]. Another example is the exception handling in programming languages. The "rule + exception" models correspond to the cognitive style that a human expert most likely uses to organize and represent knowledge.

The combination of rules and exceptions to rules provides a concise, economic, and comprehensive way of knowledge representation. "Rule + exception" strategies lead naturally to a multiple level organization of knowledge [27]. Instead of using a larger set of more specific rules without exceptions at the same level, one may use a smaller set of more general rules with exceptions at higher levels. On one hand, a general rule with less conditions is normally applicable to more cases and easy to understand by a human user. On the other hand, the modification by exceptions to rules at lower levels ensures that the accuracy of the rule is not compromised. One may move to a lower level to examine exceptions when more accurate knowledge is needed.

3   Three "Rule + Exception" Models

The three models reviewed represent different important aspects of "rule + exception" strategies. They demonstrate the psychological plausibility, the cognitive basis, and the economy of "rule + exception" strategies, as well as the human adoption of these strategies in learning, knowledge management, and reasoning.

3.1   Rule-Plus-Exception Model of Human Classification Learning

The rule-plus-exception model (RULEX) was proposed by Nosofsky *et al.* for modeling human classification learning [21]. The basic assumption of the model is that people tend to form simple logical rules and memorize occasional exceptions to those rules when learning to classify objects [21]. The learning process of RULEX consists of constructing a decision tree and testing for exceptions at each node. The criterion used is that the learner only needs to memorize minimum information. The decision tree is developed on a trial-by-trial basis using induction over examples [21].

The RULEX model is designed to investigate the psychological plausibility of such a "rule + exception" learning strategy. It is in fact found that the model accounts for many fundamental classification phenomena. Moreover, individuals vary greatly in their choices of rules and exceptions to the rules, which lead to different patterns of generalization [21].

3.2   Ripple-Down Rule Model for Knowledge Base Maintenance

Ripple-down rule model was introduced by Compton and Jansen as a tool for the acquisition and maintenance of large rule-based knowledge base [5]. The model explores the notions of rules and exceptions from a different point of view. In particular, the ripple-down rule model captures the ways in which experts perform knowledge acquisition and maintenance tasks.

The ripple-down rule model is motivated by the observation that people deal with complex large knowledge structures by making incremental changes within a well-defined context. The context consists of a sequence of rules whose applications lead to an incorrect interpretation and thus require a change. The effect of changes is therefore locally contained in such a well-defined manner [7]. In contrast to other knowledge base maintenance methods, rules in the ripple-down rule model are never directly corrected or changed. Corrections are instead contained in new rules which represent exceptions to the existing rules and are added to the knowledge base. This provides another way to cope with rules and exceptions.

Two types of exceptions can be identified: the cases with incorrect interpretations or conclusions produced by the existing rules, and the cases for which the existing rules fail to produce interpretations or conclusions [5,7]. They are referred to, respectively, as the false positives and false negatives by some authors [6,7]. We refer to them as incorrectly covered exceptions and uncovered exceptions of the rules.

To cope with the two types of exceptions, a two-way dependency relation between rules are created. An "if-true" dependency links a rule with a set of rules that handle its incorrectly covered exceptions, and an "if-false" dependency links a rule with a set of rules that handle its uncovered exceptions. Each exception rule can also have its exceptions linked by the two types of links. Through the dependency links, ripple-down rules in fact form a different type of binary decision tree. Each node in the decision tree is labeled by a rule, the left subtree deals with incorrectly covered exceptions, and the right subtree processes uncovered exceptions. The decision procedure is different from a standard decision tree [7]. If the rule at the root can be applied, one must search recursively its left subtree to see if a more specific rule can be applied. If no contradiction arrives from its left subtree, the conclusion of the root is used, otherwise, the conclusion from the left subtree is used. If the rule at the root can not be applied, one searches for the right subtree. The conclusion is given by the last successful rule.

3.3 Default Hierarchy of Classifiers in Genetic Algorithms

The ideas of "rule + exception" have been investigated in classifier systems, a machine learning model investigated in genetic algorithms [8,10]. By considering general rules (classifiers) as defaults and specific rules as exceptions, the multi-level layout of rules forms a default hierarchy.

A classifier system consists of a set of classifiers, a message list, an input interface and an output interface [10]. A classifier is a string rule made up by a condition and an action. At any given point of time, if the condition part of a classifier is satisfied by a message in the message list, the classifier is fired and its action part specifies a message to be placed on the message list. A set of classifiers can be organized into a default hierarchy, ordered by their generalities.

The default hierarchy offers an alternative way to represent "rule + exception" type knowledge. In some sense, a default hierarchy is related to a ripple-down rule, if only the uncovered exceptions are considered in the latter. With a default hierarchy, the number of rules needed is smaller than the number of rules in a perfect rule set [8]. This achieves the goal of economy of defaults and exceptions [10]. Moreover, rules, when being organized into default hierarchies and operating in parallel, can be used to build mental models [10]. The classifier systems are concrete examples of such mental models.

4 "Rule + Exception" Strategies in Knowledge Discovery

This section first reviews the "rule + exception" strategies for knowledge discovery derived from the applications of the principles and ideas of the three models, and then briefly summarizes related studies.

4.1 Applications of the Three Models

Application of RULEX model. The findings from the RULEX model have significant implications for knowledge discovery. First, human classification learning involves forming simple rules and memorizing occasional exceptions, which is natural, economic, and comprehensive. Accordingly, knowledge discovery systems should explore the "rule + exception" type knowledge. Second, individuals vary greatly when forming rules and exceptions. Each piece of resulting "rule + exception" knowledge may reveal a particular aspect of the data. Therefore, knowledge discovery algorithms need to deal with different combinations of rules and exceptions.

Based on the RULEX model, Wang *et al.* proposed an algorithm to discover rules and exceptions using the theory of rough sets [27,31]. The algorithm first selects a set of attributes in order to construct a set of rules. The set of attributes induces a boundary region for which certain, i.e., 100% correct, rules do not exist. The algorithm then attempts to describe the boundary region by using rule and exception pairs. With the two types of control, namely, the selection of attribute sets, and the selection of rule and exception pairs, the algorithm is able to produce a multi-level summarization of data [27].

In order to choose a suitable set of attributes, user preference of attributes is used. The principle for the selection of rule and exception pairs is consistent with the RULEX model. The rules should be chosen in a way so that their exceptions are minimum.

In knowledge discovery, one may consider two types of rules [28]. The low order rules focus on the knowledge about a single object. Classification rules and association rules are examples of low order rules. Such a rule typically involves the determination of the class of an object, or its value on a different set of attributes, based on its value on a set of attributes. The high order rules focus on the knowledge about a pair of objects. Instance functional dependency in database is a typical example of high order rules. An instance functional dependency states that if two objects have the same value on one set of attributes, they have the same value on another set of attributes [2].

The method proposed by Wang *et al.* discovers low order rules with exceptions. A method for discovering high order rules with exceptions was introduced by Berzal *et al.* [2]. The notion of partial instance functional dependency is introduced. A partial instance functional dependency can be precisely presented by a pair of full instance functional dependency and a set of exceptions. An exception is a tuple that breaks the instance functional dependency. The criterion for finding a set of exceptions is similar to the RULEX model, namely, the number of exceptions must be minimum.

Application of ripple-down rule model. There are several advantages of the ripple-down rule model. It provides a systematic way to represent and organize the "rule + exception" type knowledge. Its binary decision tree representation is not only easy to understand, but also codes the context in which exceptions occur. Moreover, the construction of the decision tree is seamlessly tied together with the knowledge updating process. Those salient features make the model a good candidate for knowledge discovery. In fact, the model can be easily adopted for knowledge discovery [7,29].

Gaines and Compton applied a machine learning algorithm, called Induct, for the induction of ripple-down rules [7]. The Induct algorithm is an extension of Cendrowka's PRISM algorithm [4], which applies naturally to the discovery of ripple-down rules. The experiments show that ripple-down rules are much easier to understand and are in very economic forms, namely, the number of rules and the number of attributes in each rule are smaller than rules obtained using other machine learning algorithms.

Application of default hierarchy. The notion of default hierarchies can be discussed in a wide context, in connection to default reasoning [23]. General rules represent general conditions and produce certain default expectations. More specific rules cover exceptions. The default expectation derived from general rules can be overridden by more specific rules, representing the exceptions to the default expectations. The result can be overridden again by even more specific rules.

Mollestad and Skowron proposed a framework for mining default rules based on the theory of rough sets [20]. They suggested that a default rule may be constructed to account for the normal situation, and further exception rules can be constructed when more specific knowledge becomes available. The rules discovered by their method may be organized into simple default hierarchies.

4.2 Additional Studies on "Rule + Exception" Strategies

Suzuki introduced the notion of exception rules [25,26]. An exception rule is associated with a general association rule as the modification of the latter. Rule and exception rule pairs present "rule + exception" type knowledge. It is related to the formulation of Wang *et al.* for mining rule and exception pairs [27,31], and the formulation of default rule and exception pairs by Mollestad and Skowron for mining default rules [20].

Li suggested building classification trees with exception annotations [15]. In the decision tree construction process, a node is checked to see if it needs exception annotation. A node is deemed exceptional if one particular class is dominant. That is, the dominant class may be viewed as the decision of the current node, and the instances of other classes as exceptions. The result is a concise decision tree, although may not be very accurate. Exception rules are mined from these exception nodes. Li's method therefore provides another way for implementing the "rule + exception" strategy, based on a modification of classical decision tree construction methods.

Liu *et al.* proposed to use general rules and exceptions, called GE patterns, as intuitive representation of a decision tree [16,17]. A general rule may have none or a list of exceptions, which in turn may have further exceptions. The GE patterns are obtained by post-processing a decision tree generated by a tree induction algorithm. A decision tree is transformed into a much more concise GE tree. The GE tree shares some common features with ripple-down rules, in terms of knowledge representation and reasoning method.

Although both methods of Li and Liu *et al.* involve the adoption of classical decision tree learning, there is a subtle and important difference. The annotation operation is performed during the construction of the decision tree. This allows us to consider explicitly the "rule + exception" strategies in the learning process. In contrast, an GE tree is the result of post-processing a decision tree, without considering the "rule + exception" strategies in the tree construction stage. It is desirable for a tree induction algorithm to use a heuristic that is directly linked to the "rule + exception" strategy.

The topic of subgroup discovery is related to the "rule + exception" strategies [14]. One of the criteria discussed by Lavrač *et al.* for subgroup discovery is consistent with the "rule + exception" strategies [14]. Instead of requiring the rule to be as accurate as possible, new heuristics for subgroup discovery aim at finding "best" subgroups in terms of rule coverage. Consequently, such a rule may introduce exceptions. The trade-off of generality and accuracy of the rule reflects the basic principle of "rule + exception" strategies.

4.3 Discussion

The investigations of "rule + exception" are related to, and different from, the outlier analysis and peculiarity-oriented data mining [13,30]. In many classical outlier analysis methods, outliers or exceptions are treated as noise due to human or measurement error, which are to be removed. It is recently realized in data mining that exceptional instances are in fact true descriptions of the real world. It is therefore necessary to identify and examine such exceptional and peculiar cases [9,13,30,31].

The "rule + exception" strategies deal with a new type of knowledge. There exist two types of exceptions to a rule, the incorrectly covered exceptions and uncovered exceptions. The presentation of exceptions in a well-constructed context may provide more insights into the understanding of general knowledge and its exceptions. While rules and exception rules cover subsets of instances, exceptions are instances. The rules, exceptions rules, and exceptions can be organized into a multi-level structure, which provides a multi-level view of the data.

Algorithms for discovering "rule + exception" typ knowledge must use new heuristics. In contrast to a standard criterion that emphasizes the accuracy of discovered rules, "rule + exception" strategies aim at easy understandable, approximate rules. The new heuristics can be characterized by softened criteria discussed by Kacprzyk and Szkatula for inductive machine learning [12]. The partial completeness criterion requires that the rules must correctly describe most of the positive examples. The partial consistency criterion requires that the rules must describe almost none of the negative examples [12]. Obviously, such criteria implement the principles of RULEX model.

For a given set of data, there exist different combinations of rules, exception rules and exceptions. Each of them leads to a different view of data or a different knowledge structure. A commonly accepted criterion is related to the economy of knowledge representation, namely, the rules must be as simple as possible, and at the same time, the number of exceptions must be as small as possible.

Algorithms for the discovery of "rule + exception" type knowledge can be obtained by adopting existing algorithms with explicit consideration of "rule + exception" strategies. Currently, we are in the process of designing and evaluating algorithms based on existing algorithms, such as PRISM [4], Induct [6,7], and ART [3]. The results of learning are expressed as a binary decision tree, in the same way ripple-down rules are represented. An initial study of these algorithms suggests that the "rule + exception" strategies can be easily incorporated.

5　Conclusion

"Rule + exception" strategies lead to a concise and comprehensive way of knowledge representation. They have been explored either explicitly or implicitly in many fields. Knowledge discovery needs to consider such strategies.

In contrast to algorithm-centered approaches, this paper focuses more on the conceptual understanding of "rule + exception" strategies. As a first step, we argue for the study of such strategies and review existing studies. Although the underlying idea of "rule + exception" is easy to understand or elementary, its significance should not be overlooked. The view, provided by the "rule + exception" strategies, offers new opportunities for knowledge discovery. By pooling together scattered research efforts in many fields, it is hoped that a new research topic can be emerged and receive its due attention.

There are advantages of the "rule + exception" strategies. They are related to the ways in which human learning and organize knowledge. The use of "rule + exception" leads to understandability and economy in knowledge representation. This provides not only insights into the problem itself, but also guidelines for the design of actual algorithms. Existing algorithms can be easily adopted to discover "rule + exception" type knowledge.

The conceptual investigation of the paper establishes a solid basis for the further study of rules, exception rules, and exceptions in knowledge discovery. With respect to the "rule + exception" strategies, it is necessary to modify existing algorithms, design new algorithms, as well as to test these algorithms on real world data.

References

1. Anderberg, M.R. *Cluster Analysis for Applications*, Academic Press, New York, 1973.
2. Berzal, F., Cubero, J.C., Cuenca, F. and Medina, J.M. Relational decomposition through partial funcational dependencies, *Data and Knowledge Engineering*, **43**, 207-234, 2002.
3. Berzal, F., Cubero, J.C., Sánchez, D., and Serrano, J.M. ART: a hybrid classification model, *Machine Learning*, **54**, 67-92, 2004.
4. Cendrowska, J., PRISM: an algorithm for inducing modular rules, *International Journal of Man-Machine Studies*, **27**, 349-370, 1987.
5. Compton, P. and Jansen, B. Knowledge in context: a strategy for expert system maintenance, *The Second Australian Joint Conference on Artificial Intelligence*, 292-306, 1988.
6. Gaines, B.R. The trade-off between knowledge and data in knowledge acquisition, in: *Knowledge Discovery in Databases*, Piatetsky-Shapiro, G. and Frawley, W.J. (Eds.), AAAI/MIT Press, Menlo Park, California, 491-506, 1991.
7. Gaines, B.R. and Compton, P. Induction of ripple-down rules applied to modeling large databases, *Journal of Intelligent Information Systems*, **5**, 211-228, 1995.
8. Goldberg, D.E. *Genetic Algorithms in Search, Optimization, and Machine Learning*, Addison-Wesley, Reading, Massachusetts, 1989.
9. Han, J. and Kamber, M. *Data Mining: Concept and Techniques*, Morgan Kaufmann Publisher, 2000.
10. Holland, J.H., Holyoak, K.J., Nisbett, R.E. and Thagard, P.R. *Induction: Processes of Inference, Learning, and Discovery*, The MIT Press, Cambridge, Massachusetts, 1986.
11. Hsieh, C.C., Tsai, T.H., Wible, D. and Hsu, W.L. Exploiting knowledge representation in an intelligent tutoring system for English lexical errors, *International Conference on Computers in Education (ICCE'02)*, 115-116, 2002.
12. Kacprzyk, J. and Szkatula, G. A softened formulation of inductive learning and its use for coronary disease data, *Foudations of Intelligent System, 15th International Symposium*, LNAI 3488, 200-209, 2005.

13. Knorr, E.M. and Ng, R.T. A unified notion of outliers: properties and computation, *Proceedings of KDD'97*, 219-222, 1997.
14. Lavrač, N., Kavšek, B., Flach, P. and Todorovski, L. Subgroup discovery with CN2-SD, *Journal of Machine Learning Research*, **5**, 153-188, 2004.
15. Li, J. *Constructing Classification Trees with Exception Annotations for Large Datasets*, M.Sc. Thesis, Simon Fraser University, 1999.
16. Liu, B., Hu, M. and Hsu, W. Intuitive representation of decision trees using general rules and exceptions, *Proceedings of AAAI-2000*, 615-620, 2000.
17. Liu, B., Hu, M. and Hsu, W. Multi-level organization and summarization of the discovered rules, *Proceedings of SIGKDD-2002*, 20-23, 2002.
18. Michalski, R.S., Bratko, I. and Kubat, M. (Eds.) *Machine Learning and Data Mining: Methods and Applications*, Wiley, New York, 1998.
19. Mitchell, T.M. *Machine Learning*, McGraw-Hill, Boston, 1997.
20. Mollestad, T. and Skowron, A. A rough set frameworkf for data mining of propositional default rules, *Foundations of Intelligent Systems, 9th International Symposium, ISMIS'96*, LNAI 1079, 448-457, 1996.
21. Nosofsky, R.M., Palmeri, T.J. and McKiley, S.C. Rule-plus-exception model of classification learning, *Psychological Review*, **101**, 53-79, 1994.
22. Rector, A. Defaults, context, and knowledge: alternatives for OWL-indexed knowledge bases, *Pacific Symposium on Biocomputing 2004*, 226-237, 2004.
23. Reiter, R. A logic for default reasoning, *Artificial Intelligence*, **13**, 81-132, 1980.
24. Russell, S. and Norvig, P. *Artificial Intelligence, A Modern Approach*, Prentice Hall, 1995.
25. Suzuki, E. Autonomous discovery of reliable exception rules, *Proceedings of KDD'97*, 259-262, 1997.
26. Suzuki, E. and Żytkow, J.M. Unified algorithm for undirected discovery of exception rules, *Proceedings of PKDD-2000*, 169-180, 2000.
27. Wang, J., Zhao, M., Zhao, K. and Han S. Multilevel data summarization from information system: a "rule + exception" approach, *AI Communications*, **16**, 17-39, 2003.
28. Yao, Y.Y. Ming high order decision rules, in: *Rough Set Theory and Granular Computing*, Inuiguchi, M., Hirano, S. and Tsumoto, S. (Eds.), Springer, Berlin, 125-135, 2003.
29. Yoshida, T. and Motoda, H. Performance evaluation of fuzing two different knowledge sources in ripple down rules method, *Proceedings of the 2005 International Conference on Active Media Technology*, 69-74.
30. Zhong, N., Yao, Y.Y. and Ohshima, M. Peculiarity oriented multidatabase mining, *IEEE Transactions on Knowledge and Data Engineering*, **15**, 952-960, 2003.
31. Zhou Y. and Wang J. Rule+exception modeling based on rough set theory, *Rough Sets and Current Trends in Computing, Proceedings of First International Conference (RSCTC'98)*, LNAI 1424, 529-536, 1998.

Outlier Detection Using Rough Set Theory[*]

Feng Jiang[1,2], Yuefei Sui[1], and Cungen Cao[1]

[1] Key Laboratory of Intelligent Information Processing,
Institute of Computing Technology, Chinese Academy of Sciences,
Beijing 100080, P.R. China
[2] Graduate School of Chinese Academy of Sciences,
Beijing 100039, P.R. China
jiangkong@163.net, {yfsui, cgcao}@ict.ac.cn

Abstract. In this paper, we suggest to exploit the framework of rough set for detecting outliers — individuals who behave in an unexpected way or feature abnormal properties. The ability to locate outliers can help to maintain knowledge base integrity and to single out irregular individuals. First, we formally define the notions of exceptional set and minimal exceptional set. We then analyze some special cases of exceptional set and minimal exceptional set. Finally, we introduce a new definition for outliers as well as the definition of exceptional degree. Through calculating the exceptional degree for each object in minimal exceptional sets, we can find out all outliers in a given dataset.

1 Introduction

Rough set theory introduced by Z. Pawlak [1,2,3], is as an extension of set theory for the study of intelligent systems characterized by insufficient and incomplete information. It is motivated by the practical needs in classification and concept formation. The rough set philosophy is based on the assumption that with every objects of the universe there is associated a certain amount of information (data, knowledge), expressed by means of some attributes used for object description. Objects having the same description are indiscernible (similar) with respect to the available information. In recent years, there has been a fast growing interest in this theory. The successful applications of the rough set model in a variety of problems have amply demonstrated its usefulness and versatility.

In this paper, we suggest a somewhat different usage of rough set. The basic idea is as follows. For any subset X of the universe and any equivalence relation on the universe, the difference between the upper and lower approximations constitutes the boundary region of the rough set, whose elements can not be characterized with certainty as belonging or not to X, using the available information (equivalence relation). The information about objects from the boundary

---

[*] This work is supported by the National NSF of China (60273019 and 60073017), the National 973 Project of China (G1999032701), Ministry of Science and Technology (2001CCA03000) and the National Laboratory of Software Development Environment.

D. Ślęzak et al. (Eds.): RSFDGrC 2005, LNAI 3642, pp. 79–87, 2005.

region is, therefore, inconsistent or ambiguous. When given a set of equivalence relations (available information), if an object in X always lies in the boundary region with respect to every equivalence relation, then we may consider this object as not behaving normally according to the given knowledge (set of equivalence relations) at hand. We call such objects outliers. An outlier in X is an element that always can not be characterized with certainty as belonging or not to X, using the given knowledge.

Recently, the detection of outlier (exception) has gained considerable interest in KDD. Outliers exist extensively in real world, and they are generated from different sources: a heavily tailed distribution or errors in inputting the data. While there is no single, generally accepted, formal definition of an outlier, Hawkins' definition captures the spirit: "an outlier is an observation that deviates so much from other observations as to arouse suspicions that it was generated by a different mechanism" [4]. Finding outliers is important in different applications, such as credit fraud detection and network intrusion detection. Outlier detection has a long history in statistics [4, 5], but has largely focused on univariate data with a known distribution. These two limitations have restricted the ability to apply these types of methods to large real-world databases which typically have many different fields and have no easy way of characterizing the multivariate distribution of examples. Other researchers, beginning with the work by Knorr and Ng [6,7,8], have taken a non-parametric approach and proposed using an example's distance to its nearest neighbors as a measure of unusualness [9,10,11]. Eskin et al. [12], and Lane and Brodley [13] applied distance-based outliers to detecting computer intrusions from audit data. Although distance is an effective non-parametric approach to detect outliers, the drawback is the amount of computation time required. Straightforward algorithms, such as those based on nested loops, typically require $O(N^2)$ distance computations. This quadratic scaling means that it will be very difficult to mine outliers as we tackle increasingly larger datasets.

In this paper, we formally state the ideas briefly sketched above within the context of Pawlak's rough set theory. Our goal is to develop a new way for outlier definition and outlier detection. The remainder of this paper is organized as follows. In the next section, we present some preliminaries of rough set theory that are relevant to this paper. In Section 3, we give formal definitions of concepts of exceptional set and minimal exceptional set, and discuss basic properties about them. In Section 4, we analyze some special cases of exceptional set and minimal exceptional set. Section 5 introduces a new definition for outliers along with the definitions of exceptional degree (degree of outlier-ness). Conclusions are given in Section 6.

2   Preliminaries

Let U denote a finite and nonempty set called the universe, and $\theta \subseteq U \times U$ denote an equivalence relation on U. The pair $apr = (U, \theta)$ is called an approximation space. The equivalence relation θ partitions the set U into disjoint subsets. Such a partition of the universe is denoted by U/θ . If two elements x, y in U belong to the same equivalence class, we say that x and y are indistinguishable. The equivalence classes of θ and the empty set $\emptyset$ are called the elementary or atomic sets in the approximation space.

Given an arbitrary set $X \subseteq U$, it may be impossible to describe X precisely using the equivalence classes of θ. In this case, one may characterize X by a pair of lower and upper approximations:

$$\underline{X}_\theta = \bigcup\{[x]_\theta : [x]_\theta \subseteq X\},$$
$$\overline{X}_\theta = \bigcup\{[x]_\theta : [x]_\theta \cap X \neq \emptyset\},$$

where $[x]_\theta = \{y \mid x\theta y\}$ is the equivalence class containing x. The pair $(\underline{X}_\theta, \overline{X}_\theta)$ is called the rough set with respect to X. The lower approximation $\underline{X}_\theta$ is the union of all the elementary sets which are subsets of X, and the upper approximation $\overline{X}_\theta$ is the union of all the elementary sets which have a nonempty intersection with X. An element in the lower approximation necessarily belongs to X, while an element in the upper approximation possibly belongs to X.

3   Exceptional Set and Minimal Exceptional Set

In contrast to current methods for outlier detection, we will take a two step strategy. First, we find out all exceptional sets and minimal exceptional sets in a given dataset X. Second, we detect all outliers in X from minimal exceptional sets of X. Here we assume that all outliers in X must belong to some minimal exceptional set of X. That is, if an object in X doesn't belong to any minimal exceptional set of X, then we can conclude that it is not an outlier of X. What we need to do is to judge whether an object from a minimal exceptional set is an outlier of X.

In the rest of this paper, given a finite and nonempty universe U, we will not only consider one equivalence relation on U at one time, but also consider an amount of equivalence relations on U simultaneously, which denoted by set $R = \{r_1, r_2, ..., r_m\}$. First, we give the definition of exceptional set.

Definition 1 [Exceptional Set]. Given an arbitrary set $X \subseteq U$, and a set $R = \{r_1, r_2, ..., r_m\}$ of equivalence relations on U. Let $e \subseteq X$ be a subset of X. If for every equivalence relation $r_i \in R$, $e \cap B_i^X \neq \emptyset$, $i = 1, 2, ..., m$, then e is called an exceptional set of X with respect to R, where $B_i^X = BN_i(X) \cap X = X - \underline{X}_i \neq \emptyset$. $\underline{X}_i$ and $\overline{X}_i$ are respectively the lower approximation and the upper approximation of X with respect to r_i. $BN_i(X) = \overline{X}_i - \underline{X}_i$ is called the boundary of X with respect to r_i.

We call B_i^X the inner boundary of X with respect to r_i. When X is clear from the context, we simply use B_i to denote B_i^X.

If an exceptional set $e \subseteq \bigcup_{i=1}^{m} B_i^X$, then e is called a type 1 exceptional set, else e is called a type 2 exceptional set.

In order to define the concept of minimal exceptional set, we give the following two definitions first.

Definition 2. Given an arbitrary set $X \subseteq U$, and a set $R = \{r_1, r_2, ..., r_m\}$ of equivalence relations on U. Let $e \subseteq X$ be an exceptional set of X with respect to R. For any $x \in e$, if $e - \{x\}$ is also an exceptional set of X with respect to R, then the element x is called dispensable in the set e with respect to R, otherwise x is indispensable.

Definition 3. Let $e \subseteq X$ be an exceptional set of X with respect to R. If all the elements of e are indispensable in e with respect to R, then exceptional set e is called independent with respect to R, otherwise e is dependent.

Now we can define minimal exceptional set as an exceptional set which is independent with respect to the corresponding set R of equivalence relations.

Definition 4 [Minimal Exceptional Set]. Let $e \subseteq X$ be an exceptional set of X with respect to R. If $f = e - e'(e' \subseteq e)$ is an independent exceptional set of X with respect to R, then f is called a minimal exceptional set of X with respect to R in e . We use $Min(e)$ to denote the set of all minimal exceptional sets of X with respect to R in e.

It is not difficult to prove that the exceptional set and minimal exceptional set have the following basic properties.

Proposition 1. Given an arbitrary set $X \subseteq U$, and a set $R = \{r_1, r_2, ..., r_m\}$ of equivalence relations on U. If $e \subseteq X$ is an exceptional set of X with respect to R, then there exists at least one minimal exceptional set f in e.

Proposition 2. Given an arbitrary set $X \subseteq U$, and a set $R = \{r_1, r_2, ..., r_m\}$ of equivalence relations on U. If $e \subseteq X$ is an exceptional set of X with respect to R and f is a minimal exceptional set in e, then

(i) $f \subseteq e$;

(ii) $f \subseteq \bigcup_{i=1}^{m} B_i$, where B_i denotes the inner boundary of X with respect to equivalence relation r_i, $i = 1, 2, ..., m$.

Proposition 3. Let E be the set of all exceptional sets of X with respect to R and F be the set of all minimal exceptional sets of X with respect to R, denoted by $F = \bigcup_{e \in E} Min(e)$, where $Min(e)$ is the set of all minimal exceptional sets in e. Then

(i) $F \subseteq E$;

(ii) For any $e, e' \subseteq X$, if $e \in E$ and $e \subseteq e'$čňthen $e' \in E$;

(iii) For any $e, e' \subseteq X$, if $e' \notin E$ and $e \subseteq e'$, then $e \notin E$;

(iv) For any $e \in E$, $e \neq \emptyset$, that is, exceptional set can not be empty;

(v) For any $e, e' \in E$, if $e \subseteq e'$, then all minimal exceptional sets in e are also minimal exceptional sets in e'.

Proposition 4. If E is the set of all exceptional sets of X with respect to R and F is the set of all minimal exceptional sets of X with respect to R, then

(i) For any $e_1, e_2 \in E$, $e_1 \cup e_2 \in E$;

(ii) For any $e_1, e_2 \in F$, if $e_1 \neq e_2$, then $e_1 \cap e_2 \notin E$.

Proof.

(i) Given any $e_1, e_2 \in E$, for every $1 \leq i \leq m$, $e_1 \cap B_i \neq \emptyset$ and $e_2 \cap B_i \neq \emptyset$, where B_i denotes the inner boundary of X with respect to equivalence relation r_i. Therefore for every $1 \leq i \leq m$, $(e_1 \cup e_2) \cap B_i = (e_1 \cap B_i) \cup (e_2 \cap B_i) \neq \emptyset$. So $e_1 \cup e_2$ is an exceptional set of X with respect to R by Definition 1, that is, $e_1 \cup e_2 \in E$;

(ii) (Proof by contradiction) Assume that $e_1 \cap e_2 \in E$. Since $e_1 \neq e_2$, $e_1 \cap e_2 \subset e_1$ and $e_1 \cap e_2 \subset e_2$. Therefore $e_1 - (e_1 \cap e_2) \neq \emptyset$, that is, there exists a $x \in (e_1 - (e_1 \cap e_2))$. Furthermore, $e_1 \in F \subseteq E$ and $e_1 \cap e_2 \in E$. So x is dispensable in the set e_1 with respect to R, e_1 is dependent with respect to R, that is, e_1 is not a minimal exceptional set of X with respect to R. This contradicts with the condition $e_1 \in F$. So if $e_1 \neq e_2$, then $e_1 \cap e_2 \notin E$. $\square$

Proposition 5. Given an arbitrary set $X \subseteq U$, and a set $R = \{r_1, r_2, ..., r_m\}$ of equivalence relations on U. Let F be the set of all minimal exceptional sets of X with respect to R and $B = \{B_1, B_2, ..., B_m\}$ be the set of all inner boundaries of X with respect to each equivalence relations in R. The union of all minimal exceptional sets in F equals to the union of all inner boundaries in B, that is,

$$\bigcup_{f \in F} f = \bigcup_{i=1}^{m} B_i.$$

4 Some Special Cases

From above we can see, mostly, we get an amount of exceptional sets and minimal exceptional sets from a given X and R. In order to detect all outliers in X from these minimal exceptional sets, it is necessary to investigate some special cases of them first.

At first, we define a concept of boundary degree.

Definition 5 [Boundary Degree]. Given an arbitrary set $X \subseteq U$, and a set $R = \{r_1, r_2, ..., r_m\}$ of equivalence relations on U. Let $B = \{B_1, B_2, ..., B_m\}$ be the set of all inner boundaries of X with respect to each equivalence relations in R. For every object $x \in X$, the number of different inner boundaries which contain x is called the boundary degree of x, denoted by $Degree\_B(x)$.

Then, we can consider a special kind of minimal exceptional set which contains the least elements with respect to other minimal exceptional sets. We define it as the shortest minimal exceptional set.

Definition 6 [The Shortest Minimal Exceptional Set]. Given an arbitrary set $X \subseteq U$, and a set $R = \{r_1, r_2, ..., r_m\}$ of equivalence relations on U. Let F be the set of all minimal exceptional sets of X with respect to R. If there exists a minimal exceptional set $f' \in F$ such that for any $f \in F$, $|f'| \leq |f|$, where $|p|$ denotes the cardinal number of p. Then f' is called the shortest minimal exceptional set of X with respect to R.

Next, we give an algorithm which can find out the shortest minimal exceptional set of X with respect to R.

Algorithm 1. Find out the shortest minimal exceptional set of X with respect to R.

    Input: Inner boundaries set $B = \{B_1, B_2, \ldots, B_m\}$

    Output: The shortest minimal exceptional set f'

    (1) $f' = \emptyset$ // Initialize f' as an empty set;

    (2)   While ($B \neq \emptyset$) do {

    (3)   For each $B_i \in B$

    (4)   For each $x \in B_i$

    (5)   Compute the boundary degree of x // $Degree\_B(x)$;

    (6)   Find an element y which has the biggest boundary degree in all $B_i \in B$
        (if there exist more than one such elements, Select one randomly);

    (7) $f' = f' \cup \{y\}$;

    (8)   Delete all the inner boundaries which contain y from B;

    (9)   }

    (10)   Return f'.

We can also define two special kinds of exceptional set—the greatest exceptional set and the least exceptional set.

Definition 7 [The Greatest Exceptional Set]. Given an arbitrary set $X \subseteq U$, and a set $R = \{r_1, r_2, ..., r_m\}$ of equivalence relations on U. If E is the set of all exceptional sets of X with respect to R, then the union of all elements in E is called the greatest exceptional set of X with respect to R, denoted by $GES_R(X) = \bigcup\limits_{e \in E} e$.

Proposition 6. The greatest exceptional set of X with respect to R is unique and equals to X itself, that is, $\bigcup\limits_{e \in E} e = X$.

Definition 8 [The Least Exceptional Set]. Given an arbitrary set $X \subseteq U$, and a set $R = \{r_1, r_2, ..., r_m\}$ of equivalence relations on U. Let E be the set of all exceptional sets of X with respect to R. If there exists a set $l \in E$ such that for any $e \in E$, $l \subseteq e$. Then l is called the least exceptional set of X with respect to R.

Proposition 7. Let E be the set of all exceptional sets of X with respect to R and F be the set of all minimal exceptional sets of X with respect to R. If l is the least exceptional set of X with respect to R, then

    (i) l is also a minimal exceptional set of X, that is, $l \in F$;

    (ii) l is not empty and unique;

    (iii) l equals to the intersection of all the elements in E, denoted by $l = \bigcap\limits_{e \in E} e$.

Since the least exceptional set is the intersection of all exceptional sets. But the intersection of all exceptional sets may be empty. So when do we have the least exceptional set? The next proposition gives an answer.

Proposition 8. Let E be the set of all exceptional sets of X with respect to R, and F be the set of all minimal exceptional sets of X with respect to R. If and only if there is only one element in F, the least exceptional set of X with respect to R exists, and the only element in F just is the least exceptional set.

5   Defining Outliers

Most current methods for outlier detection give a binary classification of objects (data points): is or is not an outlier. In real life, it is not so simple. For many scenarios, it is more meaningful to assign to each object a degree of being an outlier. Therefore, M. M. Breunig proposed a method for identifying density-based local outliers [14]. He defines a local outlier factor (LOF) that indicates the degree of outlier-ness of an object using only the object's neighborhood. The outlier factor of object p captures the degree to which we call p an outlier.

We define two types of exceptional degree respectively for object and set.

Definition 9 [Exceptional Degree of Object]. Given an arbitrary set $X \subseteq U$, and a set $R = \{r_1, r_2, ..., r_m\}$ of equivalence relations on U. Let $B = \{B_1, B_2, ..., B_m\}$ be the set of all inner boundaries of X with respect to each equivalence relations in R. For any object $x \in X$, the cardinal number of set B (equals to m) divided by the boundary degree of x (namely $Degree\_B(x)$) is called the exceptional degree of x with respect to R, denoted by $ED\_Object(x) = \dfrac{Degree\_B(x)}{m}$.

Obviously, $0 \leq ED\_Object(x) \leq 1$.

When we have worked out the exceptional degree for all objects in minimal exceptional sets of X, it is not difficult to find out all outliers in X with respect to R. We can assume that all the objects in minimal exceptional sets whose exceptional degree is greater than a given threshold value are outliers. And the other objects in minimal exceptional sets are not outliers.

Definition 10 [Outlier]. Given an arbitrary set $X \subseteq U$, and a set $R = \{r_1, r_2, ..., r_m\}$ of equivalence relations on U. Let F be the set of all minimal exceptional sets of X with respect to R. For any object $o \in \bigcup_{f \in F} f$, if $ED\_Object(o) \geq \mu$ then object o is called an outlier in X with respect to R, where μ is a given threshold value.

Definition 11 [Exceptional Degree of Set]. Given an arbitrary set $X \subseteq U$, and a set $R = \{r_1, r_2, ..., r_m\}$ of equivalence relations on U. For any set $Y \subseteq X$, the sum on the exceptional degree of all objects in Y divided by the cardinal number of Y is called the exceptional degree of set Y, denoted by $ED\_Set(Y) = \dfrac{\sum_{y \in Y} ED\_Object(y)}{|Y|}$.

Obviously, $0 \leq ED\_Set(Y) \leq 1$.

Proposition 9. Given an arbitrary set $X \subseteq U$, and a set $R = \{r_1, r_2, ..., r_m\}$ of equivalence relations on U. Let $B = \{B_1, B_2, ..., B_m\}$ be the set of all inner boundaries of X with respect to each equivalence relations in R. If $\bigcap_{i=1}^{m} B_i \neq \emptyset$ then $ED\_Set(\bigcap_{i=1}^{m} B_i) = 1$.

Proof.

Since $\bigcap_{i=1}^{m} B_i \neq \emptyset$, there exists an $x \in \bigcap_{i=1}^{m} B_i$, that is, for every $B_i \in B$, $x \in B_i$, where $i = 1, 2, ..., m$. Therefore for any $y \in \bigcap_{i=1}^{m} B_i$, $Degree\_B(y) = m$ and $ED\_Object(y) = 1$. Let $Y = \bigcap_{i=1}^{m} B_i$, then $ED\_Set(Y) = \dfrac{\sum_{y \in Y} ED\_Object(y)}{|Y|} = \dfrac{\sum_{y \in Y} 1}{|Y|} = 1$. So $ED\_Set(\bigcap_{i=1}^{m} B_i) = 1$. □

6   Conclusion

Finding outliers is an important task for many KDD applications. In this paper, we present a new method for outlier defining and outlier detection. The method exploits the framework of rough set for detecting outliers. The main idea is that objects in boundary region have more likelihood of being an outlier than objects in lower approximations.

There are two directions for ongoing work. The first one is to analyze the complexity of our method. The second one is to make a comparison between our method and other outlier detection methods.

References

1. Pawlak, Z.: "Rough sets", *International Journal of Computer and Information Sciences*, **11** (1982) 341–356
2. Pawlak, Z.: Rough sets: Theoretical Aspects of Reasoning about Data, (Kluwer Academic Publishers, Dordrecht,1991)
3. Pawlak, Z., Grzymala-Busse, J.W., Slowinski, R., and Ziarko, W.: "Rough sets", Comm. ACM, **38** (1995) 89–95
4. Hawkins, D.: *Identifications of Outliers*, (Chapman and Hall, London, 1980)
5. Barnett, V., and Lewis, T.: *Outliers in Statistical Data*, (John Wiley & Sons, 1994)
6. Knorr, E., and Ng, R.: "A Unified Notion of Outliers: Properties and Computation", Proc. of the Int. Conf. on Knowledge Discovery and Data Mining, (1997) 219–222
7. Knorr, E., and Ng, R.: "Algorithms for Mining Distance-based Outliers in Large Datasets", VLDB Conference Proceedings, (1998)
8. Knorr, E., and Ng, R.: "Finding intensional knowledge of distance-based outliers". In Proc. of the 25th VLDB Conf., (1999)
9. Angiulli, F., and Pizzuti, C.: "Fast outlier detection in high dimensional spaces", In Proc. of the Sixth European Conf. on the Principles of Data Mining and Knowledge Discovery, (2002) 15–226

10. Ramaswamy, S., Rastogi, R., and Shim, K.: "Efficient algorithms for mining outliers from large datasets". In Proc. of the ACM SIGMOD Conf., (2000)
11. Knorr, E., Ng, R. and Tucakov, V.: "Distance-based outliers: algorithms and applications", VLDB Journal: Very Large Databases, 8(3-4) (2000) 237–253
12. Eskin, E., Arnold, A., Prerau, M., Portnoy, L., and Stolfo, S.: "A geometric framework for unsupervised anomaly detection: Detecting intrusions in unlabeled data", In Data Mining for Security Applications, (2002)
13. Lane, T., and Brodley, C.E.: "Temporal sequence learning and data reduction for anomaly detection", ACM Transactions on Information and System Security, 2(3) (1999) 295-331
14. Breunig, M.M., Kriegel, H.P., Ng, R.T., and Sander, J.: "LOF: Identifying density-based local outliers", In Proc. ACM SIGMOD Conf., (2000) 93–104

Reverse Prediction

Julia Johnson and Patrick Campeau

Department of Mathematics and Computer Science,
Laurentian University,
Sudbury, Ontario P3E 2C6, Canada
{julia, pcampeau}@cs.laurentian.ca

Abstract. Rough set reverse method enables prediction of the best values for condition attributes given values for the decision attributes. Reverse prediction is required for many problems that do not lend themselves to being solved by the traditional rough sets forward prediction. The RS1 algorithm has been rewritten using better notation and style and generalized to provide reverse prediction. Rough Set Reverse Prediction Algorithm was implemented and evaluated on its ability to make inferences on large data sets in a dynamic problem domain.

1 Introduction

In the traditional rough set forward prediction process, given attribute values for each condition attribute, the decision attribute can be predicted following the decision rules. In this research, we do the opposite. Given a value for the decision attribute, decision rules are followed by which the attribute value for each condition attribute that best implies the decision attribute can be predicted. The two scenarios are illustrated as follows:

Forward Prediction: $C_1[\text{given}], C_2[\text{given}], \ldots, C_n[\text{given}] \rightarrow D[\text{predict}]$. Given attribute values for each condition attribute, a value for the decision attribute is predicted.

Reverse Prediction: $D[\text{given}] \leftarrow C_1[\text{predict}], C_2[\text{predict}], \ldots \ldots, C_n[\text{predict}]$. Given a value for the decision attribute, we predict the attribute value for each condition attribute that best implies the value of the decision attribute.

Reverse prediction is required for many problems that do not lend themselves to being solved by a forward prediction method. For example, for Internet business applications, we know the decision attribute (we want most customers to be satisfied) and we want to find the condition attributes (characteristics of the product) that would lead to most customers being satisfied.

We develop a new rough set algorithm, the Rough Set Reverse Predicting Algorithm (RSRPA) which takes as input a decision table and the decision (e.g., most people satisfied) that we aim for. Output is a set of the predicted best condition attribute values (soft values, e.g., low, high, instead of numeric values) required to achieve that aim.

D. Ślęzak et al. (Eds.): RSFDGrC 2005, LNAI 3642, pp. 88–97, 2005.

2 Related Work

In this section, we review rough set software systems to contrast with our own that implements many of the same features but with addition of reverse prediction. We review uncertain reasoning using a different approach than a rough set one. We chose Bayesian reasoning for comparison. The relationship of Rough Sets to the Bayesian approach is a well researched topic in itself. We review results relevant to the notion of reverse prediction and suggest how the reverse prediction method relates.

2.1 Rough Set Software Systems

The commercially available Windows based ROSETTA system [9] provides a complete software environment for rough set operations. The RS1 algorithm is central to most rough set engines including ROSETTA since Wong and Ziarko developed the algorithm in the mid eighties. RS1 synthesizes decision rules from an information table. ROSETTA generates if-then rules also providing validation and analysis of the rules. Additionally, an unsupervised mode of operation is supported which finds general patterns in data.

ROSETTA has been put to use recently in the area of medical biology [7]. Microarray technology generates vast amounts of data in the process of measuring the behavior of thousands of genes simultaneously. Supervised learning is being studied for selecting genes that discriminate between tumor subtypes.

The Rough Set Exploration System (RSES) is software for data analysis and classification, free for non-commercial use [1]. It has been put to use, for example, for analysis of data from a real medical project STULONG [8] which concerns a twenty year longitudinal study of the risk factors of atherosclerosis.

2.2 Uncertain Reasoning Within a Bayesian Approach

Explicit management of uncertainty based on probability theory has been used for neurophysiological problems [13,14] requiring the analysis of vast amounts of data generated by dynamic brain imaging techniques. The foundation for this work is Bayes' theorem whose central insight is that a hypothesis is confirmed by any body of data that its truth renders probable [4]. The neurophysiological work involves a fundamental problem known as the source separation problem.

The source separation problem is one of inductive inference where insufficient information must be used to infer the most probable solution. There are multiple signal sources recorded by multiple detectors. Each detector records a mixture of the original signals. The goal is to recover estimates of the original signals. In what is called the *forward problem* one knows the regions of activity or sources in the brain, and the objective is to calculate the magnetic fields on the surface of the head. In the *inverse problem*, from the magnetic fields one must calculate the locations and orientations of the sources. Knuth states that "inverse problems are notoriously more difficult to solve than forward problems." [6]

Consider Bayes' theorem as a natural starting point for solving either an inductive or deductive inference problem.

$$P_{data,I}(model) = \frac{P_{model,I}(data)P_I(model)}{P_I(data)}$$

where *model* describes the model or model parameters used to describe the physical situation, *data* represents any data or new information obtained in an experiment, and I denotes any additional prior information one may have about the problem.

The probability on the left hand side of the equation is called the posterior probability. It describes the degree to which one believes the model accurately describes the physical situation given the data and all prior knowledge. The second probability in the numerator is the prior probability. It describes one's prior knowledge regarding the probability that the model adequately describes the physical situation of interest. (adapted from [6])

Before being applied to a forward source separation problem, the theorem must be recast to a more useful form by modeling the physical situation using mixed signals and original source waveforms, and by accounting for amplitude of the source signals and signal propagation in the prior probability. In the end we have a derivation within a Bayesian framework of a pre-existing algorithm for source separation expressed as a forward problem.

2.3   Reverse Prediction in Relation to Bayesian Methodology

Extensive work has been done to understand the relationship between rough sets and Bayesian reasoning [3,11,12]. The certainty and coverage associated with a decision rule have been shown to satisfy BayesŠ theorem. This result makes way for the use of BayesŠ theorem to discover patterns in data without referring to prior and posterior probabilities. That leaves the first probability in the numerator $P_{model,I}(data)$ the likelihood, that describes how well the model can predict the data, and evidence $P_I(data)$ in the denominator that describes the predicting power of the data. There is a form of Bayes theorem that is particularly useful for inferring causes from their effects. Pawlak uses this theorem (with probability concepts coverage and certainty factored out) for providing a way of explaining decisions by deductive inference [10,11].

There is generally a difficult issue with inverse problems (e.g., from the magnetic fields one must calculate the locations and orientations of the sources). "The only hope is that there is additional information available that can be used to constrain the infinite set of possible solutions to a single unique solution. This is where Bayesian statistics will be useful." [6] It may well be possible to derive the reverse prediction algorithm within a Bayesian framework (as was Rough Bayesian Model derived for Rough Set model [16]). If so, reverse prediction would be formulated as a forward problem, not an inverse problem.

Although we cannot be certain given the proprietary nature of the product, it appears from the literature that rules predicting causes from effects in the nature of learning Bayesian networks from data is not supported in ROSETTA. Neither does it appear that the modest generalization of RS1 developed here in which we consider any subset of attributes of the decision table to be the decision attribute, has been incorporated in ROSETTA. However, the unsupervised learning of which ROSETTA is capable may be related to rough set reverse prediction. Deductive rules derived within a Bayesian framework for explaining decisions in RSES are expected shortly.

3   Rough Set Algorithms

Rough set algorithms generate a set of decision rules that model all concepts in a decision table. This set is only a subset of all possible decision rules. The algorithms attempt to model a given concept by using the least rules possible. For each concept, if possible, only deterministic rules are generated to explain the concept. If the attributes do not hold enough knowledge to be explained deterministically, then non-deterministic rules are also generated.

3.1   RS1 Algorithm

In this project, the rough set algorithm used is known as the RS1 inductive learning algorithm [17]. The RS1 algorithm has been rewritten by changing the notation and describing the steps in a more user friendly way. The RS1 algorithm is illustrated in the next section by pointing out the sections of RSRPA that are taken directly from RS1 and highlighting the new sections that are unique to RSRPA. Whereas RS1 generates decision rules to model all concepts in the decision table, in RSRPA, RS1 is used to model a given concept. The statements unique to RSRPA are highlighted in bold with the exception of statement labels which also appear in bold. The remaining statements are stylistic and notational improvements of those of RS1.

3.2   Notations

A concept X can be defined approximately by two exact sets called the lower approximation $P_L X$ of X and the upper approximation $P^U X$ of X. The discriminant index is a quality measure of the ability of one or many attributes to approximate or explain a certain concept. Discriminant index is denoted as αP where P is a set of attributes and U is the universe of entities.

$$\alpha P(X) = 1 - \frac{|P^U X - P_L X|}{|U|}$$

Given a set of condition attributes P, we generate m indiscernibility classes by intersecting the indiscernibility classes for each attribute. Let those indiscernibility classes be denoted as $Q_1, Q_2 \ldots Q_m$. Given a set of decision attributes, we can generate n indiscernibility classes or concepts. Let them be denoted as $X_1, X_2 \ldots X_n$. A decision rule links the ith indiscernability class to the jth concept in the form $\{r_{ij} : \text{Des}(Q_i) \Rightarrow \text{Des}(X_j) | Q_i \cap X_j \neq \phi\}$ which is to say that any given rule exists if at least a single object in Q_i is in X_j.

3.3   RSRPA Algorithm

INPUT
    Decision Table
    V = Attribute value of concept

SETUP
    1. Let U be the universe of objects.
    2. Let C be the set of condition attributes.
    3. Let X be given concept with attribute value V.
    4. Let BCR = ϕ **be a set of decision rules.**

STEP 0
    Let $C^1 = C$

STEP 1
    $U^1 = U$
    $X^1 = X$
    $P = \phi$ (Pivot)

STEP 2
    Let max $= -1$
    Let $best_c = \phi$
    For all $c \in C^1$
        Let $P_t = P \cup \{c\}$
        Compute the discriminant index $\alpha P_t(X)$
        If $\alpha P_t(X) > \max$
            $\max = \alpha P_t(X)$
            $best_c = \{c\}$
    Let $P = P \cup best_c$

STEP 3
    If $P_L X = \phi$
        Goto STEP 4
    Else
        For each equivalence class $Q_\#$ that was used to derive $P_L X$
            Output deterministic decision rule in the form $\text{Des}(Q_\#) \Rightarrow \text{Des}(X)$

    If more then one rule generated
        Pick the rule R with the highest coverage.

    For each condition attribute C_v covered by the rule R
        $C^1 = C^1 - C_v$

    BCR = **BCR**$\cup R$

    If $C = \phi$
        Goto STEP 6
    Else
        Goto STEP 2

STEP 4

Let $U^1 = U^1 - [(U^1 - P^U X) \cup P_L X]$

Let $X = X - P_L X$

If $U^1 = \phi$

   Goto STEP 6

Else

   Let $C^1 = C^1 - \text{best}_c$

   If $C^1 \neq \phi$

      Goto STEP 2

STEP 5

For each equivalence class $Q_\#$ that was used to derive $P^U X$

Output non-deterministic decision rule in form $\text{Des}(Q_\#) \Rightarrow \text{Des}(X)$

* Comment: RS1 ends here. Normally, RS1 would branch back to Step 2.

If more then one rule generated

   Pick the rule R with the highest certainty

   BCR = BCR$\cup$R

END

The RSRPA algorithm begins by executing the RS1 algorithm on the decision table (for the given concept). The execution of RS1 terminates when one or more rules get generated in a single step. If more then one rule is generated, the best one is picked using either coverage or certainty. This rule is added to the set of Best Condition attribute Rules (BCR). Each condition attribute that is covered by this rule is removed from the set of condition attributes (i.e., the column in the decision table that represents the removed attribute is no longer considered). If the set of condition attributes still has some attributes in it, the RS1 algorithm is restarted on the columns of the decision table that represent the remaining condition attributes. This process continues until the set of condition attributes is empty at which time the set BCR contains rules with the strongest condition attribute values implying the given concept.

At the end of STEP 5 the set BCR contains rules that are mutually exclusive with respect to the condition attributes they cover. Because an attribute is removed from the condition attribute set only when a rule covering it is generated, no two rules in BCR cover the same attribute. Also, since the only way to remove an attribute value from the set of attributes is to generate a rule for it, each condition attribute will be covered by one rule in BCR. The set BCR therefore contains one attribute value for each condition attribute. These attribute values are the ones that RSRPA predicts best imply the concept.

RSGUI. RSRPA was embedded in a system referred to as RSGUI that provides an effective graphical user interface that facilitates use of the system for experimentation. Facility was provided in RSGUI to consider any subset of attributes in the decision table as the decision attribute, the remainder being considered as condition attributes. A feedback loop provides the user with the opportunity to view the rules generated as a result of the current choice of decision attributes and modify the choice of decision attributes to obtain better rules on a subsequent execution. Hence, the outer loop of RS1 that generates one concept after another is replaced by the feedback loop in RSGUI in which the user initiates generation of the next concept of choice to be explained.

4   Evaluation

An application needing dynamic decision making was developed to test RSRPA. Our application is a hockey game. Each team consists of five artificial players.

4.1   Hockey Game Application

Each player A is in one of four distinct states which are listed as follows together with an abbreviation that we will be using later to refer to the state. 1) the puck is in A's possession (*mine*), 2) the puck is in A's teammate's possession (*mate's*), 3) the puck is in A's opposing team's possession *foe's*), 4) the puck is free (*fate's*).

The notion of a state is important for predicting behaviors of dynamic objects, but rather than using the decision attribute for recording states as in [15], characteristics of the hockey game application require that the condition attributes incorporate information about states. In the game of hockey, we know the decision attribute (we want our team to win) and we want to find the condition attributes (behaviors of the individual team members) that would lead to a win.

Unlike past work [5] where the behavior of objects is given by data collected by a human watching the program, the behaviors in this research are the actual methods coded in a programming language to perform the behavior. Codes of the more popular behaviors, their meanings and abbreviated names are as follows: A1 - the player chases the puck (short name Chaser), A4 - the player predicts how he will get to the puck (Psychic Chaser), B1 - the player shoots the puck directly on the net (Random Shooter), B3 - the player shoots the puck off the boards onto the net (Bounce Shooter), E6 - a player is kept between the puck and his own net (N & P Defense), I1(1) - this behavior takes in one other behavior as parameter. The behavior codes refer to methods coded in Java. The logic for I1(1) follows: If close to top or bottom boards use behaviour 1 else if in above half of rink skate upwards else skate downwards. The complete set of 34 behavior codes, their descriptions and the situations to which they apply are given in [2].

The hockey game runs in two modes: Decision table creation mode and testing mode. Let us first examine the form of the information table created by the hockey game.

Information Table Creation. There are four states per player and five players per team from which 20 condition attributes can be derived. A row in the decision table output by the hockey game follows: $< t\_91, D2, E6, C7, E6, F1, C2, A1, G1, I2[I1[D2]], E6, C2, E9, H3[B3, F1], C5, C6, E2, F1, C4, H1[A1, E6], H1[A4, C1],$

Table 1. Winning team predicted using rough set reverse prediction algorithm. This team is called the Rough Set team. The game was run many times pitting the newly created Rough Set team against teams with random behaviors.

Results from RSRPA - This is NOT the Decision Table			
player #	mine	mate's	foe's	fate's
1	$I1[B1]$	$C1$	$H1[A1, C7]$	$A4$
2	$B2$	$C2$	$H1[A1, C6]$	$A4$
3	$F1$	$H1[A1, C7]$	$G1$	$A4$
4	$12[B3]$	$E6$	$E6$	$E6$
5	$B3$	$E9$	$E9$	$H2[A4, E9]$

$WIN >$. The first field of every row is a unique row identifier. Player 1's behaviors are in fields 2 to 5, player 2's behaviors in fields 6 to 9, and so on. The first field for each player codes the behavior that the given player uses when he has the puck in his possession (*mine*), the second field is the behavior he uses when one of his teammates has the puck (*mate's*), the third field the behavior he uses in state *foe's*, and the fourth field the behavior he uses in state *fate's*. A decision attribute that measures the success or failure of a combination of behaviors for each player in each state completes the decision table.

Evaluation of Predictions. The hockey game can be run in a mode that allows us to enter a team's behaviors and run that team against hundreds of other randomly generated teams. The best set of behaviors to achieve a win was predicted for each player on the team using rough set reverse prediction algorithm. Quantitative measures of RSRPA's success at making the right predictions were obtained by computing the percentage of games won by the team predicted by RSRPA. The higher the winning percentage, the more successful was the prediction.

4.2 Results

We ran our new Rough Set team against 1000 other randomly generated teams. The results were impressive. The Rough Set team won 788 of those 1000 games, lost 144 and tied 68. Excluding the ties the Rough Set team won 84.5 % of its games. We tested the same Rough Set team using B3 for the attribute #1 value for player 4. The team improved, winning 835 of the 1000 games but also tying 133 of them. This resulted in a 96.4 winning percentage. Although B2 was the expert's choice as the best behavior for that player, we also tested the team with behavior D2 as the attribute #1 value. Surprisingly, this team was the best of the three tested. It won 862 games, lost only 10 and tied 127. That is a 98.9 winning percentage. The testing demonstrated that an expert can better predict the best combinations of behaviors with the support of a decision aid.

4.3 Efficiency

In this subsection, a word on performance as we observed it from executing the algorithm. To make data collection easy, several options were added to the game.

For example, the game can be executed with graphics off. By not generating the graphics, a game takes on average, just over one second to execute (as opposed to over 10 minutes with graphics on). This is an empirical analysis.

5   Summary and Conclusions

We have shown within a rough sets approach how to predict the best condition attribute values given values for the decision attributes. A procedure to generate decision rules using reverse prediction was specified and implemented.

A method of testing the accuracy of the rough set reverse prediction method was devised that not only showed that RSRPA can be used with high success in a problem domain to accomplish preset goals, but showed it in an objective, quantitative way.

RSRPA was compared with the original rough set rule induction algorithm RS1. The rules are optimized in the same way for reverse prediction as in the classical algorithms for rough set rule induction (for example, those implemented in RSES[1] or ROSETTA[9]). This was illustrated by showing where RS1 ends and the super-algorithm RSRPA begins.

Since the Bayesian philosophy requires our assumptions to be made explicit, the model, the probability assignments, or a simplifying assumption may be modified to more appropriately reflect a given problem. However, an algorithm such as RS1 is not intended to be modified to suit a particular application. Bayesian reasoning may have advantage over rough set approach for including reverse prediction because the former is more general. It is hard to modify an algorithm (e.g., RS1) and know what we have done, but not so hard to modify a formulation of a problem based on probability theory.

Researchers are struggling with the accuracy of predicting a class with a group of attributes. Is it possible to do it reversely, i.e., predict a group of attributes with a single class label? Should this question come to the reader's mind, let us be reminded that we are providing reverse prediction, not inverse inference. Forward Prediction: $C_1[\text{given}], C_2[\text{given}], \ldots, C_n[\text{given}] \rightarrow D[\text{predict}]$. Reverse Prediction: $D[\text{given}] \leftarrow C_1[\text{predict}], C_2[\text{predict}], \ldots \ldots, C_n[\text{predict}]$.

Pawlak has provided a way of explaining decisions deductively based on probability theory. Here we have taken the approach of modifying RS1 directly without first formulating the problem using Bayes' theorem. That means that we are providing reverse prediction by solving an inductive inference problem. It remains to be seen if a formulation of RSRPA within a Bayesian framework will result in Pawlak's deductive rules for explaining decisions.

References

1. Bazan, J.G., Szczuka, M.: Rough Set Exploration System (RSES). Transactions on Rough Sets III. Peters, J.F., Skowron, A., van Albada, D. (eds.): Lecture Notes in Computer Science. Vol. 3400. Springer-Verlag, (2005) 37-56
2. Campeau, P.: Predicting the Most Favorable Behavior of Artificial Objects using Rough Sets. Honor's Thesis. Département de mathématiques et d'informatique, Université Laurentienne. Sudbury, Le Canada. (2000)

3. Greco, S., Pawlak, Z., Slowinski, R.: Bayesian Confirmation Measures within Rough Set Approach. In: Tsumoto, S., Slowinski, R., Komorowski, J., Grzymala-Busse, J.W. (Eds.) Rough Sets and Current Trends in Computing (2004) 264-273
4. Joyce, J.: Bayes' Theorem. In: Edward N. Zalta (ed.): The Stanford Encyclopedia of Philosophy (2003)
5. Karimi, K., Johnson, J.A., Hamilton, H.J.: Including Behavior in Object Similarity Assessment with Examples from Artificial Life. In: Ziarko, W., Yao, Y. (eds.): Lecture Notes in Artificial Intelligence. Vol. 2005. Springer-Verlag, (2000) 642-651
6. Knuth, K.H.: A Bayesian Approach to Source Separation. In: Cardoso,J.F., Jutten, C., Loubaton, P. (eds.): Proceedings of the First International Workshop on Independent Component Analysis and Signal Separation: ICA'99 (1999) 283-288.
7. Midelfart, H., Komorowski, J., Nørsett, K., Yadetie, F., Sandvik, A.K., Laegreid, A.: Learning Rough Set Classifiers from Gene Expressions and Clinical Data. In: Fundamenta Informaticae. 53:2 (2002) 155-183
8. Nguyen, H. S.: Nguyen S. H.: Analysis of STULONG Data by Rough Set Exploration System (RSES). In: Berka, P. (Ed.). Proc. ECML/PKDD Workshop (2003) 71-82.
9. Öhrn, A., Komorowski, J., Skowron, A., and Synak, P.: The Design and Implementation of a Knowledge Discovery Toolkit based on Rough Sets: The ROSETTA system. In: Polkowski, L., Skowron, A. (eds.): Rough Sets in Knowledge Discovery 1: Methodology and Applications. Heidelberg: Physica-Verlag (1998) 376-399
10. Pawlak, Z.: Flow Graphs and Data Mining. Transactions on Rough Sets III. Peters, J.F., Skowron, A., van Albada, D. (eds.): Lecture Notes in Computer Science. Vol. 3400. Springer-Verlag, (2005) 1-36
11. Pawlak, Z: A rough set view on Bayes' Theorem. Int. J. Intelligent Systems 18:5 (2003) 487-498
12. Pawlak, Z. : Combining Rough Sets and Bayes' Rules. Computational Intelligence 17:3 (2001) 401-408
13. Shah, A.S., Knuth, K.H., Lakatos, P., Schroeder, C.E.: Lessons from applying differentially variable component analysis (dVCA) to electroencephalographic activity. In: Erickson, G.J., Zhai, Y. (eds.): Bayesian Inference and Maximum Entropy Methods in Science and Engineering, AIP Conference Proc. 707 (2003) 167-181
14. Shah, A.S., Knuth, K.H., Truccolo, W.A., Ding, M., Bressler, S.L., Schroeder, C.E. A Bayesian approach to estimating coupling between neural components: evaluation of the multiple component event related potential (mcERP) algorithm. In: Williams, C. (ed.): Bayesian Inference and Maximum Entropy Methods in Science and Engineering, AIP Conference Proc. 659 (2002) 23-38
15. Shen, L., Tay, F., Qu, L., Shen, Y.: Fault Diagnosis using Rough Sets Theory. Computers in Industry. 43:1 (2000) 61-72
16. Ślęzak, D.: Rough Sets and Bayes' Factor: Transactions on Rough Sets III. Peters, J.F., Skowron, A., van Albada, D. (eds.): Lecture Notes in Computer Science. Vol. 3400. Spring Verlag, (2005) 202-229
17. Wong, S.K.M., Ziarko, W.: Algorithm for Inductive Learning. Bulletin of Polish Academy of Sciences. 34:5 (1986) 271-276

Prediction Mining – An Approach to Mining Association Rules for Prediction*

Jitender Deogun and Liying Jiang

Department of Computer Science and Engineering,
University of Nebraska - Lincoln,
Lincoln, NE, 68588-0115, USA
{deogun, ljiang}@cse.unl.edu

Abstract. An interesting application of association mining in the context temporal databases is that of prediction. Prediction is to use the antecedent of a rule to predict the consequent of the rule. But not all of association rules may be suitable for prediction. In this paper, we investigate the properties of rules for prediction, and develop an approach called *prediction mining* — mining a set of association rules that are useful for prediction. Prediction mining discovers a set of prediction rules that have three properties. First, there must be a time lag between antecedent and consequent of the rule. Second, antecedent of a prediction rule is the minimum condition that implies the consequent. Third, a prediction rule must have relatively stable confidence with respect to the time frame determined by application domain. We develop a prediction mining algorithm for discovering the set of prediction rules. The efficiency and effectiveness of our approach is validated by experiments on both synthetic and real-life databases, we show that the prediction mining approach efficiently discovers a set of rules that are proper for prediction.

1 Introduction

Association rule mining is an important theme in data mining. Association rules are dependency rules that describe the occurence of an itemset based on the occurrences of other itemsets. When considered in the context of temporal databases, some association rules also reveal the purported cause-effect relation between antecedent and consequent, that is, the occurrence of the antecedent implies the occurrence of the consequent. We may take the antecedent as cause and the consequent as result, a natural and interesting application of association rules is that of making prediction. However, not all association rules are suitable for prediction, there are several specialties for prediction rules.

First, we consider the prediction rule in the context of temporal databases. Traditional association rule mining seeks co-occurrence relationships among data

---

* This research was supported in part by NSF Digital Government Grant No. EIA-0091530, USDA RMA Grant NO. 02IE08310228, and NSF EPSCOR, Grant No. EPS-0091900.

D. Ślęzak et al. (Eds.): RSFDGrC 2005, LNAI 3642, pp. 98–108, 2005.

while does not take temporal features into consideration. However, for prediction purpose, in many cases, temporal factors are not only important but necessary. For example, weather greatly inpacts on corn yields. We expect to predict corn yields based on weather indices that reflect weather changes. It is found that similar weather indices values in April and in June may have different influences on corn yields. In addition, the variations of weather indices in April may affect corn yields in August, which indicates weather variations and corn yields are not simultaneous and there is a time lag between them. It is natural to use the events that have already happened to predict the events that might happen in the future, a reasonable request for prediction rule is that there must be a time lag between the antecedent and consequent in a prediction rule, which indicates the consequent happens some time later than the antecedent. Antecedent or consequent of a rule may comprise several events, in such cases, it is needed to define the maximal time span constraint within antecedent or consequent, which is the allowed time length between the occurrence of the first event and the last event in the antecedent or consequent.

Since we predict the consequent based on the occurrence of the antecedent of a rule, a prediction rule can be applied only if its antecedent is satisfied at present. The more number of items (events) that an antecedent comprises, the more difficult the antecedent is satisfied, and thus the more restricted that a rule can be applied. Highly restricted rules may not be as useful as less restricted rules in terms of prediction. For prediction rules, we are looking for rules, antecedent of which includes only the most important factors that can bring out the consequent so that the antecedent includes as small number of items as possible. E.g.,if two rules, $A_1 \Rightarrow B$ and $A_1 A_2 \Rightarrow B$, both have higher confidence than threshold, the first rule is better than the second for prediction purpose, because to predict the same consequent, the first rule can be applied if we detect the occurrence of A_1, while for the second needs to assure the occurence of both A_1 and A_2. We formalize our thought process of discovering the most informational rule in [1] and propose *maximal potentially useful* (MaxPUF) association rules model. MaxPUF rules are a set of most informational and useful rules, characterized by the minimum antecedent among rules of the same consequent.

The confidence of a rules denotes the strength of association between antecedent and consequent, and high confidence value implies strong association. Thus high confidence rules are desired for prediction. However, the confidence of a rule may vary as time changes. If a rule does not maintain high confidence all through, using such rules for prediction maybe not reliable, because it is not sure whether the association between antecedent and consequent is still strong in the future. Therefore, we require that a prediction rule should show the trend of maintaining high confidence. We test whether the confidence of a rule varies seviously over time frames determined by application domains, less variation on confidence means the rule have the same or similar confidence value in different time frames and implies that the rule is very likely to have similar confidence value in the future as it has now. We define *high confidence stable rule* (HCSR) as the rules that have high confidence in all time division frames, and *partial high confidence stable rules* (PHCSR) as the rules that have high confidence in most of the time division frames. These two kinds of rules approximately have stable high confidence value and thus are proper for prediction.

2   Related Works

Some efforts have been investigated on making use of association rule for prediction with intertransaction rules [2,3,4]. Traditional association rules are looking for co-occurrence relation within the pale transactions, thus also called intratransaction rules. For prediction purpose, we instead are looking for cause-effect relationships that are time-ordered and beyond the boundary of transactions. A new type of rules called intertransaction rules are developed to break the barrier of transactions to discover interesting rules [5,6]. For example, inter-transaction rules may describe the case like "If the prices of IBM and SUN go up, Microsoft's will most likely (80% of the time) goes up 2 days later", where the event "IBM and SUN go up" and "Microsoft́fs goes up" are in different transactions and thus can not be discovered with the notion of intra-transaction rules. Intertransaction rule mining extends the traditional association mining by looking for associations across transactions. However, the purpose of intertransaction rule is not reflecting cause-effect relations, instead, it is looking for the co-occurrence relations in a wider transaction spaces. Some intertransaction rules maybe suitable for prediction, while some may not. In [2,3,4], the authors discuss to use intertransaction rules for some specific prediction tasks. Different from previous work, in the paper, we specifically investigate the properties of rules suitable for prediction and proposes approach to efficiently discover such rules. For example, our work considers the prediction rule in the context of temporal rules, while intertransaction rules generally are not. We point out that the antecedent of a rule should be minimum to make rules more applicable for prediction, and we develop the model of MaxPUF rules for this objective. We also measure the stability of a rule to assure the precision of prediction.

3   Prediction Rules

In temporal databases, each item is associated with a time stamp that indicates the occurrence time. We therefore call each item an *event* and denote it as a pair (e, t), where $e \in E$ and E is a set of different type of events, and t is the occurrence time of event of type e. In this paper, we may use *item e* and *event of type e* interchangeably. A sequence is a sequence of events [7]. The antecedent and consequent of a temporal rules are either an event or a sequence. Temporal databases are represented as event sequences. As there is no clear notion of transactions in temporal databases, to count *support*, a widely used method is *sliding window* [8]. Each *window* is a a slice of an event sequence, formally, window $w = [t_s, t_e)$ where t_s and t_e are start time and end time of the window. The size of window w is t if $t = t_e - t_s$. When we place a window of size t along the sequence, and move the window forward with one more event at a time, then the sequence is segmented into fragments of event sequences, and the whole sequence can be deemed as a series of partially overlapping windows. All the fragments of event sequences can be used to simulate the transactions in the temporal sequences. Support and confidence are then be computed based on transactions.

3.1   Time Lag Constraints for Prediction Rules

Prediction rules are a set of temporal association rules that must have time lag between antecedent and consequent. We use $tl_{A \Rightarrow B}$ to denote the time lag between antecedent and consequent of a rule $A \Rightarrow B$. To put restrictions on $tl_{A \Rightarrow B}$, we consider two thresholds, one is called *minimum time lag threshold*, denoted as tl_{min}, and the other is *maximum time lag threshold*, denoted as tl_{max}. tl_{min} controls that the consequent should occurr later than the antecedent at least tl_{min} time long, and tl_{max} controls that the consequent should occur after the antecedent at no more than tl_{max} time length. If an antecedent (consequent) is an event sequence, that is, there is more than one events in the antecedent, then we also need to consider the temporal constraint within the antecedent (consequent), which is denoted as tl_w. tl_w restricts the maximal time length between the first event and the last event within the antecedent (consequent). Moreover, we define the time stamp of a sequence equal to the time stamp of the first event in the sequence. E.g., for a rule $A \Rightarrow B$, if both A and B consist one event, then $tl_{A \Rightarrow B} = t_B - t_A$; otherwise, if $B = \{b_1, ..., b_n\}$ and $A = \{a_1, ..., a_m\}$, $tl_{A \Rightarrow B} = t_{b_1} - t_{a_1}$. To sum up, a prediction rule $A \Rightarrow B$ satisfies the temporal constraints that $tl_{min} \leq tl_{A \Rightarrow B} \leq tl_{max}$, and $t_{a_m} - t_{a_1} \leq t_w$ and $t_{b_n} - t_{b_1} \leq t_w$, where $B = \{b_1, ..., b_n\}$, $A = \{a_1, ..., a_m\}$. tl_{min}, tl_{max} and t_w are user-defined parameters. Figure 1 shows the relationships among these constraints.

3.2   MaxPUF Property for Prediction Rules

A rule becomes more restricted as the antecedent includes more items. In discovering prediction rules, we do not want to generate many rules, each of which reflects a restricted case, as restricted cases may rarely happen again in the future and thus rules reflecting such cases may be less interesting in terms of prediction. We need to match antecedent of a rule for prediction, thus we expect the antecedent of a prediction rule should include only the most important factors while ignore the minors, in other words, the antecedent is minimum in terms of the number of items it includes. The model of MaxPUF rule we develop in [1] is proper for this objective, which we give a briefly introduction here. A *concept* P is one or conjunction of predicate symbols. If P is a concept, then $[P] = r \ (0 \leq r \leq 1)$ is an elementary

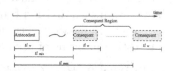

Fig. 1. Time Lag Constraints

pattern, where operation "[ ]" computes the probability of a proposition over a set of objects. If P, Q are concepts and $P \neq \emptyset$, then $[Q|P] = r$ is a conditional pattern. Q is called conSequent Concept (SC), and P conDition Concept (DC) of the pattern. Probability r is called confidence of the pattern, and $r = \frac{[QP]}{[P]}$. We can logically formulate an association rule as a conditional pattern. DC of the conditional pattern represents the *antecedent* of the rule and SC represents the *consequent* of the rule. *Probability* of the pattern denotes the *confidence* of the rule. *Support* of the antecedent, the consequent and the rule is equal to the *probability* of the corresponding elementary patterns. E.g., a rule $A \Rightarrow B$ with confidence c and support s, then the corresponding conditional pattern is $[B|A] = c$, and $sup(A) = [A]$, $sup(B) = [B]$, $s = sup(AB) = [AB]$.

Definition 1. MaxPUF patterns and Valid DC. *Let c_{min} be the user-defined minimum confidence threshold. If a pattern $[B|A] = r$ where $r \geq c_{min}$, and there is no patterns in the form of $[B|A'] = r'$ so that $r' \geq c_{min}$ and $A' \subset A$, then $[B|A] = r$ is a MaxPUF pattern of B, and A is called a* valid DC *of B.*

Among all high-confidence patterns of a certain SC, MaxPUF patterns are the patterns DC of which has the smallest number of items. A *Valid DC* is the minimal condition such that the SC occurs at high enough probability and *Valid DC* is the set of main condition factors to assure the occurrence of the consequent concept [1]. MaxPUF rules utmost avoid over-restricted conditions and are more applicable for prediction. We require the prediction rules to be MaxPUF rules, in other words, prediction rules obtain MaxPUF property.

3.3   Stable High Confidence Property for Prediction Rules

Prediction rules should reflect strong cause-effect association between antecedent and consequent, and moreover preserved the strong association in the future. This is a problem to test whether the confidence of a rules changes significantly with respect to the time. Our method is to check confidence of a rule against multiple time division frames, and examine the variations of the confidence. For example, if a given dataset is collected in time period of t, we compute the confidence over the time period t for each rule. Then we divide t into n time frames, $t_1, t_2, ..., t_n$ ($\sum_{i=1}^{n} t_i = t$), and compute the confidence in each of time division frames. The optimal case is a rule has invariant confidence. Due to noises, it is usually rare that rule has unaltered confidence value all along. We therefore propose two approximate stable confidence rule models.

If a rule R does not have identical confidence in different time division frames, however, in each division frame t_i and in t, R has confidence higher than threshold, then R shows the trend to have high confidence always. Such rules are interesting in terms of prediction and we call them *high confidence stable rules*.

Definition 2. High Confidence Stable Rules (HCSR). *Let t_i be a time division and $\sum_{i=1}^{n} t_i = t$, $conf_x(R)$ is confidence of rule R in time division x, and c_{min} is user-defined minimum threshold. Rule R is a high confidence stable rule if $conf_t(R) \geq c_{min}$ and $conf_{t_i}(R) \geq c_{min}$ for $1 \leq i \leq n$.*

If a rule R does not have high confidence in all the time division frames, but does in most of them, such rules are till statistically significant and can be selected for predicting purpose.

Definition 3. Partial High Confidence Stable Rules (PHCSR). *Rule R is a PHCSR if* $\frac{|\{i|conf_{t_i}(R) \geq c_{min}, 1 \leq i \leq n\}|}{n} \geq \alpha$. α *is the significant level,* $0 < \alpha \leq 1$.

If we define α equal to 100%, the set of PHCSR is equivalent to the set of HCSR. PHCSR have better tolerance for noise, and it can control the level of noise tolerance by adjusting the significant level α. Larger α value reduces the number of rules qualified and vice versa.

Definition 4. Prediction Rules. *Prediction rules are rules satisfying MaxPUF property, time lag constraints between and within antecedent and consequent, and are (partial) high confidence stable rules.*

4   Prediction Mining Algorithm

The algorithm includes two phases. First is to discover a set of candidate prediction rules, which satisfying MaxPUF property and time lag constraints. Second is to select HCSR or PHCSR from the candidate rules as prediction rules.

4.1   Discover Candidate Prediction Rules

Mining Schema. To discover candidate rule, we consider to push tl_w, tl_{min} and tl_{max} constraints and MaxPUF property. We can make use of the constraints to prune more unlikely candidates during the mining and improve mining efficiency. Since association rules can be represented as patterns as stated in Section 3.1, we may interchangeably use patterns and rules in the following discussions. We first introduce a Lemma on association rule.

Lemma 1. *The necessary condition that a pattern* $[X_1 X_2 ... X_n | A] \geq c_{min}$ *holds is that* $\forall X_i$, $[X_i | A] \geq c_{min}$ *for* $1 \leq i \leq n$ *holds, where* X_i *is a 1-itemset concept.*

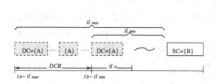

Fig. 2. tl_{min} and tl_{max}

If a pattern $[A|B] \geq c_{min}$, we say $[A|B]$ is a valid pattern referring to c_{min}. We adopt level-wise method to generate candidate patterns, i.e., first discover 1-itemset SC patterns, then 2-itemset SC patterns and etc. Lemma 1 says that the validity of the patterns with k-itemset SC depends on the valid patterns with 1-itemset SC. For discovering valid k-itemset SC patterns, only if two or more valid 1-itemset SC patterns have DC in common, we can generate a possible candidate pattern as follows: DC of the candiate pattern is the common DC, and SC is the combination of SCs from those 1-itemset SCs patterns. We can see the discovery of 1-itemset SC patterns can be separated from the discovery of k-itemset SC patterns, and the latter process is dependent on the former one. We design a new discovery schema that includes two steps. First step is called DC-*expansion*, which is to discover valid patterns of 1-itemset SC. The second step is called

SC-expansion, which is to discover k-itemset SC patterns based on 1-itemset SC patterns discovered in the first step. In *DC-expansion*, for each 1-itemset SC, find DCs that compose valid patterns with the 1-itemset SC. *DC-expansion* adopts level-wise method that checks from 1-itemset DCs to k-itemset DCs. Each level loop includes three steps. First is to generate k-itemset candidate DCs using $(k-1)$-itemset DCs. Second is to evaluate the patterns that are composed with the generated k-itemset DC candidates and the 1-itemset SC, and select the valid DCs. The last step is to select k-itemset DCs for generating $(k+1)$-itemset candidate DCs in the next level loop. The process begins with 1-itemset DCs, and loops until there is no candidate DCs are generated. In *DC-expansion*, we can make use of time lag constraints and MaxPUF property to prune DC candidates, and we discuss these in details later in the paper. *SC-expansion* is to discover k-itemset SC patterns where $2 \leq k \leq n$. Again, we use level wise method to generate SC candidates from 2-itemsets to n-itemsets.

Implement tl_w Constraint. In temporal rule mining, it adopts *sliding window* for counting *support* of events [9]. The support of a event sequence equals to the number of windows passing by it. Only events within a window are counted together. By controlling the window size, we control the allowed number of events that are counted together. Assume each event has one unit time duration, then the number of events of an event sequence equals to its time span length. If we set up the sliding window size equal to or less than tl_w, we then make sure that the antecedent and consequent will satisfy the requirement of tl_w.

Implement tl_{min} and tl_{max} constraints. We first consider to push these constraints in 1-itemset SC patterns, e.g., $[B|A]$ where $B=(B, t_B)$ and B includes one event. In order to satisfy $tl_{min} \leq tl_{A \Rightarrow B} \leq tl_{max}$, A should only include events that are in the time region $[t_B - tl_{max}, t_B - tl_{min}]$, as shown in Figure 2. For each SC, there is a time region where the DC candidates should be constructed from and we call the region DC *Constraint Region* (DCR). A pattern $[B|A]$ is said valid refering to the time lag constraints if $A \in DCR_B$.

Setting $DCR = [t_B - tl_{max}, t_B - tl_{min}]$, however, might cause problem in *SC-expansion*. The error cases occur when a k-itemset SC pattern is valid but not all of of its related 1-itemset SC patterns are valid. For example, assume $[B_1, B_2, ..., B_k|A] \geq c_{min}$, and the time stamp of the SC is t_{B_1}. If pattern $[B_1, B_2, ..., B_k|A]$ is valid, then $t_A \in [t_{B_1} - tl_{max}, t_{B_1} - tl_{min}]$. We can deduce that $[B_1|A]$ is valid, but we do not know whether all others $[B_2|A], ..., [B_k|A]$ are valid. If any $[B_i|A]$ is not valid, pattern $[B_1, B_2, ..., B_k|A]$ cannot be discovered because $[B_i|A]$ is not discovered in *DC-expansion*. To solve this, we instead use $DCR = [t_B - tl_{max} + t_w, t_B - tl_{min} + t_w]$ in constructing DC candidates. We broaden DCR to ensure that those 1-itemset SC patterns, which might be needed to generate the corresponding patterns with k-itemset SC, are generated.

Implement MaxPUF Property. To discover patterns that satisfy MaxPUF property, it is a process to find *Valid DC*s for each SC. Actually, based on the definition of MaxPUF rules, for any SC, if a k-itemset DC is a Valid DC of the SC, then none of its (k-1)-itemset subconcepts are Valid DCs of the SC. Therefore, a k-itemset DC should be a candidate only if none of its $(k-1)$-itemset subconcepts are *Valid DCs*. Thus in generating k-itemset candidate DCs, only use those $(k-1)$-itemset DCs that are not *Valid DCs*.

4.2   Select Stable Rules

To check the stability of rules, we need to set up a time division schema. There are two kinds of time division schemas. One is evenly distributed division, which evenly divides a period of length t into n divisions and each division frame is of length $\frac{t}{n}$. A more complex schema is unevenly distributed division, which divides a period into division frames of various lengths. Unevenly distributed division schema provides more flexibilities, for example, when discovering rules from a weather database, rules about the event of rain may have dense distributions from June to August, while sparse distributions in other months. In such case, we may need to design a time schema that has more divisions from June to August and less divisions in other months. Generally, time-division schema is application dependent. Given a time division schema, for each candidate prediction rule generated in Phase I, we compute the confidence of the rule in each time division frame, and select HCSR and PHCSR referring to α as prediction rules.

5   Experiments and Analysis

The experiments are designed to test effectiveness and efficiency of prediction mining approach. We compare effect of different parameter, and evaluate the set of generated prediction rules for making prediction. A set of comprehensive performance studies are conducted on both synthetic and real-life datasets. The synthetic dataset generator is retrieved from IBM Almaden research center. The programs are coded in C++, and experiments are conducted on a 950 MHz Intel Pentium-III PC with 512 MB main memory. Figure 3 to 7 show experimental results on synthetic dataset T25D100kI10. Table 1 presents experimental results on a real weather database.

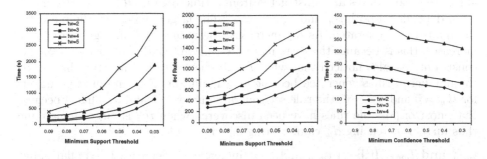

Fig. 3. Sup vs. Time   **Fig. 4.** Sup vs. # Rules   **Fig. 5.** Conf vs. Time

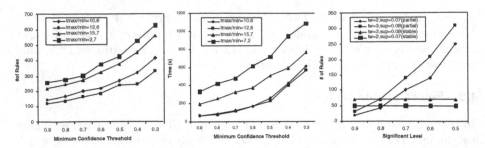

Fig. 6. tmin/tmax vs. # Rules   **Fig. 7.** tmin/tmax vs. Time   **Fig. 8.** vs. # Rules

5.1   Analaysis of Effects of Different Constraints

s_{min} **and** c_{min} When s_{min} decreases, the running time greatly increases, since more itemsets satisfy s_{min}, sometimes almost exponentially more candidate itemsets are generated; the number of rules generated also slowly increases as support decreases, it is not significant because the number of rules is also decided by confidence threshold, and c_{min} has more to do with it than s_{min}. As c_{min} increases, the number of candidate prediction rules generated decreases.

From Figure 5, we see as c_{min} decreases, the running time slowly decreases. This is different from Apriori algorithm, for which the time increases as confidence decreases. To explain this, we notice that c_{min} affects on checking MaxPUF property. On one hand, as c_{min} decreases, for each SC, it is more likely that its *Valid DC*s appear in earlier level loops in the *DC-expansion*, and thus less DC candidates are generated in later loops. On the other hand, in *SC-expansion*, larger c_{min} blocks more SC candidates earlier, and thus less time is needed. But *DC-expansion* is more time consuming than *SC-expansion*, so as a whole the running time decreases as c_{min} decreases. It is deserved to point out that compared with s_{min}, c_{min} has less affection on running time.

tl_w **constraint.** tl_w has great affection on running time from two aspects. On one hand, larger tl_w has less restrictions for constructing antecedent and consequent, thus more candidates are generated and more running time is needed. on the other hand, sine support counting time is proportional to sliding window size, larger tl_w results in support counting more time-consuming. In *DC-expansion*, antecedent candidates are constructed from a time region DCR, and the size of DCR depends on both tl_w and $t_{max} - t_{min}$. The larger the tl_w is, the more DC candidates are generated. As tl_w increases, the number of rules generated also increases, this is because there are more DC and SC candidates satisfy time lag constraint. We also noticed that when tl_w reaches certain value, the changes on the number of rules generated become less significant. E.g., in our experiments for $tl_w = 5$ and $tl_w = 6$, the rule set generated are very similar. This is because that most of possible rules have been discovered when tl_w is large enough and thus further increasing tl_w cannot bring out more rules.

t_{min} **and** t_{max}. If both t_{min} and t_{max} increases or decrease by similar value, the running time does not change significantly. Actually the gap between t_{min}

and t_{max} that have more affections on running time. Time increases as the gap is larger. DC and SC candidates are constructed from the gap regions between t_{min} and t_{max}, and larger gap means less regions are in the sequence. In terms of the number of rules generated, as the gap increase, less rules are generated.

5.2 Evaluation of Prediction Rules

To further evaluate the precision of prediction rules discovered, we evaluate the rules generated from real databases. The data is collected from the weather station at Clay Center, Nebraska. We intend to discover rules that demonstrate the relations between climatic events and drought events and can be used for prediction. To evaluate the set of rules generated, we use *precision* metrics, which is a widely used quality metrics in *information retrieval*. Precision is defined as the percentage of interesting rules discovered among all the rules discovered by an algorithm, i.e., $precision = \frac{\#\ of\ interesting\ rules\ discovered}{\#\ of\ rules\ discovered}$. The larger the precision value is, the more precise and better the rule set discovered is. The summarized result in Table 1, where the prediction rules discovered are HCSR and PHCSR, and interesting rules are identified by the domain experts. From the results, we can see as for different α value, the precision is different. For this dataset, in general, as α decrease, more prediction rules are discovered, but the precision value decreases. In general, higher α value is preferred.

Table 1. Evaluation of Prediction Rule Set

$c_{min} = 0.8, s_{min} = 0.5, t_w = 2$				$c_{min} = 0.8, s_{min} = 0.5, t_w = 3$			
# of HCSR =15				# of HCSR =19			
α	#PHCSR	# Interest. Rules	Precision(%)	α	#PHCSR	# Int. Rules	Precision(%)
0.9	20	28	28/35=0.8	0.9	30	30	30/49=0.61
0.7	31	31	31/46=0.67	0.7	46	35	35/65=0.53
0.5	63	35	35/78=0.44	0.5	83	39	39/102=0.38

6 Conclusion

In this paper, we propose prediction mining approach to discover a set of association rules that are proper for prediction. We discuss the properties of prediction rules, based on which we develop the model of prediction rules. An algorithm for mining prediction rules is proposed. Experimental results shows that the proposed algorithm can efficiently discover a set of prediction rules, and experiments on real database show the set of prediction rules discovered can be used for prediction with relatively good precision.

References

1. Deogun, J., Jiang, L.: Discovering Maximal Potentially Useful Association Rules Based on Probability Logics. Rough Sets and Curr. Trends in Computing (2004)

2. Berberidis, C., and et al: Inter-Transaction Association Rules Mining for Rare Events Prediction. Proc. 3rd Hellenic Conference on Artificial Intellligence (2004)
3. Feng, L., Dillon, T., Liu, J.: Inter-Transactional Association Rules for Multidimensional Contexts for Prediction and their Applications to Studying Meteological Data. International Journal of Data and Knowledge Engineering (2001)
4. Lu, H. and et al: Stock movement prediction and n-dimensional inter-transaction association rules. Proc. ACM SIGMOD Workshop on Research Issues on Data Mining and Knowledge Discovery (1998)
5. Lu, H. and et al.: Beyond intratransaction association analysis: mining multidimensional intertransaction association rules. ACM Trans. Inf. Syst. (2000)
6. Tung, A., Lu, H., Han, J., Feng, L.: Efficient Mining of Intertransaction Association Rules. IEEE Trans. Knowl. Data Eng (2003)
7. Ale, J., Rossi, G.: An approach to discovering temporal association rules. SAC '00: Proceedings of the 2000 ACM symposium on Applied computing (2000)
8. Mannila, H., Toivonen, H., Verkamo, A.: Discovery of Frequent Episodes in Event Sequences. Data Mining and Knowledge Discovery (1997)
9. Harms, S. and et al.: Building knowledge discovery into a geo-spatial decision support system. ACM symposium on Applied computing (2003)

A Rough Set Based Model to Rank
the Importance of Association Rules

Jiye Li[1] and Nick Cercone[2]

[1] School of Computer Science, University of Waterloo,
200 University Avenue West, Waterloo, Ontario, Canada N2L 3G1
j27li@uwaterloo.ca
[2] Faculty of Computer Science, Dalhousie University,
6050 University Avenue, Halifax, Nova Scotia, Canada B3H 1W5
nick@cs.dal.ca

Abstract. Association rule algorithms often generate an excessive number of rules, many of which are not significant. It is difficult to determine which rules are more useful, interesting and important. We introduce a rough set based process by which a rule importance measure is calculated for association rules to select the most appropriate rules. We use ROSETTA software to generate multiple reducts. Apriori association rule algorithm is then applied to generate rule sets for each data set based on each reduct. Some rules are generated more frequently than the others among the total rule sets. We consider such rules as more important. We define rule importance as the frequency of an association rule among the rule sets. Rule importance is different from rule interestingness in that it does not consider the predefined knowledge on what kind of information is considered to be interesting. The experimental results show our method reduces the number of rules generated and at the same time provides a measure of how important is a rule.

Keywords: Rough Sets, Association Rules, Rule Importance Measure.

1 Introduction

Rough sets theory was first presented by Pawlak in the 1980's [1]. He introduced an early application of rough sets theory to knowledge discovery systems, and suggested that rough sets approach can be used to increase the likelihood of correct predictions by identifying and removing redundant variables. Efforts into applying rough sets theory to knowledge discovery in databases has focused on decision making, data analysis, discovering and characterizing the inter-data relationships, and discovery interesting patterns [2].

Although the rough sets approach is frequently used on attribute selection, little research effort has been explored to apply this approach to association rules generation. The main problem of association rules algorithm is that there are usually too many rules generated, and it is difficult to process the large amount of rules by hand. In the data preprocessing stage, redundant attributes

D. Ślęzak et al. (Eds.): RSFDGrC 2005, LNAI 3642, pp. 109–118, 2005.

can be found by a rough sets approach. By removing the redundant attributes, association rules generation will be more efficient and more effective.

Klemettinen introduced the concept of rule templates [3]. Properly defined rule templates can be helpful on generating desired association rules to be used in decision making and collaborative recommender systems [4], [5].

We discuss how the rough sets theory can help generating important association rules. We are interested in applying these rules for making decisions. Therefore, the type of rules we are looking for are rules which have, on the consequent part, the decision attributes, or items that can be of interest for making decisions. We propose a new rule importance measure based on rough sets to evaluate the utilities of the association rules. This method can be applied in both decision making and recommender system applications.

We discuss related work on association rules algorithm, the rough sets theory on rule discovery and recommender system in Section 2. In Section 3 we show our approach to generate reduct sets, and introduce the new rule importance measure. In Section 4, we describe our experiments on an artificial data set and a sanitized geriatric care data set. Finally we summarize our contributions and discuss next step work in Section 5.

2   Related Work

2.1   Association Rules Algorithm

An association rules algorithm helps to find patterns which relate items from transactions. For example, in market basket analysis, by analyzing transaction records from the market, we could use association rules algorithm to discover different shopping behaviors. Association rules can then be used to express these kinds of behaviors, thus helping to increase the number of items sold in the market by arranging related items properly.

An association rule [6] is a rule of the form $\alpha \rightarrow \beta$, where α and β represent itemsets which do not share common items. The association rule $\alpha \rightarrow \beta$ holds in the transaction set L with confidence c, $c = \frac{|\alpha \cup \beta|}{|\alpha|}$, if c% of transactions in L that contain α also contain β. The rule $\alpha \rightarrow \beta$ has support s, $s = \frac{|\alpha \cup \beta|}{|L|}$, if s% of transactions in L contain $\alpha \cup \beta$. Here, we call α antecedent, and β consequent. Confidence gives a ratio of the number of transactions that the antecedent and the consequent appear together to the number of transactions the antecedent appears. Support measures how often the antecedent and the consequent appear together in the transaction set.

A problem of using association rules algorithm is that there are usually *too many rules generated* and it is difficult to analyze these rules. Rule interestingness measures have been proposed to reduce the number of rules generated.

2.2   Rough Sets Theory and Rule Discovery

Rough Sets was proposed to classify imprecise and incomplete information. Reduct and core are two important concepts in rough sets theory. A reduct is a subset of attributes that are sufficient to describe the decision attributes. Finding all the reduct sets for a data set is a NP-hard problem [7]. Approximation algorithms are used to obtain the reduct set [8]. All reducts contain core. Core represents the most important information of the original data set. The intersection of all the possible reducts is the core.

Hu et al. [9] introduced core generation and reduct generation algorithms based on the rough sets theory and efficient database operations.

Procedure 1. Core Generating Algorithm
Input: Decision table $T(C, D)$. Output: Core attributes.
(1) $Core \leftarrow \phi$
(2) For each attribute $A \in C$
(3)   If $Card(\Pi(C - A + D)) \neq Card(\Pi(C - A))$
(4)   Then $Core = Core \cup A$

where C is the set of condition attributes, and D is the set of decision attributes. $Card$ denotes the count operation, and Π denotes the projection operation.

There have been contributions on applying rough sets theory to rule discovery. Rules and decisions generated from the reduct are representative of the data set's knowledge. In [10], two modules were used in the association rules mining procedure for supporting organizational knowledge management and decision making. Self-Organizing Map was applied to cluster sale actions based on the similarities in the characteristics of a given set of customer records. Rough sets theory was used on each cluster to determine rules for association explanations. Hassanien [11] used rough sets to find all the reducts of data that contain the minimal subset of attributes associated with a class label for classification, and classified the data with reduced attributes.

Rough sets can be used to determine whether there is redundant information in the data and whether we can find essential data needed for our applications. We expect fewer rules will be generated due to fewer attributes.

2.3   Recommender Systems

Not many research efforts are found on applying association rules algorithms for collaborative filtering recommender systems, one of the two types of recommender systems of interest. The rule templates [3] can be appropriately defined to extract rules that match the templates in the post processing of the association rules generation. Therefore this method can increase both the efficiency and the accuracy of recommendations. In our experiment, we define rule template, and generate rules with only decision attributes on the consequent part. This type of recommendation rules can be used to make decisions.

3   Rules, Measures and Templates

3.1   Motivation

In medical diagnosis, a doctor requires a list of symptoms in order to make a diagnosis. For different diseases, there are different patient symptoms to examine.

However, there are some routine exams that the doctor must perform for all the patients, such as the age of the patient, the blood pressure, the body temperature and so on. There are other symptoms that doctors may take into consideration, such as whether the patients have difficulty walking, whether the patients have bladder problems and so on. We would like to find the most important symptoms for diagnoses. We know that the symptoms that are checked more frequently are more important and essential for making diagnoses than those which are considered less frequently. However, both the symptoms that require frequent checking and the symptoms that are checked less frequently are included in the list of checkup symptoms. In this way, the doctor will make a precise diagnose based on all possible patient information.

3.2   Rule Importance

The medical diagnosis process can be considered as a decision making process. The symptoms can be considered as the condition attributes. The diagnosed diseases can be considered as the decision attributes. Since not all symptoms need to be known to make a diagnosis, the essential symptoms are considered as representative. These symptoms can be selected by a reduct generation algorithm.

All the patient information can also be represented in a transaction data set, with each patient's record considered to be an item set. Association rules algorithm can be applied on this transaction data set to generate rules, which have condition attributes on the antecedent part and decision attributes on the consequent part of the rules. Rules generated from different reduct sets can contain different representative information. If only one reduct set is being considered to generate rules, other important information might be omitted. Using multiple reducts, some rules will be generated more frequently than other rules. We consider the rules that are generated more frequently more important.

We propose a new measure, *Rule Importance*, to evaluate the importance of rules. A rule is defined to be important by the following definition.

Definition 1. *If a rule is generated more frequently across different rule sets, we say this rule is more important than other rules.*

Rule importance measure is defined as follows,

Definition 2.

$$Rule\ Importance\ Measure = \frac{Number\ of\ times\ a\ rule\ appears\ in\ all\ rule\ sets}{Number\ of\ reduct\ sets}$$

Suppose for a certain data set, there are 3 reducts used for rule generation. For $reduct_1$, the rule set generated is $\{a, b \rightarrow 1; a \rightarrow 0; b, c \rightarrow 1\}$; for $reduct_2$, the rule set generated is $\{b \rightarrow 1; b, c \rightarrow 1; c, d \rightarrow 0\}$; for $reduct_3$, the rule set generated is $\{a, c, d \rightarrow 1; b, c \rightarrow 1; c, d \rightarrow 0\}$. Rule $b, c \rightarrow 1$ is generated from all the 3 reducts, and its rule importance is $3/3 = 100\%$. Rule $c, d \rightarrow 0$ is generated from 2 reducts, therefore its importance is $2/3 = 66.67\%$. The rest rules are only generated once among the 3 rule sets. Their rule importance are $1/3 = 33.33\%$.

Rule importance is different from rule interestingness since it does not require predefined knowledge of what is interesting. Without considering people's interests, rule importance provides diverse choices of how important is a rule.

3.3 Specifying Rule Templates for Wanted and Subsumed Rules

Apriori association rules algorithm is used to generate rules. Because our interest is to make decisions or recommendations based on the condition attributes, we are looking for rules with only decision attributes on the consequent part. Therefore, we specify the following rule templates for extracting rules we want.

$$\langle Attribute_1, Attribute_2, ..., Attribute_n \rangle \rightarrow \langle DecisionAttribute \rangle$$

This template specifies only decision attributes can be on the consequent of a rule, and $Attribute_1$, $Attribute_2$,..., $Attribute_n$ lead to a decision of $DecisionAttribute$.

We specify the rules to be removed. For example, given rule

$$\langle Attribute_1, Attribute_2 \rangle \rightarrow \langle DecisionAttribute \rangle$$

the following rules

$$\langle Attribute_1, Attribute_2, Attribute_3 \rangle \rightarrow \langle DecisionAttribute \rangle$$

$$\langle Attribute_1, Attribute_2, Attribute_6 \rangle \rightarrow \langle DecisionAttribute \rangle$$

can be removed because they are subsumed.

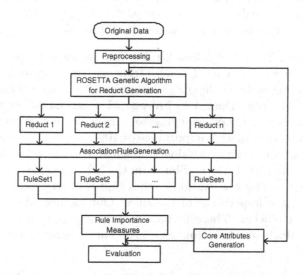

Fig. 1. Experiment Procedure

3.4   Experiment Procedure

In our experiments, we first preprocess the original data set. Then the data is imported to ROSETTA [12] for reduct generation. Association rules algorithm is applied to generate multiple rule sets for multiple reducts. Rule templates are used in the rule generation stage. The rule importance measure is used to rank these rules. Core attributes are generated from the preprocessed data set to help evaluating the rules. The following experimental procedure in Figure 1 shows the proposed rough sets based model to rank the importance of association rules.

4   Experiment

We experiment on two data sets. ROSETTA GUI version 1.4.41[1] is used for reduct generation. The apriori algorithm [13] for large item sets generation and rule generation is performed on Sun Fire V880, four 900MHz UltraSPARC III processors, with 8GB of main memory.

4.1   Experiment on a Car Data Set

The first data set we experiment on is an artificial data set about cars [14], as shown in Table 1. It is used to decide the mileage of different cars. The condition attributes are *make_mode, cyl, door, displace, compress, power, trans, weight*. *Mileage* is the decision attribute. There are 14 instances. The data set does not contain missing attribute values.

For the car data set, the core attributes are, *make_model*, and *trans*. ROSETTA generates 4 reducts as shown in Table 2. We then generate the rule sets based on these 4 reduct sets with $support = 1\%, confidence = 100\%$, and we also rank their rule importance, as shown in Table 3.

Discussion. From Table 3, the first 2 rules have an importance of 100%. This matches our experiences on cars. The auto transmission cars usually have a lower mileage than the manual cars. Japanese cars are well known for using less gas and higher mileage. The rule "Door_4 → Mileage_Medium" has a lower importance because the number of doors belonging to a car does not affect car mileage. We noticed that two rules with importance of 100% contain core attributes and only core attributes to make a decision of mileage. For the rest of the rules with importance less than 100%, the attributes on the left hand side of a rule contains non-core attributes. This observation implies that core attributes are important when evaluating the importance of the rules. Our method of generating rules with reduct sets is efficient. There are 6327 rules generated from the original data without using reducts or rule templates. 13 rules are generated using reducts and rule templates.

---

[1] ROSETTA provides approximation algorithms for reduct generation: Johnson's algorithm, Genetic algorithm and others. Johnson's algorithm returns a single reduct. Genetic algorithm returns multiple reducts. We use genetic algorithm with the option of full discernibility.

Table 1. Car Data Set

make_model	cyl	door	displace	compress	power	trans	weight	mileage
USA	6	2	Medium	High	High	Auto	Medium	Medium
USA	6	4	Medium	Medium	Medium	Manual	Medium	Medium
USA	4	2	Small	High	Medium	Auto	Medium	Medium
...	...	...	...	...	...	...	...	...
Japan	4	2	Small	Medium	Low	Manual	Medium	High
Japan	4	2	Small	High	Medium	Manual	Medium	High
USA	4	2	Small	High	Medium	Manual	Medium	High

Table 2. Reduct Sets Generated by Genetic Algorithm for Car Data Set

No.	Reduct Sets
1	{make_model, compress, power, trans}
2	{make_model, cyl, compress, trans}
3	{make_model, displace, compress, trans}
4	{make_model, cyl, door, displace, trans, weight}

Table 3. The Rule Importance for the Car Data Set

No.	Selected Rules	Rule Importance
1	Trans_Auto → Mileage_Medium	100%
2	JapanCar → Mileage_High	100%
3	USACar, Compress_Medium → Mileage_Medium	75%
4	Compress_High, Trans_Manual → Mileage_High	75%
5	Displace_Small, Trans_Manual → Mileage_High	50%
6	Cyl_6 → Mileage_Medium	50%
...	...	...
12	Door_4 → Mileage_Medium	25%
13	Weight_Light → Mileage_High	25%

4.2 Experiment on a Medical Data Set

In this experiment, a sanitized geriatric care data set is used as our test data set. This data set contains 8547 patient records with 44 symptoms and their survival status. The data set is used to determine the survival status of a patient giving all the symptoms he or she shows. We use *survival status* as the decision attribute, and the 44 symptoms of a patient as condition attributes, which includes *education level, the eyesight, the age of the patient at investigation* and so on. [2] There is no missing value in this data set. Table 4 gives selected data records of this data set.

There are 12 inconsistent data entries in the medical data set. After removing these instances, the data contains 8535 records. [3]

---

[2] Refer to [15] for details about this data set.

[3] Notice from our previous experiments that core generation algorithm can not return correct core attributes when the data set contains inconsistent data entries.

Table 4. Geriatric Care Data Set

edulevel	eyesight	health	trouble	livealone	cough	hbp	heart	...	studyage	sex	livedead
0.6364	0.25	0.25	0.00	0.00	0.00	0.00	0.00	...	73.00	1.00	0
0.7273	0.50	0.25	0.50	0.00	0.00	0.00	0.00	...	70.00	2.00	0
0.9091	0.25	0.00	0.00	0.00	0.00	1.00	1.00	...	76.00	1.00	0
0.5455	0.25	0.50	0.00	1.00	1.00	0.00	0.00	...	81.00	2.00	0
0.4545	0.25	0.25	0.00	1.00	0.00	1.00	0.00	...	86.00	2.00	0
...	...	...	...	...	...	...	...	...	...	...	...

Table 5. Reduct Sets for the Geriatric Care Data Set after Preprocessing

No.	Reduct Sets
1	{edulevel,eyesight,hearing,shopping,housewk,health,trouble,livealone, cough,sneeze,hbp,heart,arthriti,eyetroub,eartroub,dental, chest,kidney,diabetes,feet,nerves,skin,studyage,sex}
...	...
86	{edulevel,eyesight,hearing,shopping,meal,housewk,takemed,health, trouble,livealone,cough,tired,sneeze,hbp,heart,stroke,arthriti, eyetroub,eartroub,dental,chest,stomach,kidney,bladder,diabetes, feet,fracture,studyage,sex}

There are 14 core attributes generated for this data set. They are *eartroub, livealone, heart, hbp, eyetroub, hearing, sex, health, edulevel, chest, housewk, diabetes, dental, studyage*. Table 5 shows selected reduct sets among the 86 reducts generated by ROSETTA. All of these reducts contain the core attributes. For each reduct set, association rules are generated with *support* = 30%, *confidence* = 80%. [4]

Discussion. There are 218 rules generated and ranked according to their rule importance as shown in Table 6. We noticed there are 8 rules having importance of 100%. All attributes contained in these 8 rules are core attributes. These 8 rules are more important when compared to other rules. For example, consider rule No.5 and No.11. Rule No.11 has an importance measure of 95.35%. The difference between these two rules is that rule No.5 contains attribute *Livealone, HavingDiabetes, HighBloodPressure*, and rule No. 11 contains the first 2 attributes, and instead of *HighBloodPressure, SeriousNerveProblem* is considered to decide whether the patient will survive. Generally high blood pressure does affect people's health condition more than nerve problem in combination with the other 2 symptoms. Rule No.11 are more important than rule No.218 because in addition to the *NerveProblem*, whether a patient is able to take medicine by himself or herself is not as fatal as whether he or she has diabetes, or lives alone without care. With the same support and confidence, 2, 626, 392 rules

---

[4] Note that the value of support and confidence can be adjusted to generate as many or as few rules as required.

Table 6. The Rule Importance for the Geriatric Care Data Set

No.	Selected Rules	Rule Importance
1	SeriousChestProblem → Dead	100%
2	SeriousHearingProblem, HavingDiabetes → Dead	100%
3	SeriousEarTrouble → Dead	100%
4	SeriousHeartProblem → Dead	100%
5	Livealone, HavingDiabetes, HighBloodPressure → Dead	100%
...	...	...
11	Livealone, HavingDiabetes, NerveProblem → Dead	95.35%
...	...	...
217	SeriousHearingProblem, ProblemUsePhone → Dead	1.16%
218	TakeMedicineProblem, NerveProblem → Dead	1.16%

are generated from the original medical data set without considering reduct sets or rule templates. Our method efficiently extracts important rules, and at the same time provides a ranking for important rules. Johnson's reduct generation algorithm [12] generates one reduct with the minimum attributes. 16 rules are generated using this reduct [15]. The 8 rules with 100% importance in Table 6 are also generated. Although the reduct generated by Johnson's algorithm can provide all the 100% importance rules, the result does not cover other important rules. A doctor may be interested to know a patient is not in a good condition, if he is living alone, has diabetes and also coughs often. This information is more important than whether a patient has diabetes and loses control of the bladder. The experimental results show that considering multiple reducts gives us more diverse view of the data set, the rule importance measure provides a ranking of how important is a rule. Important rules consist of only core attributes.

5   Conclusions

We introduced a rough set based model which provides an automatic and effi-cient way of ranking important rules for decision making applications. The core attributes should be taken into consideration while choosing important and use-ful rules. By considering as many reduct sets as possible, we try to cover all representative subsets of the original data set.

This method can be combined with other human specified interestingness measures to evaluate rules. In the future, we are interested in studying this rule importance measure on large recommender system to improve the quality of the recommendations.

Acknowledgements

We gratefully acknowledge the financial support of the Natural Science and En-gineering Research Council (NSERC) of Canada.

References

1. Pawlak, Z.: Rough Sets. In Theoretical Aspects of Reasoning about Data. Kluwer, Netherlands, 1991.
2. Pawlak, Z., Grzymala-Busse, J., Slowinski, R., Ziarko, W.: Rough Sets. Communications of the ACM, Vol.38, No. 11, November (1995)
3. Klemettinen, M., Mannila, H., Ronkainen, R., Toivonen, H., Verkamo, A.I.: Finding interesting rules from large sets of discovered association rules. CIKM'94,401–407
4. Li, J., Tang, B., Cercone, N.: Applying Association Rules for Interesting Recommendations Using Rule Templates. PAKDD 2004, pp. 166 – 170.
5. Lin, W., Alvarez, S., Ruiz, C.: Efficient adaptive-support association rule mining for recommender systems. Data Mining and Knowledge Discovery (2002) 6:83–105
6. Agrawal, R., Srikant, R.: Fast Algorithms for Mining Association Rules. Proceedings of 20th International Conference Very Large Data Bases, Santiago de Chile, Chile, Morgan Kaufmann, (1994) 487–499
7. Kryszkiewicz, M., Rybinski, H.: Finding Reducts in Composed Information Systems, Rough Sets, Fuzzy Sets Knowldege Discovery. In W.P. Ziarko (Ed.), Proceedings of the International Workshop on Rough Sets, Knowledge Discovery pp. 261 – 273. Heidelberg/Berlin: Springer-Verlag, 1994.
8. Bazan, J., Nguyen, H.S., Nguyen, S.H., Synak, P., and Wroblewski, J.: Rough set algorithms in classification problems. In Polkowski, L., Lin, T.Y., and Tsumoto, S., editors, Rough Set Methods and Applications: New Developments in Knowledge Discovery in Information Systems, Vol. 56 of Studies in Fuzziness and Soft Computing, pages 49-88. Physica-Verlag, Heidelberg, Germany, 2000
9. Hu, X., Lin, T., Han, J.: A New Rough Sets Model Based on Database Systems. Fundamenta Informaticae 59 no.2-3 (2004), pp.135-152.
10. Huang, Z, Hu, Y.Q.: Applying AI Technology and Rough Set Theory to Mine Association Rules for Supporting Knowledge Management. Proc. of the 2nd Int'l Conference on Machine Learning and Cybernetics, Xi'an. November (2003).
11. Hassanien, A.E.: Rough Set Approach for Attribute Reduction and Rule Generation: A Case of Patients with Suspected Breast Cancer. Journal of The American Society for Information Science and Technology, 55(11):954-962. (2004)
12. Aleksander Ohrn: Discernibility and Rough Sets in Medicine: Tools and Applications. PhD Thesis, Department of Computer and Information Science, Norwegian University of Science and Technology, Trondheim, Norway, NTNU report 1999:133, IDI report 1999:14, ISBN 82-7984-014-1, 239 pages. 1999.
13. Borgelt, C.: Efficient Implementations of Apriori and Eclat. Proceedings of the FIMI'03 Workshop on Frequent Itemset Mining Implementations. CEUR Workshop Proceedings (2003) 1613-0073
14. Hu, X.: Knowledge Discovery in Databases: an Attribute-Oriented Rough Set Approach. PhD Thesis, University of Regina, 1995.
15. Li, J. and Cercone, N.: Empirical Analysis on the Geriatric Care Data Set Using Rough Sets Theory. Technical Report, CS-2005-05, School of Computer Science, University of Waterloo, 2005.

A Hierarchical Approach to Multimodal Classification

Andrzej Skowron[1], Hui Wang[2], Arkadiusz Wojna[3], and Jan Bazan[4]

[1] Institute of Mathematics, Warsaw University, Banacha 2, 02-097 Warsaw, Poland
skowron@mimuw.edu.pl
[2] School of Computing and Mathematics, University of Ulster at Jordanstown,
Northern Ireland, BT37 0QB, United Kingdom
h.wang@ulst.ac.uk
[3] Institute of Informatics, Warsaw University, Banacha 2, 02-097 Warsaw, Poland
wojna@mimuw.edu.pl
[4] Institute of Mathematics, University of Rzeszów,
Rejtana 16A, 35-310 Rzeszów, Poland
bazan@univ.rzeszow.pl

Abstract. Data models that are induced in classifier construction often consists of multiple parts, each of which explains part of the data. Classification methods for such models are called the multimodal classification methods. The model parts may overlap or have insufficient coverage. How to deal best with the problems of overlapping and insufficient coverage? In this paper we propose hierarchical or layered approach to this problem. Rather than seeking a single model, we consider a series of models under gradually relaxing conditions, which form a hierarchical structure. To demonstrate the effectiveness of this approach we implemented it in two classifiers that construct multi-part models: one based on the so-called lattice machine and the other one based on rough set rule induction. This leads to hierarchical versions of the classifiers. The classification performance of these two hierarchical classifiers is compared with C4.5, Support Vector Machine (SVM), rule based classifiers (with the optimisation of rule shortening) implemented in Rough Set Exploration System (RSES), and a method combining k-nn with rough set rule induction (RIONA in RSES). The results of the experiments show that this hierarchical approach leads to improved multimodal classifiers.

Keywords: Hierarchical classification, multimodal classifier, lattice machine, rough sets, rule induction, k-NN.

1 Introduction

Many machine learning methods are based on generation of different models with separate model parts, each of which explains part of a given dataset. Examples include decision tree induction [24], rule induction [1] and the lattice machine [21]. A decision tree consists of many branches, and each branch explains certain number of data examples. A rule induction algorithm generates a set of rules as

D. Ślęzak et al. (Eds.): RSFDGrC 2005, LNAI 3642, pp. 119–127, 2005.
© Springer-Verlag Berlin Heidelberg 2005

a model of data, and each rule explains some data examples. The lattice machine generates a set of hypertuples as a model of data, and each hypertuple covers a region in the data space. We call this type of learning *multimodal learning* or *multimodal classification*.

In contrast some machine learning paradigms do not construct models with separate parts. Examples include neural networks, support vector machines and Bayesian networks.

In the multimodal learning paradigm the model parts may overlap or may have insufficient coverage of a data space, i.e., the model does not cover the whole data space. In a decision tree the branches do not overlap and cover the whole data space. In the case of rule induction, the rules may overlap and may not cover the whole data space. In the case of lattice machine the hypertuples overlap and the covering of the whole data space is not guaranteed too.

Overlapping makes it possible to label a data example by more than one class whereas insufficient coverage makes it possible that a data example is not labeled at all. How to deal best with the overlapping and insufficient coverage issues?

In this paper we consider a hierarchical strategy to answer this question. Most machine learning algorithms generate different models from data under different conditions or parameters, and they advocate some conditions for optimal models or let a user specify the condition for optimal models. Instead of trying to find the 'optimal' model we can consider a series of models constructed under different conditions. These models form a hierarchy, or a layered structure, where the bottom layer corresponds to a model with the strictest condition and the top layer corresponds to the one with the most relaxed condition. The models in different hierarchy layers correspond to different levels of pattern generalization.

To demonstrate the effectiveness of this strategy we implemented it in two classifiers that construct multi-part models: one based on the lattice machine, and the other one based on rough set rule induction. This leads to two new classification methods.

The first method, called HCW, is a hierarchical version of the CASEEx-TRACT/CE (or CE/CE for short) classifier – the operations in the lattice machine [21]. As mentioned earlier, the lattice machine generates hypertuples as model of data, but the hypertuples overlap (some objects are multiply covered) and usually only a part of the whole object space is covered by the hypertuples (some objects are not covered). Hence, for recognition of uncovered objects, we consider some more general hypertuples in the hierarchy that covers these objects. For recognition of multiply covered objects, we also consider more general hypertuples that cover (not exclusively) the objects. These covering hypertuples locate at various levels of the hierarchy. They are taken as neighbourhoods of the object. A special voting strategy has been proposed to resolve conflicts between the object neighbourhoods covering the classified object.

The second method, called RSES-H, is a hierarchical version of the rule-based classifier (hereafter referred to by RSES-O) in RSES [23]. RSES-O is based on rough set methods with optimisation of rule shortening. RSES-H constructs a hierarchy of rule-based classifiers. The levels of the hierarchy are defined by different levels of minimal rule shortening [2,23]. A given object is classified by the classifier from the hierarchy that recognizes the object and corresponds to the minimal generalisation (rule shortening) in the hierarchy of classifiers.

We compare the performance of HCW and RSES-H with the well known classifiers C5.0 [13], SVM [17], and also with CE/C2 [18,20], RSES-O, and RIONA that is a combination of rough sets with k-nn [7,23]. The evaluation of described methods was done through experiments with benchmark datasets from UCI Machine Learning Repository. The results of experiments show that in many cases the hierarchical approach leads to improved classification accuracy.

It is necessary to note that our hierarchical approach to multimodal classification is different from the classical hierarchical classification framework (see, e.g., [6,16,12,5,3,4,8]), which aims at developing methods to learn complex, usually hierarchical, concepts. In our study we do not consider the hierarchical structure of the concepts in question; therefore our study is in fact a *hierarchical approach to flat classification*.

2 HCW: Hierarchical Lattice Machine

In this section we present one implementation of our hierarchical approach to multimodal classification. This is a hierarchical version of the CE/C2 algorithm in the lattice machine, referred to by HCW.

A lattice machine [18,21] is a machine learning paradigm that constructs a generalised version space from data, which serves as a model (or hypothesis) of data. A model is a hyperrelation, or a set of hypertuples (patterns), such that each hypertuple in the hyperrelation is equilabelled, supported, and maximal. Being equilabelled means the model is consistent with data (i.e., matches objects with the same decision only); being maximal means the model has generalisation capability; and being supported means the model does not generalise beyond the information given in the data. When data come from Euclidean space, the model is a set of hyperrectangles consistently, tightly and maximally approximating the data. Observe that, this approach is different from decision tree induction, which aims at partition of the data space. Lattice machines have two basic operations: a construction operation to build a model of data in the form of a set of hypertuples, and a classification operation that applies the model to classify data. The LM algorithm [19] constructs the unique model but it is not scalable to large datasets. The efficient algorithm CASEEXTRACT presented in [18] constructs such a model with the maximal condition relaxed. When such a model is obtained, classification can be done by the C2 algorithm [20]. C2 distinguishes between two types of data: those that are covered by at least one hypertuple (primary data), and those that are not (secondary data). Classification is based on two measures. Primary data t is put in the same class as the hypertuple that covers t, and secondary data are classified with the use of these two measures. Some variants of C2 are discussed in [21]. However, the classification accuracy is still not desirable for secondary data. Table 1 shows some experimental results by CE/C2. We can see clearly that C2 performed extremely well on primary data. Since the overall performance is the weighted average of those of primary and secondary data, it is clear that C2 performed poorly on secondary data.

We implement the hierarchical strategy in the lattice machine with the expectation that the classification accuracy of the lattice machine can be improved. Here is an outline of the solution.

We apply the CASEEXTRACT algorithm repeatedly to construct a hierarchy of hypertuples. The bottom layer is constructed by CASEEXTRACT directly from data. Then those data that are covered by the hypertuples with small coverage are marked out in the dataset, and the algorithm is applied again to construct a second layer. This process is repeated until a layer only with one hypertuple is reached. At the bottom layer all hypertuples are equilabelled, while those at higher layers may not be equilabelled.

To classify a data tuple (query) we search through the hierarchy to find a hypertuple at the lowest possible layer that covers the query. Then all data (including both marked and unmarked) covered by the hypertuple are weighted by an efficient counting-based weighting method. The weights are aggregated and used to classify the query. This is similar to the weighted k-nearest neighbour method, but it uses counting instead of distance to weigh relevant data.

2.1 Counting-Based Weighting Measure

In this section we present a counting-based weighting measure, which is suitable for use with hypertuples.

Suppose we have a neighbourhood D for a query tuple (object) t and elements in D may come from any class. In order to classify the query based on the neighbourhood we can take a majority voting with or without weighting. This is the essence of the well-known k-nearest neighbour (kNN) method [11,10].

Weighting is usually done by the reverse of distance. Distance measures usually work for numerical data. For categorical data we need to transform the data into numerical form first. There are many ways for the transformation (see for example [15,9,22]), but most of them are task (e.g., classification) specific.

We present a general weighting method that allows us to count the number of all hypertuples, generated by the data tuples in a neighbourhood of a query tuple t, that cover both t and any data tuple x in the neighbourhood. Intuitively the higher the count the more relevant this x is to t, hence x should play a bigger role (higher weight). The inverse of this count can be used as a measure of distance between x and t. Therefore, by this count we can order and weight the data tuples. This counting method works for both numerical and categorical data in a conceptually uniform way. We consider next an efficient method to calculate this count.

As a measure of weighting we set to find out, for tuples t and x in D, the number of hypertuples that cover both t and x. We call this number the *h-count* of t and x, denoted by $cnt(t, x)$. The important issue here is how to calculate the h-count for every tuple in D.

Consider two simple tuples $t = < t_1, t_2, \cdots, t_n >$ and $x = < x_1, x_2, \cdots, x_n >$. t is a simple tuple to be classified (query) and x is any simple tuple in D. What we want is to find all hypertuples that cover both t and x. We look at every attribute and explore the number of subsets that can be used to generate a hypertuple covering both t and x. Multiplying these numbers across all attributes gives rise to the number we require.

Consider an attribute a_i. If a_i is numerical, N_i denotes the number of intervals that can be used to generate a hypertuple covering both t_i and x_i. If a_i is categorical, N_i denotes the number of subsets for the same purpose:

$$(1) \quad N_i = \begin{cases} (\max(a_i) - \max(\{x_i, t_i\}) + 1) \times (\min(\{x_i, t_i\}) - \min(a_i) + 1) \\ \qquad \text{if } a_i \text{ is numerical} \\ 2^{m_i - 1} \quad \text{if } a_i \text{ is categorical and } x_i = t_i \\ 2^{m_i - 2} \quad \text{if } a_i \text{ is categorical and } x_i \neq t_i. \end{cases}$$

where $\max(a_i)$, $\min(a_i)$ are the maximal and the minimal value of a_i, respectively, if a_i is numerical, and $m_i = |dom(a_i)|$, if a_i is categorical.

The number of covering hypertuples of t and x is $cnt(t, x) = \prod_i N_i$.

A simple tuple $x \in D$ is then weighted by $cnt(t, x)$ in a kNN classifier. More specifically, we define

$$K(t, q) = \sum_{x \in D_q} cnt(t, x).$$

where D_q is a subset of D consisting of all q class simple tuples. $K(t, q)$ is the total of the h-counts of all q class simple tuples. Then the weighted kNN classifier is the following rule (WKNN rule):

t is classified by q_0 that has the largest $K(t, q)$ for all q.

We now present a classification procedure, called, *hierarchical classification based on weighting* (HCW).

Let D be a given dataset, let HH be a hierarchy of hypertuples constructed from D, and let t be a query – a simple tuple to be classified.

Step 1. Search HH in the bottom up order and stop as soon as a covering hypertuple is found at layer l. Continue searching layer l until all covering hypertuples are found. Let S be a set of all covering hypertuples from this layer;

Step 2. Let $N \leftarrow \{\underline{h} : h \in S\}$, a neighbourhood of the query;

Step 3. Apply WKNN to classify t.

Note that $\underline{h}$ is the set of simple tuples covered by h.

3   RSES-H: Hierarchical Rule-Based Classifier

In this section we present another implementation of our hierarchical approach to multimodal classification. This is a hierarchical version of RSES-O, referred to by RSES-H.

In RSES-H a set of minimal decision rules [1,23] is generated. Then, different layers for classification are created by rule shortening. The algorithm works as follows:

1. At the beginning, we divide original data sets into two disjoint parts: train table and test table.
2. Next, we calculate (consistent) rules with a minimal number of descriptors for the train table (using covering method from RSES [1,23]). This set of rules is used to construct the first (the bottom) level of our classifier.
3. In the successive steps defined by the following thresholds (for the positive region after shortening): $0.95, 0.90, 0.85, 0.80, 0.75, 0.70, 0.65, 0.60$, we generate a set of rules obtained by shortening all rules generated in the previous step. The rules generated in the i-th step are used to construct the classifier with the label $i + 1$ in the classifier hierarchy.
4. Now, we can use our hierarchical classifier in the following way:
   (a) For any object from the test table, we try to classify this object using decision rules from the first level of our classifier.
   (b) If the tested object is classified by rules from the first level of classifier, we return the decision value for this object and the remaining levels of our classifier are not used.
   (c) If the tested object can not by classified by rules from the first level, we try to classify it using the second level of our hierarchical classifier, etc.
   (d) Finally, if the tested object can not be classified by rules from the level with the label 9, then our classifier can not classify the tested object. The last case happens seldom, because higher levels are usually sufficient for classifying any tested object.

4   Evaluation

The two hierarchical classifiers described in Section 2.1 (HCW) and in Section 3 (RSES-H) were evaluated by experiments on some popular benchmark datasets from UCI Machine Learning Repository[1]. Each classifier was tested 10 times on each dataset with the use of 5-fold cross-validation. The average results are shown in Table 1.

For comparison, we also include experimental results by the well-known decision tree C5.0 [13] and support vector machine (SVM) [17], the two non-hierarchical methods CE/C2 and RSES-O based on rules, and RIONA.

CE/C2 is a lattice machine based classifier [21]. The CASEEXTRACT algorithm builds, as a classifying function, a set of overlapping hypertuples and the C2 algorithm classifies a data example.

RSES-O implemented in RSES [2,23] is a rule based method with the rule shortening optimization. It is based on the decision rules with the minimal number of descriptors and the operation of rule shortening [1]. The classifier is constructed over the set of rules obtained by shortening these minimal rules using the optimal threshold.

RIONA [7] is another classification algorithm implemented in RSES [2,23] that combines the k nearest neighbor method with rule induction. The method induces a distance measure and distance-based rules. For classification of a given

---

[1] http://www.ics.uci.edu/~mlearn/MLRepository.html

Table 1. General information on the datasets and the 5-fold cross validation success rate of C5.0, SVM, CE/C2 on all data, CE/C2 on primary data, HCW, RSES-H, RSES-O and RIONA. The "PP" column is the percentage of primary data. Note that the SVM results for "German", "TTT" and "Vote" are not available because they have categorical attributes and this method does not work with categorical attributes directly. For HCW, RSES-H and RSES-O the standard deviations are also provided. In the columns HCW and RSES-H the superscripts denote the levels of statistical significance of difference between these classifiers and RSES-O: 5 is 99.5%, 4 is 99%, 3 is 97.5%, 2 is 95%, 1 is 90% and 0 is below 90%. Plus indicates that the average accuracy of the method is higher than in RSES-O and minus otherwise.

Data	General Info			5CV success rate								%PP
	Att	Exa	Cla	C5.0	SVM	CE/C2	Prim.	HCW	RSES-H	RSES-O	RIONA	
Anneal	38	798	6	96.6	91.3	96.8	97.6	$96.0\pm0.4^{+5}$	$96.2\pm0.5^{+5}$	94.3 ± 0.6	92.5	93.4
Austral	14	690	2	90.6	85.3	83.5	95.1	$92.0\pm0.4^{+5}$	$87.0\pm0.5^{+3}$	86.4 ± 0.5	85.7	87.2
Auto	25	205	6	70.7	68.3	76.1	86.8	$76.5\pm1.4^{+5}$	$73.7\pm1.7^{+5}$	69.0 ± 3.1	76.7	56.1
Diabetes	8	768	2	72.7	77.7	71.0	71.7	72.6 ± 0.8^{-5}	73.8 ± 1.2^{0}	73.8 ± 0.6	75.4	66.8
German	20	1000	2	71.7		72.5	72.6	71.4 ± 0.9^{-4}	$73.2\pm0.9^{+5}$	72.2 ± 0.4	74.4	65.4
Glass	9	214	3	62.4	63.9	64.0	69.6	$71.3\pm1.2^{+5}$	$63.4\pm1.8^{+3}$	61.2 ± 2.5	66.1	79.4
Heart	13	270	2	77.0	83.3	77.0	82.1	79.0 ± 1.0^{-5}	$84.0\pm1.3^{+0}$	83.8 ± 1.1	82.3	61.5
Hepatitis	19	155	2	80.0	80.7	81.2	84.1	78.7 ± 1.2^{-5}	81.9 ± 1.6^{-0}	82.6 ± 1.3	82.0	69.0
Iris	4	150	3	94.7	94.0	92.7	97.6	94.1 ± 0.4^{-1}	$95.5\pm0.8^{+0}$	94.9 ± 1.5	94.4	82.7
Sonar	60	208	2	71.6	72.2	69.7	81.4	73.7 ± 0.8^{-0}	$75.3\pm2.0^{+0}$	74.3 ± 1.8	86.1	59.2
TTT	9	958	2	86.2		83.5	96.2	95.0 ± 0.3^{-5}	$99.1\pm0.2^{+1}$	99.0 ± 0.2	93.6	94.9
Vehicle	18	846	4	71.9	76.8	75.7	76.7	$67.6\pm0.7^{+5}$	$66.1\pm1.4^{+4}$	64.2 ± 1.3	70.2	61.7
Vote	18	232	2	96.5		94.2	98.5	95.4 ± 0.5^{-5}	$96.5\pm0.5^{+0}$	96.4 ± 0.5	95.3	89.7
Average success rate				80.20	79.35	79.84	85.38	81.79	81.98	80.93	82.67	

test object the examples most similar to this object vote for decisions but first they are compared against the rules and the examples that do not match any rule are excluded from voting.

On average HCW and RSES-H outperform C5.0, SVM, CE/C2 and RSES-O and are almost the same as RIONA (the advantage of RIONA is only due to the dataset *Sonar*). To provide more details on the benefit from hierarchical approach we compared HCW and RSES-H against the non-hierarchical RSES-O (on average RSES-O gives better accuracy than than CE/C2) and computed the statistical significance of their difference using the one-tail unpaired Student's t-test [14].

Comparing RSES-H against RSES-O one can see that for 6 datasets RSES-H dominates with at least 97.5% confidence level and there is no dataset on which RSES-H was significantly worse.

The comparison between HCW and RSES-O does not show supremacy of any method. However, for some datasets (*Australian, Auto* and *Glass*) HCW provided significantly better results than both RSES-H and RSES-O. Moreover, it outperformed CE/C2 in 9 out of 13 datasets. The best improvements were for the datasets *TTT* (11.5%), *Australian* (8.5%) and *Glass* (7.3%). It is interesting to note that the performance of CE/C2 on the *Vehicle* dataset was significantly better (8.1%) than the performance of HCW. Observe also (see column Prim in Table 1) that CE/C2 performed extremely well on primary data, i.e., data covered by hypertuples induced by lattice machine.

The experiments confirmed our original expectation that the performance of CE/C2 and RSES-O can be improved by our hierarchical approach. The cost is some extra time to construct the hierarchy and to test some new objects using this hierarchy.

Observe also that for most of the tested datasets the best method selected from the discussed rough set methods (RSES-O, RSES-H), combination of rough sets with k-nn (RIONA), and lattice machine (CE/C2,HCW) outperforms the methods C5.0 and SVM.

5   Conclusions

The experimental study has shown that the discussed hierarchical approach leads to improvement of classification accuracy. We plan to develop more advanced methods for hierarchical classification in incremental learning.

Acknowledgements. The research has been supported by the grants 4 T11C 040 24 and 3 T11C 002 26 from Ministry of Scientific Research and Information Technology of the Republic of Poland.

References

1. J. G. Bazan, M. Szczuka, J. Wróblewski. A New Version of Rough Set Exploration System, Proc. of RSCTC'2002, Lecture Notes in Artificial Intelligence 2475, Springer-Verlag, Heidelberg, 397-404, 2002.
2. J. Bazan, M. Szczuka, A. Wojna, M. Wojnarski. On the evolution of Rough Set Exploration System, Proc. of RSCTC'2004, Lecture Notes in Artificial Intelligence 3066, Springer, Heidelberg, 592–601, 2004.
3. J. Bazan, S. Hoa Nguyen, H. Son Nguyen, A. Skowron. Rough set methods in approximation of hierarchical concepts. *Proc. of RSCTC'2004*, Lecture Notes in Artificial Intelligence 3066, Springer, Heidelberg, 346–355, 2004.
4. J. Bazan. Classifiers based on two-layered learning. Lecture Notes in Artificial Intelligence 3066, Springer, Heidelberg, 356–361, 2004.
5. S. Behnke. Hierarchical Neural Networks for Image Interpretation. Lecture Notes in Artificial Intelligence 2766, Springer, Heidelberg, 2003.
6. T. G. Dietterich. Ensemble Learning. In M.A. Arbib (Ed.), The Handbook of Brain Theory and Neural Networks, Second edition, Cambridge, MA: The MIT Press, 405-408, 2002.
7. G. Góra and A. G. Wojna. RIONA: a new classification system combining rule induction and instance-based learning. *Fundamenta Informaticae*, 51(4):369–390, 2002.
8. S. Hoa Nguyen, J. Bazan, A. Skowron, H. Son Nguyen. Layered learning for concept synthesis. Lecture Notes in Artificial Intelligence 3100, *Transactions on Rough Sets I*:187–208, Springer, Heidelberg, 2004.
9. S. Cost, S. Salzberg. A weighted nearest neighbor algorithm for learning with symbolic features. *Machine Learning*, 10:57–78, 1993.
10. S. A. Dudani. The distance-weighted k-nearest-neighbor rule. *IEEE Trans. Syst. Man Cyber.*, 6:325–327, 1976.

11. E. Fix and J. L. Hodges. Discriminatory analysis, nonparametric discrimination: Consistency properties. Technical Report TR4, USAF School of Aviation Medicine, Randolph Field, TX, 1951.
12. T. Poggio, S. Smale. The Mathematics of Learning: Dealing with Data. *Notices of the AMS* 50(5):537-544, 2003.
13. R. Quinlan. Rulequest research data mining tools. http://www.rulequest.com/.
14. G. W. Snedecor, W. G. Cochran. Statisitical Methods, Iowa State University Press, Ames, IA, 2002, eighth edition.
15. C. Stanfill and D. Waltz. Toward memory-based reasoning. *Communication of ACM*, 29:1213–1229, 1986.
16. P. Stone. *Layered Learning in Multi-agent Systems: A Winning Approach to Robotic Soccer*. MIT Press, Cambridge, MA, 2000.
17. V. N. Vapnik. *Statistical learning theory*. Wiley New York, 1998.
18. H. Wang, W. Dubitzky, I. Düntsch, and D. Bell. A lattice machine approach to automated casebase design: Marrying lazy and eager learning. In *Proc. IJCAI99*, Stockholm, Sweden, 254–259, 1999.
19. H. Wang, I. Düntsch, D. Bell. Data reduction based on hyper relations. *Proceedings of KDD98, New York*, 349–353, 1998.
20. H. Wang, I. Düntsch, G. Gediga. Classificatory filtering in decision systems. *International Journal of Approximate Reasoning*, 23:111–136, 2000.
21. H. Wang, I. Düntsch, G. Gediga, A. Skowron. Hyperrelations in version space. *International Journal of Approximate Reasoning*, 36(3):223–241, 2004.
22. D. R. Wilson and T. R. Martinez. Improved heterogeneous distance functions. *Journal of Artificial Intelligence Research*, 6:1–34, 1997.
23. RSES: Rough set exploration system. http://logic.mimuw.edu.pl/~rses, Institute of Mathematics, Warsaw University, Poland.
24. R. Quinlan. Improved Use of Continuous Attributes in C4.5. Journal of Artificial Intelligence Research, 4:77-90, 1996.

Rough Learning Vector Quantization Case Generation for CBR Classifiers*

Yan Li[1], Simon Chi-Keung Shiu[1],
Sankar Kumar Pal[2], and James Nga-Kwok Liu[1]

[1] Department of Computing, Hong Kong Polytechnic University,
Kowloon, Hong Kong
{csyli, csckshiu, csnkliu}@comp.polyu.edu.hk
[2] Machine Intelligence Unit, Indian Statistical Institute,
Kolkata 700 035, India
sankar@isical.ac.in

Abstract. To build competent and efficient CBR classifiers, we develop a case generation approach which integrates fuzzy sets, rough sets and learning vector quantization (LVQ). If the feature values of the cases are numerical, fuzzy sets are firstly used to discretize the feature spaces. Secondly, a fast rough set-based feature selection method is built to identify the significant features. The representative cases (prototypes) are then generated through LVQ learning process on the case bases after feature selection. These prototypes can be also considered as the extracted knowledge which improves the understanding of the case base. Three real life data sets are used in the experiments to demonstrate the effectiveness of this case generation approach.

1 Introduction

Case-based Reasoning (CBR) [1] is a reasoning methodology that based on prior experience and examples. Compared with rule-based systems, CBR systems usually require significantly less knowledge acquisition, since it involves collecting a set of past experiences (called case base) without the added necessity of extracting a formal domain model from these cases. The CBR systems used in classification problems are called CBR classifiers.

The performance of CBR classifiers, in terms of classification accuracy and efficiency, closely depends on the competence and size of the case base. The competence of a case base is the range of unseen cases which the case base can correctly classify. In general, the more competent the case base, the higher the classification accuracy of the CBR classifier. On the other hand, it is obvious that the larger the size of a case base, the lower the case retrieval speed. The reduction of cases will improve the efficiency but may hurt the case base competence. In this research, we attempt to make a trade-off between the classification accuracy and efficiency by building both compact and competent case bases for CBR classifiers.

---

* This work is supported by the Hong Kong government CERG research grant BQ-496.

D. Ślęzak et al. (Eds.): RSFDGrC 2005, LNAI 3642, pp. 128–137, 2005.

We achieve this goal by developing a rough learning vector quantization (LVQ)-based case generation approach. A few of prototypes are generated to represent the entire case base without loss the competence of the original case base.

As a necessary preprocessing of LVQ-based case generation, a fast rough set-based method is developed to select the relevant features and eliminate the irrelevant ones. Rough sets [2] allow the most informative features to be detected and then selected through the reduct computation. There is much research work in rough set-based feature selection [3,4,5,6], most of which are computational intensive. To reduce the computational load inherent in such methods, a new concept called approximate reduct is introduced. Other primary concepts in rough sets, such as dispensable (indispensable) attribute and core, are also modified. Using these extended concepts, we develop a fast rough set based approach to finding the approximate reduct. The computational load is linear with the number of cases and features. In this feature selection process, fuzzy sets are used to discretize the numerical attribute values to generate indiscernibility relation and equivalence classes of the given case base.

Learning vector quantization is then applied to extract the representative cases (also called prototypes) to represent the entire case base. LVQ is a competitive algorithm, which is considered to be a supervised version of the Self-Organizing Map (SOM) algorithm [7]. Mangiameli et al. [8] demonstrated that SOM is a better clustering algorithm than hierarchical clustering with irrelevant variables or different sized populations. Pal et al. used SOM to extract prototypical cases in [9] and reported a compact representation of data. However, Kohonen pointed out in [7], decision and classification processes should use Learning Vector Quantization (LVQ) in stead of SOM. Since we focus on the classification problems in this paper, LVQ is used to generate prototypical cases. LVQ has similar advantages of SOM, such as the robustness with noise and missing information.

After applying the case selection approach, the original case base can be reduced to a few prototypes which can be directly used to predict the class label of the unseen cases. These prototypes can be regarded as the specific domain knowledge which is extracted from the case base. This will speed up the case retrieval and make the case base be more easily understood. On the other hand, since the most representative cases are generated, case base competence can be also preserved.

2   Fuzzy Discretization of Feature Space

The rough set-based feature selection methods are all built on the basis of indiscernibility relation. If the attribute values are continuous, the feature space needs to be discretized for defining the indiscernibility relations and equivalence classes on different subset of attribute sets. In this paper, fuzzy sets are used for the discretization by partition each attribute into three levels: Low (L), Medium (M), and High (H). Finer partitions may lead to better accuracy at the cost of higher computational load. The use of fuzzy sets has several advantages over the traditional "hard" discertizations, such as handling the overlapped clusters and linguistic representation of data [9].

Triangular membership functions are used to define the fuzzy sets: L, M and H. There are three parameters C_L, C_M, and C_H for each attribute which should be determined beforehand. They are considered as the centers of the three fuzzy sets. In this paper, the center of fuzzy set M for a given attribute a is the average value of all the values occurring in the domain of a. Assume V_a is the domain of attribute a, then $C_M = \sum_{y \in V} y / |V_a|$, where $| * |$ is the cardinality of set $*$.

C_L and C_M are computed as $C_L = (C_M - Min_a)/2$ and $C_H = (Max_a - C_M)/2$, where $Min_a = min\{y|y \in V_a\}$ and $Max_a = max\{y|y \in V_a\}$.

3   Feature Selection Based on Approximate Reduct

In this section, we develop a fast feature reduction method based on the concept of approximate reduct. Before we present the proposed algorithm, the rough set-based feature selection methods are briefly reviewed.

3.1   Traditional Rough Set-Based Feature Selection Methods

The discernibility function-based reduct computation algorithms belong to the traditional rough set-based feature selection methods. They are built on the concepts of indiscernibility relation, set approximations, dispensable and indispensable attributes, reduct and core [2].

The reduct computation is directly based on discernibility matrix [5]. Assume IS is an information system which can be represented by a triplet $IS = (U, A, f)$, where U is a finite nonempty set of n objects $\{x_1, x_2, ..., x_n\}$; A is a finite nonempty set of m attributes (features) $\{a_1, a_2, ..., a_m\}$; $f_a : U \to V_a$ for any $a \in A$, where V_a is called the domain of attribute a. The discernibility matrix is defined as a $n \times n$ matrix represented by (dm_{ij}), where $dm_{ij} = \{a \in A : f_a(x_i) \neq f_a(x_j)\}$ for $i, j = 1, 2, ..., n$.

All reducts are hidden in some discernibility function induced by the discernibility matrix. If there are n objects in the IS, m attributes in $A \cup \{d\}$, the computation complexity of these methods is $O(n^2 \times m)$.

3.2   Relative Dependency-Based Reduct Computation

To reduce the computational load of the discernibility function-based methods, Han et al. [10] have developed a reduct computation approach based on the concept of relative attribute dependency. Given a subset of condition attributes, B, the relative attribute dependency is a ratio between the number of distinct rows in the sub-decision table corresponding to B only and the number of distinct rows in the sub-decision table corresponding to B together with the decision attributes, i.e., $B \cup \{d\}$. The larger the relative attribute dependency value (i.e., close to 1), the more useful is the subset of condition attributes B in discriminating the decision attribute values. To evaluate the generated approximate reducts, Bazan et al. [11] used a quality measure for reducts based on the number of rules generated by the reducts. In this paper, we do not need to obtain the optimal approximate reduct, which requires much more computational effort. In the following sections, a feature selection method will be built based on the work of Han et al. Some pertinent concepts are defined as:

Definition 1. (Projection) [10] Let $P \subseteq A \cup D$, where $D = \{d\}$. The projection of U on P, denoted by $\Pi_P(U)$, is a sub table of U and is constructed as follows: 1) remove attributes $A \cup D - P$; and 2) merge all indiscernible rows.

Definition 2. (Relative Dependency Degree) Let $B \subseteq A$, A be the set of conditional attributes. D is the set of decision attributes. The *relative de-pendency degree* of B w.r.t. D is defined as δ_B^D, $\delta_B^D = |\Pi_B(U)|/|\Pi_{B \cup D}(U)|$, where $|\Pi_X(U)|$ is the number of equivalence classes in $U/IND(X)$.

δ_B^D can be computed by counting the number of equivalence classes induced by B and $B \cup D$, i.e., the distinct rows in the projections of U on B and $B \cup D$.

Definition 3. (Consistent Decision Table) A decision table DT or U is consistent when $\forall x, y \in U$, if $f_D(x) \neq f_D(y)$, then $\exists a \in A$ such that $f_a(x) \neq f_a(y)$.

It can be easily induced that $\delta_A^D = 1$ when U is consistent. A subset of attributes $B \subseteq A$ is found to be a reduct, if the sub-decision table is still consistent after removing the attributes in $A - B$. This is given as Theorem 1.

Theorem 1. If U is consistent, $B \subseteq A$ is a reduct of A w.r.t. D, if and only if $\delta_B^D = \delta_A^D = 1$ and for $\forall Q \subset B$, $\delta_Q^D \neq \delta_A^D$. (See [10] for the proof)

Theorem 1 gives the necessary and sufficient conditions for reduct computation and implies that the reduct can be generated by only counting the distinct rows in some projections. The computational load is linear to the number of cases, n, and the number of attributes, m.

3.3 Feature Selection Based on Approximate Reduct

From Section 3.2, we notice that, although the relative dependency-based reduct computation is fast, U is always assumed to be consistent in theorem 1. This assumption is not necessarily true in real life applications. In this section, we relax this condition by finding approximate reduct instead of exact reduct. The use of a relative dependency degree in reduct computation is extended to inconsistent in-formation systems. Some new concepts, such as the β-*dispensable attribute*, β-*indispensable attribute*, β-*reduct* (i.e., approximate reduct), and β-*core* are introduced to modify the traditional concepts in rough set theory. The parameter is used as the consistency measurement to evaluate the goodness of the subset of attributes currently under consideration. These are explained as follows.

Definition 4. (β-dispensable attribute and β-indispensable attribute) If $a \in A$ is an attribute that satisfies $\delta_{A-\{a\}}^D \geq \delta \cdot \delta_A^D$, a is called a δ-*dispensable* attribute in A. Otherwise, a is called a β-*indispensable* attribute.

The parameter β, $\beta \in [0, 1]$, is called the consistency measurement.

Definition 5. (β-reduct/approximate reduct and β-core) B is called a β-*reduct* or *approximate reduct* of conditional attribute set A if B is the minimal subset of A such that $\delta_B^D \geq \beta \cdot \delta_A^D$. The β-*core* of A is the set of β-indispensable attributes.

The consistency measurement β reflects the relationship of the approximate reduct and the exact reduct. The larger the value of β, the more similar is the approximate reduct to the exact reduct computed using the traditional discernibility function-based methods. If $\beta = 1$ (i.e., attains its maximum), the two reducts are equal (according to theorem 1). The reduct computation is implemented by counting the distinct rows in the sub-decision tables of some sub-attribute sets. β controls the end condition of the algorithm and therefore controls the size of reduced feature set. It can be determined beforehand by experts or can be learned during the feature selection process. Based on Definitions 4-5, the rough set-based feature selection algorithm in our developed approach is given as follows.

Feature Selection Algorithm

Input: U - the entire case base; A - the entire condition attribute set; D - the decision attribute set.
Output: R - the approximate reduct of A.

Step 1. Initialize R=empty set;
Step 2. Compute the approximate reduct.

> While A is not empty
> 1. For each attribute $a \in A$
>   Compute the significance of a;
> 2. Add the most significant one, q, to R: $R = R \cup \{q\}$;
> $A = A - q$;
> 3. Compute the relative dependency degree δ_R^D for current R;
> 4. If $\delta_R^D > \beta$, return R and stop.

Since the computation of approximate reduce does not increase the computational load to the method of Han et al., the computation complexities of the feature selection algorithms is also $O(n \times m)$, where m is the number of features in $A \cup D$, n is the number of objects in U.

4 LVQ-Based Case Generation

After the approximate reduct-based feature selection, the supervised learning process of LVQ is used for generating prototypes which represent the entire case base.

4.1 Learning Vector Quantization

LVQ derives from the Self-organizing map (SOM) which is an unsupervised learning and robust to handle noisy and outlier data. The SOM can serve as a clustering tool of high-dimensional data. For classification problems, supervised learning LVQ should be superior to SOM since the information of classification results is incorporated to guide the learning process. LVQ is more robust to redundant features and cases, and more insensitive to the learning rate.

4.2 Rough LVQ Algorithm

Although LVQ has similar advantages of SOM, such as the robustness with noise and missing information, it does not mean that the data preprocessing is not required before the learning process. Since the basic assumption of LVQ is that similar feature values should lead to similar classification results, the similarity computation is critical in the learning process. Feature selection is one of the most important preparations for LVQ which can achieve better clustering and similarity computation results.

Different subset of features will result different data distribution and clusters. Take the Iris data [12] for example. Based on the two subsets of features, LVQ is applied to learn three prototypes for the Iris data. The generated representative cases are shown in Table 1-2. It shows that different subset of attributes can affect the LVQ learning process and different prototypes are generated. According to the classification accuracy, the feature set of {PL, PW} is better than {SL, SW}.

Table 1. Prototypes extracted using PL and PW

Prototypes	SL	SW	PL	PW	Class label
P1	0.619	0.777	0.224	0.099	1
P2	0.685	0.613	0.589	0.528	2
P3	0.766	0.587	0.737	0.779	3

Classification accuracy using P1 P2 and P3: 0.98

Table 2. Prototypes extracted using SL and SW

Prototypes	SL	SW	PL	PW	Class label
P1	0.649	0.842	0.211	0.094	1
P2	0.712	0.550	0.572	0.212	2
P3	0.980	0.840	1.096	1.566	3

Classification accuracy using P1, P2 and P3: 0.80

In this paper, the feature selection is handled using the approximate reduct-based method which given in the previous section. LVQ is then applied to generate representative cases for the entire case base. Here the learning rate α is given in advance, and only the distance between the winning node and the given input vector is updated in each learning step. The number of weight vectors is determined as the number of classes in the given case base. The learning process is ended with a fixed number of iterations T, say, 5000 in this paper. Assume the given case base has n cases which represented by m features, and there are c classes. R is the approximate reduct computed by the feature selection process. The LVQ algorithm is given as follows:

Step 1. Initialize c weight vectors $[v_1, v_2, ..., v_c]$ by randomly selecting one case from each class.

Step 2. Generate prototypes through LVQ.

$t \leftarrow 1$;
    While $(t \leq T)$
        for $k = 1$ to n
            $x \in U$, $x_k \leftarrow x$, $U \leftarrow U - x_k$;
            1. Compute the distances $D = \{\|x_k - v_{i,t-1}\|_R : 1 \leq i \leq c\}$;
            2. Select $v_{win,t-1} = arg\{v_{i,t-1} : \|x_k - v_{i,t-1}\|_R = min\{d \in D\}\}$;
            3. If $Class(v_{win,t-1}) = Class(x_k)$
                Update $v_{win,t} = v_{i,t-1} + \alpha(x_k - v_{win,t-1})$;
            4. Output $V = [v_{1,T-1}, v_{2,T-1}, ..., v_{c,T-1}]$.

The output vectors are considered to be the generated prototypes which represent the entire case base. Each prototype can be used to describe the corresponding class and regarded as the cluster center.

5   Experimental Results

To illustrate the effectiveness of the developed rough LVQ case selection method, we describe here some results on three real life data [12]: Iris, Glass, and Pima. In all the experiments, 80% cases in each database are randomly selected for training and the remaining 20% cases are used for testing.

In this paper, four indices are used to evaluate the rough LVQ case generation method. The classification accuracy is one of the important factors to be considered for building classifiers. On the other hand, the efficiency of CBR classifiers in terms of case retrieval time should not be neglected. The storage space and clustering performance (in terms of intra-similarity and inter-similarity) are also tested in this section. Based on these evaluation indices, comparisons are made between our developed method and others such as basic SOM, basic LVQ and Random case selection methods.

In the experiments of this section, the parameter β is determined during the testing through populating the points in the interval [0.5, 1]. Initially, β is set to be 0.5. In each step, the β value increase at a constant rate 0.01 and this value is used in the feature selection process and being tested. The steps stop when attains 1. The value which can achieve the highest classification accuracy is selected as the suitable β. The learning rates for the three data sets are: $\alpha= 0.8$ (Iris data), $\alpha= 0.8$ (Glass data) and $\alpha= 0.5$ (Pima data).

5.1   Classification Accuracy

In this section, the results of classification accuracy for the three databases and four case selection methods are demonstrated and analyzed.

If the training cases are used for classify the testing cases, the classification accuracies on the three databases are: 0.980 (Iris), 0.977 (Glass), 0.662 (Pima). These accuracy values are called the original classification accuracies. The experimental results of using the generated prototypes are demonstrated in Table 3. Here we test the accuracy using both the testing cases and all cases, denoted by $Accu_{Test}$ and $Accu_{All}$, respectively. It is observed that after the case generation,

Table 3. Classification accuracy using different case generation methods

Methods	Iris data		Glass data		Pima data	
	$Accu_{Test}$	$Accu_{All}$	$Accu_{Test}$	$Accu_{All}$	$Accu_{Test}$	$Accu_{All}$
Random	0.760	0.746	0.860	0.864	0.597	0.660
SOM	0.920	0.953	0.930	0.925	0.688	0.730
LVQ	0.980	0.953	0.930	**0.935**	0.708	**0.743**
Rough LVQ	**1.000**	**0.960**	0.930	**0.935**	**0.714**	0.740

the original accuracies are preserved and even improved. The rough LVQ method can achieve the highest classification accuracy in most of the testing. The basic LVQ method performs better than the other methods: Random and SOM.

5.2   Reduced Storage Space of Rough LVQ-Based Method

Due to both the feature selection and case selection processes, the storage space with respect to the features and cases is reduced substantially. Subsequently, the average case retrieval time will decrease. These results are shown in Table 4, where

$$Reduced\ features = (1 - \frac{|Selected\ features|}{|Original\ features|}) \times 100\%,$$
$$Reduced\ cases = (1 - \frac{|Prototypes|}{|Entire data|}) \times 100\%,$$
$$Saved\ time\ of\ case\ retrieval = (t_{train} - t_p),$$

where t_{train} is the case retrieval time using the training cases; t_p is the case retrieval time using the extracted prototypes. The unit of time is second.

Table 4. Reduced storage and saved case retrieval time

Data set	Reduced features	Reduced cases	Saved time of case retrieval
Iris	50%	97.0%	0.600 sec
Glass	60%	98.8%	0.989 sec
Pima	50%	99.6%	0.924 sec

From Table 4, the storage requirements of features and cases are reduced dramatically. For example, the percentage of reduced features is 60% for Glass data, and the percentage of reduced cases is 99.6% for Pima data. The case retrieval time also decreases because that there are much fewer features and cases after applying the rough LVQ-based case selection method.

5.3   Intra-similarity and Inter-similarity

Intra-similarity and inter-similarity are two important indices to reflect the clustering performance. They are used in this section to prove that the developed rough LVQ-based approach can achieve better clustering than using random selected prototypes. Since the similarity between two cases is inverse proportional to the distance between them, we use inter-distance and intra-distance to describe the inter-similarity and intra-similarity. Assume there are K classes for a given case base, $C_1, C_2, ..., C_K$. The intra-distance and inter-distance of the case base are defined as:

$$Intra\text{-}Distance = \sum_{x,y \in C} d(x,y),$$
$$Inter\text{-}Distance = \sum_{x \in C, y \in C} d(x,y), i,j = 1, 2, ..., K, i \neq j$$
$$Ratio = Intra\text{-}Distance / Inter\text{-}Distance.$$

The lower the intra-distance and the higher the inter-distance, the better is the clustering performance. Therefore, it is obvious that the higher the ration between the inter-distance and the intra-distance, the better is the clustering performance. The results are shown in Table 5. Rough LVQ method demonstrates higher Ratio values and therefore achieves better clustering result.

Table 5. Inter-distance and inter-distance: Comparisons between the Random and Rough LVQ methods.

Data set	Methods	Inter-Distance	Intra-Distance	Ratio
Iris	Random	1284.52	102.13	12.577
	Rough LVQ	1155.39	51.99	22.223
Glass	Random	8640.20	4567.84	1.892
	Rough LVQ	7847.37	3238.99	2.423
Pima	Random	56462.83	54529.05	1.035
	Rough LVQ	28011.95	25163.45	1.113

6   Conclusions

In this paper, a rough LVQ approach is developed to address the case generation for building compact and competent CBR classifiers. Firstly, the rough set-based feature selection method is used to select features for LVQ learning. This method is built on the concept of approximate reduct instead of exact reuduct. It is a generalization of traditional discernibility matrix-based feature reduction. LVQ is then used to extract the prototypes to represent the entire case base. These prototypes are not the data points in the original case base, but are modified during the LVQ learning process. They are considered as the most representative cases for the given case base, and used to classify the unseen cases. Through the experimental results, using much fewer features (e.g., 40% of the original features for Glass data), the classification accuracies for the three real life data are higher using our method than those using methods of Random, basic SOM and LVQ. The case retrieval time for predicting class labels of unseen cases is also reduced. Furthermore, higher intra-similarity and lower inter-similarity are achieved using the rough LVQ approach than that using the random method.

References

1. Kolodner, J.: Case-Based Reasoning. Morgan Kaufmann, San Francisco, (1993).
2. Pawlak, Z.: Rough sets: Theoretical aspects of reasoning about data. Kluwer Academic Publishers, Boston, (1991).
3. Nguyen, H. S. and Skowron, A.: Boolean reasoning for feature extraction problems. Proceedings of the 10th International Symposium on Methodologies for Intelligent Systems, (1997), 117–126.
4. Wang, J. and Wang, J.: Reduction algorithms based on discernibility matrix: The ordered attributes method. Journal of Computer Science & Technology, Vol. 16, **6**, (2001), 489–504.
5. Skowron, A. and Rauszer, C.: The discernibility matrices and functions in information systems. In: K. Slowinski (ed.): Intelligent Decision Support-Handbook of Applications and Advances of the Rough Sets Theory. Kluwer, Dordrecht, (1992), 331–362.
6. Shen, Q. and Chouchoulas, A.: A rough-fuzzy approach for generating classification rules. Pattern Recognition, Vol. 35, (2002), 2425–2438.
7. Kohonen, T.: Self-organizing maps. New York, Springer-Verlag, (1997).
8. Mangiameli, P., Chen, S. K. and West, D.: A comparison of SOM neural network and hierarchical clustering methods. European Journal of Operational Research, Vol. 93, (1996), 402–417.
9. Pal, S. K., Dasgupta, B. and Mitra, P.: Rough-self organizing map. Applied Intelligence, Vol. 21, **3**, (2004), 289–299.
10. Han, J., Hu, X. and Lin, T. Y.: Feature subset selection based on relative dependency between attributes. Proceedings of the 4th International Conference of Rough Sets and Current Trends in Computing (RSCTC04), Springer-Verlag, Berlin, (2004), 176–185.
11. Bazan, J., Nguyen, H. S., Nguyen, S. H., Synak, P., Wróblewski, J.: Rough Set Algorithms in Classification Problem. In: Polkowski, L., Tsumoto, S. and Lin, T.Y. (eds.): Rough Set Methods and Appli-cations. Physica-Verlag, Heidelberg, New York, (2000), 49–88.
12. UCI Machine Learning Data Repository: http://www.ics.uci.edu/ mlearn/MLRepository.html

ML-CIDIM: Multiple Layers of Multiple Classifier Systems Based on CIDIM*

Gonzalo Ramos-Jiménez, José del Campo-Ávila, and Rafael Morales-Bueno

Departamento de Lenguajes y Ciencias de la Computación,
E.T.S. Ingeniería Informática, Universidad de Málaga, Málaga 29071, Spain
{ramos, jcampo, morales}@lcc.uma.es

Abstract. An active research area in Machine Learning is the construction of multiple classifier systems to increase learning accuracy of simple classifiers. In this paper we present a method to improve even more the accuracy: ML-CIDIM. This method has been developed by using a multiple classifier system which basic classifier is CIDIM, an algorithm that induces small and accurate decision trees. CIDIM makes a random division of the training set into two subsets and uses them to build an internal bound condition. ML-CIDIM induces some multiple classifier systems based on CIDIM and places them in different layers, trying to improve the accuracy of the previous layer with the following one. In this way, the accuracy obtained thanks to a unique multiple classifier system based on CIDIM can be improved. In reference to the accuracy of the classifier system built with ML-CIDIM, we can say that it competes well against bagging and boosting at statistically significant confidence levels.

1 Introduction

Classification and prediction tasks are two of the most popular activities in Machine Learning. There are many approaches that try to extract knowledge from data. These approaches are very diverse, but one of the most active research area is composed by multiple classifier systems. They have benefited from the idea of using a committee or ensemble of models to do cited tasks.

Many kind of models can take part into a multiple classifier system (homogeneous or heterogeneous). Decision trees are widely used on Machine Learning community (CART [1], ID3 [2], C4.5 [3], ITI [4], VFDT [5] ...) and they have some positive characteristics. They have the ability of splitting the hyperspace into subspaces and fitting each space with different models. They also have a good feature: the understandability.

In the literature we can find many approaches to define a multiple classifier system. Thus, we have methods that mainly reduce variance, such as bagging [6] or boosting [7], and methods that reduce bias, such as stacked generalization [8].

---

* This work has been partially supported by the MOISES project, number TIC2002-04019-C03-02, of the MCyT, Spain.

D. Ślęzak et al. (Eds.): RSFDGrC 2005, LNAI 3642, pp. 138–146, 2005.

Other multiple classifier methods, such as cascading [9], generate new attributes from the class probability estimation. Delegating [10] is another method and it works with examples in the dataset, using part of them in each classifier and delegating the rest of examples to the next classifier. In short, there are many methods for generating multiple models.

Taking this into account, we can use a very simple method to induce a multiple classifier that uses CIDIM as the basic classifier. CIDIM (Control of Induction by sample DIvision Methods) [11] is an algorithm that induces small and accurate decision trees, dividing the training set into two subsets and using them to build an internal bound condition. What we present in this paper is another level over this multiple classifier system. ML-CIDIM induces multiples layers of multiple classifiers trying to improve the previous one with the following one.

The paper is organized as follows. In Section 2 we will briefly describe CIDIM and its utilization in a multiple classifier system. We will introduce ML-CIDIM and how this method can improve the accuracy achieved by a multiple classifier in section 3. Some experimental results are shown in section 4. Finally, in section 5, we summarise our conclusions and suggest future lines of research.

2   Simple Multiple Classifier System Based on CIDIM

We have divided this section in two parts. Firstly, we briefly present the CIDIM algorithm in Subsection 2.1. Then, we describe a simple multiple classifier system that uses CIDIM as the basic classifier in Subsection 2.2.

2.1   CIDIM

CIDIM (Control of Induction by sample DIvision Methods) [11] was developed to induce accurate and small decision trees. It divides the training set into two subsets and uses them to define an internal bound condition for expansion. Let us comment these characteristics with more detail:

- The top down induction of decision trees (TDIDT) algorithms [2,3], generally, divides the set of examples into two subsets: the training subset (used to induce the tree) and the test subset (used to test the results). CIDIM makes an additional division. It divides the training subset into two new subsets with the same class distribution and similar size: the construction subset (called CNS) and the control subset (called CLS). Every node has its corresponding CNS and CLS subsets. When an expansion is made, CNS and CLS subsets of the parent node are divided into multiple CNS and CLS subsets, each one corresponding to the appropriate child node. Thus, the size of CNS and CLS decreases as the node is deeper in the tree. CNS and CLS are used in the expansion process.
- Usually, the expansion of the tree finishes when all examples associated with a node belong to the same class, yielding too large trees. In order to avoid this overfitting, external conditions are considered by different algorithms (C5, an updated version of C4.5, demands that at least two branches have

at least a pre-configurable number of examples). CIDIM uses the following as an internal condition: a node is expanded only if its expansion improves the accuracy calculated on CLS. Tree expansion supervision is local for every node and it is driven by two indexes: the absolute index I_A and the relative index I_R (see equations (1)). For every step, a node is expanded only if one or both indexes are increased. If one index decrease, expansion is not made. The absolute and relative indexes are defined as

$$I_A = \frac{\sum_{i=1}^{N} CORRECT(e_i)}{N} \quad \text{and} \quad I_R = \frac{\sum_{i=1}^{N} P_{C(e_i)}(e_i)}{N} . \tag{1}$$

where N is the number of examples in CLS, e a single example, $C(e)$ the class of the e example, $P_m(e)$ the probability of m class for the e example, and $CORRECT(e) = 1$ if $P_{C(e_i)} = max\{P_1(e), P_2(e), ..., P_k(e)\}$ or 0 otherwise.

A description of CIDIM can be seen in Figure 1.

---

1. CNS (*ConstructioN Subset*) and CLS (*ControL Subset*) are obtained by a random division of the set of examples used to induce the tree
2. **for** each non-leaf node **do**:
   2.1. Select the best splitting (considering a given disorder measure)
   2.2. **if** splitting does not improve prediction
        then Label node as a leaf-node
   2.3. **if** splitting improves prediction
        then Expand node

Fig. 1. CIDIM algorithm

Decision trees generated by CIDIM are usually smaller than those obtained with other TDIDT algorithms. This allows the induction of more general trees, more understandable for human experts. At the same time, accuracy of the induced trees keeps similar to decision trees induced by other TDIDT algorithms.

CIDIM can be applied to any problem with a finite number of attributes. These attributes must be nominal and can be ordered or not. If the problem has continuous attributes, they can be discretized, resulting ordered nominal attributes. The class attribute must have a finite number of unordered classes.

These advantages have been used to solve real problems, such as system modelling [12] or modelling of prognosis of breast cancer relapse [13].

2.2 Simple Multiple Classifier

Improving the generalization of classifiers is an aim of Machine Learning. Voting methods tries to achieve this improvement. Many algorithms have been developed [14,15,16,6] and numerous studies have been made about them [17,18,19].

We can divide these algorithms into two categories: those that change the dataset distribution depending on the previous steps of the algorithm and those that do not change the cited distribution.

Algorithms in the first group are usually called *boosting algorithms* [14,15,16]. Breiman uses a least known term: Arcing (Adaptively Resample and Combine) [20]. Some algorithms in this group are AdaBoost (Adaptive Boosting) [16] also known as AdaBoost.M1, and Arc-x4 [16].

The second group is usually called *bagging algorithms* (Bootstrap Aggregating) [6], although Breiman sets it into a larger family *P&C* (Perturb and Combine). One variant of bagging is wagging (Weight aggregation) [18] that makes a random variation of weights instead of a simple resampling perturbation.

Our simple multiple classifier system is based on the bagging scheme. It uses CIDIM as the basic classifier, and it induces a pre-configured number of decision trees to make the ensemble. CIDIM – as a the algorithm that makes a random division of the training set into two subsets (CNS and CLS) – suits very well with the bagging scheme. Our multiple classifier uses uniform voting to predict.

3   ML-CIDIM

Once we have described the multiple classifier system that it is used by ML-CIDIM, we explain in this section how it tries to improve the performance of the multiple classifier system.

Layered learning is a machine learning paradigm defined as a set of principles for construction of a hierarchical, learned solution to a complex task [21]. The key principles of layered learning (also known as many-layered learning [22]) are: breaking a problem down into several layers following a bottom-up strategy; and learning each of them separately, but using contents of one layer in a next one.

Systems that use layered learning usually have different layers to model different tasks, and they are applied in the context of robots and agents [23,24,25]. We are interested in only one task: classification; and the layered learning is used to produce successive refinements of multiple classifier systems.

ML-CIDIM is composed of a number (l) of multiple layers (*Layers*). Each of them consists of a multiple classifier system based on CIDIM. For the construction of the first layer, examples in the training set are used to induce a multiple classifier. Then, while constructing the second layer, every example in the training set is modified incorporating new induced attributes. These new attributes describe the classification given by every CIDIM tree in the first layer. Once we have the training set with the modified examples, ML-CIDIM induces the multiple classifier system based on CIDIM for the second layer. This process is iterative and it continues until no improvement is possible (it can be improved if the last layer misclassifies examples and there are discrepancies in the voting produced by the multiple classifier system) or until a pre-configured number of layers (*Maximum_number_of_layers*) are induced. Thus, every layer is built using the examples in the training set plus the classification information contained in the previous layers. A description of ML-CIDIM can be seen in the Figure 2.

1. *Layers* it is initialized with the first multiple classifier system based on CIDIM
2. $l = 1$
3. **while** (*Layers* can be improved) and
   ($l < Maximum\_number\_of\_layers$) **do**:
   3.1.   A new multiple classifier system based on CIDIM is built using
           new examples. These examples incorporate information of
           the classification made in the last layer (new induced attributes)
   3.2.   Add the new multiple classifier system based on CIDIM into *Layers*
   3.3. $l = l + 1$

Fig. 2. ML-CIDIM algorithm

Although we have used ML-CIDIM to improve the performance of a multiple classifier system based on CIDIM, the basic idea can be used to improve any other multiple classifier system based on other classifiers.

The prediction process used in ML-CIDIM is very simple. The prediction given for an example is the prediction given by the first layer in which there is no discrepancy about the classification. If all layers disagree, the prediction given is the one of the last layer.

4   Experimental Results

The experiments we have done and the results we have obtained are now exposed. Before we go on to deal with particular experiments, let us explain some issues:

– The five datasets we have used are summarised in Table 1 that shows the number of examples, the number of attributes, and the number of values for the class. All these datasets have been taken from the *UCI Machine Learning Repository* [26] and are available online. All the datasets used have a common feature: all variables are nominal variables. We have used these because CIDIM is designed for dealing with these kinds of variables. Discretizing real variables to nominal variables is a way for using any dataset, but we have opted to use the datasets exactly as they are.

– ML-CIDIM has been compared with other well-known methods: bagging [6], boosting [7] and a rough set based method [27]. For the experiments, we have used the implementation of bagging and boosting implemented in Weka [28]. These two algorithms have been executed using J48 (implementation of C4.5 in Weka) as the their basic classifier. We have configured bagging and boosting with 10 iterations (default configuration). Considering this, ML-CIDIM has been configured to induce multiple classifier systems with 10 trees. Rose2 [29,30] has been the implementation that we have selected to do the experiments with a rough set based method and it has been configured with the default configuration.

– For every experiment, the presented values for accuracy have been obtained from a 10 x 10 fold cross-validation. Average and standard deviation values are given. To compare results, a statistical test must be made [31]. A t-test

Table 1. Summary table for the datasets used in experiments

Name	UCI Repository Name	Examples	Variables	Classes
Cancer	Breast Cancer	286	9	2
Car	Car Evaluation	1728	6	4
KR-vs-KP	Chess (king-rook-vs-king-pawn)	3196	36	2
Mushroom	Mushroom	8124	22	2
Nursery	Nursery	12960	8	5

Table 2. Comparison between bagging, boosting, rough set based method (Rose2) and ML-CIDIM. Average values and standard deviations are given for accuracy. Significance tests are with respect to ML-CIDIM with two layers (ML-CIDIM-2).

	Cancer	Car	KR-vs-KP	Mushroom	Nursery
BAGGING	**72.98** ± 1.06 ⊕	93.27 ± 0.48 ⊙	99.38 ± 0.08 ⊙	100.00 ± 0.00 ⊙	97.33 ± 0.06 ⊖
BOOSTING	66.73 ± 1.97 ⊖	**95.83** ± 0.26 ⊕	**99.62** ± 0.07 ⊕	100.00 ± 0.00 ⊙	**99.53** ± 0.06 ⊕
ROSE2	68.90 ± 1.03 ⊖	94.33 ± 0.34 ⊕	99.51 ± 0.11 ⊙	100.00 ± 0.00 ⊙	98.75 ± 0.09 ⊕
ML-CIDIM-1	69.96 ± 0.49 ⊙	89.56 ± 0.89 ⊖	98.76 ± 0.47 ⊖	99.998 ± 0.01 ⊙	97.52 ± 0.11 ⊖
ML-CIDIM-2	70.01 ± 1.14	93.40 ± 0.33	99.41 ± 0.08	100.00 ± 0.00	98.38 ± 0.11
ML-CIDIM-3	70.05 ± 0.89 ⊙	94.50 ± 0.31 ⊕	99.46 ± 0.10 ⊙	100.00 ± 0.00 ⊙	98.64 ± 0.12 ⊕
ML-CIDIM-4	69.40 ± 2.62 ⊙	94.81 ± 0.28 ⊕	99.50 ± 0.10 ⊕	100.00 ± 0.00 ⊙	98.78 ± 0.13 ⊕
ML-CIDIM-5	69.36 ± 2.48 ⊙	95.04 ± 0.32 ⊕	99.53 ± 0.09 ⊕	100.00 ± 0.00 ⊙	98.79 ± 0.14 ⊕

has been conducted using the results of the cited 10 x 10 fold cross-validation. The t-test values have been calculated using the statistical package R [32]. A difference is considered as significant if the significance level of the t-test is better than 0.05. We have selected the results obtained by ML-CIDIM with two layers as the reference value. Thus, in Table 2, ⊕ indicates that the accuracy is significantly better than the accuracy of ML-CIDIM with two layers. ⊖ signifies that the accuracy is significantly worse than the accuracy of ML-CIDIM with two layers and ⊙ signifies that there is no significant difference. In addition to this comparisons, the best result for each experiment has been emphasized using numbers in boldface.

Once we have established the datasets and the configuration used for each algorithm we can continue talking about the experiments. Having obtained the results shown in Table 2, we can reach some conclusions:

 – Accuracy reached with ML-CIDIM is comparable with accuracy reached by bagging and boosting. Neither of them (bagging or boosting) is always better than ML-CIDIM. In none dataset, ML-CIDIM gets the worst accuracy, and its results are always between the results achieved by bagging and boosting (when ML-CIDIM uses two or more layers). Results of rough set based method is usually better than the results of ML-CIDIM with one layer, but, when ML-CIDIM uses more layers, the results change and ML-CIDIM finishes getting more accurate results than rough set based method.

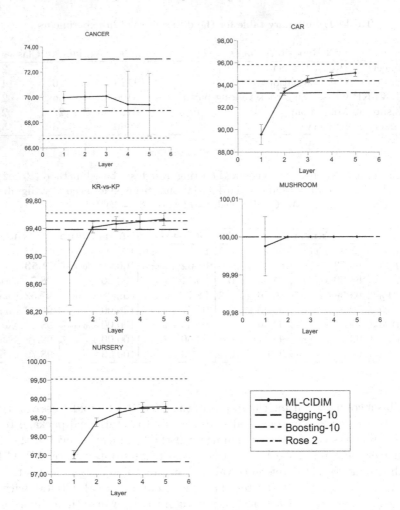

Fig. 3. Accuracy of bagging, boosting and ML-CIDIM with different number of layers

- In almost every dataset, ML-CIDIM performs better when the number of layers is increased. When it has only one layer, it can be worse than bagging and boosting at the same time (car, kr-vs-kp or mushroom for example), but, when we increase the number of layers, the accuracy gets better and it approximates to the best accuracy achieved by bagging or boosting. Thus, we can see that ML-CIDIM improves the performance of an isolated multiple classifier system. It combines some of these multiple classifiers in different layers and add information to the process (new induced attributes).
- When there is no possible improvement, none layer is added. In mushroom dataset, ML-CIDIM induces a maximum of two layers, although we have configured a maximum of five. When ML-CIDIM classifies all the examples correctly, no more layers are needed.

5   Conclusions

This paper introduces ML-CIDIM, a method that improves the performance of a multiple classifier system that uses CIDIM as its basic classifier. As we have seen in experimental section, the performance of ML-CIDIM is stable for every experiment that we have done: ML-CIDIM never gets the worst accuracy and, although it never gets the best one, it usually approximates it to the most accurate results by adding new layers. The algorithm we present uses CIDIM because this classifier induces accurate and small decision trees, what can lead to simpler multiple classifier systems.

The method we propose in this paper to improve multiple classifier systems based in CIDIM can also be extended to any other system. Thus, one of our future lines of research is the study of the improvement that can be achieved by using this method in other multiple classifier systems. Our aim of improving ML-CIDIM involves two issues:

- We are working to improve our algorithm CIDIM providing it the ability of working with continuous attributes. In this way, we will not have to discretize real variables to ordered nominal variables and an automatic execution of CIDIM (or ML-CIDIM) will be possible.
- We are also working to automatically detect the best number of layers to induce. Thus, it would not be necessary to configure the number of layers. The method would induce layers as they are needed.

References

1. Breiman, L., Friedman, J.H., Olshen, R.A., Stone, C.J.: Classification and Regression Trees. Wadsworth (1984)
2. Quinlan, J.R.: Induction of decision trees. Machine Learning **1** (1986) 81– 106
3. Quinlan, J.R.: C4.5: Programs for Machine Learning. Morgan Kaufmann (1993)
4. Utgoff, P.E., Berkman, N.C., Clouse, J.A.: Decision tree induction based on efficient tree restructuring. Machine Learning **29** (1997) 5– 44
5. Domingos, P., Hulten, G.: Mining high-speed data streams. In: Proc. of the 6th Intern. Conf. on Knowledge Discovery and Data Mining, ACM Press (2000) 71–80
6. Breiman, L.: Bagging predictors. Machine Learning **24** (1996) 123–140
7. Freund, Y., Schapire, R.E.: Experiments with a new boosting algorithm. In: Proc. of 13th Intern. Conf. on Machine Learning, Morgan Kauffmann (1996) 146– 148
8. Wolpert, D.: Stacked generalization. Neural Networks **5** (1992) 241–260
9. Gama, J., Brazdil, P.: Cascade generalization. Machine Learning **41** (2000) 315– 343
10. Ferri, C., Flach, P., Hernández-Orallo, J.: Delegating classifiers. In: Proc. of the 21st International Conference on Machine Learning, Omnipress (2004)
11. Ramos-Jiménez, G., Morales-Bueno, R., Villalba-Soria, A.: CIDIM. Control of induction by sample division methods. In: Proc. of the Intern. Conf. on Artificial Intelligence. (2000) 1083–1087
12. Ruiz-Gómez, J., Ramos-Jiménez, G., Villalba-Soria, A.: Modelling based on rule induction learning. In: Computers and Computacional Engineering in Control. World Scientific and Engineering Society Press, Greece (1999) 158–163

13. Jerez-Aragonés, J.M., Gómez-Ruiz, J.A., Ramos-Jiménez, G., Muñoz Pérez, J., Alba-Conejo, E.: A combined neural network and decision trees model for prognosis of breast cancer relapse. Artificial Intelligence in Medicine **27** (2003) 45–63

14. Schapire, R.E.: The strength of weak learnability. Machine Learning **5** (1990) 197–227

15. Freund, Y.: Boosting a weak learning algorithm by majority. Information and Computation **121** (1995) 256–285

16. Freund, Y., Schapire, R.E.: The strength of weak learnability. Journal of Computer and System Sciences **55** (1997) 119–139

17. Aslam, J.A., Decatur, S.E.: General bounds on statistical query learning and PAC learning with noise via hypothesis boosting. Information and Computation **141** (1998) 85–118

18. Bauer, E., Kohavi, R.: An empirical comparison of voting classification algorithms: Bagging, boosting and variants. Machine Learning **36** (1999) 105–139

19. Kearns, M.J., Vazirani, U.V.: On the boosting ability of top-down decision tree learning algorithms. Journal of Computer and System Sciences **58** (1999) 109–128

20. Breiman, L.: Arcing classifiers. Technical report, Berkeley: Statistics Department. University of California (1996)

21. Stone, P.: Layered Learning in Multi-Agent Systems. PhD thesis, School of Computer Science, Carnegie Mellon University, Pittsburgh (1998)

22. Utgoff, P.E., Stracuzzi, D.J.: Many-layered learning. Neural Computation **14** (2002) 2497–2529

23. Stone, P., Veloso, M.: A Layered Approach to Learning Client Behaviors in the RoboCup Soccer Server. Applied Artificial Intelligence **12** (1998) 165–188

24. Takahashi, Y., Asada, M.: Multi-layered learning systems for vision-based behavior acquisition of a real mobile robot. In: Proc. of SICE Annual Conference. (2003) 2937–2942

25. Whiteson, S., Stone, P.: Concurrent layered learning. In: Second International Joint Conference on Autonomous Agents and Multiagent Systems. (2003)

26. Blake, C., Merz, C.J.: UCI repository of machine learning databases. University of California, Department of Information and Computer Science (2000)

27. T. Y. Lin, N. Cercone, eds.: Rough Sets and Data Mining: Analysis of Imprecise Data. Kluwer Academic Publishers, Norwell, MA, USA (1996)

28. Witten, I.H., Frank, E.: Data Mining: Practical machine learning tools with Java implementations. Morgan Kaufmann, San Francisco (2000)

29. Predki, B., Slowinski, R., Stefanowski, J., R. Susmaga, Sz. Wilk: ROSE - Software Implementation of the Rough Set Theory. In: Rough Sets and Current Trends in Computing. LNAI. Volume 1424. Springer-Verlag, Berlin (1998) 605–608.

30. Predki, B., Wilk, S.: Rough Set Based Data Exploration Using ROSE System. In: Foundations of Intelligent Systems. LNAI. Volume 1609. Springer-Verlag, Berlin (1999) 172–180

31. Herrera, F., Hervás, C., Otero, J., Sánchez, L.: Un estudio empírico preliminar sobre los tests estadísticos más habituales en el aprendizaje automático. In: Tendencias de la Minería de Datos en España. (2004)

32. R Development Core Team: R: A language and environment for statistical computing. R Foundation for Statistical Computing, Vienna, Austria. (2004) 3-900051-07-0. http://www.R-project.org.

Constructing Rough Decision Forests

Qing-Hua Hu, Da-Ren Yu, and Ming-Yang Wang

Harbin Institute of Technology, China
huqinghua@hcms.hit.edu.cn

Abstract. Decision forests are a type of classification paradigm which combines a collection of decision trees for a classification task, instead of depending on a single tree. Improvement of accuracy and stability is observed in experiments and applications. Some novel techniques to construct decision forests are proposed based on rough set reduction in this paper. As there are a lot of reducts for some data sets, a series of decision trees can be trained with different reducts. Three methods to select decision trees or reducts are presented, and decisions from selected trees are fused with the plurality voting rule. The experiments show that random selection is the worst solution in the proposed methods. It is also found that input diversity maximization doesn't guarantee output diversity maximization. Hence it cannot guarantee a good classification performance in practice. Genetic algorithm based selective rough decision forests consistently get good classification accuracies compared with a single tree trained by raw data as well as the other two forest constructing methods.

1 Introduction

Overfitting and stability are persistent problems in using tree-based learner or classifier. It's proven to be a promising technique to improve the classification performance by training multiple trees and combining their decisions with a certain decision fusion scheme. This is called a decision forest. A decision forest is a classifier consisting of a collection of tree-structured classifiers and each tree casts a unit vote for the most popular class of the input [4]. Significant improvement in classification accuracy was observed, independent of tree construction algorithms. CART, ID3 and C4.5 were employed to train the component trees. Ho [1,2] proposed that combining multiple trees, which were constructed in randomly selected subspaces, can achieve nearly monotonic improvement in generalization. Breiman presented a series of techniques to produce random forests. Due to the good performance, decision forests are made to wide-range applications. Tong combined multiple independent decision tree models for prediction of binding affinity of 232 chemicals to the estrogen receptor; consistent and significant improvement in both training and testing steps was observed [5]. Hong applied the decision forests to analyze microarray data and got a high accuracy more than 95%. Applications such as handwritten word recognition [6], digital photographs classification [7], and face recognition [8] were reported in papers.

D. Ślęzak et al. (Eds.): RSFDGrC 2005, LNAI 3642, pp. 147–156, 2005.

Roughly speaking, there are two kinds of methods to construct a decision forest for a given pattern recognition task. One is to generate multiple sample subsets from the original samples. The other is to construct trees in distinct feature subspaces. We name the first one as sample subset method (SSM) and the second feature subset method (FSM). As to SSM, the most prevailing techniques are Bagging and Boosting. Bagging randomly produces several training subsets from the original sample set [3] and train multiple trees with the subsets. While boosting generates a sequence of trees, whose training sets are determined by the performance of the former ones, where training samples misclassified will be selected in the next training set with a great probability [9]. AS to FSM, Dietterich proposed a method based on random split selection, where at each node the split is selected at random from among the K best splits [10]. As there are some data sets with very high dimensionality and small size, Ho [1,2] presented a series of random-subspace methods. These techniques randomly generate some distinct subsets of the original feature set and train the classifiers in different subspaces. SSM is applicable to the case there are a lot of samples and FSM works in many-features cases. there exists a similar problem of the two methods, namely, the methods cannot guarantee the diversity between the trained trees. It is well-accepted that the performance of multiple classifier systems (MCS) depends not only on the performance of individual classifiers in the system, but also on the diversities between them. A multiple classifier system with diverse classifiers has a good potential to improve the classification performance compared with the non-diverse ones [16].

As we know, in real-world applications a lot of data is with tens, even hundreds of reducts when a rough-set based reduction is conducted. Each reduct is considered as a minimal representation of the raw decision table without loss of the information in the rough-set view of point. Therefore each reduct can be utilized to train a decision tree. Then a series of decision trees will be built. Wu [18] presented a scheme to make full use of the total reducts without selecting. Here we will propose a selective solution for the reducts. Rough decision forests are a kind of classification systems based on a team of decision trees, where each tree is trained with a rough set based reduct of a decision table, and the decisions from the trees are combined with plurality voting or majority voting. In essence, rough decision forests are a kind of multiple classifier system based on feature subset method. Compared with random forests, one advantage of the proposed method is that training trees with reducts can guarantee good performance of all of the trees, for reducts are the minimal presentations of data without information loss.

As Zhou [13] pointed out that selectively ensembling some of the trained classifiers will lead to a good performance, instead of ensembling all of the classifiers. Especially when there are a lot of classifiers at hand, combining some of them will get a perfect performance compared with combing all of the classifiers. Experiments show that selective ensemble not only reduces the size of classification systems, but also gets higher accuracies with neural network and decision tree based classifiers. Here we will present three solutions to building rough decision forests with a philosophy that selective ensemble of some trained trees is better than the ensemble of all trees. Some numeric experiments will show the properties of the techniques. The rest of the paper is organized as follows. Section 2 will show three techniques to building a rough decision forest. Experiments will be presented in section 3. Conclusions and future work are given in section 4.

2   Three Techniques to Construct Rough Decision Forests

There are four main procedures in constructing a selective rough decision forest: reduction, training decision trees, selecting trees and combining the selected trees. Dimensionality reduction based on rough set theory is a mature technique. Several greedy reduction algorithms were proposed to search a minimal reduct or a reduct set.An extensive review about rough set based reduction and feature selection was given in [12,17]. There are several algorithms to train a decision tree. CART, ID3, C4.5, See5.0 etc perform well in different applications. Here we use CART to train decision trees. As to decision fusion, plurality voting is employed. In this paper we will focus on the techniques to select classifiers. Three methods will be presented in this section: random selection, input diversity maximization and genetic algorithm.

2.1   Random Rough Decision Forests

Ho [2] constructed decision forests in randomly selected subspaces. This technique produces diversity between classifiers by training trees with different feature vectors. As there is an exponent combination of attributes, a great number of decision trees trained in different subspaces can be built. However, how can the accuracy of an individual be guaranteed? Obviously, the performance of a decision forest depends on the individuals as well as the diversity between the trees.

Reducts of a decision table are the attribute subsets which have the same discernibility as the whole attribute set. Theoretically, this property guarantees that all of the reducts have sufficient information to build satisfactory classifiers. Although good performance of the individuals is not a sufficient condition for constructing a good decision forest, combining good individuals has more chances to build a good ensemble system. Reduction presents a feasible solution to producing multiple feature subsets.

As there are hundreds of reducts for some data sets, it is unnecessary, sometimes impossible, to train trees with all of the reducts and combine them. Random Rough Decision Forests are a kind of multiple classifier system, in which decision trees are trained by part of rough set based reducts randomly selected from the whole reducts. Compared with existing random forests, random rough decision forests are trained with rough set based reducts.

2.2   Rough Decision Forests with Input Diversity Maximization

Improvement of classification performance brought by a multiple classifier system will be contributed to the diversity among the individuals in the system [16].

The diversity makes them complement and leads to good generalization. It's observed that great diversity between individuals will make great improvement in ensemble systems. Therefore, it is vital to build decision trees with great diversity and little correlate for a successful decision forest. Bagging and boosting belong to one kind of methods to produce diversity based on different training samples. At another angle, we can make diversity among individual trees by using different training attributes. Diversity in attribute sets will lead to diversity in tree structures and then lead to diversity in decision. So finding a group of reducts with great diversity in feature set may get improvement of classification performance.

To get a great diversity in decision trees by input space diversity maximization, a clustering algorithm is designed. The reducts with similar attribute subsets are grouped into a cluster, and then some delegates of the cluster are chosen from distinct clusters.

The similarity of reducts A and B is defined as

$$SIM(A, B) = \frac{|A \cap B|}{|A| + |B| - |A \cap B|}. \tag{1}$$

where $| \bullet |$ denotes the number of elements in the set. The demonstration is shown as figure 1. The metric of similarity has the following properties:

1) $\forall A, B, SIM(A, B) \in [0, 1]$;
2) $Reflexivity : \forall A, SIM(A, A) = 1$;
3) $Symmetry : \forall A, B, SIM(A, B) = SIM(B, A)$.

Assumed there are n reducts for a given data set, computing similarity between each reduct pair, a fuzzy similar relation matrix is produced:$M = (s_{ij})_{nn}$.Here s_{ij} denotes the similarity of reducts i and j, and we have $s_{ii} = 1$ and $s_{ij} = s_{ji}$.A fuzzy equivalence relation will produce when a max-min transitivity closure operation is performed on a fuzzy similarity relation. Performing a-cuts, we will get a series of partitions of the reduct sets. Reducts from different clusters have great diversity, so input space diversity maximization can be reached by selecting reducts from different branches of the clustering tree.

2.3   Genetic Algorithm Based Rough Decision Forests

Searching the optimal ensemble of multiple classifier systems, here decision forests, is a combinational optimization problem. Genetic algorithms make a good performance in this kind of problems. The performance of decision forests not only depends on power of individuals, but also is influenced by the independence between classifiers. The idea of genetic algorithms is to survive the excellent individuals with a great probability during evolution. Some excellent population will be produced after a number of inheritance, crossover and mutation.

GA rough decision forest is a selective decision tree ensemble, where individual trees are trained by a rough set based reduction, and only parts of trained trees are included in the ensemble system with a genetic algorithm based selection.

Simple genetic algorithms can be defined as an 8-tuple:

$$SGA = (C, E, P_0, M, \Phi, \Gamma, \Psi, T)$$

where C is the coding method for individual, E is the evaluating function for a gene, P_0 is the initiation population; M is the size of population; Φ is the selecting operator, Γ is crossover operator, Ψ is mutation operator and T is the terminating condition.

In this application, the binary coding is used, namely, the classifier selected is labeled with 1, otherwise 0. And the accuracy of ensemble system on validation set is taken as the fitness function, $M = 20$. The number of maximal generation is 100. The program stops when the maximal generation reaches or improvement is less than a predefined little number. Computation of finding optimal decision forests with genetic algorithm is not time-consuming in practices.

GA based rough decision forest

Input: decision table T, reducer R, learner L
Output: ensemble C
1. reduce decision table T with R, and get N reducts
2. train N classifiers with N reducts based on learner L
3. initialize genetic algorithm (GA), generate a population of bit strings
4. evolve the population with GA, and the fitness is the accuracy of the forest
5. output the best individuals and ensemble C

It requires less than 20 generations when there are 20 decision trees to be selected.

3   Experiments

Some experiments were conducted to test and compare the proposed methods. The data sets used are from UCI databases (www. Ics.uci.edu / ~ mlearn / ML-Summary.html). The description of data is shown in table 1. There are numeric attributes in some data sets. To discretize the numeric features, a clustering operations based on FCM are conducted on each numeric attribute, and the numeric attributes are divided into three intervals. Some forest construction methods are compared. All the trees are trained with CART algorithm and two thirds samples in each class are selected as training set, the rest are test set.

The numbers of attributes of the selected data sets vary from 13 to 35, and the numbers of reducts range between 24 and 229 in table 1, which show that there are a great number of reducts for some data sets in practice. If we just make use of one of the reducts, much useful information hidden in other reducts will do no favor for the classification task. Multiple classifier system will improve classification by combining a series of classifiers.

Here, for simplicity, 20 reducts are randomly extracted from the reduct sets of all data sets at first, respectively. Subsequent experiments are conducted on

Table 1. Data set and their numbers of reducts

Data Name	Abbreviation	Size	Attributes	reducts
Dermatology Database	Der.	366	34	44
Heart Disease Databases	Heart	270	14	24
Ionosphere database	Ionos	351	35	194
Wisconsin Diagnostic Breast Cancer	WDBC	569	32	211
Wine recognition data	Wine	168	13	135
Wisconsin Prognostic Breast Cancer	WPBC	198	34	229

Table 2. Randomly select five reducts for ensemble

	Base1	Base2	Base3	Base4	Base5	Ensemble
Der	0.88793	0.75862	0.7931	0.65517	0.66379	0.8448
Heart	0.84286	0.82857	0.85714	0.74286	0.8	0.8286
Ionos	0.84158	0.9802	0.9604	0.83168	0.90099	0.9604
WDBC	0.91716	0.90533	0.95858	0.89941	0.91716	0.9290
Wine	0.70833	0.75	0.72917	0.70833	0.72917	0.8958
WPBC	0.61765	0.55882	0.58824	0.55882	0.44118	0.5882

the extracted 20 reducts. The first method is randomly to choose some of the reducts and train trees with them. In my experiments, five reducts are included in ensemble systems. The accuracy of individuals and the forests are shown in table 2.

Compared the decision forests with their individuals; it is easy to find that there is not significantly improvement at angle of classification accuracy except data wine. We can conclude that a fine decision forest should be elaborately constructed. Roughly combining some classifiers will even produce performance decrease. Therefore, it is important to select a number of appropriate classifiers to build an effective decision forest.

Table 3 shows the classification accuracy of decision forests with input space diversity maximization. Three, five or seven reducts are selected from the clustering trees, respectively.

Size and accuracy of three kinds of rough decision forests are shown in table 4. The first one is size and accuracy of ensemble system combining all decision trees at hand. The second are with genetic algorithms and the third are with n top classifiers, n is the corresponding size of GAS decision forests.

We can get that GA rough decision forests make a good performance not only compared with the forests combining all trees, but also with the forests combining the several best classifiers. Moreover, consistent improvement is observed for each data set.

Accuracy of individual classifiers and the selected classifiers are showed as figures 2,3,4. We find that genetic algorithms don't choose all of the classifiers with best performance. While some bad decision trees are included in the forests,

Table 3. Select reducts with input diversity maximization

	Base1	Base2	Base3	Base4	Base5	Base6	Base7	Ensemble
Der	0.7155	0.8017	0.7155	0.6207	0.8966	-	-	0.8362
Heart	0.8429	0.7714	0.8571	0.8429	0.8143	0.7857	0.8286	0.8571
Ionos	0.8317	0.8614	0.9406	0.9208	0.9901	-	-	0.9307
WDBC	0.8935	0.8935	0.9053	-	-	-	-	0.9349
Wine	0.7917	0.8125	0.8542	-	-	-	-	0.9583
WPBC	0.5588	0.5294	0.6765	0.5441	0.5588	0.6765	0.6176	0.6324

Table 4. Comparison of decision forests

	All		GAS		Top	
	size	accuracy	size	accuracy	size	accuracy
Der	20	0.9052	10	0.9310	10	0.91379
Heart	20	0.8429	6	0.8857	6	0.85714
Ionos	20	0.9406	8	0.9901	8	0.94059
WDBC	20	0.9349	7	0.9704	7	0.94675
Wine	20	0.7292	7	1	7	0.97917
WPBC	20	0.5882	9	0.75	9	0.70588
Aver.	20	0.8235	7.8333	0.9212	7.8333	0.8906

Table 5. Comparison of classification accuracy based on different methods

	Original	Min-reduct	Forest 1	Forest 2	Forest 3	All-reducts	GAS
Der	0.9483	0.7155	0.8448	0.8362	0.91379	0.9052	0.9310
Heart	0.8429	0.7429	0.8286	0.8571	0.85714	0.8429	0.8857
Ionos	0.8119	0.8317	0.9604	0.9307	0.94059	0.9406	0.9901
WDBC	0.8757	0.8757	0.9290	0.9349	0.94675	0.9349	0.9704
Wine	0.7083	0.7083	0.8958	0.9583	0.97917	0.7292	1.0000
WPBC	0.5735	0.5147	0.5882	0.6324	0.70588	0.5882	0.7500
Aver.	0.7934	0.7315	0.8411	0.8583	0.8906	0.8235	0.9212

which shows the performance of individuals can not guarantee the performance of decision forests.

The comparison of all classification accuracy is shown in table 5. Original denotes classification accuracy with a single decision tree trained by the original data set. Min-reduct denotes the results with a single tree trained by the minimal reduct. Decision forest with random reduct selection is labeled as forest 1; decision forest with input space diversity maximization is labeled as forest 2, decision forests with some top classifiers is labeled as forest 3 and forests with GA selective ensemble is labeled as GAS. All-reducts denotes the performance of

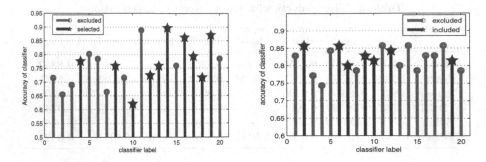

Fig. 1. Left: Der data set; ten trees are included in the decision forest. Right: Heart data set; seven trees are included in the decision forest.

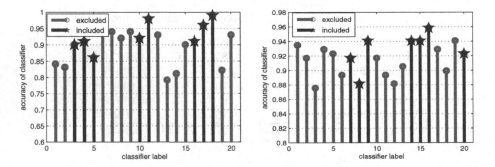

Fig. 2. Left: Ionos data set; 8 decision trees are included in the decisionforest. Right: WDBC data set; 7 decision trees are included in the decision forest.

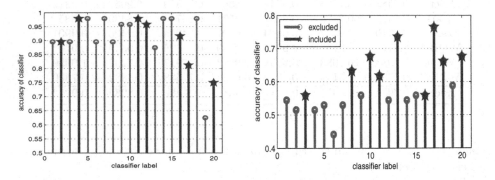

Fig. 3. Left: Wine data set; 7 decision trees are in included in the decision forest. Right: WPBC data set; 9 decision trees are included in the forest.

the decision forests combining all decision trees. We can find the decision trees trained with minimal reducts make a worst performance as for all of data sets. The best classification paradigm is GA rough decision forest, which get nearly 20% improvements relative to the minimal reducts. The second is decision forests constructed with the best decision trees, which means that the performance of individuals has great influence on the forests, but is not a sufficient condition. The average accuracy of the forests made up of all trees is worse than that of other ensemble, which shows selective ensemble is a good solution for MCS.

4   Conclusion and Future Work

Some techniques to construct rough decision forests are proposed in this paper. On one hand, as a generalization of random forests, rough decision forests can guarantee the performance of individual trees; on the other hand, rough decision forests can make full use of the output of reduction algorithms. Multiple trees are trained with different reducts and a decision forest is constructed by combining some of the trained trees. Three methods are proposed to construct a selective rough decision forest. Random selection, input space diversity maximization and genetic algorithms are tried and compared. The experimental results show that the selective decision forests are better than the decision forests combining all classifiers. GA rough decision forests get the best performance relative to the other forests.

Although good performance is produced in the experiments, the explanation of GA rough decision forests as good multiple classification systems is not clear. There are several diversity measures to analyze the properties of multiple classifier systems. We will cover a way to understand the behaviors of rough decision forests and try to propose a method for getting a consistent improvement.

References

1. Ho T. K.: Random decision forests. 3rd international conference of document analysis and recognition. 278–282
2. Ho T. K.: The random subspace method for constructing decision forests. IEEE Transactions on pattern analysis ans machine intelligence. **20** (1998) 832–844
3. Breiman L.: Bagging predictors. Machine Learning. **26** (1996) 123–140
4. Breiman L.: Random forests. Machine learning. **45** (2001) 5-32
5. Tong W., Hong H., Fang H., Xie Q., Perkins R.: Decision forest: combining the predictions of multiple independent decision tree models. Journal of chemical information ans computer sciences. **43** (2003) 525-531
6. Gunter S., Bunke H.: Handwritten word recognition using classifier ensembles generated from multiple prototypes. International journal of pattern recognition and artificial intelligence. **18** (2004) 957-974
7. Schettini R.: Automatic classification of digital photographs based on decision forests. International journal of pattern recognition and artificial intelligence. **18** (2004) 819-845

8. Cheng J., Liu Q., Lu H., et al.: Random independent subspace for face recognition. Lecture notes in computer science. **3214** (2004) 352-358
9. Freund Y., Schapire R. E.: a decision-theoretic generalization of on -line learning and application to boosting. the 2nd European conference on computational learning theory. (1995) 23-37
10. Dietterich T.: An experimental comparison of three methods for constructing ensembles of decision trees: Bagging, boosting and randomization. Machine Learning. (1998) 1-22
11. Gunter S., Bunke H.: Feature selection algorithms for the generation of multiple classifier systems and their application to handwritten word recognition. Pattern recognition letters. **25** (2004) 1323-1336
12. Swiniarski R., Skowron A.: Rough set methods in feature selection and recognition. Pattern recognition letters. **24** (2003) 833-849
13. Zhou Z., Wu J., Tang W.: Ensembling neural networks: Many could be better than all. Artificial intelligence. **137** (2002) 239-263
14. Hu Q., Yu D., Bao W.: Combining multiple neural networks for classification based on rough set reduction. Proceedings of the 2003 International Conference on Neural Networks and Signal processing. **1** (2003) 543 - 548
15. Hu Q., Yu D.: Entropies of fuzzy indiscernibility relation and its operations. International Journal of uncertainty, fuzziness and knowledge based systems. **12** (2004) 575-589
16. Kittler J., Hatef M., Duin R., et al.: On combining classifiers. IEEE Transactions on pattern analysis ans machine intelligence. **20** (1998) 226-239
17. Wang J., Miao D.: Analysis on attribute reduction strategies of rough set. Journal of computer science and technology. **13** (1998) 189-193
18. Wu Q., Bell D., Mcginnity M.: Multiknowledge for decision making. Knowledge and information systems. **7** (2005) 246-266

Attribute Reduction in Concept Lattice Based on Discernibility Matrix

Wen-Xiu Zhang[1], Ling Wei[1,2], and Jian-Jun Qi[3]

[1] Faculty of Science, Institute for Information and System Sciences,
Xi'an Jiaotong University, Xi'an 710049, P.R. China
wxzhang@mail.xjtu.edu.cn
[2] Department of Mathematics, Northwest University,
Xi'an 710069, P.R. China
qjjwv@nwu.edu.cn
[3] Institute of Computer Architecture & Network, Xi'an Jiaotong University,
Xi'an 710049, P.R. China
qjjwv@21cn.com

Abstract. As an effective tool for knowledge discovery, concept lattice has been successfully applied to various fields. One of the key problems of knowledge discovery is knowledge reduction. This paper studies attribute reduction in concept lattice. Using the idea similar to Skowron and Rauszer's discernibility matrix, the discernibility matrix and function of a concept lattice are defined. Based on discernibility matrix, an approach to attribute reduction in concept lattice is presented, and the characteristics of core attribute are analyzed.

1 Introduction

Concept lattice stems from the so-called formal concept analysis proposed by Wille in 1982 [1]. A concept lattice is an ordered hierarchical structure of formal concepts that are defined by a binary relation between a set of objects and a set of attributes. Each formal concept is an (objects, attributes) pair, which consists of two parts: the extension (objects covered by the concept) and intension (attributes describing the concept). As an effective tool for data analysis and knowledge processing, concept lattice has been applied to various fields, such as data mining, information retrieval, software engineering, and so on.

Most of the researches on concept lattice focus on such topics as [2]: construction of concept lattice [3,4,5], pruning of concept lattice [6], acquisition of rules [4,5], relationship with rough set [7,8,9,10,11], and applications [6,12]. Although rough set theory [13] and formal context analysis are different theories, they have much in common, in terms of both goals and methodologies. In this paper, we study attribute reduction in concept lattice. The attribute reduction in concept lattice is to find the minimal sets of attributes, which can determine a concept lattice isomorphic to the one determined by all attributes while the object set remains unchanged. It makes the discovery of implicit knowledge in data easier and the representation simpler, and extends the theory of concept lattice.

D. Ślęzak et al. (Eds.): RSFDGrC 2005, LNAI 3642, pp. 157–165, 2005.

The paper is organized as follows. Section 2 recalls basic definitions in formal concept analysis. Section 3 gives the definitions and properties about attribute reduction in concept lattice. Section 4 introduces the discernibility matrix and function of concept lattice, and then discusses the approach to reduction as well as the characteristics of core attribute. Finally, Section 5 concludes the paper.

2   Basic Definitions of Formal Concept Analysis

To make the paper self-contained, we introduce the basic notions of formal concept analysis [14].

Definition 1. *A triple (U, A, I) is called a formal context, if U and A are sets and $I \subseteq U \times A$ is a binary relation between U and A. $U = \{x_1, \ldots, x_n\}$, each $x_i(i \leq n)$ is called an object. $A = \{a_1, \ldots, a_m\}$, each $a_j(j \leq m)$ is called an attribute.*

In a formal context (U, A, I), if $(x, a) \in I$, also written as xIa, we say that the object x has the attribute a, or that a is possessed by x. In this paper, $(x, a) \in I$ is denoted by 1, and $(x, a) \notin I$ is denoted by 0. Thus, a formal context can be represented by a table only with 0 and 1.

With respect to a formal context (U, A, I), a pair of dual operators are defined by: for $X \subseteq U$ and $B \subseteq A$,

$$X^* = \{a \in A | (x, a) \in I \text{ for all } x \in X\}, \tag{1}$$

$$B^* = \{x \in U | (x, a) \in I \text{ for all } a \in B\}. \tag{2}$$

X^* is the set of all the attributes shared by all the objects in X, and B^* is the set of all the objects that possess all the attributes in B. We write $\{x\}^*$ as x^* for $x \in U$, and write $\{a\}^*$ as a^* for $a \in A$.

Definition 2. *Let (U, A, I) be a formal context. A pair (X, B) is called a formal concept, for short, a concept, of (U, A, I), if and only if,*

$$X \subseteq U, \quad B \subseteq A, \quad X^* = B, \quad \text{and} \quad X = B^*.$$

X is called the extension and B is called the intension of the concept (X, B).

The concepts of a formal context (U, A, I) are ordered by

$$(X_1, B_1) \leq (X_2, B_2) \Leftrightarrow X_1 \subseteq X_2 (\Leftrightarrow B_1 \supseteq B_2), \tag{3}$$

where (X_1, B_1) and (X_2, B_2) are concepts. Furthermore, (X_1, B_1) is called a sub-concept of (X_2, B_2), and (X_2, B_2) is called a super-concept of (X_1, B_1). The set of all concepts form a complete lattice called the concept lattice of (U, A, I) and denoted by $L(U, A, I)$. The infimum and supremum are given by:

$$(X_1, B_1) \wedge (X_2, B_2) = (X_1 \cap X_2, (B_1 \cup B_2)^{**}), \tag{4}$$

$$(X_1, B_1) \vee (X_2, B_2) = ((X_1 \cup X_2)^{**}, B_1 \cap B_2). \tag{5}$$

With respect to a formal context (U, A, I), the following properties hold: for all $X_1, X_2, X \subseteq U$ and all $B_1, B_2, B \subseteq A$,

1. $X_1 \subseteq X_2 \Rightarrow X_2^* \subseteq X_1^*, \quad B_1 \subseteq B_2 \Rightarrow B_2^* \subseteq B_1^*.$
2. $X \subseteq X^{**}, \quad B \subseteq B^{**}.$
3. $X^* = X^{***}, \quad B^* = B^{***}.$
4. $X \subseteq B^* \Leftrightarrow B \subseteq X^*.$
5. $(X_1 \cup X_2)^* = X_1^* \cap X_2^*, \quad (B_1 \cup B_2)^* = B_1^* \cap B_2^*.$
6. $(X_1 \cap X_2)^* \supseteq X_1^* \cup X_2^*, \quad (B_1 \cap B_2)^* \supseteq B_1^* \cup B_2^*.$
7. (X^{**}, X^*) and (B^*, B^{**}) are all concepts.

3 Definitions and Properties of Attribute Reduction in Concept Lattice

Definition 3. *Let $L(U, A_1, I_1)$ and $L(U, A_2, I_2)$ be two concept lattices. If for any $(X, B) \in L(U, A_2, I_2)$ there exists $(X', B') \in L(U, A_1, I_1)$ such that $X' = X$, then $L(U, A_1, I_1)$ is said to be finer than $L(U, A_2, I_2)$, denoted by:*

$$L(U, A_1, I_1) \leq L(U, A_2, I_2). \tag{6}$$

If $L(U, A_1, I_1) \leq L(U, A_2, I_2)$ and $L(U, A_2, I_2) \leq L(U, A_1, I_1)$, then these two concept lattices are said to be isomorphic to each other, denoted by:

$$L(U, A_1, I_1) \cong L(U, A_2, I_2). \tag{7}$$

Let (U, A, I) be a formal context. For any $D \subseteq A$ and $I_D = I \cap (U \times D)$, (U, D, I_D) is also a formal context. For any $X \subseteq U$, X^* is represented by X^* in (U, A, I) and by X^{*D} in (U, D, I_D). It is clear that $I_A = I$, $X^{*A} = X^*$, $X^{*D} = X^{*A} \cap D = X^* \cap D$, and $X^{*D} \subseteq X^*$.

Theorem 1. *Let (U, A, I) be a formal context. For any $D \subseteq A$ such that $D \neq \emptyset$, $L(U, A, I) \leq L(U, D, I_D)$ holds.*

Proof. Suppose $(X, B) \in L(U, D, I_D)$. We have $(X^{**}, X^*) \in L(U, A, I)$ by property 7. By property 2, we have $X^{**} \supseteq X$. On the other hand, $X^* \supseteq X^{*D} = B$ implies that $X^{**} \subseteq B^* = X$. It follows that $X^{**} = X$ and $(X, X^*) \in L(U, A, I)$. Thus $L(U, A, I) \leq L(U, D, I_D)$.

Definition 4. *Let (U, A, I) be a formal context. If there exists an attribute set $D \subseteq A$ such that $L(U, D, I_D) \cong L(U, A, I)$, then D is called a consistent set of (U, A, I). And further, if $L(U, D - \{d\}, I_{D-\{d\}}) \not\cong L(U, A, I)$ for all $d \in D$, then D is called a reduct of (U, A, I). The intersection of all the reducts of (U, A, I) is called the core of (U, A, I).*

The following result can be easily verified.

Theorem 2. *Let (U, A, I) be a formal context, $D \subseteq A$ and $D \neq \emptyset$. Then,*

$$D \text{ is a consistent set } \Leftrightarrow L(U, D, I_D) \leq L(U, A, I).$$

Similar to the rough set theory proposed by Pawlak [13], we define three types of attributes in a formal context.

Definition 5. *Let (U, A, I) be a formal context, the set $\{D_i | D_i$ is a reduct, $i \in \tau\}$ (τ is an index set) includes all reducts of (U, A, I). Then A is divided into the following three parts:*

1. *Absolute necessary attribute (core attribute) $b : b \in \bigcap\limits_{i \in \tau} D_i$.*
2. *Relative necessary attribute $c : c \in \bigcup\limits_{i \in \tau} D_i - \bigcap\limits_{i \in \tau} D_i$.*
3. *Absolute unnecessary attribute $d : d \in A - \bigcup\limits_{i \in \tau} D_i$.*

The attribute not in the core is called unnecessary attribute $e : e \in A - \bigcap\limits_{i \in \tau} D_i$, which is either a relative necessary attribute or an absolute unnecessary attribute. Let b be an absolute necessary attribute, c a relative necessary attribute, and d an absolute unnecessary attribute, it is clear that $b^* \neq c^*, c^* \neq d^*, b^* \neq d^*$.

Theorem 3. *The reduct exists for any formal context.*

Proof. Let (U, A, I) be a formal context. If $L(U, A - \{a\}, I_{A-\{a\}}) \ncong L(U, A, I)$ for all $a \in A$, then A itself is a reduct. If there exists an attribute $a \in A$ such that $L(U, A - \{a\}, I_{A-\{a\}}) \cong L(U, A, I)$, then we study $B_1 = A - \{a\}$. Further, if $L(U, B_1 - \{b_1\}, I_{B_1-\{b_1\}}) \ncong L(U, A, I)$ for all $b_1 \in B_1$, then B_1 is a reduct, otherwise we study $B_1 - \{b_1\}$. Repeating the above process, since A is a finite set, we can find at least one reduct of (U, A, I).

Generally speaking, it is possible that a formal context has multiple reducts. Let (U, A, I) be a formal context. Clearly, we have the following results.

Corollary 1. *The core is a reduct $\Leftrightarrow$ there is only one reduct.*

Corollary 2. *$a \in A$ is an unnecessary attribute $\Leftrightarrow A - \{a\}$ is a consistent set.*

Corollary 3. *$a \in A$ is a core attribute $\Leftrightarrow A - \{a\}$ is not a consistent set.*

Example 1. Table 1 shows a formal context (U, A, I), in which,

$$U = \{1, 2, 3, 4\}, \quad A = \{a, b, c, d, e\}.$$

The concept lattice of (U, A, I) is showed in Fig. 1. There are 6 concepts: $(1, abde), (24, abc), (13, d), (124, ab), (U, \emptyset), (\emptyset, A)$, which are labelled as FCi (i=1,2,...,6) respectively. (U, A, I) has two reducts: $D_1 = \{a, c, d\}$ and $D_2 = \{b, c, d\}$. Thus, c, d are absolute necessary attributes, a, b are relative necessary attributes, e is absolute unnecessary attribute, and a, b, e are unnecessary attributes. The concept lattice of (U, D_1, I_{D_1}) is showed in Fig. 2. It is easy to see that the two concept lattices are isomorphic to each other.

Table 1. A formal context (U, A, I)

	a	b	c	d	e
1	1	1	0	1	1
2	1	1	1	0	0
3	0	0	0	1	0
4	1	1	1	0	0

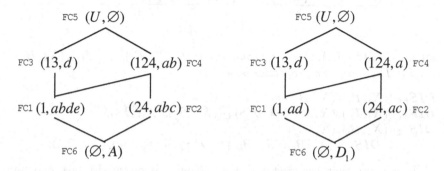

Fig. 1. The concept lattice of (U, A, I) **Fig. 2.** The concept lattice of (U, D_1, I_{D_1})

4   Approach to Attribute Reduction in Concept Lattice

Using an idea similar to Skowron and Rauszer's discernibility matrix [15], this section introduces the discernibility matrix and discernibility function of a concept lattice, gives an approach to attribute reduction, and discusses the characteristics of core attribute.

Definition 6. *Let (U, A, I) be a formal context, (X_i, B_i), $(X_j, B_j) \in L(U, A, I)$. Then*

$$DIS_{FC}((X_i, B_i), (X_j, B_j)) = B_i \cup B_j - B_i \cap B_j \tag{8}$$

is called the discernibility attributes set between (X_i, B_i) and (X_j, B_j), and

$$\Lambda_{FC} = (DIS_{FC}((X_i, B_i), (X_j, B_j)), (X_i, B_i), (X_j, B_j) \in L(U, A, I)) \tag{9}$$

is called the discernibility matrix of the concept lattice $L(U, A, I)$.

In the discernibility matrix Λ_{FC}, only those non-empty elements are useful to reduction. We also denote the set of non-empty elements in the matrix by Λ_{FC}. It is easy to see the meaning of Λ_{FC}. In fact, $DIS_{FC}((X_i, B_i), (X_j, B_j)) \neq \emptyset$ is equivalent to $(X_i, B_i) \neq (X_j, B_j)$.

Example 2. Table 2 gives the discernibility matrix of the concept lattice showed in Fig. 1.

Table 2. The discernibility matrix of the concept lattice in Fig. 1

	$FC1$	$FC2$	$FC3$	$FC4$	$FC5$	$FC6$
$FC1$	$\emptyset$					
$FC2$	$\{c,d,e\}$	$\emptyset$				
$FC3$	$\{a,b,e\}$	$\{a,b,c,d\}$	$\emptyset$			
$FC4$	$\{d,e\}$	$\{c\}$	$\{a,b,d\}$	$\emptyset$		
$FC5$	$\{a,b,d,e\}$	$\{a,b,c\}$	$\{d\}$	$\{a,b\}$	$\emptyset$	
$FC6$	$\{c\}$	$\{d,e\}$	$\{a,b,c,e\}$	$\{c,d,e\}$	A	$\emptyset$

Theorem 4. Let (U, A, I) be a formal context, $(X_i, B_i), (X_j, B_j), (X_k, B_k) \in L(U, A, I)$. The following properties hold:

1. $DIS_{FC}((X_i, B_i), (X_i, B_i)) = \emptyset$.
2. $DIS_{FC}((X_i, B_i), (X_j, B_j)) = DIS_{FC}((X_j, B_j), (X_i, B_i))$.
3. $DIS_{FC}((X_i, B_i), (X_j, B_j))$
   $\subseteq DIS_{FC}((X_i, B_i), (X_k, B_k)) \cup DIS_{FC}((X_k, B_k), (X_j, B_j))$.

Proof. It is clear that the first two hold. Now, we prove the last one. Suppose $a \in DIS_{FC}((X_i, B_i), (X_j, B_j))$. We have $a \in B_i \cup B_j$ and $a \notin B_i \cap B_j$. Without loss of generality, suppose $a \in B_i$ and $a \notin B_j$. If $a \notin B_k$, then $a \in DIS_{FC}((X_i, B_i), (X_k, B_k))$; if $a \in B_k$, then $a \notin DIS_{FC}((X_i, B_i), (X_k, B_k))$, but $a \in DIS_{FC}((X_k, B_k), (X_j, B_j))$. Thus,

$$a \in DIS_{FC}((X_i, B_i), (X_k, B_k)) \cup DIS_{FC}((X_k, B_k), (X_j, B_j)).$$

Theorem 5. Let (U, A, I) be a formal context. For any $D \subseteq A$ such that $D \neq \emptyset$, the following assertions are equivalent:

1. D is a consistent set.
2. For all $(X_i, B_i), (X_j, B_j) \in L(U, A, I)$, if $(X_i, B_i) \neq (X_j, B_j)$, then $B_i \cap D \neq B_j \cap D$.
3. For all $(Y_m, C_m), (Y_n, C_n) \in L(U, A, I)$, if $DIS_{FC}((Y_m, C_m), (Y_n, C_n)) \neq \emptyset$, then $D \cap DIS_{FC}((Y_m, C_m), (Y_n, C_n)) \neq \emptyset$.
4. For all $B \subseteq A$, if $B \cap D = \emptyset$, then $B \notin \Lambda_{FC}$.

Proof. $1 \Rightarrow 2$. Suppose $(X_i, B_i), (X_j, B_j) \in L(U, A, I)$ and $(X_i, B_i) \neq (X_j, B_j)$. Since D is a consistent set, we have $L(U, D, I_D) \leq L(U, A, I)$. There exist $C_i, C_j \subseteq D$ such that $(X_i, C_i), (X_j, C_j) \in L(U, D, I_D)$ and $(X_i, C_i) \neq (X_j, C_j)$. Hence, $C_i = X_i^{*_D} = X_i^* \cap D = B_i \cap D$, $C_j = X_j^{*_D} = X_j^* \cap D = B_j \cap D$ and $C_i \neq C_j$. Thus, $B_i \cap D \neq B_j \cap D$.

$2 \Rightarrow 1$. If for all $(X, B) \in L(U, A, I)$, $(X, B \cap D) \in L(U, D, I_D)$ hold, then $L(U, D, I_D) \leq L(U, A, I)$. Thus, D is a consistent set. We need only to prove that for all $(X, B) \in L(U, A, I)$, $X^{*_D} = B \cap D$ and $(B \cap D)^* = X$ hold. First, we have $X^{*_D} = X^* \cap D = B \cap D$. Second, suppose $(B \cap D)^* \neq X$. Since $((B \cap D)^*, (B \cap D)^{**}) \in L(U, A, I)$, we have $(X, B) \neq ((B \cap D)^*, (B \cap D)^{**})$, which implies that $B \cap D \neq (B \cap D)^{**} \cap D$. On the one hand,

$$B \cap D \subseteq B \Rightarrow (B \cap D)^* \supseteq B^* = X$$
$$\Rightarrow (B \cap D)^{**} \subseteq X^* = B$$
$$\Rightarrow (B \cap D)^{**} \cap D \subseteq B \cap D.$$

On the other hand, $B \cap D \subseteq (B \cap D)^{**} \Rightarrow B \cap D = B \cap D \cap D \subseteq (B \cap D)^{**} \cap D$. Thus, $B \cap D = (B \cap D)^{**} \cap D$, which is a contradiction. So $(B \cap D)^* = X$.

$2 \Rightarrow 3$. For $(Y_m, C_m), (Y_n, C_n) \in L(U, A, I)$, if $DIS_{FC}((Y_m, C_m), (Y_n, C_n)) \neq \emptyset$, then $(Y_m, C_m) \neq (Y_n, C_n)$, which implies that $C_m \cap D \neq C_n \cap D$. We have $C_m \cap D - C_n \cap D = D \cap C_m \cap \overline{C_n} \neq \emptyset$ or $C_n \cap D - C_m \cap D = D \cap C_n \cap \overline{C_m} \neq \emptyset$. Thus,

$$D \cap DIS_{FC}((Y_m, C_m), (Y_n, C_n))$$
$$= D \cap (C_m \cup C_n - C_m \cap C_n)$$
$$= D \cap (C_m \cup C_n) \cap (\overline{C_m \cup C_n})$$
$$= (D \cap C_n \cap \overline{C_m}) \cup (D \cap C_m \cap \overline{C_n}) \neq \emptyset.$$

$3 \Rightarrow 2$. Suppose $(X_i, B_i), (X_j, B_j) \in L(U, A, I)$. If $(X_i, B_i) \neq (X_j, B_j)$, then $DIS_{FC}((X_i, B_i), (X_j, B_j)) \neq \emptyset$, which implies $D \cap DIS_{FC}((X_i, B_i), (X_j, B_j)) \neq \emptyset$. Hence, there exists $a \in D$ such that $a \in DIS_{FC}((X_i, B_i), (X_j, B_j))$, which implies that $a \in B_i \cup B_j$ and $a \notin B_i \cap B_j$. Thus, if $a \in B_i$ and $a \notin B_j$, then $a \in D \cap B_i$ and $a \notin D \cap B_j$; if $a \in B_j$ and $a \notin B_i$, then $a \in D \cap B_j$ and $a \notin D \cap B_i$. It follows that $B_i \cap D \neq B_j \cap D$.

$3 \Leftrightarrow 4$. Obvious.

Theorem 6. *Let (U, A, I) be a formal context, $a \in A$. Then,*
a is a core attribute $\Leftrightarrow$ there exist $(X_i, B_i), (X_j, B_j) \in L(U, A, I)$ such that
$$DIS_{FC}((X_i, B_i), (X_j, B_j)) = \{a\}.$$

Proof. By Corollary 3 and Theorem 5, we have,
    a is a core attribute
$\Leftrightarrow A - \{a\}$ is not a consistent set
$\Leftrightarrow$ there exist $(X_i, B_i), (X_j, B_j) \in L(U, A, I)$ such that
    $DIS_{FC}((X_i, B_i), (X_j, B_j)) \neq \emptyset$ and
    $DIS_{FC}((X_i, B_i), (X_j, B_j)) \cap (A - \{a\}) = \emptyset$
$\Leftrightarrow$ there exist $(X_i, B_i), (X_j, B_j) \in L(U, A, I)$ such that
    $DIS_{FC}((X_i, B_i), (X_j, B_j)) = \{a\}.$

Theorem 5 shows that to find a reduct of a formal context is to find a minimal subset D of attributes such that $D \cap H \neq \emptyset$ for all $H \in \Lambda_{FC}$. Theorem 6 shows that if some $H \in \Lambda_{FC}$ has only one element a then a is a core attribute.

Example 3. We can find the reducts of the formal context in Table 1 based on the discernibility matrix in Table 2. Specifically:

$$\Lambda_{FC} = \{\{c\}, \{d\}, \{a, b\}, \{d, e\}, \{c, d, e\}, \{a, b, e\}, \{a, b, c\}, \{a, b, d\},$$
$$\{a, b, d, e\}, \{a, b, c, d\}, \{a, b, c, e\}, \{a, b, c, d, e\}\}.$$

Consider $D_1 = \{a, c, d\}$. It satisfies $D_1 \cap H \neq \emptyset (\forall H \in \Lambda_{FC})$. In addition, for any set $Z \subsetneq D_1$, there is an element W in Λ_{FC} such that $Z \cap W = \emptyset$. For instance consider $\{a, c\}, \{a, d\}, \{c, d\}$, there exist corresponding elements $\{d\}, \{c\}, \{a, b\}$ in Λ_{FC} such that the intersection is empty, respectively. Thus, D_1 is a reduct.

Consider $D_2 = \{b, c, d\}$. It also satisfies $D_2 \cap H \neq \emptyset (\forall H \in \Lambda_{FC})$. On the other hand, for its subsets $\{b, c\}, \{b, d\}, \{c, d\}$, there exist corresponding elements $\{d\}, \{c\}, \{a, b\}$ in Λ_{FC} such that the intersection is empty, respectively. Hence, D_2 is a reduct.

Definition 7. *Let (U, A, I) be a formal context. The discernibility function of (U, A, I) is defined as:*

$$f(\Lambda_{FC}) = \bigwedge_{H \in \Lambda_{FC}} \left(\bigvee_{h \in H} h \right). \tag{10}$$

By absorption law and distributive law, the discernibility function $f(\Lambda_{FC})$ can be transformed to a minimal disjunctive normal form [15], whose items can form all the reducts of (U, A, I).

Example 4. We continue Example 3 and calculate the discernibility function.
$$
\begin{aligned}
f(\Lambda_{FC}) &= \bigwedge_{H \in \Lambda_{FC}} \left(\bigvee_{h \in H} h \right) \\
&= (d \vee e) \wedge c \wedge (c \vee d \vee e) \wedge (a \vee b \vee c \vee e) \wedge (a \vee b \vee c \vee d \vee e) \\
&\quad \wedge (a \vee b \vee c \vee d) \wedge (a \vee b \vee c) \wedge (a \vee b \vee e) \wedge (a \vee b \vee d \vee e) \\
&\quad \wedge (a \vee b \vee d) \wedge (a \vee b) \wedge d \\
&= c \wedge d \wedge (a \vee b) \\
&= (a \wedge c \wedge d) \vee (b \wedge c \wedge d).
\end{aligned}
$$

In the final minimal disjunctive normal form, there are two items $(a \wedge c \wedge d)$ and $(b \wedge c \wedge d)$. So the formal context has two reducts, they are $\{a, c, d\}$ and $\{b, c, d\}$.

5   Conclusion

The theory of concept lattice is an effective tool for knowledge representation and knowledge discovery, and is applied to many fields. This paper examined the attribute reduction in concept lattice. The attribute reduction in concept lattice is to find a minimal attribute set, which can determine all concepts and their hierarchy in a formal context. The attribute reduction in concept lattice makes the representation of implicit knowledge in a formal context simpler. The results of this paper extend the theory of concept lattice. The introduced notions of discernibility matrix and function of a formal context are useful in knowledge discovery. In fact, an approach to reduction is introduced and the characteristics of core attribute are studied.

Acknowledgements

The authors gratefully acknowledge the support of the National 973 Program of China (No.2002CB312200), and the Natural Scientific Research Project of the Education Department of Shaanxi Province in China (No.04JK131).

References

1. Wille, R.: Restructuring lattice theory: an approach based on hierarchies of concepts. In: Ivan Rival (ed.), Ordered sets, Reidel, Dordrecht-Boston (1982) 445-470
2. Hu, K.Y., Lu, Y.C., Shi, C.Y.: Advances in concept lattice and its application. Journal of Tsinghua University (Science & Technology), 40(9) (2000) 77-81
3. Ho, T.B.: An approach to concept formation based on formal concept analysis. IEICE Trans. Information and Systems, E782D(5) (1995) 553-559
4. Carpineto, C., Romano, G.: GALOIS: An order-theoretic approach to conceptual clustering. In: Utgoff, P. (ed.), Proceedings of ICML 293. Amherst, Elsevier (1993) 33-40
5. Godin, R.: Incremental concept formation algorithm based on Galois (concept) lattices. Computational Intelligence, 11(2) 1995 246-267
6. Oosthuizen, G.D.: The Application of Concept Lattice to Machine Learning. Technical Report, University of Pretoria, South Africa, (1996)
7. Yao, Y.Y.: Concept lattices in rough set theory. In: Dick, S., Kurgan, L., Pedrycz, W. and Reformat, M. (eds.), Proceedings of 2004 Annual Meeting of the North American Fuzzy Information Processing Society (NAFIPS 2004). IEEE Catalog Number: 04TH8736, June 27-30 (2004) 796-801
8. Oosthuizen, G.D.: Rough sets and concept lattices. In: Ziarko, W.P. (ed.), Rough Sets, and Fuzzy Sets and Knowledge Discovery (RSKD'93). London, Springer-Verlag (1994) 24-31
9. Deogun, J.S., Saquer, J.: Concept approximations for formal concept analysis. In: Stumme, G. (ed.), Working with Conceptual Structures. Contributions to ICCS 2000. Verlag Shaker Aachen (2000) 73-83
10. Düntsch, I., Gediga, G.: Algebraic aspects of attribute dependencies in information systems. Fundamenta Informaticae, 29(1-2) (1997) 119-133
11. Pagliani, P.: From concept lattices to approximation spaces: Algebraic structures of some spaces of partial objects. Fundamenta Informaticae, 18(1) (1993) 1-25
12. Grigoriev, P.A., Yevtushenko, S.A.: Elements of an Agile Discovery Environment. In: Grieser, G., Tanaka, Y. and Yamamoto, A. (eds.), Proc. 6th International Conference on Discovery Science (DS 2003). Lecture Notes in Artifical Intelligence, 2843 (2003) 309-316
13. Pawlak, Z.: Rough sets. International Journal of Computer and Information Sciences, 11 (1982) 341-356
14. Ganter, B., Wille, R.: Formal Concept Analysis, Mathematical Foundations. Springer, Berlin (1999)
15. Skowron, A., Rauszer, C.: The discernibility matrices and functions in information systems. In: Slowinski, R. (ed.), Intelligent Decision Support: Handbook of Applications and Advances of the Rough Set Theory. Kluwer Academic Publishers, Dordrecht (1992) 331-362

Reducing the Storage Requirements of 1-v-1 Support Vector Machine Multi-classifiers

Pawan Lingras[1] and Cory J. Butz[2]

[1] Department of Math and Computer Science, Saint Mary's University,
Halifax, Nova Scotia, Canada, B3H 3C3
Pawan.Lingras@stmarys.ca
[2] Department of Computer Science, University of Regina,
Regina, Saskatchewan, Canada S4S 0A2
butz@cs.uregina.ca

Abstract. The methods for extending binary support vectors machines (SVMs) can be broadly divided into two categories, namely, 1-v-r (one versus rest) and 1-v-1 (one versus one). The 1-v-r approach tends to have higher training time, while 1-v-1 approaches tend to create a large number of binary classifiers that need to be analyzed and stored during the operational phase. This paper describes how rough set theory may help in reducing the storage requirements of the 1-v-1 approach in the operational phase.

1 Introduction

While support vector machines (SVMs) improve traditional perceptrons [6,10] by using a higher dimensional space and identifying planes that provide maximal separation between two classes, they are essentially binary classifiers. In order to increase the applicability of SVMs, it is necessary to extend them to multi-classification. Vapnik [11] proposed the 1-v-r (one versus rest) approach, which involves constructing a binary classifier for each class that separates objects belonging to one class from objects that do not. If we assume that there are N classes, the 1-v-r approach will create N binary classifiers. Knerr, et al. [4] suggested the use of 1-v-1 (one versus one) approach, whereby a separate SVM is constructed for every pair of classes. This approach has been further investigated by many researchers. The 1-v-1 approach involves creating binary classifiers for each pair of classes, thus creating $N \times (N - 1)/2$ classifiers. Platt, et al. [9] proposed the use of directed acyclic graphs, referred to as DAGSVM, to reduce the number of computations when deciding classification of objects during the testing and operational phases. Similar to the classical 1-v-1 approach, however, DAGSVMs need to store $N \times (N-1)/2$ SVMs [1]. Lingras and Butz [5] provided interpretation of the binary classification resulting from a SVM in terms of interval or rough sets. This paper extends the formulation proposed by Lingras and Butz for multi-classification using the 1-v-1 approach. The paper also explores the advantages of such a formulation, which include the same time complexity during operational phase as the DAGSVM, but significantly lower storage requirements.

D. Ślęzak et al. (Eds.): RSFDGrC 2005, LNAI 3642, pp. 166–173, 2005.

This paper is organized as follows. Section 2 reviews support vector machines for binary classification. A rough sets approach to support vector machine binary classification is given in Section 3. In Section 4, we present a rough set approach to 1-v-1 support vector machine multi-classifiers. Conclusions are made in Section 5.

2 Support Vector Machines for Binary Classification

Let $\mathbf{x}$ be an input vector in the input space X. Let y be the output in $Y = \{+1, -1\}$. Let $S = \{(x_1, y_1), (x_2, y_2), \ldots, (x_i, y_i), \ldots\}$ be the training set used for supervised classification. Let us define the inner product of two vectors $\mathbf{x}$ and $\mathbf{w}$ as:

$$< \mathbf{x}, \mathbf{w} > \quad = \quad \sum_j x_j \times w_j,$$

where x_j and w_j are components of the vectors $\mathbf{x}$ and $\mathbf{w}$, respectively. If the training set is linear separable, the perceptron learning algorithm will find the vector $\mathbf{w}$ such that:

$$y \times [\; < \mathbf{x}, \mathbf{w} > + b \,] \; \geq \; 0, \qquad (1)$$

for all $(\mathbf{x}, y) \in S$. SVMs overcome the shortcomings of linear separability in the perceptron approach by using a mapping Φ of the input space to another feature space with higher dimension. Equation (1) for perceptrons is then changed as follows:

$$y \times [\; < \Phi(\mathbf{x}), \Phi(\mathbf{w}) > + b \,] \; \geq \; 0, \qquad (2)$$

for all $(\mathbf{x}, y) \in S$. Usually, a high dimensional transformation is needed in order to obtain reasonable classification [2]. Computational overhead can be reduced by not explicitly mapping the data to feature space, but instead just working out the inner product in that space. In fact, SVMs use a kernel function K corresponding to the inner product in the transformed feature space as: $K(\mathbf{x}, \mathbf{w}) = < \Phi(\mathbf{x}), \Phi(\mathbf{w}) >$. Polynomial kernel is one of the popular kernel functions. Let us derive the polynomial kernel function of degree 2 for two dimensional input space. Let $\mathbf{x} = (x_1, x_2)$ and $\mathbf{w} = (w_1, w_2)$:

$$
\begin{aligned}
K(\mathbf{x}, \mathbf{w}) \quad &= \quad < \mathbf{x}, \mathbf{w} >^2 \\
&= \quad (x_1 w_1 + x_2 w_2)^2 \\
&= \quad (x_1^2 w_1^2 + x_2^2 w_2^2 + 2 x_1 w_1 x_2 w_2) \\
&= \quad < x_1^2 + x_2^2 + \sqrt{2} x_1 x_2, \; w_1^2 + w_2^2 + \sqrt{2} w_1 w_2 > \\
&= \quad < \Phi(\mathbf{x}), \Phi(\mathbf{w}) > .
\end{aligned}
$$

The dimensionality rises very quickly with the degree of polynomial. For example, Hoffmann [3] reports that for an original input space with 256 dimensions, the transformed space with second degree polynomials was approximately

33,000, and for the third degree polynomials the dimensionality was more than a million, and fourth degree led to a more than billion dimension space. This problem of high dimensionality will be discussed later in the paper.

The original perceptron algorithm was used to find one of the possibly many hyperplanes separating two classes. The choice of the hyperplane was arbitrary. SVMs use the size of margin between two classes to search for an optimal hyperplane. The problem of maximizing the margin can be reduced to an optimization problem [2,11]: minimize $< \mathbf{x}, \mathbf{w} >$ such that

$$\mathbf{y} \times [\ < \mathbf{x}, \mathbf{w} > + b \ ] \ \geq \ 0, \tag{3}$$

for all $(\mathbf{x}, \mathbf{y}) \in S$. SVMs attempt to find a solution to such an optimization problem.

The problem of multi-classification, especially for systems like SVMs, does not present an easy solution [9]. It is generally simpler to construct classifier theory and algorithms for two mutually-exclusive classes than it is for N mutually-exclusive classes. Platt [8] claimed that constructing N-class SVMs is still an unsolved research problem. The standard method for N-class SVMs [11] is to construct N SVMs. The ith SVM will be trained with all of the examples in the ith class with positive labels, and all other examples with negative labels. Platt et al. [9] refer to SVMs trained in this way as 1-v-r SVMs (short for one versus rest). The final output of the N 1-v-r SVMs is the class that corresponds to the SVM with the highest output value. Platt et al. [9] list the disadvantages of 1-v-r approach as follows. There is no bound on the generalization error for the 1-v-r SVM, and the training time of the standard method scales linearly with N.

Another method for constructing N-class classifiers from SVMs is derived from previous research into combining two-class classifiers. Knerr et al. [4] suggested constructing all possible two-class classifiers from a training set of N classes, each classifier being trained on only two out of N classes. Thus, there would be $N \times (N - 1)/2$ classifiers. Platt et al. [9] refer to this as 1-v-1 SVMs (short for one-versus-one). Platt et al. [9] proposed DAGSVM, which uses directed acyclic graphs to reduce the number of SVMs that need to be used during the testing and operational phase. Chang et al. [1] studied one-against-one and DAGSVM. In the training phase, both methods require solving $N \times (N-1)/2$ binary classification problems. In the testing phase, the one-against-one technique conducts $N \times (N-1)/2$ classifications, while the DAGSVM technique employs a directed acyclic graph that has $N \times (N-1)/2$ nodes and N leaves, reducing the number of classifications to $N - 1$. Both methods are subject to the drawback that, when the number of classes N is large, they incur exhaustive amount of training time and produce an extremely large set of support vectors [1].

The 1-v-r approach creates N SVMs as opposed to $N \times (N - 1)/2$ SVMs created and stored for 1-v-1 and DAGSVM methods. The training of 1-v-1 is computationally less expensive, since only a subset (corresponding to the pair of classes involved) of the training sample is used. This paper describes a rough set based scheme that makes it possible to reduce the training set size, provides a possible semantic description for the multiclassification, and makes the testing and operational phase more streamlined.

3 Rough Sets Based on Binary Support Vector Machine Classification

This section describes a rough set interpretation of SVM binary classification proposed by Lingras and Butz [5]. A certain familiarity with *rough set theory* [7] is assumed. We will first consider the ideal scenario, where the transformed feature space is linear separable and the SVM has found the optimal hyperplane by maximizing the margin between the two classes. There are no training examples in the margin. The optimal hyperplane gives us the best possible dividing line. However, if one chooses to not make an assumption about the classification of objects in the margin, the margin can be designated as the boundary region. This will allow us to create rough sets as follows.

Let us define b_1 as: $\mathbf{y} \times [\ < \mathbf{x}, \mathbf{w} > + \ b_1\ ] \geq 0$, for all $(\mathbf{x}, \mathbf{y}) \in S$, and there exists at least one training example $(\mathbf{x}, \mathbf{y}) \in S$ such that $y = 1$ and $\mathbf{y} \times [\ < \mathbf{x}, \mathbf{w} > + b_1\ ] = 0$. Similarly, b_2 is defined as: $\mathbf{y} \times [\ < \mathbf{x}, \mathbf{w} > + b_2\ ] \geq 0$, for all $(\mathbf{x}, \mathbf{y}) \in S$, and there exists at least one training example $(\mathbf{x}, \mathbf{y}) \in S$ such that $y = -1$ and $\mathbf{y} \times [\ < \mathbf{x}, \mathbf{w} > + b_2\ ] = 0$. It can be easily seen that b_1 and b_2 correspond to the boundaries of the margin. The modified SVM classifier can then be defined as follows:

$$\text{If} < \mathbf{x}, \mathbf{w} > + \ b_1 \geq 0, \text{ classification of } \mathbf{x} \text{ is } +1. \tag{R1}$$
$$\text{If} < \mathbf{x}, \mathbf{w} > + \ b_2 \geq 0, \text{ classification of } \mathbf{x} \text{ is } -1. \tag{R2}$$
$$\text{Otherwise, classification of } \mathbf{x} \text{ is uncertain.} \tag{R3}$$

The proposed classifier will allow us to create three equivalence classes, and define a rough set based approximation space. This simple extension of an SVM classifier provides a basis for a more practical application, when the SVM transformation does not lead to a linear separable case. Cristianini [2] list disadvantages of refining feature space to achieve linear separability. Often this will lead to high dimensions, which will significantly increase the computational requirements. Moreover, it is easy to overfit in high dimensional spaces, i.e., regularities could be found in the training set that are accidental, which would not be found again in a test set. The soft margin classifiers [2] modify the optimization problem to allow for an error rate. The rough set based rules given by (R1)-(R3) can still be used by empirically determining the values of b_1 and b_2. For example, b_1 can be chosen in such a way that, for an $(\mathbf{x}, \mathbf{y}) \in S$, if $< \mathbf{x}, \mathbf{w} > + \ b_1 \geq 0$, then y must be $+1$. Similarly, b_2 can be chosen such that, for an $(\mathbf{x}, \mathbf{y}) \in S$, if $< \mathbf{x}, \mathbf{w} > + \ b_2 \leq 0$, then y must be -1. Assuming there are no outliers, such a choice of b_1 and b_2 would be reasonable. Otherwise, one can specify that the requirements hold for a significant percentage of training examples. For example, b_1 can be chosen in such a way that, for an $(\mathbf{x}, \mathbf{y}) \in S$, if $< \mathbf{x}, \mathbf{w} > + \ b_1 \geq 0$, then in at least 95% of the cases y must be $+1$. Similarly, b_2 can be chosen in such a way that, for an $(\mathbf{x}, \mathbf{y}) \in S$, if $< \mathbf{x}, \mathbf{w} > + \ b_2 \leq 0$, then in at least 95% of the cases y must be -1.

The extension proposed by Lingras and Butz [5] can be easily implemented after the soft margin classifier determines the value of $\mathbf{w}$. All the objects in the training sample will be sorted based on the values of $< \mathbf{x}, \mathbf{w} >$. The value of b_1 can be found by going down (or up if the positive examples are below the hyperplane) in the list until 95% of the positive examples are found. The value of b_2 can be found by going up (or down if the positive examples are below the hyperplane) in the list until 95% of the negative examples are found.

4   Rough Sets Based on the 1-v-1 Approach

The terminologies for rules (R1)-(R3) from the previous section need be slightly modified for pairwise classifications between classes i and j. Let us assume that +1 corresponds to class i and -1 corresponds to class j. We can define equivalence classes corresponding to rules (R1)-(R3). Let $E_{ij}(i)$ be the set of $\mathbf{x}$ (or region) that follows rule (R1), $E_{ij}(j)$ be the set of $\mathbf{x}$ that follows rule (R2), and $E_{ij}(BND)$ be the set of $\mathbf{x}$ that follows rule (R3). The lower bound for class i will be $E_{ij}(i)$ and the upper bound will be $E_{ij}(i) \cup E_{ij}(BND)$. Similarly, the lower bound for class j will be $E_{ij}(j)$ and the upper bound will be $E_{ij}(j) \cup E_{ij}(BND)$. In some cases, this would mean the use of soft margin classifiers.

Figure 1 shows a classification problem with three classes. It is assumed that the objects have already been mapped using the same mapping Φ to transform the problem to a linear separable case. Figure 2 shows the 1-v-1 classification for classes (1,2). Similarly, Figures 3 and 4 show the 1-v-1 classifications for the pairs (1,3) and (2,3), respectively. The equivalence classes for each pair (i, j) will be used to calculate the overall lower bounds of N classes as shown in Eq. (4).

$$\underline{A}(class_i) \quad = \quad \bigcap_{j=1}^{N} E_{ij}(i), \tag{4}$$

where $j \neq i$.

We now show that the lower bounds of every class are mutually exclusive. Consider any pair of classes (i, j). By definition, $E_{ij}(i) \cap E_{ij}(j) = \emptyset$. By Eq. (4),

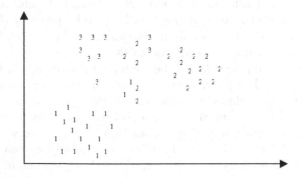

Fig. 1. A classification problem involving three classes 1, 2 and 3

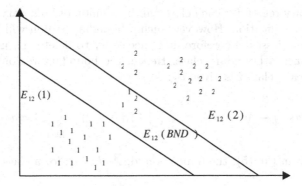

Fig. 2. A rough set approach to 1-v-1 classification for classes 1 and 2

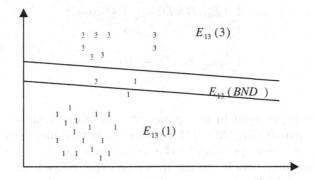

Fig. 3. A rough set approach to 1-v-1 classification for classes 1 and 3

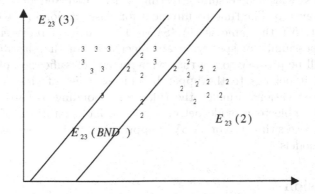

Fig. 4. A rough set approach to 1-v-1 classification for classes 2 and 3

we can conclude that $\underline{A}(class_i) \subseteq E_{ij}(i)$ and $\underline{A}(class_j) \subseteq E_{ij}(j)$. Therefore, $\underline{A}(class_i) \cap \underline{A}(class_j) = \emptyset$.

The boundary region for each class will be a union of boundary regions from each pairwise classification. However, such a boundary region will include lower bounds of other classes. Therefore, it is necessary to delete the union of lower bounds from such a boundary class. Hence, the boundary region, $\overline{A}(class_i) - \underline{A}(class_i)$, for each class i is given by:

$$\overline{A}(class_i) - \underline{A}(class_i) \;=\; \bigcup_{j=1}^{N} E_{ij}(BND) - \bigcup_{k=1}^{N} \underline{A}(class_k), \qquad (5)$$

where $j \neq i$. From Eq. (5), the upper bound, $\overline{A}(class_i)$, for a class i is given by:

$$\begin{aligned}
\overline{A}(class_i) \;&=\; \bigcup_{j=1}^{N} E_{ij}(BND) - \bigcup_{k=1}^{N} \underline{A}(class_k) + \underline{A}(class_i) \\[2mm]
&=\; \bigcup_{j=1}^{N} E_{ij}(BND) - \bigcup_{j=1}^{N} \underline{A}(class_j) \\[2mm]
&=\; \bigcup_{j=1}^{N} (E_{ij}(BND) - \underline{A}(class_j)), \qquad (6)
\end{aligned}$$

where $j \neq i$.

The approach proposed in this paper uses the same training time as the classical 1-v-1 approach or DAGSVM. However, only two rules need to be stored for each class, one corresponding to the lower bound $\underline{A}(class_i)$, given by Eq. (4), and another corresponding to the upper bound $\overline{A}(class_i)$, given by Eq. (6). Therefore, a total of $2N$ rules are stored for the testing and operational phases, as opposed to $N \times (N-1)/2$ SVMs stored by 1-v-1 and DAGSVM approaches. Moreover, during the operational phase, the determination of membership of an object in a class will involve simply testing which lower and/or upper bounds the object belongs to. The time requirement for classification in the operational phase will be $O(N)$, the same as DAGSVM. The rough set representation also provides the possibility of specifying an uncertainty in the classification. For example, it will be possible to say that while precise classification of the object is not known, it belongs to the upper bounds of a list of classes, i.e., a list of possible classifications. Finally, the rules corresponding to lower and upper bounds may be able to provide better semantic interpretations of the multi-classification process than the other SVM approaches, which have been regarded as black-box models.

5   Conclusion

The approaches for extending binary classifications obtained from support vector machines (SVMs) to multi-classification can be divided into two categories, 1-v-r (one versus rest) and 1-v-1 (one versus one). 1-v-r classification technique involves creating a separate SVM for every class using the members of the class as positive instances and non-members as negative instances. This approach requires a large training time. The 1-v-1 approach involves creating and storing $N \times (N - 1)/2$ SVMs. The time requirement in the operational phase for 1-v-1 approach can be reduced using directed acyclic graphs leading to DAGSVMs. However, the storage requirement for DAGSVM is still the same as the classical 1-v-1 approach, i.e., $N \times (N - 1)/2$. This paper describes an extension of 1-v-1 approach using rough or interval sets. The use of rough sets may make it possible to provide a semantic interpretation of the classification process using rule-based approach, which may be an advantage over the black-box SVM models. It is shown that during the operation phase, the proposed approach has the same $O(N)$ time requirement as DAGSVM. However, it only requires storage of $2N$ rules as opposed to $N \times (N-1)/2$ SVMs stored by the DAGSVM and the classical 1-v-1 approach. Our approach also makes it possible to introduce uncertainty in describing classifications of objects.

References

1. Chang, F., Chou, C.-H., Lin, C.-C., and Chen, C.-J.: A Prototype Classification Method and Its Application to Handwritten Character Recognition. Proceedings of IEEE Conference on Systems, Man and Cybernetics (2004) 4738-4743
2. Cristianini, N.: Support Vector and Kernel Methods for Pattern Recognition. http://www.support-vector.net/tutorial.html (2003)
3. Hoffmann, A.: VC Learning Theory and Support Vector Machines. http://www.cse.unsw.edu.au/~cs9444/Notes02/Achim-Week11.pdf (2003)
4. Knerr, S., Personnaz, L., and Dreyfus, G.: Single-layer learning revisited: A stepwise procedure for building and training a neural network. In Fogelman-Soulie and Herault, editors, Neurocomputing: Algorithms, Architectures and Applications, NATO ASI. Springer (1990)
5. Lingras P. and Butz, C.J.: Interval Set Classifiers using Support Vector Machines. Proceedings of 2004 conference of the North American Fuzzy Information Processing Society, Banff, AB., June 27-30 (2004) 707-710
6. Minsky, M.L. and Papert, S.A.: Perceptrons, MIT Press, Cambridge, MA. (1969)
7. Pawlak, Z.: Rough Sets: Theoretical Aspects of Reasoning about Data. Kluwer Academic Publishers (1992)
8. Platt, J.C.: Support Vector Machines. http://research.microsoft.com/users/jplatt/ svm.html (2003)
9. Platt, J.C., Cristianini, N., and Shawe-Taylor, J.: Large margin DAG's for multiclass classification. In: Advances in Neural Information Processing Systems, MIT Press, Cambridge, MA, (2000) 547-553
10. Rosenblatt, F.: The perceptron: A perceiving and recognizing automaton. Technical Report 85-460-1, Project PARA, Cornell Aeronautical Lab (1957)
11. Vapnik, V.: Statistical Learning Theory. Wiley, NY. (1998)

A Possibilistic Approach to RBFN Centers Initialization

A. Guillén, I. Rojas, J. González, H. Pomares, L.J. Herrera,
O. Valenzuela, and A. Prieto

Department of Computer Architecture and Computer Technology,
Universidad de Granada, Spain

Abstract. Clustering techniques have always been oriented to solve classification and pattern recognition problems. This clustering techniques have been used also to initialize the centers of the Radial Basis Function (RBF) when designing an RBF Neural Network (RBFNN) that approximates a function. Since classification and function approximation problems are quite different, it is necessary to design a new clustering technique specialized in the problem of function approximation. In this paper, a new clustering technique it is proposed to make the right initialization of the centers of the RBFs. The novelty of the algorithm is the employment of a possibilistic partition of the data, rather than a hard or fuzzy partition as it is commonly used in clustering algorithms. The use of this kind of partition with the addition of several components to use the information provided by the output, allow the new algorithm to provide better results and be more robust than the other clustering algorithms even if noise exits in the input data.

1 Introduction

The function approximation problem can be formulated as, given a set of observations $\{(\boldsymbol{x}_k; y_k), k = 1, ..., n\}$ with $y_k = F(\boldsymbol{x}_k) \in \mathbb{R}$ and $\boldsymbol{x}_k \in \mathbb{R}^d$, it is desired to obtain a function $\mathcal{G}$ so $y_k = \mathcal{G}(\boldsymbol{x}_k) \in \mathbb{R}$ with $\boldsymbol{x}_k \in \mathbb{R}^d$. To solve this problem, Radial Basis Function Neural Networks (RBFNN) are used because of their capability as universal approximators [5,11].

The design of a RBFNN is performed by following several steps, in which the initialization of the centers of the RBFs is the first one. The use of a clustering algorithm is a common solution for a first initialization of the centers [9,15]. These clustering algorithms were designed for classification problems [8] instead of for the function approximation problem so the results they provide can be improved significantly. Clustering algorithms try to classify the set of input data assigning a set of predefined labels, however, in the function approximation problem, the output of the function belongs to a continuous interval. Clustering algorithms do not use the information provided by the function output ignoring the variability of the function. In the function approximation problem, the information provided by the output of the function to be approximated is needed to obtain a correct placement of the centers. Centers must be placed in the areas where the function

D. Ślęzak et al. (Eds.): RSFDGrC 2005, LNAI 3642, pp. 174–183, 2005.

is more variable and therefore, it will be needed more RBFs to be able to model the variations of the function, meanwhile, in the areas where the function is not that variable, less centers will be needed to approximate the function.

It is necessary to design a clustering algorithm oriented to the function approximation problem in order to make a right initialization of the RBFs centers. In this paper, a new algorithm to solve this task is proposed. It is based on a mixed fuzzy-possibilistic approach improving results, as it will be shown in the experiments section, in comparison with traditional clustering algorithms and clustering algorithms designed specifically for the function approximation problem.

2   RBFNN Description

A RBFNN $\mathcal{F}$ with fixed structure to approximate an unknown function F with n entries and one output starting from a set of values $\{(\boldsymbol{x}_k; y_k); k = 1, ..., n\}$ with $y_k = F(\boldsymbol{x}_k) \in \mathbb{R}$ and $\boldsymbol{x}_k \in \mathbb{R}^d$, has a set of parameters that have to be optimized:

$$\mathcal{F}(\boldsymbol{x}_k; C, R, \Omega) = \sum_{j=1}^{m} \phi(\boldsymbol{x}_k; \boldsymbol{c}_j, r_j) \cdot \Omega_j \tag{1}$$

where $C = \{\boldsymbol{c}_1, ..., \boldsymbol{c}_m\}$ is the set of RBF centers, $R = \{r_1, ..., r_m\}$ is the set of values for each RBF radius, $\Omega = \{\Omega_1, ..., \Omega_m\}$ is the set of weights and $\phi(\boldsymbol{x}_k; \boldsymbol{c}_j, r_j)$ represents an RBF. The activation function most commonly used for classification and regression problems is the Gaussian function because it is continuous, differentiable, it provides a softer output and improves the interpolation capabilities [3,13]. The procedure to design an RBFNN for functional approximation problem is shown below:

1. Initialize RBF centers $\boldsymbol{c}_j$
2. Initialize the radius r_j for each RBF
3. Calculate the optimum value for the weights Ω_j.

The first step is accomplished by applying clustering algorithms, the new algorithm proposed in this paper will initialize the centers, providing better results than other clustering algorithms used for this task.

3   Previous Clustering Algorithms

This section will describe several clustering algorithms that have been used to determine the centers when designing RBFNN for functional approximation problems.

3.1   Fuzzy C-Means (FCM)

This algorithm uses a fuzzy partition of the data where an input vector belongs to several clusters with a membership value. The objective function to be minimized is:

$$J_h(U, C; X) = \sum_{k=1}^{n} \sum_{i=1}^{m} u_{ik}^h \|x_k - c_i\|^2 \tag{2}$$

where $X = \{x_1, x_2, ..., x_n\}$ are the input vectors, $C = \{c_1, c_2, ..., c_m\}$ are the centers of the clusters, $U = [u_{ik}]$ is the matrix where the degree of membership is established by the input vector to the cluster , and h is a parameter to control the degree of the partition fuzziness. After applying the minimum square method to minimize the function in Equation 2 [2], we get the equations to reach the solution trough and iterative process:

$$u_{ik} = \left(\sum_{j=1}^{m} \left(\frac{D_{ikA}}{D_{jkA}} \right)^{\frac{2}{h-1}} \right)^{-1} \tag{3}$$

$$c_i = \frac{\sum\limits_{k=1}^{n} u_{ik}^h x_k}{\sum\limits_{k=1}^{n} u_{ik}^h} \tag{4}$$

where $D_{jkA} = \|x_k - c_j\|^2$, and $\| \cdot \|$ is the inner product norm in $\mathbb{R}^d$. Using this iterative process we calculate matrix U from matrix C or vice versa starting from a random initialization of any of the matrices: ($C_{t-1} \rightarrow U_t \rightarrow C_t$ or $U_{t-1} \rightarrow C_t \rightarrow U_t$). The stop criteria is usually considered as $\|C_{t-1} - C_t\| < threshold$, this is, when the centers do not move significantly.

3.2   Improved Possibilistic C-Means (IPCM)

The Possibilistic C-means [10] determines a possibilistic partition of the data, in which a possibilistic membership measures the absolute degree of typicality of a point to a cluster. This approach is robust because noisy points will not affect significantly the possibilistic partition as they would in a fuzzy partition. This algorithm tends to find identical clusters [1] so an improved version of this algorithm is proposed in [14]. This new approach combines a fuzzy partition with a possibilistic partition determining the following function to be minimized:

$$J_h(U^{(p)}, U^{(f)}, C; X) = \sum_{k=1}^{n} \sum_{i=1}^{m} (u_{ik}^{(f)})^{h_f} (u_{ik}^{(p)})^{h_p} d_{ik}^2 + \sum_{i=1}^{m} \eta_i \sum_{k=1}^{n} (u_{ik}^{(f)})^{h_f} (1 - u_{ik}^{(p)})^{h_p} \tag{5}$$

where:

- $u_{ik}^{(p)}$ is the possibilistic membership of x_k in the cluster i.
- $u_{ik}^{(f)}$ is the fuzzy membership of x_k in the cluster i.
- h_p and h_f are the weighting exponents for the possibilistic and the fuzzy membership functions.
- η_i is a scale parameter that is calculated using:

$$\eta_i = \frac{\sum\limits_{k=1}^{n} (u_{ik}^{(f)})^{h_f} (u_{ik}^{(p)})^{h_p} d_{ik}^2}{(u_{ik}^{(f)})^{h_f} (u_{ik}^{(p)})^{h_p}} \tag{6}$$

As in the previous algorithms, an iterative process drives to the solution.

3.3 Clustering for Function Approximation (CFA)

This algorithm uses the information provided by the objective function output in such a way that the algorithm will place more centers where the variability of the output is higher instead of where there are more input vectors.

To fulfill this task, the CFA algorithm defines a set $O = \{o_1, ..., o_m\}$ that represents a hypothetic output for each center. This value will be obtained as a weighted mean of the output of the input vectors belonging to a center.

CFA defines an objective function that has to be minimized in order to converge to a solution:

$$\frac{\sum\limits_{j=1}^{m} \sum\limits_{x_k \in C_j} \|x_k - c_j\|^2 \omega_{kj}}{\sum\limits_{j=1}^{m} \sum\limits_{x_k \in C_j} \omega_{kj}} \tag{7}$$

where ω_{kj} weights the influence of each input vector in the final position a center.

The CFA algorithm is structured in three basic steps: Partition of the data, centers and estimated output updating and a migration step.

The partition is performed as it is done in Hard C-means [4], thus, a Voronoi partition of the data is obtained. Once the input vectors are partitioned, the centers and their estimated outputs have to be updated, this process is done iteratively using the equations shown below:

$$c_j = \frac{\sum\limits_{x_k \in C_j} x_k \omega_{kj}}{\sum\limits_{x_k \in C_j} \omega_{kj}} \qquad o_j = \frac{\sum\limits_{x_k \in C_j} F(x_k) \omega_{kj}}{\sum\limits_{x_k \in C_j} \omega_{kj}} . \tag{8}$$

The algorithm, to update centers and estimated outputs, has an internal loop that iterates until the total distortion of the partition is not decreased significantly.

The algorithm has a migration step that moves centers allocated in input zones where the target function is stable, to zones where the output variability is higher. The idea of a migration step was introduced in [12] as an extension of Hard C-means and the objective is to find an optimal vector quantization where each center makes an equal contribution to the total distortion [5].

3.4   Fuzzy Clustering for Function Approximation (FCFA)

The FCFA algorithm [6,7] is based in the CFA and FCM. The main difference between CFA and FCFA is the application of fuzzy logic to the algorithm. FCFA performs a fuzzy partition of the data and iterates in the same way as FCM does, thus, it improves the speed of the algorithm in comparison with CFA because it only needs one step of actualization instead of an internal loop. The algorithm considers the input data as the input data vectors concatenated with their outputs. Proceeding like this, the expected output of a center correspond with its last coodinate. FCFA also makes a modification in the migration process performing a pre-selection of the centers to be migrated modifying the criteria used to decide if a center should be migrated or not. This pre-selection is based on a fuzzy ruled system.

4   Possibilistic Centers Initializer (PCI)

The new algorithm proposed uses a possibilistic partition and a fuzzy partition, combining both approach as it was done in [14]. The objective function $J_h(U^{(p)}, U^{(f)}, C, W; X)$ to be minimized is defined as:

$$\sum_{k=1}^{n}\sum_{i=1}^{m} (u_{ik}^{(f)})^{h_f}(u_{ik}^{(p)})^{h_p}D_{ikW}^2 + \sum_{i=1}^{m}\eta_i\sum_{k=1}^{n}(u_{ik}^{(f)})^{h_f}(1 - u_{ik}^{(p)})^{h_p} \qquad (9)$$

where:

- $u_{ik}^{(p)}$ is the possibilistic membership of x_k in the cluster i.
- $u_{ik}^{(f)}$ is the fuzzy membership of x_k in the cluster i.
- D_{ikW} is the weighted euclidean distance.
- η_i is a scale parameter that is calculated using:

$$\eta_i = \frac{\sum\limits_{k=1}^{n} (u_{ik}^{(f)})^{h_f} d_{ik}^2}{(u_{ik}^{(f)})^{h_f}} \qquad (10)$$

This function is obtained by replacing de distance measure in the FCM algorithm by the objective function of the PCM algorithm, obtaining a mixed approach. The scale parameter determines the relative degree to which the second term in the objective function is compared with the first. This second term forces to make the possibilistic membership degree as big as possible, thus, choosing this value for η_i will keep a balance between the fuzzy and the possibilistic memberships. When calculating η_i, the distance is not weighted because the estimated outputs, in the initialization of the algorithm, are not appropriate to calculate w.

4.1   Weighting Parameter

To make the output of the target function to be approximated influence the placement of the centers, it is necessary to change the similarity criteria in the clustering process. The combination of the possibilistic and the fuzzy approach has to be influenced by the output of the function to be minimized. In order to do this, the euclidean distance used as the similarity criteria will be weighted using the parameter w. The calculation of w is obtained by:

$$w_{kj} = |F(\boldsymbol{x}_k) - o_j| \tag{11}$$

where o_j represents the expected output of a center, this is, the hypothetic position of the center c_j in the output axis. The euclidean distance d_{ij} between a center i and an input vector will be weighted using the following equation:

$$D_{ijW} = d_{ij} \cdot w_{ij}. \tag{12}$$

Proceeding this way, D_{ijW} will be small if the center is near the input vector and they have similar output values. Thus a center can own input vectors that are far from him if they have similar output values, and will not own input vectors that, even though are near the center, have a big difference in the output values. This will allow the algorithm to place more centers where the output of the target function to be approximated is more variable.

4.2   Iterative Process

As in all the previous algorithms based on a fuzzy or a possibilistic partition, the solution is reached by an alternating optimization approach where all the elements defined in the function to be minimized (Equation 9) are actualized iteratively. For the new algorithm proposed in this paper, the equations are:

$$u_{ik}^{(p)} = \frac{1}{1 + \left(\frac{D_{ikW}}{\eta_i}\right)^{\frac{1}{h_p-1}}} \tag{13}$$

$$u_{ik}^{(f)} = \frac{1}{\sum_{j=1}^{m} \left(\frac{(u_{ik}^{(p)})^{(h_p-1)/2}D_{ikW}}{(u_{jk}^{(p)})^{(h_p-1)/2}D_{jkW}}\right)^{\frac{2}{h_f-1}}} \tag{14}$$

$$c_i = \frac{\sum_{k=1}^{n} (u_{ik}^{(p)})^{(h_p)}(u_{ik}^{(f)})^{(h_f)}x_k w_{ik}^2}{\sum_{k=1}^{n} (u_{ik}^{(p)})^{(h_p)}(u_{ik}^{(f)})^{(h_f)}w_{ik}^2} \tag{15}$$

$$o_i = \frac{\sum_{k=1}^{n} (u_{ik}^{(p)})^{(h_p)}(u_{ik}^{(f)})^{(h_f)}Y_k d_{ik}^2}{\sum_{k=1}^{n} (u_{ik}^{(p)})^{(h_p)}(u_{ik}^{(f)})^{(h_f)}d_{ik}^2} \tag{16}$$

These equations are obtained by differentiating $J_h(U^{(p)}, U^{(f)}, C, W; X)$ (Equation 9) with respect $u_{ik}^{(p)}$, $u_{ik}^{(f)}$, c_i and o_i. This approach is the same followed in FCM, IPCM and the convergence is guaranteed.

4.3   General Scheme

The PCI algorithm follows the scheme shown below to place the centers:

Initialize C_1 using Fuzzy C-means
Initialize O_1 using fuzzy membership function
Do
    Calculate w
    Calculate the distance between C_i and X
    Calculate the new U_i
    Calculate the new C_i from U_i
    Calculate the new O_i from C_i
    i=i+1
While(abs(C_{i-1}-C_i<*threshold*)

As in [14], the FCM algorithm is used to find a proper start point, making the algorithm much more robust. In the first step, the expected output o_i of each center c_i will correspond with the output value of the input vector that belongs to c_i with the highest membership value.

5   Experimental Results

The experiment will consists in the approximation of the function f_1 represented in Fig. 1, that has been generated using an RBFNN with the following parameters:

centers	radii	weights
119.029	15.595	-3.748
175.106	4.279	-1.016
39.796	16.350	3.855
71.087	9.164	1.857
93.030	37.518	4.095

200 points uniformly distributed were generated between the interval [1,399] using the RBFNN described above with a gaussian activation function . The function has been designed to show the importance of the output variability on the target function. In this function there is an interval where the variability of the output is high and another interval where the function is almost constant. This fact will make the initialization of the centers very important because the centers will have to be concentrated in the areas where the function is more variable.

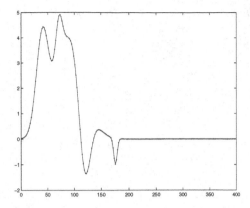

Fig. 1. Target Function (blue line) and training set (red dots)

Table 1. Mean and Standard Deviation of the approximation error (NRMSE) for function f_1

Clusters	FCM	IPCM	CFA	FCFA	PCI
4	0.633(0.002)	0.592(2E-4)	0.595(0.022)	0.361(0.035)	0.444(1E-4)
5	0.619(0.001)	0.584(0.001)	0.515(0.035)	0.345(0.034)	0.343(0.001)
6	0.544(0.003)	0.537(0.001)	0.412(0.041)	0.312(0.046)	0.287(3E-4)

Table 2. Mean and Standard Deviation of the approximation error (NRMSE) for function f_1 after local search algorithm

Clusters	FCM	IPCM	CFA	FCFA	PCI
4	0.182(0.011)	0.187(0.015)	0.186(0.012)	0.149(0.030)	0.100(1E-4)
5	0.308(0.001)	0.256(0.026)	0.178(0.045)	0.104(0.043)	0.048(0.022)
6	0.187(0.069)	0.125(0.045)	0.098(0.071)	0.082(0.019)	0.0002(3E-4)

Once the clustering algorithm were executed and the corresponding RBFNNs were generated, the normalized root mean squared error (NRMSE) has been used in order to determine the quality of the approximation.

The radii of the RBFs were calculated using the k-neighbors algorithm with k=1. The weights were calculated optimally by solving a linear equation system.

FCM, IPCM, CFA, FCFA and PCI were executed several times providing the results shown in Table 1. In this table it is shown the approximation error right after the initialization procedure. In Table 2 are shown the results after applying a local search algorithm (Levenberg-Marquardt) to make a fine tune of the RBF centers and radii. The results are depicted in Fig. 2.

The results show how there is a need of using specific clustering algorithms to initialize the centers when designing an RBFNN for the functional approxi-

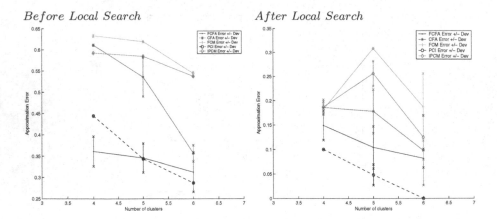

Fig. 2. Mean and Standard Deviation of the approximation error (NRMSE) before and after local search algorithm

mation problem. Classical clustering do not use the information provided by the output of the target function to be approximated. Thus they are not able to detect the areas where the output is more variable, providing poor results. The approximation error decreases significantly when specific clustering algorithms designed for this task are employed.

The new algorithm proposed in this paper has shown that can performs better than all the previous clustering. PCI not only performs better, but is more robust because the standard deviations of the solutions are very small, indicating that it finds the same configuration on each execution of the algorithm. The previous clustering algorithms for functional approximation were not too robust, so it can be appreciated how a mixed fuzzy-possibilistic approach can solve that problem.

6   Conclusions

RBFNNs provides good results when they are used for functional approximation problems. The first step in the design of those RBFNNs was performed by clustering algorithms. In this paper, a new clustering algorithm designed specifically for the center initialization task has been presented. The novelty of this algorithm in comparison with other clustering algorithms designed for this task, is the use of a mixed possibilistic and fuzzy approach when making the partition of the data. The results shown how this approach allow to make a better initialization of the centers, providing better results when approximating functions.

References

1. M. Barni, V. Capellini, and A. Mecocci. Comments on 'A posibilistic approach to clustering'. *IEEE Transactions on Fuzzy Systems*, 4:393–396, June.
2. J. C. Bezdek. *Pattern Recognition with Fuzzy Objective Function Algorithms*. Plenum, New York, 1981.

3. A. G. Bors. Introduction of the Radial Basis Function (RBF) networks. *OnLine Symposium for Electronics Engineers*, 1:1–7, February 2001.
4. R. O. Duda and P. E. Hart. *Pattern classification and scene analysis*. New York: Wiley, 1973.
5. A. Gersho. Asymptotically Optimal Block Quantization. *IEEE Transanctions on Information Theory*, 25(4):373–380, July 1979.
6. A. Guillén, I. Rojas, J. Gonzalez, H. Pomares, and L. J. Herrera. Clustering based algorithm for rfbs centers initialization. In *XI SIGEF Congress, Techniques and Methodologies for the Information and Knowledge Economy*, pages 44–63, Reggio Calabria-Messina, November 2004.
7. A. Guillén, I. Rojas, J. Gonzalez, H. Pomares, L.J. Herrera, and A. Prieto. Using a new clustering algorithm to design rbf networks for functional approximation problem. In *Proceedings of the Learning'04 International Conference*, pages 19–24, Elche, October 2004.
8. J. A. Hartigan. *Clustering Algorithms*. New York: Wiley, 1975.
9. N. B. Karayannis and G. W. Mi. Growing radial basis neural networks: Merging supervised and unsupervised learning with network growth techniques. *IEEE Transactions on Neural Networks*, 8:1492–1506, November 1997.
10. R. Krishnapuram and J. M. Keller. A Possibilistic Approach to Clustering. *IEEE Transactions on Fuzzy Systems*, 1(2):98–110, May 1993.
11. J. Park and J. W. Sandberg. Universal approximation using radial basis functions network. *Neural Computation*, 3:246–257, 1991.
12. G. Patanè and M. Russo. The Enhanced-LBG algorithm. *Neural Networks*, 14(9):1219–1237, 2001.
13. I. Rojas, M. Anguita, A. Prieto, and O. Valenzuela. Analysis of the operators involved in the definition of the implication functions and in the fuzzy inference proccess. *Int. J. Approximate Reasoning*, 19:367–389, 1998.
14. J. Zhang and Y. Leung. Improved possibilistic C–means clustering algorithms. *IEEE Transactions on Fuzzy Systems*, 12:209–217, 2004.
15. Q. Zhu, Y. Cai, and L. Liu. A global learning algorithm for a RBF network. *Neural Networks*, 12:527–540, 1999.

Intelligent Information Retrieval Based on the Variable Precision Rough Set Model and Fuzzy Sets

Ming He and Bo-qin Feng

Department of Computer Science and Technology,
Xi'an Jiaotong University, Xi'an 710049, China
ming_he1314@163.com

Abstract. In this paper, an information retrieval methodology and model based on variable precision rough set model (VPRSM) are proposed through combining rough sets and fuzzy sets. In the methodology, the documents are represented as fuzzy index terms, the queries are defined with a rough set and that each document has an approximation in this set. The experimental results compared with vector space model (VSM) are presented.

1 Introduction

With the explosive growth and widespread of the Internet and World Wide Web, there is great increase in interest in information retrieval. The three classic models in information retrieval are called Boolean, vector, and probabilistic respectively [1]. Among the information retrieval techniques developed in the past, the rough sets-based, non-pattern matching approach proposed by Das-Gupta [2] deserves particular attention and further investigation. The theoretical basis for Gupta's approach is developed around the original rough sets (RS) theory as proposed by Pawlak [3,4]. Advantages offered by the theory are: the implicit inclusion of Boolean logic; term weighting; and the ability to rank retrieved documents. However, the main limitation of this ranking procedure is that it ranks documents into very few rank levels thus making it impossible to determine the differences in relevance status between many documents belonging to the same rank level.

The classic models in information retrieval consider that each document is described by a set of representative keywords called index terms, which are used to index and summarize the document contents. Given a set of index terms for a document, however, not all terms are equally useful for describing the document. In fact, there are index terms which are simply vaguer than others, namely, distinct index terms have varying relevance when used to describe document contents. Consequently, it is an important issue to decide the importance of a term for summarizing the contents of a document.

In this paper, we propose a rough fuzzy information retrieval model (RFIRM) that can retrieve needed documents more promptly and accurately by replacing

D. Ślęzak et al. (Eds.): RSFDGrC 2005, LNAI 3642, pp. 184–192, 2005.
© Springer-Verlag Berlin Heidelberg 2005

common index terms with fuzzy index terms, which can represent the semantics of document more precisely. Furthermore, instead of using the original equivalence RS model based on using equivalence relations, we use variable precision rough set model (VPRSM) [5], which can produce finer ranking and more accurate relevance judgments. Related work on applying RS theory to information retrieval was reported in [6,7,8,9].

2   Information Retrieval Model Based on VPRSM

Let $X \subseteq U$ be a subset of the universe U and let R be an equivalence relation on U with the equivalence classes (elementary sets) $E \subseteq U$. We assume that all sets under consideration are finite and non-empty. Each elementary E can be assigned a measure of overlap with set X by the function $P(X|E) = \frac{|X \cap E|}{|E|}$, referred here as conditional probability function.

The VPRSM [5] is an extension of the RS model aimed at increasing its discriminator capabilities by using parameter-controlled grades of conditional probability associated with the elementary sets. The asymmetric VPRS generalization [10] is based on the lower and upper limit certainty threshold parameters l and u, which satisfy the constraints $0 \le l < P(X) < u \le 1$.

The u-positive, l-negative and (l, u)-boundary regions are given, respectively, by

$$POS_u(X) = \cup\{E : P(X|E) \ge u\} \tag{1}$$

$$NEG_l(X) = \cup\{E : P(X|E) \le u\} \tag{2}$$

$$BND_{l,u}(X) = \cup\{E : P(X|E) \in (l, u)\} \tag{3}$$

In the context of information retrieval VPRSM ability to flexibly control approximation regions' definitions allows for capturing probabilistic relations existing in information. It is clear that the original RS model is a special case of VPRSM, for $l=0$ and $u=1$. Usually, however, more interesting results are expected for non-trivial settings, tuned to particular data and satisfying the constrains $0 \le l < P(X) < u \le 1$.

Definition 1. *A generalized information retrieval model is a quadruple [1]* $\Re = [\mathbf{D}, \mathbf{Q}, F, R(q_i, d_j)]$ *where*

1. $\mathbf{D}$ *is a set composed of representations for the documents in the collection.*
2. $\mathbf{Q}$ *is a set composed of representations for the user information needs, such representations are called queries.*
3. *F is a framework for modelling document representation, queries, and their relations.*
4. $R(q_i, d_j)$ *is a ranking function which associates a real number with a query ordering among the documents with regard to the query $q_i \in \mathbf{Q}$ and a document representation $d_j \in \mathbf{D}$.*

Definition 2. *On this basis, the information retrieval model based on VPRSM may be defined by* $\Re=[U,A,X,V_q,f_q]$ *where*

1. *U is a finite set of documents, which is the universe of discourse.*
2. *A is a finite set of attributes, which composed of index terms of documents in a collection.*
3. *X denotes set of documents to be retrieved, which for the user information need.*
4. *V_q is the range of value of the attribute q and represents the documents that contain the index term, where $q \in A$.*
5. *$\forall q \in A, \exists f_q : X \times U \to V_q$.*

Using the query index terms X in information retrieval, $POS_u(X)$ denotes selected documents, $BND_{l,u}(X)$ represents optional documents and $NEG_l(X)$ means the documents fail to be selected.

3   Document and Query Representation

To build a model, we think first of representation for the documents and query for the user information need. In traditional information retrieval, representing documents in a collection and queries through index terms descriptions, which are only partially related to the real semantic contents of the respective documents and queries. Moreover, the matching of a document to the query terms is approximate (or vague). Any collection of semantic indexes corresponds to a family of sets of respective defining index terms. It can be assumed, without loss of generality, that all these sets are disjoint as otherwise more basic semantic indexes corresponding to atoms of the algebra of sets can be used for document and query representation.

In this paper, we adopt fuzzy index terms based on fuzzy sets theory [10,11] to represent documents, which can represent the semantics of original documents more precisely and facilitate information retrieval. In addition, we consider that each query term defines a rough sets and that each document has an approximation in this set. Assembling index terms into index terms set is a feasible way to reduce the time complexity of the information retrieval system which computing expense maps to the number of the index terms increases.

Definition 3. *A thesaurus is constructed in this paper by defining a term-term correlation matrix $\overrightarrow{c}$ (called keyword connection matrix in [12]) whose rows and columns are associated to the index terms in the document two term k_i and k_l can be defined by*

$$c_{i,l} = \frac{n_{i,l}}{n_i + n_l - n_{i,l}} \tag{4}$$

where $n_{(i)}$ is the number of document of documents which contain the term k_i, n_l is the number of documents which contain the term k_l, $n_{i,l}$ is the number of documents which contain both terms. Such a correlation metric is quite common and has been used extensively with clustering algorithms [1].

Definition 4. *We can use the term correlation matrix $\overleftrightarrow{c}$ to define a fuzzy index terms, which can be comprised of a monotonic decreasing sequence by their fuzzy membership function values. Assume that there are N index terms, $[Index_1, Index_2, , Index_N]$, in one document and their memberships are defined by*

$$\mu_D(indx_i) = \frac{\sum_{i=1}^{n} c_{i,l}}{N} \tag{5}$$

Let $A = (U, R)$ be an approximation space on the universe U of fuzzy index terms used for defining semantic indexes and for indexing documents. The equivalence relation R represents the partition of U into disjoint sets corresponding to semantic indexes. In rough sets theory terminology, each semantic index is an elementary set in A whereas each queries Q is a rough set in A. A query Q initially expressed as a set of index terms is a rough sets in the same approximation space A. What it means is that the original query, the subset of index terms, can be represented by standard semantic indexes as defined in the approximation space A. In this representation, the query is perceived as a pair $(\overline{R}Q, \underline{R}Q)$ of rough approximations of the original set of index terms forming the query. The query is considered to be with certainty about subjects corresponding to semantic indexes included in the lower approximation of the query terms and it is possibly about subjects corresponding to semantic indexes included in the upper approximation of the query terms. In particular, the query can be expressed by specifying some semantic indexes rather than index terms. In such case, the query is a precise set in the approximation space A and it is with certainty about subjects corresponding to semantic indexes contained in the query definition [13].

4   Information Retrieval Architecture Based on VPRSM

Given above representation, we then conceive the framework in which they can be modeled. Architecture of RFIRM is described in Figure 1.

First of all, each document and a query are represented as collections of higher order, composite semantic indexes each of which reflects some information about the meaning of the document. With very large document collections, however, even modern computers might have to reduce the set of representative index terms. This can be accomplished through the elimination of stop words, the use of stemming, and the identification of noun groups. Further, compression might be employed. Finally, we use fuzzy index terms to represent semantics of document. These operations procedure are called document pre-processing, which reduce the complexity of the document.

Given that the document collections are indexed, the retrieval process can be imitated. The user first specifies a user need which is then parsed and transformed by the same document operations applied to the document. Then, query operations might applied before the actual query, which provides a system representation for the user need, is generated. The query is then processed to obtain the retrieved documents. Fast query processing is made possible by the index

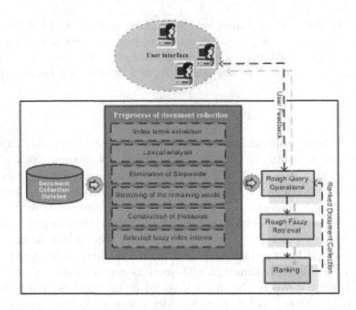

Fig. 1. RFIRM architecture

structure previously built. Before been sent to the user, the retrieved documents are ranked according to a likelihood of relevance. The user then examines the set of ranked documents in the search for useful information. At this point, he might pinpoint a subset of the document seen as definitely of interest and initiate a user feedback cycle.

5   Key Algorithms

The key algorithms constructing the rough fuzzy information retrieval are listed as follows:

Algorithm 1: Fuzzy index terms selected algorithm.

Input: Document collections U, index terms of each document and threshold θ.

Output: The universe Ψ of fuzzy index terms.

1. Let $N = |U|$ denote the number of document collections, $\Psi = \emptyset$ and $j = 1$;
2. Calculate degree of membership of each index term and construct term-term correlation matrix $\vec{c}$;
3. While $j \leq n$ add the index terms whose degree of membership $\geq \theta$ to Ψ, $j = j + 1$;
4. Return Ψ.

Algorithm 2: Approximation query algorithm.

Input: $A = (U, R), l, u(0 \leq l < u \leq 1)$ and Query Q.

Output: Approximation sets of query Q.

1. Calculate equivalence class (partitions) U of with R: $\{E_1, E_2, ..., E_m(0 < m \le |U|)\}, i = 1$;
2. While $(i \le m)$ Calculate lower and upper approximation set of Q respectively:
   $$\overline{R}(Q) = \cup\{E_i : P(X|E_i) \ge u\}, \underline{R}(Q) = \cup\{E_i : P(X|E_i) \le l\}, i = i + 1;$$
3. Return $\overline{R}(Q)$ and $\underline{R}(Q)$.

Algorithm 3: Rough fuzzy information retrieval algorithm.

Input: $A = (U, R), l, u \ (0 \le l < u \le 1)$, S_0 (similarity threshold) and Query Q.

Output: The retrieved document collections R_D.

1. Let $N = |U|$ denotes the number of the document collections, $R_D = \emptyset$ and $i = 1$;
2. While$(i \le N)$ calculate similarity S between Q and document candidate document $D_i \in U$:

$$S = \cos(D_i, Dj) = \frac{\sum_{i=1}^{n} d_{ik} \cdot d_{jk}}{\sqrt{\sum_{i=1}^{n} (d_{ik})^2 \cdot (d_{jk})^2}} \tag{6}$$

3. If $(S \ge S_0)$ then add the current retrieval results R_i to $R_D, R_D := R_D + R_i, i = i + 1$;
4. Return R_D.

Algorithm 4: Retrieved document collections approximate ranking.

Input: The retrieved document collections R_D. equivalence relation R, parameters $l, u(0 \le l < u \le 1)$.

Output: The ranked document collections R'_D.

1. Let $N = |R_D|$ denotes the number of the Retrieved document collections;
2. Calculate similarity between $D_i, D_j \in R_D(1 \le i, j \le N)$:

$$SIM = SIM_{l,u}(D_i, D_j) = \overline{SIM}_l(D_i, D_j) + \underline{SIM}_u(D_i, D_j) \tag{7}$$

where $\overline{SIM}_l(D_i, D_j) = |\frac{\overline{R}_l(D_i) \cap \overline{R}_l(D_j)}{\overline{R}_l(D_i) \cup \overline{R}_l(D_j)}|, \underline{SIM}_u(D_i, D_j) = |\frac{\underline{R}_u(D_i) \cap \underline{R}_u(D_j)}{\underline{R}_u(D_i) \cup \underline{R}_u(D_j)}|$;
3. Return R'_D.

The higher value of the similarity SIM leads to a higher rank for the corresponding fetched document. These similarity measures can be used only after the retrieved.

The time complexity of the rough fuzzy information retrieval algorithm is $O(log_2|M|)$, where $|M|$ is the number of rough fuzzy sets instead of the number of the document collections.

6 Experiments

In the experiments conducted for this project, the value of the parameter u is set arbitrarily to 0.5 and the value of l is 0, which are same as [13]. With these settings, the original definition of upper approximation was preserved whereas the lower approximation included all elementary sets (semantic indexes) which contained no less than 50% of its defining terms in common with the document or query index terms [13].

We have implemented the whole model of rough fuzzy information retrieval based on Java/XML Web Service and tomcat 4.0 for rough fuzzy information retrieval platform which is a test bed for performance evaluation and internal use, after integration testing we will publish the whole system for scientific researchers to receive useful and fresh information. The system treats each Web page as a document. Fig.2 is the new and refresh retrieved information results.

Fig. 2. RFIRM Experimental Platform: New and Refresh Retrieval Results

The VSM is used as an experimental benchmark to compare it with the RFIRM for Web page ranking. The dataset used in our experiment is taken from the website http://www.research.att.com/ lewis/reuters21578.html. Based on the experiments we noted the following:

First, when proceeding with our examination of the ranking generated, we can plot a curve of precision versus recall as illustrated in Fig.3. The RFIRM-ranked query results demonstrate better recall-precision performance than the VSM-ranked query at each recall level.

Second, Table 1 shows that when the number of retrieved Web pages is small, the recall-precision is approximate to the RFIRM and VSM. As the number of retrieved Web pages increases, the RFIRM produces better results than the VSM

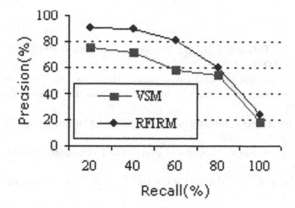

Fig. 3. Recall-precision performance comparison between VSM and RFIRM

Table 1. Recall-precision performance comparison between VSM and RFIRM

The Number of	Recall(%)		Average Precision(%)	
Retrieved Web Page	VSM	RFIRM	VSM	RFIRM
20	89	91	31	33
40	80	82	55	62
500	60	62	58	79
1250	35	40	70	89
2000	20	26	75	91

queries, since the RFIRM has a higher precision value than the VSM for a fixed recall value. The average precision improvements range from 2% to 21% for the sample query.

7   Conclusions

In this paper we combine rough sets with fuzzy sets to propose a new information retrieval model, in which a new algorithm is used to improve the effectiveness of information retrieval. The results of experiments indicated better performance of the rough fuzzy sets-based method over VSM. With the rapid increase of electronic documents and development of information science, there is a wide foreground for application of the rough fuzzy information retrieval.

Acknowledgment

The research reported in this article was supported by the National High-Tech Research and Development Plan of China under Grant No. 2003AA1Z2610.

References

1. Baeza-Yates, R., Ribeiro-Neto, B.: Modern Information Retrieval. Beijing: China Machine Press (2004)
2. Das-Gupta, P.: Rough Set and Information Retrieval. In: Proc. of the 11th conference on Research and Development in Information Retrieval, Grenoble, France (1996) 567-581
3. Pawlak, Z.: Rough Sets. International Journal of Computer and Information Science, 11(5) (1982) 341-356
4. Pawlak, Z.: Rough Sets: Theoretical Aspects of Reasoning about Data. Kluwer, Dordrecht (1991)
5. Ziarko, W.: Variable Precision Rough Set Model. Journal of Computer and Systems Sciences, 46(1) (1993) 39-59
6. Ho, T.B., Furakoshi, K.: Information Retrieval using Rough Set. Journal of Japanese Society for AI, 23(102) (1990)
7. Wong, S.K.M., Ziarko, W.: A Machine Learning Approach to Information Retrieval. In: Proc. of 1986 ACM SIGIR Conference, Italy (1986) 228-233
8. Srinivasan, P.: Intelligent Information Retrieval Using Rough set Approximations. Information Processing and Management: an International Journal, 25(4) (1989) 347-361
9. Green, J., Horne, N., Orlowska, E.: A rough set model of information retrieval. Fundamenta Informaticae, 28(3-4) (1996) 273-296.
10. Zadeh, L.A.: Fuzzy set. Information and control, 8 (1965) 338-353
11. Zadeh, L.A.: Fuzzy set. Readings in Fuzzy set for Intelligent Systems, Morgan Kaufmann (1993)
12. Ogawa, Y., Morita, T., Kobayashi, K.: A fuzzy document retrieval system using the keyword connection matrix and a learning method. Fuzzy set and Systems, 39 (1991) 163-179
13. Ziarko, W., Fei, X.: VPRSM approach to WEB searching. In: Proc. of the Third Intl. Conference on Rough Sets and Current Trends in Computing. Penn State University, USA, Springer Verlag LNAI 2475 (2002) 514-521

A Comprehensive OWA-Based Framework
for Result Merging in Metasearch

Elizabeth D. Diaz, Arijit De, and Vijay Raghavan

Center of Advanced Computer Studies,
University of Louisiana at Lafayette,
Lafayette, LA 70504
elidiaz@bellsouth.net
{axd9142, raghavan}@cacs.louisiana.edu

Abstract. When a query is passed to multiple search engines, each search engine returns a ranked list of documents. The problem of result merging is to fuse these ranked lists such that optimal performance is achieved as a result of the combination. In this paper, our primary contribution is a result merging method, based on fuzzy set theory that adapts the quantifier-guided, Ordered Weighted Averaging (OWA) operators introduced by Yager. The proposed framework is more comprehensive than the existing OWA operator based method, as our investigation evaluates alternative heuristics for missing documents (those existing exist in some, but not all, ranked lists) in order to place such documents into the ranked lists before merging. It shows that the effectiveness of the merging process is improved over the based strategy known as Borda-fuse.

1 Introduction

A metasearch engine is a system that supports unified access to multiple existing search engines. When a query is passed to a metasearch engine, it dispatches the query to a set of search engines, extracts results from the returned pages, and merges them into a single ranked list. In this paper we propose a result-merging algorithm for the meta-search process. Our algorithm is unique as it handles missing documents thereby dealing with one of the biggest challenges in the result-merging [7,8]. A missing document is a document that has been retrieved by some search engines, but not by others. Therefore they appear in some ranked lists, but not in others. A document might be missing from a ranked list if the search engine (a) does not retrieve it, (b) does not index it, (c) if it does not covered it. Handling missing documents also involves a way to compute the position of missing documents in the ranked lists where they are missing. This paves the way for inserting missing documents into the ranked lists in an effort to come up with a more homogenous environment for merging. In this paper we propose (1) a comprehensive method for result-merging that is based on the OWA operators and (2) two different heuristics for handling missing documents.

D. Ślęzak et al. (Eds.): RSFDGrC 2005, LNAI 3642, pp. 193–201, 2005.

2 Related Work

Data fusion techniques for result merging, in the context of metasearch, have been well explored by researchers. Thompson [12], Fox & Shaw [5], Alvarez'[1] have all explored this area. Other models include the Logistic Regression Model [6], and the Linear Combination Model.

Aslam and Montague proposed two models [2]. The first model, Borda-Fuse, (based on the political election strategy Borda Count) works by assigning points to each document in each of the lists to be merged, is optimal [11, 17] in comparison to standard voting methods but has demonstrated limitations[9] with respect to both the Condorcet Principle and Order, and the Increasing and Decreasing Principles. The second method, the Weighted Board-Fuse, a weighted version of Borda-Fuse requires training to determine the best weights for the performance of the search engines but performs better than Borda-Fuse.

Recently, Bordogna proposed a method, named SOFIA [3], which merges the lists from the different search engines by using OWA operators and the fitness scores for each search engine. However SOFIA does not attempt to estimate a value for missing documents. On the contrary, it punishes a missing document by assigning a zero value. Bordogna [3] while reporting the SOFIA method presents experimental results based on only 15 search engines showing any type of comparison to other related methods. Also in SOFIA the fitness scores for various search engines are based on training by means of user feedback. Also SOFIA is a method that uses training to determine the fitness scores of search engines.

3 Merging Approach

In this section we discuss the proposed method for merging documents; the OWA method. We also describe two heuristic strategies for handling missing documents.

3.1 Positional Value and Heuristics for Handling Missing Document

The positional value (PV) of a document d_i in the resulting list l_k returned by a search engine s_k is defined as

$$(n - r_{ik} + 1) \tag{1}$$

where, r_{ik} is the rank of d_i in search engine s_k and n is the total number of documents in the result.

Let PV_i be the positional values for a document d in the ith search engine. Let m be the total number of search engines. Let r be the number of search engines in which d appears. Let j denote a search engine not among the r search engines where d appears.

In heuristic H1 PV_j for all j is denoted by the average of the positional values of the documents in r search engines. Equation (2) denotes this.

$$PVj = \frac{\sum_{i=1}^{r} PV_i}{r} \tag{2}$$

$$PVj = \frac{\sum_{i=1}^{r} PV_i}{m} \tag{3}$$

In heuristic H2 PV_j for all j is denoted by the average of the positional values of the documents in m search engines in which d appears. Equation (3) denotes this.

3.2 OWA Operator

Our OWA approach is based on the OWA operators proposed by Yager. An OWA operator, F, of dimension n is a mapping $F: R^n \rightarrow R$ which has an associated weighting vector, $W = [w_1, w_2, \ldots w_n]^T$, given by

$$w_j \varepsilon [0,1] \text{ and } \sum_{j=1}^{n} w_j = 1 \tag{4}$$

$$F(a_1, a_2, \ldots, a_n) = \sum_{j=1}^{n} w_j b_j, \text{ where } b_j \text{ is the } j^{th} \text{ largest } a_i. \tag{5}$$

It can be seen that the OWA operators depend on the weighing function. A number of special cases have been listed in the literature [16]. We point out three special cases of the OWA operators, distinguished by the weighting vector W:

$$\text{Max: } F(a_1, a_2, a_n) = \max\{a_1, a_2, \ldots, a_n\} \text{ where } W = [1,0,\ldots,0]^T \tag{6}$$

$$\text{Min: } F(a_1, a_2, \ldots, a_n) = \min\{a_1, a_2, \ldots, a_n\} \text{ where } W = [0,0,\ldots,1]^T \tag{7}$$

$$\text{Average: } F(a_1, a_2, \ldots, a_n) = \frac{a_1 + a_2 + \ldots a_n}{n} \tag{8}$$

$$\text{where } W = [\frac{1}{n}, \frac{1}{n}, \ldots \frac{1}{n}]^T$$

OWA operators, introduced by Yager, can be characterized by three measures. These are the "or", the "and" and the "disp" operators.

$$\text{orness (w)} = \frac{1}{n-1} \sum_{i=1}^{n} (n-i)w_i. \tag{9}$$

$$\text{andness (w)} = 1 - \text{orness}(w_i). \tag{10}$$

$$\text{disp (w)} = -\sum_{i=1}^{n} w_i \ln(w_i). \tag{11}$$

3.3 Definition of Weights for OWA

The weights used for the aggregation using the OWA operator can be either generated from a learning mechanism or be associated with a linguistic quantifier [4, 16] according to the formula shown in equation 12. Here Q is the associated linguistic quantifier and n is the number of criteria in the merging process.

$$w_i = Q(\frac{i}{n}) - Q(\frac{i-1}{n}).1 \le i \le n. \tag{12}$$

Thus, if we have 4 search engines, then the weights for the quantifier Q (r) = r^α where $\alpha \ge 0$, is calculated as:

$$w_1 = \left[\frac{1}{4}\right]^\alpha, w_2 = \left[\frac{2}{4}\right]^\alpha - \left[\frac{1}{4}\right]^\alpha,$$

$$w_3 = \left[\frac{3}{4}\right]^\alpha - \left[\frac{2}{4}\right]^\alpha, w_4 = \left[\frac{4}{4}\right]^\alpha - \left[\frac{3}{4}\right]^\alpha. \tag{13}$$

Thus, the process used in quantifier-guided aggregation is to use the quantifier Q to generate a set of OWA weights, $w_1 \ldots w_n$ where n is the number of alternatives and then (2) for each alternative calculate the overall importance or satisfaction as F (d_1, d_2, ..., d_n)) where F is an OWA aggregation using the weights found in equation (5).

3.4 Application of OWA for Result Merging

In this section we discuss our proposed application of the OWA operator to result merging. We have a finite number of search engines (m) each of which returns a ranked list of documents for a query. We merge the lists into a single ranked list by representing a document d as a set of positional values, S as shown in equation 14.

$$S = \{ PV_j | \forall j \ 1 \le j \le m\} \tag{14}$$

Here m is the number of search engines and PV_j is the position of document d in the ranked list returned by search engine j. We define an OWA operator F for a document d as shown in equation 15. Here w_j is the weight derived from equation (12).

$$F(d) = \sum_{j=1}^{m} w_j * PV_j \tag{15}$$

The OWA operator, from equation (15), provides an overall PV for any document d in the merged list. Four steps must be followed for aggregating the results from different search engines. (1) Calculate the position values (PV's) for each document in different search engines, based on the rank of the document as defined in this section. Consider one of the alternatives as stated above for calculating the position values (PV's) of a missing document in the list of results returned by a search engine. (2) For each search engine, arrange the position values (PV's) of each of the documents in descending order to obtain an m tuple for each document. (3) Calculate weights for each search engines from the formula as given in equation (12). (4) Apply the OWA operator F on the tuples to get a rank for each document and arrange the documents in the descending order of their ranks.

Example: OWA with Missing Document Heuristic: H1
Table 1(a) shows the results from four search engines for a query q. The rows in the table represent the documents retrieved by these search engines in the descending order of their local similarity. M indicates that the particular document is missing in the search engine. In the first step, the PVs of the documents returned by a search engine are calculated based on their positional values as defined before. The results are shown in Table 1(b). Each column in the table represents the PVs of a particular document. In step 2 the PVs of each of the documents is arranged in descending order as shown in Table 1(c). Each column in the table represents the PVs of a particular document, in the descending order. In step 3 the weights for the algorithm are derived from the equations (12) and (13). Table 1(d) shows the value when the weights of $\alpha = 0.5$. In step 4 the OWA operator F, defined as in equation 15 is applied on the tuples in Table 1(e) to obtain an overall rank for each document.

Table 1. This table shows the five steps in computing the document weights and corresponding document ranks using the OWA method

Table 1(a). Results from four search engines.

Se_1	D_2	D_1	D_3	D_4	D_5
Se_2	D_2	D_3	D_4	M	M
Se_3	D_2	D_5	D_4	D_1	M
Se_4	D_5	D_3	D_2	D_4	D_1

Table 1(b). Positional Values of the documents in the four search engines.

	D_1	D_2	D_3	D_4	D_5
Se_1	4	5	3	2	1
Se_2	2 (M)	3	2	1	3(M)
Se_3	1	4	3 (M)	2	3
Se_4	1	3	4	2	5

Table 1(c). PVs of the documents in the four search engines sorted in descending order.

D_1	D_2	D_3	D_4	D_5
4	5	4	2	5
2	4	3	2	3
1	3	3	2	3
1	3	2	1	1

Table 1(d). Weights calculated as per step 3

w_1	w_2	w_3	w_4
0.5	0.21	0.16	0.13

Table 1(e) Document ranks calculated and sorted

D_2	D_5	D_3	D_1	D_4
4.2	4	3.4	2.71	1.9

4   Experiments and Results

We used the data set TREC 3 obtained from TREC, (Text Retrieval Conference). The data set contains 50 topics (analogous to queries) numbered 151-200 and 40 systems (analogous to search engines). Thus, topics (queries) are passed onto a system (search engine). The search engines then return a set of documents in the form of a ranked list. Each document is either relevant (represented by 1), highly relevant (represented by 2) or not relevant (represented by 0). Search engines return up to 1000 documents when queried with a certain topic. We also used the recall based precision method for evaluation of each strategy. The theory for recall based precision can be found in [10]. We used recall values of 0.25, 0.5, and 1 to do our evaluations.

Below is a list the steps performed to obtain the experimental results.

1. Pick a number m [2, 12], where m is the number of search engines to be searched/merged.
2. Pick a query q [151, 200] at random, and submit/dispatch q to the m search engines selected in the previous step.
3. Use either OWA/Borda-fuse for merging the results from the m search engines employing a heuristic (either H1 or H2) for handling missing documents and a value of α quantifier for the OWA method.
4. Calculate the average precision for the documents in the merged list.
5. Repeat steps 2 – 4 in order to replicate 200 times.
6. Repeat steps 2 – 5 and obtain an average precision for each m.

We ran our experiments comparing the OWA method, with quantifier values of 0.5, 1, 2, and 2.5 to the Borda Method when both heuristic H1 and H2 we used to handle missing documents.

Figure 1 shows the variation in RB-precision of the merged list when the number of search engine result sets being merged increases from 2 to 12. The number of search engines being merged is represented in the X-axis while RB-precision is

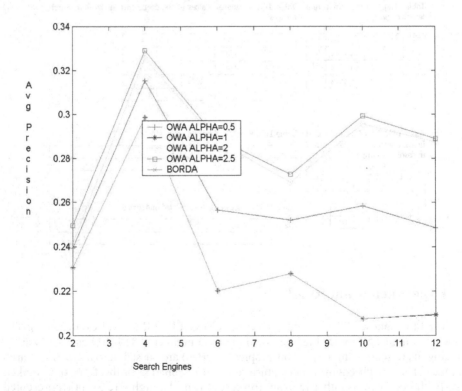

Fig. 1. The figure displays a graph that shows how the OWA method compares against the BORDA method when using heuristic H1 for handling missing documents

represented in the Y-axis. The graph shows variation in RB-precision of the merged list with the number of search engines being merged for BORDA and OWA with quantifiers of 0.5,1,2 and 2.5. Here heuristic H1 is used to handle missing documents in case of both BORDA and OWA. RB-precision increases as the number of search engine result sets being merged increases from 2 to 4. A peak value is reaches at this point. Following this the value decreases and increases somewhat periodically. Also in this case the OWA methods do significantly better than the BORDA method.

Figure 2 shows a graphical plot similar to Figure 1. The only difference in this case is that the heuristic H2 is employed. Notice that as the number of search engines increases, the BORDA method does worse while the OWA method with different quantifiers does better. When more than 8 search engines are merged the OWA method with different quantifiers do better than the BORDA method.

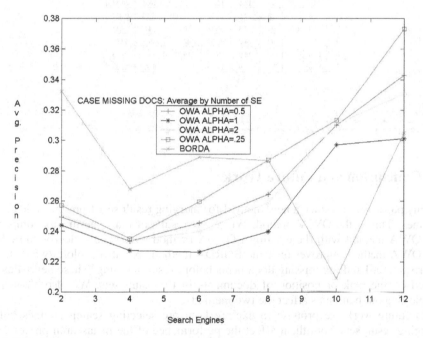

Fig. 2. This figure shows a graph that compares the OWA and Borda when using heuristic H2 to handle missing documents

Table 2 summarizes the improvement of the OWA method, for quantifier values of 0.5,1,2 and 2.5, over the BORDA method when using each of the two heuristics H1 and H2 when merging between 2 and 12 search engine result sets.

In general OWA improves over BORDA mainly when eight or more search engines are being merged, irrespective of what the quantifier value for OWA is and what heuristic we are employing. The OWA method shows greater improvement over the BORDA method when employing the heuristic H2. In case of heuristic H1 the OWA method with quantifier value of 2.5 gives the best results, followed by OWA with quantifier value of 2, 0.5 and 1. Similar results are observed for heuristic H2.

Table 2. Improvement of OWA over BORDA for different heuristics when using different values of alpha quantifier

SE	%Improvement of OWA over BORDA when using H1				%Improvement of OWA over BORDA when using H2			
α→	0.5	1	2	2.5	0.5	1	2	2.5
2	3.82	0	4.8	8.21	-24.90	-26.52	-24.5	-22.6
3	5.22	0.04	8.1	10.6	-18.05	-19.72	-18.1	-17
4	5.59	0	9	10.2	-12.90	-15.18	-12.7	-12.2
5	8.48	0.38	11	15.5	50.59	46.92	48.2	51.8
6	16.5	0.01	31	31.2	-15.08	-21.8	-17.1	-10.2
7	8.15	-0.1	15	17.6	16.51	10.71	16.4	20.33
8	10.6	0	18	19.6	-7.84	-16.44	-9.73	0.072
9	14.4	0.01	28	28.8	69.27	50.07	64.8	79.32
10	24.5	0	42	44.2	48.33	42.17	48.8	49.88
11	10.8	0	17	18.9	28.39	19.37	26.5	34.33
12	18.6	0	37	37.9	12.39	-1.20	8.37	22.35

5 Conclusion and Future Work

In this paper we introduce a new method for merging result sets from multiple search engines. This is the OWA method. We report results of our experiments comparing the OWA method with the existing BORDA method. Our results clearly show how the OWA method improves over the BORDA method. We also explore two different heuristics for handling missing documents before result merging. These heuristics are based on the rank or position of documents in the result sets. We also show how employing our heuristics affect the two methods.

In future work we propose to explore how pre selecting search engines before merging result sets from them affect the performance of the metasearch process. We explore strategies for pre selecting search engines for result merging.

References

[1] S. A. Alvarez, Web Metasearch as Belief Aggregation, AAAI-2000 Workshop on Artificial Intelligence for Web Search, Austin, TX, July 2000.

[2] J. A. Aslam , M. Montague, Models for Metasearch, Proceedings of the 24th annual international ACM SIGIR conference on Research and development in information retrieval, New Orleans, Louisiana, United States, September 2001, pp. 276-284.

[3] G. Bordogna, Soft Fusion of Information Accesses, Proceedings of the IEEE Int. Conf. On Fuzzy Systems 2002, Honolulu, Hawaii, USA, May 2002, pp. 24-28.

[4] C. Carlson, R.Fullér and S.Fullér, OWA operators for doctoral student selection problem, in: R. R. Yager and J. Kacprzyk, *The ordered weighted averaging operators: Theory, Methodology, and Applications*, Kluwer Academic Publishers, Boston, 1997, pp. 167-178.

[5] E. A. Fox and J. A. Shaw, Combination of multiple searches, Proceedings of the 2nd Text Retrieval Conference (TREC-2), National Institute of Standards and Technology Special Publication 500-215, 1994, pp. 243-252.

[6] D. A. Hull, J. O. Pedersen, H. Schütze, Method combination for document filtering, Proceedings of the 19th annual international ACM SIGIR Conference on Research and Development in Information Retrieval,   August 18-22, 1996, Zurich, Switzerland, pp. 279-287.

[7] W. Meng., C. Yu, K. Liu, Building Efficient and Effective Metasearch engines, ACM Computing Surveys, March 2002, pp. 48-84.

[8] W. Meng, C. Yu, K. Liu. A Highly Scalable and Effective Method for Metasearch, ACM Transactions on Information Systems, pp. 310-335, July 2001.

[9] J.R. Parker, Multiple Sensors, Voting Methods and Target Value Analysis, Computer Science Technical Report, 1998, February 1, 1998, University of Calgary, Laboratory for Computer Vision, pp. 615-06.

[10] V. Raghavan, G. Jung, A Critical Investigation of Recall and Precision as Measures of Retrieval System Performance. Proceedings of the 1989 ACM Transactions on Information Systems, Vol 7, No 3, July 1989, pp. 205-229.

[11] F. Roberts, *Discrete Mathematical Models*, Prentice Hall, Inc., 1976.

[12] P. Thompson, A combination of expert opinion approach to probabilistic information retrieval, part 1: The conceptual model, Information Processing and Management: an International Journal, v.26 n.3, pp. 371-382, 1990.

[13] R.R. Yager, V. Kreinovich, On how to merge sorted lists coming from different web search tools, Soft Computing Research Journal 3,1999, pp. 83-88.

[14] R.R. Yager, On ordered weighted averaging aggregation operators in multicriteria decision making, Fuzzy Sets and Systems, vol. 10, 1983, pp. 243-260.

[15] R.R. Yager, Aggregating evidence using quantified statements, *Information Sciences*, vol. 36, no. 1, 1985, pp. 179-206.

[16] R.R. Yager, Quantifier guided Aggregating using OWA operators, International Journal of Intelligent Systems 11, 1996 pp. 49-73.

[17] F. Zachary, Lansdowne, Outranking Methods for Multicriterion Decision Making: Arrow's and Raynaud's Conjecture"; Social Choice and Welfare; Vol. 14, No. 1; January, 1997, pp 125-128; #2431.

[18] E.D. Diaz, A. De, V. V. Raghavan, On Selective Result Merging in a Metasearch Environment. Workshop on Web-based Support Systems, 2004: pp. 52-59.

[19] E. Diaz, Selective Merging of Retrieval Results for Metasearch Environments: Ph.D. Dissertation, The Center of Advanced Computer Studies, University of Louisiana at Lafayette, Register of Copyrights, USA, # TX 6-0400305, November 6, 2004.

Efficient Pattern Matching of Multidimensional Sequences*

Sangjun Lee[1], Kyoungsu Oh[1], Dongseop Kwon[2], Wonik Choi[3], Jiman Hong[4],
Jongmoo Choi[5], and Donghee Lee[6]

[1] Soongsil University
{sjlee, oks}@computing.ssu.ac.kr
[2] Seoul National University
dongseop@gmail.com
[3] Thinkware Systems Corporation
styxii@db.snu.ac.kr
[4] Kwangwoon University
gman@daisy.kw.ac.kr
[5] Dankook University
choijm@dankook.ac.kr
[6] University of Seoul
dhlee@venus.uos.ac.kr

Abstract. We address the problem of the similarity search in large multidimensional sequence databases. Most of previous work focused on similarity matching and retrieval of one-dimensional sequences. However, many new applications such as weather data or music databases need to handle multidimensional sequences. In this paper, we present the efficient search method for finding similar sequences to a given query sequence in multidimensional sequence databases. The proposed method can efficiently reduce the search space and guarantees no false dismissals. We give preliminary experimental results to show the effectiveness of the proposed method.

1 Introduction

A time series (or time sequence) database is a collection of data that are generated in series as time goes on. Typical examples include stock price movements, financial information, weather data, biomedical measurements, music data, video data, etc. The similarity search in time series databases is essential in many applications, such as pattern matching, data mining and knowledge discovery [1][2].

Although the sequential scanning can be used to perform the similarity search, it is obvious that it would be time consuming and inefficient as the size of time series databases increases. Therefore, it is important to reduce the search space for efficient processing of the similarity search in large time series databases. In general, an indexing scheme is used to support fast retrieval of

---

* This work is supported by the Korea Research Foundation Grant (KRF-2004-005-D00198).

D. Ślęzak et al. (Eds.): RSFDGrC 2005, LNAI 3642, pp. 202–210, 2005.

similar sequences to a given query sequences. However, a naive indexing of high-dimensional data such as sequences suffers from performance deterioration due to the *dimensionality curse* [3][7] of the index structures. The general approaches of the similarity search in time series databases performs the feature extraction as dimensionality reduction to avoid the dimensionality curse, and index the features using a spatial access method such as R-tree [5] or R*-tree [6] in the feature space. The important issue in indexing time series using dimensionality reduction methods is that these methods must guarantee no false dismissals. That is, the distance between dimensionality reduced sequences should be the lower bound of the distance between original sequences (lower bound condition) [3].

Most of existing similarity models or search techniques in time series databases does not consider multidimensional sequences where an element in a sequence is composed of two or more attributes. Many new applications need to deal with multidimensional sequences. For example, we may want to find all regions that have weather patterns similar to a given region. Such weather patterns may refer to both temperature and humidity.

In this paper, we present the efficient search method to find all sequences similar to a given query sequence. The proposed method uses the lower dimensional transform to map multidimensional sequences into one-dimensional sequences and extracts the features from those one-dimensional sequences. Our proposed method can efficiently reduce the search space and guarantees no false dismissals.

The remainder of this paper is organized as follows. Section 2 provides a survey of the related work. Section 3 explains the similarity model for multidimensional sequences. Our proposed approach is described in Section 4. Section 5 presents preliminary experimental results for evaluating the effectiveness of the proposed approach. Finally, several concluding remarks are given in Section 6.

2 Related Work

Various methods have been proposed for fast matching and retrieval of similar sequences in one-dimensional time series databases. The main focus is to improve the search performance. The search performance using spatial access methods shows the rapid deterioration as the dimensionality of data increases, eventually, it becomes worse than the sequential scanning. To avoid this problem, various feature extraction methods have been used to reduce the dimensionality of sequences, including the Discrete Fourier Transform [3][4][15], the Discrete Wavelet Transform [16][22], the Singular Value Decomposition [11], and the Piecewise Aggregate Approximation [17][20], etc.

Another important issue of the similarity search in time series databases is to provide a more intuitive notion of the similarity between sequences to users. The notion of the similarity can be subjective to the users' perspectives. Various transformations and similarity models have been proposed to satisfy users' perspectives, including normalization [8][9], scaling and shifting [14], moving average [15], time warping [12][19][21], individual distance of the slope [13], and landmark model [18], etc.

Though there have been many methods to process the similarity search in time series databases, most of the previous work focused on one-dimensional sequences. The similarity search for multidimensional sequences is not fully studied in database communities. There are just a few works on such sequences.

In [23], the authors propose the indexing method of multidimensional sequences based on the sum of distances of multidimensional data objects. They introduced the normalized distance $D_{norm}()$ for efficient processing of the similarity search. However, the method using $D_{norm}()$ can generate false alarms. In [25], the authors address the problem of the similarity search considering the shifting and scaling in multidimensional sequences. In [24], the authors propose the indexing method of multidimensional sequences based on the LCSS (Longest Common Subsequence) model used in [9]. The problem of the LCSS model is that it requires high computational complexity.

The above similarity models for multidimensional sequences are essentially based on the distance between two elements in sequences. That is, the similarity models for multidimensional sequences are the sum of distance between two elements [23] or its derivatives [25] and the LCSS model based on the distance between two elements [24]. The similarity models of above approaches are only suitable when the distance between elements has the meaningful notion of the distance such as the trajectory matching [24].

The limitation of the current models for multidimensional sequences is that there is no consideration for attributes' sequences. The multidimensional sequences are composed of several attributes' sequences. Since the users may want to find the similar patterns considering attributes's sequences, it is more appropriate to consider the similarity between two multidimensional sequences in the viewpoint of attributes' sequences. For example, we may want to find similar songs to the given song in music databases and the music data may be composed of rhythms and intervals. In this case, the song would be classified as similar or dissimilar by considering their rhythms and intervals.

3   Multidimensional Sequences and Similarity Model

The problem we focus on is the design of efficient retrieval of total-similar multidimensional sequences in time series databases. The multidimensional sequence S of length n is defined as follows: Each of $S_j[i]$ represents the $i-th$ element of the $j-th$ attribute's sequence.

Definition 1 (Multidimensional Sequences). *The m-dimensional sequence S of length n is defined as follows.*

$$S = \begin{bmatrix} sensing\ time \\ first\ attribute \\ second\ attribute \\ \cdots \\ m-th\ attribute \end{bmatrix} \begin{bmatrix} t_1 \\ S_1[1] \\ S_2[1] \\ \cdots \\ S_m[1] \end{bmatrix} \begin{bmatrix} t_2 \\ S_1[2] \\ S_2[2] \\ \cdots \\ S_m[2] \end{bmatrix} \begin{bmatrix} t_3 \\ S_1[3] \\ S_2[3] \\ \cdots \\ S_m[3] \end{bmatrix} \cdots \begin{bmatrix} t_n \\ S_1[n] \\ S_2[n] \\ \cdots \\ S_m[n] \end{bmatrix}$$

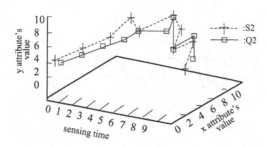

Fig. 1. Example of two-dimensional sequences

Figure 1 shows the example of two-dimensional sequences. Sequences $S2$ and $Q2$ are displayed in sensing time - attribute x - attribute y space, respectively.

The multidimensional sequences are composed of several attributes' sequences and it is more appropriate to consider the similarity between two multidimensional sequences in the viewpoint of attributes' sequences. We define the total-similarity between two multidimensional sequences by using the weighted sum of Euclidean distances for attributes' sequences. Specifically, the total- similarity model between two multidimensional sequences $D_{total}(S, Q)$ is defined as follows.

Definition 2 (Total-similarity model). *The total-similarity between two m-dimensional sequences Q and S of length n is defined by the weighted sum of Euclidean distances for attributes' sequences as follows.*

$$D_{total}(S, Q) = \sum_{j=1}^{m} \lambda_j (\sum_{i=1}^{n} |S_j[i] - Q_j[i]|^2)^{1/2}$$

λ_j denotes the weighting factor for $j - th$ attribute since it is necessary to normalize the effect of each attribute on the total-similarity above defined. Two multidimensional sequences are said to be total-similar if their weighted sum of Euclidean distances for attributes' sequences is within a user-defined threshold ϵ_{total}. Using the total-similarity model, we can process the similarity-based query in multidimensional sequence databases

4   Proposed Approach

The naive and obvious method for multidimensional sequences may be to use the individual index for each attribute's sequences. This method is to construct the individual index structure for each attribute's sequences. We call this approach as the *Individual Index Method*. The critical problem of the above approach is that it cannot deal with k-nearest neighbor query or ranking query such as *find 10 nearest neighbor song similar to the given song considering both their rhythms and intervals in music databases or show me the top-10 songs ranked by*

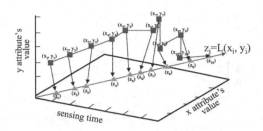

Fig. 2. Example of mapping two-dimensional sequence into one-dimensional sequence

the similarity to the given song. Since the individual index for each attribute's sequences is independent from each other and the closeness for one attribute does not always mean the closeness for another attribute, so it is hard to retrieve all sequences which are total-similar to a given query sequence. Moreover, this method may be impractical and inefficient in space and processing since we have to build m index structures for m-dimensional sequences. This method would be a straightforward solution when the query conditions are given for attributes separately. However, this type of queries is not our focus and we do not consider this approach any more in this paper.

To overcome the shortcomings of the *Individual Index Method*, it is highly required to build the unified framework for multidimensional sequences. We propose the *Unified Index Method (UIM)* for multidimensional sequences. It uses lower dimensional transform $L()$ mapping high-dimensional sequences into low-dimensional ones. For example, Figure 2 shows the case of mapping two-dimensional sequence into one-dimensional sequence. Note that the dimensionality reduction in this method means the reduction of the number of sequence's attributes and the length of a sequence is maintained after the lower dimensional transformation. Various methods can be used to reduce the number of attributes if they satisfy the lower bound condition. In this paper, we used the summation of attributes' elements in a sequence as a lower dimensional transform $L()$.

After the lower dimensional transformation, feature vectors are extracted from dimensionally reduced sequences to construct a unified index structure using a spatial access method such as the R-tree. The similarity search can be performed against the query sequence using the unified index structure.

In order to guarantee no false dismissals, we must construct a distance measure $D_{low}(L(S), L(Q))$ defined for dimensionality reduced sequences, which has the following property.

$$D_{low}(L(S), L(Q)) \le D_{total}(S, Q)$$

The distance measure between dimensionally reduced sequences is defined as
$D_{low}(L(S), L(Q)) =$

$$= \{\sum_{i=1}^{n} |(\lambda_1 S_1[i] + \cdots + \lambda_m S_m[i]) - (\lambda_1 Q_1[i] + \cdots + \lambda_m Q_m[i])|^2\}^{1/2}$$

We must show that the distance between dimensionality reduced sequences is the lower bound of that of between original multidimensional sequences as follows.

Theorem 1. *The distance measure $D_{low}(L(S), L(Q))$ is the lower bound of the total similarity $D_{total}(S, Q)$ and it guarantees no false dismissals.*

Proof. Let the $\vec{V_j}$ denote the vector of differences measures with respect to the $j-th$ attribute, $j = 1, \ldots, m$. The unit vector $\vec{e_i}, i = 1, \ldots, n$ represents the basis vector for i-dimension. We obtain:

$$\vec{V_j} = \lambda_j (\sum_{i=1}^{n} (S_j[i] - Q_j[i]) \vec{e_i})$$

By using the triangular inequality, Theorem 1 is proven as follows:

$$|\vec{V_1} + \vec{V_2} + \cdots + \vec{V_m}|^2$$
$$= |\vec{V_1}|^2 + \cdots + |\vec{V_m}|^2 + 2|\vec{V_1}||\vec{V_2}| \cos \theta_1 + \cdots + 2|\vec{V_{m-1}}||\vec{V_m}| \cos \theta_{m(m-1)/2-1}$$
$$\leq |\vec{V_1}|^2 + \cdots + |\vec{V_m}|^2 + 2|\vec{V_1}||\vec{V_2}| + \cdots + 2|\vec{V_{m-1}}||\vec{V_m}|$$
$$= (|\vec{V_1}| + |\vec{V_2}| + \cdots + |\vec{V_m}|)^2 \qquad \qquad \square$$

After an index structure has been built, we can perform the similarity search against a given query sequence. The search processing consists of two main parts. The first is for candidate selection via the index traversal and the other is for postprocessing to remove false alarms from candidate sequences. Some false alarms may be included in the results of candidate selection. The actual distance between a query sequence and candidate sequences are computed and only those within the threshold are reported as the query results.

5   Performance Evaluation

In this section, we will present the some experimental results to analyze the performance of the *Unified Index Method (UIM)*. To verify the effectiveness of the proposed method, we compared the *Unified Index Method* with the sequential scanning in terms of the search space ratio to test the filtering effect of removing irrelevant sequences in the process of the index searching by varying the threshold. The search space ratio is defined as follows.

$$search \ space \ ratio = \frac{the \ number \ of \ candidate \ sequences}{the \ number \ of \ sequences \ in \ a \ database}$$

Note that the search space ratio is related to only the feature vectors and independent of implementation factors such as hardware·software platforms, etc. This approach to evaluate the indexing scheme appears in [10][20].

For the experiments, we have generated two-dimensional and three-dimensional sequences of length 64 using the random walk model following [3]

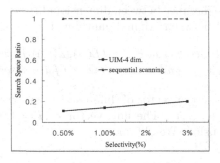

Fig. 3. Search space ratio by varying threshold for 2d-sequences

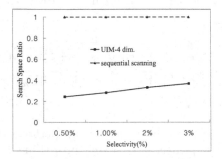

Fig. 4. Search space ratio by varying threshold for 3d-sequences

for the lack of real multidimensional sequence dataset. More specifically, each attribute's sequence was generated by the following formula.

$$S_m[i] = S_m[i-1] + \alpha \cdot z_i$$
$$where \quad S_m[0] \sim U(-500, 500), \ z_i \sim N(-500, 500),$$
$$and \ \alpha = 0.05$$

The weighting factor λ_j for $j - th$ attribute can be adjusted by considering users' preferences for certain attributes and the range of values in attribute's sequences, etc. For simplicity, all weighting factors for normalizing the effect of each attribute on the total-similarity are set to 1 in our experiments. The size of each dataset was set to 10,000. The Discrete Wavelet Transform is used for feature extraction from dimensionality reduced sequences. An important parameter is the dimensionality of feature vectors and we used 4-dimensions in our experiments. The query ranges were chosen such that the average selectivity of query results be 0.5%, 1%, 2% and 3% for datasets. We ran 50 random queries over synthetic dataset to find similar sequences and took the average of query results. The query sequences were also generated in the same way of data sequences by the random walk model. The results show that our proposed method can efficiently reduce the search space without false dismissals.

6   Conclusion

Most of previous work on the similarity search in time series databases is concentrated on one-dimensional sequences and does not take into account more dimensions corresponding to two or more attributes. In this paper, we considered the problem of efficient matching and retrieval of multidimensional sequences. The proposed method uses the lower dimensionality transform to map multidimensional sequences into one-dimensional sequences and extracts the features from those one-dimensional sequences. To show the soundness of our approach, we have proven that the proposed method does not produce any false dismissal. We have performed the experiments on synthetic random work data, and evaluated the search space ratio of our proposed method. The experiments show that our approach can efficiently reduce the search space.

References

1. Agrawal, R., Imielinski, T., Swami, A.N.: Database Mining: A Performance Perspective. IEEE Transactions on Knowledge and Data Engineering, Vol.5, No.6 (1993) 914-925
2. Fayyad, U.M., Piatetsky-Shapiro, G., Smyth, P.: Knowledge Discovery and Data Mining: Towards a Unifying Framework. In: Proceedings of International Conference on Knowledge Discovery and Data Mining (1996) 82-88
3. Agrawal, R., Faloutsos, C., Swami, A.N.: Efficient Similarity Search In Sequence Databases. In: Proceedings of International Conference on Foundations of Data Organization and Algorithms (1993) 69-84
4. Faloutsos, C., Ranganathan, M., Manolopoulos, Y.: Fast Subsequence Matching in Time-Series Databases. In: Proceedings of ACM SIGMOD International Conference on Management of Data (1994) 419-429
5. Guttman, A.: R-trees: A Dynamic Index Structure for Spatial Searching. In: Proceedings of ACM SIGMOD International Conference on Management of Data (1984) 47-57
6. Beckmann, N., Kriegel, H.P., Schneider, R., Seeger, B.: The R*-tree: An Efficient and Robust Access Method for Points and Rectangles. In: Proceedings of ACM SIGMOD International Conference on Management of Data (1990) 322-331
7. Faloutsos, C., Lin, K.I.: Fastmap: A Fast Algorithm for Indexing, Data-mining and Visualization of Traditional and Multimedia Datasets. In: Proceedings of ACM SIGMOD International Conference on Management of Data (1995) 163- 174
8. Goldin, D.Q., Kanellakis, P.C.: On Similarity Queries for Time-Series Data: Constraint Specification and Implementation. In: Proceedings of International Conference on Constraint Programming (1995) 137-153
9. Das, G., Gunopulos, D., Mannila H.: Finding Similar Time Series. In: Proceedings of European Conference on Principles of Data Mining and Knowledge Discovery (1997) 88-100
10. Hellerstein, J.M., Koutsoupias, E., Papadimitriou, C.H.: On the Analysis of Indexing Schemes. In: Proceedings of ACM SIGACT-SIGMOD-SIGART Symposium on Principles of Database Systems (1997) 249-256
11. Korn, F., Jagadish, H.V., Faloutsos, C.: Efficiently Supporting Ad Hoc Queries in Large Datasets of Time Sequences. In: Proceedings of ACM SIGMOD International Conference on Management of Data (1997) 289-300

12. Yi, B.K., Jagadish, H.V., Faloutsos, C.: Efficient Retrieval of Similar Time Sequences Under Time Warping. In: Proceedings of International Conference on Data Engineering (1998) 201-208
13. Lam, S.K., Wong, M.H.: A Fast Projection Algorithm for Sequence Data Searching, Data and Knowledge Engineering, Vol.28, No.3 (1998) 321-339
14. Chu, K.K.W., Wong, M.H.: Fast Time-Series Searching with Scaling and Shifting. In: Proceedings of ACM SIGACT-SIGMOD-SIGART Symposium on Principles of Database Systems (1999) 237-248
15. Rafiei, D.: On Similarity-Based Queries for Time Series Data. In: Proceedings of International Conference on Data Engineering (1999) 410-417
16. Chan, K.P., Fu, A.W.: Efficient Time Series Matching by Wavelets. In: Proceedings International Conference on Data Engineering (1999) 126-133
17. Yi, B.K., Faloutsos, C.: Fast Time Sequence Indexing for Arbitrary Lp Norms. In: Proceedings of International Conference on Very Large Data Bases (2000) 385-394
18. Perng, C.S., Wang, H., Zhang, S.R., Parker, D.S.: Landmarks: a New Model for Similarity-based Pattern Querying in Time Series Databases. In: Proceedings of International Conference on Data Engineering(2000), 33-42
19. Kim, S.W., Park S., Chu, W.W.: An Index-Based Approach for Similarity Search Supporting Time Warping in Large Sequence Databases. In: Proceedings of International Conference on Data Engineering (2001) 607-614
20. Keogh, E.J., Chakrabarti, K., Mehrotra, S., Pazzani, M.J.: Locally Adaptive Dimensionality Reduction for Indexing Large Time Series Databases. In: Proceedings of ACM SIGMOD International Conference on Management of Data (2001) 151-162
21. Keogh, E.J.: Exact Indexing of Dynamic Time Warping. In: Proceedings of International Conference on Very Large Data Bases (2002) 406-417
22. Popivanov, I., Miller, R.J.: Similarity Search Over Time-Series Uisng Wavelets. In: Proceedings of International Conference on Data Engineering (2002) 212-221
23. Lee, S.L., Chun, S.J., Kim, D.H., Lee, J.H., Chung, C.W.: Similarity Search for Multidimensional Data Sequences. In: Proceedings of International Conference on Data Engineering (2000) 599-608
24. Vlachos, M., Kollios, G., Gunopulos, D.: Discovering Similar Multidimensional Trajectories. In: Proceedings of International Conference on Data Engineering (2002) 673-684
25. Kahveci, T., Singh, A., Gurel, A.: Similairty Searching for Multi-attribute Sequences. In: Proceedings of International Conference on Scientific and Statistical Database Management (2002) 175-184

HQC: An Efficient Method for ROLAP with Hierarchical Dimensions

Xing-Ye Dong, Hou-Kuan Huang, and Hong-Song Li

School of Computer and IT, Beijing Jiaotong University,
Beijing 100044, China
dong.xingye@163.com, hkhuang@center.njtu.edu.cn, mlhs@163.com

Abstract. A useful concept called cover equivalence was proposed recently. By using this concept, the size of data cube can be reduced, and quotient cube was proposed. The scheme of ROLAP put forward in this paper is called HQC, in which a cover window is set and hierarchical dimensions are introduced. By using the concept of cover window, the size of data cube can be reduced further. E.g, for the Weather dataset, there are about 5.7M aggregated tuples in quotient table, but only about 0.18M in HQC when the cover window is 100. At the same time, the query performance can be improved. By using hierarchical dimensions, the size of HQC can be reduced without information being lost. This paper also illustrates a construction algorithm and a query algorithm for HQC. Some experimental results are presented, using both synthetic and real-world datasets. These results show that our techniques are effective.

1 Introduction

Data cube [1] is an important operator for data warehousing and OLAP. Generally speaking, a data cube is a multi-level, multi-dimensional dataset with multiple granularity aggregates. It is a generalization of the relational group-by operator, and contains group-bys corresponding to all possible combinations of a list of dimensions. If there is no hierarchy in any dimension, there will be 2^n group-bys in a n dimensional data cube. In practice, a data cube lattice is often huge. Issues related to the size of data cubes have attracted much attention of researchers. Various algorithms have been developed aiming at fast computation of large sparse data cube [2, 3, 4, 5] and various structures have been put forward for reducing the size of data cube, such as condensed cube [6] and Dwarf [7]. Recently, researchers began to focus attention on extracting more "semantics" from a data cube. E.g., [8] studies most general contexts under which observed patterns occur and [9] generalizes association rules to a much broader context by using the cube structure. [10] and [11] put forward a data cube called quotient cube and an efficient summary structure called QC-trees. Quotient cube can be stored in a table called quotient table. [12] brings forward a data cube called closed data cube. In summary, all of them compress the size of data cube by sharing common tuples, and needn't real-time aggregation.

D. Ślęzak et al. (Eds.): RSFDGrC 2005, LNAI 3642, pp. 211–220, 2005.

This paper proposes a method for ROLAP with hierarchical dimensions called HQC (Hierarchical Quotient Cube). This method fully utilizes the function of relational database and reduces the size of data cube by sharing common tuples, partially materializing and reducing the number of dimensions. And this method improves the query performance.

The remainder of the paper is organized as follows. Section 2 gives some related basic concepts. Section 3 presents our partially materializing strategy. Section 4 and 5 give a construction algorithm and a query algorithm for HQC respectively. Experimental results are presented in section 6. We discuss the related work in section 7, and conclude the paper in section 8.

2   Basic Concepts

The size of data cube is closely relevant to the number of dimensions. It can be reduced effectively by reducing the number of dimensions. E.g., we may use three dimensions, i.e., country, province and city, to store area information. If this information is stored in one hierarchical dimension having three levels, then two dimensions will be reduced, and great mass of storage space will be saved. In order to implement a hierarchy of dimension, a code format of dimension needs to be defined.

Definition 1 (Code Format of Hierarchical Dimension). *Let $P_j^i = (v_1, v_2, \ldots, v_{k_i})$ is the code of the ith level of the jth dimension. k_i denotes the number of digits of level i. P_j^i can roll up to "*", which denotes the special value "All" of level i. "*" is less than any other value of this level. The code of hierarchical dimension is arranged by such code from higher level to lower level, namely, the code format is $(P_j^m, P_j^{m-1}, \ldots, P_j^1)$ if the jth dimension has m levels.*

According to the definition, for hierarchical dimension, it does not roll up to "All" directly from the most detail level, but rolls up level by level. E.g., an area dimension has three levels: country, province and city, then the roll up sequence is city, province, country and "All".

Example 1. Sales information. Area dimension has two levels: country and city. Each level is presented by one digit. Time dimension has two levels: quarter and month. The quarter level is presented by one digit while the other two digits. Product dimension has no hierarchy. Shown as the following tables.

AID	Area	TID	Time	PID	Product	AID	TID	PID	Sale
10	China	100	1st quarter	1	Product 1	11	101	1	10
11	Beijing	101	Jan	2	Product 2	11	102	2	7
12	Shanghai	102	Feb	3	Product 3	12	101	2	12

The code of dimension can be different schemes. It is numeric in this example. According to the highly relevance between every two levels, it is easy to see that the number of tuples in a data cube by using non-hierarchical dimensions is the same as that by using hierarchical ones. Hence, the size of data cube can be reduced. The data cube lattice produced from the base table in Example 1 is illustrated in Fig. 1, where the aggregate function is sum.

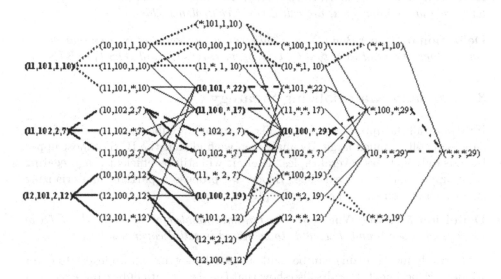

Fig. 1. Lattice of the data cube produced from Example 1. Cover equivalence classes are shown in different broad-brush line and upper bounds in bold.

From Fig. 1 we can find that the tuples connected by different broad-brush line must have the same aggregate measure value for they are aggregated from the same set of base tuples. E.g., those tuples connected by broad solid line are all aggregated from the base tuple (12,101,2,12).

In the following definitions, C denotes the data cube produced from base table $R(d_1, d_2, \ldots, d_n, M)$, where $d_i (1 \le i \le n)$ denotes dimensions and M denotes measure items.

Definition 2 (Cover Relation). *For $t_1 \in C$, $t_2 \in C$, $\forall d_i$, $1 \le i \le n$, t_2 covers t_1 or t_1 is covered by t_2 if they satisfy the following conditions: if $t_2(d_i)$ is at the lowest level, then $t_1(d_i) = t_2(d_i)$; otherwise, $t_1(d_i)$ can be any value which is at lower level and belongs to $t_2(d_i)$.*

E.g., (11,100,1) covers (11,101,1). If there is another tuple (11,204,1), then (11,100,1) does not cover it, for 204 belongs to the second quarter, not the first, though it is at one level lower than that of 100 locates.

Definition 3 (Base Tuple Set, BTS). *The base tuple set of tuple $t \in C$ is $BTS(t) = \{t' | t' \in R,\ t \in C,\ t\ covers\ t'\}$.*

E.g., in Example 1, BTS((10,101,*))={(11,101,1,10), (12,101,2,12)}. According to the definition, if t_2 covers t_1 then BTS(t_1) $\subseteq$ BTS(t_2).

Definition 4 (Cover Equivalence Relation). *There exists cover equivalence relation between t_1 and t_2 if BTS(t_1)=BTS(t_2).*

Definition 5 (Cover Equivalence Class). *The tuples, which have cover equivalence relation among them, are called cover equivalence class.*

Definition 6 (Upper Bound). *t_1 is called an upper bound of a cover equivalence class if there does not exist $t_2 \in C$, $t_1 \neq t_2$, t_1 covers t_2, and BTS(t_1)=BTS(t_2).*

3   Partially Materializing Strategy

If we store all the upper bounds, just like the quotient cube does, the size of data cube will still be much large. By analyzing, we find that the BTS of most upper bounds only includes several tuples. Then, it will still be efficient if aggregating these upper bounds in real time. Hence, we propose a partially materializing strategy based on the following concept.

Definition 7 (Cover Window). *The minimal number of tuples in the BTS of aggregated upper bound that needs to be stored is called cover window.*

Partially materializing can be implemented by setting an appropriate cover window. Experimental results also show that the size of data cube can be reduced greatly and the query performance can be improved efficiently by setting an appropriate cover window.

4   Construction Algorithm of HQC

Definition 8 (Hierarchical Quotient Cube, HQC). *HQC consists of two relational tables. They store base tuples and aggregated upper bounds which satisfy the cover window requirement separately. And hierarchical dimensions are considered by using the code format defined by definition 1.*

HQC stores the aggregated upper bounds and the base tuples in two separate relational tables. For the base table in Example 1, HQC tables store 7 tuples (the tuples in bold in Fig. 1), 3 base tuples and 4 aggregated tuples, where the cover window is 2. Moreover, HQC can solve more general problems because the hierarchical dimension is considered.

In order to construct HQC tables, the upper bounds need to be aggregated. Since the tuples in base table must be upper bounds, only the aggregated upper bounds need to be found. The rule of aggregating upper bounds is as follows: aggregating the tuples in the BTS of a class, if those tuples in the BTS have the same value on a certain dimension, then the upper bound has the same value on the corresponding dimension; otherwise, the value of the upper bound is set to the one that at the lowest possible level on condition that it covers all the tuples in BTS. E.g., in Fig. 1, (11,101,1,10) and (12,101,2,12) are tuples in the BTS of certain class. They have different values on the first dimension, and they have the same value 10 when being rolled up one level, so the value of the upper bound on this dimension is set to 10; the value of the upper bound on the second dimension is 101 because all the tuples in BTS have the same value on this dimension; the value of the upper bound on the third dimension is "*" for the tuples in BTS have different values on this dimension. Hence, the upper bound of the class is (10,101,*,22).

The process of constructing HQC tables is an iterative procedure. The basic concept is computing from (*,*,...,*), drilling down step by step, partitioning the base table, and aggregating the upper bound, then checking if the upper bound had been aggregated and storing it if not. The meanings of the parameters of the algorithm are as follows: c is an aggregated tuple; B_c is the BTS of c and it has been sorted in ascending order according to the field denoted by parameter k and those fields after k; k denotes the current solving field; w denotes the size of the cover window. The initial value of these parameters are: $c=$(*,*,...,*), B_c is the whole base table, k is 1 and w is a number which is larger than 1. The algorithm is described in pseudo code as follows.

Algorithm (Constructing HQC Tables from Base Table)
ConstructHQC(c,B_c,k,w)
1. Compute the upper bound d from B_c, include the measure value of d;
2. if (exists $1 \leq j < k$, the level of $c[j]$ is higher than that of $d[j]$)
3.   return; // for tuple d must have been aggregated
4. Save tuple d to HQC table;
5. for(each dimension $k \leq i \leq n$, $d[i]$ is not at the lowest level)
6. {
7.   if(exists $k \leq j < i$, $d[j]$ is not at the lowest level)
8.   Sort B_c in ascending order by the ith dimension and those after ith;
9.   for(each x belonged to $d[i]$ and x is one level lower than $d[i]$)
10.   {
11.   Produce $e = d$, other than $e[i] = x$, produce its BTS B_e;
12.   if(the number of tuples in B_e is not less than w)
13.   ConstructHQC(e,B_e,i,w);
14.   }
15. }

For the base table in Example 1, the stored aggregated tuples are (10,100,*,29), (11,100,*, 17), (10,101,*,22) and (10,100,2,19) when the cover window is 2. When the cover window is 3, the stored aggregated tuple is only (10,100,*,29).

According to the algorithm, it is easy to understand that the stored tuples will not duplicate. The virtue of this algorithm is that the constructing speed and the size of data cube can be adjusted by adjusting the size of the cover window.

5   Query Performance

For answering query, the method of finding the upper bound of the class that the given tuple belongs to is needed. Firstly, a method of retrieving upper bound is described as follows.

If the upper bound of the class that the given tuple t belongs to exists in HQC tables, the upper bound tuple can be retrieved by the following method: generate query conditions according to the value of every dimension of tuple t, then sort the satisfied tuples which in the table storing aggregated tuples in ascending order, and if there exists any tuple, the upper bound must be the first tuple; otherwise, query satisfied tuples in the table storing base tuples and aggregate the upper bound in real time. Note that the special value "*" is less than any other value. The method of generating query conditions is as follows: if the value of the ith dimension is "*", then there is no condition on this dimension; if the value of the ith dimension is not "*" and not at the lowest level, suppose at level k and the code is $(P_i^m, \ldots, P_i^k, *, \ldots, *)$, then the query condition is the pattern of "$d_i \geq (P_i^m, \ldots, P_i^k, *, \ldots, *)$ and $d_i \leq$ the largest code which belongs to $(P_i^m, \ldots, P_i^k, *, \ldots, *)$"; if the value of the ith dimension is at the lowest level, then the query condition is "$d_i = (P_i^m, \ldots, P_i^1)$". The full query conditions can be formed by connecting these conditions by using operator "and".

E.g., when the cover window is 2, for tuple (10,102,*) in Example 1, the query conditions are the pattern of "AID $\geq$ 10 and AID $\leq$ 12 and TID = 102". There is no satisfied tuple in the the table storing aggregated tuples, then perform another query in the table storing base tuples and get the result tuple (11,102,2,7). When querying the upper bound of tuple (10,101,*), where the cover window is 3, the result (10,101,*,22) can be aggregated in real time.

The query can be classified into point query and range query. There are three cases when performing a point query in HQC tables: (1) the upper bound can be found in the table storing aggregated tuples; (2) the previous case is not satisfied, but the upper bound can be aggregated in real time; (3) the BTS of the given tuple is empty, so the query result is null. The query strategies can be formed easily for these three cases, and detailed algorithm is omitted here.

For range query, the difference compared with point query is that the query conditions on some dimensions are given in enumerative pattern. E.g., the given tuple is $t = (\{v_{11}, \ldots, v_{1i}\}, \{v_{21}, \ldots, v_{2j}\}, \ldots, \{v_{k1}, \ldots, v_{kz}\}, a_1, \ldots, a_{n-k})$. The idea of the range query algorithm will be illustrated through an example and the detailed algorithm will be omitted here. E.g., for tuple $t=(\{10,11\},\{101, 102\},*)$, there can be generated four point queries, (10,101,*), (10,102,*), (11,101,*) and (11,102,*), and these tuples form a query list. The upper bound being found according to the first tuple in the query list is (10,101,*,22). For the values on each dimension of these two tuples are equal, we only need to delete tuple (10,101,*) from the query list. The upper bound being found according to tuple (10,102,*) is (11,102,2,7). Because the values on certain dimension of these two tuples are not identical, those tuples cover (11,102,2) and covered by (10,102,*) are deleted from the query list, that is, tuple (10,102,*) and (11,102,*) are deleted. The tuple left in the query list is (11,101,*) now. Query the upper bound according to it and the result is tuple (11,101,1,10). Now sort these results and delete duplicate tuples. The result of this range query is {(10,101,*,22),(11,101,1,10),(11,102,2,7)}. As we can see, tuple (10,102,*) and (11,102,*) have common upper bound, so it is enough to query only once.

6   Experimental Results

In order to verify the validity of HQC data cube, we carry out a series of experiments, using synthetic data and real world data. The aggregate function is sum. The experiments are conducted on a Pentium IV 2.8G PC with 512M main memory and running windows 2000 server version. All algorithms are implemented in C++ and the database is SQL Server 2000. Only the size of HQC tables with different cover windows is compared here, because [11] has compared the size of quotient table with that of complete data cube, and the size of HQC tables is equal to that of the quotient table when the cover window is 2. Moreover, the time of constructing HQC data cube and query performance with different cover windows are also compared. The synthetic dataset are generated by random. It includes 6 dimensions. Each dimension has 99 different values. The first and second dimension are highly relevant and can be replaced by one hierarchical dimension with two levels. The third and fourth dimension, the fifth and sixth dimension are in the same case. There are no duplicate tuples in the synthetic dataset and the number of tuples in the base table is increased from 2M to 8M at 2M interval. The real world dataset is Weather [13].

The first experiment uses synthetic data. Fig. 2 illustrates the construction time on condition that each dimension has no hierarchies ($d = 6$) and on condition that each dimension has hierarchies ($d = 3$), where the cover window is 2, while Fig. 3 illustrates the corresponding results where the cover window is 15. From Fig. 2 and Fig. 3, we can see that the construction time is reduced dramatically while the cover window is set to a larger number. The reason is that the number of aggregated tuples in the data cube is reduced dramatically. Fig. 4 and Fig. 5 illustrate the number of aggregated tuples in the data cube where the cover window is set to 2 and to 15 respectively. We can see that the aggregated tuples in HQC while the cover window is set to 15 is much fewer than that in quotient table. E.g., when there are 2M tuples in the base table, there will be about 4.4M aggregated tuples in the quotient table (from Fig. 4, note that the size of HQC is equal to that of quotient table when the cover window is 2), while only about 0.059M in HQC when the cover window is 15 (from Fig. 5). Moreover, we can see that the construction time is reduced greatly by using hierarchical dimensions from Fig. 2 and Fig. 3.

The real world dataset Weather is adopted by many experiments. It has 1,015,376 tuples, 9 dimensions. We examined the effect of different cover windows on the construction time. Fig. 6 illustrates the changing trend of construction time with the change of the cover window. Fig. 7 illustrates the changing trend of the number of aggregated tuples in HQC with the change of the cover window. From Fig. 6 we can see that the reducing of the construction time is slowed down

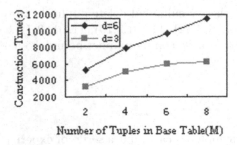

Fig. 2. Construction time (synthetic data) Cover Window is 2

Fig. 3. Construction time (synthetic data) Cover Window is 3

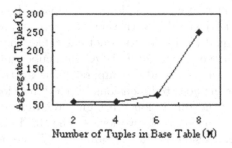

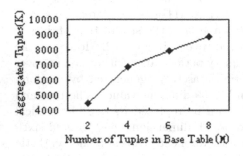

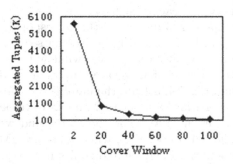

Fig. 4. Number of aggregated upper bounds, synthetic data, cover window is 2

Fig. 5. Number of aggregated upper bounds, synthetic data, cover window is 15

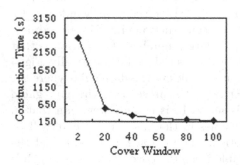

Fig. 6. Construction time (Weather data)

Fig. 7. Number of aggregated upper bounds (Weather data)

with the increasing of the cover window. The reason is that the Weather dataset has some skew, and with the increasing of the cover window, the reducing speed of aggregated tuples in HQC is slowed down, as shown in Fig. 7. Also, we can see from Fig. 7 that the aggregated tuples in quotient table is about 5.7M, while only about 0.18M in HQC when the cover window is set to 100.

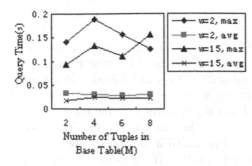
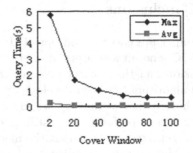

Fig. 8. Query performance (synthetic data)   **Fig. 9.** Query performance (Weather data)

In order to verify query performance, we generate 1000 point queries for synthetic data and Weather data respectively. Fig. 8 shows the maximum and average query time on the synthetic data where the hierarchy of dimensions is considered (the number of dimension is 3) on condition that the cover window is set to 2 and to 15 separately. Cover window is denoted by w, maximum query time is denoted by max and average query time is denoted by avg. The maximum query time fluctuates quite much in experiments, and a representative group of data are used in this figure. The Weather data is used in Fig. 9. It illustrates the effect of different cover windows on the query performance. We can see that the query performance can be improved by setting an appropriate cover window. Also, we can see that, from Fig. 9, the query performance is quite bad when storing too many aggregated tuples.

7   Related Work

The work presented in this paper is relevant to [6,7], and highly relevant to [10,11,12]. [6] presents a concept of BST (Base Single Tuple), and the size of data cube based on this concept is reduced. The concept of cover equivalence presented by [10] puts this still further and the quotient cube stores only upper bounds. Actually, the data cube based on BST stores the upper bounds where the number of tuples in BTS is one and all other aggregated tuples. The Dwarf structure presented by [7] compresses the data cube by using prefix and suffix coalescing. The Dwarf structure is a special chain and it is difficult to be implemented. The QC-trees structure presented by [11] is also a special chain. The HQC presented by this paper is simply two relational tables.

Definition 2, 4, 5 and 6 are relevant to the concepts presented by [11] and [12]. Definition 3 is relevant to [12]. Our definitions expand their content, and they are suitable for dimensions with hierarchies.

The algorithm of constructing HQC table is highly relevant to the algorithm presented in [11]. Our research is that the new algorithm can solve hierarchical dimensions and the cover window is considered, so it can solve more general problems more efficiently. The algorithm of query bears little relation to [12].

8   Conclusions

This paper presents the concept of HQC data cube, an algorithm of constructing HQC, and an algorithm of query, also describes the concept of hierarchical dimension and the concept of cover window. No efficient incremental maintenance algorithm has been developed yet, but we can reconstruct the data cube in a short period of time by setting a little larger cover window on condition that the query performance is still acceptable. The theoretical analysis and the experimental results show that the methods proposed in this paper are quite effective. Moreover, the simplicity and maturity of ROLAP make the scheme more practicable. Our further work is to develop an efficient incremental maintenance algorithm, and automatically selecting an appropriate cover window is also an interested problem.

References

1. J. Gray et al. Data cube: A relational aggregation operator generalizing group-by, cross-tab and sub-total. In ICDE'96, 152-159
2. S. Agarwal, R. Agrawal, P. Deshpande, A. Gupta, J. F. Naughton, R. Ramakrishnan, and S. Sarawagi. On the computation of multidimensional aggregates. In VLDB'96, 506-521
3. Y. Zhao, P. Deshpande, and J. F. Naughton. An array-based algorithm for simultaneous multidimensional aggregates. In SIGMOD'97, 159-170
4. K. A. Ross and D. Srivastava. Fast computation of sparse datacubes. In VLDB'97, 116-185
5. K. S. Beyer and R. Ramakrishnan. Bottom-up computation of sparse and iceberg cubes. In SIGMOD'99, 359-370
6. W. Wang, J. Feng, H. Lu, and J. Xu Yu. Condensed Cube: An Effective Approach to Reducing Data Cube Size. In ICDE'02
7. Y. Sismanis, A. Deligiannakis. Dwarf: Shrinking the PetaCube. ACM SIGMOD'02, 464-475
8. G. Sathe and S. Sarawagi. Intelligent Rollups in Multidimensional OLAP Data. VLDB'01, 531-540
9. T. Imielinski et al. Cubegrades: Generalizing Association Rules. Tec. Rep., Rutgers U., Aug. 2000
10. L.V.S. Lakshmanan, J. Pei, and J. Han. Quotient Cube: How to Summarize the Semantics of a Data Cube. Proceedings of the 28th VLDB Conference, Hong Kong, China, 2002
11. L.V.S. Lakshmanan, J. Pei, and Y. Zhao. QC-Trees: An Efficient Summary Structure for Semantic OLAP. SIGMOD 2003, 64-75
12. S.-E. Li, S. Wang. Research on closed data cube technology. Journal of Software. Journal of Software, 2004,15(8), 1165-1171 (in Chinese with English abstract)
13. C. Hahn, S. Warren, J. London. Edited synoptic cloud reports from ships and land stations over the globe. 1996. http://cdiac.esd.ornl.gov/cdiac/ndps/ndp026b.html

Knowledge Discovery Based Query Answering
in Hierarchical Information Systems

Zbigniew W. Raś[1,2], Agnieszka Dardzińska[3], and Osman Gürdal[4]

[1] Univ. of North Carolina, Dept. of Comp. Sci., Charlotte, N.C. 28223
[2] Polish Academy of Sciences, Institute of Comp. Sci.,
Ordona 21, 01-237 Warsaw, Poland
[3] Bialystok Technical Univ., Dept. of Math.,
ul. Wiejska 45A, 15-351 Bialystok, Poland
[4] Johnson C. Smith Univ., Dept. of Comp. Sci. and Eng.,
Charlotte, NC 28216

Abstract. The paper concerns failing queries in incomplete Distributed
Autonomous Information Systems ($DAIS$) based on attributes which are
hierarchical and which semantics at different sites of $DAIS$ may differ.
Query q fails in an information system S, if the empty set of objects
is returned as an answer. Alternatively, query q can be converted to
a new query which is solvable in S. By a refinement of q, we mean a
process of replacing q by a new relaxed query, as it was proposed in [2],
[7], and [8], which is similar to q and which does not fail in S. If some
attributes listed in q have values finer than the values used in S, then
rules discovered either locally at S or at other sites of $DAIS$ are used
to assign new finer values of these attributes to objects in S. Queries
may also fail in S when some of the attributes listed in q are outside the
domain of S. To resolve this type of a problem, we extract definitions of
such attributes at some of the remote sites for S in $DAIS$ and next use
them to approximate q in S. In order to do that successfully, we assume
that all involved information systems have to agree on the ontology of
some of their common attributes [14], [15], [16]. This paper shows that
failing queries can be often handled successfully if knowledge discovery
methods are used either to convert them to new queries or to find finer
descriptions of objects in S.

1 Introduction

Distributed Autonomous Information System ($DAIS$) is a system that connects
a number of information systems using network communication technology. Some
of these systems have hierarchical attributes and information about values of attributes for some of their objects can be partially unknown. Our definition of
system incompleteness differs from the classical approach by allowing a set of
weighted attribute values as a value of an attribute. Additionally, we assume
that the sum of these weights has to be equal 1. If we place a minimal threshold
for weights to be allowed to use, we get information system of type λ. Its definition and also the definition of a distributed autonomous information system

D. Ślęzak et al. (Eds.): RSFDGrC 2005, LNAI 3642, pp. 221–230, 2005.

used in this paper was given by Raś and Dardzińska in [15]. Semantic inconsistencies among sites are due to different interpretations of attributes and their values among sites (for instance one site can interpret the concept *young* differently than another one). Ontologies ([1], [6], [9], [10], [17], [18], [19], [21]) can be used to handle differences in semantics among information systems. If two systems agree on the ontology associated with attribute *young* and its values, then attribute *young* can be used as a semantical bridge between these systems. Different interpretations are also due to the way each site is handling null values. Null value replacement by a value predicted either by statistical or some rule-based methods [3] is quite common before queries are answered by QAS. In [14], the notion of *rough semantics* was introduced and used to model semantic inconsistencies among sites due to different interpretations of incomplete values.

There are cases when a classical Query Answering System (QAS) fails to return an answer to a submitted query but still a satisfactory answer can be found. For instance, let us assume that an information system S has hierarchical attributes and there is no single object in S which description matches a query q. Assuming that a distance measure between objects in S is defined, then by generalizing q, we may identify objects in S which descriptions are nearest to the description q. Another example of a failing query problem is when some of the attributes listed in a query are outside the domain of S. The way to approach this problem, proposed by Ras [13], is to extract definitions of such attributes at remote sites for S (if S is a part of a distributed information system) and next used them in S. This problem is very similar to the problem when the granularity of an attribute value used in a query q is finer than the granularity of the corresponding attribute used in S. By replacing such attribute values in q by more general values used in S, we retrieve objects from S which may satisfy q. Alternatively, we can compute definitions of attribute values used in q, at remote sites for S, and next use them by QAS to enhance the process of identifying objects in S satisfying q. This can be done if collaborating systems also agree on the ontology of some of their common attributes [14], [15], [16]. Additionally, the granularity level of the attribute which definition is remotely computed should be the same at the remote site and in q. This paper presents a new methodology, based on knowledge discovery, for the failing query problem.

2   Query Processing with Incomplete Data

Information about objects is collected and stored in information systems which are usually autonomous and reside at different locations. These systems are often incomplete and the same attribute may have different granularity level of its values at two different sites. For instance, at one information system, concepts *child, young,middle-aged, old, senile* can be used as values of the attribute *age*. At the other system, only integers are used as the values. If both systems agree on a semantical relationship among values of attributes belonging to these two granularity levels (their ontology), then they can use this attribute to communicate with each other. It is very likely that an attribute which is missing in one information system may occur at many others. Assume that user submits a query q to a Query Answering System (QAS) of S (called a client) and some of the attributes used in q either are not present in S or their granularity is more specific than the granularity of the same attributes at S. In both cases, S may look for a definition of each of these attributes at other information systems in $DAIS$ assuming that the granularity level of these attributes in these systems is matching their granularity level in q. All these definitions are stored in the knowledge base for S and next used to chase (see [4]) the missing values and, if needed, to refine the current values of attributes at S. Algorithm Chase for $DAIS$, based on rules, was given by Dardzińska and Raś in [5]. This algorithm can be modified easily and used for refinement of object descriptions in S.

Definition 1:
We say that $S = (X, A, V)$ is a partially incomplete information system of type λ, if the following four conditions hold:

- X is the set of objects, A is the set of attributes, and $V = \bigcup\{V_a : a \in A\}$ is the set of values of attributes,

- $(\forall x \in X)(\forall a \in A)[a_S(x) \in V_a$ or $a_S(x) = \{(v_i, p_i) : 1 \leq i \leq m\}]$,

- $(\forall x \in X)(\forall a \in A)[(a_S(x) = \{(v_i, p_i) : 1 \leq i \leq m\}) \rightarrow \sum_{i=1}^{m} p_i = 1]$,

- $(\forall x \in X)(\forall a \in A)[(a_S(x) = \{(v_i, p_i) : 1 \leq i \leq m\}) \rightarrow (\forall i)(p_i \geq \lambda)]$.

An example of an information system of type $\lambda = \frac{1}{4}$ is given in Table 1.

Table 1. Information System S

X	a	b	c	d	e
x_1	$\{(a_1, \frac{1}{3}), (a_2, \frac{2}{3})\}$	$\{(b_1, \frac{2}{3}), (b_2, \frac{1}{3})\}$	c_1	d_1	$\{(e_1, \frac{1}{2}), (e_2, \frac{1}{2})\}$
x_2	$\{(a_2, \frac{1}{4}), (a_3, \frac{3}{4})\}$	$\{(b_1, \frac{1}{3}), (b_2, \frac{2}{3})\}$		d_2	e_1
x_3		b_2	$\{(c_1, \frac{1}{2}), (c_3, \frac{1}{2})\}$	d_2	e_3
x_4	a_3		c_2	d_1	$\{(e_1, \frac{2}{3}), (e_2, \frac{1}{3})\}$
x_5	$\{(a_1, \frac{2}{3}), (a_2, \frac{1}{3})\}$	b_1	c_2		e_1
x_6	a_2	b_2	c_3	d_2	$\{(e_2, \frac{1}{3}), (e_3, \frac{2}{3})\}$
x_7	a_2	$\{(b_1, \frac{1}{4}), (b_2, \frac{3}{4})\}$	$\{(c_1, \frac{1}{3}), (c_2, \frac{2}{3})\}$	d_2	e_2
x_8		b_2	c_1	d_1	e_3

Assume now that the set $\{S_i, i \in J\}$, where $S_i = (X_i, A_i, V_i)$, represents information systems at all sites in $DAIS$. Query language for $DAIS$ is built, in a standard way (see [16]), from values of attributes in $\bigcup\{V_i : i \in J\}$ and from the functors *or* and *and*, denoted in this paper by $+$ and $*$, correspondingly.

To be more precise, by a query language for $DAIS$ we mean the least set Q satisfying the following two conditions:

- if $v \in \bigcup\{V_i : i \in J\}$, then $v \in Q$,
- if $t_1, t_2 \in Q$, then $t_1 * t_2, t_1 + t_2 \in Q$.

For simplicity reason, we assume that user is only allowed to submit queries to QAS in Disjunctive Normal Form (DNF).

The semantics of queries for $DAIS$ used in this paper was proposed by Raś & Joshi in [16]. It has all the properties required for the query transformation process to be sound [see [16]]. For instance, they proved that the following distributive property holds: $t_1 * (t_2 + t_3) = (t_1 * t_2) + (t_1 * t_3)$.

To recall their semantics, let us assume that $S = (X, A, V)$ is an information system of type λ and t is a term constructed in a standard way (for predicate calculus expression) from values of attributes in V seen as *constants* and from two functors $+$ and $*$. By $N_S(t)$, we mean the standard interpretation of a term t in S defined as:

- $N_S(v) = \{(x, p) : (v, p) \in a(x)\}$, for any $v \in V_a$,
- $N_S(t_1 + t_2) = N_S(t_1) \oplus N_S(t_2)$,
- $N_S(t_1 * t_2) = N_S(t_1) \otimes N_S(t_2)$,

where, for any $N_S(t_1) = \{(x_i, p_i)\}_{i \in I}$, $N_S(t_2) = \{(x_j, q_j)\}_{j \in J}$, we have:

- $N_S(t_1) \oplus N_S(t_2) =$
  $\{(x_i, p_i)\}_{i \in (I-J)} \cup \{(x_j, p_j)\}_{j \in (J-I)} \cup \{(x_i, max(p_i, q_i))\}_{i \in I \cap J}$,
- $N_S(t_1) \otimes N_S(t_2) = \{(x_i, p_i \cdot q_i)\}_{i \in (I \cap J)}$.

So, it means that the interpretation N_S is undefined for queries outside the domain V. To have such queries processed by QAS, they have to be converted to queries built only from attribute values in V.

Assume now that two information systems $S_1 = (X, A, V_1)$, $S_2 = (X, A, V_2)$ are partially incomplete and they are both of type λ. Although attributes in S_1, S_2 are the same, they may still differ in granularity of their values. Additionally, we assume that the set $\{a_{1i} : 1 \leq i \leq m\}$ contains all children of a_1 which means that semantically a_1 is equivalent to the disjunction of a_{1i}, where $1 \leq i \leq m$. Saying another words, we assume that both systems agree on the ontology related to attribute a and its values which is represented as a tree structure in Fig. 1.

Two types of queries can be submitted to S_1.

The first type is represented by query $q_1 = q_1(a_3, b_1, c_2)$ which is submitted to S_1 (see Fig. 1). The granularity level of values of attribute a used in q_1 is more general than their granularity level allowed in S_1. It means that $N_{S_1}(q_1)$ is not defined. In this case q_1 can be replaced by a new query $q_2 = q(\sum\{a_{3i} : 1 \leq i \leq m_3\}, b_1, c_2)$ which is in the domain of N_{S_1} and the same can be handled by QAS for S_1.

The second type is represented by query $q = q(a_{31}, b_1, c_2)$ which is submitted to S_2 (see Fig. 1). The granularity level of values of the attribute a used in q is finer than their granularity level allowed in S_2. It means that $N_{S_2}(q)$ is not

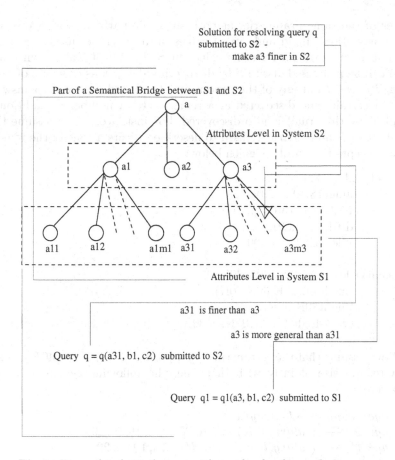

Fig. 1. Hierarchical attribute a with two levels of granularity

defined. The problem now is more complex but still it can be solved. Namely, it is sufficient to learn definitions of a_{31} at other sites of $DAIS$ in terms of b_1 and c_1 or in terms of values which are finer than b_1 and c_1. When this is done, the objects in S_2 having property a_{31} can be identified by following the query processing strategy similar to the one presented in [16].

3 How to Handle Failing Queries in DAIS

In this section, the problem of failing queries in $DAIS$ is presented in a more detailed way. Namely, let us assume that a query $q(B)$ is submitted to an information system $S = (X, A, V)$, where B is the set of all attributes used in q and $A \cap B \neq \emptyset$. All attributes in $B - [A \cap B]$ are called foreign for S. If S is a part of $DAIS$, then for definitions of foreign attributes for S we may look at its remote sites (see [14]). We assume here that two information systems can collaborate in solving q only if they agree on the ontology related to attributes used in both of them. Clearly, the same ontology does not mean that a common attribute has values of the same granularity at both sites. Similarly, as we have seen in the previous section, the granularity of values of an attribute used in a query may differ from the granularity of its values in S. In [14], it was shown that query $q(B)$ can be processed at site S by discovering definitions of values of attributes from $B - [A \cap B]$ at any of the remote sites for S and use them to answer $q(B)$. With a certain rule discovered at a remote site, a number of additional rules (implied by that rule) is also discovered. For instance, let us assume that two attributes *age* and *salary* are used to describe objects at one of the remote sites which accepts the ontology given below:

- age(child($\leq$17),
         young(18,19,...,29),
         middle-aged(30,31,...,60),
         old(61,62,...,80),
         senile(81,82,...,$\geq$100))

- salary(low(10K,20K,30K,40K),
          medium(50K,60K,70K),
          high(80K,90K,100K),
          very-high(110K,120K,$\geq$130K))

Now, assume that the certain rule $(age, young) \longrightarrow (salary, 40K)$ is extracted at a remote site. Jointly with that rule, the following certain rules are also discovered:

- $(age, young) \longrightarrow (salary, low)$,
- $(age, N) \longrightarrow (salary, 40K)$, where $N = 18, 19, ..., 29$,
- $(age, N) \longrightarrow (salary, low)$, where $N = 18, 19, ..., 29$.

The assumption that the extracted rules have to be certain, in order to generate from them additional rules of high confidence, can be relaxed to "almost" certain rules. Stronger relaxation is risky since, for instance, the rule $r = [(age, N) \longrightarrow (salary, 40K)]$ may occur to be a surprising rule, as defined by Suzuki [20]. If both attributes *age* and *salary* are local in $S = (X, A, V)$ and the granularity of values of the attribute *salary* in S is more general than the granularity of values of the same attribute used in some rules listed above, then these rules can be used to convert S into a new information system which has finer information about objects in X than the information about them in S with respect to attribute *salary*. Clearly, this step will help us to solve $q(B)$ in a more precise way. Otherwise, we have to replace the user query by a more general one to match the granularity of values of its attributes with a granularity used in S. But, clearly, any user prefers to see his query unchanged.

Assume now that $D_{S'}$ is a set of all rules extracted at a remote site S' for $S = (X, A, V)$ by the algorithm $ERID(S', \lambda_1, \lambda_2)$ [4]. Parameters λ_1, λ_2 represent thresholds for minimum support and minimum confidence of these rules. Additionally, we assume that $L(D_{S'}) = \{(t \rightarrow v_c) \in D_{S'} : c \in G(A, q(B))\}$, where $G(A, q(B))$ is the set of all attributes in $q(b)$ which granularity of values in S is more general than their granularity in $q(B)$ and S'. The type of incompleteness in [15] is the same as in this paper but we also assume that any attribute value a_1 in S can be replaced by $\{(a_{1i}, 1/m) : 1 \leq i \leq m\}$, where $\{a_{1i} : 1 \leq i \leq m\}$ is the set of all children of a_1 in the ontology associated with a_1 and accepted by S.

By replacing descriptions of objects in S by new finer descriptions recommended by rules in $L(D_{S'})$, we can easily construct a new system $\Phi(S)$ in which $q(B)$ will fail (QAS will return either the empty set of objects or set of weighted objects with weights below the threshold value provided by user). In this paper we propose an automated refinement process for object descriptions in S which guarantees that QAS will not fail on $\Phi(S)$ assuming that it does not fail on S. But before we continue this subject any further, another issue needs to be discussed first.

Foreign attributes for S can be seen as attributes which are 100% incomplete in S, that means values (either exact or partially incomplete) of such attributes have to be ascribed to all objects in S. Stronger the consensus among sites in $DAIS$ on a value to be ascribed to x, *finer* the result of the ascription process for x can be expected.

We may have several rules in the knowledge-base $L(D_{S'})$, associated with information system S, which describe the same value of an attribute $c \in G(A, q(B))$. For instance, let us assume that $t_1 \rightarrow v_c$, $t_2 \rightarrow v_c$ are such rules. Now, if the granularity of attribute c is the same in both of these rules, the same in a query $q(B) = v_c * t_3$ submitted to QAS, and at the same time the granularity of c is more general in S, then these two rules will be used to identify objects in S satisfying $q(B)$. This can be done by replacing query $q(B)$ by $t_3 * (t_1 + t_2)$. Then, the resulting term is replaced by $(t_3 * t_1) + (t_3 * t_2)$ which is legal under semantics N_S. If the granularity level of values of attributes used in $t_3 * (t_1 + t_2)$ is in par with granularity of values of attributes in S, then QAS can answer $q(B)$.

Let us discuss more complex scenario partially represented in Figure 2. As we can see, attribute a is hierarchical. The set $\{a_1, a_2, a_3\}$ represents the values of attribute a at its first granularity level. The set $\{a_{[1,1]}, a_{[1,2]}, ..., a_{[1,m_1]}\}$ represents the values of attribute a at its second granularity level. The set $\{a_{[3,1]}, a_{[3,2]}, ..., a_{[3,m_3]}\}$ represents the remaining values of attribute a at its second granularity level. We assume here that the value a_1 can be refined to any value from $\{a_{[1,1]}, a_{[1,2]}, ..., a_{[1,n_1]}\}$. Similar assumption is made for value a_3. The set $\{a_{[3,1,1]}, a_{[3,1,2]}, a_{[3,1,3]}\}$ represents the values of attribute a at its third granularity level which are finer than the value $a_{[3,1]}$.

Finally, the set $\{a_{[3,1,3,1]}, a_{[3,1,3,2]}, a_{[3,1,3,3]}, a_{[3,1,3,4]}\}$ represents the values of attribute a at its forth granularity level which are finer than the value $a_{[3,1,3]}$.

Now, let us assume that query $q(B) = q(a_{[3,1,3,2]}, b_1, c_2)$ is submitted to S_2 (see Figure 2). Also, we assume that attribute a is hierarchical and ordered. It basically means that the difference between the values $a_{[3,1,3,2]}$ and $a_{[3,1,3,3]}$ is smaller than between the values $a_{[3,1,3,2]}$ and $a_{[3,1,3,4]}$. Also, the difference

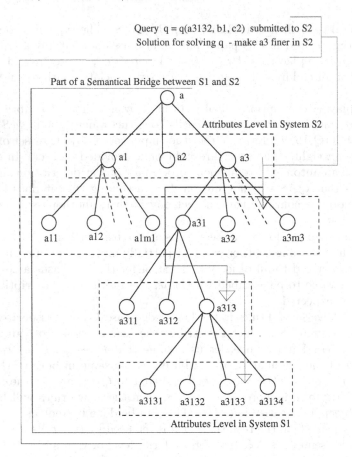

Fig. 2. Hierarchical attribute a with four levels of granularity

between any two elements in $\{a_{[3,1,3,1]}, a_{[3,1,3,2]}, a_{[3,1,3,3]}, a_{[3,1,3,4]}\}$ is smaller than between $a_{[3,1,3]}$ and $a_{[3,1,2]}$.

Now, we outline a possible strategy which QAS can follow to solve $q = q(B)$. Clearly, the best solution for answering q is to identify objects in S_2 which precisely match the query submitted by user. If this step fails, we should try to identify objects which match query $q(a_{[3,1,3]}, b_1, c_2)$. If we succeed, then we try queries $q(a_{[3,1,3,1]}, b_1, c_2)$ and $q(a_{[3,1,3,3]}, b_1, c_2)$. If we fail, then we should succeed with $q(a_{[3,1,3,4]}, b_1, c_2)$. If we fail with $q(a_{[3,1,3]}, b_1, c_2)$, then we try $q(a_{[3,1]}, b_1, c_2)$ and so on. Clearly, an alternate strategy is to follow the same steps in a reverse order. We start with a highest generalization of q which is $q(b_1, c_2)$. If we succeed in answering that query, then we try $q = q(a_{[3]}, b_1, c_2)$. If we succeed again, we try $q = q(a_{[3,1]}, b_1, c_2)$ and so on.

But before we follow the above process, we have to discover rules at these sites of $DAIS$ which are remote for S_2 and which agree with S_2 on the ontology of attributes in $\{a, b, c\}$. These rules should describe values of any granularity of attribute a in terms of values of attributes b, c which granularity is consistent with their granularity in S_2. Clearly, if a rule $t_1 \rightarrow a_{[3,1,3,4]}$) is discovered, then also the rules $t_1 \rightarrow a_{[3,1,3]}$), $t_1 \rightarrow a_{[3,1]}$), $t_1 \rightarrow a_{[3]}$) are discovered as well.

4 Conclusion

This paper shows how to solve the failing query problem if queried information system S is a part of $DAIS$. This is done by extracting certain groups of rules in $DAIS$ and next using them by QAS to make descriptions of objects in S finer and the same way to get more precise match between them and a query.

References

1. Benjamins, V. R., Fensel, D., Pérez, A. G. (1998) Knowledge management through ontologies, in *Proceedings of the 2nd International Conference on Practical Aspects of Knowledge Management (PAKM-98)*, Basel, Switzerland.
2. Chu, W., Yang, H., Chiang, K., Minock, M., Chow, G., Larson, C. (1996) Cobase: A scalable and extensible cooperative information system, in *Journal of Intelligent Information Systems*, Vol. 6, No. 2/3, 223-259
3. Dardzińska, A., Raś, Z.W. (2003) Rule-Based Chase Algorithm for Partially Incomplete Information Systems, in **Proceedings of the Second International Workshop on Active Mining (AM'2003)**, Maebashi City, Japan, October, 42-51
4. Dardzińska, A., Raś, Z.W. (2003) On Rules Discovery from Incomplete Information Systems, in **Proceedings of ICDM'03 Workshop on Foundations and New Directions of Data Mining**, (Eds: T.Y. Lin, X. Hu, S. Ohsuga, C. Liau), Melbourne, Florida, IEEE Computer Society, 31-35
5. Dardzińska, A., Raś, Z.W. (2003) Chasing Unknown Values in Incomplete Information Systems, in **Proceedings of ICDM'03 Workshop on Foundations and New Directions of Data Mining**, (Eds: T.Y. Lin, X. Hu, S. Ohsuga, C. Liau), Melbourne, Florida, IEEE Computer Society, 24-30
6. Fensel, D., (1998), *Ontologies: a silver bullet for knowledge management and electronic commerce*, Springer-Verlag, 1998
7. Gaasterland, T. (1997) Cooperative answering through controlled query relaxation, in *IEEE Expert*, Vol. 12, No. 5, 48-59
8. Godfrey, P. (1997) Minimization in cooperative response to failing database queries, in *International Journal of Cooperative Information Systems*, Vol. 6, No. 2, 95-149
9. Guarino, N., ed. (1998) Formal Ontology in Information Systems, IOS Press, Amsterdam
10. Guarino, N., Giaretta, P. (1995) Ontologies and knowledge bases, towards a terminological clarification, in *Towards Very Large Knowledge Bases: Knowledge Building and Knowledge Sharing*, IOS Press
11. Pawlak, Z. (1991) Rough sets-theoretical aspects of reasoning about data, Kluwer, Dordrecht
12. Pawlak, Z. (1991) Information systems - theoretical foundations, in **Information Systems Journal**, Vol. 6, 205-218
13. Raś, Z.W. (1994) Dictionaries in a distributed knowledge-based system, in **Concurrent Engineering: Research and Applications**, Conference Proceedings, Pittsburgh, Penn., Concurrent Technologies Corporation, 383-390

14. Raś, Z.W., Dardzińska, A. (2004) Ontology Based Distributed Autonomous Knowledge Systems, in **Information Systems International Journal**, Elsevier, Vol. 29, No. 1, 47-58
15. Raś, Z.W., Dardzińska, A. (2004) Query answering based on collaboration and chase, in **Proceedings of FQAS 2004 Conference**, Lyon, France, LNCS/LNAI, No. 3055, Springer-Verlag, 125-136
16. Raś, Z.W., Joshi, S. (1997) Query approximate answering system for an incomplete DKBS, in **Fundamenta Informaticae Journal**, IOS Press, Vol. 30, No. 3/4, 313-324
17. Sowa, J.F. (2000a) Ontology, metadata, and semiotics, in B. Ganter & G. W. Mineau, eds., *Conceptual Structures: Logical, Linguistic, and Computational Issues*, LNAI, No. 1867, Springer-Verlag, 55-81
18. Sowa, J.F. (2000b) Knowledge Representation: Logical, Philosophical, and Computational Foundations, Brooks/Cole Publishing Co., Pacific Grove, CA.
19. Sowa, J.F. (1999a) Ontological categories, in L. Albertazzi, ed., *Shapes of Forms: From Gestalt Psychology and Phenomenology to Ontology and Mathematics*, Kluwer Academic Publishers, Dordrecht, 307-340.
20. Suzuki E., Kodratoff Y. (1998), Discovery of Surprising Exception Rules Based on Intensity of Implication, in **Proceedings of the Second European Symposium, PKDD98**, LNAI, Springer-Verlag
21. Van Heijst, G., Schreiber, A., Wielinga, B. (1997) Using explicit ontologies in KBS development, in *International Journal of Human and Computer Studies*, Vol. 46, No. 2/3, 183-292

A Content-Based Image Quality Metric*

Xinbo Gao, Tao Wang, and Jie Li

School of Electronic Engineering, Xidian Univ.,
Xi'an 710071, P.R. China

Abstract. image quality assessment plays an important role in relevant fields of image processing. The traditional image quality metric, such as PSNR, cannot reflect the visual perception to the image effectively. For this purpose, based on the fuzzy Sugeno integral a novel image quality assessment measure, called content-based metric (CBM), is proposed in this paper. It fuses the amount and local information into the similarity of the image structural information and gives a comprehensive evaluation for the quality of the specified image. The experimental results illustrate that the proposed metric has a good correlation with the human subjective perception, and can reflect the image quality effectively.

1 Introduction

Image quality assessment plays an important role in relevant fields of image processing. The problem of image quality evaluation is involved in many applications, such as image compression, communication, storage, enhancement, watermarking and *etc*. A quality assessment metric can be used to guide the construction and adjustment of image processing systems, or to optimize the processing algorithms and the parameter settings. The most reliable way of assessing the quality of an image is subjective evaluation, because human beings are the ultimate receivers in most applications. The mean opinion score (MOS), which is a subjective quality measurement obtained from a number of human observers, has been regarded for many years as the most reliable form of quality measurement. But it is too inconvenient to apply for most applications. So, an appropriate objective image quality assessment metric is demanded to be designed for approximating the subjective perception.

According to the availableness of the original image, the objective image quality metrics can be classified into three types of models: full-reference model(FR), no-reference model (NR) and reduced-reference model (RR)[1]. This paper focuses on the investigation of the full-reference image quality assessment. The mean squared error (MSE), and peak signal-to-noise ratio (PSNR) are the most widely used full-reference quality metrics, because they are simple to calculate, have clear physical meanings, and are mathematically convenient in the context of optimization. But they are not very well matched to perceived visual quality.

* This work was supported by the National Natural Science Foundation of China (No.60202004) and the Key project of Chinese Ministry of Education (No.104173).

D. Ślęzak et al. (Eds.): RSFDGrC 2005, LNAI 3642, pp. 231–240, 2005.

In the last three decades, a great deal of effort has gone into the development of image quality assessment methods that take advantage of known characteristics of the human visual system (HVS). The Daly visible differences predictor and Sarnoff visual discrimination model are two of the leading image quality models in these methods [2]. All of these methods are based on error sensitivity and must rely on a number of strong assumptions and generalizations [3]. In fact, they are complicated, but none of them in the literature has shown any clear advantage over simple mathematical measures such as PSNR under strict testing conditions and different image distortion environments [4]. In view of this, Zhou Wang *et. al.* proposed a new philosophy in designing image quality metrics. They mentioned that *the main function of the human eyes is to extract structural information from the viewing field, and the human visual system is highly adapted for this purpose.* Therefore, a measure of structural distortion should be a good approximation of perceived image distortion. Based on the new philosophy, they constructed *structural-similarity-based*(SSIM) image quality measure [3,5,6]. But, in [7], it was concluded that the "amount of error", the "location of error", and the "structure of error" are three essential factors of distortion. For this purpose, an image coding quality assessment based on fuzzy integral (FE) is proposed, which inducts the participation of human knowledge and experience by fuzzy integral [8]. Compared with the available metric, the FE-based image quality assessment method achieved better performance.

To fully incorporate more distortion information with human knowledge and construct a more reasonable and sensitive image quality metric, we proposed a new metric based on the content of images in this paper. In our approach, an image is partitioned into three parts: edges, textures and flat regions as the method proposed in [8]. Then Sugeno fuzzy integral is used to fuse the SSIM in the three parts respectively. Finally, the measurements of three parts are weighting averaged as the metric of the image quality, which is called content-based metric (CBM). Obviously the CBM fully considers the effects of the "amount of error", "location of error", and "structure of error" on the image quality. A lot of experiments illustrate that the proposed metric approximates the MOS more closely than the metrics of the SSIM and the FE.

2   Fuzzy Measure and Fuzzy Integral

The theory of fuzzy measures and fuzzy integrals was first introduced by Sugeno [9]. A fuzzy measure is used to express an evaluation, which is heavily subject to human perception as the "grade of importance", or "grade of beauty", and *etc.* In mathematical terms, a fuzzy measure is a set functions with monotonicity but not always additivity. Based on the notion of fuzzy measure, a fuzzy integral is a functional with monotonicity, which is used for aggregating information from multiple sources with respect to the fuzzy measure.

Definition 2.1: Let X be an arbitrary set and $\mathbf{B}$ be a Borel field of X. A set function g defined on $\mathbf{B}$ is a fuzzy measure if it satisfies the following conditions.

1) Boundary: $g() = 0, g(X) = 1$
2) Monotonicity: $g(A_1) \leq g(A_2)$, if $A_1 \subset A_2$ and $A_1, A_2 \in \mathbf{B}$
3) Continuity: if $A_1 \subset A_2 \subset \cdots \subset A_n \subset \cdots, A_n \in \mathbf{B}$, then $g(\bigcup_{n=1}^{\infty} A_n) = \lim_{n \to \infty} g(A_n)$

While the conventional Lebesgue measures assume additivity, fuzzy measures assume only monotonicity. The detailed discussion can be found in [10].

Definition 2.2: Let $(X, \mathbf{B}, g)$ be a fuzzy measure space and $f : X \to [0, 1]$ be a $\mathbf{B}$-measurable function. Sugeno fuzzy integral over $A \subseteq X$ of the function f with respect to g a fuzzy measure is defined by

$$(S) \int_A f(x) dg = \sup_{E \subseteq X} [\min(\min_{x \in E} f(x), g(A \cap E))]$$

$$= \sup_{\alpha \subseteq [0,1]} [\min(\alpha, g(A \cap F_\alpha(f)))], \tag{1}$$

where (S) denotes Sugeno fuzzy integral and $F_\alpha(f) = \{x | f(x) \geq \alpha\}$. The following is the interpretation of the fuzzy integral that will be adopted in this paper [11]. Suppose that an object is evaluated from the point of views of a set of quality factors X. Let $f(x) \in [0, 1]$ denote the quality evaluation on the object when quality factor is considered and let $g(\{x\})$ denote the degree of importance of this quality factor $x \in X$. Now, suppose an object is evaluated using quality factors from $A \subseteq X$. It is reasonable to consider $W(A) = \min_{x \in A} f(x)$ a quantity as the best-secured quality evaluation that the object provides and $g(A)$, which is called importance measure in this paper, expresses the grade of importance of this subset of quality factor. The value obtained from comparing these two quantities in terms of the "min" operator is interpreted as the grade of agreement between real possibilities $f(x)$, and the expectations g. Hence fuzzy integration is interpreted as searching for the maximal grade of agreement between the objective evidence and the expectation.

3 Content-Based Metric for Image Quality Assessment

For the applications of image coding, Miyahara *et al.* [7] proposed an objective assessment metric, picture quality scale (PQS), and concluded that the "amount of error", the "location of error", and the "structure of error" are three essential factors of distortion. To construct a more reasonable and effective image quality measure, we proposed a content-based metric (CBM) for objective image quality assessment based on the above conclusion.

The new metric CBM is constructed on the basis of the SSIM measure. First, the local structure similarity information is extracted for each pixel pair from the original and the distortion images respectively. Then, by analyzing the content of the original and distortion images, all the pixels of the given image are partitioned into three parts: edges, textures and flat regions with the method in [8]. Secondly the similarity measurement of each part is calculated by synthesizing the SSIMs of all the pixels in corresponding region with Sugeno integral. Finally, an overall image quality is evaluated with the weighting average

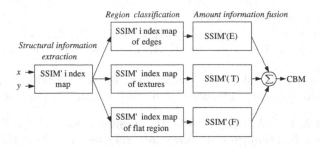

Fig. 1. Diagram of the proposed image quality assessment system based on CBM

of the similarities in above three regions. The new metric fuses the amount and local information into the similarity of the image structural information. The system diagram of the proposed image quality assessment system is shown in Fig.1, which consists of three basic modules: structural information extraction, region classification and amount information fusion.

3.1   Structural Information Extraction

Zhou Wang *et al.* proposed the SSIM metric [6]. They indicated that the luminance of the surface of an object being observed is the product of the illumination and the reflectance, but the structures of the objects in the scene are independent of the illumination. Consequently, the structural information is defined as those attributes that represent the structure of objects in the scene, independent of the average luminance and contrast. In [6], the luminance, contrast and structure comparison function are respectively defined as follows.

$$l(x,y) = \frac{2\mu_x\mu_y + C_1}{\mu_x^2 + \mu_y^2 + C_1}, c(x,y) = \frac{2\sigma_x\sigma_y + C_2}{\sigma_x^2 + \sigma_y^2 + C_2}, s(x,y) = \frac{\sigma_{xy} + C_3}{\sigma_x\sigma_y + C_3}, \quad (2)$$

where (x,y) represents the corresponding point pair from the original and distortion images respectively. μ_x is the local mean intensity at x, which is an estimation of the luminance at x; σ_x is the local standard deviation at x, which is an estimation of the contrast at x; σ_{xy} is the local correlation coefficient between x and y, which is an estimation of the similarity between x and y. The constant C_1, C_2 and C_3 are included to avoid instability when the denominators are very close to zero. Where C_1, C_2 and C_3 are small constants given by

$$C_1 = (K_1L)^2, \qquad C_2 = (K_2L)^2, \qquad C_3 = C_2/2 \qquad (3)$$

$K_1 << 1, K_2 << 1$ and L is the dynamic range of the pixel values. The general form of the structural similarity (SSIM) index between x and y is defined as

$$\text{SSIM}(x,y) = [l(x,y)]^\alpha \cdot [c(x,y)]^\beta \cdot [s(x,y)]^\gamma, \qquad (4)$$

where $\alpha > 0$, $\beta > 0, \gamma > 0$. And the SSIM index satisfies the following conditions.

1) Symmetry: $\text{SSIM}(x, y) = \text{SSIM}(y, x)$;
2) Boundedness: $\text{SSIM}(x, y) \leq 1$;
3) Unique maximum: $\text{SSIM}(x, y) = 1$ if and only if $x = y$.

Specifically, we set $\alpha = \beta = \gamma = 1$, and the resulting SSIM index is given by

$$\text{SSIM}(x, y) = \frac{(2\mu_x\mu_y + C_1)(\sigma_{xy} + C_2)}{(\mu_x^2 + \mu_y^2 + C_1)(\sigma_x^2 + \sigma_y^2 + C_2)}, \tag{5}$$

In [6], an 11×11 circular-symmetric Gaussian weighting function $w = \{w_i | \sum_{i=1}^{N} w_i = 1, i = 1, 2, \cdots N\}$ is used, with standard deviation of 1.5 samples, which moves pixel-by-pixel over the entire image. At each step, the local statistics and SSIM index are calculated within the local window. The estimations of local statistics, μ_x, σ_x and σ_{xy} are then modified accordingly as

$$\mu_x = \sum_{i=1}^{N} w_i x_i, \quad \sigma_x = \left(\sum_{i=1}^{N} w_i(x_i - \mu_x)^2\right)^{\frac{1}{2}}, \quad \sigma_{xy} = \sum_{i=1}^{N} w_i(x_i - \mu_x)(y_i - \mu_y)$$

With above steps, a SSIM index map is obtained between the original and the distortion images. Then a mean SSIM (MSSIM) index is used to evaluate the overall image quality. Where, M represents the amount of points in the SSIM index map. The source code of the SSIM algorithm is available online [12].

$$\text{MSSIM} = \frac{1}{M} \sum_{j=1}^{M} \text{SSIM}(x_j, y_j) \tag{6}$$

In the SSIM metric, we find that $l(x, y), c(x, y) \in [0, 1]$, while $s(x, y) \in [-1, 1]$, which is not convenient for the following Sugeno integral. As shown in Fig.2, (b) is the negative image of (a). In fact, according to (1), the structural information similarity of them is $s = -1$, namely (b) negatively correlates with (a). From the point of view of information representation, it can be considered that the structural information which is represented in the two images is the same, and the difference between them lies in their luminance and contrast. So we redefine the structural information similarity as

(a) "couple" image   (b) negative of "couple" image

Fig. 2. Comparison of the structural information of "couple" images

$$s'(x,y) = \frac{|\sigma_{xy}| + C_3}{\sigma_x \sigma_y + C_3} \tag{7}$$

Thus, $s'(x,y) \in [0,1]$. The left two components in SSIM, $l(x,y)$ and $c(x,y)$ are unchanged. Then we redefine (4) as

$$\text{SSIM}'(x,y) = [l(x,y)]^\alpha \cdot [c(x,y)]^\beta \cdot [s'(x,y)]^\gamma \tag{8}$$

With (8), we can get the SSIM$'$ index map according to the above steps. In this module, we mainly utilized the "structural information of error".

3.2   Region Classification

In this module, an image is partitioned into three parts: edges, textures and flat regions, according to their contents. The importance of edges, textures and flat regions is gradually decreasing to human perception, which corresponds to their gradual decline of gradient magnitudes in the image gradient field. So the three parts can be determined by the gradient magnitudes. We also partition the above parts based on the same way in [8].

1) Convolute the original image and the distortion one with Sobel mask individually to obtain two gradient fields, and pixel-by-pixel compute the gradient magnitudes of the two gradient fields.

2) Compute the thresholds for partition $T_1 = 0.12 g_{max}$ and $T_2 = 0.06 g_{max}$, where g_{max} is the maximal gradient magnitude of the original image.

3) Determine the pixels of edges, textures, and flat regions. Assume that the gradient of pixel at (x,y) of the original image is $p_o(x,y)$ and the gradient of pixel at (x,y) of the distortion image is $p_d(x,y)$. The pixel classification is carried out according to the following rules.

R1: if $p_o(x,y) > T_1$ or $p_d(x,y) > T_1$, then it is considered as an edge pixel.
R2: if $p_o(x,y) < T_2$ and $p_d(x,y) \leq T_1$, then it belongs to a flat region.
R3: if $T_1 \geq p_o(x,y) \geq T_2$ and $p_d(x,y) \leq T_1$, then it is a texture pixel.

As the above steps, the SSIM$'$ index map can be partition into the SSIM$'$ maps of the edge, texture and flat regions, which are denoted by E, T and F. Here, we mainly utilized the "location information of error", namely error occurring in different regions is perceived differently by human eyes.

3.3   The Proposed Image Quality Metric

In this subsection, let $X = \{x_i | i = 1, 2, \cdots, N\}$ and $Y = \{y_i | i = 1, 2, \cdots, N\}$ denote two sets, which consist of the pixels correspond to an region A in the original and distortion image. Let $S = \{s_i = \text{SSIM}'(x_i, y_i) | i = 1, 2, \cdots, N\}$, then the overall structural information similarity of A is computed as

$$\text{SSIM}'(A) = (S) \int_A \text{SSIM}'(x_i, y_i) dg = \sup_{s_i \in S}[\min(s_i, g(F_{S_i}(S)))], \tag{9}$$

where $F_{S_i}(S) - \{s_k|s_k \geq s_i, s_k \in S\}$, $g(K) = |K|/N$. $|K|$ denotes the cardinality of the set K. g denotes some importance of the set K, and reflects the distortion degree in amount. Thus, we get the SSIM$'(A)$, $A \in \{E, T, F\}$.

Finally, the overall image quality CBM is computed as follows.

$$CBM = \sum_{A \in \{E,T,F\}} w_A \cdot SSIM'(A), \qquad (10)$$

where $w_E + w_T + w_F = 1$. Obviously, CBM $\in [0, 1]$, and it gets the maximum 1, just when the distortion image is the same as the original one.

4   Experimental Results and Analysis

To verify the rationality and validity of the proposed image quality metric CBM, we conducted the following three experiments. (1) the consistency test experiment of the CBM with the subjective quality measurement MOS; (2) the validity test experiment; (3) the sensitivity test experiment. The parameters used in the experiments are listed in Table 1.

Table 1. The Parameters Used in Experiments

K_1	K_2	L	α	β	γ	w_E	w_T	w_F
0.01	0.03	255	1	1	1	0.462	0.337	0.201

4.1   The Consistency Test Experiment of the CBM with MOS

We test the consistency of CBM with MOS on LIVE quality assessment database [13]. In the database, twenty-nine high-resolution RGB color images were compressed at a range of quality levels using either JPEG or JPEG2000, producing a total of 175 JPEG images and 169 JPEG2000 images. The distribution of subjective quality scores was approximately uniform over the entire range. The subjective quality scores and other information of the database are also included in the given Database.

First, variance-weighted regression analysis are used in a fitting procedure to provide a nonlinear mapping between the objective/subjective scores. Then three metrics are used as evaluation criterions [3]. Metric 1 is the correlation coefficient (CC) between objective/subjective scores after variance-weighted regression analysis, which provides an evaluation of *prediction accuracy*. Metric 2 is the Spearman rank-order correlation coefficient between the objective/subjective scores, which is considered as a measure of prediction monotonicity. Finally, metric 3 is the outlier ratio (percentage of the number of predictions outside the range of 2 times of the standard deviations) of the predictions after the nonlinear mapping, which is a measure of prediction consistency. We also calculated the mean absolute error (MAE), and root mean square error (RMS) after the nonlinear mapping. The evaluation results for all the objective image quality assessment models being compared are given in Table 2 and Fig.3.

Table 2. The Consistency Test of CBM with MOS

Model	CC	MAE	RMS	ROCC	OR
PSNR	0.9265	6.883	8.978	0.8956	0.1424
FE	0.9269	5.445	6.799	0.8932	0.0860
MSSIM	0.9606	5.432	6.745	0.9447	0.0698
CBM	0.9756	4.129	5.100	0.9631	0.0116

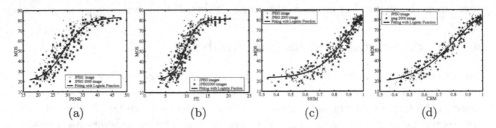

(a)   (b)   (c)   (d)

Fig. 3. Scatter plots of subjective mean opinion score (MOS) versus model prediction

4.2   The Validity Test Experiment of the CBM

As shown in Fig.4, the CBM scores of "Lena" image with different types of distortions: (a) blurring (with smoothing window of $W \times W$); (b) impulsive salt-pepper noise (density=D); (c) additive Gaussian noise (mean=0,variance=V); and (d) JPEG compression (compression rate=R), always drop with the increasing intensity of the above distortions. It is accord with the tendency of the decreasing image quality in fact.

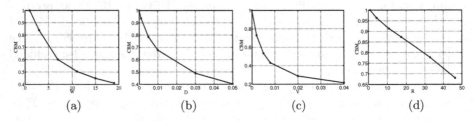

(a)   (b)   (c)   (d)

Fig. 4. the CBM scores of "Lena" with different types of distortions. (a) Blurring; (b) Impulsive Salt-Pepper Noise; (c) Additive Gaussian Noise; (d) JPEG Compression.

4.3   The Sensitivity Test Experiment of the CBM

As shown in Fig.5, the PSNR of "couple" with different types of distortion (Fig5(b-h)) are almost the same (PSNR=26.08dB), but the perceived qualities of them are various in fact. The metric CBM shown in Table 3 can distinguish them more preferably.

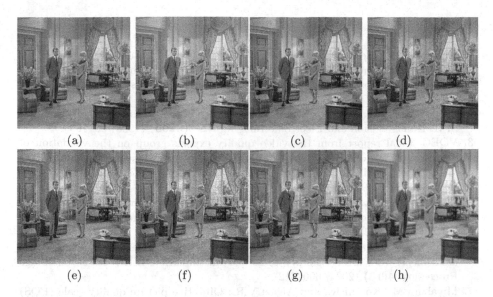

Fig. 5. "couple" image with different perceived quality and the same PSNR. (a) The original "couple" image; (b) Contrast stretching; (c) Mean shift; (d) Impulsive salt-pepper noise; (e) Additive Gaussian noise; (f) Multiplicative speckle noise; (g) JPEG compression; (h) Blurring.

Table 3. The CBM Scores of The Images in Fig5

IMAGE	(a)	(b)	(c)	(d)	(e)	(f)	(g)	(h)
CBM	1.000	0.9614	0.9609	0.7486	0.7125	0.7100	0.6665	0.6434

5   Conclusion and Discussion

In this paper, the irrationality of the negative image structural similarity to representation of the image structural information is first analyzed, and based on which, the modified structural similarity (SSIM) is redefined for image quality metric. Then, the specified image is partitioned into three parts: edges, textures and flat regions, according to their contents. Next, in each part, the Sugeno integral with the amount information is made as the fuzzy measure to get the similarity of each part. Finally the weighted average of the fuzzy measures in three parts is computed as a final image quality metric named CBM. Experimental results illustrate that the proposed metric is more highly correlated to the results of the human visual perception than the SSIM and FE.

The proposed CBM metric is mainly applicable to full-reference (FR) gray image quality assessment. Whereas human is sensitive to color images. So the novel quality metric for color images and the no-reference (NR) metric are the following research topics.

References

1. Kusuma, T.M., Zepernick, H.J.: A reduced-reference perceptual quality metric for in-service image quality assessment. Proc. Joint First Workshop on Mobile Future and IEEE Symposium on Trends in Communications, Bratislava, Slovakia, IEEE Press (2003) 71–74
2. Bei Li, Meyer W., Klassen Victor R.: Comparison of two image quality models. SPIE Human Vision and Electronic Imaging III, **2(3299)** (1998) 98–109
3. VQEG: Final report from the video quality experts group on the validation of objective models of video quality assessment. http://www.vqeg.org/, **3** (2000)
4. Wang Z. and Bovik A.C.: A universal image quality index. IEEE Signal Processing Letters, **3(9)** (2002) 81–84
5. Wang Z., Bovik A.C. and Lu L.: Why is image quality assessment so difficult. Proc. IEEE Int. Conf. on Acoustics, Speech, and Signal Processing, Orlando, Florida, IEEE Press (2002) 3313–3316
6. Wang Z., Bovik A.C., Sheikh Hamid R. and Simoncelli Eero P.: Image quality assessment: from error visibility to structural similarity. IEEE Trans. on Image Processing, **4(13)** (2004) 600–612
7. Miyahara M., Kotani K., and Algazi V.R.: Objective picture quality scale (PQS) for image coding. IEEE Trans. on Commun., **9(46)** (1998) 1215–1226
8. Junli Li, Gang Chen, Zheru Chi, and Chenggang Lu.: Image coding quality assessment using fuzzy integrals with a three-component image model. IEEE Trans. on Fuzzy Systems, **1(12)** (2004) 99–106
9. Sugeno M.: Theory of fuzzy integrals and its application. PhD dissertation, Tokyo institute of technology, Japan (1974)
10. Klir G.J. and Wang Z.: Fuzzy Measure Theory. Norwell, MA: Kluwer (2001)
11. Tahani H. and Keller J.M.: Information fusion in computer vision using the fuzzy integral. IEEE Trans. on Syst., Man, Cybern., **(20)3** (1990) 733–741
12. Wang Z.: the SSIM index for image quality assessment. http://www.cns.nyu.edu/ lcv/ssim/
13. Sheikh H.R., Wang Z., Bovik A.C. and Cormack L.K.: Image and video quality assessment research at LIVE. http://live.ece.utexas.edu/research/quality/

A Novel Method of Image Filtering
Based on Iterative Fuzzy Control*

Rui-hua Lu[1], Ming Yang[2], and Yu-hui Qiu[2]

[1] School of Electronic Information Engineering,
Southwest China Normal University,
400715 Chongqing, China
chenlr@swnu.edu.cn
[2] School of Computer and Information Science,
Southwest China Normal University,
400715 Chongqing, China
{yangming, yhqiu}@swnu.edu.cn

Abstract. A novel method of iterative fuzzy control-based filtering (IFCF) is proposed in this paper. The proposed method has outstanding characteristics of removing impulse noise and smoothing out Gaussian noise while preserving edges and image details effectively. This filtering approach is mainly based on the idea of not letting each point in the area of concern being uniformly fired by each of the basic fuzzy rules. The extended iterative fuzzy control-based filter (EIFCF) and the modified iterative fuzzy control-based filter (MIFCF) are presented in this paper too. EIFCF is mainly based on the idea that in each iteration the universe of discourse gets more shrunk and by shrinking the domains of the fuzzy linguistics, i.e., by compressing their membership function the number of fired fuzzy rules will be forced to keep unchanged in order to preserve the ability of the filter. MIFCF aims to enhance the property of the IFCF via increasing the iteration number without loosing edge information. Experiment results show that the proposed image filtering method based on iterative fuzzy control and its different modifications are very useful for image processing.

1 Introduction

Any digitized image transmitted over a noisy channel cannot avoid degradation. Removal of such degradation with preserving the completeness of the original image is a very important problem in image processing[1]. The key to the settlement of the problem lies in image filtering which aims at removing impulse noise, smoothing non-impulse noise and enhancing edges or certain prominent structures of the input image. So called noise filtering can be regarded as replacing the grey-level value of each pixel in the image by a new value relying on

---

* Supported in part by the fund of the Applied Fundamental Research of Chongqing Science and Technology Committee under Grant 2000-6968; Supported by the fund of University Science and Technology under Grant SWNU 2004006.

D. Ślęzak et al. (Eds.): RSFDGrC 2005, LNAI 3642, pp. 241–250, 2005.

the local context. An ideal filtering algorithm varies from pixel to pixel based on the local context. For instance, if the local region is relatively smooth, the new value of the pixel is determined by averaging adjacent pixels values. And, if the local region holds within itself edge or impulsive noise pixels, a different type of filtering should be applied. However, it is very difficult, if not impossible, to set the conditions under which a certain filter should be chosen, because the local conditions can be evaluated only vaguely in some parts of an image [2]. For this reason, a filtering system should be capable of performing reasoning with uncertain information, which is a common usage of fuzzy logic.

Edge enhancement and noise smoothing are considered as two inherently conflicting processes. Smoothing a region might ruin an edge while enhancing edges might cause unnecessary noise. To resolve this problem, a number of techniques have been presented in the research works [3],[4],[5]. In this paper, we propose a novel image filtering method based on iterative fuzzy control. The proposed method can remove impulse noise and smooth Gaussian noise while edges and image details can be preserved effectively.

This paper consists of five sections besides introduction. In section 2 iterative fuzzy control-based filter(IFCF) is presented. Section 3 shows the experimental results, including the influence of Gaussian noise variance on the performance of IFCF. Section 4 gives a brief description of extended IFCF. In section 5 modified IFCF is shown. Finally, in section 6 the conclusion is made.

2   Iterative Fuzzy Control-Based Filter

2.1   Fuzzy Control and Image Processing

Fuzzy logic-based fuzzy control is a new type of control method relying on the fuzzy mathematical theory. The theory and implementation technique of this method are totally different in comparison with traditional control theory and technique. Fuzzy set theory is provided with great potential capability of efficiently representing input/output relationships of dynamic systems, so it has obtained popularity in many aspects. In the well-known rule-based method of image processing [6], one may employ human intuitive knowledge expressed heuristically in linguistic terms. This is highly nonlinear in nature and cannot be easily characterized by traditional mathematical modelling. Furthermore, this method allows one to incorporate heuristic fuzzy rules into conventional methods, leading to a more flexible design technique. For example, Russo presented fuzzy rule-based operators for smoothing, sharpening and edge detection [7],[8]. References [9],[10] presented an image enhancement method based on fuzzy rules. It is necessary to point out that so called fuzzy control applies fuzzy mathematical theory only in control methods, and the work that is done by fuzzy control yet is certain. Fuzzy control can either implement successfully its purpose or imitate human thought. It can run efficiently control over procedures for which it is impossible to make mathematical modelling [11].

2.2 Iterative Fuzzy Control-Based Filter

In this paper, in image processing system we adopt the general structure of fuzzy if-then rule mechanism. The core of image filtering method based on iterative fuzzy control lies in the idea of not letting each point in the area of concern being uniformly fired by each of the basic fuzzy rules, such as:

Rule 1: IF(**more** of x_i are NB) THEN y is NB
Rule 2: IF(**more** of x_i are NM) THEN y is NM
Rule 3: IF(**more** of x_i are NS) THEN y is NS
Rule 4: IF(**more** of x_i are PS) THEN y is PS
Rule 5: IF(**more** of x_i are PM) THEN y is PM
Rule 6: IF(**more** of x_i are PB) THEN y is PB
Rule 0: ELSE y is Z

Here all the x_i's indicate the luminance differences between adjacent pixels (laid in a window of size $N \times N$) and the central pixel I , i.e., $x_i = I_i - I$. The output variable y is the quantity which is added to I for giving the resulting pixel luminance I'.The term sets NB (Negative Big), NM (Negative Medium), NS (Negative Small), PS (Positive Small), PM (Positive Medium) and PB (Positive Big) are the fuzzy sets that represent the proper fuzzy dividing of input and output spaces, whose fine choice of membership functions with the general triangular shape is shown in Fig. 1. Fig. 1 indicates membership functions of fuzzy quantity drawn with the elements in the universe of discourse as horizontal coordinate and the membership degrees as vertical coordinate in the universe of discourse after quantization. These values are the linguistic values of the linguistic variables x_i and y in the universe of discourse [-256,256]. The term **more** represents a S-type fuzzy function and may be described by the following formula:

$$\mu_{more}(t) = \begin{cases} 0 & t < a \\ 0.5\left\{1 - \cos\left[\frac{\pi(t-a)}{b-a}\right]\right\} & a < t < b \\ 1 & t > b \end{cases} \tag{1}$$

The values used in the experiment are $a = 0.2$ and $b = 0.8$.

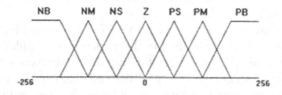

Fig. 1. Membership function of NB,NM,NS,PS,PM and PB

2.3 Degree of Activity of the If-Then Rules

Activity degree of Rule 1 is calculated by the following relationship (the other if-then rules' degrees of activity are computed similarly).

$$\lambda_1 = min[\mu NB(x_i) : x_i \in support(NB)]$$
$$\times \mu_{more} \left[\frac{number\ of\ x_i \in support(NB)}{total\ number\ of\ x_i} \right] \tag{2}$$

For the ELSE rule, i.e., Rule 0, the degree of activity is evaluated by the following formula:

$$\lambda_0 = max \left\{ 0, 1 - \sum_{i=1}^{6} \lambda_i \right\} \tag{3}$$

In order to reason the output numerically from the fuzzy rules, the correlation-product inference mechanism is employed as follows [5]:

$$y = \frac{\sum\limits_{i=0}^{6} C_i W_i \lambda_i}{\sum\limits_{i=0}^{6} W_i \lambda_i} \tag{4}$$

Here C_i and W_i are respectively the center point and the width of the membership function used in the ith fuzzy rule. Because all the W_i's are equal and $C_0 = 0$, equation (4) can be simplified as the following:

$$y = \sum_{i=1}^{6} C_i \lambda_i \tag{5}$$

2.4 Performance of IFCF

To show the performance of IFCF in a Gaussian noise case, Lena image is considered as a case study. Let the image first be corrupted by the Gaussian noise with $\mu = 0, \sigma^2 = 400$. Then, the proposed filter is used. The outcome of filtering procedure is shown in Fig.2(a). It is easy to observe from this curve that the more the number of iterations is, the better image restoration becomes in the sense of mean square error(MSE).

In order to demonstrate the performance of the proposed filter in the mixed noise environment, the image studied in this experiment is added by [%2.5,%2.5] impulse noise (the notation [%p,%q] for impulse noise means that p% of the image pixels were contaminated by positive noise and q% of the image pixels were corrupted by negative impulse noise). The result is shown in Fig.2(b). From these two results in cases of Gaussian noise and mixed noise we know that the proposed filter has good ability of image restoration as the number of iterations increases.

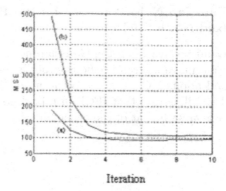

Iteration

Fig. 2. Performance of IFCF on 256×256 Lena image corrupted by Gaussian noise with $\mu = 0$, $\sigma^2 = 400$: (a)without impulse noise; (b)with[%2.5,%2.5]impulse noise.

3   Experimental Results

3.1   Influence of Gaussian Noise Variance on the Performance of IFCF

In order to demonstrate how Gaussian noise variance affects the performance of IFCF, Lena image corrupted by zero mean Gaussian noise with different variances ($\sigma^2 = 0, 100, 200, 300, 400$) is used again in the experiment. The MSE of the restored image as a function of the variance of Gaussian noise and comparison of the performance of IFCF with that of fuzzy weighted median filter(FWMF) [12] and edge-preserving smoothing filter (EPSF) [13] are shown in Fig.3. The results indicate that the performance of IFCF is rather satisfactory.

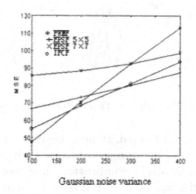

Gaussian noise variance

Fig. 3. MSE as a function of Gaussion noise variance,calculated for Lena image

3.2 Influence of Gaussian Noise Variance on the Performance of IFCF in a Mixed Noise Environment

To show how IFCF would behave when the Gaussian noise variance changes in a mixed noise case, Lena image used in previous experiment is mixed by [%2.5, %2.5] impulse noise and applied as an input to the filter. The results in image restoration shown in Fig.4 illustrate that IFCF in mixed noise case has the best performance in comparison with that of the other filters.

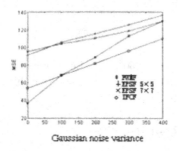

Gaussian noise variance

Fig. 4. MSE of restored image with different filters for Lena image contaminated by mixed noise(Gaussian noise and [%2.5,%2.5]impulse noise)

4 Extended Iterative Fuzzy Control-Based Filter

EIFCF is mainly based on the idea that in each iteration the universe of discourse gets more shrunk, as shown in Fig.5. This allows the filter to preserve its filtering performance during iterations. The core of this idea is that in each

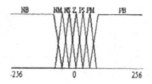

Fig. 5. Membership functions after several iterations

iteration the image gets more filtered. Hence, the amount of noise in the sense of average and peak values will be decreased and by shrinking the domains of the fuzzy linguistics, in other words, by compressing their membership functions, the number of fired fuzzy rules will be forced to keep unchanged in order to preserve the ability of the filter.

Let us do a new experiment, comparing the performance of EFICF with that of IFCF as the number of iterations increases. Here both filters are applied to Lena image corrupted by Gaussian noise with variance $\sigma^2 = 400$ and

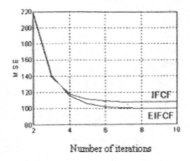

Fig. 6. Comparison of IFCF and EIFCF on the degraded Lena image for different number of iterations

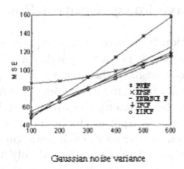

Fig. 7. MSE of restored image of different filters for Lena image corrupted by Gaussian noise

[%2.5, %2.5] impulse noise, and the MSE of both filters in each iteration is calculated. Fig.6 shows the experimental results. It is easy to find that at the beginning both filters respond uniquely, but after several iterations only EIFCF keep its capability of filtering. Further observation shows that running the filtering algorithm more than 6 iterations does not give effect any more, for there is no extra image enhancement. This experiment aims to demonstrate how the noise variance affects performance of EIFCF. Lena image corrupted by zero mean Gaussian noise with different variances ($\sigma^2 = 100, 200, 300, 400, 500, 600$) is taken for the test study. Fig.7 illustrates the MSE of the restored image as a function of Gaussian variance and compares the performance of EIFCF with that of FWMF, EPSF, ENHANCE F[7] and IFCF. Results show that the performance of EIFCF is satisfactory. In order to demonstrate how EIFCF would behave during the changing of the Gaussian noise variance in a mixed noisy case, the image in previous experiment is mixed by [%2.5,%2.5] impulse noise and used as an input to the filter. The outcomes in image restoration shown in Fig. 8 illustrate that EIFCF in a mixed noise case displays the best performance in comparison with that of the other filters above-mentioned.

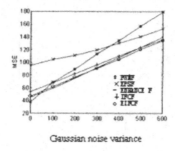

Gaussian noise variance

Fig. 8. MSE of restored image with different filters for Lena image contaminated by mixed noise Gaussian noise and [%2.5,%2.5]impulse noise

5   Modified Iterative Fuzzy Control-Based Filter

It is a pity that observation from several test experiments shows that in each iteration the output image edges get a little indistinct. Therefore, the more iteration number is, the more unsharp the image gets. In particular for low noise cases, this makes the image, after some iterations, more degraded instead of getting enhanced. To resolve this problem, the **more** function in each step should be tuned in a way that it gets sharper at the boundaries as shown in Fig.9. The range of activity becomes narrower as in each iteration the shape of the **more** function gets distinct. Thus, the Rules 1-6 are fired only in those regions in which they have higher possibility of firing and after several iterations these rules do not activate for most image pixels. Such a characteristic allows us to raise the number of iterations without having any edge vague problem. In this way we can achieve the goal of enhancing the property of IFCF via increasing the iteration number without loosing edge information. To demonstrate the better performance of MIFCF in comparison with that of IFCF, in particular for low noise cases, Lena image is considered as corrupted by additive Gaussian noise with different variances ($\sigma^2 = 100, 200, 300, 400, 500, 600$). The MSE of the restored image got by these two filters are illustrated in Fig.10. For a mixed noise case, the [%2.5,%2.5] impulse noise is added to the previous image and the outcomes are shown in Fig.11. Both two figures show that MIFCF has better performance than that of IFCF, especially in a low noise environment.

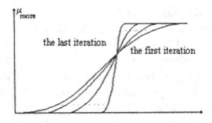

Fig. 9. The change of the shape of the **more** function during iterations

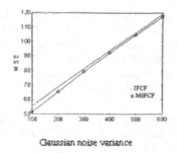

Fig. 10. MSE as a function of Gaussian noise variance,calculated for Lena image by IFCF and MIFCF with 3 × 3 window size

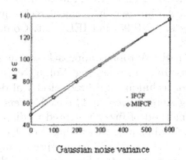

Fig. 11. MSE of restored image of IFCF and MIFCF with 3 × 3 window size for Lena image contaminated by mixed noise(Gaussian noise and [%2.5,%2.5] impulse noise)

6   Conclusion

In this paper a novel method of image filtering based on iterative fuzzy control is proposed. This method possesses the distinguishing properties of removing impulse noise and smoothing out Gaussian noise while preserving edges and image details effectively. The proposed method and its different modifications are very useful for image processing. This method is suitable to other fields of image processing. Now we are applying the proposed filtering thoughts to image segmentation. And we are also working for the optimization of fuzzy rules using some other aspects of computational intelligence.

References

1. Arakawa K.: Digital signal processing based on fuzzy rules. In: Proceedings of the Fifth IFSA World Congress (1994) 1305-1308
2. Mancuso M., Poluzzi R., Rizzotto G.: A fuzzy filter for dynamic range reduction and contrast enhancement. In: Proceedings of FUZZ-IEEE'94 3rd IEEE Int. Conf. Fuzzy Systems (1994) 264-267

3. Mastin G.A.: Image Processing.Adaptive filters for digital image noise smoothing: an evaluation, Computer Vision, Graphics, Vol. 31. (1985) 103-121
4. Pal S.K.: Fuzzy sets in image processing and recognition. In:Proceedings of FUZZ-IEEE'92 First IEEE Int. Conf. Fuzzy Systems (1992) 119-126
5. Krishnapuram R., Keller M.: Fuzzy sets theoretic approach to computer vision: an overview. In: Proceedings of FUZZ-IEEE'92 First IEEE Int. Conf. Fuzzy Systems (1992) 135-142
6. Chen B.T., Chen Y., Hsu W.: Image processing and understanding based on the fuzzy inference approach. In: Proceedings of FUZZ-IEEE'94 3rd IEEE Int. Conf. Fuzzy Systems (1994) 279-283
7. Russo F., Ramponi G.: Edge detection by FIRE operators. In: Proceedings of FUZZ-IEEE'94 3rd IEEE Int. Conf. Fuzzy Systems (1994) 249-253
8. Russo F.: A user-friendly research tool for image processing with fuzzy rules. In: Proceedings of FUZZ-IEEE'92 First IEEE Int. Conf. Fuzzy Systems (1992) 561-568
9. Russo F., Ramponi G.: An image enhancement technique based on the FIRE operator. In: Proceedings of ICIP'95 2nd IEEE Int. Conf. Image Processing, Vol.1 (1995) 155-158
10. Choi Y., Krishnapuram R.: A robust approach to image enhancement based on fuzzy logic. IEEE Trans. Image Processing, Vol. 6, No. 6 (1997) 808-825
11. Yu Y.-Q.: Fuzzy control technique and fuzzy electrical devices for home-use. Publishing House of Beijing Aeronautical and Space University, Beijing (2000) 102-106
12. Taguchi A.: A design method of fuzzy weighted median fillers. In: Proceedings of ICIP'96 3rd IEEE Int. Conf. Image Processing, Vol. 1 (1996) 423-426
13. Muneyasu M., Wada Y., Hinamoto T.: Edge-preserving smoothing by adaptive nonlinear filters based on fuzzy control laws. In: Proceedings of ICIC'96 3rd IEEE Int. Conf. Image Processing, Vol. 1 (1996) 785-788

Land Cover Classification of IKONOS
Multispectral Satellite Data: Neuro-fuzzy,
Neural Network and Maximum Likelihood Methods

JongGyu Han, KwangHoon Chi, and YeonKwang Yeon

Korea Institute of Geosciences & Mineral Resources,
305-350, 30 Gajung-dong Yusong-ku Daejeon, Republic of Korea
{jghan, khchi, ykyeon}@kigam.re.kr

Abstract. We present the results of a study of performance of neuro-fuzzy method derived from a generic model of a three-layer fuzzy perceptron, and compare it with conventional statistical and artificial intelligent methods: maximum likelihood and neural network. The land cover classification is performed using multispectral IKONOS satellite data of the part of Daejeon City in Korea. Land cover classification results of satellite image data are usually summarized as confusion matrices. The results of the classification and method comparison show that the neuro-fuzzy method is the most accurate. Thus, the neuro-fuzzy model is more suitable for classifying a mixed-composition area such as the natural environment of the Korean peninsula. And the neuro-fuzzy classifier is superior in its suppression of classification errors for mixed land cover signatures. The classified land cover information is important when the results of the classification are integrated into a geographical information system.

1 Introduction

The classification of aerial or satellite multispectral image data has become an important tool for generating ground cover maps. Many classification techniques exist. These include conventional statistical algorithms such as discriminate analysis, and the maximum likelihood classification scheme, which allocates each image pixel to the land cover class in which it has the highest probability of membership (Mather, 1997). The application of this type of conventional statistical classification to problems, particularly in relation to assumed normal distributions, and also to the integration of ancillary data, particularly if the data is incomplete (or acquired at low measurement precision), has prompted the development of an alternative classification approach (Peddle, 1993). Recently, there has been much research on remotely sensed data sets processed by neural network-based classifiers that have included images acquired by the Landsat MSS (Multispectral Scanner) (Lee et al., 1990), by the Landsat TM (Thematic Mapper) (Yoshida and Omatu, 1994), by synthetic aperture radar (Hara et al., 1994), by SPOT HRV(High Resolution Visible sensor) (Tzeng et al., 1994), by AVHRR (Advanced Very High Resolution Radiometer data) (Gopal et al., 1994) and by aircraft scanner data (Benediktsson et al., 1993). Although there are many instances when both conventional and alternative classification techniques have

D. Ślęzak et al. (Eds.): RSFDGrC 2005, LNAI 3642, pp. 251–262, 2005.
© Springer-Verlag Berlin Heidelberg 2005

been used successfully in the accurate mapping of land cover, they are not always appropriate for land cover mapping applications. As the number of successful applications of neural network classifications increases, it seems increasingly clear that neural network-based classification can produce more accurate results than conventional approaches for remote sensing. The reasons for this include: 1) neural network classifiers are distribution free, and can detect and exploit nonlinear data patterns; 2) neural network classification algorithms can easily accommodate ancillary data; 3) neural network architectures are quite flexible, and can be easily modified to optimise performance; and 4) neural networks are able to handle multiple subcategories per class. Much of the neural network classification work in remote sensing has used multi-layer feed-forward networks that are trained using the back propagation algorithm based on a recursive learning procedure using a gradient descent search (Gopal, 1999).

In this study, for comparison and evaluation of neuro-fuzzy, neural network, and maximum likelihood classifiers, a land cover classification was performed. For this purpose, a neuro-fuzzy classifier program was developed by modification of an existing program and applied to a land cover classification. The neuro-fuzzy classifier program has a three-layer feed-forward architecture that is derived from a generic fuzzy perceptron (Halgamuge and Glesner, 1994). Using the program, an IKONOS image of the part of Daejeon City in Korea, was processed to acquire land cover classification data. For the purpose of evaluating classifiers, three types - neuro-fuzzy, neural network and maximum likelihood - were compared using the study area

2 Classification Methods

2.1 Maximum Likelihood

The maximum-likelihood classifier is a parametric classifier that relies on the second-order statistics of a Gaussian probability density function model for each class. The class probability density functions usually are assumed to be normal, then the discriminant function becomes

$$g^i = p(X \mid w_i) p(w_i)$$

$$= p_i (2\pi)^{-n/2} |\Sigma_i|^{-1/2} \bullet \exp\left\{ -\frac{1}{2}(X - M_i)'\Sigma_i^{-1}(X - M_i) \right\}$$

where n is the number of bands, X is the data vector, M_i is the mean vector of class i, and Σ_i is the covariance matrix of class i,

$$X = \begin{bmatrix} x_i \\ x_i \\ x_i \\ \vdots \\ x_i \end{bmatrix} \qquad M_i = \begin{bmatrix} \mu_{i1} \\ \mu_{i2} \\ \mu_{i3} \\ \vdots \\ \mu_{in} \end{bmatrix} \qquad \Sigma_i = \begin{bmatrix} \sigma_{i11} & \sigma_{i12} & \sigma_{i13} & \cdots & \sigma_{i1n} \\ \sigma_{i21} & \sigma_{i22} & \sigma_{i23} & \cdots & \sigma_{i2n} \\ \sigma_{i31} & \sigma_{i32} & \sigma_{i33} & \cdots & \sigma_{i3n} \\ \vdots & \vdots & \vdots & \ddots & \vdots \\ \sigma_{in1} & \sigma_{in2} & \sigma_{in3} & \cdots & \sigma_{inn} \end{bmatrix}$$

In the maximum-likelihood classification, pixels are allocated to their most likely class of membership. Given equal *a priori* probabilities, this can be achieved by allocating each case to the class with the highest probability density function, or equivalently, by allocating each pixel to the class with which it has the highest *a posteriori* probability of membership. For equal *a priori* probabilities, the *a posteriori* probabilities are assessed as the probability density of a case relative to the sum of the densities (Roger, 1996).

2.2 Neural Network

Neural networks have recently become popular as pattern classification. Pattern classification is usually accomplished by means of a feed-forward architecture which has its processing elements organized in layers. Feed-forward neural networks are often used as mapping mechanisms from the feature space to the category space (Wassserman, 1989). In back-propagation neural networks (Rumelhart, 1986), there are usually three layers of neurons. The bottom layer accepts the inputs and distributes these to the next layer of processing elements. The units in the next layer typically gather values from all input units and pass the net input an activation function which calculates the output for each unit. In our research, the number of neurons in the first layer equals the number spectral bands. The third layer, the output layer, represents the category space. The optimal number of neurons in the second layer has to be determined by training. In the training phase, feature vectors of training pixels are presented to the network and propagate through it, one vector at a time. The weights are adjusted so that eventually they represent the desired mapping. The weights determine the activation levels of the neurons of the second layer. The entire training set has to be presented, and weights have to be adjusted many times. In back-propagation networks, the learning rules assure that, in the limit, the network will function as a least squares classifier for the pixels of the training set, i.e. it will minimize the value of S:

$$S = \sum_{j=1}^{NC}\sum_{i=1}^{n}(T_{ji} - M_{ji})^2$$

where NC is the number of categories, n is the number of samples in the training set, T_{ji} is the desired target of feature vector i, and M_{ji} is the actual mapping of the ith feature vector. Since the weights and the activation laws of the neurons in this network are continuous, new vectors, that closely surround an example vector in the feature space, will point to the same category.

2.3 Neuro-fuzzy Approach

This theory facilitates analysis of non-discrete natural processes (or phenomena) using mathematical formulas. In classical set theory, membership in a set is limited to either 1 or 0 (true or false, respectively), while membership in a fuzzy set can have any real value between 0 (full non-membership) and 1 (full membership). A fuzzy set may be viewed as a general form of a classical set whose membership only has two values {0,1}. A fuzzy set, F, is represented as

$$F = \left\{ \mu_{f(x)} \middle| x \in X \right\}$$

where X is a collection of objects denoted generically by x, and u(x) maps X to the membership space that is called the membership function of x. A fuzzy membership function can be regarded as a possibility distribution function, where the possibility distribution is similar to, but different from, the mathematical probability distribution.

The general concept of using "multi-layer neuro-fuzzy" as a pattern classification is to create fuzzy subsets of the pattern space in the hidden layer, and then to aggregate the subsets to form a final decision in the output layer. The proposed neuro-fuzzy classification system has a three-layer feed-forward architecture that is derived from a generic fuzzy perceptron (Fig. 1).

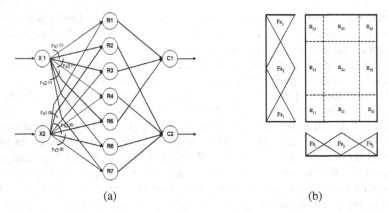

(a)   (b)

Fig. 1. (a) A three layer feed-forward architecture of the neuro-fuzzy model, (b) Fuzzy rules indicated in the corresponding fuzzy subspaces.

A fuzzy perceptron can be viewed as a normal three-layer perceptron that is fuzzified to a certain extent. Only the weights, the net inputs and the activations of the output units are modelled as fuzzy sets. A fuzzy perceptron is like the normal kind of perceptron that is used for function approximation. The advantage lies within the interpretation of its structure in the form of linguistic rules, because the fuzzy weights can be associated with the linguistic terms. The network can also be created partly or wholly from linguistic (fuzzy IF-THEN) rules. The neuro-fuzzy classifier considered here is based on the technique of distributed fuzzy IF-THEN rules where grid-type fuzzy partitions on the pattern space are used. To adapt its fuzzy sets, the learning algorithm of the neuro-fuzzy classification system repeatedly performs through the learning set by repeating the following steps until a given end criterion is reached.

1. Select the next pattern from the learning set R_s and propagate it.
2. Determine the delta value $\delta_{ci} = t_i - a_{ci}$
3. For each rule unit R with $a_R > 0$

$$\delta_R = a_R (1 - a_R) \sum_{c \in U_3} W(R, c) \delta_c$$

    a.   Determine the delta value

    b.   Find x' such that

$$W(x', R)(a_{x'}) = \min_{x \in U_1} \{W(x, R)(a_x)\}$$

c.   For the fuzzy set $W(x',R)$, determine the delta values for its parameter a, b, c using the learning rate $\sigma > 0$:

$$\delta_b = \sigma \cdot \delta_R \cdot (c - a) \cdot \mathrm{sgn}(a_{x'} - b)$$

$$\delta_a = -\sigma \cdot \delta_R \cdot (c - a) + \delta_b$$

$$\delta_c = \sigma \cdot \delta_R \cdot (c - a) + \delta_b$$

and apply the changes to $W(x',R)$.

4. If an epoch was completed, and the end criterion is met, then stop; otherwise proceed with step.

Using the neuro-fuzzy algorithm, a classifier program was developed by modification of an existing program and applied to the land cover classification (Fig. 2).

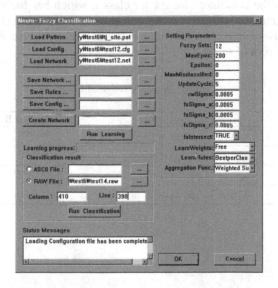

Fig. 2. Neuro-fuzzy classification program developed in this study

3 Data Processing and Comparison

The satellite image used in our research was acquired with the IKONOS satellite. It is imaged over the part of Daejeon city, Korea, and selected for the primary comparison of the neuro-fuzzy, neural network and maximum-likelihood classification methods. Familiarity with this area is allowed for accurate class training and test site identification. The image used consists of 399 lines, with 550 pixels per line, a pixel size of about 4×4 m, and the three visible and the one near-infrared band. The spectral ranges of IKONOS are listed in Table 1, and the image of channel 1, 2, 3 and 4 used in this research shows in Fig. 3 respectively. Fig. 4 presents two-dimensional scatter plots between spectral channels for the IKONOS image, which mean spectral correlation between channels. It is used for selection of training data for land cover classification. For the comparison of accuracy, the same training sites are used by the neuro-fuzzy, neural network and maximum-likelihood classifier. We determine that nine classes covered the majority of land cover feature in the test image. Fig. 5 shows training sites for getting training data set. A set of similar-sized training regions are defined by visual interpretation of the image. Ground field survey data such as topographic map(Fig. 6) compiled by geographer are also used for calculation of classification accuracy. Table 2 shows the separability betweens classes of training data. The separability measure is calculated using the following formula.

$$SM(i,j) = 2*[1-exp(-a(i,j))]$$
$$a(i,j) = 0.125*T[M(i)-M(j)]*Inv[A(i,j)]*[M(i)-M(j)]$$
$$+ 0.5 \ *ln\{det(A(i,j))/SQRT[det(S(i))*det(S(j))]\}$$

where, $M(i)$ is the mean vector of class i, where the vector has the number of channel elements, $S(i)$ is the covariance matrix for class i, which has the number of channel, $Inv[]$ is the inverse of matrix, $T[]$ is the transpose of matrix, $A(i,j)$ is $0.5*[S(i)+S(j)]$, $det()$ is the determinant of a matrix, $ln\{\}$ is the natural logarithm of scalar value and $T[]$ is the square root of scalar value.

Table 1. Spectral range of IKONOS

Channel No.	Spectral Range	Spatial Resolution
1	0.45 μm ~ 0.52 μm (Blue)	4m/pixel
2	0.52 μm ~ 0.60 μm (Green)	4m/pixel
3	0.63 μm ~ 0.69 μm (Red)	4m/pixel
4	0.76 μm ~ 0.90 μm (Near-IR)	4m/pixel

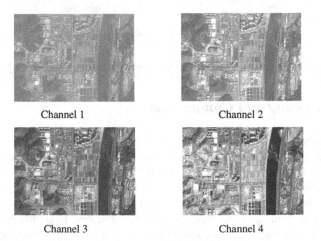

Channel 1   Channel 2

Channel 3   Channel 4

Fig. 3. IKONOS satellite image used in this study

Table 2. Separability measures betweens classes of training data

C1: Water, C2: Forest, C3: Dried Grass, C4: Green House with Vinyl, C5: Asphalt Road, C6: Bare Soil, C7: Building, C8: Crop Land, C9: Shadow

	C1	C2	C3	C4	C5	C6	C7	C8
C2	1.9876							
C3	1.9999	1.8343						
C4	1.9995	1.9919	1.9841					
C5	1.9544	1.9993	1.9882	1.7890				
C6	2.0000	2.0000	1.8365	2.0000	1.9999			
C7	1.8346	1.7261	1.5045	1.4244	1.3899	1.9138		
C8	1.9997	1.4565	0.9629	1.9045	1.9950	1.9864	1.4666	
C9	1.4177	1.9969	1.9998	1.9984	1.8839	2.0000	1.8005	1.9996

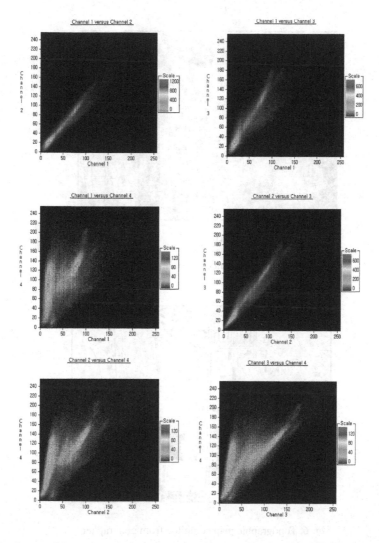

Fig. 4. Two-dimensional scatter plots between spectral channels of IKONOS image

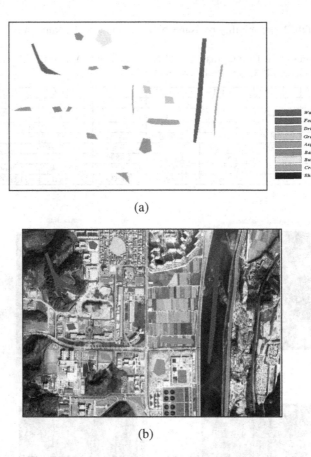

	Water
	Forest
	Dried grass
	Greenhouse with vinyl
	Asphalt road
	Bare soil
	Building
	Crop land
	Shadow

(a)

(b)

Fig. 5. Training sites selected for land cover classification

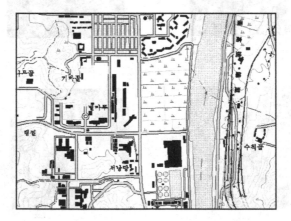

Fig. 6. Topographic map compiled from geographer

Land cover classification is the procedure most often used for quantitative analysis of remote sensing image data. It rests upon using suitable algorithms that label the pixels in an image as representing particular ground cover types. The steps for land cover classification are as follows:

Step 1. Decide on the set of ground cover types into which the image is to be classified. These are the information classes, which for example could be water, grass, etc.

Step 2. Choose representative or prototype pixels from each of the desired sets of classes. These pixels are said to form training data. Training sets for each class can be established using site visits, maps, air photographs, or even from the photo-interpretation of a colour composite product formed from the image data.

Step 3. Use the training data to estimate the parameters of the particular classifier algorithm to be used. These parameters will be the properties of the probability model used, or will be equations that define the partitions in the multispectral space. The set of parameters for a given class is sometimes called the signature of that class.

Step 4. Using the trained classifier, label, or classify, every pixel in the image into one of the desired ground cover types.

Step 5. Produce thematic (class) maps that summarize the results of the classification.

The maximum likelihood classification is applied to the IKONOS image, and the land cover classification map is generated as Fig. 7. The overall accuracy of the maximum likelihood method is 76.2% and kappa coefficient is 0.73. The classification result map of neural network method shows in Fig. 8. The overall accuracy of the neural network method is 79.0% and kappa coefficient is 0.76. In Fig. 9, the classification map shows the result of the neuro-fuzzy method applied to the same data. First, we developed classification software based on the neuro-fuzzy model, and by modifying existing software, we applied this to the system. For the neuro-fuzzy learning process the patterns of training sets are ordered alternatively within the training sets to classify the image. The domains of the four input bands were initially each partitioned by 12 equally distributed fuzzy sets. The neuro-fuzzy classifier selected 20 fuzzy sets, and 218 fuzzy rules out of the 732 fuzzy rules produced to classify the test image from the training sets. The learning of the fuzzy sets stopped after 745 epochs, because the error did not decrease after 612 epochs.

Fig. 7. Land cover classification map using Maximum Likelihood method

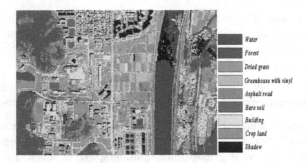

Fig. 8. Land cover classification map using Neural Network method

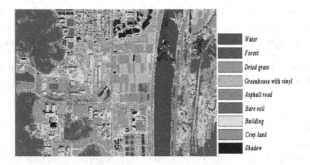

Fig. 9. Land cover classification map using Neuro-fuzzy method

Table 3. Classification results obtained with the Maximum Likelihood method

Classified Data	Reference Data									Row Total	User's Acc. (%)
	C1	C2	C3	C4	C5	C6	C7	C8	C9		
C1	131	11	21	0	5	23	0	6	6	203	64.5
C2	12	124	11	2	2	1	11	1	1	165	75.2
C3	4	7	101	11	1	6	3	2	0	135	74.8
C4	1	2	5	98	4	11	8	9	0	138	71.0
C5	0	14	2	3	103	8	1	8	3	142	72.5
C6	0	1	0	1	0	114	0	11	9	136	83.8
C7	4	3	7	0	0	1	132	4	2	153	86.3
C8	2	0	0	2	1	3	0	106	8	122	86.9
C9	0	0	0	3	4	6	0	2	50	65	76.9
Column Total	154	162	147	120	120	173	155	149	79	1259	
Producer's Acc. (%)	85.1	76.5	68.7	81.7	85.8	65.9	85.3	71.1	63.3		

After the learning process, 34 out of the 1,024 patterns from the training set were wrongly classified. The overall accuracy of the neuro-fuzzy method is 85.6% and kappa coefficient is 0.83.

While comparing the classification accuracy, the neuro-fuzzy classifier was the most accurate method. Thus, the neuro-fuzzy model is more suitable for classifying a mixed-composition area such as the natural environment of the Korean peninsula.

Table 4. Classification results obtained with the Neural Network method

Classified Data	Reference Data									Row Total	User's Acc. (%)
	C1	C2	C3	C4	C5	C6	C7	C8	C9		
C1	132	9	11	1	2	23	0	5	4	187	70.6
C2	9	129	9	1	1	1	7	4	1	162	79.6
C3	5	6	117	5	0	6	1	1	1	142	82.4
C4	2	5	3	101	7	11	5	7	0	141	71.6
C5	3	5	5	1	108	5	1	5	3	136	79.4
C6	0	5	0	2	0	115	0	9	7	138	83.3
C7	0	3	2	2	0	3	137	5	6	158	86.7
C8	2	0	0	5	0	2	2	105	7	123	85.4
C9	1	0	0	2	2	7	2	8	50	72	69.4
Column Total	154	162	147	120	120	173	155	149	79	1259	
Producer's Acc. (%)	85.7	79.6	79.6	84.2	90.0	66.5	88.4	70.5	63.3		

Table 5. Classification results obtained with the Neuro-fuzzy method

Classified Data	Reference Data									Row Total	User's Acc. (%)
	C1	C2	C3	C4	C5	C6	C7	C8	C9		
C1	138	5	8	1	3	7	0	4	4	170	81.2
C2	6	134	7	1	2	0	5	0	0	155	86.5
C3	1	5	119	9	0	1	3	2	1	141	84.4
C4	3	3	3	103	2	4	6	2	4	130	79.2
C5	1	3	2	2	112	3	4	8	3	138	81.2
C6	0	1	0	1	0	156	0	6	5	169	92.3
C7	2	3	5	0	0	0	137	4	2	153	89.5
C8	2	5	1	2	0	0	0	121	2	133	91.0
C9	1	3	2	1	1	2	0	2	58	70	82.9
Column Total	154	162	147	120	120	173	155	149	79	1259	
Producer's Acc. (%)	89.6	82.7	81.0	85.8	93.3	90.2	88.4	81.2	73.4		

Table 6. Performance of Maximum Likelihood, Neural Network and Neuro-fuzzy methods

Methods	Classification Performance	
	Overall Accuracy (%)	Kappa Coefficient
Maximum Likelihood	76.2	0.73
Neural network	79.0	0.76
Neuro-fuzzy	85.6	0.83

4 Conclusion and Discussion

In this study, the neuro-fuzzy, neural network and maximum likelihood classification algorithms were compared using the land use classification processed IKONOS image of the part of Daejeon City in Korea. For this, the neuro-fuzzy classification system had to be developed, and the classification system was initialized by prior knowledge using fuzzy If-Then rules. These were interpreted after the learning process, and created fuzzy rules by learning from its fuzzy sets from adapting the parameters of its membership functions. The neuro-fuzzy method were compared with a neural network method using a back-propagation algorithm, and with a maximum likelihood method, a widely used standard method that yields the minimum total classification error for Gaussian distributions. The results show that the neuro-fuzzy method was considerably more accurate than other methods on mixed composition areas such as "bare soil" and "crop land". These classes were classified in accuracy over 90%. The neural network method's accuracy was between that of the neuro-fuzzy and the maximum likelihood methods for all the land cover classes. Thus, the neuro-fuzzy model can be used to classify mixed composition areas such as the natural environment of the Korean peninsula. This method was superior in the suppression of classification errors for mixed land cover signatures.

The classified land cover information will be important when the results of the classification are to be integrated into a Geographical Information System (GIS). The classified information can be used for land use management, and for planning from the detection of any changes. For future work, a refinement of the classification algorithms for the whole system is needed.

Acknowledgement. IKONOS image was supported by e-HD.com for the research.

References

1. Benediktsson, J. A., Swain, P. H. and Ersoy, O. K.: Conjugate-gradient Neural Networks in Classification of Multisource and Very-high-dimensional Remote Sensing Data. Int. J. of Remote Sensing 14 (1993) 2883–2903
2. Gopal, S., Sklarew, D. M. and Lambin, E.: Fuzzy-neural Networks in Multi-temporal Classification of Land-cover Change in the Sahel. Proc. of the DOSES Work-shop on New Tools for Spatial Analysis (1994) 55–68
3. Gopal, S., Woodcock, C., Strahler, A.: Fuzzy Neural Network Classification of Global Land Cover from a AVHRR Data Set. Remote Sensing of Environment 67 (1999) 230-243
4. Halgamuge, S. K., Glesner, M.: Neural Networks in Designing Fuzzy Systems for Real World Applications. Fuzzy Sets and Systems 65 (1994) 1-12
5. Hara, Y., Atkins, R. G., Yueh, S. H., Shin, R. T. and Kong, J. A.:Application of Neural Networks to Radar Image Classification. IEEE Tran. on Geosci. and Remote Sensing 32 (1994) 100–111
6. Lee, J., Weger, W. C., Sengupta, S. K., Welch, R. M.: Neural Network Approach to Cloud Classification. IEEE Tran. on Geoscience and Remote Sensing 28 (1990) 846–855
7. Mather, P. M.: Computer Processing of Remotely Sensed Images. Chichester, Wiley (1997)
8. Peddle, D. R.: Empirical Comparison of Evidential Reasoning, Linear Discriminant Analysis and Maximum Likelihood Algorithms for Land Cover Classification. Canadian Journal of Remote Sensing 19 (1993) 31-44
9. Tzeng, Y. C., Chen, K. S., Kao, W. L., Fung, A. K.: Dynamic Learning Neural Network for Remote Sensing Applications. IEEE Tran. on Geoscience and Remote Sensing 32 (1994) 1096–1103
10. Yoshida, T., Omatu, S.: Neural Network Applications to Land-cover Mapping. IEEE Tran. on Geoscience and Remote Sensing 32 (1994) 1103–1109
11. Roger, R. E.: Sparse Inverse Covariance Matrices and Efficient Maximum Likelihood Classification of Hyperspectral Data. Int. J. Remote Sensing 17 (1996) 589-613
12. Wasserman, P. D.: Neural Computing, Theory and Practice. New York: Vain Nostrand Reinhold (1989)
13. Rumelhart, D.E., Hinton, G. E., Williams, R. J.: Learning Internal Representations by Error Propagation. Parallel Distributed Processing, Cambridge, MA: MIT Press (1986) 318-362

Rough Set Approach to Sunspot Classification Problem

Sinh Hoa Nguyen[1], Trung Thanh Nguyen[2], and Hung Son Nguyen[3]

[1] Polish-Japanese Institute of Information Technology,
Koszykowa 86, 02-008, Warsaw, Poland
[2] Department of Computer Science, University of Bath,
Bath BA2 7AY, United Kingdom
[3] Institute of Mathematics, Warsaw University,
Banacha 2, 02-097 Warsaw, Poland

Abstract. This paper presents an application of hierarchical learning method based rough set theory to the problem of sunspot classification from satellite images. The Modified Zurich classification scheme [3] is defined by a set of rules containing many complicated and unprecise concepts, which cannot be determined directly from solar images. The idea is to represent the domain knowledge by an ontology of concepts – a treelike structure that describes the relationship between the target concepts, intermediate concepts and attributes. We show that such ontology can be constructed by a decision tree algorithm and demonstrate the proposed method on the data set containing sunspot extracted from satellite images of solar disk.

Keywords: Hierarchical learning, rough sets, sunspot classification.

1 Introduction

Sunspots that appear as dark spots on the solar surface, have been the subject of interest to astronomers and astrophysicists for many years. Sunspot observation, analysis and classification form an important part in furthering knowledge about the Sun, the solar weather, and its effect on earth [8]. Certain categories of sunspot groups are associated with solar flares. Observatories around the world track all visible sunspots in an effort to early detect flares. Sunspot recognition and classification are currently manual and labor intensive processes which could be automated if successfully learned by a machine.

Some initial attempts at automatic sunspot recognition and classification were presented in [4]. Several learning algorithms were examined to investigate the ability of machine learning in dealing with the problem of sunspot classification. The experiment showed that it is very difficult to learn the classification scheme using only visual properties as attributes. The main issue is that many characteristics of sunspots can not be precisely determined from digital images.

To improve the classification accuracy we experimented with classification learning in combination with clustering and layered learning methods. It was

D. Ślęzak et al. (Eds.): RSFDGrC 2005, LNAI 3642, pp. 263–272, 2005.

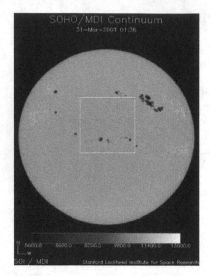 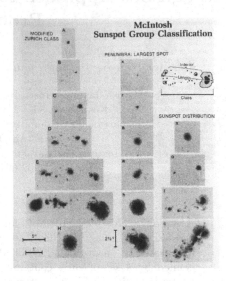

Fig. 1. Left: The SOHO/MDI satellite image of the solar disk, showing sunspots. Right: the McIntosh Sunspot Classification Scheme. (Courtesy P.S. McIntosh, NOAA(1990).

concluded that one possible way of improving accuracy is to embed the domain knowledge into the learning process. In previous papers we have considered the case where domain knowledge was given in a form of concept ontology and have presented a rough set and layered learning based method that successfully makes use of such kind of domain knowledge [5] [7]. In this paper, that approach is applied to the sunspot classification problem with an exception that the concept ontology is *not given* but constructed by a supervised learning method. The proposed solution has been implemented and the experimental results show many advantages in comparison with standard learning algorithms.

2   Sunspot Classification Schemes

Sunspots appear on the solar disk as individual spots or as a group of spots. Larger and more developed spots have a dark interior called the *umbra*, surrounded by a lighter area referred to as *penumbra*. Sunspots have strong magnetic fields. *Bipolar* spots have both magnetic polarities present, whereas *unipolar* have only one. Within complex groups the *leading spot* may have one polarity and the following spots the reverse, with intermediate a mixture of both. Sunspot groups can have an infinite variety of formations and sizes, ranging from small solo spots to giant groups of spots with complex structure. Despite such a diversity of shapes and sizes astronomers have been able to define broad categories of sunspot groups. Using the McIntosh Sunspot Classification Scheme [3] spots are classified according to three descriptive codes. The first code is a modification of the old Zurich scheme, with seven broad categories:

A: Unipolar group with no penumbra, at start or end of spot group's life

B: Bipolar group with penumbrae on any spots

C: Bipolar group with penumbra on one end of group, usually surrounding largest of leader umbrae

D: Bipolar group with penumbrae on spots at both ends of group, and with longitudinal extent less than 10 arc seconds (120 000 km)

E: Bipolar group with penumbrae on spots at both ends of group, and with longitudinal extent between 10 and 15 arc seconds

F: Bipolar group with penumbrae on spots at both ends of group, and length more than 15 arc seconds (above 180 000 km)

H: Unipolar group with penumbra. Principal spot is usually the remnant leader spot of pre-existing bipolar groups

The second code describes the penumbra of the largest spot of the group and the third code describes the compactness of the spots in the intermediate part of the group [3]. Up to sixty classes of spots are covered, although not all code combinations are used. A particular spot or group of spots may go through a number of categories in their lifetime. Solar flares are usually associated with large groups. When attempting automated classification the following issues need to be considered:

1. **Interpreting classification rules:** As only broad forms of classification exist there is a large allowable margin in the interpretation of classification rules. The same group may be assigned a different class depending on the expert doing the classification. Observatories share information and cross-check results regularly to form an opinion.

2. **Individual spots and groups:** Sunspot classification schemes classify sunspot groups not individual spots. When sunspots are extracted from digital images they are treated as individual spots. Hence further information is required to group spots together to form proper sunspot groups.

3. **Dealing with groups migration:** Sunspots have their own life-cycle and migrate across the Sun's surface. They start their life as small tiny spots that usually continue to form pairs and evolve into groups. Once a group attains its maximum size it starts to decay. As a result, a particular group may change its class assignment several times during its lifetime. A reliable method to keep track of those changes must be devised to correctly follow a group during its lifetime. It may be difficult to decide exactly when the change occurs. An individual image of a solar disk containing sunspots has no information about their previous and future class. Moreover, as groups approach the edge of the visible solar disk their shape appears compacted making classification based solely on digital images difficult.

4. **Availability of data:** The average number of visible sunspots varies over time, increasing and decreasing on average over 11.8 years. As each cycle progresses sunspots gradually start to appear closer to the Sun's equator while forming larger and more complex groups. This creates an issue when deciding on the input data range for a *training dataset*. For example by

taking observations only from a short period at solar maximum, where there are likely to be more sunspots groups class D, E, F, an unbalanced training sample may be obtained.

5. **Quality of input data:** For automatic recognition and classification systems to perform well they need a consistent set of high quality input images, free of distortions and of fairly high resolution. Images should be taken from one source and the same instrument to reduce the variability. Thus satellite images are more suitable than photographs taken from the ground. Note that some sunspots can be very small and may not be captured at all.

The automated sunspot classification system that we propose consist of two modules: the image processing module and the classification module. The aim of the former is to handle the input image, extracting spots and their properties. The classification module is responsible for predicting the spot's class and grouping them together.

Our current system is able to import digital images of solar disks from NASA SOHO/MDI satellite, separate individual spots from their background using a custom threshold function and extract their features to a text file to build a matrix of instances and attributes. Such a flat-file can be imported to machine learning tools (such as WEKA, RSES) for building a classifier. A future objective would be to build a complete system whose input is an image and output are sunspot groups marked and classified.

3   Learning Sunspot Classification

Data mining and machine learning techniques can help to find the set of rules that govern classification and deal with the margin that exists for the interpretation of sunspot classification rules. This is achieved by learning from actual data and the past experience of expert human astronomers who have been classifying sunspots manually for years.

The standard learning algorithms that used only visual properties to predict classification scheme proved to be inadequate, especially for robust and accurate daily prediction. To improve the classification accuracy, it is necessary to embed the domain knowledge into the learning process. This paper presents a learning method to sunspot classification based on rough sets and layered learning approach. Layered learning [11] is an alternative approach to concept approximation. Given a hierarchical concept decomposition, the main idea is to synthesize a target concept gradually from simpler ones. One can imagine the decomposition hierarchy as a treelike structure containing the target concept in the root. A learning process is performed through the hierarchy, from leaves to the root, layer by layer. At the lowest layer, basic concepts are approximated using feature values available from a data set. At the next layer more complex concepts are synthesized from basic concepts. This process is repeated for successive layers until the target concept is achieved. In previous papers (see [6] [5]) we presented a hierarchical learning approach to concept approximation based on rough set theory. The proposition was performed with an assumption that the concept ontology already exists. This assumption is not satisfied in the case of sunspot classification problem. One of the main issues of this contribution is the construction of concept ontology from the domain knowledge. Our solution to sunspot classification problem consists of four main steps:

1. recognize single sunspots using image processing techniques and create decision table describing their classification made by experts;
2. group daily sunspots into clusters and create decision table for those clusters;
3. create a concept ontology from the domain knowledge;
4. apply hierarchical learning method based on rough set theory to learn the Zurich sunspot classification scheme.

3.1 Sunspot Recognition and Data Preparation

The process of constructing the *training dataset* consisted of gathering data from two sources: the NASA/SOHO website and the ARMaps pages from the Hawaii University website. The method of sunspot recognition and extraction from digital images of solar disk was described in [4]. The resulting data set consists of sunspots as objects, their visual properties (size, shape, etc.) as attributes and the Zurich classification (made by experts from ARMaps) as the class label.

Attribute Selection: The features extracted by the image processing method were shape descriptors describing the shape of single sunspots and information about spot's neighbours. The following sunspot features were extracted: x and y coordinates of a spot center; *area* of a spot; *perimeter* length around a spot; spot's *angle* to the main axis; spot's *aspect ratio*, *compactness*, and *form factor*; spot's *feret's diameter*; spot's *circularity*; count of how many neighbouring spots are within a specified *radii* (nine radii were selected).

Data Preparation: The following manual classification process was repeated for all training images: Found an ARMap that fitted the corresponding drawing of detected sunspots using the date and the filename of a drawing. Looked at the regions marked on the ARMap and matched them with the regions of spots detected in the drawings. All regions on the ARMap were numbered - to be annotated. All spots that fell within each identified region were selected. Since each spot is numbered, it was possible to assign the ARMap region number to those spots in the main flat file. All spots with an identical ARMap region number were assigned the class of the ARMap region.

3.2 Sunspot Clustering

For each image, individual spots were grouped together using a simple hierarchical agglomerative clustering algorithm. The objective was to obtain groups which closely matched real life sunspot groups. Three different methods were used and compared: single-link, complete-link and group average [2]. The Euclidean distance was used to calculate the dissimilarity measure. The clustering process starts with all spots within a single image. Spots are then merged into groups until the stop condition is triggered. The stop condition was based on the total distance of all spots within a single cluster. If at any iteration that total distance across all clusters exceeded a predefined threshold then the process is stopped and groups produced.

3.3   Construction of the Concept Ontology

The main goal of sunspot classification problem is to classify recognised sunspots into one of the seven classes $\{A, B, C, D, E, F, H\}$. After the clustering step, the task is restricted to classification of sunspot groups. In our system, every cluster is characterised by about 40 attributes. These attributes describe not only properties of whole groups, but also features of the largest spots in a group.

In Section 1 we have presented the original sunspot classification scheme. This scheme seems to be complicated but, in fact, the classification can be described by some simpler concepts:

1. **Magnetic type of groups:** there are two possible types called *unipolar* and *bipolar*;
2. **Group span:** a heliographical distance of two farthest spots in a group; there are three spanning degrees, i.e., *NULL* (not applicable), *small* (less than 10 h.degs. or 120000 km), *large* (more than 15 h.degs. or 180000 km) and *middle* (between 10 h.degs and 15 h.degs.);
3. **Penumbra type of the leading spot:** there are four possible types called *no penumbra, rudimentary, asymmetric, and symmetric*;
4. **Penumbra size of the leading spot:** there are two possible values *small* (less than 2,5 h.degs. or 30000km), and *large* (more than 2,5 h.degs.);
5. **Distribution of spots inside a group:** there are four possible values called *single, open, intermediate, and compact.*

If we consider all situations described by those five concepts, one can see that there are 60 possible situations only. Every situation is characterized by those concepts (which can be treated as attributes) and can be labeled by one of seven letters $\{A, B, C, D, E, F, H\}$, accordingly to the Zurich classification scheme. Therefore we have a decision table with 60 objects, 5 attributes, 7 decision classes. The idea is to create a decision tree for the described above decision table. The resulting tree computed by the decision tree induction method, which is implemented in Weka [14] as J48 classifier, is presented in Figure 2.

This decision tree leads the following observations, which are very useful for concept decomposition process: (1) Classes D, E and F are similar on almost all attributes except attribute **group span**; (2) Classes A, H have similar magnetic type (both are unipolar), but they are discerned by the attribute **penumbra type**; (3) Classes B, C have similar magnetic type (both are bipolar), but they are discerned by the attribute *penumbra size*.

The final concept ontology of target concept has been build from those observations. Figure 3 presents the main part of this ontology which was created by including the following additional concepts to the decision tree in Fig. 2:

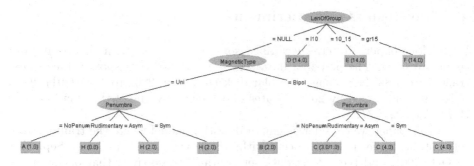

Fig. 2. The Zurich classification scheme represented by a decision tree

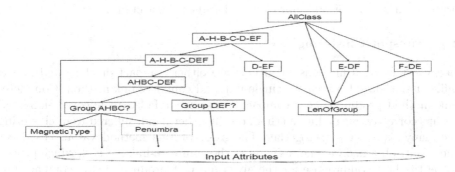

Fig. 3. The concept hierarchy for sunspot classification problem

- **Group AHBC?**: does a sunspot cluster belong to one of classes A, B, C, H?
- **Group DEF?**: does a sunspot cluster belong to one of classes D, E, F?
- **AHBC-DEF**: the classification distinguishing $\{A, B, C, H\}$ and $\{D, E, F\}$;
- **A-H-B-C-DEF**: the classification that groups classes D, E, F together;
- **A-H-B-C-D-EF**: the classification that groups classes E, F together;
- **D-EF, E-DF, F-DE**: classification problems that distinguish one class from the rest for three decision classes D, E, F;
- **target classes**: what is the label of a sunspot cluster?

The synthesis process is performed through the concept hierarchy, from leaves to the root as it has been presented in [5]. The learning algorithm, for every node N of the concept hierarchy, produces the rough membership function for every decision class that occurs in N. Later, the extracted membership functions are used as attributes to construct the rough membership function for those concepts occurring in the next level of the hierarchy.

We have shown that rough membership function can be induced by many classifiers, e.g., k-NN, decision tree or decision rule set. The problem is to chose the proper type of classifiers for every node of the hierarchy. In experiments with sunspot classification, we have applied the rule based classification algorithm and the modified nearest neighbor algorithms that were implemented in RSES [13].

4   The Results of Experiments

In previous paper, we have performed some experiments with classification of single sunspots. The prepared data set contains 2589 sun spots (objects) extracted from 89 daily images of solar disk (from Sep 2001 to Nov 2001). Each object was described by 20 attributes and labeled by one of the decision class A, B, C, D, E, F, H.

In this paper we consider a temporal testing model where the training data set contains those spots that occur within first two months, i.e., from Sep. 2001 to Oct. 2001, and the testing data set contains those spots that occur in the last month, i.e., in Nov. 2001. Classification accuracies of standard learning algorithms for such data sets are very poor and oscillate about 38%. Applying the proposed method one can improve the classification accuracy.

4.1   Sunspot Clustering

Because most real life sunspot groups are either compact or elongated it was difficult to choose between the single-link and complete-link method. Complete-link method produced more compact clusters but failed to uncover elongated groups correctly. Single-link method, on the other hand, suffered from clustering too many distinct groups together. The group average method was also used but the results obtained were not as good as the complete-link method, which proved to be the best compromise for the given data. It produced many compact but correct groups contained within larger elongated groups instead of small number of large but incorrect elongated groups.

Since sunspot groups have dimension limits the sum of all spot distances within a cluster was used for a stopping condition. If a diameter of a cluster grows too large the clustering process is stopped. The experiments were made to obtain the best threshold value. A performance measure used for obtaining the best threshold value was a cluster purity measure. For each cluster produced by the clustering algorithm a comparison was made with the reference cluster to identify how many spots were in fact correctly grouped. A 100% pure cluster is the cluster which had all the spots correctly grouped. So to find the best threshold value for the dataset the cluster purity measure was calculated for each cluster and the average obtained for the whole dataset for every threshold value. The threshold value which produced the best average was ultimately chosen.

4.2   Classification of Sunspot Clusters

For each daily image of solar disk in the three month period from September 2001 to November 2001, we have applied the sunspot recognition algorithm and the described above clustering algorithm to extracted sunspots. Total of 494 sunspot clusters were obtained. The train set (obtained from September and October 2001) consists of 366 clusters, while the test set (November 2001) contains 128 sunspot clusters. The distribution of decision classes in training and testing data is presented in Table 1.

Table 1. The distribution of decision classes on training and test data sets

Train/Test table	No of obj.	Zurich's classes						
		A	B	C	D	E	F	H
Train set	366	0,8%	2,2%	9,6%	30,6%	19,7%	21,9%	15,3%
Test set	128	0%	1,6%	7,8%	36,7%	18,8%	18%	17,2%

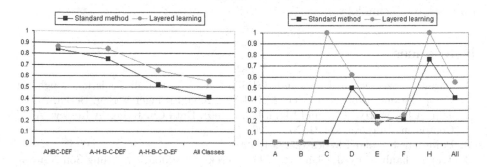

Fig. 4. Left: The classification accuracy of standard and layered method for some concepts in the ontology presented in Fig. 3. Right: the classification accuracy of standard and layered method for particular decision classes.

We have performed some experiments with learning the sunspot classification to compare accuracy of two methods, i.e., the standard rule based method and the proposed method based on layered learning idea. Experimental results are shown in Figure 4. A considerable improvement was obtained by applying the proposed method based on rough sets and layered learning approach compared to standard methods. The highest improvements were achieved for classes C and H that were recognized by the layered learning method with 100% accuracy, see Fig. 4 (right). Classes A and B were too small to be evaluated. Also, the accuracy of the recognition problem: "whether a cluster belongs to one of three classes D, E, F" was very high (about 98%). The main problem here was how to separate those three classes. The decision tree presented in Fig. 2 suggests that these classes can be separated by the cluster span. Unfortunately, our clustering algorithm tends to form smaller groups compared to the real ones. Therefore some large clusters may have been divided into a few smaller ones, and this could have been the reason for low classification accuracy of classes D, E, F.

5 Conclusions

We have demonstrated that automated classification of sunspots is possible and the results show that higher accuracy can be achieved through a layered learning approach and sunspot clustering. In future work we are planning to improve the image processing module to extract additional attributes and enriching the training dataset with new examples. These changes should help to improve the accuracy of classification further and address some of the shortcomings in the current training data. We are also planing to improve clustering algorithms to increase the classification quality of three classes D, E, F.

Acknowledgement. The research has been partially supported by the grant 3T11C00226 from Ministry of Scientific Research and Information Technology of the Republic of Poland and the research grant of Polish-Japanese Institute of Information Technology.

References

1. Bazan J., Szczuka M. RSES and RSESlib - A Collection of Tools for Rough Set Computations, Proc. of RSCTC'2000, LNAI 2005, Springer Verlag, Berlin, 2001
2. Jain, A.K., Murty M.N., and Flynn P.J. (1999): Data Clustering: A Review, ACM Computing Surveys, Vol 31, No. 3, 264-323
3. P. McIntosh, Solar Physics 125, 251, 1990.
4. Trung Thanh Nguyen, Claire P. Willis, Derek J. Paddon, and Hung Son Nguyen. On learning of sunspot classification. In Mieczyslaw A. Klopotek, Slawomir T. Wierzchon, and Krzysztof Trojanowski, editors, *Intelligent Information Systems, Proceedings of IIPWM'04, May 17-20, 2004, Zakopane, Poland*, Advances in Soft Computing, pages 59–68. Springer, 2004.
5. Sinh Hoa Nguyen, Jan Bazan, Andrzej Skowron, and Hung Son Nguyen. Layered learning for concept synthesis. In Jim F. Peters, Andrzej Skowron, Jerzy W. Grzymala-Busse, Bozena Kostek, Roman W. Swiniarski, and Marcin S. Szczuka, editors, *Transactions on Rough Sets I*, volume LNCS 3100 of *Lecture Notes on Computer Science*, pages 187–208. Springer, 2004.
6. Sinh Hoa Nguyen and Hung Son Nguyen. Rough set approach to approximation of concepts from taxonomy. In *Proceedings of Knowledge Discovery and Ontologies Workshop (KDO-04) at ECML/PKDD 2004, September 24, 2004, Pisa, Italy*, 2004.
7. Sinh Hoa Nguyen and Hung Son Nguyen. Learning concept approximation from uncertain decision tables. In Monitoring, Security, and Rescue Techniques in Multi-agent Systems Dunin-Keplicz, B.; Jankowski, A.; Skowron, A.; Szczuka, M. (Eds.), Advances in Soft Computing, Springer-Verlag 2005, page 249–260.
8. K. J. H. Phillips. *Guide to the Sun.* Cambridge University Press, 1992.
9. J. R. Quinlan. Induction of decision trees. *Machine Learning*, 1(1):81–106, 1986.
10. P. H. Scherrer, et al., Sol. Phys., 162, 129, 1995.
11. P. Stone. *Layered Learning in Multi-Agent Systems: A Winning Approach to Robotic Soccer.* The MIT Press, Cambridge, MA, 2000.
12. I. H. Witten and Frank E. *Data Mining: practical machine learning tools and techniques with Java implementations.* Morgan Kaufmann Publishers, San Francisco, CA., 2000.
13. The RSES Homepage, http://logic.mimuw.edu.pl/~rses
14. The WEKA Homepage, http://www.cs.waikato.ac.nz

Jacquard Image Segmentation Method Based on Fuzzy Optimization Technology

Zhilin Feng[1,2], Jianwei Yin[2], Jiong Qiu[2],
Xiaoming Liu[2], and Jinxiang Dong[2]

[1] College of Zhijiang, Zhejiang University of Technology,
Hangzhou 310024, China
[2] State Key Lab of CAD & CG, Zhejiang University,
Hangzhou 310027, China

Abstract. Automatic pattern segmentation of jacquard images is a challenging task for jacquard pattern analysis. In this paper, the phase field model was introduced to extract specific pattern structures within jacquard images. A novel fuzzy optimization method, namely, Multi-start Fuzzy Optimization Method (MSFOM) was proposed for numerical solving of the phase field model. The proposed method was a hybrid algorithm combining fuzzy logic and genetic algorithms, which was able to find global minimum of the phase field model with low computational cost. Experimental results on synthetic and jacquard images demonstrate the efficacy of the proposed method.

1 Introduction

Jacquard images are fabric images which contain elaborately figured designs with geometric motifs [1]. Simple geometric motifs include such stylized flowerlike figures as crescents, stars, rosettes, and leaves. More complex geometric motifs combine elements such as gracefully curving and intertwined geometric patterns. Jacquard images differ from traditional fabric images in that they contain many serpentine curves, regular or irregular geometric shapes, symmetrical or unsymmetrical patterns [2]. Fig. 1 shows some examples of jacquard images.

Traditional fabric images have regular periodic texture patterns produced during manufacturing. Hence, the segmentation process of such images can be formulated as a texture classification problem. To achieve that, autocorrelation function, local integration and gray level difference method have been used to extract statistical texture features for fabric segmentation [3,4]. However, the above fabric segmentation algorithms have difficulty in capturing complex structure of visual features, such as the complex contours of jacquard patterns. Actually, poor image quality, low contrast, and complex nature of the shapes of jacquard patterns may lead to poor accuracy or robustness of existing segmentation algorithms for jacquard images. Active contour models [5,6] are more widely adopted approaches for pattern contour extraction, which are usually constructed by a series of connected curves conforming to the object's boundary under internal

D. Ślęzak et al. (Eds.): RSFDGrC 2005, LNAI 3642, pp. 273–282, 2005.

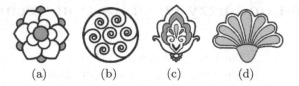

(a)   (b)   (c)   (d)

Fig. 1. Examples of jacquard images

and external forces. However, in a jacquard image, consistently strong edge information is not always presented along the entire boundary of the contours to be segmented. Moreover, if the available jacquard image is heavily corrupted by noise, the performance of the active contour models is often inadequate.

Phase field models [7,8,9,10] are commonly used methods for complex pattern segmentation, which are more immune to noise than the active contour models. The phase field models provide a well-established framework for the mathematical description of free boundary problems of phase transitions [7]. The diffuse interface is represented by the level sets of a function, called order parameter or phase field, which identifies the phases at particular points in space and time [8,9]. The evolution of the order parameter is described by non-linear parabolic differential equations and can be obtained by minimizing a suitable, non-convex total free energy [9]. The phase field models allow topological changes of the interface, and they have attracted a lot of interest in the field of nonlinear analysis for many years [10]. Gajewski et al. [11] regarded an image as binary grey alloy of a black and a white component, and used a nonlocal phase separation model to describe the task of image segmentation. The phase field models can also be viewed as physically motivated level set methods. Instead of choosing an artificial smoothing function for the interface in level set method, the phase field model describes the interface by a mixing energy. Benes et al. [12] presented an algorithm of image segmentation based on the level set solution of phase field equation. The approach can be understood as a regularization of the level set motion by means of curvature, where a special forcing term is imposed to enforce the initial level set closely surrounding the curves of patterns with different shapes.

Since the introduction of the theory of fuzzy logic by Zadeh [13], many different applications of this fuzzy theory have been developed. Of all these applications, the concept of fuzzy logic is adopted to describe some uncertain properties in an analysis. Rao et al. [14] applied these concepts to a static finite element analysis. In this paper, we propose a fuzzy-based optimization method to solve the phase field model on piecewise linear finite element spaces. Experimental results show that the proposed method works well on extraction of complex patterns of jacquard images with good accuracy, and can significantly improve the integrity of segmentation performance.

The rest of this paper is organized as follows. Section 2 describes the phase field model for segmentation. Section 3 is devoted to discussing the implementation of the proposed method. Some experimental results and evaluations are presented in Section 4. Finally, we give a brief conclusion of this research.

2 Phase Field Model for Segmentation

Image Segmentation is an important technique applied in image processing to identify the objects in an image. In some sense, image segmentation involves the recovery of the structure of interest in an image domain, such as pattern contours or detailed edges. Traditionally, phase transitions for the task of image segmentation can be expressed mathematically by free boundary problems, where the interface between regions of different phases is represented by a sharp surface of zero thickness [12].

Let $\Omega \subset R^2$ be a bounded open set and $g \in L^\infty(\Omega)$ represent the original image intensity. The function g has discontinuities that represent the contours of objects in an image. Let $u = u(x,t) \in R$ be an image field, which stands for the state of the image system at the position $x \in \Omega$ and the time $t \geq 0$, and K be the set of discontinuity points of u . Here, we assume that our image field has two stable states corresponding to $u = +1$ and $u = -1$. In this case, the phase-field energy of the image system is often given as follows:

$$E_\varepsilon(u, K) = \int_{\Omega \setminus K} \left(\frac{\varepsilon}{2} (\Psi(\nabla u(x)))^2 + \frac{1}{\varepsilon} F(u(x)) \right) dx \tag{1}$$

where $F(u) = (u^2 - 1)^2/4$ is a double well potential with wells at -1 and $+1$ (i.e., a non-negative function vanishing only at -1 and $+1$). Here, the value $u(x)$ can be interpreted as a phase field (or order parameter), which is related to the structure of the pixel in such a way that $u(x) = +1$ corresponds to one of the two phases and $u(x) = -1$ corresponds to the other. The set of discontinuity points of u parameterizes the interface between the two phases in the corresponding configuration and is denoted by a closed set K.

Ψ is a positive function satisfying $\Psi(\overrightarrow{p}) = |\overrightarrow{p}| \Psi(\overrightarrow{p}/|\overrightarrow{p}|)$, which specifies the anisotropy of the diffuse interface, and helps determine the magnitude of that interfacial energy. If Ψ is isotropic (i.e. $\Psi(\overrightarrow{n}) = 1$) for every unit vector $\overrightarrow{n}$, then the gradient flow for E_ε in the L^2 inner product with mobility $\frac{1}{\varepsilon}$ produces solutions to the Allen-Cahn equation [15]

$$u_t = \Delta u - \frac{1}{\varepsilon^2} F'(u), u_0 = g \tag{2}$$

and these solutions converge to motion by weighted mean curvature as ε goes to zero.

Heuristically, we expect solutions to Eq. (1) to be smooth and close to the image g at places $x \notin K$, and K constitutes edges of the image. To show existence of solutions to Eq. (1), a weak formulation was proposed by De Giorgi et al. [16] by setting $K = S_u$ (the jumps set of u) and minimizing only over $u \in GSBV$, the space of functions of bounded variation. We recall some definitions and properties concerning functions with bounded variation.

Definition 1. *Let $u \in L^1(\Omega; R^2)$. We say that u is a function with bounded variation in Ω , and we write $u \in BV(\Omega; R^2)$, if the distributional derivative Du of u is a vector-valued measure on Ω with finite total variation.*

Definition 2. Let $u \in L^1(\Omega; R^2)$ be a Borel function. Let $x \in \Omega$, we define the approximate upper and lower limits of u as $y \to x$, and abbreviate the approximate limit to $'ap - \lim'$.

$$ap - \limsup_{y \to x} u(y) = \inf\{t : \{u > t\} \text{ has density } 0 \text{ in } x\}$$
$$ap - \liminf_{y \to x} u(y) = \sup\{t : \{u > t\} \text{ has density } 1 \text{ in } x\}$$

We define $u^+(x) = ap - \limsup_{y \to x} u(y)$ and $u^-(x) = ap - \liminf_{y \to x} u(y)$, and say that u is approximately continuous at x if $u^+(x) = u^-(x)$. In this case, we denote the common value by $\tilde{u}(x)$. Finally, we define the jump set of u by $S_u = \{x \in \Omega : \tilde{u}(x) \text{ does not exist}\}$, so that $\tilde{u}(x)$ is defined on $\Omega \backslash S_u$.

Proposition 1. If $u \in BV(\Omega)$, then S_u turns out to be countably $(H^1, 1)$ rectifiable, i.e., $S_u = N \cup (\underset{i \in \mathbb{N}}{\cup} K_i)$, where $H^1(N) = 0$, and each K_i is a compact set contained in a C^1-hypersurface.

Definition 3. Let $u \in BV(\Omega)$. We define three measures $D^a u$, $D^j u$ and $D^c u$ as follows. By the Radon-Nikodym theorem, we set $Du = D^a u + D^s u$ where $D^a u$ is the absolutely continuous part of Du , $D^s u$ is the singular part of Du . $D^s u$ can be further decomposed into the part supported on S_u (the jump part $D^j u$) and the rest (the Cantor part $D^c u$): $D^j u = D^s u|_{S_u}$ and $D^c u = D^s u|_{\Omega \backslash S_u}$. Thus, we can then write $Du = D^a u + D^j u + D^c u$.

Definition 4. A function $u \in L^1(\Omega; R^2)$ is a special function of bounded variation on Ω if its distributional derivative can be written as $Du = f L_n + g H^{n-1}|_K$ where $f \in L^1(\Omega; R^2)$, K is a set of $\sigma-$finite Hausdorff measure, and g belongs to $u \in L^1(\Omega; R^2)$. The space of special functions of bounded variation is denoted by $SBV(\Omega)$.

Definition 5. A function $u \in L^1(\Omega; R^2)$ is a generalized function of bounded variation on Ω , if for each $T > 0$ the truncated function $u_T = (-T) \vee (T \wedge u)$ belongs to $SBV(\Omega)$. The space of these functions will be denoted by $GSBV(\Omega)$.

Proposition 2. Every $u \in GSBV(\Omega) \cap L^1_{loc}(\Omega)$ has an approximate gradient $\nabla u(x)$ for a.e. $x \in \Omega$, and a countably $(H^1, 1)$ rectifiable discontinuity set S_u . Moreover, $\nabla u_k \to \nabla u$ a.e. in Ω, $H^1(S_{u_k}) \to H^1(S_u)$, as $k \to \infty$.

De Giorgi et al. [16] proved that

Theorem 1. Let Ω be an open subset of R^2 and let $\{u_k\}$ be a sequence in $GSBV(\Omega)$. Suppose that there exists $p \in [1, \infty)$ and a constant C such that

$$\int_{\Omega \backslash K} \left(\frac{\varepsilon}{2} (\Psi(\nabla u(x)))^2 + \frac{1}{\varepsilon} F(u(x)) \right) dx \leq C < +\infty \tag{3}$$

for every k . Then there exists a subsequence and a function $u \in GSBV(\Omega) \cap L^2(\Omega)$ such that

$$u_k(x) \to u(x) \text{ a.e. in } \Omega,$$
$$\nabla u_k \to \nabla u \text{ weakly in } L^2(\Omega; R^2) ,$$
$$H^1(S_u) \leq \liminf_{k \to +\infty} H^1(S_{u_k}) .$$

By theorem 1, we can give the weak formulation of the original problem (1) as follows:

$$E(u, K) = E(u, S_u) \qquad (4)$$

and easily prove that minimizers of the weak problem (4) are minimizers of the original problem (1). However, from a numerical point of view, it is not easy to compute a minimizer for Eq. (4), due to the term $H^1(S_u)$, and to the fact that this functional is not lower-semicontinuous with respect to S_u. It is natural to try to approximate Eq. (2) by simpler functionals defined on $GSBV$ spaces. Ambrosio and Tortorelli [17] showed that Eq. (4) can be approximated by a sequence of elliptic functionals which are numerically more tractable. The approximation takes place in the sense of the $\Gamma-$ convergence.

The theory of $\Gamma-$ convergence, introduced by De Giorgi *et al.* [16], is designed to approximate a variational problem by a sequence of regularized variational problems which can be solved numerically by finite difference/finite element methods.

Definition 6. *Let X be a metric space, let $\{F_k\}$ be a sequence of functions defined in X with values in R . Let us set*

$$\Gamma-\liminf_{k \to +\infty} F_k(u) := \inf_{u_k \to u} \left\{ \liminf_{k \to +\infty} F_k(u_k) : \{u_k\} \to u \right\},$$

$$\Gamma-\limsup_{k \to +\infty} F_k(u) := \inf_{u_k \to u} \left\{ \limsup_{k \to +\infty} F_k(u_k) : \{u_k\} \to u \right\} .$$

If $\Gamma-\liminf\limits_{k \to +\infty} F_k(u) = \Gamma-\limsup\limits_{k \to +\infty} F_k(u) = F(u)$ for all $u \in X$, we say that F is the $\Gamma-$ limit of $\{F_k\}$, and we write $F(u) = \Gamma-\lim\limits_{k \to +\infty} F_k(u)$.

In this paper, we consider numerical approximation of the phase-field model, in the sense of $\Gamma-$ convergence, by a sequence of discrete models defined on finite elements spaces over structured and adaptive triangulation.

Let $\Omega = (0,1) \times (0,1)$, let $T_\varepsilon(\Omega)$ be the triangulations and let ε denote the greatest length of the edges in the triangulations. Moreover let $V_\varepsilon(\Omega)$ be the finite element space of piecewise affine functions on the mesh $T_\varepsilon(\Omega)$ and let $\{T_{\varepsilon_j}\}$ be a sequence of triangulations with $\varepsilon_j \to 0$.

Modica [18] proved that

Theorem 2. *Let $BVC(\Omega) = \{\psi \in BV(\Omega) : \psi(\Omega) \subset \{-1, +1\}\}$, and let $W : R \to [0, +\infty)$ be a continuous function such that $\{z \in R : W(z) = 0\} = \{-1, +1\}$, and $c_1(|z|^\gamma - 1) \leq W(z) \leq c_2(|z|^\gamma + 1)$ for every $z \in R$, with $\gamma \geq 2$.*
Then, the discrete functionals

$$E_\varepsilon(u, T) = \begin{cases} \int_{\Omega \setminus K} \left(\frac{\varepsilon}{2}(\Psi(\nabla u_T(x)))^2 + \frac{1}{\varepsilon}F(u_T(x)) \right) dx, u \in V_\varepsilon(\Omega), T \in T_\varepsilon(\Omega) \\ +\infty, otherwise \end{cases} \quad (5)$$

$\Gamma-$ converge as $\varepsilon \to 0$ to the functional $E(u) = c_0 \int_\Omega \Phi(u)dx$ for every Lipschitz set Ω and every function $u \in L^1_{loc}(R^2)$, where $c_0 = \int_{-1}^1 \sqrt{F(u)}du$, and

$$\Phi(u) = \begin{cases} H^1(S_u), u \in BVC(\Omega) \\ +\infty, otherwise \end{cases} \quad (6)$$

3 Segmentation Method Using Fuzzy Optimization Technology

In order to arrive at the joint minimum (u, T) of Eq. (5), we propose a novel numerical method to implement the solving of Eq. (5). The numerical method for the task of segmentation is summarized as follows:

1. Initialize iteration index: $j \leftarrow 0$,
2. Set initial ε_j and u_j,
3. Generate the adapted triangulation T_{ε_j} by the mesh adaptation algorithm, according to u_j,
4. Minimize $E_{\varepsilon_j}(u_j)$ on the triangulation T_{ε_j} by the MSFOM algorithm,
5. Update the current index: $j \leftarrow j + 1$,
6. Generate a new ε_j,
7. If $|\varepsilon_j - \varepsilon_{j-1}| > \mu$, return to Step 3. Otherwise, goto Step 8,
8. Stop.

In the above method, a scheme for the mesh adaptation is first enforced to refine and reorganize a triangular mesh to characterize the essential contour structures of jacquard patterns. Then, the MSFOM algorithm is applied to find the absolute minimum of the discrete version of the functional at each iteration.

Fuzzy Optimization Method (FOM) is a modified version of the steepest descent method (SDM), in which searching direction vector at n*th* step is constructed by use of convex conjugation between (n-1)*th* searching direction vector and n*th* searching direction vector used in SDM [19,20]. The coefficient of convex conjugation is computed by use of stochastic fuzzy estimation based on data resulting from (n-1)*th* and (n-2)*th* searching direction vectors. Originally, FOM is invented as a local minimizer search algorithm. In order to look for a global minimizer, Multi-start Fuzzy Optimization Method (MSFOM), which is a hybrid algorithm with FOM and Genetic Algorithms (GAs), has been developed on the basis of FOM. GAs is used to scatter the set of quasi-local maximizers, i.e., restarting points to the next down-hill procedure, into much higher positions and to let the set of quasi-local maximizers escape completely from the hole. The three fundamental functions in GAs play an important role in the following way: the selection operation in GAs aids the complete climb up to the summits of the target manifold or cross the ridge. The cross over and mutation operations contribute to the optimal rearrangement of the set of restarting initial points.

Let us define operators F, M and R as follows.

- F : Algorithm due to Fuzzy Optimization Method. This procedure is a down-hill process on the cost manifold.
- M : Mountain crossing algorithm. This procedure is a up-hill process on the cost manifold.
- R: Rearrangement algorithm by GAs. In this procedure, starting points for the next down-hill process are rearranged by use of GAs.

Then, the algorithm of Multi-start FOM is summarized as follows:

1. Give an initial population W^0 of $E_\varepsilon(u)$(the set of searchers),
2. Evaluate W^0 , and compute $U^n := FW^n$ (the set of local minimizers obtained),
3. Compute $V^n := MU^n$ (the set of quasi-local maximizers obtained),
4. Compute $W^n := RV^n$ (the set of rearranged searchers),
5. Increase generation number $n := n + 1$ and repeat steps from 2 to 4 until the generation number n is beyond the preset one.

The computational complexity of the proposed method can be estimated by studying the underlying two algorithms, e.g., the mesh adaptation algorithm and the MSFOM algorithm. Since the mesh adaptation algorithm is a linear-time algorithm, the overall computational complexity is dominated by the MSFOM algorithm, which is $O[n^2(n-1)]$.

4   Experimental Results

In this section, we applied the proposed method to some experimental applications to evaluate its effectiveness. We carried out segmentation experiments on some synthetic and real jacquard images. Fig. 2 illustrated the segmentation results of two synthetic images by applying the method. Fig. 2(a)-(b) gived two synthetic images with different shapes respectively. After 8 mesh adaptation processes, the final foreground meshes of Fig. 2(a)-(b) were shown in Fig. 2(c)- (d).

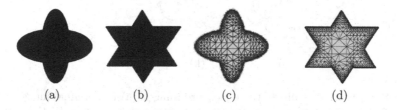

(a)   (b)   (c)   (d)

Fig. 2. Segmentation of synthetic images. (a)-(b) synthetic images. (c)-(d) final foreground meshes.

We also conducted experiments on several real jacquard images. Fig. 3 illustrated segmentation results of three jacquard images using the proposed method. Fig. 3(a)-(c) gived original jacquard images. Fig. 3(d)-(f) and Fig. 3(g)-(i) showed nodes of Delaunay triangulation and the final foreground meshes of Fig. 3(a)-(c) after 8 mesh adaptation processes. The segmented edge sets of Fig. 3(a)-(c) were shown in Fig. 3(j)-(l).

The following experiments were designed for comparing accuracy and efficiency of the proposed method with a popular level set method for Allen-Cahn model, i.e., Benes et al.'s method [12]. We adopted two indirect measures to

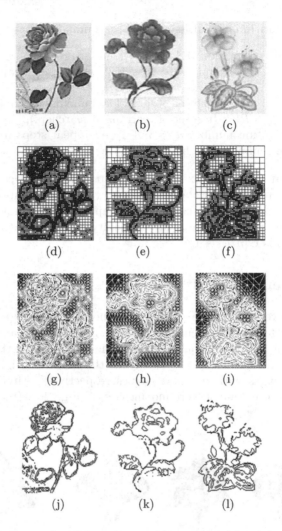

Fig. 3. Segmentation results of three jacquard images. (a)-(c): original images, (d)-(f): nodes of Delaunay triangulation, (g)-(i): final foreground meshes, (j)-(l): segmented edge sets.

evaluate the objective performance of fine image segmentation: the number of segmented regions, and the mean square error (MSE) between the original image and the segmented image. Since MSE represented the degree of segmented region homogeneity for a given number of regions, it could be used as an indirect measure of segmentation efficiency if we considered the number of regions simultaneously. The segmentation results in Table 1 demonstrated that the proposed method improved the fine segmentation performance since it produced better objective segmentation quality in terms of MSE even with a smaller number of regions compared with the Benes *et al.*'s method.

Table 1. Number of regions and MSE comparison between the Benes *et al.*'s method and the proposed method

	Benes *et al.*'s method		Proposed method	
	Number of regions	MSE	Number of regions	MSE
Fig.2 (a)	459	34.25	402	28.17
Fig.2 (b)	620	53.32	540	41.28
Fig.2 (c)	507	41.65	457	32.58

5   Conclusions

In this paper, we presented a novel segmentation method for jacquard images which is based on fuzzy optimization technology. In this method, multi-start fuzzy optimization algorithm is applied to find the minimum of discrete phase field model. Future work would look into learning patterns of variability from a training set and exploiting prior knowledge to provide more robust and accurate results.

References

1. Ngan, H.Y.T., Pang, G.K.H., Yung, S.P., Michael, K.N.: Defect detection on patterned jacquard fabric. In: proceedings of SPIE Conference on Applied Imagery Pattern Recognition. (2003) 163–168
2. Bodnarova, A., Bennamoun, M., Latham, S.J.: Flaw detection in jacquard fabrics using Gabor filters. In: proceedings of SPIE Conference on Intelligent Robots and Computer Vision XVIII: Algorithms, Techniques, and Active Vision.(1999) 254–269
3. Unser, M.: Texture classification and segmentation using wavelet frames. IEEE Transaction on Image Processing. **4** (1995) 1549–1560
4. Soria-Frisch, A., Koppen, M., Nickolay, B.: Aggregation as similarity in a morphological framework for the processing of textile images. In: proceedings of IEEE International Conference on Fuzzy Systems. (2004) 1739–1744
5. Ginneken, B.V., Frangi, A.F., Staal, J.J., Viergever, M.A.: Active shape model segmentation with optimal features. IEEE Transactions on Medical Imaging. **21** (2002) 924–933
6. Xiao, H., Xu, C.Y.: A topology preserving level set method for deformable models. IEEE Transaction on Pattern Analysis and Machine Intelligence. **25** (2003) 755–768
7. Kichenassamy, S., Kumar, A., Olver, P.J., Tannenbaum, A., Yezzi, A.: Conformal curvature flows: from phase transitions to active vision, Archive for Rational Mechanics and Analysis. **134** (1996) 257–301
8. Nestler, B., Wheeler, A.A.: Phase-field modeling of multi-phase solidification. Computer Physics Communications. **147** (2002) 230–233
9. Barles, G., Soner, H.M., Sougandis, P.E.: Front propagation and phase field theory. SIAM Journal on Control and Optimization. **31** (1993) 439–469
10. Capuzzo, D., Finzi, V., March, R.: Area-preserving curve-shortening flows: From phase separation to image processing. Interfaces and Free Boundaries. **31** (2002) 325–343

11. Gajewski, H., Gartner, K.: On a nonlocal model of image segmentation, Weierstrass Institute for Applied Analysis and Stochastics. **762** (2002) 87–107
12. Benes, M., Chalupecky, V., Mikula, K.: Geometrical image segmentation by the AllenÍCCahn equation. Applied Numerical Mathematics. **51** (2004) 187–205
13. Zadeh, L.A.: Fuzzy sets, Information and Control. **8** (1965) 338–353
14. Rao, S.S., Sawyer, J.P.: Fuzzy Finite Element Approach for the Analysis of Imprecisely Defined Systems. AIAA Journal. **33** (1995) 2364–2370
15. Allen, M., and Cahn, W.: A microscopic theory for antiphase boundary motion and its application to antiphase domain coarsening. Applied Physics. **27** (1979) 1085–1095
16. De Giorgi, E., Carriero, M., Leaci, A.: Existence theorem for a minimum problem with free discontinuity set. Archive for Rational Mechanics and Analysis. **1** (1990) 291–322
17. Ambrosio, L., and Tortorelli, V.M.: Approximation of functionals depending on jumps by elliptic functionals via Γ-convergence. Communications on Pure and Applied Mathematics. **43** (1990) 999–1036
18. Modica, L.: The gradient theory of phase transitions and the minimal interface criterion. Archive for Rational Mechanics and Analysis. **98** (1987) 123–142
19. Kawarada, H., Suito, H.: Fuzzy Optimization Method, Computational Science for the 21st Century. John Wiley & Sons, 1997.
20. Kawarada, H., Ohtomo, T., Suito, H.: Multi-Start Fuzzy Optimization Method, GAKUTO International Series. Mathematical Sciences and Applications. **11** (1997) 26–78

Intelligent Algorithms for Optical Track Audio Restoration

Andrzej Czyzewski, Marek Dziubinski,
Lukasz Litwic, and Przemyslaw Maziewski

Multimedia Systems Department, Gdansk University of Technology,
ul. Narutowicza 11/12, 80-952 Gdansk, Poland
ac@pg.gda.pl

Abstract. The Unpredictability Measure computation algorithm applied to psychoacoustic model-based broadband noise attenuation is discussed. A learning decision algorithm based on a neural network is employed for determining audio signal useful components acting as maskers of the spectral components classified as noise. An iterative algorithm for calculating the sound masking pattern is presented. The routines for precise extraction of sinusoidal components from sound spectrum were examined, such as estimation of pitch variations in the optical track audio affected by parasitic frequency modulation. The results obtained employing proposed intelligent signal processing algorithms will be presented and discussed in the paper.

1 Introduction

An approach of spectral subtraction, employing perceptual filtering driven by an intelligent algorithm, used for signal enhancement is presented in this paper. A neural network is a main part of the decision system employed to classify noisy patterns (see [11] for more details). The idea of applying psychoacoustic fundamentals for signal enhancements in terms of perceptual filtering was also demonstrated by others [8]. Number of methods related to noise reduction problem have been proposed, among which Wiener and Kalman adaptive filtration, or spectral subtraction belong to the most frequently applied [4]. However, these methods do not take into account some subjective proprieties of human auditory system [5] successfully exploited in some audio coding standards [2,3]. Additionally, adaptive noise reduction (Wiener and Kalman) suffers from several drawbacks such as: computational complexity, problems in estimation of filter parameters and slow convergence of parameters, which in case of dynamically varying signals (music) result in significant distortions [24,28,25,26]. Spectral subtraction techniques, which are computationally efficient and do not face slow convergence problems, are far more popular in acoustic noise reduction [27]. However, these methods may suffer from artifacts produced by non-ideal estimation of signal and noise estimation in the frequency domain. Both adaptive and spectral subtraction do not employ proprieties of sinusoidal components versus components with chaotic phase in the signal's and noise parameters estimation.

D. Ślęzak et al. (Eds.): RSFDGrC 2005, LNAI 3642, pp. 283–293, 2005.

As it was reported in earlier work [7], employing human auditory system models for parasite noise reduction may be very effective. Application of precise sound perception modeling appears to be necessary for this task and as discussed in [10], it requires implementation of a complex psychoacoustic model [6] rather than the simplified one exploited in the MPEG standard [3].

Another problem related to archive audio recorded in optical tracks is parasitic frequency modulation originated from motor speed fluctuations, tape damages and inappropriate editing techniques. This kind of distortion is usually defined as wow or flutter, or modulation noise (depending on the frequency range of the parasitic modulation frequency). As particularly wow leads to undesirable changes of all of the sound frequency components, sinusoidal sound analysis originally proposed by McAulay and Quatieri [12] was found to be very useful in the defects evaluation. In such approach tracks depicting tonal components changes are processed to obtain precise wow characteristics [13,14,15,16,17]. Notwithstanding all of the cited proposals there is still a need for further algorithmic approach to the wow restoration as it can be very complex sharing periodic or accidental nature. Therefore this paper, similarly as the previous one [16] addresses the problem of wow extraction, however in this case also employing soft computing.

2   Noise Removal Algorithm

The masking phenomena are fundamental for contemporary audio coding standards [2,3], although it can be also exploited in noise reduction [7,10]. More detailed information on psychoacoustics principles of signal processing can be found in abundant literature [5,6,9] also including our papers [7,10,11].

Significant role in the psychoacoustic modeling play tonality descriptors of spectral components. The tonality may be represented by the *Unpredictability Measure* parameter [1] used for calculation of the masking offset. Masking offset for the excitation of b_x Barks at frequency of b_x Barks is given by the formula:

$$O_{k,x} = \alpha_k^t \cdot (14.5 + bark(x)) + (1 - \alpha_k^t) \cdot 5.5 \tag{1}$$

The tonality index α_x^t of the excitation of b_x Barks is assumed to be directly related to the *Unpredictability Measure* parameter $(\alpha_k^t = c_k^t)$, where c_k^t is calculated in the following way:

$$c_k^t = \frac{\sqrt{(r_k^t \cdot \cos \Phi_k^t - \hat{r}_k^t \cdot \cos \hat{\Phi}_k^t)^2 + (r_k^t \cdot \sin \Phi_k^t - \hat{r}_k^t \cdot \sin \hat{\Phi}_k^t)^2}}{r_k^t + |\hat{r}_k^t|} \tag{2}$$

for r_k^t denoting spectral magnitude and Φ_k^t denoting phase, both at time t , while $\hat{r}_k^t$ and $\hat{\Phi}_k^t$ represent the predicted values of Φ_k^t , and are referred to the past information (calculated for two previous signal sample frames):

$$\begin{cases} \hat{r}_k^t = r_k^{t-1} + (r_k^{t-1} - r_k^{t-2}) \\ \hat{\Phi}_k^t = \Phi_k^{t-1} + (\Phi_k^{t-1} - \Phi_k^{t-2}) \end{cases} \Rightarrow \begin{cases} \hat{r}_k^t = 2r_k^{t-1} - r_k^{t-2} \\ \hat{\Phi}_k^t = 2\Phi_k^{t-1} - \Phi_k^{t-2} \end{cases} \tag{3}$$

Thus, based on the literature [6], the masking threshold of the Basilar membrane T, stimulated by the single excitation of b_x Barks and of magnitude equal to S_x is calculated with regard to:

$$\begin{cases} T_{i,x} = S_i \cdot 10^{-s_1 \cdot (b_x - b_i)/10 - O_{i,x}}, & b_x \leq b_i \\ T_{j,x} = S_j \cdot 10^{-s_2 \cdot (b_j - b_x)/10 - O_{j,x}}, & b_x > b_j \end{cases} \qquad (4)$$

where S_i, S_j are magnitudes related to excitations b_i, b_j and global masking threshold is obtained by summing up all of individual excitations.

2.1 Perceptual Noise Reduction System

In the perceptual noise reduction system (Fig. 1), published first at the KES'2004 conference [11], it is assumed that noise is of additive type. Spectral representation of the disturbance is calculated with regard to spectral subtraction techniques [4].

Because noise suppression in this approach is based on masking some spectral components of the disturbing noise, it is necessary to determine which components should be masked and which should act as maskers. For this reason, so called rough estimate $\hat{X}^{ref}(j\omega)$ of the clean signal's spectrum is obtained with accordance to spectral subtraction method [4] based on the iterative algorithm represented by the Noise Masking block in Fig. 1.

The proposed algorithm [7,10] has been recently improved and extended with a learning decision algorithm. The new *Decision System* module [11] containing a neural network is responsible for determining which components are going to be treated as maskers U (*useful* components), and which represent distortions and are going to be masked D (*useless* components). The basic classification (without neural network application described in Sect. 4) can be carried out on the basis of the following expressions:

$$U = \{\hat{X}_i^{ref}; \quad |\hat{X}_i^{ref}| > T_i^{ref} \wedge |Y_i| > T_i^Y, 1 \leq i \leq N/2\} \qquad (5)$$

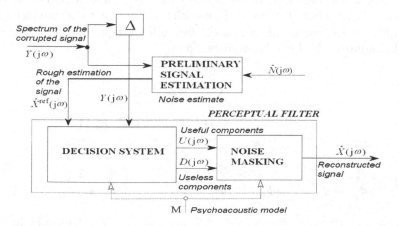

Fig. 1. General lay-out of noise reduction system

$$D = \{Y_i; \quad |\hat{X}_i^{ref}| \le T_i^{ref} \vee |Y_i| \le T_i^Y, 1 \le i \le N/2\} \tag{6}$$

where i denotes spectrum component indexes, U and D are sets containing useful and useless information. T^{ref} is the masking threshold caused by the presence of $\hat{X}^{ref}(j\omega)$, and T^Y is the masking threshold of the input signal: $Y^{ref}(j\omega)$.

Lowering of the masking threshold preserves more noise of the input signal, so the influence of the reconstruction filter is significantly smaller than it is in case of the uplifting method, giving less distorted output signal. Modified global masking threshold T_x^β at barks can be calculated with regard to formula:

$$T_x^\beta = \sum_{j \in U_L(x)} T_{j,x} + \sum_{j \in D_L(x)} T_{j,x}^\beta + \sum_{i \in U_H(x)} T_{i,x} + \sum_{i \in D_H(x)} T_{i,x}^\beta \tag{7}$$

where $T_{i,x}^\beta$ and $T_{j,x}^\beta$ represent new masking thresholds, caused by reduced single excitations and β is vector containing reduction factor values for the noisy components. $U_L(x)$ and $U_H(x)$ (similarly $D_L(x)$ and $D_H(x)$) denote subset of U(or subset of D) containing elements with frequencies lower or equal (L) to b_x barks, and frequencies higher than b_x barks (H).

Since values of β may differ for the elements of D, and changing each value affects T_x^β , thus it is impractical to calculate all reducing factor values directly. For this reason sub-optimal iterative algorithm was implemented [11].

2.2   Unpredictability Measure Application

Calculation of the masking offset, described by (1) plays a significant role in the masking threshold calculation. In noisy signals, tonal components that are occurring just above the noise floor, may be not very well represented by the *Unpredictability Measure* (*UM*) parameter due to the strong influence of the noisy content. A practical solution to this problem is extending time domain resolution, by increasing overlap of the frames used only for unpredictability calculation. Standard *Unpredictability Measure* (2-3) refers to the fragment of the signal represented by 3 consecutive frames, i.e. beginning of this fragment (T_{start}) is at the beginning of the frame with $t - 2$ index and the end of the fragment (T_{start}) is at the end of frame with t index, with accordance to (3). Consequently, the same fragment is divided into N equally spaced frames, so that the improved UM can be expressed as:

$$\bar{c}_k^t = \frac{1}{N-2} \sum_{n=1}^{N-2} c_k^{t^n} \tag{8}$$

$$\text{where} \quad c_k^{t^n} = \frac{dist\left((\hat{r}_k^{t^n}, \hat{\Phi}_k^{t^n}), (r_k^{t^n}, \Phi_k^{t^n})\right)}{r_k^{t^n} + |\hat{r}_k^{t^n}|} \tag{9}$$

$$\text{and} \quad \begin{cases} \hat{r}_k^{t^n} = r_k^{t^n-1} + (r_k^{t^n-1} - r_k^{t^n-2}) \\ \hat{\Phi}_k^{t^n} = \Phi_k^{t^n-1} + (\Phi_k^{t^n-1} - \Phi_k^{t^n t-2}) \end{cases} \Rightarrow \begin{cases} \hat{r}_k^{t^n} = 2r_k^{t^n-1} - r_k^{t^n-2} \\ \hat{\Phi}_k^{t^n} = 2\Phi_k^{t^n-1} - \Phi_k^{t^n-2} \end{cases} \tag{10}$$

while $T_{start} \le t^n - 2 < t^n - 1 < t^n \le T_{stop}$ and $c_k^t = \bar{c}_k^t$. Additionally, classification of the spectrum components in non-linear spectral subtraction, can be extended by some psychoacoustic parameters, i.e. the tonality description values. By analyzing time-frequency domain behavior of the *UM* vectors calculated for each frame, it is easy to spot tracks representing harmonic content of the signal. Basing on this observation, artificial neural network was deployed as the decision system for classifying, c_k^{tn} patterns. A set of training data was obtained from the noise fragment and from the noisy signal - c_k^{tn} vectors of the noise represented useless components, while those obtained from the noisy input signal, classified as useful components with standard spectral subtraction algorithm, represented patterns of the useful signal. A three-layer neural network of the feed-forward type was used in the experiments. Its structure was defined as follows:

- Number of neurons in the initial layer is equal to the number of elements in the feature vector
- Number of neurons in the hidden layer is equal to the number of neurons in the initial layer
- Output layer contained one neuron in the output neurons in the initial and the output layers have log-sigmoid transfer functions, while neurons in the hidden layer have tan-sigmoid transfer functions.The weights and biases, were updated during the training process, according to Levenberg-Marquardt optimization method. A method of controlling the generalization process was also used. Such an approach is very effective for recovering sinusoidal components, however it does not significantly improve recovery of non-tonal components. Therefore it should be considered as an extension to the spectral subtraction decision process. The algorithm was verified experimentally (the results are discussed in Sect. 4).

3   Parasitic Modulation Compensating Algorithm

The proposed algorithm (presented in Fig.2) for wow defect evaluation is to estimate the pitch variation function $p_w(n)$ from the contaminated (wow) input signal $x_w(n)$ [23]. The first stage of the algorithm, depicted as STFT in Fig.2, results in a time-frequency representation of the input signal. The distorted input signal, initially divided into time-frames (with an appropriate overlapping) is windowed with the Hamming window for better side-lobe suppression. To gain frequency resolution the windowed signal is zero-padded and then it is packed into the buffer for a zero phase spectrum [18]. Finally, Discrete Fourier Transform (DFT) is evaluated for every time-frame buffer to obtain the time-frequency representation.

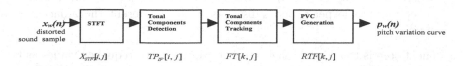

Fig. 2. Block diagram of wow estimation process

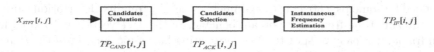

Fig. 3. Structure of the Tonal Components Detection Block

The next stage of the algorithm (presented in Fig.3) is to detect tonal components of the signal. In the first step candidates for tonal components are detected as local maxima (peaks) of a magnitude spectrum stored in X_{STFT}. Since these peaks result either form the main-lobes or the side-lobes of the spectral components it is necessary to exclude the latter ones. It also essential to reject the peaks resulting from localized noise [23]. This task has to be performed according to an appropriate criterion. The most intuitive, an amplitude threshold, recognizes component as a tonal peak when its amplitude is above the certain threshold. As this criterion suffers from many drawbacks other criteria for peak validation have been proposed [19,20,23]. Nevertheless, none is enough sufficient by oneself for distorted and noisy musical signals which are of interest of this paper.

We propose an intelligent algorithm, depicted as Candidates Selection block in Fig.2, containing three independent criteria. Those are as follow:

- Sinusoidal Likeness Measure (SLM) - the criterion assumes the tonal peaks in analysis spectrum provide the result of multiplication of the tonal components by the window function. Thus the maxima of cross-correlation function of the main-lobe's spectrum of the candidate and the analysis window would indicate the presence of a sinusoidal components [21]:

$$\Gamma(\omega) = \Big| \sum_{\substack{k \\ |\omega - \omega_k| < B}} X(\omega_k) W(\omega - \omega_k) \Big| \qquad (11)$$

where X and W are spectra of analyzed signal and window respectively, B is the low-pass bandwidth within the cross-correlation evaluated.

The main drawback of this preliminary criterion is that it may acknowledge a side-lobe component as a tonal part.

- Phase Measure - this criterion assumes that the phase of the tonal component's main-lobe varies significantly less than those resulted from noise. This criterion validates the result of the SLM criterion selection.

- Relative Amplitude Threshold [21] - this criterion can discard some side-lobes as well as components of a minor significance:

$$h(k_p) = |X(k_p)| - 0,5 \cdot |X(k_{v+})| + |X(k_{v-})| \qquad (12)$$

where X represents the DFT array, k - the frequency bin index, subscript p represents the peak, and subscripts v^+, v^- represent the adjacent local minima.

The next step is to estimate their true (instantaneous) frequency values as they are relevant due to the time-frequency resolution trade-off in the STFT representation. As mentioned earlier, the zero padding was applied to gain frequency resolution but still this resolution is constant over the signal bandwidth. Moreover, for signals that are non-stationary within the analysis frame, inter-frame modulations, which effect in peaks smearing may occur [24].

To overcome above mentioned drawbacks, the spectral reassignment method, depicted as Instantaneous Frequency Estimation block (Fig. 3), is employed. This method [22] assigns the tonal component's value to the STFT frequency bin's center of gravity:

$$\hat{\omega}(x;t,\omega) = \omega + \Im\left\{\frac{STFT_{dw}(x;t,\omega)}{STFT_w(x;t,\omega)}\right\} \tag{13}$$

where $STFT_w$ is STFT using analysis window w, $STFT_{dw}$ is STFT employing the first derivative of a window function.

After the tonal components detection the tracking stage (presented in Fig.4), in which the peaks are linked to create trajectories is launched. Since the pitch

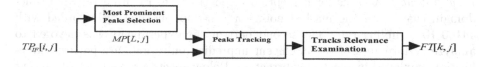

Fig. 4. Structure of the Tonal Components Tracking Block

variation curve $p_w(n)$ is evaluated from the trajectories it is proposed to take into account only the relevant tracks, that can depict the wow defect well. Therefore it is reasonable to form only these trajectories which are based on the most prominent tonal peaks from the magnitude spectrum. The idea for joining tonal components together applies the following frequency criterion [12]:

The $K - th$ tonal component $TP_{IF}[K,j]$ is joined together with the $P - th$ track $FT[P,j]$ when:

$$|TP_{IF}[K,j] - FT[P,j-1]| = min(|TP_{IF}[:,j] - FT[P,j-1]|) \tag{14}$$

$$\text{and} \quad |TP_{IF}[K,j] - FT[P,j-1]| < f_{Dev} \tag{15}$$

where $min(\cdot)$ denotes minimal value and f_{Dev} is the maximum frequency deviation.

The most prominent tonal components, stored in MP matrix, correspond to the peaks of the greatest magnitude hence are considered to be the most perceivable ones. A new track is "born" only from the components stored in MP matrix that were not fitted to any existing tracks. A track is "dead" when there is no continuation according to the frequency criterion.

The last stage of the presented algorithm, according to the diagram in Fig.2, is the PVC generation stage in which the pitch variation function $p_w(n)$ is computed. First, the relative frequencies are calculated for all of the tracks stored in the FT matrix. Next, RFT (Relative Frequency Tracks) matrix is obtained by dividing each track frequency values by the preceding point values. Secondly, median is calculated in RTF columns (i.e. discrete time moments) [16]. Finally, $p_w(n)$ is obtained as a cumulative product of the mean values computed for each discrete time moment.

Since the optimal values of Sinusoidal Likeness Measure (SLM), Phase measure, and Relative Amplitude Threshold are unknown, we applied standard fuzzy logic reasoning to determining the tonal components $TP_{ACK}[i,j]$ true (instantaneous) frequency values. Due to space limitation, more details on that are discussed during the paper presentation at the RSFDGrC 2005 in Regina, Canada.

4   Experiments and Results

4.1   Experiments Concerning Noise Reduction

It is important to notice, that for the comparison purposes in the informal subjective tests the same spectral subtraction algorithm was used to calculate the *rough estimate* $\hat{X}^{ref}$ as for perceptual reconstruction. Figure 5 presents time-domain changes of the masked noise for a saxophone melody recorded with 44100 Hz sampling rate. The second part of the experiments was devoted to analyze performance of the intelligent unpredictability measure pattern classification employed in spectral subtraction. Below spectrograms (Fig. 6) present signal recovered with standard linear spectral subtraction method, and with spectral subtraction improved by UM vector classification system (as described in Sect. 2.2).

4.2   Experiments Concerning Wow Compensation

The proposed wow compensating algorithm was tested on several archival sound samples recorded in the Polish National Film Library and the Documentary and

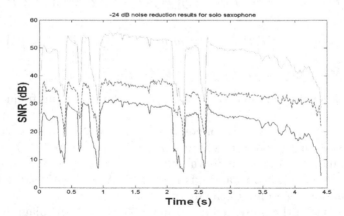

Fig. 5. Time varying SNR for 24 dB noise attenuation, calculated for each processing frame, for input signal (solid line), for perceptually reconstructed signal (dashed line) and for signal restored with spectral subtraction (dotted line), which was used as the *rough estimate* of the restored signal

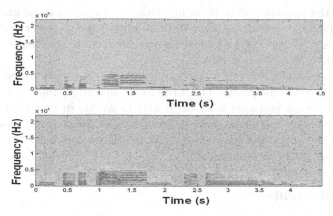

Fig. 6. Spectrograms of signal restored with spectral subtraction (upper plot), and with spectral subtraction enhanced by intelligent pattern recognition system (lower plot)

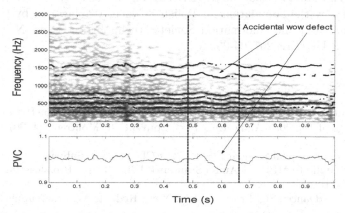

Fig. 7. Tracks detected by the algorithm plotted on the spectrogram with the simultaneously plotted pitch variation curve

Feature Film Studio. Presented example epitomize obtained results. Figure 7 depicts the spectrogram of the sample simultaneously with the detected tracks and the evaluated pitch variation curve (PVC). As can be noticed from the spectrogram only the most relevant tracks are taken into account for the PVC extraction.

Example presented in Fig.7 clearly demonstrates computed PVC and wow defect convergence. It is also worth to mention that the obtained PVC characteristics were successfully utilized in restoration process.

5 Conclusions

The Unpredictability Measure (UM) intelligent pattern recognition system involving UM for spectrum components classification has been presented as an extension of the spectral subtraction algorithms. Applying some properties of the human auditory system to noise reduction allows one to preserve much more of the input signal's energy and consequently enables decreasing unfavourable influence of the reconstruction filter.

As experiments resulted in satisfactory wow defect evaluation, the presented approach appears to be valid. The presented algorithm manages to detect changes of the pitch variation function $p_w(t)$. However, in case of strong variations of $p_w(t)$ (e.g. accidental wow defect), it still needs to be more robust, especially at the pitch variation tracking stage. Therefore, a further development of this algorithm is underway.

Acknowledgments

Research funded by the Commission of the European Communities, Directorate-General of the Information Society within the Integrated Project No. FP6-507336 entitled: "PRESTOSPACE - Preservation towards storage and access. Standardised Practices for Audio-visual Contents Archiving in Europe". The research was also subsidized by the Foundation for Polish Science, Warsaw and by the Ministry of Science and and Information Society Technologies - Dec. No. 155/E-359/SPB/6.PR UE/DIE 207/04-05.

References

1. Brandenburg, K.: Second Generation Perceptual Audio Coding: The Hybrid Coder. Proceedings of the 90th Audio Eng. Soc. Convention, Montreux (1990) Preprint No. 2937
2. MPEG-4, International Standard ISO/IEC FCD 14496-3, Subpart 4 (1998)
3. Shlien, S.: Guide to MPEG-1 Audio Standard. IEEE Trans. Broadcasting, Vol.40, (1994) 206-218
4. Vaseghi, S.: Advanced Sig. Proc. and Dig. Noise Reduct., Wiley&Teubner, N.York (1997)
5. Zwicker, E., Zwicker, T.: Audio Engineering and Psychoacoustics: Matching Signals to the Final Receiver,the Human Auditory System. J. of Audio Eng. Soc, Vol. 39, No. 3, (1991) 115-126
6. Beerends, J., Stemerdink, J.: A Perceptual Audio Quality Measure Based on a Psychoacoustic Sound Representation. J. of Audio Eng. Soc., Vol. 40, No. 12, (1992) 963-978
7. Czyzewski, A., Krolikowski, R.: Noise Reduction in Audio Signals Based on the Perceptual Coding Approach. Proceedings of the IEEE Workshop on Applications of Signal Processing to Audio and Acoustics, October, New Paltz, New York (1999) 147-150
8. Tsoukalas, D., et al.: Perceptual Filters for Audio Sig. Enh, J. of Audio. Eng. Soc., Vol.45, No.1/2, (1997) 22-36
9. Humes, L.: Models of the Additivity of Masking. J. Ac. Soc. Of Am., Vol. 85,(1989) 1285-1294
10. Krolikowski, R., Czyzewski A.: Noise Reduction in Acoustic Signals Using the Perceptual Coding. 137th Meeting, Acoust. Soc. Of Am., Berlin, Germany, (1998) CD-Preprint

11. Czyzewski, A., Dziubinski, M.: Noise Reduction in Audio Employing Spectral Unpredictability Measure and Neural Net. Knowledge-Based Intelligent Information and Engineering Systems: 8th International Conference, KES'04, LNAI [Lecture Notes in Artificial Intelligence] 3213, Springer - Verlag, Berlin, Heidelberg, Wellington, New Zealand, September (2004), Part I: 743-750

12. McAulay, J., Quatieri, T.F.: Speech analysis/synthesis based on a sinusoidal representation. IEEE Trans. on Acoustics, Speech, and Signal Processing, Vol. 34, No. 4, August, (1986) 744-754

13. Godsill, J. S., Rayner, J. W.: The restoration of pitch variation defects in gramophone recordings. Proceedings of the IEEE Workshop on Applications of Signal Processing to Audio and Acoustics, October, New Paltz, New York (1993)

14. Godsill, J. S.: Recursive restoration of pitch variation defects in musical recordings, Proc. International Conference on Acoustics, Speech, and Signal Processing, Vol. 2, April, Adelaide, (1994) 233-236

15. Walmsley, P. J., Godsill, S. J., Rayner, P. J. W.: Polyphonic pitch tracking using joint Bayesian estimation of multiple frame parameters. Proc. 1999 IEEE Workshop on Applications of Signal Processing to Audio and Acoustics,October, New Paltz, New York (1999)

16. Czyzewski, A., et. al.: Wow detection and compensation employing spectral processing of audio. 117 Audio Engineering Society Convention, Convention Paper 6212, October, San Francisco (2004)

17. Nichols, J.: An interactive pitch defect correction system for archival audio. AES 20th International Conference, October, Budapest (2001)

18. Serra, X.: Musical Sound Modeling with Sinusoids plus Noise. In: Pope, S., Picalli, A., De Poli, G., Roads, C. (eds.): Musical Signal Processing, Swets & Zeitlinger Publishers, (1997)

19. Rodet, X.: Musical Sound Signal Analysis/Synthesis: Sinusoidal + Residual and Elementary Waveform Models. Proc. IEEE Symp. Time-Frequency and Time-Scale Analysis, (1997)

20. Lagrange, M., Marchand, S., Rault, J.B.: Sinusoidal parameter extraction and component selection in a non-stationary model. Proc. of the 5th Int. Conference on Digital Audio Effects, September, Hamburg (2002)

21. Masri, P.: Computer Modeling of Sound for Transformation and Synthesis of Musical Signals, PhD thesis, University of Bristol, (1996)

22. Auger, F., Flandrin, P.: Improving the readability of time-frequency and time-scale representations by the reassignment method. IEEE Trans. on Signal Processing, Vol.43, No. 5, May (1995) 1068-1089

23. Czyzewski, A., et. al.: New Algorithms for Wow and Flutter Detection and Compensation in Audio. Paper to be presented (material submitted to pre-printing) for the 118th Audio Engineering Society Conv., May, Barcelona (2005)

24. Ifeachor, E., Jervis, B.: Digital Signal Processing. A Practical Approach, Addison-Wesley Publishing Company, (1993)

25. Kalman, R.: A New Approach to Linear Filtering and Prediction Problems. Trans. of the ASME, J. of Basing Engineering, Vol. 82, March (1960) 34-35

26. Moghaddamjoo, A., Kirlin, L.: Robust Kalman Filtering with Unknown Inputs. IEEE Trans. on Acoustics, Speech, and Signal Processing, Vol. 37, No. 8, August (1989) 1166-1175

27. Vaseghi, S., Frayling-Cork, R.: Restoration of Old Gramophone Recordings. J. of Audio Eng. Soc., Vol. 40, No. 10, October (1997) 791-800.

28. Widrow, B., Stearns, S.: Adaptive Signal Processing, Prentice-Hall Intl. Inc., New Jersey (1985)

Multiresolution Pitch Analysis of Talking, Singing, and the Continuum Between

David Gerhard

Department of Computer Science, University of Regina,
Regina, Saskatchewan, S4S 0A2 Canada
gerhard@cs.uregina.ca

Abstract. Talking and singing seem disparate, but there are a range of human utterances that fall between them, such as poetry, chanting, and rap music. This paper presents research into differentiation between talking and singing, development of feature-based analysis tools to explore the continuum between talking and singing, and evaluating human perception of this continuum as compared to these analysis tools. Preliminary background is presented to acquaint the reader with some of the science used in the algorithm development. A corpus of sounds was collected to study the differences between singing and talking, and the procedures and results of this collection are presented. A set of features is developed to differentiate between talking and singing, and to investigate the intermediate vocalizations between talking and singing. The results of these features are examined and evaluated. The perception of speech is heavily influenced by the pitch, which in the english language carries no lexicographic information but can carry higher-level semiotic information and can contribute to disambiguation.

1 Introduction

The difference between talking and singing can be compared to the difference between walking and dancing: a certain "style" or "presence" has been added to the one which makes it qualitatively different from the other. Part of the motivation of this research is to try to understand and quantify some of these differences. A difficulty is that these differences seem to be ill-defined and subjective. As will be seen in Section 3, people disagree on what is singing when compared to talking, and on what features and characteristics can be used to define the differences. Part of the problem is likely to be linguistic: when describing subjective phenomena, words may mean different things to different people. When describing an utterance, people appear to agree on general concepts, but when they are asked to define the concepts and why they made these decisions, people's understandings start to differ.

Musical instruments often produce constant pitches held for a duration. Instruments such as the piano cannot change the pitch of a single note. Human singing is, on the other hand, not dependent on steady pitches and in fact it is very difficult and often undesirable for human song to have a perfectly constant

D. Ślęzak et al. (Eds.): RSFDGrC 2005, LNAI 3642, pp. 294–303, 2005.

pitch. Rather, a more perceptually pleasant human song style has a pitch track that uses vibrato, a pseudo-sinusoidal pitch track oscillation.

Modern computing methods such as soft computing [1] and chaos theory [2] have been used to study sound, and human categorical perception [3] is an appropriate venue to consider fuzzy classification. As will be seen in Section 2, there are many ways to consider a classification space in which a continuum between disparate classes is apparent.

This paper concentrates on pitch-based differences. The pitch feature is used to extract timing and rhythmic information as well as stylistic additions like vibrato. This is not to advance the opinion that pitch is the only relevant feature. Indeed, pitch is only the means to an end in several of the features discussed in this paper. Rather, pitch is such a fundamental difference between speaking and singing that the question arose whether it could on its own fully differentiate between speech and song. A set of features based on a single quantity means that the base feature extraction engine can be optimized. What is shown is not that pitch is necessary, but that it is sufficient.

2 Human Utterance Continua

Many human utterances are not strictly classifiable as talking or singing. Utterances like poetry, chant and rap music fall somewhere between speaking and singing, with characteristics of each [4, 5]. Another intermediate utterance is *sprechstimme* or *sprechgesang* (speech-song), developed by the composer Arnold Schoenberg and used later by his student Alban Berg. It is a vocal musical style characterized by widely varying pitches, with the singer approximating the pitch instead of singing the exact note.

When considering a classification domain with intermediate utterances between two classes, there are several ways to proceed, three of which are hard classification, continuum classification, and sub-category hard classification.

Hard classification. The traditional classification paradigm, where each new data point must be assigned to exactly one class. In the case of speech versus song, a single two-class discrimination will not accurately describe utterances that fall between speech and song. A two-class paradigm might be a beneficial starting point for classifying intermediate utterances, since the two-class features can be extended by assigning a confidence metric to each feature measurement.

Continuum classification. Also called fuzzy classification, soft classification or confidence classification, this method assumes that each incoming data point can have membership in all available classes to some degree. The terminology of these various techniques differs but the result is primarily the same. In confidence classification, each data point is assigned to one class, with an associated confidence metric indicating the "good-ness" of the classification. If all relevant features agree with a classification, the confidence would be high, while disagreement in feature results would result in a lower confidence.

Sub-category hard classification. Create a set of classes between speech and song and require that each new clip be assigned to one of these classes. This removes the extra computation that is required with continuum classification while acknowledging the range of possible utterances between speech and song.

This work compares hard classification and continuum classification for differentiation between speech and song. Sound files considered to be speaking or singing (without membership in the other category) are used to develop features which are then evaluated on similar files to determine if they can make a hard classification. These same features are then used on sound clips with partial membership in both categories, such as poetry or chanting, and the results are compared to human assessment of class membership.

3   Audio Data Corpus

For audio research in a specific domain, the most desirable option is often to find a corpus of data that has been collected previously and is in use by other researchers, as this provides a place to start and a set of colleagues with whom to compare results. If the domain is new, obscure or specific, such a corpus may not exist. Intermediate utterances between speech and song is such a data domain. There exist many corpora of speaking only[1], and some corpora including sung clips, but searching the current literature did not uncover any corpora containing intermediate clips between speaking and singing, or clips of the same phrase spoken and sung by one individual. Both of these would be valuable to speech/song research.

This corpus is primarily monolingual, with a small collection of other languages. A larger multilingual corpus may be collected in the future, to expand the current research and results to other languages. The corpus contains 90.3% (756 files) English language utterances with the remainder of the clips (82 files) in languages including French, Italian, Swedish, Gaelic, Japanese, Mandarin Chinese, Rumanian, Hungarian, German, Latin, Iroquois[2], Mon-kmer[3] and Zunian[4]. Some clips have no language, such as whistling or humming. Clips were extracted from existing media as well as solicited from 50 subjects using a set of prompts designed to produce speech, song, and intermediated utterances

3.1   Features Identified by Listeners

Many listeners describe features that they consider relevant for speech or singing, usually in the context of singing as it compares to speech. The most common features are pitch (also described as tone and melody) and rhythm (also described

---

[1] The Linguistics Data Consortium (http://www.ldc.upenn.edu) is a thorough repository of such corpora, and does not, as of this writing, contain data sets of this type.
[2] The Iroquois are a collection of aboriginal american tribes from the north-easter United States, Quebec and Ontario.
[3] Mon-kmer is the language of the Kmhmu people, an aboriginal tribe from Laos.
[4] The Zuni are an american aboriginal tribe originating in New Mexico and Arizona.

as beat, speed, and patterns of rhythm). Some listeners also consider rhyme and repetition as features of song. Other listeners chose to describe speech as it compares to singing, but the same basic features were used, and the listeners described speech as the absence of the features necessary for singing, like pitch, rhythm, and vibrato. These features are described in more detail in Section 4.

Some listeners describe the differences between speech and song using more elusive terms which do not relate to a definable feature. These include "emotion", "flow" and "feeling". Some example comments are:

232 "There's something in the amount of 'feeling' behind what is being said that pushes it toward speech. Good luck quantifying that!"

236 "The process of identifying speech and singing is subjective to the listener as well as to the person who's voice is being heard."

347 "Near the end I became aware of a dimension of clarity and sharpness of pitch that characterizes singing."

4   Pitch and Fundamental Frequency

As discussed in the previous section, many perceptual differences between talking and singing rely on the perception of the pitch of the utterance. Indeed, perceptual differences such as rhythm and repetition can also be inferred from the pitch track of the utterance. The pitch is the perceptual analogue of the fundamental frequency (f_0) of the signal, the lowest frequency at which the signal repeats. Most higher harmonics of a periodic signal are related in frequency to the f_0 by whole-number ratios, and have less energy than the f_0.

Only periodic or pseudo-periodic waveforms can have a valid f_0. Perceptually, periodic and pseudo-periodic signals have a pitch. These are not, however, the only signals that can produce the perception of pitch. Filtered noise in specific contexts can seem pitch-like. For the remainder of the discussion, however, we will restrict our subject to periodic and pseudo-periodic signals

It should be noted here that while aperiodic signals can give the perception of pitch, as in the case of filtered noise, the human voice can produce musical notes with lyrics only when a glottal pulse is active—only when a voiced phoneme is being produced. One cannot sing whispered notes, unless lyrics are abandoned. The pitch of a sung note is determined by the frequency of the glottal pulse driving the vocalization. When whispering, a chaotic airflow is passed through the vocal tract instead of a glottal pulse, and this airflow has no inherent pitch. Only by manipulating the resonant frequencies of the vocal tract can a person impart a perception of pitch on the chaotic airflow, and that vocal tract then cannot be used to generate the resonant frequencies necessary for phoneme production.

Periodic signals exactly repeat to infinity ($w(t + \tau) = w(t)$) with a period of τ and $f_0 = \tau^{-1}$ for the largest value of τ. Pseudo-periodic signals *almost* repeat ($w(t + \tau) = w(t) + \epsilon$). There is a slight variation in the waveform from period to period, but it can still be said to have $f_0 = \tau^{-1}$, corresponding to the longest period τ at which the waveform repeats within some tolerance ϵ.

Table 1. Feature labels

Label	Feature
V_{AC}	Vibrato, using autocorrelation
V_{FT}	Vibrato, using fast Fourier transform
$M(f_0)$	Maximum f_0
$m(f_0)$	Minimum f_0
$\mu(f_0)$	Mean f_0
$\sigma(f_0)$	Standard deviation of f_0
$M(f_0')$	Maximum f_0'
$\mu(f_0')$	Mean f_0'
$\sigma(f_0')$	Standard deviation of f_0'
R_s	Segment f_0 track repetition
$\mu_s(f_0)$	Segment-based mean f_0
$\sigma_s(f_0)$	Segment-based standard deviation of f_0
PV_{f_0}	f_0-based proportion of voiced frames
PU_{f_0}	f_0-based proportion of unvoiced frames

Extracting f_0 from a signal will only make sense if the waveform is periodic. f_0 detectors often serve a dual purpose in this case—if the detected f_0 makes sense for the rest of the signal, then the signal is considered to be periodic. If the f_0 appears to vary randomly or if the detector provides an impossible or invalid result, the signal is considered to be aperiodic. Often, programmers will build into their algorithms some measure of periodicity detection, and the system will produce an impossible value, such as "0", when the algorithm determines that the waveform is aperiodic. For this work, the YIN f_0 estimator [6] was used, which also provides a confidence measure.

Pitch as a feature in sound classification systems has considerable precident. In the multimedia database system, described in [7], f_0 is an important feature for distinguishing between pieces of music. Speech word boundaries are detected using f_0 in [8], with the reasonable assumption that large variations in f_0 are unlikely to happen in the middle of a word.

The features used in this work which are based on the pitch of the signal and are presented in Table 1. The pitch of the signal is used to infer characteristics of rhythm, pitch continuity, and syllable duration. These features consider the pitch of the signal at multiple resolutions: Simple pitch statistics such as $\mu(f_0)$ consider the pitch at frame-sized time instances. The Segment-based features such as R_s examine the pitch track over a syllabic segment, like a note or phoneme, broken by non-pitched frames. The vibrato features, and the proportion of voiced and unvoiced frames, consider the entire length of the signal.

5 Training

The features were trained on clips with membership in only one class (talking or singing). Gaussian mixture models (GMMs) were generated as probability density function estimators for the feature values for each class (talking, singing) and the GMMs were compared.

5.1   Gaussian Mixture Models

For a random variable, the probability density function is a measure of the likelihood that a measurement of that variable will fall within a specified range. Equation 1 shows the calculation of a probability from a PDF $f(x)$:

$$P(a < X < b) = \int_a^b f(x)dx. \tag{1}$$

The estimation of a PDF is the opposite problem: given a set of measurements $x_1, x_2, \ldots$ of a random variable X, estimate the probability density at every point in the range of possible values of X. The resulting function is called a *probability density estimation* (PDE) and is notated by " ˆ ". Gaussian mixture models are a specific example of the kernel method [9] of generating a PDE.

The set of measurements (represented by a series of delta functions) is convolved with a gaussian kernel, $w(x)$, of appropriate size, as in Equation 2. The effect is that a gaussian range of probability is added to the PDE for each measurement. These gaussians "pile up" where they are close together, indicating high probability density, and where the measurements are far apart, the gaussians are separate, indicating low probability. The gaussians can be approximated by any easily-generated bell-shaped curve, and for the talking and singing PDEs in this work, a hann window[5] [10] was used.

$$\hat{P_X} = \frac{(\delta \times \{x1, x2, \ldots\}) \otimes w[n]}{\sum_{-\infty}^{\infty}((\delta \times \{x1, x2, \ldots\}) \otimes w[n])} \tag{2}$$

The denominator term is added to satisfy the requirement that $\int(\hat{P_X})dx = 1$. A number of improvements to the kernel method are presented in [9], but it was judged that the improvements in theoretical accuracy are small compared to the required increase in computational complexity.

5.2   Class-Specific Feature Model Generation

Once the PDEs have been calculated, one each for the talking and singing classes, the next step is to compare them. First, Kolmogorov-Smirnov (K-S) [11] statistics are calculated to determine if there is a significant difference between the two mixture models. If there is no significant difference, the feature is considered not useful for a classification scheme. For those features with a significant K-S distance, the PDEs are compared by taking the log difference between them, as shown in Equation 3:

$$\hat{P}_{s-t} = \log(\hat{P}_s) - \log(\hat{P}_t) = \log\frac{\hat{P}_s}{\hat{P}_t}. \tag{3}$$

---

[5] The hann window is similar to the more commonly used hamming window. These windows are calculated as $w[n] = a - b\cos(2\pi n/M)$, $0 \le n \le M$ with $a = 0.5, b = 0.5$ for the hann window and $a = 0.54, b = 0.46$ for the hamming window.

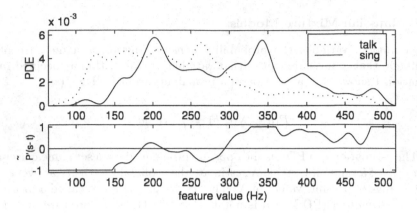

Fig. 1. Feature model of maximum f_0, $[M(f_0)]$

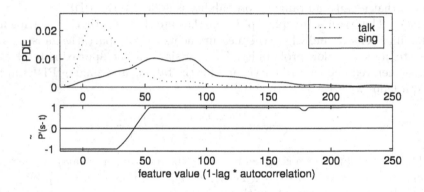

Fig. 2. Feature model of autocorrelation-based vibrato measure, $[V_{AC}]$

Here, $\hat{P}_t$ is the PDE for the talking files, $\hat{P}_s$ is the PDE for the singing files, and $\hat{P}_{s-t}$ is the comparative PDE used to judge fuzzy class membership.

In some situations, one or the other of the PDEs may be equal to zero, in which case $\hat{P}_{s-t}$ would approach $\pm\infty$. To avoid this, the comparative PDE is hard-limited to ± 1, with the following justification: Since $\int(\hat{P}_X)dx = 1$, $\hat{P}_X \leq 1$, and $\log(a \leq 1) \leq 0$. Further, in comparing the two PDEs we are interested in their relative values only where one PDE does not clearly dominate over the other. If $|\hat{P}_{s-t}| > 1$, one PDE clearly dominates and the limit of ± 1 is justified. The improved formula $\hat{P}'_{s-t}$ is presented in Equation 4:

$$\hat{P}'_{s-t} = \begin{cases} 1, & \log(\hat{P}_s) - \log(\hat{P}_t) \geq 1, \\ -1, & \log(\hat{P}_s) - \log(\hat{P}_t) \leq -1, \\ \log(\hat{P}_s) - \log(\hat{P}_t), & \text{otherwise}. \end{cases} \tag{4}$$

Thus when $|\hat{P}_{s-t}| < 1$, soft or fuzzy membership is appropriate. Figures 1 and 2 show examples of these feature models.

6   Results: Feature Accuracy

The comparative PDE $\hat{P}'_{s-t}$ is used to evaluate each feature model against individual sound files with *a-priori* known ratings. For each evaluation file being tested, each feature extractor is applied to obtain a set of feature values. Each feature x generates a speech/song rating $\hat{P}'_{s-t}(x)$. This rating is evaluated in two ways: absolute and relative correctness.

The *absolute correctness* is calculated thus: If the *a-priori* class of the file is talking, and $\hat{P}'_{s-t}(x) < 0$, the feature model behaved correctly for that file, and is given a value of 1. If not, the feature model is given a value of 0.

The *relative correctness* of $\hat{P}'_{s-t}(x)$ is calculated by comparing the value of $\hat{P}'_{s-t}(x)$ to the *a-priori* rating for the file. An *a-priori* rating of 5 (pure singing) compared to $\hat{P}'_{s-t}(x) = 4.5$ for a given feature, gives a correctness of 0.9, since the difference between the target rating and the PDE is 10%.

The corpus was divided into sections, with the files from each section used to develop separate versions of the system. This testing was done in two sessions, first with four sections and then with ten sections. With four sections, four separate systems were developed (using 75% of the corpus) and tested (on the remaining 25%) for absolute and relative correctness.

The mean results from these four systems are presented in Table 2a, sorted by absolute correctness. In the same way, ten separate systems were developed and tested, and the mean results are presented in Table 2b.

Table 2. Feature correctness results for separated development and test data

(a) four sets:

Feature	Relative	Absolute
V_{AC}	0.7937	0.8071
R_s	0.7800	0.7886
V_{FT}	0.6415	0.7064
$\mu(f_0)$	0.6549	0.6779
PU_{f_0}	0.6234	0.6560
$\mu_s(f_0)$	0.5798	0.6376
PV_{f_0}	0.5556	0.6191
$M(f_0)$	0.5785	0.5839
$m(f_0)$	0.5665	0.5755
$\mu(f_0')$	0.5423	0.5755
$\sigma(f_0)$	0.5542	0.5722
$M(f_0')$	0.5194	0.5571
$\sigma_s(f_0)$	0.5207	0.5537
$\sigma(f_0')$	0.4860	0.4513

(b) ten sets:

Feature	Relative	Absolute
V_{AC}	0.7921	0.8034
R_s	0.7823	0.7966
V_{FT}	0.6421	0.7153
$\mu(f_0)$	0.6616	0.6881
PU_{f_0}	0.6309	0.6627
$\mu_s(f_0)$	0.5786	0.6339
PV_{f_0}	0.5564	0.6186
$M(f_0)$	0.5850	0.6170
$m(f_0)$	0.5754	0.6000
$\mu(f_0')$	0.5504	0.5814
$\sigma(f_0)$	0.5491	0.5678
$M(f_0')$	0.5178	0.5492
$\sigma_s(f_0)$	0.5182	0.5458
$\sigma(f_0')$	0.4955	0.5017

7 Feature Models Applied to Intermediate Vocalizations

As a final evaluation of the developed feature models, intermediate vocalizations from the speech-song corpus are tested. These clips were rated between speaking and singing by listeners in the user study.

The intermediate vocalizations are considered to have fuzzy membership between speaking and singing, with a target membership provided by user ratings. The goal therefore is to approach these target ratings with the features extracted from the sound. Fuzzy membership in one class is considered to be equivalent to the complementary membership in the other class. This is not a limitation of the system but a consideration for simplicity - the class membership could be separated, although a new set of data from human listeners would have to be collected, with a pair of prompts (how song-like, how speech-like) instead of a single continuum rating.

For each intermediate utterance clip, a feature value is calculated according to the feature extractor algorithm. The feature value is then applied to the feature model to generate a computed measure (M_c) between -1 and 1. This rating is compared to the human measure (M_h), being the mean listener rating for that clip, a value between 1 and 5. (The mean rating result is scaled to match the feature result range), and the euclidean distance is calculated between these ratings. If the computed measure and the human measure match, the distance will be zero. If they are opposite, e.g. if $M_c = -1$ indicating talking and $M_h = 5$ indicating singing, the (maximal) distance will be 2.

The human measure is compared to the computed measure for each intermediate file applied to each feature, and the mean distances for all intermediate files are presented in Table 3.These distances show that while no individual feature model duplicates the human perception of intermediate vocalizations between speech and song, some features do provide encouraging results. All features perform better than chance.

Table 3. Feature model results compared to human ratings of intermediate files

Feature	Mean Distance
V_{FT}	0.4122
$\mu_s(f_0)$	0.5189
V_{AC}	0.5241
R_s	0.5498
PU_{f_0}	0.5762
PV_{f_0}	0.5804
$\sigma(f_0')$	0.5956
$\sigma_s(f_0)$	0.6007
$\mu(f_0')$	0.6212
$m(f_0)$	0.6643
$M(f_0')$	0.7162
$M(f_0)$	0.7958
$\sigma(f_0)$	0.8068
$\mu(f_0)$	0.8148

8 Conclusions

The analysis of human utterances using pitch-based metrics can provide sufficient information for placing an utterance along a continuum between speaking
and singing, such that a sound thus classified has membership in both categories
to a degree. This is the basis of fuzzy classification, and removes the requirement of forcing an "in-between" sound into one of two hard categories. Partial
membership in both categories also allows for the possible refinement of the
continuum into a set of sub-categories around which similar sounds may be clustered, such as poetry, rap and chant. The pitch-based features which have been
discussed are evaluated in isolation and found to produce reasonable levels of
correctness. Used in a multi-dimensional system, it is expected that an accurate
human utterance classification will be possible.

References

[1] Kostek, B.: Soft Computing in Acoustics, Applications of Neural Networks, Fuzzy
    Logic and Rough Sets to Musical Acoustics, Studies in Fuzziness and Soft Com-
    puting. Physica Verlag Heidelberg, New York (1999)
[2] Schroeder, M.R.: Fractals, Chaos, Power Laws: Minutes from an Infinite Paradise.
    W.H.Freeman, New York (1991)
[3] Levitin, D.J.: Absolute pitch: Self-reference and human memory. International
    Journal of Computing and Anticipatory Systems 4 (1999) 255–266
[4] List, G.: The boundaries of speech and song. In McAllester, D., ed.: Readings in
    Ethnomusicology. Johnson Reprint Co. (1971) 253–268
[5] Mang, E.H.S.: Speech, Song and Intermediate Vocalizations: A Longitudinal
    Study of Preschool Children's Vocal Development. PhD thesis, University of
    British Columbia (1999)
[6] de Cheveigné, A., Kawahara, H.: Yin, a fundamental frequency estimator for
    speech and music. Journal of the Acoustical Society of America 111 (2002)
[7] Wold, E., Blum, T., Keislar, D., Wheaton, J.: Content-based classification, search
    and retrieval of audio. IEEE MultiMedia (1996) 27–37
[8] Rao, G.R., Srichand, J.: Word boundary detection using pitch variations. In:
    Fourth International inproceedings on Spoken Language Processing. Volume 2.
    (1996) 813–816
[9] Silverman, B.W.: Density estimation for statistics and data analysis. Monographs
    on Statistics and Applied Probability (1986)
[10] Oppenheim, A.V., Schafer, R.W.: Discrete-Time Signal Processing. Prentice Hall,
     Nwe Jersey (1999)
[11] Press, W.H., Teukolsky, S.A., Vetterling, W.T., Flannery, B.P.: Numerical Recip-
     ies in C. Cambridge University Press (1992)

Toward More Reliable Emotion Recognition of Vocal Sentences by Emphasizing Information of Korean Ending Boundary Tones

Tae-Seung Lee, Mikyoung Park, and Tae-Soo Kim

CAD/CAM Research Center, Korea Institute of Science and Technology,
39-1, Hawolgok-dong, Seongbuk-gu, Seoul, 136-791, Republic of Korea
thestaff@hitel.net, {miky, ktaesoo}@kist.re.kr

Abstract. Autonomic machines interacting with human should have capability to perceive the states of emotion and attitude through implicit messages for obtaining voluntary cooperation from their clients. Voice is the easiest and the most natural way to exchange human messages. The automatic systems capable of understanding the states of emotion and attitude have utilized features based on pitch and energy of uttered sentences. Performance of the existing emotion recognition systems can be further improved with the support of linguistic knowledge that specific tonal section in a sentence is related to the states of emotion and attitude. In this paper, we attempt to improve the recognition rate of emotion by adopting such linguistic knowledge for Korean ending boundary tones into an automatic system implemented using pitch-related features and multilayer perceptrons. From the results of an experiment over a Korean emotional speech database, a substantial improvement is confirmed.

1 Introduction

Humans interact in two kinds of channels: one transmits explicit messages about information of a certain purpose; the other implicit messages about the people themselves [1]. The explicit messages require conducting substantial behaviors, while the implicit messages solicit to understand the ones' motivational states. Most of studies conducted until now have focused on analyzing the explicit messages for grammatical rules. In social relationships, however, voluntary cooperation cannot be offered without understanding motivational states of the others. With the advent of the ubiquitous world, it is required that autonomic machines interacting with human have capability to perceive the implicit messages, i.e. the states of emotion and attitude.

Voice is the easiest and the most natural way to exchange the two kinds of messages. During last three decades, many studies have been attempted in automatic speech recognition systems to analyze the explicit messages spoken by human, finding out the linguistic structure [2]. As compared, it has been only a few years since the implicit messages were taken an interest in to process paralinguistic meaning of spoken language [3], [4]. Representative tools for processing paralinguistic information are pitch and energy of uttered speech sentences.

D. Ślęzak et al. (Eds.): RSFDGrC 2005, LNAI 3642, pp. 304–313, 2005.
© Springer-Verlag Berlin Heidelberg 2005

Approaches to measuring paralinguistic information can be classified into static and dynamic methods. Features for recognizing the states of emotion and attitude are statistics of pitch and energy in static method [5] and contours of pitch and energy in several differential orders in dynamic method [6] from the entire sentence. Recently a novel approach was attempted to involve linguistic information into emotion recognition and reported lower errors than those of static and dynamic methods [7].

The outcome of [7] suggests the necessity of adopting linguistic knowledge in processing paralinguistic information to enhance reliability of recognizing the states of emotion and attitude. O'Connor and Arnold [8] said that there were seven nuclear tones in English and each tone meant the emotional and attitudinal states of speakers such as earnest, calm, surprise, etc. Jun [9] and Lee [10] argued that meaning of ending boundary tones in Korean sentences was especially related with emotional and attitudinal states. From the results of those studies, more reliable recognition of emotional and attitudinal states would be obtainable if importance is put more on the nuclear tones in English and the ending boundary tones in Korean.

In this paper we attempt to improve the performance of the existing automatic emotion recognition system based on static method by putting more weight on the statistics from the ending boundary tones in Korean sentences. In our emotion recognition system each Korean sentence is divided into two parts: leading body and ending tail. Body has double length of tail and the tail includes the ending boundary tone. An optimal ratio of weights of body and tail is searched for to get the best emotion recognition rate on a Korean emotional speech database. The improvement in recognition rate is reported by applying the optimal ratio of weights to the existing emotion recognition system.

2   Effect of Korean Ending Boundary Tones on Expression and Perception of Emotion

Humans express their emotions in many ways such as speech, facial expression, tear, gesture, etc. Among them speech is the most natural and versatile tool to express emotions. Though the external expression and the internal state for an emotion do not always coincide, hearers try to guess through the utterance what the emotion is. Intonation is one of the most important means to verbalize emotional states. In this section, we attempt to understand the relationship between intonation and emotion in English and Korean languages through literatures.

The relationship between intonations and their corresponding intentions has been studied since an interest for intonational phonology was taken. O'Connor and Arnold [8] said that English sentences consisted of one or more tones and each tone had components of pre-head, head, and nuclear tone. There are seven nuclear tones in English: low falling, high falling, low rising, full rising, rising-falling, falling-rising, and middle-level. O'Connor and Arnold argued the nuclear tones were related to speaker's emotional and attitudinal states such as earnest, calm, surprise, etc. From their point of view, it can be inferred that the relation of intonation to emotion and attitude is very close.

In another view of intonational phonology by Pierrehumbert and Hirschberg [10], a sentence can have one or more intonational phrases (IPs). A boundary tone is marked and realized in the final syllable of IP. There are nine boundary tones and they are separated into two groups; one group includes the labels, L%, HL%, LHL%, HLHL%, LHLHL%; the other H%, LH%, HLH%, LHLH%, where L designates the low tone, H the high tone, and % the ending of sentence. It should be noted that the boundary tones are the same concept as the nuclear tones. Pierrehumbert and Hirschberg investigated that the boundary tones delivered information about pragmatic meaning like emotion, attitude, modality, etc., as well as the type of sentence such as declarative, imperative, interrogative, etc.

One of the characteristics of Korean language is the left branching, which means that the most important grammatical constituent is placed at the right position of the others. In this way, the boundary tones at the ending of a sentence have possibility to be combined with the meaning of the whole sentence. Therefore, in Korean language ending boundary tones are important to understand the relationship between intonations and their meanings.

Several Korean researchers have sought for the effect of the ending boundary tones on emotion and attitude of speakers. Jun [9] described meanings of some Korean ending boundary tones, especially in consideration of emotion or attitude, as follow:

1) LHL% - persuasive, insistent, confirmative, annoyed, irritative;
2) LH% - annoyed, unpleasant, unbelievable;
3) HLH% - confident so expecting listener's agreement;
4) LHLH% - annoyed, irritative, unbelievable;
5) HLHL% - confirmative, insistent, nagging, persuasive;
6) LHLHL% - more intensive emotion than being annoyed.

Lee [11] suggested application of the intonational phonology into Korean language to study the attitudinal functions of the ending boundary tones. He mentioned the functions of Korean ending boundary tones by relating them to emotion and attitude as

1) Low level - conclusive, cold;
2) High level - interested, surprised.

From the results of the studies having been conducted in intonational phonology, it is known that the boundary tones are very important to grasp the emotional states of a sentence uttered by a certain speaker. Especially in Korean language, the key effects raised by intonation are concentrated on the ending boundary tones of a sentence. Therefore, more reliable recognition of emotional states would be obtainable if importance is concentrated more on the boundary tones in English and the ending boundary tones in Korean. In the next section, adopting the intonational phonological knowledge about Korean ending boundary tones we will investigate the effect on improvement of emotion recognition capability by experiment.

3   Experiment

To adopt the linguistic knowledge reviewed in Section 2 into automatic emotion recognition system, we implemented a system based on the existing static featuring method and multilayer perceptrons (MLPs), and made the system have more importance on the statistics from the vocal section including the ending boundary tones than on those from the other section. This implemented system is evaluated on a Korean emotional speech database and an optimal weight imposed on the ending boundary tones is searched for to achieve the best recognition rate.

3.1   Implemented System

The emotion recognition system implemented in this paper uses pitch-related features and MLP as emotional parameters and pattern recognition method, respectively. The system goes through four procedures: isolating speech sentences, analyzing the sentences for pitch contour, calculating emotional features, and learning and classifying emotions.

It is essential to isolate a speech sentence from input sound signal because features to recognize emotions should be extracted from the sentence. To achieve this work, an endpoint detection algorithm based on the method of Rabiner and Sambur [12] is developed in our system. This algorithm uses signal energy and zero-crossing rate as speech-detection parameters, and has a characteristic of real-time processing. This algorithm goes through seven states as depicted in Fig. 1: algorithm launching (START), silence (SILENCE), starting of voiceless sound suspected (VL_START_SUS), starting of voiced sound suspected (V_START_SUS), starting of speech determined (S_START_DET), ending of speech suspected (S_END_SUS), and ending of speech determined (STOP).

Pitch contour is extracted from the sentence isolated in the previous procedure. The pitch extraction algorithm in our system is adopted and partly modified from the algorithm proposed by David and Niederjohn [13]. In the original pitch extraction algorithm, the standard short-time autocorrelation function is calculated for each successive 30 ms speech segment. Successive segments are overlapped by 66.7%. Based on the original algorithm, we modified the method

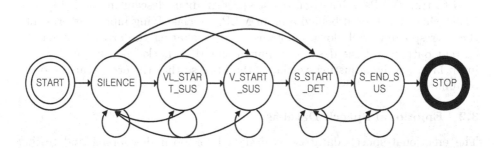

Fig. 1. State diagram for isolating a speech sentence from input sound signal

Table 1. Pitch-related features used in the implemented system

Feature No.	Description
1	Mean of pitches
2	Standard deviation of pitches
3	Maximum of pitches
4	Relative position of the maximum to the length of the entire sentence
5	Minimum of pitches
6	Relative position of the minimum to the length of the entire sentence
7	Maximum in rising gradients
8	Mean of rising gradients
9	Maximum in falling gradients
10	Mean of falling gradients
11	Mean of gradients
12	Area formed by pitch contour whose bottom line is the minimum

to determine voicing of the signal by using energy spectrums from low and high frequency bands. If the energy of high band is larger than that of low band, it can be inferred that the segment is not part of voiced sound and the segment is discarded to skip the extraction of pitch.

In many emotion recognition systems based on static method, speech energy as well as pitch is used for the ingredient of emotional features. However, our system uses only pitch-related features because speech energy is apt to be distorted by amplification of microphone and distance between source and destination of utterance. The twelve pitch-related features used in our system are selected from ones used in [5] and [7]. They are described in Table 1.

Using the twelve features as input patterns, MLPs learn full-blown emotions of speakers by the patterns and classify newly incoming patterns into the emotions. An MLP consists of one input layer, more than zero hidden layer(s) and one output layer [14]. The input layer receives the patterns, the hidden layer determines the learning capability for the network's behavior and the output layer presents the recognized scores of modeled emotions. Each layer consists of one or more computational nodes and all nodes in a layer are fully connected with the nodes of the facing layers. Error backpropagation (EBP) algorithm widely used to train MLPs is based on the steepest gradient descent method [14]. The EBP achieves a desired behavior of an MLP, i.e. classifying input patterns into the corresponding full-blown emotions, by propagating the error between the current output and the desired output of the MLP back from output layer to input layer and by adjusting weights of the MLP so that the error reaches to the minimum.

3.2   Emotional Speech Database

The emotional speech database is designed for both developing and testing speaker and sentence independent emotion recognition system. The emotions targeted by the database include joy, sadness, anger, and neutral. The sentences are thirty-one declarative and fourteen interrogative Korean sentences, and each is uttered three times by three males and three females who are all Korean amateur actors. Each uttered sentence is recorded in a calm office room by using a digital audio taperecorder with the sampling rate of 16 kHz and the quantization of 16 bits. There are silent durations of about 50 ms before and after each sentence. A subjective listening test conducted to another thirteen Korean audience using this emotion speech database presented the recognition rate of 78.2%.

3.3 Experiment Conditions

To confirm the effect of the ending boundary tones on emotion recognition, three conditions of experiment are set up. First, an ordinary evaluation is conducted to obtain the basis performance for the emotional speech database. Under this condition, the emotion label recognized is determined by

$$L = SelMax(M_i(F_{whole})), \qquad i \in \{joy, sadness, anger, neutral\} \qquad (1)$$

where F_{whole} stands for feature vector of the whole sentence, M_i for output vector for the emotions modeled, $SelMax$ for function to select the label L of the maximum output. Second, separation of sentences into leading bodies and ending tails, where each body has double length of tail, is performed to identify the higher importance of tails, which include ending boundary tones, to those of bodies. Under this condition, the emotion label recognized is determined by

$$\begin{cases} L_{body} = SelMax(M_i(F_{body})) \\ L_{tail} = SelMax(M_i(F_{tail})) \end{cases}, \qquad i \in \{joy, sadness, anger, neutral\} \qquad (2)$$

where L_{body} is the label selected for the feature vector F_{body} of body and L_{tail} for the feature vector F_{tail} of tail. Third, the optimal ratio of weights on recognition outcomes for bodies and tails is searched for to get the best recognition rate of emotions. Under this condition, the emotion label recognized is determined by

$$L = SelMax(a \cdot M_i(F_{body}) + b \cdot M_i(F_{tail})), \quad i \in \{joy, sadness, anger, neutral\} \qquad (3)$$

where a and b are the weights on the output vectors of MLPs for body and tail, respectively.

Evaluation results are taken for each speaker with all the forty-five sentences in the emotional speech database. Two of three utterances for each sentence and emotion are used for training MLPs and the other for testing. Therefore, there are 360 (45 sentences * 2 times * 4 emotions) utterances used for training and 180 (45 * 1 * 4) for testing for each speaker. All results presented are the averages of the outcomes which are obtained by ten times of training and testing an MLP.

The MLP used in this experiment consists of input layer, one hidden layer, and output layer. Input layer has twelve input points corresponding to the pitch-related features, hidden layer fifty nodes, and output layer four nodes corresponding to the kinds of emotions to be recognized. All the patterns used for training and testing are normalized to have the range from -1.0 to +1.0. Learning rate of 0.05 and objective error energy of 0.05 are taken as learning parameters for EBP.

3.4 Results

The experimental results under the three conditions mentioned above are presented in Fig. 2. The first row is for the ordinary evaluation, the second and third rows for bodies and tails, respectively, on separation and the fourth row for the searched optimal weighting ratio on bodies and tails. It is noted that the total recognition rate under the optimal weighting condition was 4% higher than that under the ordinary condition, as well as individual recognition rates were increased for all the emotions.

The changing curve of recognition rates is depicted in Fig. 3, when different weight pairs are applied to bodies and tails. The figure shows that when more importance is imposed on the tails of sentences the recognition rates are higher than that under the ordinary condition and the system achieves the best recognition rate at the weight pair [0.5, 0.5]. Tables 2 and 3 provide the confusion matrices, in which the numbers are the counts of output labels recognized for each input emotional label of bodies and tails, respectively. Except the emotional state joy, the confusions of all emotional states for tails became lower than those for bodies.

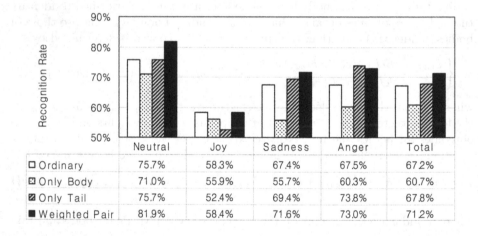

	Neutral	Joy	Sadness	Anger	Total
□ Ordinary	75.7%	58.3%	67.4%	67.5%	67.2%
▨ Only Body	71.0%	55.9%	55.7%	60.3%	60.7%
▨ Only Tail	75.7%	52.4%	69.4%	73.8%	67.8%
■ Weighted Pair	81.9%	58.4%	71.6%	73.0%	71.2%

Fig. 2. Average recognition rates for each emotion and for the whole emotions under three experimental conditions

4   Discussion

Boundary tones have been known to play an important role in verbal emotion communication. Intonation at boundary tones is very important to express and percept emotional states of oneself and any other speakers. In Korean language, ending boundary tones have been reported to have an effective function on communicating emotion due to the left branching characteristic of Korean. If the

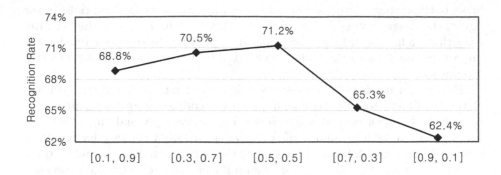

Fig. 3. Change of recognition rates according to various weight pairs in [body, tail]

Table 2. The counts of utterances recognized as output labels for each input emotional label in the evaluation for bodies

Input \ Output	Neutral	Joy	Sadness	Anger
Neutral	**32.0**	2.7	8.7	1.7
Joy	2.2	**25.2**	2.9	14.8
Sadness	10.5	6.0	**25.1**	3.4
Anger	1.5	14.5	1.8	**27.2**

Table 3. The counts of utterances recognized as output labels for each input emotional label in the evaluation for tails

Input \ Output	Neutral	Joy	Sadness	Anger
Neutral	**34.1**	3.4	5.6	1.9
Joy	2.5	**23.6**	3.3	15.6
Sadness	5.9	3.8	**31.2**	4.1
Anger	0.8	10.0	1.1	**33.2**

researched results of intonational phonology are verifiable in real-world systems, it is probably arguable to adopt the linguistic knowledge into the existing emotion recognition systems to get higher reliability on recognition performance. The experiment results presented in Section 3 are the good grounds of the argument.

In Fig. 2, we can notice that the contribution of tails to emotion recognition is over that of bodies for all emotions except joy. It might be inferred that the performance result under the ordinary condition is based on that of tails. In the experiment most of tails include Korean ending boundary tones, so the results in intonational phonology are confirmed with this outcome.

The higher recognition rates for the whole emotions were acquired when higher weights were imposed on sections of tails as seen in Fig. 3. The point of

[0.66, 0.34] is where the equal importance is imposed on bodies and tails. In the figure, the range of weight pairs from [0.1, 0.9] to [0.6, 0.4] covers higher rates than that under the ordinary condition. It implies the method of adjusting the importance on tails to the higher is effective to achieve more reliable emotion recognition.

However, it needs to be more studied that a different situation was occurred at the emotional state joy. Although there were confusable emotion pairs in the results, i.e. between neutral and sadness, and between joy and anger, only the joy showed poorer hit count in the evaluation for tails than that for bodies as seen in Tables 2 and 3. It may be caused by the reason that other boundary tones as well as the ending boundary tone had influence on the emotional expression and perception in Korean. The effect from more weighting tails held good even in the joy but the improvement was so trivial. A hierarchical weighting method can be devised to amend this problem.

5 Conclusion

We have investigated so far the application of intonational phonological knowledge for Korean ending boundary tones to an automatic emotion recognition system based on static method to enhance the reliability of emotion recognition. The effect of Korean ending boundary tones on emotional behavior was proved through the higher recognition rates of tails, which include the ending boundary tones. In consequence, more credible result for recognizing emotions was obtained by inflicting more significance on tails. This research has a significant meaning and necessity for adopting intonational phonology into practical emotion recognition systems. In the future work, the role of general boundary tones in automatic recognition of emotions will need to be more explored for vocal sentences in English as well as in Korean.

Acknowledgement

This research was supported by Responsive Cyber Space project.

References

1. Cowie, R., Douglas-Cowie, E., Tsapatsoulis, N., Votsis, G., Kollias, S., Fellenz, W., Taylor, J. G.: Emotion Recognition in Human-Computer Interaction. IEEE Signal Processing Magazine 18 (2001) 32-80
2. Gauvain, J., Lamel, L.: Large-Vocabulary Continuous Speech Recognition: Advances and Applications. Proceedings of the IEEE 88 (2000) 1181-1200
3. Yoshimura, T., Hayamizu, S., Ohmura, H., Tanaka, K.: Pitch Pattern Clustering of User Utterances in Human-Machine Dialogue. International Conference on Spoken Language 2 (1996) 837-840
4. Dellaert, F., Polzin, T., Waibel, A.: Recognizing Emotion in Speech. International Conference on Spoken Language 3 (1996) 1970-1973

5. Bhatti, M. W., Wang, Y., Guan, L.: A Neural Network Approach for Human Emotion Recognition in Speech. International Symposium on Circuits and Systems **2** (2004) 181-184
6. Schuller, B., Rigoll, G., Lang, M.: Hidden Markov Model-Based Speech Emotion Recognition. IEEE International Conference on Acoustics, Speech, and Signal Processing **2** (2003) 1-4
7. Schuller, B., Rigoll, G., Lang, M.: Speech Emotion Recognition Combining Acoustic Features and Linguistic Information in a Hybrid Support Vector Machine-Belief Network Architecture. IEEE International Conference on Acoustics, Speech, and Signal Processing **1** (2004) 577-580
8. O'Connor, J. D., Arnold, G. F.: Intonation of Colloquial English. 2nd eds. Longmans, London (1961)
9. Jun, S.: K-ToBI Labelling Conventions. Ver. 3.1. http://www.linguistics.ucla.edu/people/jun/ktobi/K-tobi.html (2000)
10. Pierrehumbert, J., Hirschberg, J.: The Meaning of Intonation Contours in the Interpretation of Discourse. In: Cohen, P., Morgan, J., Pollack, M. (eds): Intentions in Communication. MIT Press, Cambridge (1990) 271-323
11. Lee, H.: The Structure of Korean Prosody. Doctoral Dissertation, University of London (1990)
12. Rabiner, L., Sambur, M.: An Algorithm for Determining the Endpoints of Isolated Utterances. Bell System Technical Journal **54** (1975) 297-315
13. Krubsack, D. A., Niederjohn, R. J.: An Autocorrelation Pitch Detector and Voicing Decision with Confidence Measures Developed for Noise-Corrupted Speech. IEEE Transactions on Signal Processing **39** (1991) 319-329
14. Bengio, Y.: Neural Networks for Speech and Sequence Recognition. International Thomson Computer Press, London Boston (1995)

Some Issues on Detecting Emotions in Music

Piotr Synak and Alicja Wieczorkowska

Polish-Japanese Institute of Information Technology,
Koszykowa 86, 02-008 Warsaw, Poland
{synak, alicja}@pjwstk.edu.pl

Abstract. Investigating subjective values of audio data is both interesting and pleasant topic for research, gaining attention and popularity
among researchers recently. We focus on automatic detection of emotions
in songs/audio files, using features based on spectral contents. The data
set, containing a few hundreds of music pieces, was used in experiments.
The emotions are grouped into 13 or 6 classes. We compare our results
with tests on human subjects. One of the main conclusions is that multi-
label classification is required.

Keywords: Music information retrieval, sound analysis.

1 Introduction

Automatic recognition of emotions in music is a difficult task because of many
reasons. First of all, there is no any universal way or any standard of describing
sound files. Several kind of descriptors can be generated from sounds without
any warranty that they reflect any emotions. Moreover, especially in the case
of emotions, any classification (also subjective one) can be ambiguous – every
subject may classify emotions in a little bit different way. However, for listeners
from similar cultural background, one may expect to obtain similar classification.
Therefore, we considered this topic worth investigations.

We present some initial experiments performed on a database of 870 sound
files classified to 13 or 6 classes of emotions. To describe the files we used a
number of spectral descriptors. In the paper, we discuss the obtained results and
draw the conclusions how to detect the emotions better.

2 Data Parametrization

Automatic parametrization of audio data for classification purposes is hard because of ambiguity of labeling and subjectivity of description. However, since a
piece of music evokes similar emotions in listeners representing the same cultural
background, it seems to be possible to obtain parametrization that can be used
for the purpose of extracting emotions. Our goal was to check how numerical
parameters work for classification purposes, how good or low is classification
accuracy, and how it is comparable with human performance.

D. Ślęzak et al. (Eds.): RSFDGrC 2005, LNAI 3642, pp. 314–322, 2005.
© Springer-Verlag Berlin Heidelberg 2005

Objective descriptors of audio signal characterize basic properties of the investigated sounds, such as loudness, duration, pitch, and more advanced properties, describing frequency contents and its changes over time. Some descriptors come from speech processing and include prosodic and quality features, such as phonation type, articulation manned etc. [12]. Such features can be applied to detection of emotions in speech signal, but not all of them can be applied to music signals, which require other descriptors. Features applied to music signal include structure of the spectrum - timbral features, time domain features, time-frequency description, and higher-level features, such as rhythmic content features [7], [9], [13], [14].

When parameterizing music sounds for emotion classification, we assumed that emotions depend, to some extend, on harmony and rhythm. Since we deal with audio, not MIDI files, our parametrization is based on spectral contents (chords and timbre). Western music, recorded stereo with 44100 Hz sampling frequency and 16-bit resolution was used as audio samples. We applied long analyzing frame, 32768 samples taken from the left channel, in order obtain more precise spectral bins, and to describe longer time fragment. Hanning window was applied, and spectral components calculated up to 12 kHz and no more than 100 partials, since higher harmonics did not contribute significantly to the spectrum.

The following set of 29 audio descriptors was calculated for our analysis window [14]:

- *Frequency*: dominating fundamental frequency of the sound
- *Level*: maximal level of sound in the analyzed frame
- *Tristimulus*$1, 2, 3$: Tristimulus parameters calculated for *Frequency*, given by [10]:

$$Tristimulus1 = \frac{A_1^2}{\sum_{n=1}^{N} A_n^2} \tag{1}$$

$$Tristimulus2 = \frac{\sum_{n=2,3,4} A_n^2}{\sum_{n=1}^{N} A_n^2} \tag{2}$$

$$Tristimulus3 = \frac{\sum_{n=5}^{N} A_n^2}{\sum_{n=1}^{N} A_n^2} \tag{3}$$

where A_n denotes the amplitude of the nth harmonic, N is the number of harmonics available in spectrum, $M = \lfloor N/2 \rfloor$ and $L = \lfloor N/2 + 1 \rfloor$
- *EvenHarm* and *OddHarm*: Contents of even and odd harmonics in the spectrum, defined as

$$EvenHarm = \frac{\sqrt{\sum_{k=1}^{M} A_{2k}^2}}{\sqrt{\sum_{n=1}^{N} A_n^2}} \tag{4}$$

$$OddHarm = \frac{\sqrt{\sum_{k=2}^{L} A_{2k-1}^2}}{\sqrt{\sum_{n=1}^{N} A_n^2}} \tag{5}$$

– *Brightness*: brightness of sound - gravity center of the spectrum, defined as

$$Brightness = \frac{\sum_{n=1}^{N} n\,A_n}{\sum_{n=1}^{N} A_n} \tag{6}$$

– *Irregularity*: irregularity of spectrum, defined as [5], [6]

$$Irregularity = \log\left(20\sum_{k=2}^{N-1}\left|\log\frac{A_k}{\sqrt[3]{A_{k-1}A_k A_{k+1}}}\right|\right) \tag{7}$$

– *Frequency*1, *Ratio*1, ..., 9: for these parameters, 10 most prominent peaks in the spectrum are found. The lowest frequency within this set is chosen as *Frequency*1, and proportions of other frequencies to the lowest one are denoted as *Ratio*1, ..., 9
– *Amplitude*1, *Ratio*1, ..., 9: the amplitude of *Frequency*1 in decibel scale, and differences in decibels between peaks corresponding to *Ratio*1, ..., 9 and *Amplitude*1. These parameters describe relative strength of the notes in the music chord.

3   Experiment Setup

Investigations on extracting emotions from music data were performed on a database of 870 audio samples. The samples represented 30 seconds long excerpts from songs and classic music pieces. This database was created by Dr. Rory A. Lewis from the University of North Carolina at Charlotte. Therefore, all audio file were labeled with information about emotions by a single subject. The pieces were recorded in MP3 format and next converted to au/snd format for parametrization purposes. Sampling frequency 44100 Hz was chosen. Parametrization was performed for 32768 samples (2^{15}) frame length. The data set is divided into the following 13 classes, covering wide range of emotions [7]:

1. frustrated,
2. bluesy, melancholy,
3. longing, pathetic,
4. cheerful, gay, happy,
5. dark, depressing,
6. delicate, graceful,
7. dramatic, emphatic,
8. dreamy, leisurely,
9. agitated, exciting, enthusiastic,
10. fanciful, light,
11. mysterious, spooky,
12. passionate,
13. sacred, spiritual.

Class	No. of objects	Class	No. of objects
Agitated	74	Graceful	45
Bluesy	66	Happy	36
Dark	31	Passionate	40
Dramatic	101	Pathetic	155
Dreamy	46	Sacred	11
Fanciful	38	Spooky	77
Frustrated	152		

Fig. 1. Representation of classes in the 870-element database

Number of samples in each class is shown in Figure 1.

Some classes are underrepresented, whereas others are overrepresented in comparison with the average number of objects in a single class. Moreover, labeling of classes is difficult in some cases, since the same piece may evoke various emotions. Therefore, we decided to join the data into 6 superclasses as follows (see [7]):

1. happy and fanciful,
2. graceful and dreamy,
3. pathetic and passionate,
4. dramatic, agitated, and frustrated,
5. sacred and spooky,
6. dark and bluesy.

The classification experiments were performed using k-NN algorithm, with k varying within range 1..20, and the best k in each experiment was chosen. We decided to use k-NN because in the first experiments it outperformed classifiers of other types. For training purposes, 20% of the data set was removed and then used as test data after finishing training; this procedure was repeated 5 times (i.e., standard CV-5 procedure was applied). Next, the results were averaged. In order to compare results with Li and Ogihara [7], we performed experiments for each class separately, recognizing them in a binary way - one class against the rest of the data. The binary classification can be a good basis for construction of a general classifier, based on a set of binary classifiers [1].

4   Results

The experiments described in the previous section were first performed on a smaller data set, containing 303 objects, as presented in Figure 2. These experiments yielded results presented in Figure 3.

The results can be well compared with the results obtained by Li and Ogihara [7]. They obtained accuracy ranging from 51% to 80% for various classes and 30-element feature vector, with use of 50% of data for training and the remaining 50% of the data set, consisting of 599 audio files, also labeled by a single subject into the same 3 classes, and then into 6 classes, as described in section 3. We

Class	No. of objects	Class	No. of objects
Agitated	16	Graceful	14
Bluesy	18	Happy	24
Dark	6	Passionate	18
Dramatic	88	Pathetic	32
Dreamy	20	Sacred	17
Fanciful	34	Spooky	7
Frustrated	17		

Fig. 2. Representation of classes in the collection of 303 musical recordings for the research on automatic classifying emotions

Class	No. of objects	k-NN	Correctness
1. happy, fanciful	57	k=11	81.33%
2. graceful, dreamy	34	k=5	88.67%
3. pathetic, passionate	49	k=9	83.67%
4. dramatic, agitated, frustrated	117	k=7	62.67%
5. sacred, spooky	23	k=7	92.33%
6. dark, bluesy,	23	k=5	92.33%

Fig. 3. Results of automatic classification of emotions for the 303-element database using k-NN

Class	No. of objects	Correctness
1. happy, fanciful	74	95.97%
2. graceful, dreamy	91	89.77%
3. pathetic, passionate	195	71.72%
4. dramatic, agitated, frustrated	327	64.02%
5. sacred, spooky	88	89.88%
6. dark, bluesy,	97	88.80%

Fig. 4. Results of automatic classification of emotions for the 870-element database

also performed experiments for the same 6 classes, using k-NN classifier, i.e., examining all 6 classes in parallel. These experiments yielded 37% correctness (and 23.05% for 13 classes), suggesting that further work was needed. Since we suspected that uneven number of objects in classes and not too big data set could hinder classification, the 870-element data set was used in further experiments.

The results of experiments with binary classification performed on the full data set, containing 870 audio files, are presented in Figure 4. The best results of experiments were obtained in k-NN for $k = 13$. As we can see, the results have been even improved comparing to the small data set. However, general classification for all classes examined in parallel was still low, comparable with results for 303-element data set, since we obtained 20.12% accuracy for 13 classes and 37.47% for 6 classes.

Because of the low level of accuracy in general classification, we decided to compare the results with human performance. Two other subjects with musical background were asked to classify a test set of 39 samples, i.e., 3 samples for each class. The results convinced us that the difficulty is not just in the parametrization or method of classification, since the correctness of assessment yielded 24.24% and 33.33%, differing essentially on particular samples. This experiment suggests that multi-class labeling by a few subjects may be needed, since various listeners may perceive various emotions while listening to the same file, even if they represent the same cultural and musical background.

5   Multi-class Labeling

In our experiments we used a database of music files collected by a professional musician acting as an expert. Every file was labeled and classified to exactly one class representing particular kind of emotion. One of the first remarks of the expert was that in several cases it is impossible to classify a song to exactly one class. First of all, the nature of the song and the melody can be labeled by more than one adjective. Secondly, labeling is very subjective and different people may use various associations. This is because the perception of sounds by humans is not uniform. The perception can be dominated by different factors, e.g., by particular instrument or by vocal, and thus, different labels can be attached to the same piece of sound.

The results of our initial experiments (i.e., with 13 decision classes) one may interpret as not satisfactory. One reason of low results is that the set of used descriptors is relatively small. However, we claim that the most important factor is that the files were initially classified to single classes only. To confirm this we conducted the following experiment. We asked another two musicians (female and male) to classify the sound files to the same categories as the initial labeling. As we stated in the previous section, the results were very surprising in that the quality of recognition by a human was worse than one obtained by k-NN.

From the discussions with the experts it follows that the main difficulty while performing the classification was that they had to choose one class only, whilst in most cases they found at least two class labels appropriate. Therefore, we suggest to use multi-class labeling, i.e., to allow labeling each piece of sound with any number of labels.

The data that can be classified to more than one class are known in the literature as multi-label data [2,8,4]. This kind of data is often being analyzed in text mining and scene classification, where text documents or pictures may have been attached several labels describing their contents.

There are several problems related to multi-label data analysis, including: selecting training model with multi-label data, using testing criteria, and evaluating multi-label classification results.

5.1   Training Models

One of the basic questions of training phase of classifier's induction is how to use training examples with multiple labels? There are a few models commonly used.

The simplest model (*MODEL-s*) assumes labeling of data by using single label – the one which is most likely.

MODEL-i assumes ignoring all the cases with more than one label. That means that there can no data to be used in the training phase if there are no data with single label.

In *MODEL-n* there are created new classes for each combination of labels occurring in the training sample. The main problem of this model is that the number of classes easily becomes very large, especially when we consider not only two, but three and more labels attached to one sample. Therefore, the data become very sparse, and, as result of that, several classes can have very few training samples.

The most efficient model seems to be *MODEL-x*, **cross**-training, where samples with many labels are used as positive examples, and not as negative examples, for each class corresponding to the labels.

5.2   Testing Criteria

We assume that we build models for each base class only, and not for combination of classes (*MODEL-n*) because of sparseness of data as discussed above. As an exemplary classifier we use Support Vector Machines (SVM) [3] as they are recognized to give very good results in text and scene classification, i.e., in multi-label data.

Now, let us see how can we obtain multiple labels from the outputs of each of the models. In standard 2-class SVM the positive (negative) output of a SVM for a testing object means that it is a positive (negative) example. In the case of multi-class problems there are several SVMs built – one for each class. The highest positive output of SVMs determines the class of a testing object. However, it can happen that no SVM gives positive output. This approach can be extended to multi-label classification.

Let us consider the following three testing (labeling) criteria.

P-criterion labels the testing object with all classes corresponding to positive output of SVM. If no output is positive than the object is unlabeled.

T-criterion works similarly to *P-criterion*, however, if no output is positive than the top value is used for labeling.

C-criterion evaluates top values that are close each other no matter whether they are positive or negative.

5.3   Evaluating Classification Results

Evaluation of results differs from the classical case of single-label classification, where testing object is classified either correctly or incorrectly. In the case of multi-label data classification we can have more cases. If all the labels assigned to a testing object are proper then it is classified correctly – if all are wrong then incorrectly. However, what makes it different from single-label classification, only some of the labels can be attached properly – this is the case of partial correctness.

Thus, except standard measures of quality of classification like precision or accuracy, we need additional ones that take into account also partial correctness. Some examples of such measures, for example one-error, coverage, and precision, have been proposed in the literature (see, e.g., [11]). In [2] there are proposed two methods, α-*evaluation* and *base class evaluation* of multi-label classifier evaluation that make it possible to analyze results of classification in a wide range of settings.

6   Conclusions and Future Work

Difficult task of automatic recognition of emotions in music pieces was investigated in our research. The purpose of this investigations was not only testing how numerical parameters perform in objective description of subjective features, but also assessment of the recognition accuracy, and comparison of results with human subjects. The obtained accuracy is not high, but is of the same quality as human assessment. Since humans differ in their opinions regarding emotions evoked by the same piece, inaccuracies in automatic classification are not surprising.

In the next experiments we plan to apply multi-class labeling of sounds and develop the methodology for multi-label data classification.

We also plan to extend the set of descriptors used for sounds parametrization. In particular, we want to investigate how values of particular parameters change with time and how it is related to any kind of emotions.

Acknowledgements

This research was partially supported by the National Science Foundation under grant IIS-0414815, by the grant 3 T11C 002 26 from Ministry of Scientific Research and Information Technology of the Republic of Poland, and by the Research Center at the Polish-Japanese Institute of Information Technology, Warsaw, Poland.

The authors express thanks to Dr. Rory A. Lewis from the University of North Carolina at Charlotte for elaborating the audio database for research purposes.

References

1. Berger, A.: Error-correcting output coding for text classification. IJCAI'99: Workshop on machine learning for information filtering. Stockholm, Sweden (1999). Available at http://www-2.cs.cmu.edu/aberger/pdf/ecoc.pdf
2. Boutell, M., Shen, X., Luo, J., Brown, C.: Multi-label Semantic Scene Classification. Technical Report, Dept. of Computer Science, U. Rochester, (2003).

3. Burges, C.J.: A tutorial on support vector machines for pattern recognition. Data mining and knowledge discovery **2(2)** (1998) 121–167.
4. Clare, A., King, R.D.: Knowledge Discovery in Multi-label Phenotype Data. Lecture Notes in Computer Science **2168** (2001) 42–53.
5. Fujinaga, I., McMillan, K.: Realtime recognition of orchestral instruments. Proceedings of the International Computer Music Conference (2000) 141–143
6. Kostek, B., Wieczorkowska, A.: Parametric Representation Of Musical Sounds. Archives of Acoustics **22, 1** (1997) 3–26
7. Li, T., Ogihara, M.: Detecting emotion in music. 4th International Conference on Music Information Retrieval ISMIR, Washington, D.C., and Baltimore, MD (2003). Available at http://ismir2003.ismir.net/papers/Li.PDF
8. McCallum, A.: Multi-label Text Classification with a Mixture Model Trained by EM. AAAI'99 Workshop on Text Learning, (1999).
9. Peeters, G. Rodet, X.: Automatically selecting signal descriptors for Sound Classification. ICMC 2002 Goteborg, Sweden (2002)
10. Pollard, H. F., Jansson, E. V.: A Tristimulus Method for the Specification of Musical Timbre. Acustica **51** (1982) 162–171
11. Schapire, R., Singer, Y.: Boostexter: a boosting-based system for text categorization. Machine Learning **39(2/3)** (2000) 135–168
12. Tato, R., Santos, R., Kompe, R., Pardo, J. M.: Emotional Space Improves Emotion Recognition. 7th International Conference on Spoken Language Processing ICSLP 2002, Denver, Colorado (2002).
13. Tzanetakis, G., Cook, P.: Marsyas: A framework for audio analysis. Organized Sound **4(3)** (2000) 169-Ű175. Available at http://www-2.cs.cmu.edu/gtzan/work/pubs/organised00gtzan.pdf
14. Wieczorkowska, A., Wroblewski, J., Synak, P., Slezak, D.: Application of temporal descriptors to musical instrument sound recognition. Journal of Intelligent Information Systems **21(1)**, Kluwer (2003), 71–93

A Global-Motion Analysis Method via Rough-Set-Based Video Pre-classification

Zhe Yuan, Yu Wu, Guoyin Wang, and Jianbo Li

Institute of Computer Science and Technology,
Chongqing University of Posts and Telecommunications,
Chongqing 400065, P.R. China

Abstract. Motion information represents semantic conception in video to a certain extent. In this paper, according to coding characteristics of MPEG, a global-motion analysis method via rough-set-based video pre-classification is proposed. First, abnormal data in MPEG stream are removed. Then, condition attributes are extracted and samples are classified with rough set to obtain global-motion frames. Finally, their motion models are built up. So the method can overcome disturbance of local motion and promote veracity of estimations for six-parameter global motion model. Experiments show that it can veraciously distinguish global and non-global motions.

1 Introduction

With the development of network, computer and multimedia technologies, the demands for video become greater. People attempt to find a quick way to obtain interested material from video. Obviously, traditional retrieval based on text can't meet these demands, so content-based video retrieval has been proposed as a solution to address this problem. This technology is relative with objects instead of identifiers, with which video features, such as colors, textures and motion types, are extracted from multimedia data to retrieve similar video data from multimedia databases.

As the unique feature of video, motion information of objects and backgrounds is essential in the research of video retrieval. As a result, motion-information-based video retrieval has had broad attention. Video motions can be divided into two types, global and local. The global motions are caused by camera movements, and there are six motion types defined in MPEG-7, including panning, titling, zooming, tracking, booming, and dollying. In recent years, several parameter estimation methods for global motions in the uncompressed domain have been proposed [1] [2] [3]. On the other hand, Tan and Saur [4] proposed a quick parametric-global motion estimate algorithm by extracting motion vectors of macroblocks from compressed data, and a video retrieval system based on global motion information [5] was founded by Tianli Yu. However, the above methods are unreliable if there are local motions or coding errors. In this paper, we propose a new method to cope with these matters. Video frames are

D. Ślęzak et al. (Eds.): RSFDGrC 2005, LNAI 3642, pp. 323–332, 2005.

firstly classified before global-motion analysis, and non-global motion ones from classification results won't be processed.

Nevertheless, the classification may bring uncertainty and inconsistency. For example, there are almost similar motion features between frames of two motion types. Therefore, the theory of rough set as following may be useful. Rough set theory [6] was proposed by Z Pawlak in 1982 as a powerful mathematical analysis tool to process incomplete data and inaccurate knowledge. It's a new hot spot in the artificial intelligence field at present and has been widely used in knowledge acquisition, knowledge analysis, decision analysis and so on [7]. Without any mathematical description of attributes and features of detected objects in advance, directly from given knowledge classification, it determines the knowledge reduction and educes decision rules via indiscernibility relations and classes. Since there are uncertainty and inconsistency in the classification of global and non-global motions, the rough set method is adopted to construct a better global motion model.

2   Rough-Set-Based Video Pre-classification Modeling

2.1   Modeling Method

As for MPEG, each video sequence is composed of a series of Groups of Pictures (GOP's), in which "I" frames are intracoded, "P" frames are predictively coded, and "B" frames are bi-directionally predictive coded. The first frame in a GOP is always the I frame intra coded by DCT. P frames are coded by taking the previous I frame or P frame as reference frames while B frames are coded by taking the nearest P frames and I frames as reference frames. Thus, the P frame can best represent movements of the whole GOP. In this paper, video is pre-classified just by analyzing information of P frames in the compressed domain.

The decision rules of video pre-classification depend on the foundation of video information system, which is a 4-tuple, $IS = (U, A, V, f)$. U is a finite set of objects (universe), describing examples of P frames. A is a finite set of attributes, that is $A = \{a_1, a_2, \ldots, a_n\}$ or $A = C \bigcup D$, where C denotes the condition attributes of P frames, and D denotes the decision attributes, whose values are motion types of P frames. V_a is the domain of the attribute a. For each $a \in A$, an information function is defined as $f_a : U \rightarrow V_a$. This information system can be also described using a two-dimensional decision information table, in which each column denotes one example of U, each row denotes one attribute of A, and each element denotes the value of one attribute that is the value of information function f_a.

Therefore, in order to complete an information table we need to extract information data U and determine an attribute set A.

2.2   Extraction of U

For universality of samples, various test sequences are chosen, including cartoon clips, advertisement clips, news clips. Then, after extracting many P frames (there are 1367 frames in our experiments), motion types of these P frames are added by hand to form information data U.

2.3   Determination of A

The attribute set A is determined via analyzing many P frames. For our information system, the analyzed data are extracted from P frames in the compressed domain, including macroblock types and motion vectors.

The macroblock types are denoted as the field *macroblock_type* in MPEG stream. However, the field is just used in video decoding, but hardly in video retrieval. To exploit temporal redundancy, MPEG adopts macroblock-level motion estimation. During motion estimation, the encoder first searches for the best match of a macroblock in its neighborhood in the reference frame. If the prediction macroblock and the reference macroblock are not in the same positions of the frames, motion compensation is applied before coding. Given that *No_MC* means no motion compensation, when a macroblock has no motion compensation, it is referred as a *No_MC* macroblock. Generally, there are two kinds of *No_MC*, which are intra-coded *No_MC* and inter-coded *No_MC*. In typical MPEG encoder architecture, there exists an inter/intra classifier. The inter/intra classifier compares the prediction error with the input picture elements. If the mean squared error of the prediction exceeds the mean squared value of the input picture, the macroblock is then intra-coded; otherwise, it is inter-coded. In fact, in a special case, when the macroblock perfectly matches its reference, it is skipped and not coded at all. Furthermore, they can be divided into three types, which are low change (L), middle change (M) and high change (H). So the change ranges of frames are shown in the field *macroblock_type* in a certain degree.

Via the field *macroblock_type*, ratios of macroblock types are defined as follows:

$$RateH = Hcount/Tcount. \tag{1}$$

$$RateM = Mcount/Tcount. \tag{2}$$

$$RateL = Lcount/Tcount. \tag{3}$$

Where *Tcount* is the whole count of a P frame, and the other *Xcount* are the count of the macroblock type X.

In order to correctly process motion vectors, global and local abnormal data need to be removed at first. Assumed that all motion vectors of a P frame are based on Gaussian distributions, one motion model will be directly built up. Motion vectors here are extracted via block matching algorithm, which tries to find the best matches. However, there still exist random errors in low texture areas of frames that are called abnormal data.

The coordinate system for a P frame where the original point is in the center is shown in Fig. 1, in which the rectangle denotes a 16*16 macroblock, whose coordinate is (i, j). The line emitting from the rectangle center denotes the motion vector of the macroblock. We define:

$$E_{ij} = \sqrt{v_{ijx}^2 + v_{ijy}^2}. \tag{4}$$

$$\theta_{ij} = angle. \tag{5}$$

where v_{ijx} is horizontal motion vector of macroblock (i, j) and v_{ijy} is the vertical, E_{ij} is its movement energy and θ_{ij} is its movement direction.

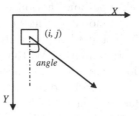

Fig. 1. Movement energy and direction of the macroblock

The energy of the macroblock can be characterized by several levels. In order to match human optical features, here it is non-uniformly quantified as five degrees: $0 \sim 8$, $8 \sim 16$, $16 \sim 32$, $32 \sim 64$, ≥ 64. Then we define:

$$ratio[i] = count[i]/sum. \tag{6}$$

where sum denotes the sum of macroblocks with motion vectors, and $count[i]$, $ratio[i]$ respectively denote the count and ratio of macroblocks in level i. A proper threshold 7% is set here, which means that if $ratio[i]$ is smaller than the threshold, all motion vectors in qualified level i are set to zero.

For global motions, the movement trend of neighbor macroblocks is always changed gradually. So are the local motions sometimes, but it becomes the fastest in parts where different objects with different motions are tangent. As a result, we use 3*3 detection matrixes to trim local abnormal data. The center of matrixes as a reference point is compared with other eight macroblocks by the energy and direction. Then sudden changed ones are removed during processing. After this step, the following is defined:

$$RateM1 = Mcount1/Tcount. \tag{7}$$

where $Mcount1$ is the count of macroblocks having motion vectors after deletion of abnormal data, not as the definition in (2).

Sequentially, macroblocks are clustered by checking whether they are neighboring. Class S_k is defined as:

$$S_k = \{(i,j)|(i,j) \text{ are neighboring and } E_{ij} \neq 0\}. \tag{8}$$

Since the motion model of each clustered class is unique, we adopt a six-parameter affine model to describe the movement of each class. The optimal motion parameters as follows are calculated by using the least square method:

$$u = a_0 x + b_0 y + z_0. \tag{9}$$

$$v = a_1 x + b_1 y + z_1. \tag{10}$$

where x and y are the horizontal and vertical coordinate of macroblocks, u and v are the horizontal and vertical motion vector, a_0, b_0, z_0, a_1, b_1, z_1 are six motion parameters describing models: a_0, b_0, a_1, b_1 describe the depth of motion scenes and z_0, z_1 describe 2-D global or local motion [8]. Therefore, classes with the similar motion models can be clustered further by taking six parameters above into account. The count of final motion models is defined as $ModuleNum$.

A motion activity description is recommended in MPEG-7, in which the describing of spatial distribution of motion activity represents motion density, motion rhythm and so on. It can also be indirectly scaled with intensity of motion vectors in the MPEG stream as follows [9]:

$$C_{mv,avg} = \frac{1}{IJ} \sum_{i=-I/2}^{I/2} \sum_{j=-J/2}^{J/2} E_{ij}. \tag{11}$$

where I and J are the width and height of a P frame in unit of a macroblock.

Referring to the literature [10], the motion centroid Com and motion radii Rog are calculated as follows:

$$m_{pq} = \sum_{i=-I/2}^{I/2} \sum_{j=-J/2}^{J/2} i^p j^q f(i,j), \text{ where } f(i,j) = \begin{cases} 0 & \text{if } E_{ij} = 0 \\ 1 & \text{if } E_{ij} \neq 0 \end{cases}. \tag{12}$$

$$Com_x = \frac{m_{10}}{m_{00}}, \; Com_y = \frac{m_{01}}{m_{00}}, \; Com = \sqrt{Com_x^2 + Com_y^2}. \tag{13}$$

$$Rog_x = \sqrt{\frac{m_{20}}{m_{00}}}, \; Rog_y = \sqrt{\frac{m_{02}}{m_{00}}}, \; Rog = \sqrt{Rog_x^2 + Rog_y^2}. \tag{14}$$

Next, feature attributes of information system need to be chosen. Due to correlations among $RateH$, $RateM$ and $RateL$, only $RateH$ and $RateL$ are selected to describe ratios of different types of macroblocks together with $RateM1$. $ModuleNum$ is used to denote the count of main motions in a frame. The four attributes above are computed not only by analyzing motion vectors but also by extracting the field $macroblock\_type$ in MPEG steam. The field $macroblock\_type$ is hardly referred in literatures, but it is crucial for us to distinguish global motion frames from non-global motion frames in our experiments. So $RateH$, $RateM$, $RateL$ and $ModuleNum$ are defined for the first time. Referred to [9] and [10], Cmv, avg, Com, Rog are also selected. Above all, seven feature attributes are defined in order to construct the video pre-classification condition attribute set $C = \{RateH, RateM1, RateL, ModuleNum, Cmv, avg, Com, Rog\}$. The seven attributes can show differences between global motion model and non-global motion model, such as ratios of different motions, the count of motions and movement characteristics. As a result, those attributes are quite enough for video classification. The decision attribute of the decision table is described that global motion type is 1 and non-global motion type is 2. As an example, Table 1 shows a decision table for example.

Table 1. Example of decision table in video pre-classification system

RateH	RateM1	RateL	ModuleNum	$C_{mv,avg}$	Com	Rog	Type
0.167	0.121	0.712	1	3.320	0.279	3.732	2
0.179	0.129	0.692	3	1.909	0.192	2.067	2
0.475	0.25	0.275	2	4.427	0.136	2.269	1
0.636	0.053	0.311	1	2.867	0.61	5.734	2
0.863	0.0542	0.083	1	0.338	0.121	0.937	1
0.106	0.053	0.819	1	0.211	0.531	1.131	2
0.159	0.25	0.591	1	0.962	0.102	0.452	1
0.004	0	0.996	0	0	0	0	2
0.285	0.135	0.579	2	0.989	0.020	1.122	2

2.4 Extraction of Decision Rules Based on Rough Set

Extraction of decision rules via rough set theory includes the following steps.

Data Preprocessing. It includes deleting repeated records, filling missing data and discretization. Comparison experiments show that Nguyen improved greedy algorithm achieves the best result.

Reduction of Attributes. Here the reduction algorithm based on condition information entropy is adopted.

Reduction of Values. The reduction algorithm based on decision matrixes is adopted.

Obtaining Logic Rules According to Reduction of Values. Combined with logic meanings of attributes, the rules derived from reduction of attributes are analyzed to form logic rules, which are validated later taking coding features of P frames into account.

3 Experiments and Analysis of Results

As said above, many kinds of video clips are selected for our experiment. 1367 P frames extracted from them are taken as the data set U, 440 of which are global motion frames and the others are non-global. 400 samples are randomly selected from them as train data, in which 146 are global. Then, in order to produce the video classification decision table used for rule obtainment, feature attributes of those frames are extracted one by one according to attribute descriptions above.

In our experiments, RIDAS system is adopted as data mining platform, which is developed by Institute of Computer Science and Technology, Chongqing University of Posts and Telecommunications in China [11]. The system integrates almost 30 classical algorithms regarding rough set theory.

Since values of attributes are unique, there's nothing missing in the information table and the filling of missing data isn't needed. Types of most data are float, so discretization for data is necessary. Via Nguyen improved greedy algorithm, the broken set can be obtained as listed in Table 2. From each broken set,

Table 2. Values of intervals of attributes after discretization

Attribute	Count of interval	Broken set
$RateH$	2	*, 0.223, *
$RateM1$	4	*, 0.082, 0.138, 0.170, *
$RateL$	4	*, 0.330, 0.499, 0.671, *
$ModuleNum$	2	*, 1.5, *
$C_{mv,avg}$	5	*, 0.136, 0.218, 0.529, 1.243, *
Com	4	*, 0.206, 0.241, 0.441, *
Rog	6	*, 0.661, 0.889, 1.096, 1.193, 2.452, *

Table 3. Distribution of recognition ratio

	Right recognition	Wrong recognition	Unknown recognition
Recognition count	797	142	28
Percentage (%)	82.4	14.7	2.9

Table 4. Distribution of Wrong recognition

Original type	Count	Recognition type	Count	Percentage (%)
		Global motion	232	79
Global motion	294	Non-global motion	56	19
		Unknown recognition	6	2
		Non-global motion	565	84
Non-global motion	673	Global motion	86	12.8
		Unknown recognition	22	3.2

Table 5. Accuracy with each classifier

	Global motion Acc.	Non-global motion Acc.	Total motion Acc.
Roughset	79%	84%	82.4%
Decision tree	74.5%	80.2%	78.4%
SVMs	71%	83.6%	79.8%

intervals can be easily got. For example, the broken set "*, 0.223, *" means that there are 2 intervals, including [*, 0.223] and [0.223, *]. All condition attributes are reserved after reduction of attributes, which indicates that they are all partly necessary attributes, which means the decision attributes educed by them are accordant with that educed by all attributes.

After value reduction, totally 97 rules are obtained from the video pre-classification information table. Some rules covering over 20 samples are listed as follows.

$$\text{rule1: } C_{mv,avg}(4) \bigcup ModuleNum(1) \bigcup RateM1(1) \rightarrow D2$$

rule2: $C_{mv,avg}(0) \bigcup Rog(0) \rightarrow$D2
rule3: $ModuleNum(0) \bigcup Rog(3) \bigcup RateM(3) \rightarrow$ D1
rule4: $Com(0) \bigcup RateL(3) \bigcup RateM(0) \rightarrow$ D2

By analyzing rules that cover many samples, we find some useful knowledge below. If global motion is dominant in a P frame, there is much energy and few motion models, for example often only one model; its motion centroid is near the center; and there are many intra-coded macroblocks in the case of few motion vectors. If local motion is dominant in a P frame, there is little energy and more than two motion models; its motion centroid is far from the center; its motion radii is long; and the ratio of low-changed macroblocks is high.

Next 937 P frames are used as test data for our experiment. These data make rule-match via majority priority strategy [12] to cope with conflict and inconsistency among them. The results are listed in Table 3. Furthermore, distribution information of wrong recognition of two types of P frames is listed in Table 4.

In addition, we have designed experiments to compare rough-set-based method adopted in the paper with other solutions. One is decision tree with ID3 algorithm [13]; another is the SVMs(Support Vector Machines) classifier [14]. These classifiers are test with the same test set. The accuracy with each classifier is shown in Table 5. By observing three parameters of accuracy in Table 5, we can conclude that the rough-set-based method is better than the other two algorithms and more helpful for global-motion analysis of video.

4   Conclusions

Video classification rules may be rather important and useful in video retrieval, especially for parameter extraction in video retrieval system that is based on motion features. In a video retrieval system based on global motion information, we may just consider those P frames with global motions, so that disturbance of local motions can be well overcome for building up a more precise motion model. In this case, video classification rules are very helpful. In this system, video are divided into sequential shots at first. Then feature attributes are extracted from representative P frames of shots, and they are used with classification rules proposed in the paper to check motion types of shots. If they are shots with global motion, their motion models are formed. When users input samples to retrieve video, the features of these samples are compared with those of video shots by use of the shot distance algorithm. Most similar shots are output and display as results. In addition, the numbers of global motion frames and non-global motion frames of a video clip can be taken as feature attributes in the sequential pattern data mining method [15] for video classification.

In conclusion, as unique information of video data, motion information plays an important part in video retrieval. Unfortunately, video data analysis is not robust due to disturbance of coding at present, which are avoided only through transcendent knowledge. In this paper, according to characteristics of MPEG coding, a novel robust analysis method of global motion via rough-set-based pre-classification is presented. In this method, condition attributes of video are extracted by analyzing motion vectors and *macroblock_type* fields, which are crucial but usually ignored. Then, P frames are classified as global type and non-global type via the rough set classifier, so that global motion models with more precise parameters can be built up. Meanwhile, the rules constructed by rough set system can be used to instruct classification of video, which is our future work.

Acknowledgements

This paper is supported by the following foundations or programs, including Program for New Century Excellent Talents in University (NCET), National Natural Science Foundation of China (No.60373111), Science and Technology Research Program of the Municipal Education Committee of Chongqing of China.

References

1. F. Dufaux, J. Konrad: Efficient, Robust, and Fast Global Motion Estimation for Video Coding. IEEE Trans. on Image Process. **9** (2000) 497–501
2. G. Giunta, U. Mascia: Estimation of Global Motion Parameters by Complex Linear Regression. IEEE Trans. on Image Process. **8** (1999) 1652–1657
3. K.Y. Yoo, J.K. Kim: A New Fast Local Motion Estimation Algorithm Using Global Motion. Signal Processing. **68** (1998) 219–224
4. Y.P. Tan, D.D. Saur, S.R. Kulkarni, P.J. Ramadge: Rapid Estimation of Camera Motion from Compressed Video with Application to Video Annotation. IEEE Tans. on Circuits Syst. Video Techo. **10** (2000) 133–145
5. T.L. Yu, S.J. Zhang: Video Retrieval Based on the Global Motion Information. Acta Electronica Sinica. **29** (2001) 1794–1798
6. Z. Pawlak, J. Grzymala-Busse, R. Slowinski: Rough Sets. Communications of the ACM. **38** (1995) 89–95
7. G.Y. Wang, J. Zhao, J.J. An, Y. Wu: Theoretical Study on Attribute Reduction of Rough Set Theory: in Algebra View and Information View. Third International Conference on Cognitive Informatics. (2004) 148–155
8. G. Sudhir, J.C.M. Lee: Video Annotation by Motion Interpretation Using Optical Flow Streams. Journal of Visual Communication and Image Representation. **7** (1996) 354–368
9. A. Divakaran, H. Sun: Descriptor for Spatial Distribution of Motion Activity for Compressed Video. SPIE. **2972** (2000) 392–398
10. Y.F. Ma, H.J. Zhang: Motion Pattern Based Video Classification and Retrieval. EURASIP JASP. **2** (2003) 199–208
11. G.Y. Wang, Z. Zheng, Y. Zhang: RIDAS– A Rough Set Based Intelligent Data Analysis System. Proceedings of the First Int. Conf. on Machine Learning and Cybernetics. (2002) 646–649
12. G.Y. Wang, F. Liu, Y. Wu: Generating Rules and Reasoning under Inconsistencies. Proceedings of IEEE Intl. Conf. on Industrial Electronics, Control and Instrumentation. (2000) 646–649

13. D.S. Yin, G.Y. Wang, Y. Wu: A Self-learning Algorithm for Decision Tree Pre-pruning. Proceedings of the Third International Conference on Machine Learning and Cybernetics. (2004) 2140–2145
14. O. Chapelle, P. Haffner, V.N. Vapnik: Support Vector Machines for Histogram-Based Image Classification. IEEE Trans. On Neural Networks. **10** (1999)
15. S.H. Lee, S.J. Bae, H.J. Park: A Compact Radix –64 54*54 CMOS Redundant Binary Parallel Multiplier. IEICE Trans. ELENCTRON. (2002)

Analysis and Generation of Emotionally-Charged Animated Gesticulation

Bożena Kostek and Piotr Szczuko

Multimedia Systems Department,
Gdansk University of Technology
{bozenka, szczuko}@sound.eti.pg.gda.pl

Abstract. Computer-animated sequences of emotionally-charged gesticulation are prepared using keyframe animation method. This method consists in creating an animation by changing the properties of objects at key moments over a time sequence. Such a sequence is analyzed in terms of locations and spacing of the keyframes, shapes of interpolation curves, and emotional features present in them. In the paper the keyframe method serves for creating animated objects characterized by differentiating emotions. On the basis of the analysis of these computer-animated sequences several parameters are derived. Then decision tables are created containing feature vectors describing emotions related to each object at key moments. This system serves for derivation of rules related to various categories of emotions. Rules are analyzed, and significant parameters are discovered. Conclusions and future experiments are also outlined.

1 Introduction

Traditional animation and computer keyframe animation are governed by their own rules and principles [2]. Both aim at animating a character with a highly human appearance, personality and emotions though using different artistic and technical means [9,11]. The simplest definition of the animation process is creation by changing the properties of objects over time. A keyframe is a time point when a property has been set or changed. In traditional animation master animators draw the keyframes and assistants do the in-between frames. In computer animation in-between frames are calculated or interpolated by the computer. Although computer animation process is much faster than traditional one, the quality of computer animations still lacks naturalness.

In our work an attempt is done to design an expert system based on animation rules used in traditional animation, capable of creating realistic animated characters according to the animator's requirements. One can analyze and parameterize features of hand-made animation and then translate them into the description of emotional features. These data can be utilized for the creation of the knowledge base containing feature vectors derived from the analysis of animated character emotions. In such a way the user's tasks could be limited to designing a simple animated sequence, and to delivering a description of the

D. Ślęzak et al. (Eds.): RSFDGrC 2005, LNAI 3642, pp. 333–341, 2005.

desired emotions to the expert system. These data could next be processed in the fuzzy logic module of the system, in which the animation parameters are modified, and as a result an emotionally charged animation is generated. The last phase is the evaluation of the conveyed emotion rendered into the animation.

2 Animation of Realistic Motion of Character

In the beginning of XX century, simultaneously with the invention of the movie, the animation was born. At the very early stage of animation, to create the animated motion, a small black-and-white picture was drawn on several layers of celluloid. Continuity of motion was achieved by introducing very small changes between each frame (cel), drawn one after one. Later the color drawing on papers and on foils attached to the peg was invented. Therefore it was possible to create frames in varied order - first the most important and powerful poses were designed, then transitional frames were filled in, called also in-betweens [2]. The same approach is utilized in the computer animation systems with keyframes [11]. An animator first sets up main poses in time and space then the system fills in the transitional frames by interpolating locations, rotations and torque of objects and characters' bones. The animator can influence the interpolation process, therefore the acceleration, slow-in and slow-out phases can be changed, and keyframes inserted or transposed.

2.1 Animation Rules

Correct utilization of poses and transitions between them can implicate different emotional features of the character's motion. As a result of experience derived from the first years of traditional animation the animation rules were created in 1910, by the art designers from the Walt Disney studio. These rules state how to achieve specific features, utilizing posing, keyframes, and phases of motion [9,11].

One of the basic rules is anticipation. This refers to preparation for an action. For every action there is an equal and opposite reaction. Before the main action starts there should always be a preparation for it, which is a slight movement in a direction opposite to the direction of the main action. If the preparation phase is long, the performing character will be perceived as weak, or hesitating. Short anticipation gives effect of a self-confident, strong character.

Follow-through is a rule related to physics of the moving body. The motion always starts near the torso: first the arm moves, then the forearm, and the last is hand. Therefore keyframes for bones in the forearm and hand should be delayed comparing to the arm bone. The delay adds a whip-like effect to the motion, and the feeling of the elasticity and flexibility.

Another rule connected to the physical basis of motion is overshoot. The last bone in the chain, for example hand, cannot stop instantly. It should overpass target position, and then goes back to it and slowly stops.

Stops are never complete. A rule called moving hold is related to keeping character in a pose for some time. Very small movements of head, eyes, and limbs should be introduced to maintain the life-like character.

Natural motion almost always goes along curve. Only a vertically falling object moves absolutely straight. Joints in human body implicate curve moves, but also head movement from left to right if straight, will not appear to be natural.

Other rules, not mentioned here, are related to staging, i.e. posing a character in front of the camera, exaggeration of motion, squashing and stretching for achieving cartoon-like effects, and so on. However, these rules do not fall within the scope of the objectives of this research study.

The know-how of hand-made animation and the rules being passed through generations of animators, have a subjective nature, and have never been analyzed by scientific means.

2.2 Computer Animation Methods

Many attempts were done to achieve a realistic motion with computer methods. Physical simulations of a human body motion were created, resulting in a realistic motion during flight, free fall, etc. [4]. It is necessary to assign boundary conditions such as how the motion starts, when and where it should stop, and on this basis the transitional phase is calculated. Such a method makes the animation realistic but neglects emotional features.

An attempt was also done to connect emotions with energy, therefore a very energy consuming motion was assumed as happy and lively, and a low energy consuming motion as tired and sad. In self-teaching algorithms the energy consumption was assumed to be the target function. The method was tested on 4-legged robot creature, and is still in research phase [6].

Genetic algorithms and neural networks were applied to create a model of human, and to teach it to move and react in a human-like way [10]. Data related to physiology of the human body were gathered and the target functions were composed related to keeping vertical position, not to falling over, and reaching a desired location on foot. A system developed for this purpose was trained to accomplish these tasks. Various behaviors were implemented, such as walking, falling, running, limping, jumping, reacting to being hit by different forces, but the method developed actually lacks emotional acting.

There were also some efforts to create new controllers for the animation process. For example a recorded motion of the pen drawing on the computer tablet is mapped to some motion parameters, like changes of location, rotation and speed of selected character's bone, or the movement of character's eyes. It gives the animator new technical means to act intuitively with the controller, and map that action onto the character [8].

A very similar and well-known method is the motion capture [3], consisting in the registration of sensor motions, which are attached to the key parts of the performer's body. It is possible to use a single sensor as a controller for the selected motion parameter [7]. Unfortunately this method is expensive, and the processing of the captured data is very unintuitive and complex, and editing by hand is then nearly impossible.

3   Case Study

In this paper it is assumed that animated motion could be described in a similar way as the animator does it. This means that using data of character's bones in keyframes along with the interpolation data is sufficient to comprehensively analyze and generate the realistic and emotionally charged motion. It is assumed that the animation rules presented earlier are related to these data, thus it is desirable to treat them as a knowledge base, and to evaluate both their correspondence to emotional features of a motion, and the effectiveness of the parametrization performed in terms of its categorization.

4   Preliminary Emotional Feature Evaluation

For the purpose of this research work one of the authors, a semi-professional animator, basing on traditional animation rules, created a series of animations. These animation objects present two arm gestures expressing picking up hypothetical thing and pointing at hypothetical thing with fear, anger, sadness, happiness, love, disgust and surprise. Animations consist of rotations of the joints as shown in Figure 1. In such a case none of other bone parameters are changed. 36 test animations were prepared.

It is assumed that each animation should clearly reproduce the emotion prescribed according the the rule applied. However taking into account subjectivity of emotions, an additional evaluation of perceived emotions is needed. This may help to verify the emotional definition of each sequence.

The following subjective test was conducted. For each animation, presented in a random order, viewers were supposed to give an answer as to what kind of emotion is presented by indicating only one emotion from the list. This was done by assigning answers from 3-point scale (1 - just noticeably, 2 - noticeably, 3 - definitely). Additional features were also evaluated: strength of emotion, naturalness of motion, its smoothness, and lightness, all of which have a 5-point scale assigned to them (e.g. 1 - unnatural, 3 - neutral, 5 - natural). 12 non-specialists, students from the Multimedia Systems Department of the Gdansk University of Technology took part in the tests. This was the typical number

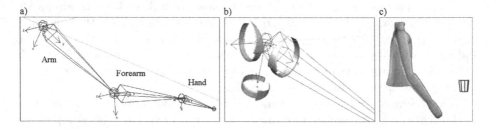

Fig. 1. Presentation of a chain of bones (a), possible bone rotations (b), torso with animated arm (c)

of subjects taking part in such an evaluation [5]. Students were not trained to make these evaluations.

In the first attempt of evaluation, 17 of 36 animations were described by participants as having different emotion than the animator aimed at. Therefore in the next stage all gathered answers were analyzed, but not taking into account the prior assumptions about emotions. The results obtained revealed also some difficulty in selecting only one description. Participants reported similarity of gestures, e.g. similarities between 'negative' emotions like fear, surprise, and anger. 27.9% of acquired data describes anger emotion, 19.4% fear, 16.5% happiness, 13.3% love, and others like disgust, sadness and surprise were the remaining emotions indicated. It was also checked that after training, subjects were more consistent in their answers, thus in future tests a training session will be carried out prior to the evaluation tests.

5   Parametrization of Animation Data

For the purpose of analysis of animation data various parameters of the keyframed motion are proposed. These parameters are related to the process of creating animation. The starting point of the animation process is very simple

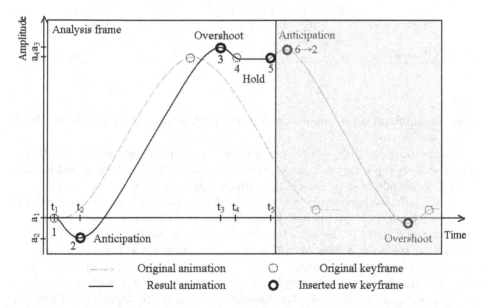

Fig. 2. Presentation of animation parameters. Original animation is without important elements such as anticipation and overshoot. Result animation is a variation of the original one, with anticipation and overshoot inserted. For that purpose it is necessary to add new keyframes, which change the curve of motion amplitude. Keyframes times are marked as t_i, and values of amplitude associated with them as a_i.

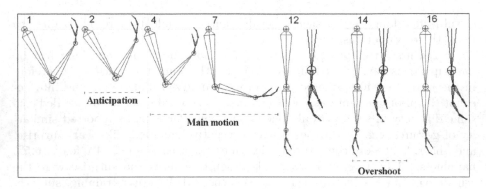

Fig. 3. Animation utilizing bone rotations with frame numbers and motion phases marked. Anticipation is very short (2 frames long) and subtle motion in direction opposite to main motion. Main phase usually extends across many frames and changes of rotation for bones are distinct. The overshoot is a short phase before the complete stop, when last bones in chain overpass target position (hand bones are magnified to visualize the overpass in frame 14).

Table 1. Decision table

Bone Rot	A_m	t_m	V_m	A_a	t_a	V_a	A_o	t_o	V_o	t_h	A_a/A_m	t_a/t_m	Decision
Arm Rot$_X$	1.2	2	0.6	1	1	1	0.5	1	0.5	2	0.83	0.5	Surprise
Hand Rot$_Y$	1	2	0.5	2	2	1	2	1	2	3	2	1	Fear
...	...	...	...	...	...	...	...	...	...	...	...	...	...
Hand Rot$_Z$	2	2	1	1	2	0.5	0.2	1	0.2	2	0.5	1	Happiness

and the animator adds important elements such as anticipation and overshoot later (see Figure 2).

Animations for the test were prepared utilizing only rotation of bones, therefore there are separate keyframes for rotations along X-, Y-, Z-axes, and in such a case amplitude literally means the rotation angle (see Figure 3).

Long animated sequences are segmented into parts with one main motion phase and one hold phase (see Figure 2, 'Analysis frame'). Each segment is analyzed and included as a pattern in the decision table (Table 1). For each animation segment, values of animation parameters are calculated related to amplitudes of particular phases ($A_a = a_2 - a_1, A_m = a_3 - a_2, A_o = a_4 - a_3$), their lengths ($t_m = t_3 - t_2, t_a = t_2 - t_1, t_o = t_4 - t_3, t_h = t_5 - t_4$), and speeds ($V_m = A_m/t_m, V_a = A_a/t_a, V_o = A_o/t_o$). Variables a_i and t_i are depicted in Figure 2. The decision parameter for an animation segment is the emotion assigned most often by the participants of a test while rating the animation.

This table serves as an input to the rough set system. The system task is to evaluate rules describing interrelations between the calculated parameters and features of motion.

6   Data Mining

For the generation of rules based on the decision table, the Rough Set Exploration System can be used [1]. During the processing, the automatic discretization of parameter values is performed. In the case of experiments performed the local discretization method was used. Some parameters were excluded at this level as not important for defining the searched relations. 12 parameters were left in the decision table: *Bone, Rotation axis*, amplitude for first keyframe a_1, length and amplitude of anticipation phase t_a, A_a, amplitude for anticipation keyframe a_2, length and speed of main motion phase t_m, V_m, time for overshoot keyframe t_3, length of hold phase t_h, speed of overshoot phase V_o, and time for ending keyframe t_5.

With utilization of the genetic algorithm available in the Rough Set Exploration System there were 1354 rules generated containing the above given parameters. Total coverage was 1.0, and total accuracy in classification of objects from decision table was equal to 0.9. The shortening of the rules resulted in a set of 1059 rules, giving total coverage 0.905, and accuracy for classification was equal to 0.909.

An attempt was done to lower the number of used parameters. Therefore from 12 parameters, only 6 were chosen. There were such as follows: *Bone*, and ones having more than three discretization ranges: a_1, t_a, t_m, t_3, t_h. This resulted in generation of 455 rules with total coverage 1.0 and accuracy equal to 0.871. After additional shortening, 370 rules were left, resulting in lower coverage (0.828) and accuracy of 0.93.

After discarding a_1, when only *Bone* and time parameters have been left, results not changed much: there were 197 rules, with coverage 1.0 and accuracy of approx. 0.871. Also after shortening, when only 160 rules left, coverage was the same as before (0.828), and accuracy was equal to 0.933. The resulting confusion matrix is presented in Table 2. It should be noted that the a_1 parameter is discretized into 10 ranges, and consecutively t_a into 12, t_m into 6, t_3 into 7, and t_h into 5 ranges.

Further attempts to reduce the number of parameters resulted in great accuracy loss.

Table 2. Results of classification of objects with derived set of 160 rules

		Predicted:						
		Anger	Sadness	Love	Happiness	Fear	Surprise	Disgust
Actual:	Anger	103	0	0	0	0	0	0
	Sadness	4	31	0	0	0	0	0
	Love	0	0	37	0	0	0	0
	Happiness	0	0	0	50	3	0	0
	Fear	0	0	8	0	57	0	4
	Surprise	0	0	0	0	0	16	0
	Disgust	0	4	0	0	0	0	24

It may be said that these results are very satisfying, namely it was discovered that time parameters are especially important for defining emotions in motion. In the derived 160 rules generated for 5 parameters, 100 of them use only time parameters. 102 rules have a size of 2, and 58 rules have a size of 3. Maximal support for the rule is 29, minimal 3, and mean is 5.7.

For rules, related to each class, parameter values were analyzed, resulting in creation of representative sets. For example for *surprise* emotion, most objects in decision table have $t_a=(7.5,8.5)$, $t_m=(17.5,\text{Inf})$, $t_3=(45.5,51.5)$, $t_h=(18.5,19.5)$ for all bones, and $t_a=(16.5,19.5)$, $t_m=(17.5,\text{Inf})$, $t_3=(36.0,45.5)$, $t_h=(19.5,21.0)$ for *love*. This information could be utilized later in a fuzzy logic module, for generating variations of animations introducing desired emotional features.

Examples of the rules derived are: IF (Bone=Forearm) AND $(t_m=(-\text{Inf},5.5))$ THEN (Decision=Anger), and IF $(t_a=(16.5,19.5))$ AND $(t_m=(-\text{Inf},5.5))$ THEN (Decision=Anger), which can be rewritten in natural language as follows: *"if the forearm main motion phase is very short then emotion is anger"*, and *"if anticipation in motion is long and the main motion phase is very short then emotion is anger"*.

Next for each discretization range appropriate linguistic description should be subjectively selected, and used as membership function name. Tests will be needed to choose functions for ranges of e.g. *short*, *medium* and *long* anticipation.

7   Conclusions and Future Experiments

It is assumed that most of the rules generated in the rough set analysis are closely congruent to the animation rules derived from the traditional animation. The presented here work will be continued in order to create tools for realistic and emotionally charged animation generation.

Results presented verify a very important fact known to the animators, namely that timing of keyframes is important for defining the emotion in animation. Interrelation between emotions and amplitudes gives possibilities to introduce many constrains to motion, such as exact specification of target position for grabbing, or walking sequence. In such case the amplitudes may remain unchanged to satisfy constrains, but timing may vary, resulting in different emotional features.

The rules generated could be used in the expert system containing a fuzzy logic module. The rough set measure can be applied as the weight in the fuzzy processing. The input parameters fed to the system may consist of data obtained from keyframes of a simple animation created for easy manipulation along with the description of the desired emotional feature. Output parameters are the ones needed for creating realistic motion sequence: positions of keyframes and lengths of anticipation and overshoot phases. For each parameter, membership functions should be defined, correlated to discretization cuts acquired in the rough set rule generation process (e.g. for animation parameters), or triangle membership functions covering ranges from 0 to 100 (e.g. for animation features).

For any simple animation, a set of modifications could be created, utilizing different values of emotional descriptions. With the output parameters from the fuzzy logic module, changes can be introduced to the animation, resulting in new keyframes, insertion of anticipation and overshoot phases. It is planned to generate sequences with the same emotional features as the ones prepared by the animator in the first stage, and verify their emotional quality and naturalness. The results obtained may be utilized for derivation of better rules, and the effectiveness of the system can increase.

The methodology outlined can also be extended to other parts of the human body, and this is planned as the future aim. The practical utility of this research is to enhance computer-based animation features in order to create animation more realistic and human-like.

References

1. Bazan, J.G., Szczuka, M.S., Wróblewski, J.: A new version of rough set exploration system. In: Alpigini, J.J, Peters, J.F., Skowron, A., Zhong, N. (eds.): RSCTC'2002. Lecture Notes in Artificial Intelligence, Vol. 2475. Springer-Verlag, Malvern (2002) 397–404
2. Blair, P.: Cartoon Animation. Walter Foster Publishing, Laguna Hills (1995)
3. Bruderlin, A., Williams, L.: Motion signal processing. Computer Graphics **29** (1995) 97–104
4. Fang, A.C., Pollard, N.S.: Efficient Synthesis of Physically Valid Human Motion. ACM Transactions on Graphics, Vol. 22. ACM (2003) 417–426
5. Kostek, B.: Soft Computing in Acoustics, Applications of Neural Networks, Fuzzy Logic and Rough Sets to Musical Acoustics, Physica Verlag, Heidelberg, NY (1999).
6. Park, J., Kang, Y., Kim, S., Cho, H.: Expressive Character Animation with Energy Constraints. Proc. Edu+Compugraphics '97. Vilamoura, Portugal (1997) 260–268
7. Popović, J., Seitz, S.M., Erdmann, M.: Motion Sketching for Control of Rigid-Body Simulations. ACM Transactions on Graphics, Vol. 22. ACM (2003) 1034–1054
8. Terra, S.C.L., Metoyer, R.A.: Performance Timing for Keyframe Animation. Proc. Eurographics/SIGGRAPH Symposium on Computer Animation (2004) 253–258
9. Thomas F., Johnston O.: Disney Animation - The Illusion of Life. Abbeville Press, New York (1981)
10. Whitepaper: Dynamic Motion Synthesis. NaturalMotion Ltd., Oxford (2004)
11. Williams, R.: The Animator's Survival Kit: A Manual of Methods, Principles, and Formulas for Classical, Computer, Games, Stop Motion, and Internet Animators. Faber & Faber (2002)

Handling Missing Attribute Values
in Preterm Birth Data Sets

Jerzy W. Grzymala-Busse[1], Linda K. Goodwin[2],
Witold J. Grzymala-Busse[3], and Xinqun Zheng[4]

[1] Department of Electrical Engineering and Computer Science,
University of Kansas, Lawrence, KS 66045, USA
[2] Institute of Computer Science, Polish Academy of Sciences,
01-237 Warsaw, Poland
Jerzy@ku.edu, http://lightning.eecs.ku.edu/index.html
[3] Nursing Informatics Program, Duke University,
Durham, NC 27710, USA
Linda.Goodwin@duke.edu
[4] Filterlogix, Lawrence, KS 66049, USA
WBusse@FilterLogix.com
[5] PC Sprint, Overland Park, KS 66211, USA
Xinqun.Zheng@mail.sprint.com

Abstract. The objective of our research was to find the best approach
to handle missing attribute values in data sets describing preterm birth
provided by the Duke University. Five strategies were used for filling in
missing attribute values, based on most common values and closest fit
for symbolic attributes, averages for numerical attributes, and a special
approach to induce only certain rules from specified information using
the MLEM2 approach. The final conclusion is that the best strategy was
to use the global most common method for symbolic attributes and the
global average method for numerical attributes.

1 Introduction

Predicting preterm birth risk among pregnant women is a difficult problem.
Diagnosis of preterm birth is attributed with a positive predictive value (the
ratio of all true positives to the sum of all true positives and false positives) only
between 17 and 38% [7].

The main objective of our research was to find the best approach to handling
missing attribute values in data sets describing preterm birth. These data, collected at the Duke University, were affected by vast quantity of missing attribute
values. Additionally, in spite of the fact that many attributes were numerical,
these data sets were inconsistent, another complication for data mining.

Additionally, the best approach to missing attribute values must be selected
taking into account that the main criterion of quality is not the smallest error
rate but the sum of sensitivity (conditional probability of diagnosis of preterm
birth) and sensitivity (conditional probability of diagnosis of fullterm birth). In

D. Ślęzak et al. (Eds.): RSFDGrC 2005, LNAI 3642, pp. 342–351, 2005.

order to increase sensitivity, an additional technique of changing rule strength
was applied [6]. Another important criterion of rule quality is the area under the
curve for the ROC graph.

2   Missing Attribute Values

In this paper we will discuss only methods dealing with incomplete data sets
(with missing attribute values) based on conversion of incomplete data sets into
complete data sets, without missing attribute values. Such a conversion is conducted before the main process of rule induction, therefore it is a kind of preprocessing.

2.1   Global Most Common Attribute Value for Symbolic Attributes, and Global Average Value for Numerical Attributes (GMC-GA)

This method is one of the simplest methods among the methods to deal with
missing attribute values. For symbolic attributes, every missing attribute value
should be replaced by the most common attribute value; for numerical attributes,
every missing value should be replaced by the average of all values of the corresponding attribute.

2.2   Concept Most Common Attribute Value for Symbolic Attributes, and Concept Average Value for Numerical Attributes (CMC-CA)

This method may be considered as the method from Subsection 2.1 restricted
to concepts. A concept is a subset of the set of all cases with the same outcome.
In preterm birth data sets there were two concepts, describing preterm and
fullterm birth. In this method, for symbolic attributes, every missing attribute
value should be replaced by the most common attribute value that occurs for the
same concept; for numerical attributes, every missing values should be replaced
by the average of all values of the attributed, restricted to the same concept.

2.3   Concept Closest Fit (CCF)

The closest fit algorithm [4] for missing attribute values is based on replacing a
missing attribute value with an existing value of the same attribute from another
case that resembles as much as possible the case with missing attribute values.
When searching for the closest fit case, we need to compare two vectors of attribute
values of the given case with missing attribute values and of a searched case.

During the search, for each case a proximity measure is computed, the case
for which the proximity measure is the smallest is the closest fitting case that is
used to determine the missing attribute values. The proximity measure between
two cases x and y is the Manhattan distance between x and y, i.e.,

$$distance(x, y) = \sum_{i=1}^{n} distance(x_i, y_i),$$

where

$$distance(x_i, y_i) = \begin{cases} 0 & \text{if } x_i = y_i , \\ 1 & \text{if } x \text{ and } y \text{ are symbolic and } x_i \neq y_i, \\ & \text{or } x_i =? \text{ or } y_i =?, \\ \frac{|x_i - y_i|}{r} & \text{if } x_i \text{ and } y_i \text{ are numbers and } x_i \neq y_i , \end{cases}$$

where r is the difference between the maximum and minimum of the known values of the numerical attribute with a missing value. If there is a tie for two cases with the same distance, a kind of heuristics is necessary, for example, select the first case. In general, using the global closest fit method may result in data sets in which some missing attribute values are not replaced by known values. Additional iterations of using this method may reduce the number of missing attribute values, but may not end up with all missing attribute values being replaced by known attribute values.

3   Duke Data Sets

The preterm birth data were collected at the Duke University Medical Center. This data set includes a sample of 19,970 ethnically diverse women and includes 1,229 variables. The data set was partitioned into two parts: training (with 14,977 cases) and testing (with 4,993 cases). Three mutually disjoint subsets of the set of all 1,229 attributes were selected, the first set contains 52 attributes, the second 54 attributes and the third subset contains seven attributes; the new data sets were named Duke-1, Duke-2, and Duke-3, respectively. The Duke-1 set contains laboratory test results. The Duke-2 test represents the most essential remaining attributes that, according to experts, should be used in diagnosis of preterm birth. Duke-3 represents demographic information about pregnant women. All the three data sets are large, have many missing attribute values, are unbalanced, many attributes are numerical, and the data sets are inconsistent. Tables 1 and 2 outline the basic characteristics of these three data sets.

Table 1. Duke training data sets

	Duke-1	Duke-2	Duke-3
Number of cases	14,997	14,997	14,997
Number of attributes	52	54	7
Number of concepts	2	2	2
Consistency level	42.18%	47.61%	95.95%
Number of cases in the basic class	3,116	3,116	3,069
Number of cases in the complementary class	11,861	11,861	11,908
Number of missing atribute values	503,743	291,338	4,703

Table 2. Duke testing data sets

	Duke-1	Duke-2	Duke-3
Number of cases	4,993	4,993	4,993
Number of attributes	52	54	7
Number of concepts	2	2	2
Consistency level	42.34%	52.29%	98.52%
Number of cases in the basic class	1,010	1,010	1,057
Number of cases in the complementary class	3,983	3,983	3,936
Number of missing attribute values	168,957	97,455	1,618

4   Data Mining Tools

In our experiments, for rule induction the algorithm LEM2 (Learning from Examples Module, version 2) was used [2]. LEM2 is a component of the LERS (Learning from Examples based on Rough Sets) data mining system. Additionally, a modified version of LEM2, called MLEM2, was also used for some experiments [3]. The classification system of LERS is a modification of the bucket brigade algorithm. The decision to which concept a case belongs is made on the basis of three factors: strength, specificity, and support. They are defined as follows: *Strength* is the total number of cases correctly classified by the rule during training. *Specificity* is the total number of attribute-value pairs on the left-hand side of the rule The third factor, *support*, is defined as the sum of scores of all matching rules from the concept, where the score of the rule is the product of its strength and specificity. The concept for which the support is the largest is the winner and the case is classified as being a member of that concept.

5   Criteria Used to Measure the Rule Set Quality

Several criteria were used to measure the rule set quality in our experiments: error rate, sensitivity and specificity, and the area under curve (AUC) of the receiver operating Characteristic (ROC) [8]. For unbalanced data sets, error rate is not a good indicator for rule set quality. *Sensitivity + Specificity − 1* is a better indicator as well as the Area Under Curve of Receiver Operating Characteristic.

5.1   Error Rate

In medical diagnosis, the objective is not to achieve a small error rate. Diagnosticians are interested mostly in correctly diagnosing the cases that are affected by disease. Moreover, frequently medical data sets are unbalanced: one class is represented by the majority of cases while the other class is represented by the minority. Unfortunately, in medical data the smaller class—as a rule—is more important. We will call this class basic, and the other class complementary. Consequently, the error rate in the original rule sets is not a good indicator of rule set quality [6].

5.2 Sensitivity and Specificity

The set of all correctly classified (preterm) cases from the basic concept are called true-positives, incorrectly classified basic cases (i.e., classified as fullterm) are called false-negatives, correctly classified complementary (fullterm) cases are called true-negatives, and incorrectly classified complementary (fullterm) cases are called false-positives.

Sensitivity is the conditional probability of true-positives given basic concept, i.e., the ratio of the number of true-positives to the sum of the number of true-positives and false-negatives. It will be denoted by $P(TP)$. Specificity is the conditional probability of true-negatives given complementary concept, i.e., the ratio of the number of true-negatives to the sum of the number of true-negatives and false-positives. It will be denoted by $P(TN)$. Similarly, the conditional probability of false-negatives, given actual preterm, and equal to $1 - P(TP)$, will be denoted by $P(FN)$ and the conditional probability of false-positives, given actual fullterm, and equal to $1 - P(TN)$, will be denoted by $P(FP)$.

In Duke's prenatal training data, only 20.7% of the cases represent the basic concept, preterm birth. During rule induction, the average of all rule strengths for the bigger concept is also greater than the average of all rule strengths for the more important but smaller basic concept. During classification of unseen cases, rules matching a case and voting for the basic concept are outvoted by rules voting for the bigger, complementary concept. Thus the sensitivity is poor and the resulting classification system would be rejected by diagnosticians.

Therefore it is necessary to increase sensitivity by increasing the average rule strength for the basic concept. In our research we selected the optimal rule set by multiplying the rule strength for all rules describing the basic concept by

Table 3. Duke-1, only certain rules

	GMC-GA	CMC-CA	CCF-CMC-CA	CCF-CMC	CCF-MLEM2
Initial error rate	21.29%	20.25%	64.65%	20.89%	20.39%
Critical error rate	40.48%	N/A	N/A	61.39%	56.68%
MAX $P(TP) - P(FP)$	0.156	0	-0.469	0.0782	0.1062
MIN $P(TP) - P(FP)$	-0.009	-0.122	-0.4845	-0.0895	-0.0588
Critical rule strength multiplier	7.7	N/A	N/A	13.38	6.5
AUC	0.5618	0.4563	0.2602	0.4878	0.5197

Table 4. Duke-2, only certain rules

	GMC-GA	CMC-CA	CCF-CMC-CA	CCF-CMC	CCF-MLEM2
Initial error rate	21.37%	20.23%	21.91%	20.83%	21.41%
Critical error rate	51.79%	N/A	N/A	41.1%	50.47%
MAX $P(TP) - P(FP)$	0.1224	0.0026	-0.0025	0.057	0.1419
MIN $P(TP) - P(FP)$	0.0007	-0.0028	-0.0166	-0.0813	-0.0109
Critical rule strength multiplier	6.6	N/A	N/A	12.07	5
AUC	0.5505	0.5013	0.4952	0.496	0.5624

the same real number called a strength multiplier. In general, the sensitivity increases with the increase of the strength multiplier. At the same time, specificity decreases. An obvious criterion for the choice of the optimal value of the strength multiplier is the maximum of the difference between the relative frequency of true positives, represented by *Sensitivity*, and the relative frequency of false positives, represented by *Specificity* − *1*. Thus we wish to maximize

$$Sensitivity + Specificity - 1 = P(TP) - P(FP)$$

This criterion is based on an analysis presented by Bairagi and Suchindran [1]. For each rule set, there exists some value of the strength multiplier, called *critical* (or *optimal*), for which the values of $P(TP) - P(FP)$ is maximum. The total error rate, corresponding to the rule strength multiplier equal to one, is called *initial*; while the total arror rate, corresponding to the critical strength multiplier, is called *critical*.

5.3 The Area Under Curve (AUC) of Receiver Operating Characteristic (ROC) Graph

The ROC graph is a plot of sensitivity versus one minus specificity. The major diagonal, a line that goes through (0, 0) and (1, 1), represents a situation in which the hit and false-alarm are equal. It corresponds to making a random diagnosis. Thus the ROC curve should be located above the main diagonal, the further from the diagonal the better [8]. The bigger the AUC value, the better the quality of the rule set. Apparently, $AUC = 0.5$ corresponds to random diagnosis. So, $AUC > 0.5$ means the result is better than the random diagnosis, and $AUC < 0.5$ means the result is worse than the random diagnosis.

6 Experiments

First, for the three Duke data sets, missing attribute values were replaced using the five methods. The first two methods were GMC-GA and CMC-CA. Since

Table 5. Duke-3, only certain rules

	GMC-GA	CMC-CA	CCF-CMC-CA	CCF-CMC
Initial error rate	22.33%	22.37%	22.55%	22.63%
Critical error rate	48.65%	47.03%	47.45%	50.09%
MAX $P(TP) - P(FP)$	0.1524	0.1578	0.1608	0.1473
MIN $P(TP) - P(FP)$	0.0102	0.0124	0.0122	0.0108
Critical rule strength multiplier	12	11	10	10
AUC	0.5787	0.5888	0.5854	0.5821

Table 6. Only possible rules

	Duke-1		Duke-2		Duke-3	
	GMC-GA	CCF-CMC	GMC-GA	CCF-CMC	GMC-GA	CCF-CMC
Initial error rate	21.95%	20.81%	21.53%	20.85%	23.79%	23.91%
Critical error rate	56.19%	43.98%	53.74%	59.80%	34.15%	31.32
MAX $P(TP) - P(FP)$	0.0894	0.1427	0.0818	0.0522	0.1412	0.1383
MIN $P(TP) - P(FP)$	-0.0437	-0.2114	0.0046	-0.091	0.0193	0.0157
Critical rule strength multiplier	4	6.8	2.1	12.28	10	8
AUC	0.5173	0.5528	0.5383	0.49	0.5707	0.5714

the missing attribute value rates were so high, applying the concept closest fit algorithm (CCF) could not fill in all the missing attribute values in these three data sets. So, the concept most common method for symbolic attributes and the concept average value method for numerical attributes (CMC-CA), and concept most common for both symbolic and numerical attributes method (CMC) were used respectively followed by the method of concept closest fit. For the same reason, the MLEM2 algorithm for Duke-1 and Duke-2 was tested after the concept closest fit algorithm (CCF) was applied.

To reduce the error rate during classification a very special discretization method for Duke-1 and Duke-2 was used. First, in the training data set, for any numerical attribute, values were sorted. Every value v was replaced by the interval $[v, w)$, where w was the next larger value than v in the sorted list. This discretization method was selected because the original data sets, with numerical attributes, were inconsistent.

Table 7. First certain rules, then possible rules

	Duke-1		Duke-2		Duke-3	
	GMC-GA	CCF-CMC	GMC-GA	CCF-CMC	GMC-GA	CCF-CMC
Initial error rate	21.89%	21.03%	21.65%	20.91%	23.91%	24.03%
Critical error rate	41.0%	59.74%	51.67%	41.04%	34.97%	38.33%
MAX						
$P(TP) - P(FP)$	0.155	0.0841	0.1135	0.0533	0.1329	0.1823
MIN						
$P(TP) - P(FP)$	-0.0099	-0.0837	0.002	-0.085	0.0157	0.0142
Critical rule						
strength multiplier	7.7	13.37	6.6	12.07	13	16
AUC	0.562	0.4929	0.5454	0.4929	0.5623	0.5029

In the experiments, four combinations of using rule sets were applied: *using only certain rules, using only possible rules, using certain rules first then possible rules if necessary,* and *using both certain and possible rules.* The option *complete matching, then partial matching if necessary* is better than the option *using both complete matching and partial matching* [5], so only that first option was used.

For training data sets Duke-1 and Duke-2, the consistency levels were 100% after replacing missing attribute values by methods CMC-CA and by CCF-CMC-CA, so no possible rules were induced. We used MLEM2 only to induce certain rules. Thus in Tables 6–8, only two methods are listed: GMC-GA and CCF-CMC.

From Tables 4 and 5 it is clear that by using methods CMC-CA and CCF-CMC-CA for Duke-1 and Duke-2 the worst results were obtained. Comparing CCF-MLEM2 and CCF-CMC (Tables 3 and 4) based on the $P(TP) - P(FP)$, we can see that the CCF-MLEM2 method provided slightly better results.

Comparison of the four strategies to deal with certain and possible rules was conducted for two methods: GMC-GA and CCF-CMC. The GMC-GA method was the simplest method of the five methods tested and this method produced better results than CCF-CMC (based on the value of $P(TP) - P(FP)$ and AUC). This can be verified by the Wilcoxon matched-pairs signed rank test (5% significance level).

For Duke-3, the four methods GMC-GA, CMC-CA, CCF-CMC-CA, CCF-CMC produced roughly the same results in each classification strategy, see Tables 5–8. The explanation of this result may be that the attributes with missing values were not critical attributes so that any filling in missing values used before rule induction may not affect the quality of rule set greatly.

In order to make the best use of certain and possible rule sets induced by LEM2 from inconsistent data, four different strategies of classification were tested in the experiments. From experiments on Duke-3, see Tables 5–8, it could be seen that using only certain rules provided the biggest value of $P(TP)-P(FP)$ among

Table 8. Union of certain and possible rules

	Duke-1		Duke-2		Duke-3	
	GMC-GA	CCF-CMC	GMC-GA	CCF-CMC	GMC-GA	CCF-CMC
Initial error rate	21.79%	20.95%	21.65%	20.83%	23.47%	23.89%
Critical error rate	53.23%	49.35%	43.44%	41.78%	31.18%	30.64%
MAX $P(TP) - P(FP)$	0.0999	0.1175	0.1532	0.0525	0.1456	0.1366
MIN $P(TP) - P(FP)$	-0.0263	-0.0467	0.0073	-0.0906	0.0227	0.0139
Critical rule strength multiplier	4.3	8.21	2.3	12.17	8	8
AUC	0.5305	0.5304	0.5681	0.4903	0.5707	0.5704

the four strategies based on each of the four filling in missing attribute value methods: GMC-GA, CMC-CA, CCF-CMC-CA, and CCF-CMC. This shows that for low consistency level data sets, certain rules are more important than possible rules.

7   Conclusions

Among the five different filling in missing values methods tested, our results show that for DukeŠs data, GMC-GA provided the best results. This is a result of the poor quality DukeŠs data sets, where the missing rate is very high for many numerical attribute values. For the same reason, applying CMC-CA directly or followed by CCF for DukeŠs data sets, provides worse results.

MLEM2 usually induces fewer rules than other rule induction methods. But it did not produce good results for data sets that have low consistency levels. However, for data sets with high consistency levels, MLEM2 induced high quality rule sets.

By comparing the four strategies of classification methods, the only conclusion is that for low consistency level data sets, certain rules are better than possible rules. On the other hand, for high consistency level data sets, there is no one single best strategy.

References

1. Bairagi, R. and Suchindran C.M.: An estimator of the cutoff point maximizing sum of sensitivity and specificity. Sankhya, Series B, Indian Journal of Statistics 51 (1989) 263–269.
2. Grzymala-Busse, J. W.: LERS—A system for learning from examples based on rough sets. In Intelligent Decision Support. Handbook of Applications and Advances of the Rough Sets Theory. Slowinski, R. (ed.), Kluwer Academic Publishers, 1992, 3–18.

3. Grzymala-Busse, J.W.:. MLEM2: A new algorithm for rule induction from imperfect data. Proceedings of the 9th International Conference on Information Processing and Management of Uncertainty in Knowledge-Based Systems, IPMU 2002, July 1–5, Annecy, France, 243–250.

4. Grzymala-Busse, J. W., Grzymala-Busse, W. J. and Goodwin, L. K.: A closest fit approach to missing attribute values in preterm birth data. Proc. of the Seventh Int. Workshop on Rough Sets, Fuzzy Sets, Data Mining and Granular-Soft Computing (RSFDGrC'99), Ube, Yamaguchi, Japan, November 8Ű10, 1999. Lecture Notes in Artificial Intelligence, No. 1711, Springer Verlag, 1999, 405–413.

5. Grzymala-Busse, J.W. and Zou X.: Classification strategies using certain and possible rules. Proc. of the First International Conference on Rough Sets and Current Trends in Computing, Warsaw, Poland, June 22–26, 1998. Lecture Notes in Artificial Intelligence, No. 1424, Springer Verlag, 1998, 37–44.

6. Grzymala-Busse, J. W., Goodwin, L.K., and Zhang, X.: Increasing sensitivity of preterm birth by changing rule strengths. Proceedings of the 8th Workshop on Intelligent Information Systems (IIS'99), Ustronie, Poland, June 14–18, 1999, 127–136.

7. McLean, M., Walters, W. A. and Smith, R.:. 1993. Prediction and early diagnosis of preterm labor: a critical review. Obstetrical & Gynecological Survey 48 (1993) 209–225.

8. Swets, J.A. and Pickett, R.M.: Evaluation of Diagnostic Systems. Methods from Signal Detection Theory. Academic Press, 1982.

Attribute Selection and Rule Generation Techniques for Medical Diagnosis Systems

Grzegorz Ilczuk[1] and Alicja Wakulicz-Deja[2]

[1] HEITEC AG Systemhaus fuer Automatisierung und Informationstechnologie,
Werner-von-Siemens-Strasse 61, 91052 Erlangen, Germany
Grzegorz.Ilczuk@ilczuk.com
[2] Institute of Informatics University of Silesia,
Bedzinska 39, 41-200 Sosnowiec, Poland
wakulicz@us.edu.pl

Abstract. Success of many learning schemes is based on selection of a small set of highly predictive attributes. The inclusion of irrelevant, redundant and noisy attributes in the process model can result in poor predictive accuracy and increased computation. This paper shows that the accuracy of classification can be improved by selecting subsets of strong attributes. Attribute selection is performed by using the Wrapper method with several classification learners. The processed data are classified by diverse learning schemes and generated "if-then" rules are supervised by domain experts.

1 Introduction

Nowadays medical information systems contain patient information that can be used by decision systems to improve medical care, uncover new relations among data and reveal new patterns that identify diseases or indicate certain treatments. Unfortunately the information needed by decision systems is often written in free-text form instead of coded form and therefore seldom used by computer-aided decision tools. Also the quality of information collected mainly not for data mining purposes results in noisy, unreliable, irrelevant and redundant data what makes knowledge discovery more difficult. One of the possible solution is to identify and remove as much of the irrelevant and redundant information as possible by selecting for the further processing only a limited subset of attributes. Attribute selection prior to learning can be beneficial because reducing the dimensionality of the data reduces the size of the hypothesis space and allows algorithms to operate faster and more effectively. In many cases accuracy on future classification can be improved any the result is a more compact, easily interpreted representation of the target concept.

At present most research effort in machine learning is directed toward the invention of new algorithms and much less into gaining experience in applying them to important practical applications. Therefore in our research we focus on developing a system for doctors and clinicians which provides an insight into understanding the relations between complex medical data. Main functional blocks of the system and their functions are:

D. Ślęzak et al. (Eds.): RSFDGrC 2005, LNAI 3642, pp. 352–361, 2005.
© Springer-Verlag Berlin Heidelberg 2005

1. Import the data from medical information systems
2. Convert information extracted from narrative text into a data understandable by standard machine learning algorithms. Information extracted this way should include not only knowledge directly retrieved from the free-text reports but also draw conclusions from the retrieved information
3. Based on the input entered by an user perform attribute selection for further rule generation data processing. The process of attribute selection will be divided into two parts: grouping of binary attributes according to a background knowledge from domain experts and reduction of redundant and noisy attributes. The selected attribute subset(s) will be used for rule generation.
4. Post-processing of generated decision rules. We presented entry results for the LEM2 algorithm in [7].
5. Visualization of the knowledge discovery in an easily understandable by humans form.

The main objective of this study is the third point of the described system. We use the Wrapper method with various learning schemes to select subsets of strong attributes from a data set with binary attributes, then compare these results with results achieved for a data with a limited, suggested by domain experts set of grouped attributes. Both data sets are then used as a train data for several rule-based learning algorithms. Accuracy of generated by each method 'if-then" rules is validated using 10-times repeated 10-fold cross-validation. Appliance of generated decision rules is verified by domain experts.

2   Material and Method

2.1   Dataset Preparation

The data used in our research was obtained from Electrocardiology Clinic of Silesian Medical Academy in Katowice-the leading Electrocardiology Clinic in Poland specializing in hospitalization of severe heart diseases. We made our experiments on a data set of 2039 patients in average age over 70 hospitalized between 2003 and 2004. The data about current patient state was written in original clinical dataset in a form of free-text reports. In order to extract this information was to transform the original data into ICD-10 codes by assigning proper codes to original phrases found in diagnosis e.g. a found phrase "Morbus ischaemicus cordis" resulted in a value of the I25.1 being set to 1 (this process will be extended and automatized in the final version of the described system). We followed the similar proceeding to extract information about patient's drug treatment. In this paper we presents experimental results for two main groups of drugs prescribed against heart diseases:

ACE Inhibitors which open wider blood vessels so blood can flow through more easily. These drugs act by blocking formation of angiotensin, a hormone that causes tightening of arteries and sodium retention,
Beta-blockers change force and frequency of the heartbeat thus reducing workload and pressure on the heart and blood vessels,

This data pre-processing phase ended up with a data set containing 2039 objects described by a value of 84 binary attributes. A value of each attribute was set to 1 if a disease was diagnosed and to 0 otherwise. We included into this data set two binary decision attributes: **cACE** and **cBBloker**, whose value was set to 1 if a correlative drug was prescribed to a patient and to 0 otherwise. The data set with the described two decision attributes was splitted into two separate data sets called: *D-84-ACE* (cACE class) and *D-84-BBloker* (cBBloker class).

Based on these two data sets and with a help from the domain experts we joined binary attributes into 14 grouped attributes thus creating two additional data sets: *D-14-ACE* and *D-14-BBloker* with following attributes:

AVBL - Atrioventricular block [0–3]
DIAB - Diabetes [0,1]
PTACH - Paroxysmal tachycardia [0–3]
HYPERCHOL - Hypercholesterolaemia [0,1]
CARDIOMYO - Cardiomyopathy [0,1]
ATHEROSC - Atherosclerosis [0,1]
AFF - Atrial fibrillation and flutter [0–2]
HYPERTEN - Hypertension (High Blood Pressure) [0,1]
CIHD - Chronic ischaemic heart disease [0–3]
OBESITY - Obesity [0,1]
SSS - Sick Sinus Syndrome [0–6]
PACEMAKER - Pacemaker stimulation [0,1]
TYROIDG - Disorders of thyroid gland [0–3]
MIOLD - Myocardial infarction in past [0,1]

If specified in parentheses integer value of attribute is greater then 1 then it indicates the severity of the diagnosed disease.

2.2 Experimental Environment

We used a freely available, powerful open-source machine learning workbench called Weka (Waikato Environment for Knowledge Analysis), developed at the University of Waikato, New Zealand, in version 3.4.3. This written in Java, and therefore available at any computer that has a Java run time environment installed, package brings together many machine learning algorithms and tools under a common framework with an intuitive graphical user interface. Weka offers two different graphic environments: a data exploration mode and an experiment mode. The data exploration mode called "Explorer" allows an user to select easily each data preprocessing, learning, attribute selection and data visualization functions implemented in Weka and thus encourages initial exploration of the data. The other mode called "Experimenter" is used both to perform large scale experiments on several data sets and to analyze retrieved results. In our experiments we used Weka to reduce unnecessary attributes from our initial data sets and to test the accuracy of selected classifiers. In our study we selected a following set of classifiers, which have been already successfully applied in medical decision systems:

1. Decision Table an implementation of Decision Table Majority (DTM) algorithm, which as shown in [8] in discrete spaces shows accuracy sometimes higher then state-of-art induction algorithms.
2. Ridor (RIpple-DOwn Rule learner) has been successfully tested in medical knowledge acquisition system [11] and its principle to generate general rule and exceptions should simplify human analysis.
3. JRip a rule learner proposed by Cohen [3] as an optimized version of IREP.
4. J48 Decision tree (C4.5 release 8) an algorithm derived from Quinlan's ID3 induction system using the standard TDIDT (top-down induction of decision trees) approach, recursively partitioning the data into smaller subsets, based on the value of an attribute [14]. The "pruned" version of J48 reduces the chances of over-fitting [4] the data.
5. PART decision list learner uses a divide-and-conquer rule to build a partial C4.5 decision tree in each iteration and makes the "best" leaf into a rule.
6. LEM2 this proposed by Grzymala-Busse [5] and based on Pawlak's Rough Set theory [10] rule generation algorithm, which has be successfully used in many medical decision systems [15]. Because this classifier is not implemented in Weka we used the RSES (Rough Set Exploration System) [2] environment to compare its accuracy and performance. Other methods implemented in the RSES system are beyond the scope of this paper.

We selected rule-based algorithms for our study (J48 decision tree can be easily convertible to decision rules) not only because these algorithms perform better in discrete/categorical attribute space [1] but also because discovered from data knowledge must be verifiable by humans.

Performance of the classifiers was tested using 10-times repeated 10-fold cross-validation with instance randomization after each run. This methodology provides a very stable replicability as shown in [13,12]. In case of LEM2 we performed non-repeated 10-fold cross-validation in RSES and therefore the results for this method are not directly comparable with other implemented in Weka classifiers.

3   Results

3.1   Wrapper Attribute Selection

The Wrapper attribute selection estimates the worth of attribute subsets by using a target learning algorithm. This method uses cross-validation (in our study five-fold CV) to provide an estimate for the accuracy of a classifier on the data when using only the attributes in a given subset. The CV is repeated as long as the standard deviation over the runs is greater than one percent of the mean accuracy or until five repetitions have been completed [9]. For searching the space of attribute subsets the BestFirst method was applied, which in our case always started with an empty set of attributes and searched forward by considering all possible single attribute additions. The wrapper attribute selection method was selected over filter based methods because the interaction between the search and the learning scheme gives as presented in [6] better results at the cost of computational expense.

In our case we used the WrapperSubsetEval implemented in the WEKA package with Decision Table, JRip, Ridor and J48 as a learning algorithms. The results for four input data sets and names of data subsets generated after attribute reduction are shown in the table 1. Subsets generated for the cACE class with J48 and JRip were identically thus only one data subset D-14-ACE-5 was created.

Table 1. Reduction of attributes using the WrapperSubsetEval method

Learning scheme	Selected Generated attributes data set	Best merit	Number of subsets evaluated
Entry data set: D-84-ACE, decision class the cACE			
DecisionTable	6 D-84-ACE-6	0.224	864
J48	7 D-84-ACE-7	0.221	936
JRip	10 D-84-ACE-10	0.217	1144
Ridor	11 D-84-ACE-11	0.218	1213
Entry data set: D-14-ACE, decision class the cACE			
DecisionTable	3 D-14-ACE-3	0.228	99
J48	5 D-14-ACE-5	0.228	96
JRip	5 D-14-ACE-5	0.229	149
Ridor	6 D-14-ACE-6	0.226	119
Entry data set: D-84-BBloker, decision class the cBBloker			
DecisionTable	12 D-84-BBloker-12	0.306	1281
J48	16 D-84-BBloker-16	0.298	1607
JRip	13 D-84-BBloker-13	0.300	1427
Ridor	10 D-84-BBloker-10	0.297	1219
Entry data set: D-14-BBloker, decision class the cBBloker			
DecisionTable	6 D-14-BBloker-6DT	0.316	117
J48	7 D-14-BBloker-7	0.300	119
JRip	6 D-14-BBloker-6JRIP	0.309	126
Ridor	5 D-14-BBloker-5	0.318	108

From the table 1 it can be seen that the smallest attribute subset for the cACE decision class was achieved when DecisionTable was used as a target learning algorithm. Next in the ranking were J48 and JRip with subsets a bit longer then generated by DecisionTable. Ridor appears quite low on the ranking because it has produced slightly larger subsets of attributes than the other schemes. The results for the cBBloker class are somewhat different than for the cACE. In this case the smallest subset of attributes is generated by Ridor. Second in the ranking are DecisionTable and JRip with their subsets being just a bit longer. It appears that for the cBBloker decision class J48 scored the worst. We analyzed these contradicting results with the best merit value for selected attribute subsets. In this comparison DecisionTable generates most times the shortest subset of attributes with the best merit. From this table it can be also seen that the number of evaluated subsets is more then ten times greater for data sets with 84 attributes what also results in longer calculation times. Results for data sets with grouped attributes were calculated faster and the average merit value for selected subsets of attributes were higher. Achieved results emphasize the importance of data pre-processing prior to data mining. In the next chapter we describe classification results for both original data sets and reduced data sets.

3.2 Classification

The table 2 presents the percentage of correct classifications for the selected classifiers trained with both full and reduced sets of attributes. We used 10-times repeated 10-fold cross-validation with instance randomization to test classifier accuracy. Results for LEM2 are separated in all comparison because for that method we used 10-fold CV implemented in other software package (RSES). Average number of generated rules (for J48 it is a number of nodes) are shown in the table 3.

Table 2. Results of correctly classified instances [%] for the cACE class

Data set	Decision Table	JRip	Ridor	PART	J48	LEM2
D-84-ACE	75.74	76.06	74.59	68.70	75.26	72.10
D-84-ACE-11	76.75	77.86	77.69	77.64	77.89	76.60
D-84-ACE-10	76.62	78.14	78.02	77.65	77.87	76.30
D-84-ACE-7	76.83	77.63	77.63	77.73	77.93	75.50
D-84-ACE-6	77.54	77.69	77.62	77.69	77.65	76.70
D-14-ACE	76.03	76.25	76.16	73.38	76.21	68.00
D-14-ACE-6	76.94	76.72	77.07	77.09	77.15	73.90
D-14-ACE-5	76.95	76.83	77.09	77.08	77.15	74.70
D-14-ACE-3	77.16	76.90	77.03	77.16	77.16	76.50

From the table 2 it can be seen that the accuracy of classification for data sets with 14 grouped attributes is better then for data sets with 84 binary attributes. It can be also observed that percent of correctly classified instances increases with a reduction of attribute subsets. The best performance of J48 in this ranking could be attributable to its ability to identify attribute dependencies. Reduced subsets of attributes containing strongly interacting attributes increase the likelihood that J48 will discover and use these interactions early on in the tree construction before the data becomes too fragmented. The results show that in general, all classifiers have comparable accuracy but as shown in the table 3 they need different number of rules to achieve it. The smallest number of rules generated JRip and Ridor. PART and J48 both using C4.5 decision tree produced similar results. The largest number of rules created DecisionTable but these rules as shown in the table 2 did not increase the accuracy. The number of rules for LEM2 for all reduced data sets lied between the results for J48 and DecisionTable with comparable accuracy.

Table 3. Average number of generated rules for the cACE class

Data set	Decision Table	JRip	Ridor	PART	J48	LEM2
D-84-ACE	113.69	3.59	6.54	163.26	51.68	814
D-84-ACE-11	35.85	2.04	4.54	7.53	8.88	18
D-84-ACE-10	29.75	2.06	3.25	5.96	10.35	16
D-84-ACE-7	22.34	2.00	4.09	6.08	7.00	13
D-84-ACE-6	21.64	2.21	5.24	7.95	7.94	7
D-14-ACE	53.73	4.51	7.94	97.39	22.39	733
D-14-ACE-6	14.85	2.29	6.57	6.08	5.03	17
D-14-ACE-5	14.54	2.44	5.98	4.98	5.03	13
D-14-ACE-3	7.96	2.00	3.77	3.00	3.99	5

Table 4. Wins versus losses in correctly classified instances for the cACE class

Scheme	Wins–Looses	Wins	Looses
J48	15	18	3
Ridor	4	8	4
JRip	-1	9	10
PART	-7	8	15
DecisionTable	-11	5	16

In the table 4 a pairwise comparison between Weka schemes is shown. The number of times each scheme is significantly more or less accurate than another is recorded and the schemes are ranked by the total number of "wins" and "losses". From this table it can be seen that the J48 classifier outperform its competitors with 18 wins and only three losses and Ridor is the only other scheme that has more wins than losses.

Results in the table 5 for the cBBloker shows the same tendency as the results for the cACE that accuracy of classification is higher for the data sets with grouped attributes in compare to the data sets with a lot of binary attributes. Overall accuracy of classification oscillates around 69% (76% for the cACE) what could be attributable to increased complexity of correct prediction and thus resulting in more decision rules as shown in the table 6. The total number of rules increased but again the smallest number of rules generated JRip followed by Ridor. Similar to the results for the cACE class PART and J48 generated larger sets of rules but again most rules needed DecisionTable. Ranking of classifiers based on their accuracy shown in the table 7 clearly documents that J48 with 21 wins and only 8 looses scored the best. Not surprisedly PART based also on C4.5 decision tree took the second place in this ranking. LEM2 classifying the cBBloker class with a similar accuracy to the other algorithms needed to achieve it for data sets after attribute selection less rules then Decision Table was confirms the importance of data pre-processing for this based on Rough Sets method.

Table 5. Results of correctly classified instances [%] for the cBBloker class

Data set	Decision Table	JRip	Ridor	PART	J48	LEM2
D-84-BBloker	66.18	66.96	64.78	63.56	65.13	60.00
D-84-BBloker-16	68.29	68.48	68.36	69.46	69.70	65.40
D-84-BBloker-13	68.54	69.33	68.81	69.92	69.80	66.80
D-84-BBloker-12	68.96	69.01	69.17	69.40	69.09	67.50
D-84-BBloker-10	68.42	69.24	69.63	69.48	69.36	65.80
D-14-BBloker	67.74	67.05	65.30	64.70	67.43	61.90
D-14-BBloker-7	68.53	68.20	67.36	69.56	70.20	65.00
D-14-BBloker-6DT	68.79	68.25	68.08	69.56	69.38	66.70
D-14-BBloker-6JRIP	67.65	68.82	67.39	68.58	68.89	66.50
D-14-BBloker-5	68.61	68.25	68.06	70.11	69.50	67.20

Table 6. Number of generated rules for the cBBloker class

Data set	Decision Table	JRip	Ridor	PART	J48	LEM2
D-84-BBloker	188.17	5.21	10.99	123.39	55.14	921
D-84-BBloker-16	141.35	5.20	7.36	20.02	28.08	125
D-84-BBloker-13	159.83	5.31	9.18	26.02	28.95	85
D-84-BBloker-12	110.30	5.43	8.93	22.38	24.97	28
D-84-BBloker-10	151.39	5.18	10.53	30.44	25.45	42
D-14-BBloker	218.60	4.64	9.24	182.91	115.14	802
D-14-BBloker-7	76.60	3.79	5.34	5.10	10.95	163
D-14-BBloker-6DT	84.12	3.92	5.30	6.16	10.56	91
D-14-BBloker-6JRIP	129.89	4.39	7.92	19.46	15.91	74
D-14-BBloker-5	121.89	4.25	8.54	23.02	19.90	75

Table 7. Wins versus losses in correctly classified instances for the cBBloker class

Scheme	Wins–Looses	Wins	Looses
J48	19	22	3
PART	13	21	8
JRip	-2	10	12
DecisionTable	-12	7	19
Ridor	-18	3	21

The presented results show that in general accuracy of tested classifiers is comparable but they need different number of rules to achieve it. Because we were looking for an algorithm, which is not only accurate but also easily verifiable by human we asked domain experts from Electrocardiology Clinic of Silesian Medical Academy in Katowice for their opinion. According to their considerations DecisionTable generates verifiable rules if only the number of generated rules is not to high (this was an issue for the cBBloker class). To solve this problem a method to generalize or join the rules would be appreciated. Such methods are available in the RSES package and when they are used on rules generated by the LEM2 algorithm the small number of decision rules is easily verifiable and accurate. Ridor and JRip generate short rules but the acceptance of their short, except rules in medical domain is low. This can be attributable to the fact that except rules represent collected knowledge in a way which is uncommon for medical experts and therefore hard to interpret. PART and J48 both based on the C4.5 decision tree generate small number of short and easily verifiable rules. Domain experts especially appreciated by the rule verification the possibility to visualize a decision tree generated by J48.

As our experiment results show the accuracy of selected top-down algorithms is comparable so that the decision which classifier should be used depends on generated decision rules. In our study a few easily verifiable rules generated by LEM2 and C4.5 based algorithms: PART and J48 favored usage of these methods in medical decision systems. An additional advantage in 'what-if' reasoning is a possibility to visualize decision trees generated by J48.

4   Conclusions

In this paper we shown that performed prior to data mining pre-processing of data increase future classification accuracy and dramatically decrease computation time. Our experiments indicate that by using Wrapper attribute reduction method it was possible to find reducts which either increase classification accuracy or achieve similar accuracy with a much reduced attribute sets. In our study we concluded that accuracy is not the ultimate measurement when comparing the learner's credibility. Especially in medical domain computed results must be easily understandable and verifiable by humans and therefore a number of generated rules and their testability is an important criteria. This criteria can not be fulfilled by data sets with a lot of binary attributes because this knowledge fragmentation leads to too many specialized rules (Decision Table) or irrelevant to practice rule exceptions (JRip, Ridor). Our results indicate that LEM2 algorithm offers acceptable accuracy and a small number of decision rules if only data sets with strong attribute subsets are used. The best accuracy performance results are achieved for J48 implementation of the C4.5 decision tree what more its hierarchical result representation allows knowledge management at different levels of details in a way which is more suitable for human consumption.

Acknowledgment

We would like to thank Rafal Mlynarski from Electrocardiology Clinic of Silesian Medical Academy in Katowice, Poland for providing us the data and giving us feedbacks.

References

1. Tan, A.C., Gilbert, D.: An empirical comparison of supervised machine learning techniques in bioinformatics Proc. 1st Asia Pacific Bioinformatics Conference (2003) 219–222
2. Bazan, J.G., Szczuka, M.S.: Rses and rseslib - a collection of tools for rough set computations. Lecture Notes in Computer Science **2005** (2000) 106–113
3. Cohen, W.: Fast Effective Rule Induction. Proc. of the 12th International Conference on Machine Learning (1995) 115–123
4. Cohen, P.R., Jensen, D.: Overfitting Explained. Preliminary Papers of the Sixth International Workshop on Artificial Intelligence and Statistics (1997) 115–122
5. Grzymala-Busse, J.W.: A new version of the rule induction system lers. Fundamenta Informatica **31** (1997) 27–39
6. Hall, M., Holmes, G.: Benchmarking Attribute Selection Techniques for Discrete Class Data Mining. IEEE Transactions on knowledge and data engineering **15** (2003) 1437–1447
7. Ilczuk, G., Wakulicz-Deja, A.: Rough Sets approach to medical diagnosis system. (2005)
8. Kohavi, R.: The Power of Decision Tables. Lecture Notes in Artificial Intelligence **914** (1995) 174–189
9. Kohavi, R., John, G.H.: Wrappers for feature subset selection. Artificial Intelligence **97** (1997) 273–324
10. Pawlak, Z., Grzymala-Busse, J.W., Slowinski, R., Ziarko, W.: Rough sets. Commun. ACM **38** (1995) 88–95
11. Preston, P., Edwards, G., Compton, P.: Rule Expert System Without Knowledge Engineers. Second World Congress on Expert Systems (1993)
12. Bouckaert, R.: Choosing between two learning algorithms based on calibrated tests. (2003)
13. Bouckaert, R., Eibe F.: Evaluating the Replicability of Significance Tests for Comparing Learning Algorithms. (2004)
14. Quinlan, J.R.: C4.5, Programs for Machine Learning. Morgan Kauffman, San Mateo, California, USA (1993)
15. Wakulicz-Deja A., Paszek, P.: Applying rough set theory to multi stage medical diagnosing. Fundamenta Informatica **54** (2003) 387–408

Relevant Attribute Discovery in High Dimensional Data Based on Rough Sets and Unsupervised Classification: Application to Leukemia Gene Expressions

Julio J. Valdés and Alan J. Barton

National Research Council Canada, M50, 1200 Montreal Rd.,
Ottawa, ON K1A 0R6
{julio.valdes, alan.barton}@nrc-cnrc.gc.ca
http://iit-iti.nrc-cnrc.gc.ca

Abstract. A pipelined approach using two clustering algorithms in combination with Rough Sets is investigated for the purpose discovering important combination of attributes in high dimensional data. In many domains, the data objects are described in terms of a large number of features, like in gene expression experiments, or in samples characterized by spectral information. The Leader and several k-means algorithms are used as fast procedures for attribute set simplification of the information systems presented to the rough sets algorithms. The data submatrices described in terms of these features are then discretized w.r.t the decision attribute according to different rough set based schemes. From them, the reducts and their derived rules are extracted, which are applied to test data in order to evaluate the resulting classification accuracy. An exploration of this approach (using Leukemia gene expression data) was conducted in a series of experiments within a high-throughput distributed-computing environment. They led to subsets of genes with high discrimination power. Good results were obtained with no preprocessing applied to the data.

1 Introduction

As a consequence of the information explosion and the development of sensor and observation technologies, it is now common in many domains to have data objects characterized by an increasingly larger number of attributes, leading to high dimensional databases in terms of the set of fields. A typical example is a gene expression experiment, where the genetic content of samples of tissues are obtained with high throughput technologies (microchips). Usually, thousands of genes are investigated in such experiments. In other bio-medical research contexts, the samples are characterized by infrared, ultraviolet, and other kinds of spectra, where the absorbtion properties, with respect to a large number of wavelengths, are investigated. The same situation occurs in other domains, and the common denominator is to have a set of data objects of a very high dimensional nature.

This paper investigates one, of the possibly many approaches to the problem of finding relevant attributes in high dimensional datasets. The approach is based on a combination of clustering and rough sets techniques in a high throughput distributed

D. Ślęzak et al. (Eds.): RSFDGrC 2005, LNAI 3642, pp. 362–371, 2005.

computing environment, with low dimensional virtual reality data representations aiding data analysis understanding. The goals are: *i)* to investigate the behavior of the combination of these techniques into a knowledge discovery process, and *ii)* to perform preliminary comparisons of the experimental results from the point of view of the discovered relevant attributes, applied to the example problem of finding relevant genes.

2   Experimental Methodology

2.1   Clustering Methods

Clustering with classical partition methods constructs crisp (non overlapping) subpopulations of objects or attributes. Two such classical algorithms were used in this study: the Leader algorithm [1], and several variants of k-means [2].

The leader algorithm operates with a dissimilarity or similarity measure and a preset threshold. A single pass is made through the data objects, assigning each object to the first cluster whose leader (i.e. representative) is close enough to the current object w.r.t. the specified measure and threshold. If no such matching leader is found, then the algorithm will set the current object to be a new leader; forming a new cluster. This technique is fast; however, it has several negative properties. For example, *i)* the first data object always defines a cluster and therefore, appears as a leader, *ii)* the partition formed is not invariant under a permutation of the data objects, and *iii)* the algorithm is biased, as the first clusters tend to be larger than the later ones since they get first chance at "absorbing" each object as it is allocated. Variants of this algorithm with the purpose of reducing bias include: *a)* reversing the order of presentation of a data object to the list of currently formed leaders, and *b)* selecting the absolute best leader found (thus making the object presentation order irrelevant).

The k-means algorithm is actually a family of techniques, where a dissimilarity or similarity measure is supplied, together with an initial partition of the data (e.g. initial partition strategies include: random, the first k objects, k-seed elements, etc). The goal is to alter cluster membership so as to obtain a better partition w.r.t. the measure. Different variants very often give different partition results. However, in papers dealing with gene expression analysis, very seldom are the specificities of the k-means algorithm described. For the purposes of this study, the following k-means variants were used: Forgy's, Jancey's, convergent, and MacQueen's [2].

The classical Forgy's k-means algorithm consists of the following steps: *i)* begin with any desired initial configuration. Go to *ii)* if beginning with a set of seed objects, or go to *iii)* if beginning with a partition of the dataset. *ii)* allocate each object to the cluster with the nearest (most similar) seed object (centroid). The seed objects remain fixed for a full cycle through the entire dataset. *iii)* Compute new centroids of the clusters. *iv)* alternate *ii)* and *iii)* until the process converges (that is, until no objects change their cluster membership). In Jancey's variant, the first set of cluster seed objects is either given or computed as the centroids of clusters in the initial partition. At all succeeding stages each new seed point is found by reflecting the old one through the new centroid for the cluster. MacQueen's method is composed of the following steps: *i)* take the first k data units as clusters of one member each. *ii)* assign each of the remaining objects to the cluster with the nearest (most similar) centroid. After each assignment, recompute the centroid of the gaining cluster. *iii)* after all objects have been assigned in step *ii)*, take the existing cluster centroids as fixed points and make one more pass through the dataset assigned each object to the nearest (most similar) seed object. A so called convergent k-means is defined by the following steps: *i)* begin with an initial partition like in Forgy's and Jancey's methods (or the output of MacQueen's method). *ii)* take each object in sequence and compute the distances (similarities) to all cluster centroids; if the nearest (most similar) is not that of the object's parent cluster, reassign the object and update the centroids of the losing and gaining clusters. *iii)* repeat steps *ii)* and *iii)* until convergence is achieved (that is, until there is no change in cluster membership).

The leader and the k-means algorithms were used with a similarity measure rather than with a distance. In particular Gower's general coefficient was used [3], where the similarity [4] between objects i and j is given by $S_{ij} = \sum_{k=1}^{p} s_{ijk} / \sum_{k=1}^{p} w_{ijk}$ where the weight of the attribute (w_{ijk}) is set equal to 0 or 1 depending on whether the comparison is considered valid for attribute k. For quantitative attributes (like the ones of the dataset used in the paper), the scores s_{ijk} are assigned as $s_{ijk} = 1 - |X_{ik} - X_{jk}|/R_k$, where X_{ik} is the value of attribute k for object i (similarly for object j), and R_k is the range of attribute k.

2.2 Rough Sets

The Rough Set Theory [5] bears on the assumption that in order to define a set, some knowledge about the elements of the data set is needed. This is in contrast to the classical approach where a set is uniquely defined by its elements. In the Rough Set Theory, some elements may be indiscernible from the point of view of the available information and it turns out that vagueness and uncertainty are strongly related to indiscernibility. Within this theory, knowledge is understood to be the ability of characterizing all classes of the classification. More specifically, an information system is a pair $\mathbf{A} = (U, A)$ where U is a non-empty finite set called the universe and A is a non-empty finite set of attributes such that $a : U \to V_a$ for every $a \in A$. The set V_a is called the value set of a. For example, a decision table is any information system of the form $\mathbf{A} = (U, A \cup \{d\})$, where $d \in A$ is the decision attribute and the elements of A are the condition attributes. For any $B \subseteq A$ an equivalence relation $IND(B)$ defined as $IND(B) = \{(x, x') \in U^2 | \forall a \in B, a(x) = a(x')\}$, is associated. In the Rough Set Theory a pair of precise concepts (called lower and upper approximations) replaces each vague concept; the lower approximation of a concept consists of all objects, which surely belong to the concept, whereas the upper approximation of the concept consists of all objects, which possibly belong to the concept. A *reduct* is a minimal set of attributes $B \subseteq A$ such that $IND(B) = IND(A)$ (i.e. a minimal attribute subset that preserves the partitioning of the universe). The set of all reducts of an information system $\mathbf{A}$ is denoted $RED(A)$. Reduction of knowledge consists of removing superfluous partitions such that the set of elementary categories in the information system is preserved, in particular, w.r.t. those categories induced by the decision attribute. In particular, minimum reducts (those with a small number of attributes), are extremely important, as decision rules can be constructed from them [6]. However, the problem of reduct computation is NP-hard, and several heuristics have been proposed [7].

2.3   Experimental Methodology

The datasets consist of information systems with an attribute set composed of ratio and interval variables, and a nominal or ordinal decision attribute. More general information systems have been described in [8]. The general idea is to construct subsets of relatively similar attributes, such that a simplified representation of the data objects is obtained by using the corresponding attribute subset representatives. The attributes of these simplified information systems are explored from the point of view of their reducts. From them, rules are learned and applied systematically to testing data subsets not involved in the learning process (Fig-1). The whole procedure can be seen as a pipeline.

In a first step, the objects in the dataset are shuffled using a randomized approach in order to reduce the possible biases introduced within the learning process by data chunks sharing the same decision attribute. Then, the attributes of the shuffled dataset are clustered using the two families of fast clustering algorithms described in previous sections (the leader, and k-means). Each of the formed clusters of attributes is represented by exactly one of the original data attributes. By the nature of the leader algorithm, the representative is the leader (called an *l-leader*), whereas for a k-means algorithm, a cluster is represented by the most similar object w.r.t. the centroid of the corresponding cluster (called a *k-leader*). This operation can be seen as a filtering of the attribute set of the original information system. As a next step, the filtered information

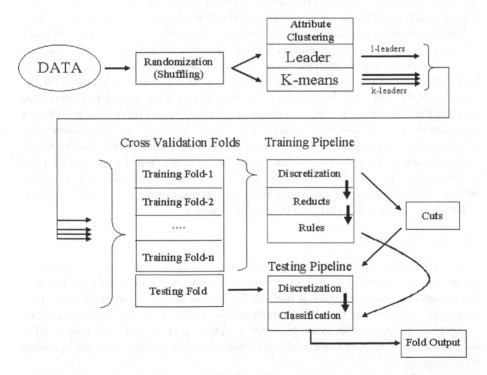

Fig. 1. Data processing strategy combining clustering with Rough Sets analysis and cross validation

system undergoes a segmentation with the purpose of learning classification rules, and testing their generalization ability in a cross-validation framework. N-folds are used as training sets; where the numeric attributes present are converted into nominal attributes via a discretization process (many possibilities exist), and from them, reducts are constructed. Finally, classification rules are built from the reducts, and applied to a discretized version of the test fold (according to the cuts obtained previously), from which the generalization ability of the generated rules can be evaluated. Besides the numeric descriptors associated with the application of classification rules to data, use of visual data mining techniques, like the virtual reality representation (section 2.4), enables structural understanding of the data described in terms of the selected subset of attributes and/or the rules learned from them. Each stage feeds its results to the next stage of processing, yielding a pipelined data analysis stream.

2.4   Virtual Reality Representation of Relational Structures

A virtual reality, visual, data mining technique extending the concept of 3D modelling to relational structures was introduced in http://www.hybridstrategies.com and [9]. It is oriented to the understanding of *i)* large heterogeneous, incomplete and imprecise data, and *ii)* symbolic knowledge. The notion of data is not restricted to databases, but includes logical relations and other forms of both structured and non-structured knowledge. In this approach, the data objects are considered as tuples from a heterogeneous space [8], given by a Cartesian product of different source sets like: nominal, ordinal, real-valued, fuzzy-valued, image-valued, time-series-valued, graph-valued, etc. A set of relations of different arities may be defined over these objects. The construction of a VR-space requires the specification of several sets and a collection of extra mappings, which may be defined in infinitely many ways. A desideratum for the VR-space is to keep as many properties from the original space as possible, in particular, the similarity structure of the data [10]. In this sense, the objective of the mapping is to maximize some metric/non-metric structure preservation criteria [11], or minimize some measure of information loss. In a supervised approach, when a decision attribute is used explicitly, measures of class separability can be used for constructing virtual reality spaces with nonlinear features maximizing the differentiation of the data objects from the point of view of the classes of the decision attribute. This technique was used as a visual data mining aid for the interpretation of the datasets described only in terms of the subsets of attributes resulting from the data processing pipelines.

2.5   Implementation

A detailed perspective of data mining procedures provides insight into additional important issues to consider (e.g. storage/memory/communication/management/time/etc) when evaluating a computational methodology; consisting of combined techniques. This study presents one possible implementation, from which more software development may occur in order to integrate better and/or different tools. In addition, all of these issues become even more pronounced when, as in this study, a complex problem is investigated.

The implementation is in the paradigm of a high throughput pipeline (Fig-2) consisting of many co-operating programs, which was automatically generated. The file

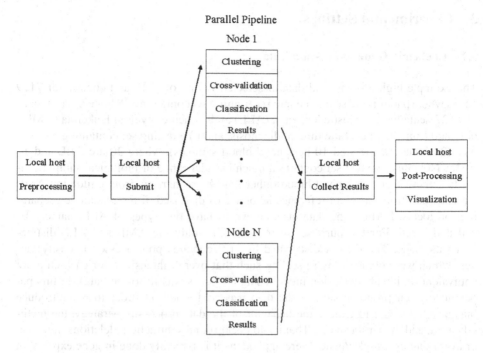

Fig. 2. Automatically generated high throughput pipeline oriented towards the Condor distributed computing environment

generation program (written in Python and running on the local host) created a pipeline oriented towards Condor (http://www.cs.wisc.edu/condor/), a distributed computing environment developed by the Condor Research Project at the University of Wisconsin-Madison (UW-Madison). Condor is a specialized workload management system for compute-intensive jobs. Like other full-featured batch systems, Condor provides a job queueing mechanism, scheduling policy, priority scheme, resource monitoring, and resource management.

The initial preprocessing stage of the pipe, occurring on the local host after generation of files, involves shuffling the input data records as described previously and in Fig-1. The shuffled data is stored on the local host's disk, in order to provide the same randomized data to the next stage of processing, which occurs on the remote hosts (Fig- 2).

A Condor submission program, which was also automatically generated, is used to specify all of the data and configuration files for the programs that will execute on the remote host. The submission process enables Condor to *i)* schedule jobs for execution, *ii)* check point them (put a job on hold), *iii)* transfer all data to the remote host, and *iv)* transfer all generated data back to the local host (submitting machine).

The final postprocessing stage of the pipe involves collecting all of the results (parsing the files) and reporting them in a database. These results may then be queried and visualized using a high dimensional visualization system (as described in the VR section above) for the purpose of aiding results interpretation.

3 Experimental Settings

3.1 Leukemia Gene Expression Data

The example high dimensional dataset selected is that of [12], and consists of 7129 genes where patients are separated into i) a training set containing 38 bone marrow samples: 27 acute lymphoblastic leukemia (ALL) and 11 acute myeloid leukemia (AML), obtained from patients at the time of diagnosis, and ii) a testing set containing 34 samples (24 bone marrow and 10 peripheral blood samples), where 20 are ALL and 14 AML. Note that, the test set contains a much broader range of biological samples, including those from peripheral blood rather than bone marrow, from childhood AML patients, and from different reference laboratories that used different sample preparation protocols. Further, the dataset is known to have two types of ALL, namely B-cell and T-cell. For the purposes of investigation, only the AML and ALL distinction was made. The dataset distributed by [12] contains preprocessed intensity values, which were obtained by re-scaling such that overall intensities for each chip are equivalent (A linear regression model using all genes was fit to the data). In this paper no explicit preprocessing of the data was performed, in order to not introduce bias and to be able to expose the behavior of the data processing strategy, the methods used, and their robustness. That is, no background subtraction, deletions, filtering, or averaging of samples/genes were applied, as it is typically done in gene expression experiments.

3.2 Settings

The pipeline (Fig-1) was investigated through the generation of 480 k-leader and 160 l-leader for a total of 640 experiments (Table-1).

The discretization, reduct computation and rule generation algorithms are those included in the Rosetta system [13]. This approach leads to the generation of 74 files per experiment, with 10-fold cross-validation.

Table 1. The set of parameters and values used in the experiments using the distributed pipeline environment

Algorithm/Parameter	Values
Leader	ReverseSearch, ClosestSearch
Leader Similarity Threshold	0.7, 0.8, 0.9, 0.95, 0.99, 0.999, 0.9999, 0.99999
K-Means	Forgy, Jancey, Convergent, MacQueen
Cross-validation	10 folds
Discretization	BROrthogonalScaler, EntropyScaler, NaiveScaler, SemiNaiveScaler
Reduct Computation	JohnsonReducer, Holte1RReducer
Rule Generation	RSESRuleGenerator

4   Results

From the experiments completed so far, one was chosen which illustrates the kind of results obtained with the explored methodology. It corresponds to a leader clustering algorithm with a similarity threshold of 0.99 (leading to 766 l-leader attributes), used as input to the data processing pipeline containing 38 samples. The results of the best 10 fold cross-validated experiment has a mean accuracy of 0.925 and a standard deviation of 0.168. This experiment led to 766 reducts (all of them singleton attributes), which was consistent across each of the 10 folds. The obtained classification accuracy represents a slight improvement over those results reported in [14] (0.912). It was conjectured in that study that the introduction of a cross-validated methodology could improve the obtained classification accuracies, which is indeed the case. It is interesting to observe that all of the 7 relevant attributes (genes) reported in [14] are contained (subsumed) within the single experiment mentioned above. Moreover, they were collectively found using both the leader and k-means algorithms, with different dissimilarity thresholds and number of clusters, whereas with the present approach, a single leader clustering input was required to get the better result. Among the relevant attributes (genes) obtained, many coincide with those reported by [12], [15], and [14].

At a post-processing stage, a virtual reality representation of the above mentioned experiment is shown in Fig-3. Due to the limitations of representing an interactive vir-

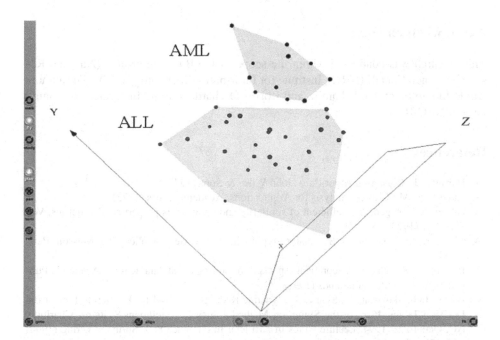

Fig. 3. Snapshot of the Virtual Reality representation of the union of all of the reducts obtained from 10 fold cross-validation input (38 samples with 766 genes). The leader clustering algorithm was used with a similarity threshold of 0.99. The ALL and the AML classes are perfectly separated. Representation error = 0.0998.

tual world on static media, a snapshot from an appropriate perspective is presented. Sammon's error [11] was used as criteria for computing the virtual reality space, and also Gower's similarity was used for characterizing the data in the space of the 766 selected genes. After 200 iterations a satisfactory error level of 0.0998 was obtained. It is interesting to see that the ALL and AML classes can be clearly differentiated.

5 Conclusions

Good results were obtained with the proposed high throughput pipeline based on the combination of clustering and rough sets techniques for the discovery of relevant attributes in high dimensional data. In particular, the introduction of a fast attribute reduction procedure aided rough set reduct discovery in terms of computational time, of which the former is further improvable via its amenability for parallel and distributed computing. Cross-validated experiments using Leukemia gene expression data demonstrates the possibilities of the proposed approach. More thorough studies are required to correctly evaluate the impact of the experimental settings on the data mining effectivity. Visual exploration of the results (when focusing on selected genes) was very useful for understanding the properties of the pipeline outputs, and the relationships between the discovered attributes and the class structure. Further experiments with this approach are necessary.

Acknowledgements

This research was conducted within the scope of the BioMine project (National Research Council Canada (NRC), Institute for Information Technology (IIT)). The authors would like to thank Fazel Famili, and Robert Orchard from the Integrated Reasoning Group (NRC-IIT).

References

1. Hartigan, J.: Clustering Algorithms. John Wiley & Sons (1975)
2. Anderberg, M.: Cluster Analysis for Applications. Academic Press (1973)
3. Gower, J.C.: A general coefficient of similarity and some of its properties. Biometrics, Vol. 1, No. 27 (1973) 857–871
4. Chandon, J.L. and Pinson, S.: Analyse typologique. Théorie et applications: Masson, Paris (1981)
5. Pawlak, Z.: Rough sets: Theoretical aspects of reasoning about data. Kluwer Academic Publishers, Dordrecht, Netherlands (1991)
6. Bazan, J.G., Skowron, A., Synak, P.: Dynamic Reducts as a Tool for Extracting Laws from Decision Tables. Proc. of the Symp. on Methodologies for Intelligent Systems. Charlotte, NC, Oct. 16-19 1994. Lecture Notes in Artificial Intelligence 869, Springer-Verlag (1994) 346–355
7. Wróblewski, J.: Ensembles of Classifiers Based on Approximate Reducts. Fundamenta Informaticae 47 IOS Press, (2001), 351–360
8. Valdés, J.J.: Similarity-Based Heterogeneous Neurons in the Context of General Observational Models. Neural Network World. Vol 12, No. 5 (2002) 499–508

9. Valdés, J.J.: Virtual Reality Representation of Relational Systems and Decision Rules: An exploratory Tool for understanding Data Structure. In Theory and Application of Relational Structures as Knowledge Instruments. Meeting of the COST Action 274 (Hajek, P. Ed). Prague, November 14-16 (2002)

10. Borg, I. and Lingoes, J.: Multidimensional similarity structure analysis. Springer-Verlag, New York, NY (1987)

11. Sammon, J.W.: A non-linear mapping for data structure analysis. IEEE Trans. on Computers C18 (1969) 401–409

12. Golub, T.R., etal.: Molecular classification of cancer: class discovery and class prediction by gene expression monitoring. Science, Vol. 286 (1999) 531–537

13. Øhrn, A. and Komorowski, J.: Rosetta- A Rough Set Toolkit for the Analysis of Data. Proc. of Third Int. Join Conf. on Information Sciences (JCIS97), Durham, NC, USA, March 1-5 (1997) 403–407

14. Valdés, J.J. and Barton, A.J.: Gene Discovery in Leukemia Revisited: A Computational Intelligence Perspective. Proceedings of the 17th International Conference on Industrial & Engineering Applications of Artificial Intelligence & Expert Systems, May 17-20, 2004, Ottawa, Canada. Lecture Notes in Artificial Intelligence LNAI 3029, Springer-Verlag, (2004) 118–127

15. Famili, F. and Ouyang, J.: Data mining: understanding data and disease modeling. In Proceedings of the 21st IASTED International Conference, Applied Informatics, Innsbruck, Austria, Feb. 10-13, (2003) 32–37

A Hybrid Approach to MR Imaging Segmentation Using Unsupervised Clustering and Approximate Reducts

Sebastian Widz[1], Kenneth Revett[2], and Dominik Ślęzak[3]

[1] Deforma Sebastian Widz, Warsaw, Poland
[2] University of Westminster, London, UK
[3] University of Regina, Regina, Canada

Abstract. We introduce a hybrid approach to magnetic resonance image segmentation using unsupervised clustering and the rules derived from approximate decision reducts. We utilize the MRI phantoms from the Simulated Brain Database. We run experiments on randomly selected slices from a volumetric set of multi-modal MR images (T1, T2, PD). Segmentation accuracy reaches 96% for the highest resolution images and 89% for the noisiest image volume. We also tested the resultant classifier on real clinical data, which yielded an accuracy of approximately 84%.

Keywords: MRI segmentation, rough sets, approximate decision reducts, self-organizing maps, magnitude histogram clustering.

1 Introduction

Segmentation is the process of assigning the class labels to data containing spatially varying information. For Magnetic Resonance Imaging (MRI), we have a 3D data set (a volume) collected as a series of 2D slices. The goal is to classify every voxel within a slice to one of the tissue classes. We focus on three classes of a clinical interest: cerebrospinal fluid (CSF), grey matter (GM), and white matter (WM). It has been demonstrated repeatedly in the literature that relative distribution of these classes is diagnostic for specific diseases such as stroke, Alzheimer's disease, various forms of dementia, and multiple sclerosis [6,7]. An automated method for segmenting tissue would provide a useful adjunct to clinical radiology for the effective diagnosis of disease.

Rough sets [1,9,14] provide powerful methodology for constructing classification models, useful also for image segmentation (cf. [5]). In our approach, we create a decision table with objects corresponding to voxels and decisions derived from the Simulated Brain Database (SBD) of fully segmented images[1] [2,12]. To define conditional attributes, we employ two unsupervised clustering algorithms – the self-organizing map and our own, simple method for the

---

[1] Provided by Montreal Neurological Institute http://www.bic.mni.mcgill.ca/ brainweb

D. Ślęzak et al. (Eds.): RSFDGrC 2005, LNAI 3642, pp. 372–382, 2005.

magnitude histogram clustering. Using an order-based genetic algorithm (o-GA) [4,22], we search for the optimal R-approximate reducts – irreducible subsets of conditional attributes, which approximately preserve the data-based global relative gain of decision [17,18]. From the best found reducts we generate (possibly inexact) "if...then..." rules applicable to classification of voxels in new slices.

There are several imaging parameters that affect resolution of MRI: slice thickness, noise levels, bias field inhomogeneities (INU), partial volume effects, imaging modality. These factors should be incorporated into an automated segmentation system in order for it be clinically relevant. Hence, we verify the usage of reducts learned over the slices from a high resolution image volume (1mm, 3% noise, 20% INU) also for images with possibly higher noise (up to 9%) and INU (up to 40%). Comparing to our previous research [19,20], where the obtained decision rules were tested only against the SBD data, we applied our segmentation algorithm on real clinical images (T2-weighted, 5mm thick slices with relatively low noise and bias). Despite differences in characteristics of the training and testing images, we obtained a segmentation accuracy of approximately 84% on clinical images. We believe this is a result of both appropriately derived attributes and robustness of short rules induced from approximate reducts.

The paper is organized as follows: In Section 2, we describe the basic data preparation techniques. In Section 3, we introduce the details of the applied unsupervised clustering algorithms. In Section 4 we discuss the foundations of the applied approximate attribute reduction method. In Section 4, we present the experimental results. In Section 5 we summarize our work.

2   Data Preparation

The primary source of information obtainable from an MR Image is the magnitude value for a given voxel. For reasonably good MR images, for every considered modality, the voxels form a series of Gaussian distributions corresponding to the tissue classes. In a typical MR image of the brain, there are generally the following classes: bone, Cerebral Spinal Fluid (CSF), Grey Matter (GM), White Matter (WM), as well as fat, skin, muscle and background. An example of magnitude histogram is illustrated in Fig. 1. In this study, we focus on CSF, GM, and WM exclusively. Therefore, the first processing step was to remove all voxels that do not belong to the actual brain. Background is removed automatically by applying a simple mask algorithm. Bone, fat, skin and muscles are removed manually, basing on information about the SBD image crisp phantom.

To apply the segmentation procedure based on decision rules derived from data, we must first generate the training data set. Following the standards developed within the theory of rough sets [14], we form a decision table $\mathbb{A} = (U, A \cup \{d\})$, where each attribute $a \in A \cup \{d\}$ is a function $a : U \to V_a$ from the universe U into the value set V_a. The elements of U are voxels taken from MR images. Each SBD data set is a series of 181 217x181 images. We use a range <61;130> of slices where we have good representation of all tissue classes. The decision attribute $d \notin A$ represents the ground truth, which is necessary during

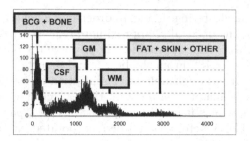

Fig. 1. A single bin frequency histogram from a T1 SBD slice #81 (1mm slice thickness, 3% noise and 20% INU). The x-axis values are 12 bit-unsigned integers, corresponding to the magnitude of the voxels from the raw image data. The histogram's peaks are likely to correspond to particular decision/tissue classes.

the classifier training phase. The set A should contain the attributes labeling the voxels with respect to the available MRI modalities. Further, we characterize the method we employed to extract the attributes in A from the MRI images.

Edge attributes are denoted by $edgeT1$, $edgeT2$, $edgePD$. They are derived using a simple *Discrete Laplacian* method – a general non-directional gradient operator determining whether the neighborhood of a voxel is homogenous. For instance, $edgeT1$ takes the value 0 for a given voxel, if its neighborhood for T1 is homogeneous, and 1 otherwise. We apply the 3x3 window to determine the voxel neighbors. We use a threshold determined by the noise level parameter estimated by running various tests on T1, T2 and PD training images, respectively. For each parameter value at the range [0,0.5] we run a test measuring correctness of recognized edges versus the phantom edges. Generally, the optimal noise parameter setting for T1 is 0.08, while for T2 and PD it is 0.13. The edge attributes provide information that may be subject to a *partial volume effect* (PVE) – It can be used also in the future studies on PVE.

Magnitude attributes are denoted by $hcMagT1$, $hcMagT2$, $hcMagPD$, as well as $somMagT1$, $somMagT2$, $somMagPD$. They are derived using the *histogram clustering algorithm* HCLUSTER (prefix 'hc') and self-organizing map SOM (prefix 'som') for all three image modalities. SOM and HCLUSTER perform the unsupervised segmentation of the image – they are discussed later in Section 3. The results of such segmentation are recorded as the corresponding attribute values. In our previous work [19,20], we employed a manually based approach using polynomial interpolation to find the *Full-Width Half-Maximum* (FWHM) value for each of the histogram peaks (cf. [2]). We find HCLUSTER and SOM techniques more autonomous and accurate than FWHM.

Neighbor attributes are denoted by $hcNbrT1$, $hcNbrT2$, $hcNbrPD$, as well as $somNbrT1$, $somNbrT2$, $somNbrPD$, They are derived as follows:

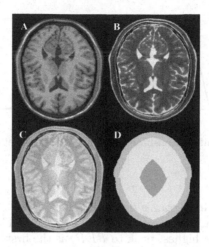

Fig. 2. Modalities T1 (Picture A), T2 (B), and PD (C) from the SBD slice #81 (thickness 1mm, 3% noise, 20% INU). Picture D presents the mask obtained for this case.

If ($EDGE == 0$)
    NBR = the same class as in case of the MAG attribute
Else // $EDGE == 1$
    NBR = major class value appearing in the neighborhood

Naturally, for hc-attributes we use the class values derived from the HCLUSTER algorithm, and for som-attributes – those provided by SOM. For example, the value of $hcNbrT1$ is calculated from $edgeT1$ (EDGE) and $hcMagT1$ (MAG).

Mask attribute is denoted as msk. It is used to mask the brain area. It can happen that two different tissues have similar voxel value and appear on the histogram in one peak. Knowing the relative position of a voxel may help in removing the resulting classification ambiguity. It provides us with extra information about the voxel location (e.g. CSF tissue is located more in the middle of the brain). For the exact algorithm of deriving the mask values we refer to our previous work [19,20]. Here, we illustrate its appearance in Fig. 2D.

3 Histogram Clustering and Self-organizing Maps

We propose a simple method for clustering the magnitude histograms, referred as HCLUSTER. Let us denote the value of the i-th histogram's position by h_i. We define the distance $dist(i, j)$ between positions i and j as the length of the path between points (i, h_i) and (j, h_j) with the histogram. Let's assume that $i < j$. We have $dist(i, j) = \sum_{k=i}^{j-1} \sqrt{1 + (h_k - h_{k+1})^2}$, as illustrated by Figure 3. The algorithm is controlled by parameters α and β, which influence the number of found clusters, as well as sensitivity to the histogram's peaks.

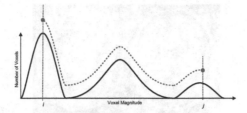

Fig. 3. Illustration of histogram-based distance $dist(i, j)$ between positions i and j

(α, β)-HCLUSTER

1. Let DOM be the histogram's domain, REP – the set of the cluster representatives, and CAN – the set of candidates. Put $CAN = DOM$, $REP = \emptyset$.
2. Add position of the highest peak to REP, as the first cluster representative.
3. *while* $(\max_{i \in CAN} (\min_{j \in REP} dist(i, j) + \alpha * h_i) \geq \beta)$
   $i_{rep} = argmax_{i \in CAN} (\min_{j \in REP} dist(i, j) + \alpha * h_i)$
   $CAN = CAN \setminus \{i_{rep}\}$
   $REP = REP \cup \{i_{rep}\}$
4. Put every element of DOM to the cluster corresponding to its closest (due to distance $dist$) element of REP.

For every modality, the obtained cluster numbers correspond to the magnitude attribute values in the decision table. For instance, if the PD-magnitude of the given voxel $u \in U$ drops into the 3rd cluster (counting from left hand side of the PD's histogram), then we get the value $hcMagPD(u) = 2$.

The self-organizing map (SOM) is employed to automate the association of a class label based on the magnitude of a voxel in a similar way as HCLUSTER. The network consists of 12 nodes, each initialized with normalized random weights. The inputs are normalized magnitude values of voxels extracted from images. The whole framework may work with either single or multiple modalities, although, in this paper, we apply it only separately to T1, T2 and PD.

The SOM is trained on a single row in the middle of the randomly selected slice from SBD. The weights are updated using the least mean square algorithm. The training is terminated when the error is below a user specified level (0.01). After training, the network is used to classify and generate values for $somMag$ and $somNbr$ attributes for all voxels within the given volume.

Due to space constraints, we do not discuss how to adjust parameters of the self-organizing map (like neighborhood, learning rate, maximum number of learning cycles, etc.) and HCLUSTER (α and β). In the same way, we will not discuss parameters of the genetic algorithm described in the next section. All these settings are adjusted due to our experience with data processing.

4   Approximate Reduction

When modeling complex phenomena, one must strike a balance between accuracy and computational complexity. This balance can be achieved through the use of a *decision reduct*: an irreducible subset $B \subseteq A$ determining d in decision table $\mathbb{A} = (U, A \cup \{d\})$. The obtained decision reducts are used to produce the decision rules from the training data. Reducts generating smaller number of rules seem to be better as the corresponding rules are more general and applicable.

Sometimes it is better to remove more attributes to get even shorter rules at the cost of their slight inconsistencies. One can specify an arbitrary data-based measure M which evaluates a degree of influence $M(d/B)$ of subsets $B \subseteq A$ on d. Then one can decide which attributes may be removed from A without a *significant* loss of M. Given the approximation threshold $\varepsilon \in [0, 1)$, let us say that $B \subseteq A$ is an (M, ε)-*approximate decision reduct*, if and only if it satisfies inequality $M(d/B) \geq (1 - \varepsilon) * M(d/A)$ and none of its proper subsets does it. For an advanced study on such reducts we refer the reader to [15,16]. Here we consider the *multi-decision relative gain measure* [17,18]:

$$R(d/B) = \sum_{\text{rules } r \text{ induced by } B} \left(\frac{\text{number of objects recognizable by } r}{\text{number of objects in } U} * \right.$$

$$\left. \max_i \frac{\text{probability of the } i\text{-th decision class induced by } r}{\text{prior probability of the } i\text{-th decision class}} \right) \quad (1)$$

Measure (1) expresses the average gain in determining decision classes under the evidence provided by the rules generated by $B \subseteq A$. It can be used, e.g., to evaluate the potential influence of a particular attributes on the decision. The quantities of $R(d/\{a\})$, $a \in A$, reflect the average information gain obtained from one-attribute rules. They are, however, not enough to select the *subsets* of relevant attributes. For instance, several attributes $a \in A$ with low values of $R(d/\{a\})$ can create together a subset $B \subseteq A$ with high $R(d/B)$.

The problems of finding approximate reducts are generally hard (cf. [15]). Therefore, for the decision table with attributes described in the previous sections, we prefer to consider the use of a heuristic rather than an exhaustive search. We adapt the *order based genetic algorithm (o-GA)* for searching for minimal decision reducts [22] to find heuristically (sub)optimal (R, ε)-approximate decision reducts. We follow the same way of extension as that proposed in [16], also used by ourselves in the previous papers on MRI segmentation [19,20]. As a *hybrid algorithm* [4], the applied o-GA consists of two parts:

1. *Genetic part*, where each chromosome encodes a permutation of attributes
2. *Heuristic part*, where permutations τ are put into the following algorithm:

(R, ε)-REDORD algorithm (cf. [16,22])

1. Let $\mathbb{A} = (U, A \cup \{d\})$ and $\tau : \{1, .., |A|\} \to \{1, .., |A|\}$ be given; Let $B_\tau = A$;
2. For $i = 1$ to $|A|$ repeat steps 3 and 4;
3. Let $B_\tau \leftarrow B_\tau \setminus \{a_{\tau(i)}\}$;
4. If B_τ does not satisfy inequality $R(d/B) \geq (1 - \varepsilon) * R(d/A)$, undo step 3.

We define fitness of a given permutation-individual τ due to the quality of B_τ resulting from (R, ε)-REDORD. As mentioned before, we would like to focus on reducts inducing possibly low numbers of rules. Therefore, we use the following:

$$fitness(\tau) = 1 - \frac{\text{number of rules derived from } B_\tau}{\text{number of rules derived from the whole set } A} \quad (2)$$

To work on permutations-individuals, we use the order cross-over (OX) and the standard mutation switching randomly selected genes [4,13]. It is important that the results are *always* (R, ε)-approximate decision reducts.

5 Results of Experiments

All the classification tests were performed using the following procedure:

1. Generate the approximate reducts using o-GA based on (R, ε)-REDORD for a given $\varepsilon \in [0, 1)$. Leave out ten reducts related to the best fitness (2).
2. For every reduct (out of ten left) generate (possibly inexact) decision rules. Filter the rules according to their coverage measure.
3. For every new voxel, vote using the confidence of all applicable rules.

Reducts and rules were generated using 10 slices chosen randomly from the SBD database, for the slice range [61, 130], 1mm thickness, 3% noise, and 20% INU. The resulting classifier were tested against 20 slices (always different than those chosen for training) from the same range, taken from the following volumes:

- Volume 1: 1mm thickness, 3% noise, 20% INU
- Volume 2: 1mm thickness, 9% noise, 20% INU
- Volume 3: 1mm thickness, 9% noise, 40% INU

Obviously, the segmentation is more challenging when applied to slices with a higher noise/INU. Figure 4 presents the average (for 10 experiments repeated with different training/testing slices) accuracy (the number of correctly recognized voxels divided by the number of total number of voxels) and coverage (the number of recognized voxels divided by the total number of voxels).

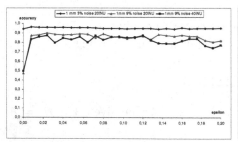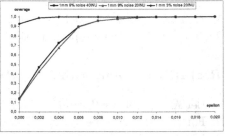

Fig. 4. Accuracy and coverage for the SBD volumes 1,2,3, given different values of ε

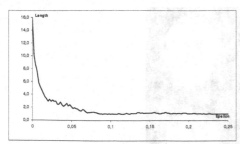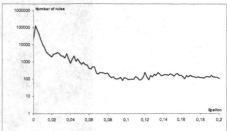

Fig. 5. Average reduct length and number of generated rules for different values of ε

	Manual Segm.		Autom. Segm.	
Tissue Category	Image 1	Image 2	Image 1	Image 2
Whole Brain	5080	5058	5114	5170
CSF	280	541	200 (1.6%)	403 (2.8%)
GM	2382	2457	2801 (8.2%)	2777 (6.3%)
WM	2409	1707	2113 (5.8%)	2090 (7.6%)
Total Error			15.5%	16.7%

Fig. 6. Comparison between manual and automated segmentation on the T2-weighted axial images. The values in the segmentation columns refers to the total number of voxels n that class and the values in parentheses represents the difference between the manual and automated classification (the associated error) expressed as a percentage of the total number of manually segmented (clinical) voxels.

For this particular data, given $\varepsilon = 0$, there is only one reduct – the set of all attributes. The corresponding rules are then too specific and, therefore, coverage is very low. While increasing ε, the reducts become shorter and the number of generated rules decreases, as shown in Figure 5. Coverage grows fast to 1.00 (note that in Figure 4 the range for coverage is 0.00-0.02, while the range for accuracy is 0.0-0.2). The best accuracy is obtained for the following settings:

- Volume 1: 96% for $\varepsilon = 0.010$
- Volume 2: 91% for $\varepsilon = 0.052$
- Volume 3: 88% for $\varepsilon = 0.108$

Let us note that the above results are significantly better than those obtained in [19,20] (95.1%, 84.4%, 78.7%) using the FWHM-based attributes. Also notice that when the noise and INU increase, higher ε gives better performance.

We tested the segmentation accuracy also on a sample of T2-weighted images acquired from a clinical environment. The images were acquired using a transmit and receive birdcage head coil imaged in the axial plane, using an interleaved spin-echo pulse sequence (TR = 130 ms and TE = 3000 ms), 96x96 matrix, slice thickness of 5mm with 1mm inter-slice gap, field of view = 24x24cm with an in-plane resolution of 3.24mm^2 (1.8 x 1.8mm). No preprocessing of the images was performed. Manual segmentation was performed by a domain expert. Differences

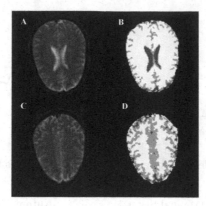

Fig. 7. Real T2-weighted images (A,C) and corresponding segmentation results (B,D)

between the classifier based segmented tissue classes and clinical tissue classes are reported in Fig. 6. Segmented images are illustrated in Fig. 7.

6   Conclusions and Discussion

The segmentation algorithm developed in this paper was tested on the SBD data sets, producing a maximal accuracy on the order of 96%. We also tested the accuracy of the rule set generated from training on the SBD volumes on real clinically derived T2-weighted images, producing the average accuracy ca. 84%. The primary factor influencing the classification accuracy of the clinical images appears to be directly related to partial volume effect (PVE) – as most voxels that were misclassified were edge voxels – principally between GM and CSF and also between GM and WM. These edge effects are difficult to manually classify – as the domain expert also will face difficulties in deciding, without any preprocessing of the images – which category a voxel belongs to.

A favorable factor is that any errors produced by PVE will be systematic – and with respect to comparing segmentation results – one would expect the bias to occur consistently between manual and artificially segmented images. In order to reduce this burden on segmentation accuracy, and to improve the accuracy of our automated segmentation algorithm, we will employ methods that reduce the partial volume effect in our future work. We also plan to train the system on more different data sets. We think that doing that and tuning the parameters better would significantly improve the results.

Our automated MR image segmentation was substantially improved comparing to previous version [19,20]. A principal change is the automation of the magnitude attribute extraction, previously performed manually through the use of a polynomial interpolation technique. We implemented two automated unsupervised clustering techniques: one based on a derivation of histogram clustering and the other based on a self-organizing map. Because of the lack of space, we did not present the results related to relative importance of the obtained attributes in reducts and rules. Our general observation is that the best classification performance is provided by diversified ensembles of the attribute sets, generated from both applied clustering methods in the same time.

Acknowledgments. The third author was partially supported by the research grant of the Natural Sciences and Engineering Research Council of Canada.

References

1. Bazan, J.G., Nguyen, H.S., Nguyen, S.H, Synak, P., Wróblewski, J.: Rough Set Algorithms in Classification Problem. In: Polkowski, L., Tsumoto, S., Lin, T.Y. (eds): Rough Set Methods and Applications: New Developments in Knowledge Discovery in Information Systems. Physica Verlag (2000) pp. 49–88.
2. Cocosco, C.A., Zijdenbos, A.P., Evans, A.C.: Automatic Generation of Training Data for Brain Tissue Classification from MRI. In: Proc. of MICCAI'2002 (2002).
3. Collins, D.L., Zijdenbos, A.P., Kollokian, V., Sled, J.G., Kabani, N.J., Holmes, C.J., Evans, A.C.: Design and Construction of a Realistic Digital Brain Phantom IEEE Transactions on Medical Imaging 17(3) (1998) pp. 463–468.
4. Davis, L. (ed.): Handbook of Genetic Algorithms. Van Nostrand Reinhold (1991).
5. Hirano S.,Tsumoto S.: Segmentation of Medical Images Based on Approximations in Rough Set Theory. In: Proc. of RSCTC'2002. Malvern, USA (2002).
6. Kamber, M., Shinghal, R., Collins, L.: Model-based 3D Segmentation of Multiple Sclerosis Lesions in Magnetic Resonance Brain Images. IEEE Trans Med Imaging 14(3) (1995) pp. 442–453.
7. Kaus, M., Warfield, S.K., Nabavi, A., Black, P.M., Jolesz, F.A., Kikinis, R.: Automated Segmentation of MRI of Brain Tumors. Radiology 218 (2001) pp. 586–591.
8. Kollokian, V.: Performance Analysis of Automatic Techniques for Tissue Classification in Magnetic Resonance Images of the Human Brain. Master's thesis, Concordia University, Montreal, Canada (1996).
9. Komorowski, J., Pawlak, Z., Polkowski, L., Skowron, A.: Rough sets: A tutorial. In: S.K. Pal, A. Skowron (eds): Rough Fuzzy Hybridization – A New Trend in Decision Making. Springer Verlag (1999) pp. 3–98.
10. Kovacevic, N., Lobaugh, N.J., Bronskill, M.J., Levine, B., Feinstein, A., Black, S.E.: A Robust Extraction and Automatic Segmentation of Brain Images. NeuroImage 17 (2002) pp. 1087–1100.
11. Kwan, R.K.S., Evans, A.C., Pike, G.B.: An Extensible MRI Simulator for Post-Processing Evaluation. Visualization in Biomedical Computing (VBC'96). Lecture Notes in Computer Science, vol. 1131. Springer-Verlag, (1996) pp. 135–140
12. Kwan, R.K.S., Evans, A.C., Pike, G.B.: MRI Simulation-Based Evaluation of Image-Processing and Classification Methods. Neuroimage 10 (1999) pp. 417–429.
13. Michalewicz, Z.: Genetic Algorithms + Data Structures = Evolution Programs. Springer-Verlag (1994).
14. Pawlak, Z.: Rough sets – Theoretical aspects of reasoning about data. Kluwer (1991).
15. Ślęzak, D.: Approximate Entropy Reducts. Fundamenta Informaticae (2002).
16. Ślęzak, D., Wróblewski, J.: Order-based genetic algorithms for the search of approximate entropy reducts. In: Proc. of RSFDGrC'2003. Chongqing, China (2003).
17. Ślęzak, D., Ziarko, W.: Attribute Reduction in Bayesian Version of Variable Precision Rough Set Model. In: Proc. of RSKD'2003. Elsevier, ENTCS 82(4) (2003).

18. Ślęzak, D., Ziarko, W.: The investigation of the Bayesian rough set model. Int. J. of Approximate Reasoning, in press.
19. Widz, S., Revett, K., Ślęzak, D.: Application of Rough Set Based Dynamic Parameter Optimization to MRI Segmentation. In: Proc. of 23rd International Conference of the North American Fuzzy Information Processing Society (NAFIPS'2004). Banff, Canada, June 27-30 (2004).
20. Widz, S., Ślęzak, D., Revett, K.: An Automated Multispectral MRI Segmentation Algorithm Using Approximate Reducts. In: Proc. of the 4th International Conference on Rough Sets and Current Trends in Computing (RSCTC'2004). Uppsala, Sweden, June 1-5. Springer Verlag, LNAI 3066 (2004) pp. 815-824.
21. Vannier, M.W.: Validation of Magnetic Resonance Imaging (MRI) Multispectral Tissue Classification. Computerized Medical Imaging and Graphics 15(4) (1991) pp. 217-223.
22. Wróblewski, J.: Theoretical Foundations of Order-Based Genetic Algorithms. Fundamenta Informaticae 28(3-4) (1996) pp. 423-430.
23. Xue, J.H., Pizurica, A., Philips, W., Kerre, E., Van de Walle, R., Lemahieu, I.: An Integrated Method of Adaptive Enhancement for Unsupervised Segmentation of MRI Brain Images. Pattern Recognition Letters 24(15) (2003) pp. 2549-2560.

Analysis of Gene Expression Data: Application of Quantum-Inspired Evolutionary Algorithm to Minimum Sum-of-Squares Clustering

Wengang Zhou, Chunguang Zhou, Yanxin Huang, and Yan Wang

College of Computer Science and Technology, Jilin University,
Changchun 130012, P.R. China
wgzhou@email.jlu.edu.cn

Abstract. Microarray experiments have produced a huge amount of gene expression data. So it becomes necessary to develop effective clustering techniques to extract the fundamental patterns inherent in the data. In this paper, we propose a novel evolutionary algorithm so called quantum-inspired evolutionary algorithm (QEA) for minimum sum-of-squares clustering. We use a new representation form and add an additional mutation operation in QEA. Experiment results show that the proposed algorithm has better global search ability and is superior to some conventional clustering algorithms such as k-means and self-organizing maps.

1 Introduction

In the field of bioinformatics, clustering algorithms have received renewed attention due to the breakthrough of microarrays data. Microarrays experiments allow for the simultaneous monitoring of the expression patterns of thousands of genes. Since a huge amount of data is produced during microarray experiments, clustering methods are essential in the analysis of gene expression data. The goal is to extract the fundamental patterns inherent in the data and to partition the elements into subsets referred to as clusters. Two criteria should be satisfied: homogeneity - elements in the same cluster are highly similar to each other; and separation - elements from different clusters have low similarity to each other. In gene expression, elements are usually genes. The vector of each gene contains its expression levels under each of the monitored conditions.

Several clustering algorithms have been proposed for gene expression data analysis, such as hierarchical clustering [1], self-organizing maps [2], k-means [3], and some graph theoretic approaches: HCS, CAST, CLICK [4], MST [5], and many others. In general, these approaches can not be compared directly, since there is no unique measure quality.

In this paper, we propose a novel evolutionary algorithm so called quantum-inspired evolutionary algorithm (QEA) for minimum sum-of-squares clustering. Experiment results show that the proposed algorithm is superior to conventional clustering algorithms such as k-means and self-organizing maps.

D. Ślęzak et al. (Eds.): RSFDGrC 2005, LNAI 3642, pp. 383–391, 2005.

2   Minimum Sum-of-Squares Clustering

Clustering can be considered as a combinatorial optimization problem [6], in which an assignment of data vectors to clusters is desired, such that the sum of distance square of the vectors to their cluster mean (centroid) is minimal. Let P_k denote the set of all partitions of X with $X = \{x_1, \ldots, x_n\}$ denoting the data set of vectors with $x_i \in R^m$ and C_i denoting the i_{th} cluster with mean $\hat{x}_i$. Thus the objective function becomes:

$$min_{p \in P_k} \quad \sum_{i=1}^{K} \sum_{x_j \in C_i} d^2(x_j, \hat{x}_i) \tag{1}$$

$$with \quad \hat{x}_i = \frac{1}{|C_i|} \sum_{x_j \in C_i} x_j \tag{2}$$

where $d(.,.)$ is the Euclidean distance in R^m. Alternatively we can formulate the problem as the search for an assignment p of the vectors to the clusters with $C_i = j \in \{1, \ldots, n\} | p[j] = i$. Thus the objective function becomes:

$$min_p \quad \sum_{i=1}^{n} d^2(x_i, \hat{x}_{p[i]}) \tag{3}$$

This combinatorial optimization problem is called the minimum sum-of-squares clustering (MSSC) problem and has been proven to be NP-hard [7]. The k-means algorithm is a heuristic approach which minimizes the sum-of-squares criterion provided an initial assignment of centroids. It can in fact be regarded as a local search algorithm for this hard combinatorial optimization problem. This fact demonstrates the importance of effective global optimization methods from the field of evolutionary computation.

Since the novel quantum-inspired evolutionary algorithm has better global search ability and has been shown to be effective as compared to the conventional genetic algorithm [8], the application of QEA to the MSSC appears to be promising.

3   Quantum-Inspired Evolutionary Algorithm

Quantum-inspired evolutionary algorithm (QEA) is based on the concept and principles of quantum computing such as a quantum bit and superposition of states [9]. Like other evolutionary algorithms, QEA is also characterized by the representation of the individual, the evaluation function and the population dynamics. The smallest unit of information stored in a two-state quantum computer is called a quantum bit or qubit [10]. A qubit may be in the '1' state, in the '0' state, or in any superposition of the two. The state of a qubit can be represented as:

$$|\psi\rangle = \alpha|0\rangle + \beta|1\rangle \tag{4}$$

where α and β are complex numbers that specify the probability amplitudes of the corresponding states. $|\alpha|^2$ gives the probability that the qubit will be found in the '0' state and $|\beta|^2$ gives the probability that the qubit will be found in the '1' state. Normalization of the states to unity guarantees the following equation:

$$|\alpha|^2 + |\beta|^2 = 1 \tag{5}$$

A number of different representations can be used to encode the solutions onto individuals in evolutionary computation. Inspired by the concept of quantum computing, QEA uses a new representation, called a Q-bit, for the probabilistic representation that is based on the concept of qubits, and a Q-bit individual as a string of Q-bits. A Q-bit is defined as the smallest unit of information in QEA, which is defined with a pair of numbers (α, β) as $\begin{bmatrix} \alpha \\ \beta \end{bmatrix}$, where α and β satisfy the equation (2). A Q-bit individual is defined as:

$$\begin{bmatrix} \alpha_1 | \alpha_2 | \dots | \alpha_m \\ \beta_1 | \beta_2 | \dots | \beta_m \end{bmatrix} \tag{6}$$

The state of a Q-bit can be changed by the operation with a quantum gate, such as NOT gate, Rotation gate, and Hadamard gate, etc. Rotation gate is often used to update the Q-bit as follows:

$$\begin{bmatrix} \alpha_i' \\ \beta_i' \end{bmatrix} = \begin{bmatrix} \cos(\Delta\theta_i) & -\sin(\Delta\theta_i) \\ \sin(\Delta\theta_i) & \cos(\Delta\theta_i) \end{bmatrix} \begin{bmatrix} \alpha_i \\ \beta_i \end{bmatrix} \tag{7}$$

where $|\alpha_i|^2 + |\beta_i|^2 = 1$, $i = 1, 2, \dots, m$.

The angle parameters used for rotation gate are shown in Table 1. Where x_i and b_i are the i_{th} bit of the best solution b and the binary solution x respectively; $f(.)$ is the objective function defined in Eq. (3).

Table 1. The angle parameters used for rotation gate

x_i	b_i	$f(x) \geq f(b)$	$\Delta\theta_i$	x_i	b_i	$f(x) \geq f(b)$	$\Delta\theta_i$
0	0	false	θ_1	1	0	false	θ_5
0	0	true	θ_2	1	0	true	θ_6
0	1	false	θ_3	1	1	false	θ_7
0	1	true	θ_4	1	1	true	θ_8

The structure of QEA is described in the following:

Procedure QEA
begin
$t \leftarrow 0$
initialize $Q(t)$
make $P(t)$ by observing the states of $Q(t)$
evaluate $P(t)$
store the best solutions among $P(t)$ into $B(t)$

while (not termination-condition) do
begin
$t \leftarrow t + 1$
make $P(t)$ by observing the states of $Q(t-1)$
evaluate $P(t)$
update $Q(t)$ using Q-gates
store the best solutions among $B(t-1)$ and $P(t)$ into $B(t)$
store the best solution b among $B(t)$
if (global migration condition)
then migrate b to $B(t)$ globally
else if (local migration condition)
then migrate b_j^t in $B(t)$ to $B(t)$ locally
end
end

A migration in QEA is defined as the copying of b_j^t in $B(t)$ or b to $B(t)$. A global migration is implemented by replacing all the solutions in $B(t)$ by b and a local migration is implemented by replacing some of the solutions (local group) in $B(t)$ by the best one of them. The local group size is often set as $max(round(n/5), 1)$, where n is the population size.

4   The Gene Expression Data Sets

The first data set denoted as HL-60 is described in the work by Tomayo [11] and it contains data from macrophage differentiation experiments. The data set consists of 7229 genes and expression levels at 4 time points including 0, 0.5,4 and 24 hours. We apply a variation filter which discards all genes with an absolute change in maximum and minimum expression level less than 30. The number of genes which pass the filter is 2792. The vectors are then normalized to have mean 0 and variance 1.

The second data set denoted as Yeast is described in the work by Cho [12]. It consists of 6602 yeast genes including some reduplicate ones measured at 17 time points over two cell cycles. The 90-minute and 100-minute time points are excluded because of difficulties with scaling. Afterwards, we use a variation filter to discard all genes with an absolute expression level change less than or equal to 100, and an expression level of max/min<2.0 or min=0. The number of genes that pass the filter is 2947. Again, the vectors are normalized to have mean 0 and variance 1.

The number of clusters for the clustering is taken from Ref. [11] for the HL-60 data set and from Ref. [12] for the Yeast data set, the cluster number is 12 and 30 respectively.

5   QEA for Clustering Gene Expression Data

In our experiments, we compare quantum-inspired evolutionary algorithm (QEA) with the multi-start k-means (MS+k-means) and self-organizing maps

(SOM) algorithms. Multi-start k-means produces the best solution by running k-means algorithm many times with randomly generating initial centroid. QEA and multi-start k-means algorithms are implemented in Matlab 6.5. The self-organizing maps algorithm is available in the software package Gene Cluster 2.0. In the experiments, the default values of Gene Cluster are used.

5.1 Initialization

The k-means algorithm is first run ten times and so ten initial solutions are produced for each data set. Each solution is composed of n mean vectors and n is the number of clusters for each data set. Given the mean vectors, the cluster memberships can be calculated by calculating the nearest distance of each gene vector with all mean vectors. Therefore it is not necessary to store the cluster memberships in the Q-bit individuals.

5.2 Representation and Fitness Function

The representation used in QEA is straightforward. There are $10 \times n$ mean vectors in all for the ten initial solutions. Then we number each mean vector as $1, 2, 3, \ldots, 10 \times n$ and put them into the set V where $V = (v_1, v_2, \ldots, v_{10 \times n})$. So $10 \times n$ Q-bits are used in each Q-bit individual. A Q-bit individual has the following form in the t_{th} generation:

$$\begin{bmatrix} \alpha_1^t | \alpha_2^t | \ldots | \alpha_n^t | \alpha_{n+1}^t | \ldots | \alpha_{2 \times n}^t | \ldots | \alpha_{9n+1}^t | \ldots | \alpha_{10 \times n}^t \\ \beta_1^t | \beta_2^t | \ldots | \beta_n^t | \beta_{n+1}^t | \ldots | \beta_{2 \times n}^t | \ldots | \beta_{9n+1}^t | \ldots | \beta_{10 \times n}^t \end{bmatrix} \tag{8}$$

where α is given as a random number between 0 and 1 initially and then β could be computed according to Eq. (5). The fitness function used in QEA is the MSSC error provided in Eq. (3).

5.3 Make and Repair Operation

To obtain the binary string, the step of "Make(x)" by observing the states of Q-bit can be implemented for each Q-bit individual as follows:

Procedure Make (x)
begin
$i \leftarrow 0; k \leftarrow 0;$
while $i < n \times 10$ do
begin
if $random(0, 1) < |\beta_i^2|$ and $k < n$
then $x(i) \leftarrow 1; k \leftarrow k + 1;$
else $x(i) \leftarrow 0;$
$i \leftarrow i + 1;$
end
end

where the variant k is used to guarantee that the number of '1' in each binary string must be less than or equal to n. Afterwards, an additional operation "Repair (x)" should be done to be sure there should be and only be n '1' in each binary string. That is if the number of '1' is less than n in some strings, there must be stochastic search operation to increase the number of '1' for each Q-bit individual as follows:

Procedure Repair(x)
begin
calculate the number of '1' as k;
while $k < n$ do
begin
$randpos \leftarrow random(1, n \times 10)$;
if $x(randpos) = 0$
then $x(randpos) \leftarrow 1$;
$k \leftarrow k + 1$;
end
end

It can be seen that the repair (mutation) operation can intensify the local search ability of the algorithm and it has similar function of the mutation operation in GA. After obtaining the repaired binary string, we can choose n mean vectors from the set V by observing the binary string for each individual. If the i_{th} bit of the string is equal to '1', then the i_{th} mean vector is chosen. So each Q-bit individual corresponds to different n mean vectors. It is represented as follows:

$$Individual_i \Rightarrow (v_{i1}, v_{i2}, \ldots, v_{in}).v_{ik} \in V, k = 1, \ldots, n. \tag{9}$$

5.4   Evaluate and Update Operation

Then the evaluate operation is executed to calculate the fitness value according to Eq. (3) for each Q-bit individual represented by Eq. (9) and so the best individual can be selected. The update operation is used to update Q-bit states of each individual by rotation gate in Eq. (7). It is like to the crossover operation in GA for the global search. In this experiment, the global migration period in generation is 10, the local migration period is 1, and the local group size is set to 5 according to others experience [13]. The angle parameter in Table 1 is set as follows according to our experiment observation:

$$If \ \alpha \times \beta > 0 \ then \ \theta_3 = 0.01\pi; \ \theta_5 = -0.01\pi;$$
$$If \ \alpha \times \beta < 0 \ then \ \theta_3 = -0.01\pi; \ \theta_5 = 0.01\pi;$$
$$If \ \alpha \times \beta = 0 \ then \ \theta_3 = \pm0.01\pi; \ \theta_5 = \pm0.01\pi.$$

6   Experiment Results

In all the experiments, QEA is run with a population size of 20. The k-means and QEA algorithms are all terminated when the maximum generation of 50

Table 2. Experiment results for the two data sets

Data set	Algorithm	Best obj	Avg obj	Excess
HL-60	QEA	1514.3	1598.5	5.56%
	MS+k-means	1514.6	1604.3	5.92%
	3×4-SOM	1523.2	1624.0	6.62%
Yeast	QEA	15741.0	15860.0	0.76%
	MS+k-means	15752.0	15905.0	0.97%
	3×4-SOM	15801.0	16002.0	1.27%

is arrived. The three algorithms are all run ten times, and the best and the average objective value are produced. In Table 2, the results are displayed for the described two gene expression data sets. The objective value is the minimum sum-of-squares referred in Eq. (3). Excess value is the percentage of the average objective value above the best objective value. The smaller excess value means better performance of the algorithm.

The proposed QEA algorithm performs better than other two algorithms even with a small population. The QEA can find best solutions in each data set in spite of it's slowly convergence speed sometimes. For the HL-60 data set, the best solutions found by all algorithms have similar fitness, so we believe the best solutions found by the algorithms are optimal. But the excess value of QEA is smaller. For the Yeast data set, the k-means solution is close to the best solution found by QEA, and it seems that the data set is fit for k-means search.

In order to observe the convergence rate, the curve of fitness change is given for the HL-60 and Yeast data sets in Figure 1. The results show the superiority of QEA compared to multi-start k-means and self-organizing maps algorithms. It also shows that QEA can always adjust all individuals to the direction of better solution and find the (near) optimum or best-known solutions to the NP-hard clustering problem. In addition, the k-means algorithm performs better than self-organizing maps for all the two data sets.

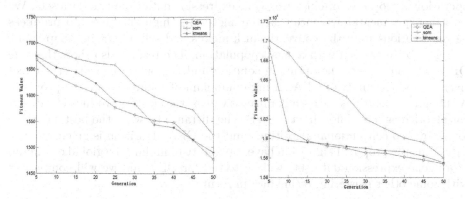

Fig. 1. Fitness changes for the HL-60 (left) and Yeast (right) data sets

Table 3. The distances to the best-known solutions found by QEA

Data set	Algorithm	Distance value
HL-60	MS+k-means	41.97
	3×4-SOM	56.08
Yeast	MS+k-means	487.31
	3×4-SOM	677.70

From the biologists' point of view, it is important how the cluster membership of the genes change if QEA is used instead of other clustering algorithms. But it is often the case that although the solutions have similar fitness values, the clusters produced by different algorithms may differ drastically. Since the cluster memberships are more important, the distance to the best-known solutions found by QEA for the k-means and SOM algorithms are provided in Table 3. The distance of two solutions is defined as follows:

$$D(p, q) = \sum_{i=1}^{n} d^2(\hat{x}_{p[i]}, \hat{x}_{q[i]}). \tag{10}$$

For the Yeast and HL-60 data set, however, solutions obtained using the two algorithms appear to be far away from the best-known solutions in terms of cluster memberships. Hence, the previously proposed heuristic method is not sufficient to arrive at optimum clustering solution. The QEA algorithm has been shown to perform well and be more robust in finding better solutions.

7   Conclusions

In this paper, we first introduce a novel evolutionary algorithm so called quantum-inspired evolutionary algorithm, and then quantum-inspired evolutionary algorithm (QEA) with a new representation form and an additional mutation operation is proposed for clustering gene expression data from two data sets. We present experimental evidence that our method is high effective and produces better solutions than the conventional k-means and self-organizing maps clustering algorithms even with a small population. The results also show that the QEA can converge to the optimum solution and demonstrate clearly the effectiveness and feasibility of QEA for minimum sum-of-squares clustering problem. Although the solutions have similar fitness values, the clusters produced by different algorithms may differ drastically. So the distance between the best solutions found by two conventional algorithms and the QEA algorithm is given. It indicates that the proposed algorithm have the ability of finding the global optimum. More gene expression data sets will be tested for QEA and we will compare it with some other clustering techniques in future work.

Acknowledgements

This work is supported by the National Natural Science Foundation of China under Grant No. 60433020 and the Key Laboratory of Symbol Computation and Knowledge Engineering of the Ministry of Education.

References

1. Eisen, M., Spellman, P., Botstein, D.: Cluster Analysis and Display of Genome-wide Expression Patterns. Proceedings of the National Academy of Sciences (1998) 14863-14867
2. Kohonen, T.: Self-Organizing Maps. Berlin Springer (1997)
3. Tavazoie S., et al.: Systematic Determination of Genetic Network Architecture. Nat. Genet., 22 (1999) 281-285
4. Shamir, R., Sharan, R.: Algorithmic Approaches to Clustering Gene Expression Data. In: T. Jiang et al. (eds): Current Topics in Computational Molecular Biology. MIT Press (2002) 269-299
5. Xu, Y., Olman, V., Xu, D.: Clustering Gene Expression Data Using a Graph-theoretic Approach: An Application of Minimum Spanning Trees. Bioinformatics, 18 (2002) 536-545
6. Merz, P.: Analysis of Gene Expression Profiles: An Application of Memetic Algorithms to the Minimum Sum-of-squares Clustering Problem. Biosystem, 72 (2003) 99-109
7. Brucker, P.: On the Complexity of Clustering Problems. Lecture Notes in Economics and Mathematical Systems, 157 (1978) 45-54
8. Han, K., Kim, J.: Quantum-inspired Evolutionary Algorithm for a Class of Combinatorial Problem. IEEE transactions on evolutionary computation, 6 (2002) 580-593
9. Han, K., Kim, J.: Genetic Quantum Algorithm and Its Application to Combinatorial Optimization Problem. Proceedings of the Congress on Evolutionary Computation (2000) 1354-1360
10. Hey, T.: Quantum Computing: An Introduction. Computing & Control Engineering Journal, 10 (1999) 105-112
11. Tamayo, P., Slonim, D., et al.: Interpreting Patterns of Gene Expression with Self-organizing Maps: Methods and Application to Hematopoietic Differentiation. Proceedings of the National Academy of Sciences (1999) 2907-2912
12. Cho, R.J., Winzeler, E.A., Davis, R.W.: A Genome-wide Transcriptional Analysis of the Mitotic Cell Cycle. Mol. Cell, 2 (1998) 65-73
13. Han, K., Kim, J.: On Setting the Parameters of Quantum-inspired Evolutionary Algorithm for Practical Applications. Proceedings of the Congress on Evolutionary Computation (2003) 178-184

An Open Source Microarray Data Analysis System with GUI: Quintet

Jun-kyoung Choe[1,*], Tae-Hoon Chung[1,*], Sunyong Park[1],
Hwan Gue Cho[2], and Cheol-Goo Hur[1,**]

[1] Laboratory of Plant Genomics, KRIBB, 52 Eoeun-dong, Yuseong-gu,
Daejeon 305-333, Korea
{jkchoe, thcng, psy, hurlee}@kribb.re.kr
http://genepool.kribb.re.kr
[2] Department of Computer Science, Pusan National University,
San-30, Jangjeon-dong, Keumjeong-gu, Pusan 609-735, Korea
hgcho@pusan.ac.kr
http://pearl.cs.pusan.ac.kr

Abstract. We address Quintet, an R-based unified cDNA microarray
data analysis system with GUI. Five principal categories of microarray
data analysis have been coherently integrated in Quintet: data processing
steps such as faulty spot filtering and normalization, data quality assessment
(QA), identification of differentially expressed genes (DEGs), clustering
of gene expression profiles, and classification of samples. Though
many microarray data analysis systems normally consider DEG identification
and clustering/classification the most important problems, we
emphasize that data processing and QA are equally important and should
be incorporated into the regular-base data analysis practices because microarray
data are very noisy. In each analysis category, customized plots
and statistical summaries are also given for users convenience. Using
these plots and summaries, analysis results can be easily examined for
their biological plausibility and compared with other results. Since Quintet
is written in R, it is highly extendable so that users can insert new
algorithms and experiment them with minimal efforts. Also, the GUI
makes it easy to learn and use and since R-language and its GUI engine,
Tcl/Tk, are available in all operating systems, Quintet is OS-independent
too.

1 Introduction

DNA microarray is the standard technology for high-throughput functional genomics
in the post-genomic era. Since the microarray experiment is highly
evolved and requires multiple handling steps each of which is a potential source
of fluctuation which undermines the reliability of the data itself [1], much effort
has been exerted to understand the sources of variability and minimize them to
produce high-quality reproducible data.

---

* These authors contributed equally to this work.
** Corresponding author.

D. Ślęzak et al. (Eds.): RSFDGrC 2005, LNAI 3642, pp. 392–401, 2005.
© Springer-Verlag Berlin Heidelberg 2005

In order for this technology to be fruitful, however, reliable analysis of the data is as important as the production of high-quality data itself. Due to the high-throughput character of the microarray data, this requires maturity in numerous statistical techniques, not to mention the data processing chores. Also required is the dexterity in scrutinizing various pertinent biological information so that one can successfully reconstruct the "big picture" of biological processes fragmentally reflected in the data. Considering these, a system that can provide analytic capability as well as informatic capability is crucial for an effective, versatile analysis of microarray data. In addition, since many new approaches appear almost daily by researchers, an ideal system should be extendable enough so that new techniques can be experimented with minimal efforts.

In this article, we present an R-based unified cDNA microarray data analysis system, Quintet, the first result of our on-going project to build up a customized microarray data analysis suite. As the name suggests, the five indispensable categories of data analysis have been coherently integrated in Quintet: data processing including filtering and normalization, customized set of data quality assessments (QAs), identification of differentially expressed genes (DEGs), clustering of gene expression profiles, and classification of samples using a small set of gene expression patterns.

Though many microarray data analysis systems claim DEG identification and clustering/classification the most important problems, we emphasize that data processing and QA are equally important and should be incorporated into the regular-base data analysis practices because the microarray data are quite noisy [1,2]. Under this rationale, some set of data processing and QA procedures is implemented in Quintet and constitutes the core functionality module of Quintet. Quintet is written in R which is virtually the standard platform for microarray data analysis now. Since many new algorithms are also written in R, they can be inserted into Quintet without much trouble and users can extend its functionality for their own needs. The GUI makes it easy to learn and use Quintet. Furthermore, Quintet is OS-independent since R-language and its GUI engine adapted for Quintet, Tcl/Tk, are available in all operating systems.

2   Overview of Quintet: Data Analysis Model

A simplified data analysis model we have projected in Quintet is depicted in Figure 1 (a). In this Figure, procedures that are carried out in Quintet are depicted in grey boxes. We have projected in Quintet, a simplified data analysis model. We have not implemented any image analysis functionality in Quintet and the data analysis starts from a set of text slide data files. According to our experience, the absence of image analysis module does not cause much trouble since every scanning software has a mechanism to export slide data into text format files and detailed examination of data variables, not the visual inspection of microarray images, provide thorough understanding of microarray data. Quintet retains all the variables that scanning softwares provide for each gene since previously unused variables may turn out to be important for particular purposes,

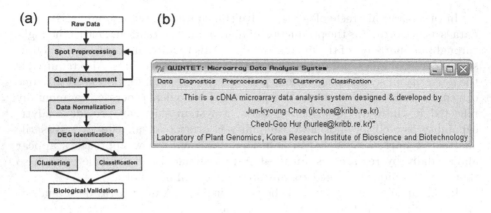

Fig. 1. (a) Simplified data analysis model and (b) screen shot of our system

especially in QA steps. For example, popular microarray image analysis software from Axon Instruments, GenePix, provides 43 variables for each gene, which enables a detailed understanding of spot intensities and their characteristics.

For each slide data, we first mark genes that are doubted to be erroneous from various criteria. Then, we check the quality of each slide data using various plots and statistical summaries. The error spot flagging and QA procedures should be iterated until no further quality improvements are evidenced. We consider the inter-operation of data processing and quality improvement check is very important to avoid data"over-processing" since any data processing can introduce unwanted artifacts which cannot be amended in downstream analysis steps. We apply normalization procedures to remaining genes according to the algorithm developed by Yang *et al.* [3]. This is an effort to remedy systematic artifacts that may have been introduced by signal extraction procedures. Normalized data are the basis for downstream analysis steps like DEG identification and clustering/classification.

Downstream analysis steps are quite straightforward. First, DEGs are identified. Since DEGs constitute basic elements for subsequent analysis steps, reliable identification of DEGs is of utmost importance. Furthermore, since different algorithms produce different DEG sets, multiple algorithms are supplied in Quintet and users can select their own DEG set among them based on the statistical characteristics revealed by auxiliary plots provided in Quintet. Using the identified DEGs, a gene expression matrix is constructed and clustering/classification is carried out. As such, the DEG identification procedure is a dimension-reduction step in this sense. In clustering/classification, we also supplied multiple algorithms and users can experiment different algorithms to survey possible variations in clustering/classification results.

Now, Quintet is not able to communicate with databases. However, we have been using Quintet practically for much of microarray analyses domestically, for examples, human or mouse cDNA chip experiments for DEG selection by heavy metal poisoning or for deciphering the effects of pharmaceutical plants,

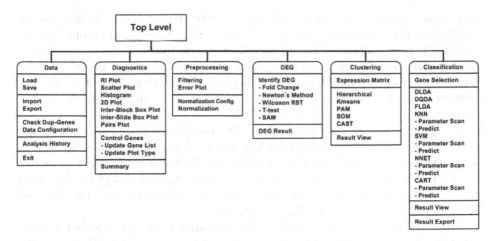

Fig. 2. Layout of the overall Quintet system

those results are not published yet and have a store of analysis results at the GENEPOOL database (http://genepool.kribb.re.kr).

3   Data Organization

In general, a microarray experiment is composed of multiple stages. For example, each time point can be considered as a stage in the case of time-series experiments [4] and each individual condition can be considered as a stage in the case of experiments composed of multiple conditions [5]. Furthermore, each stage is usually composed of multiple slides. Some slides in the stage can be replicates and the others can be dye-swaps.

Since the number of stages and data compositions in each stage can be arbitrary, we needed a simple but flexible method to import all necessary slides at one stroke. At the same time, the stage-slide relationship should be stored also. For this purpose, simple configuration file approach is used in Quintet. In Quintet, stage information appears in the first column, experiment types (replicate/dye-swap) in the second, full paths of slide data file in the third and slide aliases to be used internally in Quintet in the last column. Replicates are designated by 'A' while dye-swaps are designated by 'B' in the second column. Using this information, all relevant slide data are imported into Quintet in a batch mode. The data organization is stored for later use also. Users can store the initial data format setted up for use of Quintet by R format exporting. It enable users import the saved format for later analysis which remove teasing process of data resetting.

4   QA Module

QA of microarray data has not been considered as an important problem of micorarray data analysis by itself, which explains the lack of established standard procedure for QA. However, QA can be a decisive factor in establishing the reliability of analysis results performed using highly evolved algorithms because 'nothing can compensate for poor-quality data regardless of the sophistication of the analysis' [2]. Furthermore, QA itself is very important in constructing large centralized databases and collecting gene expression data on a comprehensive scale since data sharing can be drastically restricted without quality assurance [6].

In Quintet, QA module is one of the five core functional module. Although there is no established procedure for QA and methods implemented in Quintet are rather exploratory, QA methods implemented in Quintet were very successful in understanding the data quality according to our experience. QA module relies heavily on various statistical plots and summaries of particular variables like spot intensities, background intensities and log ratios.

In assessing the data quality of a slide, replicated genes can provide the clearest information since, though spotted at various positions within the same slide, they should show very similar behavior in every aspect. Position-dependent dissimilarity and variability between variables of the same replicated genes can be used as a quality measure. Because of this, we implemented two special menus to examine the characteristics of replicated genes. We classify replicated genes into two types: controls and simple duplicates. Genes that are repeatedly spotted for special purposes are called controls and genes that are replicated without such consideration are called simple duplicates. Therefore, by comparing the observed differential expression levels of control genes with their expected differential expression levels and by measuring the variability of observed differential expression levels over control genes representing the same reference level, we can estimate the quality of accuracy in differential expression levels recorded for a slide. Contrary to this, simple duplicates cannot be used to estimate the data quality by measuring discrepancy between the observed and expected differential expression levels, However, they can be used in assessing data quality by examining the correlation of variables between values obtained from different positions.

5   Data Processing Module

Quintet's data processing module is composed of two parts: spot preprocessing and data normalization. In spot preprocessing part, Quintet filters out faulty spots that can undermine the reliability of analysis results. What actually takes place is that Quintet marks suspicious spots based on several criteria separately and keeps all the mark results so that users can select a suitable combination of error flags under their own discretion. In normalization part, Quintet carries out the local regression (LOWESS) fit normalization procedures developed by Yang et al. [3] to remaining spots.

Following list of flagging criteria are supplied in Quintet: Background error, Maximum intensity error, Control spots, Original error, SNR (signal-to-noise ratio) error, Outlier error [2], Median-vs-mean ratio error [7] and Foreground-vs-Background error [8].

After removing error spots, remaining data should be normalized to minimize systematic variations in the measured gene expression levels. What we hope is that biological differences can be more easily distinguished, as well as the comparison of expression levels across slides can be accomplished more easily as a result of normalization. The procedure that is implemented in Quintet is basically the one developed by Yang *et al.* [3]. This normalization procedure is composed of three parts: pin-block centering, pin-block scaling and file scaling.

To these basic normalization procedures, we supplemented another step in Quintet: global normalization of average intensity A. This is motivated by the fact that the DEG identification in cDNA microarrrays should be based on comparison between values of $\log_2 R$ and $\log_2 G$. However, if only log ratio M values are normalized, large variations in average intensities will mask the true difference between $\log_2 R$ and $\log_2 G$, which would result in high levels of false positives and false negatives. To avoid this problem, we should normalize average intensities as well as log ratios.

The global normalization of average intensity is performed to all slides under analysis in Quintet. However, other three basic normalization procedures are selectively applied to individual slides based on a user-specified configuration. Based on QA results, users should classify slides into three groups: pin-block centering group, pin-block scaling group and removal group. This classification is possible since QA results give clear view of the type of normalization procedures that should be applied to individual slides.

6   DEG Identification Module

One perplexing factor while implementing DEG identification algorithms in Quintet is the number of replicates in each comparison unit since some algorithms can be applied only to single slides (single-slide algorithms) while others intrinsically need multiple slides (multiple-slide algorithms). Therefore multiply-replicated comparison units cause another complication for single-slide algorithms. Furthermore, since we cannot measure the level of confidence without replicates [9], single-slide algorithms are of limited value compared with multiple-slide algorithms. Nevertheless, we have included some single-slide algorithms in Quintet since, in general, they are easy to implement and their results are easy to interpret and gain in reliability can be achieved by imposing more stringent cutoff values. In addition, the absence of statistical significance should not prevent single-slide algorithms from being utilized because comparison units in most published microarray data so far are single slides whose results have been quite successful in elucidating various previously unknown global genetic pictures.

Currently, the following algorithms are implemented in Quintet: Fold change type (Generic algorithm, Z-test type [2,3], Sapir-Churchill algorithm [11]), Newton's algorithm [12], T-test, Wilcoxon rank sum test (RST) [13] and Significance analysis of microarrays (SAM) [14].

Since these algorithms are based on statistical arguments, false positives and false negatives cannot be avoided. Furthermore, according to our experience, different algorithms produce different DEG results, which make the identification of optimal DEG set very difficult. Therefore one should be very careful in interpreting the result of any single algorithm and we strongly recommend users to try to use as many different algorithms as possible and compare them very cautiously to get a robust result. For this reason, we are trying to implement as many available DEG identification algorithms as possible in Quintet. In addition, we are developing a method to integrate the results of individual algorithms, hoping to get more robust set of DEGs thinking that only robust DEGs not false positives and false negatives of each algorithm will be selected by many different algorithms.

7   Clustering Module

Clustering is one of the most widely used methods in gene expression analysis [2,4]. As transcription is regulated mainly by the binding of transcription factors (TFs) to the promoter region, clustering of gene expression profiles can be very useful in identifying cis-regulatory elements in the promoters, providing more insight to gene function and regulation networks.

Since the seminal work of Eisen et al. [4], clustering has been extensively used in microarray data analysis and culminated a lot of successful results. This entails novel algorithms such as self-organizing maps (SOM), clustering affinity search technique (CAST) [15], minimum spanning tree (MST) as well as conventional algorithms such as hierarchical clustering [4], k-means clustering and partitioning around medoids (PAM) clustering [17] and to mention a few. Because of this, many non-commercial and commercial systems regard clustering module as their core functionality [16] and Quintet provides them.

Clustering results are presented in several different forms in Quintet. First, individual clusters are reported in separate text format external files with corresponding differential expression levels so that users can scrutinize individual genes contained within each cluster in detail and use clustering results in other programs. Second, clusters are depicted in several plots. Typical plots normally adopted in cluster representation are shown in Figure 3. The dendrogram attached 2D image plot shown in Figure 3(a) is the most well-known representation format of hierarchical clustering. For non-agglomerative clustering algorithms like K-means clustering, only the 2D image plot is shown in Quintet.

8   Classification Module

There are many good candidate classifiers already [18] and the following list of algorithms is implemented in Quintet: Fisher linear discriminant analysis (FLDA), Maximum likelihood discriminant analysis (MLDA), K-nearest neighbor (KNN) method, Classification and regression tree (CART), Artificial neural network (ANN) [19] and Support vector machine (SVM) [20,21].

Though Quintet can handle only two-class classification problems now, efforts to incorporate multiple-class classification problems are underway. In the course

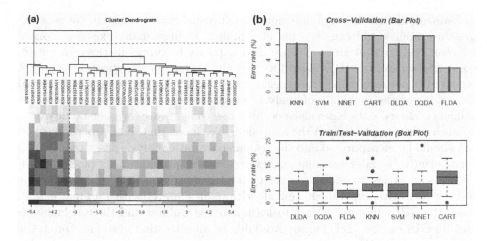

Fig. 3. Typical clustering and classification result presentation plots. (a) Dendrogram with 2D image plot for clustering module (b) Auxiliary plots for classification module.

of refining classifiers in learning phase, one needs to minimize errors between known class assignments and predicted classes. Since only the class assignments of learning set is usually known, one randomly splits the learning set into two classes, pseudo learning set and pseudo test set, constructs classifiers using the pseudo learning set only and estimates the error rate using the pseudo test set. In Quintet, the random separation of learning set can be selected between two different ways: cross-validation and test-train set type. In the cross-validation type learning, the learning set is divided into K subsets (K-fold cross validation) of equal size from the start. The classifier is then learned at K times, each time using one subset in turn as a test set. To the contrary, in the test-train set type learning the learning set is divided at every turn into two different subsets (pseudo learning set and pseudo test set) and the classifier is learned using the pseudo learning set while the error rate is estimated on the pseudo test set. This whole process is repeated a number of times to calculate the error rate distribution.

Besides the core classification functional module, Quintet supplies auxiliary plots to be used in assessing the performance of specific classifiers. In Quintet, we show the error rate profiles calculated through cross-validation and train-test set type learning as the parameter K is varied in KNN classification. The error rate profiles across different classification algorithms at their respective optimum parameters are shown in Figure 3(b).

9   Conclusion

Quintet is an unified cDNA microarray data analysis system capable of carrying out five indispensable categories of microarray data analysis seamlessly: data processing steps such as faulty spot filtering and normalization, data quality assessment, identification of differentially expressed genes, clustering of gene expression profiles and classification of samples. Though many existing tools of microarray data analysis emphasize their capacity to carry out three core categories of data analysis (DEG identification, clustering and classification), Quintet is geared to perform data preprocessing and QA also. In particular, QA is crucial for enhancing the reliability of analysis results and sharing gene expression data using centralized data bases since nothing can compensate for poor-quality data no matter how sophisticated the analysis is. We insist that data processings and QA should be incorporated into the regular-base data analysis practices. To help users intuitively understand data characteristics, we provide lots of plots and statistical summaries. In addition, since Quintet is written in R, it is highly flexible so that users can experiment new algorithms in Quintet with minimal efforts. Also, the GUI will make it easy to learn and use Quintet and since R-language and its GUI engine, Tcl/Tk, are available in all operating systems, Quintet is OS-independent. We have next version system in contemplation, that is able to communicate with database. We will improve Quintet with that system that can analyze easily microarray data imported from our GENEPOOL database or other microarray databases.

Acknowledgements. We acknowledge the following R-language software packages: BioConductor project, cluster, e1071, GeneSom, lattice, MASS, mva, nnet, rpart, sma. This work was supported by a grant (PF003301-00) from Plant Diversity Research Center of 21st Century Frontier Research Program funded by Ministry of Science and Technology of Korean Government.

References

1. Draghici S, Kuklin A, Hoff B, Shams S: Experimental design, analysis of variance and slide quality assessment in gene expression arrays. Curr Opin Drug Discov Devel 2001, 4:332-337
2. Quackenbush J: Microarray data normalization and transformation. Nat Genet 2002, Supple 32:496-501
3. Yang YH, Dudoit S, Luu P, Lin DM, Peng V, Ngai J, Speed TP: Normalization for cDNA microarray data: a robust composite method addressing single and multiple slide systematic variation. Nucleic Acids Res 2002, 30:e15
4. Eisen MB, Spellman PT, Brown PO, Botstein D: Cluster analysis and display of genome-wide expression patterns. Proc Natl Acad Sci USA 1998, 95:14863-14868
5. Gasch AP, Spellman PT, Kao CM, Carmel-Harel O, Eisen MB, Storz G, Botstein D, Brown PO: Genomic expression programs in the response of yeast cells to environmental changes. Mol Biol Cell 2000, 11:4241-4257
6. Becker KG: The sharing of cDNA microarray data. Nat Rev Neurosci 2001, 2:438-440
7. Tran PH, Peiffer DA, Shin Y, Meek LM, Brody JP, Cho KWY: Microarray optimizations: increasing spot accuracy and automated identification of true microarray signals. Nucleic Acids Res 2002, 30:e54

8. Delenstarr G, Cattell H, Connell S, Dorsel A, Kincaid RH, Nguyen K, Sampas N, Schidel S, Shannon KW, Tu A, Wolber PK: Estimation of the confidence limits of oligonucleotide microarray-based measurements of differential expression. in Microarrays: Optical Technologies and Informatics. ed. by Bittner M, *et al.* Proceedings of SPIE 2001, 4266:120-131

9. Lee MLT, Kuo FC, Whitmore GA, Sklar J: Importance of replication in microarray gene expression studies: statistical methods and evidence from repetitive cDNA hybridizations. Proc Natl Acad Sci USA 2000, 97:9834-9839

10. Yang IV, Chen E, Hasseman JP, Liang W, Frank BC, Wang S, Sharov V, Saeed AI, White J, Li J, Lee NH, Yeatman TJ, Quackenbush J: Within the fold: assessing differential expression measures and reproducibility in microarray assays. Genome Biol 2002, 3:research0062.1-0062.12

11. Sapir M and Churchill GA: Estimating the posterior probability of differential gene expression from microarray data. Poster 2000
[http://www.jax.org/research/churchill/pubs/index.html]

12. Newton MA, Kendziorski CM, Richmond CS, Blattner FR, Tsui KW: On differential variability of expression ratios: improving statistical inference about gene expression changes from microarray data. J Comput Biol 2001, 8:37-52

13. Troyanskaya OG, Garber ME, Brown PO, Botstein D, Altman RB: Nonparametric methods for identifying differentially expressed genes in microarray data. Bioinformatics 2002, 18:1454-1461

14. Benjamini Y and Hochberg Y: Controlling the false discovery rate: a practical and powerful approach to multiple testing. J Roy Stat Soc B 1995, 57:289-300

15. Ben-Dor A, Shamir R, Yakhini Z: Clustering gene expression patterns. J Comput Biol 1999, 6:281-297

16. Yeung KY, Medvedovic M, Bumgarner RE: Clustering gene-expression data with repeated measurements. Genome Biol 2003, 4:R34

17. Kaufman L and Rousseeuw PJ: Finding Groups in Data: an Introduction to Cluster Analysis. John Wiley & Sons; 1990

18. Dudoit S, Fridlyand J, Speed TP: Comparison of discrimination methods for the classification of tumors using gene expression data. JASA 2002, 97:77-87

19. Khan J, Wei JS, Ringner M, Saal LH, Ladanyi M, Westermann F, Berthold F, Schwab M, Antonescu CR, Peterson C, Meltzer PS: Classification and diagnostic prediction of cancers using gene expression profiling and artificial neural networks. Nat Med 2001, 7:673-679

20. Vapnik V: The Nature of Statistical Learning Theory. Springer-Verlag; 1995

21. Zien A, Ratsch G, Mika S, Scholkopf B, Lemmen C, Smola A, Lengauer T, Muller K: Engineering support vector machine kernels that recognize translation initiation sites. Bioinformatics 2000, 16:799-807

Similarity Index for Clustering DNA Microarray Data Based on Multi-weighted Neuron

Wenming Cao

Institute of Intelligent Information Systems, Information College
Zhejiang University of Technology, Hangzhou 310032, China
csann@zjut.edu.cn

Abstract. A common approach to the analysis of gene expression data is to define clusters of genes that have similar expression. A critical step in cluster analysis is the determination of similarity between the expression levels of two genes. We introduce a non-linear multi-weighted neuron-based similarity index and compare the results with other proximity measures for Saccharomyces cerevisiae gene expression data. We show that the clusters obtained using Euclidean distance, correlation coefficients, and mutual information were not significantly different. The clusters formed with the multi-weighted neuron-based index were more in agreement with those defined by functional categories and common regulatory motifs.

1 Introduction

DNA microarray technology has enabled the study of large-scale gene expression data. A number of analytical methodologies have been introduced to analyze gene expression patterns, and cluster analysis [1] has played a prominent role. Cluster analysis usually requires two steps. The first step is to measure relations (e.g., distance or similarity) of gene expression by a pre-specified measure, in a pairwise fashion. The second step is to cluster the genes based on the measures derived in the first step. In this paper, we trained multi-weighted neuron [2][3][4] to classify a gene expression pattern as being similar to a pre-specified one ("target"), and therefore created a neural network-based proximity measure. We used the assessed proximity measures in a simple threshold clustering algorithm to verify whether the multi-weighted neuron-based measure could result in clusters that resembled those formed using functional categories and common regulatory motifs. We also evaluated clusters derived from Euclidean distance, correlation coefficients, and mutual information.

2 Materials and Methods

We used S. cerevisiae gene expression data consisting of 79 measurements of 2467 genes.[1] Briefly, they were obtained during the diauxic shift, the mitotic cell division cycle, sporulation, and temperature and reducing shocks [5].

---

[1] http://genome-www4.stanford.edu/MicroArray/SMD/index. html

D. Ślęzak et al. (Eds.): RSFDGrC 2005, LNAI 3642, pp. 402–408, 2005.

2.1 Proximity/Distance Measures

Euclidean distance (normalized vector): Distance was calculated based on the normalized dispersion in expression level of each gene across the measurement points (s.d./mean). This normalized expression level is obtained by subtracting the mean across the measurement points from the expression level of each gene, and dividing the result by the standard deviation across the time points:

$$d(x, \bar{x}) = ||x - \bar{x}|| = \frac{|x - \bar{x}|}{1/N\sqrt{\sum_1^N (x - \bar{x})^2}} \tag{1}$$

where x is the normalized expression level, x is a vector of expression data of a series of N conditions in gene x, and $\bar{x}$ is the mean of x.

Correlation coefficient: The correlation coefficient was calculated as in [5]:

$$s(x, y) = \frac{1}{N} \sum_{i=1,N} (\frac{x_i - x_{offset}}{\Phi_x})(\frac{y_i - y_{offset}}{\Phi_y}) \tag{2}$$

$$Ml = H(x) + H(y) - H(x, y), \ H(x) = -\sum_{i=1}^{n} p(x_i) \log_2(p(x_i)) \tag{3}$$

where $H(x) = -\sum_{i=1}^{n} p(x_i) \log_2(p(x_i))$. $H(x)$ is the entropy of a gene expression pattern of a series of N conditions in gene x, and H(x,y) is the joint entropy of genes x and y defined as in [10]:

$$H(x, y) = -\sum_{i=1}^{n} \sum_{j=1}^{N} p(x_i, y_j) \log_2(p(x_i, y_j)) \tag{4}$$

where p(x,y) is the joint probability of x and y. Note that the number of distinct expression patterns in a neighbor list increases as the threshold becomes large. We counted the number of distinct gene expressions in a neighbor gene list at different proximity thresholds. The thresholds were selected so that the number of distinct expression patterns ranged from 50 to 300 by intervals of 10.

2.2 Simple Threshold Clustering: Neighbor Gene Lists

We applied a simple threshold clustering method to the data after calculation of the proximity/distance between all pairs of gene expressions by each of the four measures. For each pattern, we generated a list of neighbors. In this context, "neighbor" means a gene that has similar expressions and it does not mean either physical location of the genes in the genome or similarity of DNA sequences. An element of the neighbor gene list is a set that contains genes within a proximity threshold (radius) from a reference gene (center). In other words, the genes in a set show similar expression patterns to the reference gene expression pattern and the degree of similarity is within the proximity threshold from the reference gene expression pattern.

3   Multi-weighted Neurons

Usually, in neural networks, neurons are based on single-weighted vectors which can only reach the simple and regular shapes. In fact, the real shapes of some patterns in the feature space, such as a given person's face images, are irregular and complicated. A novel method using multi-weighted vector neurons [2][3][4] is capable to deal with such shapes.

If different samples belong to the same class, then they should be in the same, possibly irregular, connected region. The aim of pattern recognition is to find such regions or use geometric shapes to approximate them well enough. DBF is one typical method which use "hypersphere" to approximate real shape [2][3], however, few real shapes induced by the same class samples are exactly hyperspheres. In our approach, all samples of the same class should be included in the shape covered by a neuron, so when this shape is different from the real shape, it must be bigger than the real one and it not only covers samples of this class but also those from other classes. Then the error recognition rate will increase. A different approximation will result in different error recognition rate.

Fig. 1. Hypersphere and hyper-sausage

As an example, hypersphere can be considered as topologic product of a point (0-dimensional manifold) and n-dimensional hypersphere. It can be actualized by a single-weighted neuron. Mathematic expression of such neuron's shape is:

$$|\vec{X} - \vec{W}|^2 = k \tag{5}$$

In Fig.1, hypersphere is compared to hyper-sausage – topologic product of line segment (1-dimensional manifold) and hypersphere. The line segment's end-points are decided by study samples A and B; it is actualized by a two-weighted neuron. The shape covered by hyper-sausage is the union of the three following parts $S = \bigcup_{i=1}^{3} S_i$, and called pS_i3 neuron: S_1 is the set of points whose distances to the line segment equal a certain constant k; S_2 is the set of points whose distances to a sample point A equal k; S_3 is the set of points whose distances to a sample point B equal k:

$$S_1 : |\vec{X} - \vec{W_1}|^2 - \left[(\vec{X} - \vec{W_1}) \times \frac{\vec{W_2} - \vec{W_1}}{|\vec{W_2} - \vec{W_1}|} \right]^2 = k$$

$$S_2 : |\vec{X} - \vec{W_1}|^2 = k \qquad S_3 : |\vec{X} - \vec{W_2}|^2 = k \tag{6}$$

According the theory of high-dimension space geometry [4], the volume of a hypersphere in k dimensions is:

$$V_1 = \begin{cases} \frac{\pi^{\frac{k}{2}}}{(\frac{k}{2})!} r_1^k, & k = 2m \\ \frac{2^{\frac{k+1}{2}} \pi^{\frac{k-1}{2}}}{k!} r_1^k, & k = 2m+1 \end{cases} \tag{7}$$

and the volume of a hyper-sausage (hyper cylinder) is

$$V_2 = \begin{cases} \dfrac{2^{\frac{k}{2}} \pi^{\frac{k-2}{2}}}{(k-1)!} r_2^{(k-1)} \times h, & k = 2m \\ \dfrac{\pi^{\frac{k-1}{2}}}{(\frac{k-1}{2})!} r_2^{(k-1)} \times h, & k = 2m+1 \end{cases} \tag{8}$$

where r_2 is the radius of the cylinder's bottom, which is (k-1)-dimensional hypersphere; h is its altitude. Comparing to Fig.1, r_1 is the radius of k-dimensional hypersphere (at the left); r_2 is the radius of hyper-sausage's bottom, which is $(k-1)$-dimensional hypersphere (at the right); h is hyper-sausage's altitude. We suppose $h = 2r_1$ and $r_2 = r_1/2$. We can find that if $k = 100$, then $V_1/V_2 \approx 2^{100}$. So if we use hyper-sausage, the error recognition rate may decrease largely.

Generally, the expression of a multi-weighted neuron is:

$$Y = f[\Phi(W_1, W_2, ..., W_m, X)] \tag{9}$$

where $W_1, W_2, ..., W_m$ are m weights vectors and are decided by a group of study samples vectors $S_1, S_2, ...S_m$; X is the input vector; Φ is a function decided by a multi-weighted neuron; f is step function, which is equal to 1 when $x \leq k$ and equal to 0 when $x > k$.

4   Proposed Method of Clustering DNA Microarray Data

The task of multi-weighted neuron is to cover a given expression pattern by a chain units with a minimum sum of volumes via determining the end points of each line segment and the radius of each hyper-sausage. At first, we constructed one manifold for each expression pattern, or "target pattern" (e.g., one manifold pS_i3 for pattern ATP3: ATP synthesis). The goal of each network was to determine the proximity of an expression pattern to the target pattern. If using manifolds of type pS_i3, every neuron may be described as follows:

$$Y = f[\Phi(X, W_1, W_2, W_3) - Th] \tag{10}$$
$$\Phi(X, W_1, W_2, W_3) = \|X - \theta_{(W_1, W_2, W_3)}\| \tag{11}$$

where Th is its threshold, $\theta_{(W_1, W_2, W_3)}$ denotes a finite triangle area, which is enclosed by three points (W_1, W_2, W_3). We can represent it as:

$$\theta_{(W_1, W_2, W_3)} = \{Y | Y = \alpha_2[\alpha_1.W_1 + (1 - \alpha_1) W_2] + (1 - \alpha_2) W_3, \alpha_1, \alpha_2 \in [0, 1]\} \tag{12}$$

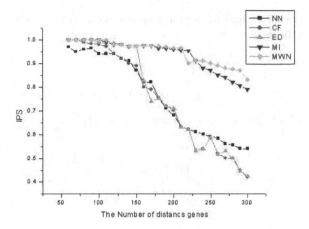

Fig. 2. Comparison of performance based on motifs. On the x-axis: proximity thresholds are represented by the number of distinct expression patterns. On the y-axis: the performance in integrated performance score (IPS) is shown. The multi-weighted neuron-derived measure was superior in all IPS scores (p 0:01 by the modified log-rank test). There was no significant statistical difference in the IPSs of the neighbor gene lists produced using neural networks (NN), correlation coefficients (CF), Euclidean distance (ED), mutual information (MI), and multi-weighted neuron (MWN).

Then, $\Phi(X, W_1, W_2, W_3)$ actually is the Euclidean distance from X to the triangle area of the pS_i3 neuron. The model of activation function is:

$$f(x) = \begin{cases} 1, x \leq Th \\ -1, x > Th \end{cases} \tag{13}$$

In multi-dimensional space, we use every three sample points of the same class to construct a finite 2D plane, namely, a triangle. Then several 2D spaces can be constructed – we cover these planes by the pS_i3 neuron to approximate the complicated "shape", which is formed by many sample points of the DNA multi-dimensional space.

4.1   Construction of Multi-weighted Neuron

Step 1: Let the sample points of the training set are $\alpha = A_1, A_2, ... A_N$; N is the number of the total sample points. To figure out the distances between points, two points having the least distance are defined as B_{11} and B_{12}. Let B_{13} denote the nearest point away from B_{11} and B_{12}. Obviously, B_{13} is not in the line formed by B_{11} and B_{12}. In this way, B_{11}, B_{12}, and B_{13} construct the first triangle plane represented as θ_1, which is covered by a pS_i3 neuron. The covering area is:

$$P_1 = \left\{ X | \rho_{X\theta_1} \leq Th, X \in R^n \right\} \tag{14}$$

$$\theta_1 = \left\{ Y | Y = \alpha_2 \left[\alpha_1 . B_{11} + (1 - \alpha_1) B_{12} \right] + (1 - \alpha_2) B_{13}, \alpha_1, \alpha_2 \in [0, 1] \right\} \tag{15}$$

where Th is its threshold, and $\rho_{X\theta_1}$ denotes the distance from X to θ_1.

Step 2: Firstly, the points contained in P_1 should be removed. Then, according to the method of step 1, define the nearest point away from B_{11}, B_{12}, and B_{13} as B_{21}. Among B_{21}, B_{22}, and B_{23} , two nearest points away from are denoted as B_{22}, and B_{23}. B_{21}, B_{22}, and B_{23} construct the second triangle defined as θ_2, which is covered by another pS_i3 neuron. The covering area is described as follows:

$$P_2 = \{X | \rho_{X\theta_2} \leq Th, X \in R^n\} \tag{16}$$

$$\theta_2 = \{Y | Y = \alpha_2 [\alpha_1 B_{21} + (1 - \alpha_1) B_{22}] + (1 - \alpha_2) B_{23}, \alpha_1, \alpha_2 \in [0, 1]\} \tag{17}$$

where Th is its threshold, and $\rho_{x\theta_2}$ denotes the distance from X to θ_2.

Step 3: Remove the points contained in the covering area of previous $(i - 1)$ pS_i3 neurons. Let B_{i1} denotes the nearest point from the remained points to the three vertexes of the triangle. Two nearest vertexes of the $(i-1)th$ triangle away from B_{i1} are represented as B_{i2} and B_{i3}. Then, B_{i1}, B_{i2}, and B_{i3} construct the i-th triangle, defined as θ_3. In the same way, θ_3 is covered by a pS_i3 neuron. The covering area is

$$P_i = \{X | \rho_{X\theta_3} \leq Th, X \in R^n\} \tag{18}$$

$$\theta_3 = \{Y | Y = \alpha_2 [\alpha_1 B_{i1} + (1 - \alpha_1) B_{i2}] + (1 - \alpha_2) B_{i3}, \alpha_1, \alpha_2 \in [0, 1]\} \tag{19}$$

where Th is its threshold, and $\rho_{x\theta_3}$ denotes the distance from X to θ_3.

Step 4: Repeat the step 3 until all sample points are conducted successfully. Finally, there are m pS_i3 neurons, and their mergence about covering area is the covering area of every DNAs' class. That is $P = \bigcup_{i=1}^{m} P_i$.

4.2   Clustering Based on Multi-weighted Neuron

Taking $Th = 0$, the pS_i3 neuron can be described as follows:

$$\rho = \|X - \theta_{(W_1, W_2, W_3)}\| \tag{20}$$

The output ρ is the distance from X to the finite area $\theta_{(W_1, W_2, W_3)}$. The distance called ρ_i from the sample DNA waiting for being recognized to the covering area of the i-th class is:

$$\rho_i = \min_{j=1}^{M_i} \rho_{ij}, i = 1, \cdots, 2467 \tag{21}$$

where M_i is the number of pS_i3 neurons covered by the i-th class DNAs, ρ_{ij} is the distance between the DNA sample waiting for being recognized and the neural network's i-th neuron's covering range covered by the j-th class DNAs. X will be classified to the DNA class corresponding to the least ρ_i. Namely:

$$j = \min_{j=1}^{2467} \rho_i, j = (1, \cdots, 2467). \tag{22}$$

5   Results and Discussion

Using *Saccharomyces* cerevisiae gene expression data, we compared the performances of the multi-weighted neuron-based similarity index and other similarity (or distance) measures in forming clusters that resemble those defined by functional categories or the presence of common regulatory motifs. A simple clustering method based on similarity thresholds was used for comparison. The clusters obtained using Euclidean distance, correlation coefficients, and mutual information were not significantly different. The clusters formed with the neural network-based index were more in agreement with those defined by functional categories or common regulatory motifs. Non-linear similarity measures such as the one proposed may play a role in complex microarray data analysis. Further studies are necessary to demonstrate their applicability beyond this "proof-of-concept" experiment.

6   Conclusion

In this study, we developed a multi-weighted neuron-based measure of gene expression proximity and evaluated its performance in a single dataset. The clusters were based on simple proximity threshold cutoffs. We tested these measures on data consisting of 79 measurements from 10 different experimental conditions. The cluster performance was evaluated based on the motif DNA sequences and MIPS functional categories. The performance was compared statistically. There was no significant difference among results obtained using Euclidean distance, correlation coefficients, and mutual information. The performance of the multi-weighted neuron-based measure was significantly different. Non-linear proximity multi-weighted neuron methods such as the one derived from high dimensional space may play a role in the analysis of gene expression data.

References

1. Aldenderfer, M.S., Blashfield, R.K.: Cluster Analysis. Sage, Newbury Park, CA (1984)
2. Wang, S.: A New Development on ANN in China - Biomimetic Pattern Recognition and Multi Weight Vector Neurons. In: Proc. of RSFDGrC (2003) 35-43
3. Cao, W., Hao, F., Wang, S.: The application of DBF neural networks for object recognition. Inf. Sci., 160 (2004) 153-160
4. Cao, W., Wang, S.: Study of Adaptive Equalizers Based on Two Weighted Neural Networks. CIT (2004) 612-615
5. Herwig, R., et al: Genome Res., 9 (1999) 1093-1105

Screening for Ortholog Clusters
Using Multipartite Graph Clustering
by Quasi-Concave Set Function Optimization

Akshay Vashist[1,*], Casimir Kulikowski[1], and Ilya Muchnik[1,2]

[1] Dept. of Computer Science, Rutgers University,
Piscataway NJ 08854, USA
[2] DIMACS, Rutgers University, Piscataway NJ 08854, USA

Abstract. Finding orthologous genes, similar genes in different genomes, is a fundamental problem in comparative genomics. We present a model for automatically extracting candidate ortholog clusters in a large set of genomes using a new clustering method for multipartite graphs. The groups of orthologous genes are found by focusing on the gene similarities across genomes rather than similarities between genes within a genome. The clustering problem is formulated as a series of combinatorial optimization problems whose solutions are interpreted as ortholog clusters. The objective function in optimization problem is a quasi-concave set function which can be maximized efficiently. The properties of these functions and the algorithm to maximize these functions are presented. We applied our method to find ortholog clusters in data which supports the manually curated Cluster of Orthologous Genes (COG) from 43 genomes containing 108,090 sequences. Validation of candidate ortholog clusters was by comparison against the manually curated ortholog clusters in COG, and by verifying annotations in Pfam and SCOP - in most cases showing strong correlations with the known results. An analysis of Pfam and SCOP annotations, and COG membership for sequences in 7,701 clusters which include sequences from at least three organisms, shows that 7,474(97%) clusters contain sequences that are all consistent in at least one of the annotations or their COG membership.

1 Introduction

Genes related through evolution are called homologous genes. They provide a good basis for extrapolating our knowledge from well-studied organisms to new ones, as in functional annotation of their genes. An important class of homologous sequences is that of orthologous genes, or gene sequences present in different genomes that have arisen through vertical descent from a single ancestral gene in the last common ancestor [1]. Such genes usually perform the same function(s) in different organisms but the degree of sequence similarity across the organisms varies, and usually depends on the time elapsed since their divergence. Ortholog

---

* The author was supported, in part, by the DIMACS graduate students award.

D. Ślęzak et al. (Eds.): RSFDGrC 2005, LNAI 3642, pp. 409–419, 2005.

detection is a fundamental problem in estimating traces of the vertical evolution of genes; its practical purpose include gene function annotation and finding targets for experimental studies.

While many ortholog detection procedures have been proposed [2], [3], [4], [5], [6], they suffer from limitations that present real challenges. Ortholog detection in [5] is limited to a pair of genomes, [6] requires phylogenetic information which may not be reliable, [4] can handle only small sized data. COG [3] and KEGG [2] are the most widely used and trusted databases of orthologous groups but they require manual curation step(s) by experts and this is a rate limiting factor to address the current demand. Automatic procedures of ortholog screening, grounded on methodologies that can tackle the problem as completely as possible, while ensuring the sensitivity of the orthologous groups produced, could therefore be valuable adjuncts to speedup the process.

In the proposed method, we require that a gene has to be similar in sequence to most genes from other genomes within its ortholog cluster. We have designed a new kind of similarity function (linkage function) to capture the relationship between a gene and a subset of genes. The similarity relationships among genes from multiple genomes are represented as a multipartite graph, where nodes in a partite set correspond to genes in a genome. To this we apply a new clustering method for multipartite graphs. The method is fast and enables us to extract ortholog clusters from a large sets of genomes. The key to the efficiency of the procedure is a particular property of the objective function, which is based on the linkage function.

We evaluate the performance of our method on the data set used to construct the COG [3], [7] database. In order to have reliable estimates of association between ortholog clusters in COG and ortholog clusters extracted by our method, we use statistical coefficients and calculate several indices of comparison, each of which reflects a particular aspect of similarity between the two classifications. The ortholog clusters produced by the method are evaluated based on the protein family annotation in Pfam [8] and structural annotation in SCOP [9]. Validation of clusters using these independent sources reveals that sequences within clusters share annotations provided by these sources.

The presentation of the remaining paper is as follows. In section 2 we present quasi-concave set functions and their maximizers which are then used to extract an optimal subset as a "quasi-clique" on a graph. Section 3 specifies the method to extract a cluster on a multipartite graph, and its extension to extract a sequence of clusters. In section 3.1 ortholog clusters are modeled as clusters in a multipartite graph, by specifying the similarity function between a gene and a set of genes. In section 4, we describe the results of applying the procedure to the data used for ortholog clustering in the COG database. The comparative analysis of our ortholog clusters with those in COG is presented in section 5. This is followed by conclusions in section 6.

2 ⋃-Maximizer of a Quasi-Concave Set Function as a Cluster

Suppose $V = \{1, 2, \ldots, i, \ldots, n\}$ is a set of n elements in which we intend to find a cluster. Further, assume that relationships among elements in V are represented by the undirected edge weighted graph $G^1 = (V, E, W)$, where E is the set of edges, and the weight, $w_{ij} \in W$ on the edge $e_{ij} \in E$ is interpreted as a degree of similarity between elements i and j. As a cluster, we intend to extract a subset whose elements are similar to each other. If we let the set function $F(H)$ [1] denote a measure of proximity among elements in the subset H, then as a cluster we wish to obtain a subset H^* of V that maximizes $F(H)$ i.e.,

$$H^* = \arg \max_{H \subseteq V} F(H) \qquad (1)$$

The specific realization of the function $F(H)$ expresses the notion of similarity between elements and determines the efficiency of finding the optimal set H^*. Let us introduce a function $\pi(i, H)$ which measures similarity between an element, i, and a subset of elements, H. This linkage function $\pi(i, H)$ may be interpreted as measuring a degree of membership of the element i to the subset H, where $i \in H \subseteq V$. Using the linkage function, the function $F(H)$ is defined as

$$F(H) = \min_{i \in H} \pi(i, H), \quad \forall i \in H \text{ and } \forall H \subseteq V \qquad (2)$$

In other words, $F(H)$ is defined as the $\pi(i, H)$ value of the least similar element in the subset H. Then, according to (1), the subset, H^* contains elements such that the similarity of the least similar element in H^* is maximum. This criteria has been used to explore the structure of data in [10]. The optimization problem defined as in (1), when $F(H)$ is expressed as in (2) is very hard, in general. However, the problem becomes efficiently solvable, if we require the function $\pi(i, H)$ to be monotone.

Definition 1. *A linkage function, $\pi : V \times \{2^V \setminus \emptyset\} \to \mathbf{R}$, is monotone increasing if it satisfies the inequality:*

$$\pi(i, H) \geq \pi(i, H_1) \quad \forall i, \forall H_1, \forall H : i \in H_1 \subseteq H \subseteq V \qquad (3)$$

Definition 2. *A set function F is quasi-concave if it satisfies*

$$F(H_1 \cup H_2) \geq \min(F(H_1), F(H_2)) \quad \forall H_1, H_2 \subseteq V \qquad (4)$$

Proposition 1. *The set function $F(H)$ as defined in (2) is quasi-concave, if and only if the linkage function is monotone increasing.*

Proposition 2. *For a quasi-concave set function $F(H)$ the set of all its maximizers, H^*, as defined by (1), is closed under the set union operation.*

---

[1] The argument $H \subseteq V$ is a set and $F : \{2^V \setminus \emptyset\} \to \mathbf{R}$.

We omit the proofs of these propositions due to space constraints.

Definition 3. *A maximizer of $F(H)$ that contains all other maximizers is called the $\cup$-maximizer.*

We denote the $\cup$-maximizer by $\hat{H}$. It is obvious from proposition 2 that $\hat{H}$ is the unique largest maximizer.

The algorithm for finding the $\cup$-maximizer of $F(H)$ is iterative and begins with the calculation of $F(V)$, and the set, M_1, containing elements that satisfy $F(V) = \pi(i, V)$, i.e., $M_1 = \{i \in V : \pi(i, V) = F(V)\}$. The elements in the set M_1 are removed from the set V to produce the set $H_2 = V \setminus M_1$, $(H_1 = V)$. At the iteration t, it considers the set H_{t-1} as input, calculates $F(H_{t-1})$ and identifies the set of elements M_t such that $F(H_{t-1}) = \pi(i_t, H_{t-1})$, $\forall i_t \in M_t$ and removes them from H_{t-1} to produce $H_t = H_{t-1} \setminus M_t$. The algorithm terminates at iteration T when $H_T = \emptyset$ outputting the extremal subset $\hat{H}$ as the subset, H_j with smallest j, such that $F(H_j) \geq F(H_i) \ \forall i \in < 1, 2, \ldots, T >$, $i \neq j$. The pseudocode for this algorithm is given in Table 1.

We introduce some notation that facilitates the understanding of the algorithm and helps in proving its correctness. By $\mathcal{H} = \{H_1, H_2 \ldots, H_T\}$ we denote a sequence of nested subsets of V such that $H_T \subset H_{T-1} \subset \ldots \subset H_2 \subset H_1 = V$, where, $H_t \setminus H_{t+1} = M_t = \{i : \pi(i, H_t) = \min_{j \in H_t} \pi(j, H_t)\}$. Additionally, $\Gamma = \{\Gamma_1, \Gamma_2, \ldots, \Gamma_p\}$ represents another sequence of nested subsets of V (actually a subsequence of $\mathcal{H}$), where $\Gamma_p \subset \Gamma_{p-1} \subset \ldots \Gamma_2 \subset \Gamma_1 = V$, and $F(\Gamma_1) < F(\Gamma_2) < \ldots < F(\Gamma_p)$. In fact, each Γ_i, $i = < 1, 2, \ldots, p >$ is equal to some H_j, $j = < i, i+1, \ldots, T >$.

Table 1. Pseudocode to extract the $\cup$-maximizer of $F(H)$

```
Input : monotone linkage function π(i, H), i ∈ H ⊆ V.
Output: Sequence of nested subsets H = {H₁, H₂ ..., H_T}
    s.t. H_T ⊂ H_{T-1} ⊂ ... ⊂ H₂ ⊂ H₁ = V
    along with a sequence of values
    F = {F₁, F₂, ..., F_T} s.t. F(H_t) = F_t, t =< 1, 2, ..., T >
    Another sequence of nested subsets, Γ = {Γ₁, Γ₂, ..., Γ_p}
    where Γ_p ⊂ Γ_{p-1} ⊂ ... Γ₂ ⊂ Γ₁ = V
    and F(Γ₁) < F(Γ₂) < ... < F(Γ_p)
Step 0: Set t := 1; s := 1; H₁ := V; Γ₁ := V;
Step 1: Find M_t := {i : π(i, H_t) = min π(j, H_t)};
                                      j∈H_t
Step 2: if (H_t \ M_t = ∅) STOP.
        else H_{t+1} := H_t \ M_t; F_{t+1} := F(H_{t+1}); t := t + 1;
        if (F_t > F(Γ_s)) s := s + 1; Γ_s = H_t;
        go to Step 1.
```

Theorem 1. *The subset Γ_p output by the above algorithm is the $\cup$-maximizer for F in the set V.*

Proof. According to the algorithm $F(\Gamma_p) = \max_{H_i \in \mathcal{H}} F(H_i)$. Let us begin by proving that Γ_p is a maximizer, i.e., $F(\Gamma_p) \geq F(H) \ \forall H \subseteq V$. The proof is divided into two cases: (i) $H \setminus \Gamma_p \neq \emptyset$ and, (ii) $H \subseteq \Gamma_p$.

Case (i) $[H \setminus \Gamma_p \neq \emptyset]$: Let H_i be the smallest set in the sequence $\mathcal{H}$ that contains the given set H, so that $H \subseteq H_i$ but $H \not\subseteq H_{i+1}$. According to the algorithm, $M_i = H_i \setminus H_{i+1}$, so there is at least one element in M_i which also belongs to H, say $i_H \in H$, and $i_H \in M_i$. By definition of $F(H_i)$, we have

$$F(H_i) = \min_{i \in H_i} \pi(i, H_i) = \pi(i^*, H_i) \tag{5}$$

By construction of M_i (step 1 of the pseudocode), all i^* satisfying (5) belong to M_i, so, $\pi(i^*, H_i) = \pi(i_H, H_i)$. Then, by monotonicity of $\pi(i, H)$ we get

$$\pi(i_H, H_i) \geq \pi(i_H, H) \geq \min_{i \in H} \pi(i, H) = F(H) \tag{6}$$

Using (5) and (6) we obtain $F(H_i) \geq F(H)$. According to the algorithm $F(\Gamma_p) > F(H_i), \forall \Gamma_p \subset H_i$, so we prove that

$$F(\Gamma_p) > F(H), \ \forall H \setminus \Gamma_p \neq \emptyset \tag{7}$$

Case (ii) $[H \subseteq \Gamma_p]$: Similar to the previous case, there exists a smallest subset H_i in the sequence $\mathcal{H}$ that includes H. So, the inequalities in (6) hold here too, and we could write $F(H_i) \geq F(H)$. On the other hand, $F(\Gamma_p) \geq F(H_i)$, which in conjunction with the previous inequality this means

$$F(\Gamma_p) \geq F(H), \ \forall H \subseteq \Gamma_p \tag{8}$$

It is obvious that a maximizer which satisfies both the inequalities (7) and (8) is the $\cup$-maximizer.

3   Quasi-Concave Set Functions on a Multipartite Graph

We now extend the above formulations for a multipartite graph. Consider a family of sets, $G = \{G_1, G_2, \ldots, G_k\}$, where $G_s, s \in <1, 2, \ldots, k>$ is a set; let $H = \{H_1, H_2, \ldots, H_k\}$ be a family of subsets where $H_s \subseteq G_s, s \in <1, 2, \ldots, k>$. We will also use G to denote the set containing elements of all its member sets and H to denote the set containing elements of its member sets [2]. The usage should be clear from the context.

A weighted multipartite graph related to the family of sets, G, is represented by $G^k = (G, E, W) = (G_1 \cup G_2 \cup \ldots \cup G_k, E, W)$, where members of G are considered as partite sets in the graph and the set of edges E represents the similarity relations between elements from different partite sets. The weight $w_{ij}^{st} \in W$ on an edge $e_{ij}^{st} \in E$ represents the strength of similarity between a node, $i \in G_s$ and $j \in G_t$ where $s, t = <1, 2, \ldots, k>$ and $s \neq t$.

---

[2] In this case, G is identified with a single set $V = \{1, 2, \ldots, i, \ldots, n\}$ of all the considered elements in all, $G_s, s = <1, 2, \ldots, k>$; a similar analogy holds for H.

The formulation of an optimization problem to extract a multipartite cluster requires the design of a linkage function that would appropriately capture the idea of similar elements in different partite sets of G. For any $i_s \in H_s$, $s =< 1, \ldots, k >$ and all H_t, $t =< 1, 2, \ldots, k >$, $s \neq t$, consider the linkage function, $\pi_{st}(i_s, H_t)$ which satisfies the monotonicity condition $\pi_{st}(i_s, H_t) \geq \pi_{st}(i_s, H'_t) \; \forall H'_t \subseteq H_t$. Using this family of linkage functions as basic components, we build a multipartite linkage function as

$$\pi_{mp}(i, H) = \begin{cases} \sum_{\substack{s=1 \\ s \neq t}}^{k} \pi_{st}(i_s, H_t), & \text{if} \quad (i = i_t) \; \wedge \; (\exists t : H_t \neq \emptyset) \\ 0, & \text{otherwise} \end{cases} \quad (9)$$

It follows that $\pi_{mp}(i, H)$ is also a monotone function. According to (9), an element $i_t \in H_t$ is not influenced by any of the elements from its own partition H_t and the multipartite linkage function considers similarity values between elements belonging to different families in the set. Furthermore, analogous to the objective function for a general graph, the *multipartite objective function* is defined as $F_{mp} = \min_{i \in H} \pi_{mp}(i, H)$. Then a multipartite cluster is defined as

$$\hat{H} = \arg \max_{H \subseteq G} F_{mp}(H) \quad (10)$$

Since the multipartite linkage function is also monotonically increasing, we can obtain the optimal solution for (10) using the procedure given in Table 1. This procedure outputs one multipartite cluster in the set G. However, many such clusters are likely to be present in the set G. If we assume that these clusters are unrelated to one another, we can remove the elements belonging to the first cluster $\hat{H}$ from G and extract another multipartite cluster in the set $G \setminus \hat{H}$. This idea can be iteratively applied to find all multipartite clusters. The procedure given in Table 2 formalizes this idea. It produces an ordered set,

Table 2. Pseudocode to extract a series of multipartite clusters

Initialization: $G^0 := G$; $m := 0$; $C = \emptyset$;
Step 1: Extract $\hat{H}^m$ from G^m using (1); Add $\hat{H}^m$ to C;
Step 2: $G^{m+1} := G^m - \hat{H}^m$; $m := m + 1$;
Step 3: if ($(G^m = \emptyset) \vee (\pi_{mp}(i, H) = 0 \; \forall i \in H \subseteq G^m)$)
$\quad\quad\quad$ Output C, G^m as R, and m; STOP;
$\quad\quad$ else go to step 1

$C = \{\hat{H}^0, \hat{H}^1, \ldots, \hat{H}^m\}$, of m clusters, and a set of residual elements $R = \{i : i \in G \setminus C\}$. The number, m, of non-trivial clusters is determined by the method automatically. Every cluster in C contains at least two elements from at least two different partite sets of G. Clusters from C and R form a partition of the set of genes. A cluster, $\hat{H}_i$, produced at the iteration i, has the position i in the order set, C and satisfies $F(\hat{H}_i) > F(\hat{H}_{i+1})$, $i =< 1, \ldots, m >$.

3.1   Modeling Ortholog Clusters

Known complete methods to find clusters of orthologous genes have at least two
stages - automatic and manual. The role of the latter is to correct the results of
the first stage which is a clustering procedure. Although specific implementations
of clustering procedures in different methods vary, most successful methods include some critical steps such as build clusters based on a set of "mutually most
similar pairs" of genes from different genomes. These pairs are called BBH (bi-
directional best hits [5], [3]). This preprocessing is time intensive and not robust -
small changes in the data or in free parameters used in the procedure can alter
the results. So, the current status of the problem to extract groups of orthologous genes has at least three bottlenecks: (a) the manual curation, (b) time
complexity, and (c) the hyper-sensitivity of the automatic stage to parameter
changes. Our approach tries to resolve these three tasks.

Since orthologous genes must be present in different organisms, our definition
of ortholog clusters ignores similarity among genes within a genome and focuses
on similarity values between genes from different organisms only. For the ortholog
clustering problem, the family of sets $G = \{G_1, G_2, \ldots, G_k\}$ corresponds to the
set of k different complete genomes under consideration, where G_l is the lth
genome and the nodes in the partite set, G_l, correspond to genes in that genome.
Let $M^{st} = ||m_{ij}^{st}||$ represent the matrix of similarities (computed using Blast [11])
between genes $i \in G_s$ and $j \in G_t, s \neq t$, then the pair-wise linkage function for
genes in genomes G_s and G_t is defined as

$$\pi_{st}(i_s, H_t) = \sum_{j_t \in H_t} m_{ij}^{st} \tag{11}$$

Using this function, the multipartite linkage function $\pi_{mp}(i, H)$ is defined as in
(9). Following the definition of the multipartite objective function, an orthologous group is extracted as a multipartite cluster $\hat{H}$ in (10).

The method is robust to slight variations in pair-wise similarities because
the linkage function value depends on many pair-wise similarities. The method
automatically determines the number of ortholog clusters. It does not require
a high quality of "completeness" of the considered genomes, indeed, the linkage
function integrates similarity values from one gene to many genes, so it is unlikely
that results might change considerably for a small variation in the sets of genes
in the considered genomes. A few tests of such perturbation in the input data
have been performed and they show that results are very stable.

4   Experimental Results

We applied the proposed method to the data set used to construct the Cluster of Orthologous Groups, COG database (version updated Feb. 2003, http:
//www.ncbi.nlm.nih.gov/COG/) [3], [7]. This database of orthologs was constructed from 43 complete genomes containing 104,101 protein sequences. Some
of these proteins are multi-domain sequences (two or more subunits, each with

an independent biological role) and are manually divided based on domains, as a consequence there are 108,091 sequences used to construct COGs. The construction procedure for COGs requires that orthologous genes be present in three or more organisms, and, as a result only 77,114 sequences corresponding to 74,059 genes, or about 71% of all sequences in the 43 complete genomes, belong to 3,307 ortholog clusters in the COG database. More precisely, the COGs are made up of 26 groups derived from 43 genomes by combining similar genomes into "hyper-genomes". In other words, all genes from genomes within a group are considered as genes in the corresponding hyper-genome. Furthermore, similar genes in each of the 26 groups of genomes are grouped together as *paralogs* and considered as single units when producing ortholog clusters in COG.

Pair-wise similarity values between sequences, computed using Blast [11], are available at the COG website. We use these pre-computed similarity scores. The raw pair-wise similarity values are made symmetric by $sim(i,j) = \max (s(i,j), s(j,i))$, where $s(i,j) = -\log\{e\text{-}value(i,j)\}$.

In contrast to COG, which was constructed on 26 groups of genomes, we applied our procedure to all 108,091 sequences in the 43 complete genomes. The procedure produced 38,285 clusters including 13,202 singletons, 16,806 clusters of size 2, while 8,277 clusters contain at least 3 sequences. The singletons, by definition, cannot be ortholog clusters and are removed from further analysis. The 8,277 clusters contain 576 clusters which contain sequences from 2 organisms, and 7,701 clusters containing sequences from at least 3 organisms. We call these 7,701 clusters, the MPC clusters and focus our analysis on them.

To assess the conservation among sequences within MPC clusters, we used their Pfam and SCOP annotations. These annotations were obtained through HMM search performed using HMMER [12]. In the set of 7,701 clusters with sequences from at least 3 organisms, only 61 clusters contain sequences that are related to different Pfam families. There are 541 clusters, with no sequence associated with a Pfam family and 5,901 clusters with all their sequences annotated with a single Pfam family. Comparisons with SCOP annotations show that only 52 clusters contain sequences that are related to different SCOP super-families, and 4,946 clusters have all their sequences annotated by a single SCOP superfamily, while sequences in 1,884 clusters could not be annotated with any SCOP superfamily. As in the case of clusters with size 2, we found that clusters produced earlier while iteratively generating clusters are those highly correlated with a single Pfam family, or SCOP superfamily annotation.

5   Comparative Analysis

The 7,701 ortholog clusters contain 51,134 sequences. Among the 7,701 of our ortholog clusters, 7,101 (92%) contain sequences from a single COG, but there are 7,474 (97%) clusters whose sequences are consistent in at least one of the annotations - Pfam, SCOP or COG membership. The set of all sequences in our ortholog clusters are mostly contained (98%) in the set of all sequences in COGs. There are 104 COGs that are found to match our clusters exactly.

To estimate the association between clusters in COG and MPC clusters, we calculate several statistical parameters. We use the *rand index* [13] and its normalized variant *adjusted rand index* [14] to quantify the relatedness of the two classifications. These indices involve counting the number of agreements between the two classifications based on how each pair of elements from the underlying set is assigned to classes (clusters) by the two classification schemes. We obtained a value of 0.804 for the rand index which can be interpreted as : more than 80% of all pairs of sequences in our clustering results agree with ortholog clusters in COG. When the number of agreement pairs are normalized with the expected value of the number of agreement pairs in a random classification (the adjusted rand index) we obtained a value of 0.665, suggesting a high degree of correlation between the MPC clusters and manually curated clusters in COGs.

For the average index measuring the fraction of the number of sequences in our clusters that do not belong to any COG cluster, we obtain a value of 0.021, suggesting that it is very rare that sequences in an MPC-cluster do not belong to any COG. The average number of different COGs that overlap with an MPC-cluster, is 1.087 which indicates that most our clusters contain sequences from a single COG cluster. The average of the number of MPC cluster present in COG clusters is 2.463. This is consistent with the fact that there are 7,701 MPC clusters and 3,307 COG clusters.

A comparison of distribution of the size of MPC clusters with the size of COG clusters reveals that our clusters are smaller in size. MPC clusters are usually sub-clusters of COG and contain elements from evolutionarily closely related organisms. For instance, there are 10 MPC-clusters that contain genes from all organisms from 2 kingdoms, however, most (7) of these are fragments of COGs that contain genes from the 3 kingdoms. This effect is probably due to the stringent criteria used in our ortholog clustering formulation.

Clusters containing sequences from a single COG are evidently homogeneous and contain orthologous genes. Then, from an evaluation perspective it is interesting to analyze MPC clusters that overlap with more than one COG clusters. Such clusters might naively be considered as spurious, but a careful analysis shows that sequences in these clusters share important biological signals. There are 78 large clusters (size≥20) that overlap with more than one COG. We found that annotations for different COGs that overlap with an MPC cluster are highly related, moreover, all sequences in this class of clusters share Pfam and SCOP annotations. In many cases, these clusters correspond to COGs whose annotations have keywords like *ABC transporters* (*ATPases* and *GTPases*), *dehydrogenases*, *regulatory genes for transcription*, DNA binding domains, etc. These annotations are related to some the largest group of paralogs, and are known to be hard to distinguish based on pair-wise sequence similarity scores [15].

6   Conclusions

The problem of finding orthologous clusters in a large number of complete genomes is modeled as clustering on a multipartite graph (MPC). Such modeling abstracts the problem and allows us to focus on multipartite graph clustering. We have designed a new measure of similarity between an entity and a subset using the monotone linkage function for multipartite graphs. The multipartite graph clustering problem is formulated as a combinatorial optimization problem using a quasi-concave function induced over the linkage function. This enables us to get a cluster in the multipartite graph, and it is shown that this scheme can be used, sequentially, to cluster the graph. The method is efficient for ortholog studies in a large data set and does not require any thresholds. Since the optimal set is related to the similarity structure present in the data, the proposed method has an added advantage of discovering the number of clusters in the data which is a feature well suited to ortholog clustering.

We have applied the method to screening for orthologous genes in a large number of prokaryote genomes. The analyses of the results shows that orthologous clusters obtained using the MPC approach show a high degree of correlation with the manually curated ortholog clusters in one of the most trusted databases of ortholog clusters, COG.

The multipartite graph clustering method produces smaller but conserved orthologous clusters. This feature ensures that clusters contain sequences which share an orthologous relationship, and is critical to balance for the manual curation of orthologous clusters. On the other hand, related conserved clusters can be merged, using a variant of the proposed method, to obtain a desired level of aggregation. This could be useful to biologists who search genomic data to discover relationships between genes in related organisms.

References

1. Fitch, W.M.: Distinguishing homologous from analogous proteins. Syst Zool. **19** (1970) 99–113
2. Fujibuchi, W., Ogata, H., Matsuda, H., Kanehisa, M.: Automatic detection of conserved gene clusters in multiple genomes by graph comparison and P-quasi grouping. Nucleic Acids Res. **28** (2002) 4096–4036
3. Tatusov, R., Koonin, E., Lipmann, D.: A genomic perspective on protein families. Science **278** (1997) 631–637
4. Strom, C.E., Sonnhammer, E.L.: Automated ortholog inference from phylogenetic trees and calculation of orthology reliability. Bioinformatics **18** (2002) 92–99
5. Remm, M., Strom, C.E., Sonnhammer, E.L.: Automatics clustering of orthologs and in-paralogs from pairwise species comparisons. J Mol Biol. **314** (2001) 1041–1052
6. Zmasek, C.M., Eddy, S.R.: RIO: Analyzing proteomes by automated phylogenomics using resampled inference of orthologs. BioMed Central Bioinformatics **3** (2002)
7. Tatusov, R.L., Galperin, M.Y., Natale, D.A., Koonin, E.V.: The COG database: a tool for genome-scale analysis of protein function and evolution. Nucleic Acids Res. **28** (2000) 33–36
8. Bateman, A., Coin, L., Durbin, R., Finn, R.D., Hollich, V., Griffiths-Jones, S., Khanna, A., Marshall, M., Moxon, S., Sonnhammer, E.L.L., Studholme, D.J., Yeats, C., Eddy, S.R.: The Pfam protein families database. Nucleic Acids Res. **32** (2004) 138–141

9. Andreeva, A., Howorth, D., Brenner, S.E., Hubbard, T.J.P., Chothia, C., Murzin, A.G.: SCOP database in 2004: refinements integrate structure and sequence family data. Nucleic Acids Res. **32** (2004) 226–229

10. Mirkin, B., Muchnik, I.: Layered clusters of tightness set functions. Appl. Math. Lett. **15** (2002) 147–151

11. Altschul, S., Madden, T., Schaffer, A., Zhang, J., Zhang, Z., Miller, W., Lipman, D.: Gapped BLAST and PSI-BLAST: a new generation of protein database search programs. Nucleic Acids Res. **25** (1997) 3389–3402

12. Eddy, S.R.: A review of the profile HMM literature from 1996-1998. Bioinformatics **14** (1998) 755–763

13. Rand, W.M.: Objective criterion for the evaluation of clustering methods. J. Am. stat. Assoc. **66** (1971) 846–850

14. Hubert, L.J., Arabie, P.: Comparing partitions. Journal of Classification **2** (1985) 193–218

15. Tomii, K., Kanehisa, M.: A comparative analysis of ABC transporters in complete microbial genomes. Genome Res. **8** (1998) 1048–59

An Ontology-Based Pattern Mining System for Extracting Information from Biological Texts

Muhammad Abulaish[1] and Lipika Dey[2]

[1] Department of Mathematics, Jamia Millia Islamia (A Central University),
New Delhi-110025, India
mdabulaish@rediffmail.com
[2] Department of Mathematics, Indian Institute of Technology, Delhi,
Hauz Khas, New Delhi - 110 016, India
lipika@maths.iitd.ac.in

Abstract. Biological information embedded within the large repository of unstructured or semi-structured text documents can be extracted more efficiently through effective semantic analysis of the texts in collaboration with structured domain knowledge. The GENIA corpus houses tagged MEDLINE abstracts, manually annotated according to the GENIA ontology, for this purpose. However, manual tagging of all texts is impossible and special purpose storage and retrieval mechanisms are required to reduce information overload for users. In this paper we have proposed an ontology-based biological Information Extraction and Query Answering (BIEQA) system that has four components: an ontology-based tag analyzer for analyzing tagged texts to extract Biological and lexical patterns, an ontology-based tagger for tagging new texts, a knowledge base enhancer which enhances the ontology, and incorporates new knowledge in the form of biological entities and relationships into the knowledge base, and a query processor for handling user queries.

Keywords: Ontology-based text mining, Biological information extraction, Automatic tagging.

1 Introduction

The collection of research articles in the field of Molecular Biology is growing at such a tremendous rate, that without the aid of automated content analysis systems designed for this domain, the assimilation of knowledge from this vast repository is becoming practically impossible [10]. The core problem in designing content analysis systems for text documents arises from the fact that these documents are usually unstructured or semi-structured in nature. Recent efforts at consolidating biological and clinical knowledge in the structured form of ontologies however have raised hopes of realizing such systems. Since ontology specifies the key concepts in a domain and their inter-relationships to provide an abstract view of an application domain [1], ontology-based Information Extraction (IE) schemes can help in alleviating a wide variety of natural language ambiguities present in a given domain.

D. Ślęzak et al. (Eds.): RSFDGrC 2005, LNAI 3642, pp. 420–429, 2005.

Let us illustrate our point of view through an example. Suppose a user poses a query like *"What are the biological substances activated by CD28?"*, then a specific answer like, *"Differential regulation of proto-oncogenes c-jun and c-fos in T lymphocytes activated through CD28,"* can be extracted from the repository provided the system knows that *proto-oncogenes, c-jun* and *c-fos* are biological substances. Kim et al. [7] suggest that such an answer can be produced if the elements in the text are appropriately annotated. Though this scheme can solve the information extraction problem very effectively, some of the key challenging tasks towards designing such systems are: (i) recognition of entities to be tagged (ii) automatic tagging of identified entities (iii) choosing a base ontology that can be used to annotate the text effectively (iv) assimilate new domain knowledge.

In this paper we have proposed an ontology-based Biological Information Extraction and Query Answering (BIEQA) System that tries to address the above problems within a unified framework. The system exploits information about domain ontology concepts and relations in conjunction with lexical patterns obtained from biological text documents. It extracts and structures information about biological entities and relationships among them within a pre-defined knowledge base model. The underlying ontology is enhanced using knowledge about feasible relations discovered from the texts. The system employs efficient data structures to store the mined knowledge in structured form so that biological queries can be answered efficiently.

The rest of the paper is organized as follows. We review some related works on biological information extraction in section 2. The architecture of the complete system is presented in section 3. Sections 4 through 7 present functional details of each module. The performance of the system is discussed in section 8. Finally, we conclude and discuss future work in section 9.

2   Related Work

A general approach to perform information extraction from biological documents is to annotate or tag relevant entities in the text, and reason with them. Most of the existing systems focus on a single aspect of text information extraction. The tagging is often done manually. A significant effort has gone towards identifying biological entities in journal articles for tagging them. Su et al. [11] have proposed a corpus-based approach for automatic compound extraction which considers only bigrams and trigrams. Collier et el. [2] have proposed a Hidden Markov Model (HMM) based approach to extract the names of the genes and gene products from Medline abstracts. Fukuda et al. [5] have proposed a method called PROtein Proper-noun phrase Extracting Rules (PROPER) to extract material names from sentences using surface clue on character strings in medical and biological documents.

Reasoning about contents of a text document however needs more than identification of the entities present in it. Kim et el. [7] have proposed the GENIA ontology of substances and sources (substance locations) as a base to fix the class of molecular biological entities and relationships among them. The GE-

NIA ontology is widely accepted as a baseline for categorizing biological entities and reasoning with them for inferring about contents of documents. There also exists a GENIA corpus created by the same group, which contains 2000 manually tagged MEDLINE abstracts, where the tags correspond to GENIA ontology classes. Tags can be both simple or nested, where simple tags have been awarded to single noun phrases, whereas nested tags are for more complex phrases. Tags can help in identification of documents containing information of interest to a user, where interest can be expressed at various levels of generalization. Extracting contents from text documents based on relations among entities is also another challenge to text-mining researchers. Craven and Kumlien [3] have proposed identification of possible drug-interaction relations between protein and chemicals using a bag of words approach applied at the sentence level. Ono et al. [8] report on extraction of protein-protein interactions based on a combination of syntactic patterns. Rinaldi et al. [9] have proposed an approach to automatically extract some relevant relations in the domain of Molecular Biology, based on a complete syntactic analysis of existing corpus. Friedman et al. [4] has proposed GENEIS - a natural language processing system for extracting information about molecular pathways from texts.

3   Architecture of the BIEQA System

In contrast to the systems discussed earlier, BIEQA is conceived as a completely automated information extraction system that can build a comprehensive knowledge base of biological information to relieve users from information overload. The system uses the GENIA ontology as its starting domain knowledge repository.

Fig. 1 represents the complete architecture of the BIEQA system. Though the primary role of the system is to answer queries efficiently, initially the system is trained to tag new documents automatically, for the ease of information extraction. The system has four main components. The first component, Tag Analyzer, has dual responsibilities. During system training, it operates on a set of tagged texts to extract relationships between tags and other lexical patterns within texts. Tag Analyzer also extracts key biological information from tagged texts in the form of entities and their relations. This is stored in the knowledge base to answer user queries efficiently. The second module, Tag Predictor, tags new documents using the knowledge about tagging extracted by the analyzer. This module uses a combination of table look-up and maximum-likelihood based prediction techniques. The system is equipped with a powerful entity recognizer for identifying candidate phrases in new documents for both simple and nested tagging. One of the unique aspects of our system is the integration of a module called Knowledge Base Enhancer which has the capability to enhance existing ontological structures with new information that is extracted from documents. Query Processor, the fourth module, extracts relevant portions of documents from a local database, along with their MEDLINE references. User interaction with the system is provided through a guided query interface. The interface al-

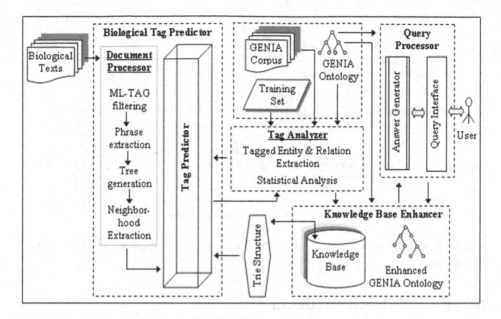

Fig. 1. System Architecture

lows users to pose queries at various levels of specificity including combinations of entities, tags and/or relations. Further details of each module is presented in the following sections.

4   Tag Analyzer

As already mentioned, the Tag Analyzer has two main functions. During training, the analyzer helps in extracting statistical information about tag-word co-occurrences from manually tagged documents. To start with, the Tag Analyzer filters stop words from the corpus. We have considered most of the stop words used by PubMed database. After that, it assigns a document id, a name (Medline number), and a line number to every sentence of the corpus. Then it extracts contents of a sentence and stores them in a tree structure, which is defined as follows:

```
struct tag{
char * name;
struct tag * lchild; struct tag * rchild; struct tag *InnerTag;}
struct segment {
char *non_tagged_text; struct tag *tags;}
struct segment sentence[no_of_segments]
```

This tree is used by Tag Predictor and Knowledge Base Enhancer. Fig. 2 shows a sample tree structure created by Tag Analyzer corresponding to a tagged sentence picked up from MEDLINE:95197524.

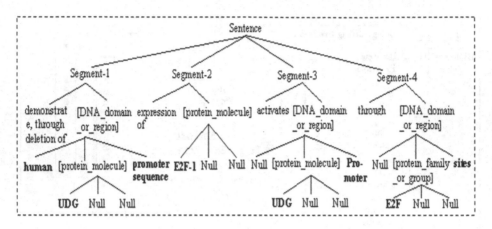

Fig. 2. Tree structure generated with a sample sentence. [] indicates tags. Entities are in boldface.

5 Biological Tag Predictor

The main function of this module is to locate entities in the biological document and tag them according to GENIA ontology. During the training phase of the system, this module works on the tree structure generated by Tag Analyzer to extract statistical information for tagging. After training, it applies the extracted statistical knowledge to tag the biological entities appearing in a document. To identify entities from documents, this module also implements a document processor. Since tagging is based on neighboring words, hence, it also includes a neighborhood extractor which stores information about occurrences of terms surrounding an entity. We outline the functions of each of these components in the following subsections.

5.1 Document Processor for Entity Recognition

The main function of this module is to locate entities. Since entities are either nouns or noun phrases, the document processor consists of a Parts-Of-Speech (POS) Tagger that assigns parts of speech to English words based on the context in which they appear. We have used a web-based Tagger, developed by the Specialized Information Services Division (SIS) of the National Library of Medicine[1] (NLM), to locate and extract noun phrases that are present in the text document. In addition to identification of nouns and noun phrases as named entities, this module also consists of a set of rules to handle special characters which are very common in biological documents. Gavrilis et el. [6] have proposed a rule set for pre-processing biological documents. We have modified this rule set including some new ones. These rules have been identified after analysis of 100 manually tagged documents picked at random from the GENIA corpus. The

---

[1] http://tamas.nlm.nih.gov

Rules

1. $<W>-<S><D> \rightarrow <S>-<D>$
2. $<w1><S>(<w2>)-<D> \rightarrow <w_1>-<D><S>(<w_2>-<D>)$
3. $<W><D>/<D> \rightarrow <W><D>/<S><W><D>$
4. $<w_1>-, <w_2>-,.., \text{ and } <w_n>-<w_m> \rightarrow <w_1>-<w_m>, <w_2><w_m>,.., \text{ and } <w_n><w_m>$
5. $<w_1>-, <w_2>-,..., \text{and} <w_n>-<w_m> \rightarrow <w_1>-<w_m>, <w_2><w_m>,..., \text{ or } <w_n><w_m>$
6. $<w_m>-<w_1>, -<w_2>,.. \text{ and } -<w_n> \rightarrow <w_m>-<w_1>, <w_m>-<w_2>,.. \text{ and } <w_m><w_n>$
7. $<w_m>-<w_1>, -<w_2>,..., \text{ or } -<w_n> \rightarrow <w_m>-<w_1>, <w_m>-<w_2>,..., \text{ or } <w_m><w_n>$
8. $<w_1>-<w_2>$ AND $<w_2>$: induc*, activat*, bind*, inhibit*, regulat*, transcri*, phospho*, suppress*, indepen*, specifi* $\rightarrow <w_1><S>-<S><w_2>$

Identified entities in a Medline abstract sentence [MEDLINE: 95369245] by Phraser

IL-2 gene expression and NF-kappa B activation through CD28 requires reactive
N   N   N   C   J   N   N   R   N   V   J
oxygen production by 5-lipoxygenase.
N   N   R   N

[[IL-2 gene] expression] and [[NF-kappa B] activation] through [CD28] requires [reactive oxygen production] by [5-lipoxygenase].

Legend
$<W>=(a-z, A-Z)^+$; $w=w_1+w_2+...+w_n \in W$; $<D>=(0-9)^+$; $<S>=\{$White space chars.$\}$

Fig. 3. Entity recognition rules and a sample sentence with entities identified for tagging indicated by [ ]

modified rule set is shown in Fig. 3. These rules help in generating equivalent names from a number of different appearances of Biological names, or even extract different instances from concatenations and commonly used abbreviations. For example, concatenated instances like *B- and T-cell* or *gp350/220* are converted into *B-cell and T-cell*, and *gp350/gp250* respectively. The complete list of entities are identified by applying the above-mentioned rules in conjunction with the identified noun phrases. Our method is capable of identifying both simple and nested entities to be tagged. All stop words are filtered from the documents and the processed document is passed on to the Neighborhood Extractor for extraction of bigrams. The pre-processor also assigns a document id and name (generally Medline number) and breaks the document into sentences and assigns them a unique line number within the document so that the combination of the document id and line number form a primary key.

Initially, each entity is assigned an arbitrary tag. This tag acts as a placeholder which helps in identifying locations in the sentence where tags will be inserted. The lower box in Fig. 3 shows a sample sentence along with its entities identified and marked for tag prediction. The sentence with expected tag positions marked, is now converted into a tree structure similar to the one stated in section 4, though tag names are not known now. This tree encodes all needed information about an entity and its neighboring terms in a sentence, which is used for predicting its tag.

5.2   Statistical Prediction of Tags for Entities

GENIA ontology defines 36 tag classes, including the "other_name" tag. Tag Predictor has been implemented to predict the most likely and most specific tag from this collection. For all known entities, the tag is looked up from the knowledge base. Otherwise, the tag prediction process uses a maximum likelihood based model to predict an entity E's tag based on the information about its neighboring words. The task is to maximize $\beta(T|E_n)$, where T stands for a tag and E_n for the neighbourhood of the entity. $\beta(T|E_n)$ is computed using bigrams of words and/ or tags. We define E_n as a 4-tuple (two left words and two right words), that surround entity E that is to be tagged. A 4-tuple denoted by - $< LHW-1, LHW, RHW, RHW+1 >$ specifies the state of the system. Tag Predictor generates the 4-tuple set for E through *preorder traversal* of the tree mentioned earlier. The likelihood of tag T_i, is computed using the following equation:

$$\beta(T_i|LHW-1, LHW, RHW, RHW+1) = \\ P(T_i|LHW-1) + P(T_i|LHW) + P(T_i|RHW) + P(T_i|RHW+1)$$

where $P(|)$ is calculated from training data as follows:

$$P(T_i|t) = N(T_i, t)/\Sigma_{j=1to36}N(T_j, t)$$

where $N(T_k/t)$ represents the number of times a tag T_k is observed in combination with term t in the given position, in training data.

For any entity, one or more of its neighboring words may be entities themselves, which need to be tagged. In this case we have considered the tag, which has the maximum probability of occurrence in the corresponding position as obtained from training data. The tag with maximum likelihood value which is greater than a given threshold value is assigned to the new entity. If an entity cannot be associated with any tag the entity is tagged with "other_name".

6   Knowledge Base Enhancer

Knowledge Base Enhancer conducts *postorder traversal* of the tree to extract information about entities occurring in documents. While an ontology provides useful domain knowledge for extracting information from unstructured texts, it also becomes necessary at times to enhance existing domain knowledge with additional information extracted from the text sources.

GENIA ontology specifies concept taxonomy over molecular biological substances and their locations only. Our system applies statistical analysis on the tagged documents to extract information about other possible biological relations among substances, or locations or among substances and locations. This is accomplished through extraction of relational verbs from documents and analysing their relationships with surrounding tagged entities. To identify feasible relations to enhance the ontology structure, we have focused on recognition of relational verbs in the neighborhood of the entities. After analyzing the whole collection, those relational verbs which occur with maximal frequencies surrounded by ontology tags are accepted for inclusion into the ontology. Some example relations extracted for incorporation to enhance the ontological structure are: *inhibitors_of*(other_organic_compound, protein_molecule), *inducers_of*(lipid,protein_complex), *induces_in*(mono_cell, protein_molecule), *activates*(protein_molecule, protein_molecule) etc. It may be noted that prepositions determine the role of a concept in a relation. Information about all known entities and documents in which they are occurring are stored separately in a trie structure, and not in the ontology. For each entity in the collection it stores the corresponding tag and its locations in the corpus.

7   Query Processor

Query processing is a two-step process - acceptance and analysis of the user query and then finding the relevant answer from the structured knowledge base. Query Processor uses the enhanced ontology structure to allow the user to formulate queries at multiple levels of specificity. For example, a user may specify an entity name and ask for documents containing it. However, a user can be more generic and post a query like that shown earlier "What are the *biological substances* activated by CD28", which is a combination of generic concepts like *biological substances*, specific instances like *CD 28* and a specific relation *activated by*, which should relate these elements in the document.

Our system stores various permissible templates to enable users to formulate feasible queries at multiple levels of specificity. As the user formulates a query, the most appropriate template is selected by the system. Templates could be of the form <*,relation,Entity>, or <Entity,*, Tag>, or <Tag,relation, Tag> etc. A query is analyzed and processed by the Answer Generator module to extract the relevant information from the knowledge base. The query presented above is passed on to system through template <*,relation=activated,Entity=CD28>. Two of the responses extracted from the local knowledge base are:

1. MEDLINE:95081587: Differential regulation of proto-oncogenes c-jun and c-fos in T lymphocytes activated through CD28.
2. MEDLINE:96322738: The induction of T cell proliferation requires signals from the TCR and a co-receptor molecule, such as CD28, that activate parallel and partially cross-reactive signaling pathways.

Another query "How are HIV-1 and cell_type related?" instantiates the template <Entity=HIV-1,relation=*,Tag=Cell_type>. Some corresponding abstracts extracted for this are:

1. MEDLINE:95187990: HIV-1 Nef leads to inhibition or activation of T cells depending on its intracellular localization.
2. MEDLINE:94340810: Superantigens activate HIV-1 gene expression in monocytic cells.

8   System Performance Analysis

To judge the performance of the system, we have randomly selected 10 documents from the GENIA corpus that consist of 80 sentences and 430 tags. These documents were cleaned by removing tags from them. Table 1 summarizes the performance of entity recognition process over this set. It is observed that precision is somewhat low due to the fact that there are many noun phrases that are not valid entities. To evaluate the effectiveness of Tag Predictor, we have blocked the table look-up process because in this case all entities can be found in the knowledge base. Table 2 summarizes the performance of Tag Predictor in the form of a misclassification matrix. We have considered the fact that along with the assignment of correct tags to relevant entities, the system should tag those entities which are not Biological as *other_name*. Computation of precision takes this into account.

Table 1. Misclassification Matrix for Entity Recognition

Module	Relevant Phrases extracted	Nonrelevant phrases extracted	Relevant phrases missed	Prec-ision	Re-call
Entity Recognizer	417	50	13	89.29	96.98

Table 2. Misclassification Matrix for Tag Predictor

Module	Correct prediction	Wrong prediction	Right prediction of othername	Wrong prediction of othername	Prec-ision	Re-call
Tag Predictor	389	27	9	42	90.47	92.29

9   Conclusions and Future Work

In this paper we have presented an ontology-based deep text-mining system, BIEQA, which employs deep text mining in association to information about the likelihood of various entity-relation occurrences to extract information from biological documents. User interaction with the system is provided through an ontology-guided interface, which enables the user to pose queries at various levels of specification including combinations of specific entities, tags and/or relations. One of the unique aspects of our system lies in its capability to enhance existing ontological structures with new information that is extracted from documents. Presently, we are working towards generating a fuzzy ontology structure, in which, relations can be stored along with their strengths. Strength of relations can thereby play a role in determining relevance of a document to a user query. Query Processor is also being enhanced to tackle a wide range of structured natural language queries. Further work on implementing better entity recognition rules is also on.

Acknowledgements. The authors would like to thank the Ministry of Human Resources and Development, Government of India, for providing financial support for this work (#RP01537).

References

1. Broekstra, J., Klein, M., Decker, S., Fensel, D., van Harmelen, F., Horrocks, I.: Enabling Knowledge Representation on the Web by Extending RDF Schema. In Proceedings of the 10th Int. World Wide Web Conference, Hong Kong (2001) 467-478

2. Collier, N., Nobata C., Tsujii J.: Extracting the Names of Genes and Gene Products with a Hidden Markov Model. In Proceedings of the 18th Int. Conference on Computational Linguistics (COLING'2000), Saarbrucken Germany (2000) 201-207

3. Craven, M., Kumlien, J.: Constructing Biological Knowledge Bases by Extracting Information from Text Sources. In Proceedings of the 7th Int. Conference on Intelligent Systems for Molecular Biology (ISMB'99), Heidelburg Germany (1999) 77-86

4. Friedman, C., Kra, P.,Yu, H., Krauthammer, M., Rzhetsky, A.: GENIES: A Natural-Language Processing System for the Extraction of Molecular Pathways from Biomedical Texts. Bioinformatics 17 (2001) 74-82

5. Fukuda, K., Tsunoda, T., Tamura, A., Takagi, T.: Toward Information Extraction: Identifying Protein Names from Biological papers. In Pacific Symposium on Biocomputing, Maui Hawaii (1998) 707-718

6. Gavrilis, D., Dermatas, E., Kokkinakis, G.: Automatic Extraction of Information from Molecular Biology Scientific Abstracts. In Proceedings of the Int. Workshop on SPEECH and COMPUTERS (SPECOM'03), Moscow Russia (2003)

7. Kim, J.D., Ohta, T., Tateisi, Y., Tsujii, J.: GENIA corpus - A Semantically Annotated Corpus for Bio-Textmining. Bioinformatics 19(1) (2003) 180-182

8. Ono, T., Hishigaki, H., Tanigami, A., Takagi, T.: Automated Extraction of Information on Protein-Protein Interactions from the Biological Literature. Bioinformatics 17(2) (2001) 155-161

9. Rinaldi, F., Scheider, G., Andronis, C., Persidis, A., Konstani, O.: Mining Relations in the GENIA Corpus. In Proceedings of the 2nd European Workshop on Data Mining and Text Mining for Bioinformatics, Pisa Italy (2004) 61-68

10. Stapley, B.J., Benoit, G.: Bibliometrics: Information Retrieval and Visualization from Co-occurrence of Gene Names in MedLine Abstracts. In Proceedings of the Pacific Symposium on Biocomputing, Oahu Hawaii (2000) 529-540

11. Su, K., Wu, M., Chang, J.: A Corpus-Based Approach to Automatic Compound Extraction. In Proceedings of the 32nd Annual Meeting of the Association for Computational Linguistics (ACL'94), Las Cruses New Maxico USA (1994) 242-247

Parallel Prediction of Protein-Protein Interactions Using Proximal SVM

Yoojin Chung[1,*], Sang-Young Cho[1], and Sung Y. Shin[2]

[1] Computer Science & Information Communications Engineering Division,
Hankuk University of Foreign Studies, Yongin, Kyonggi-do, Korea
{chungyj, sycho}@hufs.ac.kr
[2] EE and Computer Science Department, South Dakota State University,
Brookings SD 57007
Sung.Shin@sdstate.edu

Abstract. In general, the interactions between proteins are fundamental to a broad area of biological functions. In this paper, we try to predict protein-protein interactions in parallel on a 12-node PC-cluster using domains of a protein. For this, we use a hydrophobicity among protein's amino acid's physicochemical feature and a support vector machine (SVM) among machine learning techniques. According to the experiments, we get approximately 60% average accuracy with 5 trials and we obtained an average speed-up of 5.11 with a 12-node cluster using a proximal SVM.

1 Introduction

A major post-genomic scientific pursuit is to describe the functions performed by the proteins encoded by the genome. The goal of proteomics is to elucidate the structure, interactions and functions of all proteins within cells and organisms. The expectation is that this gives full understanding of cellular processes and networks at the protein level, ultimately leading to a better understanding of disease mechanisms.

The interactions between proteins are fundamental to the biological functions such as regulation of metabolic pathways, DNA replication, protein synthesis, etc [3]. But, biologists used experimental techniques to study protein interactions such as two-hybrid screens. And these experimental techniques are labor-intensive and potentially inaccurate. Thus, many bioinformatic approaches has been taken to predict protein interactions.

Among them, Bock and Gough [4] and Chung et al. [6] proposed a method to predict protein interactions from primary structure and associated physicochemical features using SVM. It is based on the following postulate: knowledge of the amino acid sequence alone might be sufficient to estimate the propensity for two proteins to interact and effect useful biological function. The postulate

---

* This work was supported by grant NO. R01-2004-000-10860-0 from the Basic Research Program of the Korea Science& Engineering Foundation.

D. Ślęzak et al. (Eds.): RSFDGrC 2005, LNAI 3642, pp. 430–437, 2005.

is suggested by the virtual axiom that sequence specifies conformation [9]. Here, primary structure of a protein is the amino acid sequence of the protein. And Chung et al. [7] proposed a parallel method to predict protein interactions using a proximal SVM [5].

In this paper, we also use a proximal SVM for parallel processing. But we develop various methods to make a feature vector of SVM using domains of a protein and hydrophobicity and and measure speedup and performances on various configurations.

2   Our Domain-Based Protein-Protein Interaction System

SVM learning is one of statistical learning theory, it is used many recent bioinformatic research, and it has the following advantages to process biological data [4]:

- SVM generates a representation of the nonlinear mapping from residue sequence to protein fold space [11] using relatively few adjustable model parameters.
- SVM provides a principled means to estimate generalization performance via an analytic upper bound on the generalization error. This means that a confidence level may be assigned to the prediction and alleviates problems with overfitting inherent in neural network function approximation [12].

In this paper, we use TinySVM among diverse implementations of SVM and its web site is http://cl.aist-nara.ac.jp/ taku-ku/software/TinySVM. TinySVM uses many techniques to make large-scale SVM learning practical and thus, it is good for our application with large dimensions of a feature vector of SVM and huge amount of data sets. Because [14] shows that 10 is about the right number of folds to get the best estimate of error, we do our experiments using a 10-fold Cross-Validation [13].

SVM is a supervised learning method. Thus we need both positive and negative examples to train SVM. We obtained positive examples (that is interacting proteins) from the Database of Interacting Proteins (DIP for short) and its web site is http://www.dip.doe-mbi.ucla.edu/. At the time of our experiments, the DIP database has 15117 entries. And each entry represents a pair of interacting proteins. We make negative examples by using global shuffling to the pairs not in DIP. Here, interacting mean that two amino acid chains were experimentally identified to bind to each other. Our system generate a discrete, binary decision, that is, interaction or no interaction.

Testing sets are not exposed to the system during SVM learning. The database is robust in the sense that it represents protein interaction data collected from diverse experiments. There is a negligible probability that the learning system will learn its own input on a narrow, highly self-similar set of data examples. This enhances the generalization potential of the trained SVM.

DIP database dose not have any domain information. We get this domain information from PIR (Protein Information Resource) [1] which we get using cross references in DIP. We make a feature vector of SVM by combining these domain informations with protein's amino acid sequence.

Now, we will explain how to make a feature vector of SVM. A protein has a various length of an amino acid sequence and its length is from several hundreds to several thousands. Thus, the first step is to normalize the length of each amino acid sequence of a protein. And then, we simply concatenate these two normalized amino acid sequences of protein pair which is interacting or non-interacting. And finally, we replace each amino acid in the concatenated sequence with its feature value according various methods which is described in Subsection 4.1.

We evaluate the performance of SVM using accuracy, precision, and recall. Their definitions are as follows.

- Accuracy = (pp+nn) / (pp+np+pn+nn)
- Precision = pp / (pp+pn)
- Recall = pp / (pp+np),

where p indicates positive, which means there is an interaction, and n indicates negative, which means there is no interaction. And pp is true positive, pn is false positive, np is false negative, and nn is true negative because the right side value is a real value and the left side value is a SVM's predicted value.

The accuracy is the percentage of correct predictions among all the testing set, the precision is the percentage of true positive among all the predicted positive, and the recall is the percentage of true positive among all the real positive testing data. Note that if accuracy is high, recall is an important factor to be a computational screening technique that narrow candidate interacting proteins.

3   Our Parallel Method

Now, we will explain our parallel domain-based method to predict protein-protein interactions. Fig. 1 is the configuration of our 12-node PC-cluster, which consists of one master node and 12 computing nodes. Each PC has a Pentium III processor and they are connected by gigabit ethernet. Each PC has 256M byte memory. Note that memory size is a main constraint to deal with very large dimensions of a feature vector of SVM in our PC-cluster system.

To do SVM training in parallel, we mainly refer to Fung and Mangasarian's Incremental SVM [5] and its parallel implementation [8]. Now, we will explain the main idea of proximal SVM.

3.1   Proximal SVM

We consider the problem of classifying m points in the n dimensional input space R^n, represented by the $m \times n$ matrix A, according to membership of each point A_i in the class $A+$ or $A-$ as specified by a given $m \times m$ diagonal matrix D with plus ones or minus ones along its diagonal. For this problem, the standard SVM with a linear kernel is given by the following quadratic program with paramenter $\nu > 0$ [5]:

Number of nodes	12 computing nodes
	1 master nodes
Processor	Inter Pentium III coppermine 866Mhz
	(32KB L1, 256KB L2 cache)
Main memory	256MB SDRAM
Hard disk	30GB EIDE HDD
Network	3com Gigabit Ethernet switch
	100 Base-T Ethernet NIC
OS	Redhat Linux
Language	MPICH
Physical size	W 180cm × D 60cm × H 130cm

Fig. 1. The configuration of our 12-node PC-cluster

$$\min_{(\omega,\nu,y)\in R^{n+1+m}} \nu e'y + \frac{1}{2}\omega'\omega \tag{1}$$
$$\text{s.t. } D(A\omega - e\gamma) + y \geq e,$$
$$y \geq 0.$$

ω is the normal to the bounding planes:

$$x'\omega = \gamma + 1 \tag{2}$$
$$x'\omega = \gamma - 1$$

that bound most of the sets $A+$ and $A-$ respectively. The constant γ determines their location relative to the origin. When the two classes are strictly linearly separable, that is the the error variable $y = 0$ in (1), the plane $x'\omega = \gamma + 1$ bounds all of the class $A+$ points, while the plane $x'\omega = \gamma - 1$ bounds all of the class $A-$ points as follows:

$$A_i\omega \geq \gamma + 1, \text{ for } D_{ii} = 1, \tag{3}$$
$$A_i\omega \leq \gamma - 1, \text{ for } D_{ii} = -1.$$

Consequently, the plane

$$x'\omega = \gamma, \tag{4}$$

midway between the bounding planes in (2), is a separating plane that separates $A+$ from $A-$ completely if $y = 0$, else only approximately. The quadratic term in (1), which is twice the reciprocal of the square of the 2-norm distance $\frac{2}{\|\omega\|}$ between the two bounding planes of (2), maximizes this distance, often called the "margin". Maximizing the margin enhances the generalization capability of SVM. If the classes are linearly inseparable, then the two planes bound the two classes with a "soft margin" (i.e. bound approximately with some error) determined by the nonnegative error variable y, that is:

$$A_i\omega + y_i \geq \gamma + 1, \text{ for } D_{ii} = 1, \tag{5}$$
$$A_i\omega - y_i \leq \gamma - 1, \text{ for } D_{ii} = -1.$$

The 1-norm of the error variable y is minimized parametrically with weight ν in (1), resulting in an approximate separating plane. This plane acts as a linear classifier as follows:

$$sign(x'\omega - \gamma) \begin{cases} = 1, & \text{then } x \in A+, \\ = -1, & \text{then } x \in A-. \end{cases} \tag{6}$$

Fund and Mangasarian [5] make a very simple change in the numerical formulation of a standard SVM and changes the nature of an optimization problem of a standard SVM significantly and it is called a proximal SVM. This change can be applied only to a linear kernel of a standard SVM. Two planes are not bounding planes anymore. But, they can be thought of as 'proximal' planes, that is, around the planes the points of each class are clustered, and the two planes are pushed as far apart as possible.

Given m data points in R^n represented by the $m \times n$ matrix A and a diagonal matrix D of $\pm$ labels denoting the class of each row of A, the linear proximal SVM generates classifier (6) as follows.

- Define $E = [A - e]$ where e is an $m \times 1$ vector of ones. Compute

$$\begin{bmatrix} \omega \\ \gamma \end{bmatrix} = (\frac{1}{\nu} + E'E)^{-1}E'De \tag{7}$$

for some positive γ. Typically γ is chosen by means of a tuning set.
- Classify a new x by using (6) and the above solution $\begin{bmatrix} \omega \\ \gamma \end{bmatrix}$.

Then, a proximal SVM can be generated by using a simple procedure to the proximal SVM. A proximal SVM can process data using a divide-and-conquer approach and thus it can be implemented in parallel directly. Tveit and Engum [8] implement it and we use it for our experiments.

4   Experiments

4.1   Sequential Method

We use hydrophilic values of Hopp and Woods [2] for our experiments. We use a protein database of DIP, a protein-protein interaction database of Yeast, and a protein database of PIR. The data used for our experiments are as follows.

- The protein DB that we use for our experiments has 17000 proteins at the time of our experiments but among them, the number of the proteins which have domains in domain DB are only 2811.
- DIP DB has 15409 interacting protein-protein pairs but among them only 2481 pairs have domains in domain DB.
- Thus, the number of proteins used for our experiments are 2811 and the number of pairs in DIP used for positive examples for SVM is 2481.

For each try of experiments, we select pairs of proteins of yeast in DIP randomly. We use the following 6 methods using domains.

- Method 1: We use both hydrophobicity and polarity of a protein's amino acid's features. For this experiment, we do 60 trials.
- Method 2: We replace domains with 1 and the others with 0 in a protein's amino acid sequence.
- Method 3: We use only the hydrophobicity of domain's amino acid in a protein's amino acid sequence.
- Method 4: We replace the amino acids with hydrophobicity in a domain with 1, the amino acids without hydrophobicity in a domain with 0, and the others in a protein's amino acid sequence with 2.
- Method 5: We replace all the amino acids in a domain with the domain's id and the others with 0 in a protein's amino acid sequence.
- Method 6: We use only the interacting protein-protein pairs which has domains in DIP.

Table 1 shows experimental results of 6 methods using a domain. According to the experiments, Method 1 shows the best average accuracy 76.8 % but it shows the worst precision. And Method 1 shows the best recall 39.8 % among them but it is not a good value. Method 4 shows the best precision 53.4 %.

Table 1. Comparing 6 methods using domains (unit:%)

Methods	accuracy	precision	recall
Method 1	76.6	27.2	39.8
Method 2	65.6	34.5	37.1
Method 3	65.9	36.1	36.7
Method 4	52.4	53.4	37.6
Method 5	62.9	48.9	20.1
Method 6	57.1	43.2	21.5

4.2   Parallel Method

As different values of ν in (7) in subsection 3.1 can give difference in accuracy in the classification, we use ν value of 100 for our experiments according to Chung et al. [6]. And we do our experiments using a 10-fold Cross-Validation [13] because [14] shows that 10 is about the right number of folds to get the best estimate of error.

For our parallel experiments, we use Method 5 in Subsection 4.1, i.e., we replace all the amino acids in a domain with the domain's id and the others with 0 in protein's amino acid sequence. Our PC-cluster has 12 nodes and we get experimental results using 2 nodes, 4 nodes, 8 nodes, and 12 nodes respectively. Table 2 shows the accuracy of each trial with the various number of nodes when using a proximal SVM. For each trial, we use 4000 protein pairs and we do 5 trials.

Table 2. Accuracies with various number of nodes

Trial	1-node	2-node	4-node	8-node	12-node
1	60.62%	58.88%	58.27%	57.23%	58.79%
2	59.98%	56.32%	54.81%	56.84%	57.47%
3	58.32%	54.11%	55.83%	52.13%	55.21%
4	61.03%	58.61%	59.31%	53.74%	57.22%
5	59.02%	55.33%	54.09%	57.84%	55.87%
average	59.79%	56.65%	56.46%	55.55%	56.91%

Table 3. Processing time with various number of nodes (unit: sec)

Trial	1-node	2-node	4-node	8-node	12-node
1	217	192	122	51	41
2	210	188	121	51	42
3	219	195	127	51	41
4	217	191	127	51	43
5	212	190	120	51	41
average	215	191	123	51	42

According to the experiments, our method using a proximal SVM shows average accuracy of 59.79% using 1 node, 56.65% using 2 node, and so on. Thus, accuracies are almost the same regardless of the number of nodes as proved in the numerical formulation of a proximal SVM [5].

Table 3 shows the speed-up of processing time when increasing the number of nodes. The average speed-up is 1.12 with 2-node, 1.74 with 4-node, 4.21 with 8-node and 5.11 with 12-node cluster.

5   Conclusion

In this work, we devised 6 methods to predict protein-protein interactions using domains and showed experimental results comparing them. Moreover, we showed how to predict protein-protein interactions in parallel using proximal SVM and showed various experimental results. The results are not so good and we want to improve our domain-based protein-protein interaction prediction system. With experimental validation, further development may produce a robust computational screening techniques that narrow the range of candidate interacting proteins.

But, the most difficult thing in using a supervised learning method such as a SVM to predict protein-protein interactions is to find negative examples of interacting proteins, i.e., non-interacting protein pairs. If such a database of non-interacting protein pairs are constructed, the better method to predict protein-protein interactions can be developed.

References

1. http://pir.georgetown.edu/.
2. T.P. Hopp and K.R. Woods.: Predicting of protein antigenic determinants from amino acid sequences, *Proc. Natl. Acad. Sci.* USA, 7 8 (1981) 3824-3828.
3. B. Alberts, D. Bray, J. Lewis, M. Raff, K. Roberts, and J. D. Watson.: *Molecular Biology of the Cell*, Garland, New York, 2nd edn. (1989).
4. J. R. Bock and D. A. Gough.: Predicting protein–protein interactions from primary structure, *Bioinformatics* 17 (2001) 455–460.
5. G. Fung and O. L. Mangasarian.: Incremental support vector machine classification, In *2nd SIAM int'l. Conf. on Data Mining*, SIAM (2002) 247-260.
6. Y. Chung, G. Kim, Y. Hwang, and H. Park.: Predicting protein–protein interactions from one feature using svm, In *IEA/AIE'04 Conf. Proc.*, Ottawa, Canada, May (2004).
7. Y. Chung, S. Cho and C. Kim.: Predicting Protein-Protein Interactions in Parallel. In *PARA'04 Cong. Proc.*, Lingby, Denmark, June (2004).
8. A. Tveit and H. Engum.: Parallelization of the Incremental Proximal Support Vector Machine Classifier using a Heap-based Tree Topology, Technical Report, IDI, NTNU, Trondheim, Norway, August (2003).
9. C. B. Anfinsen.: Principles that govern the folding of protein chains, *Science*, 81(1) (1973) 223–230.
10. T. Joachims.: Making large-scale support vector machine learning practical. In *Advances in Kernel Methods-Support Vector Learning*, Chap. 11, MIT Press, Cambridge, MA (1999) 169–184.
11. P. Baldi and S. Brunak.: Bioinformatics: the machine learning approach. In *Adaptive Computation and Machine learning*, MIT press, Cambridge, MA (1998).
12. C. Bishop.: In *Neural networks for pattern recognition*, Oxford University Press, UK (1996).
13. P. Cohen.: In *Empirical methods for artificial intelligence*, Chap. 6.10, MIT Press, (1995) 216–219.
14. I. Witten and E. Frank.: In *Data mining: Practical machine learning tools with Java implementations*, Chap. 5.3, Morgan Kaufmann Publishers (2000) 125–127.

Identification of Transcription Factor Binding Sites Using Hybrid Particle Swarm Optimization

Wengang Zhou, Chunguang Zhou, Guixia Liu, and Yanxin Huang

College of Computer Science and Technology, Jilin University,
Changchun 130012, P.R. China
wgzhou@email.jlu.edu.cn

Abstract. Transcription factors are key regulatory elements that control gene expression. Recognition of transcription factor binding sites (TFBS) motif from the upstream region of genes remains a highly important and unsolved problem particularly in higher eukaryotic genomes. In this paper, we present a new approach for studying this challenging issue. We first formulate the binding sites motif identification problem as a combinatorial optimization problem. Then hybrid particle swarm optimization (HPSO) is proposed for solving such a problem in upstream regions of genes regulated by octamer binding factor. We have developed two local search operators and one recombination mutation operator in HPSO. Experiment results show that the proposed algorithm is effective in obtaining known TFBS motif and can produce some putative binding sites motif. The results are highly encouraging.

1 Introduction

The publication of a nearly complete draft sequence of the human genome is an enormous achievement, but characterizing the entire set of functional elements encoded in the human and other genomes remains an immense challenge [1]. Two of the most important functional elements in any genome are transcription factors and the sites with the DNA which they bind. Transcription factors are usually proteins that stimulate or repress gene transcription and their binding sites are usually short sequence fragment located in upstream of the coding region of the regulated gene. A more complete understanding of transcription factors and their binding sites will permit a more comprehensive and quantitative mapping of the regulatory pathways within cells [2].

Because of the significance of this problem, many computational methods for identification of transcription factor binding sites have been proposed [3-5]. The prediction and computational identification of regulatory elements in higher eukaryotes is more difficult than in model organisms partly because of the larger genome size and a larger portion of noncoding regions. Furthermore, even the general principles governing the locations of DNA regulatory elements in higher eukaryotic genomes remain unknown. Existing methods [6] often converge on sequence motifs that are not biologically relevant. So the enrichment of computational methods is necessary for an efficient search.

D. Ślęzak et al. (Eds.): RSFDGrC 2005, LNAI 3642, pp. 438–445, 2005.
© Springer-Verlag Berlin Heidelberg 2005

In this paper, we first formulate the binding sites identification problem as a combinatorial optimization problem. Then hybrid particle swarm optimization is proposed for finding regulatory binding sites motif in upstream regions of coexpressed genes. We have developed two local search operators and one recombination mutation operator to intensify the ability of local search and increase the variance of population in HPSO. This method can identify conserved TFBS motif across multiple sequences without pre-alignment.

2   Hybrid Particle Swarm Optimization

Particle swarm optimization (PSO) is an evolutionary computation technique first introduced by Kennedy and Eberhart [7] in 1995. The position and the velocity of the particle in the n-dimensional search space can be represented as $X_i = (x_{i1}, x_{i2}, \ldots, x_{in})$ and $V_i = (v_{i1}, v_{i2}, \ldots, v_{in})$ respectively. The velocity and position vector is calculated according to the following equations:

$$V_i = w \cdot V_i + c_1 \cdot rand() \cdot (P_i - X_i) + c_2 \cdot rand() \cdot (P_g - X_i) \qquad (1)$$

$$X_i = X_i + V_i \qquad (2)$$

Where c_1 and c_2 are constants and are known as acceleration coefficients, w is called the inertia weight, $rand()$ generate random numbers in the range of $[0, 1]$.

We propose a hybrid particle swarm optimization (HPSO) by incorporating local search operation and recombination mutation operation. In local search operation, nine offspring individuals are produced by using two operators for each parent individual before updating its position. Then the best individual is chosen to replace the original one. In recombination mutation operation, two individuals chosen at random with equal probabilities from the population are executed the operation in a user-defined probability to increase the population variance. The details are shown in section 4.

3   Transcription Factor Database

TRANSCompel database is originated from the COMPEL [8] and provides information of composite regulatory elements which contain two closely situated binding sites for distinct transcription factors. It contains 256 experimentally validated composite elements from which we choose one transcription factor, octamer-binding factor (Oct) as test example. This transcription factor is chosen because its binding mechanism is well studied and many known genes in the downstream regulatory pathways have been verified experimentally. The seven genes regulated by transcription factor Oct with known binding sites motif in their 1kb upstream region are shown in table 1. In our experiment, the 1kb regions upstream to the transcription start site for each of these genes are searched for identification of binding sites.

Table 1. Genes with experimentally validated Oct binding sites

TF	Gene Name	Accession No	Species	Sequence Motif
Oct	U2 small nuclear RNA	C00039	Homo sapiens	ATGCAAAT
Oct	Unknown protein	C00043	Mouse virus	ATGTAAAT
Oct	Surface antigen	C00048	Human virus	ATGTAAAT
Oct	Immunoglobulin chain	C00049	Mus musculus	ATGCAAAT
Oct	Immunoglobulin chain	C00050	Mus musculus	ATGCAAAG
Oct	Interleukin-2	C00158	Mus musculus	ATGTAAAA
Oct	Interleukin-3	C00169	Homo sapiens	ATGCAAAT

4   Hybrid PSO for TFBS Motif Identification

TFBS motif consists of a set of windows with one window for each sequence. Identification of TFBS motif can be formulated as a combinatorial optimization problem. That is we choose one window from each sequence, then the aim of our algorithm is to find the optimum combination of these windows that can maximize the fitness function. The number of possible combination (search space) is computed according to the formula:

$$p = (l - d)^s \tag{3}$$

Where l is the length of the sequences, d is the width of the window being used, and s is the number of sequences. The algorithm is implemented in Matlab 6.5.

4.1   Population Initialization

In this experiment, we use a fixed TFBS window size of eight. A single candidate solution represents a set of windows randomly placed over the 1kb upstream sequences with only one window per sequence. Thus the i_{th} particle is initialized as a vector with the following form: $X_i = (x_{i1}, x_{i2}, x_{i3}, x_{i4}, x_{i5}, x_{i6}, x_{i7})$. Where x_{ik} is a random number from 1 to 993 (because the sequence length is one thousand and the window size is equal to eight) and it represents the initial position of the k_{th} window. The details are shown in figure 1.

```
C00039: AGGAGGGGTCCAGCCCTCAGCGATGGGATTTCAGAGCGGG
C00043: ACTATTTTTACTCAAATTCAGAAGTTAGAAATGGGAATAGA
C00048: ATGCTGTAGCTCTTGTTCCCAAGAATATGGTGACCCGCAA
C00049: ACAATAACATTTTATGTATATGTCTATCCATATATGTGTAAA
C00050: ACTCTTACATCTTTTTAGATAAACATGTGAGATCAATGGAC
C00158: ACAGGAGAGAAGTTACTAGCAAGAGTTGGTCTCTGACCTC
C00169: TTTTTATCCCATTGAGACTATTTATTTATGTATGTATGTATT
```

Fig. 1. The individual $X_i = (11, 21, 30, 15, 6, 20, 35)$ represents the set of windows which consist of these short sequences with bold font

4.2   Local Search Operation

For the purpose of enlarging search space and intensifying the ability of local search, we have developed two variation operators: window position change and A+T percentage measure. Before updating the position of each individual (particle), we use the two operators to generate nine offspring solutions for each individual and select the best one from the total ten individuals (one parent and nine offspring) to replace the original individual. We first generate a random number from the range [1, 3] which decides to how many times we use the two operators. Each time an operator is required, the choice on the type of variation operators is made according to the user-defined probabilities for each operator. This process is repeated until the maximum times are reached. The main pseudo-code is summarized as follows:

Procedure Local search (population P)
begin
For each individual P_j with $1 \leq j \leq popsize$ in the population P
initialize $n = 1$;
while $n \leq 9$ do (generate nine offspring solutions)
generate a random number $ntime$ from the range [1, 3];
for $i = 1$ to $ntime$
if $rand() < 0.2$ (user-defined probability)
use the window position change operator;
else use the A+T percentage measure operator;
increase n;
calculate the fitness value for the ten individuals;
select the individual $lbest$ with the maximum fitness;
replace the original individual P_j with $lbest$;
end

One window in the parent solution is chosen randomly for modification. When we use the window position change operator, the chosen window is moved either to the left or to the right across the 1kb upstream region with equal probability. A choice of new window position is chosen at random from the range [1, n], where n represents the maximum number of nucleotides in that direction. In our experiment, n is equal to 993 (sequence length - window width + 1) with the sequence starting from the 5' end.

If the A+T percentage measure operator is used, the average A+T percentage is first computed for all windows except the window being modified. Then a percentage similarity to this average is calculated for all possible windows in the full 1000 nucleotide sequence for the window being modified. All the window positions are stored with A+T similarity equal to or greater than a user-defined threshold. We set the threshold to 1 in all the experiments. From this set of window positions, a new location for the window being modified is chosen with equal probability.

4.3   Fitness Evaluation

In order to evaluate each individual well, we introduce two criteria: similarity and complexity [9]. The total fitness of each individual is calculated according to the following formula:

$$Fitness(i) = w_1 \times Similarity(i) + w_2 \times Complexity(i) \qquad (4)$$

where w_1 and w_2 are used to balance the importance of similarity and complexity. In our experiment, $w_1 = 0.6$ and $w_2 = 0.4$ have generated better results.

There are many methods to calculate similarity [10]. In this paper, we first get a likelihood matrix by calculating the frequency of A, T, G, and C at each column. The greatest value of each column in the likelihood matrix is subtracted from 1 and the absolute value of the result is stored. Then we calculate the sum of each column in the subtraction matrix and a difference of 1 minus the sum is got. The sum of the difference value for each column is the final similarity.

The average complexity for all windows represents the total complexity score for each individual solution. Complexity of a window can be calculated according to the following formula:

$$Complexity = \log_{10}^{d!/\prod n_i!} \qquad (5)$$

where d is the window width, and n_i is the number of nucleotides of type i, $i \in \{A, T, G, C\}$. In the worst cases, a window sequence has only one type of nucleotides, thus its complexity is zero.

4.4   Update Position X and Velocity V

The velocity V of each individual is initialized in the first generation as a seven-dimensional vector and each element in the vector has the range $[1, 8]$. Then V can be updated according to the Eq. (2) and X can be updated according to Eq. (1). We limit the maximum and the minimum velocity for each particle in order to avoid missing the global optima or entrapping in the local optima soon. So any window in the individual can move one window width at most one time either to the left or to the right. In addition, the position X should be modified when the particle escapes from the boundary. The pseudo code for modifying velocity and position is shown as follows:

Procedure Update (X,V)
begin
For each particle in the population P
Calculate V according to Equation (1);
for $k=1$ to 7
if $V_{ik} > 8$ then $V_{ik} = 8$; if $V_{ik} < -8$ then $V_{ik} = -8$;
Update X according to Equation (2);
for k=1 to 7
if $X_{ik} < 1$ then $X_{ik} = 1$; if $X_{ik} > 993$ then $X_{ik} = 993$;
end

4.5   Recombination Mutation

Basing on simulations, we notice that there may be some duplicate individuals in each generation. These duplicate solutions can induce premature convergence to local optima, so it is important to maintain the variance of the population. We propose a recombination mutation operator to increase this variance. After updating the X value for all individuals, two of them, chosen at random with equal probabilities from the population, are treated with recombination mutation with a user-defined probability. A random recombination mutation point is selected from the range [1, 7]. Individuals' information is exchanged after this mutation point. Details are shown in figure 2.

Particle I			Particle J		
$X_i = (170, 39, 287, 605, 216, 308, 915)$			$X_j = (93, 762, 900, 416, 153, 320, 676)$		
Seq. 1	(170,177)	TCTGCACG	Seq. 1	(93,100)	GGGGCGCG
Seq. 2	(39,46)	AGAAAATA	Seq. 2	(762,769)	CGTGTGTT
Seq. 3	(287,294)	TCTTGTAA	Seq. 3	(900,907)	AAAACGAG
Seq. 4	(605,612)	CCAATATT	Seq. 4	(416,423)	CAGAAGAA
Seq. 5	(216,223)	AGAAAATA	Seq. 5	(153,160)	CTGATCAC
Seq. 6	(308,315)	AACCCTTC	Seq. 6	(320,327)	GAATTTGT
Seq. 7	(915,922)	GACCATGT	Seq. 7	(676,683)	TCAACATC
Recombination mutation point=random number from the range [1, 7]=6					
$X_i'=(170,39,287,605,216,\mathbf{320,676})$			$X_j'=(93,762,900,416,153,\mathbf{308,915})$		
Seq. 1	(170,177)	TCTGCACG	Seq. 1	(93,100)	GGGGCGCG
Seq. 2	(39,46)	AGAAAATA	Seq. 2	(762,769)	CGTGTGTT
Seq. 3	(287,294)	TCTTGTAA	Seq. 3	(900,907)	AAAACGAG
Seq. 4	(605,612)	CCAATATT	Seq. 4	(416,423)	CAGAAGAA
Seq. 5	(216,223)	AGAAAATA	Seq. 5	(153,160)	CTGATCAC
Seq. 6	(320,327)	**GAATTTGT**	Seq. 6	(308,315)	**AACCCTTC**
Seq. 7	(676,683)	**TCAACATC**	Seq. 7	(915,922)	**GACCATGT**

Fig. 2. Recombination mutation. Two particles X_i and X_j represent a set of short sequence fragments which are extracted from the seven upstream sequences.

5   Experiment Results

In all experiments, the proposed HPSO is run with a population size of 30. The algorithm is terminated after 500 generations. Three parameters in Eq. (1) are set to as follows: $c_1 = c_2 = 2$, $w = 0.6$. They are tuned repeatedly with respect to the known TFBS information and the observation from the experiment results. In table 2(a), the best solution in all the runs is shown, and it is identical with the known TFBS motif. Other good solutions are grouped by similar TFBS motif for all sequences, shown in table 2(b). These putative motifs for each sequence are slightly different from the known motif. It is reasonable because one transcription factor can bind to many different sites.

Table 2. (a - left) The best solution for the Oct sequence set; (b - right) Putative binding sites discovered by HPSO.

Accession No	Location	Sequence Motif	Accession No	Putative Motif
C00039	(786,793)	ATGCAAAT	C00039	CGAGACAG, CGAAGTAA
C00043	(681,688)	ATGTAAAT	C00043	TTAGAAAT, TCAGAAGT
C00048	(97,104)	ATGTAAAT	C00048	ATGCTGTA, ATGCGCTA
C00049	(946,953)	ATGCAAAT	C00049	ATGATTAA, AACAATAT
C00050	(484,491)	ATGCAAAG	C00050	ATGCAGCT, ATACAAGA
C00158	(921,928)	ATGTAAAA	C00158	ATGTTAAA, ATGTGCAC
C00169	(905,912)	ATGCAAAT	C00169	AGCCATGT, AGCCAGAT

Table 3. (a - left) X_1=(786,681,97,116,484,384,905); (b - right) X_2=(786,681,97,183, 484,921,389).

Accession No	Location	Sequence Motif	Accession No	Location	Sequence Motif
C00039	(786,793)	ATGCAAAT	C00039	(786,793)	ATGCAAAT
C00043	(681,688)	ATGTAAAT	C00043	(681,688)	ATGTAAAT
C00048	(97,104)	ATGTAAAT	C00048	(97,104)	ATGTAAAT
C00049	(116,123)	**ATGAAAAT**	C00049	(183,190)	**ATTAAAAT**
C00050	(484,491)	ATGCAAAG	C00050	(484,491)	ATGCAAAG
C00158	(384,391)	**ATGTTAAA**	C00158	(921,928)	ATGTTAAA
C00169	(905,912)	ATGCAAAT	C00169	(389,396)	**TTGAAAAT**

Because of many local optima for this problem, any evolutionary algorithm may converge to such optima from random solutions of low fitness. Two near optimum solutions (X_1 and X_2), which our method often converges to, are shown in tables 3(a) and 3(b), respectively. These binding sites represented by two particles are identical with the known TFBS shown in table 1 except the motifs written in bold font. However, capturing information included in these solutions is as important as capturing the global optimum. These near optimum solutions can more probably present novel TFBS that are not discovered yet. We notice that different binding sites for the gene C00049 are found in two solutions. It is also difficult to find true TFBS motif for the gene C00158 and the gene C00169. These problems may be overcome by appropriate tuning the several probability parameters used in our algorithm. In addition, more known TFBS information should also be incorporated in future experiments.

6   Conclusions

In this paper, we first formulate the identification of TFBS motif as a combinatorial optimization problem. Then hybrid particle swarm optimization is proposed to solve it. We suggest two operators for intensifying the local search and one recombination mutation operator for increasing the variance of the population in HPSO. The simulation results show that the proposed algorithm can be successfully applied to discover binding sites motif from the upstream region of coexpressed genes regulated by Oct. The advantage of this algorithm is that it runs very fast compared to other evolutionary algorithms and it can get better solutions with small search space. This study demonstrates the feasibility of heuristic methods and provides a new perspective for discovery of transcription factor binding sites motif.

The problem of TFBS motif identification may be dealt with exhaustive research method if the sequence length is relative short. But when the sequence length and the number of sequence increase, the potential search space will increase exponentially. For the seven sequences with 1000 nucleotides, the search space of exhaustive method will be nearly 10^{21} (according to Eq. 3). However, by using our algorithm, we can get the global optima in the successful run and get the near optimum solutions in most of the runs with a small search space about 10^5. The result is highly encouraging.

Acknowledgements

This work is supported by the National Natural Science Foundation of China under Grant No. 60433020 and the Key Laboratory of Symbol Computation and Knowledge Engineering of the Ministry of Education.

References

1. Collins, F., Green, E., Guttmacher, A., Guyer, M.: A Vision for the Future of Genomics Research. Nature, 422 (2003) 835-847
2. Lockhart, D., Winzeler, E.: Genomics, Gene Expression and DNA Arrays. Nature, 405 (2000) 827-836
3. Qin Z., McCue L., Thompson, W., Mayerhofer, L., Lawrence, C., Liu, J.: Identification of Co-regulated Genes Through Bayesian Clustering of Predicted Regulatory Binding Sites. Nature Biotechnology, 21 (2003) 435-439
4. Olman V., et al: Identification of Regulatory Binding Sites Using Minimum Spanning Trees. Proceedings of Pacific Symposium on Biocomputing (2003) 327-338
5. Cora, D., DiCunto, F., Provero, P., Silengo, L., Caselle, M.: Computational Identification of Transcription Factor Binding Sites by Functional Analysis of Sets of Genes Sharing Overrepresented Upstream Motifs. BMC Bioinformatics, 5 (2004) 57
6. Bailey, T., Elkan, C.: Fitting A Mixture Model by Expectation Maximization to Discover Motifs in Biopolymers. Proceedings of International Conference on Intelligent Systems for Molecular Biology (1994) 28-36
7. Kennedy, J., Eberhart, R.C.: Particle Swarm Optimization. Proceedings of the IEEE International Conference on Neural Networks (1995) 1942-1948
8. Kel-Margoulis, O.V.: COMPEL: A Database on Composite Regulatory Elements Providing Combinatorial Transcriptional Regulation. Nucleic Acids Research, 28 (2003) 311-315
9. Fogel, G.B.: Discovery of Sequence Motifs Related to Coexpression of Genes Using Evolutionary Computation. Nucleic Acids Research, 32 (2004) 3826-3835
10. Rasmussen, T.K., Krink, T.: Improved Hidden Markov Model Training for Multiple Sequence Alignment by A Particle Swarm Optimization. Biosystems, 72 (2003) 5-17

A Grid Computing-Based Monte Carlo Docking Simulations Approach for Computational Chiral Discrimination

Youngjin Choi[1], Sung-Ryul Kim[2], Suntae Hwang[3], and Karpjoo Jeong[4,*]

[1] Department of Microbial Engineering, Konkuk University,
Seoul 143-701, Korea
[2] Department of Internet and Multimedia & Center for Advanced
e-System Integration Technology, Konkuk University,
Seoul 143-701, Korea
[3] Department of Computer Science, Kookmin University,
Seoul 136-702, Korea
[4] Department of Internet and Multimedia & Applied Grid Computing Center,
Konkuk University, Seoul 143-701, Korea
jeongk@konkuk.ac.kr

Abstract. A validity of Grid computing with Monte Carlo (MC) docking simulations was examined in order to execute prediction and data handling for the computational chiral discrimination. Docking simulations were performed with various computational parameters for the chiral discrimination of a series of 17 enantiomers by β-cyclodextrin (β-CD) or by 6-amino-6-deoxy-β-cyclodextrin (am-β-CD). Rigid-body MC docking simulations gave more accurate predictions than flexible docking simulations. The accuracy was also affected by both the simulation temperature and the kind of force field. The prediction rate of chiral preference was improved by as much as 76.7% when rigid-body MC docking simulations were performed at low temperatures (100 K) with a sugar22 parameter set in the CHARMM force field. Our approach for Grid-based MC docking simulations suggested the conformational rigidity of both the host and guest molecule.

1 Introduction

Separation of chiral compounds is of great interest to researchers because the majority of biomolecules, such as proteins and carbohydrates, are chiral. In nature, these biomolecules only exist in one of the two possible enantiomeric forms, and living organisms show different biological responses to each pair of the enantiomers in drugs, pesticides, and waste compounds [1]. For effective chiral separation, numerous kinds of chiral stationary phases (CSP) or mobile phase additives have been developed since the 1960s. There are five categories of CSPs: Perkle, Cellulose, Inclusion complex, Ligand exchange, and Protein types. Among these

---

* Corresponding author.

D. Ślęzak et al. (Eds.): RSFDGrC 2005, LNAI 3642, pp. 446–455, 2005.

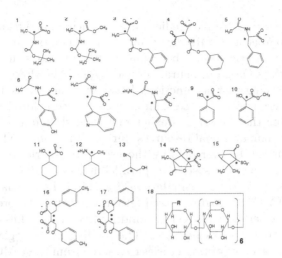

Fig. 1. Chiral guests and host cyclodextrins considered in this work: 1. N-t-Boc-alanine; 2. N-t-Boc-alanine methyl ester; 3. N-Cbz-alanine; 4. N-Cbz-aspartic acid; 5. N-acetyl-phenylalanine; 6. N-acetyl-tyrosine; 7. N-acetyl-tryptophan; 8. Gly-Phe; 9. mandelic acid; 10. mandelic acid methyl ester; 11. hexahydromandelic acid; 12. 1-cyclohexylethylamine; 13. 3-bromo-2-methyl-1-propanol; 14. camphanic acid; 15. camphorsulfonic acid; 16. O,O'-toluoyl-tartaric acid; 17. O,O'-dibenzoyl-tartaric acid; 18. β-cyclodextrin (R = OH) and 6-amino-6-deoxy-β-cyclodextrin (R = NH_3^+).

CSPs, cyclodextrins (CDs) and their derivatives are one of the most important inclusion complex forming agents in enantio-separation fields [2].

In this research, we attempted to apply the Grid-based Monte Carlo (MC) docking simulations method to predict the chiral recognition between a guest enantiomer and the host CD at a molecular level. These force field-based calculations could be advantageous for analyzing molecular mechanisms as well as for effective conformational searching because these approaches can reproduce various ensembles for the enantio-selective conformations induced by the inclusion complexation [3]. Moreover, the molecular MC simulations give us valuable insights on the physiological biomolecular conformations even though at high- or low- temperature [4]. In this study, either β-cyclodextrin (β-CD) or 6-amino-6-deoxy-β-cyclodextrin (am-β-CD) were used as hosts and 17 series of chiral compounds were used as guests (Fig. 1), since these molecules were experimentally well-validated candidates for predicting the chiral preference [5].

In the chiral recognition process, the enantiomers are identical and have the same size, the same shape, the same molecular electrostatics, etc.; therefore, they can only be distinguished when giving rise to slightly different diastereomeric responses upon associating with another chiral object or environment [6]. The intermolecular forces responsible for enantio-differentiation are the same as those in other cases of molecular recognition, but the differences of corresponding binding free energies are usually much smaller in magnitude.

This is why enantio-selective prediction is so much more difficult than typical computational approaches [7]. Recently, numerous attempts to develop predictive models of enantio-selectivity have been made with traditional molecular modeling strategies such as QSAR or neural network types [8,9]. However, these methods require developing scoring functions based on exact molecular descriptors for the chiral discrimination process. In contrast, force field-based calculations did not suffer from the necessity of exact molecular descriptors, although they do require many computational resources during simulations. These computing resource problems can be overcome by the use of high-performance computing equipment, such as the Grid system or parallel machines [10].

In this study, MC docking simulations for chiral discrimination were performed using CHARMM program based on Grid system. The prediction of chiral preference was performed based on binding free energy differences between each chiral guest and host cyclodextrin. The binding free energies are obtained using an ensemble average of trajectories extracted from these MC docking simulations. Such calculations require a very large amount of computing time on a single computer, which is impossible to handle in practice. In order to address this challenging computation requirement, we have developed a computational Grid system, called MGrid, to process a large number of force field calculations simultaneously. The MGrid system was designed to support remote execution, file transfers, and standard interface to legacy MPI (Message Passing Interface) applications to run successful MC docking simulations.

2   MC Docking Simulations and Grid Computing

2.1   Molecular Models and Protocols of MC Docking Simulations

The starting configuration of the β-CD for MC simulations was taken from X-ray crystal structure, and the am-β-CD was prepared by amino-deoxy modification for template β-CD using the InsightII/Builder module (version 2000, Accelrys Inc. San Diego USA). The following missing hydrogen atoms in X-ray coordinates were built with the InsightII program. The 17 series of chiral guest molecules were built with the InsightII/Biopolymer module. The initial conformations of each chiral guest were determined using simulated annealing molecular dynamics (SA-MD) simulations for geometry optimization. Simulations were performed using the molecular modeling program CHARMM (version 28b2), with a parm22 all-atom force field. In SA-MD simulations, temperature was alternated between 300 K and 1000 K and this was repeated ten times. Total time for SA-MD simulation was 3,000 ps. Ten structures were saved and fully energy-minimized at the end of each production phase at 300 K, and the lowest-energy conformation among the ten structures was selected for the initial structure of the next SA-MD cycle. The starting configurations of guest compounds for the MC docking simulations were taken from the SA-MD conformations with the lowest-energy value. Their two-dimensional molecular structures are depicted in Fig. 1.

The MC docking simulations were performed using the "MC" module of CHARMM. The parameter values for the β-CD were modified according to a revised carbohydrate parameter set (carbohydrate solution force field or sugar22 force field) of the CHARMM. The short-range nonbonded interactions were truncated with a 13-A cutoff. An implicit solvent water model was used with a distance-dependent dielectric constant. The docking process was assumed to be a 1:1 interaction between each host and chiral guest during the MC runs. The initial configuration of each host and guest molecule was positioned arbitrarily within a neighboring distance. Trials to a new configuration were accomplished by changing each move set of a guest molecule. The MC move set for flexible docking was composed of rigid translations, rigid rotations, and rotations of freely rotatable dihedral angles of the guest. For rigid-body docking, dihedral rotations of the MC move set were interrupted. A single step consists of picking a random conformer, making a random move, minimizing the energy of a new conformer, and then checking the energy with a Metropolis [12] criterion. This process uses a combined methodology consisting of Metropolis criterion for a global optimization and an energy minimization method for a local optimization. Host CDs were weakly fixed using a harmonic positional restraint of CHARMM to maintain backbone integrity. The MC-minimized structures were saved every 20 steps for 20,000 trials. These MC processes produced various docked structures for each host with its chiral guest.

The MM-PBSA methodology [13], which was originally developed for molecular dynamics simulations by P. A. Kollman et al., was applied to the analysis of our MC trajectories. The method estimates the free energies of binding by combining the absolute energies in the gas phase (EMM), solvation free energies (GPB + Gnonpolar), and entropy changes (TS) for each guest, host, and complex. The interaction energy and the difference of binding free energy between the R-enantiomer and S-enantiomer complexes are defined as:

$$\Delta\Delta G_{binding} = \Delta G_S - \Delta G_R \tag{1}$$

$$\Delta G_{binding} = \Delta G_{(complex)} - [\Delta G_{(host)} + \Delta G_{(guest)}] \tag{2}$$

$$G_{molecule} = <E_{MM}> + <G_{PB}> + <G_{nonpolar}> -TS \tag{3}$$

$$E_{MM} = E_{vdw} + E_{elec} \tag{4}$$

$$\Delta E_{interaction} = \Delta E_{(complex)} - [\Delta E_{(host)} + \Delta E_{(guest)}] \tag{5}$$

where $<>$ denotes an average over a set of snapshots along an MC trajectory. E_{vdw} and E_{elec} denote van der Waals and electrostatic energies, respectively. The polar contribution to the solvation free energy (GPB) was calculated by solving the Poisson-Boltzmann equation with the "PBEQ" module of CHARMM. For the PBEQ calculations, the grid spacing was set at 0.5Å, the molecule was filled with the grid box, and 2,000 iterations were performed to ensure the maximum change in potential was less than $2 \times 10^{-6} kT/e$. The dielectric constant inside and outside the molecule was 1.0 and 80.0, respectively. The nonpolar solvation contribution includes cavity creation in water and vdW interactions between the modeled nonpolar molecule and water molecules. This term can be imagined as transferring a nonpolar molecule with the shape of the host or guest from vacuum to water. This transfer of free energy is described as [14]: $\Delta G_{nonpolar} = \gamma A + b$,where A is the solvent-accessible surface area calculated by CHARMM, and γ and b are 0.00542 kcal/mol·$Å^2$ and 0.92 kcal/mol, respectively, derived from the experimental transfer energies of hydrocarbons. The probe radius was 1.4Å. In eq. (3), S is the entropy change for the host-guest complexation. The solvent entropy changes caused by polarization and cavity formation are included in the polar and nonpolar solvation-free energy terms. The solute entropy changes are almost identical for the structural properties of each are identical in enantiomers. Thus, in this study the entropy change of each enantiomeric complex upon binding is assumed to be equal [15].

2.2 Molecular Grid System (MGrid)

In addition to the development of these novel simulation techniques for the prediction of chiral discrimination, we have also constructed a computational Grid system called MGrid(http://service.mgrid.or.kr) [11]. This computing system is motivated by the large number of required force field calculations that are, in practice, impossible to handle with a single computer. The MGrid system is designed to allow us to execute a number of simulation jobs on remote computers simultaneously and to examine the results in a user-friendly Web-based problem-solving environment. In addition, MGrid automatically stores these simulation results in databases for later retrieval and supports various searching methods. A prototype system was installed and implemented on Konkuk University's Linux cluster, which has 30 nodes with dual Xeon 2.0 GHz CPUs. We used the MGrid system to run the entire MC simulation on a number of computers simultaneously and, as a result, were able to reduce simulation time significantly. The MGrid system also helped us manage a number of jobs and their results in a simple and secure manner via an easy-to-use Web-based user interface. With this Linux cluster, it took about 15,000 hours to produce the simulation results presented in this paper. Currently, the MGrid system is being ported to the testbed (http://testbed.gridcenter.or.kr/eng/), which is a cluster of Linux clusters and supercomputers at a number of universities and research institutes. Once this porting is finished, the MGrid system will be able to provide much more computing power and will allow us to tackle more challenging problems.

3 Computational Chiral Discrimination

3.1 Rigid-Body vs. Flexible Docking Simulations

We define chiral prediction rate as percentage of correctly predicted preferences between R- and S-enantiomers in 30 systems of chiral complexes. We predict chiral preferences in one pair of enantio-complexes based on the MC docking simulations. Table 1 lists the binding free energy differences for chiral discrimination and the prediction rate in MC docking simulations based on conjugate gradient energy-minimization with a carbohydrate solution force field (CSFF).

Table 1. Binding free energies (kcal/mol) of inclusion complexes of chiral guests with β-CD or am-β-CD from MC docking simulations based on flexible- or rigid-body docking. Keys: 1. N-t-Boc-alanine / β-CD; 2. N-t-Boc-alanine methyl ester / β-CD; 3. N-Cbz-alanine / β-CD; 4. N-Cbz-aspartic acid / β-CD; 5. N-acetyl-phenylalanine / β-CD; 6. N-acetyl-tyrosine / β-CD; 7. N-acetyl-tryptophan / β-CD; 8. Gly-Phe / β-CD; 9. mandelic acid / β-CD; 10. mandelic acid methyl ester / β-CD; 11. hexahydromandelic acid / β-CD; 12. 3-bromo-2-methyl-1-propanol / β-CD; 13. camphanic acid / β-CD; 14. camphorsulfonic acid / β-CD; 15. O,O'-toluoyl-tartaric acid / β-CD; 16. O,O'-dibenzoyl-tartaric acid / β-CD; 17. N-t-Boc-alanine / am-β-CD; 18. N-t-Boc-alanine methyl ester / am-β-CD; 19. N-Cbz-alanine / am-β-CD; 20. N-acetyl-phenylalanine / am-β-CD; 21. N-acetyl-tyrosine / am-β-CD; 22. N-acetyl-tryptophan / am-β-CD; 23. Gly-Phe / am-β-CD; 24. mandelic acid / am-β-CD; 25. hexahydromandelic acid / am-β-CD; 26. 1-cyclohexylethylamine / am-β-CD; 27. 3-bromo-2-methyl-1-propanol / am-β-CD; 28. camphanic acid / am-β-CD; 29. camphorsulfonic acid / am-β-CD; 30. O,O'-dibenzoyl-tartaric acid / am-β-CD.

Complex	Experiment				Flexible Docking				Rigid-body Docking			
	ΔG_R	ΔG_S	$\Delta\Delta G$	P_{obs}	ΔG_R	ΔG_S	$\Delta\Delta G$	P_{cal}	ΔG_R	ΔG_S	$\Delta\Delta G$	P_{cal}
1	-3.54	-3.50	+0.04	R	-4.53	-3.98	+0.55	R	-6.99	-4.40	+2.59	R
2	-3.85	-3.77	+0.08	R	-11.39	-11.57	-0.18	S	-12.42	-11.12	+1.30	R
3	-2.96	-2.95	+0.01	R	1.59	-6.13	-7.72	S	-6.77	-6.60	+0.17	R
4	-2.52	-2.55	-0.03	S	18.52	16.92	-1.60	S	9.75	18.50	+8.75	R
5	-2.43	-2.49	-0.06	S	-3.99	-2.83	+1.16	R	-5.02	-5.42	-0.40	S
6	-2.85	-2.88	-0.03	S	-2.22	-7.06	-4.84	S	-3.12	-1.70	+1.42	R
7	-1.51	-1.68	-0.17	S	-6.86	-4.00	+2.86	R	-3.90	-3.18	+0.72	R
8	-2.28	-2.36	-0.08	S	0.34	-7.09	-7.43	S	-3.25	-4.37	-1.12	S
9	-1.41	-1.29	+0.12	R	2.55	3.00	+0.45	R	2.51	2.52	0.01	-
10	-2.49	-2.53	-0.04	S	-7.50	-7.32	+0.18	R	6.99	-6.63	+0.36	R
11	-3.84	-3.79	+0.05	R	-1.87	-2.25	-0.38	S	-1.95	-1.59	+0.36	R
12	-2.94	-2.93	+0.01	R	-7.39	-5.75	+1.64	R	-6.44	-6.13	+0.31	R
13	-3.07	-3.16	-0.09	S	-8.21	-11.45	-3.24	S	-10.70	-10.22	+0.48	R
14	-3.75	-3.67	+0.08	R	-7.46	-5.34	+2.12	R	-6.94	-4.96	+1.98	R
15	-2.76	-2.70	+0.06	D	-1.69	1.85	+3.54	D	-1.90	-0.48	+1.42	D
16	-2.06	-1.77	+0.29	D	-1.72	4.68	+6.4	D	-0.34	0.42	+0.76	D
17	-3.88	-3.78	+0.10	R	-6.31	-5.70	+0.61	R	-5.69	-2.70	+2.99	R
18	-3.54	-3.47	+0.07	R	-10.33	-11.05	-0.72	S	-12.23	-12.06	+0.17	R
19	-3.09	-3.05	+0.04	R	-6.91	-6.60	+0.31	R	-3.58	-2.69	+0.89	R
20	-2.41	-2.58	-0.17	S	-3.30	-2.66	+0.64	R	-1.99	-5.05	+3.06	R
21	-2.81	-2.90	-0.09	S	-1.52	-2.17	-0.65	S	-0.05	-1.15	-1.10	S
22	-1.63	-1.94	-0.31	S	-0.36	-0.52	-0.16	S	3.94	-1.52	-5.46	S
23	-2.17	-2.21	-0.04	S	0.50	-0.54	-1.04	S	-4.26	-4.51	-0.25	S
24	-2.37	-2.25	+0.12	R	-1.84	3.47	+5.31	R	4.31	4.28	-0.03	S
25	-4.58	-4.33	+0.25	R	-0.61	-1.11	-0.50	S	-1.28	0.09	+1.37	R
26	-3.10	-3.12	-0.02	S	-0.63	2.08	+2.71	R	5.28	1.51	-3.77	S
27	-2.81	-2.80	+0.01	R	-7.21	-7.50	-0.29	S	-6.34	-6.55	-0.21	S
28	-3.05	-3.16	-0.11	S	-10.11	-4.74	+5.37	R	-7.18	-7.38	-0.20	S
29	-3.95	-3.99	-0.04	S	-3.71	-5.14	-1.43	S	-7.09	-4.26	-2.83	R
30	-2.45	-2.24	+0.21	D	4.90	11.75	-6.85	L	5.52	6.10	+0.58	D
Prediction Rate (%)					56.7				66.7			

Experimental and calculated binding free energies were present at the same order of magnitude in most cases. The error ranges of absolute binding free energies in the calculated results were reasonable compared with the ones obtained from the general MM-PBSA (Molecular Mechanics / Poisson-Boltzmann Surface Area) approach reported in [16]. The binding free energies were calculated from two different docking approaches: rigid-body or flexible MC docking simulations. In rigid-body docking, the ligand enantiomers were regarded as rigid solid bodies, so just one conformer with the lowest-potential energy was evaluated for docking simulations. Flexible docking, on the other hand, allowed the evaluation for multiple conformers of ligands using dihedral angle rotations [17]. The backbone integrity of host CD molecules was maintained using a rigid harmonic constraint. The rigid-body MC docking simulations gave the prediction rate as 66.7%, while flexible docking showed a 56.7% accuracy at room temperature (298 K). The rigid-body docking method might be preferred to the flexible docking method for the accurate chiral discrimination process. This accuracy might originate from characteristics of the chiral recognition process, which is driven by rigid three-point interaction [18]. Based on those results, the rigid-body docking method combined with an energy-minimization method was adopted as a basic MC docking protocol for the prediction of chiral recognition by cyclodextrins.

3.2   Acceptance Probability During the MC Simulation

We optimized an acceptance probability, which is defined as the ratio of accepted moves to trial moves during MC simulations. The acceptance probability is an important quantity for understanding the efficiency of MC simulations because the RMSD (root mean squared deviation) and displacements of each MC move are varied as a function of the acceptance probability [19]. These quantities should go to zero for a small acceptance probability, since most moves are rejected, and also for a high acceptance probability, since each trial move is too small [20]. Thus, acceptance probability is often adjusted during MC simulations so that about half of the trial moves are rejected [21]. The prediction rates for the acceptance probability of 0.1, 0.3, 0.5, and 0.7 in our Grid-based MC docking simulations were estimated to be 63.3, 60.0, 66.7, and 60.0%, respectively. The accuracy was lowered when the acceptance probability was either higher or lower than 0.5. Thus, an optimal acceptance probability of 0.5 was selected for our MC docking simulations for predicting chiral preference.

3.3   Temperature and Parameter Set for the Accurate Prediction

Binding free energies and interaction energies of inclusion complexes of chiral guests with β-CD or am-β-CD were computed by MC docking simulations using the CSFF parameter set at 100K, 300K, 500K, and 700K. Criteria based both on interaction energy ($\Delta E_{interaction}$) and binding free energy ($\Delta G_{binding}$) were examined. In the interaction energy-based prediction, a maximum accuracy of 63.7% was obtained with 700 K of high simulation temperature. In the chiral prediction based on binding free energy, a maximum prediction rate of 66.7% was obtained at a temperature of 300 K, where binding free energy was calculated from interaction energy with solvation energy terms. Hard calculations for solvation energy terms did not affect the prediction rate at any temperature on the carbohydrate solution force field (CSFF). Since the prediction rate was not optimized by adjusting the simulation temperature, the CSFF parameter set used in MC simulations was changed to a sugar22 parameter as an alternative carbohydrate force field developed for CHARMM. The sugar22 parameter set used in CHARMM normally supports the increased force constant in the hydroxymethyl dihedral angle (O5-C5-C6-O6), in contrast to the CSFF parameter. We then examined the temperature effect on the prediction rate based on interaction energy criterion and binding free energy criterion with this sugar22 parameter set. In chiral prediction based on interaction energy, the prediction rate reached a range of 50.0–56.7% without being significantly affected by temperature. However, the accuracy increased to as high as 76.7% in the binding free energy-based prediction for rigid-body MC docking simulations at 100 K. This result suggests that the prediction of chiral discrimination could be optimized at low-temperatures with solvation contribution.

According to the accepted theory for chiral recognition, three simultaneous interactions between the chiral stationary phase (CSP) and at least one of the chiral guests are required, and one of these interactions must be stereochemically dependent [14]. Cyclodextrins can distinguish enantiomers by the presence or absence of a third intermolecular interaction. Therefore, it is expected that the conformationally rigid CSP interacts strongly with the guest compound in the chiral recognition process. At lower temperatures, a large portion of high-energy structures are rejected while a few are accepted during the Metropolis

Table 2. Summarized results for the predictions rates (%) of the enantiodifferences of chiral guests with β-CD and am-β-CD from binding energy criterion at different temperatures

Chiral Guest	CSFF				avg.	Sugar22				avg.
	100	300	500	700		100	300	500	700	
N-t-Boc-alanine	91.7	100	100	100	97.9	100	100	100	100	100
N-t-Boc-alanine-Me	50.0	0.0	25.0	41.7	29.2	50.0	16.7	100	41.8	52.1
N-Cbz-alanine	0.0	0.0	0.0	66.7	16.7	58.3	0.0	25.0	0.0	20.8
N-Cbz-aspartic acid	0.0	0.0	0.0	16.7	4.2	0.0	50.0	0.0	66.7	29.2
N-acetyl-phenylalanine	100	83.3	100	83.3	91.7	100	100	100	100	100
N-acetyl-tyrosine	33.3	41.7	91.7	33.3	50.0	100	83.3	100	83.3	91.7
N-acetyl-tryptophan	50.0	50.0	83.3	83.3	66.7	100	41.7	83.3	50.0	68.8
Gly-Phe	100	75.0	58.3	66.7	75.0	50.0	50.0	0.0	66.7	41.7
mandelic acid	100	25.0	41.7	25.0	47.9	100	91.7	100	50.0	85.4
mandelic acid methyl ester	0.0	50.0	0.0	16.7	16.7	0.5	8.3	0.0	16.7	6.4
hexahydromandelic acid	50.0	100	58.3	66.7	68.8	83.3	83.3	0.0	66.7	58.3
1-cyclohexylethylamine	0.0	33.3	83.3	100	54.2	41.7	41.7	33.3	41.7	39.6
3-bromo-2-methyl-1-propanol	91.7	16.7	50.0	66.7	56.3	50.0	100	100	58.3	77.1
camphanic acid	0.0	0.0	16.7	16.7	8.4	0.0	0.0	0.0	8.3	2.1
camphorsulfonic acid	50.0	66.7	50.0	41.7	52.1	100	50.0	91.7	66.7	77.1
O,O'-toluoyl-tartaric acid	66.7	100	100	100	91.7	50.0	50.0	100	50.0	62.5
O,O'-dibenzoyl-tartaric acid	100	100	100	100	100	100	100	100	100	100
Average accuracy (%)	52.0	49.5	56.4	60.3	54.5	63.8	56.9	60.8	56.9	59.7

MC docking simulations. Therefore, the low-temperature simulations with rigid-body docking conditions might increase the conformational rigidity of both host and guest to enhance the chiral recognition process.

Table 2 summarizes results of prediction of the chiral discrimination for each enantiomeric guest with different ensemble average ranges.

4   Conclusions

Our MC docking simulation method revealed that the conformational rigidity of both the host and guest plays a key role in chiral discrimination predicting. This is because the rigid-body docking and low-temperature condition with the sugar22 parameter set resulted in the most accurate prediction of chiral preference. The CSFF is a specially designed parameter set to describe the correct hydroxymethyl conformer distribution of glucopyranose residue in water by decreasing the force constant in the hydroxymethyl dihedral angle (O5-C5-C6-O6) [22]. That decreases in the dihedral parameters acts as an incentive to more flexible conformational behavior of cyclodextrins during MC docking simulations based on the CSFF parameter. This reduction of steric hindrance could cause increased ambiguity [18] in the computational prediction of chiral discrimination based on force field calculation. That is why CSFF is less accurate than the sugar22 parameter set.

References

1. Cabusas, M.E.: Chiral Separations on HPLC Derivatized Polysaccharide CSPs: Ph. D. Thesis, Virginia Polytechnic Institute and State University, USA (1998) 1-9.
2. Lee, S., Yi, D.H., Jung, S.: NMR Spectroscopic Analysis on the Chiral Recognition of Noradrenaline by ĕâ-Cyclodextrin and Carboxymethyl- ĕâ-cyclodextrin. Bull. Korean Chem. Soc. 25 (2004) 216-220.
3. Choi, Y.H., Yang, C.H., Kim, H.W., Jung, S.: Monte Carlo simulations of the chiral recognition of fenoprofen enantiomers by cyclomaltoheptaose. Carbohydr. Res. 328 (2000) 393-397.
4. Bouzida, D., Rejto, P.A., Verkhivker, G.M.: Monte Carlo Simulations of Ligand-Protein Binding Energy Landscapes with the Weighted Histogram Analysis Method. Int. J. Quant. Chem. 73 (1999) 113-121.
5. Rekharsky, M.V., Inoue, Y.J.: Complexation and Chiral Recognition Thermodynamics of 6-Amino-6-Deoxy-Beta-Cyclodextrin with Aanionic, Cationic, and Neutral Chiral Guests: Counterbalance between van der Waals and Coulombic Interactions. J. Am. Chem. Soc. 124 (2002) 813-826.
6. Lipkowitz, K.B., Coner, R., Peterson, M.A.: Locating Regions of Maximum Chiral Discrimination: A Computational Study of Enantioselection on a Popular Chiral Stationary Phase Used in Chromatography. J. Am. Chem. Soc. 119 (1997) 11269-11276.
7. Dodziuk, H., Lukin, O.: The Dependence of the Average Energy Difference for the Diastereomeric Complexes of α-Pinene Enantiomers with α-Cyclodextrin on the Length of Dynamic Simulations. Chem. Phys. Lett. 327 (2000) 18-22.

8. Wolbach, J.P., Lloyd, D.K., Wainer, I.W.: Approaches to Quantitative Structure Enantio-selectivity Relationships Modeling of Chiral Separations Using Capillary Electrophoresis. J. Chromatogr. A. 914(2001) 299-314.

9. Booth, T.D., Azzaoui, K., Wainer, I.W.: Prediction of Chiral Chromatography Separations by Combined Multivariate Regression Neural Networks. Anal. Chem. 69 (1997) 3879-3883.

10. Natrajan, A., Crowley, M., Wilkins-Diehr, N., Humphrey, M.A., Fox, A.D. Grimshaw, A.S., Brooks: C.L.III. Studying Protein Folding on the Grid: Experiences Using CHARMM on NPACI Resources under Legion. Concurr. Computat. Pract. Exper. 16 (2004) 385-397.

11. Jeong, K., Kim, D., Kim, M., Hwang, S., Jung, S., Lim, Y., Lee, S.: A Workflow Management and Grid Computing Approach to Molecular Simulation-Based Bio/Nano Experiments. Lecture Notes in Computer Science, Vol. 2660. Springer-Verlag, Berlin Heidelberg (2003) 1117-1126.

12. Metropolis, N., Rosenbluth, A.W., Rosenbluth, M.N., Teller, A.H., Teller, E.: Equation of State Calculation by Fast Computing Machines. J. Chem. Phys. 21 (1953) 1087-1092. Solvation Correction. Comput. Chem. 18 (1997) 723-743.

13. Srinivasan, J., Cheatham, T.E., Cieplak, P., Kollman, P.A., Case, D.A.: Continuum Solvent Studies of the Stability of DNA, RNA, and Phosphoramidate-DNA Helices. J. Am. Chem. Soc. 120 (1998) 9401-9409.

14. Sitkoff, D., Sharp, K.A., Honig, B.: Accurate Calculation of Hydration Free Energies Using Macroscopic Solvent Models. J. Phys. Chem. 98 (1994) 1978-1988. Growth Hormone-Receptor Complex. J. Comput. Chem. 23 (2002) 15-27.

15. Choi, Y., Jung, S.: Molecular Dynamics Simulations for the Prediction of Chiral Discrimination of N-acetylphenylalanine Enantiomers by Cyclomaltoheptaose Based on the MM-PBSA Approach. Carbohydr. Res. 339 (2004) 1961-1966.

16. Bea, I., Jaime, C., Kollman, P.A.: Molecular Recognition by β-Cyclodextrin Derivatives: FEP vs MM/PBSA Goals and Problems. Theor. Chem. Acc. 108 (2002) 286-292.

17. Halperin, I., Ma, B., Wolfson, H. Nussinov, R.: Principles of Docking: An Overview of Search Algorithms and a Guide to Scoring Functions. Proteins 47 (2002) 409-443.

18. Ahn, S., Ramirez, J., Grigorean, G., Lebrilla, C.B.: Chiral Recognition in Gas phase Cyclodextrin: Amino Acid Complexes. J. Am. Soc. Mass Spec. 12 (2001) 278-287.

19. Mbamala, E.C., Pastore, G.: Optimal Monte Carlo Sampling for Simulation of Classical Fluids. Phys. A. 313 (2002) 312-320.

20. Bouzida, D., Kumar, S., Swendsen, R.H.: Efficient Monte Carlo Methods for the Computer Simulation of Biological Molecules. Phys. Rev. A. 45 (1992) 8894-8901.

21. Allen, M.P., Tildesley, D.J.: Computer Simulations of Liquids, Oxford University Press, New York (1987)

22. Kuttel, M., Brady, J.W.; Naidoo, K.J.: Carbohydrate Solution Simulations: Producing a Force Field with Experimentally Consistent Primary Alcohol Rotational Frequencies and Populations. J. Comput. Chem. 23 (2002) 1236-1243.

Web Mining of Preferred Traversal Patterns in Fuzzy Environments

Rui Wu[1,2], Wansheng Tang[1], and Ruiqing Zhao[1]

[1] Institute of Systems Engineering, Tianjin University,
Tianjin 300072, P.R. China
[2] Shanxi Teachers University, Shanxi 041004, P.R. China
wurui1971@eyou.com
{tang, zhao}@tju.edu.cn

Abstract. In this paper, the linguistic evaluations and time duration on web pages are characterized as fuzzy variables in the web mining of preferred traversal patterns. The concept of fuzzy web page preference function which is a function of fuzzy linguistic evaluations, fuzzy time duration and access frequency is proposed to replace the traditional concept of confidence. The fuzzy web page preference function can be used as a judgment criterion to reveal users interest and preference. The structure of <u>F</u>requent <u>L</u>ink and <u>A</u>ccess <u>T</u>ree (FLaAT) which stores all user access information is introduced to avoid the loss of important information. Furthermore, an algorithm based on the fuzzy web page preference function is developed for mining users preferred traversal patterns from the structure of FLaAT. Finally an example is provided to illustrate the proposed approach.

1 Introduction

Web mining can be divided into three classes: web content mining, web structure mining and web usage mining [5]. Web usage mining is an application of data mining algorithm to web logs to find trends and regularities in web users traversal patterns. Many algorithms have been proposed to deal with specific aspects of web usage mining for the purpose of automatically discovering user profiles. Schechter et al [11] proposed a method of using path profiles for describing HTTP request behavior to improve web server system performance. Perkowita and Etzioni [10] investigated adaptive web sites to mine the data buried in web server logs to produce more easily navigable web sites. Chen et al [2] and Cohen et al [4] introduced the concept of using maximal forward references to break down user sessions into transactions for easily mining traversal patterns.

Fuzzy theory provides a natural framework for dealing with uncertainty and impreciseness. Arotaritei and Mitra [1] provided a survey of the available literature on fuzzy web mining. In Hong et al [6], the *confidence* was determined by two factors, linguistic evaluations and access frequency. The authors adopted fuzzy set concepts to model linguistic evaluations given by experts. Lo et al [9] used fuzzy set method to transform the numerical time duration to the corresponding linguistic values for more easily describing the discovered patterns.

D. Ślęzak et al. (Eds.): RSFDGrC 2005, LNAI 3642, pp. 456–465, 2005.
© Springer-Verlag Berlin Heidelberg 2005

In order to make our results more reasonable, fuzzy variables are used to characterize the factors, linguistic evaluations, and time duration on web pages due to their uncertainties and impreciseness. By their expected values, their fuzzy features can vividly described. *Fuzzy web page preference function*, as a function of linguistic evaluations, time duration, and access frequency, is proposed to be a judgement criterion replacing *preference* (considering two factors, time duration, and access frequency) in Xing [13] to measure users interest and preference under special web environment. Since linguistic evaluations, time duration, and access frequency are main factors disclosing the users interest and preference, the results based on the judgement of *fuzzy web page preference function* are more reasonable. And the structure FLaAT which stores all user access information is provided to replace PNT introduced in Xing [13] to ensure the integrity of the mined patterns. Finally an algorithm based on the *fuzzy web page preference function* is developed for mining preferred traversal patterns from the FLaAT instead of original web logs. By the analysis of the data given in the example, our proposed algorithms are feasible and the results are reasonable.

The paper is organized as follows. The concepts of fuzzy variable are introduced in Section 2, while the concept of fuzzy web page preference function is defined in Section 3. Section 4 presents the algorithm for mining preferred traversal patterns. An example is provided to illustrate the feasibility of the proposed algorithm in Section 5. Finally, Section 6 draws a conclusion.

2   Fuzzy Variable and Its Expected Value

Let ξ be a fuzzy variable on a possibility space $(\Theta, \mathcal{P}(\Theta), \mathrm{Pos})$, where Θ is a universe, $\mathcal{P}(\Theta)$ the power set of Θ, and Pos a possibility measure defined on $\mathcal{P}(\Theta)$. The *possibility, necessity*, and *credibility* of a fuzzy event $\{\xi \geq r\}$ can be represented by

$$
\begin{aligned}
\mathrm{Pos}\{\xi \geq r\} &= \sup_{u \geq r} \mu_\xi(u), \\
\mathrm{Nec}\{\xi \geq r\} &= 1 - \sup_{u < r} \mu_\xi(u), \\
\mathrm{Cr}\{\xi \geq r\} &= \frac{1}{2}\left[\mathrm{Pos}\{\xi \geq r\} + \mathrm{Nec}\{\xi \geq r\}\right],
\end{aligned}
\tag{1}
$$

respectively, where μ_ξ is the membership function of ξ.

The credibility of a fuzzy event is defined as the average value of its possibility and necessity. Thus the credibility measure is self dual. A fuzzy event may fail though its possibility reaches 1 and may hold even though its necessity is 0. However, the fuzzy event must hold if its credibility is 1 and fail if its credibility is 0. It will play an important role in the definition of expected value operator.

Definition 1. *(Liu and Liu [8]) The expected value of a fuzzy variable ξ is defined as*

$$
E[\xi] = \int_0^\infty \mathrm{Cr}\{\xi \geq r\}\mathrm{d}r - \int_{-\infty}^0 \mathrm{Cr}\{\xi \leq r\}\mathrm{d}r
\tag{2}
$$

provided that at least one of two integrals is finite.

Example 1. (Liu and Liu [8]) The expected value of a triangular fuzzy variable (r_1, r_2, r_3) is defined as follows

$$E[\xi] = \frac{1}{4}(r_1 + 2r_2 + r_3).$$ (3)

Example 2. (Liu and Liu [8]) The expected value of a trapezoid fuzzy variable (r_1, r_2, r_3, r_4) is defined as follow

$$E[\xi] = \frac{1}{4}(r_1 + r_2 + r_3 + r_4).$$ (4)

The expected value of a fuzzy variable can characterize this fuzzy variable by numerical value.

3   Fuzzy Web Page Preference Function

The web page preference is determined by the following three factors, fuzzy linguistic evaluations, time duration and access frequency of this web page.

Let ξ_{ki} denote a linguistic evaluation given by the ith expert on the kth web page, $i = 1, 2, \cdots, N, k = 1, 2, \cdots, m$, respectively. Here the linguistic evaluations ξ_{ki} are fuzzy variables. The membership function of ξ_{ki} can be obtained by adept experts or from the methods introduced in [3] and [12]. Thus the evaluation W_k denoting the importance of the kth web page can be defined as

$$W_k = \frac{1}{N} \sum_{i=1}^{N} E[\xi_{ki}],$$ (5)

where N denotes the total numbers of fuzzy linguistic evaluations on the kth web page.

The time duration on a web page is another important factor to measure users interest and preference. A linguistic term characterized as a fuzzy variable is used to depict the characteristic of the time duration on a web page. The method of denoting the time duration on a web page k by a linguistic term (characterized as a fuzzy variable) is as follows.

Step 1.   Assume that the domain of the time duration on all web pages is divided into l fuzzy regions depicted by l different linguistic terms. Every linguistic term is characterized as a corresponding fuzzy variable $\eta_j, j = 1, 2, \cdots, l$.

Step 2.   for all time durations $t_1, t_2, \cdots, t_v$ on the web page k, calculate the membership degrees $\mu_{\eta_j}(t_i)$ in every fuzzy region $j(j = 1, 2, \cdots, l)$, respectively. Then calculate the scalar cardinality $Count_j$, which definition is as

$$Count_j = \sum_{i=1}^{v} \mu_{\eta_j}(t_i), \qquad (6)$$

Step 3. The fuzzy variable corresponding the largest scalar cardinality $Count_k$, $j = 1, 2, \cdots, l$ is selected to depict the time duration on the web page k (Without loss of generality, this fuzzy variable is also denoted by η_k).

Assume that T_{max} is the given maximal time duration on web pages, then the relative time duration T_k of the web page k can be described as follows

$$T_k = \frac{E[\eta_k]}{T_{max}}. \qquad (7)$$

The third factor reflecting users interest and preference is access frequency. Many algorithms adopt the absolute browsing times to determine whether a web page is preferred [2,6,9]. Xing [13] used the relative browsing times to reflect users interest and preference which were more reasonable in specific web framework. Here, we adopt the definition of Xing [13]. The access frequency S_k of the kth web page is defined as

$$S_k = \frac{n \times C_k}{\sum_{i=1}^{n} C_i}, \qquad (8)$$

where C_k is the absolute browsing times from the parent web page to the kth child web page. There are n different choices from the parent web page to child web page.

Based on the above mentioned consideration, the *fuzzy web page preference function* P_k of the kth web page is defined as

$$P_k = V_k \times T_k \times S_k. \qquad (9)$$

Because the three factors satisfy the relationship of intersection, the style of product is adopted. According to the above definition, *fuzzy web page preference function* embodies integrated influence of the three factors on users interest and preference. The higher the *fuzzy web page preference function* is, the more he prefers.

4   Mining Preferred Traversal Patterns Based on Fuzzy Web Page Preference Function

This section describes the proposed algorithms of mining preferred traversal patterns based on *fuzzy web page preference function*. The preferred traversal patterns can be mined from a structure of FLaAT using a Depth First Traversal strategy.

4.1   FLaAT

FLaAT is a combination of the frequent link and the access tree. Its definition is as follows.

The structure of an access tree is defined as:

```
TYPE  Nodeptr =^ Nodetype;
        Nodetype=RECORD
                URL: string;
                Count: integer;
                Selection preference: real;
                Fuzzy preference: real;
                Next,Child,Younger: Nodeptr;
                END.
```

Frequent Link is a one-dimension array whose structure is:

```
TYPE FLTYPE=FrequentLink[1..n]: Itemtype;
        Itemtype=RECORD
                URL: string;
                Count: integer;
                Fuzzy evaluation:real;
                Relative time duration:real;
                First: Nodeptr;
                END.
```

URL denotes the name of current visited web page. Count is the absolute access frequency of current URL. Next is a pointer pointing to next node with the same URL in the access tree. Child points to a child node, while Younger points to a brother node in the access tree. First is a pointer in the frequent link pointing to the first node with the same URL in the access tree. The definition of the Selection preference, Fuzzy preference, Fuzzy evaluation and Relative time duration can be seen in section 3.

4.2   Construction of FLaAT

If the user sessions from web logs have already been well identified and stored in user access database D_s. Then the algorithm is to scan user access database D_s and to construct a FLaAT.

Algorithm 1. **Algorithm for Construction of FLaAT**
Input. User access session database D_s
Output. FLaAT
1) Initialize a one-dimension array FL[1..m].
2) Create a root node.
    Its Count is the number of user session in D_s.
3) For $i = 1$ to the number of user session in D_s Do

4) Let current pointer p point to the root node.

5) For $j = 1$ to the size of user session S_i Do

6) Do case

7) case1: (p^ .URL==S_{ij}.URL) p^ .Count++.

8) case2: (p^ .child==Null)

create p^ .child; p^ .child. URL=S_{ij}.URL and p^ .child. Count=1;

9) otherwise

if URL of a Younger==S_{ij}.URL, the Count of this younger increase 1; else

create p^ .Younger; p^ .Younger. URL=S_{ij}.URL; p^ .Younger. Count=1;

EndIf

10) Endcase

11) Store the gained the fuzzy web page preference function P_k by Eq.9 in the corresponding item.

12) Let p point to the current node.

13) Search FL, the condition is FL[k].URL= S_{ij}.URL.

If not exists then

compute the fuzzy evaluation and relative time duration by Eq.5 and Eq.7 and store them into the corresponding items;

FL[k].Count=1;

insert this current node (child or younger) into the link of the FL[k].First;

else modify the relative time duration and FL[k].Count add 1;

EndIf.

14) EndFor.

15) EndFor.

16) END.

4.3   Mining Preferred Traversal Patterns from the FLaAT

A node in FLaAT is said to be a preferred node if its *fuzzy web page preference function* and *count* are higher than the given thresholds. A branch is called a preferred traversal pattern if all nodes in it are preferred. Preferred traversal patterns could be mined from FLaAT instead of the user session database D_s.

Algorithm 2. **Algorithm for Mining Preferred Traversal Patterns Based on FLaAT**

Input.   A FLaAT, fuzzy web page preference function threshold ($P_{threshold}$), support threshold ($S_{threshold}$)

Output. User preferred traversal patterns

Let R be a pointer pointing to the root node of the FLaAT, O an auxiliary stack and Q an auxiliary queue, PP an auxiliary space to store the preferred traversal patterns.

1) O=NULL, Q=NULL, PP=NULL.

2) Search the first node whose Count is no less than the $S_{threshold}$ in the FL, then let p point to p^ .first.

3) While (p≠ NULL) and (its Fuzzy web page preference function $\geq P_{threshold}$)

and (p^ .Count $\geq S_{threshold}$)

Push p into O, insert p into Q, p← Child(p).
EndWhile.
4) p=p←(Younger)p; If p≠NULL goto 3) EndIf.
5) If Q is not the subset of pp then output Q in pp EndIf.
6) pop(O,p); delete(Q); p=p←(Younger)p;
7) If not empty(O) then goto 3) EndIf.
8) Repeat 2)-7) until no new preferred traversal pattern is produced.
9) Search FL;
   While exists (FL[k].count≥ $S_{threshold}$) and (FL[k].URL is not included in pp)
   mergesameroute();//merge the same sub-paths
   if the merged route satisfies the given condition store the route in pp;
   search FL;
   EndWhile.
10)END.

Xing [13] created a structure of PNT (that is similar to our defined the access tree) to store all users access information and the mining algorithm is similar to our algorithm from step 1 to 8. The major difference to our algorithm is that the same patterns were not merged in Xing [13]. Besides, he proposed a judgement criteria *preference* that only considered the two factors, time duration and access frequency to reveal users interest and preference.

5   An Example

Am example is given to discover users preferred traversal patterns from the web browsing log data with our proposed algorithms.

We extract browsing sequences from a log data shown in Table 1 to illustrate the mining process. A web log data is composed of user sessions. The sets of several (URL, time duration) make up a user session. URL denotes the current visited web page. Time duration denotes time spending on the current visited web page.

Here the linguistic evaluations on eight web pages by three experts are shown in Table 2.

Table 1. Browsing sequences from the log data

Client Id	Browsing sequences
1	(A,23), (B,68), (D,98), (E,130)
2	(A,45), (B,89), (D,102)
3	(A,27), (B,56), (F,86)
4	(A,32), (B,87), (D,45), (G,115), (H,118)
5	(A,30), (C,65), (H,78), (C,34), (G,32)
6	(A,78), (C,89), (G,110), (H,123)
7	(A,10), (B,24), (G,45), (H,34)

Table 2. Fuzzy linguistic evaluations on web pages given by experts

web page	manager1	manager2	manager3
A	important	important	important
B	important	important	important
C	very important	important	important
D	ordinary	ordinary	important
E	unimportant	unimportant	unimportant
F	unimportant	ordinary	ordinary
G	unimportant	unimportant	ordinary
H	ordinary	unimportant	unimportant

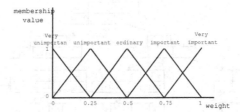

Fig. 1. The membership functions of fuzzy linguistic evaluations

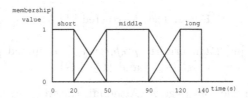

Fig. 2. The membership functions of the time duration

Assume that the fuzzy linguistic evaluations on web pages are classified into five different categories by experts, the membership functions of these fuzzy variables given by experts are depicted in Fig.1.

It is assumed that the membership functions of the time duration on all web pages given by experts here are shown in Fig.2. And the maximal time duration is set to be 140s.

According to the Algorithm 1, the constructed FLaAT from Table 1 is shown in Fig.3, in which the width of the arrow is determined by the *fuzzy web page preference function* of the target node.

Assume that the *support* threshold and *fuzzy web page preference function* threshold are set to be 2 and 0.3, respectively. Thus all mined preferred traversal patterns are $\{B \to D\}$, $\{C \to G\}$ and $\{G \to H\}$ by the algorithm 2.

In Xing [13], the algorithm was testified superior to previous works. His algorithm used a Depth First Traversal strategy to mine preferred traversal patterns

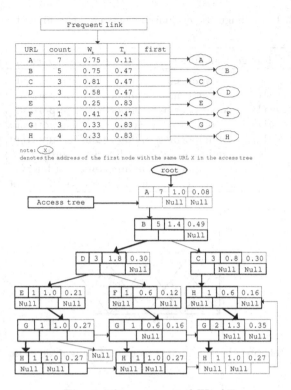

Fig. 3. The constructed FLaAT

from PNT by the judgment criteria *preference*. The mined preferred traversal patterns in Xing [13] were $\{B \to D\}$ and $\{C \to G\}$.

(1) Let us consider the web page A. Although the web page A is the most frequently visited page and has higher linguistic evaluations, its time duration is very short. It is clear that the web page A is an essential page to access a target page in the special web site frame. Users show little interest and preference in it. The result is more logical and reasonable.

(2) All possible sensitive factors are considered to reveal users interest and preference including the linguistic evaluations on web pages, time duration, and access frequency of web pages. Besides, fuzziness method is applied to process linguistic evaluation of experts and numeric time duration, which is more reasonable and similar to human reasoning.

(3) According to the example, the preferred traversal pattern $\{G \to H\}$ can not be discovered from the algorithm in Xing [13] because the prefixes of the pattern are different and merging the same route were not considered in [13], which results in the loss of important information. Therefore, our proposed algorithm is more accurate.

(4) The expansibility of our algorithm is very good. Once the FLaAT is constructed, it doesn't need to be reconstructed. Only modification to the corresponding route is needed. And searching the whole FLaAT isn't needed.

6   Conclusions

In this paper, a new concept of *fuzzy web page preference function* is proposed as a judgement criterion to replace the traditional *confidence* when preferred traversal patterns are mined. The *fuzzy web page preference function* considers all possible factors influencing the users interest and preference. Besides, fuzziness method is applied to deal with uncertain and imprecise factors, linguistic evaluations and time duration on web pages. According to the proposed judgement criterion an effective algorithm is developed to mine the preferred traversal patterns from the structure of FLaAT, from which we can find more integrated and accurate traversal patterns.

Acknowledgments

This work was supported by the National Natural Science Foundation of China Grant No.70471049 and China Postdoctoral Science Foundation No.2004035013.

References

1. Arotaritei, D., Mitra, S.: Web mining: a survey in the fuzzy framework. Fuzzy Sets and Systems. 148 (2004) 5-19
2. Chen, M., Park, J., Yu, P.: Efficient data mining for path traversal patterns. IEEE Transaction on Knowledge Data and engineering. 10 (1998) 209-221
3. Civanlar, M., Trussel, H.: Constructing membership function using statistical data. Fuzzy Sets and Systems. 18 (1986) 1-13
4. Cohen, E., Krishnamurthy, B., Rexford, J.: Efficient algorithm for predicting requests to web servers. The eighteenth IEEE Annual Joint Conference on Computer and Communications Societies, New York (1999) 284-293
5. Cosala, R.: Web mining research: a survey. Acm Sigkdd. 1 (2000) 1-15
6. Hong, T., Chiang, M., Wang, S.: Mining weighted browsing patterns with linguistic minimum supports. 2002 IEEE International Conference on Systems, Man and Cybernetics, Tunisia, 4 (2002) 6-9
7. Liu, B.: Theory and Practice of Uncertain Programming, Physica-Verlag, Heidelberg (2002)
8. Liu, B., Liu Y.: Expected value of fuzzy variable and fuzzy expected value models. IEEE Transactions on Fuzzy Systems. 10 (2002) 445-450
9. Lo, W., Hong, T., Wang, S.: A top-down fuzzy cross-level Web-mining approach. 2003 IEEE International Conference on Systems, Man and Cybernetics, United States, 3 (2003) 2684-2689
10. Perkowitz, M., Etzioni, O.: Towards adaptive web sites: conceptual framework and case study. Artificial Intelligence 118 (2000) 245-275
11. Schechter, S., Krishnan, M., Smith, M.: Using path profiles to predict HTTP requests. Computer Networks and ISDN Systems 30 (1998) 457-467
12. Wang X., Ha, M.: Note On maxmin u/E estimation. Fuzzy Sets and Systems. 94 (1998) 71-75
13. Xing, D., Shen, J.: Efficient data mining for web navigation patterns. Information and Software Technology. 46 (2004) 55-63
14. Zadeh, L.: Fuzzy sets. Information and Control. 8 (1965) 338-353

Discovering Characteristic Individual Accessing Behaviors in Web Environment

Long Wang[1,2] Christoph Meinel[2] and Chunnian Liu[3]

[1] Computer Science Department, Trier University, Campus II, 54296 Trier, Germany
Long.wang@hpi.uni-potsdam.de
[2] Hasso Plattner Institut, Potsdam University, 14482 Potsdam, Germany
Meinel@hpi.uni-potsdam.de
[3] Beijing Municipal Key Lab. of Multimedia and Intelligent Software Technology,
Beijing University of Technology, 100022 Beijing, China
cslcn@but.edu.cn

Abstract. Discovering diverse individual accessing behaviors in web environment is required before mining the valuable patterns from behaviors of groups of visitors. In this paper, we investigate the data preparation in web usage mining, and especially focus on discovering characteristic individual accessing behaviors and give a systematic and formalized study on this topic. Based on the target usage patterns, individual user behavior through the web site can be discovered into five different categories: granular accessing behavior, linear sequential behavior, tree structure behavior, acyclic routing behavior and cyclic routing behavior. We also give different algorithms for discovering different kinds of behaviors. The experimental studies show that our discovery of individual behavior is very useful and necessary in web usage mining.

1 Introduction

It is necessary to clean and collect usage data for different visitors before mining usage pattern in web environment. Different web service providers use different methods to record the tracks of their visitors, such as web server logs, cookies functions, personalized agents [10] or other interactive scripts. Traditional mining tools such as association rules, sequential patterns, and classification help much to find the usage patterns, but there are some other typical web characteristics that could be revealed from visitors accessing by these tools, such as revisiting and routing.

Many other experts have made great works on mining characteristic patterns in web environment. In [9], the user browsing model is built based on classifying the objects (pages) into content page and auxiliary page. The format of user browsing model is represented by a sequence, so the main contribution of such representation is to mine the usage patterns as association rules and frequent traversal paths. In [7], a maximal forward reference is formed from the start of an access till the occurring of revisiting a previously visited object by the same access. And the large reference sequences are used to depict the path traversal patterns and mined from maximal forward references. In [1,4], web access pattern

D. Ślęzak et al. (Eds.): RSFDGrC 2005, LNAI 3642, pp. 466–476, 2005.
© Springer-Verlag Berlin Heidelberg 2005

is the sequence of accesses pursued frequently by many visitors which may exist repeated objects.

Characteristic usage patterns are mined from the personalized individual accessing behaviors, so it is necessary to investigate individual accessings, which is far more than the above defined usage patterns. In this paper, we give a new view on discovering individual accessing behavior in web environment. An individual accessing behavior is beyond the visited objects and also the routing process among these objects. Based on the target mined patterns, an individual accessing behavior can be discovered into five different categories: granular accessing behavior, linear sequential behavior, tree structure behavior, acyclic behavior and cyclic routing behavior. In these methods, discovering individual behaviors are combined in the process of session reconstruction.

Individual accessing behaviors are discovered from reconstructed sessions. A session is defined as a group of requests made by a single user for a single navigation purpose [11]. This definition gives a better illustration on "session", but "session" is firstly refereed to a time concept, which means that a session must have happened within a couple of time boundaries.

There are different methods to rebuild sessions from web logs. In [2], timeout method is used to identify different session. In this method, a session shift is identified between two requests if the time interval between two requests is more than a predefined threshold. In [9], a single visitor can be identified by IP address, client information and even the direct links from any of the objects visited by the same IP and client information. And two timeouts are used to identify individual sessions from all the objects accessed by each visitor. While in [6], proactive strategies like cookie-based identification were used to reconstruct session. A method named maximal forward reference is used in [7]. And in [11], Zhang used a statistical language modelling to identify sessions from web logs.

In [6], it is showed that there is no best method for session reconstruction. In our experiments, we refereed the method from [9] to identify different visitors and different sessions. The problem of session identification is beyond our discussion in this paper, our contribution concerns on recovering individual accessing behaviors from reconstructed sessions. In this paper, our work is done based on the assuming that the sessions are already identified.

Different from [9] in session reconstruction, we don't care if there is hyperlink between two successively accessed objects, because it is possible for a visitor to use bookmark or URL hints cached by browser within a session. And also unrelated information should be removed from sessions. If an object was accessed *continuously* within a session, we omit the repeat happenings. The reason for the continuously repeat happenings of the same object is mainly due to "reloading or refreshing the same object" or "the existence of hyperlink to itself".

The rest of the paper is organized as follows. In section 2, we present the necessary terminology and formally define individual behavior. Section 3 gives a detailed view on the algorithms of discovering individual accessing behavior. We analysis our experiment results on three different kind of web sites in section 4. Section 5 provides a conclusion and overview on the future works.

2   Problem Statements

Let W be the target web site that gives us the web usage logs, and L be the target cleaned logs. Let V be the set of all visitors identified from L and T be the set of all time requests recorded in L, and O be the set of possible object requests in W. An object is a page, media file or a visitor's action captured by the web server.

L is a list of actual object requests from V, and each of these object requests is recorded as a logline entry termed as l. So L can be regarded as a set, but all the loglines are ordered by the timestamp of their invocation. We use $l.visitor$ to denote the visitor of the logline $l \in L$, and $l.time$ to denote the request time of l, and l.url to denote the URL request in l and $l.obj$ to denote the object requested by $l.visitor$. It is obvious that for each logline l, $l.visitor \in V$, $l.time \in T$, and $l.obj \in O$.

A session s is denoted:

$$s = \{l_1, \ldots, l_m\} : l \le i < j \le m, l_i.visitor = l_j.visitor, l_i.time < l_j.time.$$

And also s should satisfy the following conditions:

$$\forall i (1 \le i < m) : l_{i+1}.time - l_i.time \le Timeout1, l_m.time - l_1.time \le Timeout2.$$

$Timeout1$ and $Timeout2$ are the two time thresholds needed to identify sessions, and $Timeout1$ is the threshold that constraints the time delay between two continuously accessed objects and $Timeout2$ aims to constrain the time duration of a session. As the same definition for logline l, we also denote $s.visitor$ the visitor of this session, and $s.length$ the number of objects in s.

With the above definition, we can map web logs L into a session set S, for each logline $linL$, l belongs to exactly one session, and this ensures that S partitions L in an order-preserving way.

We give a function to get the ith accessed object in a session s:

$$Object(s, j) = l_i.obj : l_i ins.(*)$$

(1) The firstly accessed object in a session s:

$$EntranceObject(s) = l_1.obj : l_1 ins.$$

(2) The last accessed object in a session s:

$$ExistObject(s) = l_{s.length}.obj : l_{s.length} ins.$$

We call the object obj_j "target object" of object obj_i and obj_j "source object" of obj_j, if obj_j is accessed after obj_i. And we also call the last accessed object "final target object" of a session.

(3) The set of repeated objects in a session s:

$$Repeated(s) = \{obj_1, \ldots, obj_k\}, \forall i (1 \le i \le k), \exists i', j' (1 \le i' <> j' \le s.length) :$$
$$Object(s, i') = Object(s, j') = obj_i.$$

(4) The set of access objects in a session s:

$$ObjectSet(s) = \{obj_1, \ldots, obj_k\},$$
$$\forall i, j (1 \leq i <> j \leq k), \exists i', j' (1 \leq i' <> j' \leq s.length) :$$
$$Object(s, i') = obj_i, Object(s, j') = obj_j, obj_i <> obj_j.$$

(5) An access sequence in a session s:

$$Sequence(s) = obj_1 obj_2 \ldots obj_k,$$
$$\forall i, j (1 \leq i < j \leq k), \exists i', j' (1 \leq i' < j' \leq s.length) :$$
$$Object(s, i') = obj_i, Object(s, j') = obj_j, obj_i <> obj_j, obj_i.time < obj_j.time.$$

(6) An access path in a session s:

$$Path(s) = obj_1 obj_2 \ldots obj_k,$$
$$\exists i' (1 \leq i' < s.length), \forall i, j (1 \leq i <> j \leq k) :$$
$$Object(s, i + j') = obj_i, Object(s, j + i') = obj_j, obj_i <> obj_j.$$

From the definition (5) and (6), the difference between accessed sequence and path is that all the objects in a sequence are accessed in the same time order as in the original session, while in a path, all the objects must be *continuously* accessed one by one as the order in the session. So access path can be seen as the special access sequence. Even with removing continuously repeatedly accessed objects in the raw session, it doesn't affect the final results of finding sequences and paths in a session.

We use $q.length$ and $p.length$ to denote the lengths of a sequence and a path. And the definitions for the ith object in a sequence and a path are the same as in (*), which only the parameter "s" is replaced by "q" or "p".

Access sequence $Seq' = obj'_1 obj'_2 \ldots obj'_k$ is called a subsequence of access sequence $Seq = obj_1 obj_2 \ldots obj_n$ and Seq a super-sequence of Seq', denoted as $Seq' \subseteq Seq$, if and only if there exist $1 \leq i_1 < i_2 < \ldots < i_k \leq n$, such that $obj'_j = obj_{i_j}$ for $(1 \leq j \leq k)$. Access path $P' = obj'_1 obj'_2 \ldots obj'_k$ is called a sub path of access path $P = obj_1 obj_2 \ldots obj_n$ and P a super-path of P', denoted as $P' \subseteq P$, if and only if there exist a const c, such that $obj'_j = obj_{j+c}$ for $(1 \leq j \leq k)$.

It is well acknowledged that a web site is a complex graph, and any kind of information can find its position in this graph. In our study, we take the objects accessed by visitors as the basic unit, then these objects are the vertices and the hyperlinks among them are edges in this graph. The relationships among the accessed objects in a session, such as tree structure, undirected and directed graph, are hidden in a session which is a form of sequence. Tree structure relationship is characterized by the nodes that lead to different objects in a session, which mean divert or different paths after an object. Thus we call this tree structure relationship "divert path tracking" in web usage. Furthermore, in the routing on a graph, it is popular that there is more than one path between two selected vertices, which looks like a rhombus structure. And we call this relationship "parallel path tracking" in web usage.

(7) A circle path in a session s:

$$CirclePath(s) = obj_1 \ldots obj_k,$$
$$\exists i'(1 \leq i' < s.length), \forall i(1 \leq i \leq k) : Object(s, i + i') = obj_i, obj_1 = obj_k.$$

(8) The diverged paths in a session s:

$$DivertPath(s) = \{Path(s)_1, \ldots, Path(s)_k\},$$
$$\forall i, j(1 \leq i <> j \leq k) : Object(P_i, 1) = Object(P_j, 1).$$

(9)The parallel paths in a session s:

$$ParallelPath(s) = \{Path(s)_1, \ldots, Path(s)_k\}, \forall i, j(1 \leq i <> j \leq k) :$$
$$Object(P_i, 1) = Object(P_j, 1), Object(P_i, P_i.length) = Object(P_j, P_j.length).$$

The above definitions reveal the diversities of the usage activities endowed with the special characteristics in web environment, such as entrance page, hyperlinks, backtracking, revisiting and so on. It is possible for an individual accessing session to be interpreted with one of these definitions or the combination of several definitions, which is far more than object sets and sequences patterns as discussed in [4,9]. We use a plain term "Action" to uniform these 9 different basic functions, because each of them characterizes the unique activity perfumed by a visitor on some objects in a session. So an action of a visitor is embodied with the organization of some objects in a session.

We now give the definition of individual accessing behavior: *An individual accessing behavior is the combination of several actions performed by a visitor during his session with the web server.*

3   Discovery Algorithms

An individual accessing behavior is the combination of actions extracted from a session and it displays not only the accessed objects and part of site structure, but also the concept hierarchies and the routing activities on these objects.

Individual accessing behavior can be discovered by using several recovery techniques. The choice of proper discovering method is decided by what kind of access patterns we want to mine in the next step. From simple to complex, we show here some strategies of behaviors discovery. We illustrate this problem by using a real session reconstructed from our server logs. The objects here are the web pages, so in the rest of the paper, we replace the term "object" with "page", and every page is titled with its ID. This session is listed as following:

$$s = \{0, 292, 300, 304, 350, 326, 512, 510, 513, 512, 515, 513, 292, 319, 350, 517, 286\}.$$

0 and 286 were accessed separately as entrance and leaving pages, and $Repeated(s) = \{292, 350, 513, 512\}$. Any piece of session without repeated pages can form a path, for example:

$$Path_1(s) = 300\text{-}304\text{-}350\text{-}326\text{-}512, \text{ and } Path_2(s) = 512\text{-}515\text{-}513\text{-}292.$$

3.1 Simple Behaviors Discovery

This strategy overlooks all the repeated pages in a session. The behavior of this visitor can be simply discovered into the largest set of accessed objects, and the longest access sequence. We also call the largest set of accessed objects "granular behavior" and longest access sequence "linear sequential behavior". These two kinds of behaviors are the extensions of the definitions of "set of access objects" and "access sequence" in section 3; and the former is defined as $ObjectSet_L(s)$ and the latter is $Seq_L(s)$. To discover the longest accessed sequence, we choose the first request time as the time for the same repeated pages in a session. For the above session, we remove the 10th, 12th, 13th, and 15th pages:

$ObjectSet_L(s) = \{0, 286, 292, 300, 304, 319, 326, 350, 510, 512, 513, 515, 517\}$.
$Seq_L(s) = < 0-292-300-304-350-326-512-510-513-515-319-517-286 >$.

We can see that any sub set of $ObjectSet_L(s)$ is one of the sets of accessed objects by this visitor. Any subsequence of $Seq_L(s)$ is one of the accessed sequences in this session.

Motivated by other data mining applications in [4,9], given a large group of accessed objects and accessed sequences by different sessions, we can mine the most popular set of accessed objects and the most popular accessed sequences.

3.2 Tree Structure Behaviors Discovery

The tree structure behavior is characterized by diverged paths in a session defined in (8). From this definition, some paths in a session can form diverged path because they share the start accessed object. Though all the accessed objects are ordered by timestamp in a sequence, we can find those repeated objects that lead to different target objects. Tree structure behaviors displayed not only the visiting patterns, but also some conceptual hierarchy on site semantics.

To discover tree structure t from a session s, a pointer pr is used to point to the last read node in t. Every page is read in the same order as in s and this page is inserted as the child node of pr if it firstly happens in t; but if the same page already exits in t, we do nothing but only setting pr point to this page in t.

The tree structure behaviors for the above session can be discovered with our strategy as the figure 1.

Based on this algorithm, there is some property in the discovered tree structure behaviors:

Property 1: Given a discovered tree structure behavior, the nodes that lead to diverged paths are the repeated objects in this session.

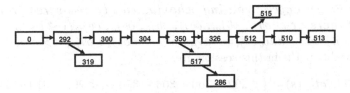

Fig. 1. Tree Structure Behavior

The diverged path in this session is:

$$DivertPath_1(s) = \{< 292 - 300 - 304 - 350 >, < 292 - 319 >\},$$
$$DivertPath_2(s) = \{< 350 - 326 - 512 >, < 350 - 517 - 286 >\},$$
$$DivertPath_3(s) = \{< 512 - 510 - 513 >, < 512 - 515 >\}.$$

Similar from [8], given a large group of discovered individual tree behaviors, the most popular tree structure access patterns can be mined.

3.3 Acyclic Routing Behaviors Discovery

"Acyclic routing behavior" means that in a session, there exist at least two different pages between which there are at least two different access paths. This kind of behavior is characterized by the parallel paths in a session. It shows that a visitor can access the same target object from the same start object but via different paths. With acyclic routing behaviors, we can further query the shortest path and most popular path between two pages. Because this discovered behavior has a lattice structure, we also call it semi-lattice behavior.

The final discovered behavior is like a lattice structure defined as l, and we used pr pointing to the last read node in l. The pages are read in the same sequence as in s, and for every page, we check if the same page exits in l. If this page firstly happens in l, we insert this as a new child node of pr, and let pr point to this new node. If this page already exits in l, there are four different relations between this page and the last read page:

- This page is the same as pr:
  1. Do nothing.
- This page can be backward tracked from pr:
  1. Set pr point to this page.
- This page can be forward tracked from pr:
  1. Build new edge directed from pr to this page, if there is not directed edge from pr to this page,
  2. Set pr point to this page.
- This can not be tracked from pr:
  1. Build new edge directed from pr to this page,
  2. Set pr point to this page.

Figure 2 displays the recovered acyclic routing behavior from the above session. It is clear that if an acyclic routing behavior can be discovered from a session, the session must have the following property:

Property 2: An acyclic routing behavior can be recovered from a session s iff there exist obj_i, obj_m, obj_j, obj_v, obj_k, obj_w $(1 \leq i < m < j < v < w \leq s.length)$ **in** s, **and** $obj_i == obj_v$; $obj_j == obj_w$; $obj_m <> obj_k$.

The parallel paths in this session are:

$$ParallelPath_1(s) = \{< 292 - 300 - 304 - 350 >, < 292 - 319 - 350 >\},$$
$$ParallelPath_2(s) = \{< 512 - 515 - 513 >, < 512 - 510 - 513 >\}.$$

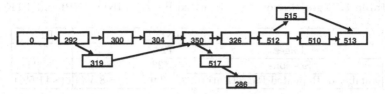

Fig. 2. Acyclic Routing Behavior

3.4   Cyclic Routing Behaviors Discovery

If there are back tracked or revisited objects in a session, directed links will be built from every revisited objects to one of its source object. From the semantic level, we call these two object can be mutually heuristically evoked. So in this situation, the individual behavior can be discovered as cyclic routing behavior and this kind of behavior is characterized by the circle path hidden in the session.

The strategy for discovering cyclic routing behavior is similar to but more complicate than discovering acyclic routing. The following figure shows cyclic routing behaviors discovered from the same example.

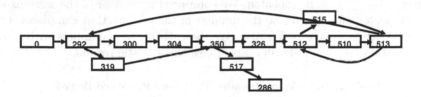

Fig. 3. Cyclic Routing Behavior

The circle paths in this session are:

$$CirclePath_1(s) = 292 - 300 - 304 - 350 - 326 - 512 - 510 - 513 - 292,$$
$$CirclePath_2(s) = 512 - 510 - 513 - 512.$$

4   Experiment Results

Our experiment data was taken from three web sites: www.informatik.uni-trier.de (INFO), www.hpi.uni-potsdam.de (HPI) and www.tele-task.de (TTK). These three sites are chosen because of their differences: INFO is a well frame based site, and TTK is a site dedicated to multimedia lectures and HPI has launched a new version. The time durations for these logs are one month for INFO and HPI, and 12 months for TTK because of the small access count.

The distribution of repeated pages is closely related with the web structure. It is clear that a structure with many pages has more repeated pages than those with small number of pages. It can be seen from the different distribution that TTK has a small number of repeated pages than INFO and HPI. But for the ratio of repeated pages, the simple structure has a higher possibility of repeated

Table 1. Pages, Sessions and Repeated Pages on INFO, HPI and TTK

	INFO	HPI	TTK
Pages	728	253	52
Sessions	5828	28308	33894
Number of Repeated Pages(Ratio)	29(~3.9%)	21(~8.3%)	6(~11.5%)

happenings than complicate structure; the reason is that a visitor could have more choices in a site with many pages which could reduce the happening of repeated visits. Another factor is related site structures, the difference of the number of repeated pages from INFO and HPI is not as so big as the number of total pages on this two sites, this is because the a big part of pages from INFO are those with few links in their contents and are seen as the bottom pages or the leaf pages on the site graph.

The average of the length of session is 3~4. It has been discussed in the previous parts that for every session a granular behavior and linear sequence behavior can be discovered, but for tree structure behavior there must be repeated objects in a session, and for semi-lattice structure behavior, two or more different objects must be repeated. We compute the number of the sessions with 1 or 2 repeated pages, and also the number of the sessions that can discover tree and semi-lattice behaviors. We also give the ratio of these numbers with respect to the session set. The following table gives the statistic results.

Table 2. Statistics of Repeated Pages and Recovered Behaviors

	INFO	HPI	TTK
Sessions with 1 R-Page (ratio)	701(~12%)	3998(~14.1%)	1319(~3.9%)
Sessions with 2 R-Pages (ratio)	350(~6%)	2493(~8.8%)	237(~0.7%)
Sessions with T-Behavior (ratio)	642(~11%)	3911(~13.8%)	1085(~3.2%)
Sessions with L-Behavior (ratio)	72(~1.2%)	402(~1.4%)	22(~0.06%)

From the table2, we found that tree behaviors and semi-lattice behaviors exist in some sessions, and their hosts are the most valuable visitors for the sites. And the visiting behavior is closely related with site structure and content. Firstly, the more complex of the web site, the more complex of the behavior; secondly, most of the sessions with repeated pages can discover tree behavior, but great drawdown of semi-lattice behavior from sessions with 2 or more pages, which is due to the constraints among objects in a lattice behavior. And also, HPI has more complex link relations than INFO, so in HPI the lattice behavior happens frequently than in INFO.

Based on the discovered individual behaviors, we further mine the popular and characteristic web usage patterns. By analyzing the accessing information of entrance page and exit page, these three different sites have the same accessing distribution: the entrance pages concentrate on a very few number of pages, which have much higher popularities than other pages accessed as entrance page.

The exit pages concentrated on a number of pages, while the difference on accessing popularity is not as violently as on entrance page. This phenomenon gives us the hint that the exit page plays more important on discriminating visitors from different interests. The analysis on mining popular co-accessed pages and popular sequences from discovered simple behavior set is the same as that from other researchers, so we don't give the mined examples here. Mining complex patterns from discovered complex behaviors such as tree behaviors and semi-lattice behaviors, we build a complex tree structure named DIXT (Double Index Three-Dimension Tree) to index and agglomerate individual behaviors, and this will be detailed discussed in another paper. Based on the properties analysis in the above sections, one required conditions for recovering tree structure behavior is the existence of at least 1 repeated object in a session; and one required conditions for recovering lattice behavior is the existence of at least 2 different repeated objects in a session.

We now give some general statistics on the mined popular tree patterns and parallel patterns on these tree sites separately with different support thresholds.

Table 3. Statistic on Tree Patterns

	INFO	HPI	TTK
Sessions with T-Behavior	642	3911	1085
Tree Patterns (sup=0.005)	21	48	23
Tree Patterns (sup=0.01)	6	11	8

Table 4. Statistic on Lattice Patterns

	INFO	HPI	TTK
Sessions with L-Behavior	72	402	22
Lattice Patterns (sup=0.02)	64	7	14
Lattice Patterns (sup=0.05)	3	0	3

For further analysis, lattice behavior surely includes its corresponding tree structure if we keep only one incoming connection for a node that is repeatedly accessed from different nodes. A tree pattern is shared by two individual tree structure behaviors, if both of them have one same node that connects to at least two same nodes. If one parallel path in a discovered individual lattice behavior shares the same start node and also the same end node with another parallel path in another individual behavior, we call these two behaviors share the same parallel path, while we don't care if the middle nodes on separate path for two parallel path are the same or not. From above two tables about distribution of tree patterns and parallel patterns, we find that both of them are the rare patterns, which can be seen as the unexpected patterns in web usage mining; and also the complexity of such behaviors makes it less possible to find tree patterns or semi-lattice patterns. We can also further find from these two tables that the number of semi-lattice patterns is larger than that of tree patterns while the former support number is also larger than the later, one reason for this phenomenon is that our constraint for a semi-lattice patterns is less stricter than that of tree patterns, and the second reason is that more complex of individual behavior, and more impossible to find dominated popular complex patterns, although the size of discovered tree behavior set is larger than that of discovered semi-lattice behavior set. So the support number on thousands of individual tree behaviors is set smaller than that of hundreds or less than hundred of individual semi-lattice behaviors. A circle path is a special sequence, which the start node is the same as the end node, so mining circle paths is the same as mining the largest forward paths from other researchers.

5   Conclusion

The bottleneck of enlarging the mining applications in web usage field is the exploding of web knowledge and the specialities of web environment, which attract us to deeply investigate the individual access behavior.

In this paper, we discuss the individual access behavior through the web, and how to discover these behaviors from web logs. The complexity of web structure and the variety of visitors, and also the target patterns pursued decide that access behaviors can not be simplified into one category, and we define five different categories of individual access behavior. Before these behaviors were given, we also define 9 different basic actions that could be performed during a session. And individual access behavior is the combination of these basic actions. The experiment results show that our defined actions and behavior universally exist in many websites. And they are the necessary for mining the useful usage patterns with web characteristics in the following mining steps.

References

1. B. Berendt and M. Spiliopoulou: Analysis of navigation behavior in web sites integrating multiple information systems, The VLDB Journal, (2000).
2. D. He and A. Goker: Detecting Session Boundaries from Web User Logs, 22nd Annual Colloquium on IR Research, (2000).
3. J. Srivastava, R. Cooley, M. Deshpande and P. Tan: Web Usage Mining: Discovery and Application of Usage Patterns from Web Data, ACM SIGKDD, (2000).
4. J. Pei, J. Han, B. Mortazavi-Asl and H. Zhu: Mining Access Patterns Efficiently from Web Logs, PAKDD, (2000).
5. J. Pei, J. Han and W. Wang: Mining Sequential Patterns with Constraints in Large Databases, ACM CIKM, (2002).
6. M. Spiliopoulou, B. Mobasher, B. Berendt and M. Nakagawa: A Framework for the Evaluation of Session Reconstruction Heuristics in Web Usage Analysis, INFORMS Journal on Computing, (2003).
7. M. Chen, J. Park and P. Yu: Data Mining for Path Traversal Patterns in a Web Environment, 16th International Conference on Distributed Computing Systems, (1996).
8. M. J. Zaki: Efficiently Mining Frequent Trees in a Forest, ACM SIGKDD, (2002).
9. R. Cooley, B. Mobasher and J. Srivastava: Data Preparation for Mining World Wide Web browsing Patterns, Knowledge and Information System, Journal of Knowledge and Information System, (1999).
10. T. Joachims, D. Freitag and T. Mitchell: WebWatcher: A Tour Guide for the World Wide Web, IJCAI, (1997).
11. X. Huang, F. Peng, A. An and D. Schuurmans: Dynamic Web Log Session Identification with Statistical Language Models, Journal of Information Science and Technology, (2004).

An Efficient and Practical Algorithm for the Many-Keyword Proximity Problem by Offsets

Sung-Ryul Kim[1,*] and Jiman Hong[2]

[1] Division of Internet & Media and CAESIT,
Konkuk University
kimsr@konkuk.ac.kr
[2] School of Computer Science and Engineering,
Kwangwoon University
gman@daisy.kw.ac.kr

Abstract. One of the most important relevance factors in the Web search context is the proximity score, i.e., how close the keywords appear together in a given document. A basic proximity score is given by the size of the smallest range containing all the keywords in the query. We generalize the proximity score to include many practically important cases and present an $O(n \log k)$ time algorithm for the generalized problem, where k is the number of keywords and n is the number of occurrences of the keywords in a document.

1 Introduction

When using a search engine, because the number of keywords in the query to a search engine is usually small, there are a tremendous number of search results unless the query contains a very specific combination of keywords. For example, when the query is "apple computer support," what the user intended is most likely the customer support page in the Apple computer site. However, some other documents may contain all three keywords in totally different contexts (irrelevant results). So the issue for the search engine is to find the relevant documents and show the relevant ones first. Many heuristics are used to compute the relevance of a document. Examples include the *PageRank* model [2] and the *hub and authority* model [4], both based on the links between the documents. Also, the content of a document and the *anchor text* (the text that appears close to the link to the document from some other document) are used to determine the relevance. Some examples are the relative frequency of the keywords and the location of keywords (in the title or close to the start of a document).

We focus on the textual information, particularly how close the keywords appear together (i.e., the *proximity*) in a document, which makes a good measure of relevance. If the proximity is good, then it is more likely that the keywords have combined meaning in the document. Proximity score cannot be computed off-line because we can't predict all possible combinations of keywords practically. Therefore, we need to compute the proximity score very efficiently.

---

* Corresponding author.

D. Ślęzak et al. (Eds.): RSFDGrC 2005, LNAI 3642, pp. 477–483, 2005.

In this paper we define the generalized k-keyword proximity problem and present an $O(n \log k)$-time algorithm for the problem, where k is the number of keywords and n is the number of occurrences of the keywords in a document. Our main contribution is an algorithm that retains the same time complexity as the best previous result while solving a more general problem. An important application of our algorthms can be found in computational biology. In biology context, keywords correspond to motifs and the proximity score gives some hints on how similar different genes are.

2   Problem Definition

The *offset* of a word in a document is defined to be the distance from the start of the document, which is measured by the number of words. A *range* in a document is a contiguous portion of the document. The *size* of a range is the number of words in it. Given a set of keywords, the *basic proximity score* is defined to be the size of the smallest range in the document containing all of the keywords.

In some cases, the basic proximity score is not enough. In the previous "apple computer support" query, the two keywords 'apple' and 'computer' has a stronger combined meaning than 'computer' and 'support.' So even if the basic proximity score is similar for two documents, one document might have 'apple' and 'computer' in close proximity while the other does not. In this case, we have to give a higher overall score to the first document. This case leads to the definition of *proximity score with partial keyword set* where the score is defined to be the size of the the smallest range in the document that contains k' $(\leq k)$ distinct keywords. It can be used in combination with the basic proximity score to refine overall score for a document.

Consider the query "johnson and johnson." This is another case the basic proximity score does not work because the same keyword 'johnson' must appear twice in a range. This leads to the definition of the *proximity requiring repetitions of keywords* where we are given the number of required occurrences of each keyword. The score is defined to be the size of the smallest range in the document that contains each keyword the specified number of times.

Most search engines use inverted file structures to store documents. In an inverted file structure, the database is organized first by keywords. The entry for each keyword contains a list of document IDs that contain the keyword. Also, there is a list for each document ID that contains the offsets where the

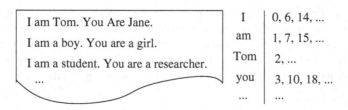

Fig. 1. A simple example

keyword appears in the document. Inverted file structures are useful because we can find the set of documents that contain all of the keywords very efficiently, thus reducing the number of documents to consider. Fig. 1 is an example where a particular document and the lists of offsets are shown. Because search engines use very complicated ranking algorithms, inverted file structure may not provide all of the information that a ranking algorithm requires. However, because most search engines use inverted file structure, we believe that our algorithms have practical implications.

Because of the inverted file structure we may assume that the sorted lists of offsets, rather than the whole document, is given as the input. The following is the definition of the generalized k-keyword proximity problem that combines all three kinds of proximity scores mentioned above.

Definition 1. *Given k keywords $w_1, w_2, \ldots, w_k$, a set of lists $K = \{K_1, K_2, \ldots, K_k\}$ where $K_i = \{o_{i1}, o_{i2}, \ldots, o_{ij_i}\}$ $(1 \le i \le k)$ is the sorted list of the offsets of the i-th keyword w_i, and positive integers $R_1, R_2, \ldots, R_k$, and k' $(\le k)$, the generalized k-keyword proximity problem is to find the smallest range that contains k' distinct keywords w_i $(1 \le i \le k)$ that appear at least R_i times each in the range.*

Let n be the total number of offsets given in the input. Note that the generalized problem becomes the basic score problem when all $R_i = 1$ $(1 \le i \le k)$ and $k' = k$. Also it becomes proximity with partial keyword set (respectively, proximity requiring repetition) when all $R_i = 1$ for $1 \le i \le k$ (respectively, $k' = k$).

3   Previous Works

There are some results on finding k keywords within a given maximum distance d. Gonnet et al. [3] proposed an algorithm for finding two keywords P_1 and P_2 within distance d in $O(m_1 + m_2)$ time, where $m_1 < m_2$ are the numbers of occurrences of the two keywords. Baeza-Yates and Cunto [1] proposed the abstract data type Proximity and an $O(\log n)$-time algorithm, but the construction takes $O(n^2)$ time. Manber and Baeza-Yates [7] also proposed an $O(\log n)$-time algorithm, but it takes $O(dn)$ space. However all of the above does not directly deal with the problem of this paper because they assume that the maximum distance d is known in advance. Sadakane and Imai proposed an $O(n \log k)$-time algorithm for a restricted version of the problem [8]. Their version of the problem corresponds to the basic proximity score. As far as we know, this is the only result for the k-keyword proximity problem. Our algorithm achieves the same time complexity while dealing with a generalized version of the problem.

4   Algorithm

The algorithm consists of two stages. In the first stage, called the *preprocessing*, we merge the lists of offsets into a new sorted list. Each offset is labeled with the

Query = "A B C"

Document   A ? ? ? C B A ? ? A C ? B

Merged list

offset	0	4	5	6	9	10	12
ki	1	3	2	1	1	3	2

Fig. 2. Example merged list (?'s are the places where none of three keywords appear)

keyword index (i if the keyword is w_i) during the merge. Because the input lists are already sorted, it is easy to show that the first stage takes $O(n \log k)$ time. The merged list is denoted by $L[0..n-1]$. Each entry in the list has two fields denoted by $L[x].offset$ (the offset) and $L[x].ki$ (the keyword index). Let (x, y) be the range starting at $L[x].offset$ and ending at $L[y].offset$. See Fig. 2 for an example, where the query consists of three keywords. The second stage is the main part of the algorithm. The second stage takes $O(n)$ time.

Before describing the main algorithm, we need to define a few terms. Then we will prove the key lemmas.

Definition 2. *A* candidate range *is a range containing at least k' distinct keywords w_i ($1 \le i \le k$) that appear at least R_i times each in the range.*

Lemma 1. *The solution to the generalized k-keyword proximity problem is the smallest of the candidate ranges.*

Proof. Immediate from the definition of the problem.

The number of candidate ranges is less than $n(n-1)/2$. Now we will reduce the number of candidate ranges we have to consider. We consider only the *minimal* candidate ranges because we want to find the smallest one.

Definition 3. *A* critical range *is a candidate range that does not properly contain other candidate ranges.*

Lemma 2. *The solution to the generalized k-keyword proximity problem is a critical range.*

Proof. Suppose that the solution is not a critical range. Then the solution properly contains a smaller candidate range. A contradiction to Lemma 1.

Fig. 3 illustrates the difference between critical ranges and candidate ranges. Assume that we are given the query "A A B C," and $k' = k = 3$. (A has to appear at least twice while B and C may appear only once.) Range 1 is a candidate range, but not a critical range. (Range 1 contains candidate ranges 2 and 3). Ranges 2 and 3 are critical ranges since there are no ways to make them smaller while satisfying the given condition. Now we bound the number of critical ranges.

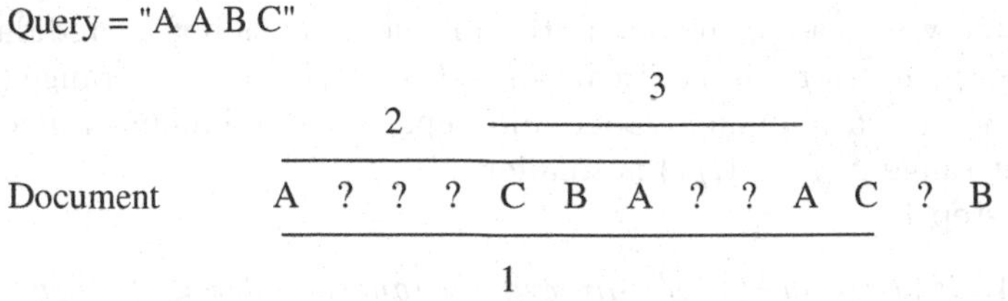

Query = "A A B C"

Document   A ? ? ? C B A ? ? A C ? B

Fig. 3. Critical ranges and candidate ranges. ?'s are the places where none of three keywords appear. Note that this range does not contain offsets.

Lemma 3. *There are at most n critical ranges.*

Proof. Two different critical ranges cannot share starting offsets because if they do, one of the critical ranges is properly contained in the other. Because there are at most n starting offsets, there are at most n critical ranges.

The algorithm works by maintaining a current range. By Lemma 2 it is enough to consider only the critical ranges. We find all the critical ranges by scanning the merged list of offsets from left to right and whenever we find a critical range, we compare it with the smallest one up to that point. When the scanning is finished, we have the solution of the generalized k-proximity problem.

We use two position numbers of the merged list to indicate where the current range is: p_ℓ is for the starting offset and p_r is for the ending offset of the current range, respectively. For each keyword w_i ($1 \leq i \leq k$), we maintain a counter c_i which indicates the number of times w_i appears in the current range. There is another counter h which indicates the number of c_i's ($1 \leq i \leq k$) larger than or equal to R_i. Initially $p_\ell = h = 0$, $c_i = 0$ for all $1 \leq i \leq k$, and $p_r = -1$.

Whenever we increase a position number by one in the following algorithm, we modify at most two counters, namely, one of c_i is increased or decreased by one and h is adjusted accordingly, to update the status of the current range.

- Assume that we have increased p_r by one and let i be $L[p_r].ki$. Because w_i is added to the current range we increase c_i by one. If c_i equals R_i at this point, we increase h by one also.
- Assume that we have increased p_ℓ by one and let j be $L[p_\ell - 1].ki$. Because w_j is removed from the current range we decrease c_j by one. If c_j equals $R_j - 1$, we decrease h by one.

One can easily verify that each c_i ($1 \leq i \leq k$) indicates the number of occurrences of w_i in the current range, respectively, and that h corresponds to the number of keywords w_j ($1 \leq j \leq k$) which appear at least R_j times in the current range. Thus the current range is a candidate range only if $h \geq k'$.

Main Algorithm

1. Repeatedly increase p_r by one until current range is a candidate range or we have passed the end of the list.
2. If we have passed end of the list, finish.

3. Repeatedly increase p_ℓ by one until current range is not a candidate range.
4. The range $(p_\ell - 1, p_r)$ is a critical range. Compare the size of range $(p_\ell - 1, p_r)$ with the stored minimum range and replace the minimum range with the current range if $(p_\ell - 1, p_r)$ is smaller.
5. Go to step 1.

Lemma 4. *If (x, y) and (x', y') are critical ranges and $x < x'$, then $y < y'$.*

Proof. Obvious from the fact that the critical ranges are not nested.

We show that the algorithm works correctly. All we have to show is that the algorithm identifies each critical range after step 3. We consider two cases.

- The first case is the initial case and we show that the algorithm finds the first critical range (x, y), i.e., the critical range with smallest x and y whose existence is implied by Lemma 4. Note that $(0, y')$ for $y' < y$ cannot be a candidate range because then it would contain a critical range, contradicting the assumption that (x, y) is the first critical range. Also note that $(0, y)$ is a candidate range. Thus we have verified that step 1 stops when p_r reaches y. For step 3, note that (x', y) is a candidate range if $x' \leq x$ and it is not, otherwise. Thus, we have verified that step 3 stops when p_ℓ reaches $x + 1$.
- The other case is searching for the next candidate range after finding one. Let (x, y) be the critical range we have just identified and let (x'', y'') be the next critical range, i.e., the one with smallest $x'' - x \ (> 0)$ and smallest $y'' - y \ (> 0)$ whose existence is implied by Lemma 4. When step 1 starts $p_\ell = x + 1$ and $p_r = y$. Note that $(x + 1, y')$ is not a candidate range if $y' < y''$ because otherwise, it must contain a critical range, contradicting the assumption on (x'', y''). Also note that $(x + 1, y'')$ is a candidate range. Thus we have verified that step 1 stops when p_r reaches y''. We can show that step 3 stops when p_ℓ reaches $x'' + 1$ in the same way as in previous case.

Example 1. Suppose we have a query "A A B C" and three lists of offsets $K_1 = \{0, 2, 4, 5\}$, $K_2 = \{1, 6, 7\}$ and $K_3 = \{3, 8\}$. Then we have four critical ranges I_1, I_2, I_3 and I_4 as indicated in Fig. 4. The solution is I_1, I_2 or I_3. A dashed arrow indicates the changes made to p_r in one execution of step 1 and a dotted arrow indicates the changes made to p_ℓ in one execution of step 3.

We show that the time complexity of the second stage is $O(n)$. Since the two position numbers are only increased, they are increased at most n times. Each time a position number is increased, we access at most two counters. Thus the time complexity for accessing counters is $O(n)$. Steps 2, 4, and 5 are performed once for each critical range. Since there are at most n critical ranges by Lemma 3, they are performed at most n times. The space complexity of the (whole) algorithm is easily shown to be $O(n + k)$ since the only additional space we use are the $k + 1$ counters.

Theorem 1. *The generalized k-keyword proximity problem can be solved in $O(n \log k)$ time with $O(n + k)$ space.*

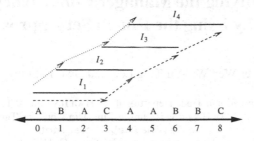

Fig. 4. Finding the solution for Example 1

5   Conclusion

We presented an $O(n \log k)$ time algorithm for the generalized k-keyword proximity problem. To compute s proximity scores for varying values of $R_1, R_2, \ldots, R_k$, and k', the preprocessing stage may be performed only once. So, the time complexity is $O(n \log k + sn)$. To find m smallest ranges, the time complexity is $O(n(\log k + \log m))$. When k is a constant, the algorithm runs in linear time. The algorithm has been implemented and is currently being used in the WiseNut search engine, which is now part of LookSmart Corporation [6]. Our implementation of the algorithm uses less than 1% of the total query processing time on the average.

An open problem is to identify a lower bound. We conjecture that the lower bound is $\Omega(n \log k)$, i.e., the algorithm given in the paper is optimal.

References

1. Baeza-Yates, R., and Cunto, W.: The ADT proximity and text proximity problems, *IEEE String Processing and Information Retrieval Symposium (SPIRE '99)*, 24–30, 1999.
2. Brin, S., and Page, L.: The anatomy of a large-scale hypertextual web search engine, *Computer Networks and ISDN Systems*, 30(1-7):107–117, 1998.
3. Gonnet, G. H., Baeza-Yates, R., and Snider, T.: New indices for text: PAT trees and PAT arrays, *Information retrieval: algorithms and data structures*, ed. Frakes, W. and Baeza-Yates., R., Prentice-Hall, 66–82, 1992
4. Kleinberg, J.: Authoritative sources in a hyperlinked environment, *Proc. the 9th Annual ACM-SIAM Symposium on Discrete Algorithms*, 668–677, 1998.
5. Lawrence, S., and Giles, C. L.: Searching the web: general and scientific information access, *IEEE Communications*, Vol. 37., Num. 1, 116–122, 1999.
6. LookSmart Inc.: http://www.looksmart.com/
7. Manber, U., and Baeza-Yates, R.: An algorithm for string matching with a sequence of don't cares, *Information Processing Letters*, Vol. 37, 133–136, Feb. 1991.
8. Sadakane, K., and Imai, H.: Fast algorithms for k-word proximity search, *IEICE Trans. Fundamentals*, Vol. E84-A, No.9, 312–319, Sep. 2001.

Simplifying the Manager Competency Model
by Using the Rough Set Approach

Wei-Wen Wu, Yu-Ting Lee, and Gwo-Hshiung Tzeng

International Trade Department, Ta Hwa Institute of Technology,
1. Ta Hwa Road, Chiung-Lin, Hsin-Chu 307, Taiwan
miketina@ms5.hinet.net
Distinguished Chair Professor G.-H. Tzeng,
National Chiao Tung University, Institute of Management of Technology,
1001 Ta-Hsueh Road, Hsinchu 300, Taiwan
Department of Business Administration, Kainan University,
No.1 Kainan Rd, Shinshing Tsuen, Luchu Shiang, Taoyuan 338, Taiwan
ghtzeng@cc.nctu.edu.tw

Abstract. It is now a leading company strategy to apply competency models for identifying and developing capabilities of their managers. However, a competency model usually contains too many intended competencies to be implemented. Recently, some scholars and experts argue that eight is the maximum for managers to assess. Hence, how to simplify the manager competency model is becoming an important issue. Well known as data mining techniques, the rough sets theory is a relatively new approach and good at data reduction in qualitative analysis, so that the rough set approach is suitable for dealing with the qualitative problem in simplifying the competency model. The aim of this paper is to mining the minimal set of competencies through using the rough set approach to help companies for better utilizing the competency model. The results show that the "self-management" competency is the most indispensable portion to a manager competency model.

1 Introduction

In order to meet the impact of existing and future competition advancements, it is important to develop manager competency models, and also apply the competencies in all major human resource fields, including recruitment, selection, assessment, development, appraisal, and rewards [29], [14], [30]. The competency model is a set of competencies, namely success factors which include the key behaviors required for excellent performance in a particular role [29]. Moreover, the competency model can be used to identify the competencies which employees need to improve performance in their current job or to prepare for other jobs; in particular, employees' competencies may be compared to the appropriate model to detect where the gaps exist, hereby individual training and development plans may be developed to bridge the gaps [30].

However, a competency model usually contains too many intended competencies to be implemented. Recently, some scholars and experts argue that eight is the maximum for managers to assess [6], [37]. Hence, how to slim the manager competency model is becoming an important issue. In addition, dealing with this kind

D. Ślęzak et al. (Eds.): RSFDGrC 2005, LNAI 3642, pp. 484–494, 2005.

of issue is a qualitative problem. Well known as data mining techniques, the rough sets theory is a relatively new approach and good at data reduction in qualitative analysis, which was originally introduced by [22] to help for dealing with these problems such as inductive reasoning, automatic classification, pattern recognition, learning algorithms, etc. The rough sets theory (RST) is particularly useful to deal with imprecise or vague concepts [25]. Unlike a conventional data analysis which uses statistical inferential technique, whereas the rough sets approach is based on data-mining techniques to discover knowledge [9]. The RST has been successfully applied in a variety of fields [32], [5], [2], [9], [36]. Since the rough set approach has these advantages, it is suitable for solving the problem in simplifying the manager competency model.

The aim of this paper is to mining the minimal set of required competencies through using the rough set approach to help companies for better utilizing the competency model. The rest of this paper is organized as follows. In section 2, some of the prior literatures related to the competency model are reviewed. In section 3, the basic of rough sets theory is presented. In section 4, the research design and results are illustrated. Finally, based upon the findings of this research, conclusions and suggestions are depicted.

2 Slimming the Manager Competency Model

In order to be smart for launching competency applications effectively, it is a favorable way that focusing on some urgent competencies and implementing them with a stepwise mode. The concept of a competency model and the issue of the competency implementation are discussed below.

2.1 Concepts of the Competency Model

Modern managers are required to possess multiple managerial competencies in order to meet the pressing business challenges. The concept of competency has been developed by McClelland and the McBer and Company. Especially, McClelland's paper, "Testing for Competence Rather Than Intelligence" [18], started the competency movement in 1970s. As most know, competencies are characteristics of people that differentiate performance in a specific job or role [15], [18]. Indeed, the definition of what a competency is has still not reached unanimity over the years. Recently, competencies are commonly conceptualized as a measurable pattern of knowledge, skills, abilities, behaviors, and other characteristics (KSAOs) that differentiate high from average performance [20], [1], [28].

The competency model is a set of success factors, which contribute to achieving high performance and concrete results. [17] states that a competency model is a detailed description of behaviors which requires employees to have the ability to be effective in a job. Competency models are often developed by studying what top performers do in the defined job context. For developing a competency model, the essential data may be collected in a variety of ways, including employee questionnaires, focus groups, and interviews with managers and employees [30]. The competency model is important because it provides a road map for the range of behaviors that produce excellent performance [29].

2.2 The Issue of the Competency Implementation

Concerning the methods for developing competency models, [33] mention that: competency studies are most cost-effective when they focus on value-added jobs; full-scale classic studies are relatively expensive and take two or three months; and expert panel based studies are suitable for analysis of large numbers of less critical jobs. Moreover, [13] deems that: the classic method is more workable for analysis of specific roles, but it requires much effort and expense; and the simple method is more suitable for analysis of regular or general roles. Importantly, as [30] emphasize, in order to overcome significant barriers and to improve impact of competency interventions, there are some important matters to consider with regard to model building, such as: it is need to ensure the linkage between competency initiatives and organization strategies; and it is better to keep models simple at launch, and leverage tools and databases to "quick start" model building. Especially important is that, even if competency methods require so much time and cost, there is still no promising that it is a "best fit" for organizations with rapidly changing environments. Further, the competency models are required to be timely reformed for adapting to the changeable environment; the fact is particularly evident to the high-tech companies [1].

There are several useful manager competency models, such as proposed by [3], [33], [27], [12]. But there is no single one which can be suitable for all different types of companies because competency models are required to reflect the unique of each individual company. Most importantly, some scholars and experts recently argue that a competency model usually contains too many intended competencies to be implemented [6], [37]. The above competency models, they all contain many detailed managerial competencies in each cluster. [37] suggests that it had better implementing the competency model gradually and involving less than eight competencies at a time. Moreover, [6] emphasizes that too many competencies is unfavorable to implement and the six is the maximum. In this sense, how to slim the manager competency model for better implementation is becoming an important issue.

3 The Basics of Rough Sets Theory

RST was firstly introduced by Pawlak in 1982 [22], [23], as a valuable mathematical tool to deal with vagueness and uncertainty [25]. In the Rough Set approach, any vague concept is characterized by pair of precise concepts, that is the lower and upper concept approximation [25]. Using lower and upper approximation of a set, the accuracy and the quality of approximation can be defined, as well as the knowledge hidden in the data table may be discovered and expressed in the form of decision rules [19]. The basic concepts of rough sets theory and the analytical procedure of data analysis are discussed as follows.

3.1 Information System and Indiscernible Relation

Rough set-based data analysis starts from a data table called an information system which contains data about objects of interest characterized in terms of some attributes or features [26]. An information system is used to construct the approximation space. The information system can be viewed as an application such that each object is described by a set of attributes [25].

According to [23], [25], an information system is defined as the quadruple $S = (U,Q,V,\rho)$, where the universe U is a finite set of objects, the Q is a finite set of attributes, the $V = \bigcup_{q \in Q} V_q$ is the set of values of attributes and V_q is the domain of the attribute q; $\rho : U \times Q \to V$ is a description function such that $\rho(x,q) \in V_q$ for every $q \in Q$, $x \in U$.

It is hard to distinguish objects on the basis of imprecise information is the starting point of the rough sets theory [25]. In other words, the imprecise information causes the indiscernibility of objects in terms of available data. Moreover, the indiscernible relation is used to define two main operations on data, namely, lower and upper approximation of a set. By using the lower and upper approximation of a set, we can define the accuracy and the quality of approximation [23].

3.2 Decision Table and the Analytical Procedure

The decision table describes decisions in terms of conditions that must be satisfied in order to carry out the decision specified in the decision table [26]. An information system can be seen as the decision table in the form of $S = (U, C \cup D, V, \rho)$, in which $C \cup D = Q$ and means that condition attributes C and decision attributes D are two disjoint classes of attributes [11]. Through analyzing the decision table, valuable decision rules can be extracted.

Especially, the Covering Index (CI) is a rather valuable way to evaluate the quality of the decision rule [21]. Let the decision attributes D is a singleton $D = \{d\}$, the d – elementary sets in S are denoted by $Y_i \in \{Y_1, Y_2, ..., Y_m\}$ and called the decision classes of the classification; let the condition attribute $A \subseteq C$ and its domain V_{a_j} of the attribute $a_j \in A$.

Then, the CI can be expressed as $\mathrm{CI}\,(V_{a_j}, Y_i) = card(V_{a_j} \wedge Y_i) / card(Y_i)$, where the " $\wedge$ " is the operator of conjunction. The CI represents a ratio called the covering ratio which indicates the degree of that how many objects with the same attribute value matching the decision class in contrast with that how many objects belonging to the same decision class. The rough sets theory provides a relatively new technique of reasoning from vague and imprecise data; specially, it has several advantages and noticeable features [16], [8], [31], [34], [7]. In practice, for the analysis of decision table, there are some main steps mentioned by [35]. Similarly, for the data analysis in rough set approach, we suggest the three-step analytical procedure: (1) calculating the approximation; (2) finding the reducts of attributes and the core of attributes; and (3) creating the decision rules.

4   Research Design and Results

The study attempted to mining the minimal set of required competencies through using the rough set approach, and hereby to achieve the aim of simplifying the manager competency model. The survey design, sampling, data analysis, and discussions are presented as follows

4.1 Survey Design

For this study, the questionnaire was developed based on the rough set approach to collect data of expert judgments. The study was conducted with two stages. In the first stage, through an intensive literature review and the significant discussions with six experts, the content of the questionnaire was confirmed, including: selection of the manager competency model proposed by [12] and design of the measurement scale. The manager competency model [12] contains six clusters of manager competency; moreover, there are several detailed managerial competencies within each cluster of the manager competency model. As shown in Table 1, six clusters of manager competency are used as condition attributes, and the detailed managerial competencies in each cluster are used as the condition attribute values (alphabetic symbols from A to S) for rough set analysis. In addition, the decision attribute in terms of the management level are divided into three classes: (1) senior manager, (2) middle manager, and (3) first-line manager.

Table 1. Condition attributes and decision attributes

The condition attributes:	4. the Strategi c Action competency cluster
1. the Communication competency cluster	(K) understanding the industry
(A) informal communication	(L) understanding the organization
(B) formal communication	(M) taking strategic actions
(C) negotiation	5. the Global Awareness competency cluster
2. the Planning and Administration competency cluster	(N) integrity and ethical conduct
(D) information gathering, analysis, and problem solving	(O) cultural openness and sensitivity
(E) planning and organizing projects	6 . the Self Management competency cluster
(F) time management	(P) cultural knowledge and understanding
(G) budgeting and financial management	(Q) personal drive and resilience
3. the Teamwork competency cluster	(R) balancing work and life demands
(H) designing teams	(S) self awareness and development
(I) creating a supportive environment	**The decision attributes:**
(J) managing team dynamics	(1) senior manager;
	(2) middle manager;
	3) first line manager.

The questionnaire contained two portions: one portion is the basic information, and another portion is the serial questions about the topic issue. Data were collected through the nominal scale with the values by the alphabetic symbols (from A to S). Specifically, the basic information portion was used to ask the respondents about the information concerning respondents' management position and their company profile including product category. In the topic issue portion, the respondents were asked to indicate which detailed managerial competency is most important within each cluster. For example, a question was like that "In the Communication competency cluster, which of the following competencies is most significant?", with answer choices: (A) informal communication, (B) formal communication, and (C) negotiation.

4.2 Sampling

The science-based industrial park gathering high-tech companies performs as a powerful tractor, tugging economic development and industrial innovation. In Taiwan, the first science-based industrial park is the Hsin-Chu Science-Based

Industry Park (HSIP) introduced in 1980, and it has contributed greatly to the development of Taiwan's high-tech industries. Especially, these enterprises in HSIP are representative high-technology industries of Taiwan. In recent years, these enterprises in HSIP have been facing competitive price cutting and lower margins, so they have a great need to apply competencies in order to optimize utilization of human resources for the purpose of enhancing labor productivity, and global competitiveness.

Due to this urgent need of utilizing the competency models, the Taiwan Style Competency Study Group (TSCSG) holding 54 members, was established in 2003 to promote the use of competency for those companies in HSIP. The TSCSG belongs to the Hsin-Chu Human Resource Management Association (HC-HRMA) which is mainly composed of HR managers from the HSIP. We targeted the members of TSCSG for conducting this research. Through telephone to invite and explain the purpose of the research, there are 50 participants willing to join. These participants all are HR professionals and have experience in developing competency models for their companies. Then, in November 2004 we mailed the questionnaire to those participants of TSCSG members. This almost covered the whole TSCSG members in HC-HRMA. By December 2004, in total, 43 valid responses were obtained with a response rate of 86% which is acceptable level for this research. Concerning the position of the respondents, there were the senior manager (10), the middle manager (14), and the first-line manager (19). The respondents came from such industry categories as: Integrated Circuits (13), Computers and Peripherals (8), Telecommunications (5), Optoelectronics (11), and other (6). Addition, the majority of respondents were from the Integrated Circuits industry and the Optoelectronics industry.

4.3 Data Analysis

The implementation of data analysis is performed through our suggested three-step analytical procedure with the help of the software ROSE (Rough Sets Data Explorer). ROSE is software that implementing basic elements of the rough set theory and rule discovery techniques. Before the data analysis, it is required to construct the decision table. As shown in Table 2, the decision table contains 43 records characterized by one decision attribute (Dec) and six condition attributes (six competency clusters): communication (Comm), planning and administration (Plan), teamwork (Team), strategic action (Stra), global awareness (Glob), and self-management (Self). Further, the seven attributes and their values are denoted as follows: $V_{Comm} = \{A,B,C\}$, $V_{Plan} = \{D,E,F,G\}$, $V_{Team} = \{H,I,J\}$, $V_{Stra} = \{K,L,M\}$, $V_{Glob} = \{N,O\}$, $V_{Self} = \{P,Q,R,S\}$, and $V_{Dec} = \{1,2,3,4\}$.

Step 1: Calculating the approximation.

The first step of data analysis using rough set theory is to calculate the approximations of decision classes. As shown in Table 3, each decision class is well describable due to its high accuracy of 1.000 shown in the last column. This is to say that all three decision classes are characterized exactly by those data in the decision table. In addition, there are totally 36 atoms in the decision table. On the whole, the accuracy of the entire classification is 1.000, and also the quality of the entire classification is 1.000.

Table 2. The decision table

Object	Dec	Comm	Plan	Team	Stra	Glob	Self	Object	Dec	Comm	Plan	Team	Stra	Glob	Self
1	1	C	D	J	M	O	S	23	3	C	D	H	K	N	P
2	2	A	D	H	L	N	S	24	3	B	F	J	L	O	Q
3	2	A	D	H	L	O	S	25	3	A	E	I	K	N	P
4	1	C	D	J	M	O	Q	26	3	B	E	I	K	N	Q
5	1	C	D	I	L	O	Q	27	3	B	E	I	K	O	Q
6	1	C	D	J	M	O	Q	28	3	B	E	I	K	N	Q
7	1	C	D	J	M	O	Q	29	3	C	G	H	M	O	S
8	1	C	D	J	M	O	Q	30	3	B	E	I	L	O	R
9	1	C	D	J	L	N	S	31	3	B	F	I	K	O	R
10	2	A	E	H	L	O	S	32	3	B	F	H	K	N	R
11	2	A	E	H	L	O	Q	33	3	B	F	I	K	N	S
12	2	A	E	H	M	O	Q	34	3	B	F	J	M	N	R
13	3	C	D	H	M	N	Q	35	2	B	D	I	L	N	S
14	1	C	D	J	M	O	Q	36	3	B	F	I	L	N	R
15	2	A	E	H	K	O	S	37	1	A	D	J	L	O	R
16	2	A	E	H	K	O	Q	38	2	A	E	H	M	O	S
17	2	A	E	H	L	N	S	39	3	B	D	J	K	O	R
18	1	C	D	J	M	O	Q	40	3	B	D	I	L	O	R
19	2	A	D	J	K	O	S	41	2	A	E	H	L	O	S
20	3	B	F	H	M	N	S	42	2	A	E	H	K	N	S
21	3	B	F	J	M	O	Q	43	2	C	D	J	K	N	R
22	3	A	D	H	L	O	P								

Table 3. The lower and upper approximations

Class number	Number of objects	Lower approx.	Upper approx.	Accuracy
1	10	10	10	1.000
2	14	14	14	1.000
3	19	19	19	1.000

<u>Step 2</u>: Finding the reducts of attributes and the core of attributes.

In this step, the indiscernibility relation method is used for dealing with the reduction of attributes and finding the core of attributes, due to all the condition attributes are nominal attributes (unordered qualitative attributes) with linguistic values. Employing the indiscernibility relation method, it may find all potential reducts in the information table. As a result, we obtained four reducts of attributes and one core of attributes. These four reducts are: {Comm, Plan, Glob, Self}, {Comm, Plan, Team, Stra}, {Comm, Team, Stra, Self}, and {Plan, Team, Stra, Glob, Self}. Especially, the core of attributes is the only one, namely the attribute {Self}. This means that the attribute "self-management" is the most meaningful attribute among those six attributes.

<u>Step 3</u>: Creating the decision rules.

The most important step of data analysis is to generate decision rules. In order to find the minimal covering rules, the minimal covering method is employed, which attempts to find the minimal number of attribute values for a decision rule. As a result, 10 rules are created. These 10 exact rules are shown in Table 4, from which we can acquire several valuable implications for making decisions. In particular, we can find the most important determinant for each decisions class through using the covering ratio of Covering Index (CI).

Table 4. The exact rules

Rule number	The minimal covering rule	Covering ratio
Rule 1.	(Comm = C) & (Team in {J, I}) & (Stra in {M, L}) => (Dec = 1)	90.00%
Rule 2.	(Comm = A) & (Team = J) & (Stra = L) => (Dec = 1)	10.00%
Rule 3.	(Comm = A) & (Self in {S, Q}) => (Dec = 2)	85.71%
Rule 4.	(Comm = B) & (Plan = D) & (Glob = N) => (Dec = 2)	7.14%
Rule 5.	(Comm = C) & (Self = R) => (Dec = 2)	7.14%
Rule 6.	(Comm = B) & (Glob = O) => (Dec = 3)	36.84%
Rule 7.	(Comm = B) & (Plan in {F, E}) => (Dec = 3)	63.16%
Rule 8.	(Self = P) => (Dec = 3)	15.79%
Rule 9.	(Plan = G) => (Dec = 3)	5.26%
Rule 10.	(Stra = M) & (Glob = N) => (Dec = 3)	15.79%

For decisions class 1, obviously the rule 1={C, J, I, M, L} holds the higher covering ratio of 90.00% than the rule 2={A, J, L} with the covering ratio of 10.00% (Table 4). This means that the majority 90.00% of the senior managers considered that those competencies are relatively significant in the manager competency model, including (C) negotiation, (I) creating a supportive environment, (J) managing team dynamics, (L) understanding the organization, and (M) taking strategic actions. Similarly, for decisions classes 2, the rule 3={A, S, Q} holds the highest covering ratio of 85.71% than both the rule 4 and the rule 5 with the lower covering ratio of 7.14%. This means that the majority 85.71% of the middle managers considered that those competencies were relatively significant in the manager competency model, including (A) informal communication, (Q) personal drive and resilience, and (S) self-awareness and development. As for decisions classes 3, the rule 7={D, G, K, O} holds the highest covering ratio of 63.16% than the remaining classes. The decisions classes 3 involved with more the number of rules than the decisions classes 1 and the decisions classes 2. This implies that the opinions of the first-line managers were highly different than those of the senior managers or the middle managers, concerning the question "which competency is most significant?" According to the rule 7, it indicates that the 63.16% of the middle managers consider that those competencies are relatively important in the competency model, including (D) information gathering, analysis, and problem solving, (G) budgeting and financial management, (K) understanding the industry, and (O) cultural openness and sensitivity.

4.4 Discussions

For reducing the competency model effectively, the rough sets approach is a wise option. The rough sets approach is different from the quantitative-oriented statistical technique. In contrast to classical statistical techniques such as discriminant analysis, the strength of RST is that it requires no underlying statistical assumptions, especially the RST can provide rules which cover only subsets of the basic objects or data records available [4]. It is not only free from such the unrealistic assumption of statistical hypotheses [5], but also it has no need of a huge data. In particular, it can directly analyze the original data with either quantitative attributes or qualitative attributes, as well as does not need additional information. Hence, using the rough sets approach is an advantageous way to solve qualitative problems. Although the

RST has been successfully applied to a variety of areas, such as data mining or classification in marketing, finance, banking, and manufacturing fields, it is still rare to be applied in human resource field.

Therefore, for solving the problem of reducing the competency model, which characterizing complex and multi-attribute, in this study we employ the rough set approach to aim at mining the minimal set of required competencies. According to the results of the empirical study, we are able to derive many implications about business management as follows.

Firstly, the attribute "self-management" was the core attribute in the manager competency model. This reflects that most managers consider the "self-management" competency is commonly essential for every manager. It also implies that the "self-management" competency is the most indispensable attribute to a manager competency model. Secondly, four reducts of attributes are obtained through the rough sets approach, and these four reducts may regard as four sets of primary attributes that can be chose optionally, in terms of constructing a manager competency model. For example, if the reduct={Comm, Plan, Glob, Self} is selected, this means that a practical manager competency model is required to contain these four competencies including the "Communication", the "Planning and Administration", the "Global Awareness", and the "Self-Management". Thirdly, concerning the opinions of which detailed competency is most required, it is rather varied due to different management level. In view of the covering ratio, if constructing a manager competency model for the senior managers, there are some competency elements required to be built inside, such as: (C) negotiation, (I) creating a supportive environment, (J) managing team dynamics, (L) understanding the organization, and (M) taking strategic actions. Similarly, constructing a manager competency model for the middle managers, it needs to include essential competency elements, such as: (A) informal communication, (Q) personal drive and resilience, and (S) self-awareness and development. As for the first-line managers, the manager competency model is necessary to comprise these competency elements, such as: (D) Information gathering, analysis, and problem solving, (G) budgeting and financial management, (K) understanding the industry, and (O) cultural openness and sensitivity.

To sum up, for simplifying the manager competency model, the result of this study is satisfactory. By utilizing the advantage features of the rough set approach, the study was successfully conducted to mining the minimal set of required competencies, and hereby achieved the aim to slim the manager competency model. This study has obtained some meaningful facts, but it has the limitation of that the sample size is small and lacks great statistical significance. The above findings reflect the situation that several Taiwan high-tech companies in HSIP, concerning how they think about the important elements of manager competency models. Also, this study is presented as a test case to extend practical applications of RST in human resource field.

5   Conclusions

The aim to help companies to simplify and better utilize the manager competency model, we researched into reducing the manager competency model for Taiwan high-tech companies in HSIP, and employed the rough set approach for data analysis.

Eventually, the result of this study is satisfactory and it brings out many implications in terms of the use of the manager competency model. For example, due to the "self-management" is the core attribute in the manager competency model, this reflects that most managers consider the "self-management" competency is commonly essential for every manager, and it is the most indispensable attribute to a manager competency model. Moreover, there are no published works using the rough set approach to deal with the kind issue of the competency model. Hence, this study has contributed to extend practical applications of RST in human resource field. Further, using our suggested analytical procedure, it can effectively handle any problem of reducing a complex and multi-attribute model for mining the minimal set of significant elements.

References

1. Athey, T.R. & Orth, M.S.: Emerging Competency Methods for the Future. Human Resource Management. **38** (3) (1999) 215-226
2. Beynon, M.J. & Peel M.J.: Variable precision rough set theory and data discretisation: an application to corporate failure prediction. Omega: International Journal of Management Science. **29** (6) (2001) 561-576
3. Boyatzis, R.E.: The competent manager: A model for effective performance. New York: John Wiley & Sons (1982)
4. Curry, B.: Rough sets: current and future developments. The International Journal of Knowledge Engineering and Neural Networks. **20** (5) (2003) 247-250
5. Dimitras, A.I., Slowinski, R., Susmaga, R. & Zopounidis, C.: Business failure prediction using rough sets. European Journal of Operational Research. **114** (2) (1999) 263-280
6. Dive, B.: Education Management. Auckland: New Zealand Management (2004)
7. Doumpos, M. & Zopounidis, C.: Rough Sets and Multivariate Statistical Classification: A Simulation Study. Computational Economics. **19** (3) (2002) 287-301
8. Dubois, D. & Prade, H.: Putting rough sets and fuzzy sets together. In: Slowinski, R. (Ed). Intelligent Decision Support: Handbook of Applications and Advances of the Rough Sets Theory. Dordrecht: Kluwer Academic Publishers (1992) pp. 203-232
9. Goh, C. & Law, R.: Incorporating the rough sets theory into travel demand analysis. Tourism Management. **24** (5) (2003) 511-517
10. Greco, S., Matarazzo, B. & Slowinski, R.: A new rough set approach to evaluation of bankruptcy risk. In: Zopounidis, C. (Ed). Operational Tools in the Management of Financial Risks. Dordrecht: Kluwer Academic Publishers (1998) pp. 121-136
11. Greco, S., Matarazzo, B. & Slowinski, R.: Rough sets methodology for sorting problems in presence of multiple attributes and criteria. European Journal of Operational Research. **138** (2) (2002) 247-259
12. Hellriegel, D., Jackson, S.E. & Slocum, J.W.: Management: A Competency-Based Approach. Cincinnati: South-Western College Pub (2004)
13. Japanese Style Competency Study Group: A Proposal for Japanese Style Competency Model. Tokyo: Japan Productivity Center for Socio-Economic Development (2000)
14. JPC-SED: The Fifth Survey on Changes in the Japanese-style Personnel System. Tokyo: Japan Productivity Center for Socio-Economic Development (2002)
15. Kelner, S.P.: A Few Thoughts on Executive Competency Convergence. Center for Quality of Management Journal. **10** (1) (2001) 67-72
16. Krusinska, E., Slowinski, R. & Stefanowski, J.: Discriminat versus rough set approach to vague data analysis. Applied Stochastic Models and Data Analysis. **8** (1) (1992) 43-56

17. Mansfield, R.S.: Building Competency Models: Approaches for HR Professionals. Human Resource Management. **35** (1) (1996) 7-18
18. McClelland, D.C.: Testing for competence rather than for intelligence. American Psychologist. **28** (1) (1973) 1-24
19. Mi, J.S., Wu, W.Z. & Zhang, W.X.: Approaches to knowledge reduction based on variable precision rough set model. Information Sciences. **159** (3-4) (2004) 255-272
20. Mirable, R.: Everything You Wanted to Know About Competency Modeling. Training and Development. **51** (8) (1997) 73-77
21. Mori, N., Tanaka, H. & Inoue, K.: Rough sets and KANSEI: knowledge acquisition and reasoning from KANSEI data. Japan, Tokyo: Kaibundo (2004)
22. Pawlak, Z.: Rough sets. International Journal of Computer and Information Science. **11** (5) (1982) 341-356
23. Pawlak, Z.: Rough Classification. International Journal of Man-Machine Studies. **20** (5) (1984) 469-483
24. Pawlak, Z.: Rough Sets: Theoretical Aspects of Reasoning about Data. Norwell, MA: Kluwer Academic Publishers (1992)
25. Pawlak, Z.: Rough Sets. In: Lin, T. Y. & Cercone, N. (Eds.). Rough Sets and Data Mining: Analysis for Imprecise Data. Norwell, MA: Kluwer Academic Publishers (1997)
26. Pawlak, Z.: Rough sets, decision algorithms and Bayes' theorem. European Journal of Operational Research. **136** (1) (2002) 181-189
27. Quinn, J.B., Anderson, P. & Syndey, F.: Managing professional intellect: Making the most of the best. Harvard Business Review. **74** (2) (1996) 71-80
28. Rodriguez, D., Patel, R., Bright, A., Gregory, D. & Gowing, M.K.: Developing Competency Models to Promote Integrated Human Resource. Human Resource Management. **41** (3) (2002) 309-324
29. Schoonover, S.C., Schoonover, H., Nemerov, D. & Ehly, C.: Competency-Based HR Applications: Results of a Comprehensive Survey. Andersen/Schoonover/SHRM (2000)
30. Sinnott, G.C., Madison, G.H. & Pataki, G.E.: Competencies: Report of the Competencies Workgroup, Workforce and Succession Planning Work Groups. New York State Governor's Office of Employee Relations and the Department of Civil Service (2002)
31. Skowron, A. & Grzymala-Busse, J.W.: From the rough set theory to the evidence theory. In: Fedrizzi, M., Kacprzyk, J., Yager, R.R. (Eds.). Advances in the Dempster–Shafer Theory of Evidence. New York: John Wiley & Sons (1993) pp. 295-305
32. Slowinski, R. & Zopounidis, C.: Application of the rough set approach to evaluation of bankruptcy risk. International Journal of Intelligent Systems in Accounting, Finance and Management. **4** (1) (1995) 27-41
33. Spencer, L.M. & Spencer, S.M.: Competence at work: Model for superior performance. New York: John Wiley & Sons (1993)
34. Tay, F.E.H. & Shen, L.: Economic and financial prediction using rough sets model. European Journal of Operational Research. **141** (3) (2002) 641-659
35. Walczak, B. & Massart, D.: Rough sets theory. Chemometrics and Intelligent Laboratory Systems. **47** (1) (1999) 1-16
36. Wang, Y.F.: Mining stock price using fuzzy rough set system. Expert Systems with Applications. **24** (1) (2003) 13-23
37. Works Institute: What is the competency? Works. **57** (1) (2003) 1-47, Japan: Recruit

Financial Risk Prediction Using Rough Sets Tools: A Case Study

Santiago Eibe[1], Raquel Del Saz[1], Covadonga Fernández[1], Óscar Marbán[1,*], Ernestina Menasalvas[1], and Concepción Pérez[2]

[1] DLSIS, Facultad de Informática, Universidad Politécnica de Madrid, Madrid, Spain
{seibe, cfbaizan, omarban, emenasalvas}@fi.upm.es,
rdel_saz@mixmail.com
[2] Departamento de Informática Escuela Técnica Superior de Ingenieros Industriales e Informáticos, Universidad de Oviedo, Spain
cpllera@uniovi.es

Abstract. Since the Rough Sets Theory was first formulated in 1982, different models based on it have been proposed to be applied in economic and financial prediction. Our aim is to show the development of a method of estimation of the financial risk when a credit is granted to a firm, having into account its countable status. This is a classical example of inference of classification/prediction rules, that is the kind of problem in which the adequacy of Rough Sets methods has been proved. Coming from data concerning industrial companies that were given to us by the Banks that granted the credits, we have obtained a set of classification rules to be used to predict the result of future credit operations.

Keywords: Financial risk, Prediction rules, Classification rules, Rough Sets, Machine Learning, Data Mining.

1 Introduction

When different firms need a credit, they attend to the banks or any other financial entities. Then, the bank has to choose between to grant or to deny the credit. This is a difficult choice, because it could happen that some firms will not return the lent sum, thus producing a negative result for the bank. Financial data of the firms are used to decide the credit grant, but there is not an infallible formula.

Traditionally, financial analysts' experience was the unique basis to take a decision, but later, statistic tools have been used to face the problem. We have used data provided by the banks about enterprises that were granted a credit, to infer knowledge and to predict the result of future operations.

There are some ratios calculated from the data, that are the condition variables that will allow us to classify a firm as "solvent" or "defaulter" (decision categories).

Tools based in Rough Sets Theory allow us to infer rules from data contained in a decision table.

* The work presented in this paper has been partially supported by UPM project ERDM - ref. 14589.

D. Ślęzak et al. (Eds.): RSFDGrC 2005, LNAI 3642, pp. 495–502, 2005.

The rest of the paper is organized as follows: First section is the state of the art of Rough Sets applied to "Business failure" prediction. Second section is the statement of the problem (case under study). In the third section are explained the variables taken into account. The fundamentals of Rough Sets are explained in the following section. The two next sections show us how to preprocess data for this particular problem. How rules are inferred is explained in section eight. Finally, same conclusions are drawn in section nine.

2   Mining Business Data: A Brief Overview on Financial Prediction Tools

The application of Data Mining tools to a variety of domains in business has greatly improved the quality of firm's decisions. Among these tools, methods based on Rough Sets Model, have the following advantages:

- The use of external information becomes unnecessary
- They are suitable for analyzing quantitative and qualitative values
- Discovered facts hidden in data, are expressed by means of rules, thus being easy of understand

Financial organizations need methods for evaluating risk before granting a credit to a firm.

Dimitras et al [2] gave a complete review of the methods used for this kind of prediction. In this report, Rough Sets Model appears to be an adequate tool for the analysis of financial tables describing a set of objects (firms) by means of a set of attributes (financial ratios).

The application of the Rough Sets approach in business failure prediction was investigated by Slowinski et al. [7] and Dimitras et al. [3]. In these works, the Rough Sets approach was compared with three other methods: C4.5 inductive algorithm, discriminant analysis and logit analysis. The study was carried out on a sample of 40 failed (defaulter) firms and 40 healthy (solvent) firms from 13 different industrial areas, meeting the following criteria:

- Having been in business for more than 5 years
- Data availability

The financial expert selected a set of 12 ratios to compose the information table with a bi-valued decision attribute:

- 1 (healthy)
- 0 (failed)

They used a distance measure based on a valued closeness relation [7] to decide which decision class an object belongs to in the case of no rules matching this object.

The decision rules generated from reducts selected by the expert, were applied to the validation data sets, which were comprised of the previous three years data of the same firms.

Having into account the predictive accuracy, Rough Sets approach was found to be better than the classical discriminant analysis. It also outperformed the C4.5 inductive algorithm as far as the classification accuracy is concerned.

Rough Sets approach was also better than logit analysis in relation with this prediction problem.

In another comparative study described by Szladow and Mills [8], Rough Sets Model made 97% of correct predictions (failed firms having into account five financial ratios). By applying multi-variable discriminant analysis, the percentage was 96%.

Since Rough Sets Theory was first formulated (1982), different models based on it have been proposed: DataLogic, Dominance relation, Rough Das and Profit, Hybrid model (for a comparative study, see [10]).

Our study has been carried out by using a tool developed in the University of Oviedo, that is based on Ziarko's VPRS Model and allows for the extraction of discrimination rules.

3   Statement of the Problem

Data provided to us by the banks that granted the credits were the starting point of our work. We have taken into account the following common characteristics:

- Short term credit operations (deadline 1 year)
- Business operations involving each firm and bank under analysis, had a turnover greater than 150,000 €
- All the firms under analysis, were anonymous or limited companies.

Once reached the corresponding deadline, firms were classified as:

- Solvent, if the nominal value as well as the interests of the credit have already been paid
- Defaulter, in the opposite case.

4   Variables Taken into Account

Financial experts use up to 34 ratios to grant or to deny a credit. These ratios, in our Rough Sets approach, are the condition variables that will allow us to classify a firm as "solvent" or "defaulter" (decision categories). We only will mention how the ratios are grouped:

- Liquidity (R1-R4)
- Indebtedness (R5-R12)
- Activity (R13,R14)
- Structure (R15-R19)
- Turnover (R20-R24)
- Resource generation (R25-R28)
- Profitability (R29-R34).

5   Fundamentals of Rough Sets Theory

Rough Sets Theory has been proposed by Z. Pawlak [5]. A further "practical" version, the Variable Precision Rough Sets Model (VPRS), has been proposed by W. Ziarko [9].

Tools based in this Theory allow us to infer rules from data contained in a decision table.

We can to infer characterization and/or discrimination rules. A discrimination rule contains in its antecedent pairs (attribute, value) from the condition set and in its consequent the pair (attribute, value) from the decision, that is the description of the concept.

When dealing with Rough Sets, we consider that all the attributes are monovalued. A monovalued attribute induces a partition in the universe of objects. Having this into account, the attribute may be considered as the name of an equivalence relation and the partition may be seen as the quotient set induced in the universe of objects. Any combination of monovalued attributes also defines an equivalence relation (the indiscernibility relation). Let U be the universe of objects. Let C be the condition set and let D be the decision attribute. The corresponding quotient sets, are the following:

$$
\begin{aligned}
U/C &= \{X_1, X_2, \dots, X_n\} \\
U/D &= \{Y_1, Y_2, \dots, Y_m\}
\end{aligned}
\tag{1}
$$

And the positive region of D:

$$
POSC(D) = \bigcup \{X_i \in U/C : \exists Y_i \in U/D, X_i \subseteq Y_i\}
\tag{2}
$$

The dependence degree of D from C, k, is calculated by dividing the number of elements of the positive region by the number of elements of U, and the corresponding dependence is $C \Rightarrow k_D$.

To obtain rules from dependencies the decision table may be binarized. Another procedure, based on the deletion of superfluous values in the condition set, is described in [5].

In this work, we have used a tool developed in the University of Oviedo, that is based on the VPRS Model and allows for the extraction of discrimination rules.

6   Preprocessing Data: Discretization and Estimation of Reducts

6.1   Discretization

For each ratio, the following four intervals were defined:

1. Value $<=$ mean $-$ deviation
2. mean $>=$ Value $>$ mean $-$ deviation
3. mean $+$ deviation $>=$ Value $>$ mean
4. Value $>$ mean $+$ deviation.

6.2 Estimation of Reducts

Once the table has been discretized, the following step is to simplify it by extracting a reduct from the set of condition attributes (and deleting the columns labelled by the remaining ones).

A reduct is a subset of the condition attributes preserving the classification power. If at least a reduct exits, it usually means the existence of interdependencies in the previous condition set.

Reducts provide for more simple and "readable" rules. We have obtained the following reduct:

$$\{R_2, R_4, R_{10}, R_{13}, R_{20}, R_{24}, R_{33}\}. \tag{3}$$

7 More About Discretization Process

When defining intervals for each ratio, we have calculated the mean having previously deleted some examples (rows) to enforce the "skewness" and the asymmetry coefficient in such a way that values range between -2 and +2, that is a necessary condition for the distribution be normal.

A previous discretization was done having into account only a crosspoint defining two intervals corresponding to "Solvent" and "Defaulter". This was an excessive simplification that hid the semantic of the problem.

Statistical discretization in four intervals was a noticeable improvement of the process, especially with regard to the confidence of rules.

7.1 Discretization of R1: A Short Description of the Process

R_1 is the solvency ratio and it is perhaps the more general one. In the following, we will briefly show how the corresponding discretization was done.

Table 1. Statistical data of R1

Mean	1,231167685	Minimum	0,396232383
Characteristic error	0,056358901	Maximum	4,212148567
Median	1,086023543	Sum	162,5141344
Standard deviation	0,64751447	Count	132
Variance of the sample	0,419274989	Greatest (1)	4,212148567
Skewness	8,776575672	Smallest (1)	0,396232383
Asymmetry coefficient	2,676238479	Confidence level (95,0%)	0,111491284
Range	3,815916184		

So, we obtained the following classes and the corresponding histogram (see figures 1 and 2).

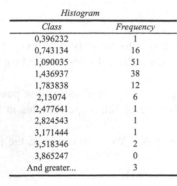

Histogram	
Class	Frequency
0,396232	1
0,743134	16
1,090035	51
1,436937	38
1,783838	12
2,13074	6
2,477641	1
2,824543	1
3,171444	1
3,518346	2
3,865247	0
And greater...	3

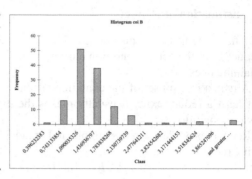

Fig. 1. Classes histogram

DISCRETIZATIÓN of R1 having into
account the mean obtained from all the
values
0,583653 <= mean – desv.std
1,231168 > mean – desv and <= **mean**
1,878682 > mean and <= mean + desv

Class	Frequency
0,583653	6
1,231168	83
1,878682	33
and greater ...	10

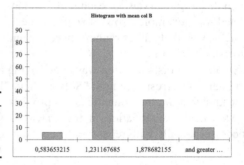

Fig. 2. Classes histogram

To enforce skewness and asymmetry coefficient in such a way the distribution of the R_1 was normal, we have deleted values greater than 2.3806954.

Deletions was 7, that represents only a 9.24% of the sample. All of the deleted elements, were solvent firms. And these are the new statistical data and histogram:

Table 2. New statistical data of R1

Mean	1.105625283	Minimum	0.396232383
Characteristic error	0.031331007	Maximum	2.3806954
Median	1,054060519	Sum	138.2031603
Standard deviation	0.350291312	Count	125
Variance of the sample	0.122704003	Greatest	2.3806954
Skewness	0.972310681	Smallest	0.396232383
Asymmetry coefficient	0.726057661	Confidence level (95.0%)	0.062012797
Range	1.984463017		

Histogram

Class	Frequency
0,39623238	1
0,57663811	5
0,75704384	13
0,93744957	16
1,1178553	38
1,29826103	21
1,47866676	14
1,65907248	8
1,83947821	3
2,01988394	5
2,20028967	0
And greater...	1

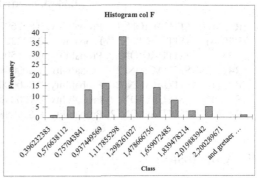

Fig. 3. Classes histogram

DISCRETIZATIÓN of R1 having into account the mean obtained from selectec values
  0,75533397 <= mean R1 – desv R1
  1,10562528 > mean R1 – desv R1 y <= **mean R1**
  1,45591659 > mean R1 y <= mean R1 + dev R1

Class	Frequency
0,75533397	19
1,10562528	52
1,45591659	36
and greater...	18

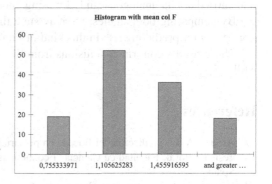

Fig. 4. Classes histogram

8 Inferred Rules

We have obtained 37 rules, 16 corresponding to solvent firms and 21 to defaulter ones.

Probability ranges from 0.636364 to 1 for solvent firms and from 0.619048 to 1 for defaulter ones. The average probability is 0.801982. Some of the inferred rules are shown in table 3.

It has been used a method to calculate a way of validation, called Stochastic Validation, that makes the cross validation with $N = 10$ for eleven times.

In the first validation it is used for generating rules the method of approaching of the Rough Sets Theory. In each one of the ten left repetitions it is used the stochastic approaches method for β values between 0.9 and 0.5 (0.9, 0.95, 0.8, ..., 0.5) and $\alpha = 1 - \beta$.

This way of validation has been included to compare the results obtained with the stochastic approaching using different values for β, with the result of the traditional method.

For the 10 validations it is used the same random reorganization that the original data sets.

Table 3. Inferred rules

(R2, 4) → (SITUACION, 1) Probability: 0.807692 Specificity: 1 Strength: 21 TrMatch: 26
(R20, 4) → (SITUACION, 1) Probability: 0.722222 Specificity: 1 Strength: 13 TrMatch: 18
(R33, 3) → (SITUACION, 1) Probability: 0.687500 Specificity: 1 Strength: 22 TrMatch: 32
(R4, 1) → (SITUACION, 2) Probability: 1.000000 Specificity: 1 Strength: 8 TrMatch: 8
(R2, 1) → (SITUACION, 2) Probability: 0.880000 Specificity: 1 Strength: 22 TrMatch: 25
(R20, 1) → (SITUACION, 2) Probability: 0.700000 Specificity: 1 Strength: 14 TrMatch: 20
(R10, 3) → (SITUACION, 2) Probability: 0.619048 Specificity: 1 Strength: 26 TrMatch: 42

9 Conclusion

Our study has been done by analyzing real data. This provided us for the possibility of checking our "predictions" with real results.

A research group from the Economics School of the University of Murcia (Spain), had carried out an analogous study by using classical multidimensional analysis [1].

By comparing both studies, we may state that Rough Sets provide for simple and good tools for predicting risk in this kind of financial operations.

These results confirm conclusions from Slowinski et al. [7] and from Szladow and Mills [8].

References

1. Arques, A. La predicción del fracaso empresarial: Aplicación al riesgo crediticio bancario. Tesis Doctoral, Facultad de Ciencias Económicas y Empresariales, Universidad de Murcia, Spain (1999)
2. Dimitras, A.I., Zanakis, S.H, Zopounidis, C.: A survey of business failure with an emphasis on prediction methods and industrial applications. European Journal of Operational Research 90 (1996) 487-513
3. Dimitras, A.I., Slowinski, R., Susmaga, R., Zopounidis, C.: Business failure prediction using Rough Sets. European Journal of Operational research 114 (1999) 263-280
4. Fernández, C., Menasalvas, E., Pérez, C., Del Saz, R.: Rough Sets as a tool to predict risk in finantial operations. Proc. Int. Conf. on Recent Advances in Computer Sciences (RASC'04), Nottingham (U.K.) (2004) 477-482
5. Pawlak, Z.: Rough Sets: Theoretical aspects of reasoning about data. Kluwer academic publishers (1991)
6. Slowinski, R.: Rough Sets learning of preferential attitudes in multi-criteria decision making. In: Komorowski, J. and Ras, Z. (eds): Methodologies for Intelligent Systems. Springer-Verlag, Berlin (1993) 642-651
7. Slowinski, R., Zopounidis, C., Dimitras, A.I., Susmaga, R.: Rough Sets predictor of business failure. In: Ribeiro, R.R., Yager, R.R., Zimmermann, H.J., Kacprzyk, J. (eds): Soft Computing in Financial Engineering. Physica-Verlag, Heidelberg (1999) 402-424
8. Szladow, A., Mills, D: Tapping financial databases. Business Credit 7 (1993)
9. Ziarko, W.: Variable precision Rough Sets Model. Journal of Computer & System Sciences 46 (1991) 39-49
10. Tay, F.E., Shen, L.: Economic and financial predictions using Rough Sets Model. European Journal of Operational Research 141 (2002) 641-659

Using Rough Set and Worst Practice DEA in Business Failure Prediction

Jia-Jane Shuai[1,2] and Han-Lin Li[2]

[1] Department of Information Management,
Ming-Hsin University of Science and Technology,
Hsin-Feng, Hsinchu 304, Taiwan
jjs@mis.must.edu.tw
[2] Institute of Information Management,
National Chiao-Tung University, Hsinchu 300, Taiwan
hlli@cc.nctu.edu.tw

Abstract. This paper proposes a hybrid approach that predicts the failure of firms based on the past business data, combining rough set approach and worst practice data envelopment analysis (DEA). The worst practice DEA can identify worst performers (in quantitative financial data) by placing them on the frontier while the rules developed by rough set uses non-financial information to predict the characteristics of failed firms. Both DEA and rough set are commonly used in practice. Both have limitations. The hybrid model Rough DEA takes the best of both models, by avoiding the pitfalls of each. For the experiment, the financial data of 396 Taiwan firms during the period 2002-2003 were selected. The results show that the hybrid approach is a promising alternative to the conventional methods for failure prediction.

1 Introduction

Corporate bankruptcy always brings huge economic losses to investors and others, together with a substantial social and economical cost to the nation. Numerous researchers have studied bankruptcy prediction over the last decades. As a result, various theories have evolved in an effort to explain or distinguish between firms that have failed. Altman [1] used multivariate discriminant analysis to differentiate between failed and non-failed US firms. Following the study of Altman, a large number of methods such as logit analysis, probit analysis and linear programming have been applied to model this problem. These conventional statistical methods, however, have some restrictive assumptions such as the linearity, normality and independence among predictor or input variables. Considering that the violation of these assumptions for independent variables frequently occurs with financial data, these methods can have limitations to obtain the effectiveness and validity. Recently, a number of new techniques emerging to assist the failure prediction, such as expert systems, neural networks, rough set theory and genetic programming. A key advantage of these contemporary methods over their traditional counterparts is that they do not require pre-specification

D. Ślęzak et al. (Eds.): RSFDGrC 2005, LNAI 3642, pp. 503–510, 2005.
© Springer-Verlag Berlin Heidelberg 2005

of a function form, nor the adoption of restriction assumptions concerning the distributions of model variables and errors. However, most classification systems lack the ability to systematically conduct sensitivity analysis. Sensitivity analysis in bankruptcy prediction problem has several decision support advantages. This information, if available, provides substantial decision support advantages for investors as well as managers. Recently, Troutt *et al.* [2] and Seiford and Zhu [3] showed that the DEA model can be used for classification. Pendharkar [4] showed how to use the sensitivity analysis procedure in DEA model to solve the inverse classification on bankruptcy prediction. Cielen *et al.* [5] compared the bankruptcy classification performance of a linear programming model, a DEA model and a rule induction (C5.0) model. Paradi *et al.* [6] use a layered worst practice DEA technique, where the sequential layers of poor performance are found with decreasing risk rating. This layering technique enables incorporation of risk attitudes and risk-based pricing. A limitation of these DEA studies is that the difficulty to treat qualitative data, therefore all these studies use quantitative financial data.

On the other hand, rough set theory has been applied to a wide variety of financial decision analysis problems. A limitation of rough set is that the continuous data used to derive the rough set rules, have been discretised with the aid of a selected expert. Rough set analysis produces better results when the attribute domains for continuous variables are finite sets of low cardinality. Therefore it is necessary to recode continuous variables, such as financial ratios, into qualitative terms such as 'low, medium, high'. Using sorting rules developed by rough sets may lead to a burdensome situation where a new case does not match any of the sorting or classification rules. In this paper we propose a hybrid system combining rough set approach and DEA. Our system has two agents: one is a visual display agent that helps users monitor the risk by placing the distressed firms on layered frontiers based on how efficient they are at being bad. At the prediction step, the mining agent apply the rules developed by rough set, and help users make decision about the risk analysis. The effectiveness of our hybrid approach was verified with experiments that compared to the worst DEA model.

In the following we briefly present the idea of rough DEA by introduce an example. Suppose the following financial data is given for five firms (A, B, C, D and E). Suppose there is one decision rule generated from previous year (if C1=1 and C2 =1 then D = failure.). In Fig.1 the worst practice DEA is illustrated with two outputs and fixed inputs. The units A and B are on the frontier and thus the companies have the highest liabilities (Y1) and receivable days (Y2). When removing these frontier units and running the DEA model again, a second layer of frontier units, C and D are identified. The companies on the first layer are the companies with the highest risk and the companies on the second layer are assumed to have a lower risk rating on DEA. However, the DEA model contains only quantitative data; with the decision rule generated from rough set we can identify that firm C also have high risk since the firm changed auditor and financial manager recently. Information like this can be used to determine which companies at risk and the risk level.

Table 1. Rough DEA example

	A	B	C	D	E	Variables
X1: Profit	1	1	1	1	1	DEA input variable
Y1: Liabilities	2	8	3	5	2	DEA output variable
Y2:Receivable days	8	3	4	2	2	DEA output variable
C1:Auditor changed	1	1	1	0	0	Rough condition var.
C2:CFO changed	1	0	1	1	0	Rough condition var.
D :Failure Risk	High	High	High	Medium	Low	Rough decision var.

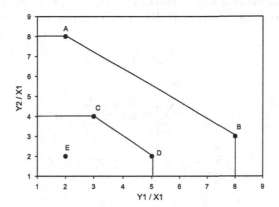

Fig. 1. The worst practice DEA and the layering technique

The remainder of this paper is organized as follows. Section 2 and 3 review the rough set and DEA methodology. The details of the proposed hybrid approach are presented in Section 4. It is followed by the empirical illustration in Section 5. A summary and conclusions are then given in Section 6.

2   Rough Set

The concept of rough sets theory [7] is based on the assumption that every object of the universe is associated with some information. Objects characterized by the same information are indiscernible (similar) in view of their available information. The rough sets theory provides a technique of reasoning from imprecise data, discovering relationships in data and generating decision rules.

Slowinski and Zopounidis [8] first employed rough set approach for a sample of 39 Greek firms. They used 12 financial ratios and compared rough set approach with statistical approach for business failure prediction. Dimitras *et al.* [9] employed indiscernibility relationships for a sample of 80 Greek firms even though variables were preference ordered. The comparison of predictive accuracy with the discriminant analysis also showed that the rough sets approach was a strong alternative. More recently, Beynon and Peel [10] employed the variable precision rough sets model to predict between failed and non-failed UK companies. The results are com-pared to those generated by the classical logit and multivariate discriminant analysis, together with non-parametric decision tree methods.

3 Worst Practice DEA

The DEA [11] is a nonparametric approach that does not require any assumptions about the functional form of the production function. It is assumed that there are Decision-Making Units (DMUs), with m inputs and p outputs, while the efficiency evaluation model of DMU can be defined as following:

$$\max S_k = \sum_{r=1}^{p} u_r y_{rk} \tag{1}$$

$$s.\ t. \qquad \sum_{r=1}^{p} u_r y_{rk} - \sum_{i=1}^{m} v_i x_{ik} \tag{2}$$

$$\sum_{i=1}^{m} v_i x_{ik} = 1, k = 1, 2, ..., m \tag{3}$$

$$u_r \geq \varepsilon \geq 0, r = 1, 2, ..., p; \qquad v_i \geq \varepsilon \geq 0, i = 1, 2, ..., m. \tag{4}$$

Where, x_{ik} is the ith input value for k^{th} DMU, y_{rk} is the rth output value for the kth DMU, u_r and v_i are the virtual multiplier of the output and input, respectively, and is a very small positive value. Where S_k is the efficiency value for k^{th} DMU. DEA does not use common weight, as do multiple criteria decision models. In DEA, the weights vary among the units: this variability is the essence of DEA. The worst practice DEA uses the same model formulation, but instead of picking out the good performers, the goal is to identify the bad performer. This is achieved by select variables reflect poor utilization of resources as output.

4 The Structure of Rough Set DEA System

The proposed system solves failure prediction problem in a hierarchical framework, as illustrated in Fig. 2.

4.1 Data Collection

In the analysis, we are considering data for the year prior to failure, that is the 2002 data for the companies that went bankrupt during 2003 and their control group, 2003 data for the 2004 bankruptcies. For DEA analysis, 9 financial ratios were selected because they proved to be efficient to predict bankruptcy in prior research. For the rough set analysis, four variables (conditional attributes) were collected for potential rule generation. Table 2 contains the variable definitions and the corporate attributes they refer to.

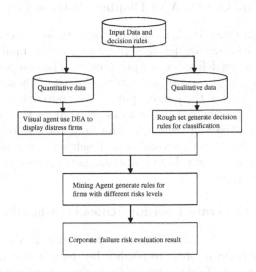

Fig. 2. The proposed rough set DEA system

Table 2. Definition of variables

Attribute Description	Variables value	DEA
Financial structure		
C1	Liabilities/assets ratio (%)	output
Solvency		
C2	Current ratio (%)	input
C3	Quick ratio (%)	input
Management Quality		
C4	Average accounts receivable collection days	output
C5	Average inventory days	output
C6	Fixed assets turnover (times)	input
C7	Total assets turnover (times)	input
Profitability		
C8	Operating income to paid-in capital (%)	input
C9	Return on shareholders' equity (%)	input
Non-financial Qualitative data for Rough set analysis		
C10	1 if abnormal changed CEO in previous year	
C11	1 if changed financial manager in previous year	
C12	1 if auditor qualified audit report, 0 otherwise	
C13	1 if changed auditor in previous year, 0 otherwise	

4.2   Visual Agent Use DEA to Display Distress Firms

By using a worst practice DEA model, financial ratios with a positive correlation to a healthy firm are defined as input factors. The financial ratios with a negative correlation are defined as output factors. The companies that make up the frontier in this analysis are those with the lowest of those good inputs while having the highest level of the bad outputs. This approach is an ideal fit for the failure risk evaluation, where it is the worst companies that need to be clearly identified. Using the layering technique, the firms on the frontier are removed, after which the model is run a second time resulting a new set of frontier units and so on. Thereby sequential layers of worst performance can be found which have changing risk rating.

4.3   Rough Set Generate Decision Rules for Classification

The rough set is used to provide a set of rules able to discriminate between healthy and failing firms in order to predict business failure. The four variables (C10-C13) described in Table 2 relate to various non-financial corporate attributes which have been found to be associated with corporate failure. The first two variables (C10, C11) are binary in nature and relate to the management quality and fraud detection since several Taiwanese firms declare bankruptcy after the abnormal change of chief executive and/or financial officers. The final two variables (C12, C13) are related to auditor characteristics. The first is the auditor opinion signaling for going-concern problems. The second is whether or not a company had changed its auditor the previous year. Previous studies have reported that failing firms are more likely to switch auditor, largely in consequence of disputes between auditors and managers over disagreements in respect of audit opinions/qualifications. In this study, data are analyzed using Rough Set Data Explorer (ROSE) system [12].

4.4   Mining Agent Generate Rules for Firms with Different Risks Levels

Using the layering technique enables a more flexible approach to classification which can take into managerial judgment and risk attitude. The more risk aversion the institution is, the more layers in the worst practice models should be considered. The decision rules generated by rough set can identify potential risky firms for each risk level as well as get the change curve with multi period comparison.

5   Experiments

A large number of firms which failed in Taiwan in the year 2003-2004 were collected. We drew a state-based sample instead of a pure random sample. A pure random selection would lead to a very small sample of failed companies and inaccurate parameter estimation in the models. The resulting sample comprises

Table 3. Out of sample bankruptcy and non-bankruptcy classification accuracies

	Bankruptcy Classification			Non-Bankruptcy Classification		
	Layer 1 (%)	Layer 2 (%)	Layer 3 (%)	Layer 1 (%)	Layer 2 (%)	Layer 3 (%)
Worst DEA	38	54	82	80	85	100
Rough DEA	67	92	100	87	93	100

Table 4. Decision rules deducted from rough set

Rule	
1	(CFO = same) & (opinion = unqualified) ⇒ (failure = no)
2	(CEO = same) & (auditor = unchanged) ⇒ (failure = no)
3	(CEO = same) & (CFO = changed) & (opinion = unqualified) & (auditor = unchanged) ⇒ (failure = no)
4	(CFO = changed) & (opinion = qualified) ⇒ (failure = yes)
5	(opinion = qualified) & (auditor = changed) ⇒ (failure = yes)

396 annual reports broken down in two subsets running: 352 and failed: 44. The best classification results are achieved when combining the rough set with the worst practice DEA model. This gives an impressive 100% bankruptcy classification accuracy as well as 100% non-bankrupt classification accuracy as shown on Table 3. The decision rules generated by rough set for the first level worst practice firms are shown in Table 4.

6 Conclusion

We used a hybrid rough DEA model instead of the traditional methods. This gives the user the opportunity to view and evaluate the potential failure risk of firms. Inclusion of non-financial characteristics in the financial prediction has already been recommended in several other studies in order to improve the validity of the decision rules model. The rough DEA approach adapts very easily to this need since it accepts both qualitative and quantitative attributes. Experimental results demonstrated the applicability and effectiveness of the proposed approach.

References

1. Altman, E.I.: Financial ratios, discriminant analysis and the prediction of corporate bank-ruptcy. Journal of Finance **4** (1968) 589–609
2. Troutt, M.D., Rai, A., Zhang, A.: The potential use of DEA for credit applicant acceptance systems. Computers and Operations Research, **23** (1996) 405–408
3. Seiford, L.M., Zhu, J.: An acceptance system decision rule with data envelopment analysis. Computers and Operations Research, **25** (1998) 329–332

4. Pendharkar, P.C.: A potential use of data envelopment analysis for the inverse classifica-tion problem. Omega (2002) 243–248
5. Cielen, A., Peeters, L., Vanhoof, K. : Bankruptcy prediction using a data envelopment analysis. European Journal of Operational Research, **154** (2004) 526–532
6. Paradi, J.C., Asmild, M., Simak, P.C. : Using DEA and worst practice DEA in credit risk evaluation. Journal of Productivity Analysis. **21** (2004) 153–165
7. Pawlak, Z.: Rough sets. International Journal of Computer and Information Sciences **11** (1982) 341–356
8. Slowinski, R., Zopounidis, C. : Business failure prediction using rough sets. International Journal of Intelligent Systems in Accounting, Finance and Management **4** (1995) 27–41
9. Dimitras, A.I., Slowinski, R., Susmaga, R., Zopounidis, C.: Business failure prediction using rough sets. European Journal of Operational Research, **114** (1999) 263–280
10. Beynon, M.J., Peel, M.J. : Variable precision rough set theory and data discretisation: an application to corporate failure prediction, Omega: (2001) 561–576
11. Charnes, A., Cooper, W.W., Rhodes, E. : Measuring the efficiency of decision making units. European Journal of Operational Research **30** (1984) 1078–1092
12. Predki, B., Slowinski. R., Stefanowski. J., Susmaga. R., Wilk. S.Z. : ROSE - software implementation of the rough set theory. In: Polkowski L, Skowron A. (eds.): *Rough sets and Current Trends in Computing, Lecture Notes in Artificial Intelligence*, Berlin Heidelberg New York, Springer-Verlag, (1998) 605–608

Intrusion Detection System
Based on Multi-class SVM

Hansung Lee, Jiyoung Song, and Daihee Park

Dept. of computer & Information Science, Korea Univ., Korea
{mohan, songjy, dhpark}@korea.ac.kr

Abstract. In this paper, we propose a new intrusion detection system: MMIDS (Multi-step Multi-class Intrusion Detection System), which alleviates some drawbacks associated with misuse detection and anomaly detection. The MMIDS consists of a hierarchical structure of one-class SVM, novel multi-class SVM, and incremental clustering algorithm: Fuzzy-ART. It is able to detect novel attacks, to give detail informations of attack types, to provide economic system maintenance, and to provide incremental update and extension with a system.

1 Introduction

Recently threat elements and criminal behaviors against computer and information resources on networks appears to increase and communize rapidly to the extent harming on household computers. Threat elements against computer resources are expanded to a variety of types of attack ranging from simple intrusion by use of scripts to misuse of computers by use of malware equipped with multiple functions, and the scale of damage also increases rapidly [1]. Hence, it is necessary to develop more effective intrusion detection algorithms in order to detect malicious behaviors and intrusions being expanded to a variety of range.

Intrusion detection is the art of detecting unauthorized, inappropriate, or anomalous activity on computer systems. There are two major paradigms for intrusion detection methods according to general strategy for detection: misuse detection and anomaly detection. The misuse detection model establishes a rule base by way of a detail analysis on the attack type, and performs the detection on the basis of it. This model has an intrinsic disadvantage that the rule base should be manually updated for new types of attack in order to deal with them. The anomaly detection model detects attacks by determining data deviated at a great extent from the profile including normal behavior as abnormal behavior. This model is useful to detect new types of attack, but has an unavoidable limit that it can not take a proper action against the intrusion because it lacks detail information about the detected type of attack [2].

According an investigation on latest research literatures, there are many ongoing attempts to apply data mining and machine learning techniques to the intrusion detection systems in order to design more intelligent intrusion detection model. Recently, the support vector learning method, featuring superior

D. Ślęzak et al. (Eds.): RSFDGrC 2005, LNAI 3642, pp. 511–519, 2005.

performance at some issues such as pattern classification and function approximation, has grown up as a viable tool in the area of intrusion detection systems. The intrusion detection model based on SVM (support vector machine) is mainly classified into three types. The first type [3] divides data into normal data and attack data using characteristics of the binary classifier SVM, and the second type [4] implements an anomaly detection model using one-class SVM. All of both methods described above, however, can not offer additional information about detected type of attack, only but distinguish normal data and abnormal data. Finally, the third type [5] establishes multi-class SVM at the form of combining many binary classifiers, namely, SVMs and divides data into normal data and four types of attack data. Since this type has many problems including that system performance of which is completely dependent on the quality of training data and training time of which take a long time, it can not be used as practical intelligent intrusion detection system although it is more advanced one in comparison with other two methods.

In this paper, we propose a novel intrusion detection model, which keeps advantages of existing misuse detection model and anomaly detection model and resolves their problems. This new intrusion detection system, named to MMIDS (Multi-step Multi-class Intrusion Detection System), was designed to satisfy all the following requirements by combining one-class SVM, proposed novel multi-class SVM and Fuzzy-ART that is a incremental clustering algorithm, hierarchically: 1)Fast detection of new types of attack unknown to the system; 2) Provision of detail information about the detected types of attack; 3) cost-effective maintenance due to fast and efficient learning and update; 4) incrementality and scalability of system.

The organization of this paper is as follows. Section 2 explains the new-proposed multi-class SVM, and Section 3 describes the proposed intrusion detection model: MMIDS. The experimental results are given in Section 4, and conclusions are made in Section 5.

2   Multi-class SVM Based on One-Class SVM

Recently, the support vector learning method has grown up as a viable tool in the area of intelligent systems. It shows an excellent performance at the pattern classification and function approximation by ensuring global optimum for a given problems. However, it is difficult to apply SVM at real world applications, most of which are as to the multi-class classification, because it has a structural limit of the binary classifier. How to effectively extend it for multi-class classification is still an ongoing research issue. Currently, there are three major types of approaches for multi-class SVM: one-against-all, one-against-one, and DAGSVM [6].

As for the intrusion detection, the volume of data necessary for the training varies depending on each type of attack. Hence, the training result for a type of attack may be affected by other types of attack data owing to the unbalanced size of training data. In addition, it can not be said that current training data represents for the whole class, because new types of attack, included in one attack class, are increasingly emerged. So, the binary classifier SVM may be subject to misclassification for novel attack data by creating decision boundary including unobserved area. It is preferable, therefore, to select the decision boundary using one-class SVM [8] that expresses only the corresponding class independently. In this paper, we propose a multi-class SVM that can classify various types of attack on the basis of one-class SVM.

Given K-data set of N_k patterns in d-dimensional input space, $D_k = \{x_i^k \in R^d | i = 1, \ldots, N_k\}; k = 1, \ldots, K$, multi-class SVM to classify each class is defined as a problem to obtain a sphere that minimizes the volume with it including the training data, and it is formalized through the following optimization problem.

$$min \quad L_0(R_k^2, a_k, \xi_k) = R_k^2 + C \sum_{i=1}^{N_k} \xi_i^k \qquad (1)$$

$$s.t. \quad \|x_i^k - a_k\|^2 \le R_k^2 + \xi_i^k, \xi_i^k \ge 0, \forall i.$$

Where, a_k is the center of the sphere that expresses k-th class, R_k^2 is the square value of sphere radius, ξ_i^k is the penalty term that shows how far i-th training data x_i^k pertained to k-th class is deviated from the sphere, and C is the trade-off constant.

By introducing a Lagranger multiplier for each inequality condition, we obtain the following Lagrange function:

$$L(R_k^2, a_k, \xi_k, \alpha_k, \eta_k) = R_k^2 + C \sum_{i=1}^{N_k} \xi_i^k \qquad (2)$$

$$+ \sum_{i=1}^{N_k} \alpha_i^k \left[(x_i^k - a_k)^T (x_i^k - a_k) - R_k^2 - \xi_i^k \right]$$

$$- \sum_{i=1}^{N_k} \eta_i^k \xi_i^k$$

where $\alpha_i^k \ge 0, \eta_i^k \ge 0, \forall i$.

From the saddle point condition, the equation (2) has to be minimized with respect to R_k^2, a_k and ξ_i^k and maximized with respect to α_k and η_k [7,8]. The optimal solution of (1) should satisfy the following:

$$\frac{\partial L}{\partial R_k^2} = 0 : \sum_{i=1}^{} N_k a_i^k = 1. \qquad (3)$$

$$\frac{\partial L}{\partial \xi_i^k} = 0 : C - \alpha_i^k - \eta_i^k = 0 \quad \therefore \alpha_i^k \in [0, C], \forall i.$$

$$\frac{\partial L}{\partial a_k} = 0 : a_k = \sum_{i=1}^{} N_k \alpha_i^k x_i^k.$$

With substitution of the above into Lagrange function L, we obtain the following dual problem:

$$min_{\alpha_k} \quad \sum_{i=1}^{N_k}\sum_{j=1}^{N_k} \alpha_i^k \alpha_j^k <x_i^k, x_j^k> - \sum_{i=1}^{N_k} \alpha_i^k <x_i^k, x_i^k> \tag{4}$$

$$s.t. \quad \sum_{i=1}^{N_k} \alpha_i^k = 1, \alpha_i^k \in [0, C], \forall i.$$

Since, each class can express more complex own decision boundary in respective feature space F [7,8], training of the system is done with solving the following QP problem by considering independency of the feature space to which each class is mapped.

$$min_{\alpha_k} \quad \sum_{i=1}^{N_k}\sum_{j=1}^{N_k} \alpha_i^k \alpha_j^k K_k(x_i^k, x_j^k) - \sum_{i=1}^{N_k} \alpha_i^k K_k(x_i^k, x_i^k) \tag{5}$$

$$s.t. \quad \sum_{i=1}^{N_k} \alpha_i^k = 1, \alpha_i^k \in [0, C], \forall i.$$

When the gaussian function is chosen for the kernel, we always have $K(x, x) = 1$ for each $x \in R^d$. Thus, the above problem can be further simplified as follows:

$$min_{\alpha_k} \quad \sum_{i=1}^{N_k}\sum_{j=1}^{N_k} \alpha_i^k \alpha_j^k K_k(x_i^k, x_j^k) \tag{6}$$

$$s.t. \quad \sum_{i=1}^{N_k} \alpha_i^k = 1, \alpha_i^k \in [0, C], \forall i.$$

Note that in this case, the decision function of each class can be summarized as follows

$$f_k(x) = R_k^2 - \left(1 - 2\sum_{i=1}^{N_k} \alpha_i^k K_k(x_i^k, x) + \sum_{i=1}^{N_k}\sum_{j=1}^{N_k} \alpha_i^k \alpha_j^k K_k(x_i^k, x_j^k)\right) \geq 0 \tag{7}$$

Since the output $f_k(x)$ of one-class SVM that is defined on different feature space means absolute distance between corresponding data and decision boundary in each feature space, it is not recommended to determine pertained class by comparing absolute distances on different feature spaces. Accordingly, we calculate the relative distance $\hat{f}_k(x) = f_k(x)/R_k$ by dividing the absolute distance $f_k(x)$ on the feature by the radius R_k of the sphere that is defined on the feature space, and decide the class having maximum relative distance as one to which the input data x is pertained.

$$Class \ of \ x \equiv arg \ max_{k=1,...,k}\hat{f}_k(x) \tag{8}$$

$$where \ \hat{f}_k(x) = f_k(x)/R_k$$

Remark: To show its effectiveness, we compare the proposed method with other methods with respect to complexity analysis. Let's assume k classes and n training data per class in order to compare the multi-class SVM that we propose and conventional methodologies. For one-against-all, total number of data for the training is nk^2 because the number of SVMs to be trained is k and each SVM has to train data amounting to nk. For one-against-one and DAG, the number of SVMs to be trained is $k(k-1)/2$ and $2n$ data contributes to the training of each SVM. Total number of data to be trained is, therefore, $nk^2 - nk$. For the proposed method, with total number of data involved in the training being nk because k SVMs are trained and n data per SVM is involved, the proposed algorithm delivers a faster training speed. If one new class is added into the multi-class SVM that has already been trained, $k+1$ SVMs should be trained newly for one-against-all and k SVMs should be trained again for one-against-one, respectively. In the case of DAG, not only k SVMs should be trained again but also additional cost for reconstructing the graph is required. Whereas, the proposed algorithm is very cost-effective in terms of system reconstruction because it trains only added SVM. The Complexity Analysis of conventional Multi-Class SVMs and proposed method are summarized in Table 1.

Table 1. Complexity Analysis of Multi-Class SVMs

	The number of training SVMs	The number of training data per SVM	The number of training SVMs when a class is added	The number of test SVMs
one-against-all	k	nk	$k+1$	k
one-against-one	$k(k-1)/2$	$2n$	k	$k(k-1)/2$
DAG	$k(k-1)/2$	$2n$	$k+DAG$	k
Proposed Method	k	n	1	k

3 MMIDS (Multi-step Multi-class Intrusion Detection System)

In this section, we propose a new intrusion detection model, which keeps advantages of existing misuse detection model and anomaly detection model as they are and resolves their problems. The new intrusion detection system, named to MMIDS, is designed to satisfy all the following requirements: 1) Fast detection of new types of attack unknown to the system; 2) Provision of detail information about the detected types of attack; 3) cost-effective maintenance due to fast and efficient learning and update; 4) incrementality and scalability of system.

As shown in Figure 1, MMIDS consists of three main components; one-class SVM that distiguishes normal data and attack data; multi-class SVM classifies the attack data into one of DOS (denial of service), R2L (remote to local), U2R (user to root) and Probing attacks; Fuzzy-ART that carries out detail clustering

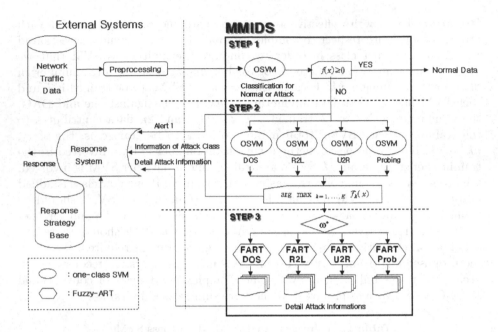

Fig. 1. The Architecture of MMIDS

for each type of attack. There are three phases in the procedure of intrusion detection for the test data. We take a look at them closely here.

Phase 1: One-class SVM that has been trained by normal data classifies normal data and attack data at the first stage. The training process requires only normal data without need to prepare attack data, ensuring a faster training speed. The one-class SVM, as an anomaly detection model, detects novel attack without additional process for normal data on the system operation. When attack data is detected, it generates first alarm to the intrusion response system and steps into the phase 2.

Phase 2: The multi-class SVM classifies the attack data detected at phase 1 into one of DOS, U2R, R2L and Probing, and provides the intrusion response system with additional information about the type of attack. For the update of the novel attack data to the system, only classifier of the corresponding class rather than whole system is retrained. It allows the maintenance cost on the on-site system operation to be reduced.

Phase 3: If more detail information about incoming attack is required, Fuzzy-ART performs clustering for each type of attack. Detail data for each attack is not much enough to train classifiers such as SVM, and it is difficult to predict its type as well. Thus it is recommended to carry out classification by attack using the unsupervised learning, namely, clustering.

4   Experimental Results

To evaluate the effectiveness of the intrusion detection system, MMIDS, KDD CUP 1999 data [10] were used for the experiments. In order to make accurate analysis on the experiment result, we used only Corrected-labeled data set among KDD CUP 99 data which was collected through the simulation on the U.S. military network by 1998 DARPA Intrusion Detection Evaluation Program, aiming at obtaining the benchmark data set in the field of intrusion detection. The used data amounting to 311,029 consists of 9 symbolic attributes and 32 numeric attributes. The data is mainly divided into four types of attack: DOS, R2L, U2R and probing, and subsidiary types of attack by main attack amounts to 37 including 6 Probing attacks such as ipsweep and saint.

4.1   Comparison with Other Intrusion Detection Algorithms

Because many research results of intrusion detection have been reported recently, we compare our performance with other Intrusion Detection Algorithms. Table 2 shows classification capability of each research for normal data and 4 types of attack. The multi-class classifier proposed in this paper has superior classification capability to conventional researches as a whole, as shown in Table 2. It should be observed that all research results show considerable inferior performance only at the classification capability as to R2L and U2R. As shown in Table 2, our method can provide superior performance in separating these two patterns. In particular in the comparison between this experiment and Ambwani [5] that used one-against-one multi-class SVM targeting at same data as ours, the experiment results of this methodology shows much enhanced performance. It can be explained as follows;

Note that R2L and U2R are host-based attacks which exploit vulnerabilities of operating systems, not of network protocol. Therefore, these are very similar to the "normal" data in the KDD CUP 99 data collected from network packets. And depending on type of attack, the size of data available for the training is quite different. The size of U2R or R2L attack data, for example, is smaller than that of other types of attack. Hence at the conventional multi-class SVM that trains decision boundary for each class after mapping all classes into the same feature space, the class, size of which is relatively larger, may deliver more impact on the training result than others. It can be said, therefore, that the strategy of multi-class SVM employed in this paper, that is to enhance classification performance

Table 2. Comparison with Other Intrusion Detection Algorithms

	Bernhard [10]	W. Lee [11]	Y. Liu [12]	Kayacik [13]	Ambwani [5]	MMIDS
Normal	99.5%	-	-	95.4%	99.6%	**96.74%**
DOS	97.1%	79.9%	56%	95.1%	96.8%	**98.24%**
R2L	**8.4%**	**60.0%**	**78%**	**9.9%**	**5.3%**	**35.00%**
U2R	**13.2%**	**75.0%**	**66%**	**10.0%**	**4.2%**	**85.23%**
Probing	83.3%	97.0%	44%	64.3%	75.0%	**98.27%**

for own-class and minimizes the effect from unbalanced size of training data (see Eq. 6), is turned out to be very efficient.

4.2 Clustering of Attack Data

In addition, we performed the clustering for each of 4 types of attack using Fuzzy-ART in order to verify detailed separation capability corresponding to phase 3 of MMIDS. Table 3 shows the results from the Probing attack. According to the experimental results of Table 3, detailed separation capability of MMIDS is relatively good.

Table 3. Experimental Results of Probing Attack

Attacks	Detection Ratio	Attacks	Detection Ratio
ipsweep	95.0%	satan	91.7%
saint	17.2%	mscan	88.2%
portsweep	96.0%	nmap	20.0%

5 Conclusions

In this paper, we proposed a new intrusion detection model so that it keeps advantages of existing misuse detection model and anomaly detection model and resolves their problems. This novel intrusion detection system, named to MMIDS, was designed to satisfy all the following requirements by combining one-class SVM, proposed multi-class SVM and Fuzzy-ART that is an incremental clustering algorithm, hierarchically: 1) Fast detection of new types of attack unknown to the system; 2) Provision of detail information about the detected types of attack; 3)cost-effective maintenance due to fast and efficient learning and update; 4) incrementality and scalability of system.

Comprehensive researches that consider organic relationship between two systems: IDS and response system, including the method of utilizing detail information about attacks detected by the intrusion detection system for establishing policy of intrusion detection system, may be required for future works.

References

1. E. Skoudis and L. Zeltser: Malware - Fighting Malicious Code, Prentice Hall, 2004.
2. S. Noel, D. Wijesekera, and C. Youman: 'Modern Intrusion Detection, Data Mining, and Degrees of Attack Guilt', in Applications of Data Mining in Computer Security, Kluwer Academic Publisher, pp. 1-31, 2002.
3. W.H. Chen, S.H. Hsu, and H.P. Shen: 'Application of SVM and ANN for intrusion detection', Computers & Operations Research, ELSEVIER, Vol. 32, Issue 10, pp. 2617-2634, 2005.

4. K.L. Li, H.K. Huang, S.F. Tian, and W. Xu: 'Improving one-class SVM for anomaly detection', International Conference on Machine Learning and Cybernetics, Vol. 5, pp. 3077-3081, 2003.
5. T. Ambwani: 'Multi class support vector machine implementation to intrusion detection', Proceedings of the International Joint Conference on Neural Networks, Vol. 3, pp. 2300-2305, 2003.
6. C.W. Hsu and C.J. Lin.: 'A comparison of methods for multi-class support vector machines', IEEE Transactions on Neural Networks, Vol. 13, pp. 415-425, 2002.
7. N. Cristianini and J. Shawe-Taylor: 'An introduction to support vector machines and other kernel-based learning methods', Cambridge University PRESS, pp. 93-124, 2000.
8. D.M.J. Tax and R.P.W. Duin: 'Uniform Object Generation for Optimizing One-class Classifiers', Journal of Machine Learning Research, Vol. 2, Issue 2, pp. 155-173, 2001.
9. J. Huang, M. Georgiopoulos, and GL Heileman: 'Fuzzy ART properties', Neural Networks, Vol. 8, No. 2, pp. 203-213, 1995.
10. Results of the KDD'99 Classifier Learning Contest, Available in http://www-cse.ucsd.edu/users/elkan/clresults.html
11. W. Lee, S.J. Stolfo, and K.W. Mok: 'A data mining framework for building intrusion detection models', Proceedings of the 1999 IEEE Symposium on Security and Privacy, pp. 120-132, 1999.
12. Y. Liu, K. Chen, X. Liao, and W. Zhang: 'A Genetic Clustering Method for Intrusion Detection', Pattern Recognition, Vol. 37, Issue 5, pp. 927-942. 2004.
13. H.G. Kayacik, A.N. Zincir-Heywood, and M.I. Heywood: 'On the capability of an SOM based intrusion detection system', Proceedings of the International Joint Conference on Neural Networks, Vol. 3, pp. 1808-1813, 2003.

A Development of Intrusion Detection and Protection System Using Netfilter Framework*

Min Wook Kil[1], Seung Kyeom Kim[2], Geuk Lee[2],
and Youngmi Kwon[3]

[1] Dept. of Computer & Image Information,
Mun Kyung College, Mun Kyung,
South Korea
mwkil@mkc.ac.kr
[2] Dept. of Computer Engineering,
Hannam University, Daejeon,
South Korea
{codekim, leegeuk}@hannam.ac.kr
[3] Dept. of InfoCom, Chungnam National University,
Daejeon, South Korea
ymkwon@cnu.ac.kr

Abstract. Information can be leaked, changed, damaged and illegally used regardless of the intension of the information owner. Intrusion Detection Systems and Firewalls are used to protect the illegal accesses in the network. But these are the passive protection method, not the active protection method. They only react based on the predefined protection rules or only report to the administrator. In this paper, we develop the intrusion detection and protection system using Netfilter framework. The system makes the administrator's management easy and simple. Furthermore, it offers active protection mechanism against the intrusions.

1 Introduction

Rapid growth of network and Internet market comes along with the positive aspects in the perspective business area based on the information communications, but with the negative aspects in the harmful intrusion into the network systems. The information can be leaked, changed, damaged and illegally used regardless of the intension of the information owner [1].

The Security Systems have been developed to prevent these harmful hazards, but it is not sufficient to solve the problems. Monitoring the information systems, the Intrusion Detection System (IDS) analyzes and detects the trials of attacks on real time. However, it is hard for IDS to do the session-based detection which uses multiple packets [2]. Network IDS can detect the real-time packets coming from the outer world, but it is also problematic that the network IDS is lack of

---

* This work was supported by a grant No.R12-2003-004-02002-0 from Korea Ministry of Commerce, Industry and Energy.

D. Ślęzak et al. (Eds.): RSFDGrC 2005, LNAI 3642, pp. 520–529, 2005.
© Springer-Verlag Berlin Heidelberg 2005

the blocking the attacks. Because the IDS can detect the packets on the network, but can't block the attacks, almost packets may go to the destined victims and be successful to penetrate the systems. Further, the intrusion detection systems and firewalls which are used to protect the illegal accesses in the network are the passive protection method, not the active protection method. They only react based on the predefined protection rules or only report to the administrator [3].

To compensate for the IDS and firewalls' limitations with speeding up the prompt reactions to the attacks, and to supply the administrators with convenient management environments, we developed a real-time packet-blocking system using Netfilter framework. Our intrusion detection and protection system can block the incoming packets as soon as the attacks are detected without the intervention of the administrator. The proposed system makes the administrator's management easy and simple. Furthermore, it can make a rapid response actively on the intrusions. The structure of this paper is as follows: in section 2, we analyzed the existing Intrusion Detection System and Intrusion Protection System. In section 3, we explained the system design and described the principals of the system processes. Finally, we will give a conclusion of the work in section 4.

2   Related Works

This section describes an overview of the existing techniques which are necessary for the development of intrusion detection and protection system.

2.1   Intrusion Detection System (IDS)

Intrusion is an action to attack the integrity, confidentiality and availability of the system resources. IDS is to detect the unprivileged access and keep the system from the illegal access effectively. It monitors, analyzes, detects and responds to the intrusions to the information systems [4].

Limitations of IDS: Some limitations may take place because of a design oriented only to detection. Misdetection and failure-of-detection can occur. As the attack-trails increased, it became difficult for network IDS or host IDS to detect the attacks with a limited capability [5].

Further, the IDS cannot prevent the attacks in real-time. The reason is that it can detect the suspicious packets, but not prevent those packets. Almost suspicious packets may come to the victim system before the system blocks them. Many systems tried to compensate for those limitations. But misdetection, a bulky log and real-time prevention problems have not been solved easily.

2.2   Intrusion Protection System (IPS)

This type of system (also called firewall) is a device which controls the internal networks and external networks to prevent the illegal access or hackers' attack [6]. It establishes the gate between two networks and then controls that communication route. By locating the IPS at the bottleneck point of the bidirectional traffics, the internal networks can be protected from the exposure of system's weak points to the outer world. When we install the router or application gateway having the firewall function on the boundary of the internal network and outer Internet, all the data communications can go only through these devices.

Limitations of IPS: The principle of firewall is to block the packets coming from the outer network based on the predefined rules. IPS has passive characteristics such that is can prevent only the predefined rules and filter some kinds of packets [7]. So the firewall has following limitations:

- It should open some inevitable service ports.
- It has deficiency of active prevention.
- It can prevent restrictively the known attack types.
- It can not detect the attacks started from the inner site.
- It does not have a capability of attack-reports.

2.3 Netfilter

Netfilter is a framework for packet mangling. It resides at the outside of the standardized Berkeley socket interface, in the Linux kernel internals. It provides the extensible NAT and packet filtering functions [8].

In the packet filtering function, the packet header is inspected first and the reaction is decided whether the packet will be dropped, accepted, or treated for the other purposes. The kernel has an initial filter table having the fundamental three chains: INPUT, OUTPUT and FORWARD.

The Process of Packet Filtering: Netfilter inspects the packet header and decide the next action to the packet. The packet can be denied (DROP), accepted (ACCEPT), or may be treated according to the other purposes.

- ACCEPT: proceed the packet
- DROP: deny the packet
- STOLEN: steal the packet. That is, the packet is not forwarded.
- QUEUE: send a packet to the queue.

Kernel has three fundamental chains in 'filter' table: INPUT, OUTPUT and FORWARD chain. In figure 1, three circles show three fundamental chains. When a packet comes to a chain, its next action is decided on that chain. If a chain decides to 'DROP', then that packet is deleted on that spot. Or if a chain decides to 'ACCEPT', then that packet is transferred to the next step. In a chain, more than one rule(s) can be assigned. Each rule specifies the condition that the packets should meet. And it also describes the (target) actions when the condition is satisfied. If a packet does not meet one rule's condition, then it references the next rule. If the rule is the last one, then the filtering process decides the next step of the packet based on the packet's default policy. Basically, the existing rule should not be eliminated.

Incoming packets to the filtering system pass through the 'INPUT' chain, and out-going packets from the system pass through the 'OUTPUT' chain. The packets flowing in one inner network pass through 'FORWARD' chain.

If the command to insert the rules to the chain is executed, then the new rules are appended at the bottommost of the chain.

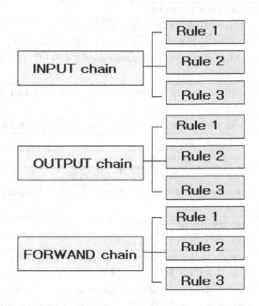

Fig. 1. Basic Three Chains

iptables: 'iptables' is a user tool to insert and/or delete the filtering rules into/from the *Packet Filtering Table* in the kernel [9]. 'iptables' is not a packet filtering tool itself. It is just a command tool of the Netfilter imported in the kernel, and we should use this tool to make rules to reflect current intrusion aspects. The commands used for the operation of iptables are shown in table 1 [10]. The system accepts or prevents packets with these iptables commands. When it configures the iptables for the web-server (port range: 1 65535), it sets a port of 21 to be open for ftp, 22 for ssh, 23 for telnet, 80 for http and 111 for portmap (NFS) as following.

- iptables -A INPUT -p tcp –dport 21 -j ACCEPT
- iptables -A INPUT -p tcp –dport 22 -j ACCEPT
- iptables -A INPUT -p tcp –dport 23 -j ACCEPT
- iptables -A INPUT -p tcp –dport 80 -j ACCEPT
- iptables -A INPUT -p tcp –sport 111 -j ACCEPT

The results of these commands are shown in figure 2.

To block all the packets from specific IP address, for example, 203.247.42.156, the following command is used, and the result is shown in figure 3.

iptables -A INPUT -s 203.247.156 -j DROP

Table 1. iptables commands

Command	Description
N	Create new chain
X	Delete an empty chain
P	Change the basic principle of already existing chains
L	List the rule items
F	Eliminate all the rules in chain
A	Decide if the rules of chain will be applied or not when it choose the result as one of INPUT, OUTPUT, FORWAND
I	Apply the newly inserted rule earlier than other existing rules
R	Relocate the existing rule to another position
D	Delete a rule
s	Specify a source IP address
d	Specify a destination IP address
p	Specify one protocol among TCP, UDP, and ICMP protocols
i	Specify input interface
o	Specify output interface
j	Decide how manages the packet. Generally, the choices is one of ACCEPT (an option to accept a packet option), DENY (an option to bounce a packet without accepting a packet), and DROP (an option to discard a packet)

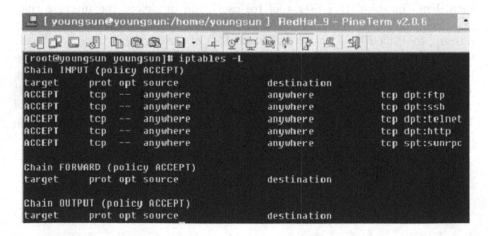

Fig. 2. Configuration of Web-Server iptables

Fig. 3. Configuration to prevent packets from a specific IP address

3   The Development of Intrusion Detection and Protection System

3.1   Algorithm Design

The intrusion detection and protection system consists of three modules in a large abstract view. One is the *Analysis Module for Input Packet* module.

This module collects and filters the input packets. Another is the *Detection Module for Intrusion Packet* module. This module classifies the input packets and analyzes if it is suspicious or not. And the other is the *Management Module for Intrusion Protection* module. This module operates a management process by setting the rules for intrusion protection and recording the log. The overall algorithm design is shown in figure 4.

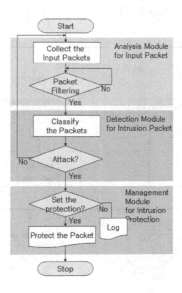

Fig. 4. The Algorithm Design

3.2   System Module Design

Figure 5 shows an overall block diagram of system modules and figure 6 is a detailed system configuration. The proposed intrusion detection and protection system is located between the internal network and external networks. Packets coming from the external networks are classified and analyzed according to the protocols in the *Analysis Module for Input Packet* module. The *Detection Module for Intrusion Packet* module detects the existence of intrusions by comparing the decomposed packets with the Rule DB. If this module detects some suspicious packet, then it sends an "Information of Protection Establishment" to the *Management Module for Intrusion Protection* module. The *Management Module for Intrusion Protection* module sets the rules for intrusion protection based on the configuration information passed from the *Detection Module for Intrusion Packet* module and records the log to the corresponding packet. The *Information of Protection Establishment* informs if the intrusion should be blocked or not, if the log should be recorded in the warning message, and how the level of reaction should be decided.

The detailed descriptions of each module are following in the subsections.

Analysis Module for Input Packet: This module decomposes the packet into each layer's header and analyzes the packets according to the network interface layer, internet layer, transport layer and application layer. The related functions are Analyze_Ethernet_packet(), Analyze_IP_Packet(), Analyze_TCP_Packet(), Analyze_UDP_Packet(), and Analyze_ICMP_Packet().

- *Analyze_Ethernet_Packet()*: Cast the type of input packet to the Ethernet structure. Store the hardware address and upper layer protocol identification.
- *Analyze_IP_Packet()*: Cast the type of input packet to the IP structure. Store the IP header contents. Analyze the packets based on the one of upper layer protocols: TCP, UDP and ICMP.

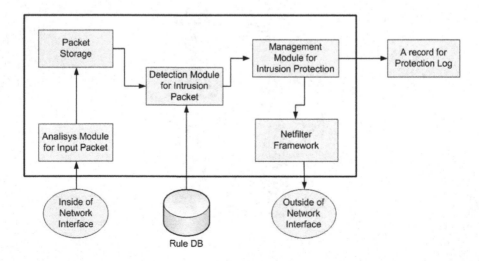

Fig. 5. Block Diagram of the System Modules

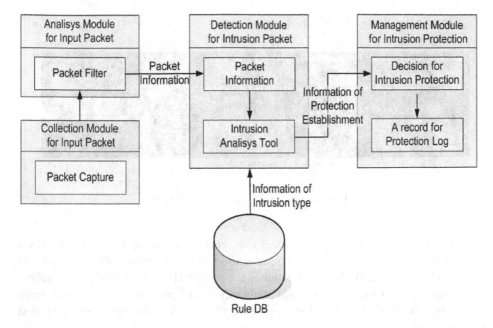

Fig. 6. A Detailed System Configuration

- *Analyze_TCP_Packet()*: Analyze the TCP Packet Header
- *Analyze_UDP_Packet()*: Analyze the UDP Packet Header
- *Analyze_ICMP_Packet()*: Analyze the ICMP Packet Header

Detection Module for Intrusion Packet: The *Detection Module for Intrusion Packet* module detects the existence of intrusions by comparing the decomposed packets with the Rule DB. If this module detects some suspicious packet, then it sends an *Information of Protection Establishment* to the *Management Module for Intrusion Protection* module. The related functions are Parse_Rule_DB() and Check_Rule().

- *Parse_Rule_DB()*: Read the rules line by line from the Rule DB and store the type of attack information into the inner structure.
- *Check_Rule()*: Detect the attacks by comparing the header information of the input packet with the type of attack information.

Management Module for Intrusion Protection: The *Management Module for Intrusion Protection* module sets the rules for intrusion protection based on the *Information of Protection Establishment* passed from the *Detection Module for Intrusion Packet* module and records the log to the corresponding packet. The *Decision for Intrusion Protection* module decides if the intrusion should be blocked instantly or not, if the log should be recorded in the form of warning message, and how the level of reaction should be activated. And the level information how seriously the system will react against the attacks is also decided. This module uses a libiptc library to interact with a Netfilter framework. libiptc is a library to set the packet filtering function in the Netfilter framework. The related functions in this module are Set-Intrusion_Detection() and log().

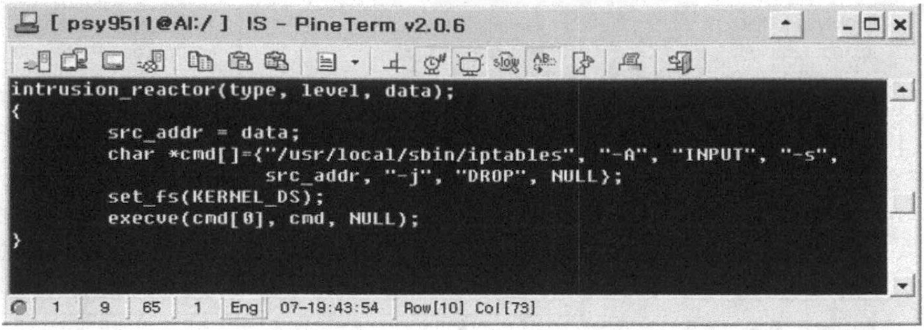

```
[ psy9511@AI:/ ]  IS - PineTerm v2.0.6

intrusion_reactor(type, level, data);
{
        src_addr = data;
        char *cmd[]={"/usr/local/sbin/iptables", "-A", "INPUT", "-s",
                     src_addr, "-j", "DROP", NULL};
        set_fs(KERNEL_DS);
        execve(cmd[0], cmd, NULL);
}

  1    9   65   1   Eng   07-19:43:54   Row[10] Col[73]
```

Fig. 7. A reaction code for intrusions

- *Set_Intrusion_Detection()*: protect the attacks according to the *Information of protection Establishment*. libiptc is used in this function. The *Information of Protection Establishment* includes the source IP address and port number.
- *Log()*: record logs for the packets classified and analyzed by an upper layer protocol. And the *Information of Protection Establishment* is also recorded as a log.

According to the information from the *Information of Protection Establishment*, the *Decision for Intrusion Protection* module updates intrusion status information and creates rule for intrusion protection. This rule is inserted into *Packet Filtering Table* to activate protection process. Figure 7 is a part of reaction code for intrusions. It creates new protection rule for the *Packet Filtering Table* automatically.

4   Conclusions

In this paper, we develop the intrusion detection and protection system which uses Netfilter to improve the stability and safety in network environment. This system performs the detection and protection functions simultaneously based on the Rule DB. When the intrusion detection module detects some possibility of new attacks, it records some rules, and the protection module uses those rules on real-time without administrator's intervention. This means that the system becomes to have active protection mechanism and real-time protection functionality by virtue of prompt and automatic updates for the protection rules.

The proposed system will be the basis for the secure, stable and reliable services. It will also improve the packet processing capability, and makes the administration easy and simple.

The proposed system runs at the application level. So the speed and performance of the collecting and analyzing the packets may be worse than that of the kernel-mode systems. So porting the intrusion detection and protection system into the kernel level is required as a further work.

References

1. Schupp, S.: Limitation of Network Intrusion Detection. http://www.sans.org/rr/whitepapers/detection/
2. Bace, R.G.: Intrusion Detection. Macmillan Technical Pub (2000)
3. Esmaili, M., Safavi-Naini, R., Pieprzyk, J.: Intrusion Detection: a Survey. Proceedings of ICCC (1995) 409-414
4. Jeong, B.H., Kim, J.N., Sohn, S.W.: Current Status and Expectation of Techniques for Intrusion Protection System. http://kidbs.itfind.or.kr/WZIN/jugidong/1098/109801.htm
5. Shim, D.C.: A trend of Intrusion Detection System. KISDI IT FOCUS 4. Korea Information Strategy Development Institute (2001) 61-65
6. Alan, J.: Netfilter and IPTables: A Structural Examination. http://www.sans.org/rr/whitepapers/firewalls/1392.php
7. Cho, D.I., Song, K.C., Noh, B.K.: Handbook of Analysis for Detection of Network Intrusion and Hacking. Infobook (2001)
8. Russell, R., Welte, H.: Linux netfilter Hacking HOWTO. http://www.netfilter.org/documentation/HOWTO/netfilter-hacking-HOWTO.html
9. Cohen, F.: 50 ways to Defeat Your Intrusion Detection System. http://www.mjidor.com/50dis.shtml
10. Andreasson, O.: iptables-tutorial. http://www.0kr.net/files/iptables-tutorial.html

A Group Decision-Making Model
of Risk Evasion in Software Project Bidding
Based on VPRS

Gang Xie[1], Jinlong Zhang[1], and K.K. Lai[2]

[1] School of Management, Huazhong University of Science and Technology,
430074 Wuhan, China
xgbill@hotmail.com, jlzhang@mail.hust.edu.cn
[2] Department of Management Sciences, City University of Hong Kong,
Hong Kong and College of Business Administration, Hunan University, China
mskklai@cityu.edu.hk

Abstract. This study develops a group decision-making model based on Variable Precision Rough Set, which can be used to adjust classification error in decision tables consisting of risk-evading level (REL) of software project bidding. In order to reflect experts' ability, impartiality and carefulness roundly during the course of group decision-making, a weight is endowed with each expert. Integrated risk-evading level (IREL) of projects and risk indices are computed. Then, risk-evading measures, the rank of risk-evading strength and risk-evading methodology are discussed.

1 Introduction

Risk evasion, including risk identification, risk assessment, risk analysis, risk reduction and risk monitoring, is an approach to prevent and remove the risk in software project bidding, and its purpose is to achieve the success of the bidding. Based on the experts' experience, subjective judgement and sensibility, risk evasion is a complex, unstructured or semi-structured decision-making process. Risk-evading level (REL) of software project bidding is the experts' evaluation on risk-evading strength project and indices needed. Because of evaluating error, practical risk-evading strength is always different from that which the projects really need: If bidders' risk-evading strength is too high, they will refuse to bid for software projects with lower risk than their evaluation, or it will cost more to develop and implement the software projects. On the other hand, if their risk-evading strength is too lower, bidders will erroneously accept software projects with higher risk than expected, which causes the failure of projects without precaution. In the same way, improper risk-evading measures also result in the bidding failing. In this study, successful bidding refers to not only achieving the contract but also the profitable development and implementation of software projects. As a matter of fact, risk evasion is a prerequisite of successful bidding,

D. Ślęzak et al. (Eds.): RSFDGrC 2005, LNAI 3642, pp. 530–538, 2005.

which needs proper risk-evading measures and strength. Therefore, a group decision pattern is adopted to gain comprehensive and precise decisions, since this makes the best use of experts' knowledge and experience.

With the development of communication, computation and decision support in information technology, related demand accelerates the study in the field of group decision support system, and facilitates expert groups with different knowledge structures and experience to work together in the process of unstructured and semi-structured decision-making problems [1,2]. Integrated risk-evading level (IREL) is the aggregation of all expert's evaluation of REL. As a rule, IREL of risk indices decides the strength of corresponding risk-evading measures. The IREL of a project decides the risk-evading strength of the project.

Under a group decision pattern, experts score the REL that software projects and the indices need, based on which decision tables are established. This paper makes use of VPRS [3,4] as a data mining tool to process the data in decision tables, remove noise in the data by setting an approximate precision factor $\beta(0.5 < \beta \leq 1)$, and endows each expert with a weight. Then, REL of experts is aggregated into IREL. Relationship among IREL, risk-evading measures, risk-evading strength and risk-evading methodology are discussed.

2 Group Decision-Making Model

Suppose $C, D \subseteq A$ are the condition attribute set and the decision attribute set respectively, and A is a finite set of attributes, U is the object set. Then with $Z \subseteq U$ and $P \subseteq C, Z$ is partitioned into three regions:

$$POS_P^\beta(Z) = \bigcup_{Pr(Z|X_i) \geq \beta} \{X_i \in E(P)\}$$
$$NEG_P^\beta(Z) = \bigcup_{Pr(Z|X_i) \leq 1-\beta} \{X_i \in E(P)\} \qquad (1)$$
$$BND_P^\beta(Z) = \bigcup_{1-\beta < Pr(Z|X_i) < \beta} \{X_i \in E(P)\}$$

where $E(\cdot)$ denotes a set of equivalence classes, i.e. the condition classes based on P. The significance of P to D, also the quality of classification, is defined as

$$\gamma^\beta(P, D) = \frac{card(POS_P^\beta(Z))}{card(U)} \qquad (2)$$

where $Z \in E(D)$ and $P \subseteq C$.

Suppose there are m experts, n risk factors, which are independent with each other, in the risk index system. P_i denotes the ith risk factor in the system, $i = 1, 2, \ldots, n$. Decision table is established based on the experts' score of the REL of each software project bid (see Table 1). From formula (2), the significance of P_{ki} to D is

$$\gamma^\beta(P_{ki}, D) = \frac{card(POS_{P_{ki}}^\beta(Z))}{card(U)} \qquad (3)$$

where P_{ki} is the score that the kth expert ($k = 1, 2, \ldots, m$) evaluates the REL of P_i.

Generally, experts' weight is assumed same for convenient. In this paper, we divide experts' weight into subjective weight s_k and objective weight o_k. s_k is endowed according to the advantages of the experts, such as competence, speciality, fame, position, etc. o_k is decided according to the score of experts [5]. As subjectivity and randomness exists in s_k, this study mainly discusses using distance matrix theory to decide experts' o_k.

Combining AHP [6] and VPRS, from formula (3), taking expert k as an example, we construct judgment matrix B as follow.

$$B = \begin{bmatrix} b_{11} & b_{12} & b_{13} & \cdots & b_{1n} \\ b_{21} & b_{22} & b_{23} & \cdots & b_{2n} \\ \vdots & \vdots & \vdots & & \vdots \\ b_{n1} & b_{n2} & b_{n3} & \cdots & b_{nn} \end{bmatrix}$$

We can see that b_{ij} is the element of the ith row and jth column in judgment matrix B, and it denotes the relative significance between risk indices P_i and P_j.

$$b_{ij} = \frac{\gamma^\beta(P_{ki}, D)}{\gamma^\beta(P_{kj}, D)} = \frac{card(POS^\beta_{P_{ki}}(Z))/card(U)}{card(POS^\beta_{P_{kj}}(Z))/card(U)}$$

$$= \frac{card(POS^\beta_{P_{ki}}(Z))}{card(POS^\beta_{P_{kj}}(Z))} \tag{4}$$

As $b_{ij} \times b_{jk} = b_{ik}$, B is a matrix with complete consistency. Obviously, the judgment matrix is always complete consistency when VPRS and AHP are combined to compute the weight of attributes.

We obtain a priority vector for each expert after processing the data in decision table (Table 1). A distance matrix [7,8] is constructed to reflect difference between the score of experts, and we obtain o_k. According to the REL of the risk indices scored by expert k, the geometric mean is used to obtain priority vector W_k. After normalization, the weight of P_{ki} is defined as

$$W_{ki} = \frac{(\prod\limits_{j=1}^{n} b_{ij})^{\frac{1}{n}}}{\sum\limits_{i=1}^{n}(\prod\limits_{j=1}^{n} b_{ij})^{\frac{1}{n}}} \tag{5}$$

where W_{ki} is the weight of P_i decided by expert k, so the priority vector consisting of the weight of n risk indices is

$$W_k = (W_{k1}, \ldots, W_{ki}, \ldots, W_{kn})^T \tag{6}$$

Repeat formula (4)-(6), priority vector of each expert is computed. And the distance between two experts' priority vectors, for example, W_a and $W_b(a, b = 1, 2, \ldots, m)$ is defined as

$$d(W_a, W_b) = \sqrt{\frac{1}{2}\sum_{i=1}^{l}(W_{ai} - W_{bi})^2} \tag{7}$$

where $d(W_a, W_b)$ indicates the difference between the decision-making of expert a and that of expert b. To reflect the judgment difference from one expert to the others, we construct distance matrix D as

$$D = \begin{bmatrix} 0 & d(W_1, W_2) & d(W_1, W_3) & \cdots & d(W_1, W_m) \\ & 0 & d(W_2, W_3) & \cdots & d(W_2, W_m) \\ & & 0 & \cdots & \\ & & & \ddots & \\ & \text{symmetry} & & & 0 \end{bmatrix}$$

Let $d_k = \sum_{j=1}^{m} d(W_k, W_j)$, where d_k denotes the difference in degree between W_k and other priority vectors. The objective weight of expert k shows the evaluating difference of expert k from other experts, and o_k decreases in d_k. Based on this theory, o_k is defined as

$$o_k = \frac{1/d_k}{\sum_{k=1}^{m} (1/d_k)} \tag{8}$$

In particular, when $d_k = 0$, this means that all experts' evaluation is exactly the same. However, this result seldom happens, but if it does, the experts should be reorganized to evaluate the REL once again, and go on the procedure.

The weight of expert k is defined as

$$\gamma_k = cs_k + do_k \tag{9}$$

where $c + d = 1$. We let subjective weight of experts s_k a constant in this paper. By changing the values of c and d, we can adjust the proportion of s_k and o_k within the weight of experts, which means that the model can be applied to different kinds of group decision patterns. Clearly, $\sum_{k=1}^{m} s_k = 1, \sum_{k=1}^{m} o_k = 1, \sum_{k=1}^{m} \gamma_k = 1$.

According to above analysis, experts score the REL of all bidding projects (decision attributes) and their indices (condition attributes). After processing the data in decision table consisting of REL, we obtain the IREL of software projects and their indices. The IREL of index P_i is defined as

$$U_i = \sum_{k=1}^{m} P_{ki} \gamma_k W_{ki} \tag{10}$$

The IREL of project i is defined as

$$V_i = \sum_{k=1}^{m} D_{ki} \gamma_k \tag{11}$$

where D_{ki} is the REL of the ith project that expert k scores. U_i and V_i integrate the evaluation of all experts. U_i decides the risk-evading strength of corresponding risk-evading measures, while V_i indicates the risk of the project and is used to decide whether bidders should bid for the projects or not.

According to above analysis, the algorithm is designed as the following 12 steps:

- Experts are invited to evaluate the REL and decision table is established.
- Choose the variable precision factor β.
- Compute $\gamma^\beta(P_{ki}, D)$ for each risk index P_i, if $\gamma^\beta(P_{ki}, D) = 0$, then remove the indices that meet $\gamma^\beta(P_{ki}, D) = 0$ and define $W_{ki} = 0$.
- Compute relative significance b_{ij} between risk indices for the same expert.
- Establish judgment matrixes based on b_{ij} .
- Compute the significance of each risk index.
- Create priority vectors of all experts.
- Construct the distance matrix.
- Compute the objective weight o_k of expert k: if $d_k = 0$, return to the first step.
- Establish the weight of expert k according to some proportion of s_k and o_k.
- Compute the IREL of projects and their indices.
- Sort the risk-evading strength adopted to corresponding risk-evading measures.

Some literature discusses risk-evading measures in bidding [9]. Generally speaking, risk-evading measures of software project bidding can be summarized as follows:

- (i) mechanism. According to software engineering and experience, a good mechanism is established to improve efficiency of software development and implementation.
- (ii) offer. If the competition is serious, reduce the offer, or else, if the risk of project management is serious, enhance the offer or do not take part in the bid.
- (iii) service. By improving service such as by upgrades, maintenance frees and so on, bidders reinforce their competitiveness to win the bidding.
- (iv) contract. The contract regulates the force majeures and the obligations of each side involved in software projects. So when the force majeure comes into play, bidders do not respond with damages. What is more, the contract can prevent the risk from clients who do not fulfil their obligations.
- (v) outsourcing. Risk can be evaded by outsourcing some part of software projects that bidders are not accomplished in.
- (vi) cooperation. If the project is too large for any one company, bidders may cooperate with other IT companies to finish part or whole of a software project. Complementing each others' advantage, they coordinate to pool their risk.

3   Example

An IT company lists 10 software projects from those are inviting public bids as its bidding objects. Four experts are invited to evaluate the REL of the projects and their indices. The expert team analyzes the risk existing in the software project bidding, and establishes the index system, which includes 5 main risk indices: client risk P_1, ability risk P_2, market risk P_3, development and implementation risk P_4, technology risk P_5. The score includes four levels: 1, 2, 3, 4, where 1 denotes light, 2 denotes moderate, 3 denotes some serious, 4 denotes serious. After assessment of REL, decision table is established (see Table 1).

Table 1. Decision table consisting of REL

U	E_1						E_2						E_3						E_4					
	P_1	P_2	P_3	P_4	P_5	D	P_1	P_2	P_3	P_4	P_5	D	P_1	P_2	P_3	P_4	P_5	D	P_1	P_2	P_3	P_4	P_5	D
1	1	2	1	1	1	1	2	2	2	1	1	2	1	1	1	2	1	1	2	1	2	1	2	2
2	1	2	2	1	1	2	1	2	1	1	1	1	1	1	3	1	2	2	1	2	1	1	1	1
3	1	1	2	2	3	2	1	1	1	1	1	1	2	1	1	1	1	2	1	2	2	1	2	2
4	1	1	1	2	3	1	1	1	1	2	1	1	2	2	1	2	2	2	2	1	1	2	1	1
5	2	2	1	1	3	2	2	2	1	2	3	2	2	3	2	2	1	3	1	2	2	1	1	2
6	2	3	1	1	2	2	3	2	2	2	3	3	2	3	2	2	2	3	2	2	2	2	2	2
7	2	2	1	3	2	3	2	2	2	2	3	3	3	3	2	3	2	3	2	2	2	3	2	3
8	3	4	3	4	3	3	3	3	4	4	3	4	4	4	3	4	4	4	3	3	4	4	3	4
9	3	4	3	3	4	3	3	3	3	4	2	4	4	3	4	2	3	3	4	3	3	4	3	3
10	4	3	3	3	4	4	4	3	3	3	4	4	4	4	4	2	3	3	3	4	4	4	4	4

Here, $m = 4, n = 5$, let $c = d = 0.5, s_k = 0.25, \beta = 0.8$. Based on Table 1 and the algorithm, the objective weight of the four experts are: $o_1 = 0.247, o_2 = 0.328, o_3 = 0.231, o_4 = 0.194$, then we get the weight of experts: $\gamma_1 = 0.2485, \gamma_2 = 0.289, \gamma_3 = 0.2405, \gamma_4 = 0.222$, respectively. So the IREL of software project bidding is as follows in Table 2.

Table 2. IREL, risk-evading measures and strength sorting

U	P_1	P_2	P_3	P_4	P_5	D	measures and strength (descending)
1	0.334	0.386	0.515	0.206	0.086	1.511	(ii) (iii) (vi) (iv) (i) (v)
2	0.220	0.399	0.518	0.153	0.112	1.489	(ii) (iii) (vi) (iv) (i) (v)
3	0.234	0.271	0.523	0.184	0.086	1.711	(ii) (iii) (vi) (iv) (i) (v)
4	0.276	0.324	0.322	0.306	0.112	1.241	(vi) (ii) (iii) (i) (iv) (v)
5	0.398	0.582	0.528	0.261	0.108	2.241	(vi) (ii) (iii) (i) (iv) (v)
6	0.514	0.644	0.582	0.275	0.162	2.530	(vi) (ii) (iii) (i) (iv) (v)
7	0.455	0.554	0.582	0.405	0.162	3.000	(ii) (iii) (vi) (iv) (i) (v)
8	0.675	0.850	1.169	0.612	0.256	3.752	(ii) (iii) (vi) (iv) (i) (v)
9	0.717	0.783	1.033	0.474	0.198	3.289	(ii) (iii) (vi) (iv) (i) (v)
10	0.838	0.825	1.172	0.420	0.230	3.760	(ii) (iii) (vi) (iv) (i) (v)

4 Discussion

From above analysis, we continue our discussion about IREL, risk-evading strength, risk-evading measures and risk-evading methodology.

4.1 IREL

REL is the evaluation on the risk-evading strength of projects and their indices by each expert. In order to enhance the precision of software project bidding risk evasion, group decision-making pattern is used, under which knowledge of multi-expert is integrated, to form IREL.

4.2 Risk-Evading Strength

Risk-evading strength of measures is implemented according to IREL to reduce the risk. According to the experts' experience, the software projects are divided into 3 types and 3 corresponding IREL intervals respectively. In Type I, IREL $\in (1,1.5]$, the projects have low risk. Type II, IREL $\in (1.5,3.5]$, are middle risk. Type III, IREL $\in (3.5,4.0]$, are high risk. The intervals can also be adjusted according to the detail situation.

From Table 2, we see that for projects of type I, for example, projects 2 and 4, the IREL is on the low side. Hence, they need the least risk-evading strength, and the cost of risk evasion can be reduced on this type of project. The IREL of type III projects is very high (for example, projects 8 and 10) and therefore they need the highest risk-evading strength. It is difficult to accomplish the type III projects, and to work out which will most probably have the largest budget deficits. We should reject these types of projects, i.e. not bid for them. A majority of projects have normal IREL, such as projects 1, 3, 5, 6, 7 and 9, and these are type II projects. The IREL of some indices is low (such as P_4 and P_5) which indicates that the indices are less important in the system, i.e. the impact of these indices on the risk-evading strength is low. On the other hand, some of the indices have the greater IREL (for example P_3) which indicates that this index is the most important in the system and it influences the risk-evading measures and their strength most.

4.3 Risk-Evading Measures

Each risk index corresponds to some kind of risk-evading measures. The risk-evading measures are mainly implemented to the projects of type I and II. The study shows: Client risk (P_1) is caused by the tenderee, such as by lack of management support, improper demand orientation, financial crisis and uncoordinated personnel, and the risk-evading measure can be (iv). Capability risk (P_2) includes bidders' assets, relative experience and understanding of clients' demand, and (vi) is a good measure. When there are many bidders, market risk (P_3) is serious, and risk-evading measures (ii) and (iii) are appropriate, i.e. adjusting the offer and improving service. Development risk (P_4) always occurs because of a lack of a good mechanism, and risk-evading measure (i) is needed to improve the situation. If technology risk (P_5) appears, it may cost too much time to continue the project through learning or cooperation, so (v) is a proper risk-evading measure. For a software project, there may be many other risk-evading measures. While, the measures are not always used separately, if all of them are used, their strength should be different. Thus, the risk-evading strength of the measures is sorted, which will help managers know the significance of the measures in practice (see Table 2).

4.4 Risk-Evading Methodology

Patterson and Neailey [10] consider that the project risk management is a circular procedure. The risk management system consists of various tools, techniques and methods underlying the process. They construct the risk register database system within risk reduction stage, and this risk register can be updated as an ongoing and dynamic process. Based on the methodology, the intellectualized risk-evading system (IRES) can be established using expert group decision-making pattern. The IRES can monitor the whole circular process of risk evasion, and process correlative information continuously. As a part of the system, experts make their decisions on the five stages online. Data is updated according to experts' decision-making in each stage within a new circulation, and new knowledge is mined in databases, which means that the decision-making is always the optimal within the context of the current knowledge background. The methodology is a mechanism that system owns the ability of self-study and intellectualised information process.

5 Conclusion

VPRS is a good tool to remove the data noise in the information system, which improves the precision of decision-making. Under the pattern of expert group decision-making, experts are endowed with a weight, which can reduce the negative effect caused by differences in experts' subjectivity and ability difference. The risk-evading strength of the measures increases in IREL of corresponding risk indices, while the risk-evading strength of a project increases in IREL of the bidding project. Sometimes, software projects have too high risk-evading strength to bid for since the IREL is too high and no surplus is expected. Generally, if proper risk-evading measures and strength are implemented for software projects with corresponding IREL, the efficiency of risk evasion will be improved greatly.

Acknowledgement

This project is supported by National Natural Science Foundation of China (70271031) and Ministry of Education (20010487015) and the grant from the NNSF of China and RGC of Hong Kong Joint Research Scheme (Project No. N_CityU103/02). We thank Hubei Bidding Company for providing us with the data used in our experiments.

References

1. Gerardine, D., Brent, G.R.: A foundation for the study of group decision support systems. Management Science, **33(5)** (1987) 589-609
2. Bidgoli, H.: Group decision support system. Journal of System Management, **14(1)** (1996) 56-62
3. Ziarko, W.: Variable precision rough set model. Journal of Computer and System Sciences, **46(1)** (1993) 39-59
4. Beynon, M.: The Elucidation of an Iterative Procedure to ęÂ-Reduct Selection in the Variable Precision Rough Sets Model. LNAI, Springer-Verlag Berlin Heidelberg, **3066** (2004) 412-417
5. Ramanathan, R., Ganesh, L.S.: Group preference aggregation methods employed in AHP: An evaluation and an intrinsic process for deriving members' weightages. European Journal of Operational Research, **79** (1994) 249-265
6. Saaty, T.L.: The Analytic Hierarchy Process. McGraw-Hill, New York, (1980)
7. Hayden, T.L., Tarazaga, P.: Distance matrices and regular figures, Linear Algebra Appl., **195** (1993) 9-16
8. Trosset, M.W.: Distance Matrix Completion by Numerical Optimization, Computational Optimization and Applications, **17** (2000) 11-22
9. Wu, Q.L.: Risk analysis before tender, Chinese Cost Management of Railway Engineering, **1** (2000) 21-24
10. Patterson, F.D., Neailey, K.: A risk register database system to aid the management of project risk, International Journal of Project Management, **20** (2002) 365-374

Research on Risk Probability Estimating Using Fuzzy Clustering for Dynamic Security Assessment

Fang Liu[1], Yong Chen[2], Kui Dai[1], Zhiying Wang[1], and Zhiping Cai[1]

[1] School of Computer, National University of Defense Technology, P.R. China
liufang_nudt@yahoo.com.cn
[2] Department of Computer Science, Trinity College of Ireland, Ireland

Abstract. Effective network security management requires assessment of inherently uncertain events and circumstances dynamically. This paper addresses the problems of risk probability assessment and presents an alternative approach for estimating probability of security risk associated with some interaction in ubiquitous computing. A risk probability assessment formula is proposed, and an estimating model adopting the Fuzzy C-Means clustering algorithm is presented. An experiment based on DARPA intrusion detection evaluation data is given to support the suggested approach and demonstrate the feasibility and suitability for use. The practices indicate that fuzzy clustering technique provides concepts and theoretical results that are valuable in formulating and solving problems in dynamic security assessment.

1 Introduction

Managing network security associated with the growing reliance on information technology is a continuing challenge. Ubiquitous computing is widely believed to be the Internet's next evolutionary stage, and the ubiquity of processing and communicating power will bring a great deal of risk [1]. It is no wonder that security is so difficult to manage. As an essential element of security management, security assessment provides the means by which information systems risks are identified and assessed in order to justify safeguards [2].

Currently, most traditional security risk assessment procedures follow a fairly static process and cannot satisfy the requirements of the ubiquitous computing environment [3]. Yong Chen et al. have proposed a new mechanism for estimating the risk probability of a certain interaction in a given environment using hybrid neural networks [3, 4], which helps avoid subjective judgments as much as possible.

A more flexible, dynamic risk probability assessment is needed. The objective of this study is to introduce the algorithms for solving problems of estimating risk probability, and to analyze the applicability of our approach to dynamic security assessment in ubiquitous computing. A brief introduction to challenges in risk probability assessment is presented in Section 2. A general formulation

D. Ślęzak et al. (Eds.): RSFDGrC 2005, LNAI 3642, pp. 539–547, 2005.

and definition of risk probability is proposed in Section 3. And a two-phase estimating model adopting the Fuzzy C-Means clustering algorithm (FCM) is presented in Section 4. Section 5 discusses the experiment used the approach to estimate the risk probability. Finally, conclusions deriving from the effort are presented and future work is discussed in Section 6.

2   Problems in Risk Probability Assessment

Effective security risk assessment requires typically addressing two dimensions: how likely the uncertainty is to occur (probability), and what the effect would be if it happened (impact). While unambiguous frameworks can be developed for impact assessment, probability assessment is often less clear [5].

However, proper assessment of risk probability is critical to the effectiveness of security assessment, for the following reasons: If risk probability assessment is faulty, the accuracy of risk prioritization will be affected, leading to a potential failure to select inappropriate responses results in failure to manage security effectively. Conversely if assessment of risk probability is sound, then the resulting understanding of each assessed risk will be more accurate, supporting better decisions in terms of response selection and security management strategy [5]. Therefore, it is important to be able to assess risk probability with some degree of confidence.

Assessing the probability of risks is a much more complex issue. There are a number of reasons for this.

The first problem in assessing the probability of risks is the term itself [5]. "Probability" has a precise statistical meaning, for example "A number expressing the likelihood that a specific event will occur, expressed as the ratio of the number of actual occurrences to the number of possible occurrences." [6] However its general usage is less clear, including its use within the security management process.

Setting aside the terminology issue of "probability", there is another set of problems with assessing risk probability. Ubiquitous computing itself exhibits inherent characteristics such as complexity and uncertainty, which have a significant influence over assessment of risk probability. Risk probability is always associated with some degree of uncertainty in ubiquitous computing environment where the goals, the constraints and the consequences of the possible actions are not known precisely. Consequently assessment of risk probability tends to be influenced by a wide range of unknown and unconscious factors, making it even less reliable. The use of fuzzy set theory has become increasingly popular in addressing imprecision, uncertainty and vague-ness. In this paper, fuzzy clustering algorithm has been used.

A further problem with assessing risk probability is that risks are possible future events that have not yet occurred, and as such their probability of occurrence cannot be measured but can only be estimated [5]. It is therefore not possible to measure any characteristic of a risk since it is not present in reality. It is only possible to estimate when the risk would arise.

Consequently, we present an alternative approach of estimating risk probability in an attempt to solve some problems for dynamic security assessment in ubiquitous computing. Historical data and unconscious relations have been investigated and explored as the realistic and useful approach of risk probability estimating is made.

3   Risk Probability Assessment Formula

To estimate the risk probability associated with an interaction in ubiquitous computing, we assume that any interaction in ubiquitous computing environments can be expressed as a feature vector and that the vector elements are comparable. The features must be able to describe an interaction precisely and completely.

To estimate the risk probability of a certain interaction in the feature vector space with n dimensions, the following general risk probability assessment formula is presented.

$$P^i = F(\mathbf{X}^i) + Z^i \tag{1}$$

where P^i is the risk probability of the interaction $i(i \in N)$, $\mathbf{X}^i = (x_1^i, x_2^i, ..., x_n^i)$ is the feature vector of the interaction i, and $x_j^i (j = 1, 2, ..., n)$ are its elements which consist of known parameters for this interaction. The feature elements specify the context of the interaction, participants and relevant historical memory as precisely as possible. Their values are derived from observation and collected data. Z^i is the random disturbance factor, and normally we assume it to be zero [3]. F maps the current context and interaction features to the risk probability. Its specific format may be known or unknown depending on different applications.

When the map F is known, which might be a linear or non-linear function, estimating P^i is not difficult. However, in fact, the map F is often unknown and the dimension of the features vector is very high. For this kind of situation, F is just like a black box passing the current data and historical data as inputs and outputting a risk value [3]. It is worthwhile to note that the historical data is necessary for estimating the risk of the current interaction. However, even for the historical interactions, we only know whether the result of each interaction is unexpected or not. The risk probability associated with the interactions remains unknown. If the historical features vector with confirmed risk probability were known to us, there would be means to find the map F and predict the risk probability for a new interaction.

In order to find the risk probability for each interaction, we present a general risk probability definition [4]. As any interaction is expressed as a feature vector $\mathbf{X}$ with multiple variables, an interaction could be seen a point in the n-dimension feature vector "space" R^n. The similar feature points gather round in vector space and the corresponding interactions occur closely together. Accordingly, the risk of some point depends upon its cluster and unexpected points in its neighborhood [4]. Therefore, we define a general risk probability of the cluster as follows:

$$P_r(\mathbf{X}^i) \approx \frac{U(N_r(\mathbf{X}^i))}{\|N_r(\mathbf{X}^i)\|} \tag{2}$$

where $P_r(\mathbf{X}^i)$ is the risk probability of the cluster with $\mathbf{X}^i$ among it. $N_r(\mathbf{X}^i)$ is an r-neighborhood of point $\mathbf{X}^i$,i.e. $N_r(\mathbf{X}^i) : \{\mathbf{Y} | \rho(\mathbf{X}^i, \mathbf{Y}) \leq r\}$. $\|N_r(\mathbf{X}^i)\|$ is the number of all the points in this neighborhood. $U(N_r(\mathbf{X}^i))$is the number of unexpected points in this neighborhood. Based on formula (2), $P_r(\mathbf{X}^i)$ is also the risk probability of average feature vector $\bar{X}$ in this cluster.

4   Risk Probability Estimating Model

In order to ensure the most robust assessment of risk probability, a two-phase solution is recommended.

4.1   Pre-processing Phase

Factor Analysis
As the history information is usually multitudinous, the need for powerful algorithms is paramount when reducing the data to meaningful quantities. Principal Component Analysis (PCA) technique from multivariate statistical analysis has been employed. It is often used to reduce the dimension of a data set, replacing a large number of correlated variables with a smaller number of orthogonal variables that still contain most of the information in the original data set [7]. The principal components can be shown to be the eigenvectors of the variance-covariance matrix and the eigenvalues give the amount of variation for each component. The first principal component is the eigenvector associated with the largest eigenvalue and so explains the largest amount of variation. Ideally, a small number of principal components will explain most of the variation in the original data. Examining the eigenvalues will give an indication of how many components are needed to give a reasonable representation of the data [7]. So we expand our approach [4] to integrate PCA technique to reduce the data dimensionality and improve the estimation performance.

Fuzzy C-Means Clustering
According to our risk probability definition, when a cluster is confirmed, the number of unexpected points in this cluster could be collected from historical data, from which the risk value is easy to calculate. So clustering historical interactions according to patterns is necessary as a kind of pre-processing in which distinct subclasses of patterns are discovered whose members are more similar to each other than they are to other patterns. Differently, fuzzy clustering formulation assumes that a sample can belong simultaneously to several clusters albeit with a different degree of membership [8].

Fuzzy clustering methods seek to find fuzzy partitioning by minimizing a suitable (fuzzy) generalization of the following loss cost function. The goal of minimization is to find centers of fuzzy clusters, and to assign fuzzy membership values to data points [8].

$$L = \sum_{k=1}^{m} \sum_{i=1}^{n} [u_k(x_i)]^b \ \|x_i - c_k\|^2 \tag{3}$$

where $x_1, ..., x_n$ are the training samples, m is the number of fuzzy clusters assumed to be known (pre-specified), c_k is the center of a fuzzy cluster I_k, $u_k(x_i)$ is the fuzzy membership of sample x_i to cluster I_k, and where the parameter $b > 1$ is a fixed value specified a priori. Parameter b controls the degree of fuzziness of the clusters found by minimizing (3). Typically the value of b is chosen around two [8].

Fuzzy C-Means (FCM) clustering algorithm uses the following constraints on the fuzzy membership function $u_k(x_i)$,

$$\sum_{k=1}^{m} u_k(x_i) = 1, i = 1, ..., n \tag{4}$$

where the total membership of a sample to all clusters add up to 1. The goal of FCM is minimize (3) subject to constraints (4). We can formulate necessary conditions for an optimal solution [8],

$$\frac{\partial L}{\partial c_k} = 0, \ \frac{\partial L}{\partial u_i} = 0. \tag{5}$$

Performing differentiation (5) and applying the constraints (4) leads to the necessary conditions,

$$c_k = \frac{\sum_i [u_k(x_i)]^2 x_i}{\sum_i [u_k(x_i)]^2} \tag{6}$$

$$u_k(x_i) = \frac{(1/d_{ki})}{\sum_{j=1}^{m} (1/d_{ji})}, d_{ki} = \|x_i - c_k\| \tag{7}$$

An iterative application of the conditions (6)(7) leads to a locally optimal solution. This is known as the following FCM algorithm [8].

- Set the number of clusters m and parameter b.
- Initialize cluster centers c_k.
- Update membership values $u_k(x_i)$ via (7) using current estimates of c_k.
- Update cluster centers c_k via (6) using current estimates of $u_k(x_i)$.

The two last steps are repeated until the membership values stabilize; namely the local minimum of the loss function is reached. Specifically, the algorithm alternates between estimating the cluster membership values (for the given values of cluster centers) and estimating the cluster centers (for the given membership values).

Average Risk Rate
For each cluster, the rate between the number of unexpected results of some interactions and the numbers of elements in the cluster is the risk probability of average vector $\bar{X}$, defined as the Average Risk Rate $P(\bar{X})$. We aim to make up risk probability for each vector in this cluster by $P(\bar{X})$. Intuitive idea is to see how close each vector X is to the average vector $\bar{X}$ in the cluster. In our experiment, we give the measure of the similarity for two vectors is,

$$sim(X^i, \bar{X}) = \frac{\sum\limits_{j=1}^{n} x_j^i \times \bar{x}_j}{\sqrt{(\sum\limits_{j=1}^{n} x_j^{i^2})(\sum\limits_{j=1}^{n} \bar{x}_j^2)}} \quad (8)$$

Essentially, this is Euclidean distance between two vectors. As the principal components analysis has been applied firstly for data reduction, the above formula can account for what we aim to achieve in our risk probability estimation.

Summary

We briefly summarize the pre-processing procedure as follows:

- Abstract the features from the historical data to generate the features vectors;
- Using PCA as factor analysis technique, reduce the matrices of data to their lowest dimensionality. Then get the feature vector set $C^n \subset R^n$;
- Using the feature vectors as input vectors, start the fuzzy clustering procedure. And get l cluster, i.e. $C_n = \{I_1, I_2, ... I_l\}$;
- After clustering, select every cluster set from the clustering results, for example: $I_j = \{\mathbf{X}_j^1, \mathbf{X}_j^2, ... \mathbf{X}_j^k\}((j = 1, ..., l))$. Here $\mathbf{X}_j^i(i = 1, 2, ..., k)$ is the feature vector in cluster I_j and k is the number of the features vector. From next step to the end, calculate risk probabilities for every vector in this cluster. Do the same for other clusters.
- Calculate the average risk rate of cluster $I_j((j = 1, ..., l))$, i.e. $P(\bar{X}_j)$

$$P(\bar{X}_j) = \frac{\sum\limits_{i=1}^{k} E(X_j^i)}{|I_j|} \quad (9)$$

where $|I_j|$ means the number of elements in I_j. $E(\mathbf{X}_j^i) = 1$, if the result of interaction associated with $\mathbf{X}_j^i$ is unexpected. Otherwise, $E(\mathbf{X}_j^i) = 0$.
- Calculate the similarity rate between any vector and the average vector $sim(\mathbf{X}_j^i, \bar{\mathbf{X}}_j)$ using Euclidean distance.
- Calculate risk probability for every feature vector $\mathbf{X}_j^i$

$$P(X_j^i) \approx sim(X_j^i, \bar{X}_j) \times P(\bar{X}_j). \quad (10)$$

4.2   Predicting Phase

Since we can make up risk probability for each vector of historical data, the algorithm is also able to apply to new input. The prediction procedure then comprises of following steps:

- Abstract the features from the current data to create a new vector $\mathbf{X}^p$;
- New feature vector as the input vector. Start clustering procedure;
- After clustering, $\mathbf{X}^p$ should be in one of clusters, for example $\mathbf{X}^p \in I_k$.

- Calculate similarity rate of between $\mathbf{X}^p$ and the average vector $sim(\mathbf{X}^p, \bar{\mathbf{X}}_k)$ using Euclidean distance.
- Calculate risk probability for this feature vector $\mathbf{X}^p$,

$$P(X^p) \approx sim(X^p, \bar{X}_k) \times P(\bar{X}_k) \tag{11}$$

where $P(\bar{\mathbf{X}}_k)$ is the average risk rate of cluster I_k.

In order to make the prediction more precisely, each $(\mathbf{X}^i, P^i)$, $i \in N$ could be a pair (input vector, response) with proper network behavior for BP neural network (P^i is the response of vector $\mathbf{X}^i$). Then BP neural network should be trained firstly by all the history data, which is for predicting the new vector $\mathbf{X}^j$.

5 Experiments

The experiments are based on DARPA Intrusion Detection Evaluation Data. In the 1998 DARPA intrusion detection evaluation program, an environment was set up to acquire raw TCP/IP dump data for a network by simulating a typical U.S. Air Force LAN. The LAN operated like a real environment, but being blasted with multiple attacks. For each TCP/IP connection, 41 various

Total Variance Explained

Component	Initial Eigenvalues			Extraction Sums of Squared Loadings		
	Total	% of Variance	Cumulative %	Total	% of Variance	Cumulative %
1	8.022	22.285	22.285	8.022	22.285	22.285
2	4.513	12.536	34.821	4.513	12.536	34.821
3	3.189	8.857	43.678	3.189	8.857	43.678
4	2.955	8.208	51.886	2.955	8.208	51.886
5	1.847	5.129	57.016	1.847	5.129	57.016
6	1.524	4.235	61.250	1.524	4.235	61.250
7	1.191	3.309	64.559	1.191	3.309	64.559
8	1.142	3.172	67.731	1.142	3.172	67.731
9	1.101	3.059	70.790	1.101	3.059	70.790
10	1.012	2.811	73.602	1.012	2.811	73.602
11	1.000	2.778	76.379	1.000	2.778	76.379
12	.994	2.761	79.141	.994	2.761	79.141
13	.966	2.685	81.825	.966	2.685	81.825
14	.932	2.590	84.415	.932	2.590	84.415
15	.867	2.407	86.823	.867	2.407	86.823
16	.848	2.356	89.179	.848	2.356	89.179
17	.779	2.163	91.342			
18	.727	2.019	93.361			

Extraction Method: Principal Component Analysis.

Fig. 1. Distribution of the Clustering Data

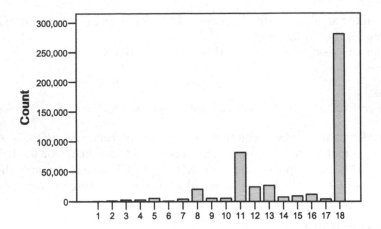

Fig. 2. Distribution of the Clustering Data

quantitative and qualitative features were extracted. The raw training data was about 4 gigabytes of compressed binary TCP dump data from 7 weeks of network traffic. This was processed into about five million connection records. Similarly, the two weeks of test data yielded around two million connection records [9].

We perform an experiment to verify the above approach, using a subset of the data which contains almost 10% of all records. These 494,021 vectors belong to a 41-dimensional space. We apply the linear PCA technique to data sets. And 16 principal components have been extracted which cover 89.179% of the total variation in the data. The result of factor analysis is given in Figure 1.

The 494,021 pieces of data are divided into 18 clusters using Fuzzy C-Means clustering algorithm. And the distribution for the data is given in Figure 2.

Each record is transformed according to the extracted 16 principal components and therefore every feature vector has 16 elements. Only 7 clusters contain unexpected connections (attacks), and the other 11 clusters are all normal connections sets with average risk rate $P(\bar{X}) = 0$. The largest cluster has almost 54% connections while it contains no attacking connection. The risk probability of connections in this cluster is 0 that means a big part of connections are normal. And similarly, we can get the risk probability of new interactions dynamically.

A true understanding for the subject can only be obtained through practical experience. Therefore the material presented here is only an introduction rather than a complete set of works.

6 Conclusion and Future Work

This paper introduces an alternative approach of estimating risk probability that follows will enhance the credibility and ultimately lead to more reliable information security assessment. The proposed approach could respond to new information interactions dynamically and avoid subjective assessment. It is also an extension of our previous work [4, 10]. We are encouraged by the initial results that show the proposed approach can be a significant tool in information security practice.

Further research would be conducted to investigate how clustering algorithm may affect the risk probability estimation. And the potential future work includes conducting sensitivity analysis to evaluate the estimating results of risk probability.

Acknowledgements

The research reported here has been supported by the National Natural Science Foundation of China (No.90104025).

References

1. Hong, J.I., Ng, J.D., Lederer, S., Landay, J.A.: Privacy Risk Models for Designing Privacy-Sensitive Ubiquitous Computing Systems, DIS 2004, August 1 (2004) Cambridge, Massachusetts, USA, ACM 1-58113-787-7/04/0008
2. Carroll, J.M.: Computer Security, Butterworth-Heinemann, Newton, MA (1996)
3. Chen, Y., Jensen, C., et al.: A General Risk Assessment of Security in Pervasive Computing. Technical Report TCD-CS-2003-45, Department of Computer Science, Trinity College Dublin, 6 November (2003).
4. Chen, Y., Jensen, C., et al.: Risk Probability Estimating Based on Clustering. In Proceedings of the 4th IEEE Annual Information Assurance Workshop, West Point, New York, U.S.A., June (2003).
5. David, A., David, T.: Assessing Risk Probability: Alternative Approaches, 2004 PMI Global Congress Proceedings, Prague, Czech Republic (2004)
6. The American Heritage® Dictionary of the English Language, Fourth Edition Copyright© (2000) by Houghton Mifflin Company
7. Multivariate Analysis-Factor Analysis and Principal Component, The Numerical Algo-rithms Group Ltd, Oxford, UK (2000)
8. Gavoyiannis, A.E., Vogiatzis, D.G., et al.: Combined Support Vector Classifiers using Fuzzy Clustering for Dynamic Security Assessment, in Proc. IEEE Power Engineering Soc. Summer Meeting, vol. 2, July (2001) pp. 1281–1286
9. http://kdd.ics.uci.edu/databases/kddcup99/task.html
10. Liu, F., Dai, K., et al.: Improving Security Architecture Development Based on Multiple Criteria Decision Making, AWCC 2004. LNCS 3309 (2004) pp. 214–218

Ensuring Data Security Against Knowledge Discovery in Distributed Information Systems

Seunghyun Im[1] and Zbigniew W. Raś[1,2]

[1] University of North Carolina at Charlotte, Department of Computer Science,
Charlotte, N.C. 28223, USA
[2] Polish Academy of Sciences, Institute of Computer Science,
Ordona 21, 01-237 Warsaw, Poland

Abstract. This paper contributes strategies that minimize the number of values which should be hidden in an Information System to guarantee that values of attributes containing sensitive information cannot be reconstructed by either Distributed or Local Chase within a Distributed Information System (DIS). The notion of the hidden attribute reconstruction by Knowledge Discovery and corresponding obstruction strategy was introduced in [1] where a minimal number of attribute values are additionally hidden to block the reconstruction of sensitive data by the rules extracted from DIS. The problem is particularly troublesome when locally generated rules restore those additionally hidden attribute values, and form a cycle of implications. The strategies in this paper complement existing Distributed Chase obstruction and work over widely used information systems.

1 Introduction

One of the frequently encountered tasks in knowledge discovery system is to protect sensitive information while providing necessary and useful knowledge. An example is that a hospital shares medical information with other health care providers to discover hidden knowledge, but would not wish to reveal sensitive patient record. The task is particularly difficult when we aim to preserve the accuracy of the knowledge. As we improve the protection on sensitive information by (1) hiding or (2) modifying the contents of the information system, more knowledge obtained through the discovery process may not reflect the actual figures. The trade-off is inevitable in most cases, and minimizing the inaccuracy is an important requirement. Between those two protection methods, hiding information from a Knowledge Discovery System is generally accepted as safer and more suitable because it is less prone to incorrect answer for critical decision problems due to the differences between the original and modified information.

In this paper, we assume that sensitive information is contained in an attribute, and the initial protection is provided by hiding the attribute. Additionally, the information system is a part of Distributed Information System (DIS) [9]. DIS is constructed by connecting a number of information systems using network communication technologies. Further assumptions include that these

D. Ślęzak et al. (Eds.): RSFDGrC 2005, LNAI 3642, pp. 548–557, 2005.
© Springer-Verlag Berlin Heidelberg 2005

systems are autonomous and incomplete. Incompleteness [3] is understood by having a set of weighted attribute values as a value of an attribute. The definition of a weighted attribute value and Distributed Information System were proposed by Ras in [7] and used later by Ras and Dardzińska in [8] to talk about semantic inconsistencies among sites of DIS from the query answering point of view. Finally, any meta-information in DIS is described by one or more ontologies [5][6][8]. Inter-ontology relationships can be seen as a semantic bridge between autonomous information systems so they can collaborate and understand each other. Under such assumptions, let's consider the following example.

Suppose an attribute d has to be hidden in an information system $S = (X, A, V)$, where X is a set of objects, A is a finite set of attributes, and V is a finite set of their values. We construct S_d by hiding d, and user queries are responded by S_d in replace of S. The question is whether hiding the attribute d is enough. In order to reconstruct d, a request for a definition of this attribute can be sent from site S_d to some of its remote sites involved in DIS. These definitions extracted or stored in the Knowledge Base (KB) can be used by Distributed Chase algorithm [4] to impute missing values for a number of objects at S_d. If this is the case, additional values of attributes for all these objects should be hidden. Hiding such attribute values in S_d is still not sufficient in cases where null value imputation by Local Chase [2] algorithm can reveal them. This results in the reconstruction of d for a substantial number of objects in X. In this paper, we examine such issues and present efficient strategies that minimize the number of values which should be additionally hidden in S_d to guarantee that values of attribute d can not be reconstructed by Distributed and Local Chase for any $x \in X$.

2   Related Work

Various authors expanded on the idea of secure multiparty protocol [10] to find globally supported rules from Distributed Knowledge Discovery System. Clifton and Kantarcioglou employed a variety of privacy preserving distributed data mining strategies [11][12] to achieve secure association rule mining in such a way that each site extracts globally supported association rules without revealing its own input to other participants. Their works include both vertically and horizontally partitioned data. Du et al, [13] pursued a similar idea, using what they termed "Commodity Server". They observed that it can be preferable to send data to a 3rd party server to improve performance which does not have to be trusted. Lindell et al, [14] discuss privacy preserving data mining for ID3 algorithm using secure multiparty protocol. They focused on improving the generic secure multiparty protocol to achieve better performance on decision tree problems. Another important aspect of research into secure knowledge discovery is sensitive rule hiding by transforming an information system from D to another D' while minimizing side effects. In [15] authors suggested a solution to protecting sensitive association rules in the form of "Sanitization Process". In their work, protection is achieved by hiding selective patterns from the frequent itemset.

Finally, there has been an interesting proposal for hiding sensitive association rules [16]. They introduced the interval of minimum support and confidence value to handle the degree of sensitive rules. The interval is specified by the user and the rules found in such interval are considered to be removed. None of the previous works had addressed the problem of hiding sensitive attribute in Distributed Information System with incomplete data, which we aim to solve in this paper.

3   Chase and Security Problem of Hidden Attributes

In this section, we present a strategy that minimizes the number of values which should be additionally hidden from an information system to guarantee that values of a sensitive attribute can not be reconstructed by Distributed and Local Chase. We present our strategy using an incomplete information system system $S = (X, A, V)$ of type $\lambda = 0.3$ shown in Table 1 as an example. An incomplete information system and its λ value [8] have the following three conditions:

- $a_S(x)$ is defined for any $x \in X$, $a \in A$,
- $(\forall x \in X)(\forall a \in A)[(a_S(x) = \{(a_i, p_i) : 1 \leq i \leq m\}) \rightarrow \sum_{i=1}^{m} p_i = 1]$,
- $(\forall x \in X)(\forall a \in A)[(a_S(x) = \{(a_i, p_i) : 1 \leq i \leq m\}) \rightarrow (\forall i)(p_i \geq \lambda)]$.

Assuming that attribute d needs to be hidden, the corresponding system S_d by applying our strategy is given in Table 2. Attribute values marked with a star character in S_d represent the attribute values that have been additionally hidden in S_d by applying our strategy. A few empty slots in S are filled in S_d by Local chase before the strategy is applied. This will ensure that maximum number of Distributed Chase rules are identified. We begin with hiding attribute values against Distributed Chase in the next subsection.

3.1   Hiding Attribute Values Against Distributed Chase

Suppose the set of rules obtained by Distributed Chase is defined as $R_{DC} = \{r = [t \rightarrow d_c] : c \in d\} \subseteq KB$ (See Table 3). The first step is to look for all rules in R_{DC}, and identify objects where the value of its hidden attribute can be reconstructed. For example, assuming that $d(x) = d_1$ for x in S, if the object x does not support any rule predicting d_1 it is ruled out because d_1 cannot be reconstructed precisely. The object supports a set of rules, it can be either $R_s(x) = \{r_1 = [t_1 \rightarrow d_1], r_2 = [t_2 \rightarrow d_1], ..., r_k = [t_k \rightarrow d_1]\}$ where the rules imply a single decision attribute value, or $\{r_1 = [t_1 \rightarrow d_1], r_2 = [t_2 \rightarrow d_2], ..., r_k = [t_k \rightarrow d_k]\}$ where the rules imply multiple decision values. If we denote support and confidence of rule r_i as $[s_i, c_i]$, and the weight of the attribute value in a slot as p_i, for $i \leq k$, the confidence for attribute value $d' \in V_d$ for x driven by KB is defined as

$$Conf_{S_d}(d', x, KB) = \frac{\sum\{[p_i] \cdot s_i \cdot c_i : [1 \leq i \leq k] \wedge [d' = d_i]\}}{\sum\{[p_i] \cdot s_i \cdot c_i : 1 \leq i \leq k\}}$$

When $d(x) = d_j$ and λ is the threshold for minimal confidence in attribute values describing objects in S_d, there are three cases in hiding attribute values.

Table 1. Information System S

X	A	B	C	D	E	F
x1	(a0,0.3)(a1,0.7)	(b1,0.7)(b2,0.3)	c1	d1	(e1,0.5)(e2,0.5)	f1
x2	(a2,0.4)(a3,0.6)	(b1,0.3)(b2,0.7)		d2	e1	f2
x3	a1	b2	(c1,0.5)(c3,0.5)	d2	e3	f2
x4	a3		c2	d1	(e1,0.7)(e2,0.3)	f2
x5	(a1,0.7)(a3,0.3)	(b1,0.5)(b2,0.5)	c2		e1	f2
x6	a2	b2	c3	d2	(e2,0.3)(e3,0.7)	f3
x7	a2	b1	(c1,0.3)(c2,0.7)	d2	e2	f3
x8	a3	b2	c1	d1	e3	f1
x9	a2	b3		d1	e3	f2
x10		(b1,0.3)(b2,0.7)		d2	e1	f2
x11	a2	b2	(c1,0.5)(c3,0.5)		e3	f4
x12	a4		c2	d1	(e1,0.7)(e3,0.3)	f4
x13	(a1,0.7)(a2,0.3)	(b1,0.5)(b2,0.5)	c2	d1	e1	f1
x14	a3	b2	c1	d2	(e1,0.3)(e2,0.7)	f3
x15	a1	b2	(c1,0.3)(c3,0.7)	d1	e3	f2
x16	(a3,0.5)(a4,0.5)	b1	c2		e3	f2

Table 2. Information System S_d

X	A	B	C	D	E	F
x1	(a0,0.3)(a1,0.7)	(b1,0.7)(b2,0.3)	c1		(e1,0.5)(e2,0.5)	f1
x2	(a2,0.4)(a3,0.6)	(b1,0.3)(b2,0.7)	c2		e1	f2
x3	a1	b2	(c1,0.5)(c3,0.5)		e3	f2
x4	a3		c2*		(e1,0.7)(e2,0.3)	f2*
x5	(a1,0.7)(a3,0.3)	(b1,0.5)(b2,0.5)	c2		e1	f2
x6	a2	b2	c3*		(e2,0.3)(e3,0.7)	f3
x7	a2	b1	(c1,0.3)(c2,0.7)		e2	f3
x8	a3	b2	c1		e3	f1
x9	a2	b3*			e3	f2*
x10		(b1,0.3)(b2,0.7)	c2		e1	f2
x11	a2	b2	(c1,0.5)(c3,0.5)		e3	f4
x12	a4	b1	c2*		(e1,0.7)(c3,0.3)	f4
x13	(a1,0.7)(a2,0.3)	(b1,0.5)(b2,0.5)	c2*		e1	f1
x14	a3	b2	c1		(e1,0.3)(e2,0.7)	f3
x15	a1	b2	(c1,0.3)(c3,0.7)		e3*	f2*
x16	(a3,0.5)(a4,0.5)	b1	c2		e3	f2

Table 3. Rules extracted from DIS by Distributed Chase algorithm

R_{DC} in KB	
$r_1 = b_3 \rightarrow d_1$ (sup = 0.15, conf = 0.90)	$r_5 = b_2 \cdot e_2 \rightarrow d_1$ (sup = 0.12, conf = 0.90)
$r_2 = a_2 \cdot c_3 \rightarrow d_2$ (sup = 0.15, conf = 0.91)	$r_6 = c_2 \cdot e_1 \rightarrow d_1$ (sup = 0.12, conf = 0.95)
$r_3 = a_3 \cdot c_2 \rightarrow d_1$ (sup = 0.15, conf = 0.92)	$r_7 = f_2 \rightarrow d_1$ (sup = 0.12, conf = 0.90)
$r_4 = b_2 \cdot e_1 \rightarrow d_2$ (sup = 0.12, conf = 0.95)	

1. if $Confs_{S_d}(d_j, x, KB) \geq \lambda$ and $(\exists d \neq d_j)[Confs_{S_d}(d, x, KB) \geq \lambda]$, we do not have to hide any additional slots for x.
2. if $Confs_{S_d}(d_j, x, KB) \geq \lambda$ and $(\forall d \neq d_j)[Confs_{S_d}(d, x, KB) < \lambda]$, we have to hide additional slots for x.
3. If $Confs_{S_d}(d_j, x, KB) < \lambda$ and $(\exists d \neq d_j)[Confs_{S_d}(d, x, KB) \geq \lambda]$, we do not have to hide additional slots for x.

Example 1. No additional slot is required to be hidden for x_8 because x_8 does not support any rule that predicts d_1. Object x_4 supports three rules, $\{r_3, r_6, r_7\}$, that predict only d_1. This indicates that $(\exists d \neq d_1)Confs_{S_d}(d, x_4, KB)$ is zero. Because $Confs_{S_d}(d_1, x_4, KB) = 1 \geq 0.3$ we need to hide an additional slot for x_4. In x_{14}, $\{r_5\}$ can reconstruct d_1, and $\{r_4\}$ can reconstruct d_2. The value of $Confs_{S_d}(d_1, x_{14}, KB) = ([1 \cdot 0.7] \cdot 0.12 \cdot 0.90)/0.109$ is 0.68, that is greater than the threshold. However, $Confs_{S_d}(d_2, x_{14}, KB) = ([1 \cdot 0.3] \cdot 0.12 \cdot 0.95)/0.109 = 0.32$ is also greater than 0.3 which makes it difficult to reconstruct d_1 precisely. We do not need to hide any additional slot in x_{14}.

Let R'_{DC} be the set of rules implying the actual decision attribute value in S_d. Then, at least one attribute value from the minimal set of attribute values covering all terms $\{t_1, t_2, ..., t_k\} \in R'_{DC}(x)$ has to be additionally hidden to block the reconstruction of hidden attribute by Distributed Chase. If we sort the attribute values $v \in R'_{DC}(x)$ by overlap frequency between rules, and start hiding them from the largest value of overlap until $Confs_{S_d}(d_j, x, R'_{DC}) < \lambda$, $d(x)$ cannot be reconstructed. This strategy is efficient in minimizing the number of hidden attribute values against Distributed Chase.

Example 2. The minimal set of attribute values covering the conditional part of $\{r_3, r_6, r_7\}$ is $\{a_3, c_2, e_1, f_2\}$ in x_4. Clearly, if we hide c_2 (largest overlap) in object x_4, d_1 cannot be predicted by two rules, $\{r_3, r_6\}$. Hiding f_2 will remove one prediction by $\{r_7\}$.

3.2 Hiding Attribute Values Against Distributed and Local Chase

Now, let's consider the rules extracted by Local Chase that restore the hidden attribute values in the previous step. In order to examine the influence of Local Chase, we first slightly modify the definition of $L(D)$ in [1] in such a way that the set of rules extracted from S_d by Chase is defined as $R_{LC} = \{(t \to v_c) : c \in A - \{d\}\} \subseteq KB$. That is, we are not only identifying the rules that reconstruct null values, but all the rules that can reconstruct attribute values in each column. The set of rules $R_{LC}(x) = \{(t \to v_c) : c \in R'_{DC}(x)\}$ contains the minimal number of rules that imply the conditional part of the global rules in x. Table 4 shows some of R_{LC} extracted by Local Chase algorithm with support = 10% and confidence = 90%. The minimum support and confidence values for R_{LC} should be carefully chosen in order to ensure protection of the information against the rules not generated by Local Chase algorithm. The most reasonable solution would be setting them to the minimum value predefined in Knowledge Discovery engine of DIS. We also assume that the owner of the database has the control

Table 4. Rules extracted from Local Information System

R_{LC}
Rules supported by x_4
$r_1 = a_3 \cdot f_2 \rightarrow c_2$ (sup $= 0.15$, conf $= 1$) $r_2 = e_1 \cdot f_2 \rightarrow c_2$ (sup $= 0.23$, conf $= 1$)
Rules supported by x_{15}
$r_1 = b_1 \cdot f_2 \rightarrow c_2$ (sup $= 0.13$, conf $= 1$) $r_2 = e_1 \cdot f_2 \rightarrow c_2$ (sup $= 0.23$, conf $= 1$)
$r_3 = b_2 \cdot c_2 \rightarrow e_1$ (sup $= 0.15$, conf $= 1$)

over support and confidence value that users can use, and only some Knowledge Discovery packages are allowed to run to extract rules.

In Example 2, two additional attribute values $\{c_2, f_2\}$ are hidden in x_5. When Local Chase algorithm using the rules in Table 4 is applied to x_4, c_2 is reconstructed by $\{r_1, r_2\}$. This means that two more hidden attribute values are needed to block the reconstruction of d_1. The total number of hidden attribute values by hiding c_2 becomes four. What if we had hidden $\{a_3, e_1\}$ instead of c_2? No additional attribute value is required to be hidden. The total number of hidden attribute value remains at three. Hiding the best attribute values for Distributed Chase does not always yields the optimal outcome when Local Chase is considered.

Before we discuss an algorithm that includes both global and local Chase rules, there are two important issues to be addressed when hiding attribute values from an information system. As the number of hidden attribute values increases, the number of local rules are most likely decreased. Several strategies have been proposed for hiding sensitive rules from information systems by hiding attribute values. Using the method presented in [15][16] we may reduce the number of hidden attribute values further. However, following such strategy does not always leads to a positive consequence for our problem because we only have to block the local rules from the objects where global rules reconstruct the hidden attribute. In fact, blocking all such local rules from the information system requires hiding more attribute values, and that is not necessary. Another issue is the number of attribute values to be hidden from a rule. Some attributes might have a unique value throughout the objects. Hiding such attribute values in the rules does not provide high level of protection against Chase. Clearly, incrementing the number of hidden attribute values in the rule decreases the possibility of reconstructing hidden attribute by replacing the hidden slot with unique value. If this is the case, security administrator with domain knowledge needs to set a minimum number of attribute values to be hidden in the rules.

Let $V_c(x) = V_c'(x) \cup V_c''(x)$, where $V_c'(x)$ is the minimal set of attribute values covering the conditional part of the terms in $\{t_1, t_2, ..., t_k\} \in R_{DC}'(x)$, and $V_c''(x)$ is the minimal set of attribute values covering conditional part of the term in $R_{LC}(x)$. For each attribute value $v_i^c \in V_c(x)$, we use the notation $|v_i^c|$ to denote the number of occurrence that v_i^c is a part of conditional attribute values. Then, $|v_i^c|$ represents the number of overlaps between conditional part of the rules. Let $V_d(x)$ be the minimal set of attribute values covering decision attribute values in $R_{LC}(x)$. We denote $|v_i^d|$ as the number of overlaps between decision part of the rules. In order to determine the most advantageous attribute values in x, each attribute value v_i is evaluated with the following weight function.

$$\omega(v_i) = |v_i^c| - |v_i^d|$$

Based on the weight, our strategy is presented in Figure 1. From $V(x) = V_c'(x) \cup V_c''(x)$, we start hiding v_i that has the maximum w and is contained in the conditional part of $R_{DC}'(x)$. This removes the largest number of local and global rules from the object. Rules that include v_i are removed from $R(x) = R_{DC}'(x) \cup R_{LC}(x)$. When two or more v_i has the equal weight, we select one in a consistent manner. (e.g. alphanumeric order of attribute). When all the rules in $R_{DC}'(x)$ are removed, yet reconstruction by Local Chase still exists, hide attribute values contained in $R_{LC}(x)$. We continue hiding attribute values until no rule in $R(X)$ reconstructs the hidden attribute values in $V(x)$, and all the rules in $R_{DC}(x)$ are removed.

Input: $R_{DC}', R_{LC}(x)$
output: $hiddenAttList$

$hiddenAttList = \phi$
begin
   $R(x) := R_{DC}' \cup R_{LC}(x)$
   get $V_c(x) = V_c'(x) \cup V_c''(x)$ from $R(x)$
   loop
      if $V_c'(x) \neq \phi$ then
         $V(x) := V(x) - (v_{max} = max(w(v_i)))$, for $v_i \in V_c'(x)$
      else
         $V(x) := V(x) - (v_{max} = max(w(v_i)))$, for $v_i \in V_c''(x)$
      end if
      $R(x) := R(x) - \{r_1..r_n\}$, where $v_{max} \in \{r_1..r_n\}$
      get new $V_c(x) = V_c'(x) \cup V_c''(x)$ from $R(x)$
      $hiddenAttList := hiddenAttList.add(v_{max})$
      exit when $r \in R(x)$ does not chase $v \in hiddenAttList$ & $R_{DC}'(x) = \phi$
   end loop
end

Fig. 1. Chase obstruction algorithm for an object x

Example 3. $R(x)$ for x_4 is $\{a_3 \cdot c_2 \rightarrow d_1, c_2 \cdot e_1 \rightarrow d_1, f_2 \rightarrow d_1, a_3 \cdot f_2 \rightarrow c_2, e_1 \cdot f_2 \rightarrow c_2\}$. The initial $V(x)$ is $\{a_3, c_2, e_1, f_2\}$, and $w(v_i)$ is $\{1, 2, 1, 3\}$ as shown in Figure 2. We first remove f_2 from $V(x)$ because it has the maximum weight among the rules in $R_{DC}(x_4)$. Also all the rules that f_2 is a part of the conditional attribute are removed from $R(x_4)$, which result in removal of all Local Chase rules from $R(x)$. Now, two Distributed Chase rules remain unblocked. From the newly generated $V(x_4) = \{a_3, c_2, e_1\}$ with weight $= \{1, 2, 1\}$, we hide c_2, that blocks all the remaining rules.

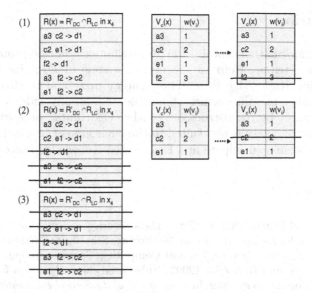

Fig. 2. An example of Chase obstruction algorithm

4   Implementation

To check what is the percentage of attribute values which have to be additionally hidden in S_d in order to guarantee that a randomly hidden attribute d can not be reconstructed by Distributed and Local Chase, we use sampling data table containing 8,000 objects described by 10 attributes. These objects are extracted randomly from a complete database describing customers of an insurance company. To build DIS environment as simple as possible (without problems related to handling different granularity and different semantics of attributes at different sites and without either using a global ontology or building inter-ontology bridges between local ontologies), this data table was randomly partitioned into 4 equal tables containing 2,000 tuples each. One of these tables is called a client and the remaining 3 are called servers. All of them represent sites in DIS. Now, for all objects at the client site, we have hidden values of one of the attributes which was chosen randomly. This attribute is denoted by d. At each server site, we learn descriptions of d using $ERID$. $ERID$ is the algorithm for discovering rules from incomplete information systems, presented by Dardzińska and Raś in [3] and used as a part of Chase algorithm in [9]. We also used $ERID$ to learn descriptions of unhidden attributes at client site. All these descriptions, in the form of rules, have been stored in KB of the client. Distributed Chase was applied to predict what is the real value of a hidden attribute for each object x at the client site. Local Chase was applied to find rules that restore the hidden attribute values by Distributed Chase. A DIS with threshold value $\lambda = 0.3$, confidence value of 85%, and support value of 3% of the rows was used in our example. Total number of attribute values required to be hidden was 1969 (9.845% of attribute values at client table).

5   Conclusion

The sensitive information contained in an attribute cannot be protected by simply hiding the attribute from an information system in DIS due to the Chase algorithm using Knowledge Base. The strategy presented in this paper minimizes the number of values which should be additionally hidden to guarantee that values cannot be reconstructed by either Distributed or Local Chase. We believe that our strategy is well suited to the environment in which a number of information systems participate in a Distributed Knowledge Discovery System.

References

1. Raś, Z.W and Dardzińska, A. (2005) Data security and null value imputation in distributed information systems, in *Monitoring, Security and Rescue Techniques in Multiagent Systems*, Advances in Soft Computing, Springer-Verlag, 2005, 133-146
2. Dardzińska, A. and Raś, Z.W. (2003) Rule-based chase algorithm for partially incomplete information systems, in *Proceedings of the Second International Workshop on Active Mining (AM'2003)*, Maebashi City, Japan, October, 2003, 42-51
3. Dardzińska, A. and Raś, Z.W. (2003) On rules discovery from incomplete information systems, in *Proceedings of ICDM'03 Workshop on Foundations and New Directions of Data Mining*, (Eds: T.Y. Lin, X. Hu, S. Ohsuga, C. Liau), Melbourne, Florida, IEEE Computer Society, 2003, 31-35
4. Dardzińska, A. and Raś, Z.W. (2003) Chasing unknown values in incomplete information systems, in *Proceedings of ICDM'03 Workshop on Foundations and New Directions of Data Mining*, (Eds: T.Y. Lin, X. Hu, S. Ohsuga, C. Liau), Melbourne, Florida, IEEE Computer Society, 2003, 24-30
5. Fensel, D., (1998) *Ontologies: a silver bullet for knowledge management and electronic commerce*, Springer-Verlag, 1998
6. Guarino, N. and Giaretta, P. (1995) Ontologies and knowledge bases, towards a terminological clarification, in *Towards Very Large Knowledge Bases: Knowledge Building and Knowledge Sharing*, IOS Press
7. Raś, Z.W. (1994) Dictionaries in a distributed knowledge-based system, in *Concurrent Engineering: Research and Applications*, Conference Proceedings, Pittsburgh, Penn., Concurrent Technologies Corporation, pp. 383-390
8. Raś, Z.W. and Dardzińska, A. (2004) Ontology based distributed autonomous knowledge systems, in *Information Systems International Journal*, Elsevier, Vol. 29, No. 1, 2004, 47-58
9. Raś, Z.W. and Dardzińska, A. (2004) Query answering based on collaboration and chase, in the *Proceedings of FQAS'04 Conference*, Lyon, France, LNCS/LNAI, Springer-Verlag, 2004
10. Yao, A. C. (1986) How to generate and exchange secrets, in *In Proceedings of the 27th IEEE Symposium on Founda- tions of Computer Science*, IEEE, 162-167
11. Clifton, C., Kantarcioglou, M., Lin, X.D. and Zhu, M.Y. (2002) in *Tools for privacy preserving distributed data mining*, SIGKDDExplorations, Vol. 4, No. 2.
12. Kantarcioglou, M. and Clifton, C. (2002) Privacy-preserving distributed mining of association rules on horizontally partitioned data, in *Proceedings of the ACM SIGMOD Workshop on Research Isuues in Data Mining and Knowledge Discovery*, 24-31.

13. Du, W.L. and Zhan, Z.J. (2002) Building decision tree classifier on private data, in *Proceedings of the IEEE ICDM Workshop on Privacy, Security and Data Mining*.
14. Lindell, Y. and Pinkas, B. (2000) *Privacy preserving data mining*, In Advances in Cryptology - CRYPTO 2000, 36-54.
15. Oliveira, S.R.M and Zaiane, O.R. (2002) Privacy preserving frequent itemset mining, in *Proceedings of the IEEE ICDM Workshop on Privacy, Security and Data Mining*, 43-54.
16. Saygin, Y., Verykios, S.V. and Elmagarmid, A.K. (2002) Privacy preserving association rule mining, in *Proceedings of the 12th International Workshop on Research Issues in Data Engineering*, 151-158.

A Scheme for Inference Problems
Using Rough Sets and Entropy

X. Chen and R. Wei*

Department of Computer Science, Lakehead Univesity,
Thunder Bay, ON, P7B 5E1, Canada
{xchen126, ruizhong.wei}@lakeheadu.ca

Abstract. The inference problem is an unauthorized disclosure of sensitive information via indirect accesses. It happens when generic users can infer classified information from the data or relations between data in a dataset available to them. This problem has drawn much attention from researchers in the database community due to its great compromise of data security. Unlike previously proposed approaches, this paper presents a new scheme for handling inference problems, which considers both security and functionality of a dataset. The scheme uses two main tools. One is the application of rough sets to form a minimal set of decision rules from the dataset. The other is the use of entropy, an important concept from information theory, to evaluate the amount of information contained in the dataset. By analyzing the changes of confidence in decision rules and in the amount of information, an optimal solution can be decided. The scheme is explicit and also easy to be implemented.

1 Introduction

The inference problem is an unauthorized disclosure of sensitive information via indirect accesses, usually via performing inference. A common representation of this problem is that the generic users infer sensitive information from data or relations between data contained in the dataset available to them. Depending on the level of accuracy by which the sensitive information is revealed, full disclosure or partial disclosure may occur.

A conventional way to deal with the inference problem is to prevent inference channels (An inference channel is a minimal set of attributes or relations between attributes needed to perform an inference) from forming. Thus at least one attribute in an inference channel should be trimmed off from the dataset for generic users. Papers considering the inference problem are often classified into two categories. One is to detect and remove the problem during database design (See [1][6][7][8][12] [13][19][20][22]). Methods in this category analyze attributes and relations between attributes. Once an inference channel is identified, one or more attributes are raised into a higher security classification, such

---

* Research supported by NSERC grant 239135-01.

D. Ślęzak et al. (Eds.): RSFDGrC 2005, LNAI 3642, pp. 558–567, 2005.

that the generic user cannot access them without being granted extra authorizations. These techniques often result in over-classification of data, and consequently reduce the availability of data. Methods in the other category deal with the inference problem in the stage of query processing (See [5][9][14][15][10][23][24][25][26]). Advocators of this category believe that this problem can be most effectively prevented since the generic users usually perform inference from the results of queries. Therefore, for a long time users' query history is intensively involved in these methods. Although these techniques allow increased data availability, an obvious weakness of them is that the system has to set up a query history for each user, and the query history of each user is infinitely growing. In other words, they are computationally expensive. In [4][21], accessing key distribution schemes are used to deal with the inference problem. Though the problem is processed in query time, both data availability and response time are considered.

In methods mentioned above, when an attribute is removed from the dataset, all the values of that attribute are hidden from the generic users. Here comes a challenge for the DBAs (database administrators). If only some values of the sensitive attribute are classified, and consequently should be hidden for the sake of security, while the others should be released for the reason of performance and functionality, then how to protect the classified values from unauthorized disclosure? The inference problem exists in this case because the relation between attributes is exposed to the generic users due to the exposure of some values in the sensitive attribute. The generic users can conclude rules from the available dataset, and then infer the missing data by applying those rules. Therefore, in most cases not only the sensitive values, but some non-sensitive values should be trimmed off from the released dataset in order to prevent the generic users from forming rules. We can easily see that there is a trade-off between functionality and security, which means more data should be released as long as the classified data is well protected. Previous efforts[2][3][11] give us inspiration for developing our scheme. In [2], decision trees analysis is used to form decision rules from dataset, and in [3], Bayesian networks is used for the same purpose. But none of them presents an integrated solution like ours in this paper. Our scheme provides explicit computational methods to evaluate both security and functionality of the dataset.

The structure of this paper is as follows. In section 2, we give an outline of our scheme. In Section 3, we show how to use rough sets to form decision rules from the dataset and to apply for inference problem. Section 4 discusses how to evaluate the amount of information of a dataset using entropy. Conclusion is given in section 5.

2 Our Scheme

In this section, we are going to present our scheme. Before getting into it, we feel worthy to dedicate some space to explain the idea of trade-off between security and functionality, which is the main motivation of our scheme.

Let's see an example, which is modified from [16]. In Table 1, attribute a represents "age" with values of "1: young, 2: pre-presbyopic, 3: presbyopic"; attribute

Table 1. Original Database

U	a b c d	e	U	a b c d	e
1	1 1 2 2	1	21	1 2 1 1	3
2	1 2 2 2	1	22	1 2 1 1	3
3	1 2 2 2	1	23	1 2 2 1	3
4	1 2 2 2	1	24	2 1 1 1	3
5	2 1 2 2	1	25	2 1 1 1	3
6	3 1 2 2	1	26	2 1 2 1	3
7	3 1 2 2	1	27	2 2 1 1	3
8	1 1 1 2	2	28	2 2 1 1	3
9	1 2 1 2	2	29	2 2 1 1	3
10	1 2 1 2	2	30	2 2 1 1	3
11	2 1 1 2	2	31	2 2 2 1	3
12	2 1 1 2	2	32	2 2 2 2	3
13	2 1 1 2	2	33	3 1 1 1	3
14	2 2 1 2	2	34	3 1 1 1	3
15	3 2 1 2	2	35	3 1 1 2	3
16	3 2 1 2	2	36	3 1 2 1	3
17	1 1 1 1	3	37	3 2 1 1	3
18	1 1 2 1	3	38	3 2 1 1	3
19	1 1 2 1	3	39	3 2 2 1	3
20	1 1 2 1	3	40	3 2 2 2	3

b means "spectacle" with values of "1: myope, 2: hypermetrope"; attribute c is "astigmatic" with values of "1: no, 2: yes"; attribute d is "tear production rate" with values of "1: reduced, 2: normal"; attribute e is "the optician's decision" with values of "1: hard contact lenses, 2: soft contact lenses, 3: no contact lenses".

Suppose for the reason of security, the value of e of patient 13 is classified as sensitive for the generic users, and the other values are not (See Table 2, in which the classified value is replaced by a question mark).

Now we examine Table 2, is the classified data actually hidden from the generic users? Obvious, this is not the case. Because among the other 39 complete records, record 11 and 12 have the same values in attributes a, b, c, d as record 13. Moreover, values of attribute e for both record 11 and 12 are the same, which is "2". Thus the generic users conclude that the value of e of patient 13 is also "2", which means that patient wears soft contact lenses. The rule can be formalized as $a_2 b_1 c_1 d_2 \rightarrow e_2$ (subscript represents the value of the attribute).

The example shows that hiding only the sensitive data sometimes can not meet the requirement of security. To protect the sensitive data from inference attack, more values should be trimmed off. One option is to hide all the relative values, in our example, all information about records 11 and 12, so that no rule could be concluded from the available dataset (In fact, we will see later that hiding records 11 and 12 will not completely eliminate the inference problem). However, in this case the generic users can no longer access any information about records 11 and 12, that reduces the availability of data, or in other words,

Table 2. Modified Database

U	a b c d	e
1	1 1 2 2	1
.	. . . .	.
9	1 2 1 2	2
10	1 2 1 2	2
11	2 1 1 2	2
12	2 1 1 2	2
13	2 1 1 2	?
14	2 2 1 2	2
15	3 2 1 2	2
.	. . . .	.
40	3 2 2 2	3

the functionality of the database. We called this dilemma the trade-off between functionality and security.

It can be seen that the optimal solution for this problem should maximize both the security and the functionality. For this purpose, we propose a new scheme. We will use rough sets and entropies for explicit computations of the security and the functionality. Based on these computations, we can obtain an optimal solution. Using our scheme, the procedure of handling the inference problem can be described as follows.

1. *Identify and trim off sensitive information from the dataset for generic users.*
   This step depends on the types of database and the users. We will not discuss this in details in this paper.
2. *Evaluate the security of the dataset.*
   Use rough sets theory to form a set of decision rules R from the dataset (See section 3). If the the sensitive information cannot be inferred by employing the decision rules, in other words, there is no inference problem existing in the dataset, end the procedure. Otherwise, go to step 3.
3. *Find out all the possible values which will course inference problem.*
   From decision rules in 2 and the sensitive values identified in 1, find out all the possible candidates which may cause the inference problem. Note that usually, there will be different choices of these values. We will discuss that in section 3.1.
4. *Choose the values to be hidden.*
   Decide the values need to be hidden for reducing the inference problem. We will use entropy functions to compute the functionality of the modified dataset and find out the right values to be hidden. The details are discussed in section 4.1
5. *Reevaluate the security of the modified dataset.*
   Use rough sets to get a new set of decision rules for the modified dataset. This would end in two possible cases. One is that the new decision rules are different from the old rules, such that the sensitive information can no longer be inferred, which means the sensitive information is well protected. The other

case is that the generic users may still infer the sensitive information by applying the decision rules, but the probability of conducting a right inference is reduced. In case that the decreasing is not satisfied, go back to step 3.
6. *Evaluate the modified dataset.*
   Considering the change in security and in functionality according to the requirements of real application. If it is viewed as balanced, end the procedure. Otherwise, repeat the procedure from step 3.

Since we want our scheme to be computational explicit, the main point is to quantify the security and the functionality of a dataset. For this purpose, we introduce rough sets and information theory to estimate these two aspects respectively. By analyzing the changes in them, the optimal solution is able to be computed.

In the next two sections, we are going to show some details of our scheme.

3   Making Decision Rules

In this section, we explain how to use rough sets to deduce decision rules from a dataset. For the definition of rough set and its application to data reasoning, readers are referred to [16].

For the sake of simplicity, we continue to use the example in section 2. We use the 39 complete records in Table 2 to form decision rules. Table 2 can be viewed as a decision table in which {a, b, c, d} are condition attributes, whereas {e} is the decision attribute. The aim is to compute the minimal set of decision rules associated with this decision table. To do that, we first simplify the decision table by eliminating duplicate rows. Since all condition attributes in the table are different, according to rough sets theory in reasoning about data, we say that there is a total dependency between the condition attributes and the decision attribute, i.e. the dependency $\{a, b, c, d\} \Rightarrow \{e\}$ is valid.

Then we need to compute the reduction of the set of condition attributes necessary to define the decision attribute. We can do that by removing one condition attribute at a time from the table, and check if the reduced table becomes inconsistent. It is readily checked that in this example none of condition attributes can be removed. Hence the set of condition attributes is e-independent.

Now we need to check whether we can eliminate some superfluous values of condition attributes. To this end, we have to find out which values of condition attributes are indispensable in order to discern the values of the decision attribute. We know the value core (see [16]) is the set of all indispensable values with respect to e. To check whether a specific value is dispensable or not, we have to remove it from the table and see if the remaining values in the same row uniquely determine the decision attribute value in this row. If not, this value belongs to the core. All core values of each decision rule are given in Table 3.

Knowing all the core values, we can easily compute reducts of each decision rule by adding to the core values of each decision rule such values of condition attributes of the rule, that the predecessor of the rule is independent and the rule is true. Reducts of each decision rule are listed in Table 4.

Table 3. Core Values of Decision Rules

U	a b c d	e	U	a b c d	e
1	- - 2 2	1	13	- - - 1	3
2	1 - 2 2	1	14	- - - 1	3
3	- 1 2 2	1	15	- - - 1	3
4	- 1 2 2	1	16	- - - 1	3
5	- - 1 2	2	17	- - - -	3
6	- - 1 2	2	18	2 2 2 -	3
7	2 - 1 2	2	19	- - - -	3
8	- - 1 2	2	20	3 1 1 -	3
9	- 2 1 2	2	21	- - - 1	3
10	- - - 1	3	22	- - - 1	3
11	- - - 1	3	23	- - - -	3
12	- - - 1	3	24	3 2 2 -	3

Table 4. Reducts of Decision Rules

U	a b c d	e	U	a b c d	e
1	x 1 2 2	1	13	x x x 1	3
1'	1 x 2 2	1	14	x x x 1	3
2	1 x 2 2	1	15	x x x 1	3
3	x 1 2 2	1	16	x x x 1	3
4	x 1 2 2	1	17	x x x 1	3
5	1 x 1 2	2	17'	2 2 2 x	3
6	1 x 1 2	2	18	2 2 2 x	3
6'	x 2 1 2	2	19	3 1 1 x	3
7	2 x 1 2	2	19'	x x x 1	3
8	2 x 1 2	2	20	3 1 1 x	3
8'	x 2 1 2	2	21	x x x 1	3
9	x 2 1 2	2	22	x x x 1	3
10	x x x 1	3	23	x x x 1	3
11	x x x 1	3	23'	3 2 2 x	3
12	x x x 1	3	24	3 2 2 x	3

It is easy to find the minimal set of decision rules now. We can get it by removing superfluous rules from Table 4. Thus the final result can be written as:

$a_1c_2d_2 \rightarrow e_1$; $b_1c_2d_2 \rightarrow e_1$

$a_1c_1d_2 \rightarrow e_2$; $a_2c_1d_2 \rightarrow e_2$; $b_2c_1d_2 \rightarrow e_2$

$d_1 \rightarrow e_3$; $a_2b_2c_2 \rightarrow e_3$; $a_3b_1c_1 \rightarrow e_3$; $a_3b_2c_2 \rightarrow e_3$

Combining all decision rules for one decision class, we get the following decision rules:

Rule 1 : $(a_1 \vee b_1)c_2d_2 \rightarrow e_1$

Rule 2 : $(a_1 \vee a_2 \vee b_2)c_1d_2 \rightarrow e_2$

Rule 3 : $d_1 \vee (a_3b_1c_1) \vee ((a_2 \vee a_3)b_2c_2) \rightarrow e_3$

3.1 Find Out Inference Values

Now we come back to the inference problem. Our purpose is to hide the rule *Rule h* : $a_2b_1c_1d_2 \rightarrow e_2$. To do that, we use the decision rules obtained to "decompose" the hiding rule as follows. Basically, we consider the "and" for *Rule h* and the decision rules of the dataset.

From *Rule 1* and *Rule h* we obtain a rule: *Rule h_1* : $b_1d_2 \rightarrow e_1 \lor e_2$.
From *Rule 2* and *Rule h* we obtain a rule: *Rule h_2* : $a_2c_1d_2 \rightarrow e_2$.
From *Rule 3* and *Rule h* we obtain a rule: *Rule h_3* : $a_2 \lor b_1c_1 \rightarrow e_2 \lor e_3$.

The decomposition gives us strong information that the rule $a_2c_1d_2 \rightarrow e_2$ causes inference problems. This rule involves records 11,12, and 14. For each of these three records, at least one value of the attributes a, c, d or e should be hidden. At this point, we still cannot decide which value to be hidden. We will discuss how to choose the values to be hidden in the next section.

After the chosen values are hidden, we repeat the above process to make the decision rules for the modified dataset. If there is some conflict in making decision rules or the new rules cannot decompose *Rule h* into a meaningful solution, then we solve the inference problem.

In Table 5, 3 more values are hidden from Table 2. Using the same method to compute the decision rules, we will find that the *Rule h_1* and *Rule h_3* are unchanged, but *Rule h_2* is changed to: $c_1d_2 \rightarrow e_2$. Therefore it is difficult to find *Rule h* from the modified dataset.

4   Quantifying Information in Database

In this section, we show how to use "entropy" to evaluate the amount of information contained in a database. In [17][18], entropy was defined as a measure of the amount of information contained in an information source. The entropy function is defined as:

$$H(p_1, \ldots, p_n) = - \sum_{i=1}^{n} p_i \log p_i$$

Where $(p_1, \ldots, p_i)$ is a probability distribution (using base 2 logarithms).

Intuitively, a table containing some missing values provides less information than a table without any missing values. We can use the probability to measure the availability of data. Suppose we select a random entry in a table. What is the probability that the value is not missing? If the table has no missing value, then the probability is 1. Otherwise, we can compute the probability by counting the missing values. However, since we are under the circumstance of databases, it is more complicated than tables or regular information source. We have to consider the distribution of missing values in rows and in columns. Therefore, we need to evaluate the amount of information with respect to both rows and columns. We use H_r and H_c to represent them respectively. If there are r rows in the dataset, then define $H_r = - \sum_{i=1}^{r} p_i \log p_i$, where p_i is the probability of availability of ith row. If no value is missing, then $p_i = \frac{1}{r}$ for each i. If some value is missing

Table 5. Further Modified Database

U	a b c d	e
1	1 1 2 2	1
.	. . . .	.
9	1 2 1 2	2
10	1 2 1 2	2
11	? 1 1 2	2
12	2 1 ? 2	2
13	2 1 1 2	?
14	2 2 1 ?	2
15	3 2 1 2	2
.	. . . .	.
40	3 2 2 2	3

in ith row, then $p_i < \frac{1}{r}$. H_c is defined in a similar way. For instance, we decide to trim the database Table 2 into Table 5.

The entropies of the Table 2 are:

$H_r = 39 \times \frac{1}{40} \times \frac{5}{5} \times \log\left(\frac{40}{1} \times \frac{5}{5}\right) + \frac{1}{40} \times \frac{4}{5} \times \log\left(\frac{40}{1} \times \frac{5}{4}\right) = 5.302$

$H_c = 4 \times \frac{1}{5} \times \frac{40}{40} \times \log\left(\frac{5}{1} \times \frac{40}{40}\right) + \frac{1}{5} \times \frac{39}{40} \times \log\left(\frac{5}{1} \times \frac{40}{39}\right) = 2.318$

The entropies of Table 5 are:

$H'_r = 36 \times \frac{1}{40} \times \frac{5}{5} \times \log\left(\frac{40}{1} \times \frac{5}{5}\right) + 4 \times \frac{1}{40} \times \frac{4}{5} \times \log\left(\frac{40}{1} \times \frac{5}{4}\right) = 5.242$

$H'_c = \frac{1}{5} \times \frac{40}{40} \times \log\left(\frac{5}{1} \times \frac{40}{40}\right) + 4 \times \frac{1}{5} \times \frac{39}{40} \times \log\left(\frac{5}{1} \times \frac{40}{39}\right) = 2.304$

The entropy function has the property that the value of the function increases when the probability becomes evener. For instance, if we hide the value of attribute a of record 12 and 14 instead, then the H'_c of Table 5 would be 2.303.

Finally, we define the information rates of the database as $IR_r = H_r/\log r$ and $IR_c = H_c/\log c$, which reflects the availability of information in a database, i.e. the functionality of a database. Therefore, $IR_r = 0.996$ and $IR_c = 0.998$, while $IR'_r = 0.985$ and $IR'_c = 0.992$.

4.1   Hiding Values

In section 3.1 we find more values should be hidden from the generic users in order to protect the classified information. So we face the challenge of how to choose those values?

We will use information rates to decide the missing values. For each of the possible choices, we compute the information rates of the modified dataset. We will choose one modification which keeps the information rate as large as possible, in other words, the modification that has the largest entropies. We know that the entropy function has the property that the evener the distribution, the larger the entropy. Let's take a look at the Table 2, from section 3.1, we decide to hide one value of attribute a, c, d or e in record $11, 12$ and 14. There are 64 $(P_4^1 P_4^1 P_4^1)$ ways to do that. Among those choices, there are 24 $(P_4^1 P_3^1 P_2^1)$ even distributions, Table 5 shows one of them. We already computed that $IR_r = 0.985$

and $IR_c = 0.992$. If we hide uneven distributed values in this example, we will find that the value of IR_c slightly smaller.

In real applications the importance of different attributes usually varies. So in practice, we can also consider that factor in determining hiding vales. By employing our method and considering the importance of attributes, an optimal solution can be decided.

5   Conclusion

In this paper, we present an integrated, computational solution for the inference problem. The solution contains two main parts. First we use rough sets to deduce the minimal set of decision rules from dataset. Then we use information rates to measure the amount of information contained in the dataset. By quantifying both security and functionality, we are able to analyze the possible changes in them. Depending on these analysis, we suggest a practical way to decide the set of values to be hidden which solves the inference problem.

Our scheme to handle the inference problem is the first one to propose computationally feasible methods for both security and functionality of a dataset. Although some other techniques, such as decision trees and Bayesian networks, were used to form decision rules, we feel that rough sets have some advantages in reasoning about data. For example, rough sets use decision tables to represent data when forming decision rules. Tabular form of representation allows us for easy computation of truth of decision rules, and consequently provides an easy way to simplify the rules. A disadvantage is that inconsistent records are abandoned when deducing decision rules in the beginning. This may cause some useful data excluded because of a small number of noisy data. One possible solution for that is to give some weight to the rules according to the number of same records.

References

1. Buczkowski L.: Database inference controller. Database Security III: Status and Prospects. North-Holland, Amsterdam (1990) 311-322
2. Chang L., Moskowitz I.: Parsimonious downgrading and decision trees applied to the inference problem . Proc. New Security Paradigms Workshop (1998)
3. Chang L., Moskowitz I.: A Bayesian network schema for lessoning database inference. International Conference on Computational Intelligence for Modeling, Control and Automation. Las Vegas, July (2001)
4. Chen X., Wei R.: A Dynamic method for handling the inference problem in multilevel secure databases. In: Proc. ITCC2005 (2005) 751-756
5. Denning D.: Commutative filters for reducing inference threats in multilevel database systems. In: Proc. IEEE Symposium on Security and Privacy (1985) 134-146
6. Goguen J., Meseguer J.: Unwinding and inference control. In: Proc. IEEE Symposium on Security and Privacy (1984) 75-86
7. Hinke T.: Inference aggregation detection in database management systems. In: Proc. IEEE Symposium on Security and Privacy (1988) 96-106

8. Hinke T. H.,Delugach H. S., Changdrasekhar A.: A fast algorithm for detecting second paths in database inference analysis. Jour. of Computer Security 3(2,3)(1995) 147-168
9. Hale J.,Shenoi S.: Catalytic inference analysis: detecting inference threats due to knowledge discovery. IEEE Symposium on Security and Privacy (1997) 188-199
10. Keef T., Thuraisingham M., Tsai W.: Secure query processing strategies. IEEE Computer 22(3) (1989) 63-70
11. Lin T. Y., Marks T. H. , Thuraisingham B.: Security and data mining. Database Security Vol. 9: Status ans Prospects, IFIP (1996) 391-399
12. Morgenstern M.: Controlling logical inference in multilevel database systems. In Proc. IEEE Symposium on Security and Privacy (1988) 245-255
13. Marks D.: Inference in MLS databse systems. IEEE Trans. Knowledge and Data Eng. 8(1)(1996) 46-55
14. Marks D., Motro A., Jajodia S.: Enhancing the controlled disclosure of sensitive information. In: Proc. European Symposium on Research in Computer Security (1996)
15. Mazumdar S., Stemple D., Sheard T.: Resolving the tension between integrity and security using a theorem prover. In: Proc. ACM Int'l Conference on Management of Data (1998) 233-242
16. Pawlak Z.: Rough sets: theoretical aspects of reasoning about data. Kluwer Academic Publishers (1992)
17. Roman S.: Coding and information theory. Springer-Verlag (1992)
18. Shannon C.: A mathematical theory of communication. Bell System Technical Journal 27(1948) 379-423, 623-656
19. Smith G.: Modeling security-relevant data semantics. In: Proc. IEEE Symposium on Research in Security and Privacy (1990) 384-391
20. Stickel M.: Elimination of inference channels by optimal upgrading. In: Proc. IEEE Symposium on Research in Security and Privacy (1994) 168-174
21. StaddonJ.: Dynamic inference control. DMKD03: 8th ACM SIGMOD Workshop on Research Issues in Data Mining and Knowledge Discovery (2003)
22. Su T., Ozsoyoglu G.: Inference in MLS database systems. IEEE Trans. Knowledge and Data Eng. 3(4)(1991) 474-485
23. Stachour P., Thuraisingham B.: Design of LDV: A multilevel secure relational database management system. IEEE Trans. Knowledge and Data Eng. 2(2)(1990) 190-209
24. Thuraisingham B.: Security checking in relational database management systems augmented with inference engines. Computers ans Security 6(1987) 479-492
25. Thuraisingham B.: Towards the design of a secure data/knowledge base management system. Data knowledge and engineering (1990)
26. Yip R., Levitt K.: Data level inference detection in database systems. IEEE Eleventh Computer Security Foundations Workshop (1998)

Towards New Areas of Security Engineering

Tai-hoon Kim, Chang-hwa Hong, and Myoung-sub Kim

San-7, Geoyeo-Dong, Songpa-Gu, Seoul, Korea
taihoon@empal.com

Abstract. Nowadays, computer systems consist of many components such as servers and clients, protocols, services, and so on. Systems connected to network have become more complex, with research focused on performance and efficiency. While most of the attention in system security has been paid to encryption technology and protocols for securing data transactions, a weakness (security hole) in any component may comprise the whole system. Security engineering is needed for eliminating such holes. This paper outlines some novel challenges of security engineering, as well as their relations to other areas of scientific research.

1   Introduction

With increasing society reliance on information, its protection constantly gains importance. Many products, systems, and services are designed to protect information. The focus of security engineering has expanded from a primary concern of safeguarding classified government data to broader applications including financial transactions, contractual agreements, personal information, and the Internet. These trends have elevated importance of security engineering [1].

ISO/IEC TR 15504, the Software Process Improvement Capability Determination (SPICE), provides a framework for the assessment of software processes, but it considers security issues incompletely [2]. They are better expressed by the evaluation criteria ISO/IEC 21827, the Systems Security Engineering Capability Maturity Model (SSE-CMM), and ISO/IEC 15408, Common Criteria (CC) [3].

The main interest of customers and suppliers may lay not in improvement of security but rather in performance and functionality. However, if we realize that a security hole can comprise the whole system, some cost-up will be appropriate. Otherwise, the resulting end product, even if well engineered, may not meet the objectives of its anticipated consumers. The IT products like firewall, intrusion detection systems, or virtual private networks, provide special functions related to security. However, they are not enough to assure global security of developed products – broader understood methodology is required.

Security engineering can be applied to software and middleware of application programs, as well as to security policies of organizations. Appropriate approaches are needed for product developers, service providers, system integrators and system administrators even though they are not security specialists. Generally, security engineering is focused on security requirements for software or related systems. Its scope is very wide and encompasses:

D. Ślęzak et al. (Eds.): RSFDGrC 2005, LNAI 3642, pp. 568–574, 2005.

- security in a complete lifecycle: concept definition, analysis of customer's requirements, high level design and low level design, development, integration, installation and generation, operation, maintenance end de-commissioning;
- requirements for product and systems developers and integrators, as well as both commercial and academic organizations that develop software and provide computer security services and solutions.

Security engineering may be applied to all kinds of organizations, dealing both with high-level issues (e.g., operational use or system architecture), and low-level issues (e.g., mechanism selection or design). Next sections illustrate various aspects of the usage of security engineering techniques.

2   Security Assurance

Software or product developers may use security engineering to gain an understanding of the customer's security needs. Optionally, the product-marketing or another group can model a hypothetical customer, if required. The main objective of security engineering here is to provide assurance about the software or system to customer. Assurance level may be a critical factor influencing purchase.

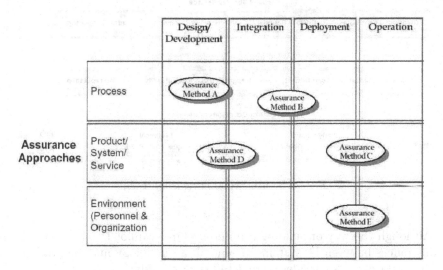

Fig. 1. Categorization of existing assurance methods

Assurance methods are classified in Fig.1 [6,7]. Depending on method's type, gained assurance is based on the assessed aspect and the lifecycle phase. Assurance approaches may examine different phases of the deliverable lifecycle or the processes producing the deliverables. Assurance analysis includes facility, development, analysis, testing, flaw remediation, operational, warranties, personnel, etc. The following novel approach using so called countermeasures is crucial for providing the customers with security assurance control.

3 Security Countermeasures

In general, threat agents' primary goals fall into three categories: unauthorized access, unauthorized modification or destruction of important information, denial of authorized access. Security countermeasures are implemented to prevent threat agents from successfully achieving these goals. It is especially important for storing and processing valuable data. Consider an example of an IT system for web-based support of decision-making. The main problem here occurs when a decision maker cannot trust the display screen or back data reported. In fact, a threat agent might comprise some components and replace some data. The owners of IT systems define security countermeasures to cope such cases.

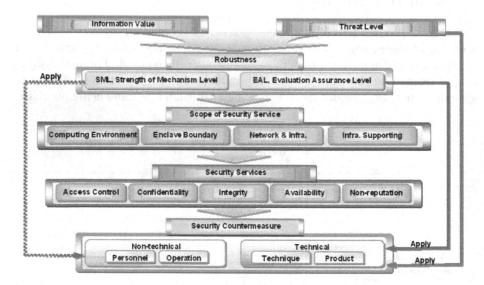

Fig. 2. Security countermeasure design

Although the way of building countermeasures cannot be universal because of differences between IT systems, a general methodology may be proposed, as in Fig.2 above. Let's consider more detailed case study:

1. Determining information value: Information may have different value levels. For instance, invest plan or financial status are very critical. Security engineers may not understand such value. Therefore, it should be decided by the information owners – customers.
2. Calculating threat level: Many people, including rival companies, want to get valuable or critical information. Then, threat agents prepare more high-tech machines and high-quality attacking tools. The level of threat is escalated. It must be calculated by security engineers.

3. Robustness (level of security countermeasures): Evaluation Assurance Level (EAL), as well as Strength of Mechanism Level (SML) for technology, operation and personnel, should be set up high to protect critical information.

4. Localization: Countermeasures cannot be implemented in all places of a system. Moreover, their implementation requests money. Discussion between the customers and security engineers is needed to locate countermeasures. In this study, imagine that we select enclave boundary.

5. Characteristics: We should select the main characteristic of the countermeasure. Here, most attacks will target information stored in databases. Therefore, we may select access control.

6. Implementation: In case of access control, we can use firewall or guard systems. But security systems are not perfect solution. All the systems must be operated by proper security policies and procedures. Firewall systems may be implemented by technical part (product and technology) and operated by non-technical part (operation policy and operator).

4 Software Engineering

The first objective of software development is perfect implementation of customer's requirements. However, if a software component has some critical security holes, the whole system becomes vulnerable. Developers and analyzers must consider some security-related factors and append security-related requirements to the customer's requirements. Fig.3 depicts the idea of the process of defining security-related requirements in combination with implementation of software itself [6,7,8]. This approach can be used, in particular, to include previously designed security countermeasures in the development process.

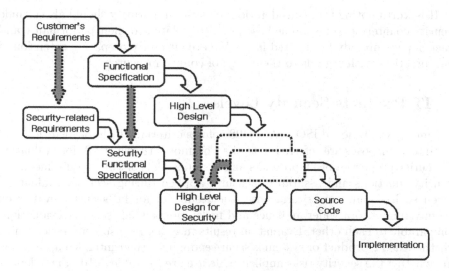

Fig. 3. Append security-related requirements

5   System Maturity

Higher quality products can be generated more cost-effectively by emphasizing maturity of the organizational practices involved [7,8]. Efficient processes are required, given the increasing cost and time required for the development of secure systems and trusted products. Maintenance of secure systems relies on the processes that link people and technology. Fig.4 presents generally accepted levels of system maturity with respect to its security capabilities.

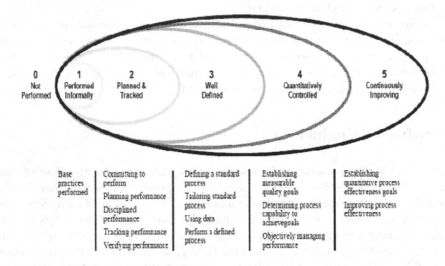

0	1	2	3	4	5
Not Performed	Performed Informally	Planned & Tracked	Well Defined	Quantitatively Controlled	Continuously Improving
Base practices performed	Committing to perform	Defining a standard process		Establishing measurable quality goals	Establishing quantitative process effectiveness goals
	Planning performance	Tailoring standard process		Determining process capability to achieve goals	Improving process effectiveness
	Disciplined performance	Using data			
	Tracking performance	Perform a defined process		Objectively managing performance	
	Verifying performance				

Fig. 4. Generally accepted levels of system maturity with respect to security

It is worth noting that considerations on system maturity should also include security countermeasures. Some base practices related to their performance and efficiency are already formulated in [1]. We are currently preparing extension of base practices with regards to the design of countermeasures.

6   IT Products Security Levels

The multipart standard ISO/IEC 15408 defines criteria, which for historical and continuity purposes are referred as to the Common Criteria (CC), for evaluation of security properties of IT products and systems. CC contains requirements for security functions and assurance measures applied during security evaluation. Given such a common criteria base, the results of an IT security evaluation are meaningful to a wider audience and make independent security evaluations comparable to each other. Evaluation results may help consumers to determine whether the IT product or system is secure enough for their intended application and whether the security risks implicit in its use are tolerable [5,10]. Fig.5 depicts generally accepted level of IT products security.

Assurance Class	Assurance Family	Assurance Components by Evaluation Assurance Level						
		EAL1	EAL2	EAL3	EAL4	EAL5	EAL6	EAL7
Configuration management	ACM_AUT				1	1	2	2
	ACM_CAP	1	2	3	4	4	5	5
	ACM_SCP			1	2	3	3	3
Delivery and operation	ADO_DEL		1	1	2	2	2	3
	ADO_IGS	1	1	1	1	1	1	1
Development	ADV_FSP	1	1	1	2	3	3	4
	ADV_HLD		1	2	2	3	4	5
	ADV_IMP				1	2	3	3
	ADV_INT					1	2	3
	ADV_LLD				1	1	2	2
	ADV_RCR	1	1	1	1	2	2	3
	ADV_SPM				1	3	3	3
Guidance documents	AGD_ADM	1	1	1	1	1	1	1
	AGD_USR	1	1	1	1	1	1	1
Life cycle support	ALC_DVS			1	1	1	2	2
	ALC_FLR							
	ALC_LCD				1	2	2	3
	ALC_TAT				1	2	3	3
Tests	ATE_COV		1	2	2	2	3	3
	ATE_DPT			1	1	2	2	3
	ATE_FUN		1	1	1	1	2	2
	ATE_IND	1	2	2	2	2	2	3
Vulnerability assessment	AVA_CCA					1	2	2
	AVA_MSU			1	2	2	3	3
	AVA_SOF		1	1	1	1	1	1
	AVA_VLA		1	1	2	3	4	4

Fig. 5. Generally accepted levels of IT products security

7   Conclusions and Future Work

As mentioned earlier, security should be considered at the starting point of all the development processes. It should be implemented and applied to the IT system or software products by using the security engineering.

In this paper, we discussed several areas of security engineering, putting a special emphasis on a novel idea of using security countermeasures. There are, however, many aspects and challenges not mentioned here. One of them is development of intelligent techniques supporting security engineers while designing optimal solutions. Nowadays, we can observe applications of such techniques to selected security topics, like e.g. intrusion detection [4], or security hole type recognition [9], which leads to automatic specification of appropriate recovery steps. However, more broad applications of data mining and intelligent design would be worth considering within security engineering methodology.

References

1. ISO. ISO/IEC 21827 Information technology - Systems Security Engineering Capability Maturity Model (SSE-CMM)
2. ISO. ISO/IEC TR 15504-2,5:1998 Information technology - Software process assessment - Parts 2,5
3. ISO. ISO/IEC 15408-1,2,3:1999 Information technology - Security techniques - Evaluation criteria for IT security - Parts 1,2,3
4. Cha, B.-R., Park, K.-W., Seo, J.-H.: Neural Network Techniques for Host Anomaly Intrusion Detection Using Fixed Pattern Transformation. In: ICCSA. LNCS 3481 (2005) 254-263
5. Kim, H.-K., Kim, T.-H., Kim, J.-S.: Reliability Assurance in Development Process for TOE on the Common Criteria. In: 1st ACIS International Conference on SERA (2003)
6. Kim, T.-H.: Approaches and Methods of Security Engineering. In: ICCMSE (2004)
7. Kim, T.-H., No, B.-G., Lee, D.-C.: Threat Description for the PP by Using the Concept of the Assets Protected by TOE. In: ICCS. LNCS 2660 (2003) 4, 605-613
8. Kim, T.-H., Lee, T.-S., Kim, M.-C., Kim, S.-M.: Relationship Between Assurance Class of CC and Product Development Process. In: The 6th Conference on Software Engineering Technology, SETC (2003)
9. Lee, W., Stolfo, S.J., Chan, P.K., Eskin, E., Fan, W., Miller, M., Hershkop, S., Zhang, J.: Real Time Data Mining-based Intrusion Detection. IEEE (2001)
10. Snouffer, R., Lee, A., Oldehoeft, A.: A Comparison of the Security Requirements for Cryptographic Modules. FIPS 140-1 and FIPS 140-2, NIST Special Publication (2001) 800-829

Application of Variable Precision Rough Set Model and Neural Network to Rotating Machinery Fault Diagnosis

Qingmin Zhou[1], Chenbo Yin[2], and Yongsheng Li[2]

[1] School of Information Science and Engineering,
Nanjing University of Technology, 210009 Nanjing, China
mse@njut.edu.cn
[2] School of Mechanical and Power Engineering,
Nanjing University of Technology, 210009 Nanjing, China
yinchenbo@njut.edu.cn

Abstract. An integration method of variable precision rough set and neural network for fault diagnosis is presented and used in rotary machinery fault diagnosis. The method integrates the ability of variable precision rough set on reduction of diagnosis information system and that of neural network for fault classification. Typical faults of rotating machinery were simulated in our rotor test-bed. The power spectrum data are used as rotating machinery fault diagnosis signal. For inconsistent data and noise data in power spectrum, variable precision rough set model allows a flexible region of lower approximations by precision variables. By attribute reduction based on variable precision rough set, redundant attributes are identified and removed. The reduction results are used as the input of neural network. The diagnosis results show that the proposed approach for input dimension reduction in neural network is very effective and has better learning efficiency and diagnosis accuracy.

1 Introduction

Fault diagnosis can generally be treated as a pattern classification task [8]. Neural network for pattern recognition has good adaptability and self-learning ability, which makes neural network to be applied in fault diagnosis [4], [11]. For applications of fault diagnosis it requires outputs with high accuracy, especially for fault diagnosis of rotating machinery. However, neural network based fault diagnosis systems is often too slow and inefficient. The main reason is that neural network can't deal with the redundant information from the fault diagnosis vibration signal. The redundant information will easily lead to some problems such as too complex network structure, long training time and even diagnosis mistakes. Because of these disadvantages the further application of neural network in the fault diagnosis is limited. Rough set theory is a mathematical tool for dealing with vagueness and uncertainty, which was introduced and studied by Z. Pawlak [9],[10]. In the rough set theory, the approximation region is determined through

D. Ślęzak et al. (Eds.): RSFDGrC 2005, LNAI 3642, pp. 575–584, 2005.

the indiscernible relations and classes. By the knowledge reduction, the redundant information is deleted and the classified knowledge rules are induced. As an extension of original rough set model, the variable precision rough set (VPRS) model is defined by W. Ziarko [6],[13]. This model inherits all basic mathematical properties of the original rough set model but allows for a predefined precision level β, which can avoid high sensitivity of computation to small misclassification errors. This is an important extension which will give us a new way to deal with the noisy data such as fault diagnosis vibration signal.

VPRS model and neural network show respectively advantages in fault diagnosis. How to integrate VPRS model and neural network together and make use of their respective advantages for fault diagnosis is an important issue. In this paper, VPRS model is taken as a preprocessing unit of fault diagnosis neural network. By VPRS model, redundant diagnosis information is reduced and the reduction results are handled as inputs of neural network. Therefore, dimensions of input data are decreased and structures of neural network are improved. For rotary machinery, typical faults were simulated in our rotor test-bed. The power spectrum data are used as rotating machinery fault diagnosis signal. For inconsistent data and noise data in power spectrum, VPRS model allows a flexible region of lower approximations by precision variables. The diagnosis results show that the proposed approach has better learning efficiency and diagnosis accuracy.

2   An Overview of Variable Precision Rough Set Model

VPRS model extends the original rough set model by relaxing its strict definition of the approximation boundary using a predefined precision level β. Hence some boundary regions are included in the positive region. It uses 'majority inclusion' relations for classification rather than 'equivalence relation' of original rough set [3]. Therefore, the VPRS model enhances discovery capabilities of the original rough set model and tolerates the inconsistent data of information system.

For a given information system $S = (U, A, V, f)$, $X \subseteq U$, $B \subseteq A$, lower approximation and upper approximation are defined with precision level β. The value β denotes the proportion of correct classifications [1], in this case, the domain of β is $0.5 < \beta \leq 1$. $\underline{B}^{\beta}(X)$ and $\overline{B}^{\beta}(X)$ are respectively called the lower and upper approximation of X with precision level β.

$$\underline{B}^{\beta}(X) = \bigcup \{[x]_B : P(X/[x]_B) \geq \beta\} \tag{1}$$

$$\overline{B}^{\beta}(X) = \bigcup \{[x]_B : P(X/[x]_B) > 1 - \beta\} \tag{2}$$

Here, $[x]_B$ is the equivalence class, $x \in U$. $P(X/[x]_B)$ is referred as conditional probability function [2],[3],[13].

$$P(X/[x]_B) = |X \cap [x]_B|/|[x]_B| \tag{3}$$

Where $|X|$ is the cardinality of the set X.

The β-positive, β-negative and β-boundary regions are defined by

$$POS_B^\beta(X) = \bigcup \{[x]_B : P(X/[x]_B) \geq \beta\} \tag{4}$$

$$NEG_B^\beta(X) = \bigcup \{[x]_B : P(X/[x]_B) \leq 1 - \beta\} \tag{5}$$

$$BN_B^\beta(X) = \bigcup \{[x]_B : P(X/[x]_B) \in (1 - \beta, \beta)\} \tag{6}$$

As β decreases, the boundary region of the VPRS model becomes narrower. That is to say, the size of the uncertain region is reduced. When $\beta = 1$, VPRS model can come back to the original rough set model.

For a given information system $S = (U, A, V, f)$, $A = C \bigcup D$, C is called condition attribute set, while D is called decision attribute set. $X \subseteq U$, $B \subseteq C$. The rough degree of uncertainty can be measured by β-accuracy $\alpha_B^\beta(x)$.

$$\alpha_B^\beta(x) = \left| \underline{B}^\beta(X) \right| \Big/ \left| \overline{B}^\beta(X) \right| \quad . \tag{7}$$

The measure of classification quality is defined by β-dependability as follows:

$$\gamma^\beta(B, D) = \frac{\left| \bigcup \{[x]_B : |X \cap [x]_B| / |[x]_B| \geq \beta\} \right|}{|U|} \quad . \tag{8}$$

The β-dependability $\gamma^\beta(B, D)$ measures the proportion of objects in the universe, for which the classification is possible with the precision level β.

In VPRS model, knowledge reduction is aimed to select the minimum attribute subsets of C which don't change the quality of classification with the precision level β[2],[13]. Assumed $red^\beta(C, D)$ is β approximate reduction, then

$$\gamma^\beta(C, D) = \gamma^\beta(red^\beta(C, D), D) \tag{9}$$

If any one attribute from $red^\beta(C, D)$ is eliminated, the formula (9) will be invalid. In other words, no proper subset of $red^\beta(C, D)$ at the same β value can also give the same quality of classification. A decision system may have many β- reductions. The intersection of all reductions is called core. People always pay attention to the minimal reduction sets that has the least attributes. However, it has been proved that the minimal reductions of the decision system are the NP-hard [12]. It is most important to find a reduction algorithm with low computation cost.

For decision system $S = (U, A, V, f)$, $A = C \bigcup D$, let $D = \{d\}$, $V_d = \{1, 2, ..., n\}$, then $U/D = \{Y_1, Y_2, ..., Y_n\}$, the decision class $Y_i = \{x \in U, d(x) = i\}$. In VPRS model, for each $x \in \underline{B}^\beta(Y_i)$ a decision rule may be generated as follows

$$\bigwedge_{r \in C} (r, r(x)) \rightarrow d(x) = i. \tag{10}$$

3 Model of VPRS and Neural Network for Fault Diagnosis

In fault diagnosis, there are not one to one definite relations between the fault reasons and the fault symptoms with relatively high information redundancy.

We always try to decrease redundance of diagnostic information by reduction. In the process of reduction, useful information is kept and redundant information is removed. However, too much absence of redundance will result in high sensitive to even small misclassification errors, which is also the essential reason in producing weak generalization and admissible error performance in original rough sets model [7]. The VPRS model can effectively eliminate the redundant information to reveal the diagnosis rules by means of reduction and mining. But it allows a predefined precision level β to deal with the noisy data, which can avoid high sensitivity of computation to small misclassification errors.

For decision system $S = (U, A, V, f)$, $A = C \bigcup D$, U is fault sample, condition attribute C is the fault symptom set; Decision attribute D corresponds with the result of the fault classification. First, we can ascertain the appropriate precision level β. For noisy domains or inconsistent data, β takes smaller value, otherwise β takes bigger value. For the discretized decision table, we calculate its upper and lower approximation sets with precision level β, β-accuracy and β-dependability. The ability of approximate classification of the decision table can be evaluated at precision level β. Subsequently, reduction of decision table is made. For condition attribute reduction, the condition attributes are checked whether all the attributes are indispensable. If the classification ability of decision table is not changed by eliminating an attribute, then this attribute can be deleted, otherwise it can't be deleted.

For neural network large number of redundance allow the system have a good performance on generalization, adaptive error, noise restrained and self-organization performance [7]. However, too much redundance results in defects of neural network, i.e., complex structure and time consuming .VPRS model can be used for attribute reduction at precision level β. By attribute reduction, unnecessary redundance is identified and removed. The reduction set of attributes can be regarded as input of neural network. The output of neural network corresponds to conclusion of the diagnostic rules. The diagnostic rules prediction accuracy can be tested by using neural network for fault testing samples. The model of fault diagnosis based on VPRS and neural network is shown in Fig.1.

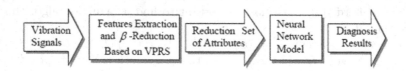

Fig. 1. The model of fault diagnosis based on VPRS and neural network

4   Application of VPRS Model and Neural Network for Rotating Machinery Fault Diagnosis

The application system of VPRS and neural network for rotating machinery fault diagnosis consists of four modules: experiment, data preparation, β-reduction based on VPRS and neural network model training. Vibration signals data from experiment are divided into two parts, that is, training samples and testing samples. Continuous attributes of training samples and testing samples must be discretized. Then the decision table is dealt with VPRS model and neural network model. Neural network is trained after being reduced. In general, the three-layer BP neural network is suitable for fault diagnosis of rotating machinery. Therefore BP neural network is used as classification model in our work. We select some of the reduction sets to train BP neural network. At last the outputs from all trained BP neural network are combined with the diagnosis classification results and are tested by fault testing samples.

4.1   Experimental Data Analysis

In fault diagnosis, many feature parameters can be used to reflect working state of equipments. But it is impossible to use all parameters to judge whether equipments work normally. We can only extract the necessary fault feature attributes and from these features obtain diagnosis rules. For fault diagnosis of rotating machinery, time domain, frequency domain and amplitude value domain can be regarded as fault features. Because the vibration signals of rotating machinery in the frequency domain are obvious, the frequency domain feature of vibration signals is regarded as main fault feature. The damage extent of fault is evaluated by energy distribution of frequency. The power spectrum data is smaller influenced by noise than the time series data. From this reason in this paper power spectrum data is used as fault diagnosis signal. Power spectrum represents the distribution of signal energy with frequency. Typical faults of rotating machinery were simulated in our rotor test-bed. Among the rotating equipments, rotor unbalance, oil-film whirl, rotor misalignment and rotor frictional impact faults are the common faults. Figures 2 ∼ 5 illustrate four typical faults power spectrum of rotor collected from our rotor experiments, where the rotor rotation speed is 4860 r/min and sampling frequency is 2560 Hz. The segment data of 0 ∼1000 Hz are given in figures.

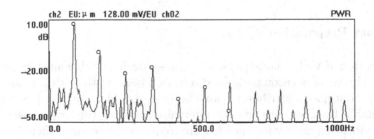

Fig. 2. Power spectrum of rotor unbalance fault

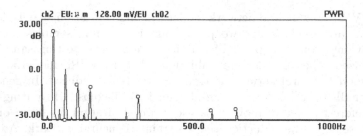

Fig. 3. Power spectrum of oil-film whirl fault

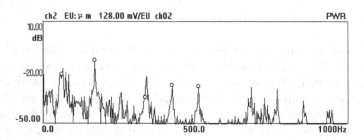

Fig. 4. Power spectrum of rotor misalignment fault

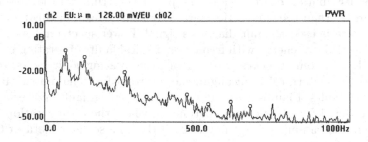

Fig. 5. Power spectrum of rotor frictional impact fault

4.2   Data Preparation

In application of VPRS model, a fault diagnosis decision table must be first built. Then, attributes of decision table are discretized because the VPRS model cannot deal with continuous attributes. Fault feature should be selected by removing unreasonable features with narrow intervals. Suppose that E_V is the average value of vibration energy for each feature frequency spectrum, then

$$E_V = \sqrt{\sum_{j=1}^{n} A_j^2} \bigg/ \sqrt{N_{BF}} \tag{11}$$

Where A_j is the amplitude of FFT spectrum; N_{BF} is the width of noise band with window (for Hamming window, $N_{BF} = 1.5$). By calculating the average value of vibration energy E_V and choosing a proper threshold μ [5], the attribute value C_i of decision table can be calculated.

If $E_V \geq \mu$ Then $C_i = "1"$ Else $C_i = "0"$
$C_i = "1"$ represents abnormal spectrum; $C_i = "0"$ represents normal spectrum.

4.3 Fault Features Reduction and Neural Network Training

Fault features are extracted by approximate reduction of VPRS model. By the reduction redundant condition attributes are deleted and important attributes which influence classification are reserved at a predefined precision level β. Several different reduction sets can be got from the fault training samples. Each reduction is a representation of the samples which don't change the quality of classification with the precision level β. BP Neural network is trained by difference reduction sets. At last the outputs from all trained BP neural network are combined with the diagnosis classification results and are tested by fault testing samples. The process of fault diagnosis based on VPRS model and neural network is shown as following steps.

Step 1. Vibration signals data from experiment are divided into training samples and testing samples. Continuous attributes are discretized.

Step 2. Fault diagnosis decision table $S = (U, A, V, f)$ is built, and the same samples are combined.

Step 3. Computing respectively all equivalence classes for fault symptom sets C and fault type sets D, namely $U/C = \{X_1, X_2, ..., X_i\}$ and $U/D = \{Y_1, Y_2, ..., Y_j\}$.

Step 4. For inconsistent equivalence class X_i, computing respectively conditional probability function $P(Y_j/X_i)$.

Step 5. The appropriate precision level β is ascertained. For a given probability value β, the β-positive region corresponding to a concept is delineated as a set of objects with conditional probabilities of allocation at least equal to β. For noisy domains or inconsistent data, β takes smaller value, otherwise, β takes bigger value.

Step 6. Lower approximation $\underline{B}^\beta(X)$ and upper approximation $\overline{B}^\beta(X)$ are calculated with precision level β. Then its β-accuracy $\alpha_B^\beta(x)$ and β-dependability $\gamma^\beta(B, D)$ are calculated.

Step 7. The fault symptom sets (condition attributes) are reduced. The core of the condition attribute reduction is calculated.

Step 8. A three-layers BP neural network is constructed that includes input layer, hidden layer and output. The training of BP neural network is performed with the reduction set. Attributes of reduction set are regarded as input layer $X_n = \{X_{n1}, X_{n2}, ..., X_{ni}\}^T$; The output layer corresponds to the conclusion of the diagnostic rules, $Y_n = \{Y_{n1}, Y_{n2}, ..., Y_{nj}\}^T$.

Step 9. In the training process of neural network, if the average quadratic error $\delta \leq 0.001$, the learning is successful. Otherwise go to step 8.

Step 10. The samples that cannot be learned by BP neural network are deleted from the training samples. And diagnostic rules are acquired.

Step 11. The diagnostic rules prediction accuracy is tested by using the BP neural network for the testing samples.

Step 12. Diagnosis results are analyzed and synthesized.

4.4 Examples

By rotor experiments 150 groups sample data of rotor fault are collected and are divided into training and testing samples. The training samples include 80 samples shown in table 1. The 70 testing samples are used for testing. $U = \{x_1, x_2, ..., x_{80}\}$ is a finite sets of the fault samples; The condition attribute $C = \{c_1, c_2, ..., c_8\}$ is the fault symptom set, and $c_1, c_2, ..., c_8$ indicate respectively frequency range, here f_0 is rotating frequency. Decision attribute D means the fault type. $D = \{1, 2, 3, 4\}$ means the sample has respectively the rotor unbalance, oil-film whirl, rotor misalignment and rotor frictional impact faults symptom.

Table 1. Fault diagnosis cases

U	0.01~ 0.39f_0 c_1	0.40~ 0.49 f_0 c_2	0.5f_0 c_3	0.51~ 0.99f_0 c_4	f_0 c_5	2f_0 c_6	3f_0 c_7	5f_0 c_8	D
x_1	-29.11	-30.65	-32.76	-11.20	9.68	-21.07	-19.18	-18.50	1
x_2	-20.19	24.05	22.86	19.06	0	-14.43	-28.81	-17.66	2
x_3	-40.12	-44.45	-47.78	-22.56	-9.83	-8.24	-19.86	-34.65	3
x_4	-42.83	-43.67	-32.71	-21.06	-5.36	-6.98	-14.29	-19.86	4
...	...	...	...	...	...	...	...	...	...
x_{80}	-34.51	-30.46	-28.77	-16.83	7.70	-23.19	-18.43	-15.32	1

Because the reference point of power spectrum obtained from the rotor test-bed does not lie in zero point, so it must be converted to zero reference point. The maximum point of absolute value of negative number is as zero point during computing. Then the attributes of decision table are discretized, the attribute value is $\{1, 0\}$, which represents respectively abnormal spectrum and normal spectrum. The decision table of fault diagnosis is built, see table 2.

Because the power spectrum data have smaller influence by noise, we take $\beta = 0.8$. Then its β-accuracy and β-dependability are calculated. When $\beta = 0.8$,

Table 2. The decision table of fault diagnosis

U	0.01~0.39f_0 c_1	0.40~0.49f_0 c_2	0.5f_0 c_3	0.51~0.99f_0 c_4	f_0 c_5	2f_0 c_6	3f_0 c_7	5f_0 c_8	D
x_1	0	0	0	1	1	0	0	0	1
x_2	0	1	1	1	0	0	0	0	2
x_3	0	0	0	1	1	1	1	0	3
x_4	0	0	0	0	1	1	1	0	4
...	...	...	...	...	...	...	...	...	...
x_{80}	0	0	0	0	1	0	0	0	1

Table 3. Classification rules for reduction subset $\{c_2, c_5, c_6, c_7\}$

Rules	
$c_2 = 0 \wedge c_5 = 1 \rightarrow D = 1$	$c_2 = 1 \wedge c_5 = 0 \rightarrow D = 2$
$c_5 = 1 \wedge c_6 = 0 \wedge c_7 = 0 \rightarrow D = 1$	$c_5 = 1 \wedge c_6 = 1 \rightarrow D = 3$
$c_2 = 1 \rightarrow D = 2$	$c_5 = 1 \wedge c_6 = 1 \wedge c_7 = 1 \rightarrow D = 4$

it results that $\alpha_B^\beta(x)$ is equal to 1.0 and $\gamma^\beta(B, D)$ to 1.0. This indicates that the approximate classification ability of decision table with precision level $\beta = 0.8$ is accord with request. We deal with the knowledge reduction with precision level $\beta = 0.8$. The reduced results of fault symptom sets are: the core of the condition attribute reduction is empty; there are six the simplest reduction subsets of condition attribute C relatively to decision attribute D. They are $\{c_2, c_5, c_6, c_7\}, \{c_3, c_5, c_7, c_8\}, \{c_6, c_7, c_8\}, \{c_2, c_4, c_5\}, \{c_3, c_5, c_6\}$ and $\{c_2, c_5, c_8\}$. The different reduction sets as inputs of BP neural network are selected and the diagnostic rules by training and learning of neural network are acquired.

Limited by the length of the paper, we only provide the rule sets for reduction subset $\{c_2, c_5, c_6, c_7\}$. The performance of the BP neural network with reduced 4-input dimension is compared with the original 8 inputs, which the number of network input nerve cells is effectively decreased. The structures of BP neural network are 4-6-4, namely, 4-input nodes, 6-hidden nodes and 4-output nodes. During training, if $\delta \leq 0.001$, then learning is successful. In the training process for reduction subsets $\{c_2, c_5, c_6, c_7\}$, diagnostic rules are acquired in table 3.

Similarly, we use this method to extract diagnostic rules for other reduction subsets. For six reduction subsets in this example, in all we extracted 21 diagnostic decision rules. These rules are tested by testing samples, where its correct rate of the diagnosis is 0.803 for all samples. Therefore, we can certain that the integration method of VPRS and neural network for rotating machinery fault diagnosis has better learning efficiency and diagnosis accuracy.

5   Conclusions

The method based on VPRS model and neural network is applied to fault diagnosis of rotating machinery, where the aim is to solve fault features extraction and diagnostic rules acquisition. The data information of fault diagnosis is obtained directly from vibration signal system in which noisy data and uncertain information exists. VPRS model can effectively eliminate the redundant fault attributes, and it allows for a precision variable to deal with the noisy data. High sensitivity of computation to small misclassification errors in diagnosis system is avoided by VPRS model. Simulation results for rotating machinery fault diagnosis show that the proposed approach is effective in reducing the redundancy of neural network and extracting the accurate diagnosis rules. The cost of computing is decreased and real-time diagnosis becomes possible. In further research, it is being considered how the precision variable in different diagnosis systems are reasonable chosen and diagnosis accuracy is further improved.

References

1. An, A., Shan, N., Chan, C., Cercone, N., Ziarko, W.: Discovering Rules for Water Demand Prediction: An Enhanced Rough-set Approach. Engineering Applications in Artificial Intelligence 9(6) (1996) 645-653
2. Beynon, M.: Reducts within the Variable Precision Rough Set Model: A Further Investigation. European Journal of Operational Research 134 (2001) 592-605
3. Beynon, M.: An Investigation of β-reduct Selection within the Variable Precision Rough Sets Model. In: Ziarko, W., Yao, Y.Y. (eds.): Proceedings of RSCTC 2000, LNAI 2005. Springer-Verlag, Berlin Heidelberg (2001) 114-122 4.
4. Depold, H. R. and Gass, F. D.: The Application of Expert Systems and Neural Networks to Gas Turbine Prognostics and Diagnostics. Journal of Engineering for Gas Turbines and Power, Transactions of the ASME 121 (1999) 607-612 5.
5. Hu, T., Lu, B.C., Chen, G.J.: A Gas Turbo Generator Fault Diagnosis New Approach Based on Rough Set Theory. Journal of Electronic Measurement and Instrument 15(1) (2001) 12-16
6. Katzberg, J.D., Ziarko, W.: Variable Precision Extension of Rough Sets. Fundamental Informatics 27 (1996)155-168
7. Liu, H.J., Tuo, H.Y., Liu, Y.C.: Rough Neural Network of Variable Precision. Neural Processing Letters, Kluwer Academic Publishers 19 (2004) 73-87
8. Liu, S.C., Liu, S.Y.: An efficient expert system for machine fault diagnosis. International Journal Advanced Manufacturing Technology 21 (2003) 691- 698
9. Pawlak, Z.: Rough sets. International Journal of Computer and Information Sciences. 11(5) (1982) 341-356
10. Pawlak, Z.: Rough sets theory and its applications to data analysis. Cybernetics and Systems 29 (1998) 661-668
11. Paya, B.A., East, I.I., Badi, M.N.: Artificial Neural Network Based Fault Diagnostics of Rotating Machinery Using Wavelet Transforms as a Preprocessor. Mechanical Systems and Signal Processing ll (1997) 751-765
12. Skowron, A., Rauszer, C.: The Discernibility Matrices and Functions in Information Systems. Intelligent Decision Support-Handbook of Applications and Advances of the Rough Sets Theory, Kluwer Academic Publishers (1992)331-362
13. Ziarko, W.: Analysis of Uncertain Information in the Framework of Variable Precision Rough Sets. Foundations of Computing And Decision Sciences 18(3-4) (1993) 381-396

Integration of Variable Precision Rough Set and Fuzzy Clustering: An Application to Knowledge Acquisition for Manufacturing Process Planning

Zhonghao Wang, Xinyu Shao, Guojun Zhang, and Haiping Zhu

School of Mechanical Science and Engineering,
Huazhong University of Science and Technology,
430074, Wuhan, The People's Republic of China
wzh_zyy@263.net

Abstract. Knowledge acquisition plays a significant role in the knowledge-based intelligent process planning system, but there remains a difficult issue. In manufacturing process planning, experts often make decisions based on different decision thresholds under uncertainty. Knowledge acquisition has been inclined towards a more complex but more necessary strategy to obtain such thresholds, including confidence, rule strength and decision precision. In this paper, a novel approach to integrating fuzzy clustering and VPRS (variable precision rough set) is proposed. As compared to the conventional fuzzy decision techniques and entropy-based analysis method, it can discover association rules more effectively and practically in process planning with such thresholds. Finally, the proposed approach is validated by the illustrative complexity analysis of manufacturing parts, and the analysis results of the preliminary tests are also reported.

1 Introduction

Knowledge processing aims at manipulating knowledge to enhance its representation and properties for better utilities in supporting decision level automation. Knowledge acquisition, however, is yet to be fully studied and remains the most difficult issue [11]. In manufacturing process planning, it undoubtedly leads to the difficulty in the uncertain manufacturing process decision.

The raw process information stored in the process database appears to be incomplete, imprecise and out-of-date. Many methods, such as ES [6], fuzzy theory [7], ANN [5], have been utilized to solve these problems, however, these approaches seem to be incapable of handling with the uncertainty happening frequently in the different phases of manufacturing process planning, saying nothing of discovering association rules from different kinds of historical process planning information. How to effectively and accurately extract the useful process knowledge from complex process information source still remains a big challenge.

The RST (rough set theory) proposed by Pawlak [8][9][10] enriches the mathematical techniques for discovering regulations and knowledge from information tables. It has attracted much attention in information processing research in recent years also. Consequently, it has been successfully introduced and applied into many real-world engineering problems, especially in the field of knowledge acquisition and

D. Ślęzak et al. (Eds.): RSFDGrC 2005, LNAI 3642, pp. 585–593, 2005.

rule induction [4][1]. Nevertheless, the classic rough set should be extended under most circumstance. Dubois [3] presented the fuzzy-rough set model based on the fuzzy theory and RST. This model has been used to deal with the practical fuzzy decision problems. Ziarko [13] put forward the VPRS (variable precision rough set) to improve the classical RST. VPRS is capable of generalizing the conclusions acquired from the objects in miniature to the objects with larger size. It has the additional desirable property of allowing for partial classification within some fault-tolerance compared to the complete classification required by RST.

The fuzzy clustering is another mature and efficient approach to knowledge discovery. In the procedure to handle with the process planning knowledge, the process designers usually analyze the similar manufacturing methods and process solutions based on the similarity measure and matching, which is the first step to cluster the analogical process solutions with fuzzy clustering. Although the similar process knowledge can be reused in this way, the decision-makers think it is impractical for them to choose solutions completely based on their experience. In most cases, they make decisions based on different decision thresholds, such as confidence, decision precision and so on. In the following sections, we synthesize the merits of both fuzzy clustering and VPRS to accomplish knowledge acquisition in manufacturing process planning.

2 Integrating Fuzzy Clustering and VPRS

Let U be a finite set of objects, as to a fuzzy relation R in $U \times U$:

(1) If $R(x,x) = 1 (\forall x \in U)$, then R is reflexive;

(2) If $R(y,x) = R(x,y)(\forall x, y \in U)$, then R is symmetrical;

(3) If $R(x,z) \geq R(x,y) \wedge R(y,z)(\forall x, y, z \in U)$, then R is transitive. If R is a reflexive, symmetrical and transitive relation, then R is referred to as a fuzzy equivalent relation [12].

Definition 1: Considering a fuzzy information system (U,R), if R is a fuzzy equivalent relation, then (U,R) is called a fuzzy equivalent relation information system.

Definition 2: Assuming that (U,R) and (U,G) are two fuzzy equivalent relation information systems, then (U,R,G) is called a fuzzy decision information system, if $R \subseteq G$, then this information system is consistent.

Definition 3: Given a fuzzy decision information system (U,R,G), as to $0 \leq \alpha, \beta \leq 1$, let us remark that:

$$R_\alpha = \{(x,y) \in U \times U : R(x,y) \geq \alpha\} \tag{1}$$

$$G_\beta = \{(x,y) \in U \times U : G(x,y) \geq \beta\} \tag{2}$$

then U can be graduated respectively as:

$$U / R_\alpha = \{[x]_\alpha : x \in U\} = \{E_1, \cdots, E_s\}, \text{ where } [x]_\alpha = \{y \in U : (x,y) \in R_\alpha\} \tag{3}$$

$$U / G_\beta = \{[x]_\beta : x \in U\} = \{D_1, \cdots, D_r\}, \text{ where } [x]_\beta = \{y \in U : (x, y) \in G_\beta\} \tag{4}$$

Formally, U / R_α and U / G_β are called the fuzzy approximation graduations.

Both of them can be induced from the fuzzy approximation Boolean matrix R_α and G_β, and α, β are the confidence values.

Definition 4: For every V, $W \in U$,

$$I(V, W) = card(V \cap W) / card(W) \tag{5}$$

is called the inclusion grade of V in W, where $card(W)$ denotes the cardinality of set W [2]. In fact, the inclusion grade can be interpreted as the conditional probability function $P(V | W)$ also [14].

Definition 5: Given a fuzzy decision information system (U, R, G), as to $0 \leq \alpha, \beta \leq 1, \gamma \in (0.5, 1]$, the lower-approximation and upper- approximation with U / R_α to U / G_β ,denoted as $\underline{R}_\gamma^\beta (X / \alpha)$ and $\overline{R}_\gamma^\beta (X / \alpha)$, are defined respectively as follows:

$$\underline{R}_\gamma^\beta (X / \alpha) = \{x \in U : I(X, [x]_\alpha) \geq \gamma, X \in [x]_\beta\} \tag{6}$$

$$\overline{R}_\gamma^\beta (X / \alpha) = \{x \in U : I(X, [x]_\alpha) > 1 - \gamma, X \in [x]_\beta\} \tag{7}$$

Where γ is the decision precision for some objects, and it is worth noting that not all the objects have the appropriate decision results unless the inclusion grade is not less than γ. From the above definition, it can be easily shown that γ links up the condition attributes and the decision attributes, and γ can be treated as the confidence for the discovered association rules. The three thresholds all together determine the rule strength of the association rules.

In the knowledge-based process planning system, the attribute values are usually miscellaneous, heterogeneous and uncertain, so it is infeasible to introduce the rough set into knowledge acquisition directly. In order to adapt to the rigorous requirements of process planning, a novel approach integrating fuzzy clustering and VPRS is proposed. It is divided into a three-step process. At first fuzzy clustering is utilized to graduate the objects with reference to the condition parts and the decision parts respectively. Secondly, the fuzzy approximation sets are obtained through VPRS model. Finally, the process association rules with different confidence are induced according to the fuzzy approximation sets. The procedure is illustrated in Fig.1. Different fuzzy approximation graduations can be acquired through setting different α as to the former attributes, it being the same case with the latter attributes by setting different β. If $x \in \underline{R}_\gamma^\beta (X / \alpha)$, some uncertain association rules can be considered as follows:

$$\bigwedge_{l=1}^{m} (a_l, f_l(x)) \rightarrow (d, j) \quad (\alpha, \beta, \gamma) \tag{8}$$

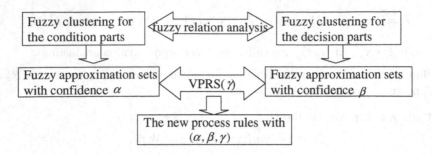

Fig. 1. The procedures to integrate fuzzy clustering and VPRS

where d denotes decision result, j is the corresponding decision values, a_l is the condition attribute, $f_l(x)$ is the corresponding attribute value and m is the number of attributes.

Proposition 1: Considering a fuzzy equivalent relation information system (U,R) and $D_k \in U / G_\beta$, $k \in \{1, \cdots, r\}$, if $\gamma = 1$, then it follows that:

$$\underline{R}_\gamma^\beta (D_k / \alpha) = \underline{R}_\alpha (D_k) = \{x \in U : [x]_\alpha \subseteq D_k\} \tag{9}$$

Proof. When $\gamma = 1$, which means $I(X,[x]_\alpha) = 1$, $X \in [x]_\beta$ and it implies $[x]_\alpha \subseteq X$. According to Eq. (4), we get $[x]_\alpha \subseteq D_k$.

As to the case of $\gamma = 1$, it is obvious that the VPRS model degenerates to the traditional rough set model, which naturally limits the application of knowledge discovery. The approach mentioned above is used to mine the individual rule for each object based on the association analysis among all the objects, while the rule representation in the following statements is applied to assess the entire information table, which is based on decision precision and rule precision.

Let us remark that

$$D(\beta / \alpha) = \frac{1}{|U|} \sum_{k=1, D_k \in U / G_\beta}^{r} |\underline{R}_\alpha (D_k)| \tag{10}$$

$$(\alpha_R, \beta_G) = \inf\{(\alpha, \beta) : D(\beta / \alpha) \geq \delta\} \tag{11}$$

then we get the following rules:

$$[x]_{\alpha_R} \to [x]_{\beta_G}^* \quad (\delta) \tag{12}$$

where δ is decision precision with confidence (α_R, β_G) for a given information table.

Let us remark that

$$D^*(\beta / \alpha) = \min\{|\underline{R}_\alpha (D_k)| / |D_k| : k \leq r\} \tag{13}$$

$$(\alpha_R, \beta_G)^* = \inf\{(\alpha, \beta) : D^*(\beta/\alpha) \ge \delta^*\} \tag{14}$$

where δ^* means rule precision with confidence $(\alpha_R, \beta_G)^*$.

3 Fuzzy Clustering-Based Graduation Algorithm

At first, the fuzzy approximation matrix $R_{n \times n}$ is built up, where n is the number of all the objects. It should be mentioned that similarity measure and distance measure are two demarcating methods applied to construct fuzzy approximation matrix in fuzzy clustering. Here the arithmetical mean least method (see Eq.15) mostly utilized in similarity measure is adopted to get the similarity coefficient r_{ij}^*, furthermore to build up fuzzy approximation matrix $R_{n \times n}$. Through calculating the transitive closure $t(R)$, we get the fuzzy equivalence matrix R.

$$r_{ij}^* = 2\sum_{l=1}^{m}(f_l(x_i) \wedge f_l(x_j)) / \sum_{l=1}^{m}(f_l(x_i) + f_l(x_j)) \tag{15}$$

Based on the fuzzy equivalence matrix R and Eq. (16), the fuzzy equivalence Boolean matrix R_α with confidence α can be gotten ultimately.

$$\begin{cases} r_{ij}=1 & r_{ij} \ge \alpha \\ r_{ij}=0 & r_{ij} < \alpha \end{cases} \forall i, j = 1, 2, \cdots, |U| \tag{16}$$

R_α is characteristic of reflexive, symmetry and transitive. Similarly, the fuzzy equivalent matrix G_β with confidence level β can be achieved. The algorithm is depicted as follows:

```
Algorithm 1:
Input: the fuzzy equivalence Boolean matrix R_α.
Output: the graduation to U as to confidence value α.
Step1: ∀x_i ∈ U , X = ∅ , Y = ∅ .
Step2: j = 0 .
Step3: if r_ij = 1 , then X = X ∪ {x_j} and Y = Y ∪ {x_j}.
Step4: j = j+1 .
Step5: if j < n , go to Step3; Otherwise go ahead.
Step6: if card(Y) > 1 , ∀x_i ∈ Y , Y = Y - {x_i} , go to Step2;
       Otherwise go ahead.
Step7: Output X and set U = U - X .
Step8: if U = ∅ complete; otherwise go back to Step1.
```

4 Lower-Approximation and Upper-Approximation in VPRS

The lower-approximation and upper-approximation are the premises for any rough set-based classification problems. The algorithm2 is similar to the traditional RST in gaining lower-approximation, and it could be found in many literatures, whereas the classification judgment criterion is different. The algorithm to get lower-approximation with confidence γ is presented as follows, with the one to get the upper-approximation being analogous.

```
Algorithm 2:
```

Input: $U / R_\alpha = \{E_1,...,E_s\}, X \in U / R_\alpha$, confidence γ.

Output: the $\underline{R}_\gamma^\beta(X / \alpha)$ lower-approximation;

Step1: $j=0$, $L=\emptyset$.

Step2: if $card(E_j \cap X) / card(E_j) \geq \gamma$, then $L \cup (E_j \cap X) \to L$.

Step3: if $j=s$, then complete, output the result L;
       Otherwise, go to Step3 to check the next E_j.

Step4: $j=j+1$, go to Step3.

5 Experiment

In manufacturing process planning, the complexity of the parts needs to be evaluated constantly, which is mainly composed of manufacturing complexity (d1), design complexity (d2) and process complexity (d3).There are many factors which result in the increase of the complexity, such as manufacturing precision, surface finish, manufacturing size and so on. While under practical circumstance, the complexity of a part is fully embodied by all the possible factors (attributes) where some redundant ones are often included. In order to carry out the knowledge discovery, we must take much time on the data pre-processing and attributes reduction. Fortunately, all these factors are manifested on the corresponding manufacturing methods and the manufacturing time spent on them indirectly. As a result, for the sake of simplicity, the manufacturing time spent on the corresponding manufacturing methods acts as the media to associate the manufacturing requirements with the part complexity. Without loss of the practicality, we only consider the most typical manufacturing methods, including lathe (a1), mill (a2), grind (a3) and trowel (a4). The attribute values denote the time or degrees some parts have spent on. Therefore, the manufacturing methods (attributes) are regarded as the kernel or cores and we need not take into account the attributes reduction any more in this paper.

In the process planning, it is intuitionist that the longer the manufacturing time is, the more complex the part is. Some researchers try to find out an efficient functional relation between the manufacturing time and the part complexity. The usual approach is based on the statistical method or entropy measure. In fact, the functional relation concluded from the entropy measure is meaningless for guiding the process decision-making and planning in practical cases.

Here, a simplified part complexity analysis table (Table 1.) is presented. There are 6 parts in it. The attribute value in the latter parts means the complexity measure corresponding to different kinds of complexity, and the bigger the attribute value is, the more complex the part is. Although the information table is presented, it is difficult for us to discover the association rule using traditional RST because of the inconsistence of the decision table. In this paper, the proposed approach directly applies the fuzzy clustering to manufacturing time and the part complexity respectively and avoids the impact of inconsistence, and then introduces the VPRS to discover the association rules between the manufacturing time and the part complexity. All these association rules can be used for reference and even be reused in other similar process decision-making.

Table 1. The part complexity analysis table

part ID	manufacturing time				complexity of the parts		
	lathe (a1)	mill (a2)	grind (a3)	trowel (a4)	manufacturing complexity(d1)	design complexity(d2)	process complexity(d3)
x1	3	5	3	6	0.9	0.2	0.5
x2	4	3	2	7	0.5	0.7	0.4
x3	0	1	4	2	0.8	0.4	0.2
x4	9	2	3	3	0.2	0.8	0.3
x5	9	3	1	3	0.1	0.3	0.9
x6	2	4	1	8	0.2	0.5	1.0

With respect to the manufacturing time, we get the transitive closure $t(R) = R^5$, and R^5 turns out to be a fuzzy equivalence matrix R. By adjusting confidence α, different fuzzy equivalent Boolean matrixes R_α are achieved. After using the Algorithm1 (see Sect .3), we obtain the following graduations:

- $U/R_{\alpha=0.91} = \{\{x1\}, \{x2\}, \{x3\}, \{x4, x5\}, \{x6\}\}$,
- $U/R_{\alpha=0.85} = \{\{x1, x2\}, \{x3\}, \{x4, x5\}, \{x6\}\}$,
- $U/R_{\alpha=0.84} = \{\{x1, x2, x6\}, \{x3\}, \{x4, x5\}\}$,
- $U/R_{\alpha=0.69} = \{\{x1, x2, x4, x5, x6\}, \{x3\}\}$.

Similarly, for the part complexity, we apply the same algorithm and have the following clusters:

- $U/G_{\beta=0.667} = \{x1, x2, x3, x4, x5, x6\}$,
- $U/G_{\beta=0.733} = \{\{x1, x2, x3, x4\}, \{x5\}, \{x6\}\} = \{D_1, D_2, D_3\}$,
- $U/G_{\beta=0.800} = \{\{x1, x3\}, \{x2\}, \{x4\}, \{x5\}, \{x6\}\} = \{D_1^*, D_2^*, D_3^*, D_4^*, D_5^*\}$.

The following results are derived from the Algorithm2 (see Sect. 4):

- $\underline{R}_{0.67}^{0.733}(D_1/0.84)=\{x1, x2, x3\}$,

- $\underline{R}_{1.00}^{0.800}(D_1^*/0.84)=\{x3\}$,

- $\underline{R}_{1.00}^{0.733}(D_1/0.85)=\{x1, x2, x3\}$.

Then we have the following rules:

- If ($a1=3$, $a2=5$, $a3=3$, $a4=6$), then ($d1=0.9$, $d2=0.2$, $d3=0.5$) (0.84, 0.733, 0.67);
- If ($a1=0$, $a2=1$, $a3=4$, $a4=2$), then ($d1=0.8$, $d2=0.4$, $d3=0.2$) (0.84, 0.800, 1.00);
and so forth.

When $\gamma=1.00$, we use Eqs. (11) and (14) as the measure of rule precision and decision precision.

- $D(0.733/0.84)=1/6$,

- $D(0.733/0.85) = D(0.733/0.91) =2/3$,

- $D(0.800/0.84) = D(0.800/0.69) =1/6$,

- $D(0.800/0.85) =1/3$,

- $D(0.800/0.91) =2/3$,

- $D^*(0.667/\alpha) =1/6$,

- $D^*(\beta \neq 0.667/\alpha) =0$.

If we choose $\delta=0.667$, then make $\alpha_R=0.85$ and $\beta_G=0.733$, which satisfies Eq. (11), and the rule is represented as:

$$[x]_{0.85} \to [x]_{0.733}^* \quad (0.667)$$

At the same time, the conclusion can be drawn from the analysis above: decision precision is not less than rule precision, represented as:

$$D(\beta/\alpha) \geq D^*(\beta/\alpha). \tag{17}$$

6   Final Remarks

This approach takes advantage of the merits of both fuzzy clustering and VPRS in knowledge discovery, so it can assist knowledge acquisition. Compared with the conventional fuzzy decision techniques and entropy-based analysis methods, this approach is more suitable and effective for discovering association rules between manufacturing time and the part complexity, especially for the evaluation of similar process solution and uncertain process decision according to the manufacturing time. The association rule is represented by three thresholds and it can guide the process decision-making based on such thresholds. The proposed approach to some extent shows its superiority, but it should be stressed specially that it is ill-considered due to the overlook of the attributes reduction. Because of the complexity of the process planning problem, all the attributes should not be merely ascribed to the manufacturing methods and the corresponding manufacturing time, but be taken into account synthetically. Consequently, the attribute reduction algorithms based on fuzzy clustering and VRPS under complex cases are the next research we will focus on.

Acknowledgements. The research reported in this article is supervised by Prof. Xinyu Shao. Meanwhile, the author wishes to acknowledge the National Key Basis Researching and Developing Planned Projects (973 programs) (No.2004CB719405). It is also supported by the financial support from National Natural Science Foundation of China (No.50275056) and National High-tech Program for CIMS (No.2003AA411042).

References

1. Bi, Y.X., Anderson, T., McClean, S.: A rough set model with ontology for discovering maximal association rules in documents collections, Knowledge-based Systems 16 (2003) 243-251.
2. Bodjanova, S.: Approximation of fuzzy concepts in decision making, fuzzy sets and systems 85 (1997) 23-29.
3. Dubois, D., Prade, H.: Twofold fuzzy sets and rough sets-some issues in knowledge representation, Fuzzy Sets and Systems 23 (1987) 3-18.
4. Jagielska, I., Mattheews, C.: An investigation into the application of neural networks, fuzzy logic, genetic algorithms and rough sets to automated knowledge acquisition for classification problems, Neurocomputing 24 (1999) 37-54.
5. Lee, J.H.: Artificial intelligence-based sampling planning system for dynamic manufacturing process, Expert systems with application 22 (2002) 117-133.
6. Ohashia, T., Motomura, M.: Expert system of cold forging defects using risk analysis tree network with fuzzy language, Journal of Materials Processing Technology 107 (2000) 260-266.
7. Ong, S.K, Vin, L.J., Nee, A.Y.C., Kals, H.J.J.: Fuzzy set theory applied to bend sequencing for sheet metal bending, Journal of Materials Processing Technology 69 (1997) 29-36.
8. Pawlak, Z.: Rough set approach to knowledge-based decision support, European Journal of Operational Research 99 (1997) 48-57.
9. Pawlak, Z.: Rough sets: Theoretical aspects of reasoning about data. MA: Kluwer Academic Publishers. Boston (1991).
10. Pawlak, Z.: Rough set, International Journal of Computer and Information Science 11 (1982) 341-356.
11. Shao, X.Y., Zhang, G.J., Li, P.G., Chen, Y.B.: Application of ID3 algorithm in knowledge acquisition for tolerance design, Journal of Materials Processing Technology 117 (2001) 66-74.
12. Wu, W.Z., Mi, J.S., Zhang, W.X.: Generalized fuzzy rough set, Information sciences 151 (2003) 263-282.
13. Ziarko, W.: Variable precision rough sets model, Journal of Computer and Systems Sciences, 46/1 (1993) 39-59.
14. Ziarko, W., Fei, X.: VPRSM Approach for web searching, RSFDGrC (2003) 514-521.

An Obstacle Avoidance Technique
for AUVs Based on BK-Product
of Fuzzy Relations

Le-Diem Bui and Yong-Gi Kim

Department of Computer Science and Research Institute of Computer
and Information Communication, Gyeongsang National University,
Jinju, Kyungnam, Korea 660-701
ygkim@gsnu.ac.kr

Abstract. This paper proposes a new heuristic search technique for
obstacle avoidance of autonomous underwater vehicles that are equipped
with a looking ahead obstacle avoidance sonar. Fuzzy relational method
of Bandler and Kohout is used as the mathematical implementation for
the analysis and synthesis of relations between the partitioned sections of
sonar and the environmental properties. For the technique used in this
paper, sonar range must be partitioned into multi equal sections and
membership functions of the properties and the corresponding fuzzy rule
bases are estimated by domain experts. The simulation result leads to the
conclusion that only with the two properties safety and remoteness and
with sonar partitioned in seven sections, the applied technique enables
AUVs to safely avoid any obstacle and to navigate on the optimal way
to goal.

1 Introduction

In recent years, autonomous underwater vehicles (AUVs) have become an in-
tense tendency of research about ocean robotics because of the commercial as
well as military potential and the technological challenge in developing them.
Navigation with an obstacle execution process is one of the many important
capabilities and behaviours of AUVs. The real time operation of this capability
is the main requirement needed within the autonomous vehicle's control management system. Many approaches to the problem have been proposed in recent
years [1][2][5][12]. Additionally, the heuristic search technique for AUVs obstacle
avoidance using BK-products was already presented in [9].

In this paper the range of obstacle avoidance sonar is required to divide into
many sections, each of which probably detects forward obstacles distinctly. A
new heuristic search technique is suggested. This is based on the fuzzy relation
between the partitioned sections of sonar range and the properties toward the
real world environment in which AUVs navigate. Because the prior knowledge
and information about underwater environment in which the AUVs operate is
often incomplete, uncertain and approximated, fuzzy logic is necessarily used to
generate the possibility of the real time environmental effects to AUVs navigation. Domain experts who are boarding a submarine recognize characteristics

D. Ślęzak et al. (Eds.): RSFDGrC 2005, LNAI 3642, pp. 594–603, 2005.

and events that can occur in the navigation environment and then analyze to figure out the rule bases and membership functions used for reasoning in this study. BK-product is applied to the above fuzzy relation and its transposed to select the optimal successive heading direction for the AUVs path planning in case that obstacles present in the planned route.

Actually, the proposed algorithm has essentially focused on horizontal movement since the translation cost for vertical movement of AUVs proved in [12] is 1.2 times greater than in horizontal movement. The turning angle of AUVs' heading is equal to the angle formed by the current heading and the selected section of sonar. In the exception case obstacle is completely filled up the sonar's coverage, AUVs must go to up one layer at a time and then apply the algorithm to find out the turning. Until obstacle clearance, AUVs are constrained to go back to the standard depth of the planned route. The first part of the paper will introduce the theory of BK-products. Then, the design of the AUV obstacle avoidance technique using BK-products is explained briefly. At last, the case study is elaborated to denote the feasible application of BK-products for this study and the experiment results are also shown in both 2D and 3D cases.

2   Fuzzy Relational Method of Bandler and Kohout

Relational representation of knowledge makes it possible to perform all the computations and decision making in a uniform relational way, by mean of special relational compositions called triangle and square products. These were first introduced by Bandler and Kohout and are referred to as the BK-products in the literature. Their theory and applications have made substantial progress since then [3][4][6][7][8].

There are different ways to define the composition of two fuzzy relations. The most popular extension of the classical circular composition to the fuzzy case is so called max-min composition [8]. Bandler and Kohout extended the classical circular products to BK-products as sub-triangle ($\triangleleft$,"included in"), super-triangle ($\triangleright$, "includes"), and square ($\square$,"are exactly the same") [13]. Assume the relations R and S are fuzzy relations, and then the R-afterset of x, xR and the S-foreset of z, Sz, obviously are fuzzy sets in Y. The common definition of inclusion of the fuzzy set xR in Y in the fuzzy set Sz in Y is given by (1).

$$xR \subseteq Sz \Leftrightarrow (\forall y \in Y)(xR(y) \leq Sz(y)) \tag{1}$$

A fuzzy implication is modeled by means of a fuzzy implication operator. A wide variety of fuzzy implication operators have been proposed, and their properties have been analyzed in detail [4][11]. For this study, we make use only of operator 5 as shown in (2).

$$a \rightarrow_5 b = \min(1, 1 - a + b) \tag{2}$$

Using (2), with n the cardinality of Y, we easily obtain the definitions for the sub-triangle and supper-triangle products in (3), (4) while the square product using the intersection and the minimum operator is shown in (5) and (6) respectively.

$$x_i(R \triangleleft S)z_j = \frac{1}{n} \sum_{y \in Y} \min(1, 1 - x_i R(y) + Sz_j(y)) \tag{3}$$

$$x_i(R \triangleright S)z_j = \frac{1}{n} \sum_{y \in Y} \min(1, 1 + x_i R(y) - Sz_j(y)) \tag{4}$$

$$x_i(R \square S)z_j = x_i(R \triangleleft S)z_j \cap x_i(R \triangleright S)z_j \tag{5}$$

$$x_i(R \square S)z_j = \min(x_i(R \triangleleft S)z_j, x_i(R \triangleright S)z_j) \tag{6}$$

Along with the above definitions, α-cut and Hasse diagram are also the two important features of this method. The α-cut transforms a fuzzy relation into a crisp relation, which is represented as a matrix [7][8]. Let R denote a fuzzy relation on the $X \times Y$, the α-cut relation of R is defined as the equation (7).

$$R_\alpha = \{(x,y)|R(x,y) \geq \alpha \text{ and } 0 \leq \alpha \leq 1\} \tag{7}$$

The Hasse diagram is a useful tool, which completely describes the partial order among the elements of the crisp relational matrix by a Hasse diagram structure. To determine the Hasse diagram of a relation, the following three steps should be adopted [10].

- **Step 1:** Delete all edges that have reflexive property.
- **Step 2:** Eliminate all edges that are implied by the transitive property.
- **Step 3:** Draw the diagraph of a partial order with all edges pointing upward, and then omit arrows from the edges.

3　Using BK-Subtriangle Product to Obstacle Avoidance of AUVs

In this study it is required that obstacle avoidance sonar range can be partitioned into several sub-ranges. One of these represents for the successive heading candidate for AUVs to go ahead. Whenever obstacle is detected, the sonar return is clustered and the sections in which obstacles present can be identified. The sonar model is illustrated as in Fig.1. Domain experts who have wide knowledge about ocean science could give the properties about the environmental effects to the of AUVs navigation.

A forward looking obstacle avoidance sonar whose coverage range can be divided into multi-sections is used to determine a heading candidate set S. Otherwise, a property set P describes the effects of AUVs toward the real time environment. The fuzzy rule base and membership function for the corresponding property can be estimated subjectively by the expert knowledge. With the set of the candidate $S = \{s_1, s_2, s_3, \ldots, s_i\}$ and the set of environmental properties $P = \{p_1, p_2, p_3, \ldots, p_i\}$, the relation R is built as (8). The elements r_{ij} of this relation means the possibility the section s_i can be characterized by the

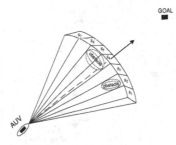

Fig. 1. A model of forward-looking obstacle avoidance sonar

property p_j. The value of r_{ij} is calculated by means of the rule bass with the membership functions.

$$R = S \times P = \begin{bmatrix} r_{11} & r_{12} & \cdots & r_{1j} \\ r_{21} & r_{22} & \cdots & r_{2j} \\ \vdots & \vdots & \ddots & \vdots \\ r_{i1} & r_{i2} & \cdots & r_{ij} \end{bmatrix} \begin{matrix} s_1 \\ s_2 \\ \vdots \\ s_i \end{matrix} \tag{8}$$
$$\begin{matrix} p_1 & p_2 & \cdots & p_j \end{matrix}$$

$$T = R \vartriangleleft R^T = \begin{bmatrix} t_{11} & t_{12} & \cdots & t_{1j} \\ t_{21} & t_{22} & \cdots & t_{2j} \\ \vdots & \vdots & \ddots & \vdots \\ t_{i1} & t_{i2} & \cdots & t_{ij} \end{bmatrix} \begin{matrix} s_1 \\ s_2 \\ \vdots \\ s_i \end{matrix} \tag{9}$$
$$\begin{matrix} s_1 & s_2 & \cdots & s_j \end{matrix}$$

$$R_\alpha = \alpha\text{-}cut(T, \alpha) = \begin{bmatrix} a_{11} & a_{12} & \cdots & a_{1j} \\ a_{21} & a_{22} & \cdots & a_{2j} \\ \vdots & \vdots & \ddots & \vdots \\ a_{i1} & a_{i2} & \cdots & a_{ij} \end{bmatrix} \begin{matrix} s_1 \\ s_2 \\ \vdots \\ s_i \end{matrix} \tag{10}$$
$$\begin{matrix} s_1 & s_2 & \cdots & s_j \end{matrix}$$

In the next step a new fuzzy relation T is computed by using sub-triangle product $\vartriangleleft$ to fuzzy relation R and R^T, the transposed relation of R. The fuzzy relation T as shown in (9) is the product relation between candidate set S that means the degree of implication among elements of candidate set. Then, the $\alpha\text{-}cut$ is applied to fuzzy relation T in order to transform into crisp relation as shown in (10). It is important to select a reasonable $\alpha\text{-}cut$ value because the hierarchical structure of candidate set depends on an applied $\alpha\text{-}cut$. Finally, we draw the Hasse diagram, which describes a partial order among elements of candidate set, that is to say, a hierarchical structure among the elements of candidate set with respect to the optimality and efficiency. Select then the top node of the Hasse diagram as the successive heading direction of AUVs.

Because the energy consumption in vertical movement of AUVs is much greater than in the horizontal movement (1.2 times)[12], this technique focus

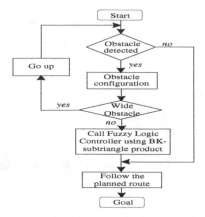

Fig. 2. A control flow of AUVs obstacle avoidance

strongly on the horizontal movement. In the case of obstacle occurrence, AUVs just turn left or right with the turning angle determined by degree from the current heading to the selected section. But in the exception case a very wide obstacle has completely filled up the sonar's coverage, AUVs must go to up one layer at a time and apply the algorithm to find out the turning. Until obstacle clearance, AUVs are constrained to go back to the standard depth of the planned route.

The algorithm of the proposed technique can summarize into five below steps and is imitated briefly in control flow as shown in Fig.2.

- **Step 1:** If AUV detects obstacle then go to next step, else go to step 5.
- **Step 2:** Determine P and configure S.
- **Step 3:** If very wide obstacle is detected in all of S then go up and return step 1; else go to next step.
- **Step 4:** Call the fuzzy logic controller using BK-subtriangle product to S and P to figure out the successive heading for obstacle avoidance.
- **Step 5:** Go on in the planned route.

4   Case Study

In the case study, assuming that sonar range can be divided into seven sections as shown in Fig.1. Actually, domain expert could determine the two fuzzy properties *Safety* and *Remoteness*. The Safety property means the degree to which each section of sonar can be characterized in case of obstacle appears within the sonar range. The Remoteness property means how far of the distance to goal if AUVs follow the direction of the section s_i. Thus, the two set S and P can be suggested as follow.

$S = \{s_1, s_2, s_3, s_4, s_5, s_6, s_7\}$: set of the heading candidate

$P = \{p_1, p_2\}$: set of the properties where p_1, p_2 is the safety and remoteness properties respectively.

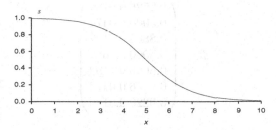

Fig. 3. The membership function of the Safety property (μ_S)

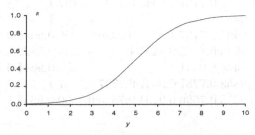

Fig. 4. The membership function of the Remoteness property (μ_R)

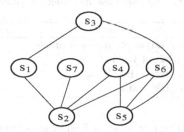

Fig. 5. Hasse Diagram

The prior knowledge and information about underwater environment in which AUVs have to operate is incomplete, uncertain. Therefore the establishment of membership functions is very important to obtain more reasonable solution using the BK's method. The design of the membership functions shown in Fig.3 and Fig.4 is subjectively calculated from experience of designer.

In this context, it was assumed that there are four levels of ambiguity as very safe (VS), safe (S), risky (R) and very risky (VR) for Safety property. It was also assumed that there are four levels of ambiguity as very far (VF), far(F), near (N) and very near (VN) according to Remoteness property. The rule bases are shown in Table 1 and Table 2 with the fuzzy degree x and y can be selected for the membership function of the safety and the remoteness respectively. It is assumed that obstacles are detected by the sections s_2, s_4, and s_5 as in Fig.1. Thus, Table 2 and Table 3 show the fuzzy membership value of the heading candidate set with respect to the safety and remoteness degree gain by the fuzzy rule bases and the membership functions.

$$R = \begin{pmatrix} 0.9526\ 0.0180 \\ 0.5000\ 0.0474 \\ 0.8808\ 0.1192 \\ 0.5000\ 0.2689 \\ 0.5000\ 0.1192 \\ 0.9526\ 0.0474 \\ 0.9820\ 0.0180 \end{pmatrix} \tag{11}$$

$$T = R \triangleleft R^T$$
$$= \begin{pmatrix} 1 & 0.7737\ 0.9641\ 0.7737\ 0.7737\ 1 & 1 \\ 0.9853\ 1 & 1 & 1 & 1 & 1 & 0.9853 \\ 0.9494\ 0.7737\ 1 & 0.8096\ 0.8096\ 0.9641\ 0.9494 \\ 0.8745\ 0.8892\ 0.9251\ 1 & 0.9251\ 0.8892\ 0.8745 \\ 0.9494\ 0.9641\ 1 & 1 & 1 & 0.9641\ 0.9494 \\ 0.9853\ 0.7737\ 0.9641\ 0.7737\ 0.7737\ 1 & 0.9853 \\ 0.9853\ 0.7590\ 0.9494\ 0.7590\ 0.7590\ 0.9853\ 1 \end{pmatrix} \tag{12}$$

Table 1. The rule base for Safety Property

Degree	Situation	Value of y
Very Safe	IF: s_i is not adjacent to any obstacle	THEN: x=1
Safe	IF: s_i is adjacent to obstacle	THEN: x=2
Risky	IF: s_i is between the obstacles	THEN: x=3
Very Risky	IF: s_i contains obstacle	THEN: x=5

Table 2. The rule base for Remoteness Property

Degree	Situation	Value of y
Very Far	IF: the distance to goal by s_i's direction is very far	THEN: y=1
Far	IF: the distance to goal in s_i's direction is far	THEN: y=2
Near	IF: the distance to goal by s_i's direction is near	THEN: y=3
Very Near	IF: the distance to goal by s_i's direction is very near	THEN: y=4

Table 3. The membership value for Safety Property

Heading Selection	Fuzzy Degree	Fuzzy Value (x)	Membership Degree (μ_S)
s_1	S	2	0.9526
s_2	VR	5	0.5000
s_3	R	3	0.8808
s_4	VR	5	0.5000
s_5	VR	5	0.5000
s_6	S	2	0.9526
s_7	VS	1	0.9820

Table 4. The membership value for Remoteness Property

Heading Selection	Fuzzy Degree	Fuzzy Value (y)	Membership Degree (μ_R)
s_1	VF	1	0.0180
s_2	F	2	0.0474
s_3	N	3	0.1192
s_4	VN	4	0.2689
s_5	N	3	0.1192
s_6	F	2	0.0474
s_7	VF	1	0.0180

The fuzzy relation R in (11) between the heading selection set S and the property set P can be done easily from the value in Table 2 and Table 3. Then, computing the new fuzzy relation T (12) uses sub triangle product $\lhd$ to the fuzzy relation R and the transposed relation R.

The Hasse diagram in Fig.5 was drawn from crisp relation R_α with $\alpha\text{-}cut =$ 0.95. It shows that the heading of AUVs could be changed from current heading direction s_4 to direction of s_3. It is the optimal way for AUVs to navigate safely in the shortest way to go ahead.

5   Experimental Results

Supposing that the AUV's velocity is 2 knots; sonar distance is 50m, sonar coverage is 70 degrees in horizontal; and the computational time of AUV is 10s. There are two scenarios suggested as follows. In the first case, AUV met four obstacles in the way to goal as shown in Fig.6. At the point A(40,0,0), obstacle A can be detected in section s_1, s_2, s_3, s_4. The section s_5 is selected as the successive heading direction. At B(150,0,0), obstacle B and C can be detected in s_1, s_4, s_5, s_6, s_7, therefore s_3 is chosen for the next turning. Similarly, at C(250,0,0), obstacle D is detected in $s_2, s_3, s_4, s_5, s_6, s_7$, and then s_1 is selected.

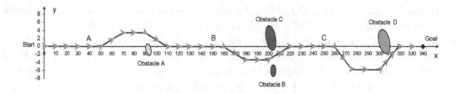

Fig. 6. Scenario of obstacle avoidance technique in 2D

In the second case, AUV could confront with very wide obstacle. The vehicle is suggested to go up. AUV starts to go up with a certain inclination angle. In the upper layer, at the position AUV has just reached, the algorithm is used to select the optimal turning angle to pass through the obstacle if certain section of sonar is detected free. If not, AUV can go to one more layer, the loop is so done until the obstacle is cleared and AUV follows the planned route of the mission.

6   Conclusions

In this paper, the obstacle avoidance capability for AUVs has been developed and verified by the new heuristic search technique. It has been shown that AUVs equipped with obstacle avoidance sonar can safely navigate in short way to the target by using BK-products. The primary requirement is that the sonar can be partitioned into many sections each of which represents for a successive heading candidate. Otherwise, the property set is also very important to collect as many characteristics of AUV toward the real time environment as possible in order to control AUVs more effectively. The more properties can be used, the more optimally and effectively AUVs can navigate. The fuzzy rule bases and membership functions play a very important role for feasibility of this study. In the scope of this study, in case of 3D scenario, we presented only how to apply the proposed technique but did not mention how to lead AUVs to go up and down. That is for the future work.

References

1. Antonelli, G., Chiaverini, S., Finotello, R. and Schiavon, R.: Real-time Path Planning and Obstacle Avoidance for RAIS: An Autonomous Underwater Vehicle, Oceanic Engineering, IEEE Journal, Vol.26, Issue 2 (2001) 216-227.
2. Anvar, A. M.,: Intelligent navigation process for autonomous underwater vehicles (AUVs) using time-based fuzzy temporal reasoning, Temporal Representation and Reasoning, 2003 and Fourth International Conference on Temporal Logic, Proceedings, 10th International Symposium on, (2003), 56-61.
3. Bandler, W. and Kohout, L. J.: Fuzzy Relational Products as a Tool for Analysis and Synthesis of the Behavior of Complex Natural and Artificial System, In: Wang, S. K, and Chang, P. P. (eds.), Fuzzy Sets: Theory and Application to Analysis and Information Systems, Plenum Press, New York (1980) 341-367.
4. Bandler, W. and Kohout, L. J.: Semantics of Implication Operators and Fuzzy Relational Products, Intl. Journal of Man-Machine Studies (1980).
5. Hyland, J.C. and Taylor, F.J.: Mine Avoidance Techniques for Underwater Vehicles, Oceanic Engineering, IEEE Journal, Vol.18, Issue 3 (1993) 340-350.
6. Kohout, L. J. and Kim, E.: Semiotic descriptors in fuzzy relational computations, In: Albus JH, Meystel A (eds) Proc IEEE Int Symp Intelligent Control, IEEE Int Symp Computational Intelligence in Robotics and Autonomous and Intelligent Systems and Semiotic (A Joint Conf Science and Technology of Intelligent Systems), Piscataway, (1998) 828-833.
7. Kohout, L. J. and Kim, E.: The role of BK-products of Relations in Soft Computing, Soft Computing 6, Springer-Verlag, (2002) 92-115.
8. Kohout, L. J., Keravnou, E. and Bandler, W.: Automatic Documentary Information Retrieval by Means of Fuzzy Relational Products, In: Gaines, B. R., Zadeh, L. A. and Zimmermann, H.J., (eds.), Fuzzy Sets in Decision Analysis, North-Holland, Amsterdam (1984) 308-404.
9. Lee, Y. I., Kim, Y. G.and Kohout, L. J.: An Intelligent Collision Avoidance System for AUVs using Fuzzy Relational Products, Information Sciences, Elsevier, Vol. 158 (2004) 209-232.

10. Lee, Y. I. and Kim, Y. G.: An Intelligent Navigation System for AUVs using Fuzzy Relational Products, IFSA World Congress and 20th NAFIPS International Conference, Joint 9th, Vol.2 (2001) 709-714.
11. Lee, Y. I., Noe, Ch. S. and Kim, Y. G.: Implication Operators in Fuzzy Relational Products for a Local Path-Planning of AUVs, Fuzzy Information Processing Society, Proceedings, NAFIPS, Annual Meeting of the North American (2002) 221-226.
12. Ong, S. M.: A Mission Planning Knowledge-based System with Three-Dimensional Path Optimization for the NPS Model 2 Autonomous Underwater Vehicle, Master's Thesis, Naval Postgraduate School (1990).
13. van de Walle, B. and van der Sluys, V.: Non-symmetric Matching Information for Negotiation Support in Electronic Markets, Proceedings of EuroFuse Workshop on Information Systems (Eds. B. De Baets, J. Fodor and G. Pasi), Italy (2002) 271-276.

SVR-Based Method Forecasting Intermittent Demand for Service Parts Inventories

Yukun Bao, Wen Wang, and Hua Zou

Department of Management Science and information System,
School of Management, Huazhong University of Science and Technology,
Wuhan 430074, China
yukunbao@mail.hust.edu.cn

Abstract. Intermittent Demand forecasting is one of the most crucial issues of service parts inventory management, which forms the basis for the planning of inventory levels and is probably the biggest challenge in the repair and overhaul industry. Generally, intermittent demand appears at random, with many time periods having no demand. In practice, exponential smoothing is often used when dealing with such kind of demand. Based on exponential smoothing method, more improved methods have been studied such as Croston method. This paper proposes a novel method to forecast the intermittent parts demand based on support vector regression (SVR). Details on data clustering, performance criteria design, kernel function selection are presented and an experimental result is given to show the method's validity.

1 Introduction

A fundamental aspect of supply chain management is accurate demand forecasting. We address the problem of forecasting intermittent (or irregular) demand. Intermittent demand appears at random, with many time periods having no demand [1]. Moreover, when a demand occurs, the request is sometimes for more than a single unit. Items with intermittent demand include service spare parts and high-priced capital goods, such as heavy machinery. Such items are often described as "slow moving". Demand that it intermittent is often also "lumpy", meaning that there is great variability among the nonzero value. An example of the difference between intermittent demand data and product demand data that is normal, or "smooth", is illustrated in the tables below:

Table 1. Intermittent Demand Data

Month	1	2	3	4	5	6	7	8	9	10	11	12	13	14	15	16	17
Demand	0	0	**19**	0	0	0	**4**	**18**	**17**	0	0	0	0	0	**3**	0	0

Table 2. Normal, Smooth Demand Data

Month	1	2	3	4	5	6	7	8	9	10	11	12	13	14	15	16	17
Demand	17	20	18	25	30	68	70	41	32	35	66	26	23	25	25	28	36

D. Ślęzak et al. (Eds.): RSFDGrC 2005, LNAI 3642, pp. 604–613, 2005.
© Springer-Verlag Berlin Heidelberg 2005

Intermittent demand creates significant problems in the manufacturing and supply environment as far as forecasting and inventory control are concerned. It is not only the variability of the demand size, but also the variability of the demand pattern that make intermittent demand so difficult to forecast [2]. The literature, that includes a relatively small number of proposed forecasting solutions to this demand uncertainty problem, can be found in [3,4,5,6]. The single exponential smoothing and the Croston methods are the most frequently used methods for forecasting low and intermittent demands [4,6]. Croston [4] proposed a method that builds demand estimates taking into account both demand size and the interval between demand incidences. Despite the theoretical superiority of such an estimation procedure, empirical evidence suggests modest gains in performance when compared with simpler forecasting techniques; some evidence even suggests losses in performance. In their experimental study, Johnston and Boylan [7], after using a wide range of simulated conditions, observed an improvement in forecast performance using the Croston method when compared with the straight Holt (EWMA) method. On the other hand, Bartezzaghi et al. [3] in their experimental simulation found that EWMA appears applicable only with low levels of lumpiness. Willemain et al. [6] concluded that the Croston method is significantly superior to exponential smoothing under intermittent demand conditions. In addition, other methods such as the Wilcox [8] and Cox Process [9] methods were also used for forecasting intermittent demand. Both methods were shown to produce poor and unreliable forecasting results after being tested on the current research data and for that reason neither is included in the study. Watson [10] found that the increase in average annual inventory cost resulted from the fluctuations in the forecast demand parameters of several lumpy demand patterns. Zhao and Lee [11] concluded in their study that forecasting errors significantly increases total costs and reduce the service level within MRP systems. Their results showed that forecasting errors increase as variations in the demand increase. The fact that the existence of forecasting error increases the total cost of MRP systems has been reported in several other studies [12,13,14].

Recently, support vector machines (SVMs) was developed by Vapnik and his co-workers [15,16]. With the introduction of Vapnik's -insensitive loss function, SVMs have been extended to solve non-linear regression estimation problems and they have been shown to exhibit excellent performance [15,16]. Our research focuses on the application of Support Vector Regression (SVR) to make a new attempt to novel forecasting method toward the intermittent parts demand.

This paper consists of five sections. Section 2 reviews the most widely used approach for forecasting intermittent demand and indicates its limitation and the direction of further improvement. General principles of SVMs regression are presented in Section 3, together with the general procedures of applying it. Section 4 and Section 5 present an experiment concerned with the detailed procedures of how to employing SVMs regression, involving data set selection, data preprocessing and clustering, kernel function selection and so on. Conclusions and discussion for further research hints are included in the last section.

2   Reviews on Forecasting Intermittent Demand Methods

Generally efforts on forecasting the intermittent demand could fall into two categories. One is to find the distribution function and the other is time series forecasting.

2.1   Demand Distribution Estimation

The inventory control method proposed here relies on the estimation of the distribution of demand for low demand parts. It is necessary to use demand distributions rather than expected values of demand because the intermittent patterns characteristic of low demand parts require a probabilistic approach to forecasting that can be incorporated into an inventory management program. Using the demand distributions, it is possible to manage the inventory to maximize readiness given a fixed inventory budget. Other optimization goals are possible as well.

The chief obstacle to reliable demand distribution estimation is the paucity of historical data available for any typical set of low demand parts. Demand typically occurs in small integer numbers of parts. Some parts may have only 3 or 4 non-zero demands among a large number of zero demand periods. This amount of data is not sufficient to construct a robust probability demand distribution. If a probabilistic model of the demand is available, such as a Weibull model or Poisson model, then it is possible to estimate the demand distribution directly from the model. If an empirical estimate of the demand distribution must derived, through bootstrapping or other means, it is necessary to group the data in a way that generates enough non-zero data points to produce robust demand distribution estimates.

2.2   Croston Method

Croston method falls into the time series forecasting category and is the most widely used method, which could be illustrated as follows.

Let Y_t be the demand occurring during the time period t and X_t be the indicator variable for non-zero demand periods; i.e., $X_t = 1$ when demand occurs at time period t and $X_t = 0$ when no demand occurs. Furthermore, let j_t be number of periods with nonzero demand during interval $[0, t]$ such that $j_t = \sum_{i=1}^{t} X_i$, i.e., j_t is the index of the the non-zero demand. For ease of notation, we will usually drop the subscript t on j . Then we let Y_j^* represent the size of the j th non-zero demand and Q_j the inter-arrival time between Y_{j-1}^* and Y_j^*. Using this notation, we can write $Y_j = X_t Y_j^*$.

Croston method separately forecasts the non-zero demand size and the inter-arrival time between successive demands using simple exponential smoothing (SES), with forecasts being updated only after demand occurrences. Let Z_j and P_j be the forecasts of the $(j+1)_{th}$ demand size and inter-arrival time respectively, based on data up to demand j. Then Croston method gives

$$Z_j = (1 - \alpha) Z_{j-1} + \alpha Y_j^* \tag{1}$$
$$P_j = (1 - \alpha) P_{j-1} + \alpha P_j \tag{2}$$

The smoothing parameter α takes values between 0 and 1 and is assumed to be the same for both Y_j^* and Q_j. Let $l = j_n$ denote the last period of demand. Then the mean demand rate, which used as the h-step ahead forecast for the demand at time $n + h$ is estimated by the ratio

$$\hat{Y}_{n+h} = Z_l / P_l \tag{3}$$

The assumptions of Croston method could be derived that (1) the distribution of non-zero demand sizes Y_j^* is iid normal;(2) the distribution of inter-arrival times Q_j is iid Geometric; and (3)demand sizes Y_j^* and inter-arrival times Q_j are mutually independent. These assumptions are clearly incorrect, as the assumption of iid data would result in using the simple mean as the forecast, rather than simple exponential smoothing, for both processes. This is the basic reason for more correction and modification toward Croston method.

3 SVR for Forecasting

Given a set of data points $G = \{(x_i, d_i)\}_l^n$ (is the input vector, is the desired value and is the total number of data patterns), SVMs approximate the function using the following:

$$y = f(x) = \omega \phi(x) + b \tag{4}$$

where $\phi(x)$ is the high dimensional feature space which is non-linearly mapped from the input space x. The coefficients ω and b are estimated by minimizing

$$R_{SVMs}(C) = C \frac{1}{n} \sum_{i=1}^{n} L_\xi(d_i, y_i) + \frac{1}{2}\|\omega\|^2, \tag{5}$$

$$L_\xi(d_i, y_i) = \begin{cases} |d - y| - \varepsilon, & \text{if } |d - y| \geq \varepsilon, \\ 0, & \text{otherwise.} \end{cases} \tag{6}$$

In regularized risk function given by Eq.(6), the first term $C\left(\frac{1}{n}\right)\sum_{i=1}^{n} L_\xi(d_i, y_i)$ is the empirical error (risk). They are measured by the ε-insensitive loss function given by Eq.(6). This loss function provides the advantage of enabling one to use sparse data points to represent the decision function given by Eq. (6). The second term $\frac{1}{2}\|\omega\|^2$, on the other hand, is the regularization term. C is referred to as the regularized constant and it determines the trade-off between the empirical risk and the regularization term. Increasing the value of C will result in the relative importance of the empirical risk with respect to the regularization term to grow. ε is called the tube size and it is equivalent to the approximation accuracy placed on the training data points. Both C and ε are user-prescribed parameters.

To obtain the estimations of ω and b, Eq.(2) is transformed to the primal function given by Eq.(4) by introducing the positive slack variables ξ_i and ξ_i^* as follows:

Minimize $R_{SVMs}\left(\omega, \xi^{(*)}\right) = C\sum_{i=1}^{n} L_\xi(\xi_i, \xi_i^*) + \frac{1}{2}\|\omega\|^2,$

Subject to $\begin{aligned} d_i - \omega\phi(x_i) - b_i &\leq \varepsilon + \xi_i, \\ \omega\phi(x_i) + b_i - d_i &\leq \varepsilon + \xi_i^*, \xi_i^* \geq 0 \end{aligned} \tag{7}$

Finally, by introducing Lagrange multipliers and exploiting the optimality constraints, the decision function given by Eq.(1) has the following explicit form [18]:

$$f\left(x, a_i, a_i^*\right) = \sum_{i=1}^{n} \left(a_i - a_i^*\right) K\left(x, x_i\right) + b \tag{8}$$

In Eq.(8), a_i and a_i^* are the so-called Lagrange multipliers. They satisfy the equalities $a_i * a_i^* = 0$, $a_i > 0$ and $a_i^* > 0$ where $i = 1, 2, \cdots, n$ and are obtained by maximizing the dual function of Eq.(4) which has the following form:

$$R\left(a_i, a_i^*\right) = \sum_{i=1}^{n} d_i \left(a_i - a_i^*\right) - \varepsilon \sum_{i=1}^{n} d_i \left(a_i + a_i^*\right)$$

$$-\frac{1}{2} \sum_{i=1}^{n} \sum_{j=1}^{n} \left(a_i - a_i^*\right) \left(a_j - a_j^*\right) K\left(x_i, x_j\right) \tag{9}$$

with the constraints

$$\sum_{i=1}^{n} \left(a_i - a_i^*\right),$$
$$0 \le a_i \le C, \quad i = 1, 2, \cdots, n \tag{10}$$
$$0 \le a_i^* \le C, \quad i = 1, 2, \cdots, n$$

Based on the Karush-Kuhn-Tucker (KKT) conditions of quadratic programming, only a certain number of coefficients $\left(a_i - a_i^*\right)$ in Eq.(8) will assume non-zero values. The data points associated with them have approximation errors equal to or larger than ε and are referred to as support vectors. These are the data points lying on or outside the ε-bound of the decision function. According to Eq.(6), it is evident that support vectors are the only elements of the data points that are used in determining the decision function as the coefficients $\left(a_i - a_i^*\right)$ of other data points are all equal to zero. Generally, the larger the ε, the fewer the number of support vectors and thus the sparser the representation of the solution. However, a larger ε can also depreciate the approximation accuracy placed on the training points.In this sense, ε is a trade-off between the sparseness of the representation and closeness to the data. $K\left(x_i, x_j\right)$ is defined as the kernel function. The value of the kernel is equal to the inner product of two vectors x_i and x_j in the feature space $\phi\left(x_i\right)$ and $\phi\left(x_j\right)$, that is, $K\left(x_i, x_j\right) = \phi\left(x_i\right) * \phi\left(x_j\right)$. The elegance of using the kernel function is that one can deal with feature spaces of arbitrary dimensionality without having to compute the map $\phi\left(x_i\right)$ explicitly. Any function satisfying Mercer's condition [17] can be used as the kernel function. The typical examples of kernel function are as follows:

Linear: $K\left(x_i, x_j\right) = x_i^T x_j$
Polynomial: $K\left(x_i, x_j\right) = \left(\gamma x_i^T x_j + r\right)^d, \gamma > 0.$
Radial basis function(RBF): $K\left(x_i, x_j\right) = \exp\left(-\gamma \|x_i - x_j\|^2\right), \gamma > 0.$
Sigmoid: $K\left(x_i, x_j\right) = \tanh\left(\gamma x_i^T x_j + r\right).$

Here, γ, r and d are kernel parameters. The kernel parameter should be carefully chosen as it implicitly defines the structure of the high dimensional feature space $\phi(x_i)$ and thus controls the complexity of the final solution. From the implementation point of view, training SVMs is equivalent to solving a linearly constrained quadratic programming (QP) with the number of variables twice as that of the training data points.

Generally speaking, SVMs regression for forecasting follows the procedures: (1) Transform data to the format of an SVM and conduct simple scaling on the data; (2) Choose the kernel functions; (3) Use cross-validation to find the best parameter C and γ; (4) Use the best parameter C and γ to train the whole training set; (5) Test.

4 Experimental Setting

4.1 Data Sets

Forecasting and inventory management for intermittent demand parts is particularly problematic because of the large number of low demand parts that must be considered. As an experiment setting, of 5,000 unique non-repairable spare parts for the Daya Bay Nuclear station in China, over half of those parts have been ordered 10 time or less in the last ten years. While many of these low demand parts are important for the safe operation of the nuclear reactor, it is simply uneconomical to stock enough spares to guarantee that every low demand part will be available when needed.Table.3 illustrates the intermittent characteristics of the spare parts according to the database of spare parts usage.

Table 3. Summary statistics for monthly intermittent demand data from 1994-2003

Statistics Indicators Values	Mean	S.D.	Max.	Min.
Zero values %	47	29	86	5
Average of nonzero demands	35	54	78	1

4.2 Clustering for Data Preprocessing

Clustering is the process of grouping parts with similar demand patterns. There are several methods to cluster data, agglomerative hierarchical clustering and c-means clustering are two typical methods. We have found that demand patterns can be robustly clustered using cumulative demand patterns. Using the cumulative demand patterns avoids problems introduced by the intermittent pattern of incremental demand. Figure 1 shows one of prototype cumulative demand patterns after clustering 4063 low demand spare parts into 10 clusters. Prototype patterns represent the typical demand pattern for each of the clusters. Also plotted are the 25th and 75th percentiles of demand gathered from the cumulative demand of the individual parts in each cluster. Note the cluster size ranges from 34 parts to 241 parts. Clustering was accomplished using a fuzzy c-means (FCM) clustering routine [18,19]. The generalized objective function subject to the same fuzzy c-partition constraints [20] is:

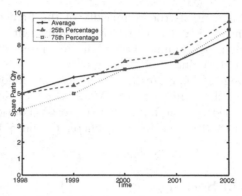

Fig. 1. Cumulative demand pattern of Cluster 1

$$\text{Min } J_m\left(U, V\right) = \sum_{i=1}^{c} \sum_{k=1}^{n} \left(\mu_{ik}\right)^m \left\| x_k - v_i \right\|^2 \qquad (11)$$

During our experiment, one of the problems associated with clustering is the difficulty in determining the number of clusters, c. Various validity measures have been proposed to determine the optimal number of clusters in order to address this inherent drawback of FCM [19,21]. In our experiment, the optimal number of terms is defined as the one that has the lowest mean squared error (MSE). The least MSE measure is also used to identify the most appropriate form of membership functions. In summary, the application procedure of the FCM has the following steps:(1) choose $c\left(2 \leq c \leq n\right), m\left(1 < m < \infty\right)$ and initialize the membership matrix. (2) Read in the data set and find the maximum and minimum values. (3) Calculate cluster centers but force the two clusters with the largest and smallest values to take the maximum and minimum domain values. (4) Update the membership matrix (5) Compute the change of each value in the membership matrix and determine whether the maximum change is smaller than the threshold value chosen to stop the iterative process (set at 0.02 throughout this study). If not, return to Step 3. (6) Redistribute erroneous membership values to the other two more appropriate terms proportional to their current membership values.

4.3   Performance Criteria

The prediction performance is evaluated using the normalized mean squared error (NMSE). NMSE is the measures of the deviation between the actual and predicted values. The smaller the values of NMSE, the closer are the predicted time series values to the actual values. The NMSE of the test set is calculated as follows:

$$\text{NMSE} = \frac{1}{\delta^2 n} \sum_{i=1}^{n} \left(y_i - \hat{y}_i\right)^2, \qquad (12)$$

$$\delta^2 = \frac{1}{n-1} \sum_{i=1}^{n} \left(y_i - \overline{y}\right)^2, \qquad (13)$$

Table 4. NMSE Values of comparative methods

Methods	NMSE
SVMs_RBF	0.3220
SVMs_Linear	0.5945
SVMs_Polynomial	0.6054
Croston	0.5730

where n represents the total number of data points in the test set. $\hat{y}_i$ represents the predicted value. $\bar{y}$ denotes the mean of the actual output values. Table 4 shows the NMSE values of different kernel functions compared with simple exponential smoothing (SES), linear exponential smoothing (LES) and tells out the best prediction method under our numerical case.

4.4 Kernel Function Parameters Selection

We use general RBF as the kernel function. The RBF kernel nonlinearly maps samples into a higher dimensional space, so it, unlike the linear kernel, can handle the case when the relation between class labels and attributes is nonlinear. Furthermore, the linear kernel is a special case of RBF as (Ref.[22]) shows that the linear kernel with a penalty parameter $\tilde{C}$ has the same performance as the RBF kernel with some parameters (C, γ). In addition, the sigmoid kernel behaves like RBF for certain parameters [23]. The second reason is the number of hyper-parameters which influences the complexity of model selection. The polynomial kernel has more hyper-parameters than the RBF kernel. Finally, the RBF kernel has less numerical difficulties. One key point is $0 < K_{ij} \leq 1$ in contrast to polynomial kernels of which kernel values may go to infinity $\left(\gamma x_i^T x_j + r > 1\right)$ or zero $\left(\gamma x_i^T x_j + r < 1\right)$ while the degree is large.

There are two parameters while using RBF kernels: C and γ. It is not known beforehand which C and γ are the best for one problem; consequently some kind of model selection (parameter search) must be done. The goal is to identify good (C, γ) so that the classifier can accurately predict unknown data (i.e., testing data). Note that it may not be useful to achieve high training accuracy (i.e., classifiers accurately predict training data whose class labels are indeed known). Therefore, a common way is to separate training data to two parts of which one is considered unknown in training the classifier. Then the prediction accuracy on this set can more precisely reflect the performance on classifying unknown data. An improved version of this procedure is cross-validation.

We use a grid-search on C and γ using cross-validation. Basically pairs of (C, γ) are tried and the one with the best cross-validation accuracy is picked. We found that trying exponentially growing sequences of C and γ is a practical method to identify good parameters (for example, $C = 2^{-5}, 2^{-3}, \cdots, 2^{15}; \gamma = 2^{-15}, 2^{-13}, \cdots, 2^3$).

5   Experimental Results

Still raise the example of Cluster 1, Figure 2 shows the experimental results by comparing the forecasting results of actual data, Croston method and SVMs regression. By summing all the clusters' result, SVMs regression method's accuracy is 12.4% higher than Croston method by the computation of standard deviation.In terms of the computational cost, SVMs takes more than Croston due to the inherent drawback of nonlinear regression and more time needed in training and parameters tuning.

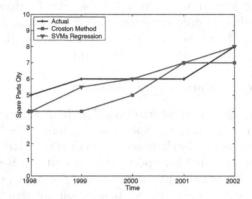

Fig. 2. Forecasting results comparison of Cluster 1

6   Conclusions

The use of SVMs regression in forecasting intermittent demand is studied in this paper. Our experiment is extremely a case study and has made a new try on applying SVMs regression as a promising alternative to forecast the intermittent demand. But further research toward an extremely changing data situation should be done, which means the data fluctuation may affect the performance of this method. Croston method still has advantages in terms of computational cost and robust. In fact, we got confused with the experimental result at the every beginning without the data clustering. Another further research hint is the knowledge priority used in training the sample and determining the function parameters. This is to say, parameters selection is free but affect the performance a lot. A good parameter selection method should be worthy of further research.

Acknowledgements. This research is granted by National Science Foundation of China, No.70401015.

References

1. Silver, E.A.: Operations research in inventory management: A review and critique. Operations Research, **29** (1981) 628-645
2. Syntetos, A.A., Boylan, J.E.: On the bias of intermittent demand estimates. International Journal of Production Economics, (2001) 457-466

3. Bartezzaghi, E., Verganti, R., Zotteri, G.A.: Simulation framework for forecasting uncertain lumpy demand. International Journal of Production Economics, **59(1-3)** (1999) 499-510
4. Croston, J.D.: Forecasting and stock control for intermittent demands. Operational Research Quarterly, **23(3)** (1972) 289-303
5. Rao, A.V.: A comment on: forecasting and stock control for intermittent demands. Operational Research Quarterly, **24(4)** (1973) 639-640
6. Willemain, T.R., Smart, C.N., Shockor, J.H., DeSautels, P.A.: Forecasting intermittent demand in manufacturing: a comparative evaluation of Croston's method. International Journal of Forecasting, **10(4)** (1994) 529-538
7. Johnston, F.R., Boylan, J.E.: Forecasting for items with intermittent demand. Journal of the Operational Research Society, **47(1)** (1996) 113-121
8. Wilcox, J.E.: How to forecast lumpy items. Production Inventory Management Journal, **11(1)** (1970) 51-54
9. Willemain, T.R., Ratti, E.W.L., Smart, C.N.: Forecasting intermittent demand using a cox process model. INFORMS Meetings, Boston, USA (1994) 1-14
10. Watson, R.B.: The effects of demand-forecast fluctuations on customer service and inventory cost when demand is lumpy. Journal of the Operational Research Society, **38(1)** (1987) 75-82
11. Zhao, X., Lee, T.S.: Freezing the master production schedule for material requirements planning systems under demand uncertainty. Journal of Operations Management, **11(2)** (1993) 185-205
12. Lee, T.S., Adam, E.E.: Forecasting error evaluation in material requirements planning (MRP) production-inventory systems. Management Science, **32(9)** (1986) 186-205
13. Sridharan, S.V., Berry, W.L.: Freezing the master production schedule under demand uncertainty. Decision Science, **21(1)** (1990) 97-120
14. Wemmerlov, U.: The behaviour of lot-sizing procedures in the presence of forecast errors. Journal of Operations Management, **8(1)** (1989) 37-47
15. Vapnik, V.N., Golowich, S.E., Smola, A.J.: Support vector method for function approximation, regression estimation, and signal processing. Advances in Neural Information Processing Systems, **9** (1996) 281-287
16. Vapnik, V.N.: The nature of statistical learning theory. New York, Springer (1995)
17. Schmidt, M.: Identifying speaker with support vector networks. Interface '96 Proceedings, Sydney (1996)
18. Dunn, J.C.: A fuzzy relative of the ISODATA process and its use in detecting compact well-separated clusters. J. Cybernet., **3** (1974) 32-57
19. Medasani, S., Kim, J., Krishnapuram, R.: An overview of membership function generation techniques for pattern recognition. International Journal of Approximation Research, **19** (1998) 391-417
20. Pal, N.R., Bezdek, J.C.: On cluster validity for the fuzzy c-means model. IEEE Trans. Fuzzy Systems, **3(3)** (1995) 370-379
21. Rezaee, M.R., Lelieveldt, B.P.F., Reiber, J.H.C.: A new cluster validity index for the fuzzy c-means. Pattern Recognition Letters, **19** (1998) 237-246
22. Haykin, S.: Neural networks: a comprehensive foundation. Englewood Cliks, NJ, Prentice Hall (1999)
23. Zhang, G.Q., Michael, Y.H.: Neural network forecasting of the British Pound=US Dollar exchange rate. Omega, **26(4)** (1998) 495-506

Fuzzy Forecast Modeling for Gas Furnace Based on Fuzzy Sets and Rough Sets Theory

Keming Xie, Zehua Chen, and Yuxia Qiu

College of Information Engineering, Taiyuan University of Technology,
030024 Taiyuan, Shanxi, P.R. China
kmxie@tyut.edu.cn

Abstract. This paper describes a new approach to generate optimal fuzzy forecast model for Box and Jenkins' gas furnace from its Input/ Output data (I/O data) by fuzzy set theory and rough set theory (RST). Generally, the nonlinear mapping relations of I/O data can be expressed by fuzzy set theory and fuzzy logic, which are proven to be a nonlinear universal function approximator. One of the most distinguished features of RST is that it can directly extract knowledge from large amount of data without any transcendental knowledge. The fuzzy forecast model determination mainly includes 3 steps: firstly, express I/O data in fuzzy decision table. Secondly, quantitatively determine the best structure of the fuzzy forecast model by RST. The third step is to get optimal fuzzy rules from fuzzy decision table by RST reduction algorithm. Experimental results have shown the new algorithm is simple and intuitive. It is another successful application of RST in fuzzy identification.

1 Introduction

System identification is a hot spot in modern control area. The traditional crisp mathematical systems theory, usually armed with linear differential equations, has been successfully applied to the problems of modeling and control of linear time-invariant systems. In many complex systems, however, Zadeh inconsistency principle exists. Zadeh's fuzzy logic system (FLS) is distinguished by its ability of emulating human thinking mechanism with linguistic fuzzy rules [1]. Fuzzy sets and fuzzy logic realize a nonlinear mapping from an input data space into an output space. And many FLS's are proven to be nonlinear universal function approximators [2]. Today, fuzzy set theory, and its combination with neural networks have become effective approaches in complex system identification, and many works have been done hitherto. Li [3] builds cement kiln model by applying fuzzy inference composition method. Li [4] gets gas furnace forecast model by fuzzy set theory and statistic method. Barada and Singh [5] get adaptive fuzzy-neural models for dynamical systems. All of them are based on the Input/Output data (I/O data) of the system, and at last, a linguistic fuzzy model is got.

Data samples can provide valuable knowledge or information about the object we want to know, and RST proposed by Pawlak [6] can explore them from large amount of data. Mrózek [7] proposed that control behavior of human beings

D. Ślęzak et al. (Eds.): RSFDGrC 2005, LNAI 3642, pp. 614–623, 2005.
© Springer-Verlag Berlin Heidelberg 2005

can be obtained from control process by RST in form of fuzzy rules If {Premise} then {Conclusion}. Obviously, RST and FST bridge the gap between the observed data of the process with the fuzzy rules, which inspired us to combine it together in fuzzy identification. As another major soft computing approach, RST is turning out to be methodologically significant in many areas besides intelligent control. Pawlak, Mrózek, Plonka, Skowron, and other scholars did much valuable work on rough and rough-fuzzy control in 1990s [8,9,10,11,12]. Rough-neural networks [13] and rough genetic algorithms [14] by Lingras are also instructive in intelligent control.

Box and Jenkins' Gas Furnace Problem [15] is a classical experiment for system identification. On ground of literature [4] and combined with RST, its fuzzy forecast model is identified in this paper. The structure of the fuzzy model is determined by the computation of the attribute importance, including the attribute combinations. The final fuzzy rules of the model are determined by the reduction algorithm of the RST. Mean square error (MSE) and the total rule number are taken as the performance index. Experimental results have shown that the new algorithm is simple, intuitive and easy to apply.

The paper is organized as follows: The background of the study and theory foundations are given in Section 2, and Section 3 explores the proposed modeling algorithm in detail by using the Box and Jenkins' Gas Furnace Problem as illustrative example. Conclusion and suggested extensions to this research are presented in Section 4.

2   Theory Foundations

2.1   Traditional Methods for Box and Jenkins' Gas Furnace Problem

Fuzzy forecast model of Box and Jenkins' Gas Furnace is got in literature [4] by correlation experiments. Through the analysis of the correlation between current output $y(t)$ with its historical process data $u(t-1), u(t-2), \ldots, u(t-9)$, $y(t-1), \ldots, y(t-3)$, the algorithm in [4] respectively counts the number of the same rules appeared in the form of fuzzy rules: if $u(t-i)$ then $y(t)$ and if $y(t-j)$ then $y(t)$, where $0 \leq i \leq 9, 0 \leq j \leq 3$. The optimal structure of the model is determined by observing how the rules scattered along the diagonal and by counting the number of the repeating rules. The optimal fuzzy forecast model of 16 fuzzy rules with structure of $< u(t-4)y(t-1), y(t) >$ is at last obtained.

This kind of fuzzy identification method is mostly based on statistical approach. The fuzzy forecast model is obtained by qualitative analysis of correlation between current output and its historical data, which is lacking of exact quantitative computation. Furthermore, the obtained rules are not the simplest ones, to some extent.

The fuzzy-neural model with good performance is got in literature [5] by finding optimal rule premise variables through modified mountain clustering (MMC) algorithm, group method of data handling (GMDH), and a search tree (ST); the optimal numbers of model rules are determined by using MMC, recursive least-squares estimation, along with parallel simulation mean square error as a performance index. However, it is relatively complex.

In this paper, fuzzy set theory and RST are together used to analyze process data so as to quantitatively determine the structure of the fuzzy forecast model, and then RST reduction algorithm is used to find the simplest fuzzy rules so as to get the optimal fuzzy forecast model with minimum MSE.

Some useful definitions such as fuzzy forecast model in fuzzy control, fuzzy decision table used in this paper and importance of attribute in RST are given in Section 2.2.

2.2   Some Definitions

Definition 1. *A group of fuzzy rules used to describe the system characteristics is called* Fuzzy Forecast Model. *It uses the input and output of the past time to forecast the current output. The forecast model which has two inputs and one output in engineering can be expressed as follows [4]:*

$$if \ u(t-k) = B_i \ and \ y(t-l) = C_i \ then \ y(t) = C_j$$

where t expresses time, u is the system input, y is that of output. $u(t-k)$ is a historical input in a certain time, $y(t-l)$ is that of output, and $y(t)$ is current output of the system. B, C are both fuzzy sets, B_i and C_j, C_s are respectively the fuzzy language variable values. Once the k and l are fixed, the structure of the model is determined.

Definition 2. *By mapping the measured I/O data into fuzzy space in form of decision table, we obtain* Fuzzy Decision Table, *marked as* $\tilde{T} = (\tilde{U}, \tilde{A}, \tilde{C}, \tilde{D}, \tilde{V})$, *where* $\tilde{U}$ *is fuzzy universe,* $\tilde{A} = \tilde{C} \cup \tilde{D}$ *is the attribute set, the fuzzy language variables in* $\tilde{C}$ *are tantamount to the classification of attributes of RST, and their corresponding values equal to the attribute values of RST.*

Fuzzy decision table makes it possible to reduce fuzzy rules by RST reduction algorithm.

Definition 3. *Let* C *and* D *be equivalence relations over* U. D-*positive region of* C *is expressed by* $pos_C(D) = \cup_{X \in U|D} C_-(X)$, *i.e. the set-theoretic sum of rough set lower approximations of classes* $X \in U|D$ *induced by* C. *When* $pos_C(D) = pos_{C\backslash r}(D)$, *we say that* $r \in C$ *is* D-*dispensable in* C, *otherwise* r *is* D-*indispensable in* C *[6].*

Definition 4. *Importance of attribute [6]:*

$$w_{c_i} = \gamma_C(D) - \gamma_{C\backslash i}(D) = \frac{cardpos_C(D) - cardpos_{C\backslash i}(D)}{cardU} \tag{1}$$

The bigger the w_{c_i}, more important the condition attribute i in C. The importance of attribute is used to determine most significant condition attributes.

2.3   Modeling Algorithms

The key for building fuzzy forecast model is to acquire a set of descriptive rules about the system according to the system I/O data. It mainly includes 4 steps.

1. Collect real I/O data, select fuzzy membership functions of U and Y in fuzzy forecast model. Give language variable table according to experience or some algorithms, and then express I/O data in form of fuzzy decision table.
2. Determine the structure of the fuzzy forecast model. Here, according to the concept of importance of attribute and attribute combination in RST, we need k and l in the fuzzy forecast model $< u(t - k)y(t - l), y(t) >$.
3. Get the smallest rule set by reduct algorithm of RST [6] with MSE and the total rule numbers as the performance index.
4. Finish with simulation and analysis.

3   Box and Jenkins' Gas Furnace Problem

The I/O data for Box and Jenkins' Gas Furnace dynamical process are found in [15], the input $u(k)$ and output $y(k)$ respectively represent gas flow rate and CO_2 concentration. 296 data records are both used for training and testing.
    Here, the algorithm mentioned above will be discussed in detail.

3.1   Expressing Measured I/O Data in Fuzzy Decision Table

To express the original data in form of decision table in RST, whose condition attributes are respectively: $u(t - 9)$, $u(t - 8)$, $u(t - 7)$, $u(t - 6)$, $u(t - 5)$, $u(t - 4)$, $u(t - 3)$, $u(t - 2)$, $u(t - 1)$, $y(t - 4)$, $y(t - 3)$, $y(t - 2)$, $y(t - 1)$, and decision attribute is $y(t)$. 296*2-size data table is turned to 287*14-size decision table.
    Fuzzy partitioning of the I/O Data. According to [4], we consider corresponding fuzzy sets B_i and C_j, where $1 \le i \le 7$, $1 \le j \le 6$. The maximum-minimum approach is used to realize fuzzification, Mamdani fuzzy inference is taken, defuzzification adapts bisector method, all of the language values are expressed by Gaussian function shown in Figure 1.
    Fuzzify the I/O data. The former decision table is now converted into the fuzzy decision table. Here $\tilde{U}$ is the fuzzy universe, $\tilde{C}$ is the condition attribute, $\tilde{D}$ is the decision attribute, i is the attribute series number. The fuzzy decision table is presented in Table 1.

3.2   Determining the Structure of the Fuzzy Forecast Model

We need to determine inputs of the fuzzy forecast model, i.e. k and l in the model "if $u(t - k) = B_i$ and $y(t - l) = C_j$ then $y(t) = C_s$". Here attribute importance is computed to determine the correlation of the historical input/output and the current output.

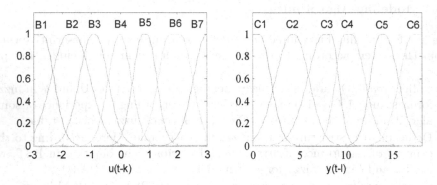

Fig. 1. Membership functions for fuzzy partition of the $u(t-k)$ and $y(t-l)$

Table 1. Fuzzy decision table of Gas Furnace Problem

			$\tilde{C}$					$\tilde{D}$
i	1	2	...	9	10	11	12	13	14
$\tilde{U}$	$u(t-9)$	$u(t-8)$		$u(t-1)$	$y(t-4)$	$y(t-3)$	$y(t-2)$	$y(t-1)$	$y(t)$
1	B4	B4		B4		C3	C3	C4	C3
2	B4	B4		B4		C3	C3	C3	C3
...									
111	B3	B2		B3		C6	C5	C5	C6
...									
287	B4	B4		B5		C5	C5	C5	C5

Table 2. $\gamma_{C_i}(D)$ and w_{C_i} for condition attributes in fuzzy decision table

Index	Variable	$\gamma_{C_i}(D)$	w_{C_i}
1	$u(t-9)$	0.94031	0.05969
2	$u(t-8)$	0.94077	0.05923
3	$u(t-7)$	0.95122	0.04878
4	$u(t-6)$	0.95122	0.04878
5	$u(t-5)$	0.94774	0.05226
6	$u(t-4)$	0.93031	0.06969
7	$u(t-3)$	0.93728	0.06272
8	$u(t-2)$	0.95122	0.04878
9	$u(t-1)$	0.94774	0.05226
10	$y(t-4)$	0.92334	0.07666
11	$y(t-3)$	0.95819	0.04181
12	$y(t-2)$	0.95122	0.04878
13	$y(t-1)$	0.95819	0.04181

1. Compute $\gamma_C(D)$ and w_{C_i}, and determine one input of the model. The computation result is listed in Table 2. In this example

$$\gamma_C^D = cardpos_C(D)/cardU = 1$$

It means that fuzzy decision table is consistent. And we have

$$\gamma_{Ci}(D) = \gamma_{C\setminus i}(D) = \frac{cardpos_{C\setminus i}(D)}{cardU} \quad (2)$$

$$w_{c_i} = \gamma_C(D) - \gamma_{C\setminus i}(D) = \frac{cardpos_C(D) - cardpos_{C\setminus i}(D)}{cardU} \quad (3)$$

here, $0.04 < w_{C_i} < 0.07$. In this condition, when $w_c \geq 0.06$, we think that corresponding attributes are more important than others. From the computation, it can be seen that for the current output, input of $u(t-3)u(t-4)$ and output of $y(t-4)$ is relative important.

2. Determine another input of the fuzzy forecast model. There exists strong correlation among the condition attributes, so after computing the attribute importance, we continue with importance of the attribute combination. According to step 1, $u(t-3)$, $u(t-4)$ and $y(t-4)$ are selected as one of the two inputs. Next we compute the importance of combinations related to the determined input. It is done according to Definition 5:

Definition 5. *(Importance of attribute combination) Let $B_{ij} = \{u(t-i), y(t-j)\}$, $1 \leq i \leq 9$, $1 \leq j \leq 4$. The importance of the attribute sets is defined as:*

$$w_{ij} = \gamma_{B_{ij}}^C(D) = \frac{cardpos_C(D) - cardpos_{C\setminus B_{ij}}(D)}{cardU} \quad (4)$$

The larger w_{ij}, the more important the correlated attributes to the output. Thus Table 3 is then obtained.

Table 3. Importance of different attribute combinations

w_{ij}	$y(t-1)$	$y(t-2)$	$y(t-3)$	$y(t-4)$
$u(t-1)$				0.07317
$u(t-2)$				0.05923
$u(t-3)$	0.08362	0.04878	0.05575	0.04878
$u(t-4)$	0.09408	0.04878	0.05575	0.05575
$u(t-5)$				0.05226
$u(t-6)$				0.07317
$u(t-7)$				0.06620
$u(t-8)$				0.04878
$u(t-9)$				0.05923

3. Select two models with biggest w_{ij} as our forecast model. It can be concluded from Table 3 that the combination of the two important attributes will not certainly result the most important combination. For example, $< u(t-3)y(t-4), y(t) >$ and $< u(t-4)y(t-4), y(t) >$ are less important than the combination of $< u(t-3)y(t-1), y(t) >$ and $< u(t-4)y(t-1), y(t) >$. Through this kind of computation, the structure of the model can be determined as $< u(t-3)y(t-1), y(t) >$ or $< u(t-4)y(t-1), y(t) >$.

3.3 Obtaining the Smallest Rule Set by RST

We rebuild two fuzzy decision tables with condition attributes, respectively, $u(t-3)y(t-1)$ and $u(t-4)y(t-1)$, and decision attribute $y(t)$. Then rough set theory is used to reduce 287 fuzzy rules to get the smallest rule set shown in

Table 4. Control rules of $< u(t-3)y(t-1), y(t) >$

	C1	C2	C3	C4	C5	C6
B1				C5	C6	C6
B2			C4	C5	C5	C6
B3			C3	C4	C5	C6
B4		C3	C3	C4	C5	C5
B5	C2	C2	C3	C4		
B6	C1	C2	C2			
B7		C2				

Table 5. Control rules of $< u(t-4)y(t-1), y(t) >$

	C1	C2	C3	C4	C5	C6
B1					C6	C6
B2				C5	C5	C6
B3		C4	C4	C4	C5	C5
B4		C3	C3	C4	C5	
B5		C2	C3	C3		
B6	C1	C2	C2			
B7	C1	C2				

Table 6. Control rules of $< u(t-4)y(t-1), y(t) >$ in [4]

	C1	C2	C3	C4	C5	C6
B1					C6	C6
B2			C4	C5	C5	C6
B3		C3	C4	C4	C5	C5
B4		C3	C3	C4	C4	C5
B5		C2	C3	C3	C4	C5
B6	C1	C2	C2	C3		
B7	C1	C1				

Table 7. Comparisons of 3 models mentioned above

	Rule number	*MSE*
$< u(t-3)y(t-1), y(t) >$	13	0.65151
$< u(t-4)y(t-1), y(t) >$	16	0.69152
$< u(t-4)y(t-1), y(t) >$	16	0.89900

Table 5. The reduction algorithm can be found in literature [6]. At last Table 4 and Table 5 are obtained. Table 6 is the analogous control table taken from literature [4].

If tables are rewritten in form of IF-THEN fuzzy rules, simpler rule set can be achieved. The total number of rules is listed in Table 7. However, to conveniently compare with Table 6, the results are also expressed in form of table.

3.4 Simulation and Analysis

To do the test experiment, the set of 296 data is used to test the forecast model derived in this paper. Figure 2 and Figure 3 are got respectively.

To compare the MSE and rule number of 3 models in Table 7, first two are computed in this paper, and the third is got in literature [4]. The MSE computation is according to the equation (5), where l represents the total measure times. And the MSE of 3 models are listed below.

$$p^2 = \frac{1}{l} \sum_{i=1}^{l} [y(t) - \hat{y}(t)]^2 \tag{5}$$

Result analysis: It can be seen through the whole modeling process that different fuzzy partitions may generate different results, however, it will not affect the

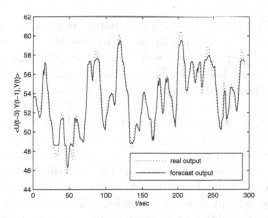

Fig. 2. Real and forecast output by using the model with $< u(t-3)y(t-1), y(t) >$

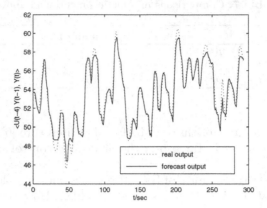

Fig. 3. Real and forecast output by using the model with $< u(t-4)y(t-1), y(t) >$

application of RST in the modeling. The fuzzification here is based on literature [4], and the model result is satisfied.

It can also be seen from the experiment that the forecast model is not unique. For example both $< u(t-3)y(t-1), y(t) >$ or $< u(t-4)y(t-1), y(t) >$ are good for engineering application, and there are only small differences between them.

Furthermore, when attribute importance of RST is used to compute the correlation of condition attribute and decision attribute, more attention should be given to the attributes combination due to its strong correlation. The combination of some most important attributes will not form the most important attributes set, on the contrary, the combination of sub optimal attributes will generate important influence on decision.

4   Conclusion

This paper describes a new approach to generate optimal fuzzy forecast model from Box and Jenkins' gas furnace dynamic process data by combining FST and RST together. Fuzzy set and fuzzy logic is firstly applied to turn I/O data into fuzzy decision table, and secondly RST is used to quantitatively determine the best structure of the forecast model and then to get the optimal rule sets by its knowledge reduction algorithm. At last, with MSE and the rule number as performance index, the optimal model is evaluated.It may be less accurate than the model in [5]. However, it is simple, intuitive and the result can be accepted by the practical engineering.

Furthermore, the concepts used here are all the basic concepts of RST, many improvements may be done. For example, to optimize the fuzzy partition in the first stage, employ entropy concept, and adopt the improved reduct algorithms to optimize the model. All these will advance the proposed algorithm. This paper just proposes a successful application of rough sets in fuzzy identification by a classical example.

Acknowledgements

This research is funded by Chinese National Natural Science Fund (60374029), and Youth Science Foundation (20041015) of Shanxi Province, P.R. China.

References

1. Zadeh, L.A.: Fuzzy Sets. Inform. Control, 8 (1965) 338–353
2. Kosko, B.: Fuzzy systems as universal approximators. IEEE Int. Conf. Fuzzy Syst. (1992) 1153–1162
3. Li, Y.S., Zhao, F.S.: A new method of system identification based on fuzzy set theory - fuzzy inference Composition. Journal of Automation, 17(3) (1991) 257–263
4. Li, B.S., Liu, Z.J.: System identification by Fuzzy set theory. Journal of Information and Control, 3 (1980) 32–38
5. Barada, S., Singh, H.: Generation Optimal Adaptive Fuzzy-Neural Models of Dynamical Systems with Applications to Control. IEEE trans. Syst., Man, Cybern., 28(3) (1998) 371–391
6. Pawlak, Z.: Rough sets: Theoretical aspects of reasoning about data. Kluwer Academic Publishers, Dordrecht, The Netherlands (1991)
7. Mrózek, A.: Rough Sets and Dependency Analysis among Attributes in Computer Implementations of Expert's Inference Models. International Journal of Man-Machine Studies, 30(4) (1989) 457–473
8. Mrózek, A., Plonka, L.: Knowledge Representation in Fuzzy and Rough Controllers. Fundam. Inform, 30(3/4) (1997) 299–311
9. Plonka, L., Mrózek, A.: Rule-Based Stabilization of the Inverted Pendulum. Computational Intelligence 11 (1995) 348–356
10. Mrózek, A., Plonka, L., Kędziera, J.: The methodology of rough controller synthesis. Proc. of the. 5th IEEE International Conference on Fuzzy Systems FUZZ-IEEE'96, September 8-11, New Orleans, Louisiana (1996) 1135–1139
11. Y.Cho, K. Lee, M. Park.: Autogeneration of fuzzy rules and membership functions for fuzzy modeling using rough set theory. IEE: Control, 45(5) (1998) 437–442
12. Peters, J.F., Skowron, A., Suraj, Z.: An Application of Rough Set Methods in Control Design. Fundam. Inform. 43(1-4) (2000) 269–290
13. Lingras, P.: Comparison of neurofuzzy and rough neural networks. Information Sciences 110 (1998) 207–215
14. Lingras, P., Davies, C.: Application of Rough Genetic Algorithms. Computational Intelligence, 17(3) (2001) 435–445
15. Box, G.E.P., Jenkins, G.M.: Time Series Analysis, Forecasting and Control. Holden Day, San Francisco (1970)

Flexible Quality-of-Control Management in Embedded Systems Using Fuzzy Feedback Scheduling

Feng Xia, Liping Liu, and Youxian Sun

National Laboratory of Industrial Control Technology,
Institute of Modern Control Engineering,
Zhejiang University, Hangzhou 310027, P.R. China
{xia, lpliu, yxsun}@iipc.zju.edu.cn

Abstract. Today's embedded systems representatively feature computing resource constraints as well as workload uncertainty. This gives rise
to the increasing demand of integrating control and scheduling in control applications that are built upon embedded systems. To address the
impact of uncertain computing resource availability on quality of control
(QoC), an intelligent control theoretic approach to feedback scheduling
is proposed based on fuzzy logic control technology. The case with one
single control task that competes for CPU resources with other non-
control tasks is considered. The sampling period of the control task is
dynamically adjusted. The goal is to provide runtime adaptation and
flexible QoC management in the presence of CPU resource constraint
and workload uncertainty. Preliminary simulation results argue that the
fuzzy feedback scheduler is effective in managing QoC in real-time embedded control applications.

1 Introduction

As embedded systems have become prevalent in today's computing community,
recent years have witnessed an increasing adoption of embedded controllers in
control applications [1,2]. It is recognized that over 99% of all microprocessors
are now used for embedded systems that control physical processes and devices
in real-time [2]. In contrast to mainstream general-purpose systems, these embedded computing platforms are often resource constrained. At the same time,
practical applications are becoming more and more complex. This leads to the
fact that several control and/or non-control tasks often share one embedded
CPU. In these cases, the system workload may exhibit uncertain characteristics
[3,4] due to: 1) task activation or termination, and 2) non-deterministic behavior
of the underlying platforms. In a resource-constrained environment, this workload uncertainty will cause the allowable CPU utilization for control purpose to
be limited and unexpectedly changeable.

From a historical perspective, control design is always dealt with as an issue
separated from task scheduling [1,5,6]. The control community generally focuses

D. Ślęzak et al. (Eds.): RSFDGrC 2005, LNAI 3642, pp. 624–633, 2005.

on developing novel control algorithms, regardless of their implementation or simply assuming that the underlying platform used to implement the control algorithms can provide real-time supports (e.g., deterministic, sufficient computing resources) as needed. However, as these control systems move from the research laboratories to real-world applications, they also become subject to the time constraints of the resource constrained environments. Although the separation of concerns allows the control community to focus on its own problem domain without worrying about how task scheduling is done, the control task does not always utilize the available computing resources in an efficient way, and the overload condition cannot be effectively addressed. As a result, the quality of control (QoC) may be significantly degraded. This is particularly serious for embedded control applications with limited computing resources. Therefore, when implementing real-time control applications over embedded systems, runtime flexibility should be provided for the sake of effective QoC management.

To address these requirements, the feedback scheduling mechanism (e.g. [6,7,8,9]) has been proposed as a promising approach to integrate feedback control and real-time scheduling. When applied in digital control systems, it is cost-effective to achieve control performance guarantees in computing resource insufficient environments. While the emerging feedback scheduling methodology is attracting more and more efforts both from the control community and the real-time scheduling community, a lot of open issues remains to be addressed in this field. For example, the computation time of a control task may vary significantly, e.g. due to the changes in the data to be processed. This makes the requested CPU time of control task(s) also uncertain. Since noises inevitably exist in the measurement of tasks' timing parameters, the measured CPU utilization is imprecise, if not unavailable.

In this work, we consider implementing real-time control applications on resource constrained embedded systems. Based on the methodology of feedback scheduling, a novel approach is proposed to provide runtime adaptation and flexible QoC management with respect to CPU resource availability variations and actual resource utilization uncertainty. Regarding the control task scheduling system as a feedback control issue, we utilize fuzzy control technology [10,11] to construct the feedback scheduler. This intelligent feedback scheduler is used to dynamically adjust the sampling period of a control task that competes for CPU time with other non-control tasks. The motivation for using fuzzy logic for feedback scheduling of control tasks is mainly raised from its inherent capacity to formalize control algorithms that can tolerate imprecision and uncertainty. Based on this intelligent control technique, we provide an innovative, systematic and scientific approach to feedback scheduling.

2   Problem Statement

In the system considered in this work, as shown in Fig.1, there is a single control task that executes concurrently on an embedded CPU together with other non-control tasks. For convenience, all these tasks are assumed to be periodic. The resource utilization of the non-control tasks may change over time. And hence the available CPU utilization for the considered control task is unexpectedly variable. According to basic real-time scheduling theory, the requested CPU utilization of the control task is $U = c/h$, where c and h are the execution time and sampling period, respectively. Let U_{sp} denote the available CPU utilization for control task execution. In order to guarantee the schedulability of the system, it must be satisfied that $c/h < U_{sp}$. Note that the CPU time can be scheduled using static or dynamic priority based scheduling algorithms, e.g. fixed priority (FP), rate monotonic (RM) or earliest dead-line first (EDF) scheduling algorithm [12]. For a specified scheduling algorithm, U_{sp} can be derived from the upper bound of the total CPU utilization in the corresponding schedulability condition. Alternatively, the CPU resource can also be allocated based on the Constant Bandwidth Server (CBS) mechanism [13]. In this case, U_{sp} can be viewed as the fraction of the CPU bandwidth assigned to the control task.

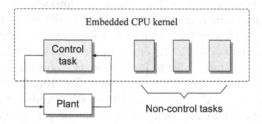

Fig. 1. The considered control task and several non-control tasks execute concurrently on one embedded CPU. The allowable CPU utilization for the control task is limited and varying.

Generally, a traditional controller is designed without taking into account computing resource availability variations. In this case, if the control task becomes unschedulable because of computing resources scarcity in real-time implementation, the control system may be destabilized [14]. In order to achieve satisfactory QoC, task schedulability should not be violated. For a well-designed control algorithm, from the control perspective, the QoC will highly depend on the sampling period h. Hence, the problem considered can be formulated as:

$$min_h \ J = \eta(h) \quad s.t. \ c/h \leq U_{sp} \tag{1}$$

where J is the control cost function with respect to h. In this work, we simply assume that h could be adjusted online and imprecise c values could be obtained through timing measurement with noise.

According to digital control theory, $\eta(\cdot)$ is a monotone decreasing function, i.e. smaller sampling period leads to better QoC. Therefore, with given execution time c, the cost function will be directly minimized by setting h to be c/U_{sp}. However, this is not so easy as it seems due to the complex uncertain characteristics of task execution time and CPU workload. On the one hand, both c

and c/U_{sp} are time-varying. On the other hand, the available values of them are imprecise due to unavoidable measurement noises. As a consequence, simply assigning h with a value of c/U_{sp} may lead to the fact that either the schedulability condition is violated, or the CPU time is not fully utilized.

In recent years, the emerging area of integrated control and scheduling has received considerable amount of attention, e.g. [4,5,6,7,8,9].In these works, the idea of feedback has been used in scheduling algorithms for applications where the dynamics of the workload cannot be characterized accurately. Marti et al [5] stress the need for new scheduling approaches able to optimize control performance according to the system dynamics. Cervin et al [6] present a scheduling architecture for real-time control tasks in which feedback information is used to adjust the workload of the processor and to optimize the overall control performance by simple rescaling of the task periods. Lu et al [8] apply a control theory based methodology to systematically design FCS algorithms to satisfy the transient and steady state performance specifications of real-time systems. Abeni et al [9] apply control theory to a reservation based scheduler and provide a precise mathematical model of the scheduler. Although these works concern dynamic computing resource availability, the inherent imprecision of the involved time parameters in feedback scheduling has not been effectively addressed. In order to achieve flexible QoC management, a more systematic and scientific approach is needed. In [4], a fuzzy feedback scheduler is proposed to improve the performance of iterative optimal control applications. As an anytime algorithm, the execution time of the controller is dynamically adjusted while the sampling period is assumed to be constant. A neural network based approach is presented in [7] to feedback scheduling of multiple control tasks. However, both scenarios considered in [4] and [7] are different from what is formulated in equation (1). In this work, we present an intelligent control theoretic approach to the above formulated problem based on fuzzy logic control technology.

3   Fuzzy Feedback Scheduling Approach

Fuzzy logic [10,11] provides a formal methodology for representing, manipulating, and implementing a human's heuristic knowledge. It provides a simple and flexible way to arrive at a definite conclusion based upon imprecise, noisy, or incomplete input information. Fuzzy logic has been proven to be an exciting problem-solving control system methodology implemented in systems ranging from simple, small, embedded controllers to large, networked, workstation-based data acquisition and control systems. In this section, we propose a novel feedback scheduling approach using fuzzy logic. First, we describe the architecture of the fuzzy feedback scheduling mechanism. Then a fuzzy feedback scheduler is designed in detail, borrowing the methodology of fuzzy control technology.

3.1   Architecture

We treat feedback scheduling as an intelligent control problem. The architecture of the fuzzy feedback scheduling methodology is given in Fig.2. From the control perspective, the scheduler can be viewed as an intelligent feedback controller [4,7]. The con-trolled variable is the CPU utilization. The sampling period of the considered control task acts as the manipulated variable. In the context of fuzzy control, the basic idea is to make use of expert knowledge and experience to build a rule base with linguistic if-then rules. Proper control actions are then derived from the rule base. Accordingly, the role of the fuzzy feedback scheduler is to control the CPU utilization to the desired level. It gathers the actual CPU utilization U and current allowable utilization U_{sp}, compares them, and then decides in an intelligent fashion what the control period should be to ensure that the performance objectives will be met. In this way, it at-tempts to minimize the control period under task schedulability constraints, thus improving the control performance to a maximum extent. Generally speaking, the feed-back scheduler can be either time-triggered or event-triggered, while we employ a periodic one in this paper. The fuzzy feedback scheduler is utilized to provide runtime adaptation to computing resource requirements of the control task. Thus there is a dynamic tradeoff between QoC improvement and task schedulability.

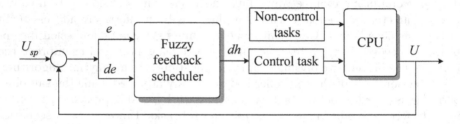

Fig. 2. Architecture of fuzzy feedback scheduling

3.2 Design Methodology

In this subsection, we detail the design of the fuzzy feedback scheduler. The internal structure of the fuzzy feedback scheduler is given in Fig.3. Similar to almost all fuzzy controllers [10], the fuzzy feedback scheduler consists of four main components: (1) The *fuzzification* is a procedure to define fuzzy sets based on system input measurements, i.e. it defines the membership mappings from the measured values of each input to a set of linguistic values. (2) The *rule base* holds the knowledge, in the form of a set of rules, of how best to control the system. (3) The *inference mechanism* evaluates which rules are relevant at the current time and then decides what the control task's period should be. And (4) the *defuzzification* interface converts the conclusions reached by the inference mechanism into the numeric output. The vast amount of knowledge and experience of fuzzy applications in control community can be borrowed in the construction of feedback schedulers. The design of the fuzzy feed-back scheduler can be conducted by the following procedures.

The first step is to identify the input and output variables, i.e. choice and scaling of the linguistic variables. There are two input variables, the error be-

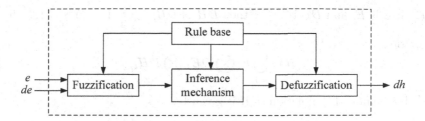

Fig. 3. Fuzzy feedback scheduler structure

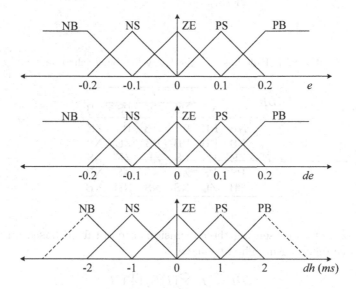

Fig. 4. Membership functions for linguistic variables

tween desired CPU utilization and actual CPU utilization, $e = U_{sp} - U$, and the change in error, $de = e_N - e_{N-1}$, where N denotes the sampling instance of the fuzzy feedback scheduler. Note that the scheduler's sampling period is different from that of the control task. The input linguistic variables are denoted by E and DE, respectively. The scheduler output is the increment of the control period dh, and the correspond-ing linguistic variable is denoted by DH. Next, we specify meaningful linguistic values and the membership functions for each linguistic variable. In this work, the linguistic values are the same for all input and output linguistic variables, i.e. negative big (NB), negative small (NS), zero (ZE), positive small (PS), and positive big (PB). Fig.4 shows the membership functions of the input and output linguistic variables.

The rule base will then be set up. Since feedback scheduling is a newly emerging research area that lacks of practical experience, we attempt to design the rule base based on our experience on simulation studies and the well-established knowledge both from control community and real-time scheduling community. Table 1 describes all possible rules. Each of them can be expressed as [11]:

R_k : if E is E_i and DE is DE_j, then DH is DH_{ij} $i = 1, \dots 5; j = 1, \dots 5.$ (2)

Therefore,

$$R = \bigcup_{i,j} E_i \otimes DE_j \otimes DH_{ij}$$ (3)

And the membership function of R is given by

$$\mu_R(e, de, dh) = \bigvee_{(i=1,j=1)}^{(i=5,j=5)} \mu_{E_i}(e) \bigwedge \mu_{DE_j}(de) \bigwedge \mu_{DH_{ij}}(dh)$$ (4)

Table 1. Rule base for the fuzzy feedback scheduler

DH		DE				
		NB	NS	ZE	PS	PB
	NB	PB	PB	PB	PS	ZE
	NS	PB	PB	PS	ZE	NS
E	ZE	PS	PS	ZE	ZE	NS
	PS	PS	ZE	NS	NS	NB
	PB	ZE	NS	NS	NB	NB

The fuzzy sets representing the conclusions are obtained based on the max-min inference mechanism. Then we have

$$DH = (E \otimes DE) \oplus R$$ (5)

And the membership function of the output variable DH is given by

$$\mu_{DH}(dh) = \bigvee_{e \in E, de \in DE} \mu_R(e, de, dh) \bigwedge \mu_E(e) \bigwedge \mu_{DE}(de)$$ (6)

In the above equations, $\bigvee$ and $\bigwedge$ are the *max* and *min* functions, respectively; $\otimes$ and $\oplus$ are fuzzy arithmetic operators.

In the defuzzification procedure, we employ the center of gravity method to pro-duce a crisp output dh. And hence

$$dh = \frac{\sum \mu(dh) \cdot dh}{\sum \mu(dh)}$$ (7)

Since the feedback scheduler will be used online and often implemented as a task that executes on the embedded CPU, it also consumes CPU time. In order for the fuzzy feedback scheduler to be cost-effective, the scheduling overhead should be relatively small. In practical applications, since R is a high order matrix, calculating a numeric output according to the above equations will demand a considerable amount of time. This is expensive for feedback scheduling of the control task on embedded systems.

For the sake of small scheduling overhead, one can easily refer to the look-up table method in the context of fuzzy feedback scheduling. The basic principle of the look-up table method is to obtain the control table through offline calculations, and store it in the memory. At run time, what the scheduler has to do is just searching the quantified output in the control table based on the quantified inputs e and de. After multiplied with the scale factor, it is exactly the scheduler's output. Thanks to that fact that the computational complexity of the loop-up table method is very low, the scheduling overhead of the fuzzy feedback scheduler can be extremely small. Furthermore, this implementation is also very simple in programming.

4   Performance Evaluation

In this section, we conduct preliminary simulations to assess the performance of the fuzzy feedback scheduler. A small DC servo motor given as $G(s) = 1000/(s^2 + s)$ is to be controlled using an embedded controller. The goal of the control is to make the servo position follow the reference position as closely as possible. The control task within the CPU executes a classical PID algorithm, which is well-designed pre-runtime to control the plant. The nominal control period $h_0 = 8$ ms. The execution time of the control task is also time varying, according to the normal distribution with a mean of 3 ms. During run time, the allowable CPU utilization varies as shown in Fig. 5. This variation is used to reflect the workload uncertainty within modern embedded systems. In this wok, two cases are simulated using Matlab/Truetime [15].

In Case I, the controller works with a fixed sampling period of 8 ms, just as in almost all current control applications. And hence the average requested CPU utilization approximates $3/8 = 0.375$ all along the simulation. In the time interval from t = 0 to 1s, as shown in Fig. 6 (dotted blue line), the DC motor performs well. Before time instance t = 1s, the available CPU resources

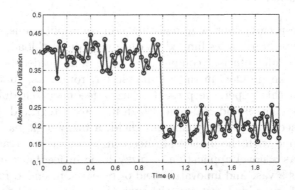

Fig. 5. Allowable CPU utilization for the controller

are sufficient in most time, notwithstanding fluctuation. However, the computing resources become scarce after time t = 1 s, which is denoted by allowable CPU utilizations smaller than what are requested. As a result, the control task becomes unschedulable, and the DC motor turns to be unstable, see Fig. 6.

Next, in Case II, a preliminary version of the fuzzy feedback scheduler presented in Section 3 is implemented to provide flexible QoC management. The control period is online adjusted in response to computing resource availability variations. The scheduler acts as a periodic task with a period of 20 ms and the scheduling overhead is neglected. The PID parameters are online updated to compensate jitters of the control period. As shown in Fig.6 (solid red line), the QoC is improved with the help of the fuzzy feedback scheduler. Because the allowable utilization is close to the requested one in Case I, the QoC improvement seems slight before t = 1s. When the CPU time becomes scarce after t = 1s, the benefit of the proposed approach is significant, and the system regains stability. It is clear that the fuzzy feedback scheduler is effective in managing uncertain resource constraints in real-time embedded control applications.

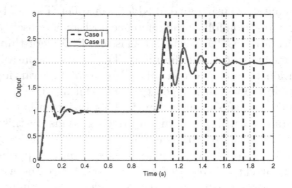

Fig. 6. Transient responses of the DC motor

5   Conclusions

In spite of widespread adoption in real-time control applications, embedded systems are prone to be resource limited. With uncertain workload, it is likely that they cannot provide sufficient computing resources as needed by control tasks. To effectively manage QoC in these dynamic environments, runtime flexibility is necessary. In this paper, we present a fuzzy feedback scheduling approach, where feedback control and real-time scheduling are integrated. In the context of feedback scheduling, a newly emerging field, a fuzzy logic based scheduler is suggested to cope with the impact of uncertain resource constraints on control performance. As a novel application of fuzzy logic in feedback scheduling, this approach opens a vast and innovative field of research intended for performance optimization of embedded systems, although there are a number of open issues that need to be critically examined. The potential benefits of the fuzzy feedback scheduler include: graceful QoC degradation under overload conditions, effectiveness in dealing with timing uncertainty inside CPU scheduling, systematic design methodology, and simple implementation. Thanks to the promising results that the fuzzy feedback scheduler exhibits, we are now working on extending the proposed approach in multitasking cases.

References

1. Arzen, K.E., Cervin, A.: Control and Embedded Computing: Survey of Research Directions. In: Proc. 16th IFAC World Congress, Prague, Czech Republic (2005)
2. Loyall, J.: Emerging Trends in Adaptive Middleware and Its Application to Distributed Real-Time Embedded Systems. LNCS **2855** (2003) 20–34
3. Buttazzo, G., Velasco, M., Marti, P., Fohler, G.: Managing Quality-of-Control Performance Under Overload Conditions. In: Proc. ECRTS, Catania, Italy (2005) 1–8
4. Xia, F., Sun, Y.: Anytime Iterative Optimal Control Using Fuzzy Feedback Scheduler. In: Proc. KES, LNCS (to appear), Springer-Verlag, Heidelberg (2005)
5. Marti, P., Yepez, J., Velasco, M., Villa, R., Fuertes, J.M.: Managing Quality-of-Control in Network-Based Control Systems by Controller and Message Scheduling Co-Design. IEEE Trans. on Industrial Electronics **51** (2004) 1159–1167
6. Cervin, A., Eker, J., Bernhardsson, B., Arzen, K.E.: Feedback-Feedforward Scheduling of Control Tasks. Real-Time Systems. **23:1** (2002) 25–53
7. Xia, F., Sun, Y.: Neural Network Based Feedback Scheduling of Multitasking Control Systems. In: Proc. KES, LNCS (to appear), Springer-Verlag (2005)
8. Lu, C., Stankovic, J., Tao, G., Son, S.: Feedback Control Real-Time Scheduling: Framework, Modeling, and Algorithms. Real-Time Systems. **23:1/2** (2002) 85–126
9. Abeni, L., Palopoli, L., Lipari, G., Walpole, J.: Analysis of a Reservation-Based Feedback Scheduler. In: Proc. 23rd IEEE RTSS, Austin, Texas (2002) 71–80
10. Passino, K., Yurkovich, S.: Fuzzy Control. Addison Wesley Longman, Menlo Park, CA (1998)
11. Li, S.: Fuzzy Control, Neurocontrol and Intelligent Cybernetics. Harbin Institute of Technology Press, Harbin, China (1998)
12. Liu, J.: Real-time systems. Prentice Hall (2000)
13. Caccamo, M., Buttazzo, G., Thomas, D.: Efficient Reclaiming in Reservation-Based Real-Time Systems with Variable Execution Times. IEEE Trans. on Computers **54** (2005) 198–213
14. Xia, F., Wang, Z., Sun, Y.: Integrated Computation, Communication and Control: Towards Next Revolution in Information Technology. LNCS **3356** (2004) 117–125
15. Henriksson, D., Cervin, A., Arzen, K.E.: True Time: Simulation of Control Loops Under Shared Computer Resources. In: Proc. 15th IFAC World Congress on Automatic Control, Barcelona, Spain (2002)

Improvement of Multicast Routing Protocol Using Petri Nets*

Dan Li, Yong Cui, Ke Xu, and Jianping Wu

Department of Computer Science, Tsinghua University, Beijing, 100084, P.R. China
{lidan, cy, xuke}@csnet1.cs.tsinghua.edu.cn
jianping@cernet.edu.cn

Abstract. Protocol Independent Multicast - Sparse Mode (PIM-SM) is the preferred multicast routing protocol currently. But it has the deficiency of high overhead of control messages and it needs to be improved. Stochastic Petri Nets is a soft computing technique that has been widely used in the area of performance evaluation. We improve PIM-SM protocol in this paper by use of Stochastic Petri Nets. The improvement mainly focuses on Register message, Join/Prune message and Bootstrap message. Experiments and analysis using Petri nets suggest that our improvement results in better performance than the current standard of PIM-SM protocol.

1 Introduction

Multicast is an efficient way for point-to-multipoint and multipoint-to-multipoint communications [1]. The function of multicast routing protocol is to maintain the multicast forwarding tree. Currently proposed multicast routing protocols include Distance Vector Multicast Routing Protocol [2], Multicast Extensions to Open Shortest Path First [3], and Protocol Independent Multicast - Dense Mode [4], Core Based Trees [5] and Protocol Independent Multicast - Sparse Mode (PIM-SM) [6]. Among all of these, PIM-SM is considered as the preferred protocol since it does not make any dependence on other unicast routing protocols, and that the multicast tree can switch from shared tree to shortest path tree.

Deployment problems of the multicast technology has been a hot topic for long [12], [13], [14], [15]. In fact, PIM-SM protocol also has the deficiency that impedes its wide deployment in Internet: the high overhead of control messages. Too many control messages lead to at least two problems, causing more router processing load and consuming more network bandwidth. Therefore, it is needed to improve PIM-SM protocol.

The analysis and improvement of PIM-SM protocol have been studied by many researchers. Billhartz compares PIM-SM protocol with Core Based Trees protocol, finding that control overhead of PIM-SM is by far more than Core Based Trees protocol [7]. Holt brings forward dynamic switching between shared

---

* This work is supported by the National Natural Science Foundation of China (No. 60473082, No. 90104002).

D. Ślęzak et al. (Eds.): RSFDGrC 2005, LNAI 3642, pp. 634–643, 2005.

tree and shortest path tree in accordance with network situations, demonstrating that control overhead can thus be reduced considerably [8]. Lin suggests period-ical relocation of Rendezvous Points according to network topology, and proves that multicast tree maintaining cost decreases a lot in this way [9].

However, as far as we know, there is not any research to improve PIM-SM protocol based on the quantitative performance analysis. Soft computing tech-niques, especially Petri nets, can help us do this. Petri nets has been widely used in the area of performance evaluation. It is powerful in describing the dynamic behavior of PIM-SM protocol. By use of Petri nets, we can find the bottle-neck of PIM-SM protocol and improve the protocol. In addition, it can help us in evaluating our improvement.

Based on the Stochastic Petri Nets (SPN) model of PIM-SM protocol and prior work on the performance analysis of different types of PIM-SM messages [10], we improve PIM-SM focusing on three types of messages: the Register message, the Join/Prune message, and the Bootstrap message. Experiments and analysis using Petri nets suggest that our improvement results in better performance.

2   Specification of PIM-SM Protocol

In a PIM-SM domain, routers running PIM-SM protocol send Hello message to neighbors periodically, so as to discover neighboring PIM-SM routers and elect the Designated Router in multi-access local area networks. the Designated Router is unique in a local area network. One function of the Designated Router is to send multicast packets to the multicast distribution tree, when there is an active multicast source in its directly connected local area network. The other function is to send Join/Prune message upstream along the multicast distribution tree, when there are members joining or leaving multicast groups.

When Join/Prune message is being sent from the Designated Router to the root of the multicast distribution tree, each router along the path builds multicast forwarding states according to the message information, leading multicast data to be forwarded downstream. Multicast forwarding states in the routers have a period of validity, so each router should send Join/Prune messages periodically to the upstream neighboring router.

When a Designated Router receives multicast data from a directly connected source, and if there is no established source-based tree, the Designated Router encapsulates the data in Register message, and unicasts the message to the Rendezvous Point of the multicast group. Upon receiving the message, the Ren-dezvous Point decapsulates the data and forwards them downstream along the shared tree to each group member, replicating at appropriate spots. At the same time, the Rendezvous Point sends Join/Prune message to join the source-based shortest path tree. When the shortest path tree has been established, multicast data are sent to the Rendezvous Point downstream along the tree, without any encapsulation. After multicast data arrive via the shortest path tree, the Ren-dezvous Point will immediately send Register-Stop message to the Designated Router as soon as receiving Register message from the Designated Router encapsulating the same data. Later, the Designated Router sends Register messages to the Rendezvous Point periodically to probe whether multicast tree works well. If so, the Rendezvous Point sends Register-Stop message to the Designated Router immediately.

PIM-SM protocol also includes the Rendezvous Point election mechanisms. the Rendezvous Point is the root node of the shared tree, and is unique for a multicast group. In a PIM-SM domain, there should be at least one router configured as the candidate Bootstrap router. All these candidate Bootstrap routers compete for a domain-unique Bootstrap Router through self-adaptive mechanisms. There can be one or more candidate Rendezvous Points configured for each multicast group, and each candidate Rendezvous Point unicasts Candidate-RP-Advertisement message to the Bootstrap Router to apply for the Rendezvous Point of a multicast group. The Bootstrap Router periodically builds Bootstrap message containing the mapping information of multicast groups and their corresponding candidate Rendezvous Points, sending the message hop by hop within the domain. Routers receiving Bootstrap message elect the Rendezvous Point for each multicast group on their own using a domain-unique hash function.

In a multicast tree, each router has a specific incoming interface for a specific group or source. In multi-access local area networks, two routers may have different upstream neighbors, so there may be redundant data in the multi-access link. When this happens, the downstream routers will receive multicast packets from a wrong incoming interface. In order to avoid data redundancy, when a router receives multicast packets from a wrong incoming interface, it sends Assert message to that interface immediately. By use of Assert message, only one router is elected to send data to that link.

Therefore, there are 7 types of messages in PIM-SM protocol: Hello message, Bootstrap message, Candidate-RP-Advertisement message, Join/Prune message, Register message, Register-stop message, and Assert message.

3   Improvement Solutions to PIM-SM Protocol

Petri nets was first put forward by C. A. Petri in his Ph.D thesis in 1962. Since then, it has been widely studied and applied in many areas [16]. It is a soft computing technique to describe and model information systems [17], [18]. The main characteristic of Petri nets is its concurrency, nondeterminacy, asynchronism, and analysis ability for distributed systems. It can simulate the dynamic behavior of real systems by the flow of the tokens [19].

The three primary elements in Petri nets are the place, the transition and the arc. Place is used to describe the possible local states of the system; transition is used to describe the event that will change the system states; and arc is used to describe the relationship between place and transition. The different states of the system are described by the tokens included in places.

Petri nets is an excellent technique in performance evaluation. With the Petri net model of PIM-SM protocol and analysis using Petri nets, we can evaluate the bottle-neck of the protocol and improve the protocol. Li has done prior work on performance analysis of PIM-SM protocol [10] by use of the Petri nets, finding that Register message and Join/Prune message cause most router processing load, while Join/Prune message and Bootstrap message consume most network bandwidth. We here improve the PIM-SM protocol using Petri nets focusing on these three types of messages.

3.1   Process Optimization of Register Message

For Register message, we optimize the router processing. In ordinary design, Register message is processed on controlling module as other types of messages. But Register message is special in that it encapsulates multicast data and arrives at the data-sending rate. To input so many Register messages encapsulating multicast data to upper layer controlling module will cause too much processing load. In our optimized design, each router processes Register message on multicast forwarding module. It avoids copying data and sending them to upper layer, which obviously reduces processing load.

3.2   Mechanism Improvement of Join/Prune Message

According to the current standard of PIM-SM protocol , additional Join/Prune messages are sent immediately each time there are multicast group members dynamically changing. We improve this mechanism as follows. When it is needed to send additional Join/Prune message upon group member change, Join/Prune message is not sent immediately, but wait for the time interval between the current time and the time to send the next periodical Join/Prune message. If the time interval exceeds a threshold value (defined as one fifth of the Join/Prune message sending period), it is sent immediately, otherwise it is to be sent along with the next periodical Join/Prune message. Through this improvement, the number of Join/Prune messages can be reduced.

3.3   Mechanism Improvement of Bootstrap Message

As for the Bootstrap message, it is formulated in the current standard of PIM-SM protocol that Candidate Rendezvous Points applies for the Rendezvous Point of a multicast group in Candidate-RP-Advertisement message sent to the Bootstrap router, then the Bootstrap router floods the mapping information of all multicast groups and their candidate Rendezvous Points in Bootstrap message hop by hop within the domain, and routers receiving Bootstrap message elect the unique Rendezvous Point for each multicast group through a domain-unique hash function on their own. We improve this mechanism as follows. The Bootstrap router elects the unique Rendezvous Point for each multicast group each time before sending Bootstrap message, and then it floods the mapping information of all multicast groups and their unique Rendezvous Point in Bootstrap message. After this improvement, the election of the unique Rendezvous Point from candidate Rendezvous Points is done by the Bootstrap router instead of by all routers on their own, and the packet size of Bootstrap message decreases. Because the computation to elect the Rendezvous Point is avoided, the router processing load of Bootstrap message will be reduced. In addition, the packet size of Bootstrap message will also decrease.

4   Experiments and Analysis

To compare the performance of PIM-SM protocol after our improvement with that of the current standard, we use the whole model of PIM-SM protocol and the multicast session established in [10]. Fig. 1 shows the SPN model of the whole PIM-SM protocol. In the model, P13 represents the arrival of Hello message; P14 represents the arrival of Bootstrap message; P15 represents the arrival of Candidate-RP-Advertisement message; P16 represents the arrival of Join/Prune message; P17 represents the arrival of Register message; P18 represents the arrival of Register-Stop message; and P19 represents the arrival of Assert message. Meanwhile, T8 represents the processing of Hello message; T9 represents the processing of Bootstrap message; T10 represents the processing of Candidate-RP-Advertisement message; T11 represents the processing of Join/Prune message; T12 represents the processing of Register message; T13 represents the processing of Register-Stop message; and T14 represents the processing of Assert message. For the significations of other places and transitions, please refer to [10].

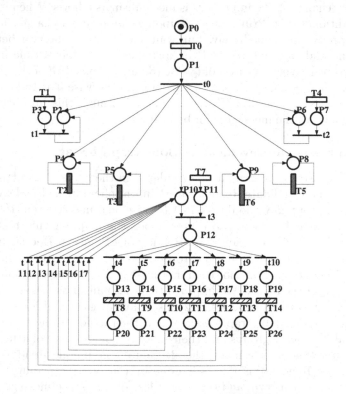

Fig. 1. The SPN model of PIM-SM

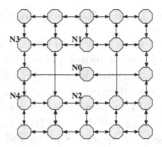

Fig. 2. Network topology of the multicast session

The multicast session runs on the network topology of Fig. 2. And Table 1 shows the assumptions on parameters of the multicast session, based on our measurement and estimation through implementation.

Among the 7 types of PIM-SM messages, Assert message only exists on multi-access local area networks, and it will disappear for long once it has corrected the redundancy. Thus, the amount of Assert messages is so small that we can ignore them for discussion. Later discussions are limited to the other 6 types of protocol messages.

After our improvement, let us discuss the performance of PIM-SM protocol from the view of the 6 types of protocol messages. Both the router processing load and the network bandwidth consumed are concerned.

Table 1. Parameters of the multicast session

Parameter Name	Value
Number of candidate Bootstrap Routers	1(N0)
Number of candidate Rendezvous Points for the multicast group	2(N1,N2)
Number of multicast sources	2 (in the local area networks where N3 and N4 stand)
Persistent time of the multicast session	2 hours
Average data sending rate of multicast sources	2Mbit/s
Average packet size	1000 bytes
Average time interval for Register message unicast from the Designated Router to the Rendezvous Point	30 milliseconds
Average time interval for the Rendezvous Point to join Source-based shortest path tree and receive data from the tree	100 milliseconds
Average Time interval for Register-Stop message unicast from the Rendezvous Point to the Designated Router	30 milliseconds
Average time interval for a router to send additional Hello messages because of network fluctuation	5 minutes
Average time interval for a router to send additional Join/Prune messages because of dynamic change of multicast group members	1 minute

4.1   Router Processing Load After Improvement

The comparative average tokens in P13~P18 of the SPN model of PIM-SM protcol stand for the comparative router processing load caused by each type of PIM-SM messages. According to the theory of Petri nets, the comparative average tokens in P13~P18 are decided by transition probabilities of t4~t10 and the transition rates of T8~T14, respectively. Since we ignore the Assert message for discussion, the transition probability of t10 is assumed as 0. Thus, we still need to quantify the transition rates of T8~T13 and the transition probabilities of t4~t9.

To compute the transition rates of T8~T13, it is needed to define the concept of effective code length. For a segment of effective code (code that is time-weighted), effective code length refers to the line number of the code after the following operations: unfolding the loop statements (bounds are assigned with reference to the multicast session on the topology above), substituting condition statements with the branch of the most probability, and substituting sub-functions with the effective code of the sub-functions (recursively until completely substituted).

After the optimized process of Register message and the improvement of the Bootstrap mechanism, we can decrease the effective code length of processing Register message from 260 to 150, and decrease that of Bootstrap message from 511 to 400. The effective code lengths of the other 4 types of messages maintain the same as before, that is, Hello message 174, Candidate-RP-Advertisement message 109, Join/Prune message 925, and Register-Stop message 89. Thus, the transition rates of T8~T13 in Fig.1 are 0.174, 0.075, 0.278, 0.033, 0.201 and 0.340, respectively.

After the improvement of Join/Prune message, the number of Join/Prune message that a router receives at most during the multicast session decreases from 720 to 654. The other 5 types of messages that a router receives at most during the multicast session remain the same, i.e., message 1056, Bootstrap

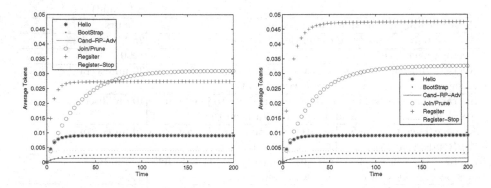

Fig. 3. Router processing load after improvement

Fig. 4. Router processing load before improvement

message 120, Candidate-RP-Advertisement message 240, Register message 3680 and Register-Stop message 900. So the transition probabilities of t4~t10 in Fig. 1 are 0.159, 0.018, 0.036, 0.099, 0.553, 0.135 and 0, respectively.

Run SPNP to simulate and we can get the result of router processing load of the 6 types of PIM-SM messages shown in Fig. 3.

Fig. 4 illustrates the router processing load of each type of message under the current standard of PIM-SM protocol, which is studied in [10]. If we compare Fig. 3 with Fig. 4, we can clearly see that the router processing load caused by Register message decreases a great deal after protocol improvement and processing optimization, and the router processing load caused by Join/Prune message and Bootstrap message is also reduced.

4.2   Network Bandwidth Consumed After Improvement

The network bandwidth each type of PIM-SM messages consumes during the multicast session is decided by its total message number and the bytes of each message.

After the improvement of Join/Prune message, the total number of Join/Prune messages on all links in the network topology during the multicast session decreases from 11040 to 9648. The total numbers of the other 5 types of protocol messages remain the same: Hello message 17952, Bootstrap message 4080, Candidate-RP-Advertisement 960, Register message 9200 and Register-Stop message 4500.

The improvement of Bootstrap message changes the payload length of Bootstrap message from 100 bytes to 76 bytes. While the payload lengths of the other 5 types of PIM-SM messages remain the same: 12 bytes for Hello message, 48 bytes for Candidate-RP-Advertisement message, 92 bytes for Join/Prune message, 8 bytes for Register message, and 44 bytes for Register-Stop message.

Therefore, we can calculate the network bandwidth consumed by each type of protocol messages during the multicast session after improvement. The network bandwidth consumed by them under the current standard of PIM-SM protocol was also studied in [10]. The comparison of the network bandwidth consumed after improvement and before improvement is shown in Table 2.

From Table 2, we can find that the network bandwidth consumed by Bootstrap message after protocol improvement is reduced by 24%, and the value for Join/Prune message also decreases by 12.6%.

Table 2. Network bandwidth consumed (bytes)

Message Type	After Improvement	Before Improvement
Hello Message	215424	215424
Bootstrap Message	310080	408000
Candidate-RP-Advertisement Message	46080	46080
Join/Prune Message	887616	1015680
Register Message	73600	73600
Register-Stop Message	198000	198000

4.3   Discussion of the Improvement Solution

As discussed above, after process optimization and mechanism improvement of PIM-SM protocol by use of Petri nets, the router processing load caused and network bandwidth consumed by PIM-SM messages are both reduced. But there are also some shortcomings of the improvement solution.

Firstly, the processing optimization for Register message partially impairs the modularity of PIM-SM message processing programs; secondly, the real time performance of Join/Prune message is degraded to some extent; and thirdly, the election of the unique Rendezvous Point from candidate Rendezvous Points is done by Bootstrap Router before periodically sending Bootstrap message, instead of by all routers after receiving Bootstrap message.

However, considering that Register messages are special in that it encapsulates multicast data and arrives at data sending rate, Join/Prune messages are much frequently sent, and the router configured as the Bootstrap Router usually performs better than other routers, the advantages of our improvement outweighs these shortcomings. Through the improvement solution, protocol performance of PIM-SM has been obviously enhanced.

5   Conclusion

PIM-SM protocol is the preferred among current proposed multicast routing protocols. But the overhead of its control messages is high. By use of the soft computing technique of Petri nets, we improve PIM-SM protocol in this paper, basing on the prior work on performance analysis of different types of PIM-SM messages. Our improvement solution mainly focuses on the three types of protocol messages which cause most router processing load and consume most network bandwidth: the Register message, the Join/Prune message, and the Bootstrap message. Experiments using Petri nets and analysis suggest that our improvement of PIM-SM protocol results in better performance than the current standard of it: in both the router processing load and the network bandwidth consumed.

References

1. Mieghem, P.V., Hooghiemstra, G., Hofstad, R.: On the Efficiency of Multicast. IEEE ACM Transactions on Networking, vol. 9, no. 6 (2001) 719-732
2. Waitzman, D., Deering, S.: Distance Vector Multicast Routing Protocol. http://www.ietf.org/rfc/rfc1075.txt (1988)
3. Moy, J.: Multicast Extensions to OSPF. http://www.ietf.org/rfc/rfc1584.txt (1994)
4. Adams, A., Nicholas, J., Siadak, W.: Protocol Independent Multicast - Dense Mode (PIM-DM):Protocol Specification (Revised). http://www.ietf.org/rfc/rfc3973.txt (2005)
5. Ballardie, A.: Core Based Trees (CBT) Multicast Routing Architecture. http://www.ietf.org/rfc/rfc2201.txt (1997)
6. Estrin, D., Farinacci, D., Helmy, A.: Protocol Independent Multicast - Sparse Mode (PIM-SM): Protocol Specification. http://www.ietf.org/rfc/rfc2362.txt (1998)

7. Billhartz, T., Cain, J., Goudreau, E.: Performance and Resource Cost Comparisons for the CBT and PIM Multicast Routing Protocols. IEEE Journal on Selected Areas in Communications, vol. 15, no. 3 (1997) 85-93
8. Holt, J., Peng W.X.: Improving the PIM Routing Protocol with Adaptive Switching Mechanism between Its Two Sparse Sub-Modes. Proceedings of IEEE ICCCN 1998, Lafayette, LA (1998) 768-773
9. Lin, Y.D., Hsu, N.B., Pan, C.J.: Extension of RP Relocation to PIM-SM Multicast Routing. IEEE ICC 2001, Helsinki, Finland, vol. 1 (2001) 234-238
10. Li, D., Wu, J., Xu, K., Cui, Y., Liu, Y., Zhang, X.: Performance Analysis of Multicast Routing Protocol PIM-SM. To appear in AICT 2005, Lisbon, Portugal (2005)
11. Lin, C.: Performance Evaluation in Computer Networks and Computer System. Tsinghua University Press (2001) 176-201
12. Mieghem, P.V., Janic, M.: Stability of a Multicast Tree. IEEE INFOCOM 2002, New York, NY, USA (2002) 1099-1108
13. Donahoo, M.J., Ainapure, S.R.: Scalable Multicast Representative Member Selection. IEEE INFOCOM 2001, Anchorage, Alaska, USA (2001) 259-268
14. Alouf, S., Altman, E., Nain, P.: Optimal On-Line Estimation of the Size of a Dynamic Multicast Group. IEEE INFOCOM 2002, New York, NY, USA, vol. 2 (2002) 1109-1118
15. Kwon, G., Byers, J.W.: Smooth Multirate Multicast Congestion Control. IEEE INFOCOM 2003, San Francisco, CA, USA, vol. 22, no. 1, (2003) 1022-1032
16. Drees, S., Gomm, D., Plunneke, H., Reisig, W., Walter, R.: Bibliography of Petri Nets. European Workshop on Applications and Theory of Petri Nets (1986) 309-451
17. Berthelot, G., Terrat, R.: Petri Nets Theory for the Correctness of Protocols. IEEE Trans. on Communications, vol. 30, no. 12, (1982) 2497-2505
18. Diaz, M.: Modeling and Analysis of Communication and cooperation Protocols Using Petri Net based Models. Computer Networks, vol. 6, no. 6, (1982) 419-441
19. Murata, T.: Petri nets: properties, analysis and applications. Proceedings of IEEE, vol. 77, no. 4, (1989) 541-580

An Efficient Bandwidth Management Scheme for a Hard Real-Time Fuzzy Control System Based on the Wireless LAN*

Junghoon Lee[1], Mikyung Kang[1], Yongmoon Jin[1],
Hanil Kim[1], and Jinhwan Kim[2]

[1] Cheju National University
{jhlee, mkkang, ymjin, hikim}@cheju.ac.kr
[2] Hansung University
kimjh@hansung.ac.kr

Abstract. This paper proposes and analyzes bandwidth allocation and reclaiming schemes on wireless media to enhance the timeliness of the real-time messages and accordingly the correctness of fuzzy control decision. Bandwidth allocation scheme generates efficient round robin polling schedule represented as a capacity vector by directly considering the deferred beacon problem. The resource reclaiming scheme reassigns unused slot time to non-real-time traffic by extending the collision period without violating the hard real-time guarantee. The simulation results show that the proposed scheme can not only enhance the schedulability of wireless network by up to 18% but also give more bandwidth to the non-real-time traffic up to 5.3%, while the resource reclaiming scheme can maximally improve the achievable throughput by 11 % for the given stream set.

1 Introduction

In a real-time system, such as a fuzzy logic control system, the current system context is perceived by one or more computing nodes to decide the appropriate control action [1]. The set of data sampled at each sensor constitutes a system context while the control decision generates a commands set to actuators. The correctness of the control decision based on fuzzy algorithms depends not only the accuracy of the control logic but also the the timeliness of the sampled data. The data are exchanged as a form of the message packet via the communication medium and the wireless network is the most promising technology for control system. Hence the message of real-time system has a hard real-time constraint that it should be transmitted within a bounded delay. Otherwise, the data is considered to be lost, and the loss of hard real-time message may jeopardize correct execution of real-time control logic or system itself [2]. Consequently, a

---

* This research was supported by the MIC (Ministry of Information and Communication), Korea, under the ITRC(Information Technology Research Center) support program supervised by the IITA (Institute of Information Technology Assessment).

D. Ślęzak et al. (Eds.): RSFDGrC 2005, LNAI 3642, pp. 644–653, 2005.

real-time message stream needs the guarantee from the underlying network that its time constraints are always met in advance of the system operation.

The IEEE 802.11 was developed as a MAC (Medium Access Control) standard for WLAN [3]. The standard consists of a basic DCF (Distributed Coordination Function) and an optional PCF (Point Coordination Function). The DCF exploits CSMA/CA (Carrier Sense Multiple Access with Collision Avoidance) protocol for non-real-time messages, aiming at enhancing their average delivery time as well as network utilization. However, packet collisions, intrinsic to CSMA protocols, make it impossible for a node to predictably access the network. After all, real-time guarantee cannot be provided without developing a deterministic access schedule on top of collision-free PCF [4]. According to the WLAN standard, the operation of PCF is left to the implementor. As an example, weighted round robin scheme makes the coordinator poll each node one by one, the polled node transmitting its message for a predefined time interval, or weight. The set of such weights is called as *capacity vector* and each element should be carefully decided according to the time constraint of respective streams.

While this scheme makes the guarantee mechanism simple and efficient, it suffers from poor utilization mainly due to both polling overhead and *deferred beacon problem* [5]. Deferred beacon problem means a situation that a non-real-time message puts off the initiation of a PCF behind the expected start time. Though the maximum amount of deferment is bounded, it seriously degrades the schedulability of real-time messages. In addition, hard real-time guarantee indispensably increases the number of unused slots as it depends on the worst case behavior. Real-time message scheduling scheme on WLAN standard should take such factors into account. Several MAC protocols have been proposed to support the hard real-time communication over a wireless channel, but they cannot be easily applied to the IEEE 802.11 WLAN standard, as they ignored the CSMA/CA part defined as mandatory in the WLAN standard, or just aimed to enhance the ratio of timely delivery for soft multimedia applications [6]. To enhance the schedulability and network utilization of IEEE 802.11 WLAN, we are to propose a bandwidth allocation scheme that decides the capacity vector for the round robin style polling mechanism. It cannot only make the guarantee scheme much simpler, but also cope with deferred beacon problem efficiently. In addition, this paper also designs a resource reclaiming scheme that improves network utilization by reallocating the network bandwidth unused by the real-time messages to non-real-time one.

This paper is organized as follows: After issuing the problem in Section 1, Section 2 introduces the related works focusing on real-time communications on the wireless medium. With the description on network and message model in Section 3, Section 4 proposes the bandwidth allocation scheme and its corresponding reclaiming procedure. Section 5 discusses the performance measurement result and then Section 6 finally concludes this paper with a brief summarization and the description of future works.

2   Related Works

Several MAC protocols have been proposed to provide bounded delays for real-time messages along with non-real-time data over a wireless channel. However, these protocols are typically based on a frame-structured access which completely removes the contention part, thus they can not conform to IEEE 802.11 standard. For example, Choi and Shin suggested a unified protocol for real-time and non-real-time communications in wireless networks [7]. In their scheme, a BS (Base Station) polls a real-time mobile station according to the non-preemptable EDF (Earliest Deadline First) policy. The BS also polls the non-real-time message according to the modified round-robin scheme regardless of a standard CSMA/CA protocol to eliminate message collision.

Most works that conform to the IEEE standard are aiming at enhancing the ratio of timely delivery for soft multimedia applications, rather than providing a hard real-time guarantee. DBASE (Distributed Bandwidth Allocation/Sharing/ Extension) is a protocol to support both synchronous and multimedia traffics over IEEE 802.11 *ad hoc* WLAN. The basic concept is that each time real-time station transmits its packet it will also declare and reserve the needed bandwidth at the next CFP. Every station collects this information and then calculates its actual bandwidth at the next cycle. This scheme can be applied to WLAN standard, but it is not essentially designed for hard real-time message streams.

In the non-academic effort, IETF has produced new drafts, EDCF (Enhanced DCF) and HCF (Hybrid Coordination Function) to replace the CSMA/CA based and centralized polling based access mechanism, respectively [8]. No guarantees of service are provided, but EDCF establishes a probabilistic priority mechanism to allocate bandwidth based on traffic categories. According to HCF, a hybrid controller polls stations during a contention-free period. The polling grants a station a specific start time and a maximum duration to transmit messages.

M. Caccamo and et. al have proposed a MAC that supports deterministic real-time scheduling via the implementation of TDMA (Time Division Multiple Access), where the time axis is divided into fixed size slots [4]. Referred as *implicit contention*, their scheme makes every station concurrently run the common real-time scheduling algorithm to determine which message can access the medium. FRASH (FRAame SHaring) is an outstanding example of resource reclaiming scheme. Its peculiarity is to increase network utilization while preserving the hard real-time guarantee. This goal is achieved by reclaiming the slots reserved but not used by the hard real-time messages. Such frames can be reassigned to aperiodic server in order to improve the responsiveness of the aperiodic messages.

3   Network Model

3.1   IEEE 802.11 WLAN

The wireless LAN operates on both CP (Collision Period) and CFP (Collision Free Period) phases alternatively in BSS (Basic Service Set) as shown in Fig. 1. Each superframe consists of CFP and CP, which are mapped to PCF and

DCF, respectively. It is mandatory that a superframe includes a CP of minimum length that allows at least one data packet delivery under DCF [3]. PC (Point Coordinator) node, typically AP (Access Point), sequentially polls each station during CFP. Even in the *ad hoc* mode, it is possible to designate a specific node to play a role of PC in a target group. The phase of network operation is managed by the exchange of control packets which have higher priority than other packets. The prioritized access is achieved by different length of IFS (InterFrame Space) the node waits before it attempts to send its packet.

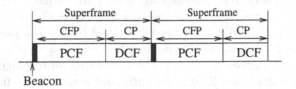

Fig. 1. Time axis of wireless LAN

The PC attempts to initiate CFP by broadcasting a *Beacon* at regular intervals derived from a network parameter of *CFPRate*. Round robin is one of the popular polling policies for CFP, in which every node is polled once a polling round. A polling round may be completed within one superframe, or spread over more than one superframe. In case the CFP terminates before all stations have been completely polled, the polling list is resumed at the next node in the ensuing CFP cycle. Only the polled node is given the right to transmit its message for a predefined time interval, and it always responds to a poll immediately whether it has a pending message or not.

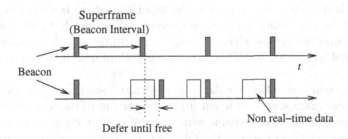

Fig. 2. Deferred beacon problem

As shown in Fig. 2, the transmission of the beacon by the coordinator depends on whether the medium is idle at the time of TBTT (Target Beacon Transmission Time). Only after the medium is idle the coordinator will get the priority due to the shorter IFS. Thus the delivery of a beacon frame can get delayed if another packet is already occupying the network, invalidating the network schedule sophisticatedly determined for hard real-time messages. As can be inferred from Fig. 2, the maximum amount of deferment coincides with the maximum length of a non-real-time packet.

3.2 Message Model

In real-time communication literature, the term real-time traffic typically means *isochronous* (or synchronous) traffic, consisting of message streams that are generated by their sources on a continuing basis and delivered to their respective destinations also on a continuing basis [9]. The stream set is fixed and known in priori of system operation, and the most important traffic characteristics of each stream are its period and message size. In case of a change in the stream set, bandwidth is to be reallocated or network schedule mode is changed [10]. This paper takes the general real-time message model which has n streams, namely, $S_1, S_2, ..., S_n$, and for each S_i, a message sized less than C_i arrives at the beginning of its period, P_i, and it must be transmitted by P_i. The period of stream, S_i, is denoted as P_i, and the maximum length of a message as C_i. The first message of each stream arrives at time 0. The destination of message can be either within a cell or outside a cell, and the outbound messages are first sent to the router node such as AP and then forwarded to the final destination.

4 Bandwidth Allocation

4.1 Basic Assumptions

As is the case of other works, we begin with an assumption that each stream has only one stream, and this assumption can be generalized with virtual station concept [9]. By allocation, we mean the procedure of determining capacity vector, $\{H_i\}$, for the given superframe time, F, and message stream set described as $\{S_i(P_i, C_i)\}$. It is desirable that the superframe time is a hyperperiod of the set and a message set can be made harmonic by reducing the period of some streams by at most half [2]. So we assume that the superframe time is also given in priori, focusing on the determination of capacity vector. For simplicity, we assume that a polling round completes within a single superframe and the assumption will be eliminated later. Ideally, CFP starts at every F interval if there is no deferred beacon.

Besides, error control issues like packet retransmission, are not considered in this paper, because they are different problems and out of the scope of this paper. We just assume that some existing error control or QoS degrading schemes can be integrated to our framework [11]. Otherwise, when experiencing packet losses above some specified threshold, the application undergoes degraded quality of service. After all, though there are many issues one needs to consider in wireless networks, we mainly focus on a significant performance issue, that is, timeliness [4].

4.2 Allocation Procedure

Allocation procedure determines capacity vector, $\{H_i\}$, for the given superframe time and message stream set. Fig. 3 illustrates that the slot size is not fixed, namely, $H_i \neq H_j$ for different i and j. It is natural that the more bandwidth is assigned to the stream with a higher utilization. At this figure, a message of size

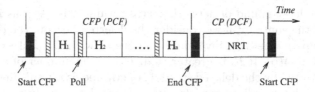

Fig. 3. Polling procedure and capacity vector

C_i is generated and buffered at regular intervals of P_i, and then transmitted by H_i every time the node receives poll from PC.

Let δ denote the total overhead of a superframe including polling latency, IFS, exchange of beacon frame, and the like, while D_{max} the maximum length of a non-real-time data packet. For a minimal requirement, F should be sufficiently large enough to make the polling overhead insignificant. In addition, if P_{min} is the smallest element of set $\{P_i\}$, F should be less than P_{min} so that every stream can meet at least one superframe within its period. For each superframe, not only the start of CFP can be deferred by up to D_{max}, but also at least a time amount as large as D_{max}, should be reserved for a data packet so as to keep compatibility with WLAN standard. After all, the requirement for the superframe time, F, can be summarized as follows:

$$\sum H_i + \delta + 2 \cdot D_{max} \leq F \leq P_{min} \tag{1}$$

The number of polls a stream meets is different period by period. Meeting hard real-time constraints for a station means that even in the period which has the smallest number of polls, the station can transmit message within its deadline. Fig. 4 analyzes the worst case available time for S_i. In this figure, a series of superframes are repeated in P_i and each period can start at any instant from the start of the superframe. Intuitively, the station can meet the smallest number of polls in the period which starts just after the end of its slot.

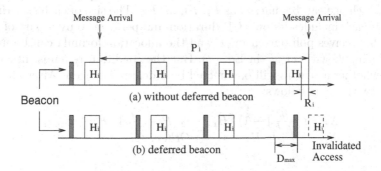

Fig. 4. Worst case analysis

In this figure, R_i is the residual obtained by dividing P_i by F, namely, $R_i = P_i - \lfloor \frac{P_i}{F} \rfloor \cdot F$. Without the deferred beacon, the CFP starts at regular intervals of

F. For S_i, the least bound of network access within P_i is $\lfloor \frac{P_i}{F} \rfloor$, as illustrated in Fig. 4(a). On the contrary, if we consider the deferred beacon, the deferred start of the last superframe may invalidate one access when R_i is less than D_{max}, as shown in Fig. 4(b). If R_i is greater than D_{max}, the number of available time slots is not affected by the delayed start of superframe. It doesn't matter whether the start of an intermediate superframe is deferred or not. In short, S_i can be affected by the deferred beacon in case R_i is less than D_{max} and the minimum value of available transmission time, X_i is calculated as Eq. (2). Namely,

$$
\begin{aligned}
X_i &= (\lfloor \tfrac{P_i}{F} \rfloor - 1) \cdot H_i \quad && if (P_i - \lfloor \tfrac{P_i}{F} \rfloor \cdot F) \leq D_{max} \\
X_i &= \lfloor \tfrac{P_i}{F} \rfloor \cdot H_i \quad && Otherwise
\end{aligned}
\tag{2}
$$

For each message stream, X_i should be greater than or equal to C_i ($X_i \geq C_i$). By substituting Eq. (2) for this inequality, we can obtain the least bound of H_i that can meet the time constraint of S_i.

$$
\begin{aligned}
H_i &= \frac{C_i}{(\lfloor \frac{P_i}{F} \rfloor - 1)} \quad && if (P_i - \lfloor \tfrac{P_i}{F} \rfloor \cdot F) \leq D_{max} \\
H_i &= \frac{C_i}{\lfloor \frac{P_i}{F} \rfloor} \quad && Otherwise
\end{aligned}
\tag{3}
$$

The allocation vector calculated by Eq. (3) is a feasible schedule if the vector meets Ineq. (1). By this, we can determine the length of CFP (T_{CFP}) and that of CP (T_{CP}) as follows:

$$
T_{CFP} = \sum H_i + \delta, \quad T_{CP} = F - T_{CFP} \geq D_{max}
\tag{4}
$$

This calculation is easily fulfilled with simple arithmetic operations. In addition, the size of time slot is different for each stream, so the capacity allocation by Eq. (3) can expect a better network utilization compared to other schemes based on fixed size slots. Finally, as this allocation scheme generates a larger T_{CP} for the given F, the network can accommodate more non-real-time messages.

In case a polling round spreads into more than one superframe, say m superframes, each one can be marked as $F_1, F_2, ..., F_m$. The size of each superframe is F, while each includes its own CP duration and performs only a part of polling round. S_i receives poll once a $m \cdot F$ and the allocation formula can be modified by replacing F with $m \cdot F$ in Eq. (2). But the condition remains intact which checks whether a stream will be affected by a deferred beacon. After all, Eq. (2) can be rewritten as follows:

$$
\begin{aligned}
X_i &= (\lfloor \tfrac{P_i}{m \cdot F} \rfloor - 1) \cdot H_i \quad && if (P_i - \lfloor \tfrac{P_i}{F} \rfloor \cdot F) \leq D_{max} \\
X_i &= \lfloor \tfrac{P_i}{m \cdot F} \rfloor \cdot H_i \quad && Otherwise
\end{aligned}
\tag{5}
$$

4.3   Bandwidth Reclaiming

Hard real-time guarantee is provided based on the worst case available transmission time as described in the previous section, so a stream can meet extra slots in some periods. Moreover, as C_i is just the upper bound of message size, some period has message to send less than C_i. So a node possibly have no pending message when it receives a poll and in that case it responds with a null frame containing no payload. Naturally, how to cope with this unused slot is critical to the network utilization. For example, FRASH reclaims such unused slots to reassign to a aperiodic server, aiming at improving the responsiveness of non-real-time messages. Whenever the transmission of the current dispatched message is over and it does not use all the reserved frames, its identifier is put in a field in the header of the last data packet of the current message. The identifier should be correctly received by all stations in the network to alleviate unnecessary contention on the slot. Furthermore, FRASH can perform properly only for TDMA protocols that operate on fixed size slots.

In the weighted round robin polling scheme, the first step to reclaim the bandwidth is to determine whether to proceed the rest of the polling or leave the slot unused. If we just proceed the polling schedule without considering the time constraint, the real-time guarantee can be broken. To describe this situation, let $P_i = k \cdot F + \Delta$, where Δ is chosen from 0 to F so that P_i and F have no common divisor. Then the number of network access within P_i is k or $k - 1$ according to whether $\Delta > D_{max}$ or not, and capacity vector is determined based on this number. If H_i moves ahead of message arrival due to the unused slot originally assigned to its predecessor, P_i loses one access, probably resulting in missing deadline of the message in that period. Fig. 5 illustrates this case specifically when k is 2 and message arrives prior to the scheduled network access by just a little amount of time.

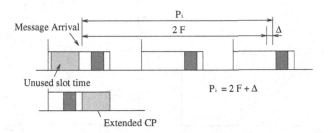

Fig. 5. Bandwidth reclaiming

In the contrary, the remaining part of polling schedule can be advanced within that superframe without violating the time constraint if all the subsequent streams have their messages to send, that is, if all of the remaining slots are not the first one of their period. As the PC can complete the polling schedule of that superframe, the length of CP can be extended to transmit more non-real-time messages and finally improve network utilization. In addition, we can increase the probability of bandwidth reclaim by rearranging the polling order. The frequency of first slot gets higher as the stream has shorter period. Therefore, it is desirable for PC to poll first the stream with shorter period.

5   Performance Measurements

A comparison with TDMA is inherently impossible because it requires so many assumptions to be decided on slot size, slot allocation scheme, and the way to cope with deferred beacon. Moreover, TDMA-based schemes excluded contention period, giving up compatibility with WLAN standard. In the mean while, other group of approaches guarantees meeting the time constraint for the hard real-time messages based on a pessimistic assumption that every stream suffers from the deferred beacon [5]. This is due to the fact that those schemes didn't accurately estimate the intervention of non-real-time message. So the first experiment compares the schedulability of our scheme with this pessimistic guarantee mechanism via simulation using ns-2 [12]. Second, we also measure the achievable bandwidth to demonstrate the effectiveness of reclaiming scheme.

For the first experiment, we have generated 2000 streams sets whose utilization has the value of 0.68 through 0.70, while the number of streams randomly distributes from 2 to 10. In the experiment, every time variable is aligned to the frame time. Accordingly, the period of each stream ranges from $5.0F$ to $10.0F$, while its message length from $0.3F$ to $3.0F$. Fig. 6 plots schedulability of proposed and pessimistic schemes changing D_{max} from 0 to $0.25F$. At low D_{max}, both schemes show equal schedulability, however, the proposed scheme improves the guarantee ratio by 18 % at maximum. In addition, the proposed scheme generates the T_{CP} up to 5.3% larger than that generated by the pessimistic scheme, enabling more non-real-time messages to occupy the network.

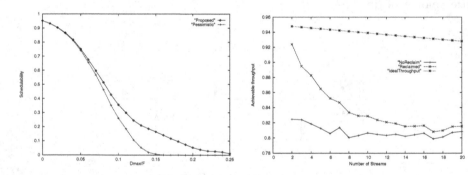

Fig. 6. Measured guarantee ratio   **Fig. 7.** Utilization improvement

Fig. 7 plots achievable bandwidth according to the average number of streams on the superframe to evaluate the performance of reclaiming scheme. We define *achievable throughput* as the virtual throughput for a given stream set without any collision even in CP. This can be estimated as the sum of both utilization of real-time message streams and ratio of average length of CP to F. Without overallocation caused by the hard real-time guarantee, the only waste is polling overhead, but overallocation makes the throughput less than ideal. However, the resource reclaiming scheme can narrow the gap between those two curves, that is, considerably relieves the problem of poor utilization of PCF operation, as shown in Fig. 7. At last, it is certain that the improvement increases when the number of streams is small, maximally 11 %.

6 Conclusion and Future Work

This paper has proposed and analyzed an hard real-time guarantee scheme based on the round robin style polling mechanism on the wireless network that conforms to the standard. The key idea is to decide the polling schedule for CFP in the form of capacity vector for the given network parameters and time constraints, after analyzing the effect of deferred beacon to the hard real-time message stream. The experiment demonstrates that the proposed scheme improves the schedulability for the experimental real-time stream sets by up to 18%. In addition, bandwidth reclaiming scheme proposed in this paper can overcome poor utilization problem of PCF in WLAN by reassigning the unused slot to non-real-time messages.

As a future work, we are planning to develop an error control scheme for dual WLANs. We believe that the dual LAN architecture can give priority in handling network errors, while the priority can be decided by the weight or urgency of messages, power management factors, and so on.

References

1. Muskinja, N.: Supervisory Control of the Real-Time Fuzzy Control Systems, Systems Analysis Modelling Simulation, Vol. 43, No. 11 (2003) 1569-1580
2. Carley, T., Ba, M., Barua, R., Stewart, D.: Contention-free periodic message scheduler medium access control in wireless sensor/actuator networks. Proc. IEEE Real-Time Systems Symposium (2003) 298-307
3. IEEE 802.11-1999: Part 11 - Wireless LAN Medium Access Control (MAC) and Physical Layer (PHY) Specifications (1999) also available at http://standards.ieee.org/getieee802.
4. Caccamo, M., Zhang, L., Sha, L., Buttazzo, G.: An implicit prioritized access protocol for wireless sensor networks. Proc. IEEE Real-Time Systems Symposium (2002)
5. Sheu, S., Sheu, T.: A bandwidth allocation/sharing/extension protocol for multimedia over IEEE 802.11 ad hoc wireless LANS. IEEE Journal on Selected Areas in Communications, Vol. 19 (2001) 2065-2080
6. Mao, S., Lin, S., Wang, Y., Panwar, S. S., Li, Y.: Multipath video transport over wireless ad hoc networks. IEEE Wireless Communications (2005)
7. Choi, S., Shin, K.: A unified wireless LAN architecture for real-time and non-real-time communication services. IEEE/ACM Trans. on Networking (2000) 44-59
8. Mangold, S. and et. al.: IEEE 802.11e Wireless LAN for Quality of Service. Proceedings of the European Wireless (2002)
9. Liu, J.: Real-Time Systems. Prentice Hall (2000)
10. Shah, S. H., Chen, K., Nahrstedt, K.: Dynamic Bandwidth Management for Single-hop Ad Hoc Wireless Networks. ACM/Kluwer Mobile Networks and Applications (MONET) Journal, Vol. 10 (2005) 199-217
11. Adamou, M., Khanna, S., Lee, I., Shin, I., Zhou, S.: Fair real-time traffic scheduling over a wireless LAN. Proc. IEEE Real-Time Systems Symposium (2001) 279-288
12. Fall, K., Varadhan, K.: Ns notes and documentation. Technical Report. VINT project. UC-Berkeley and LBNL (1997)

Application of Rough Set for Routing Selection Based on OSPF Protocol

Yanbing Liu[1,2], Hong Tang[1], Menghao Wang[1], and Shixin Sun[2]

[1] Chongqing University of Posts and Telecommunications,
Chongqing 400065, P.R. China
[2] School of Computer Science, UEST of China,
Chengdu 610010, P.R. China
liuyb@cqupt.edu.cn

Abstract. Attribute reduction is one of the most important issues and the focus of the research on efficient algorithms in rough sets. This paper focus on the routing selection algorithms and application used to compute QoS routes in OSPF protocol that are based on the rough set, which the attribute-value system about the link of network is created from the network topology. The use of rough set method can simplify enormous irregular link QoS attribute and classify the link with the link-status attribute. A illustrative example is employed to show the feasibility and effectiveness that the most excellent routing attribute set is obtained by rough set theory.

1 Introduction

IP routing protocols have long been an essential element of IP networks for many years. Recently, this technology has been the focus of new development, as routing has evolved to handle the needs of next generation networks. Traditional IP routing protocols have therefore been substantially extended in a number of areas. Data Connection provides a full range of high-function portable Unicast IP Routing software products, including BGP, OSPF and RIP for both IPv4 and IPv6 networks. With the development of network and application, the routing needs to satisfy the QoS (Quality of Service) demand. However, because the complication of many solving schemes to QoS Routing is NPC (nondeterministic polynomial time completeness), the node can't maintain the network information timely with the continual change of network state [1][2]. In order to adapt new demand on computer network, it is imperative to apply new feasible and efficient routing scheme to meet increasing demand on network.

The theory of rough sets has recently emerged as another major mathematical approach for managing uncertainty that arises from inexact, noisy, or incomplete information. Rough sets can be used for feature reduction, where attributes that do not contribute towards the classification of the given training data can be identified and removed and relevance analysis, where the contribution or significance of each attributes is assessed with respect to the classification task. The problem of finding the minimal subsets (reductions) of attributes that can describe all

D. Ślęzak et al. (Eds.): RSFDGrC 2005, LNAI 3642, pp. 654–661, 2005.

of the concepts in the given data set is NP-hard. However algorithms to reduce the computation intensity have been proposed. In one method, for example, a discernibility matrix is used to store the differences between attribute values for each pair of data samples. Rather than searching on the entire data set, the matrix is instead searched to detect redundant attributes. The work presented in this paper is to decide the link-rank by a series of the link-state attributes. The application of the rough set theory can solve this problem successfully. Usually, the link is classified by many QoS parameters such as link propagation delay, link available bandwidth, link jitter, possibility of connection and hop-counts et al. Then OSPF can select the best path with the link rank. The instance presented in this paper indicates that the reduction algorithm based on rough set offers an attractive approach to solve the feature subnet selection problem in routing-reduction table.

The remaining of this paper is organized as follows. Section 2 describes the related knowledge about OSPF. Application of rough set theory and the algorithm to select the best path are presented in Section 3. Section 4 shows a case to verify the algorithm. A conclusion is drawn in Section 5.

2 Related Knowledge

2.1 OSPF

OSPF (Open Shortest Path First) is a link-state routing protocol, which means that the routers exchange topology information with their nearest neighbors. The topology information is flooded throughout the AS, so that every router within the AS has a complete picture of the topology of the AS. This picture is then used to calculate end-to-end paths through the AS, normally using a variant of the Dijkstra algorithm. Therefore, in a link-state routing protocol, the next hop address to which data is forwarded is determined by choosing the best end-to-end path to the eventual destination. OSPF bases its path descriptions on "link states" that take into account additional network information. OSPF also lets the user assign cost metrics to a given host router so that some paths are given preference. OSPF supports a variable network subnet mask so that a network can be subdivided. The main advantage of a link state routing protocol is that the complete knowledge of topology allows routers to calculate routes that satisfy particular criteria.

2.2 OSPF Routing Algorithm

OSPF uses a link-state algorithm in order to build and calculate the shortest path to all known destinations. The algorithm by itself is quite complicated. The following is a very high level, simplified way of looking at the various steps of the algorithm[11]:

1. Upon initialization or due to any change in routing information, a router will generate a link-state advertisement. This advertisement will represent the collection of all link-states on that router.

2. All routers will exchange link-states by means of flooding. Each router that receives a link-state update should store a copy in its link-state database and then propagate the update to other routers.
3. After the database of each router is completed, the router will calculate a Shortest Path Tree to all destinations. The router uses the Dijkstra algorithm to calculate the shortest path tree. The destinations, the associated cost and the next hop to reach those destinations will form the IP routing table.
4. In case no changes in the OSPF network occur, such as cost of a link or a network being added or deleted, OSPF should be very quiet. Any changes that occur are communicated via link-state packets, and the Dijkstra algorithm is recalculated to find the shortest path.

The OSPF routing algorithm is based on Dijkstra shortest path algorithm. The term "Shortest pat" is inaccurate because what we really want to find is the "Optimum path". To find the optimum path in a network means to find a path with a minimal cost, considering factors like time , money and quality of the received data. The route is not chosen only by the cost, because in every network many constraint-attributes must be considered[11]:

- Cost-based routing metrics.
- Possibility of connection: Usually in traditional network, the possibility of link connection is high and this metric can be ignored. But in wireless network, it is a very important metric.
- Link available bandwidth: As mentioned earlier, we currently assume that most QoS requirements are derivable from bandwidth. We further assume that associated with each link is a maximal bandwidth value, e.g., the link physical bandwidth or some fraction thereof that has been set aside for QoS flows.
- Link propagation delay: This quantity is meant to identify high latency links, e.g., satellite links, which may be unsuitable for real-time requests.
- Link jitter: This quantity is used as a measure of the change of link delay. A path with a smaller jitter is more stable and typically preferable.
- Failure probability: failure probability of a single edge, the number of edges on each path, and the number of all edges shared among paths.

The main objective of QoS-based routing is to realize dynamic determination of feasible paths; QoS-based routing can determine a path, from among possibly many choices, that has a good chance of accommodating the QoS of the given flow.

2.3   Related Rough Set Theory

Rough set theory is a mathematical approach to imprecision, vague and uncertainty in information analysis [3]. It can be applied to find reduction. An attribute-value system IS is a quadruple $(U, C \cup D, V, f)$, $A = C \cup D$ is the set of all attributions which are further classified into two disjoint subsets: the condition attributes $C = \{a_i | i = 1, \cdots, m\}$ and the decision attribution $D = \{d\}$, $V = \bigcup_{a \in A} V_a$ is a set of attribute values, where $U = \{x_1, x_2, \cdots, x_n\}$ denotes the set of all objects in the set of all objects in the dataset, V_a is the domain of attribute a. $a_i(x_j)$ denotes the value of x_j on the attribution a_i. $f : U \times A \to V$ is an information function, which appoints the attribute value of every object x in U.

A discernibility matrix is a $n \times n$ matrix in which the classes are diagonal. In the matrix, the (condition) attributes which can be used to discern between the classes in the corresponding row and column are inserted. The information system's discernibility matrix $M(C_D(i,j))$ with entry $C_D(i,j)$ is defined as $\{a \in A | a(x_i) \neq a(x_j)\}$ if $d(x_i) \neq d(x_j)$, ϕ otherwise, where $i, j = 1, \cdots, n$.

The core attribute set $Core(A)$ can be defined as the set of all single element where $|C_D(i,j)| = 1$ [4,5,6].

3   Routing-Reduction Algorithm to Select the Best Path

This paper makes the elucidation of the algorithm to classify link-rank to select the best path.

1) From the historical data of routing table and the QoS information about the links, the attribute-value system about the links can be built.
2) Then we can draw the matrix about the information system and can conclude the routing-reduction table [7,8,9,10].
   Step 1: $RT = \phi$, $Core = \phi$;
   Step 2: for every $b \in A$, computing the equivalent class U/b;
   Step 3: construct discernibility matrix $M(A) = \{C_D(i,j)\}_{n \times n}$, where $1 < i, j < n$.
   Step 4: Do loop, $\forall\ C_D(i,j) \in M(A)$, if $(|C_D(i,j)| == 1)$ then $Core = Core \cup \{C_D(i,j)\}$;
   Step 5: $RT = Core$;
   Step 6: $\forall\ Core$, We set $C_D(i,j) = \phi$ when $a \in C_D(i,j)$.
3) The decision attribute with excellent routing attributes can be concluded from the routing-reduction table RT.
4) With the knowledge of OSPF, the best path can be obtained. The link state algorithm presented below is known as Dijkstra's algorithm.

```
Initialization:
        N = set of nodes in the graph; U={source node}
        for all nodes v
            if v adjacent to U
            then D(v) = c(U, v)
            else D(v) = Infinity
```

Loop
        find w not in N such that D(w) is a minimum add w to N
        for v adjacent to w and not in N update D(v):
            D(v) = min{ D(v), D(w)+c(w, v) }
      until all nodes in N.

$c(i,j)$ is the weight of the decision attributes of the link from node i to node j. $D(v)$ is cost of the path from the source node to destination v that has currently (as the iteration of the algorithm) the least cost with the most excellent routing attribute. N is set of nodes whose least-cost path from the source is definitely known.

With the help of rough set theory, the simplification of the routing-reduction table is to simplify the condition attributes in routing-reduction table, and after that the routing-reduction possesses the ability of the routing-reduction table before simplification, but possesses more important condition attributes.

4   A Case Analysis

Let us take a routing topology of network, which has ten nodes. Figure 1 is a network topology used to illustrate the above arithmetic. The number on the link denotes the link-number (link No.). Routing is determined by the link's QoS attribution parameters, such as: bandwidth, propagation delay, connection-failure possibility and bit error ratio and so on. All the values in the table 1 denote the w eight (measure) of the attributes that learn from historical records in router, which represents an equivalence class in routing table. Part of the routing-attribute conditions in network can be defined as information table IS=$(U, C \cup \{d\}, V, f)$, $C = \{a_1, a_2, a_3, a_4\}$ is a routing attribute set, in which 'a_1' represents the bandwidth of link: 1 denotes enough, 2 denotes available, 3 denotes non-enough. 'a_2' represents the propagation delay of link: 1 denotes low, 2 denotes normal, 3 denotes high. 'a_3' represents the failure probability of link: 1 denotes low, 2 denotes normal, 3 denotes under normal. 'a_4' represents the bit error ratio of the link: 1 denotes low, 2 denotes acceptable, 3 denotes insufferable. The decision attribution $D = \{d\} = \{G, N, B\}$: G denotes good, N denotes normal, B denotes bad (each of their weight is 1,2,3, respectively). The function of the information 'f' can expressed by the table 1.

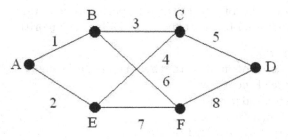

Fig. 1. The Network Topology

Table 1. Information System

Link No.	a_1	a_2	a_3	a_4	d
1	2	1	3	2	G(1)
2	2	1	1	1	G(1)
3	1	1	1	2	G(1)
4	1	2	3	2	N(2)
5	2	2	2	2	N(2)
6	1	2	3	3	B(3)
7	3	2	2	3	B(3)
8	3	3	3	1	B(3)

From Table 1, the discernibility matrix $M(C_D(i,j))$ can be given as follow:

$$
\begin{bmatrix}
\phi & a_3a_4 & a_1a_3 & a_1a_2 & a_2a_3 & a_1a_2a_4 & a_1a_2a_4 & a_1a_2a_4 \\
 & \phi & a_1a_4 & a_1a_2a_3a_4 & a_2a_3a_4 & a_1a_2a_3a_4 & a_1a_2a_3a_4 & a_1a_2a_3 \\
 & & \phi & a_2a_3 & a_1a_2a_3 & a_2a_3a_4 & a_1a_2a_3a_4 & a_1a_2a_3a_4 \\
 & & & \phi & a_1a_3 & a_4 & a_1a_4 & a_1a_2a_4 \\
 & & & & \phi & a_1a_3a_4 & a_1a_3a_4 & a_1a_2a_3a_4 \\
 & & & & & \phi & a_1 & a_1a_2a_4 \\
 & & & & & & \phi & a_2a_4 \\
 & & & & & & & \phi
\end{bmatrix}
$$

In the above matrix, $|C_D(4,6)| = 1$, $|C_D(6,7)| = 1$, we can get $Core(A) = \{a_1, a_4\}$. This means that a_1 and a_4 are the most important routing attributes. When $C_D(i,j)$ contains a_1 or a_4, then we set $C_D(i,j) = \phi$. A new simple matrix can be obtained:

$$
\begin{bmatrix}
\phi & \phi & \phi & \phi & a_2a_3 & \phi & \phi & \phi \\
 & \phi & \phi & \phi & \phi & \phi & \phi & \phi \\
 & & \phi & \phi & \phi & \phi & \phi & \phi \\
 & & & \phi & \phi & \phi & \phi & \phi \\
 & & & & \phi & \phi & \phi & \phi \\
 & & & & & \phi & \phi & \phi \\
 & & & & & & \phi & \phi \\
 & & & & & & & \phi
\end{bmatrix}
$$

The reduced attribute set can be $(a_1 \wedge a_2 \wedge a_4) \vee (a_1 \wedge a_3 \wedge a_4)$. It means the reduction attributions can be $a_1 \wedge a_2 \wedge a_4$ or $a_1 \wedge a_3 \wedge a_4$. We take $a_1 \wedge a_2 \wedge a_4$ as an example. We find that, in the initial information table 1 there are four attributes besides the decision attribute. In general, the router record these attributes by historic data, so there are some attributes that are dispensable to "Best Path". After removing the redundant attributes by rough set theory, we get the table 2.

The simplification of routing- reduction attributes needn't to select all routing-reduction attributes in the condition of keeping the consistence of routing-reduction table. That is to say, attribute reduction techniques aim at finding minimal subsets of attributes, each of which has the same discriminating

Table 2. Reduction Information System

Link No.	a_1	a_2	a_4	d
1	2	1	2	G(1)
2	2	1	1	G(1)
3	1	1	2	G(1)
4	1	2	2	N(2)
5	2	2	2	N(2)
6	1	2	3	B(3)
7	3	2	3	B(3)
8	3	3	1	B(3)

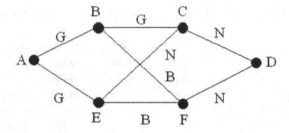

Fig. 2. The Rank of Link

power as the entire attributes. For compatible data table,the most excellent attribute set is selected by rough set theory.The links on the subnet shown Figure 1 are classified to three ranks. Based on the Dijkstra algorithm [11], we can find the best path from A to D in Figure 2 is $A \rightarrow B \rightarrow C \rightarrow D$ according to the link-rank attributes. The routing path is the best on condition that bandwidth is enough and available, bit error ratio is acceptable. After some attributes of the link aren't selected, we investigate that if the condition attribute with same row can decide the same decision value as before.

5   Conclusion and Future Work

In this paper, we have proposed a new alternate Best-path-finding algorithm for OSPF. The complication of traditional solving schemes to QoS Routing is NPC. In this paper, the link is classified to different ranks with rough set theory in terms of its QoS attributes, and OSPF based on QoS routing can be realized. Rough set theory can deal with the links with complicated QoS attributes, and can rapidly classify them to different ranks. OSPF based on rough set theory can select a path with the QoS parameters and can offer the QoS-based service in the Internet. The application of rough set theory greatly simplifies the implication of the algorithm. For further work, executing time analysis, when the connectivity and the diameter of graphs change, should be considered. Moreover, future tests in a real network environment should also be performed.

Acknowledgement

The authors would like to thank Dr. Y.Y. Yao and Dr. J.T. Yao for their help when they were in Canada. They also wish to express sincere thanks to their current and past colleagues, especially Dr. Guoyin Wang and Dr. Yu Wu, for their help and discussions. The authors thank the referees for their useful suggestions. The work is supported by the National Natural Science Foundation of China under Grant No. 90304004 , the Natural Science Foundation of CSTC and CQUPT under Grant No. A200469 and the Natural Science Foundation of CQMEC under Grant No. KJ050507.

References

1. Bruno, A. (ed.): CCIE # 2738. CCIE Routing and Switching Exam Certification Guide. Digit. Libr., 1 (2003)
2. Liu, H.S., Xu, M.W., Ke, X., Cui, Y.: Research on Internetwork Routing Protocol: a Survey. Science of Telecommunications, 19 (2003) 28-32
3. Pawlak, Z.: Rough Sets-Theoretical Aspects of Reasoning about Data. Kluwer Academic Publishers, Dordrecht, Netherlands, 1991
4. Li, P., Hong, Z., Saeid, N.: The Application of Rough Set and Kohonen Network to Feature Selection for Object Extraction. Proceedings of the second International Conference on Machine Learning and Cybernetics. November (2003) 1185-1189
5. Crawley, E., Nair, R., et al.: RFC 2386, IETF, August (1998)
6. Apostolopoulos, G., Williams, D., Kamat, S., Guerin, R., et al.: RFC 2676, IETF, August (1999)
7. Li, Y., Xiao, Z., Liu, F.S.: Classification of clients in client relationship management base on rough set theory, Proceedings of the second International Conference on Machine Learning and Cybernetics. November (2003) 242-246
8. Wang, Z.L., Meng, W.B., Gu, X.J., et al.: The Research of the Police GIS Spatial Data Classification Technology Based on Rough Set. Proceedings of the 4th Congress on Intelligent Control and Automation. June (2002) 10-14
9. Zhang, Y.: Rough Set and Genetic Algorithms in Path Planning of Robot. Proceeding of Second International Conference on Machine Learning and Cybernetics, Xi'an, Nov. (2003) 698-701
10. Wang, G.Y., Yu, H., Yang, D.C.: Decision table reduction based on information entropy (in Chinese), Chinese Journal computers, 2(7) (2002) 759-766
11. http://www.dataconnection.com/

Energy Aware Routing with Dynamic Probability Scaling*

Geunyoung Park[1], Sangho Yi[1], Junyoung Heo[1], Woong Chul Choi[2],
Gwangil Jeon[3], Yookun Cho[1], and Charlie Shim[4]

[1] Seoul National University
{gypark, shyi, jyheo, cho}@ssrnet.snu.ac.kr
[2] KwangWoon University
wchoi@daisy.kw.ac.kr
[3] Korea Polytechnic University
gijeon@kpu.ac.kr
[4] South Dakota State University
Yong.Shim@SDSTATE.EDU

Abstract. The goal of energy aware routing algorithms is to increase
the lifetime and long-term connectivity of the wireless sensor networks.
However, most of those algorithms do not use the newest states of nodes
for retrieving routing information. In this paper, we propose an efficient
energy-aware routing algorithm for wireless sensor networks. In our algorithm, the energy drain rate and residual energy of each sensor node are
used for selecting candidate routes. Information is retrieved with energy
awareness per almost every communication. Simulation results show that
our approach outperforms the previous works with respect to long term
connectivity by as much as 30%.

1 Introduction

Wireless sensor networks typically consist of hundreds or thousands of sensor
nodes deployed in a geographical region to sense events. Wireless sensor networks provide a high-level description of the events being sensed. They are used
in many applications such as environmental control, robot control, automatic
manufacturing, etc. They can be used even in harsh environment [1,2]. Therefore, their developing entails significant technical challenges due to the many
environmental constraints.

One of the most important constraints is the lack of power. Sensors in the
sensor networks are supplied with power generally by built-in battery. In addition, transmission of a packet in wireless sensor networks is expensive, because
it requires the energy consumption for both the sender and the listener. Therefore, routing, i.e. path determination, which is highly correlated with energy
consumption, is a critical factor determining the performance of network.

---

* The present research was conducted by the Research Grant of KwangWoon University in 2005, and was supported in part by the Brain Korea 21 project.

D. Ślęzak et al. (Eds.): RSFDGrC 2005, LNAI 3642, pp. 662–670, 2005.

Most previous researches on routing [3,4,5] focused on the algorithm design and performance evaluation in terms of the packet transmission overhead and loss rate. On the other hand, some routing algorithms were proposed in [1,2,6,7,8,9] in order to improve scalability of routing algorithms for large sensor networks.

Finding a route consuming the least amount of energy requires that information on all of candidate routes be known as accurately as possible. This in turn entails high cost for transmitting a single packet. Therefore, the probabilistic approach, where a route is selected based on certain criteria, is more widely used. In such cases, parameters and constraints affect performance very much.

In our proposed algorithm, the energy drain rate and the residual energy of each sensor node are used as the routing information, updated per almost every communication with energy awareness. To obtain such information, our algorithm takes advantage of the characteristic of wireless network, called overhearing. When two nodes communicate with each other, the neighboring nodes can overhear the packet being transmitted. Overhearing enables each sensor node to obtain the energy information of neighboring nodes without additional overhead. Then, they update their routing tables using this information. Therefore, our algorithm can provide longer connectivity of sensor networks through efficient use of energy among the nodes in the network.

The rest of the paper is organized as follows. In section 2 we present related works. Section 3 describes a new energy aware routing algorithm based on dynamic probability scaling. Section 4 presents and evaluates the performance of the proposed energy aware routing algorithm against the prior algorithm. Finally, some conclusions are given in Section 5.

2   Related Works

In this section, we present a brief overview of the proposed energy-aware routing algorithms. Considerable research efforts [1,2,3,4,5,6,10,11,12] have been made to determine efficient routing for wireless sensor networks.

In [6], Singh et al. proposed energy-aware routing and discussed different metrics in energy-aware routing for ad hoc networks. In [1], Shah and Rabaey proposed the use of a set of occasionally sub-optimal paths to increase the lifetime of the sensor networks. These paths are chosen by means of the probability that is dependent on the amount of energy consumed in each path.

In [3], Ganesan et al. proposed the use of braided multipaths instead of completely disjoint multipaths in order to keep the cost of maintaining the multipaths low. The costs of such alternate paths are also comparable to the primary path because they tend to be much closer to the primary path.

In [4], Chang and Tassiulas proposed an algorithm for maximizing the lifetime of a network by selecting a path whose nodes have the largest residual energy. In this way, the nodes in the primary path retain their energy resources, and thus avoid having to continuously rely on the same route. This contributes to ensuring longer life of a network.

Stojmenovic and Lin proposed the first localized energy-aware algorithm in [13]. It is unique in that it combines both energy and cost into one metric and is based on local information only. In [8], Chang and Tassiulas also applied this combined metric concept for direct routing. Their algorithm is proposed to maximize the lifetime of a network when data rate is known. The main idea is to avoid using the nodes with low energy and to choose the shortest path.

In [5], Li et al. proposed an algorithm in which the constraint of the residual energy of a route is relaxed slightly to select a more energy efficient route. It is generally known that a route with the largest residual energy for routing a packet entails high energy consumption. Therefore, there is a tradeoff between minimizing the total consumed energy and the residual energy of the network. In that paper, groups of the sensors in geographic proximity were clustered together into a zone and each zone was treated as a separate entity and allowed to determine how it will route a packet across.

To determine and manage efficient paths in networks, some protocols use artificial intelligence like fuzzy set, evolutionary computing, ants behavior, etc. In [10], Alandjani and Johnson proposed an algorithm that applies fuzzy logic to identify multiple disjoint paths, considering traffic importance and network state. Its goal is to provide high reliability for important traffic.

In [11], Liu et al. proposed a multipaths routing algorithm. It combines several network factors including the energy consumption rate and link stability based on fuzzy set theory. Then, it selects a set of paths, using those factors, to maximize network lifetime and reliability.

In [12], Carrillo et al. proposed multi-agent based routing algorithm. It was a kind of hybrid ad-hoc routing algorithm. To combine the advantages of both proactive and reactive routing algorithm, they used ant colony optimization and multi-agent system. Multi-agent system found multi-path by reactive routing manner and gave those results to the ant colony optimization. Then, ant colony optimization found the routing path by proactive routing manner.

3   Routing with Dynamic Probability Scaling

3.1   Energy Aware Routing

Energy Aware Routing (EAR) which was proposed by Shah and Rabaey [1] is one of the routing algorithms for wireless sensor networks. EAR finds multiple routes, if any, from source to destination nodes. Each route is assigned a probability of being selected to transmit a packet, based on residual energy and the energy for communications at the nodes along the route. Then, based on these probabilities, one of the candidate routes is chosen in order to transmit a packet. The probability is proportional to the energy level at each node, so the routes with higher energy are more likely to be selected. EAR protects any route from being selected all the time, preventing the energy depletion [1].

The primary goal of EAR is to improve network survivability. For this, EAR occasionally uses suboptimal paths, to slow down the depletion of the node energy across the network. As a consequence, the entire network will have a longer lifetime than that using the algorithms such as Directed Diffusion [14].

The operation of EAR consists of three phases. In *Setup phase*, a destination node initiates a route request and a routing table is built up by finding all the paths from a source to the destination and their energy cost. In *Data Communication phase*, data packets are sent from the source to the destination. Each of the intermediate nodes forwards the packet to a neighboring node, which is chosen randomly based on the probability computed in the setup phase. In *Route Maintenance phase*, local flooding is performed to keep all the paths alive [1].

3.2   Effect of Residual Energy on Route Determination

In EAR algorithm, each path is assigned a probability of being selected. This probability is inversely proportional to the "communication cost" of the path, dependent on the energy metric $Metric(i, j)$ between two neighbor nodes. The definition of energy metric is given in [1]:

$$Metric(i, j) = e_{ij}^{\alpha} R_i^{\beta}$$

Here e_{ij} is the energy used to transmit and receive on the link, R_i is the residual energy at node i normalized to its initial energy, α and β are weighting factors.

Once the path probabilities are computed, they are not changed during the data communication phase. The paths with higher probabilities are more likely to be selected, regardless of the residual energies along their nodes. As a consequence, energy of the path with lower cost will be used up quicker. To re-compute the probabilities, the setup phase must be executed again. However, flooding in this phase entails high communication cost. In this section, we propose an algorithm that can improve it by using the information of residual energies without the need of flooding. As a consequence, lifetime of entire network is enhanced.

3.3   Overhearing

In the wireless networks, radio wave is the physical media of communications. Radio wave propagates in every direction. Hence, when two nodes communicate with each other, the neighboring nodes of a sender can hear the packet being transmitted. Figure 1 shows this situation.

In Fig. 1, node A sends a packet to node B, and then all nodes in the circle with the center in A and the radius equal to the distance between A and B can hear the data packet. In general cases, packets heard unintentionally are ignored. Such *overhearing* can be exploited to compensate for a disadvantage of EAR in terms of energy consumption. In Fig. 1, for example, nodes $C \sim G$ can hear A transmitting to B, which means $C \sim G$ knows that A is consuming some amount of energy for transmitting a data packet. By using this information, each neighboring node can re-compute the current energy level for node A and itself, and then adjust probability for its route towards A.

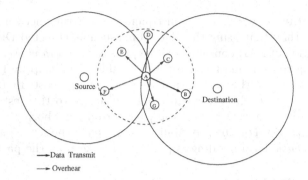

Fig. 1. Data communication in a wireless network

For a formal description of the proposed algorithm, we define the following:

1. $NodeSet(i, j)$ is the set of all nodes in the neighborhood of i, which are not more distant from i than j is.
2. $OverhearingSet(i, j) = NodeSet(i, j) - \{i, j\}$
3. $UpdateSet(A, B) = OverhearingSet(A, B) \cap$
   $NodeSet(\text{Source}, A) \cap \neg NodeSet(A, \text{Destination})$

For example, in Fig. 1 we have $NodeSet(A, B) = \{A, B, C, D, E, F, G\}$, $OverhearingSet(A, B) = \{C, D, E, F, G\}$, and $UpdateSet(A, B) = \{E, F\}$.

3.4   Our Proposed Algorithm

Finally, we describe our Energy Aware Routing with Dynamic Probability Scaling (EAR-DPS) method. The idea is to update probabilities of paths whenever they overhear communications. Similar to EAR, the operation of EAR-DPS consists of three phases: *Setup, Data Communication* and *Route Maintenance.*

Setup Phase: The same as for EAR. Destination node initiates a route request and all of intermediate nodes relay the request in towards the source node.

Data Communication Phase: After Setup is completed, each sensor, i.e. the source node, sends data that it collected to a destination node. Precisely:

1. A source node sends a data packet to any of its neighbors in the forwarding table, with the probability of the neighbor being selected set to the probability in the forwarding table [1].
2. Each intermediate node chooses the next hop among its neighbors. The probability of the neighbors being selected is set to that in the forwarding table.
3. When an intermediate node N_i selects N_j as the next hop, N_i estimates the energy needed to transmit a data packet to N_j and its residual energy after transmitting. Then, it re-computes the energy metrics for communications with its neighbors. Finally, the "cost", $Cost(N_i)$ of N_i is recomputed.

4. Node N_i forwards the data packet including its new cost.
5. Each element in $UpdateSet(N_i, N_j)$ recomputes the probability of choosing N_i as its next hop basing on new overheard $Cost(N_i)$. At this moment, the residual energy of N_i is reflected in its neighbors' forwarding tables.
6. Similarly to EAR, this process continues until the data packet reaches the destination node [1].

Route Maintenance Phase: Like in Setup, it is the same as that of EAR. Flooding is occasionally performed in order to keep all the paths alive and to compute new metrics [1]. In EAR-DPS, however, computing new metrics can be performed in the data communication phase, and thus route maintenance phase is not necessary as in EAR.

4 Simulations

4.1 Environment Setup

Our research group built simulator for both EAR and EAR-DPS. It provides basic information such as the residual energy of each node, the energy metrics between any two nodes and the communication cost of each node.

The area of the sensor networks was assumed to be 100m×100m. The number of the nodes in the network was assumed to be 100 nodes – one node is controller while the others are sensors. The controller was located at the center of the field and the sensor nodes are placed randomly in the field as shown in Fig. 2(a). All of the sensors sent data to the controller at fixed interval. The length of interval between transmissions at each node was all identical. This interval can be considered as a virtual time unit. That is, all of the sensor nodes send their data to the controller just once a single time unit.

Parameters in numeric formulas are as shown in [1]. Every node was given an identical amount, 0.05J, of initial energy. Energy for transmission was assumed 20nJ/bit + 1pJ/bit/m³. Energy for reception was assumed 30nJ/bit. The packet length was assumed 256 bytes. Energy metric function with $\alpha=1$ and $\beta=50$ was used. In this simulation, the following assumptions were made:

− Every node knows its position and distance between itself and other nodes.
− Every node has an identical maximum radio range.

4.2 Numerical Results

Figure 2(b) shows residual energy of every sensor node after 10 time units by comparing EAR-DPS with EAR. The x-axis indicates the distance between the sensor and controller or destination. Figure 2(b) shows that energies of the nodes using EAR-DPS are more uniform. Table 1 shows the statistics of residual energy of the nodes in the network for two algorithms. After 30 time units, the average residual energy of each node for EAR-DPS is ~1.29 times that for EAR. After 80 time units, the ratio exceeds over 2. It should be noted that the standard deviation of energy for EAR-DPS is much less than that for EAR, and that the

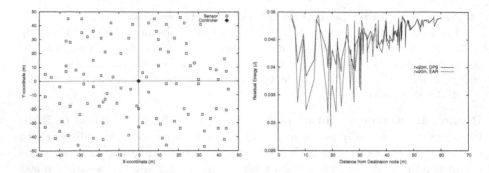

Fig. 2. (a) Layout of nodes in the network (b) Residual energy of each node

Table 1. Residual Energy Statistics

			Energy (J)		
Time	Protocol	Average	Std.Dev.	Max	Min
30	EAR-DPS	0.04495	0.003	0.049	0.036
	EAR	0.03472	0.010	0.049	0.05
80	EAR-DPS	0.03618	0.009	0.048	0.011
	EAR	0.01717	0.016	0.048	0

minimum energy for EAR-DPS is greater than that for EAR. This shows that the nodes using EAR-DPS will survive much longer than those using EAR.

Figure 3(a) shows the energy distribution at a certain time point of a network using EAR-DPS. It can be seen that the difference in energy among nodes is smaller than EAR as shown in Fig. 3(b), respectively. In addition, the energy of the entire network using EAR-DPS is still higher than that of EAR (Fig. 4(b)).

Figure 4(a) shows the number of active nodes in the network versus time. In the case a network using EAR-DPS with the maximum radio range r=20m, the first event where a node runs out of energy occurs after 100 time units, whereas in the case of EAR, it occurs after 34 time units. Then, in the case of a network using EAR-DPS with r=50m, it occurs after 86 time units and in the case of a network using EAR, after 13 time units.

In sensor networks, it is not fatal if a small number of nodes run out of energy. However, it becomes a critical problem when all of the surrounding neighboring nodes die. Therefore, in this paper, we measured the time elapsed until the energy of all the nodes which are neighbors of a destination run out. That is, the controller is no longer able to receive any more data packet and the entire network becomes useless. According to the simulation results, when the maximum radio range was assumed 20m, it occurred after 128 time units in the case of EAR-DPS, while it occurred after 93 time units for EAR. When r is 50m, it took 184 and 113 time units, respectively.

Figure 4(b) shows the average of residual energy of each node versus time. Then the total remaining energy of the network is computed by multiplying the

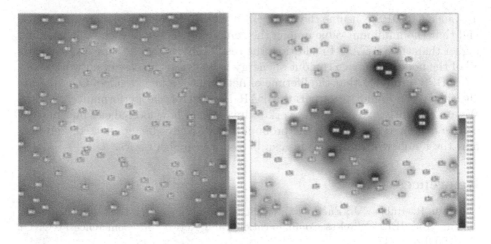

Fig. 3. (a) Energy consumption for EAR-DPS (b) Energy consumption for EAR

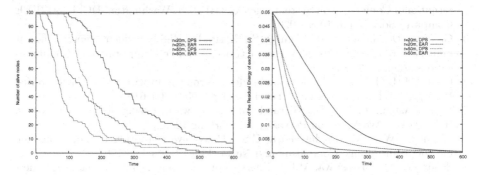

Fig. 4. (a) The number of active nodes during communication phase (b) Mean of residual energy of each node

average with the number of nodes. As we expect, the total energy of the network for EAR-DPS is greater than that for EAR.

5 Conclusion and Future Work

In this paper, we proposed an energy-aware routing algorithm with dynamic probability scaling for high survivability of wireless sensor networks. Our algorithm is based on EAR, and intended to enhance its performance. In our method, the energy drain rate and the residual energy of each sensor node were used for retrieving the energy-efficient routing information, and they were updated per almost every communication with energy awareness. By doing so, our algorithm can provide longer connectivity of sensor networks and at the same time ensure efficient use of energy among the nodes in the network.

We performed a comprehensive simulation to verify the performance of our algorithm and compared it with EAR. The results showed that the networks using our EAR-DPS consume the energy of nodes in the networks more uniformly, and that the minimum value among the remaining energy of each node sustains higher than that of EAR. In addition, the results show that the time elapsed until all of the nodes on a path run out of energy is longer in the case of network using EAR-DPS, implying that the lifetime of networks can be extended. Overall, our algorithm was found to outperform EAR in most of the performance metrics. We are currently extending our work to investigate how look-ahead information can be exploited to compute the probabilities of routes being selected, and also how the number of computations can be reduced by heuristics.

References

1. Shah, R., Rabaey, J.: Energy aware routing for low energy ad hoc sensor networks. In: Proc. IEEE Wireless Communications and Networking Conference (WCNC) (2002) 812–817
2. Heinzelman, W.R., Chandrakasan, A., Balakrishnan, H.: Energy-efficient communication protocol for wireless microsensor networks. In: Proc. the 33rd Hawaii International Conference on System Sciences (HICSS). Washington, DC, USA, IEEE Computer Society (2000) 8, 8020
3. Ganesan, D., Govindan, R., Shenker, S., Estrin, D.: Highly-resilient, energy-efficient multipath routing in wireless sensor networks. Mobile Computing and Communications Review, 5 (2001) 11–25
4. Chang, J.H., Tassiulas, L.: Maximum lifetime routing in wireless sensor networks. IEEE/ACM Transactions on Networking, 12 (2004) 609–619
5. Li, Q., Aslam, J., Rus, D.: Hierarchical power-aware routing in sensor networks. In: DIMACS Workshop on Pervasive Networking (2001)
6. Singh, S., Woo, M., Raghavendra, C.S.: Power-aware routing in mobile ad hoc networks. In: Mobile Computing and Networking.(1998) 181–190
7. Schurgers, C., Srivastava, M.B.: Energy efficient routing in wireless sensor networks. In: IEEE Military Communications Conference (MILCOM) (2001) 357–361
8. Chang, J., Tassiulas, L.: Energy conserving routing in wireless ad-hoc networks. In: IEEE Infocom. (2000) 22–31
9. Braginsky, D., Estrin, D.: Rumor routing algorithm for sensor networks. In: 1st ACM international workshop on Wireless Sensor Networks and Applications (WSNA). Atlanta, Georgia, USA, ACM Press (2002) 22–31
10. Alandjani, G., Johnson, E.E.: Fuzzy routing in ad hoc networks. In: Proc. IEEE International Conference on Performance, Computing, and Communications (2003) 525–530
11. Liu, H., Li, J., Zhang, Y.Q., Pan, Y.: An adaptive genetic fuzzy multi-path routing protocol for wireless ad-hoc networks. In: Proc. 1st ACIS International Workshop on Self-Assembling Wireless Networks (SAWN) (2005)
12. Carrillo, L., Marzo, J.L., Vilá, P., Mantilla, C.A.: Mants-hoc: A multi-agent ant-based system for routing in mobile ad hoc networks. In: Proc. Setè Congrés Català d'Intelligència Artificial (CCIA) (2004)
13. Stojmenovic, I., Lin, X.: Power aware localized routing in wireless networks. IEEE Transactions on Parallel and Distributed Systems, 12 (2001) 1122–1133
14. Intanagonwiwat, C., Govindan, R., Estrin, D.: Directed diffusion: a scalable and robust communication paradigm for sensor networks. In: Mobile Computing and Networking (2000) 56–67

Application of (Max, +)-Algebra to the Optimal Buffer Size in Poisson Driven Deterministic Queues in Series with Blocking[*]

Dong-Won Seo[1] and Byung-Kwen Song[2]

[1] College of Management and International Relations Kyung Hee University,
1 Seocheon-ri, Giheung-eup, Yongin-si, Gyeonggi-do 449-701, Korea
dwseo@khu.ac.kr
[2] Department of Information and Communication, SeoKyeong University,
16-1 Jungneung-Dong Sungbuk-Ku, Seoul 136-704, Korea
bksong@skuniv.ac.kr

Abstract. In this study, by applying (max, +)-algebra to a stochastic event graph, a special case of timed Petri nets, we consider characteristics of waiting times in Poisson driven single-server 2 queues in series with a finite buffer and having constant service times at each queue. We show that the sojourn time does not depend on the finite buffer capacity and also derive the explicit expressions of waiting times at all areas of the system as a function of the finite buffer capacity, which allow one to compute and compare waiting times under two blocking policies. Moreover, an optimization problem which determines the smallest buffer capacity satisfying a predetermined probabilistic constraint on waiting times is considered as an application of these results.

1 Introduction

As common models of telecommunication networks and manufacturing systems, queues in series with finite buffers have been widely studied. Many researchers have interests in characteristics in stochastic networks such as mean waiting times, system sojourn times, invariant probabilities, call loss (blocking) probabilities, and so forth. Since computational complexity and difficulty in the analysis of performance evaluations in stochastic networks, most studies are focused on restrictive and/or small size of stochastic networks over the past decades.

In Poisson driven 2-node tandem queues with exponential service times, Grassmann and Drekic [7] studied the joint distribution of both queues by using generalized eigenvalues. For infinite buffered queues in series with non-overlapping service times and an arbitrary arrival process, Whitt [11] studied the optimal order of nodes which minimizes the mean value of sojourn times. Nakade [9] derived bounds for the mean value of cycle times in tandem queues with general service times under communication and manufacturing blocking policies.

---

[*] This work was supported by grant No.(R01-2004-000-10948-0) from the Basic Research Program of the Korea Science & Engineering Foundation.

D. Ślęzak et al. (Eds.): RSFDGrC 2005, LNAI 3642, pp. 671–677, 2005.

Under the assumption of the capacities of buffers including the space for a customer in service and an arbitrary arrival process, Wan and Wolff [10] showed that the departure processes in tandem queues with finite buffers except for the first node and with non-overlapping service times are independent of the size of finite buffers when it is greater than 2 under communication blocking or when it is greater than 1 under manufacturing blocking. Labetoulle and Pujolle [8] gave the same results for mean response time, but derived mean waiting times at each queue under the assumption of infinite buffer capacity for all nodes. However, in our best knowledge, there is no result on waiting times in all sub-areas of finite buffered queues in series.

More generous system which so called a (max, +)-linear system has been studied. Various types of stochastic networks which are prevalent in telecommunication, manufacturing systems belong to the (max, +)-linear system. Many instances of (max, +)-linear systems can be represented by stochastic event graphs, a special type of stochastic Petri net, which allow one to analyze them. (Max, +)-linear system is a choice-free net and consists of single-server queues under FIFO(First-In First-Out) service discipline. Discrete event systems (DESs) can be properly modeled by (max, +)-algebra, involving only two operators: 'max' and '+'.

Recently, Baccelli and Schmidt [6] derived a Taylor series expansion for mean stationary waiting time with respect to the arrival rate in a Poisson driven (max, +)-linear system. Their approach was generalized to other characteristics of stationary and transient waiting times by Baccelli et al. [4], [5], Ayhan and Seo [1], [2].

By the similar way, deriving the explicit expressions of waiting times in all areas of finite buffered 2-node tandem queues is the main goal of this study. In addition, from these expressions we also disclose a relationship on waiting times under two blocking policies: communication and manufacturing. As an application of these results, moreover, we consider an optimization problem for determining the smallest buffer size which satisfies a predetermined probabilistic constraint on stationary waiting times.

Reader can refer on basic (max, +)-algebra and some preliminaries on waiting times in (max, +)-linear systems to Baccelli et al. [3] and Ayhan and Seo [1], [2] and references therein. We omit them here. This paper is organized as follows. Section 2 contains our main results. An optimization problem and a numerical example are given in section 3 and 4. Conclusion and some future research topics are mentioned in Section 5.

2   Waiting Times in Deterministic Queues in Series with a Finite Buffer

We consider Poisson driven 2 queues in series with a finite buffer and having constant service times. Each queue has its own buffer: one at the first node is infinite and the other is finite.

For the finite buffered system, we assume that the system is operated by only one of the two blocking policies, not mixed: communication and manufacturing. Under communication blocking a customer at node j cannot begin service unless there is a vacant space in the buffer at node $j + 1$. For manufacturing blocking, a customer served at node j moves to node $j + 1$ only if the buffer of node $j + 1$ is not full; otherwise the blocked customer stays in node j until a vacancy is available. During that time, node j is blocked from serving other customers.

Let σ^i and K_i be the constant service time and the buffer capacity at node i. We assume that the buffer capacity K_i includes a room for a customer in service. Before going to the finite buffered queues, it is worth to talk about the waiting times in infinite buffered system.

From the definition of D_n in [1], [2] with some algebra, the expressions on the components of random vector D_n can be obtained as

$$D_n^1 = n\sigma^1 \text{ for } n \geq 0,$$

$$D_n^2 = \sigma^1 + n \max\{\sigma^1, \sigma^2\} \text{ for } n \geq 0. \tag{1}$$

Note that the components of D_n can be written in terms of service times.

In an event graph, the finiteness can be handled by finite number of markings as shown in Figure 1 (see the details in Baccelli et al. [3]). To derive recursive equations for waiting times in a (max, +)-linear system one depicts an event graph with finite buffers and then convert it to an event graph with infinite buffers by inserting dummy nodes with zero service times. For instance, 2 queues in series with depicted in Figure 1 can be converted to the event graph with infinite buffers depicted in Figure 2 by inserting a dummy node with zero service time.

Similarly as done in infinite systems, some algebra gives the following two Propositions for the components of random vector having the same structure defined as (8) in [1] which is applicable to Corollary 3.1 in [1] and Theorem 2.3 in [2].

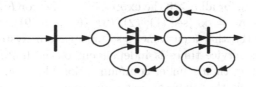

Fig. 1. 2 queues in series with a finite buffer of size 2

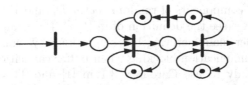

Fig. 2. 2 queues in series with infinite buffers

Proposition 1. *Under communication blocking,*

if $K_2 = 1$,

$$D_n^1 = n(\sigma^1 + \sigma^2) \text{ for } n \geq 0,$$
$$D_n^2 = \sigma^1 + n(\sigma^1 + \sigma^2) \text{ for } n \geq 0,$$

if $K_2 = 2$,

$$D_0^1 = 0,$$
$$D_n^1 = \sigma^1 + (n-1)\max\{\sigma^1, \sigma^2\} \text{ for } n \geq 1,$$
$$D_n^2 = \sigma^1 + n\max\{\sigma^1, \sigma^2\} \text{ for } n \geq 0, \tag{2}$$

if $K_2 \geq 3$,

$$D_n^1 = n\sigma^1 \text{ for } n = 0, 1, \ldots, K_2 - 1, \tag{3}$$
$$D_n^1 = \sigma^1 + \max\{(n-1)\sigma^1, (n - K_2 + 1)\sigma^2\} \text{ for } n \geq K_2, \tag{4}$$
$$D_n^2 = \sigma^1 + n\max\{\sigma^1, \sigma^2\} \text{ for } n \geq 0. \tag{5}$$

Proposition 2. *Under manufacturing blocking,*

if $K_2 = 1$,

$$D_0^1 = 0,$$
$$D_n^1 = \sigma^1 + (n-1)\max\{\sigma^1, \sigma^2\} \text{ for } n \geq 1,$$
$$D_n^2 = \sigma^1 + n\max\{\sigma^1, \sigma^2\} \text{ for } n \geq 0, \tag{6}$$

if $K_2 \geq 2$,

$$D_n^1 = n\sigma^1 \text{ for } n = 0, 1, \ldots, K_2, \tag{7}$$
$$D_n^1 = \sigma^1 + \max\{(n-1)\sigma^1, (n - K_2)\sigma^2\} \text{ for } n \geq K_2 + 1, \tag{8}$$
$$D_n^2 = \sigma^1 + n\max\{\sigma^1, \sigma^2\} \text{ for } n \geq 0. \tag{9}$$

From the above expressions, we know three facts. The first one is that under two blocking policies, for all $n \geq 0$ the expressions of D_n^2 for $K_2 \geq 2$ are the same as those of D_n^2 for $K_2 = \infty$ (see (1), (2), (5), (6), and (9)). It shows the same results in [10] and [11] that a customer's sojourn time in systems with constant or non-overlapping service times is independent of the finite buffer capacities when they are greater than 2 under communication blocking.

The second one is that one can get same expressions under two blocking policies, except for one difference in the value of finite buffer capacity at node 2, because (7) and (8) are obtained by substituting K_2 in (3) and (4) for $K_2 + 1$.

Lastly, since all components of random vector D_n and W^i are stochastically non-increasing in K_2 (see the definition of in [1], [2]), waiting times in all areas of the systems under manufacturing blocking are always smaller than or equal to those under communication blocking when buffer capacities are equal.

Now we are ready to use Corollary 3.1 in [1] and Theorem 2.3 in [2] to compute moments of waiting times and tail probabilities in a Poisson driven queues in series with a finite buffer.

3 Optimal Buffer Capacity

In this section, as an application of the expressions for D_n, we illustrate an optimization problem which minimizes the buffer capacity subject to a probabilistic constraint (like, Quality of Service) on stationary waiting times in a (max, +)-linear system where D_n sequence has the structure given in (8) of [1] (also, (2.15) of [2]).

Let $\tau \geq 0$ be a pre-specified bound on waiting time W^i for any $i = 1, 2$ and let $0 < \beta < 1$ be a pre-specified probability value. An optimal (the smallest) buffer capacity can be computed as a solution of the following optimization problem, for a given arrival rate $\lambda \in [0, a_i^{-1})$,

$$\min \; K_2$$
$$\text{s.t.} \; P(W^i > \tau) \leq \beta \qquad (10)$$
$$K_2 \in N$$

where a_i is given in the i-th component of D_n vector defined in (8) of [1] (also, (2.15) of [2]).

This type of optimization problems will arise, for example, in a telecommunication network where one would like to allocate finite resources while ensuring that a fixed percentile of call loss probabilities are less than a predetermined value. Since W^i is stochastically non-increasing in K_2, one is able to compute the smallest buffer capacity using the expressions of D_n^i together with Theorem 2.3 in [2].

4 A Numerical Example

To illustrate our results a numerical example is given in this section. Let $\sigma^1 = 1$, $\sigma^2 = 4$ be the constant service times at each node and the finite capacity be $K_2 = 5$.

Under communication blocking policy, the explicit expressions of D_n^1 are given as

$$D_n^1 = n \text{ for } n = 0, \ldots, 4,$$
$$D_n^1 = 5 + 4(n - 5) \text{ for } n \geq 5.$$

In this particular example, the maximum value a_i is 4. By using the explicit expressions of the random vector D_n^i together with Corollary 3.1 in [1] and Theorem 2.3 in [2] one is able to compute the exact value of waiting times and tail probability. The exact waiting times and simulation results for various values of arrival rate are given in the following Table 1 and Table 2. These numerical results show the accuracy of explicit expressions of random vector D_n^i and the rightness of the facts addressed in the previous section. In addition, the values of $E[W^1_{\text{Communication Blocking with } 6}]$ are exactly same as those in Table 2.

Table 1. Waiting Times Under Communication Blocking with $K_1 = \infty, K_2 = 5$

Arrival Intensity λ	$\mathbf{E}[W^1_{\text{Communication Blocking with 5}}]$	Simulation
$0.025(\rho = 0.1)$	0.01282	0.01247 ∓ 0.00147
$0.05(\rho = 0.2)$	0.02634	0.02537 ∓ 0.00156
$0.125(\rho = 0.5)$	0.08851	0.08624 ∓ 0.00641
$0.20(\rho = 0.8)$	1.68781	1.6658 ∓ 0.15152
$0.225(\rho = 0.9)$	8.35323	8.1551 ∓ 0.69208

Table 2. Waiting Times Under Manufacturing Blocking with $K_1 = \infty, K_2 = 5$

Arrival Intensity λ	$\mathbf{E}[W^1_{\text{Manufacturing Blocking with 5}}]$	Simulation
$0.025(\rho = 0.1)$	0.01282	0.01247 ∓ 0.00147
$0.05(\rho = 0.2)$	0.02632	0.02535 ∓ 0.00154
$0.125(\rho = 0.5)$	0.07629	0.07473 ∓ 0.00344
$0.20(\rho = 0.8)$	1.14075	1.1470 ∓ 0.13059
$0.225(\rho = 0.9)$	6.81748	6.6547 ∓ 0.64847

Table 3. Optimal Buffer Capacity under Communication blocking

β	$\tau = 4.5$	$\tau = 7.0$
	K_2^*	K_2^*
0.01	11	10
0.05	7	7
0.10	6	5
0.15	5	4
0.20	4	3

For optimal buffer capacity problems, one can only consider waiting times (just before the beginning of service) at the first node since the sojourn times are not dependent of the finite buffer capacity as mentioned earlier. Without the assumption for the finite capacity K_2, we can numerically solve for K_2 that satisfies $P(W^1 > \tau) \leq \beta$ for various values of τ and β by using Theorem 2.3 in [2]. The following Table 3 shows the smallest values of buffer capacity K_2^* when the arrival rate $\lambda = 0.2$, i.e. traffic intensity $\rho = 0.8$. By the relationship between two blocking policies addressed before or the same way as done in communication blocking, one is also able to determine an optimal buffer capacity for systems with manufacturing blocking policy.

5   Conclusion

In this paper, we studied waiting times in Poisson driven deterministic 2-node tandem queues with a finite buffer as a common model of telecommunication networks. The expressions for waiting times in the system with a finite buffer under communication or manufacturing blocking was obtained in (max, +)-algebra notation. From these explicit expressions we can disclose that the system sojourn time is independent of the finite buffer capacity and a relationship under two blocking rules. As an application, an optimization problem for determining the optimal buffer capacity subject to a probabilistic constraint on stationary waiting times is also considered.

These results can be extended to more complex finite buffered (max, +)-linear systems such as m-node queues in series, fork-and-join type queues and so forth. Even though it is much difficult, one may be able to find certain common patterns of the expressions for the random vector D_n^i under various types of blocking.

References

1. Ayhan, H., Seo, D. W.: Laplace Transform and Moments of Waiting Times in Poisson Driven (Max,+)-Linear Systems. Queueing Systems, Vol. 37. No. 4. (2001) 405–438.
2. Ayhan, H., Seo, D. W.: Tail Probability of Transient and Stationary Waiting Times in (Max,+)-Linear Systems. IEEE Transactions on Automatic Control. Vol. 47, No. 1. (2002), 151–157.
3. Baccelli, F., Cohen, G., Olsder, G. J., Quadrat, J-P.: Synchronization and Linearity: An Algebra for Discrete Event Systems. John Wiley & Sons, (1992)
4. Baccelli, F., Hasenfuss, S., Schmidt, V.: Transient and Stationary Waiting Times in (Max, +) Linear Systems with Poisson Input. Queueing Systems. Vol. 26. (1997) 301–342
5. Baccelli, F., Hasenfuss, S., Schmidt, V.: Expansions for Steady State Characteristics in (Max,+) Linear Systems. Stochastic Models. Vol. 14 (1998) 1–24
6. Baccelli, F., Schmidt, V.: Taylor Series Expansions for Poisson Driven (Max,+) Linear Systems. Annals of Applied Probability. Vol. 6, No. 1 (1996) 138–185.
7. Grassmann, W. K., Drekic, S.: An Analytical Solution for a Tandem Queue with Blocking. Queueing Systems. Vol. 36 (2000) 221–235
8. Labetoulle. J., Pujolle, G.: A Study of Queueing Networks with Deterministic Service and Application to Computer Networks. Acta Informatica. Vol. 7 (1976) 183–195
9. Nakade, K.: New Bounds for Expected Cycle Times in Tandem Queues with Blocking. European Journal of Operations Research. Vol. 125 (2000) 84–92
10. Wan, Y.-W., Wolff, R. W.: Bounds for Different Arrangements of Tandem Queues with Nonoverlapping Service Times. Management Science. Vol. 39, No. 9 (1993) 1173–1178
11. Whitt, W.: The Best Order for Queues in Series. Management Science. Vol. 31, No. 4 (1985) 475–487

Uncertainty Handling in Tabular-Based Requirements Using Rough Sets

Zhizhong Li and Günther Ruhe

Software Engineering Decision Support Laboratory,
University of Calgary,
2500 University Drive N.W.,
Calgary, Alberta, Canada T2N 1N4
{zhizli, ruhe}@ucalgary.ca

Abstract. Software requirements management is an essential process to better understand, identify, derive, control and improve system requirements. Typically, requirements are unclear at the beginning and evolve over time. Uncertainties usually produce conflicts among requirements. Rough set analysis (RSA) is a promising technique of granular computing. The emphasis of this paper is on formally defining three software requirements uncertainty problems and on applying RSA to solve these problems. A systematic approach called MATARS was developed for that purpose. We use a modification of a real world software requirements specification (SRS) benchmark example to illustrate main concepts and ideas of the approach.

1 Introduction and Motivation

Software requirements engineering (RE) is the process of determining what is to be produced in a software system. Requirements engineering (RE) has evolved into a key issue as one of the most difficult activities in the field of software engineering. The goal of requirements management is the development of a good requirements specification document. The IEEE guide to software requirements specifications [1] defines a good software requirements specification as being unambiguous, complete, verifiable, consistent, modifiable, traceable, and maintainable.

There are at least three challenges that are currently inherent in requirements management: firstly, it needs to transfer informal requirements, which are often vague and imprecise, to formal specification methods [2]; secondly, requirements are often conflicting with each other, and many conflicts are implicit and difficult to identify; thirdly, requirements are changing dynamically.

Rough set analysis (RSA) [3] has attracted the attention of many researchers and practitioners [4]. In applications, rough sets focus on approximate representation of knowledge derivable from data. This leads to significant results in many areas including medicine, finance, industry, multimedia systems or control theory. For an overview we refer to [4]. RSA was applied in software engineering initially in [5] to make sense out of measurement data. Since then, RSA has been successfully applied for data analysis in various areas of software engineering: software maintenance [6], software safety analysis [7], software reverse engineering [8], application run time estimation [9], and knowledge discovery for software quality.

D. Ślęzak et al. (Eds.): RSFDGrC 2005, LNAI 3642, pp. 678–687, 2005.
© Springer-Verlag Berlin Heidelberg 2005

Although RSA is used extensively as an approach to software engineering, it has rarely been applied as a systematic approach for requirements management. An objective of software requirements engineering is to improve systems modeling and analysis capabilities so that critical aspects of systems can be understood prior to system construction. A process is needed to guide the requirements engineer through requirements elicitation. The idea using RSA for requirements analysis was mentioned in [10]. In this paper, we are focusing on uncertainty problems solution and representation of tabular-based requirements.

The paper is organized into five sections. In section 2, we give a formal problem statement that will be later used to apply RSA. Section 3 provides the solution approach. This approach is illustrated in Section 4 for the modified example of A-7E requirements specification. Finally, Section 5 gives a final discussion and outlook to future research.

2 Problem Statement

2.1 Tabular-Based Requirements Management

Requirements can be represented in different ways, ranging from an informal to a more formal description. Tabular-based requirements representation is a special case of formal representation assuming that requirements specification can be done using tables. The goal of requirement management is to develop a requirement specification that contains all the needs of customers [11]. However, as time goes on, requirements change frequently or new requirements arise. Inconsistency or conflicts might result from this process. To check and handle ambiguity, incompleteness and uncertainty is of core importance for later quality of software products.

Definition 1: Tabular-based requirements
A set $R = \{A, B, \dots\}$ of requirements is said to be in tabular form if each requirement $A \in R$ is described by a set of descriptive and a set of prescriptive attributes:

- o Descriptive attributes denoted by $D_1(A), \dots, D_m(A)$ specify the conditions under which a system behaves.
- o Prescriptive attributes, denoted by $P_1(A), \dots, P_n(A)$ describe how the system should behave under the descriptive conditions $D_1(A), \dots, D_m(A)$.

Definition 2: Inconsistent requirements
Two tabular-based requirements A and B are called inconsistent to each other if they have the same value for all descriptive attributes, but are different in value for at least one prescriptive attribute. More formally,

If $D_1(A) = D_1(B), D_2(A) = D_2(B), \dots, D_m(A) = D_m(B)$
There is an attribute $j \in \{1, \dots, n\}$ so that $P_j(A) \neq P_j(B)$.

Definition 3: Redundancy between requirements
Two tabular-based requirements A and B are said to be redundant if all the descriptive and prescriptive attribute values of requirements A and B are the same. More formally,

$D_1(A) = D_1(B)$, $D_2(A) = D_2(B)$, ..., $D_m(A) = D_m(B)$ and
$P_1(A) = P_1(B)$, $P_2(A) = P_2(B)$, ..., $P_n(A) = P_n(B)$.

Definition 4: Attribute redundancy
In tabular-based requirements, certain combinations of descriptive attribute values result in certain prescriptive properties. A descriptive attribute D_p with $p \in \{1, ..., m\}$ is called redundant if the specification of the whole system remains the same after elimination of descriptive attribute D_p.

2.2 Requirements Uncertainty Problems

Uncertainty is inherent in requirements management. In this paper we will address three types of uncertainty problems as described in the following.

2.2.1 Problem 1: Inconsistency between Requirements
Inconsistency between requirements results in conflicts in the specification of the system behavior. These conflicts are the origin of software failures as typically detected in later stages. There are numerous known efforts to detect and resolve inconsistencies [12].

2.2.2 Problem 2: Missing Data in Requirements
For a tabular-based requirement, lack of information can be related to either prescriptive or descriptive attributes. Under-specification of system behavior is critical as this would force different interpretations on how the system should perform. This could result in unintended actions, causing critical system failures. The question is to suggest those values that would not create inconsistencies with existing requirements.

2.2.3 Problem 3: Redundancy
Requirements redundancy should be avoided as it is useless information. The same is true for attribute redundancy. That means the question is to detect redundancies between requirements as well as redundancies between attributes.

3 Handling Uncertainties by Using Rough Set Analysis

Tabular-based software requirements are described by descriptive and prescriptive attributes. This is very similar to the notion of condition attributes and decision attributes as used in rough set theory. Tabular-based requirements representation is mapped into an information system with the rows corresponding to the requirements and the columns corresponding to the different attributes. Descriptive and prescriptive attributes in tabular-based requirements correspond to condition respectively decision attributes as used in rough set theory.

3.1 Overview of Approach MATARS

Management of tabular-based requirements using Rough Sets (MATARS) is a method for uncertainty handling in the special case of requirements given in tabular form. MATARS has an underlying process model that is described in detail in [13]. The process here addresses the evolution of requirements as well as the overall process to handle uncertainty related to requirements. Rough set analysis plays a crucial role in MATARS. The main purpose of MATARS is to handle uncertainty in a systematic manner based on formal notation. However, we do not expect that this is completely possible without inclusion of more informal existing conflict resolution approaches as described by Robinson [12].

MATARS is focused on requirements uncertainty handling by RSA combined with existing conflict resolution approaches in requirements engineering. This process is built in order to execute requirements elicitation and resolve inconsistency with the help of RSA during evolution of requirements. The key components of MATARS are shown in Fig. 1. The stakeholders are generating requirements over time. Simultaneously, they are integral part of the resolution method.

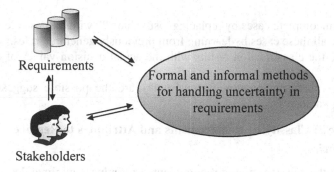

Fig. 1. Main components of MATARS

Uncertainty handling based on formal methods includes the following basic techniques described below.

3.2 Technique 1: Change of Granularity to Resolve Requirements Inconsistency

Change of granularity is one of the fundamental ideas of rough set theory. What we propose is to use this concept for resolution of conflicts in case of tabular-based requirements. Conflicts occur where different classification unions intersect with each other. Change of granularity can help to overcome these conflicts. Higher granularity with respect to one condition attribute can result in conflict resolution. We will illustrate this idea by an example in Section 4.

3.3 Technique 2: Inconsistency Check to Fill Missing Values

Incomplete data is a major problem in data analysis. Pawlak [3] and Gediga [14] present general algorithm to the treatment of missing data with classical RSA. In this paper our focus is specifically on featured tabular-based software requirements, where there are two kinds of missing value problems: missing descriptive values and missing prescriptive values. Suggestions for missing prescriptive values can be generated by learning from already specified requirements. Pawlak [3] gives four possible situations of learning from former examples.

(1) IF the new object matches exactly one of the deterministic rules
(2) THEN the classification suggestion is direct;
(3) IF the new object matches exactly one of the nondeterministic rules
(4) THEN the number (strength) of examples which support each possible category is computed. The considered object most likely belongs to the strongest category;
(5) IF the new object doesn't match any of the sorting rules
(6) THEN a set of rules 'nearest' to the description of the new object is presented;
(7) IF the new object matches more than one rule
      THEN the suggestion can be based either on the strength of possible categories or on an analysis of the objects which support each possible category.

Similarly, RSA can also help to complete missing condition values. The process is as follows:

(1) Extend incomplete cases by replacing lost value "?" with all possible values.
(2) Classify all these cases by learning from previously generated rules.
(3) Analyze the classification results with the actual decision values of extended data;
(4) All the values not creating inconsistency are the possible suggestions for missing values.

3.4 Technique 3: Classifying Requirements and Attributes to Remove Redundancies

RSA deals with the classification of requirements and induces minimal decision rules to simplify requirements representation by means of explaining prescriptive attribute values by combination of descriptive attribute values.

Discovering dependencies between attributes enables the reduction of the set of attributes. In RSA, the significance of condition attributes is of three levels.

(1) Core represents the most essential set of condition attributes.
(2) Attributes that belong to reduct are significant to represent whole system.
(3) Redundant attributes are those which do not belong to any reduct. These attributes have no contribution to classification and usually can be removed from information system.

By applying RSA, it is convenient to find condition attributes of these three levels. Redundant attributes have no contribution to classification of whole system thus they should be removed to simplify SRS. In this way we deduce attributes redundancy.

4 Illustrative Example

We consider a modification of a real world requirements benchmarking example [15] to illustrate the uncertainties management in tabular-based requirements. In this paper we use the rough set analysis tool ROSE version 2.2 developed at Technical University Poznan to analyze required tabular data [16]. This RSA tool generates decision rules using a modified version of the LEM2 Algorithm [17].

Table 1 below shows a decision table. There are four possible outside reference points for decision attribute *D*: OAP, 'fly–to point', 'target' and 'none'. Condition attributes include four Boolean attributes denoted by *C*1 to *C*4. In addition, attribute *C*5 which has six possible values (denoted by M1-M6).

Table 1. Decision table for a real world SRS [15]

Record	*C1*	*C2*	*C3*	*C4*	*C5*	*D (Decision)*
1	1	1	1	1	M1	None
2	1	1	1	0	M1	None
...	...	...	...	...	...	...
16	0	0	0	0	M1	Fly–to point
17	1	1	1	1	M2	Target
...	...	...	...	...	...	...
48	0	0	0	0	M3	OAP
49	1	1	1	1	M4	Fly-to-point
...	...	...	...	...	...	...
64	0	0	0	0	M4	Target
65	1	1	1	1	M5	Target
...	...	...	...	...	...	...
80	0	0	0	0	M5	None
81	1	1	1	1	M6	Target
82	1	1	1	0	M6	Target
...	...	...	...	...	...	...
95	0	0	0	1	M6	Fly-to-point
96	0	0	0	0	M6	OAP

To better demonstrate the proposed capabilities of MATARS, we slightly modify the original example and assume that the condition attribute *C*5 has only five groups of modes denoted by M1-M5. For that purpose, we change *C*5 value of all the last 16 requirements (from 81st till 96th) from M6 to M5. These values are shaded in Table 1. The IF-THEN rules using RSA are generated and two inconsistent rules are detected out of 14 IF-THEN rules in Table 2:

Table 2. RSA IF-THEN rules for modified SRS

Consistent rules	
(*C*1=0)(*C*5=M1) ---->(*D*=Fly-to-point)	(*C*2=1)(*C*5=M2) ---> (*D*=Target)
(*C*1=0)(*C*2=0)(*C*5=M2)-->(*D*=Fly-to-point)	(*C*2=1)(*C*5=M3) ---> (*D*=Target)
(*C*2=0)(*C*3=1)(*C*5=M3)-->(*D*=Fly-to-point)	(*C*3=0)(*C*4=0)(*C*5=M4)---> (*D*=Target)
(*C*3=1)(*C*5=M4) ---> (*D*=Fly-to-point)	(*C*2=1)(*C*5=M5) ---> (*D*=Target)
(*C*4=1)(*C*5=M4) ---> (*D*=Fly-to-point)	(*C*1=1)(*C*5=M1) ---> (*D*=None)
(*C*2=0)(*C*3=0)(*C*5=M3) ---> (*D*=OAP)	(*C*1=1)(*C*2=0)(*C*5=M2) ---> (*D*=None)
Approximate rules	
(*C*2 = 0)(*C*4 = 1)(*C*5 = *M*5) ---> (*D* = Fly-to-point) OR (*D* = None)	
(*C*2 = 0)(*C*4 = 0)(*C*5 = M5) ---> (*D* = OAP) OR (*D* = None)	

And the responding validation results in Table 3:

Table 3. Validation results for modified SRS

CLASS	Number	Lower	Upper	Accuracy
Fly-to-point	32	28	36	0.7778
OAP	8	4	12	0.3333
Target	36	36	36	1.0000
None	20	12	28	0.4286

The shaded area in both tables exposes the inconsistencies, and the accuracy is low. Obviously, if we change the granularity of $C5$ from 5 intervals back to 6, inconsistencies are removed successfully.

Another capability of RSA is the ability to handle missing values of incomplete requirements. Here from the original example in Table 1, 20 requirements were randomly selected, and they are shown in Table 4. The question is: how to complete these new cases based on the existing 76 requirements? In addition to the already introduced changes, we have added records 21 and 22 with missing condition values. All the missing values are highlighted by "?" in Table 4.

Table 4. Incomplete requirements (missing condition and decision values)

Record	C1	C2	C3	C4	C5	D
1	0	1	0	0	M1	?
...	...	...	...	...	...	?
20	1	1	0	1	M6	?
21	0	1	0	0	?	Fly-to-point
22	1	1	1	?	M2	Target

In order to accomplish decision values, we classify the twenty new objects by applying the explanation rules generated from the remaining 76 objects. The classification results are shown in Table 5. The shaded area exposes the 4 requirements (7, 9, 11 and 12) whose predicted values do not match the actual values, in other words, validation of these four cases has failed.

The two incomplete requirements can be extended by replacing lost value "?" with all possible values. Attribute $C5$ has the six levels M1-M6. Thus the first incomplete requirement can be extended to six cases from record 1 to record 6; attribute $C4$ is Boolean variable, thus the second incomplete requirement can be extended by two cases from record 7 to record 8. Table 6 shows the new complete decision table with additional eight cases.

Three shaded records (1, 7, and 8) are successfully validated, thus they are the most reasonable requirements to replace the incomplete ones. The conclusion is satisfying: record 1 and record 8 are the first two requirements in Table 5; record 7 is already inside the 76 cases of modified SRS.

Table 5. Results of ten-fold cross validation

Record	C1	C2	C3	C4	C5	D(Actual)	D(Predicted)	Matched Rule
1	0	1	0	0	M1	Fly-to-point	Fly-to-point	4
2	1	1	1	1	M2	Target	Target	9
3	0	0	0	0	M2	Fly-to-point	Fly-to-point	1
4	0	1	0	1	M2	Target	Target	9
5	0	1	0	0	M2	Target	Target	9
6	0	0	0	1	M2	Fly-to-point	Fly-to-point	1
7	0	0	1	1	M3	Fly-to-point	OAP	6
8	0	0	0	1	M3	OAP	OAP	6
9	1	0	1	0	M3	Fly-to-point	OAP	6
10	0	1	0	0	M3	Target	Target	8
11	1	0	1	1	M3	Fly-to-point	OAP	6
12	0	0	1	0	M3	Fly-to-point	OAP	6
13	1	1	1	1	M4	Fly-to-point	Fly-to-point	3
14	0	0	1	0	M4	Fly-to-point	Fly-to-point	5
15	0	1	1	1	M5	Target	Target	11
16	1	1	0	1	M5	Target	Target	11
17	1	1	1	1	M6	Target	Target	10
18	1	1	0	0	M6	Target	Target	1
19	0	0	1	0	M6	OAP	OAP	7
20	1	1	0	1	M6	Target	Target	10

Table 6. Extended decision table and validation results

Record	C1	C2	C3	C4	C5	D(Actual)	D(Predicted)	Matched Rule
1	0	1	0	0	M1	Fly-to-point	Fly-to-point	4
2	0	1	0	0	M2	Fly-to-point	Target	9
3	0	1	0	0	M3	Fly-to-point	Target	8
4	0	1	0	0	M4	Fly-to-point	Target	12
5	0	1	0	0	M5	Fly-to-point	Target	11
6	0	1	0	0	M6	Fly-to-point	Target	10
7	1	1	1	0	M2	Target	Target	9
8	1	1	1	1	M2	Target	Target	9

Finally, as part of approach we also apply RSA to simplify a decision table by reducing redundant attributes and requirements. On the basis of original example in Table 1, we added three additional attribute C6, C7 and C8, plus a requirement 97th that is exactly the same as the 96th, as shaded area shown in Table 7.

Firstly, requirement 97th is redundant and it will not affect the IF-THEN rules by RSA. Secondly, from the above table, there exists a single Core = {C1, C2, C3, C4}, together with two reducts: Reduct1 = {C1, C2, C3, C4, C5} and Reduct2 = {C1, C2,

C3, C4, C6, C7}. Attribute C8 does not belong to either reduct, thus it is redundant and can be removed from the SRS. Core = {C1, C2, C3, C4} is the most important set of attributes and each attribute inside the core is necessary to specify the requirements. However, the other three attributes $C5$, $C6$ and $C7$ are only needed in conjunction with specific reducts. For example, if we select Reduct1 then attributes {$C6$, $C7$} are superfluous; if we choose Reduct2 then attribute $C5$ becomes superfluous.

Table 7. Modified SRS with redundancies

Record	C1	C2	C3	C4	C5	C6	C7	C8	D
1	1	1	1	1	M1	0	0	1	None
2	1	1	1	0	M1	0	1	1	None
...	...	...	...	...	...	...	...	...	...
32	0	0	0	0	M2	1	2	1	Fly-to-point
...	...	...	...	...	...	...	...	...	...
96	0	0	0	0	M6	3	5	1	OAP
97	0	0	0	0	M6	3	5	1	OAP

5 Conclusions and Future Work

We have investigated the usage of rough sets for uncertainty handling for tabular-based requirements specification. This approach is part of a more comprehensive method including informal techniques as well. RSA has some fundamental conceptual advantages that can be used for conflict resolution in tabular-based requirements management. The formal approach becomes the more useful, the more complex the underlying table is. In the process of requirements elicitation and specification, RSA plays the role of an intelligent oracle answering the question for the existence of inconsistency and guiding the process to resolve it. This principle was demonstrated by an example using a modified version of the A-7E benchmark SRS.

Future research will be devoted to fully integrate RSA into the process of managing evolving requirements. MATARS is intended to be applied to further examples to validate its applicability.

Acknowledgements

The authors would like to thank the Alberta Informatics Circle of Research Excellence (iCORE) for its financial support of this research.

References

1. IEEE Guide to Software Requirements Specifications. IEEE Std 830-1984: Software Engineering Technical Committee of the IEEE Computer Society (1984)
2. Liu XF, Yen J: An Analytic Framework for Specifying and Analyzing Imprecise Requirements. In: International Conference on Software Engineering. (1996) 60-69

3. Pawlak Z (ed.): Rough Sets - Theoretical Aspects of Reasoning about Data: Kluwer Academic Publishers. (1991)
4. Komorowski J, Polkowski L, Skowron A: Rough sets: a tutorial. In: Rough-Fuzzy Hybridization: A New Method for Decision Making. Edited by Skowron SKPaA: Springer-Verlag. (1998)
5. Ruhe G: Qualitative Analysis of Software Engineering Data Using Rough Sets. In: 4th International Workshop on Rough Sets, Fuzzy Sets and Machine Discovery (RSFD'96). Tokyo, Japan. (1996) 292-299
6. Morasca S, Ruhe G: A hybrid approach to analyze empirical software engineering data and its application to predict module fault-proneness in maintenance. Journal of Systems and Software (2000) 53(3):225-237
7. Chen-Jimenez I, Kornecki A, Zalewski J: Software Safety Analysis Using Rough Sets. In: Proceedings of IEEE SOUTHEASTCON98. IEEE Press. (1998) 15-19
8. Jahnke JH, Bychkov Y: Reverse Engineering Software Architecture Using Rough Clusters. In: Proceeding of the 6th International Conference on Software Engineering & Knowledge Engineering (SEKE'04). (2004) 270-275
9. Krishnaswamy S, Loke SW, Zaslavsky A: Application run time estimation: a quality of service metric for web-based data mining services. In: Proceedings of the 2002 ACM symposium on Applied computing (SAC '02). Madrid, Spain: ACM Press. (2002) 1153-1159
10. Li Z, Ruhe G: Management of Tabular-based Requirements Using Rough Sets. In: Proceedings of the 4th ASERC Workshop on Quantitative and Soft Computing based Software Engineering (QSSE'04). Banff, Alberta, Canada. (2004) 29-34
11. Davis AM (ed.): Software Requirements: Analysis and Specification: Prentice Hall Press. (1990)
12. Robinson WN, Pawlowski SD, Volkov V: Requirements Interaction Management. ACM Comput Surv (2003) 35, no. 2:132-190
13. Li Z: Management of Tabular-based Requirements Using Rough Sets. University of Calgary (2005)
14. Gediga G, Duentsch I: Maximum Consistency of Incomplete Data via Non-Invasive Imputation: Artificial Intelligence Review (2003) 19, no. 1: 93-107
15. Heninger K, Kallander J, Parnas D, Shore J: Software Requirements for the A-7E Aircraft. In. Washington, D.C.: Naval Research Laboratory. (1978)
16. ROSE: Rough Sets Data Explorer [http://www-idss.cs.put.poznan.pl/rose/index.html]
17. Grzymala-Busse JW: LERS - A system for learning from examples based on rough sets. In: Intelligent Decision Support Handbook of Applications and Advances of the Rough Sets Theory. Edited by Slowinski R: Kluwer Academic Publishers. (1992) 3-18

Behavioral Pattern Identification Through Rough Set Modelling

Jan G. Bazan[1], James F. Peters[2], and Andrzej Skowron[3]

[1] Institute of Mathematics, University of Rzeszów,
Rejtana 16A, 35-959 Rzeszów, Poland
bazan@univ.rzeszow.pl
[2] Department of Electrical and Computer Engineering,
University of Manitoba, Winnipeg, Manitoba R3T 5V6, Canada
jfpeters@ee.umanitoba.ca
[3] Institute of Mathematics, Warsaw University,
Banacha 2, 02-097 Warsaw, Poland
skowron@mimuw.edu.pl

Abstract. This paper introduces an approach to behavioral pattern identification as a part of a study of temporal patterns in complex dynamical systems. Rough set theory introduced by Zdzisław Pawlak during the early 1980s provides the foundation for the construction of classifiers relative to what are known as temporal pattern tables. It is quite remarkable that temporal patterns can be treated as features that make it possible to approximate complex concepts. This article introduces what are known as behavior graphs. Temporal concepts approximated by approximate reasoning schemes become nodes in behavioral graphs. In addition, we discuss some rough set tools for perception modeling that are developed for a system for modelling networks of classifiers. Such networks make it possible to recognize behavioral patterns of objects changing over time. They are constructed using an ontology of concepts delivered by experts that engage in approximate reasoning on concepts embedded in such an ontology. This article also includes examples based on data from a vehicular traffic simulator useful in the identification of behavioral patterns by drivers.

Keywords: Behaviorial pattern, concept approximation, dynamical system, graph, rough sets.

1 Introduction

Many real life problems can be modelled by systems of complex objects and their parts changing and interacting over time. The objects are usually linked by some dependencies, can cooperate between themselves and are able to perform flexible autonomous complex actions (operations). Such systems are identified as *complex dynamical systems* [1,20], *autonomous multiagent systems* [15,11,13,20], or swarm intelligent systems (see, e.g., [11,13,14,18]). For example, one can consider *road traffic* as a dynamical system represented by road simulator (see,e.g. [16]). While

D. Ślęzak et al. (Eds.): RSFDGrC 2005, LNAI 3642, pp. 688–697, 2005.

driving on a road each vehicle can be treated as *an intelligent autonomous agent.*
Each agent is "observing" the surrounding situation on the road, keeping in mind
his destination and his own parameters, and makes an independent decision
about further steps by performing some maneuver such as passing, overtaking,
changing lane, or stopping.

We would like to investigate behavioral patterns of complex objects and their
parts changing over time. An identification of some behavioral patterns can
be very important for identification or prediction of behaviour of a dynamical
system, e.g., some behavioral patterns correspond to undesirable behaviours of
complex objects. If in the current situation some patterns are identified (i.e.,
they are satisfied to a satisfactory degree), then the control module can use
this information to tune selected parameters to obtain the desirable behavior of
the system. This can make it possible to overcome dangerous or uncomfortable
situations. For example, if some behaviour of a vehicle that cause a danger on
the road is identified, we can try to change its behaviour by using some suitable
means such as road traffic signalling, radio message or police patrol intervention.
Note also that the study of collective behavior in intelligent systems is now one
of the more challenging research problems (see, e.g., [11,6,12,13]), especially if
one considers the introduction of some form of learning by cooperating agents
(see, e.g., [18,4,14,5,19]).

The prediction of behavioral patterns of a complex object evaluated over
time is usually based on some historical knowledge representation used to store
information about changes in relevant futures or parameters. This information
is usually represented as a data set and has to be collected during long-term
observation of a complex dynamic system. For example, in case of road traffic,
we associate the object-vehicle parameters with the readouts of different measuring devices or technical equipment placed inside the vehicle or in the outside
environment (e.g., alongside the road, in a helicopter observing the situation
on the road, in a traffic patrol vehicle). Many monitoring devices play serve as
informative sensors such as GPS, laser scanners, thermometers, range finders,
digital cameras, radar, image and sound converters (see, e.g. [20]). Hence, many
vehicle features serve as models of physical sensors. Here are some exemplary
sensors: location, speed, current acceleration or deceleration, visibility, humidity
(slipperiness) of the road. By analogy to this example, many features of complex
objects are often dubbed sensors.

In this paper, we discuss some rough set [10] tools for perception modelling
that have been developed in our project as part of a system for modelling networks of classifiers. Such networks make it possible to recognize behavioral patterns of objects and their parts changing over time. They are constructed using
an ontology of concepts delivered by experts aiming to approximate reasoning
on concepts embedded in such an ontology. In our approach we use the notion of
temporal pattern (see Sect. 2) that express simple temporal features of objects or
groups of objects in a given complex dynamic system. Temporal patterns can be
used to approximate *temporal concepts* (see Sect. 3), that represent more complex features of complex objects. More complex behaviour of complex objects or

groups of complex objects can be presented in the form of *behavioral graphs* (see Sect. 4 and Sect. 5). Any behavioral graph can be interpreted as a *behavioral pattern* and can be used as a complex classifier for recognition of complex behaviours (see Sect. 6). Finally, we present a complete approach to the perception of behavioral patterns that is based on behavioral graphs and so called *dynamic elimination of behavioral patterns* (see Sect. 6).

This paper is a continuation of a research project in which we investigate methods for complex concept approximation using a hierarchical approach (see, e.g., [3,4,2]), and is related to companion research on interactive behavior and learning by swarms of cooperating agents (see, e.g., [11,12,13,14]).

2   Temporal Patterns

In many complex dynamic systems, there are some *elementary actions* (performed by complex objects), that is easily expressed by a local change of object parameters, measured in a very short but a registerable period. So, an elementary action should be understood as a very small but meaningful change of some sensor values such as location, distance, speed. In case of the road traffic example, we distinguish the following elementary actions such as increase in speed, decrease in speed, lane change. However, a perception of composite actions requires analyses of elementary actions performed over a longer period called a *time window*. Therefore, if we want to predict composite actions or discover a behavioral pattern, we have to investigate all elementary actions that have been performed in the current time window. Hence, one can consider the frequency of elementary actions within a given time window and temporal dependencies between them. These properties can be expressed using so called *temporal patterns*. We define a temporal pattern as a function using parameters of an object observed over a time window. In this paper we consider temporal patterns of the following types:

- *sensory pattern*. A numerical characterization of values of selected sensor from a time window (e.g., the minimal, maximal or mean value of a selected sensor, initial and final values of selected sensor, deviation of selected sensor values).
- *local pattern*. A crisp (binary) characterization of occurrences of elementary actions (e.g., action A occurs within a time window, the action B occurs in the beginning of a time window, the action C does not occur within a time window).
- *sequential pattern*. A binary characterization of temporal dependencies between elementary actions inside a time window (e.g., action A persists throughout a time window or action A begins before action B, action C occurs after action D).

One can see that any sensory pattern is determined directly by values of some sensors. For example, in case of the road traffic one can consider sensory patterns such as minimal speed and estimated speed within a time window. The value of a local or sequential pattern is determined by elementary actions registered in a time window. Local or sequential patterns are often used in queries with binary answers such as Yes or No. For example, in case of road traffic we have exemplary local patterns such as "Did vehicle speed increase in the time window?" or "Was the speed stable in the time window?" and sequential patterns such as "Did the speed increase before a move to the left lane occurred?" or "Did the speed increase before a speed decrease occurred?". We assume that any temporal pattern ought to be defined by a human expert using domain knowledge accumulated for the given complex dynamical system.

3   Approximation of Temporal Concepts

The temporal patterns mentioned in Sect. 2 can be treated as new features that can be used to approximate complex concepts. In this paper, we call them *temporal concepts*. We assume that temporal concepts are specified by a human expert. Temporal concepts are usually used in queries about the status of some objects in a particular temporal window. Answers to such queries can be of the form *Yes*, *No* or *Does not concern*. For example, in case of road traffic one can define complex concepts such as "Is a vehicle accelerating in the right lane?", "Is a vehicle speed stable while changing lanes?", or "Is the speed of a vehicle in the left lane stable?".

The approximation of temporal concepts is defined by classifiers, which are usually constructed on the basis of decision rules. However, if we want to apply classifiers for approximation of temporal concepts, we have to construct a suitable decision table called a *temporal pattern table*. A temporal pattern table is constructed from a table T that stores information about objects occurring in a complex dynamical system. Any row of table T represents information about parameters of a single object registered in a time window. Such a table can be treated as a data set accumulated from observations of the behavior of a complex dynamical system. Assume, for example, that we want to approximate a temporal concept C using table T. Initially, we construct a temporal pattern table PT as follows.

- Construct table PT with the same objects contained in table T.
- Any condition attribute of table PT is computed using temporal patterns defined by a human expert for the approximation of concept C.
- Values of the decision attribute (the characteristic function of concept C) are proposed by the human expert.

Next, we can construct a classifier for table PT that can approximate temporal concept C. Notice that many temporal concepts can be approximated using this approach. Some of these concepts are in some sense more complex than others. Therefore, usually a concept ontology for particular temporal concepts should be provided. The resulting ontology makes it possible to construct approximate reasoning (AR) schemes that can be used to approximate temporal concepts instead of simple (traditional) classifiers (see e.g. [2]).

4   Behavioral Graph for an Object

Temporal concepts defined for objects from a complex dynamical system and approximated by AR-schemes, can be treated as nodes of a graph called a *behavioral graph*, where connections between nodes represent temporal dependencies. Such connections between nodes can be defined by an expert or read from a data set that has been accumulated for a given complex dynamical system. Figure 1 presents a behavioral graph for a single object-vehicle exhibiting a behavioral pattern of vehicle while driving on a road.

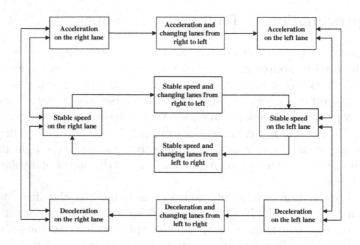

Fig. 1. A behavioral graph for a single object-vehicle

In this behavioral graph, for example, connections between node "Acceleration on the right lane" and node "Acceleration and changing lanes lanes from right to left" indicates that after an acceleration in the right lane, a vehicle can change to the left lane (maintaining its acceleration during both time windows). In addition, a behavioral graph can be constructed for different kinds of objects such as single vehicles or groups of vehicles and defined for behaviors such as driving on the strength road, driving through crossroads, overtaking, and passing. Therefore one can consider any behavioral graph as a model for behavioral patterns.

5   Behavioral Graph for a Group of Objects

In this paper, we introduce a method for approximation of temporal concepts for a group of objects based on what is known as a *group temporal pattern table*, which is constructed using the methodology presented in the Sect. 3 for the construction of the temporal pattern table, but with some important differences. To construct such a table, assume that behavioral graphs for all objects belonging to a group of objects have been constructed. For each behavioral graph we can define new temporal patterns using only two kinds of temporal patterns, namely, local patterns and sequential patterns, since information about sensors is not directly accessible.

5.1   Construction of Group Temporal Pattern Tables

A group temporal pattern table GT is constructed in the following way. Any row-object in GT is created using for any object in group G a path of nodes observed in a given behavioral graph of the object. The path in any behavioral graph should be understood as a sequence of graph nodes (temporal concepts) registered over some period, i.e., over a number of time windows. For any such path, a vector of values is computed (a vector of values of condition attributes of table GT) using temporal patterns provided by the expert for the approximation of a concept C. Additional attributes are defined using behavioral graphs of all objects simultaneously. These attributes describe temporal relations between objects in group G.

The temporal concepts defined for group of objects and approximated by AR-schemes, can be treated as nodes of a new graph, that we call as *a behavioral graph for a group of objects*. One can say, that the behavioral graph for a group of objects expresses temporal dependencies on a higher level of generalization. On lower level behavioral graphs are expressing temporal dependencies between single objects (or simpler groups of objects).

In Figure 2 we present exemplary behavioral graph for group of two objects-vehicles: vehicle A and vehicle B, related to the standard overtaking pattern. There are 6 nodes in this graph, that represent following behavioral patterns: vehicle A is driving behind B on the right lane, vehicle A is changing lanes from right to left, vehicle A is moving back to the right lane, vehicle A is passing B (when A is on the left lane and B is on the right lane), vehicle A is changing lanes from left to right and vehicle A is before B on the right lane. There are 7 connections represented spatio-temporal dependencies between behavioral patterns from nodes. For example after the node "Vehicle A is driving behind B on the right lane" the behaviour of these two vehicles can much to the pattern "Vehicle A is changing lanes from right to left and B is driving on the right lane".

6   Behavioral Patterns

In perceiving complex behaviour by individual objects or by a group of objects over a long period of time, it is possible to construct behavioral graphs to codify our observations. Such graphs facilitate observations about transitions between nodes of behavioral graph and registering a sequence of nodes that form paths in temporal patterns. If the path of temporal patterns matches a path in a behavioral graph, we conclude that the observed behaviour is compatible with the behavioral graph. In effect, we can use a behavioral graph as a complex classifier for perception of the complex behaviour of individual objects or groups

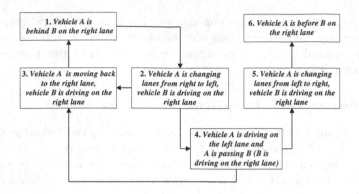

Fig. 2. A behavioral graph for the maneuver of overtaking

of objects. For this reason, a behavioral graph constructed for some complex behavior is called a *behavioral pattern*.

As an example, let us study the behavioral graph presented in Figure 2 for a group of two objects-vehicles (vehicle A and vehicle B) related to the standard overtaking pattern. We can see that the path of temporal patterns with indexes "1, 2, 3, 1, 2, 4" is matching a path from this behavioral graph, while the path with indexes: "6, 5, 4" is not matching any path from this behavioral graph (this path can match some other behavioral patterns).

A path of temporal patterns (that makes it possible to identify behavioral patterns) should have a suitable length. In the case where the length is too short, it may be impossible to discern one behavioral pattern from another pattern. For example, we can make a mistake between an overtaking a passing by a vehicle in traffic.

7   Perception of Behavioral Patterns

The construction of temporal windows is based on the notion of a temporal pattern. For any temporal pattern t_i from the family TP, we create a decision table DT_i that has only two attributes. Any object-row of the table DT_i is constructed on the basis of information registered during a time period that is typical for a given temporal pattern t_i. The second attribute of the table DT_i (the decision attribute of this table) is computed using the temporal pattern t_i. By contrast, a condition attribute registers the index of some behavioral pattern from the family BP. This index can be obtained by using some complex classifier created for some behavioral pattern from the family BP, because any complex classifier from the family BP can check single temporal window (and its time neighbourhood) whether the investigated group of objects matches to a given behavioral pattern.

Next, we compute decision rules for DT_i using methods of attribute values grouping that have been developed in the RSES system (see [17]). Any computed decision rule expresses a dependence between information about matching to some behavioral pattern and information about matching to some temporal pattern. For example, consider the problem of recognition of overtaking that can be understand as a behavioral pattern defined for a group of two vehicles. Using the methodology presented above, we can obtain the following decision rule: If the vehicle A is overtaking B then the vehicle B is driving in the right lane. After usage of a transposition low, we can obtain the following rule: If the vehicle B is not driving in the right lane then the vehicle A is not overtaking B. The last rule serves an aid to fast verification whether the behavior of a group of objects (e.g., vehicles A and B) matches the behavioral pattern of overtaking. This method only allows us to eliminate some behavioral patterns. After this elimination the complex classifiers based on a suitable behaviour graphs should be applied.

8 Experimental Results

To verify the effectiveness of classifiers based on behavioral patterns, we have implemented the algorithms in a *Behavioral Patterns* library (BP-lib), which is an extension of the RSES-lib 2.1 library forming the computational kernel of the RSES system [17]. The experiments have been performed on the data sets obtained from the road simulator (see [16]). We have applied the "train and test" method for estimating accuracy. A training set consists of 17553 objects generated by the road simulator during one thousand of simulation steps. Whereas, a testing set consists of 17765 objects collected during another(completely different) session with the road simulator.

In our experiments, we compared the quality of three classifiers: *Rough Set classifier with decomposition* (RS-D), *Behavioral Pattern classifier* (BP) and *Behavioral Pattern classifier with the dynamic elimination of behavioral patterns* (BP-E). For induction of RS-D, we employed RSES system generating the set of minimal decision rules that are next used for classification of situations from the testing data. However, we had to use the method of generating decision rules joined with a standard decomposition algorithm from the RSES system. This was necessary because the size of the training table was too large for the directly generating decision rules (see [17]). The classifiers BP and BP-E are based on behavioral patterns (see Sect. 6) but with application of dynamic elimination of behavioral patterns related to the investigated group of objects. We compared RS-D, BP and BP-E using accuracy of classification. Table 1 shows the results of applying these classification algorithms for the concept related to the *overtaking* behavioral pattern.

One can see that in case of perception of the overtaking maneuver (decision class Yes) the accuracy and the real accuracy (*real accuracy = accuracy × coverage*) of algorithm BP are higher than the accuracy and the real accuracy of algorithm RS-D for the analyzed data set. Besides, we see that the accuracy of algorithm BP-E is only 4 percent lower than the accuracy of algorithm BP. Whereas, the algorithm BP-E allows us to reduce the time of perception, because during perception we can usually identify the lack of overtaking earlier than in the algorithm BP. This means that we have not to collect and investigate the

Table 1. Results of experiments for the overtaking pattern

Decision class	Method	Accuracy	Coverage	Real accuracy
Yes	RS-D	0.800	0.757	0.606
(overtaking)	BP	0.923	1.0	0.923
	BP-E	0.883	1.0	0.883
No	RS-D	0.998	0.977	0.975
(no overtaking)	BP	0.993	1.0	0.993
	BP-E	0.998	1.0	0.998
All classes	RS-D	0.990	0.966	0.956
(Yes + No)	BP	0.989	1.0	0.989
	BP-E	0.992	1.0	0.992

whole sequence of time windows (that is required in the BP method) but only some first part of this sequence. In our experiments with the classifier BP-E it was at an average 47 percent of the whole sequence for objects from the decision class No (the lack of overtaking in the time window sequence).

9   Conclusion

In this paper, we discussed some rough set tools for perception modelling that make it possible to recognize behavioral patterns of objects and their parts changing over time. We have presented the complete approach to the perception of behavioral patterns, that is based on behavioral graphs and the dynamic elimination of behavioral patterns. Some of the tools mentioned in the paper are already implemented in our system and may be tested (see e.g. [17]). In our further work we would like to develop a complete software environment to model the perception of behavioral patterns.

Acknowledgement

The research has been supported by the grant 3 T11C 002 26 from Ministry of Scientific Research and Information Technology of the Republic of Poland. This research has also been supported by Natural Sciences and Engineering Research Council of Canada (NSERC) grant 185986 and grant T247 from Manitoba Hydro.

References

1. Bar-Yam, Y.: Dynamiocs of Complex Systems. Addison Wesley (1997)
2. Bazan, J., Skowron, A.: Classifiers based on approximate reasoning schemes. In: Dunin-Keplicz, B., Jankowski, A., Skowron, A., and Szczuka, M. (Eds.), Monitoring, Security, and Rescue Tasks in Multiagent Systems MSRAS. Advances in Soft Computing, Springer, Heidelberg (2005) 191-202

3. Bazan, J., Nguyen, S.H., Nguyen, H.S., Skowron, A.: Rough set methods in approximation of hierarchical concepts. In: Proc. of RSCTC'2004. Lecture Notes in Artificial Intelligence 3066, Springer, Heidelberg (2004) 346–355
4. Nguyen, S.H., Bazan, J., Skowron, A., Nguyen, H.S.: Layered learning for concept synthesis. Lecture Notes in Artificial Intelligence 3100, Transactions on Rough Sets, I, Springer, Heidelberg (2004) 187–208
5. Birattari, M., Di Caro, G., Dorigo, M.: Toward the formal foundation of ant programming. In: M. Dorigo, G. Di Caro, M. Sampels (Eds.), Ant Algorithms. Lecture Notes in Computer Science 2463, Springer-Verlag, Berlin (2002) 188–201
6. Bonabeau, E., Dorigo, M., Theraulaz, G.: Swarm Intelligence. From Natural to Artificial Systems. Oxford University Press, UK (1999)
7. Fahle, M., Poggio, T. (Eds.): Perceptual Learning. The MIT Press, Cambridge, MA (2002)
8. Harnad, S. (Ed.): Categorical Perception. The Groundwork of cognition. Cambridge University Press, UK (1987)
9. Pal, S.K., Polkowski, L., Skowron, A. (Eds.): Rough-Neural Computing: Techniques for Computing with Words. Cognitive Technologies. Springer, Heidelberg (2004)
10. Pawlak, Z.: Rough Sets: Theoretical Aspects of Reasoning about Data. Volume 9 of System Theory, Knowledge Engineering and Problem Solving. Kluwer Academic Publishers, Dordrecht, The Netherlands (1991)
11. Peters, J.F.: Rough Ethology: Towards a Biologically-Inspired Study of Collective Behavior in Intelligent Systems with Approximation Spaces. Transactions on Rough Sets, III, LNCS 3400 (2005) 153–174
12. Peters, J.F.: Approximation spaces for hierarchical intelligent behavioral system models. In: Dunin-Keplicz, B., Jankowski, A., Skowron, A., and Szczuka, M. (Eds.), Monitoring, Security and Rescue Techniques in Multiagent Systems. Advances in Soft Computing, Heidelberg, Physica-Verlag (2004) 13–30
13. Peters, J.F., Henry, C., Ramanna, S.: Rough Ethograms: Study of Intelligent System Behavior. In: New Trends in Intelligent Information Processing and Web Mining (IIS05), Gdańsk, Poland, June 13-16 (2005)
14. Peters, J.F., Henry, C., Ramanna, S.: Reinforcement learning with pattern-based rewards. In: Computational Intelligence (CI), Calgary, Alberta, Canada, July (2005) [to appear]
15. Luck, M., McBurney, P., Preist, Ch.: Agent Technology: Enabling Next Generation. A Roadmap for Agent Based Computing. Agent Link (2003)
16. Road simulator Homepage at
   http://logic.mimuw.edu.pl/~bazan/simulator
17. RSES Homepage at http://logic.mimuw.edu.pl/~rses
18. Dorigo, M., Birattari, M., Blum, C., Gambardella, L.M., Monada, F., Stutzle, T. (Eds.): Ant Colony Optimization and Swarm Intelligence. Lecture Notes in Computer Science 3172, Springer-Verlag, Berlin (2004)
19. Sutton, R.S., Barto, A.G.: Reinforcement Learning: An Introduction. Cambridge, MA: The MIT Press (1998)
20. Urmson, C., et al.: High speed navigation of unrehearsed terrain: Red team technology for Grand Challenge 2004. Report CMU-RI-TR-04-37, The Robotics Institute, Carnegie Mellon University (2004)
21. Zadeh, L.A.: A new direction in AI: Toward a computational theory of perceptions. AI Magazine, 22(1) (2001) 73–84

Selecting Attributes for Soft-Computing Analysis in Hybrid Intelligent Systems

Puntip Pattaraintakorn[1,2], Nick Cercone[1], and Kanlaya Naruedomkul[2]

[1] Faculty of Computer Science, Dalhousie University, Halifax, NS, Canada
{puntip, nick}@cs.dal.ca
[2] Department of Mathematics, Faculty of Science, Mahidol University, Thailand
scknr@mahidol.ac.th

Abstract. Use of medical survival data challenges researchers because of the size of data sets and vagaries of their structures. Such data demands powerful analytical models for survival analysis, where the prediction of the probability of an event is of interest. We propose a hybrid rough sets intelligent system architecture for survival analysis (HYRIS). Given the survival data set, our system is able to identify the covariate levels of particular attributes according to the Kaplan-Meier method. We use 'concerned' and 'probe' attributes to investigate the risk factor in the survival analysis domain. Rough sets theory generates the probe reducts used to select informative attributes to analyze survival models. Prediction survival models are constructed with respect to reducts/probe reducts. To demonstrate the utility of our methods, we investigate a particular problem using various data sets: geriatric data, melanoma data, pneumonia data and primary biliary cirrhosis data. Our experimental results analyze data of risk factors and induce symbolic rules which yield insight into hidden relationships, efficiently and effectively.

1 Introduction

Among prognostic modeling techniques that induce models from medical data, survival analysis warrants special treatment in the type of data required and its modeling. Data required for medical analysis includes demographic, symptoms, laboratory tests and treatment information. Special features for survival data are the events of interest, censoring, follow-up time and survival time specific for each type of disease that we will discuss. For modeling, we employ data mining to derive prediction models. While there exist techniques for processing synthetic survival data, innovative approaches that consider survival data challenges researchers. We propose a novel analysis to tackle such complexities.

Much recent research into hybrid systems tends to hybridize diverse methods which complement each other to overcome underlying individual disadvantages. From our point of view, it is difficult to gain insight into survival data. Furthermore, the presence of noisy, errorful and irrelevant data reveals the need for flexible and relaxed methods. Soft computing methodology can work synergistically with other data mining methods to provide flexible information processing

D. Ślęzak et al. (Eds.): RSFDGrC 2005, LNAI 3642, pp. 698–708, 2005.
© Springer-Verlag Berlin Heidelberg 2005

in real situations. Medsker [1] stated that soft computing differs from traditional computing in that it is tolerant of imprecision, uncertainty and partial truth. Studies have shown that soft-computing in medical is sometimes more appropriate than conventional techniques [1]. Our approach to survival analysis with attribute selection is in the initial stages. We are encouraged by our experiences with PAS (Fig. 1) [2] to examine attribute selection using soft-computing methods for survival analysis.

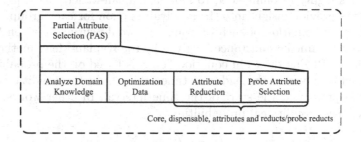

Fig. 1. Four components of PAS module [2]

We introduce in Sect. 2 preliminaries and notation of some statistics and rough sets theory for survival analysis. In Sect. 3 we propose a hybrid rough sets intelligent system for survival analysis architecture (HYRIS). We demonstrate the applicability of HYRIS on several data sets described in Sect. 4. Section 5 contains experimental results. Data evaluation is presented in Sect. 6. In Sect. 7 we add some general remarks of what next steps will be taken.

2   Preliminaries and Notation

2.1   Survival Analysis

Survival analysis describes time-to-event analysis. For example, consider the question "Is diabetes a significant risk factor for geriatric patients?" Statistics yield useful survival analysis data and theoretical tests to provide solutions. We accomplish this analysis by computing the probability the event will occur within a specific time and include a comparison among several risk factors. Frequently, however, the prediction of whether the event will eventually occur or not is of primary importance. It often happens that the study does not span enough time in order to observe the event for all patients. Thus solutions difficult using traditional statistical models such as multiple linear regressions.

Two extra factors we consider for survival analysis include: (i) survival time, commonly misleading, we mean the time patients are admitted to the study until the time to death as well as the time to particular events (e.g., recurrence of disease or time until metastatis to another organ); (ii) if any patient leaves the study for any reason, use of a censor variable is required, indicating the period of observation was cut off before the event of interest occurred. To properly address censoring, modeling techniques must take into account that for these patients the event does not occur during the follow-up period.

2.2 Kaplan-Meier Survival Analysis

In any data analysis it is always wise to perform univariate analysis before proceeding to multivariate analysis and the construction of models. In survival analysis it is highly recommended to look at Kaplan-Meier curves [3]. Kaplan-Meier curves provide insight into the survival function for each group. The proportion of the population of such patients who would survive a given length of time under the same circumstances is given by the Kaplan-Meier method or the product limit (PL) as shown in equation (1). S is based on the probability that each patient survives at the end of a time interval, on the condition that the patient was present at the start of the time interval. In other words, it is the product of these conditional probabilities.

$$\hat{S}(t) = \prod_{t_i \leq t} \left(1 - \frac{d_i}{n_i}\right) \tag{1}$$

where t_i is the period of study at point i, d_i is number of events up to point i and n_i is number of patients at risk just prior to t_i.

The method produces a table and a graph, referred to as the life time table and survival curve respectively. There are initial assumptions to make use of Kaplan-Meier method that appear in [3]. While the Kaplan-Meier method focused on a single attribute, the Cox proportional hazard model is used for multiple attributes. This model assumes a relationship between the dependent and explanatory variables and uses fine-tuned tests (cf. [4]). We handle multiple attributes with system hybridization using rough sets theory (Sect. 2.5).

2.3 Hazard Function

The hazard function is the probability that each patient will experience an event within a small time interval, given that the patient has survived up to the beginning of the interval. In general we are interested in the cumulative hazard function that is the risk of dying at time t, it is estimated by the method of Peterson [5] as:

$$\hat{H}(t) = -\ln(\hat{S}(t)) \tag{2}$$

2.4 Log-Rank Test

We also consider the log-rank [6], Brewslow [7] and Tarone-Ware tests [8] which explore whether or not to include the attribute in the prediction survival model constructions. Under the example hypotheses:

H_0: No significant difference in survival times between diabetes groups.
H_1: Significant difference in survival times between diabetes groups.

The three statistical tests differ in how they weight the examples. The log-rank test weights all examples equally, the Breslow test weights earlier periods more heavily and the Tarone-Ware test weights earlier examples less heavily than the Breslow test.

2.5   Rough Sets

Rough sets theory is the last and most important technique to turn our proposed system into a hybrid system. The purely statistical measurement gives reasonable evidence to support the hypothesis. When considering noisy real-world data, however, purely statistical measures can be less meaningful. The primary purpose of our study is to simultaneously explore the effects of several attributes on survival by using a hybrid rough sets approach. The initial study applying rough sets theory to survival analysis is [9]. They illustrated rough sets contribution to a medical expert system. Current research can be found in [10]-[11].

The rough sets principle can perform attribute selection of decision concepts that remains the same over all information. The terms probe, core and dispensable attribute, reducts and probe reducts are introduced in [2].

3   Methodology

Survival data can be analyzed using several methods and results are affected by both the analysis algorithm and the problem studied. From the architecture presented in [2], we expand the PAS. We develop and add a component to PAS to analyze domain knowledge for survival analysis (Fig. 1). Our method incorporates ad-hoc survival analysis to the previous state. The objective is to produce a hybrid rough sets intelligent system architecture for survival analysis (HYRIS) as depicted in Fig. 2.

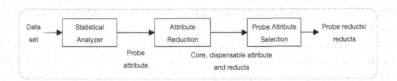

Fig. 2. A proposed hybrid rough sets intelligent system for survival analysis (HYRIS)

HYRIS is a three-module system, providing essential attributes according to the statistical functions and rough sets theory. Since, only a portion of data in the data set is relevant to a specific survival domain and survival time target concepts, an ad-hoc statistical analyzer can prune the concept space and reduce complexity. A desirable attribute selection method selects and mines the data set subject to survival domain specific objectives. Given our survival data sets, HYRIS can generate applicable and useful reducts/probe reducts as follows:

1. Preprocess survival data sets into a usable format for entry to the Statistical Analyzer module.
2. The censor and survival time attributes are used primarily in Statistical Analyzer. The Kaplan-Meier method analyzes entire survival data and generates statistical summaries (e.g., life time table, survival function, mean survival, median survival, quartiles etc.). A particular risk factor is included in Kaplan-Meier method to determine the survival and hazard curves with respect to the survival time attribute. Significance levels are tested by three prominent techniques. Overall outcomes are then considered, the probe attribute is identified for each survival data and sent to the next module.
3. It is important to reduce the number of attributes. Rough sets theory extracts core attributes, dispensable attributes and reducts. In cases that survival data have no core attributes or use all attributes as core, the probe attribute from Statistical Analyzer is used to guide generation of probe reducts.
4. If Attribute Reduction returns the most distinguished selected attributes to predict survival time, Probe Attribute Selection sets the reducts for final results. Otherwise, the probe attribute from Statistical Analyzer is added to produce most informative probe reducts.

4   Descriptions of Data Sets for Experiments

Our system was applied to several data sets - both benchmark and actual data sets (Table 1). We will explain in detail the geriatric data from Dalhousie Medical School (DalMedix). As a real-world case study, the geriatric data set contains 8546 patient records with status (dead or alive) as the censor attribute and the time lived (in months) or survival time as the target function. Due to incomplete data, we imputed the time lived in months to formulate the censor variable. For our study, all patients with status death we randomly assigned time lived in months. Since data inconsistency is an issue in rough sets and affects discernibility [11], we performed a data cleaning step to obtain consistent data. Subsequently, the data were discretized for the Statistical Analyzer. All data is discretized based on percentile groups, with each group containing approximately the same number of patients (equal density). For the geriatric data, we assigned a specification of 4 groups for survival time. Group 1 describes 1908 patients with survival time 7-17 months, 2411 patients with 18-22 months, 2051 patients with 23-48 months and 2176 patients with 49-73 months respectively.

It is commonly known that finding all reducts is NP-Hard [10], hence we focus on a reasonably fast and effective method to produce reducts. We found core attributes and dispensable attributes by using CDispro. The CDispro algorithm presented in [2] provides acceptable accuracy and achieves high dimensionality reduction as shown in Table 2. It shows the high number of condition attributes are reduced: 43 condition attributes are reduced to 17 attributes for the geriatric data set and 7 condition attributes to 3 for the melanoma data set. The CDispro algorithm produces dispensable attributes as depicted in the last column. The dispensable attributes do not contain any necessary information. The absence of these attributes is not changed by the original dependency relationship and predictive ability. Normally, in the medical domain, the adoption of dispensable attributes can minimize the expensive series of laboratory tests and medical examinations or drop high risk treatments.

Table 1. Experimental data sets

Data sets	Condition attributes	Examples	Attribute names	Descriptions of data sets
geriatric	43	8546	hbp,...,diabetes	(described in text)
melanoma* [12]	7	30	age, ini2, ..., ini4a, trt,	The survival time attribute is the time until a return to drug use and the censor attribute indicates the returning to drug use
pneumonia [13]	13	3470	agemom, alcohol, ..., birth, hos	The data contain cases from a study conducted between 1970-1985 on the University of Chicago's Billing Hospital breast cancer surgery patients
pbc** [14]	17	424	hepato, edema, bilir, ..., choles, albumin, urine, alkal, sgot	Mayo Clinic trial in pbc of the liver conducted between 1974-1984. All patients referred to Mayo Clinic during that interval, met eligibility criteria for the randomized placebo controlled trial of the drug D-penicillamine

  * exclude 2 attributes.
** exclude the additional 112 cases who did not participate in the clinical trial.

Table 2. Core attributes and dispensable attributes experimental results from CDispro

Data sets	CDispro core attributes	Dispensable
geriatric	edulevel eyesi hear shower phoneuse shopping meal housew eartroub, money health trouble livealo cough tired sneeze hbp heart walk stroke arthriti eyetroub dental chest stomac kidney bladder bowels diabetes feet nerves skin fracture age6 sex	
melanoma	age, sex, trt	none
pneumonia	all	none
pbc	none	none

5   Experimental Results

To determine the Kaplan-Meier estimate of the survivor function, we took geriatric data on the 8546 patients and formed a series of time intervals. Each of these intervals is constructed such that one observed death is contained in the interval. Status $= 0$ indicates that the example has been censored and status $= 1$ indicates death. For example, the calculation of Kaplan-Meier estimate of the survivor function is provided:

Time (months)	Status	Cumulative survival	Standard error	Cumulative event	# at risk
1	1			1	8545
1	1	.9998	.0002	2	8544
			...		
2	1			5	8523
2	1	.9993	.0003	6	8522
			...		
71	1			6685	2
71	1	.0010	.0010	6686	1
73	0			6686	0

The total number of examples is 8546, of those 1860 were censored (21.76%) leaving 6686 events (78.23%). The next results present the mean and median survival time and the respective confidence intervals. Most survival data is highly skewed, thus the median is commonly used. The median survival time is the time at which half the patients have reached the event of interest.

	Survival time	Standard error	95 % CI
Mean:	29	0	(29,29)
Median:	22	0	(22,22)

From these values we can conclude that the median survival time of patients from the geriatric data is 22 months: out of 100 patients, 50 would be dead 22 months after being admitted to our study. The estimations of quartiles are listed.

Percentiles	25	50	75
Value	29.00	22.00	19.00
Standard error	00.73	00.08	00.08

We generate the Kaplan-Meier curves by calculating the Kaplan-Meier estimate of the survivor function. A plot of this curve is a step function, in which the estimated survival probabilities are constant between adjacent death times and only decrease at each death. In Fig. 3(a), no risk factor is included, it displays one Kaplan-Meier survival curve in which all data are considered to belong to one group. In Fig. 3(b) depicts the hazard function of geriatric data. The important aspect of the survival function is to understand how it influences survival time.

After considering all data belonging to one group, we examine the effect of all suspect attributes on survival time. All condition attributes are considered to be risk factors and are included in the Kaplan-Meier method, which is used to separate the data into several subgroups. Next, Figs. 3(c) and (d) depict the analysis of diabetes and Parkinson's respectively. In Fig. 3(c) we consider two possible types of diabetes {0,1} and the same for Fig. 3(d). One can see that two curves from these groups of patients reveal different survival characteristics. We notice a slight difference between the two groups of diabetes patients and wider differences between two groups of Parkinson's. The patients who do not have diabetes and Parkinson's seem to provide better results. In other words, patients in groups that experience diabetes or Parkinson's had a higher risk of death than did other patients. However, the type without Parkinson's seem to have few censor cases left as time goes by. Initially, at time equal to zero cumulative survival is 1. In both figures, the first 15 months after admission to our study reveals very little chance of dying and two groups are visually close together. During the 15-25 month period, the hazard is clearly increased. When the curves have very good shapes, the patients start to have less risk of dying in the following 3 years. After 5 years almost all patients are dead.

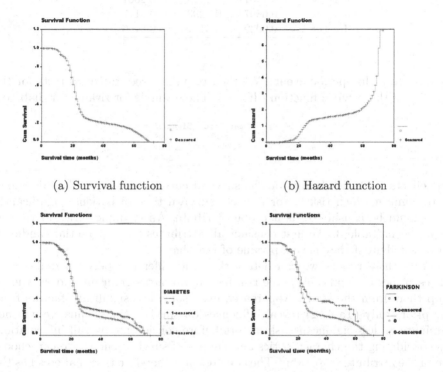

(a) Survival function

(b) Hazard function

(c) Survival function with diabetes factor (d) Survival function with Parkinson factor

Fig. 3. Survival and hazard functions of geriatric data

The interpretation of Kaplan-Meier curves is only one significant part and it is not sufficient to design the most dangerous risk factor. The comparison of the survival curves for two groups should be based on formal statistical tests, not visual impressions. We decided to run the formal hypothesis tests to see if there is any statistical evidence for two or more survival curves being different. This can be achieved using sensitive parametric methods if we have fitted a particular distribution curve to the data. In practice, the log-rank tests are used because they do not assume any particular distribution of the survivor function and are

Table 3. Test results from geriatric data

Attributes	Log-rank	Breslow	Tarone-Ware
livealone	0.4951	0.4707	0.4644
hbp	0.3502	0.1826	0.2032
Parkinson	0.0014	0.0097	0.0032
dental	0.9560	0.8999	0.9094
kidney	0.0054	0.0175	0.0088
bowels	0.0119	0.0714	0.0380
diabetes	0.0004	0.0162	0.0036
nerves	0.1107	0.2344	0.2007
skin	0.6897	0.8293	0.8117
fracture	0.0039	0.0187	0.0106

not bias to earlier period events. We then provide three statistical tests for the equality of the survival function (df = 1). The example for risk factor diabetes:

```
             Statistic  Significance
Log Rank       12.77       .0004
Breslow         5.78       .0162
Tarone-Ware     8.46       .0036
```

The effects of all risk factors on the survival curves are compared. This allows us to confirm which risk factor impacts survival time of patients significantly and should be considered as a probe attribute. An example series of tests is displayed in Table 3. We first consider all attributes to be potential candidate probe attribute if they have a p-value of less than 0.2.

From these results we can detect that the difference between diabetes in all test types is significant. Some risk factors are not significant and we should drop them from the study. Apparently, even some less significant factors from our prior study (Table 2) reveal influences on survival time. Thus we will not eliminate all less significant risk factors before considering overall information. By considering the characteristics and shapes of survival curves we can choose the probe attribute reasonably. The conclusion is therefore that diabetes has the most impact on survival time. In other word, H_1 is accepted.

In our final step, the Probe Attribute Selection module is performed to distil traditional reducts or probe reducts (Table 4). HYRIS produces probe reducts using probe attributes if it returns reducts that do not clarify pattern groups of survival. For example, the pbc data set use the alkali attribute as probe (according to the previous paradigm) for handling situation with no reducts.

6   Evaluation

All data sets are run using ELEM2 [15] for validation. The results illustrate a reduced number of total rules while keeping desired predictive ability (Table 5). We can describe particular tendencies. e.g., two exemplary prognostic rules:

```
If (edlevel = 2) ^ (eyesi ≤ 0.25) ^ (hear > 0) ^ (meal = 0) ^ (housew=0) ^ (0<health≤0.25)
 ^ (trouble=0) ^ (livealo=0) ^ (hbp>0) ^ (heart=0) ^ (stomac=0) ^ (bladder=0) ^ (diabetes=0)
         ^(skin=0) ^(age6 ≤ 3) ^ (sex = 2) then (survival time = 19-22 months)
  If (edlevel = 6) ^ (eyesi > 0.5) ^ (cough = 0) ^ (bladder = 0) ^(age6 > 4) ^ (sex = 1)
                    then (survival time = 49-73 months)
```

One interesting result of the geriatric data in Table 5 is that ELEM2 did not generate rules for survival times 7 to 22 months with all attributes while efficiently generating rules for all patient's survival times using reducts.

Table 4. Performance outcomes

Outcome	Geriatric	Melanoma	Pneumonia	PBC	Attributes
Total	800+***	16	610	83	All
# of	1600	11	610	N/A	Reducts
rules	N/A	16	N/A	6	Probe reducts
Classifi-	90.5686%	100.0000%	99.9408%	100.0000%	All
cation	83.7851%	70.0000%	99.9408%	N/A	Reducts
accuracy	N/A	100.0000%	N/A	27.7391%	Probe reducts
Average	11.4675	3.0625	8.414754	5.1687	All
length of	12.1388	2.6364	8.4148	5.1687	Reducts
the rules	N/A	3.0625	N/A	2.3333	Probe reducts
CPU	701.3	0.5	24.7	1.9	All
time	420.6	0.4	24.7	N/A	Reducts
used(s)	N/A	0.3	N/A	0.5	Probe reducts

*** ELEM2 can generate a maximum of 400 rules per decision value and generate the rules belonging to a patient's survival time between 7-22 months only.

Table 5. Reducts and probe reducts from HYRIS

Data sets	Reducts	Probe reducts
geriatric	edulevel eyesi hear shower phoneuse shopping meal housew money health trouble livealo cough tired sneeze hbp heart stroke arthriti eyetroub dental chest stomac kidney bladder bowels diabetes feet nerves skin fracture age6 sex	N/A
melanoma	age, sex, trt	age, sex, trt, ini2, ini3a
pneumonia	all	N/A
pbc	none	alkali, drug

7   Concluding Remarks and Future Works

HYRIS continues the development begun in [2] for survival analysis. HYRIS presents us with an ad-hoc tool to highlight specific survival domain knowledge. HYRIS can analyze and extract probe reducts based on statistics calculations. The performance of our approach demonstrates acceptable accuracy while reducing data dimensionality and complexity without sacrificing essential domain knowledge, both for benchmark and actual data.

We plan to improve this initial step and perform further tests using a genomic data set which is a central challenge in medical data analysis. Incorporating clustering methods to complete the PAS hybridization module will continue the development of the two remaining modules, PRS and IRQS (described in [2]). Future work will also extend to the present analysis with multiple attributes.

Acknowledgements

This research was supported by Canada's Natural Sciences and Engineering Research Council (NSERC). Thanks are also due to Arnold Mitnitski for the geriatric data set and to S. Jiampojamarn, G. Zaverucha, and the anonymous reviewers for their helpful comments.

References

1. Larry, M.R.: Hybrid Intelligent System. Kluwer Academic Publishers, Boston (1995)
2. Pattaraintakorn, P., Cercone, N., Naruedomkul, K.: Hybrid Intelligent Systems: Selecting Attributes for Soft-Computing Analysis. In: Proc. of COMPSAC'05 (2005)
3. Kaplan, E.L., Meier, P.: Nonparametric Estimation from Incomplete Observations. J. of the Amer. Stat. Asso. 53. (1958) 457-481
4. Cox, D. R.: The Analysis of Exponentially Distributed Life-times with Two Types of Failure. J. of the Royal Statistical Society 21. (1959) 411-42
5. Peterson, A.V. Jr.: Expressing the Kaplan-Meier Estimator as a Function of Empirical Subsurvival Functions. J. of the Amer. Stat. Asso. 72. (1977) 854-858
6. Peto, R., Peto, J.: Asymptotically Efficient Rank Invariant Procedures. J. of the Royal Statistical Society 135. (1972) 185-207
7. Gehan, E. A.: A Generalized Wilcoxon Test for Comparing Arbitrarily Singly-censored data. Biometrica 52. (1965) 203-223
8. Tarone, R.E., Ware, J.: On Distribution-free Tests for Equality of Survival Distributions. Biometrika 64. (1977)
9. Bazan, J., Osmolski, A., Skowron, A., Slezak, D., Szczuka, M.,S., Wroblewski, J.: Rough Set Approach to the Survival Analysis. Lecture Notes in Artificial Intelligence, Vol. 2475. Springer-Verlag, Berlin Heidelberg (2002) 522-529
10. Komorowski, J., Polkowski, L., Skowron. A.: Rough Sets: A Tutorial. In Pal, S.K., Skoworn, A. (eds.): Rough Fuzzy Hybridization: A New Trend in Decision-Making. Springer, Berlin (1999) 3-98
11. Bazan, J., Skowron, A., Slezak, D., Wroblewski, J.: Searching for the Complex Decision Reducts: The Case Study of the Survival Analysis, Lecture Notes in Artificial Intelligence, Vol. 2871. Springer-Verlag, Berlin Heidelberg (2003) 160-168
12. Lee, T. E., Wang, J. W. : Statistical Methods for Survival Data Analysis. 3rd edn. John Wiley & Sons (2003)
13. Klein, J. P., Moeschberger, M. L.: Survival Analysis: Techniques for Censored and Truncated Data. Springer (1997)
14. Murphy, P. M., Aha. D. W.: UCI Repository of Machine Learning Databases, Machine Readable Data Repository, Irvine, CA, University of California (1992)
15. An, A., Cercone, N.: ELEM2: A Learning System for More Accurate Classifications. In: Lecture Notes in Computer Science, Vol. 1418. In: 12th CSCSI. (1998) 426-441

Brain Signals: Feature Extraction and Classification Using Rough Set Methods

Reza Fazel-Rezai[1] and Sheela Ramanna[2]

[1] Department of Electrical and Computer Engineering, University of Manitoba,
Winnipeg, Manitoba R3T 5V6, Canada
reza@ee.umanitoba.ca
[2] Department of Applied Computer Science, University of Winnipeg, Winnipeg,
Manitoba R3B 2E9, Canada
s.ramanna@uwinnipeg.ca

Abstract. A brain computer interface (BCI) makes it possible to monitor conscious brain electrical activity, via electroencephalogram (EEG) signals, and detecting characteristics of brain signal patterns, via digital signal processing algorithms. Event Related Potentials (ERPs) are measures that reflect the responses of the brain to events in the external or internal environment of the organism. P300 is the most important and the most studied component of the ERP. In this paper, a new method for P300 wave detection is introduced. It consists of two components: feature extraction and classification. For feature extraction, Mexican hat wavelet coefficients provide robust features when averaged over different scales. Classification has been carried out using rough set based methods. The overall results show that P300 wave detection can be performed using only five EEG channels. This in turn reduces the computational time compared to the averaging method that uses more channels.

Keywords: Brain computer interface, classification, EEG signal, Mexican hat wavelet, P300 wave detection, rough sets.

1 Introduction

Brain Computer Interface (BCI) technology provides a direct interface between the brain and a computer for people with severe movement impairments. Considerable research has been done on BCI (see, e.g., [3,5,6,8,10]). The goal of BCI is to liberate these individuals and to enable them to perform many activities of daily living thus improving their quality of life and allowing them more independence to play a more productive role in society and to reduce social costs. A BCI involves monitoring conscious brain electrical activity, via electroencephalogram (EEG) signals, and detecting characteristics of brain signal patterns, via digital signal processing algorithms, that the user generates in order to communicate with the outside world. A particular challenge in BCI is to extract the relevant signal from the huge number of electrical signals that the human brain produces each second.

D. Ślęzak et al. (Eds.): RSFDGrC 2005, LNAI 3642, pp. 709–718, 2005.

Event related potentials (ERPs) are psychophysiological correlates of neurocognitive functioning that reflect the responses of the brain to changes (events) in the external or internal environment of the organism. ERPs have wide usage for clinical-diagnostic and research purposes. In addition, they have also been used in brain computer interfaces [4]. P300 is the most important and the most studied component of the ERP [3].

In this paper, we report results from BCI data analysis and classification using rough set methods [13]. Previous work in classifying swallowing sounds with rough set methods have shown considerable promise [9]. The objective of the study is multi-fold: i) to determine if averaging of Mexican hat wavelet coefficients is a robust technique ii) to determine the channels that are ideal for signal extraction for P300 wave detection iii) to establish a good classifier to predict the correct characters recognized by a subject. The experiments were conducted on the dataset provided by the BCI group at the Wadsworth Center, Albany, NY. This dataset represents a complete record of P300 evoked potentials recorded with BCI2000 using a paradigm described by Donchin et al., 2000. The data analysis and classification on the extracted signal data was performed using RSES [14]. Since the expected response to a particular character (and subsequently the word) is already known, rough set based supervised learning methods are ideal for predicting the correct character sequence.

We have used both standard supervised and a form of sequential character-by-character classification for this data. More recently, layered or hierarchical learning for complex concepts has been successfully applied to data from road-traffic simulator [11] and classification of sunspot data [12]. In both these cases, complex concepts are decomposed into simpler but related sub-concepts. Learning at a higher-level is affected by learning at a lower level where sub-concepts are learned independently. Incremental learning is another form of learning [16] where the structure of the decision table is changed (updated) incrementally as new data is added to the table rather than regenerating the whole table. In other words, learning occurs on a hierarchy of decision tables rather than a single table. Our work differs from both of these methods since (i) the concept (word recognition) is simple, and (ii) our table does not change over time. However, in order to determine optimal features and channels, we had to separate data for each character (row flashing and column flashing) and perform the classification in a sequential manner. The results obtained are very encouraging since two out of three words were classified with 100% accuracy. The contribution of this study is a rough set framework for demonstrating that Mexican hat wavelet coefficients provide robust features when averaged over different scales and P300 wave detection can be performed using only five EEG channels. This in turn reduces the computational time compared to the averaging method that uses more number of channels and speeds up the rate of communication.

This paper is organized as follows. An overview of BCI methodology is given in Section 2. This section also includes a brief introduction to ERP, P300, Mexican hat wavelets, signal features, and signal waveforms in 2.1, 2.2, 2.3, 2.4, and 2.5. Data analysis and classification results are reported in Section 3. Concluding remarks are given in Section 4.

2   BCI Signal Analysis

This section introduces event-related activity (ERP) of the brain, and the P300 component of the ERP.

2.1   Event-Related Activity

Fig. 1 depicts one channel of ongoing EEG activity, with stimuli presented every second.

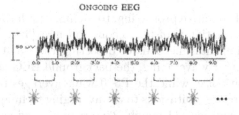

ONGOING EEG

Fig. 1. Ongoing BCI Channel Activity

As shown in this figure, there is little visible change in the ongoing EEG as a result of seeing the stimuli. This is because the ongoing EEG is composed of signals from numerous sources, and the signal related to the stimulus is buried within. If, however, one averages together many trials of the one-second of activity surrounding the stimulus, event-related activity (ERP) emerges as shown in the Visual Event-related Potential in Fig. 2.

Note that whereas the ongoing EEG activity is in the range of 50 microvolts, the ERP is much smaller. Note also that the time axis covers about one second. The "peaks" and "valleys" in the ERP are termed components, with positive deflections (downward in this picture) labelled with "P" and negative deflections (upward in this picture) labelled with "N". The N400, for example, is the negative deflection near 400 milliseconds after stimulus onset. The P300 (or P3) component is the third major positive deflection. Each component can provide a different indication of how the stimulus is processed. ERPs are measures to reflect the responses of the brain to events in the external or internal environment of the organism. Although they are not easy to be detected, they have wide usage for clinical-diagnostic and research purposes.

2.2   P300

P300 is the most important and the most studied component of the ERP [3]. It is a significant positive peak that occurs 300ms after an infrequent or significant stimulus. The actual origin of the P300 is still unclear. It is suggested that it is

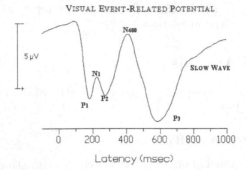

Fig. 2. Visual Event-Related Potential

related to the end of cognitive processing, to memory updating after information evaluation or to information transfer to consciousness [3,8].

One of the fundamental methods of detecting the P300 wave has been the EEG signal averaging. By averaging, the background EEG activity cancels as it behaves like random noise, while the P300 wave averages to a certain distinct visible pattern. There are limitations to the averaging technique and applications for which it is not suitable. Although P300 wave is defined as a peak at 300 ms after a stimulus, it really occurs within 300 to 400 ms [1]. This latency and also amplitude of the P300 waves change from trial to trial. Therefore, the averaging technique is not an accurate method for the P300 wave detection and there is a need for developing a technique based on advanced signal processing methods for this purpose. A method for P300 wave detection based on averaging of Mexican hat wavelet coefficients was introduced in [6]. However, the efficacy of the technique was tested using a very simple classification method. A peak of the averaged coefficients was found between 200 and 550 ms. If this peak was located between 300 and 400 ms, it was considered as target stimulus. Otherwise the stimulus was considered as a non-target.

A method for P300 wave detection based on averaging of Mexican hat wavelet coefficients is introduced.

2.3   The Mexican Hat Wavelet

Wavelet coefficients of a signal $x(t)$ at time point p are defined in Eq. 1.

$$c(s, p) = \int_{-\infty}^{\infty} x(t)\psi(s, p, t)dt \qquad (1)$$

where s is a scale number, t is a time point, and $\varphi(s, p, t)$ is an analyzing wavelet. The analyzing wavelet used is the Mexican hat is defined in Eq. 2.

$$\psi(s, p, t) = \frac{2}{\sqrt{3}}\pi^{-\frac{1}{4}}(1 - \alpha^2)e^{-\frac{1}{2}\alpha^2} \qquad (2)$$

where $\alpha = \frac{t-p}{s}$.

2.4   Signal Features and Feature Extraction

For each run, the EEG signal is stored in one big matrix (total # samples x 64 channels). One of the challenges of feature extraction is to determine which of the 64 channels (scalp positions) contain useful information. In this study, signal data from channel numbers 9, 11, 13, 34, 51 have been used. Consider the averaged coefficient curve shown in Fig. 3.

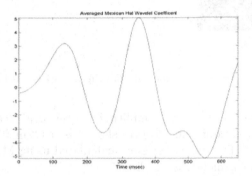

Fig. 3. Average Mexican Hat Wavelet Coefficient

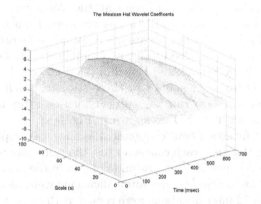

Fig. 4. 3D View of Average Mexican Hat Wavelet Coefficient

Assume that the maximum of this curve has the amplitude of A0 and it happens at time t0. Now if we find the two local minimums one just after A0 and another just before A0 with amplitudes B1 and B2 respectively, then we can define two heuristic features averaged over scales from 30 to 100 (shown in Fig. 4): Amplitude of the peak and time difference (see Eq. 3).

$$\text{Amplitude of the peak} = (A0 - B1) + (A0 - B2)$$
$$\text{Time difference} = |t0 - 300\text{msec}| / 300\text{msec} \tag{3}$$

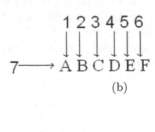

(b)

(a)

Fig. 5. (a) User Display for Spelling Paradigm, (b) Focus on a Character

Note, that to detect P300 wave, amplitude of the peak feature should have "large" value and time difference feature should be as "small" as possible (zero is considered ideal). The two features are calculated using Mexican hat wavelet from the five channels mentioned earlier.

2.5 Signal Waveform Data Characteristics

The data set provided by the BCI group at the Wadsworth Center, Albany, NY has been used in this article. EEG was recorded from 64 scalp positions (for details, see [4]). This dataset represents a complete record of P300 evoked potentials recorded with BCI2000 using a paradigm described by Donchin et al. [5], and originally by Farwell and Donchin [7]. The signals were digitized at 240Hz and collected from one subject in three sessions. Each session consisted of a number of runs. In each run, the subject focused attention on a series of characters, e.g., the word "SEND" as shown in Fig. 5(a).

When a subject focuses on one character, the matrix is displayed for a 2.5sec period, and during this time each character has the same intensity (i.e., the matrix was blank). Subsequently, each row and column in the matrix was randomly intensified for 100msec. Row/column intensifications were block randomized in blocks of 12. Sets of 12 intensifications were repeated 15 times for each character. Each sequence of 15 sets of intensifications was followed by a 2.5 s period, and during this time the matrix was blank. This period informed the user that this character was completed and to focus on the next character in the word that was displayed on the top of the screen (the current character was shown in parentheses). In other words, for each character, 180 entries of feature values are stored: 90 for row intensification and 90 for column intensification. For example, A is recognized only when row 7 and column 1 features indicate a P300 component (see Fig. 5(b)).

For each intensification/trial, events are coded using the following variables: (i) *Flashing*: 1 when row/col was intensified, 0 otherwise, (ii) *PhaseInSequence*: 1 during PreSetInterval (i.e., for each character, when matrix is blank (i.e., before row/column intensifications started)) 2 while row/columns are intensified 3 duringPostSetInterval (i.e., for each character, when matrix is blank (i.e., after row/column intensifications start). This variable can be used to determine which character was on the screen, i.e., whenever this value switches from 3 to 1, there is a new character on the screen, (iii) *StimulusCode*: 0 when no row/column is being intensified (i.e., matrix is blank) 1Ĕ6 for intensified columns (1 Ĕ left-most column) 7Ĕ12 for intensified rows (7 Ĕ upper-most row), (iv) *StimulusType*: 0 when no row/column is being intensified or intensified row/column does not contain desired character 1 when intensified row/character does contain the desired character. This variable can be used to separate the responses that did contain the desired character from the ones that did not. The signal waveforms associated with the intensification of a particular row/column were extracted using the following steps:

- Find all signal samples that hold the period after one intensification.
- Determine the *StimulusCode* for this period.
- Accumulate associate signal samples in separate buffers, one for each stimulus.

3   BCI Data Analysis and Classification

The objective of BCI data analysis and classification is two fold: to determine a good feature extraction method and which channels are ideal for signal extraction for P300 wave detection and to find a good classifier to predict the correct characters recognized by a subject. These two objectives are intertwined, since the classifier is in essence an indicator of the effectiveness of the feature extraction method. In this paper, five features (attributes) have been used: Stimulus code (character to be recognized), amplitude of the peak, time difference, ratio of amplitude to time difference and Stimulus Type (decision). The experiments were conducted using RSES [14] on 3 sets of words in uppercase: CAT, DOG and FISH. Each character is stored in a table with 90 entries for row intensification and 90 entries for column intensification. For example, the word CAT has a table with 540 entries. Discretization was used since three of the feature values are continuous. In all but one case, genetic algorithms (GA) method was used in rule derivation[15]. The experiments were conducting using 10-fold cross-validation technique. The definitions for accuracy and coverage are from RSES. The results using character -by-character learning and standard learning (the entire run of all row and column entries) for words DOG, FISH, CAT are shown in Tables 1, 2[1] and 3, respectively.

The first experiment involved feature extraction and classification with the word "CAT". One of the lessons learned was that averaging feature values over 5 channels gave a better classification result rather than separate values from each channel. Another observation was the very poor accuracy and coverage results obtained with the standard approach (all runs for the entire word "CAT").

---

[1] H col. in Table 2 uses the decomposition tree method in RSES [14].

Table 1. Word "DOG" Classification

Character	Training Set Size	Testing Set size	Accuracy	Coverage
Character-By-Character Approach				
D row	72	18	100	100
D col	72	18	100	100
O row	72	18	100	100
O col	72	18	100	100
G row	72	18	100	100
G col	72	18	100	100
Standard Approach				
"DOG"	432	108	100	100

Table 2. Word "FISH" Classification

Character	Training Set Size	Testing Set size	Accuracy	Coverage
Character-By-Character Approach				
F row	72	18	100	100
F col	72	18	100	100
I row	72	18	100	100
I col	72	18	100	100
S row	72	18	100	100
S col	72	18	100	100
H row	72	18	100	100
H col	72	18	100	100
Standard Approach				
"FISH"	476	144	100	100

Table 3. Word "CAT" Classification

Character	Training Set Size	Testing Set size	Accuracy	Coverage
Character-By-Character Approach				
C row	72	18	100	100
C col	72	18	100	100
A row	72	18	100	100
A col	72	18	100	100
T row	72	18	100	100
T col	72	18	50	50
Standard Approach				
"CAT"	432	108	79	87

Based on these observations, we had to adopt a character-by-character classification approach that isolated row and column data for each character. The character-by-character classification approach led to the conclusion that character T feature values were very poor. We also tried to include other features such as ratio of amplitude of peak to time difference to see if the classification results would improve. Based on the data analysis for "CAT", we used average feature values and character-by-character and standard approaches for the two additional words "DOG" and "FISH". These experiments reveal that P300 component was recognized perfectly for both words.

4 Conclusion

This paper introduces a new approach to P300 wave detection combined with an application of rough set methods used to classify P300 signals. For feature extraction, Mexican hat wavelet coefficients provide features when averaged over different scales. Signal classification was done using RSES [14]. Rough set methods provide a framework for verifying that Mexican Hat wavelets correctly identify BCI signals extracted from 5 channels. This approach reduces the computational time compared with the commonly used averaging method, which requires more channels for signal extraction.

Acknowledgements

The authors gratefully acknowledge the experiments and datasets provided by Wadsworth Center. The research by Sheela Ramanna is supported by a Natural Sciences and Engineering Research Council of Canada (NSERC) grant 194376. The authors also wish to thank James F. Peters for his insightful comments and suggestions.

References

1. Bayliss, J.D.: The use of the P3 evoked potential component for control in a virtual apartment. IEEE Transactions on Rehabilitation Engineering, 11(2) (2003) 113-116
2. Bazan, J.G., Szczuka, M.S., Wroblewski, J.: A new version of the rough set exploration system. In: J.J. Alpigini, J.F. Peters, A. Skowron, N. Zhong (Eds.), Rough Sets and Current Trends in Computing. Lecture Notes in Artificial Intelligence 2475, Springer-Verlag, Berlin (2002) 397-404
3. Bernat, E., Shevrin, H., Snodgrass, M.: Subliminal visual oddball stimuli evoke a P300 component. Clinical Neurophysiology, 112 (2001) 159-171
4. Blankertz, B., Müller, K.-R., Curio, G., Vaughan, T.M., Schalk, G., Wolpaw, J.R., Schlögl, A., Neuper, C., Pfurtscheller, G., Hinterberger, T., Schröder, M., Birbaumer, N.: The BCI Competition 2003: Progress and perspectives in detection and discrimination of EEG single trials. IEEE Trans. Biomed. Eng., 51 (2004) 1044-1051

5. Donchin, E., Spencer, K.M., Wijensighe, R.: The mental prosthesis: Assessing the speed of a P300-based brain-computer interface. IEEE Trans. Rehab. Eng., 8 (2000) 174-179
6. Fazel-Rezai, R., Peters, J.F.: P300 Wave Feature Eextraction: Preliminary Results, In: Proceedings of the Canadian Conference of Electrical and Computer Engineering, Saskatoon, SK, Canada (2005) 376-379
7. Farwell, L.A., Donchin, E.: Talking off the top of your head: Toward a mental prosthesis utilizing event-related brain potentials. Electroencephalogr. Clin. Neurophysiol, 70 (1988) 510-523
8. Gonsalvez, C.J., Polich, J.: P300 amplitude is determined by target-to-target interval. Psychophysiology, 39 (2002) 388-396
9. Lazareck, L., Ramanna, S.: Classification of Swallowing Sound Signals: A Rough Set Approach. In: S. Tsumoto, R. Slowinski, J. Komorowski, J.W. Grzymala-Busse (Eds.), Rough Sets and Current Trends in Computing. Lecture Notes in Artificial Intelligence 2066, Springer-Verlag, Berlin (2004) 679-684
10. Mason, S.G., Birch, G.E.: A general framework for brain-computer interface design. IEEE Transactions on Neural Systems and Rehabilitation Engineering, 11(1) (2003) 71-85
11. Nguyen, S.H., Bazan, J., Skowron, A., Nguyen, H.S.: Layered Learning for Concept Synthesis. Transactions on Rough Sets, I, LNCS 3100 (2004) 187-208
12. Nguyen, T.T., Willis, C.P., Paddon, D.J., Nguyen, H.S.: On learning of sunspot classification. In: Mieczyslaw A. Klopotek, Slawomir T. Wierzchon, and Krzysztof Trojanowski (Eds.), Intelligent Information Systems, Proceedings of IIPWM'04. Advances in Soft Computing, Springer, Berlin (2004) 58-68
13. Pawlak, Z.: Rough sets. International J. Comp. Inform. Science, 11(3) (1982) 341-356
14. The RSES Homepage at http://logic.mimuw.edu.pl/~rses
15. Wroblewski, J.: Genetic algorithms in decomposition and classification problem. In: Polkowski, L. and Skowron, A. (Eds.), Rough Sets in Knowledge Discovery, 1, Physica-Verlag, Berlin (1998) 471-487
16. Ziarko, W.: Incremental Learning with Hierarchies of Rough Decision Tables. In: Proc. North American Fuzzy Information Processing Society Conf. (NAFIPS04). Banff, Alberta (2004) 802-808

On the Design and Operation of
Sapient (Wise) Systems

René V. Mayorga

Faculty of Engineering, University of Regina,
Regina, SK, Canada
Rene.Mayorga@uregina.ca

Abstract. Recently, the author presented a Paradigm that can serve
as a general framework for the development of Intelligent and *Sapient
(Wise)* Systems. Here, under the proposed Paradigm, some performance
criteria for the proper design and operation of Intelligent and *Sapient
(Wise)* Systems are developed. These criteria are based on properly considering some characterizing matrices having a significant role on the
performance of Intelligent and *Sapient (Wise)* Systems.

1 Introduction

In recent works, [3], [5], [6], the author has presented a Paradigm that can contribute with some essential aspects to establish a baseline for the development
of *Computational Sapience (Wisdom)* as a new discipline [6]. It is demonstrated
in [3], [5], [6], that, under the proposed Paradigm, the development of *Computational Sapience (Wisdom)* methodologies can be accomplished as a natural
extension of some non-conventional (AI, Soft Computing, and Computational Intelligence) approaches. Furthermore, it is also demonstrated in [3], [5], [6], that
the Paradigm serves as a general framework for the development of Intelligent/
Sapient (Wise) Systems and *MetaBots*, [5], [7].

In [3], also some learning, adaptation, and cognition aspects are considered.
These aspects have lead the author to postulate a "formal" concept of *Computational Sapience (Wisdom)*, [3], [5], [6]. In particular, some learning, adaptation,
and knowledge (essential for cognition [11]) principles are properly addressed.
However, also the concepts of "stability", "discerning", and "inference", (as a
condition for judgment) are considered, [3]. Furthermore, it is also postulated
in [3], that under the proposed Paradigm, inferential capabilities and the ability
to determine direct and inverse relationships can contribute to built up knowledge with capacity for cognition and sound judgment; and leading to Artificial /
Computational *Sapience (Wisdom)*.

In [3], [5], [6], [7], some theoretical results for the proposed Paradigm are
presented by the author. In these works also some necessary conditions for the
implementation of general (Adaptive) Inference Systems under the proposed
Paradigm are established. It is demonstrated, [3], [5], [6], [7], that the proposed
Paradigm permits to develop simple but efficient Learning strategies for some

D. Ślęzak et al. (Eds.): RSFDGrC 2005, LNAI 3642, pp. 719–726, 2005.

Classes of (Adaptive) Inference Systems: for the case in which there is knowledge of a system input/output system relationship; and also when there is partial, or no knowledge of this relationship, [3], [5], [6], [7]. Furthermore, it is also shown that these Classes can effectively used to approximate the corresponding inverse functions characterizing this relationship, [6], [7].

Since the Proposed Paradigm enables the ability to estimate (via Adaptive Inference Systems) direct and inverse relationships; it can contribute to the construction of knowledge and the capacity for delivering sound judgment. Consequently, the Paradigm can lead to cognition [11], and *Sapience (Wisdom)*, [3].

In this article, under the proposed Paradigm, some performance criteria are established for the proper design & operation of Intelligent and *Sapient (Wise)* Systems. These criteria are based on properly considering some characterizing matrices having a significant role on the performance of Intelligent and *Sapient (Wise)* Systems. In particular, it is shown that from these characterizing matrices it is possible to establish: (a) an upper bound on a homogenized condition number; (b) a generalization of an isotropy condition; and (c) a proper bound on its rate of change. These criteria can be easily used for proper system design analysis/optimization and to determine the best regions for system operation.

2   *Sapient (Wise)* Systems Paradigm

It is important to mention that the proposed Paradigm formulation is based on the development of an inverse *effect-causal* time-variant relationship, [3], [5], [6], [7]. For a given system, at any instant of time, a set of input variables in the Plant (*causal state*) space establishes a unique set of output variables in the task/performance (*effect state*) space. At any instant of time, denote the Plant variables by $\psi_i \equiv \psi_i(t)$; $i = 1, 2, \cdots, n$. Also, define the task/performance variables describing system tasks by a vector of m variables $y_j \equiv y_j(t)$; $j = 1, 2, \cdots, m$. Also, let $t \epsilon [t_o, t_f]$ where t_o and t_f are the initial and final time of the task interval; and let $\Re^m$ and $\Re^n$ be the m-dimensional and the n-dimensional Euclidean spaces respectively. Assume that $y \equiv y(t) = [y_1, y_2, \cdots, y_m]^T \epsilon \Re^m$ and $\psi \equiv \psi(t) = [\psi_1, \psi_2, \cdots, \psi 1_n]^T \epsilon \Re^n$ are related by [9]:

$$y(t) = \mathcal{F}(\psi(t)). \tag{1}$$

In many applications it is more convenient to set the task variables (*effect state*) to follow a desired state transition, and try to calculate the corresponding Plant variables (*causal state*). This implies establishing an inverse relationship from Eq.(1). In general, this relation is nonlinear; hence an analytical inverse relationship cannot be easily obtained. Under a local approach the problem can be treated at the inverse functional and rate of change level. That is, the problem can be addressed in the following indirect fashion. By differentiating Eq.(1) with respect to time, the next equation is obtained:

$$\dot{y}(t) = J(\psi(t))\dot{\psi}(t) \tag{2}$$

where $\dot{y} \equiv \dot{y}(t) = dy(t)/dt$, $\dot{\psi} \equiv \dot{\psi}(t) = \psi(t)/dt$, and

$$J(\psi) \equiv J(\psi(t)) = \frac{\partial}{\partial \psi} \mathcal{F}(\psi(t)), \tag{3}$$

is the $(m \times n)$ Jacobian Plant matrix.

From the Eq.(2), a $\psi(t)$ plan can be computed in terms of a prescribed state transition $y(t)$. As shown in [9], a solution in an inexact context is given by:

$$\dot{\psi} = J_{wz\delta}^{+}(\psi)\dot{y} + [I - J_{wz\delta}^{+}(\psi)J(\psi)]\nu; \tag{4}$$

where $\delta > 0$, and ν is an arbitrary vector; and the weighted-augmented pseudoinverse $J_{wz\delta}^{+}(\psi)$ is given by:

$$J_{wz\delta}^{+}(\psi) = W^{-1}J^{T}(\psi)[J(\psi)W^{-1}J^{T}(\psi) + \delta Z^{-1}]^{-1} \tag{5}$$
$$= [J^{T}(\psi)ZJ(\psi) + \delta W]^{-1}J^{T}(\psi)Z; \tag{6}$$

where, the positive definite symmetric matrices W, Z, act as metrics to allow invariance to frame reference and scaling (homogenize dimensions). Notice that for $\delta = 0$ in Eq.(5), the Eq.(4) reduces to the exact solution. Also let

$$J_{wz} \equiv Z^{1/2}J(\psi)W^{-1/2}. \tag{7}$$

Also, as shown in Fig. 1, notice that the procedure to approximate a solution can be represented by considering as inputs to the system the Task variables, a "feedforward block" consisting of the computation of an approximated solution (via the augmented-weighted pseudoinverse), and an (top) "external block" containing the Jacobian matrix.

The process for approximating the Jacobian matrix, the null space vector ν (direct functions), and the augmented-weighted pseudoinverse matrix (inverse function) can be performed sequentially, and/or concurrently. Furthermore, it is this approximating process of both the direct and inverse functions that characterize a *Sapient (Wise)* system [3], [5].

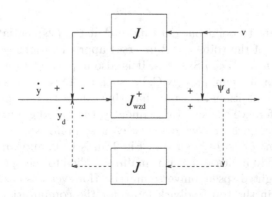

Fig. 1. Conventional Inverse Function Approximation

In [2], [3], [5], some theoretical results are presented establishing proper bounds on the norm of the difference between exact and inexact solutions (for the cases where the Jacobian matrix is entirerly known, partially known, or unknown). From the Eq.(4), it can be easily observed that the solutions depend heavily on the computation (approximation) of the pseudoinverse matrices. This computation can be performed in a conventional (numerical) manner; or as postulated in [3], it can also be approximated, as shown in Fig. 2, via non-conventional techniques (N-C.T.) such as (but not limited to) ANNs, and Adaptive Inference Systems (FIS, AFIS, CANFIS, [1]).

The theoretical results presented in [2], [3], [5], constitute the foundation of the Proposed Paradigm. In particular, the results indicate that as long as the inverse (augmented-weighted pseudoinverse matrix) function approximation is done as above, it is possible to establish finite bounds on the error on the Task variables. Furthermore, notice that the approximations for both direct (Jacobian matrix, null space vector) and inverse (augmented-weighted pseudoinverse) relationships are properly considered. These approximations can be realized (sequentially and/or concurrently) utilizing conventional (numerical) techniques, and/or via non-conventional methodologies [3], [5], [6].

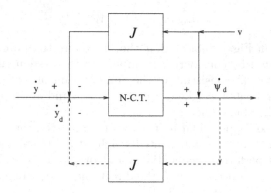

Fig. 2. Non-conventional Inverse Function Approximation

It is important to point out once more that the (sequential, and/or concurrent) realization of the (direct and inverse) approximations constitutes a characteristic of *Sapient (Wise)* Systems. It is also important to notice that the use of non-conventional techniques (N-C.T.) such as ANNs and Adaptive Inference Systems has the additional feature that they allow to incorporate adaptation, learning, and inference aspects. Consequently, the Paradigm implementation via the N-C.T. techniques, in fact constitutes a stepping stone towards the realization of *Sapient (Wise)* systems. In Fig.2 an N-C.T. appears explicitly in the feedforward loop to indicate that it is mainly applied to the approximation of the (augmented-weighted) pseudoinverse matrix. However, also as easily an N-C.T. can be utilized in the top feedback loop, for the computation of the Jacobian matrix J and (to incorporate global characteristics [3], [5], [6]) the vector ν.

An example of a Sapient (Wise) System approach is the novel procedure for global optimization of non-linear functions using Artificial Neural Networks developed by the author [4]. The procedure has shown effective, for highly non-linear functions with many local minima, such as the peaks function and the Griewank function, [4]. As shown in the figure, the technique is capable to obtain the global minimum for the peaks function, [4]. In this procedure, both the Jacobian matrix approximation as well as the inverse function approximation are done using ANNs. Furthermore, the proposed technique is shown to compare favorably with genetic algorithms and simulated annealing techniques [4].

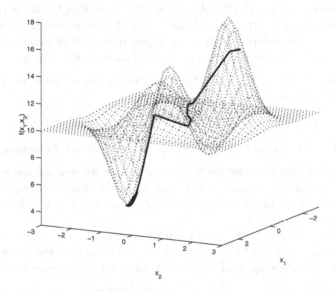

Fig. 3. Global Minimum of the peaks function

3   Performance Criteria

From the Eq.(4), it can also be easily observed that the solutions to generate plans depend heavily on the norm of the pseudoinverse matrices expressions, which in turm depends on the rank preservation of J_{wz}. Furthermore, as pointed out in [9], the condition number of a matrix it is also an appropriate criterion for measuring system performance.

As discussed in [9], it is relatively easy to define a matrix norm and a homogenized condition number on the Plant Space. This homogenized condition number can be utilized to measure task/performance invariant to frame reference selection and/or scaling; and also to deal with non-homogeneous Plant dimensions. As shown in the next development it can also serve for optimal Plant design.

First, recall that the $(m \times n)$ matrix $J_{wz}(\psi(t))$ is the weighted Jacobian matrix at any $t\epsilon[t_o, t_f]$ given by Eq.(7). Now, notice that it is relatively easy to show that

$$\|J\|_s \equiv \|J_{wz}\|_2 \equiv \|Z^{1/2}J(\psi)W^{-1/2}\|_2, \qquad (8)$$

where $\| \cdot \|_s$ represent a homogenized norm [5]. Then, the next proposition easily follows [9].

Proposition 1. *Let $\tilde{\sigma}_1 \equiv \sigma_1\{J_{wz}\}$, and $\tilde{\sigma}_m \equiv \sigma_m\{J_{wz}\}$, be the largest and smallest singular values of the matrix $[J_{wz}]$ respectively. Then, a homogenized condition number can be given by:*

$$\kappa_s \equiv \|J\|_s\|J^+\|_s = \tilde{\sigma}_1/\tilde{\sigma}_m. \tag{9}$$

Notice that in general it is quite difficult to express explicitly the condition number; then, its direct use for systems design is limited. Still, it can be used for design analysis/optimization by considering the Eq.(9) and performing an extensive simulation on the entire Task space. A better performance index can be developed by considering instead an upper bound on the condition number. From Eq.(9) it is relatively easy to show the following Proposition.

Proposition 2. *Let $\tilde{\sigma}_1$, and $\tilde{\sigma}_m$, be as in Proposition 1; then, an upper bound for the condition number is given by:*

$$\kappa_s(\psi) \equiv \tilde{\sigma}_1(\psi)/\tilde{\sigma}_m(\psi) \leq \| J_{wz}(\psi) \|_F^m /\lambda^{1/2}(\psi), \tag{10}$$

where $\lambda(\psi) = det[J_{wz}(\psi)J_{wz}^T(\psi)]$, and $\|.\|_F$ stands for the Frobenius norm.

Due to the difficulty on expressing explicitly $\lambda(\psi)$; for general cases this upper bound on the condition number can not be easily expressed explicitly either. However, it is useful for those cases ($m = 2, 3$) in which it is relatively easy to express explicitly $\lambda(\psi)$.

The above, illustrates the need to develop performance indices that can be easily expressed explicitly for general cases. For this purpose the following Propositions have been developed. Notice that it can be easily shown that:

Proposition 3. *Let $\tilde{\sigma}_1, ..., \tilde{\sigma}_m$, be as above; and $\sigma_{iso} > 0$. Then, the singular values are equal to the same value; that is, $\tilde{\sigma}_1 =, ..., = \tilde{\sigma}_m = \sigma_{iso}$; if and only if*

$$J_{wz}J_{wz}^T = \sigma_{iso}^2 I. \tag{11}$$

Furthermore, in this case, $\kappa_s = 1$.

Notice that σ_{iso} is the isotropic value of the singular values; that σ_{iso} is in fact a function of ψ. and that the Eq.(11) represents the so-called isotropic condition of a matrix. Next, the following Proposition can also be easily shown.

Theorem 1. *Consider the weighted matrix J_{wz} as given in Eq.(7). Then, an upper bound for the rate of change of its homogenized isotropic value is given by:*

$$\dot{\sigma}_{iso} \leq \beta \sum_{i=1}^{m} \sum_{j=1}^{n} |J_{wz(i,j)}| \ |\sum_{k=1}^{n} \partial J_{wz(i,j)}/\partial \psi_k|, \tag{12}$$

where $\beta = [l/\sqrt{m}\|J_{wz}\|_F]$; and $l = |\dot{\psi}|_{max}$, and $J_{wz(i,j)}$ are the elements (i,j) of the matrix J_{wz}.

Proposition 3 and Theorem 1 permit to develop performances criteria that can be easily expressed explicitly and used for systems design & operation.

4   Sapient Systems Design and Operation

Notice that the main objective for Plant Design & Operation is to ensure that the matrix J_{wz} preserves its rank and that is well conditioned on a specific region; that is, that $\|J_{wz\delta}^+\|_s$, (for $\delta \to 0$), remains bounded in that region. One of the main obstacles on developing simple and general procedures for Plant Design & Operation is the inherent difficulty to find an explicit expression for $J_{wz\delta}^+$. This explains the merit of a procedure for systems design and operation based on the isotropy condition given by Eq.(11), or the upper bound given by Ineq.(12), since the procedure relies on explicit expressions.

A conventional procedure for Plant Design & Operation based on the isotropy condition given by Eq.(11), or the upper bound given by Ineq.(12), involves a trial and error process consisting of solving a series of optimization problems. The optimization procedure normally involves formulating a constrained nonlinear programming problem which considers properly any of the above performance criteria as an objective function and subject to some parameter constraints. The solution of the optimization procedure yields some optimal systems parameters as well as some regions for best operation.

4.1   Use of Proposition 3 and Theorem 1

The Proposition 3 and Theorem 4 can be the basis for systems design analysis/optimization, as well for determining the best regions for system operation. In particular, the isotropy condition given by Eq.(11), or the upper bound given by Ineq.(12) can be used alone or in conjunction. In this case, a proper objective function can be defined only in terms of $\|J_{wz}(\psi)J_{wx}^T(\psi) - \sigma_{iso}^2(\psi)I\|_F^2$, or on the upper bound given by Ineq.(12); or by properly combining both expressions.

4.2   Non-conventional Techniques Issues

It is important to notice that the above Propositions and Theorem have been developed assuming that the weighted Jacobian matrix J_{wz} is available. However, their use remains valid in the case that an approximation (by conventional or non-conventional -ANNs, AFIS, CANFIS- techniques) to the weighted Jacobian matrix is considered.

Moreover, for Inference Systems it is possible to establish [3] a simple explicit expression that can serve to develop a non-conventional approach for Plant Design & Operation. Notice that in this case it is desired that a matrix $\Psi \approx J_{wz\delta}^+$; and that Ψ can be expressed explicitly in terms of antecedent/premise, scaling, and consequent parameters. Furthermore, in this case a proper norm of the matrix Ψ can be easily expressed explicitly in terms of the system parameters. That is, it is desired to optimize this norm (objective function) subject to some constraints in the antecedent/premise, scaling, and consequent parameters, [3].

5   Conclusions

In this article several performance criteria for the proper design and operation of Intelligent and *Sapient (Wise)* Systems are presented. These criteria are based on properly considering some characterizing matrices having a significant role on the performance of Intelligent and *Sapient (Wise)* Systems. In particular, here it is shown that from these characterizing matrices it is possible to establish: (a) an upper bound on a homogenized condition number; (b) a generalization of an isotropy condition; and (c) a proper bound on its rate of change. As discussed here, these criteria can be used for design analysis and optimization, as well for determining the best regions for system operation.

References

1. Jang, J.-S.R., Sun, C.-T., Mizutani, E.: Neuro-Fuzzy and Soft Computing: A Computational Approach to Learning and Machine Intelligence. Prentice Hall, Inc. (1997)
2. Mayorga, R.V.: The Computation of Inverse Time Variant Functions via Proper Pseudoinverse Bounding: A RBFN Approach. Int. Journal on AI Tools, 13(3) (2004)
3. Mayorga, R.V.: Towards Computational Sapience (Wisdom): A Paradigm for Sapient (Wise) Systems. In: Proc. of Int. Conference on Knowledge Intensive Multi-Agent Systems (KIMAS'2003). Cambridge MA, USA, Sept. 30 - Oct. 4 (2003)
4. Mayorga, R.V.: A Paradigm For Continuous Function Optimization: An Intelligent/Wise Systems Implementation. In: Proc. of Int. Symposium on Robotics and Automation (ISRA'2002). Toluca, Mexico, Sept. 1-4 (2002)
5. Mayorga, R.V.: Towards Computational Wisdom and MetaBotics: A Paradigm for Intelligent/Wise Systems, and MetaBots. In: Proc. of Int. Symposium on Robotics and Automation (ISRA'2000). Monterrey, Mexico, Nov. 10-12 (2000)
6. Mayorga, R.V.: Towards Computational Wisdom: Intelligent/Wise Systems, Paradigms, and MetaBots. Tutorial Notes Monograph, ANIROB, Congreso Nacional de Robotica (CONAR'99). Cd. Juarez, Dec. 13-15 (1999)
7. Mayorga, R.V.: A Paradigm for Intelligent Systems Design/Operation. In: Proc. of Int. Symposium on Robotics and Automation (ISRA'98). Saltillo, Mexico, Dec. 12-14 (1998)
8. Mayorga, R.V.: A Paradigm for Intelligent Decision and Control: Neural Nets, Fuzzy and Neuro-Fuzzy Implementations. In: Proc. of IASTED Int. Conf. on Artificial Intelligence and Soft Computing. Cancún, México, May 27-30 (1998)
9. Mayorga, R.V.: A Paradigm for Intelligent Decision and Control: An Application for the Intelligent Design of a Human-Computer Interface. Dept. of Systems Design Eng., U. of Waterloo, Tech./Res. Report, UFW-310797, July 31 (1997)
10. Meystel, A.M., Albus, J.S.: Intelligent Systems: Architecture, Design, and Control. J. Wiley & Sons (2002)
11. Perlovsky, L.I.: Neural Networks and Intellect, Oxford University Press (2001)

Three Steps to *Robo Sapiens*

José Negrete-Martínez[1,2]

[1] Departamento de Biología Celular y Fisiología,
IIBM, Unidad Periférica en Xalapa, UNAM
[2] Facultad de Física e Inteligencia Artificial,
Universidad Veracruzana, Xalapa, Veracruz, México
jnegrete@uv.mx

Abstract. In a previous paper the author posited that a sapient system would be a robot that performs abductions on a classification of concepts. In the present work, I propose the three steps that would be required for a robot to reach an initial state of sapience. Each step begins with improved mechatronics, continues with improvements in pattern recognition and ends with improvements in symbol manipulation. The first step starts with an anthropomorphic robot. I propose that if in the last step we implement adductive reasoning we have arrived at an initial sapient system. A low level robot showing the first stage evolution of a simple robot is presented. The implementation evinces many features of biological evolution such as misfitness, adaptation, exaptation, mutation, and co-evolution.

1   Introduction

Artificial Intelligence's paradigmatic game is Chess. This statement is the result of a search for a universally recognized intelligent human activity that could be played against a machine. This choice has been done in the hope of learning the system nature of human intelligence. I have been similarly motivated to search for a human activity which is recognized as Sapient. I found that the human activity to be a heuristic Meaningful Learning activity: one which constructs new meaning from experience [1]. This heuristics implies intelligent actions and thoughts leading to valuable abductions that modify the memory structure. But it is my feeling that a sapient system requires, in addition, a structural compromise with the nature of its supporting smartness, i.e. a defined composition of many single smart systems quite independent of each other; each one with its own strengths and constraints. The supporting smartness can be synthesized into three: body-brain capacity (mechatronic for a robot), formalizing capacity (symbolic for a robot) and pattern recognizing capacity (both for man and robot). The capacities evolve in the hands of the designer in lines of improvement. Each improvement in each line elicits an improvement in the other lines (co-evolution).

D. Ślęzak et al. (Eds.): RSFDGrC 2005, LNAI 3642, pp. 727–733, 2005.

2   Evolving Rules to Be Followed by the Designer

The experimenter or designer who evolves the robot must follow certain rules:

1. Any evolution starts with a given proto-robot (starting-species rule)
2. Any co-evolving step must start with a mechatronic improvement (speciation rule)
3. Any co-evolving line improvement must start "on top" of the previous advance of the line (mutation rule)
4. Before applying any mutation, the fitting of the robot must be improved through adjustment of the parameters in each line of the current co-evolution (adaptation rule)
5. In the case of reasonable behavior success of the robot in the current step, the decision to move to the next evolutionary step must be taken (fitting rule).

3   Prerequisites for a Proto-Robot

The experimenter must start with a basic robot (a proto-robot) for which I would propose the following prerequisites: it must have a mechatronic visual system and visual motor coordination; it must be implemented with arms and corresponding objects-reaching capabilities; the arms should be anthropomorphic. A head-torso configuration as in the case of the robot COG [2] with a single arm will do.

4   Evolution

Evolution can be considered as a sequence of steps driven by nature but in robots can be steps driven by a designer. We propose three steps for a designer to reach the implementation of *Robo sapiens*.

4.1   First Step

The first step starts with the "initial" mechatronic part of the robot; continues with the implementation of a network that recognizes nearby tagged objects. Since the tags can vary, the pattern recognition system should be able to learn to recognize tag variations by reinforcement (for example, see Kaelbling [3]). This stage ends by giving names to the recognized variables (for example, see Steels [4]).

4.2   Second Step

The second step starts with the implementation of new sensorial modalities in the mechatronic line, continues with improvement of the existing pattern recognition network through the addition of the new modality input so the robot can now recognize untagged objects. The learning process delineated in the previous pattern recognition step must be expanded to learn to identify shapes (for example, see Poggio [5]). The step ends with the superimposition of a formal system that represents the recognized objects by their symbols.

4.3   Third Step

The third stage starts with a new memory: a storage and retrieval electronics dedicated to representations. It continues with an adaptation of the previous network to infer objects (for example, see Kersten [6]). This step ends with the implementation of a representation of knowledge of the world and with ability to reason about it (for example, see Doyle [7]). At this point the robot is ready to explore a wider world than the one confined to the laboratory; thus, it is the moment to mutate the mechatronics, adding an all-terrain carrier and navigator that can take the robot outside the laboratory. This extension must continue with a pattern recognition adaptation focused on classifying world objects by their common features (for example, see Quinlan [8]). I propose that if in this extended stage we implement symbolic abductive reasoning (for example, see Perlovsky [9]) we have created a candidate for *Robo sapiens*.

5   A Low Level Proto-Robot: PROTO

In order to learn the nature of the co-evolution I make use of a Lynxmotion robot to develop a "PROTO", see Fig. 1

Fig. 1. A picture of PROTO from above showing on top of its hand the mobile sensor

5.1   Initial Mechatronics

PROTO has one arm with a light receptor attached to its hand tool. The arm has three sections moved by four servomotors and it is transported on top of a three wheeled vehicle (two wheels are motorized with modified servomotors). The light receptor (infrared) feeds an amplifier-filter-detector circuit (light processing circuit). A dynamic attenuator in this last circuit is implemented so the range of the sensor approaching distance to an IR light beacon can go from centimeters to milimeters without saturation. There are four microcontrollers that move each one of the arm servos stepwise; these servos are called premotor, in the sense of the premotor nuclei of the nervous system (only three are shown in Figure 2). Each microcontroller receives two kinds of signals, one that enables it and the other, a perceptual signal, coming from the pattern recognition system that provides utility information: the "utility signal". When a premotor is habilitated, it samples the present utility signal and decides to move one step in either one of two directions depending on the value of the utility signal and the previous direction of the step movement. When the utility signal is non significant, the microcontroller self inactivates [10]. Every time one of these microcontrollers moves a step, it also sends a signal that commands the utility module to sample the output of the light processing circuit (see Fig. 2).

5.2   The Initial Pattern Recognition

There is a microcontroller in PROTO called the utility module that samples, by command, the output of the light processor circuit and calculates the difference from the previously sampled value. If this difference is significant and positive (sensor approaching the light source) the sampled signal is coded as +1. When the difference is significant and negative (sensor departing from the light source) the sampled signal is coded as -1. Otherwise, the signal is coded as 0. (For a more detailed description, see Negrete-Martínez and Cruz [10].) These three values (utility signals) are the output of this microcontroller (see Fig. 2).

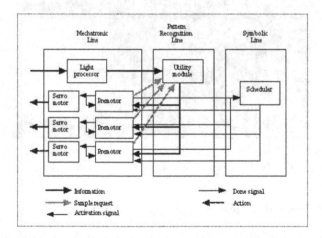

Fig. 2. Initial state of development in PROTO. In the mechatronic line there is a light processor circuit. In this mechatronic line the picture presents three premotor modules followed by its corresponding servomotors. In the pattern recognition line of development there is only one module, the utility module. The symbolic line has only one module, a scheduler program in a microcontroller.

5.3   The Initial Symbol Processing

PROTO carries a microcontroller, in which there is a program that enables the activation of a single premotor microcontroller at a time in a given cyclic schedule. The premotor microcontrollers when self-deactivated make jump to the next activation command the symbolic program (through sending a "done" signal to the scheduler, see Fig. 2 in).

5.4   Initial Behavior Performance of PROTO

PROTO extends its arm with the sensor, from 20 cm to several millimeters from the source of light.

6   First Step in PROTO

The co-evolution of PROTO in its first step is presented in incremental terms. The Fig. 3 is an extension of Fig. 2 but most of the original connectors between the blocks have been suppressed for clarity.

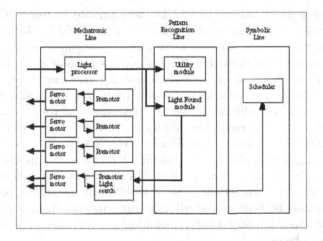

Fig. 3. First step stage of development in PROTO

6.1   First Mechatronic Improvement

To the initial mechatronics, a premotor module has been added, the light-search-and-turn module. This module activates three servomotors: one that moves the sensor and a premotor microcontroller that commands the corresponding servo and the rotating motors of the vehicle, see Fig. 3.

6.2   First Pattern Recognition Improvement

In the pattern recognition line a new module has been added, a light-finding module (microcontroller) that habilitates in turn two other premotor microcontrollers. This premotor habilitation is different from the previous kind because it is coming from the light-finding module and not from the scheduler program, see Fig. 3.

6.3   First Symbolic Improvement

In the symbolic line there is a change in the scheduler program, the function of this program is suppressed temporarily while the premotor light-search-and-turn module remains active. The improvement in the symbolic line is the inclusion of a "stop-schedule" signal for the symbolic module (notice the thick line connection in Fig. 3). The robot, at the end of this first evolving step, exhibits a new behavior that makes the sensor search for light and makes the robot turn the car toward the origin of the light when the sensor is not facing the light.

7   Discussion

The designer searches during the initial performance of the PROTO for unwanted features, misfittings of the machine to its world (in biological terms). The designer tries several corrections in pattern recognition or in the symbolic part trying to solve the misfitting. This is equivalent to adaptations in biology. In case of failure of the adaptations, the designer tries corrections in the lines (equivalent to mutations in biology). When successful, the designer is ready to move to the next co-evolution. Every mechatronic "mutation" leaves open the possibility of a pattern recognition mutation and this last mutation leaves open an opportunity for a symbolic mutation, a cascade of mutations and their corresponding adaptations. This last dynamic at times results in exaptation [11]. A simple example of exaptation was found in the implementation of mobility in the sensor. Before the implementation of mobility in the sensor, proto followed the penumbra of the beacon; but after its implementation (designed to search for light) the sensor followed a better reaching pattern, now following the center of the beacon's beam.

Abduction Failures. Corrections of abduction failures have not been specified in the candidate for *Robo sapiens* because they must take place in further evolving steps.

8   Conclusions

- Before reaching a sapient state a robot must acquire some skills in its mechatronics, pattern recognition and symbolic processing.
- The desirable final activity of a sapient system in the laboratory should combine "AI" resources among them abduction. The abduction should be performed on an explicit knowledge structure.

- The robot must perform combined actions in the physical world that would result in abductive modification in its memory structure.
- I postulate that three evolutionary steps must been taken before a robot can reach an initial state of sapience. Each step is a co-evolution process that begins with an improved mechatronics continues with improved pattern recognition and ends with an improvement in symbol manipulation.
- I found that a low level implementation of the first step can aptly illustrate the advantages of co-evolution.
- I also found that low level implementation can show several emergent biological features such as misfittings, adaptations, exaptations, mutations and co-evolution of skills.
- The presence of brainlike structures can be assimilated in the implementation of the premotor modules.
- The number of steps to reach an initial state of sapiency must not be taken literally; they only reflect mayor openings to exaptations to be exploited by the designer.

References

1. Negrete-Martínez, J: In Search of a Sapient Game. IEEE International Conferences of Knowledge Intensive Multi-Agent Systems KIMAS-2005, Boston, MA. (2005) 512-514
2. Brooks, R. A., Breazel C., Marjanowic, M., Scalssellati, B., Williamson, M. M.: The COG Project: Building a Humanoid Robot. Computation for Metaphors, Analogy, and Agents. Lecture Notes in Computer Science. Springer-Verlag Berlin Heidelberg New York **152** (1999) 52-87
3. Kaelbling, L.P.: Learning in Embedded Systems. The MIT Press (1993)
4. Steels, L.: Perceptually grounded meaning creation. Proceedings of the International Conference on Multi-Agent Systems, Menlo Park Ca. AAAI Press. (1996)
5. Poggio,T. Sung, K.: Example-based learning for view-based human face recognition. Proceedings of the Image Understanding Workshop. **11** (1994) 843-850
6. Kersten, D.: High level vision as statistical inference. In Gazzaniga, M. (ed). The Cognitive Neuroscience. Cambridge, MA., MIT Press. (1998)
7. Doyle, J.A.: Truth Maintenance System. Artificial Intelligence **12** (1979) 231-272
8. Quinlan, J.R.: Induction of Decision Trees. Machine Learning **1** (1986) 81-106
9. Perlovsky, L.I.: Neural Networks and Intellect. Oxford University Press (2001)
10. Negrete-Martínez J., Cruz, R.: Self-organized Multi-modular Robotic Control. Proceedings of the 3rd International Symposium on Robotics and Automation, IS-RAÕ2002 (2002) 421-425
11. Gould, S.J.: Challenges to Neo-Darwinism and their Meaning for a Revised View of Human Consciousness. The Tanner Lectures on Human Values. April 30, May 1,. Clare Hall Cambridge University (1984)

Author Index

Lecture Notes in Artificial Intelligence (LNAI)

Vol. 3438: H. Christiansen, P.R. Skadhauge, J. Villadsen (Eds.), Constraint Solving and Language Processing. VIII, 205 pages. 2005.

Vol. 3430: S. Tsumoto, T. Yamaguchi, M. Numao, H. Motoda (Eds.), Active Mining. XII, 349 pages. 2005.

Vol. 3419: B. Faltings, A. Petcu, F. Fages, F. Rossi (Eds.), Constraint Satisfaction and Constraint Logic Programming. X, 217 pages. 2005.

Vol. 3416: M. Böhlen, J. Gamper, W. Polasek, M.A. Wimmer (Eds.), E-Government: Towards Electronic Democracy. XIII, 311 pages. 2005.

Vol. 3415: P. Davidsson, B. Logan, K. Takadama (Eds.), Multi-Agent and Multi-Agent-Based Simulation. X, 265 pages. 2005.

Vol. 3403: B. Ganter, R. Godin (Eds.), Formal Concept Analysis. XI, 419 pages. 2005.

Vol. 3398: D.-K. Baik (Ed.), Systems Modeling and Simulation: Theory and Applications. XIV, 733 pages. 2005.

Vol. 3397: T.G. Kim (Ed.), Artificial Intelligence and Simulation. XV, 711 pages. 2005.

Vol. 3396: R.M. van Eijk, M.-P. Huget, F. Dignum (Eds.), Agent Communication. X, 261 pages. 2005.

Vol. 3394: D. Kudenko, D. Kazakov, E. Alonso (Eds.), Adaptive Agents and Multi-Agent Systems II. VIII, 313 pages. 2005.

Vol. 3392: D. Seipel, M. Hanus, U. Geske, O. Bartenstein (Eds.), Applications of Declarative Programming and Knowledge Management. X, 309 pages. 2005.

Vol. 3374: D. Weyns, H. V.D. Parunak, F. Michel (Eds.), Environments for Multi-Agent Systems. X, 279 pages. 2005.

Vol. 3371: M.W. Barley, N. Kasabov (Eds.), Intelligent Agents and Multi-Agent Systems. X, 329 pages. 2005.

Vol. 3369: V. R. Benjamins, P. Casanovas, J. Breuker, A. Gangemi (Eds.), Law and the Semantic Web. XII, 249 pages. 2005.

Vol. 3366: I. Rahwan, P. Moraitis, C. Reed (Eds.), Argumentation in Multi-Agent Systems. XII, 263 pages. 2005.

Vol. 3359: G. Grieser, Y. Tanaka (Eds.), Intuitive Human Interfaces for Organizing and Accessing Intellectual Assets. XIV, 257 pages. 2005.

Vol. 3346: R.H. Bordini, M. Dastani, J. Dix, A.E.F. Seghrouchni (Eds.), Programming Multi-Agent Systems. XIV, 249 pages. 2005.

Vol. 3345: Y. Cai (Ed.), Ambient Intelligence for Scientific Discovery. XII, 311 pages. 2005.

Vol. 3343: C. Freksa, M. Knauff, B. Krieg-Brückner, B. Nebel, T. Barkowsky (Eds.), Spatial Cognition IV. XIII, 519 pages. 2005.

Vol. 3339: G.I. Webb, X. Yu (Eds.), AI 2004: Advances in Artificial Intelligence. XXII, 1272 pages. 2004.

Vol. 3336: D. Karagiannis, U. Reimer (Eds.), Practical Aspects of Knowledge Management. X, 523 pages. 2004.

Vol. 3327: Y. Shi, W. Xu, Z. Chen (Eds.), Data Mining and Knowledge Management. XIII, 263 pages. 2005.

Vol. 3315: C. Lemaître, C.A. Reyes, J.A. González (Eds.), Advances in Artificial Intelligence – IBERAMIA 2004. XX, 987 pages. 2004.

Vol. 3303: J.A. López, E. Benfenati, W. Dubitzky (Eds.), Knowledge Exploration in Life Science Informatics. X, 249 pages. 2004.

Vol. 3301: G. Kern-Isberner, W. Rödder, F. Kulmann (Eds.), Conditionals, Information, and Inference. XII, 219 pages. 2005.

Vol. 3276: D. Nardi, M. Riedmiller, C. Sammut, J. Santos-Victor (Eds.), RoboCup 2004: Robot Soccer World Cup VIII. XVIII, 678 pages. 2005.

Vol. 3275: P. Perner (Ed.), Advances in Data Mining. VIII, 173 pages. 2004.

Vol. 3265: R.E. Frederking, K.B. Taylor (Eds.), Machine Translation: From Real Users to Research. XI, 392 pages. 2004.

Vol. 3264: G. Paliouras, Y. Sakakibara (Eds.), Grammatical Inference: Algorithms and Applications. XI, 291 pages. 2004.

Vol. 3259: J. Dix, J. Leite (Eds.), Computational Logic in Multi-Agent Systems. XII, 251 pages. 2004.

Vol. 3257: E. Motta, N.R. Shadbolt, A. Stutt, N. Gibbins (Eds.), Engineering Knowledge in the Age of the Semantic Web. XVII, 517 pages. 2004.

Vol. 3249: B. Buchberger, J.A. Campbell (Eds.), Artificial Intelligence and Symbolic Computation. X, 285 pages. 2004.

Vol. 3248: K.-Y. Su, J. Tsujii, J.-H. Lee, O.Y. Kwong (Eds.), Natural Language Processing – IJCNLP 2004. XVIII, 817 pages. 2005.

Vol. 3245: E. Suzuki, S. Arikawa (Eds.), Discovery Science. XIV, 430 pages. 2004.

Vol. 3244: S. Ben-David, J. Case, A. Maruoka (Eds.), Algorithmic Learning Theory. XIV, 505 pages. 2004.

Vol. 3238: S. Biundo, T. Frühwirth, G. Palm (Eds.), KI 2004: Advances in Artificial Intelligence. XI, 467 pages. 2004.

Vol. 3230: J.L. Vicedo, P. Martínez-Barco, R. Muñoz, M. Saiz Noeda (Eds.), Advances in Natural Language Processing. XII, 488 pages. 2004.

Vol. 3229: J.J. Alferes, J. Leite (Eds.), Logics in Artificial Intelligence. XIV, 744 pages. 2004.

Vol. 3228: M.G. Hinchey, J.L. Rash, W.F. Truszkowski, C.A. Rouff (Eds.), Formal Approaches to Agent-Based Systems. VIII, 290 pages. 2004.

Vol. 3215: M.G.. Negoita, R.J. Howlett, L.C. Jain (Eds.), Knowledge-Based Intelligent Information and Engineering Systems, Part III. LVII, 906 pages. 2004.

Vol. 3214: M.G. Negoita, R.J. Howlett, L.C. Jain (Eds.), Knowledge-Based Intelligent Information and Engineering Systems, Part II. LVIII, 1302 pages. 2004.

Vol. 3213: M.G.. Negoita, R.J. Howlett, L.C. Jain (Eds.), Knowledge-Based Intelligent Information and Engineering Systems, Part I. LVIII, 1280 pages. 2004.

Vol. 3209: B. Berendt, A. Hotho, D. Mladenic, M. van Someren, M. Spiliopoulou, G. Stumme (Eds.), Web Mining: From Web to Semantic Web. IX, 201 pages. 2004.

Vol. 3206: P. Sojka, I. Kopecek, K. Pala (Eds.), Text, Speech and Dialogue. XIII, 667 pages. 2004.